Italy (I)

	🛣️ 130	🛤️ 110	⚠️ 90	🏭 50
If towing				
	80	70	70	50
Less than three years with full licence				
	100	90	90	50
When wet				
	110	90	80	50

Some motorways with emergency lanes have speed limit of 150 kph

- 🔒 Compulsory in front seats and, if fitted, in rear
- 👶 Under 12 not allowed in front seats except in child safety seat; children under 3 must have special seat in the back. For foreign-registered cars, the country of origin's legislation applies.
- 🍷 0.05% • 0.00% for professional drivers or with less than 3 years full licence
- △ Compulsory 🧰 Recommended
- 💡 Compulsory 🦺 Recommended
- ⊖ 18 (14 for mopeds, 16 up to 125cc, 20 up to 350cc)
- 📱 Only allowed with hands-free kit
- LEZ Most northern and several southern regions operate seasonal LEZs and many towns and cities have various schemes that restrict access. There is an LEZ in the Mont Blanc tunnel
- 🔦 Compulsory outside built-up areas, in tunnels, on motorways and dual carriageways and in poor visibility; compulsory at all times for motorcycles
- ❄️ Snow chains compulsory where signs indicate 15 Oct–15 Apr. Max speed 50 kph
- ★ On-the-spot fines imposed
- ★ Radar-detection equipment is prohibited
- ★ Tolls on motorways. Blue lanes accept credit cards; yellow lanes restricted to holders of Telepass pay-toll device.
- ★ Visibility vest compulsory

Kosovo (RKS)

	🛣️ 130	🛤️ 80	⚠️ 80	🏭 50

- 🔒 Compulsory
- 👶 Under 12 must sit in rear seats in an appropriate restraint.
- 🍷 0.00% △ Compulsory 🧰 Compulsory 💡 Compulsory 🦺 Compulsory
- ⊖ 18 (16 for motorbikes under 125 cc, 14 for mopeds)
- 📋 International driving permit, locally purchased third-party insurance (green card is not recognised), documents with proof of ability to cover costs and valid reason for visiting. Visitors from many non-EU countries require a visa.
- 📱 Only allowed with a hands-free kit
- 🔦 Compulsory at all times
- ❄️ Winter tyres or snow chains compulsory in poor winter weather conditions

Latvia (LV)

	🛣️ n/a	🛤️ 100	⚠️ 90	🏭 50
If towing				
	n/a	80	80	50

In residential areas limit is 20kph • If full driving licence held for less than two years, must not exceed 80 kph

- 🔒 Compulsory in front seats and if fitted in rear
- 👶 If under 12 years and 150cm must use child restraint in front and rear seats
- 🍷 0.05% • 0.02% with less than 2 years experience △ Compulsory
- 💡 Compulsory 🦺 Recommended
- 🧰 Compulsory ⊖ 18
- 📱 Only allowed with hands-free kit
- 🔦 Must be used at all times all year round
- ❄️ Winter tyres compulsory for vehicles up to 3.5 tonnes Dec–Feb, but illegal May–Sept
- ★ On-the-spot fines imposed
- ★ Pedestrians have priority
- ★ Radar-detection equipment prohibited
- ★ Visibility vests compulsory

Lithuania (LT)

	🛣️ 130	🛤️ 110	⚠️ 70–90	🏭 50
If towing				
	n/a	70	70	50
If licence held for less than two years				
	90	90	70	50

In winter, limits are reduced by 10–20 km/h

- 🔒 Compulsory
- 👶 Under 12 or below 135 cm not allowed in front seats unless in suitable restraint; under 3 must use appropriate child seat. A rear-facing child seat may be used in front only if airbags are deactivated.
- 🍷 0.04% • 0.00% if full licence held less than 2 years
- △ Compulsory 🧰 Compulsory
- 💡 Recommended 🦺 Compulsory ⊖ 18
- 📋 Licences without a photograph must be accompanied by photographic proof of identity, e.g. a passport
- 📱 Only allowed with a hands-free kit
- 🔦 Must be used at all times
- ❄️ Winter tyres compulsory 10 Nov–1 Apr
- ★ On-the-spot fines imposed
- ★ Visibility vest compulsory

Luxembourg (L)

	🛣️ 130/110	🛤️ 90	⚠️ 90	🏭 50*
If towing				
	90	75	75	50*

If full driving licence held for less than two years, must not exceed 75 kph • *30 kph zones are progressively being introduced.

- 🔒 Compulsory
- 👶 Children under 3 must use an appropriate restraint system. Airbags must be disabled if a rear-facing child seat is used in the front. Children 3–18 and/or under 150 cm must use a restraint system appropriate to their size. If over 36kg a seatbelt may be used in the back only
- 🍷 0.049%, 0.019 for young drivers, drivers with less than 2 years experience and drivers of taxis and commercial vehicles
- △ Compulsory 🧰 Compulsory (buses)
- 🦺 Compulsory (buses, transport of dangerous goods)
- 💡 Compulsory ⊖ 18
- 📱 Use permitted only with hands-free kit
- 🔦 Compulsory for motorcyclists and in poor visibility and in tunnels for other vehicles
- ❄️ Winter tyres compulsory in winter weather
- ★ On-the-spot fines imposed
- ★ Visibility vest compulsory

Macedonia (MK)

	🛣️ 120	🛤️ 100	⚠️ 80	🏭 50
Newly qualified drivers or if towing				
	100	80	60	50

- 🔒 Compulsory
- 👶 Under 12 not allowed in front seats
- 🍷 0.05% • 0.00% for business, commercial and professional drivers and with less than 2 years experience
- △ Compulsory 🧰 Compulsory 💡 Compulsory
- 🦺 Recommended; compulsory for LPG vehicles
- ⊖ 18 (mopeds 16) 🔦 Compulsory at all times
- 📋 International driving permit; visa
- 📱 Use not permitted whilst driving
- 🔦 Compulsory at all times
- ❄️ Winter tyres or snow chains compulsory 15 Nov–15 Mar. Max speed 70 kph
- ★ GPS must have fixed speed camera function deactivated; radar detectors prohibited
- ★ Novice drivers may only drive between 11pm and 5am if there is someone over 25 with a valid licence in the vehicle.
- ★ On-the-spot fines imposed
- ★ Tolls apply on many roads
- ★ Tow rope compulsory
- ★ Visibility vest must be kept in the passenger compartment and worn to leave the vehicle in the dark outside built-up areas

Moldova (MD)

	🛣️ 90	🛤️ 90	⚠️ 90	🏭 60
If towing or if licence held under 1 year				
	70	70	70	60

- 🔒 Compulsory in front seats and, if fitted, in rear seats
- 👶 Under 12 not allowed in front seats
- 🍷 0.00% △ Compulsory
- 🧰 Compulsory 🦺 Recommended
- 💡 Compulsory
- ⊖ 18 (mopeds and motorbikes, 16; vehicles with more than eight passenger places, taxis or towing heavy vehicles, 21)
- 📋 International Driving Permit (preferred), visa
- 📱 Only allowed with hands-free kit
- 🔦 Must use dipped headlights at all times
- ❄️ Winter tyres recommended Nov–Feb

Montenegro (MNE)

	🛣️ n/a	🛤️ 100	⚠️ 80	🏭 50

80kph speed limit if towing a caravan

- 🔒 Compulsory in front and rear seats
- 👶 Under 12 not allowed in front seats. Under-5s must use an appropriate child seat.
- 🍷 0.03 %
- △ Compulsory 🧰 Compulsory
- 💡 Compulsory 🦺 Compulsory
- ⊖ 18 (16 for motorbikes less than 125cc; 14 for mopeds)
- 📋 International Driving Permit recommended
- 📱 Prohibited 🔦 Must be used at all times
- ❄️ From mid-Nov to March, driving wheels must be fitted with winter tyres
- ★ An 'eco' tax vignette must be obtained when crossing the border and displayed in the upper right-hand corner of the windscreen
- ★ On-the-spot fines imposed
- ★ Tolls on some primary roads and in the Sozina tunnel between Lake Skadar and the sea
- ★ Visibility vest compulsory

Netherlands (NL)

	🛣️ 130	🛤️ 80/100	⚠️ 80/100	🏭 50

- 🔒 Compulsory
- 👶 Under 3 must travel in the back, using an appropriate child restraint; 3–18 and under 135cm must use an appropriate child restraint. A rear-facing child seat may be used in front only if airbags are deactivated.
- 🍷 0.05% • 0.02% with less than 5 years experience or moped riders under 24
- △ Compulsory
- 🧰 Recommended 🦺 Recommended
- 💡 Recommended ⊖ 18
- 📱 Only allowed with a hands-free kit
- LEZ About 20 cities operate or are planning LEZs
- 🔦 Recommended in poor visibility and on open roads. Compulsory for motorcycles.
- ★ On-the-spot fines imposed
- ★ Radar-detection equipment is prohibited

Norway (N)

	🛣️ 90–110	🛤️ 80	⚠️ 80	🏭 30/50
If towing trailer with brakes				
	80	80	80	50
If towing trailer without brakes				
	60	60	60	50

- 🔒 Compulsory in front seats and, if fitted, in rear
- 👶 Children less than 150cm tall must use appropriate child restraint. Children under 4 must use child safety seat or safety restraint (cot). A rear-facing child seat may be used in front only if airbags are deactivated.
- 🍷 0.01% △ Compulsory
- 🧰 Recommended 🦺 Recommended
- 💡 Recommended
- ⊖ 18 (heavy vehicles 18/21)
- 📱 Only allowed with a hands-free kit
- 🔦 Must be used at all times
- ❄️ Winter tyres or summer tyres with snow chains compulsory for snow- or ice-covered roads
- ★ On-the-spot fines imposed
- ★ Radar-detectors are prohibited
- ★ Tolls apply on some bridges, tunnels and access roads into Bergen, Haugesund, Kristionsand, Oslo, Stavangar, Tonsberg and Trondheim. Several use electronic fee collection only.
- ★ Visibility vest compulsory

Poland (PL)

	🛣️	🛤️	⚠️	🏭
Motor-vehicle only roads[1], under/over 3.5 tonnes				
	130[2]/80[2]	110/80	100/80	n/a
Motor-vehicle only roads[1] if towing				
	n/a	80	80	n/a
Other roads, under 3.5 tonnes				
	n/a	100	90	50/60[3]
Other roads, 3.5 tonnes or over				
	n/a	80	70	50/60[3]
Other roads, if towing				
	n/a	60	60	30

[1]Indicated by signs with white car on blue background • [2]Minimum speed 40 kph • [3]50 kph 05.00–23.00; 60 kph 23.00–05.00; 20 kph in marked residential areas

- 🔒 Compulsory in front seats and, if fitted, in rear
- 👶 Under 12 and below 150 cm must use an appropriate child restraint. Rear-facing child seats not permitted in vehicles with airbags.
- 🍷 0.02% △ Compulsory
- 🧰 Recommended 🦺 Recommended
- 💡 Compulsory
- ⊖ 18 (mopeds and motorbikes under 125cc – 16)
- 📱 Only allowed with a hands-free kit
- 🔦 Compulsory for all vehicles
- ❄️ Snow chains permitted only on roads completely covered in snow
- ★ On-the-spot fines imposed
- ★ Radar-detection equipment is prohibited
- ★ Vehicles over 3.5 tonnes (including cars towing caravans) must have a VIAbox for the electronic toll system
- ★ Visibility vests compulsory

Portugal (P)

	🛣️ 120*	🛤️ 90/100	⚠️ 90	🏭 50/20
If towing				
	100*	90	80	50

*50kph minimum; 90kph maximum if licence held under 1 year

- 🔒 Compulsory in front seats and, if fitted, in rear
- 👶 Under 12 and below 135cm must travel in the rear in an appropriate child restraint; rear-facing child seats permitted in front for under 3s only if airbags deactivated
- 🍷 0.049% • 0.019% if full licence held less than 3 years
- △ Compulsory
- 🧰 Recommended 🦺 Recommended
- 💡 Recommended ⊖ 17
- 📋 MOT certificate for vehicles over 3 years old, photographic proof of identity must be carried at all times.
- 📱 Only allowed with hands-free kit
- LEZ An LEZ prohibits vehicles without catalytic converters from certain parts of Lisbon. There are plans to extend the scheme city-wide
- 🔦 Compulsory for motorcycles, compulsory for other vehicles in poor visibility and tunnels
- ★ On-the-spot fines imposed
- ★ Radar detectors and dash-cams prohibited
- ★ Tolls on motorways; do not use green lanes, these are reserved for auto-payment users. Some motorways require an automatic toll device.
- ★ Visibility vest compulsory
- ★ Wearers of spectacles or contact lenses should carry a spare pair

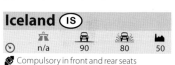

Croatia (HR)

⏱	🛣 130	⛰ 110	⚠ 90	🏙 50
Under 24				
⏱	120	100	80	50
If towing				
⏱	90	90	80	50

🛞 Compulsory if fitted

🧒 Children under 12 not permitted in front seat and must use appropriate child seat or restraint in rear. Children under 2 may use a rear-facing seat in the front only if the airbag is deactivated

🍷 0.05% · 0.00 % for drivers under 24

△ Compulsory (two if towing)

🔲 Compulsory 🔦 Compulsory

🎽 Recommended ⊖ 18

🪪 Green card recommended

📱 Only allowed with hands-free kit

🔧 Compulsory

❄ Winter tyres, snow chains and shovel compulsory in winter

★ On-the-spot fines imposed

★ Radar detectors prohibited

★ Tow bar and rope compulsory

★ Visibility vest compulsory

Czechia (CZ)

⏱	🛣 130	⛰ 90	⚠ 90	🏙 50
If towing				
⏱	80	80	80	50

🛞 Compulsory in front seats and, if fitted, in rear

🧒 Children under 36 kg and 150 cm must use appropriate child restraint. Only front-facing child retraints are permitted in the front in vehicles with airbags fitted. Airbags must be deactivated if a rear-facing child seat is used in the front.

🍷 0.00% △ Compulsory

🔲 Compulsory 🔦 Compulsory

🎽 Compulsory

⊖ 18 (17 for motorcycles under 125 cc)

🪪 Licences with a photo preferred. Paper licences should be accompanied by an International Driving Permit.

📱 Only allowed with hands-free kit

LEZ Two-stage LEZ in Prague for vehicles over 3.5 and 6 tonnes. Permit system.

🔧 Compulsory at all times

❄ Winter tyres compulsory November-March, roads are icy/snow-covered or snow is expected. Max speed 50 kph.

★ GPS must have fixed speed camera function deactivated; radar detectors prohibited

★ On-the-spot fines imposed

★ Replacement fuses must be carried

★ Spectacles or contact lens wearers must carry a spare pair in their vehicle at all times

★ Vignette needed for motorway driving, available for 1 year, 60 days, 15 days. Toll specific to lorries introduced 2006, those over 12 tonnes must buy an electronic tag

★ Visibility vest compulsory

Denmark (DK)

⏱	🛣 110-130	⛰ 80-90	⚠ 80	🏙 50*
If towing				
⏱	80	70	70	50*

*Central Copenhagen 40 kph

🛞 Compulsory front and rear

🧒 Under 135cm must use appropriate child restraint; in front permitted only in an appropriate rear-facing seat with any airbags disabled.

🍷 0.05% △ Compulsory

🔲 Recommended 🔦 Recommended

🎽 Recommended ⊖ 17

📱 Only allowed with hands-free kit

LEZ Aalborg, Arhus, Copenhagen, Frederiksberg and Odense. Proofs of emissions compliance or compliant filter needed to obtain sticker. Non-compliant vehicles banned.

🔧 Must be used at all times

Estonia (EST)

⏱	🛣 n/a	⛰ 90*	⚠ 90	🏙 50
If full driving licence held for less than two years				
⏱	90	90	90	50

*In summer, the speed limit on some dual carriageways may be raised to 100/110 kph

🛞 Compulsory if fitted

🧒 Children too small for adult seatbelts must wear a seat restraint appropriate to their size. Rear-facing safety seats must not be used in the front if an air bag is fitted, unless this has been deactivated.

🍷 0.00% △ 2 compulsory

🔲 Compulsory 🔦 Recommended

🎽 Compulsory ⊖ 18

📱 Only allowed with a hands-free kit

🔧 Compulsory at all times

❄ Winter tyres are compulsory from Dec–Mar. Studded winter tyres are allowed from 15 Oct–31 Mar, but this can be extended to start 1 October and/or end 30 April

★ A toll system is in operation in Tallinn

★ On-the-spot fines imposed

★ Two wheel chocks compulsory

★ Visibility vest compulsory

Finland (FIN)

⏱	🛣 120	⛰ 100	⚠ 80/100*	🏙 20/50
Vans, lorries and if towing				
⏱	80	80	60	20/50

*100 in summer • If towing a vehicle by rope, cable or rod, max speed limit 60 kph • Maximum of 80 kph for vans and lorries • Speed limits are often lowered in winter

🛞 Compulsory in front and rear

🧒 Below 135 cm must use a child restraint or seat

🍷 0.05% △ Compulsory

🔲 Recommended 🔦 Recommended

🎽 Recommended

⊖ 18 (motorbikes below 125cc 16)

📱 Only allowed with hands-free kit

🔧 Must be used at all times

❄ Winter tyres compulsory Dec–Feb

★ On-the-spot fines imposed

★ Radar-detectors are prohibited

★ Visibility vest compulsory

France (F)

⏱	🛣 130	⛰ 110	⚠ 80	🏙 50
On wet roads or if full driving licence held for less than 3 years				
⏱	110	100	70	50
If towing below / above 3.5 tonnes gross				
⏱	110/90	100/90	90/80	50

50kph on all roads if fog reduces visibility to less than 50m

🛞 Compulsory in front seats and, if fitted, in rear

🧒 In rear, 4 or under must have a child safety seat (rear facing if up to 9 months); if 5–10 must use an appropriate restraint system. Under 10 permitted in the front only if rear seats are fully occupied by other under 10s or there are no rear safety belts. In front, if child is in rear-facing child seat, any airbag must be deactivated.

🍷 0.049% • If towing or with less than 2 years with full driving licence, 0.00% • All drivers/motorcyclists must carry an unused breathalyser to French certification standards, showing an NF number.

△ Compulsory

🔲 Recommended 🔦 Recommended

⊖ 18 (16 for motorbikes up to 80cc)

📱 Use not permitted whilst driving

LEZ LEZs operate in the Mont Blanc Tunnel, Paris, Marseille and many other major cities. Crit'air vignettes must be displayed by compliant vehicles in such areas. Non-compliant vehicles are banned. See https://www.certificat-air.gouv.fr/en

🔧 Compulsory in poor daytime visibility and at all times for motorcycles

❄ Winter tyres recommended. Carrying snow chains recommended in winter as these may have to be fitted if driving on snow-covered roads, in accordance with signage. Max speed 50kph

★ GPS must have fixed speed camera function deactivated; radar-detection equipment is prohibited

★ Motorcyclists and passengers must have four reflective stickers on their helmets (front, back and both sides) and wear CE-certified gloves.

★ On-the-spot fines imposed

★ Tolls on motorways. Electronic tag needed if using automatic tolls.

★ Visibility vests, to be worn on the roadside in case of emergency or breakdown, must be carried for all vehicle occupants and riders.

★ Wearers of contact lenses or spectacles or lenses should carry a spare pair

Germany (D)

⏱	🛣 *	⛰ *	⚠ 100	🏙 50
If towing				
⏱	80	80	80	50

*no limit, 130 kph recommended

🛞 Compulsory

🧒 Aged 3-12 and under 150cm must use an appropriate child seat or restraint and sit in the rear. In the front, if child under 3 is in a rear-facing seat, airbags must be deactivated

🍷 0.049% • 0.0% for drivers 21 or under or with less than two years full licence

△ Compulsory 🔲 Compulsory

🔦 Compulsory 🎽 Recommended ⊖ 18

📱 Use permitted only with hands-free kit – also applies to drivers of motorbikes and bicycles

LEZ More than 60 cities have or are planning LEZs. Proof of compliance needed to acquire sticker. Non-compliant vehicles banned.

🔧 Compulsory during poor daytime visibility and tunnels; recommended at other times. Compulsory at all times for motorcyclists.

❄ Winter tyres compulsory in all winter weather conditions; snow chains recommended

★ GPS must have fixed speed camera function deactivated; radar detectors prohibited

★ On-the-spot fines imposed

★ Tolls on autobahns for lorries

★ Visibility vest compulsory

Greece (GR)

⏱	🛣 130	⛰ 110	⚠ 90	🏙 50
Motorbikes, and if towing				
⏱	90	70	70	40

🛞 Compulsory in front seats and, if fitted, in rear

🧒 Under 12 or below 135cm must use appropriate child restraint. In front if child is in rear-facing child seat, any airbags must be deactivated.

🍷 0.05% • 0.00% for drivers with less than 2 years' full licence and motorcyclists

△ Compulsory 🔲 Compulsory

🔦 Recommended 🎽 Compulsory

⊖ 17 📱 Not permitted.

🔧 Compulsory during poor daytime visibility and at all times for motorcycles

❄ Snow chains permitted on ice- or snow-covered roads. Max speed 50 kph.

★ On-the-spot fines imposed

★ Radar-detection equipment is prohibited

★ Tolls on several newer motorways.

Hungary (H)

⏱	🛣 130	⛰ 110	⚠ 90	🏙 50*
If towing				
⏱	80	70	70	50*

*30 kph zones have been introduced in many cities

🛞 Compulsory

🧒 Under 135cm and over 3 must be seated in rear and use appropriate child restraint. Under 3 allowed in front only in rear-facing child seat with any airbags deactivated.

🍷 0.00% △ Compulsory

🔲 Compulsory 🔦 Compulsory

🎽 Recommended ⊖ 17

📱 Only allowed with a hands-free kit

LEZ Budapest has vehicle restrictions on days with heavy dust and is planning an LEZ.

🔧 Compulsory during the day outside built-up areas; compulsory at all times for motorcycles

❄ Snow chains compulsory where conditions dictate. Max speed 50 kph.

★ Many motorways are toll and operate electronic vignette system with automatic number plate recognition, tickets are available for 10 days, 1 month, 13 months

★ On-the-spot fines issued

★ Radar detectors prohibited

★ Tow rope recommended

★ Visibility vest compulsory

Iceland (IS)

⏱	🛣 n/a	🚗 90	🚗 80	🏙 50

🛞 Compulsory in front and rear seats

🧒 Under 12 or below 150cm not allowed in front seat and must use appropriate child restraint.

🍷 0.05% △ Compulsory

🔲 Compulsory 🔦 Compulsory

🎽 Compulsory

⊖ 17; 21 to drive a hire car; 25 to hire a jeep

📱 Only allowed with a hands-free kit

🔧 Compulsory at all times

❄ Winter tyres compulsory c.1 Nov–14 Apr (variable). Snow chains may be used when necessary.

★ Driving off marked roads is forbidden

★ Highland roads are not suitable for ordinary cars

★ On-the-spot fines imposed

Ireland (IRL)

⏱	🛣 120	⛰ 60–100	⚠ 60–100	🏙 50*
If towing				
⏱	80	60	60	50*

*Dublin and some other areas have introduced 30 kph zones

🛞 Compulsory where fitted. Driver responsible for ensuring passengers under 17 comply

🧒 Children 3 and under must be in a suitable child restraint system. Airbags must be deactivated if a rear-facing child seat is used in the front. Those under 150 cm and 36 kg must use appropriate child restraint.

🍷 0.05% • 0.02% for novice and professional drivers △ Compulsory

🔲 Recommended 🔦 Recommended

🎽 Recommended ⊖ 17 (16 for motorbikes up to 125cc; 18 for over 125cc)

📱 Only allowed with a hands-free kit

🔧 Compulsory for motorbikes at all times and in poor visibility for other vehicles

★ Driving is on the left

★ GPS must have fixed speed camera function deactivated; radar detectors prohibited

★ On-the-spot fines imposed

★ Tolls are being introduced on some motorways; the M50 Dublin has barrier-free tolling with number-plate recognition.

Estonia section star notes:

★ Spiked tyres may be fitted 1 Nov–15 April, if used on all wheels

★ On-the-spot fines imposed

★ Radar detectors prohibited

★ Tolls apply on the Storebaeltsbroen and Oresundsbron bridges.

★ Visibility vest recommended

IV

Driving regulations

Vehicle A national vehicle identification plate is always required when taking a vehicle abroad. Fitting headlamp converters or beam deflectors when taking a right-hand drive car to a country where driving is on the right (every country in Europe except the UK and Ireland) is compulsory. Within the EU, if not driving a locally hired car, it is compulsory to have either Europlates or a country of origin (e.g. GB) sticker. Outside the EU (and in Andorra) a sticker is compulsory, even with Europlates.

Documentation All countries require that you carry a valid passport, vehicle registration document, hire certificate or letter of authority for the use of someone else's vehicle, full driving licence/International Driving Permit and insurance documentation (and/or green card outside the EU). Some non-EU countries also require a visa. Minimum driving ages are often higher for people holding foreign licences. Exit checks at the Eurotunnel and ferry terminals mean that drivers taking vehicles from the UK should allow extra time. Drivers of vehicles over three years old should ensure that the MOT is up to date, and take the certificate with them.

EHIC cards are free and give you entitlement to healthcare in other EU countries and Switzerland. *www.gov/european-health-insurance-card*

Licence A photo licence is preferred; with an old-style paper licence, an International Driving Permit (IDP) should also be carried. In some countries, an IDP is compulsory, whatever form of licence is held. Non-EU drivers should always have both a licence and and IDP. UK (except NI) drivers should check in advance whether a hire company will wish to check for endorsements and vehicle categories.

If so, visit *www.gov.uk/view-driving-licence* to create a digital code (valid for 72 hours) that allows licence details to be shared. For more information, contact the DVLA (0300790 6802, *www.dft.gov.uk/dvla*)

Insurance Third-party cover is compulsory across Europe. Most insurance policies give only basic cover when driving abroad, so you should check that your policy provides at least third-party cover for the countries in which you will be driving and upgrade it to the level that you require. You may have to take out extra cover at the frontier if you cannot produce acceptable proof of adequate insurance. Even in countries in which a green card is not required, carrying one is recommended for extra proof of insurance.

Motorcycles It is compulsory for all motorcyclists and passengers to wear crash helmets.

Other Minimum age requirements are for foreign drivers. They are not always the same as the age restrictions for nationals. In countries in which visibility vests are compulsory, one for each person should be carried in the passenger compartment, or panniers on a motorbike, where they can be reached easily. Warning triangles should also be carried in the passenger compartment .
• The penalties for infringements of regulations vary considerably from one country to another. In many countries the police may impose on-the-spot fines (ask for a receipt). Penalties can be severe for serious infringements, particularly for exceeding the blood-alcohol limit; in some countries this can result in immediate imprisonment
• In some countries, vignettes for toll roads are being replaced by electronic tags.

Symbols

🚗	Motorway
⚠	Dual carriageway
▲	Single carriageway
🚘	Surfaced road
🚙	Unsurfaced / gravel road
🏙	Urban area
Ⓢ	Speed limit in kilometres per hour (kph)
🔒	Seat belts
👶	Children
🍷	Blood alcohol level
△	Warning triangle
⛑	First aid kit
💡	Spare bulb kit
🧯	Fire extinguisher
⊖	Minimum driving age
📋	Additional documents required
📱	Mobile phones
LEZ	Low Emission Zone
◑	Dipped headlights
❄	Winter driving
★	Other information

The publishers have made every effort to ensure that the information given here was correct at the time of going to press. No responsibility can be accepted for any errors or their consequences. Please note that driving regulations may change, and that it has not been possible to cover all the information for every type of vehicle.

Andorra AND

Ⓢ	🚗	⚠	▲	🏙
	n/a	90	60/90	50

- 🔒 Compulsory
- 👶 Under 10 and below 150 cm must travel in an EU-approved restraint system adapted to their size in the rear. Airbag must be deactivated if a child is in the front passenger seat.
- 🍷 0.05% △ Compulsory
- ⛑ Recommended 💡 Compulsory
- 🧯 Recommended ⊖ 18
- 📱 Not permitted whilst driving
- ◑ Compulsory for motorcycles during day and for other vehicles during poor daytime visibility.
- ❄ Winter tyres recommended. Snow chains compulsory in poor conditions or when indicated.
- ★ On-the-spot fines imposed
- ★ Visibility vests compulsory

Austria A

Ⓢ	🚗	⚠	▲	🏙
	130	100	100	50
If towing trailer under 750kg / over 750 kg				
	100	100	100/80	50

- 🔒 Compulsory
- 👶 Under 14 and under 150cm cannot travel as a front or rear passenger unless they use a suitable child restraint; under 14 over 150cm must wear adult seat belt
- 🍷 0.049% • 0.01% if licence held less than 2 years
- △ Compulsory
- ⛑ Compulsory 💡 Recommended
- 🧯 Recommended
- ⊖ 17 (20 for motorbikes over 50cc)
- 📋 Paper driving licences must be accompanied by photographic proof of identity.
- 📱 Only allowed with hands-free kit
- LEZ Several cities and regions have LEZs affecting HGVs that ban non-compliant vehicles, impose speed restrictions and night-time bans.
- ◑ Must be used during the day by all road users. Headlamp converters compulsory
- ❄ Winter tyres compulsory 1 Nov–15 Apr

- ★ On-the-spot fines imposed
- ★ Radar detectors and dashcams prohibited
- ★ To drive on motorways or expressways, a motorway sticker must be purchased at the border or main petrol station. These are available for 10 days, 2 months or 1 year. Vehicles 3.5 tonnes or over must display an electronic tag.
- ★ Visibility vests compulsory

Belarus BY

Ⓢ	🚗	⚠	▲	🏙
	110	90	90	40*
If towing trailer under 750kg				
	90	70	70	

*In residential areas limit is 20 km/h • Vehicle towing another vehicle 50 kph limit • If full driving licence held for less than two years, must not exceed 70 kph

- 🔒 Compulsory in front seats, and rear seats if fitted
- 👶 Under 12 not allowed in front seat and must use appropriate child restraint
- 🍷 0.00% △ Compulsory
- ⛑ Compulsory 💡 Recommended
- 🧯 Compulsory ⊖ 18
- 📋 Visa, vehicle technical check stamp, international driving permit, green card, local health insurance. Even with a green card, local third-party insurance may be imposed at the border
- 📱 Use prohibited
- ◑ Compulsory during the day Nov–Mar and at all other times in conditions of poor visibility or when towing or being towed.
- ❄ Winter tyres compulsory; snow chains recommended
- ★ A temporary vehicle import certificate must be purchased on entry and driver must be registered
- ★ It is illegal for vehicles to be dirty
- ★ On-the-spot fines imposed
- ★ Radar-detectors prohibited
- ★ Road tax imposed at the border
- ★ To drive on main motorways an on-board unit must be acquired at the border or a petrol station in order to pay tolls. See www.beltoll.by/index.php/en

Belgium B

Ⓢ	🚗	⚠	▲	🏙
	120[1]	120[1]	90[2]	50[3]
If towing trailer				
	90	90	60	50[3]
Over 3.5 tonnes				
	90	90	60	50

[1]Minimum speed of 70 kph may be applied in certain conditions on motorways and some dual carriageways. [2]70 kph in Flanders. [3]20 kph in some residential areas, 30 kph near schools, hospitals and churches.

- 🔒 Compulsory
- 👶 All under 18s under 135 cm must wear an appropriate child restraint. Airbags must be deactivated if a rear-facing child seat is used in the front
- 🍷 0.049% △ Compulsory
- ⛑ Recommended 💡 Recommended
- 🧯 Compulsory
- 👕 Motorcyclists must wear fully protective clothing
- ⊖ 18
- 📱 Only allowed with a hands-free kit
- LEZ LEZs in operation in Antwerp, Brussels and areas of Flanders. Preregistration necessary and fees payable for most vehicles.
- ◑ Mandatory at all times for motorcycles and during the day in poor conditions for other vehicles
- ★ Cruise control must be deactivated on motorways where indicated
- ★ On-the-spot fines imposed
- ★ Radar detectors prohibited
- ★ Sticker indicating maximum recommended speed for winter tyres must be displayed on dashboard if using them
- ★ Visibility vest compulsory

Bosnia and Herzegovina BIH

Ⓢ	🚗	⚠	▲	🏙
	130	100	80	50

- 🔒 Compulsory if fitted
- 👶 Under 12s must sit in rear using an appropriate child restraint. Under-2s may travel in a rear-facing child seat in the front only if the airbags have been deactivated.
- 🍷 0.03% △ Compulsory

- 🔒 Compulsory 💡 Compulsory
- 🧯 Compulsory for LPG vehicles ⊖ 18
- 📋 Visa, International Driving Permit, green card
- 🚭 Prohibited
- ◑ Compulsory for all vehicles at all times
- ❄ Winter tyres compulsory 15 Nov–15 Apr; snow chains recommended
- ★ GPS must have fixed speed camera function deactivated; radar detectors prohibited
- ★ On-the-spot fines imposed
- ★ Visibility vest, tow rope or tow bar compulsory
- ★ Spare wheel compulsory, except for two-wheeled vehicles

Bulgaria BG

Ⓢ	🚗	⚠	▲	🏙
	130	90	90	50
If towing trailer				
	100	70	70	50

- 🔒 Compulsory in front and rear seats
- 👶 Under 3s not permitted in vehicles with no child restraints; 3–10 year olds must sit in rear in an appropriate restraint. Rear-facing child seats may be used in the front only if the airbag has been deactivated
- 🍷 0.049% △ Compulsory
- ⛑ Compulsory 💡 Recommended
- 🧯 Compulsory ⊖ 18
- 📋 Photo driving licence preferred; a paper licence must be accompanied by an International Driving Permit. Green card or insurance specific to Bulgaria.
- 📱 Only allowed with a hands-free kit
- ◑ Compulsory
- ❄ Winter tyres compulsory. Snow chains should be carried from 1 Nov–1 Mar. Max speed with chains 50 kph
- ★ Fee at border
- ★ GPS must have fixed speed camera function deactivated; radar detectors prohibited
- ★ On-the-spot fines imposed
- ★ Road tax stickers (annual, monthly or weekly) must be purchased at the border and displayed prominently with the vehicle registration number written on them.
- ★ Visibility vest compulsory

STOP AND GIVE WAY

Who has priority?

Make sure you keep a watchful eye on signs telling you who has priority on the road. Look for a yellow diamond sign, which tells you that traffic already on the road has priority. If you see the yellow diamond sign crossed out, then you must give way to traffic joining the road.

Priorité a droite

Despite the use of the yellow diamond signs, be aware that on some French roads (especially roundabouts in Paris), the traditional 'priorité a droite' practice is followed, even though it may no longer be legal. In theory these days, the rule no longer applies unless it is clearly signed. In practice, though, it makes sense to anticipate a driver pulling out in front of you, even though the priority may be yours.

Headlight flash

Bear in mind that the practice of flashing headlights at a junction in France does not mean the same thing as it might in the UK. If another motorists flashes his headlights at you, he's telling you that he has priority and will be coming through in front of you.

Stop means stop!

If you come to a solid white line with an octagonal 'STOP' sign, then you must come to a complete stop. In other words your wheels must stop turning. Adherence to the 'STOP' sign is generally much more rigorously enforced in European countries than you may be used to here.

HELP ME, PLEASE!

If you're in a difficult situation and need local help, then the following words and phrases might prove useful if language is a problem:

Do you speak English?	Parlez-vous anglais?	¿Habla usted inglés?	Parla inglese?	Sprechen Sie Englisch?
Thank you (very much)	Merci (beaucoup)	(Muchas) Gracias	Grazie (mille)	Danke (sehr)
Is there a police station near here?	Est-ce qu'il y a un commissariat de police près d'ici?	¿Hay una comisaría cerca?	C'e' un commissariato qui vicino?	Gibt es ein Polizeirevier hier in der Nähe?
I have lost my passport.	J'ai perdu mon passeport.	He perdido mi pasaporte	Ho perso il mio passaporto.	Ich have meinen Reisepass verloren.
I have broken down.	Je suis tombé en panne	Mi coche se ha averiado.	Ho un guasto.	Ich habe eine Panne.
I have run out of fuel.	Je suis tombé en panne d'essence.	Me he quedado sin gasolina.	Ho terminato la benzina.	Ich habe kein Benzin mehr.

WORTH KNOWING

You will need a separate GB sticker in EU countries if your car doesn't have a registration plate containing the GB euro-symbol.

Fuel is generally most expensive at motorway service areas and cheapest at supermarkets. However, these are usually shut on Sundays and Bank Holidays. So-called '24 hour' regional fuel stations in France generally accept payment by UK credit card these days, but some drivers still occasionally report difficulties. It would be better not to rely on them if your tank is running low during a night-time journey.

If you see several fuel stations in short succession before a national border, it's likely that fuel on the other side will be more expensive, so take the opportunity to fill up.

Radar speed camera detectors are illegal in most European countries.

The insurance 'green card' is no longer required for journeys in Europe, but it is important to make sure you have contact details for your insurer in case of an accident or claim.

Speed limits in France are enforced rigorously. Radar controls are frequent, and any driver (including non-residents) detected at more than 25km/h above the speed limit can have their licence confiscated on the spot. If you are caught exceeding the limit by 50km/h, even on a first offence, your car may be confiscated.

In Spain you must carry two warning triangles, plus a spare pair of glasses for every driver who needs to use them.

In Luxembourg, there are specific rules relating to how you fix a satnav device to your windscreen. Get it wrong and you could be fined on the spot.

In Germany it is against the law to run out of fuel on the motorway. If you do run out, then you face an on-the-spot fine.

Norway and Sweden have particularly low limits for drink-driving: just 20mg per 100ml of blood (compared to 80 in the UK). In Slovakia, the limit is zero.

In Hungary, the limit is also zero. If you are found to be drink-driving, your driving licence will be withdrawn by police officers on the spot.

In most countries, maps and signs will have the European road number (shown in white on a green background) alongside the appropriate national road number. However, in Sweden and Belgium only the E-road number will be shown.

Other laws and motoring advice to be aware of across Europe:

Austria Recent rules require the mandatory use of winter tyres between 1 November and 15 April. You should not use your horn when driving near hospitals. There are also restrictions on use of vehicle horns in Vienna.

Belgium You will have to pay to use most public toilets – including those at motorway service stations • You are not permitted to use cruise control on motorways when traffic is heavy • There are also specific penalties for close-following on motorways • Roadside drug-testing of drivers (using oral fluid testing devices) forms a regular part of any police controls • Drivers must carry a reflective vest in case of breakdown

Cyprus There have been important changes in how speeding and drink-driving are sanctioned. Cyprus now has a graduated system of speeding fines, ranging from one euro per km/h over the limit in marginal cases through to fines of up to €5,000 and a term of imprisonment for the most severe infringements. There are also graduated fines for drink-driving, ranging from fixed penalties for being slightly over the limit to terms of imprisonment and fines of up to €5,000 for the most severe. Eating and drinking at the wheel are both prohibited.

Denmark Cars towing caravans and trailers are prohibited from overtaking on motorways at certain times of day.

Finland Speeding fines are worked out according to your income. Access to a national database allows police at the roadside to establish a Finnish resident's income and number of dependants. Officers then impose a fine based on a specific number of days' income. The minimum speeding fine is 115 euros • If you hit an elk or deer, you must report the collision to the police.

France Legislation introduced in France in 2012 requires every driver and motorcyclist to be in possession of a valid breathalyser (displaying an 'NF' number), either electronic or chemical, to be shown to a police officer in case of control. However, the imposition of an €11 fine for failing to produce a breathalyser when required has been postponed indefinitely. So, in theory, you are required to carry a breathalyser kit, but no fine can be imposed if you don't • Motorcyclists' helmets must have four reflective stickers fitted, and there is an on-the-spot fine of €135 for non-compliance (by foreign riders as well as French). In common with other vehicle users, motorcyclists must also carry high-visibility vests to be worn on the roadside in case of emergency • Radar detectors, are banned with fines of €1500 for anyone using them • There are stiff penalties for driving while using a mobile phone. • The drink-drive limit for those who have held a licence for less than three years has been reduced to 20mg per 100ml of blood. For other drivers, the limit is 50mg. This compares with 80mg in England and Wales.

Germany Check your fuel contents regularly as it's an offence to run out of fuel on a German motorway • It's also an offence to make rude signs to other road users.

Greece Greece has one of Europe's highest accident rates in terms of the number of crashes per vehicle. Pay particular attention at traffic light junctions, as red lights are frequently ignored • Drivers detected with more than 110mg per 100ml of blood will face revocation of their licence, and possibly up to two years imprisonment • Carrying a petrol can in a vehicle is forbidden.

Ireland The drink-drive limit was reduced in 2011 from 80mg per 100ml of blood to 50mg • Beware of rural three-lane roads, where the middle overtaking lane is used by traffic travelling in both directions. On wider rural roads it's the accepted practice for slower vehicles to pull over to let faster traffic through.

Italy Police can impound your vehicle if you cannot present the relevant ownership documents when requested • You will need a red and white warning sign if you plan to use any rear-mounted luggage rack such as a bike rack • Zero alcohol tolerance is now applied for drivers who have held a driving licence for less than three years, as well as to drivers aged 18 to 21, professional drivers, taxi drivers and truckers.

Norway Under new legislation, police officers can perform roadside drug impairment saliva tests. There are specific limits set for the presence of 20 common non-alcohol drugs • You'll find what amounts to zero tolerance where drinking and driving is concerned. Only 10mg of alcohol per 100ml of blood is permitted (compared to 80mg in the UK) • Speeding fines are high. For example, a driver caught at 25 km/h over the 80 km/h speed limit on a national road could expect a fine of around £600. • No overtaking' signs apply to cars overtaking other cars and motorbikes overtaking cars, but curiously not to cars overtaking motorbikes.

Portugal If you are towing a caravan, you must have a current inventory of the caravan's contents to show a police officer if requested.

Slovakia It is mandatory to use dipped headlights on every road journey, regardless of the time of day, season or weather conditions.

Spain Motorway speed limits in Spain are 120km/h • If you need glasses for driving, then the law requires you to carry a spare pair with you in the car • It's compulsory to carry two spare warning triangles, spare bulbs for your car and reflective jackets.

Turkey Take great caution if you're driving at dusk. Many local drivers put off using their lights until it's properly dark, so you may find oncoming traffic very hard to spot • During the time of Ramadan, many people will not eat or drink between the hours of sunrise and sunset. This can seriously reduce levels of alertness, especially among people driving buses, trucks and taxis.

TOP TIPS FOR STAYING SAFE

Collisions abroad occur not just because of poor driving conditions locally, but also because we do not always take the same safety precautions as we might expect to take at home, for example by not wearing a seatbelt or by drinking and driving.

1. Plan your route before you go. That includes the journey you make to reach your destination (with sufficient breaks built in) and any excursions or local journeys you make while you're there.

2. Remember that, wherever you drive, you will be subject to the same laws as local drivers. Claiming ignorance of these laws will not be accepted as an excuse.

3. Take extra care at junctions when you're driving on the 'right side' of the road. Also, be careful if you are reversing out of a parking space on the street, as things will feel in the wrong place. If driving in a family group, involve every member in a quick 'junction safety check' to help reduce the risk of a collision. Having everybody in the car call out a catchphrase such as "DriLL DriLL DriLL" (Driver Look Left) on the approach to junctions and roundabouts is a small but potentially life-saving habit.

4. Take fatigue seriously. The excellent European motorway network means you can cover big distances with ease. But you must also make time for proper breaks (experts recommend a break of at least 15 minutes after every two hours of driving). If possible, share the driving and set strict daily limits to the number of driving hours. Watch a short video that explains the risks of driver fatigue: **www.motoringassist.com/fatigue**

5. Drink-driving limits across Europe are lower than those in the UK. The only exception is Malta, where the limit is the same. Bear this in mind if you're flying to a holiday or business destination and plan to have a drink on the plane, as the combination of unfamiliar roads and alcohol in your bloodstream is not a safe one. It's also worth remembering that drivers who cause collisions because they were drinking are likely to find their insurance policy will not cover them.

6. Expect the unexpected. Styles of driving in your destination country are likely to be very different from those you know in the UK. Drive defensively and certainly don't get involved in any altercations on the road.

7. Don't overload your car, however tempting the local bargains may appear. Make sure you have good all-round visibility by ensuring you don't pile up items on the parcel shelf or boot, and keep your windscreen clean.

8. Always wear a seatbelt and ensure everyone else on board wears one. Check specific regulations regarding the carriage of children: in some countries children under the age of 12 may not travel in the front of the car.

9. Don't use your mobile phone while driving. Even though laws on phone use while driving differ from country to country, the practice is just as dangerous wherever you are.

10. When you're exploring on foot, be wise to road safety as a pedestrian. You may get into trouble for 'jay-walking' so don't just wander across a road. Use a proper crossing, but remember that drivers may not stop for you! Don't forget that traffic closest to you approaches from the LEFT.

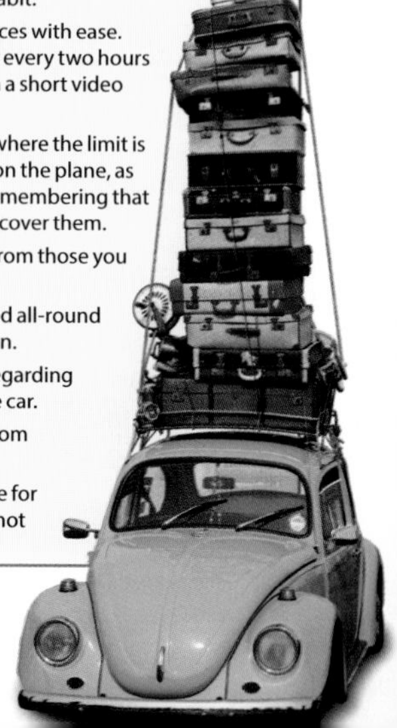

Contents

II	European driving: cut through the confusion
IV	Driving regulations
VIII	Ski resorts
X	Sights of Europe
XXIV	European politics and economics

1 Route planning maps
1 Key to route planning map pages

24 Road maps
24 Key to road map pages · Distance table

201 City plans and approach maps

Alicante C	201		Luxembourg C	215
Amsterdam C U	202		Lyon C U	215
Antwerpen C	201		Madrid U C	215
Athina U C	202		Málaga C	216
Barcelona C U	203		Marseille C	216
Basel C	203		Milano C U	217
Beograd C	205		Moskva C U	218
Berlin C U	204		München C U	218
Bordeaux C U	205		Nápoli C U	219
Bruxelles U C	205		Oslo U C	219
Budapest C U	206		Paris C U	220
Dublin C U	207		Praha C U	222
Düsseldorf C U	207		Roma C U	223
Edinburgh C	207		Rotterdam C	222
Firenze Florence C	209		Sankt Peterburg U	222
Frankfurt C	209		Sevilla C	224
Genève Geneva C	209		Stockholm C U	225
Génova Genoa C	209		Strasbourg C U	224
Göteborg C	210		Stuttgart C	224
Granada C	210		Torino U C	226
Hamburg C U	210		Venézia C	226
Helsinki C U	211		Warszawa C U	227
İstanbul U	211		Wien U C	227
København C U	212		Zagreb C	228
Köln Cologne C	212		Zürich C	228
Lisboa C U	213		C City street plan	
London C U	213		U Urban area map	

229 Index to road maps

www.philips-maps.co.uk

First published in 2007 as **Philip's EasyRead Europe** by Philip's, a division of Octopus Publishing Group Ltd
www.octopusbooks.co.uk
Carmelite House,
50 Victoria Embankment
London EC4Y 0DZ
An Hachette UK Company
www.hachette.co.uk

Ninth edition 2019, first impression 2019
ISBN 978-1-84907-501-5

While every reasonable effort has been made to ensure that the information compiled in this atlas is accurate, complete and up-to-date at the time of publication, some of this information is subject to change and the Publisher cannot guarantee its correctness or completeness.

The information in this atlas is provided without any representation or warranty, express or implied and the Publisher cannot be held liable for any loss or damage due to any use or reliance on the information in this atlas, nor for any errors, omissions or subsequent changes in such information.

The representation in this atlas of any road, drive or track is not evidence of the existence of a right of way.

The maps of Ireland on pages 26 to 30 and the urban area map and town plan of Dublin are based upon the Crown Copyright and are reproduced with the permission of Land & Property Services under delegated authority from the Controller of Her Majesty's Stationery Office, © Crown Copyright and database right 2019, PMLPA No 100503, and on Ordnance Survey Ireland by permission of the Government © Ordnance Survey Ireland / Government of Ireland Permit number 9181.

Cartography by Philip's, Copyright © Philip's 2019

Printed in Malaysia

*Independent research survey, from research carried out by Outlook Research Limited, 2005/06.

Photographic acknowledgements:
Page II: top Agencja Fotograficzna Caro / Alamy • right James Hughes • bottom Mode Images / Alamy.
Page III: centre Pete Titmuss / Alamy • bottom right Mim Friday / Alamy.

Legend to route planning maps pages 2–23

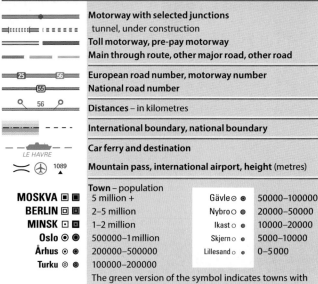

Motorway with selected junctions
 tunnel, under construction
Toll motorway, pre-pay motorway
Main through route, other major road, other road
European road number, motorway number
National road number
Distances – in kilometres
International boundary, national boundary
LE HAVRE · Car ferry and destination
Mountain pass, international airport, height (metres) · 1089

Town – population
MOSKVA 5 million +
BERLIN 2–5 million
MINSK 1–2 million
Oslo 500000–1 million
Århus 200000–500000
Turku 100000–200000
Gävle 50000–100000
Nybro 20000–50000
Ikast 10000–20000
Skjern 5000–10000
Lillesand 0–5000

The green version of the symbol indicates towns with Low Emission Zones

Scale · pages 2–23
1:3 200 000
1 in = 50.51 miles
1 cm = 32km

0 10 20 30 40 50 60 70 80 90 100 110 miles
0 20 40 60 80 100 120 140 160 180 km

Legend to road maps pages 26–200

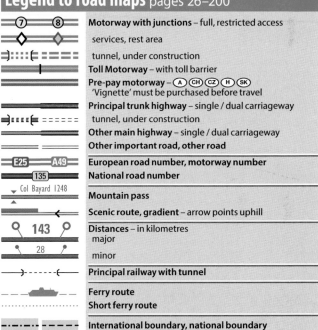

Motorway with junctions – full, restricted access
 services, rest area
 tunnel, under construction
Toll Motorway – with toll barrier
Pre-pay motorway – A CH CZ H SK
 'Vignette' must be purchased before travel
Principal trunk highway – single / dual carriageway
 tunnel, under construction
Other main highway – single / dual carriageway
Other important road, other road
E25 A49 European road number, motorway number
135 National road number
Col Bayard 1248 Mountain pass
Scenic route, gradient – arrow points uphill
143 Distances – in kilometres
 major
28 minor
Principal railway with tunnel
Ferry route
Short ferry route
International boundary, national boundary
National park, natural park

Airport
Ancient monument
Beach
Castle or house
Cave
Other place of interest
Park or garden
Religious building

Ski resort
Theme park
World Heritage site
1754 ▲ Spot height
Sevilla World Heritage town
Verona Town of tourist interest
City or town with Low Emission Zone

Scale · pages 26–181
1:753 800
1 inch = 12 miles
1 cm = 7.5km

0 2 4 6 8 10 12 14 16 18 20 22 24 26 miles
0 4 8 12 16 20 24 28 32 36 40km

Scale · pages 182–200
1:1 507 600
1 inch = 24 miles
1 cm = 15km

0 4 8 12 16 20 24 28 32 36 40 44 48 52 miles
0 8 16 24 32 40 48 56 64 72 80km

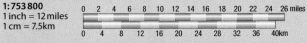

European driving:
cut through the confusion
Stay safe with GEM Motoring Assist

- Do you need advice about equipment requirements and which documents to take?
- Are you confused about European driving laws?
- How will you know what speed limits apply?
- Are you new to driving on the right hand side?
- Who do you call if you have an accident or break down?

Millions of us drive abroad on holiday each year. Perhaps it's a long motorway trip to the Mediterranean, a selection of historic cities and sites or a gentle tour along quiet country lanes. Whatever the purpose, it makes sense to ensure that both we and our vehicles are properly prepared for the journey.

It's not easy getting to grips with the finer points of driving in other countries, however experienced you may be as a motorist. Whether you have notched up thousands of miles of European driving or are preparing to make your first journey, the chances are you will always manage to find some road sign or legal requirement that will cause confusion.

What's more, 'driving in Europe' covers such a huge area. There are currently 28 countries in the European Union alone, each with its own set of road traffic laws and motoring customs. Driving in Europe can mean a spectacular and sunny coastal road that's within sight of Africa, or a snowy track amid the biting cold of the Arctic Circle, where the only others on the road are reindeer. Add to this some of the world's most congested cities, dense clusters of motorways (many with confusing numbers) and a big variation in safety standards and attitudes to risk. No wonder we often risk getting lost, taking wrong turnings or perhaps stopping where we shouldn't.

Depending on the country we're in, our errors at the wheel or our lack of familiarity with the rules of the road can sometimes bring unwelcome consequences. In any country, foreign drivers are subject to the same traffic rules as residents, enforceable in many situations by hefty on-the-spot fines and other sanctions. The situation across Europe is complex, simply because of the number of different sets of rules. For example, failure to carry a specific piece of breakdown equipment may be an offence in one country, but not in another. It's easy to see why the fun and excitement of a road trip in Europe could be spoilt by a minefield of regulations.

But we want to ensure that doesn't happen. Preparation and planning are key to a great holiday. It certainly pays to do a bit of research before you go, just to ensure you and your vehicle are up to the journey, your documents are in order and you're carrying the correct levels of equipment to keep the law enforcers happy.

Before you go
Some sensible planning will help make sure your European journey is enjoyable and – we hope – stress-free. So take some time before departure to ensure everything is in good shape: and that includes you, your travelling companions and your vehicle.

For you:
Try to become familiar with the driving laws of your holiday destination, including the local speed limits and which side of the road to drive on. You will be subject to these laws when driving abroad and if you are stopped by the police, it is not an excuse to say that you were unaware of them. Police officers in many countries have the power to impose (and collect) substantial on-the-spot fines for motoring offences, whether you are a resident or a visitor.

The European Commission's 'Driving Abroad' website http://ec.europa.eu/transport/road_safety/going_abroad gives detailed information on different road traffic rules in different European countries.

The Foreign and Commonwealth Office also gives country-specific travel advice www.gov.uk/driving-abroad with information on driving.

Passports
Check everyone's passport to make sure they are all valid.

Don't wait for your passport to expire. Unused time, rounded up to whole months (minimum one month, maximum nine months), will usually be added to your new passport.

New passports usually take two weeks to arrive. The Passport Office (0300 222 0000, www.gov.uk/renew-adult-passport) offers a faster service if you need a replacement passport urgently, but you'll have to pay a lot more.

Driving Licence
The new style photocard driving licence is currently valid in all European Union countries. Some non-EU countries may also require an International Driving Permit (£5.50, available from Post Offices). The previously used pink EU format UK paper licence is no longer a valid document. If you're planning to hire a car, the company may ask for a check code (www.gov.uk/view-driving-licence) so they can view your driving record, entitlement and any penalty points you may have. So if you haven't already done so, now is the time to update your old licence. For more information, contact the DVLA (0300 790 6802, www.gov.uk/government/organisations/driver-and-vehicle-licensing-agency)

Travel Insurance
Travel insurance is vital as it covers you against medical emergencies, accidents, thefts and cancellations, and repatriation. Ask for details before buying any travel insurance policy. Find out what it covers you for, and to what value. More important, check what's not covered. One of the key benefits of GEM membership is the excellent discount you can get on travel insurance. For more details, please visit: www.motoringassist.com/philipsmaps

European Breakdown Cover
Don't risk letting a breakdown ruin your European trip. Ensure you purchase a policy that will cover you for roadside assistance, emergency repair and recovery of your vehicle to the UK, wherever in Europe you may be heading. Once again, GEM members enjoy a specially discounted rate. You'll find the details at www.motoringassist.com/philipsmaps

EHIC
You wil need an EHIC card for everyone travelling. These are free and cover you for any medical treatment you may need during a trip to another EU or EEA country or Switzerland. However, do check at the time of requiring assistance that your EHIC will be accepted. Apply online (www.gov.uk/european-health-insurance-card), by telephone (0300 3301350) or complete an application form, available from a Post office. Allow up to 14 days for the cards to arrive.

For your vehicle:

Service
It makes sense to get your car serviced before you travel. At the very least, ensure the tyres have plenty of tread left and that coolant and oil levels are checked and topped up if required. Check them regularly during your time away.

Vehicle Registration Document
Police in many countries can demand that you prove you have the right to be driving your car. That means you need to show the registration document, or a suitable letter of authorisation if the registration document is not in your name. Remember you should never leave the registration document in the car.

Nationality plate
Your vehicle must display a nationality plate of an approved pattern, design and size.

MOT
If your car is more than three years old, make sure you take its current MOT test certificate with you.

Insurance
If you are planning a trip to Europe, you should find that your car insurance policy provides you with the minimum amount of cover you need. But it's important to contact your insurer before you go, to confirm exactly what level of cover you have and for how many days it will be valid.

Mechanical adjustments
Check the adjustments required for your headlights before you go. Beam deflectors are a legal requirement if you drive in Europe. They are generally sold at the ports, on ferries and in the Folkestone Eurotunnel terminal, but be warned – the instructions can be a little confusing! The alternative is to ask a local garage to do the job for you before you go. If you choose this, then make sure you shop around as prices for undertaking this very simple task vary enormously.

Equipment check-list
This checklist represents GEM's suggestions for what you should take with you in the car. Different countries have different rules about what's compulsory and these rules change from time to time. So it's important to check carefully before you set out. For country-by-country guidance, visit www.motoringassist.com/europe or see page IV of this atlas.

- Fire extinguisher
- First aid kit
- High-visibility jacket – one for each occupant
- Two warning triangles
- Replacement bulbs and fuses
- Spare spectacles (if worn) for each driver
- Snow chains for winter journeys into the mountains
- Camera and notebook. Keep in your glove compartment and record any collisions or damage for insurance purposes (if it is safe).

Contact details
Make sure you have all relevant emergency helpline numbers with you, including emergency services, breakdown assistance, the local British consulate and your insurance company. There are links to embassies and consulates around the world from the Foreign Office website. (www.fco.gov.uk) For information, the European emergency telephone number (our equivalent of 999) is 112.

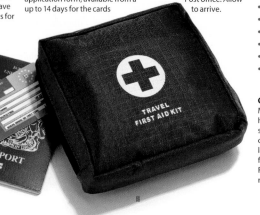

Romania (RO)

	🚗	🛣	🛤	🏭
Cars and motorcycles				
⊙	120/130	100	90	50
Vans				
⊙		110	90	80	40
Motorcycles				
⊙	100	80	80	50

For motor vehicles with trailers or if full driving licence has been held for less than one year, speed limits are 20kph lower than those listed above •Jeep-like vehicles: 70kph outside built-up areas but 60kph in all areas if diesel. For mopeds, the speed limit is 45 kph.

- Compulsory
- Under 12s not allowed in front and must use an appropriate restraint in the rear
- 🍷 0.00% △ Compulsory
- Compulsory 🧯 Compulsory
- 🔺 Compulsory ⊖ 18
- 📱 Only allowed with hands-free kit
- Compulsory outside built-up areas, compulsory everywhere for motorcycles
- ❄ Winter tyres compulsory Nov–Mar if roads are snow- or ice-covered, especially in mountainous areas
- ★ Compulsory road tax can be paid for at the border, post offices and some petrol stations. Price depends on emissions category and length of stay
- ★ It is illegal for vehicles to be dirty
- ★ On-the-spot fines imposed
- ★ Visibility vest compulsory

Russia (RUS)

	🚗	🛣	🛤	🏭
⊙	110	90	90	60/20
If licence held for under 2 years				
⊙	70	70	70	60/20

- Compulsory if fitted
- Under 12s permitted only in an appropriate child restraint
- 🍷 0.03 % △ Compulsory
- Compulsory 🧯 Compulsory
- 🔺 Compulsory ⊖ 17
- 📖 International Driving Permit with Russian translation, visa, green card endorsed for Russia, International Certificate for Motor Vehicles
- 📱 Only allowed with a hands-free kit
- Compulsory during the day
- ❄ Winter tyres compulsory 1 Dec–1 Mar
- ★ On-the-spot fines imposed
- ★ Picking up hitchhikers is prohibited
- ★ Radar detectors/blockers prohibited
- ★ Road tax payable at the border

Serbia (SRB)

	🚗	🛣	🛤	🏭
⊙	120	100	80	50
If towing				
⊙	80	80	80	50

Novice drivers limited to 90% of speed limit and not permitted to drive 11pm–5am.

- Compulsory in front and rear seats
- Age 3–12 must be in rear seats and wear seat belt or appropriate child restraint; under 3 in rear-facing child seat permitted in front only if airbag deactivated
- 🍷 0.029% • 0.0% for commercial drivers, motorcyclists, or if full licence held less than 1 year
- △ Compulsory 🧯 Compulsory
- 🧯 Compulsory 🔺 Compulsory
- ⊖ 18 (16 for motorbikes less than 125cc; 14 for mopeds)
- 📖 International Driving Permit, green card, insurance that is valid for Serbia or locally bought third-party insurance
- Compulsory
- ❄ Winter tyres compulsory Nov–Apr for vehicles up to 3.5 tonnes. Carrying snow chains recommended in winter as these may have to be fitted if driving on snow-covered roads, in accordance with signage.
- ★ 3-metre tow bar or rope
- ★ Spare wheel compulsory

- ★ On-the-spot fines imposed
- ★ Radar detectors prohibited
- ★ Tolls on motorways and some primary roads
- ★ Visibility vest compulsory

Slovakia (SK)

	🚗	🛣	🛤	🏭
⊙	130/90	90	90	50

- Compulsory
- Under 12 or below 150cm must be in rear in appropriate child restraint
- 🍷 0.0% △ Compulsory 🧯 Compulsory
- 🔺 Recommended
- ⊖ 18, 17 for motorbikes over 50cc, 15 for mopeds
- 📖 International driving permit, proof of health insurance
- 📱 Only allowed with a hands-free kit
- Compulsory at all times
- ❄ Winter tyres compulsory
- ★ On-the-spot fines imposed
- ★ Radar-detection equipment is prohibited
- ★ Tow rope recommended
- ★ Vignette required for motorways, car valid for 1 year, 30 days, 7 days; lorry vignettes carry a higher charge.
- ★ Visibility vests compulsory

Slovenia (SLO)

	🚗	🛣	🛤	🏭
⊙	130	110[1]	90[1]	50[2]
If towing				
⊙	80	80[1]	80[1]	50[2]

[1] 70 kph in urban areas, [2] 30 kph zones are increasingly common in cities. 50 kph in poor visibility or with snow chains

- Compulsory
- Below 150cm must use appropriate child restraint. A rear-facing baby seat may be used in front only if airbags are deactivated.
- 🍷 0.05% • 0.0% for commercial drivers, under 21s or less than one year with a full licence
- △ Compulsory 🧯 Compulsory
- 🧯 Compulsory 🔺 Recommended
- ⊖ 18 (motorbikes up to 125cc – 16, up to 350cc – 18)
- 📖 Licences without photographs must be accompanied by an International Driving Permit
- 📱 Only allowed with hands-free kit
- Must be used at all times
- ❄ Snow chains or winter tyres compulsory mid-Nov to mid-March, and in wintery conditions at other times. Max speed 50 kph. This limit also applies if visibility is below 50m.
- ★ On-the-spot fines imposed
- ★ Radar detectors prohibited
- ★ Vignettes valid for variety of periods compulsory for vehicles below 3.5 tonnes for toll roads. Write your vehicle registration number on the vignette before displaying it. For heavier vehicles electronic tolling system applies; several routes are cargo-traffic free during high tourist season.
- ★ Visibility vest compulsory

Spain (E)

	🚗	🛣	🛤	🏭
⊙	120*	100*	90	50*
If towing				
⊙	80	80	70	50*

*Urban motorways and dual carriageways 80 kph. 20 kph zones are being introduced in many cities

- Compulsory
- Under 135cm and below 12 must use appropriate child restraint and sit in rear.
- 🍷 0.049% • 0.029% if less than 2 years full licence or if vehicle is over 3.5 tonnes or carries more than 9 passengers
- △ Two compulsory (one for in front, one for behind)
- 🧯 Recommended 🔺 Compulsory
- 🔺 Recommended
- ⊖ 18 (21 for heavy vehicles; 16 for motorbikes up to 125cc)

- 📱 Hands-free only
- Compulsory for motorcycles and in poor daytime visibility and in tunnels for other vehicles.
- ❄ Snow chains recommended for mountainous areas in winter
- ★ Drivers who wear spectacles or contact lenses must carry a spare pair.
- ★ On-the-spot fines imposed
- ★ Radar-detection equipment is prohibited
- ★ Spare wheel compulsory
- ★ Tolls on motorways
- ★ Visibility vest compulsory

Sweden (S)

	🚗	🛣	🛤	🏭
⊙	90–120	80	70–100	30–60
If towing trailer with brakes				
⊙	80	80	70	50

- Compulsory in front and rear seats
- Under 15 or below 135cm must use an appropriate child restraint and may sit in the front only if airbag is deactivated; rear-facing baby seat permitted in front only if airbag deactivated.
- 🍷 0.019% △ Compulsory
- 🧯 Recommended 🔺 Recommended
- 🔺 Recommended ⊖ 18
- 📖 Licences without a photograph must be accompanied by photographic proof of identity, e.g. a passport
- LEZ Gothenberg, Helsingborg, Lund, Malmo, Mölndal and Stockholm have LEZs, progressively prohibiting older vehicles.
- Must be used at all times
- ❄ 1 Dec–31 Mar winter tyres, anti-freeze, screenwash additive and shovel compulsory
- ★ On-the-spot fines imposed
- ★ Radar-detection equipment is prohibited
- ★ Tow rope recommended
- ★ Visibility vest recommended

Switzerland (CH)

	🚗	🛣	🛤	🏭
⊙	120	80	80	50/30
If towing up to 1 tonne / over 1 tonne				
⊙	80	80	80/60	50/30

- Compulsory
- Up to 12 years or below 150 cm must use an appropriate child restraint. Children 6 and under must sit in the rear.
- 🍷 0.05%, but 0.0% for commercial drivers or with less than three years with a full licence
- △ Compulsory 🧯 Recommended
- 🧯 Recommended 🔺 Recommended
- ⊖ 18 (mopeds up to 50cc – 16)
- 📱 Only allowed with a hands-free kit
- Compulsory
- ❄ Winter tyres recommended Nov–Mar; snow chains compulsory in designated areas in poor winter weather
- ★ GPS must have fixed speed camera function deactivated; radar detectors prohibited
- ★ Motorways are all toll and for vehicles below 3.5 tonnes a vignette must be purchased at the border. The vignette is valid for one calendar year. Vehicles over 3.5 tonnes must have an electronic tag for travel on any road.
- ★ On-the-spot fines imposed
- ★ Pedestrians have right of way
- ★ Picking up hitchhikers is prohibited on motorways and main roads
- ★ Spectacles or contact lens wearers must carry a spare pair in their vehicle at all times

Turkey (TR)

	🚗	🛣	🛤	🏭
⊙	120	90	90	50
If towing				
⊙	80	80	80	40
Motorbikes				
⊙	80	70	70	50

- Compulsory if fitted
- Under 150 cm and below 36kg must use suitable child restraint. Under 3s can only travel in the front in a rear facing seat if the

airbag is deactivated. Children 3–12 may not travel in the front seat.

- 🍷 0.00%
- △ Two compulsory (one in front, one behind)
- 🧯 Compulsory 🔺 Compulsory
- 🔺 Compulsory ⊖ 18
- 📖 International driving permit advised, and required for use with licences without photographs; note that Turkey is in both Europe and Asia, green card/UK insurance that covers whole of Turkey or locally bought insurance, e-visa obtained in advance.
- 📱 Prohibited
- Compulsory in daylight hours
- ★ Spare wheel compulsory
- ★ On-the-spot fines imposed
- ★ Several motorways, and the Bosphorus bridges are toll roads
- ★ Tow rope and tool kit must be carried

Ukraine (UA)

	🚗	🛣	🛤	🏭
⊙	130	110	90	20/60
If towing				
⊙	80	80	80	20/60

If driving licence held less than 2 years, must not exceed 70 kph

- Compulsory in front and rear seats
- Under 12 and below 145cm must use an appropriate child restraint and sit in the rear
- 🍷 0.02% – if use of medication can be proved. Otherwise 0.00%
- △ Compulsory 🧯 Compulsory
- 🧯 Optional 🔺 Compulsory ⊖ 18
- 📖 International Driving Permit, visa, International Certificate for Motor Vehicles, green card
- 📱 No legislation
- Compulsory in poor daytime and from Oct–Apr
- ❄ Winter tyres compulsory Nov–Apr in snowy conditions
- ★ A road tax is payable on entry to the country.
- ★ On-the-spot fines imposed
- ★ Tow rope and tool kit recommended

United Kingdom (GB)

	🚗	🛣	🛤	🏭
⊙	112	112	96	48
If towing				
⊙	96	96	80	48

Several cities have introduced 32 kph (20 mph) zones away from main roads

- Compulsory in front seats and if fitted in rear seats
- Under 3 not allowed in front seats except with appropriate restraint, and in rear must use child restraint if available; in front 3–12 or under 135cm must use appropriate child restraint, in rear must use appropriate child restraint (or seat belt if no child restraint is available, e.g. because two occupied restraints prevent fitting of a third).
- 🍷 0.08% (England, Northern Ireland, Wales) • 0.05% (Scotland)
- △ Recommended 🧯 Recommended
- 🧯 Recommended 🔺 Recommended
- ⊖ 17 (16 for mopeds)
- 📱 Only allowed with hands-free kit
- LEZ London's LEZ operates by number-plate recognition; non-compliant vehicles face hefty daily charges. Foreign-registered vehicles must register.
- ★ Driving is on the left
- ★ On-the-spot fines imposed
- ★ Smoking is banned in all commercial vehicles
- ★ Some toll motorways, bridges and tunnels

Ski resorts

The resorts listed are popular ski centres, therefore road access to most is normally good and supported by road clearing during snow falls. However, mountain driving is never predictable and drivers should make sure they take suitable snow chains as well as emergency provisions and clothing. Listed for each resort are: the atlas page and grid square; the resort/minimum piste altitude (where only one figure is shown, they are at the same height) and maximum altitude of its own lifts; the number of lifts and gondolas (the total for lift-linked resorts); the season start and end dates (snow cover allowing); whether snow is augmented by cannon; the nearest town (with its distance in km) and, where available, the website and/or telephone number of the local tourist information centre or ski centre ('00' prefix required for calls from the UK).

The ❄ symbol indicates resorts with snow cannon

Andorra

Pyrenees

Pas de la Casa / Grau Roig 146 B2 ❄ 2050–2640m • 31 lifts • Dec–Apr • Andorra La Vella (30km) www.pasdelacasa.com • *Access via Envalira Pass (2407m), highest in Pyrenees, snow chains essential.*

Austria

Alps

Bad Gastein 109 B4 ❄ 1050/1100–2700m • 50 lifts • Dec–Mar • St Johann im Pongau (45km) ℹ +43 6432 3393 0 www.gastein.com/en

Bad Hofgastein 109 B4 ❄ 860–2295m • 50 lifts • Dec–Mar • St Johann im Pongau (40km) ℹ +43 6432 3393 0 www.gastein.com/en

Bad Kleinkirchheim 109 C4 ❄ 1070–2310m • 27 lifts • Dec–Mar • Villach (35km) ℹ +43 4240 8212 www.badkleinkirchheim.at

Ehrwald 108 B1 ❄ 1000–2965m • 24 lifts • Dec–Apr • Imst (30km) ℹ +43 5673 2501 www.wetterstein-bahnen.at/en

Innsbruck 108 B2 ❄ 574/850–3200m • 59 lifts • Dec–Apr • Innsbruck ℹ +43 512 5356 0 www.innsbruck.info/en/ • *Motorway normally clear. The motorway through to Italy and through the Arlberg Tunnel are both toll roads.*

Ischgl 107 B5 ❄ 1880/1400–2900m • 82 lifts • Dec–May • Landeck (25km) ℹ +43 50990 100 www.ischgl.com • *Car entry to resort prohibited between 2200hrs and 0600hrs. Lift linked to Samnaun (Switzerland).*

Kaprun 109 B3 ❄ 800/770–3030m, • 25 lifts • Nov–Apr • Zell am See (10km) ℹ +43 6542 770 www.zellamsee-kaprun.com

Kirchberg in Tirol 109 B3 ❄ 860–2000m • 197 lifts • Nov–Apr • Kitzbühel (6km) www.kitzbueheler-alpen.com/en ℹ +43 57507 2100 • *Easily reached from Munich International Airport (120 km)*

Kitzbühel (Brixen im Thale) 109 B3 ❄ 800/790–2000m • 197 lifts • Dec–Apr • Wörgl (40km) ℹ +43 57057 2000 www.kitzbueheler-alpen.com/en

Lech/Oberlech 107 B5 ❄ 1450–2810m • 97 lifts • Dec–Apr • Bludenz (50km) ℹ +43 5583 2161 0 www.lechzuers.com • *Roads normally cleared but keep chains accessible because of altitude. Linked to the other Arlberg resorts.*

Mayrhofen 108 B2 ❄ 630–2500m • 57 lifts • Dec–Apr • Jenbach (35km) ℹ +43 5285 6760 www.mayrhofen.at • *Chains rarely required.*

Obertauern 109 B4 ❄ 1740/1640–2350m • 26 lifts • Dec–Apr • Radstadt (20km) ℹ +43 6456 7252 www.obertauern.com • *Roads normally cleared but chain accessibility recommended. Camper vans and caravans not allowed; park these in Radstadt*

Saalbach Hinterglemm 109 B3 ❄ 1000/1030–2100m • 52 lifts • Nov–Apr • Zell am See (19km) ℹ +43 6541 6800 68 www.saalbach.com • *Both village centres are pedestrianised and there is a good ski bus service during the daytime*

St Anton am Arlberg 107 B5 ❄ 1300–2810m • 97 lifts • Dec–Apr • Innsbruck (104km) ℹ +43 5446 22690 www.stantonamarlberg.com • *Linked to the other Arlberg resorts.*

Schladming 109 B4 ❄ 745–1900m • 45 lifts • Dec–Mar • Schladming ℹ + 43 36 87 233 10 www.schladming-dachstein.at

Serfaus 108 B1 ❄ 1427/1200–2820m • 68 lifts • Dec–Apr • Landeck (30km) ℹ +43 5476 6239 www.serfaus-fiss-ladis.at • *Private vehicles banned from village. Use Dorfbahn Serfaus, an underground funicular that runs on an air cushion.*

Sölden 108 C2 ❄ 1380–3250m, • 33 lifts • Oct–Apr • Imst (50km) ℹ +43 57200 200 www.soelden.com • *Roads normally cleared but snow chains recommended because of altitude. The route from Italy and the south over the Timmelsjoch via Obergurgl is closed Oct–May and anyone arriving from the south should use the Brenner Pass motorway.*

Zell am See 109 B3 ❄ 750–1950m • 28 lifts • Dec–Mar • Zell am See ℹ +43 6542 770 www.zellamsee-kaprun.com • *Low altitude, so good access and no mountain passes to cross.*

Zell im Zillertal (Zell am Ziller) 109 B3 ❄ 580/930–2410m • 22 lifts • Dec–Apr • Jenbach (25km) ℹ +43 5282 7165–226 www.zillertalarena.com

Zürs 107 B5 ❄ 1720/1700–2450m • 87 lifts • Dec–Apr • Bludenz (30km) ℹ +43 5583 2161 251 www.lechzuers.com • *Roads normally cleared but keep chains accessible because of altitude. Village has garage with 24-hour self-service gas/petrol, breakdown service and wheel chains supply. Linked to the other Arlberg resorts.*

France

Alps

Alpe d'Huez 118 B3 ❄ 1860–3330m • 85 lifts • Dec–Apr • Grenoble (63km) www.alpedhuez.com • *Snow chains may be required on access road to resort.*

Avoriaz 118 A3 ❄ 1800/1100–2280m • 35 lifts • Dec–May • Morzine (14km) ℹ +33 4 50 74 02 11 www.avoriaz.com/en • *Chains may be required for access road from Morzine. Car-free resort, park on edge of village.*

Chamonix-Mont-Blanc 119 B3 ❄ 1035–3840m • 49 lifts • Dec–Apr • Martigny (38km) www.chamonix.com

Chamrousse 118 B2 ❄ 1700/1420–2250m • 26 lifts • Dec–Apr • Grenoble (30km) www.chamrousse.com • *Roads normally cleared, keep chains accessible because of altitude.*

Châtel 119 A3 ❄ 1200/1110–2200m • 41 lifts • Dec–Apr • Thonon-Les-Bains (35km) ℹ +33 4 50 73 22 44 www.chatel.com

Courchevel 118 B3 ❄ 1300–2470m • 67 lifts • Dec–Apr • Moûtiers (23km) www.courchevel.com • *Roads normally cleared but keep chains accessible. Traffic 'discouraged' within the four resort bases.*

Flaine 118 A3 ❄ 1600–2500m • 26 lifts • Dec–Apr • Cluses (25km) ℹ +33 4 50 90 80 01 www.flaine.com • *Keep chains accessible for D6 from Cluses to Flaine. Car access for depositing luggage and passengers only. 1500-space car park outside resort. Near Sixt-Fer-á-Cheval.*

La Clusaz 118 B3 ❄ 1100–2600m • 55 lifts • Dec–Apr • Annecy (32km) www.laclusaz.com • *Roads normally clear but keep chains accessible for final road from Annecy.*

La Plagne 118 B3 ❄ 2500/1250–3250m • 109 lifts • Dec–Apr Moûtiers (32km) www.la-plagne.com • *Ten different centres up to 2100m altitude. Road access via Bozel, Landry or Aime normally cleared. Linked to Les Arcs by cablecar*

Les Arcs 119 B3 ❄ 1600/1200–3230m • 77 lifts • Dec–May • Bourg-St-Maurice (15km) ℹ +33 4 79 07 12 57 www.lesarcs.com • *Four base areas up to 2000 metres; keep chains accessible. Pay parking at edge of each base resort. Linked to La Plagne by cablecar*

Les Carroz d'Araches 118 A3 ❄ 1140–2500m • 80 lifts • Dec–Apr • Cluses (13km) http://winter.lescarroz.com

Les Deux-Alpes 118 C3 ❄ 1650/1300–3600m • 55 lifts • Dec–Apr • Grenoble (75km) ℹ +33 4 76 79 22 00 www.les2alpes.com/en • *Roads normally cleared, however snow chains recommended for D213 up from valley road (D1091).*

Les Gets 118 A3 ❄ 1170/1000–2000m • 52 lifts • Dec–Apr • Cluses (18km) ℹ +33 4 50 74 74 74 www.lesgets.com

Les Ménuires 118 B3 ❄ 1815/1850–3200m • 40 lifts • Dec–Apr • Moûtiers (27km) www.lesmenuires.com • *Keep chains accessible for D117 from Moûtiers.*

Les Sept Laux Prapoutel 118 B3 ❄ 1350–2400m, • 24 lifts • Dec–Apr • Grenoble (38km) www.les7laux.com (in French only) • *Roads normally cleared, however keep chains accessible for mountain road up from the A41 motorway. Near St Sorlin d'Arves.*

Megève 118 B3 ❄ 1100/1050–2350m • 79 lifts • Dec–Apr • Sallanches (12km) www.megeve.com

Méribel 118 B3 ❄ 1400/1100–2950m • 61 lifts • Dec–May • Moûtiers (18km) ℹ +33 4 79 08 60 01 www.meribel.net • *Keep chains accessible for 18km to resort on D90 from Moûtiers.*

Morzine 118 A3 ❄ 1000–2460m • 67 lifts, • Dec–Apr • Thonon-Les-Bains (30km) ℹ +33 4 50 74 72 72 http://en.morzine-avoriaz.com

Pra Loup 132 A2 ❄ 1500–2600m • 53 lifts • Dec–Apr • Barcelonnette (10km) www.praloup.com • *Roads normally cleared but chains accessibility recommended.*

Risoul 118 C3 ❄ 1850/1650–2750m • 59 lifts • Dec–Apr • Briançon (40km) ℹ +33 4 92 46 02 60 www.risoul.com • *Keep chains accessible. Near Guillestre. Linked with Vars Les Claux*

St-Gervais Mont-Blanc 118 B3 ❄ 850/1150–2350m • 27 lifts • Dec–Apr • Sallanches (10km) ℹ +33 4 50 47 76 08 www.saintgervais.com/en

Serre Chevalier 118 C3 ❄ 1350/1200–2800m • 77 lifts • Dec–Apr • Briançon (10km) ℹ + 33 4 92 24 98 98 www.serre-chevalier.com • *Made up of 13 small villages along the valley road, which is normally cleared.*

Tignes 119 B3 ❄ 2100/1550–3450m • 87 lifts • Jan–Dec • Bourg St Maurice (26km) ℹ +33 4 79 40 04 40 www.tignes.net • *Keep chains accessible because of altitude. Linked to Val d'Isère.*

Val d'Isère 119 B3 ❄ 1850/1550–3450m • 87 lifts • Dec–Apr • Bourg-St-Maurice (30km) www.valdisere.com • *Roads normally cleared but keep chains accessible.*

Val Thorens 118 B3 ❄ 2300/1850–3200m • 29 lifts • Dec–Apr • Moûtiers (37km) ℹ +33 4 79 00 08 08 www.les3vallees.com/en/ski-resort/val-thorens • *Chains essential – highest ski resort in Europe. Obligatory paid parking on edge of resort.*

Valloire 118 B3 ❄ 1430–2600m • 34 lifts • Dec–Apr • Modane (20km) ℹ +33 4 79 59 03 96 www.valloire.net • *Road normally clear up to the Col du Galbier, to the south of the resort, which is closed from 1st November to 1st June. Linked to Valmeinier.*

Valmeinier 118 B3 ❄ 1500–2600m • 34 lifts • Dec–Apr • St Michel de Maurienne (47km) www.valmeinier.com • *Access from north on D1006 / D902. Col du Galbier, to the south of the resort closed from 1st November to 1st June. Linked to Valloire.*

Valmorel 118 B3 ❄ 1400–2550m • 90 lifts • Dec–Apr • Moûtiers (15km) www.valmorel.com • *Near St Jean-de-Belleville. Linked with ski areas of Doucy-Combelouvière and St François-Longchamp.*

Vars Les Claux 118 C3 ❄ 1850/1650–2750m • 59 lifts • Dec–Apr • Briançon (40km) ℹ +33 4 92 46 51 31 www.vars.com/en/winter • *Four base resorts up to 1850 metres. Keep chains accessible. Linked with Risoul.*

Villard de Lans 118 B2 ❄ 1050/1160–2170m • 28 lifts • Dec–Apr • Grenoble (32km) ℹ +33 4 76 95 10 38 www.villarddelans.com

Pyrenees

Font-Romeu 146 B3 ❄ 1800/1600–2200m • 25 lifts • Nov–Apr • Perpignan (87km) www.font-romeu.fr • *Roads normally cleared but keep chains accessible.*

Saint-Lary Soulan 145 B4 ❄ 830/1650/1700–2515m • 31 lifts • Dec–Mar • Tarbes (75km) ℹ +33 5 62 39 50 81 www.saintlary.com • *Access roads constantly cleared of snow.*

Vosges

La Bresse-Hohneck 106 A1 ❄ 600–1370m • 33 lifts • Dec–Mar • Cornimont (6km) ℹ +33 3 29 25 41 29 www.labresse.net

Germany

Alps

Garmisch-Partenkirchen 108 B2 ❄ 700–2830m • 38 lifts • Dec–Apr • Munich (95km) ℹ +49 8821 180 700 www.gapa.de • *Roads usually clear, chains rarely needed.*

Oberaudorf 108 B3 ❄ 480–1850m • 30 lifts • Dec–Apr • Kufstein (15km) www.oberaudorf.de • *Motorway normally kept clear. Near Bayrischzell.*

Oberstdorf 107 B5 820/830–2200m • 26 lifts • Dec–Apr • Sonthofen (15km) ℹ +49 8322 7000 www.oberstdorf.de

Rothaargebirge

Winterberg 81 A4 ❄ 700/620–830m • 19 lifts • Dec–Mar • Brilon (30km) ℹ +49 2981 925 00 www.winterberg.de (German only) • *Roads usually cleared, chains rarely required.*

Greece

Central Greece

Mount Parnassos: Kelaria-Fterolakka 182 E4 1640–2260m • 14 lifts • Dec–Apr • Amfiklia www.parnassos-ski.gr (Greek only)

Mount Parnassos: Gerondovrahos 182 E4 1800–1900m • 3 lifts • Dec–Apr • Amfiklia ℹ +30 29444 70371

Peloponnisos

Mount Helmos: Kalavrita Ski Centre 184 A3 1650–2100m • 7 lifts • Dec–Mar • Kalavrita ℹ +30 276920 24451-2 www.kalavrita-ski.gr (in Greek only)

Mount Menalo: Ostrakina 184 B3 1500–1600m • 4 lifts • Dec–Mar • Tripoli ℹ +30 27960 22227

Macedonia

Mount Falakro: Agio Pnevma 183 B6 1720/1620–2230m • 7 lifts • Dec–Apr • Drama ℹ + 30 25210 23691

Mount Vermio: Seli 182 C4 1500–1900m • 8 lifts • Dec–Mar • Kozani ℹ +30 23310 26237 www.seli-ski.gr (in Greek)

Mount Vermio: Tria-Pente Pigadia 182 C3 ❄ 1420–2005m • 5 lifts • Dec–Mar • Ptolemaida ℹ +30 23320 44464

Mount Verno: Vigla 182 C3 1650–1900m •
5 lifts • Dec–Mar • Florina ☎ +30 23850 22354
💻 www.vigla-ski.gr (in Greek)

Mount Vrondous: Lailias 183 B5
1600–1850m • 4 lifts • Dec–Mar • Serres
☎ +30 23210 53790

Thessalia

Mount Pilio: Agriolefkes 183 D5
1300–1500m • 5 lifts • Dec–Mar • Volos
☎ +30 24280 73719

Italy
Alps

Bardonecchia 118 B3 ❄ 1312–2750m •
21 lifts • Dec–Apr • Bardonecchia
💻 www.bardonecchiaski.com
• Resort reached through the 11km Frejus tunnel
from France, roads normally cleared.

Bórmio 107 C5 ❄ 1200/1230–3020m •
24 lifts • Dec–Apr • Tirano (40km)
💻 www.bormio.com • Tolls payable in Ponte del
Gallo Tunnel, open 0800hrs–2000hrs.

Breuil-Cervinia 119 B4 ❄ 2050–3500m •
21 lifts • Jan–Dec • Aosta (54km)
☎ +39 166 944311 💻 www.cervinia.it • Snow
chains strongly recommended. Bus from Milan
airport.

Courmayeur 119 B3 ❄ 1200–2760m •
21 lifts • Dec–Apr • Aosta (40km)
💻 www.courmayeurmontblanc.it
• Access through the Mont Blanc tunnel from
France. Roads constantly cleared.

Limone Piemonte 133 A3 ❄
1000/1050–2050m • 29 lifts • Dec–Apr •
Cuneo (27km) 💻 www.limoneturismo.it
• Roads normally cleared, chains rarely required.

Livigno 107 C5 ❄ 1800–3000m • 31 lifts •
Nov–May • Zernez (CH) (27km)
💻 www.livigno.com • Keep chains accessible.
The traffic direction through Munt la Schera
Tunnel to/from Zernez is regulated on Saturdays.
Check in advance.

Sestrière 119 C3 ❄ 2035/1840–2840m •
92 lifts • Dec–Apr • Oulx (22km)
💻 www.sestriere-online.com
• One of Europe's highest resorts; although roads
are normally cleared keep chains accessible.

Appennines

Roccaraso – Aremogna 169 B4 ❄
1285/1240–2140m • 24 lifts • Dec–Apr •
Castel di Sangro (7km)
💻 https://roccaraso.net (Italian only)

Dolomites

Andalo – Fai della Paganella 121 A3 ❄
1042/1050/2125m • 17 lifts • Dec–Apr • Trento
(40km) 💻 www.visitdolomitipaganella.it
☎ +39 461 585836

Arabba 108 C2 ❄ 1600/1450–2950m •
29 lifts • Dec–Mar • Brunico (45km)
☎ +39 436 79130 💻 www.arabba.it
• Roads normally cleared but keep chains
accessible.

Cortina d'Ampezzo 108 C3 ❄
1224/1050–2930m • 37 lifts • Dec–Apr •
Belluno (72km) ☎ +39 436 869086
💻 www.dolomiti.org/it/cortina
• Access from north on route 51 over the
Cimabanche Pass may require chains.

Corvara (Alta Badia) 108 C2 ❄
1568–2500m • 56 lifts • Dec–Apr • Brunico
(38km) 💻 www.altabadia.it • Roads normally
clear but keep chains accessible.

Madonna di Campiglio 121 A3 ❄
1550/1500–2600m • 72 lifts • Dec–Apr •
Trento (60km) ☎ +39 465 447501
💻 www.campigliodolomiti.it/homepage
• Roads normally cleared but keep chains
accessible. Linked to Folgarida and Marilleva.

Moena di Fassa (Sorte/Ronchi) 108 C2 ❄
1184/1450–2520m • 8 lifts • Dec–Apr •
Bolzano (40km) 💻 www.fassa.com

**Selva di Val Gardena/Wolkenstein Groden
108 C2** ❄ 1563/1570–2450m • 81 lifts •
Dec–Apr • Bolzano (40km) ☎ +39 471 777777
💻 www.valgardena.it • Roads normally cleared
but keep chains accessible.

Norway

Hemsedal 47 B5 ❄ 700/640–1450m • 24 lifts •
Nov–May • Honefoss (150km) ☎ +47 32 055030
💻 www.hemsedal.com • Be prepared for
extreme weather conditions.

Slovakia

Chopok (Jasna-Chopok) 99 C3 ❄
900/950–1840m • 17 lifts • Dec–Apr • Jasna
☎ +421 907 886644 💻 www.jasna.sk

Donovaly 99 C3 ❄ 913–1360m • 17 lifts •
Nov–Apr • Ruzomberok ☎ +421 48 4199900
💻 www.parksnow.sk/zima/en

Martinské Hole 98 B2 1250/1150–1456m •
8 lifts • Nov–May • Zilina ☎ +421 43 430 6000
💻 http://leto.martinky.com/sk (Slovak only)

Plejsy 99 C4 470–912m • 9 lifts • Dec–Mar •
Krompachy ☎ +421 53 429 8015
💻 www.plejsy.sk

Strbske Pleso 99 B4 1380–1825m •
7 lifts • Dec–Mar • Poprad ☎ +421 917 682 260
💻 www.vt.sk

Slovenia
Julijske Alpe

Kanin (Bovec) 122 A2 460/1690–2293m •
5 lifts • Dec–Apr • Bovec ☎ www.boveckanin.si

Kranjska Gora 122 A2 ❄ 800–1210m • 19 lifts
• Dec–Mar • Kranjska Gora ☎ +386 4 5809 440
💻 www.kranjska-gora.si

Vogel 122 A2 570–1800m • 8 lifts • Dec–Apr •
Bohinjska Bistrica ☎ +386 4 5729 712
💻 www.vogel.si

Kawiniške Savinjske Alpe

Krvavec 122 A3 ❄ 1450–1970m • 10 lifts •
Dec–Apr • Kranj ☎ 386 4 25 25 911
💻 http://www.rtc-krvavec.si/en

Pohorje

Rogla 123 A4 1517/1050–1500m • 13 lifts •
Dec–Apr • Slovenska Bistrica
☎ +386 3 75 77 100 💻 www.rogla.eu/en

Spain
Pyrenees

Baqueira-Beret/Bonaigua 145 B4 ❄ 1500–
2500m • 33 lifts • Dec–Apr • Vielha (15km)
☎ +34 902 415 415 💻 www.baqueira.es
• Roads normally clear but keep chains
accessible. Near Salardú.

Sistema Penibetico

Sierra Nevada 163 A4 ❄ 2100–3300m •
24 lifts • Dec–May • Granada (32km)
☎ +34 902 70 80 90 💻 http://sierranevada.es
• Access road designed to be avalanche safe and
is snow cleared.

Sweden

Idre Fjäll 199 D9 ❄ 590–890m •
33 lifts • Nov–Apr • Mora (140km)
☎ +46 253 41000 💻 www.idrefjall.se
• Be prepared for extreme weather conditions.

Sälen 49 A5 360m • 100 lifts • Nov–Apr •
Malung (70km) ☎ +46 771 84 00 00
💻 www.skistar.com/salen
• Be prepared for extreme weather conditions.

Switzerland
Alps

Adelboden 106 C2 1353m • 55 lifts • Dec–Apr
• Frutigen (15km) ☎ +41 33 673 80 80
💻 www.adelboden.ch • Linked with Lenk.

Arosa 107 C4 1800/1740–2650m • 16 lifts •
Dec–Apr • Chur (30km) ☎ +41 81 378 70 20
💻 www.arosa.ch • Roads cleared but keep
chains accessible due to high altitude.

Crans Montana 119 A4 ❄ 1500–3000m •
34 lifts • Dec–Apr, Jul-Oct • Sierre (15km)
☎ +41 848 22 10 12
💻 www.crans-montana.ch
• Roads normally cleared but keep chains
accessible for ascent from Sierre.

Davos 107 C4 ❄ 1560/1100–2840m • 38 lifts •
Nov–Apr • Davos. ☎ +41 81 415 21 21
💻 www.davos.ch

Engelberg 106 C3 ❄ 1000/1050–3020m •
26 lifts • Nov–May • Luzern (39km)
☎ +41 41 639 77 77 💻 www.engelberg.ch
• Straight access road normally cleared.

Flums (Flumserberg) 107 B4 ❄
1400/1000–2220m • 17 lifts • Dec–Apr •
Buchs (25km) ☎ +41 81 720 18 18
💻 www.flumserberg.ch • Roads normally
cleared, but 1000-metre vertical ascent; keep
chains accessible.

Grindelwald 106 C3 ❄ 1050–2950m •
39 lifts • Dec–Apr • Interlaken (20km)
☎ +41 33 854 12 12 💻 www.jungfrauregion.ch
• Linked with Wengen.

Gstaad – Saanenland 106 C2 ❄
1050/950–3000m • 74 lifts • Dec–Apr • Gstaad
☎ +41 33 748 81 81 💻 www.gstaad.ch
• Linked to Anzère.

Klosters 107 C4 ❄ 1191/1110–2840m •
52 lifts • Dec–Apr • Davos (10km).
☎ +41 81 410 20 20 💻 www.davos.ch/klosters
• Roads normally clear but keep chains
accessible.

Leysin 119 A4 ❄ 2260–2330m • 16 lifts •
Dec–Apr • Aigle (6km) ☎ +41 24 493 33 00
💻 www.aigle-leysin-lesmosses.ch

Mürren 106 C2 ❄ 1650–2970m • 12 lifts •
Dec–Apr • Interlaken (18km)
☎ +41 33 856 86 86 💻 www.muerren.ch
• No road access. Park in Strechelberg (1500 free
places) and take the two-stage cable car.

Nendaz 119 A4 ❄ 1365/1400–3300m •
20 lifts • Nov–Apr • Sion (16km)
☎ +41 27 289 55 89 💻 www.nendaz.ch
• Roads normally cleared, however keep chains
accessible for ascent from Sion. Near Vex.

Saas-Fee 119 A4 ❄ 1800–3500m • 23 lifts •
Jan–Dec • Brig (35km) ☎ +41 27 958 18 58
💻 www.saas-fee.ch/en/
• Roads normally cleared but keep chains
accessible because of altitude.

St Moritz 107 C4 ❄ 1856/1730–3300m •
24 lifts • Nov–May • Chur (89km)
☎ +41 81 837 33 33 💻 www.stmoritz.ch
• Roads normally cleared but keep chains
accessible.

Samnaun 107 C5 ❄ 1846/1400–2900m •
82 lifts • Dec–May • Scuol (30km)
☎ +41 81 861 88 30 💻 www.engadin.com/en
• Roads normally cleared but keep chains
accessible. Lift linked to Ischgl (Austria).

Verbier 119 A4 ❄ 1500–3330m • 17 lifts •
Nov–Apr • Martigny (27km)
☎ +41 27 775 38 88 💻 www.verbier.ch
• Roads normally cleared.

Villars-Gryon 119 A4 ❄ 1253/1200–2100m •
16 lifts • Dec–Apr, Jun–Jul • Montreux (35km)
☎ +41 24 495 32 32 💻 www.villars.ch
• Roads normally cleared but keep chains
accessible for ascent from N9. Near Bex.

Wengen 106 C2 ❄ 1270–2320m • 39 lifts •
Dec–Apr • Interlaken (12km)
☎ +41 33 856 85 85 💻 http://wengen.ch
• No road access. Park at Lauterbrunnen and take
mountain railway. Linked with Grindelwald.

Zermatt 119 A4 ❄ 1620–3900m • 40 lifts •
all year • Brig (42km) ☎ +41 27 966 81 00
💻 www.zermatt.ch
• Cars not permitted in resort, park in Täsch (3km)
and take shuttle train.

Turkey
North Anatolian Mountains

Uludag 186 B4 1770–2320m • 15 lifts •
Dec–Mar • Bursa (36km) 💻 http://skiingturkey.
com/resorts/uludag.html

*To the best of the Publisher's knowledge the information in this
table was correct at the time of going to press. No responsibility can
be accepted for any errors or their consequences.*

Skiing near Valmorel, France
Jacques Pierre / hemis.fr / Alamy

300 greatest sights of Europe

For entries with no website listed, use that given for the national tourist board.

Albania Shqipëria
www.albania.al

Berat
Fascinating old town with picturesque Ottoman Empire buildings and traditional Balkan domestic architecture. www.albania.al/destination/12/berati **182 C1**

Tirana Tiranë
Capital of Albania. Skanderbeg Square has main historic buildings. Also: 18c Haxhi Ethem Bey Mosque; Art Gallery (Albanian); National Museum of History. Nearby: medieval Krujë; Roman monuments. www.albania.al/destination/8/tirana **182 B1**

Austria Österreich
www.austria.info

Bregenz
Lakeside town bordering Germany, Liechtenstein, Switzerland. Locals, known as Vorarlbergers, have their own dialect. The Martinsturm Roman to 17c tower, 17c town hall and Seekapelle, Kunsthaus modern art museum, Vorarlberger Landesmuseum, Festspielhaus. www.austria.info/uk/where-to-go/cities/bregenz **107 B4**

Graz
University town, seat of imperial court to 1619. Historic centre around Hauptplatz. Imperial monuments: Burg; mausoleum of Ferdinand II; towers of 16c schloss; 17c Schloss Eggenberg (with Old Gallery). Also: 16c Town Hall; Zeughaus; 15c cathedral; New Gallery (good 19–20c); Kunsthaus (modern art). www.graztourismus.at **110 B2**

▲ Melk Abbey, Austria

Innsbruck
Old town is reached by Maria-Theresien-Strasse with famous views. Buildings: Goldenes Dachl (1490s); 18c cathedral; remains of Hofburg imperial residence; 16c Hofkirche (tomb of Maximilian I). www.austria.info/us/where-to-go/cities/innsbruck **108 B2**

Krems
On a hill above the Danube, medieval quarter has Renaissance mansions. Also: Gothic Piaristenkirche; Museumkrems; Kunsthalle (modern art). http://www.krems.gv.at/Tourismus/English_version/Tourism **97 C3**

Linz
Port on the Danube. Historic buildings are concentrated on Hauptplatz below the imperial 15c schloss.

Notable: Baroque Old Cathedral; 16c Town Hall; Old Castle Museum; Lentos Art Museum. www.linztourismus.at **96 C2**

Melk
Set on a rocky hill above the Danube, the fortified abbey is the greatest Baroque achievement in Austria – particularly the Grand Library and abbey church. www.stiftmelk.at **110 A2**

Salzburg
Set in subalpine scenery, the town was associated with powerful 16–17c prince-archbishops. The 17c cathedral has a complex of archiepiscopal buildings: the Residence and its gallery (19c); the 13c Franciscan Church (notable altar). Also: Mozart's birthplace; Schloss Mirabell; Salzburg Museum; the Hohensalzburg fortress; the Collegiate Church of St Peter (cemetery, catacombs); Museum of Modern Art at the Mönschberg and Rupertinum. www.austria.info/us/where-to-go/cities/salzburg **109 B4**

Salzkammergut
Natural beauty with 76 lakes (Wolfgangersee, Altersee, Traunsee, Grundlsee) in mountain scenery. Attractive villages (St Wolfgang) and towns (Bad Ischl, Gmunden) include Hallstatt, famous for Celtic remains. www.salzkammergut.at **109 B4**

Vienna Wien
Capital of Austria, the historic centre lies within the Ring. Churches: Gothic St Stephen's Cathedral; 17c Imperial Vault; 14c Augustine Church; 14c Church of the Teutonic Order (treasure); 18c Baroque churches (Jesuit Church, Franciscan Church, St Peter, St Charles). Imperial residences: Hofburg; Schönbrunn. Architecture of Historicism on Ringstrasse (from 1857). Art Nouveau: station pavilions, Secession Building, Postsparkasse, Looshaus, Majolicahaus. Museums: Art History Museum (antiquities, old masters), Cathedral and Diocesan Museum (15c), Albertina (graphic arts), Liechtenstein Museum (old masters), Museum of Applied Arts, Museum of Modern Art (MUMOK), Leopold Museum, Belvedere (Gothic, Baroque, 19–20c); AzW (architecture); Vienna Museum. www.wien.info **111 A3**

Belgium Belgique
http://walloniabelgiumtourism.co.uk

Antwerp Antwerpen
City with many tall gabled Flemish houses on the river. Heart of the city is Great Market with 16–17c guildhouses and Town Hall. Charles Borromeus Church (Baroque). 14–16c Gothic cathedral has Rubens paintings. Rubens also at the Rubens House and his burial place in St Jacob's Church. Excellent museums: Mayer van den Bergh Museum (applied arts); Koninklijk Museum of Fine Arts (Flemish, Belgian); MAS (ethnography, folklore, shipping); Muhka (modern art). www.visitantwerpen.be **79 A4**

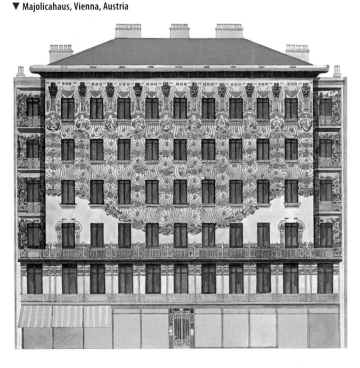

▼ Majolicahaus, Vienna, Austria

Bruges Brugge

Well-preserved medieval town with narrow streets and canals. Main squares: the Market with 13c Belfort and covered market; the Burg with Basilica of the Holy Blood and Town Hall. The collections of Groeninge Museum and Memling museum in St Jans Hospital include 15c Flemish masters. The Onze Lieve Vrouwekerk has a famous *Madonna and Child* by Michelangelo www.visitbruges.be **78 A3**

Brussels Bruxelles

Capital of Belgium. The Lower Town is centred on the enormous Grand Place with Hôtel de Ville and rebuilt guildhouses. Symbols of the city include the 'Manneken Pis' and Atomium (giant model of a molecule). The 13c Notre Dame de la Chapelle is the oldest church. The Upper Town contains: Gothic cathedral; Neoclassical Place Royale; 18c King's Palace; Royal Museums of Fine Arts (old and modern masters) Magritte Museum; MRAH (art and historical artefacts); BELvue museum (in the Bellevue Residence). Also: much Art Nouveau (Horta Museum, Hôtel Tassel, Hôtel Solvay); Place du Petit Sablon and Place du Grand Sablon; 19c Palais de Justice. https://visit.brussels/en **79 B4**

Ghent Gent

Medieval town built on islands surrounded by canals and rivers. Views from Pont St-Michel. The Graslei and Koornlei quays have Flemish guild houses. The Gothic cathedral has famous Van Eyck altarpiece. Also: Belfort; Cloth Market; Gothic Town Hall; Gravensteen. Museums: STAM Museum in Bijloke Abbey (provincial and applied art); Museum of Fine Arts (old masters). https://visit.gent.be/en **79 A3**

Namur

Reconstructed medieval citadel is the major sight of Namur, which also has a cathedral and provincial museums. www.namurtourisme.be/index.php **79 B4**

Tournai

The Romanesque-Gothic cathedral is Belgium's finest (much excellent art). Fine Arts Museum has a good collection (15–20c). www.visittournai.be/pratique/office-du-tourisme/article/tourist-office?lang=en **78 B3**

▼ Town Hall, Antwerp, Belgium

Bulgaria Bulgariya

http://bulgariatravel.org

Black Sea Coast

Beautiful unspoiled beaches (Zlatni Pyasŭtsi). The delightful resort Varna is popular. Nesebŭr is famous for Byzantine churches. Also: Danube Delta in Hungary. **17 D7**

Koprivshtitsa

Beautiful village known both for its half-timbered houses and links with the April Rising of 1876. Six house museums amongst which the Lyutov House and the Oslekov House, plus the birthplaces of Georgi Benkovski, Dimcho Debelyanov, Todor Kableshkov, and Lyuben Karavelov. http://bulgariatravel.org/en/object/18/Koprivshtica

Plovdiv

City set spectacularly on three hills. The old town has buildings from many periods: 2c Roman stadium and amphitheatre; 14c Dzumaiya Mosque; Archaeological Museum; 19c Ethnographic Museum. Nearby: Bačkovo Monastery (frescoes). http://bulgariatravel.org/en/object/306/plovdiv_grad **183 A6**

Rila

Bulgaria's finest monastery, set in the most beautiful scenery of the Rila mountains. The church is richly decorated with frescoes. www.rilamonastery.pmg-blg.com **183 A5**

Sofia Sofiya

Capital of Bulgaria. Sights: exceptional neo-Byzantine cathedral; Church of St Sofia; St Alexander Nevsky Cathedral; Boyana church; 4c rotunda of St George (frescoes); Byzantine Boyana Church (frescoes) on panoramic Mount Vitoša. Museums: National Historical Museum (particularly for Thracian artefacts); National Art Gallery (icons, Bulgarian art). http://bulgariatravel.org/en/object/234/sofia **17 D5**

Veliko Tŭrnovo

Medieval capital with narrow streets. Notable buildings: House of the Little Monkey; Hadji Nicoli Inn; ruins of medieval citadel; Baudouin Tower; churches of the Forty Martyrs and of SS Peter and Paul (frescoes); 14c Monastery of the Transfiguration. http://bulgariatravel.org/en/object/15/veliko_tyrnovo_grad **17 D6**

Croatia Hrvatska

http://croatia.hr/en-GB

Dalmatia Dalmacija

Exceptionally beautiful coast along the Adriatic. Among its 1185 islands, those of the Kornati Archipelago and Brijuni Islands are perhaps the most spectacular. Along the coast are several attractive medieval and Renaissance towns, most notably Dubrovnik, Split, Šibenik, Trogir, Zadar. **138 B2**

Dubrovnik

Surrounded by medieval and Renaissance walls, the city's architecture dates principally from 15–16c. Sights: many churches and monasteries including Church of St Blaise and Dominican monastery (art collection); promenade street of Stradun, Dubrovnik Museums; Renaissance Rector's Palace; Onofrio's fountain; Sponza Palace. The surrounding area has some 80 16c noblemen's summer villas. **139 C4**

Islands of Croatia

There are over 1,000 islands off the coast of Croatia among which there is Brač, known for its white marble and the beautiful beaches of Bol (www.bol.hr); Hvar (www.tzhvar.hr/en/) is beautifully green with fields of lavender, marjoram, rosemary, sage and thyme; Vis (www.tz-vis.hr) has the beautiful towns of Komiža and Vis Town, with the Blue Cave on nearby Biševo. **123 & 137–138**

Istria Istra

Peninsula with a number of ancient coastal towns (Rovinj, Poreč, Pula, Piran in Slovene Istria) and medieval hill-top towns (Motovun). Pula has Roman monuments (exceptional 1c amphitheatre). Poreč has narrow old streets; the mosaics in 6c Byzantine basilica of St Euphrasius are exceptional. See also Slovenia. www.istra.hr **122 B2**

Plitvička Jezera

Outstandingly beautiful world of water and woodlands with 16 lakes and 92 waterfalls interwoven by canyons. Archaeological museums; art gallery; Gallery of Ivan Meštrović. www.tzplitvice.hr **123 C4**

Split

Most notable for the exceptional 4c palace of Roman Emperor Diocletian, elements of which are incorporated into the streets and buildings of the town itself. The town also has a cathedral (11c baptistry) and a Franciscan monastery. www.visitsplit.com/en/1/welcome-to-split **138 B2**

Trogir

The 13–15c town centre is surrounded by medieval city walls. Romanesque-Gothic cathedral includes the chapel of Ivan the Blessed. Dominican and Benedictine monasteries house art collections; Ćipiko palace; Lučić palace. www.trogironline.com/tourist_info.html **138 B2**

Zagreb

Capital city of Croatia with cathedral and Archbishop's Palace in Kaptol and to the west Gradec with Baroque palaces. Donji Grad – The Lower Town – is home to the Archaological Museum, Art Pavilion, Museum of Arts and Crafts, Ethnographic Museum, Mimara Museum and National Theatre; Modern Gallery; Museum of Contemporary Art. www.infozagreb.hr/&lang=en **124 B1**

Czechia Česká Republica

www.czechtourism.com/home/

Brno

Capital of Moravia. Sights: Vegetable Market and Old Town Hall; Capuchin crypt decorated with bones of dead monks; hill of St Peter with Gothic cathedral; Church of St James; Mies van der Rohe's buildings (Bata, Avion Hotel, Togendhat House). Museums: Moravian Museum; Moravian Gallery; City Art Gallery; Brno City Museum in Spilberk Castle. www.gotobrno.cz/en **97 B4**

České Budějovice

Famous for Budvar beer, the medieval town is centred on náměsti Přemysla Otokara II. The Black Tower gives fine views. Nearby: medieval Český Krumlov. www.c-budejovice.cz/en **96 C2**

Kutná Hora

A town with strong silver mining heritage shown in the magnificent Cathedral of sv Barbara which was built by the miners. See also the ossuary with 40,000 complete sets of bones moulded into sculptures and decorations. www.czechtourism.com/t/kutna-hora **97 B3**

Olomouc

Well-preserved medieval university town of squares and fountains. The Upper Square has the Town Hall. Also: 18c Holy Trinity; Baroque Church of St Michael. http://tourism.olomouc.eu/welcome/en **98 B1**

Pilsen Plzeň

Best known for Plzeňský Prazdroj (Pilsener Urquell), beer has been brewed here since 1295. An industrial town with eclectic architecture shown in the railway stations and the namesti Republiky (main square). www.czechtourism.com/a/pilsen-area **96 B1**

Prague Praha

Capital of Czech Republic and Bohemia. The Castle Quarter has a complex of buildings behind the walls (Royal Castle; Royal Palace; cathe-

dral). The Basilica of St George has a fine Romanesque interior. The Belvedere is the best example of Renaissance architecture. Hradčani Square has aristocratic palaces and the National Gallery. The Little Quarter has many Renaissance (Wallenstein Palace) and Baroque mansions and the Baroque Church of St Nicholas. The Old Town has its centre at the Old Town Square with the Old Town Hall (astronomical clock), Art Nouveau Jan Hus monument and Gothic Týn church. The Jewish quarter has 14c Staranova Synagogue and Old Jewish Cemetery. The Charles Bridge is famous. The medieval New Town has many Art Nouveau buildings and is centred on Wenceslas Square.
www.prague.eu/en **84 B2**

Spas of Bohemia

Spa towns of Karlovy Vary (Carlsbad: www.karlovyvary.cz/en), Márianske Lázně (Marienbad: www.marianskelazne.cz) and Frantiskovy Lázně **83 B4**

Denmark Danmark

www.visitdenmark.co.uk

Århus

Second largest city in Denmark with a mixture of old and new architecture that blends well, Århus has been dubbed the culture capital of Denmark with the Gothic Domkirke; Latin Quarter; 13th Century Vor Frue Kirke; Den Gamle By, open air museum of traditional Danish life; ARoS (art museum).
www.visitaarhus.com **59 B3**

Copenhagen København

Capital of Denmark. Old centre has fine early 20c Town Hall. Latin Quarter has 19c cathedral. 18c Kastellet has statue of the Little Mermaid nearby. The 17c Rosenborg Castle was a royal residence, as was the Christianborg (now government offices). Other popular sights: Nyhavn canal; Tivoli Gardens. Excellent art collections: Ny Carlsberg Glypotek; National Gallery; National Museum.
www.visitcopenhagen.com/copenhagen-tourist **61 D2**

Hillerød

Frederiksborg (home of the national history museum) is a fine red-brick Renaissance castle set among three lakes. www.visitnorthsealand.com/ln-int/north-sealand/hilleroed **61 D2**

Roskilde

Ancient capital of Denmark. The marvellous cathedral is a burial place of the Danish monarchy. The Viking Ship Museum houses the remains of five 11c Viking ships excavated in the 1960s. www.visitroskilde.com/ln-int/roskilde-lejre/tourist **61 D2**

Estonia Eesti

www.visitestonia.com/en

Kuressaare

Main town on the island of Saaremaa with the 14c Kuressaare Kindlus. **8 C3**

Pärnu

Sea resort with an old town centre. Sights: 15c Red Tower; neoclassical Town Hall; St Catherine's Church.
www.visitparnu.com/en **8 C4**

Tallinn

Capital of Estonia. The old town is centred on the Town Hall Square. Sights: 15c Town Hall; Toompea Castle; Three Sisters houses. Churches: Gothic St Nicholas; 14c Church of the Holy Spirit; St Olaf's; Kumu Art Museum; Maritime Museum. www.visittallinn.ee/eng **8 C4**

Tartu

Historic town with 19c university. The Town Hall Square is surrounded by neoclassical buildings. Also: remains of 13c cathedral; Estonian National Museum. http://visittartu.com **8 C5**

Finland Suomi

www.visitfinland.com

Finnish Lakes

Area of outstanding natural beauty covering about one third of the country with thousands of lakes, of which Päijänne and Saimaa are the most important. Tampere, industrial centre of the region, has numerous museums, including the Tampere Art Museum (modern). Savonlinna has the medieval Olavinlinna Castle. Kuopio has the Orthodox and Regional Museums. **8 A5**

Helsinki

Capital of Finland. The 19c neoclassical town planning between the Esplanade and Senate Square includes the Lutheran cathedral. There is also a Russian Orthodox cathedral. The Constructivist Stockmann Department Store is the largest in Europe. The main railway station is Art Nouveau. Gracious 20c buildings in Mannerheimintie avenue include Finlandiatalo by Alvar Aalto. Many good museums: Art Museum of the Ateneum (19–20c); National Museum; Design Museum; Helsinki City Art Museum (modern Finnish); Open Air Museum (vernacular architecture); 18c fortress of Suomenlinna has several museums.
www.visitfinland.com/helsinki **8 B4**

Lappland (Finnish)

Vast unspoiled rural area. Lappland is home to thousands of nomadic Sámi living in a traditional way. The capital, Rovaniemi, was rebuilt after WWII; museums show Sámi history and culture. Nearby is the Arctic Circle with the famous Santa Claus Village. Inari is a centre of Sámi culture. See also Norway and Sweden.
www.lapland.fi **192–193**

France

https://uk.france.fr/en

Albi

Old town with rosy brick architecture. The vast Cathédrale Ste-Cécile (begun 13c) holds some good art. The Berbie Palace houses the Toulouse-Lautrec museum.
www.albi-tourisme.fr **130 B1**

Alps

Grenoble (www.grenoble-tourisme.com/en/), capital of the French Alps, has a good 20c collection in the Museum of Grenoble. The Vanoise Massif has the greatest number of resorts (Val d'Isère, Courchevel). Chamonix has spectacular views on Mont Blanc, France's and Europe's highest peak. **118 B2**

Amiens

France's largest Gothic cathedral has beautiful decoration. The Museum of Picardy has unique 16c panel paintings. www.visit-amiens.com **90 B2**

Arles

Ancient, picturesque town with Roman relics (1c amphitheatre), 11c cathedral, Archaeological Museum (Roman art); Van Gogh centre.
www.arlestourisme.com/en/ **131 B3**

Avignon

Medieval papal capital (1309–77) with 14c walls and many ecclesiastical buildings. Vast Palace of the Popes has stunning frescoes. The Little Palace has fine Italian Renaissance painting. The 12–13c Bridge of St Bénézet is famous.
www.ot-avignon.fr **131 B3**

Bourges

The Gothic Cathedral of St Etienne, one of the finest in France, has a superb sculptured choir. Also notable is the House of Jacques Coeur.
www.ville-bourges.fr/_en/site/tourism **103 B4**

Brittany Bretagne

Brittany is famous for cliffs, sandy beaches and wild landscape. It is also renowned for megalithic monuments (Carnac) and Celtic culture. Its capital, Rennes, has the Palais de Justice and good collections in the Museum of Brittany (history) and Museum of Fine Arts. Also: Nantes; St-Malo. www.brittanytourism.com **100–101**

Burgundy Bourgogne

Rural wine region with a rich Romanesque, Gothic and Renaissance heritage. The 12c cathedral in Autun and 12c basilica in Vézelay have fine Romanesque sculpture. Monasteries include 11c L'Abbaye de Cluny (ruins) and L'Abbaye de Fontenay. Beaune has beautiful Gothic Hôtel-Dieu and 15c Nicolas Rolin hospices.
www.burgundy-tourism.com **104 B3**

Caen

City with two beautiful Romanesque buildings: Abbaye aux Hommes; Abbaye aux Dames. The château has

▲ Abbaye aux Hommes, Caen, France

two museums (15–20c painting; history). The *Bayeux Tapestry* is displayed in nearby Bayeux. **89 A3**

Carcassonne

Unusual double-walled fortified town of narrow streets with an inner fortress. The fine Romanesque Church of St Nazaire has superb stained glass.
www.tourism-carcassonne.co.uk **130 B1**

Chartres

The 12–13c cathedral is an exceptionally fine example of Gothic architecture (Royal Doorway, stained glass, choir screen). The Fine Arts Museum has a good collection.
www.chartres.com **90 C1**

Clermont-Ferrand

The old centre contains the cathedral built out of lava and Romanesque basilica. The Puy de Dôme and Puy de Sancy give spectacular views over some 60 extinct volcanic peaks (*puys*).
www.clermontferrandtourism.com **116 B3**

Colmar

Town characterised by Alsatian half-timbered houses. The Unterlinden Museum has excellent German religious art including the famous Isenheim altarpiece. Espace André Malraux (contemporary arts).
www.tourisme-colmar.com/en/ **106 A2**

Corsica Corse

Corsica has a beautiful rocky coast and mountainous interior. Napoleon's birthplace of Ajaccio has: Fesch Museum with Imperial Chapel and a large collection of Italian art; Maison Bonaparte; cathedral. Bonifacio, a medieval town, is spectacularly set on a rock over the sea.
www.visit-corsica.com **180**

Côte d'Azur

The French Riviera is best known for its coastline and glamorous resorts. There are many relics of artists who worked here: St-Tropez has Musée de l'Annonciade; Antibes has 12c Château Grimaldi with the Picasso Museum; Cagnes has the Renoir House and Mediterranean Museum of Modern Art; St-Paul-de-Vence has the excellent Maeght Foundation and Matisse's Chapelle du Rosaire. Cannes is famous for its film festival. Also: Marseille, Monaco, Nice.
www.frenchriviera-tourism.com **133 B3**

Dijon

Great 15c cultural centre. The Palais des Ducs et des Etats is the most notable monument and contains the Museum of Fine Arts. Also: the Charterhouse of Champmol.
www.destinationdijon.com **105 B4**

Disneyland Paris

Europe's largest theme park follows in the footsteps of its famous predecessors in the United States.
www.disneylandparis.com **90 C2**

Le Puy-en-Velay

Medieval town bizarrely set on the peaks of dead volcanoes. It is dominated by the Romanesque cathedral (cloisters). The Romanesque chapel of St-Michel is dramatically situated on the highest rock.
www.ot-lepuyenvelay.fr (French only) **117 B3**

Loire Valley

The Loire Valley has many 15–16c châteaux built amid beautiful scenery by French monarchs and members of their courts. Among the most splendid are Azay-le-Rideau, Chenonceaux and Loches. Also: Abbaye de Fontévraud. www.valdeloire-france.co.uk **102 B2**

Lyon

France's third largest city has an old centre and many museums including the Museum of the History of Textiles and the Museum of Fine Arts (old masters). www.lyon-france.com **117 B4**

Marseilles Marseille

Second lagest city in France. Spectacular views from the 19c Notre-Dame-de-la-Garde. The Old Port has 11-12c Basilique St Victor (crypt, catacombs). Cantini Museum has major collection of 20c French art. Château d'If was the setting of Dumas' *The Count of Monte Cristo*.
www.marseille-tourisme.com **131 B4**

Mont-St-Michel

Gothic pilgrim abbey (11–12c) set dramatically on a steep rock island rising from mud flats and connected to the land by a road covered by the tide. The abbey is made up of a complex of buildings.
www.ot-montsaintmichel.com **101 A4**

Nancy

A centre of Art Nouveau. The 18c Place Stanislas was constructed by dethroned Polish king Stanislas.

Museums: School of Nancy Museum (Art Nouveau furniture); Fine Arts Museum. http://en.nancy-tourisme.fr **92 C2**

Nantes

Former capital of Brittany, with the 15c Château des ducs de Bretagne. The cathedral has a striking interior.
www.nantes-tourisme.com **101 B4**

Nice

Capital of the Côte d'Azur, the old town is centred on the old castle on the hill. The seafront includes the famous 19c Promenade des Anglais. The aristocratic quarter of the Cimiez Hill has the Marc Chagall Museum and the Matisse Museum. Also: Museum of Modern and Contemporary Art (especially neo-Realism and Pop Art).
http://en.nicetourisme.com/ **133 B3**

Paris

Capital of France, one of Europe's most interesting cities. The Île de la Cité area, an island in the River Seine has the 12–13c Gothic Notre Dame (wonderful stained glass) and La Sainte-Chapelle (1240–48), one of the jewels of Gothic art. The Left Bank area: Latin Quarter with the famous Sorbonne university; Museum of Cluny housing medieval art; the Panthéon; Luxembourg Palace and Gardens; Montparnasse, interwar artistic and literary centre; Eiffel Tower; Hôtel des Invalides with Napoleon's tomb. Right Bank: the great boulevards (Avenue des Champs-Élysées joining the Arc de Triomphe and Place de la Concorde); 19c Opéra Quarter; Marais, former aristocratic quarter of elegant mansions (Place des Vosges); Bois de Boulogne, the largest park in Paris; Montmartre, centre of 19c bohemianism, with the Basilique Sacré-Coeur. The Church of St Denis is the first gothic church and the mausoleum of the French monarchy. Paris has three of the world's greatest art collections: The Louvre (to 19c, *Mona Lisa*), Musée d'Orsay (19–20c) and National Modern Art Museum in the Pompidou Centre. Other major museums include: Orangery Museum; Paris Museum of Modern Art; Rodin Museum; Picasso Museum; Atelier des Lumières. Notable cemeteries with graves of the famous: Père-Lachaise, Montmartre, Montparnasse. Near Paris are the royal residences of Fontainebleau and Versailles. https://en.parisinfo.com **90 C2**

▲ Château de Chenonceaux, Châteaux of the Loire, France

Pyrenees

Beautiful unspoiled mountain range. Towns include: delightful sea resorts of St-Jean-de-Luz and Biarritz; Pau, with access to the Pyrenees National Park; pilgrimage centre Lourdes. **144–145**

Reims

Together with nearby Epernay, the centre of champagne production. The 13c Gothic cathedral is one of the greatest architectural achievements in France (stained glass by Chagall). Other sights: Palais du Tau with cathedral sculpture, 11c Basilica of St Rémi; cellars on Place St-Niçaise and Place des Droits-des-Hommes.
www.reims-tourisme.com **91 B4**

Rouen

Old centre with many half-timbered houses and 12–13c Gothic cathedral and the Gothic Church of St Maclou with its fascinating remains of a dance macabre on the former cemetery of Aître St-Maclou. The Fine Arts Museum has a good collection.
www.rouentourisme.com **89 A5**

St-Malo

Fortified town (much rebuilt) in a fine coastal setting. There is a magnificent boat trip along the river Rance to Dinan, a splendid well-preserved medieval town.
www.saint-malo-tourisme.co.uk **101 A3**

Strasbourg

Town whose historic centre includes a well-preserved quarter of medieval half-timbered Alsatian houses, many of them set on the canal. The cathedral is one of the best in France. The Palais Rohan contains several museums. www.otstrasbourg.fr/en **93 C3**

Toulouse

Medieval university town characterised by flat pink brick (Hôtel Assézat). The Basilique St Sernin, the largest Romanesque church in France, has many art treasures. Marvellous Church of the Jacobins holds the body of St Thomas Aquinas.
www.toulouse-tourisme.com **129 C4**

Tours

Historic town centred on Place Plumereau. Good collections in the Guilds Museum and Fine Arts Museum. www.tours-tourism.co.uk **102 B2**

Versailles

Vast royal palace built for Louis XIV, primarily by Mansart, set in large formal gardens with magnificent fountains. The extensive and much-imitated state apartments include the famous Hall of Mirrors and the exceptional Baroque chapel.
www.chateauversailles.fr **90 C2**

Vézère Valley Caves

A number of prehistoric sites, most notably the cave paintings of Lascaux (some 17,000 years old), now only seen in a duplicate cave, and the cave of Font de Gaume. The National Museum of Prehistory is in Les Eyzies.
www.lascaux-dordogne.com/en **129 B4**

Germany Deutschland
www.germany.travel

Northern Germany

Aachen

Once capital of the Holy Roman Empire. Old town around the Münsterplatz with magnificent cathedral. An exceptionally rich treasure is in the Schatzkammer. The Town Hall is on the medieval Market.
www.aachen-tourismus.de/en **80 B2**

Berlin

Capital of Germany. Sights include: the Kurfürstendamm avenue; Brandenburg Gate, former symbol of the division between East and West Germany; Tiergarten; Unter den

Linden; 19c Reichstag. Berlin has many excellent art and history collections. Museum Island: Pergamon Musem (classical antiquity, Near and Far East, Islam; Bode Museum (sculpture, Byzantine art); Altes Museum (Greek and Roman); New National Gallery (20th-c European); Old National Gallery (19th-c German); New Museum (Egyptian, prehistoric). Dahlem: Museum of Asian Art; Museum of European Cultures; Mueseum of Ethnology; Die Brücke Museum (German Expressionism). Tiergarten: Picture Gallery (old masters); Decorative Arts Museum (13–19c); New National Gallery (19–20c); Bauhaus Archive.

Gothic cathedral, Cologne, Germany

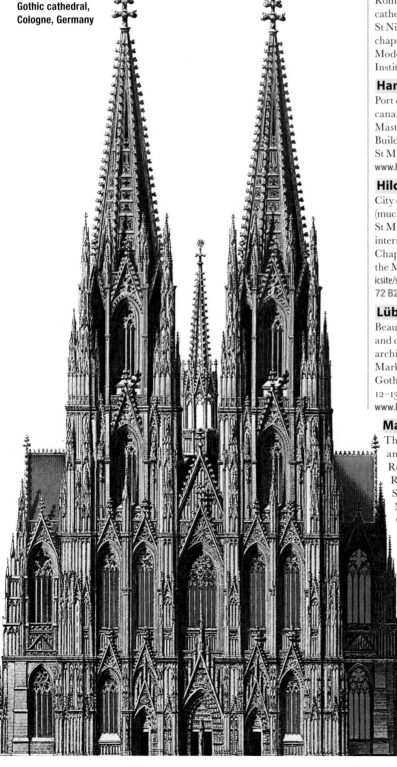

Kreuzberg: Gropius Building with Jewish Museum and Berlin Gallery; remains of Berlin Wall and Checkpoint Charlie House. Unter den Linden: German Guggenheim (commissioned contemporary works). http://visitberlin.de **74 B2**

Cologne Köln

Ancient city with 13–19c cathedral (rich display of art). In the old town are the Town Hall and many Romanesque churches (Gross St Martin, St Maria im Kapitol, St Maria im Lyskirchen, St Ursula, St Georg, St Severin, St Pantaleon, St Apostolen). Museums: Diocesan Museum (religious art); Roman-German Museum (ancient history);

Wallraf-Richartz and Ludwig Museum (14–20c art). www.cologne-tourism.com **80 B2**

Dresden

Historic centre with a rich display of Baroque architecture. Major buildings: Castle of the Electors of Saxony; 18c Hofkirche; Zwinger Palace with fountains and pavilions (excellent old masters); Albertinum with excellent Gallery of New Masters; treasury of Grünes Gewölbe. The Baroque-planned New Town contains the Japanese Palace and Schloss Pillnitz. www.dresden.de/en/tourism/tourism.php **84 A1**

Frankfurt

Financial capital of Germany. The historic centre around the Römerberg Square has 13–15c cathedral, 15c Town Hall, Gothic St Nicholas Church, Saalhof (12c chapel). Museums: Museum of Modern Art (post-war); State Art Institute. www.frankfurt-tourismus.de **81 B4**

Hamburg

Port city with many parks, lakes and canals. The Kunsthalle has Old Masters and 19-20c German art. Buildings: 19c Town Hall; Baroque St Michael's Church. www.hamburg-tourism.de **72 A3**

Hildesheim

City of Romanesque architecture (much destroyed). Principal sights: St Michael's Church; cathedral (11c interior, sculptured doors, St Anne's Chapel); superb 15c Tempelhaus on the Market Place. www.hildesheim.de/staticsite/staticsite.php?menuid=1067&topmenu=4 **72 B2**

Lübeck

Beautiful old town built on an island and characterised by Gothic brick architecture. Sights: 15c Holsten Gate; Market with the Town Hall and Gothic brick St Mary's Church; 12–13c cathedral; St Ann Museum. www.luebeck-tourism.de **65 C3**

Mainz

The Electoral Palatinate schloss and Market fountain are Renaissance. Churches: 12c Romanesque cathedral; Gothic St Steven's (with stained glass by Marc Chagall). www.mainz.de **93 A4**

Marburg

Medieval university town with the Market Place and Town Hall, St Elizabeth's Church (frescoes, statues, 13c shrine), 15–16c schloss. **81 B4**

Münster

Historic city with well-preserved Gothic and Renaissance buildings: 14c Town Hall; Romanesque-Gothic cathedral. The Westphalian Museum holds regional art. www.stadt-muenster.de/en/tourism/home.html **71 C4**

Potsdam

Beautiful Sanssouci Park contains several 18–19c buildings including: Schloss Sanssouci; Gallery (European masters); Orangery; New Palace; Chinese Teahouse. www.potsdam-tourism.com **74 B2**

Rhein Valley Rheintal

Beautiful 80km gorge of the Rhein Valley between Mainz and Koblenz with rocks (Loreley), vineyards (Bacharach, Rüdesheim), white medieval towns (Rhens, Oberwesel) and castles. Some castles are medieval (Marksburg, Rheinfles, island fortress Pfalzgrafenstein) others were built or rebuilt in the 19c (Stolzenfles, Rheinstein). **80 B3**

Weimar

The Neoclassical schloss, once an important seat of government, now houses a good art collection. Church of SS Peter and Paul has a Cranach masterpiece. Houses of famous people: Goethe, Schiller, Liszt. The Bauhaus was founded at the School of Architecture and Engineering. www.weimar.de/en/tourism **82 B3**

Southern Germany

Alpine Road
Deutsche Alpenstrasse

German Alpine Road in the Bavarian Alps, from Lindau on Bodensee to Berchtesgaden. The setting for 19c fairy-tale follies of Ludwig II of Bavaria (Linderhof, Hohenschwangau, Neuschwanstein), charming old villages (Oberammergau) and Baroque churches (Weiss, Ottobeuren). Garmisch-Partenkirchen has views on Germany's highest peak, the Zugspitze. **108 B2**

Augsburg

Attractive old city. The Town Hall is one of Germany's finest Renaissance buildings. Maximilianstrasse has several Renaissance houses and Rococo Schaezler Palace (good art collection). Churches: Romanesque-Gothic cathedral; Renaissance St Anne's Church. The Fuggerei, founded 1519 as an estate for the poor, is still in use. www.augsburg-tourismus.de **94 C2**

Bamberg

Well-preserved medieval town. The island, connected by two bridges, has the Town Hall and views of Klein Venedig. Romanesque-Gothic cathedral (good art) is on an exceptional square of Gothic, Renaissance and Baroque buildings – Alte Hofhalttung; Neue Residenz with State Gallery (German masters); Ratstube. http://en.bamberg.info **94 B2**

Black Forest Schwarzwald

Hilly region between Basel and Karlsruhe, the largest and most picturesque woodland in Germany, with the highest summit, Feldberg, lake resorts (Titisee), health resorts (Baden-Baden) and clock craft (Triberg). Freiburg is the regional capital. www.schwarzwald.de **93 C4**

Freiburg

Old university town with system of streams running through the streets. The Gothic Minster is surrounded by the town's finest buildings. Two towers remain of the medieval walls. The Augustine Museum has a good collection. https:visit.freiburg.de/en **106 B2**

Heidelberg

Germany's oldest university town, majestically set on the banks of the river and romantically dominated by the ruined schloss. The Gothic Church of the Holy Spirit is on the Market Place with the Baroque Town Hall. Other sights include the 16c Knight's House and the Baroque Morass Palace with the Museum of the Palatinate.
www.tourism-heidelberg.com **93 B4**

Lake Constance Bodensee

Lake Constance, with many pleasant lake resorts. Lindau, on an island, has numerous gabled houses. Birnau has an 18c Rococo church. Konstanz (Swiss side) has the Minster set above the Old Town. www.bodensee.eu/en **107 B4**

Munich München

Old town centred on the Marienplatz with 15c Old Town Hall and 19c New Town Hall. Many richly decorated churches: St Peter's (14c tower); Gothic red-brick cathedral; Renaissance St Michael's (royal portraits on the façade); Rococo St Asam's. The Residenz palace consists of seven splendid buildings holding many art objects. Schloss Nymphenburg has a palace, park, botanical gardens and four beautiful pavilions. Superb museums: Old Gallery (old masters), New Gallery (18–19c), Lenbachhaus (modern German). Many famous beer gardens.
www.munich-touristinfo.de **108 A2**

Nuremberg Nürnberg

Beautiful medieval walled city dominated by the 12c Kaiserburg. Romanesque-Gothic St Sebaldus Church and Gothic St Laurence Church are rich in art. On Hauptmarkt is the famous 14c Schöner Brunnen. Also notable is 15c Dürer House. The German National Museum has excellent German medieval and Renaissance art.
http://tourismus.nuernberg.de/en **94 B3**

Regensburg

Medieval city set majestically on the Danube. Views from 12c Steinerne Brücke. Churches: Gothic cathedral; Romanesque St Jacob's; Gothic St Blaisius; Baroque St Emmeram. Other sights: Old Town Hall (museum); Haidplatz; Schloss Thurn und Taxis; State Museum.
http://tourismus.regensburg.de/en **95 B4**

Romantic Road
Romantische Strasse

Romantic route between Aschaffenburg and Füssen, leading through picturesque towns and villages of medieval Germany. The most popular section is the section between Würzburg and Augsburg, centred on Rothenburg ob der Tauber. Also notable are Nördlingen, Harburg Castle, Dinkelsbühl, Creglingen.
www.romantischestrasse.de **94 B2**

Rothenburg ob der Tauber

Attractive medieval walled town with tall gabled and half-timbered houses on narrow cobbled streets. The Market Place has Gothic-Renaissance Town Hall, Rattrinke-stubbe and Gothic St Jacob's Church (altarpiece).
www.rothenburg.de/tourismus/willkommen-in-rothenburg **94 B2**

Speyer

The 11c cathedral is one of the largest and best Romanesque buildings in Germany. 12c Jewish Baths are well-preserved. www.speyer.de/sv_speyer/en/Tourism **93 B4**

Stuttgart

Largely modern city with old centre around the Old Schloss, Renaissance Alte Kanzlei, 15c Collegiate Church and Baroque New Schloss. Museums: Regional Museum; Old and New State Galleries. The 1930s Weissenhofsiedlung is by several famous architects.
www.stuttgart-tourist.de/en **94 C1**

Trier

Superb Roman monuments: Porta Nigra; Aula Palatina (now a church); Imperial Baths; amphitheatre. The Regional Museum has Roman artefacts. Also, Gothic Church of Our Lady; Romanesque cathedral.
www.trier-info.de **92 B2**

Ulm

Old town with half-timbered gabled houses set on a canal. Gothic 14–19c minster has tallest spire in the world (161m). www.tourismus.ulm.de **94 C1**

Würzburg

Set among vineyard hills, the medieval town is centred on the Market Place with the Rococo House of the Falcon. The 18c episcopal princes' residence (frescoes) is magnificent. The cathedral is rich in art. Work of the great local Gothic sculptor, Riemenschneider, is in Gothic St Mary's Chapel, Baroque New Minster, and the Mainfränkisches Museum. www.wuerzburg.de/en **94 B1**

Greece Ellas
www.visitgreece.gr

Athens Athina

Capital of Greece. The Acropolis, with 5c BC sanctuary complex (Parthenon, Propylaia, Erechtheion, Temple of Athena Nike), is the greatest architectural achievement of antiquity in Europe. The Agora was a public meeting place in ancient Athens. Plaka has narrow streets and small Byzantine churches (Kapnikarea). The Olympeum was the largest temple in Greece. Also: Olympic Stadium; excellent collections of ancient artefacts (Museum of Cycladic and Ancient Greek Art; New Acropolis Museum; National Archeological Museum; Benaki Museum). **185 B4**

Corinth Korinthos

Ancient Corinth (ruins), with 5c BC Temple of Apollo, was in 44 BC made capital of Roman Greece by Julius Caesar. Set above the city, the Greek-built acropolis hill of Acrocorinth became the Roman and Byzantine citadel (ruins). **184 B3**

Crete Kriti

Largest Greek island, Crete was home to the great Minoan civilization (2800–1100 BC). The main relics are the ruined Palace of Knossos and Malia. Gortys was capital of the Roman province. Picturesque Rethimno has narrow medieval streets, a Venetian fortress and a former Turkish mosque. Matala has beautiful beaches and famous caves cut into cliffs. Iraklio (Heraklion), the capital, has a good Archeological Museum. **185 D6**

Delphi

At the foot of the Mount Parnassos, Delphi was the seat of the Delphic Oracle of Apollo, the most important oracle in Ancient Greece. Delphi was also a political meeting place and the site of the Pythian Games. The Sanctuary of Apollo consists of: Temple of Apollo, led to by the Sacred Way; Theatre; Stadium. The museum has a display of objects from the site (5c BC Charioteer). **182 E4**

Epidavros

Formerly a spa and religious centre focused on the Sanctuary of Asclepius (ruins). The enormous 4c BC theatre is probably the finest of all ancient theatres. **184 B4**

Greek Islands

Popular islands with some of the most beautiful and spectacular beaches in Europe. The many islands are divided into various groups and individual islands: The major groups are the Kiklades and Dodekanisa in the Aegean Sea, the largest islands are Kerkyra (Corfu) in the Ionian Sea and Kriti. **182–185 & 188**

Meteora

The tops of bizarre vertical cylinders of rock and towering cliffs are the setting for 14c Cenobitic monasteries, until recently only accessible by baskets or removable ladders. Mega Meteoro is the grandest and set on the highest point. Roussánou has the most extraordinary site. Varlaám is one of the oldest and most beautiful, with the Ascent Tower and 16c church with frescoes. Aghiou Nikolaou also has good frescoes. www.meteora-greece.com **182 D3**

Mistras

Set in a beautiful landscape, Mistras is the site of a Byzantine city, now in ruins, with palaces, frescoed churches, monasteries and houses. **184 B3**

Mount Olympus Oros Olymbos

Mount Olympus, mythical seat of the Greek gods, is the highest, most dramatic peak in Greece. **182 C4**

Mycenae Mikines

The citadel of Mycenae prospered between 1950 BC and 1100 BC and consists of the royal complex of Agamemnon: Lion Gate, royal burial site, Royal Palace, South House, Great Court. **184 B3**

Olympia

In a stunning setting, the Panhellenic Games were held here for a millennium. Ruins of the sanctuary of Olympia consist of the Doric temples of Zeus and Hera and the vast Stadium. There is also a museum (4c BC figure of Hermes). **184 B2**

Rhodes

One of the most attractive islands with wonderful sandy beaches. The city of Rhodes has a well-preserved medieval centre with the Palace of the Grand Masters and the Turkish Süleymaniye Mosque
www.rhodestravels.com **188 C2**

Salonica Thessaloniki

Largely modern city with Byzantine walls and many fine churches: 8c Aghia Sofia; 11c Panaghia Halkeo; 14c Dodeka Apostoli; 14c Aghios Nikolaos Orfanos; 5c Aghios Dimitrios (largest in Greece, 7c Mosaics). **183 C5**

Hungary Magyarország
https://hellohungary.com/en

Balaton

The 'Hungarian sea', famous for its holiday resorts: Balatonfüred, Tihany, Badasconytomaj, Keszthely. **111 C4**

Budapest

Capital of Hungary on River Danube, with historic area centring on the Castle Hill of Buda district. Sights include: Matthias church; Pest district with late 19c architecture, centred on Ferenciek tere; neo-Gothic Parliament Building on river; Millennium Monument. The Royal Castle houses a number of museums: Hungarian National Gallery, Budapest History Museum; Ludwig Collection. Other museums: National Museum of Fine Arts (excellent Old and Modern masters); Hungarian National Museum (Hungarian history). Famous for public thermal baths: Király and Rudas baths, both made under Turkish rule; Gellért baths, the most visited.
www.budapest.com/ **112 B3**

Esztergom
Medieval capital of Hungary set in scenic landscape. Sights: Hungary's largest basilica (completed 1856); royal palace ruins. **112 B2**

Pécs
Attractive old town with Europe's fifth oldest university (founded 1367). Famous for Turkish architecture (Mosque of Gazi Kasim Pasha, Jakovali Hassan Mosque). www.iranypecs.hu/en/index.html **125 A4**

Sopron
Beautiful walled town with many Gothic and Renaissance houses. Nearby: Fertöd with the marvellous Eszergázy Palace. **111 B3** http://portal.sopron.hu/Sopron/portal/english

Ireland
www.ireland.com/en-gb

Aran Islands
Islands with spectacular cliffs and notable pre-Christian and Christian sights, especially on Inishmore. www.aranislands.ie **26 B2**

Cashel
Town dominated by the Rock of Cashel (61m) topped by ecclesiastical ruins including 13c cathedral; 15c Halls of the Vicars; beautiful Romanesque 12c Cormac's Chapel (fine carvings). www.cashel.ie **29 B4**

Connemara
Beautiful wild landscape of mountains, lakes, peninsulas and beaches. Clifden is the capital. www.connemara.ie/en **28 A1**

Cork
Pleasant city with its centre along St Patrick's Street and Grand Parade lined with fine 18c buildings. Churches: Georgian St Anne's Shandon (bell tower); 19c cathedral. www.corkcity.ie/traveltourism **29 C3**

County Donegal
Rich scenic landscape of mystical lakes and glens and seascape of cliffs (Slieve League cliffs are the highest in Europe). The town of Donegal has a finely preserved Jacobean castle. www.govisitdonegal.com **26 B2**

Dublin
Capital of Ireland. City of elegant 18c neoclassical and Georgian architecture with gardens and parks (St Stephen's Green, Merrion Square with Leinster House – now seat of Irish parliament). City's main landmark, Trinity College (founded 1591), houses in its Old Library fine Irish manuscripts (7c Book of Durrow, 8c Book of Kells). Two Norman cathedrals: Christ Church; St Patrick's. Other buildings: originally medieval Dublin Castle with State Apartments; James Gandon's masterpieces: Custom House; Four Courts. Museums: National Museum (archaeology, decorative arts, natural history); National Gallery (old masters, Impressionists); Museum of Modern Art; Dublin Writers' Museum. www.visitdublin.com **30 A2**

Glendalough
Impressive ruins of an important early Celtic (6c) monastery with 9c cathedral, 12c St Kevin's Cross, oratory of St Kevin's Church. www.glendalough.ie **30 A2**

Kilkenny
Charming medieval town, with narrow streets dominated by 12c castle (restored 19c). The 13c Gothic cathedral has notable tomb monuments. www.visitkilkenny.ie **30 B1**

Newgrange
Part of a complex that also includes the sites of Knowth, Dowth, Fourknocks, Loughcrew and Tara, Newgrange is one of the best passage graves in Europe, the massive 4500-year-old tomb has stones richly decorated with patterns. www.knowth.com/newgrange.htm **30 A2**

Ring of Kerry
Route around the Iveragh peninsula with beautiful lakes (Lough Leane), peaks overlooking the coastline and islands (Valencia Island, Skelling). Also: Killarney; ruins of 15c Muckross Abbey. www.ringofkerrytourism.com **29 B2**

Italy Italia
www.italia.it

Northern Italy

Alps
Wonderful stretch of the Alps running from the Swiss and French borders to Austria. The region of Valle d'Aosta is one of the most popular ski regions, bordered by the highest peaks of the Alps. **108–109 & 119–120**

Arezzo
Beautiful old town set on a hill dominated by 13c cathedral. Piazza Grande is surrounded by medieval and Renaissance palaces. Main sight: Piero della Francesca's frescoes in the choir of San Francesco. **135 B4**

Assisi
Hill-top town that attracts crowds of pilgrims to the shrine of St Francis of Assisi at the Basilica di San Francesco, comprising two churches, Lower and Upper, with superb frescoes. www.assisi-info.com **136 B1**

Bologna
Elegant city with oldest university in Italy. Historical centre around Piazza Maggiore and Piazza del Nettuno with the Town Hall, Palazzo del Podestà, Basilica di San Petronio. Other churches: San Domenico; San Giacomo Maggiore. The two towers (one incomplete) are symbols of the city. Good collection in the National Gallery (Bolognese). www.bolognawelcome.com **135 A4**

Dolomites Dolomiti
Part of the Alps, this mountain range spreads over the region of Trentino-Alto Adige, with the most picturesque scenery between Bolzano and Cortina d'Ampezzo. www.dolomiti.org/en **121 A4**

Ferrara
Old town centre around Romanesque-Gothic cathedral and Palazzo Communale. Also: Castello Estense; Palazzo Schifanoia (frescoes); Palazzo dei Diamanti housing Pinacoteca Nazion ale. www.ferraraterraeacqua.it/en **121 C4**

Florence Firenze
City with exceptionally rich medieval and Renaissance heritage. Piazza del Duomo has:13–15c cathedral (first dome since antiquity); 14c campanile; 11c baptistry (bronze doors). Piazza della Signoria has: 14c Palazzo Vecchio (frescoes); Loggia della Signoria (sculpture); 16c Uffizi Gallery with one of the world's greatest collections (13–18c). Other great paintings: Museo di San Marco; Palatine Gallery in 15–16c Pitti Palace surrounded by Boboli Gardens. Sculpture: Cathedral Works Museum; Bargello Museum; Academy Gallery (Michelangelo's *David*).

Among many other Renaissance palaces: Medici-Riccardi; Rucellai; Strozzi. The 15c church of San Lorenzo has Michelangelo's tombs of the Medici. Many churches have richly frescoed chapels: Santa Maria Novella, Santa Croce, Santa Maria del Carmine. The 13c Ponte Vecchio is one of the most famous sights. www.visitflorence.com **135 B4**

Italian Lakes
Beautiful district at the foot of the Alps, most of the lakes with holiday resorts. Many lakes are surrounded by aristocratic villas (Maggiore, Como, Garda). **120–121**

Mantua Mántova
Attractive city surrounded by three lakes. Two exceptional palaces: Palazzo Ducale (Sala del Pisanello; Camera degli Sposi, Castello San Giorgio); luxurious Palazzo Tè (brilliant frescoes). Also: 15c Church of Sant'Andrea; 13c law courts. www.turismo.mantova.it **121 B3**

Milan Milano
Modern city, Italy's fashion and design capital (Corso and Galleria Vittoro Emmanuelle II). Churches include: Gothic cathedral (1386–1813), the world's largest (4c baptistry); Romanesque St Ambrose; 15c San Satiro; Santa Maria delle Grazie with Leonardo da Vinci's *Last Supper* in the convent refectory. Great art collections, Brera Gallery, Ambrosian Library, Museum of Modern Art. Castello Sforzesco (15c, 19c) also has a gallery. The famous La Scala opera house opened in 1778. Nearby: monastery at Pavia. www.turismo.milano.it/wps/portal/tur/en **120 B2**

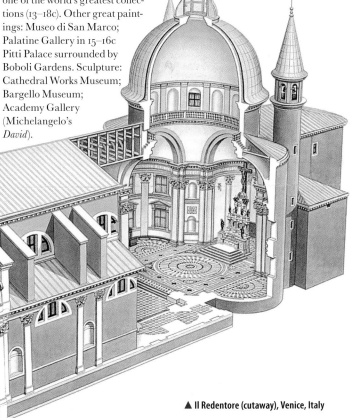

▲ Il Redentore (cutaway), Venice, Italy

Padua Pádova

Pleasant old town with arcaded streets. Basilica del Santo is a place of pilgrimage to the tomb of St Anthony. Giotto's frescoes in the Scrovegni chapel are exceptional. Also: Piazza dei Signori with Palazzo del Capitano; vast Palazzo della Ragione; church of the Eremitani (frescoes). www.turismopadova.it **121 B4**

Parma

Attractive city centre, famous for Corregio's frescoes in the Romanesque cathedral and church of St John the Evangelist, and Parmigianino's frescoes in the church of Madonna della Steccata. Their works are also in the National Gallery. www.turismo.comune.parma.it **120 C3**

Perúgia

Hill-top town centred around Piazza Quattro Novembre with the cathedral, Fontana Maggiore and Palazzo dei Priori. Also: Collegio di Cambio (frescoes); National Gallery of Umbria; many churches. www.perugiaonline.com **136 B1**

Pisa

Medieval town centred on the Piazza dei Miracoli. Sights: famous Romanesque Leaning Tower, Romanesque cathedral (excellent façade, Gothic pulpit); 12–13c Baptistry; 13c Camposanto cloistered cemetery (fascinating 14c frescoes). www.turismo.pisa.it/en **134 B3**

Ravenna

Ancient town with exceptionally well-preserved Byzantine mosaics. The finest are in 5c Mausoleo di Galla Placidia and 6c Basilica di San Vitale. Good mosaics also in the basilicas of Sant'Apollinare in Classe and Sant'Apollinare Nuovo. www.turismo.ra.it/eng **135 A5**

▼ Romanesque cathedral, Pisa, Italy

Siena

Outstanding 13–14c medieval town centred on beautiful Piazza del Campo with Gothic Palazzo Publico (frescoes of secular life). Delightful Romanesque-Gothic Duomo (Libreria Piccolomini, baptistry, art works). Many other richly decorated churches. Fine Sienese painting in Pinacoteca Nazionale and Museo dell'Opera del Duomo. www.sienaonline.com **135 B4**

Turin Torino

City centre has 17-18c Baroque layout dominated by twin Baroque churches. Also: 15c cathedral (holds Turin Shroud); Palazzo Reale; 18c Superga Basilica; Academy of Science with rich Egyptian Museum. www.turismotorino.org **119 B4**

Urbino

Set in beautiful hilly landscape, Urbino's heritage is mainly due to the 15c court of Federico da Montefeltro at the magnificent Ducal Palace (notable Studiolo), now also a gallery. www.turismo.pesarourbino.it **136 B1**

Venice Venezia

Stunning old city built on islands in a lagoon, with some 150 canals. The Grand Canal is crossed by the famous 16c Rialto Bridge and is lined with elegant palaces (Gothic Ca'd'Oro and Ca'Foscari, Renaissance Palazzo Grimani, Baroque Rezzonico). The district of San Marco has the core of the best known sights and is centred on Piazza San Marco with 11c Basilica di San Marco (bronze horses, 13c mosaics); Campanile (exceptional views) and Ducal Palace (connected with the prison by the famous Bridge of Sighs). Many churches (Santa Maria Gloriosa dei Frari, Santa Maria della Salute, Redentore, San Giorgio Maggiore, San Giovanni e Paolo) and scuole (Scuola di San Rocco, Scuola di San Giorgio degli Schiavoni) have excellent works of art. The Gallery of the Academy houses superb 14–18c Venetian art. The Guggenheim Museum holds 20c art. http://en.turismovenezia.it **122 B1**

Verona

Old town with remains of 1c Roman Arena and medieval sights including the Palazzo degli Scaligeri; Arche Scaligere; Romanesque Santa Maria Antica; Castelvecchio; Ponte Scaliger. The famous 14c House of Juliet has associations with *Romeo and Juliet*. Many churches with fine art works (cathedral; Sant'Anastasia; basilica di San Zeno Maggiore). www.tourism.verona.it/en **121 B4**

Vicenza

Beautiful town, famous for the architecture of Palladio, including the Olympic Theatre (extraordinary stage), Corso Palladio with many of his palaces, and Palazzo Chiericati. Nearby: Villa Rotonda, the most influential of all Palladian buildings. www.vicenzae.org **121 B4**

Southern Italy

Naples Napoli

Historical centre around Gothic cathedral (crypt). Spaccanapoli area has numerous churches (bizarre Cappella Sansevero, Gesù Nuovo, Gothic Santa Chiara with fabulous tombs). Buildings: 13c Castello Nuovo; 13c Castel dell'Ovo; 15c Palazzo Cuomo.

▼ Palazzo Publico, Siena, Italy

Museums: National Archeological Museum (artefacts from Pompeii and Herculaneum); National Museum of Capodimonte (Renaissance painting). Nearby: spectacular coast around Amalfi; Pompeii; Herculaneum. www.visitnaples.eu/en **170 C2**

Orvieto

Medieval hill-top town with a number of monuments including the Romanesque-Gothic cathedral (façade, frescoes). www.orvietoviva.com/en **168 A2**

Rome Roma

Capital of Italy, exceptionally rich in sights from many eras. Ancient sights: Colosseum; Arch of Constantine; Trajan's Column; Roman and Imperial fora; hills of Palatino and Campidoglio (Capitoline Museum shows antiquities); Pantheon; Castel Sant' Angelo; Baths of Caracalla). Early Christian sights: catacombs (San Calisto, San Sebastiano, Domitilla); basilicas (San Giovanni in Laterano, Santa Maria Maggiore, San Paolo Fuori le Mura). Rome is known for richly decorated Baroque churches: il Gesù, Sant'Ignazio, Santa Maria della Vittoria, Chiesa Nuova. Other churches, often with art treasures: Romanesque Santa Maria in Cosmedin, Gothic Santa Maria Sopra Minerva, Renaissance Santa Maria del Popolo, San Pietro in Vincoli. Several Renaissance and Baroque palaces and villas house superb art collections (Palazzo Barberini, Palazzo Doria Pamphilj, Palazzo Spada, Palazzo Corsini, Villa Giulia, Galleria Borghese) and are beautifully frescoed (Villa Farnesina). Fine Baroque public spaces with fountains: Piazza Navona; Piazza di Spagna with the Spanish Steps; also Trevi Fountain. Nearby: Tivoli; Villa Adriana. Rome also contains the Vatican City (Città del Vaticano). www.turismoroma.it/?lang=en **168 B2**

Volcanic Region

Region from Naples to Sicily. Mount Etna is one of the most famous European volcanoes. Vesuvius dominates the Bay of Naples and has at its foot two of Italy's finest Roman sites, Pompeii and Herculaneum, both destroyed by its eruption in 79AD. Stromboli is one of the beautiful Aeolian Islands.

Sardinia Sardegna

Sardinia has some of the most beautiful beaches in Italy (Alghero). Unique are the nuraghi, some 7000 stone constructions (Su Nuraxi, Serra Orios), the remains of an old civilization (1500–400 BC). Old towns include Cagliari and Sássari.
www.sardegnaturismo.it/en **178–179**

Sicily Sicilia

Surrounded by beautiful beaches and full of monuments of many periods, Sicily is the largest island in the Mediterranean. Taormina with its Greek theatre has one of the most spectacular beaches, lying under the mildly active volcano Mount Etna. Also: Agrigento; Palermo, Siracusa.
www.sicilytourism.com **176–177**

Agrigento

Set on a hill above the sea and famed for the Valley of the Temples. The nine originally 5c BC Doric temples are Sicily's best-preserved Greek remains. www.agrigento-sicilia.it **176 B2**

Palermo

City with Moorish, Norman and Baroque architecture, especially around the main squares (Quattro Canti, Piazza Pretoria, Piazza Bellini). Sights: remains of Norman palace (12c Palatine Chapel); Norman cathedral; Regional Gallery (medieval); some 8000 preserved bodies in the catacombs of the Cappuchin Convent. Nearby: 12c Norman Duomo di Monreale.
www.palermotourism.com **176 A2**

Syracuse Siracusa

Built on an island connected to the mainland by a bridge, the old town has a 7c cathedral, ruins of the Temple of Apollo; Fountain of Arethusa; archaeological museum. On the mainland: 5c BC Greek theatre with seats cut out of rock; Greek fortress of Euralus; 2c Roman amphitheatre; 5–6c Catacombs of St John. **177 B4**

Latvia Latvija

www.latvia.travel/en

Riga

Well-preserved medieval town centre around the cathedral. Sights: Riga Castle; medieval Hanseatic houses; Great Guild Hall; Gothic Church of St Peter; Art Nouveau buildings in the New Town. Nearby: Baroque Rundale Castle.
www.latvia.travel/en/riga **8 D4**

Lithuania Lietuva

www.lithuania.travel/en-gb

Vilnius

Baroque old town with fine architecture including: cathedral; Gediminas Tower; university complex; Archbishop's Palace; Church of St Anne. Also: remains of Jewish life; Vilnius Picture Gallery (16–19c regional); Lithuanian National Museum. http://vilnius.com **13 A6**

Luxembourg

www.visitluxembourg.com/en

Luxembourg

Capital of Luxembourg, built on a rock with fine views. Old town is around the Place d'Armes. Buildings: Grand Ducal Palace; fortifications of Rocher du Bock; cathedral. Museum of History and Art holds an excellent regional collection. **92 B2**

Macedonia Makedonija

www.exploringmacedonia.com

Ohrid

Old town, beautifully set by a lake, with houses of wood and brick, remains of a Turkish citadel, many churches (two cathedrals; St Naum south of the lake). **182 B2**

Skopje

Historic town with Turkish citadel, fine 15c mosques, oriental bazaar, ancient bridge. Superb Byzantine churches nearby. **182 A3**

Malta

http://www.visitmalta.com/en/home

Valletta

Capital of Malta. Historic walled city, founded in 16c by the Maltese Knights, with 16c Grand Master's Palace and a richly decorated cathedral; fine arts museum – Muża. **175 C3**

Monaco

www.visitmonaco.com

Monaco

Major resort area in a beautiful location. Sights include: Monte Carlo casino, Prince's Palace at Monaco-Ville; 19c cathedral; oceanographic museum. **133 B3**

Netherlands Nederland

www.holland.com

Amsterdam

Capital of the Netherlands. Old centre has picturesque canals lined with distinctive elegant 17–18c merchants' houses. Dam Square has 15c New Church and Royal Palace. Other churches include Westerkerk. The Museumplein has three world-famous museums: the newly restored Rijksmuseum (several art collections including 15–17c painting); Van Gogh Museum; Municipal Museum (art from 1850 on). Other museums: Anne Frank House; Jewish Historical Museum; Rembrandt House; Hermitage Museum (exhibitions). **70 B1**

Delft

Well-preserved old Dutch town with gabled red-roofed houses along canals. Gothic churches: New Church; Old Church. Famous for Delftware (two museums).
www.delft.nl **70 B1**

Haarlem

Many medieval gabled houses centred on the Great Market with 14c Town Hall and 15c Church of St Bavon. Museums: Frans Hals Museum; Teylers Museum.
www.haarlemmarketing.co.uk **70 B1**

The Hague Den Haag

Seat of Government and of the royal house of the Netherlands. The 17c Mauritshuis houses the Royal Picture Gallery (excellent 15–18c Flemish and Dutch). Other museums: Escher Museum; Meermanno Museum (books); Municipal Museum. **70 B1**

Het Loo

Former royal palace and gardens set in a vast landscape (commissioned by future the future King and Queen of England, William and Mary).
www.paleishetloo.nl **70 B2**

Keukenhof

In spring, landscaped gardens, planted with bulbs of many varieties, are the largest flower gardens in the world. www.keukenhof.nl **70 B1**

Leiden

University town of beautiful gabled houses set along canals. The Rijksmuseum Van Oudheden is Holland's most important home to archaeological artefacts from the Antiquity. The 16c Hortus Botanicus is one of the oldest botanical gardens in Europe. The Cloth Hall with van Leyden's *Last Judgement*.
http://leidenholland.com **70 B1**

Rotterdam

The largest port in the world. The Boymans-van Beuningen Museum has a huge and excellent decorative and fine art collection (old and modern). Nearby: 18c Kinderdijk with 19 windmills. https://en.rotterdam.info **79 A4**

Utrecht

Delightful old town centre along canals with the Netherlands' oldest university and Gothic cathedral. Good art collections: Central Museum; National Museum.
www.utrecht.nl **70 B2**

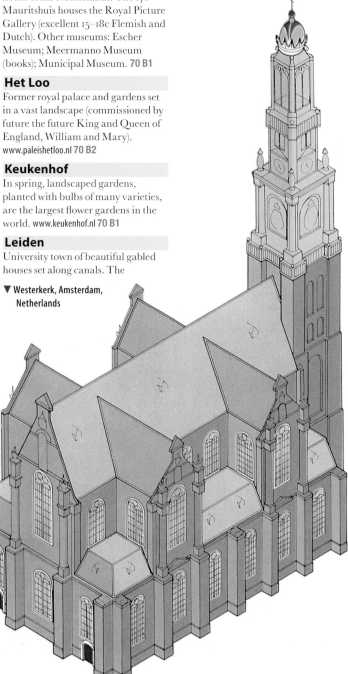

▼ Westerkerk, Amsterdam, Netherlands

Norway Norge

www.visitnorway.com

Bergen

Norway's second city in a scenic setting. The Quay has many painted wooden medieval buildings. Sights: 12c Romanesque St Mary's Church; Bergenhus fortress with 13c Haakon's Hall; Rosenkrantz Tower; Grieghallen; Bergen Art Museum (Norwegian art); Bryggens Museum.
https://en.visitbergen.com **46 B2**

Lappland (Norwegian)

Vast land of Finnmark is home to the Sámi. Nordkapp is the northern point of Europe. Also Finland, Sweden. **192–193**

Norwegian Fjords

Beautiful and majestic landscape of deep glacial valleys filled by the sea. The most thrilling fjords are between Bergen and Ålesund.
www.fjords.com **46 & 198**

Oslo

Capital of Norway with a modern centre. Buildings: 17c cathedral; 19c city hall, 19c royal palace; 19c Stortinget (housing parliament); 19c University; 13c Akershus (castle); 12c Akerskirke (church). Museums: National Gallery; Munch Museum; Viking Ship Museum; Folk Museum (reconstructed buildings).
www.visitoslo.com **48 C2**

Stavkirker

Wooden medieval stave churches of bizarre pyramidal structure, carved with images from Nordic mythology. Best preserved in southern Norway.

Tromsø

Main arctic city of Norway with a university and two cathedrals.
www.visittromso.no/en **192 C3**

Trondheim

Set on the edge of a fjord, a modern city with the superb Nidaros cathedral (rebuilt 19c). Also: Stiftsgaard (royal residence); Applied Arts Museum. www.trondheim.com **199 B7**

Poland Polska

https://poland.travel/en-gb

Częstochowa

Centre of Polish Catholicism, with the 14c monastery of Jasna Góra a pilgrimage site to the icon of the Black Madonna for six centuries.
http://jci.jasnagora.pl/?lng=en **86 B3**

Gdańsk

Medieval centre with: 14c Town Hall (state rooms); Gothic brick St Mary's Church, Poland's largest; Long Market has fine buildings (Artus Court); National Museum.
www.gdansk.pl/en **69 A3**

Kraków

Old university city, rich in architecture, centred on superb 16c Marketplace with Gothic-Renaissance Cloth Hall containing the Art Gallery (19c Polish), Clock Tower, Gothic red-brick St Mary's Church (altarpiece). Czartoryski Palace has city's finest art collection. Wawel Hill has the Gothic cathedral and splendid Renaissance Royal Palace. The former Jewish ghetto in Kazimierz district has 16c Old Synagogue, now a museum.
www.krakow.pl/english **99 A3**

Poznań

Town centred on the Old Square with Renaissance Town Hall and Baroque mansions. Also: medieval castle; Gothic cathedral; National Museum (European masters). **76 B1**

Tatry

One of Europe's most delightful mountain ranges with many beautiful ski resorts (Zakopane). Also in Slovakia. **99 B3**

Warsaw Warszawa

Capital of Poland, with many historic monuments in the Old Town with the Royal Castle (museum) and Old Town Square surrounded by reconstructed 17–18c merchants' houses. Several churches including: Gothic cathedral; Baroque Church of the Nuns of Visitation. Richly decorated royal palaces and gardens: Neoclassical Łazienki Palace; Baroque palace in Wilanów. The National Museum has Polish and European art. **77 C6**

Wrocław

Historic town centred on the Market Square with 15c Town Hall and mansions. Churches: Baroque cathedral; St Elizabeth; St Adalbert. National Museum displays fine art. Vast painting of Battle of Racławice is specially housed.
http://visitwroclaw.eu/en **85 A5**

Portugal

www.visitportugal.com/en

Alcobaça

Monastery of Santa Maria, one of the best examples of a Cistercian abbey, founded in 1147 (exterior 17–18c). The church is Portugal's largest (14c tombs).
www.mosteiroalcobaca.gov.pt/en **154 A1**

Algarve

Modern seaside resorts among picturesque sandy beaches and rocky coves (Praia da Rocha). Old towns: Lagos; Faro.
www.visitalgarve.pt/en/Default.aspx **160 B1**

Batalha

Abbey is one of the masterpieces of French Gothic and Manueline architecture (tombs, English Perpendicular chapel, unfinished pantheon).
www.mosteirobatalha.gov.pt/en **154 A2**

Braga

Historic town with cathedral and large Archbishop's Palace. **148 A1**

Coimbra

Old town with narrow streets set on a hill. The Romanesque cathedral is particularly fine (portal). The university (founded 1290) has a fascinating Baroque library. Also: Museum of Machado de Castro; many monasteries and convents. **148 B1**

Évora

Centre of the town, surrounded by walls, has narrow streets of Moorish character and medieval and Renaissance architecture. Churches: 12–13c Gothic cathedral; São Francisco with a chapel decorated with bones of some 5000 monks; 15c Convent of Dos Lóis. The Jesuit university was founded in 1559. Museum of Évora holds fine art (particularly Flemish and Portugese).
www.evora-portugal.com **154 C3**

Guimarães

Old town with a castle with seven towers on a vast keep. Churches: Romanesque chapel of São Miguel; São Francisco. Alberto Sampaio Museum and Martins Sarmento Museum are excellent.
www.visitportugal.com/en/node/73742 **148 A1**

Lisbon Lisboa

Capital of Portugal. Baixa is the Neoclassical heart of Lisbon with the Praça do Comércio and Rossío squares. São Jorge castle (Visigothic, Moorish, Romanesque) is surrounded by the medieval quarters. Bairro Alto is famous for *fado* (songs). Monastery of Jerónimos is exceptional. Churches: 12c cathedral; São Vicente de Fora; São Roque (tiled chapels); Torre de Belém; Convento da Madre de Deus. Museums: Gulbenkian Museum (ancient, oriental, European), National Museum of Ancient Art; Design Museum; Modern Art Centre; Azulego Museum (decorative tiles). Nearby: palatial monastic complex Mafra; royal resort Sintra.
www.visitlisboa.com **154 B1**

Porto

Historic centre with narrow streets. Views from Clérigos Tower. Churches: São Francisco; cathedral. Soares dos Reis Museum holds fine and decorative arts (18–19c). The suburb of Vila Nova de Gaia is the centre for port wine.
www.visitporto.travel **148 A1**

Tomar

Attractive town with the Convento de Cristo, founded in 1162 as the headquarters of the Knights Templar (Charola temple, chapter house, Renaissance cloisters). **154 A2**

Romania

http://romaniatourism.com

Bucovina

Beautiful region in northern Romanian Moldova renowned for a number of 15–16c monasteries and their fresco cycles. Of particular note are Moldovita, Voroneţ and Suceviţa. **17 B6**

Bucharest Bucureşti

Capital of Romania with the majority of sites along the Calea Victoriei and centring on Piaţa Revoluţei with 19c Romanian Athenaeum and 1930s Royal Palace housing the National Art Gallery. The infamous 1980s Civic Centre with People's Palace is a symbol of dictatorial aggrandisement. **17 C7**

Carpathian Mountains Carpaţii

The beautiful Carpathian Mountains have several ski resorts (Sinaia) and peaks noted for first-rate mountaineering (Făgă raşuiui, Rodnei). Danube Delta Europe's largest marshland, a spectacular nature reserve. Travel in the area is by boat, with Tulcea the starting point for visitors. The Romanian Black Sea Coast has a stretch of resorts (Mamaia, Eforie) between Constantaţ and the border, and well-preserved Roman remains in Histria. **17 B6**

Transylvania Transilvania

Beautiful and fascinating scenic region of medieval citadels (Timişoara, Sibiu) provides a setting for the haunting image of the legendary Dracula (Sighişoara, Braşov, Bran Castle). Cluj-Napoca is the main town. **17 B5**

Russia Rossiya

www.visitrussia.org.uk

Moscow Moskva

Capital of Russia, with many monuments. Within the Kremlin's red walls are: 15c Cathedral of the Dormition; 16c Cathedral of the Archangel; Cathedral of the Annunciation (icons), Armour Palace. Outside the walls, Red Square has the Lenin Mausoleum and 16c St Basil's Cathedral. There are a number of monasteries (16c Novodevichi). Two superb museums: Tretiakov Art Gallery (Russian); Pushkin Museum of Fine Art (European); also State Historical Museum. Kolomenskoe, once a royal summer retreat, has the Church of the Ascension. **9 E10**

Novgorod

One of Russia's oldest towns, centred on 15c Kremlin with St Sophia Cathedral (iconostasis, west door). Two other cathedrals: St Nicholas; St George. Museum of History, Architecture and Art has notable icons and other artefacts.
http://visitnovgorod.com **9 C7**

Peterhof (Petrovdorets)

Also known as Petrovdorets, Peterhof is a grand palace with numerous pavilions (Monplaisir) set in beautiful parkland interwoven by a system of fountains, cascades and waterways connected to the sea.
http://en.peterhofmuseum.ru **9 C6**

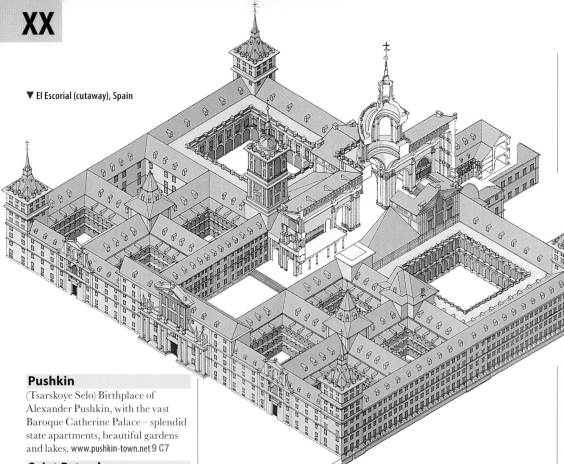

▼ El Escorial (cutaway), Spain

Pushkin

(Tsarskoye Selo) Birthplace of Alexander Pushkin, with the vast Baroque Catherine Palace – splendid state apartments, beautiful gardens and lakes. www.pushkin-town.net **9 C7**

Saint Petersburg
Sankt Peterburg

Founded in 1703 with the SS Peter and Paul Fortress and its cathedral by Peter the Great, and functioning as seat of court and government until 1918. Many of the most famous sights are around elegant Nevski Prospekt. The Hermitage, one of the world's largest and finest art collections is housed in several buildings including the Baroque Winter and Summer palaces. The Mikhailovsky Palace houses the Russian Museum (Russian art). Other sights: neoclassical Admiralty; 19c St Isaac's Cathedral and St Kazan Cathedral; Vasilievsky Island with 18c Menshikov Palace; Alexander Nevsky Monastery; 18c Smolny Convent. www.saint-petersburg.com **9 C7**

Sergiev Posad

(Zagorsk) Trinity St Sergius monastery with 15c cathedral. **9 D11**

Serbia Srbija

www.serbia.travel

Belgrade Beograd

Capital of Serbia. The largely modern city is set between the Danube and Sava rivers. National Museum; Museum of Contemporary Art. To the south there are numerous fascinating medieval monasteries, richly embellished with frescoes. www.tob.rs **127 C2**

Slovakia
Slovenska Republika

http://slovakia.travel/en

Bratislava

Capital of Slovakia, dominated by the castle (Slovak National Museum, good views). Old Town centred on the Main Square with Old Town Hall and Jesuit Church. Many 18–19c palaces (Mirbach Palace, Pálffy Palace, Primate's Palace), churches (Gothic cathedral, Corpus Christi Chapel) and museums (Slovak National Gallery). www.visitbratislava.com **111 A4**

Košice

Charming old town with many Baroque and neoclassical buildings and Gothic cathedral. **12 D4**

Spišské Podhradie

Region, east of the Tatry, full of picturesque medieval towns (Levoča, Kežmarok, Prešov) and architectural monuments (Spišský Castle). **99 B4**

Tatry

Beautiful mountain region. Poprad is an old town with 19c villas. Starý Smokovec is a popular ski resort. See also Poland. **99 B3**

Slovenia Slovenija

www.slovenia.info/en

Istria Istra

Two town centres, Koper and Piran, with medieval and Renaissance squares and Baroque palaces. See also Croatia. **122 B2**

Julian Alps Julijske Alpe

Wonderfully scenic section of the Alps with lakes (Bled, Bohinj), deep valleys (Planica, Vrata) and ski resorts (Kranjska Gora, Bohinjska Bistrica). **122 A2**

Karst Caves

Numerous caves with huge galleries, extraordinary stalactites and stalagmites, and underground rivers. The most spectacular are Postojna (the most famous, with Predjamski Castle nearby) and Škocjan. www.postojnska-jama.eu/en **123 B3**

Ljubljana

Capital of Slovenia. The old town, dominated by the castle (good views), is principally between Prešeren Square and Town Hall (15c, 18c), with the Three Bridges and colonnaded market. Many Baroque churches (cathedral, St Jacob, St Francis, Ursuline) and palaces (Bishop's Palace, Seminary, Gruber Palace). Also: 17c Križanke church and monastery complex; National Gallery and Modern Gallery show Slovene art. www.visitljubljana.com/en/visitors **123 A3**

Spain España

www.spain.info/en_GB/

Ávila

Medieval town with 2km-long 11c walls. Pilgrimage site to shrines to St Teresa of Ávila (Convent of Santa Teresa, Convent of the Incarnation). www.avila.com/avila_tourism **150 B3**

Barcelona

Showcase of Gothic ('Barri Gòtic': cathedral; Santa María del Mar; mansions on Carrer de Montcada) and *modernista* architecture ('Eixample' area with Manzana de la Discòrdia; Sagrada Familia, Güell Park, La Pedrera). Many elegant boulevards (La Rambla, Passeig de Gràcia). Museums: Modern Catalan Art, Catalan Archaeology, Picasso Museum, Miró Museum, Tàpies Museum. Nearby: monastery of Montserrat (Madonna); Figueres (Dali Museum). www.barcelonaturisme.com/wv3/en **147 C3**

Burgos

Medieval town with Gothic cathedral, Moorish-Gothic Royal Monastery and Charterhouse of Miraflores. **143 B3**

Cáceres

Medieval town surrounded by Moorish walls and with several aristocratic palaces with solars. **155 A4**

Córdoba

Capital of Moorish Spain with a labyrinth of streets and houses with tile-decorated patios. The 8–10c Mezquita is the finest mosque in Spain. A 16c cathedral was added at the centre of the building and a 17c tower replaced the minaret. The old Jewish quarter has 14c synagogue http://english.turismodecordoba.org **156 C3**

El Escorial

Immense Renaissance complex of palatial and monastic buildings and mausoleum of the Spanish monarchs. www.patrimonionacional.es **151 B3**

Granada

The Alhambra was hill-top palace-fortress of the rulers of the last Moorish kingdom and is the most splendid example of Moorish art and architecture in Spain. The complex has three principal parts: Alcazaba fortress (11c); Casa Real palace (14c, with later Palace of Carlos V); Generalife gardens. Also: Moorish quarter; gypsy quarter; Royal Chapel with good art in the sacristy. www.turgranada.es **163 A4**

León

Gothic cathedral has notable stained glass. Royal Pantheon commemorates early kings of Castile and León. **142 B1**

Madrid

Capital of Spain, a mainly modern city with 17–19c architecture at its centre around Plaza Mayor. Sights: Royal Palace with lavish apartments; Descalzas Reales Convent (tapestries and other works); Royal Armoury museum. Spain's three leading galleries: Prado (15–18c); Queen Sofia Centre (20c Spanish, Picasso's *Guernica*); Thyssen-Bornemisza Museum (medieval to modern). http://turismomadrid.es/en/ **151 B4**

Oviedo

Gothic cathedral with 12c sanctuary. Three Visigoth (9c) churches: Santullano, Santa María del Naranco, San Miguel de Lillo. **141 A5**

Palma

Situated on Mallorca, the largest and most beautiful of the Balearic islands, with an impressive Gothic cathedral and the Taller Sjert studio with works by Miró. www.palma.com **166 B2**

Picos de Europa

Mountain range with river gorges and peaks topped by Visigothic and Romanesque churches. **142 A2**

Pyrenees

Unspoiled mountain range with beautiful landscape and villages full of Romanesque architecture (cathedral of Jaca). The Ordesa National Park has many waterfalls and canyons. **144–145**

Salamanca

Delightful old city with some uniquely Spanish architecture: Renaissance Plateresque is famously seen on 16c portal of the university (founded 1215); Baroque Churrigueresque on 18c Plaza Mayor; both styles at the Convent of San Esteban. Also: Romanesque Old Cathedral; Gothic-Plateresque New Cathedral; House of Shells. www.salamanca.es/en **150 B2**

Santiago di Compostela

Medieval city with many churches and religious institutions. The famous pilgrimage to the shrine of St James the Apostle ends here in the magnificent cathedral, originally Romanesque with many later elements (18c Baroque façade). www.santiagoturismo.com **140 B2**

Segovia

Old town set on a rock with a 1c Roman aqueduct. Also: 16c Gothic cathedral; Alcázar (14–15c, rebuilt 19c); 12-sided 13c Templar church of Vera Cruz. **151 B3**

Seville Sevilla

City noted for festivals and flamenco. The world's largest Gothic cathedral (15c) retains the Orange Court and minaret of a mosque. The Alcazar is a fine example of Moorish architecture. The massive 18c tobacco factory, now part of the university, was the setting for Bizet's *Carmen*. Barrio de Santa Cruz is the old Jewish quarter with narrow streets and white houses. Casa de Pilatos (15–16c) has a fine domestic patio. The Museum of Fine Arts is in a former convent. Nearby: Roman Italica with amphitheatre. **162 A2**

Tarragona

The city and its surroundings have some of the best-preserved Roman heritage in Spain. Also: Gothic cathedral (cloister); Archaeological Museum. www.tarragonaturisme.cat/en **147 C2**

Toledo

Historic city with Moorish, Jewish and Christian sights. The small 11c mosque of El Cristo de la Luz is one of the earliest in Spain. Two synagogues have been preserved: Santa María la Blanca; El Tránsito. Churches: San Juan de los Reyes; Gothic cathedral (good artworks). El Greco's *Burial of the Count of Orgaz* is in the Church of Santo Tomé. More of his works are in the El Greco house and, with other art, in Hospital de Santa Cruz. **151 C3**

Valencia

The old town has houses and palaces with elaborate façades. Also: Gothic cathedral and Lonja de la Seda church. www.visitvalencia.com **159 B3**

Zaragoza

Town notable for Moorish architecture (11c Aljafería Palace). The Basilica de Nuestra Señora del Pilar, one of two cathedrals, is highly venerated. www.zaragoza.es/turismo **153 A3**

Sweden Sverige

https://visitsweden.com

Abisko

Popular resort in the Swedish part of Lapland set in an inspiring landscape of lakes and mountains. www.visitabisko.com **194 B9**

Gothenburg Göteborg

Largest port in Sweden, the historic centre has 17–18c Dutch architectural character (Kronhuset). The Art Museum has interesting Swedish works. www.goteborg.com/en **60 B1**

Gotland

Island with Sweden's most popular beach resorts (Ljugarn) and unspoiled countryside with churches in Baltic Gothic style (Dahlem, Bunge). Visby is a pleasant walled medieval town. http://gotland.com/en **57 C4**

Lappland (Swedish)

Swedish part of Lappland with 18c Arvidsjaur the oldest preserved Sámi village. Jokkmokk is a Sámi cultural centre, Abisko a popular resort in fine scenery. Also Finland, Norway. www.kirunalapland.se **192–193**

Lund

Charming university city with medieval centre and a fine 12c Romanesque cathedral (14c astronomical clock, carved tombs). www.visitlund.se/en **61 D3**

Malmö

Old town centre set among canals and parks dominated by a red-brick castle (museums) and a vast market square with Town Hall and Gothic Church of St Peter. www.malmotown.com/en **61 D3**

Mora

Delightful village on the shores of Siljan Lake in the heart of the Dalarna region, home to folklore and traditional crafts. **50 A1**

Stockholm

Capital of Sweden built on a number of islands. The Old Town is largely on three islands with 17–18c houses, Baroque Royal Castle (apartments and museums), Gothic cathedral, parliament. Riddarholms church has tombs of the monarchy. Museums include: National Museum; Modern Museum (one of world's best modern collections); Nordiska Museet (cultural history); open-air Skansen (Swedish houses). Baroque Drottningholm Castle is the residence of the monarchy. www.visitstockholm.com **57 A4**

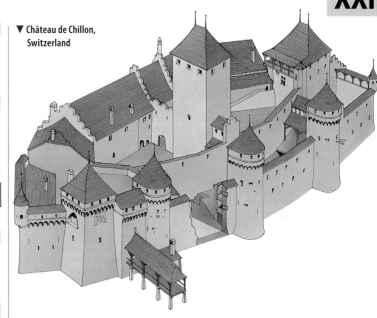

▼ Château de Chillon, Switzerland

Swedish Lakes

Beautiful region around the Vättern and Vänern Lakes. Siljan Lake is in the Dalarna region where folklore and crafts are preserved (Leksand, Mora, Rättvik). **55 B4**

Uppsala

Appealing university town with a medieval centre around the massive Gothic cathedral. www.destinationuppsala.se/en **51 C4**

Switzerland Schweiz

www.myswitzerland.com/en-gb/home.html

Alps

The most popular Alpine region is the Berner Oberland with the town of Interlaken a starting point for exploring the large number of picturesque peaks (Jungfrau). The valleys of the Graubünden have famous ski resorts (Davos, St Moritz). Zermatt lies below the most recognizable Swiss peak, the Matterhorn. **119 A4**

Basle Basel

Medieval university town with Romanesque-Gothic cathedral (tomb of Erasmus). Superb collections: Art Museum; Museum of Contemporary Art. www.basel.com/en **106 B2**

Bern

Capital of Switzerland. Medieval centre has fountains, characteristic streets (Spitalgasse) and tower-gates. The Bärengraben is famed for its bears. Also: Gothic cathedral; good Fine Arts Museum. www.bern.com/en **106 C2**

Geneva Genève

The historic area is centred on the Romanesque cathedral and Place du Bourg du Four. Excellent collections: Art and History Museum; new Museum of Modern and Contemporary Art. On the lake shore: splendid medieval Château de Chillon. www.geneve.com **118 A3**

Interlaken

Starting point for excursions to the most delightful part of the Swiss Alps, the Bernese Oberland, with Grindelwald and Lauterbrunnen – one of the most thrilling valleys leading up to the ski resort of Wengen with views on the Jungfrau. www.interlaken.ch **106 C2**

Lucerne Luzern

On the beautiful shores of Vierwaldstättersee, a charming medieval town of white houses on narrow streets and of wooden bridges (Kapellbrücke, Spreuerbrücke). It is centred on the Kornmarkt with the Renaissance Old Town Hall and Am Rhyn-Haus (Picasso collection). www.luzern.com/en **106 C1**

Zürich

Set on Zürichsee, the old quarter is around Niederdorf with 15c cathedral. Gothic Fraumünster has stained glass by Chagall. Museums: Swiss National Museum (history); Art Museum (old and modern masters); Rietberg Museum (non-European cultures). www.zuerich.com/en **107 B3**

Turkey Türkiye

www.goturkeytourism.com

Istanbul

Divided by the spectcular Bosphorus, the stretch of water that separates Europe from Asia, the historic district is surrounded by the Golden Horn, Sea of Marmara and the 5c wall of Theodosius. Major sights: 6c Byzantine church of St Sophia (converted first to a mosque in 1453 and then a museum in 1934); 15c Topkapi Palace; treasury and Archaeological Museum; 17c Blue Mosque; 19c Bazaar; 16c Süleymaniye Mosque; 12c Kariye Camii; European district with Galata Tower and 19c Dolmabahçe Palace. http://en.istanbul.com **186 A3**

Ukraine Ukraina

www.ukraine.com

Kiev Kyïv
Capital of Ukraine, known for its cathedral (11c, 17c) with Byzantine frescoes and mosaics. The Monastery of the Caves has churches, monastic buildings and catacombs. www.kiev.info 13 C9

United Kingdom

www.visitbritain.com

England
www.visitengland.com

Bath
Elegant spa town with notable 18c architecture: Circus, Royal Crescent, Pulteney Bridge, Assembly Rooms; Pump Room. Also: well-preserved Roman baths; superb Perpendicular Gothic Bath Abbey. Nearby: Elizabethan Longleat House; exceptional 18c landscaped gardens at Stourhead. https://visitbath.co.uk 43 A4

Brighton
Resort with a sea-front of Georgian, Regency and Victorian buildings, Palace Pier, i360 observation tower, and old town of narrow lanes. The main sight is the Oriental-style Royal Pavilion. Nearby: South Downs National Park. www.visitbrighton.com 44 C3

Bristol
Old port city with the fascinating Floating Harbour. Major sights include Gothic 13–14c Church of St Mary Redcliffe, SS Great Britain and 19c Clifton Suspension Bridge. http://visitbristol.co.uk 43 A4

Cambridge
City with university founded in the early 13c. Peterhouse (1284) is the oldest college. Most famous colleges were founded in 14–16c: Queen's, King's (with the superb Perpendicular Gothic 15–16c King's College Chapel), St John's (with famous 19c Bridge of Sighs), Trinity, Clare, Gonville and Caius, Magdalene. Museums: excellent Fitzwilliam Museum (classical, medieval, old masters). Kettle's Yard (20c British). www.visitcambridge.org 45 A4

Canterbury
Medieval city and old centre of Christianity. The Norman-Gothic cathedral has many sights and was a major medieval pilgrimage site (as related in Chaucer's *Canterbury Tales*). St Augustine, sent to convert the English in 597, founded St Augustine's Abbey, now in ruins. www.canterbury.co.uk 45 B5

Chatsworth
One of the richest aristocratic country houses in England (largely 17c) set in a large landscaped park. The palatial interior has some 175 richly furnished rooms and a major art collection. www.chatsworth.org 40 B2

Chester
Charming medieval city with complete walls. The Norman-Gothic cathedral has several abbey buildings. www.visitcheshire.com 38 A4

Cornish Coast
Scenic landscape of cliffs and sandy beaches with picturesque villages (Fowey, Mevagissey). St Ives has the Tate Gallery with work of the St Ives Group. St Michael's Mount is reached by causeway at low tide. www.visitcornwall.com 42 B1

Dartmoor
Beautiful wilderness area in Devon with tors and its own breed of wild pony as well as free-ranging cattle and sheep. www.dartmoor.co.uk 42 B3

Durham
Historic city with England's finest Norman cathedral and a castle, both placed majestically on a rock above the river. www.thisisdurham.com 37 B5

Eden Project
Centre showing the diversity of plant life on the planet, built in a disused clay pit. Two biomes, one with Mediterranean and Southern African focus and the larger featuring a waterfall, river and tropical trees plants and flowers. Outdoors also features plantations including bamboo and tea. www.edenproject.com 42 B2

Hadrian's Wall
Built to protect the northernmost border of the Roman Empire in the 2c AD, the walls originally extended some 120km with castles every mile and 16 forts. Best-preserved walls around Hexam; forts at Housesteads and Chesters. http://hadrianswallcountry.co.uk 37 A4

Lake District
Beautiful landscape of lakes (Windermere, Coniston) and England's high peaks (Scafell Pike, Skiddaw, Old Man), famous for its poets, particularly Wordsworth. www.lakedistrict.gov.uk 36 B3

Leeds Castle
One of the oldest and most romantic English castles, standing in the middle of a lake. Most of the present appearance dates from 19c. www.leeds-castle.com 45 B4

Lincoln
Old city perched on a hill with narrow streets, majestically dominated by the Norman-Gothic cathedral and castle. www.visitlincolnshire.com 40 B3

Liverpool
City on site of port founded in 1207 and focused around 1846 Albert Dock, now a heritage attraction. Croxteth Hall and Country Park; Speke Hall; Sudley House; Royal Liver Building; Liverpool Cathedral; Walker Art Gallery; Tate Liverpool; University of Liverpool Art Gallery. www.visitliverpool.com 38 A4

London
Capital of UK and Europe's largest city. To the east of the medieval heart of the city – now the largely modern financial district and known as the City of London – is the Tower of London (11c White Tower, Crown Jewels) and 1880s Tower Bridge. The popular heart of the city and its entertainment is the West End, around Piccadilly Circus, Leicester Square and Trafalgar Square (Nelson's Column). Many sights of political and royal power: Whitehall (Banqueting House, 10 Downing Street, Horse Guards); Neo-Gothic Palace of Westminster (Houses of Parliament) with Big Ben; The Mall leading to Buckingham Palace (royal residence, famous ceremony of the Changing of the Guard). Numerous churches include: 13–16c Gothic Westminster Abbey (many tombs, Henry VII's Chapel); Wren's Baroque St Paul's Cathedral, St Mary-le-Bow, spire of St Bride's, St Stephen Walbrook. Museums of world fame: British Museum (prehistory, oriental and classical antiquity, medieval); Victoria and Albert Museum (decorative arts); National Gallery (old masters to 19c); National Portrait Gallery (historic and current British portraiture); Tate – Britain and Modern; Science Museum; Natural History Museum. Madame Tussaud's waxworks museum is hugely popular. Other sights include: London Eye, Kensington Palace; Greenwich with Old Royal Observatory (Greenwich meridian), Baroque Royal Naval College, Palladian Queen's House; Tudor Hampton Court Palace; Syon House. Nearby: Windsor Castle (art collection, St George's Chapel). www.visitlondon.com 44 B3

◀ Salisbury Cathedral, England

Longleat

One of the earliest and finest Elizabethan palaces in England. The palace is richly decorated. Some of the grounds have been turned into a pleasure park, with the Safari Park, the first of its kind outside Africa. www.longleat.co.uk **43 A4**

Manchester

Founded on a Roman settlement of 79AD and a main player in the Industrial Revolution. Victorian Gothic Town Hall; Royal Exchange; Cathedral. Many museums including Imperial War Museum North, Lowry Centre and Manchester Art Gallery. www.visitmanchester.com **40 B1**

Newcastle upon Tyne

A key player in the Industrial Revolution with 12th century cathedral and many museums as well as strong railway heritage. www.newcastlegateshead.com **37 B5**

Norwich

Medieval quarter has half-timbered houses. 15c castle keep houses a museum and gallery. Many medieval churches include the Norman-Gothic cathedral. www.visitnorwich.co.uk **41 C5**

Oxford

Old university city. Earliest colleges date from 13c: University College; Balliol; Merton. 14–16c colleges include: New College; Magdalen; Christ Church (perhaps the finest). Other buildings: Bodleian Library; Radcliffe Camera; Sheldonian Theatre; cathedral. Good museums: Ashmolean Museum (antiquity to 20c); Museum of the History of Science; Museum of Modern Art; Christ Church Picture Gallery (14–17c). Nearby: outstanding 18c Blenheim Palace. www.experienceoxfordshire.org **44 B2**

Petworth

House (17c) with one of the finest country-house art collections (old masters), set in a huge landscaped park. www.nationaltrust.org.uk **44 C3**

Salisbury

Pleasant old city with a magnificent 13c cathedral built in an unusually unified Gothic style. Nearby: Wilton House. www.visitwiltshire.co.uk **44 B2**

Stonehenge

Some 4000 years old, one of the most famous and haunting Neolithic monuments in Europe. Many other Neolithic sites are nearby. www.english-heritage.org.uk **44 B2**

Stourhead

Early 18c palace famous for its grounds, one of the finest examples of neoclassical landscaped gardening, consisting of a lake surrounded by numerous temples. www.nationaltrust.org.uk **43 A4**

Stratford-upon-Avon

Old town of Tudor and Jacobean half-timbered houses, famed as the birth and burial place of William Shakespeare and home of the Royal Shakespeare Company. www.shakespeare-country.co.uk **44 A2**

Wells

Charming city with beautiful 12–16c cathedral (west facade, scissor arches, chapter house, medieval clock). Also Bishop's Palace; Vicar's Close. www.wellssomerset.com **43 A4**

Winchester

Historic city with 11–16c cathedral. Also: 13c Great Hall, Winchester College, St Cross almshouses. Western gateway to the South Downs National Park. www.visitwinchester.co.uk **44 B2**

York

Attractive medieval city surrounded by well-preserved walls with magnificent Gothic 13–15c Minster. Museums: York City Art Gallery (14–19c); Jorvik Viking Centre. Nearby: Castle Howard. www.visityork.org **40 B2**

Northern Ireland

http://discovernorthernireland.com

Antrim Coast

Spectacular coast with diverse scenery of glens (Glenarm, Glenariff), cliffs (Murlough Bay) and the famous Giant's Causeway, consisting of some 40,000 basalt columns. Carrickefergus Castle is the largest and best-preserved Norman castle in Ireland. http://antrimcoastandglensaonb.ccght.org http://causewaycoastaonb.ccght.org **27 A4**

Belfast

Capital of Northern Ireland. Sights: Donegall Square with 18c Town Hall; neo-Romanesque Protestant cathedral; University Square; Ulster Museum (European painting). https://visitbelfast.com **27 B5**

Giant's Causeway

Spectacular and unique rock formations in the North Antrim coast, formed by volcanic activity 50–60 million years ago. World Heritage Site. www.nationaltrust.org.uk **27 A4**

Scotland

www.visitscotland.com

Edinburgh

Capital of Scotland, built on volcanic hills. The medieval Old Town is dominated by the castle set high on a volcanic rock (Norman St Margaret's Chapel, state apartments, Crown Room). Holyrood House (15c and 17c) has lavishly decorated state apartments and the ruins of Holyrood Abbey (remains of Scottish monarchs). The 15c cathedral has the Crown Spire and Thistle Chapel. The New Town has good Georgian architecture (Charlotte Square, Georgian House). Excellent museums: Scottish National Portrait Gallery, National Gallery of Scotland; Scottish National Gallery of Modern Art. **35 C4**

Glamis Castle

In beautiful, almost flat landscaped grounds, 14c fortress, rebuilt 17c, gives a fairy-tale impression. www.glamis-castle.co.uk **35 B5**

Glasgow

Scotland's largest city, with centre around George Square and 13–15c Gothic cathedral. Fine art collections: Glasgow Museum and Art Gallery; Hunterian Gallery; Burrell Collection; Kelvingrove Art Gallery and Museum. **35 C3**

Loch Ness

In the heart of the Highlands, the lake forms part of the scenic Great Glen running from Inverness to Fort William. Famous as home of the fabled Loch Ness Monster (exhibition at Drumnadrochit). Nearby: ruins of 14–16c Urquhart Castle. www.lochness.com **32 D2**

Wales

www.visitwales.com

Caernarfon

Town dominated by a magnificent 13c castle, one of a series built by Edward I in Wales (others include Harlech, Conwy, Beaumaris, Caerphilly). www.caernarfononline.co.uk **38 A2**

Cardiff

Capital of Wales, most famous for its medieval castle, restored 19c in Greek, Gothic and Oriental styles. Also: National Museum and Gallery. www.visitcardiff.com **39 C3**

Vatican City
Città del Vaticano

http://w2.vatican.va/content/vatican/en.html

Vatican City Città del Vaticano

Independent state within Rome. On Piazza San Pietro is the 15–16c Renaissance-Baroque Basilica San Pietro (Michelangelo's dome and *Pietà*), the world's most important Roman Catholic church. The Vatican Palace contains the Vatican Museums with many fine art treasures including Michelangelo's frescoes in the Sistine Chapel. www.museivaticani.va **168 B2**

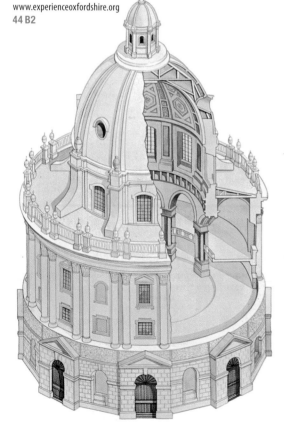

◄ Radcliffe Camera, Oxford, England

▼ The facade of Basilica San Pietro, Vatican City

European politics and economics

The figures given for capitals' populations are for the whole metropolitan area.

Albania Shqipëria

Area 28,748 km² (11,100 mi²)
Population 2,877,000
Capital Tirana / Tiranë (884,000)
Languages Albanian (official), Greek, Vlach, Romani and Slavic **GDP** $5,319 (2018)
Currency Lek = 100 Quindars
Government multiparty republic
Head of state President Ilir Meta, 2017
Head of government
Prime Minister Edi Rama, Socialist Party, 2013
Website www.kryeministria.al/en
Events In the 2005 general elections, the Democratic Party and its allies won a decisive victory on pledges of reducing crime and corruption, promoting economic growth and decreasing the size of government. The party retained power by a narrow margin in 2009, amid disputes over electoral procedure. After three years of talks, a Stabilisation and Association Agreement was signed with the EU in June 2006, and the country formally applied for membership in April 2009, the same month as it became a member of NATO. Protests at alleged official corruption and vote-rigging led to violent clashes in 2011. The Socialist Party won 53% of the vote in 2013 elections. Albania became an EU candidate member in June 2014.
Economy Although economic growth has begun, Albania is still one of the poorest countries in Europe. 56% of the workforce are engaged in agriculture. Private ownership of land has been encouraged since 1991 and foreign investment is encouraged. Public debt stands at over 70%.

Andorra Principat d'Andorra

Area 468 km² (181 mi²) **Population** 85,000
Capital Andorra la Vella (44,000)
Languages Catalan (official), French, Castilian and Portuguese **GDP** $36,987 (2016)
Currency Euro = 100 cents
Government independent state and co-principality
Head of state co-princes: Joan Enric Vives i Sicilia, Bishop of Urgell, 2003 and Emmanuel Macron (see France), 2017
Head of government Chief Executive Antoni Martí Petit, Democrats for Andorra, 2011
Website http://visitandorra.com
Events In 1993 a new democratic constitution was adopted that reduced the roles of the President of France and the Bishop of Urgell to constitutional figureheads. In 2010, the OECD removed Andorra from its list of uncooperative tax havens. Personal income tax was introduced in 2015 and in 2016 Parliament voted to end secrecy of bank accounts held by EU residents.
Economy About 80% of the work force are employed in the services sector, but tourism accounts for about 80% of GDP with an estimated 9 million visiting annually, attracted by its duty-free status and its summer and winter resorts. Agricultural production is limited (2% of the land is arable) and most food has to be imported. The principal livestock activity is sheep rearing. Manufacturing output consists mainly of cigarettes, cigars and furniture.

Austria Österreich

Area 83,859 km² (32,377 mi²)
Population 8,823,000
Capital Vienna / Wien (1,890,000)
Languages German (official)
GDP $53,764 (2016) **Currency** Euro = 100 cents
Government federal republic
Head of state President Alexander Van der Bellen, Austrian Green Party, 2016
Head of government Federal Chancellor Sebastian Kurz, Austrian People's Party, 2017
Website www.austria.org
Events Since 1999, the far right Freedom Party has made gains, but Alexander Van der Bellen unexpectedly beat its candidate in presidential elections in 2016, a result confirmed when the vote was re-run. The Austrian People's Party has ruled in coalition with the far-right Freedom Party since late 2017.
Economy Has a well-developed market economy and high standard of living. The economy contracted slightly in 2017. The leading economic activities are the manufacture of metals and tourism. Dairy and livestock farming are the principal agricultural activities.

Belarus
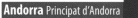

Area 207,600 km² (80,154 mi²)
Population 9,492,000
Capital Minsk (1,982,000)
Languages Belarusian, Russian (both official)
GDP $6,301 (2018)
Currency Belarussian ruble = 100 kopek
Government Republic
Head of state
President Alexander Lukashenko, 1994
Head of government Sergey Rumas, Independent, 2018
Website www.belarus.by/en/government
Events Belarus attained its independence in 1991. As a result of a referendum in 1996 the president increased his power at the expense of parliament. In 1997, Belarus signed a Union Treaty committing it to political and economic integration with Russia. Since his election in July 1994 as the country's first president, Alexander Lukashenko, has steadily consolidated his power through authoritarian means. Government restrictions on freedom of speech, the press and religion continue and in early 2005, the US listed Belarus as an outpost of tyranny. Belarus joined the EU's Eastern Partnership in 2009. In 2010, it signed a customs union with Russia and Kazakhstan. Lukashenko won a fifth term as president in October 2015, in elections seen - like those that preceded them – as corrupt. European sanctions imposed in response to earlier political clamp-downs and human-rights breaches remain.
Economy Belarus has faced problems in the transition to a free-market economy. After relaxation of currency rules in early 2011, the value of the ruble dropped sharply and the country's large foreign debts and lack of hard currency led to negotiations with Russia over substantial loans. Agriculture, especially meat and dairy farming, is important. In 2011, the country was forced to apply to the IMF for funds and for a Russian-led bailout.

Belgium Belgique

Area 30,528 km² (11,786 mi²)
Population 11,358,000
Capital Brussels/Bruxelles (1,175,000)
Languages Dutch, French, German (all official)
GDP $49,271 (2018)
Currency Euro = 100 cents
Government federal constitutional monarchy
Head of state King Philippe I, 2013
Head of government Prime Minister Charles Michel, Reformist Movement, 2014
Website www.belgium.be/en
Events In 1993 Belgium adopted a federal system of government. Elections in June 2007 led to the Christian Democrats gaining almost 30% of the vote in Flanders. An uneasy coalition was eventually formed in March 2008, but negotiations for constitutional reform stalled. Former PM Leterme replaced Herman van Rompuy when the latter became President of the European Council. The coalition collapsed in April 2010. Elections in June resulted in gains for the pro-separatist New Flemish Alliance and the Socialist Party in Wallonia. After elections in May 2014, a coalition was formed, led by Charles Michel of the Francophone Reformist Movement. In March 2016, Islamic State attacked Brussels Airport and a metro station killing 35 and wounding more than 300.
Economy Belgium is a major trading nation with a modern, private-enterprise economy, which grew slightly in 2017. The leading activity is manufacturing i.e. steel and chemicals. With few natural resources, it imports substantial quantities of raw materials and export a large volume of manufactures.

Bosnia-Herzegovina
Bosna i Hercegovina

Area 51,197 km² (19,767 mi²)
Population 3,872,000
Capital Sarajevo (643,000)
Languages Bosnian/Croatian/Serbian
GDP $4,836
Currency
Convertible Marka = 100 convertible pfenniga
Government federal republic

Head of state Chairman of the Presidency – rotates between Presidency members Bakir Izetbegović (Party of Democratic Action), Mladen Ivanić (Party of Democratic Progress) and Dragan Čović (Croatian Democratic Union of Bosnia and Herzegovina)
Head of government Prime Minister Denis Zvizdić, Party of Democratic Action, 2015
Website
www.fbihvlada.gov.ba/english/index.php
Events In 1992 a referendum approved independence from the Yugoslav federation. The Bosnian Serb population was against independence and in the resulting war occupied over two-thirds of the land. Croat forces seized other parts of the area. The 1995 Dayton Peace Accord ended the war and set up the Bosnian Muslim/Croat Federation and the Bosnian Serb Republic, each with their own president, government, parliament, military and police. There is also a central Bosnian government and rotating presidency. The office of High Representative has the power to impose decisions where the authorities are unable to agree or where political or economic interests are affected; the current incumbent, Valentin Inzko took charge in 2009. EUFOR troops took over from the NATO-led force in 2004. In 2005, agreement was reached to set up state-wide police, defence and security forces, a state court and state taxation system. In 2006, Bosnia joined NATO's Partnership for Peace programme and received its membership action plan in 2010. In 2007, the EU initiated its Stabilisation and Association Agreement with Bosnia, which was eventually signed in March 2015. In February 2016, Bosnia formally applied to join the EU.
Economy Excluding Macedonia, Bosnia was the least developed of the former republics of Yugoslavia. Currently receiving substantial aid, though this will be reduced. The country attracts considerable foreign direct investment and the Convertible Marka is Euro-pegged. The economy grew slightly in 2017.

Bulgaria Bulgariya

Area 110,912 km² (42,822 mi²)
Population 7,050,000
Capital Sofia (1,682,000)
Languages Bulgarian (official), Turkish
GDP $7,924 (2018)
Currency Lev = 100 stotinki
Government multiparty republic
Head of state President Rumen Radev, Independent, 2017
Head of government Prime Minister Boiko Borisov, Citizens for European Development of Bulgaria (GERB), 2014.
Website www.government.bg/en
Events In 1990 the first non-communist president for 40 years, Zhelyu Zhelev, was elected. A new constitution in 1991 saw the adoption of free-market reforms. Bulgaria joined NATO in 2004. The president was re-elected in 2006. Bulgaria joined the EU in January 2007, but lack of progress in tackling corruption has led to the delay, then scrapping of a large proportion of EU funding. The GERB-led coalition fell in early 2012 after street protests and was replaced in May 2013 by a technocratic government. After independent Ruman Radev beat the GERB candidate in presidential elections in early 2017, PM Boiko Borisov called snap parliamentary elections, in which he won a third term.
Economy The Lev has been pegged to the Euro since 2002. The economy has begun to attract significant amounts of foreign direct investment. Bulgaria experienced macro-economic stability and strong growth from 1996 to early 2008, and after a sharp decline in GDP in 2009, the economy returned to slight growth from 2010. Manufacturing is the leading economic activity but has outdated technology. The main products are chemicals, metals, machinery and textiles. The valleys of the Maritsa are ideal for winemaking, plums and tobacco. Tourism is increasing rapidly.

Croatia Hrvatska

Area 56,538 km² (21,829 mi²)
Population 4,154,000
Capital Zagreb (1,113,000)
Languages Croatian
GDP $14,788 (2018)
Currency Kuna = 100 lipa
Government multiparty republic
Head of state President Kolinda Grabar-Kiratovic, Independent, 2015
Head of government Prime Minister Andrej Plenkovic, Croatian Democratic Union, 2016
Website https://vlada.gov.hr/en

Events A 1991 referendum voted overwhelmingly in favour of independence from Yugoslavia.Serb-dominated areas took up arms to remain in the federation. Serbia armed Croatian Serbs, war broke out between Serbia and Croatia, and Croatia lost much territory. In 1992 United Nations peacekeeping troops were deployed.Following the Dayton Peace Accord of 1995, Croatia and Yugoslavia established diplomatic relations. An agreement between Croatia and the Croatian Serbs provided for the reintegration of Krajina into Croatia in 1998. Kolida Gravar-Kitarovic beat Ivo Josipopovic in presidential elections of 2014/15. After snap elections in September 2016, Andrej Plenkovic's Croatian Democratic Union formed a coalition with the centre-right MOST. Croatia joined NATO in 2009 and the EU in 2013.
Economy The wars badly disrupted Croatia's economy but it emerged from a mild recession in 2000, with tourism, banking and public investment leading the way. The economy continues to struggle and unemployment is high.

Czechia Česka Republica

Area 78,864 km² (30,449 mi²)
Population 10,611,000
Capital Prague/Praha (2,619,000)
Languages Czech (official), Moravian
GDP GDP $22,468 (2018)
Currency Czech Koruna = 100 haler
Government multiparty republic
Head of state President Milos Zeman, 2013
Head of government
Prime Minister Andrej Babis, ANO 2011, 2017
Website https://vlada.cz/en/
Events In 1992 the government agreed to the secession of the Slovak Republic, and on 1 January 1993 the Czech Republic was created. The Czech Republic was granted full membership of NATO in 1999 and joined the EU in May 2004. Governments have been characterized by short-lived coalitions.After 2017 elections, President Zeman asked Andrej Babis to form a government. After some months of minority rule, a coalition was formed with the Social Democrats.
Economy The country has deposits of coal, uranium, iron ore, tin and zinc. Industries include chemicals, beer, iron and steel. Private ownership of land is gradually being restored. Agriculture employs 12% of the workforce. Inflation is under control. Intensified restructuring among large enterprises, improvements in the financial sector and effective use of available EU funds served to strengthen output growth until the onset of the worldwide economic downturn, because of reduced exports. Prague is now a major tourist destination.

Denmark Danmark

Area 43,094 km² (16,638 mi²)
Population 5,786,000
Capital Copenhagen / København (1,922,000)
Languages Danish (official)
GDP $59,314 (2018)
Currency Krone = 100 øre
Government parliamentary monarchy
Head of state Queen Margrethe II, 1972
Head of government Prime Minister Lars Lokke Rasmussen, Venstre, 2015
Website www.denmark.dk/en
Events In 1992 Denmark rejected the Maastricht Treaty, but reversed the decision in a 1993 referendum. In 1998 the Amsterdam Treaty was ratified by a further referendum. In 2009 Greenland assumed responsibility for many domestic competencies. Former PM Lars Lokke Rasmussen was returned to power in parliamentary elections in 2015.
Economy Danes enjoy a high standard of living with a thoroughly modern market economy featuring high-tech agriculture, up-to-date small-scale and corporate industry, comfortable living standards and a stable currency, which is pegged to the Euro, but still independent. Economic growth gained momentum in 2004, but slowed in 2007. GDP has continued to grow slightly since 2012. Denmark is self-sufficient in oil and natural gas. Services, including tourism, form the largest sector (63% of GDP). Farming employs only 4% of the workforce but is highly productive. Fishing is also important.

Estonia Eesti

Area 45,100 km² (17,413 mi²)
Population 1,319,000
Capital Tallinn (610,000)
Languages Estonian (official), Russian
GDP $23,610 (2018) **Currency** Euro = 100 cents
Government multiparty republic
Head of state President Kersti Kaljulaid, 2016
Head of government
Prime Minister Juri Ratas, Centre Party, 2016
Website www.valitsus.ee/en
Events In 1992 Estonia adopted a new constitution and multiparty elections were held. Estonia joined NATO in March 2004 and the EU in May 2004. In 2005 a treaty defining the border with Russia was signed, but Russia refused to ratify it after Estonia introduced a reference to the Russian occupation of Estonia. Since late 2016, long-time opposition Centre Party has led a broad coalition. Estonia joined the OECD in 2010 and adopted the Euro in January 2011. Strict language laws are regarded by Russian-speakers as discriminatory. In early 2017, NATO troops were deployed to the country to counter what the alliance perceives as Russian aggression.
Economy Privatisation and free-trade reforms after independence increased foreign investment and trade. Chief natural resources are oil shale and forests. Manufactures include petrochemicals, fertilisers and textiles. Estonia has led the way among new EU states with a strong electronics and communications sector. Since the country emerged from the global financial crisis in 2010, the economy has grown erratically.

Finland Suomi

Area 338,145 km² (130,557 mi²)
Population 5,517,000
Capital Helsinki (1,471,000)
Languages Finnish, Swedish (both official)
GDP $52,422 (2018) **Currency** Euro = 100 cents
Government multiparty republic
Head of state President Sauli Niinistö, National Coalition Party, 2012
Head of government
Prime Minister Juha Sipilä, Centre Party, 2015
Website
https://valtioneuvosto.fi/en/frontpage
Events In 1986 Finland became a member of EFTA and in 1995 joined the EU. A new constitution was established in March 2000. The Finnish Parliament voted for the EU constitution in 2006. Successive governments have been in the form of multi-party coalitions. In the presidential election of 2012, Sauli Niinistö defeated Pekka-Haavisto of the Green Party.
Economy Forests are Finland's most valuable resource, with wood and paper products accounting for 35% of exports. Engineering, shipbuilding and textile industries have grown. Finland excels in high-tech exports and is a leading light in the telecoms industry. Farming employs 9% of the workforce. Unemployment remains high, although the economy returned to growth in 2011.

France

Area 551,500 km² (212,934 mi²)
Population 65,058,000
Capital Paris (12,405,000)
Languages French (official), Breton, Occitan
GDP $39,869 (2018)
Currency Euro = 100 cents
Government multiparty republic
Head of state
President Emmanuel Macron, En Marche!, 2017
Head of government Prime Minister
Edouard Philippe, Republicans, 2017
Website www.diplomatie.gouv.fr/en/
Events France was a founder member of both the EU and NATO. Its post-war governments have swung between socialist and centrist/right. François Hollande's reform of employment legislation led to widespread industrial action in 2016. Centrist Emmanuel Macron defeated Marine Le Pen of the far right National Front in the 2017 presidential elections. His public-sector employment reforms led to strikes by railway workers and air-traffic controllers, among others.
Economy France is a leading industrial nation. Industries include chemicals and steel. It is the leading producer of farm products in western Europe. Livestock and dairy farming are vital sectors. Despite a degree of recovery, unemployment remains high. It is the world's second largest producer of cheese and wine. Tourism is a major industry.

EUROPEAN UNION MEMBERSHIP

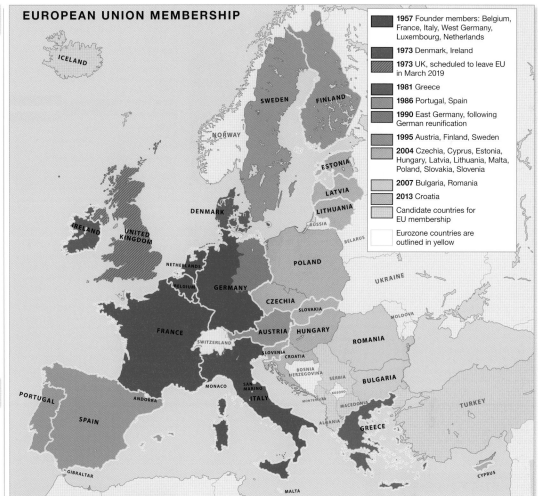

	1957 Founder members: Belgium, France, Italy, West Germany, Luxembourg, Netherlands
	1973 Denmark, Ireland
	1973 UK, scheduled to leave EU in March 2019
	1981 Greece
	1986 Portugal, Spain
	1990 East Germany, following German reunification
	1995 Austria, Finland, Sweden
	2004 Czechia, Cyprus, Estonia, Hungary, Latvia, Lithuania, Malta, Poland, Slovakia, Slovenia
	2007 Bulgaria, Romania
	2013 Croatia
	Candidate countries for EU membership
	Eurozone countries are outlined in yellow

Germany Deutschland

Area 357,022 km² (137,846 mi²)
Population 82,806,000
Capital Berlin (6,005,000)
Languages German (official)
GDP $44,550 (2018)
Currency Euro = 100 cents
Government federal multiparty republic
Head of state President Frank-Walter Steinmeier, Social Democrat, 2017
Head of government Chancellor Angela Merkel, Christian Democratic Union, 2005
Website www.bundesregierung.de
Events Germany is a major supporter of the European Union, and former chancellor Helmut Köhl was the driving force behind the creation of the Euro. The grand coalition government formed in 2005 between the CDU, CSU and Social Democrats was replaced by one of the CDU, CSU and FDP after elections in 2009. Repeated calls upon German funds in support of weaker Eurozone economies have caused widespread anger. Angela Merkel's CDU only narrowly missed winning an outright majority in 2013 elections. Immigration has become a divisive issue and in 2017 Alternative for Germany gained seats in parliamentary elections, the first extreme right party to do so since WW2.
Economy Germany has long been one of the world's greatest economic powers. The economy returned to growth in 2014. Services form the largest economic sector. Machinery and transport equipment account for 50% of exports. It is the world's third-largest car producer. Other major products include ships, iron, steel, petroleum and tyres. It has the world's second-largest lignite mining industry. Other minerals are copper, potash, lead, salt, zinc and aluminium. Germany is the world's second-largest producer of hops and beer. Other products are cheese and milk, barley, rye and pork.

Greece Ellas

Area 131,957 km² (50,948 mi²)
Population 10,768,000
Capital Athens / Athina (3,781,000)
Languages Greek (official)
GDP $20,570 (2018)
Currency Euro = 100 cents
Government multiparty republic
Head of state President Prokopis Pavlopoulos, New Democracy, 2015
Head of government Prime Minister Alexis Tsipras, Syriza, 2015
Website https://primeminister.gr/en/home
Events In 1981 Greece joined the EU, and Andreas Papandreous became Greece's first Socialist prime minister. The coalition led by Antonis Samaras fell in early 2015 because of continued discontent over the economy. The left-wing Syriza, under Alexis Tsipras, came to power on a ticket of rejecting the international donors' austerity measures. Months of negotiations over extra loans or deferment of repayments failed to reach a compromise, culminating in the Greek PM opting for a referendum on the donor's proposals, with the result being an overwhelming rejection of the EU's terms. Further bailout funds and repayment extensions were agreed in May 2016. The country exited its EU bailout programme in August 2018
Economy Greece is one of the poorest members of the European Union. Manufacturing is important. Products: textiles, cement, chemicals, metallurgy. Minerals: lignite, bauxite, chromite. Farmland covers 33% of Greece, grazing land 40%. Major crops: tobacco, olives, grapes, cotton, wheat. Livestock are raised. Tourism provides 15% of GDP. In receipt of multiple loans from Eurozone funds and the IMF, Greece has repeatedly been in danger of defaulting on debt repayments, with the possible result that it would be forced to give up the currency. Austerity measures imposed by the international community have depressed economic activity. Unemployment remains at almost 20% and over one-third of the population is below the poverty line.

Hungary Magyarország

Area 93,032 km² (35,919 mi²)
Population 9,798,000
Capital Budapest (3,304,000)
Languages Hungarian (official)
GDP $16,723 (2018) **Currency** Forint = 100 filler
Government multiparty republic
Head of state
President János Áder, Fidesz, 2012.
Head of government
Prime Minister Viktor Orban, Fidesz, 2010
Website www.kormany.hu/en
Events In 1990 multiparty elections were held for the first time. In 1999 Hungary joined NATO and in 2004 it acceded to the EU. In 2012 attempts to change the electoral system led to widespread protests, as have austerity measures imposed by successive governments. Relations with the EU bodies and IMF remain fractious because of the effect of terms imposed for Euro accession and financial bailouts.
Economy Since the early 1990s, Hungary has adopted market reforms and partial privatisation programmes. High levels of public debt meant that Hungary had to appeal for repeated loans from the IMF and EU to prevent economic collapse when the world economic crisis struck. The manufacture of machinery and transport is the most valuable sector. Hungary's resources include bauxite, coal and natural gas. Major crops include grapes for wine-making, maize, potatoes, sugar beet and wheat. Tourism is a growing sector.

Iceland Ísland

Area 103,000 km² (39,768 mi²)
Population 351,000
Capital Reykjavik (217,000)
Languages Icelandic
GDP $70,332 (2018)
Currency Krona = 100 aurar
Government multiparty republic
Head of state President Guðni Thorlacius Jóhannesson, independent, 2016
Head of government Prime Minister Katrin Jakobsdottir, Left-Green Movement, 2017
Website www.government.is
Events In 1944, a referendum decisively voted to sever links with Denmark, and Iceland became a fully independent republic. In 1946 it joined NATO. In 1970 Iceland joined the European Free Trade Association. The last post-war US military personnel left in September 2006, the same year that the government voted to resume commercial whaling. There are concerns among environmentalists about the impact of major new industrial complexes powered by Iceland's abundant thermal energy. Even though Sigurdardottir's Social Democratic Alliance had returned some stability to the economy, the Social Democrats were defeated in 2013 parliamentary elections. Snap elections called in 2017 resulted in Katrin Jakobsdottir's

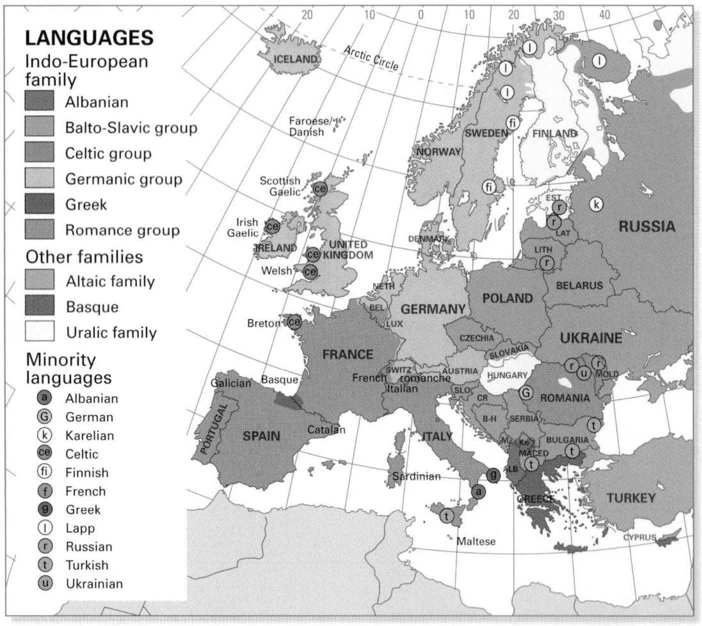
LANGUAGES
Indo-European family
Albanian
Balto-Slavic group
Celtic group
Germanic group
Greek
Romance group
Other families
Altaic family
Basque
Uralic family
Minority languages
a Albanian
G German
k Karelian
ce Celtic
fi Finnish
f French
g Greek
l Lapp
r Russian
t Turkish
u Ukrainian
Arctic Circle
ICELAND
Faroese/Danish
Scottish Gaelic
Irish Gaelic
IRELAND
UNITED KINGDOM
Welsh
Breton
SWEDEN
FINLAND
NORWAY
RUSSIA
DENMARK
EST
LAT
LITH
BELARUS
NETH
GERMANY
POLAND
BEL
LUX
CZECHIA
SLOVAKIA
UKRAINE
MOLD
FRANCE
SWITZ
Romanche
French
Italian
AUSTRIA
HUNGARY
ROMANIA
SLO
CR
B-H
SERBIA
MACED
BULGARIA
ALB
Galician
Basque
PORTUGAL
SPAIN
Catalan
ITALY
Sardinian
GREECE
TURKEY
CYPRUS
Maltese

Left-Green Movement forming a coalition with the Independence Party and Progress Party.

Economy The economy has long been sensitive to declining fish stocks as well as to fluctuations in world prices for its main exports: fish and fish products, aluminum and ferrosilicon. There has traditionally been low unemployment, and remarkably even distribution of income. Risky levels of investment in overseas companies left Iceland's banks with high debts when the global credit crunch hit, and the government had to apply for IMF funding. The economy returned to its pre-crash size in early 2015.

Ireland Eire

Area 70,273 km² (27,132 mi²)
Population 4,857,200
Capital Dublin (1,905,000)
Languages Irish, English (both official)
GDP $80,461 (2018)
Currency Euro = 100 cents
Government multiparty republic
Head of state President Michael Higgins, Independent (formerly Labour Party), 2011
Head of government Taoiseach Leo Varadkar, Fine Gael, 2017
Website www.gov.ie/en/

Events In 1948 Ireland withdrew from the British Commonwealth and joined the European Community in 1973. The Anglo-Irish Agreement (1985) gave Ireland a consultative role in the affairs of Northern Ireland. Following a 1995 referendum, divorce was legalised. Abortion remains a contentious political issue. In the Good Friday Agreement of 1998 the Irish Republic gave up its constitutional claim to Northern Ireland and a North-South Ministerial Council was established. Sinn Fein got its first seats in the European elections of June 2004. Parliamentary elections of early 2016 led to deadlock, until the two main parties reached an agreement allowing Fine Gael to become a minority government.

Economy Ireland benefited greatly from its membership of the European Union. It joined in circulating the Euro in 2002. Grants have enabled the modernisation of farming, which employs 14% of the workforce. Major products include cereals, cattle and dairy products, sheep, sugar beet and potatoes. Fishing is important. Traditional sectors, such as brewing, distilling and textiles, have been supplemented by high-tech industries, such as electronics. Tourism is the most important component of the service industry. The economy also benefited from a rise in consumer spending, construction and business investment, but growth slowed in 2007 and the country went into recession in 2008, and the joint banking and debt crisis eventually led to the government of Brian Cowen requesting a bailout from the EU and IMF. In 2013, Ireland was the first country to exit from its EU bailout programme and the economy has continued to grow since 2014.

Italy Italia

Area 301,318 km² (116,338 mi²)
Population 60,500,000
Capital Rome / Roma (4,356,000)
Languages Italian (official)
GDP $35,913 (2018)
Currency Euro = 100 cents
Government social democracy
Head of state President Sergio Mattarella, 2015
Head of government Prime Minister Giuseppe Conte, Independent, 2018

Events Since World War II Italy has had a succession of unstable, short-lived governments. Parliamentary elections of 2018 resulted in weeks of negotiations between two populist parties – the 5Star Movement and the League. Eventually they formed a coalition with Giuseppe Conti as leader.

Economy Italy's main industrial region is the north-western triangle of Milan, Turin and Genoa. It is the world's eighth-largest car and steel producer. Machinery and transport equipment account for 37% of exports. Agricultural production is important. Italy is the world's largest producer of wine. Tourism is a vital economic sector. Italy emerged from a two-year recession at the end of 2013, but unemployment remains high.

Kosovo (Republika e Kosoves/Republika Kosovo)

Area 10,887 km² (4203 mi²)
Population 1,921,000
Capital Pristina (504,000)
Languages Albanian, Serbian (both official), Bosnian, Turkish, Romani
GDP $4,140 (2018)
Currency Euro (Serbian dinar in Serb enclaves)
Government Multiparty republic
Head of state President Hashim Thaçi, Independent, 2016
Head of government Prime Minister Ramush Haradinaj, AKK, 2017
Website http://kryeministri-ks.net/en/

Events An autonomous province with a mainly ethnic Albanian Muslim popluation, Kosovo first declared independence from Serbia in 1990, leading to years of increased ethnic tension and violence. In 1998 conflict between Serb police and the Kosovo Liberation Army led to a violent crackdown by Serbia, which ceased only after more than two months' aerial bombardment by Nato in 1999, during which hundreds of thousands of Kosovo Albanians were massacred or expelled before Serbia agreed to withdraw and a UN peacekeeping force and administration were sent in, which remained in place until 2008. Talks on the status of the province took place in 2003 and 2006. In 2008, independence was declared again and a new constitution was adopted that transferred power from the UN to the ethnic Albanian government, a move that was rejected by Serbia and Russia but recognised by the US and major European countries. The International Court of Justice declared that the move was not illegal. In March 2011, direct talks between Serbia and Kosovo began. In 2013, the EU brokered an agreement on policing for the Serb minority while former wartime leader Ramush Haradinaj took over as PM after elections in 2017. Thaçi became president in early 2016.

Economy Kosovo is one of the poorest areas of Europe, with a high proportion of the population classed as living in poverty. It possesses some mineral resources but the chief economic activity is agriculture.

Latvia Latvija

Area 64,589 km² (24,942 mi²)
Population 1,953,000
Capital Riga (1,070,000)
Languages Latvian (official), Russian
GDP $18,472 (2018)
Currency Euro = 100 cents
Government multiparty republic
Head of state President Raimonds Vejonis, Green Party, 2015
Head of government Prime Minister Maris Kucinskis, Liepaja Party, 2016
Website www.mk.gov.lv/en

Events Latvia became a member of NATO and the EU in spring 2004. People applying for citizenship are now required to pass a Latvian language test, which has caused much upset amongst the one third of the population who are Russian speakers. After Ivars Godmanis resigned in February 2009 over his handling of the economic crisis, including having to apply for aid from the IMF, a 6-party coalition was approved by parliament. After the resignation of Valdis Dombrovskis in early 2014, Laimdota Straujuma was appointed PM, and the governing coalition increased its majority in elections in October. Straujuma resigned in December and was replaced by Maris Kucinskis. Latvia adopted the Euro on 1 January 2014.

Economy Latvia has to import many of the materials needed for manufacturing. It produces only 10% of the electricity it needs, and the rest has to be imported from Belarus, Russia and Ukraine. Manufactures include electronic goods, farm machinery and fertiliser. Farm exports include beef, dairy products and pork. The majority of companies, banks, and real estate have been privatised. Unemployment remains very high.

Liechtenstein

Area 157 km² (61 mi²)
Population 38,000
Capital Vaduz (5,400)
Languages German (official)
GDP $143,151 (2013)
Currency Swiss franc = 100 centimes
Government independent principality
Head of state Prince Hans Adam II (1989)
Head of government Prime Minister Adrian Hasler, Progressive Citizens Party, 2013
Website www.liechtenstein.li

Events Women finally got the vote in 1984. The principality joined the UN in 1990. In 2003 the people voted in a referendum to give Prince Hans Adam II new political powers, rendering the country Europe's only absolute monarchy with the prince having power of veto over the government. Its status as a tax haven has been criticised as it has been alleged that many billions are laundered there each year. In August 2004 Prince Hans Adam II transferred the day-to-day running of the country to his son Prince Alois, though he did not abdicate and remains titular head of state. The OECD removed Liechtenstein from its list of uncooperative tax havens in 2010. In 2013, the Progressive Citizens Party came first in parliamentary elections.

Economy Liechtenstein is the fourth-smallest country in the world and one of the richest per capita. Since 1945 it has rapidly developed a specialised manufacturing base. It imports more than 90% of its energy requirements. The economy is widely diversified with a large number of small businesses. Tourism is increasingly important.

Lithuania Lietuva

Area 65,200 km² (25,173 mi²)
Population 2,801,000 **Capital** Vilnius (805,000)
Languages Lithuanian (official), Russian, Polish
GDP $19,534 (2018) **Currency** Euro = 100 cents
Government multiparty republic
Head of state President Dalia Grybauskaite, 2009
Head of government Prime Minister Saulius Skvernelis, Peasant and Green Union, 2016
Website http://lrvk.lrv.lt/en

Events The Soviet Union recognised Lithuania's independence in September 1991. Lithuania joined NATO in March 2004 and the EU that May. Elections in autumn 2016 led to a change in the make-up of the ruling coalition. Lithuania adopted the Euro on 1 January 2015.

Economy Lithuania is dependent on Russian raw materials. Manufacturing is the most valuable export sector and major products include chemicals, electronic goods and machine tools. Dairy and meat farming and fishing are also important activities. More than 80% of enterprises have been privatised. The economy was badly hit by the 2008 global economic crisis.

Luxembourg

Area 2,586 km² (998 mi²)
Population 602,000
Capital Luxembourg (107,000)
Languages Luxembourgian / Letzeburgish (official), French, German
GDP $120,061 (2018) **Currency** Euro = 100 cents
Government constitutional monarchy (or grand duchy)
Head of state Grand Duke Henri, 2000
Head of government Prime Minister Xavier Bettel, Democratic Party, 2013
Website http://luxembourg.public.lu/en

Events Governments have mostly been coalitions led by the Christian Social People's Party under Jean-Claude Juncker. In July 2013, the Social Workers Party withdrew from the latest coalition, provoking early elections. These resulted in a coalition between the Social Democrats, Socialists and Greens.

Economy It has a stable, high-income economy, benefiting from its proximity to France, Germany and Belgium. The city of Luxembourg is a major centre of European administration and finance. In 2009, it implemented stricter laws on transparency in the banking sector. There are rich deposits of iron ore, and is a major producer of iron and steel. Other industries include chemicals, textiles, tourism, banking and electronics.

Macedonia Makedonija

Area 25,713 km² (9,927 mi²)
Population 2,104,000 **Capital** Skopje (544,000)
Languages Macedonian (official), Albanian
GDP $5,916 (2018) **Currency** Denar = 100 deni
Government multiparty republic
Head of state President Gjorge Ivanov, VMRO-DPMNE, 2009
Head of government Prime Minister Zoran Zaev, Social Democratic Union, 2017

Events In 1993 the UN accepted the new republic as a member. It formally retains the FYR prefix because of Greek fears that the name implies territorial ambitions towards the Greek region named Macedonia. In August 2004, proposed expansion of rights and local autonomy for Albanians provoked riots by Macedonian nationalists, but the measures went through. In December 2005, EU leaders conditional agreed that Macedonia should become a candidate for membership, but in 2007 expressed alarm at political developments and problems concerning rights for ethnic Albanians. In 2008 Greece vetoed NATO's invitation of membership to Macedonia, in a move ruled illegal by the International Court of Justice in 2011. Elections held in 2016 resulted in a coalition government led by Social Democrat Zoran Zaev. In July 2016 Macedonia signed an accord over the former's formal name. If approved by parliament and in a referendum, the country will be known as the Republic of North Macedonia.

Economy Macedonia is a developing country. The poorest of the six former republics of Yugoslavia, its economy was devastated by UN trade sanctions against Yugoslavia and by the Greek embargo. Economic growth remains erratic. Manufactures, especially metals, dominate exports. Agriculture employs 17% of the workforce. Major crops include cotton, fruits, maize, tobacco and wheat.

Malta

Area 316 km² (122 mi²)
Population 475,000 **Capital** Valetta (394,000)
Languages Maltese, English (both official)
GDP $30,500 (2018) **Currency** Euro = 100 cents
Government multiparty republic
Head of state President Marie Louise Coleiro Preca, Labour Party, 2014
Head of government Prime Minister Joseph Muscat, Labour Party, 2013
Website www.gov.mt

Events In 1990 Malta applied to join the EU. In 1997 the newly elected Malta Labour Party pledged to rescind the application. The Chris-

tian Democratic Nationalist Party, led by the pro-European Edward Fenech Adami, regained power in 1998 elections and won again by a narrow margin in March 2008. Malta joined the EU in May 2004 and adopted the Euro on 1 January 2008. In 2013, the Labour Party defeated Lawrence Gonzi's Nationalists to return to power for the first time in 15 years.
Economy Malta produces only about 20% of its food needs, has limited fresh water supplies and has few domestic energy sources. Machinery and transport equipment account for more than 50% of exports. Malta's historic naval dockyards are now used for commercial shipbuilding and repair. Manufactures include chemicals, electronic equipment and textiles. The largest sector is services, especially tourism.

Moldova

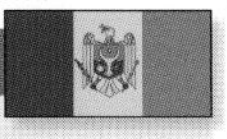

Area 33,851 km² (13,069 mi²)
Population 2,551,000
Capital Chisinau (736,000)
Languages Moldovan / Romanian (official)
GDP $2,596 (2018) **Currency** Leu = 100 bani
Government multiparty republic
Head of state President Igor Dodon, Socialist Party, 2016.
Head of government Prime Minister Pavel Filip, Democratic Party of Moldova, 2016
Website www.moldova.md
Events In 1994 a referendum rejected reunification with Romania and Parliament voted to join the CIS. A new constitution established a presidential parliamentary republic. The Transnistria region mainly inhabited by Russian and Ukrainian speakers declared independence in 1990. This independence has never been recognised and a regional referendum in Transnistria in 2006 that supported eventual union of the region with Russia is similarly being ignored. Relations between Chisinau and Moscow remain strained. Moldova joined the EU's Eastern Partnership in 2009 and signed its Association Agreement in June 2014. Elections in November resulted in pro-European parties remaining in power, although the pro-Russian Socialist Party made major gains. New PM Chiril Gaburici resigned after only a few weeks and was followed by several interim replacements before Pavel Filip was appointed in January 2016.
Economy There is a favourable climate and good farmland but no major mineral deposits. Agriculture is important and major products include fruits and grapes for wine-making. Farmers also raise livestock, including dairy cattle and pigs. Moldova has to import materials and fuels for its industries. Exports include food, wine, tobacco and textiles. The economy remains vulnerable to high fuel prices and poor agricultural weather. The economy stagnated in 2014 and then began to contract.

Monaco

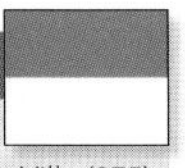

Area 1.5 km² (0.6 mi²)
Population 38,000 **Capital** Monaco-Ville (975)
Languages French (official), Italian, Monegasque
GDP $168,000 **Currency** Euro = 100 cents
Government principality
Head of state Prince Albert II, 2005
Head of government Minister of State Serge Tell, independent, 2016
Website https://en.gouv.mc/Portail-du-Gouvernement
Events Monaco has been ruled by the Grimaldi family since the end of the 13th century and been under the protection of France since 1860.
Economy The chief source of income is tourism. The state retains monopolies in tobacco, the telephone network and the postal service. There is some light industry, including printing, textiles and postage stamps. Also a major banking centre, residents live tax free. In 2010, the OECD removed Monaco from its list of uncooperative tax havens and in 2016 Monaco and the EU signed a tax transparency agreement, due to come into force in 2018.

Montenegro Crna Gora

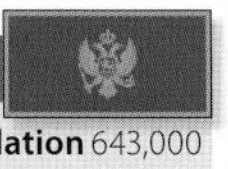

Area 13,812 km² (5,333 mi²) **Population** 643,000
Capital Podgorica (187,000)
Languages Serbian (of the Ijekavian dialect)
GDP $6,783 (2016) **Currency** Euro = 100 cents
Government federal republic
Head of state President Milo Djukanovich, Democratic Party of Socialists, 2018
Head of government Prime Minister Dusko Markovic, Democratic Party of Socialists, 2016
Website www.gov.me/en/homepage
Events In 1992 Montenegro went into federation with Serbia, first as Federal Republic of Yugoslavia, then as a looser State Union of Serbia and Montenegro. Montenegro formed its own economic policy and adopted the Deutschmark as its currency in 1999. It currently uses the Euro, though it is not formally part of the Eurozone. In 2002, Serbia and Montenegro came to a new agreement regarding continued cooperation. On 21 May 2006, the status of the union was decided as 55.54% of voters voted for independence of Montenegro, narrowly passing the 55% threshold needed to validate the referendum under rules set by the EU. On 3 June 2006 the Parliament of Montenegro declared independence. Montenegro was rapidly admitted to the UN, the World Bank and the IMF, joined NATO's Partnership for Peace and applied for EU membership. It was formally named as an EU candidate country in 2010 and accession negotiations started in 2012, just after it joined the WTO. Montenegro became a member of NATO in 2017.
Economy A rapid period of urbanisation and industrialisation was created within the communism era of Montenegro. During 1993, two thirds of the Montenegrin population lived below the poverty line. Financial losses under the effects of the UN sanctions on the economy of Montenegro are estimated to be $6.39 billion. Today there is faster and more efficient privatisation, introduction of VAT and usage of the Euro.

The Netherlands Nederland

Area 41,526 km² (16,033 mi²)
Population 17,250,000
Capital Amsterdam (2,431,000); administrative capital 's-Gravenhage (The Hague) (1,055,000)
Languages Dutch (official), Frisian
GDP $55,185 (2018) **Currency** Euro = 100 cents
Government constitutional monarchy
Head of state King Willem-Alexander, 2013
Head of government Prime Minister Mark Rutte, People's Party for Freedom and Democracy, 2010
Website www.government.nl
Events A founding member of NATO and the EU. Jan Peter Balkenende's coalition cabinet with the Labour Party and the Christian Union collapsed in early 2010 after Labour refused to sanction continued military deployment in Afghanistan. In 2010 the former junior coalition partner, the Party for Freedom and Democracy, took power, winning again in 2012 and 2017. In 2013, Queen Beatrix abdicated.
Economy The Netherlands has prospered through its close European ties. Private enterprise has successfully combined with progressive social policies. It is highly industrialised. Products include aircraft, chemicals, electronics and machinery. Agriculture is intensive and mechanised, employing only 5% of the workforce. Dairy farming is the leading agricultural activity. It continues to be one of the leading European nations for attracting foreign direct investment.

Norway Norge

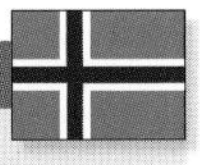

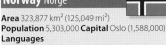

Area 323,877 km² (125,049 mi²)
Population 5,303,000 **Capital** Oslo (1,588,000)
Languages Norwegian (official), Lappish, Finnish
GDP $82,711 (2018) **Currency** Krone = 100 øre
Government constitutional monarchy
Head of state King Harald V, 1991
Head of government Prime Minister Erna Solberg, Conservative Party, 2013
Website www.norway.no/en/uk
Events In referenda in 1972 and 1994 Norway rejected joining the EU. A centre-left coalition, the Labour-led 'Red-Green Alliance' won closely contested elections in September 2005, and retained power in 2009. It was ousted by a Conservative-led minority government in 2013.
Economy Norway has one of the world's highest standards of living. Discovery of oil and gas in adjacent waters in the late 1960s boosted its economic fortunes, with its chief exports now oil and natural gas. Per capita, it is the world's largest producer of hydroelectricity. It is possible oil and gas will begin to run out in Norway in the next two decades but it has been saving its oil budget surpluses and is invested abroad in a fund, valued at more than $250 billion at its height, although this fell rapidly as a result of the global financial crisis. Major manufactures include petroleum products, chemicals, aluminium, wood pulp and paper.

Poland Polska

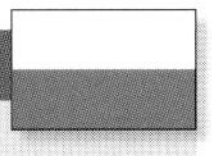

Area 323,250 km² (124,807 mi²)
Population 38,434,000
Capital Warsaw / Warszawa (3,101,000)
Languages Polish (official)
GDP $16,169 (2018)
Currency Zloty = 100 groszy
Government multiparty republic
Head of state President Andrzej Duda, Law and Justice, 2015
Head of government Prime Minister Mateusz Morawiecki, Law and Justice, 2017
Website www.premier.gov.pl/en.html
Events Poland joined the OECD in 1996, NATO in 1999 and the EU in 2004. Andrzej Duda beat Bronislaw Komorowski in presidential elections in May 2015 and Law and Justice returned to power under Beata Szydio in parliamentary polls six months later. Protests in 2017 led President Duda to veto legislation that would have given Parliament control over the judiciary. Szydio was replaced by Mateusz Morawiecki.
Economy Of the workforce, 27% is employed in agriculture and 37% in industry. Poland is the world's fifth-largest producer of lignite and ships. Copper ore is also a vital resource. Manufacturing accounts for 24% of exports. Agriculture remains important. Economic growth began to speed up in 2013.

Portugal

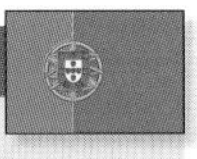

Area 88,797 km² (34,284 mi²)
Population 10,291,000
Capital Lisbon / Lisboa (2,828,000)
Languages Portuguese (official)
GDP $27,456
Currency Euro = 100 cents
Government multiparty republic
Head of state President Marcelo Rebelo de Sousa, Independent, 2016
Head of government Antonio Costa, Socialist Party, 2015
Events In 1986 Portugal joined the EU. In 2002 the Social Democrat Party won the election and formed a coalition government with the Popular Party. The opposition Socialist Party were clear victors in European elections of June 2004. After the collapse of the Socialist government in 2011, the Social Democrat-led coalition introduced strict austerity measures. Inconclusive election results in late 2015 saw the return to power of the Socialists.
Economy Portugal was badly hit by the economic downturn and in April 2011 requested a financial bailout from the IMF and Eurozone funds. Despite budget cuts, public debt remained high, but Portugal exited its bailout in May 2014. Manufacturing accounts for 33% of exports. Textiles, footwear and clothing are major exports. Portugal is the world's fifth-largest producer of tungsten and eighth-largest producer of wine. Olives, potatoes and wheat are also grown. Tourism is very important.

Romania

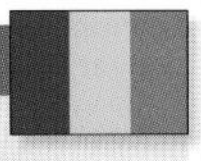

Area 238,391 km² (92,042 mi²)
Population 19,638,000
Capital Bucharest / Bucuresti (2,413,000)
Languages Romanian (official), Hungarian
GDP $12,575 (2018)
Currency Romanian leu = 100 bani
Government multiparty republic
Head of state President Klaus Iohannis, National Liberal Party, 2014
Head of government Prime Minister Vorica Danila, Social Democratic Party, 2017
Website www.gov.ro
Events A new constitution was introduced in 1991. Ion Iliescu, a former communist official, was re-elected in 2000, but barred from standing again in 2004, when he was replaced by Traian Basescu. After losing a vote of no confidence after just 10 months as PM, Boc was reappointed in December 2009. Romania joined NATO in 2004 and joined the EU in January 2007 after making progress towards tackling corruption, although because of this issue France and Germany blocked its Schengen area accession in December 2010. Klaus Iohannis beat PM Victor Ponta in presidential elections in late 2014. The latter was forced to resign in June 2015 after investigators questioned him about tax evasion, money laundering and fraud. In 2017, Vorica Danila became PM upon Mihai Tudose's resignation. Adoption of the Euro has been postponed until 2024.
Economy The currency was re-valued in 2005. Despite a period of strong economic growth, Romania's large public debt led to the need for substantial IMF loans in 2009, necessitating severe cuts in public services.

Russia Rossiya

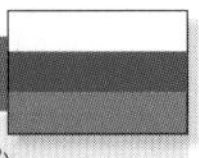

Area 17,075,000 km² (6,592,800 mi²)
Population 144,427,000
Capital Moscow / Moskva (17,100,000)
Languages Russian (official), and many others
GDP $11,946 (2018)
Currency Russian ruble = 100 kopeks
Government federal multiparty republic
Head of state President Vladimir Putin 2012
Head of government Prime Minister Dimitry Medvedev, 2012
Website http://government.ru/en/
Events In 1992 the Russian Federation became a co-founder of the CIS (Commonwealth of Independent States). A new Federal Treaty was signed between the central government and the autonomous republics within the Russian Federation, Chechnya refused to sign and declared independence. In December 1993 a new democratic constitution was adopted. Putin's chosen successor, Medvedev, was elected by a landslide in elections that were criticised by outside observers for biased media coverage. In 2011 Putin was re-elected as President, after the law that prevented serving a third term was revoked. He appointed former president Medvedev as PM. Critics allege that freedom of speech and dissent are being repressed amid crackdowns on NGOs and opponents of the ruling party. Russia joined the WTO in 2012. In 2014, Russia annexed the Crimean Peninsula and Sevastopol leading to international condemnation and sanctions. Relations with the West worsened in succeeding years and further sanctions have been imposed. Putin was re-elected in 2018, with no credible opponents allowed to stand.
Economy In 1993 mass privatisation began. By 1996, 80% of the Russian economy was in private hands. A major problem remains the size of Russia's foreign debt. It is reliant on world oil prices to keep its economy from crashing and the sudden fall in oil prices in the second half of 2008 forced it to devalue the ruble several times. The drop in oil prices from 2014 and international sanctions caused the ruble to plummet in value against other currencies. Industry employs 46% of the workforce and contributes 48% of GDP. Mining is the most valuable activity. Russia is the world's leading producer of natural gas and nickel, the second largest producer of aluminium and phosphates, and the third-largest of crude oil, lignite and brown coal. Most farmland is still government-owned or run as collectives, with important products barley, oats, rye, potatoes, beef and veal. In 2006, the ruble became a convertible currency.

San Marino

Area 61 km² (24 mi²)
Population 36,000
Capital San Marino (4,100)
Languages Italian (official)
GDP $44,947 (2017)
Currency Euro = 100 cents
Government multiparty republic
Head of state co-Chiefs of State: Stefano Palmieri and Matteo Ciacci
Head of government Secretary of State for Foreign and Political Affairs and Economic Planning Nicola Renzi, 2016
Website www.visitsanmarino.com
Events World's smallest republic and perhaps Europe's oldest state, San Marino's links with Italy led to the adoption of the Euro. Its 60-member Great and General Council is elected every five years and headed by two captains regent, who are elected by the council every six months. In 2013 a narrow majority of recorded votes were in favour of joining the EU, but the low turnout invalidated the result.
Economy The economy is largely agricultural. Tourism is vital to the state's income, contributing over 50% of GDP. The economy is generally stable.

Serbia Srbija

Area 77,474 km² (29,913 mi²), including Kosovo
Population 7,040,000
Capital Belgrade / Beograd (1,167,000)
Languages Serbian **GDP** $6,052 (2018)
Currency Dinar = 100 paras
Government federal republic
Head of state President Alexander Vucic, Progressive Party, 2017
Head of government Prime Minister Ana Brnabic, independent, 2017
Website www.srbija.gov.rs
Events Serbian attempts to control the Yugoslav federation led to the secession of Slovenia and Croatia in 1991 and to Bosnia-Herzegovina's declaration of independence in 1992 and the three-year war that ended only with the signing of the Dayton Peace Accord. Slobodan Milosovic became president of Yugoslavia in 1997. Kostunica won the elections of September 2000: Milosevic refused to hand over power, but was ousted after a week. From 2003 to 2006, Serbia was part of the State Union of Serbia and Montenegro, After a referendum in May 2006, the Parliament of Montenegro declared Montenegro independent. Serbia assumed the State Union's UN membership. In 2006 Serbia joined the NATO Partnership for Peace programme and in 2008 signed a Stability and Association Agreement with the EU, to which it applied formally for membership in December 2009. Serbia became a candidate member of the EU in 2012 and accession talks began in early 2014. In May of the latter year, the pro-EU Progressive Party scored a landslide victory in parliamentary elections.
Economy The lower-middle income economy was devastated by war and economic sanctions. Industrial production collapsed. Natural resources include bauxite, coal and copper. There is some oil and natural gas. Manufacturing includes aluminium, cars, machinery, plastics, steel and textiles. Agriculture is important. In 2008 Serbia and Russia signed an energy deal, and in October 2009 the latter granted the former a 1 billion Euro loan to ease its budgetary problems. Growth remains erratic.

Slovakia Slovenska Republika

Area 49,012 km² (18,923 mi²)
Population 5,435,000
Capital Bratislava (656,000)
Languages Slovak (official), Hungarian
GDP $20,508 (2018) **Currency** Euro = 100 cents
Government multiparty republic
Head of state President Andrej Kiska, independent, 2014
Head of government Prime Minister Peter Pellegrini, Direction – Social Democracy (Smer), 2018.
Website www.government.gov.sk
Events In 1993 the Slovak Republic became a sovereign state, breaking peaceably from the Czech Republic, with whom it maintains close relations. In 1996 the Slovak Republic and Hungary ratified a treaty confirming their borders and stipulating basic rights for the 560,000 Hungarians in the country. The Slovak Republic joined NATO in March 2004 and the EU two months later. The country adopted the Euro in January 2009. In elections in 2012 Smer returned with a parliamentary majority. SMER lost its majority in 2016. PM Robert Fico stood down in early 2018 amid protests about the death of a journalist who had been probing government corruption.
Economy The transition from communism to private ownership was initially painful with industrial output falling, unemployment and inflation rising, but the economy has become more stable. Manufacturing employs 33% of the workforce. Bratislava and Košice are the chief industrial cities. Major products include ceramics, machinery and steel. Farming employs 12% of the workforce. Crops include barley and grapes. Tourism is growing.

Slovenia Slovenija

Area 20,256 km² (7,820 mi²)
Population 2,067,000
Capital Ljubljana (538,000) **Languages** Slovene
GDP $27,535 (2018) **Currency** Euro = 100 cents
Government multiparty republic
Head of state President Borut Pahor, Social Democratic Party, 2012
Head of government Prime Minister Marjan Sarec, List of Marjan Sarac, 2018
Website www.vlada.si/en
Events In 1990 Slovenia declared itself independent, which led to brief fighting between Slovenes and the federal army. In 1992 the EU recognised Slovenia's independence. Janez Drnovsek was elected president in December 2002. Slovenia joined NATO in March 2004 and the EU two months later. In June 2004 the value of the Tolar was fixed against the Euro, which it joined in 2007. The 2008 general election resulted in a coalition government led by the Social Democratic Party. A referendum in June 2010 narrowly approved the settlement of the border dispute with Croatia. After two years of political instability, a succession of fairly short-lived coalition governments ensued. 2018 polls saw Marjan Sarec, a former comedian, political satirist and major of Kamnik elected PM.
Economy The transformation of a centrally planned economy and the fighting in other parts of former Yugoslavia caused problems for Slovenia but the economy eventually experienced strong growth in per capita GDP until this was badly hit by the gobal financial crisis. Manufacturing is the leading activity. Major manufactures include chemicals, machinery, transport equipment, metal goods and textiles. Major crops include maize, fruit, potatoes and wheat.

Spain España

Area 497,548 km² (192,103 mi²)
Population 46,700,000
Capital Madrid (6,675,000)
Languages Castilian Spanish (official), Catalan, Galician, Basque
GDP $33,000 (2018)
Currency Euro = 100 cents
Government constitutional monarchy
Head of state King Felipe VI, 2014
Head of government Prime Minister Mariano Rajoy, Spanish People's Party, 2011 (caretaker)
Website www.lamoncloa.gob.es/lang/en
Events From 1959-98 the militant Basque organisation ETA waged a campaign of terror. Its first ceasefire was broken in 2000 and a second - declared in 2006 - with a bomb attack on Madrid airport at the end of the year. A third ceasefire was declared in September 2010. In March 2004 Al qaeda-related bombers killed 191 people in Madrid, resulting in an election win for the opposition Socialist Party. In the 2008 elections, the socialists increased their numbers in Parliament, but did not gain a majority. Austerity measures brought in to tackle public debt, and as condition of the country's financial bailout, changes to pensions and benefits and rising unemployment led to widespread protests in 2010 and 2011. The Popular Party won a sweeping majority in general elections in November 2011. After inconclusive elections in 2015, Popular Party PM, Mariano Rajoy, stayed on as caretaker and gained most seats in new elections in June 2016, but resigned in 2018 because of alleged corruption in the party and was replaced by socialist, Pedro Sanchez.
Economy Spain's transformation from a largely poor, agrarian society to a prosperous nation came to an end with the economic downturn of 2008. The country's debt burden became untenable and financial bailouts from the international community in 2010 and the Eurozone in 2012 were necessary. Unemployment is more than double the European average. Agriculture now employs only 10% of the workforce and the sector is shrinking further because of recurrent droughts. Spain is the world's third-largest wine producer. Other crops include citrus fruits, tomatoes and olives. Industries: cars, ships, chemicals, electronics, metal goods, steel and textiles.

Sweden Sverige

Area 449,964 km² (173,731 mi²)
Population 10,162,000
Capital Stockholm (2,227,000)
Languages Swedish (official), Finnish
GDP $55,345 (2018)
Currency Swedish krona = 100 ore
Government constitutional monarchy
Head of state King Carl Gustaf XVI, 1973
Head of government Prime Minister Stefan Löfvén, Social Democrats, 2014
Website www.sweden.gov.se
Events In 1995 Sweden joined the European Union. The cost of maintaining Sweden's extensive welfare services has become a major political issue. In 2003 Sweden rejected adoption of the Euro. Parliamentary elections in October 2014 led to a fragile minority government being formed by the Social Democrats.
Economy Sweden is a highly developed industrial country. It has rich iron ore deposits. Privately owned firms account for about 90% of industrial output. Steel is a major product, used to manufacture aircraft, cars, machinery and ships. Forestry and fishing are important. Agriculture accounts for 2% of GDP and jobs. The Swedish central bank focuses on price stability with its inflation target of 2%.

Switzerland Schweiz

Area 41,284 km² (15,939 mi²)
Population 8,401,000 **Capital** Bern (407,000)
Languages French, German, Italian, Romansch (all official)
GDP $80,837 (2018)
Currency Swiss Franc = 100 centimes / rappen
Government federal republic
Head of state President of the Swiss Confederation Alain Berset, Social Democratic Party, 2018
Website www.admin.ch
Events Priding themselves on their neutrality, Swiss voters rejected membership of the UN in 1986 and the EU in 1992 and 2001. However, Switzerland finally became a partner country of NATO in 1997 and joined the organisation in 2002, when it also joined the UN. The federal council is made up of seven federal ministers from whom the president is chosen on an annual basis. A 2005 referendum backed membership of EU Schengen and Dublin agreements, bringing Switzerland into the European passport-free zone and increasing co-operation on crime and asylum seekers. Immigration is becoming an increasingly divisive issue.
Economy Switzerland is a wealthy and stable modern market economy with low unemployment, and per capita GDP grew strongly in 2014. Manufactures include chemicals, electrical equipment, machinery, precision instruments, watches and textiles. Livestock, notably dairy farming, is the chief agricultural activity. Tourism is important, and Swiss banks remain a safe haven for investors. In early 2015, the rapid fall of the value of the Euro on international markets led the Swiss National Bank to reverse the decision of 2011 to peg the Franc to the Euro.

Turkey Türkiye

Area 774,815 km² (299,156 mi²)
Population 80,811,000
Capital Ankara (5,445,000)
Languages Turkish (official), Kurdish
GDP $11,114
Currency New Turkish lira = 100 kurus
Government Unitary presidential constitutional republic
Head of state Recep Tayyip Erdogan, Justice and Development Party (AK), 2014
Website www.mfa.gov.tr/default.en.mfa
Events The Kurdistan Workers Party (PKK) carried out terrorist activities throughout the 1980s and 1990s, but declared a ceasefire in 1999, changed their name to Congress for Freedom and Democracy in Kurdistan (KADEK) and said they wanted to campaign peacefully for Kurdish rights. In September 2003 they ended a 4-year ceasefire, but declared another in 2006, although this did not hold. In October 2005, the EU opened accession negotiations with Ankara. Membership of the EU is an aim but human rights, the Cyprus issue and the hostility of successive French and Austrian governments are barriers, but it was announced in October that talks would recommence the following month. The escalating civil war in Syria has caused a refugee crisis on the border. In 2014, PM Erdogan won the first direct presidential election. Conflict in Syria over-spilled into the country, causing a resumption of hostilities between Kurdish and government forces. An attempted military coup in June 2016 was swiftly defeated and thousands were arrested in the ensuing crackdown. A referendum in 2017 approved a change to a presidential republic, giving Erdogan sweeping powers.
Economy Turkey is an upper-middle-income country, as classified by the World Bank. Agriculture employs 47% of the workforce, but is becoming less important to the economy. Turkey is a leading producer of citrus fruits, barley, cotton, wheat, tobacco and tea. It is a major producer of chromium and phosphate fertilisers. Tourism is a vital source of foreign exchange. In January 2005, the New Turkish lira was introduced at a rate of 1 to 1,000,000 old Turkish lira. As a result of terrorist attacks, tourist numbers had dropped by half by mid-2016, causing serious damage to the economy.

Ukraine Ukraina

Area 603,700 km² (233,088 mi²)
Population 42,418,000
Capital Kiev / Kyviv (3,375,000)
Languages Ukrainian (official), Russian
GDP $2,640 (2018)
Currency Hryvnia = 100 kopiykas
Government multiparty republic
Head of state Petro Poroshenko, independent, 2014
Head of government Vlodymyr Groysman, Petro Poroshenko Bloc, 2016
Website www.kmu.gov.ua/control/en
Events The Chernobyl disaster of 1986 contaminated large areas of Ukraine. Independence was achieved in 1991 with the dissolution of the USSR. Leonid Kuchma was elected president in 1994. He continued the policy of establishing closer ties with the West and sped up the pace of privatisation. In 2010, the coalition governent of Yulia Tymoshenko fell, and the Party of the Regions formed a coalition with the Communists and the centrist Lytvyn Bloc. Former PM Victor Yanukovic beat Tymoshenko in the presidential elections. Ukraine joined the EU's Eastern Partnership in 2009, but has abandoned plans to join NATO. President Yanukovich's decision to abandon plans for closer ties with the EU led to riots from late 2013, followed by his escape to Russia in February 2014. The following month, Russia sent forces into the Crimean Peninsula to assist separatists. A few days later, after a partially boycotted referendum, the administrations of Crimea and Sevastopol asked Russia for the right to accede, which Russia granted and annexed the region and city. Parliamentary elections in late 2014 resulted in a resounding win for pro-Western parties. Fighting continues in the east despite a fragile ceasefire brokered by France and Germany in February 2015. In July 2017, Ukraine's Association Agreement with the European Union was ratified.
Economy Ukraine is a lower-middle-income economy. Agriculture is important. It is the world's leading producer of sugar beet, the second-largest producer of barley, and a major producer of wheat. Ukraine has extensive raw materials, including coal (though many mines are exhausted), iron ore and manganese ore. Ukraine is reliant on oil and natural gas imports. The economy's dependence on steel exports made it vulnerable to the 2008 global economic downturn and it was offered a massive loan by the IMF. Economic growth remains fragile.

United Kingdom

Area 241,857 km² (93,381 mi²)
Population 66,040,000
Capital London (14,040,000)
Languages English (official), Welsh (also official in Wales), Gaelic
GDP $39,734
Currency Sterling (pound) = 100 pence
Government constitutional monarchy
Head of state Queen Elizabeth II, 1952
Head of government Prime Minister Theresa May, Conservative Party, 2016
Website www.gov.uk
Events The United Kingdom of Great Britain and Northern Ireland is a union of four countries – England, Northern Ireland, Scotland and Wales. Since 1997, Scotland and Wales have had their own legislative assemblies. In 2005 the IRA anounced a permanent cessation of hostilities and the Northern Ireland Assembly was finally reinstated in early 2007. Scotland voted against independence from the UK in September 2014. The Conservative Party won a majority in the parliamentary elections of 2015. In June 2016, voters narrowly chose to leave the EU. Uncertainty over the possible impact of leaving the EU led to sharp falls in the value of Sterling.
Economy The UK is a major industrial and trading nation. A producer of oil, petroleum products, natural gas, potash, salt and lead. Financial services and tourism are the leading service industries. The economic downturn of 2008 led to the government effectively nationalising several banks and bailing out others with huge loans. Economic growth continues to improve.

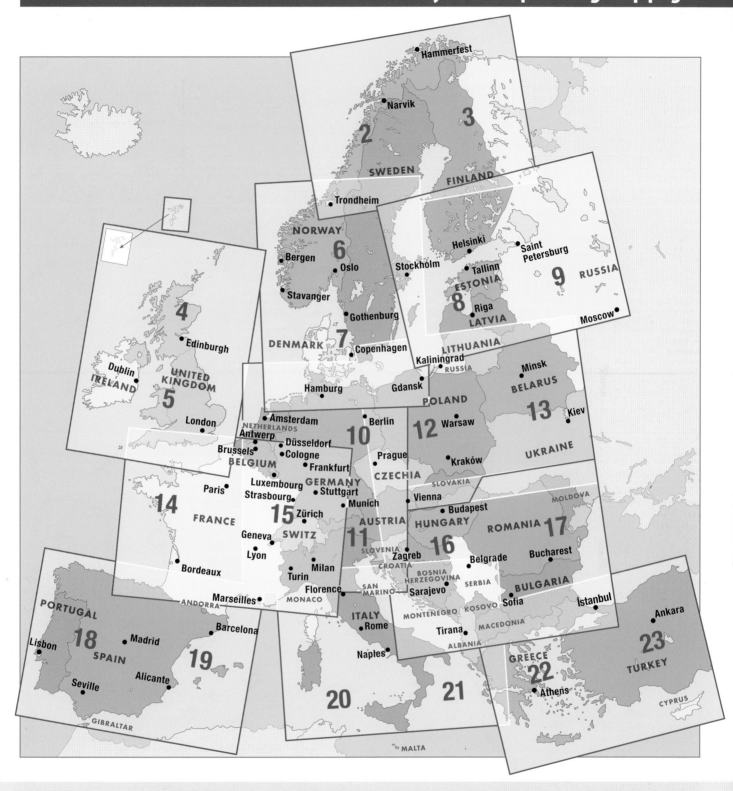

Motorway vignettes

Some countries require you to purchase (and in some cases display) a vignette before using motorways.

In Austria you will need to purchase and display a vignette on the inside of your windscreen. Vignettes are available for purchase at border crossings and petrol stations. More details from www.asfinag.at/toll/toll-sticker

In Belarus all vehicles over 3.5 tonnes and cars and vans under 3.5 tonnes registered outside the Eurasion Economic Union are required to have a *BelToll* unit installed. This device exchanges data with roadside gantries, enabling motorway tolls to be automatically deducted from the driver's account. http://beltoll.by/index.php/en/

In Czechia, you can buy a vignette at the border and also at petrol stations. Make sure you write your vehicle registration number on the vignette before displaying it. The roads without toll are indicated by a traffic sign saying "Bez poplatku". More details from www.motorway.cz

In Hungary a new e-vignette system was introduced in 2008. It is therefore no longer necessary to display the vignette, though you should make doubly sure the information you give on your vehicle is accurate. Vignettes are sold at petrol stations throughout the country. Buy online at http://toll-charge.hu/

In Slovakia, an electronic vignette must purchased before using the motorways. Vignettes may be purchased online, via a mobile app or at Slovak border crossings and petrol stations displaying the 'eznamka' logo. More details from https://eznamka.sk/selfcare/home/

In Switzerland, you will need to purchase and display a vignette before you drive on the motorway. Bear in mind you will need a separate vignette if you are towing a caravan. www.ezv.admin.ch/ezv/en/home/information-individuals/documents-for-travellers-and-road-taxes/motorway-charge-sticker--vignette-.html

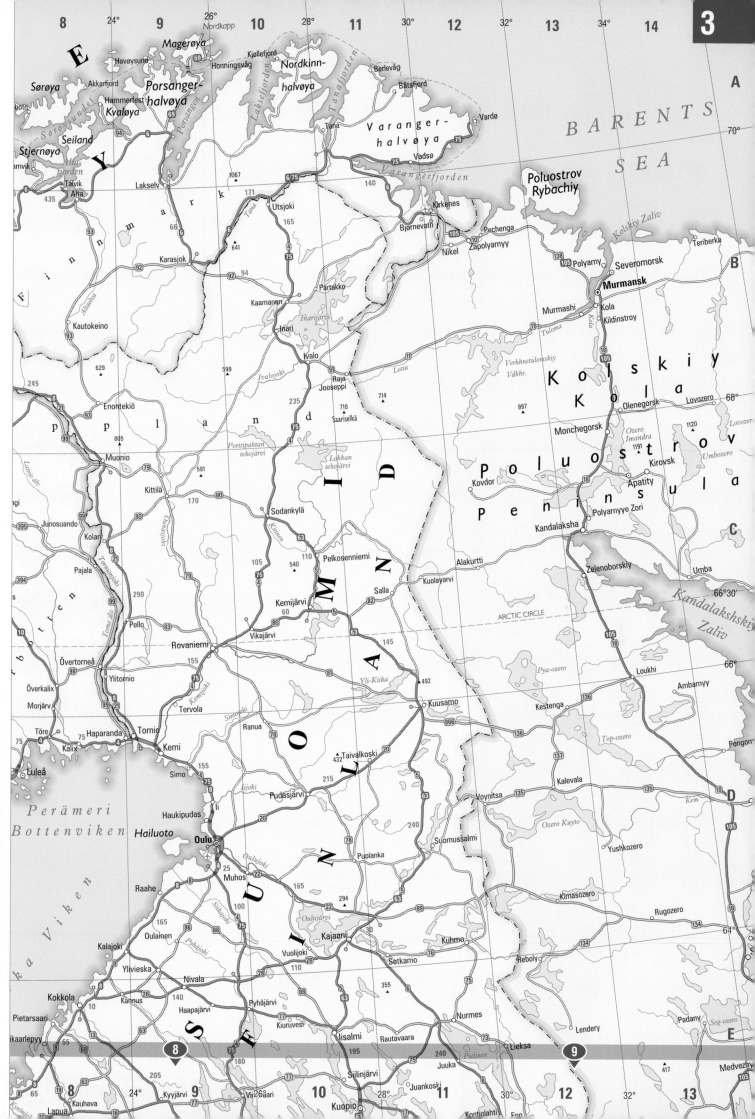

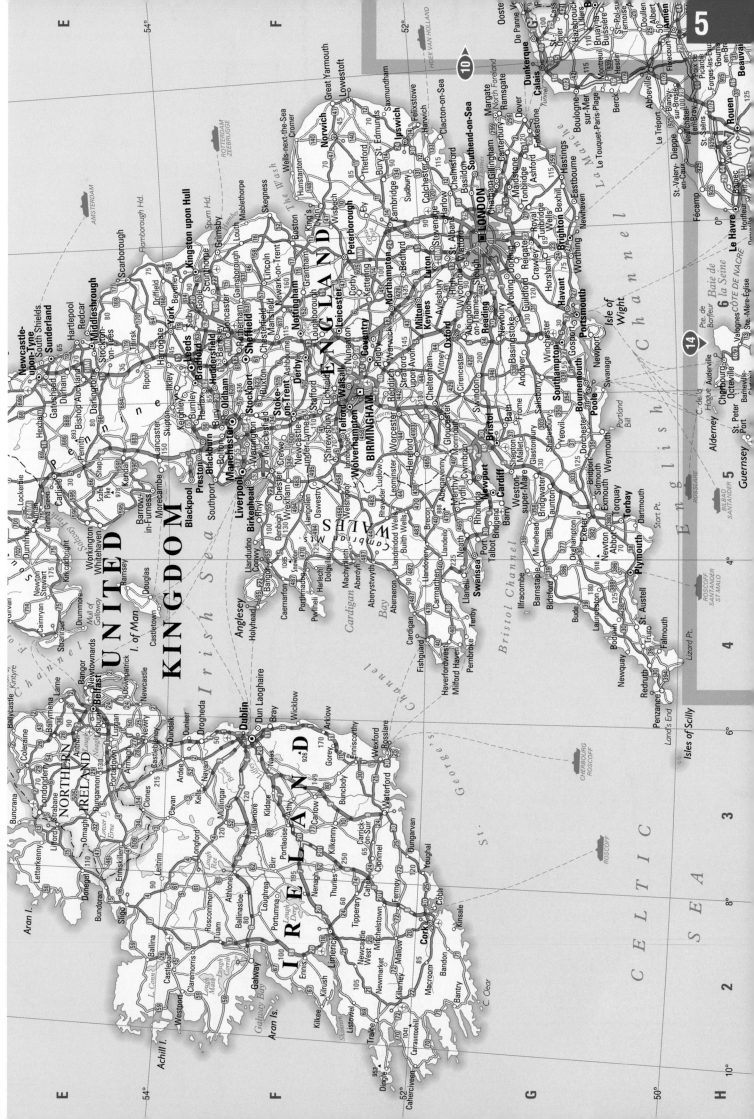

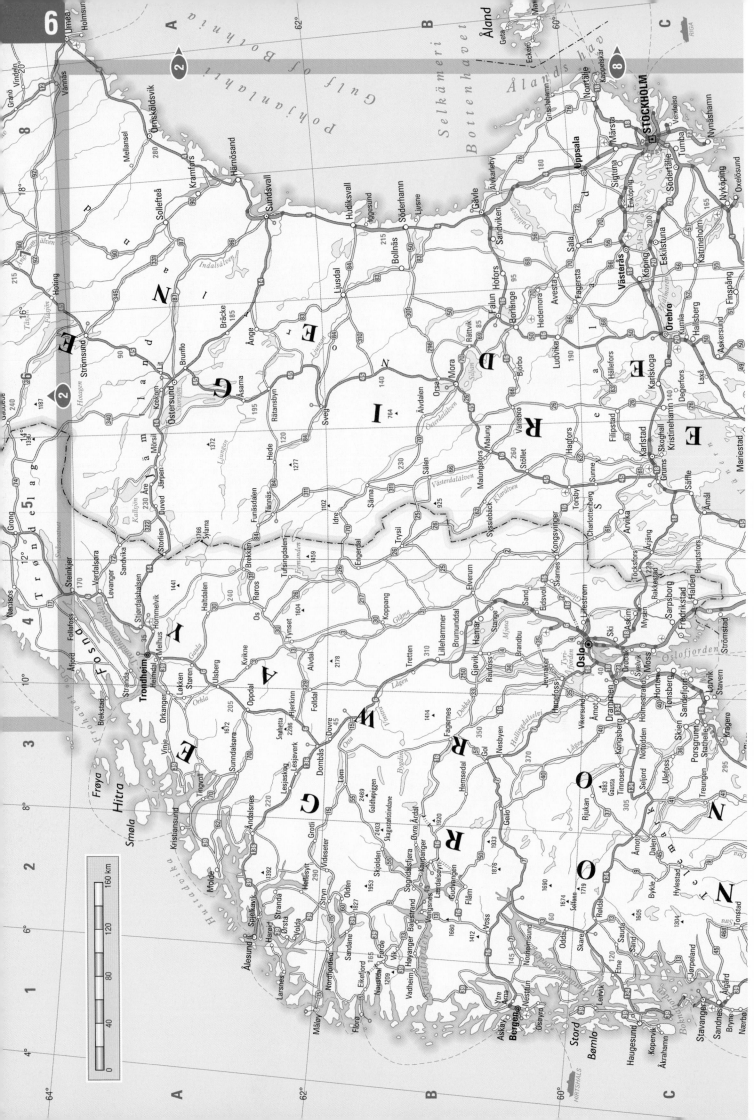

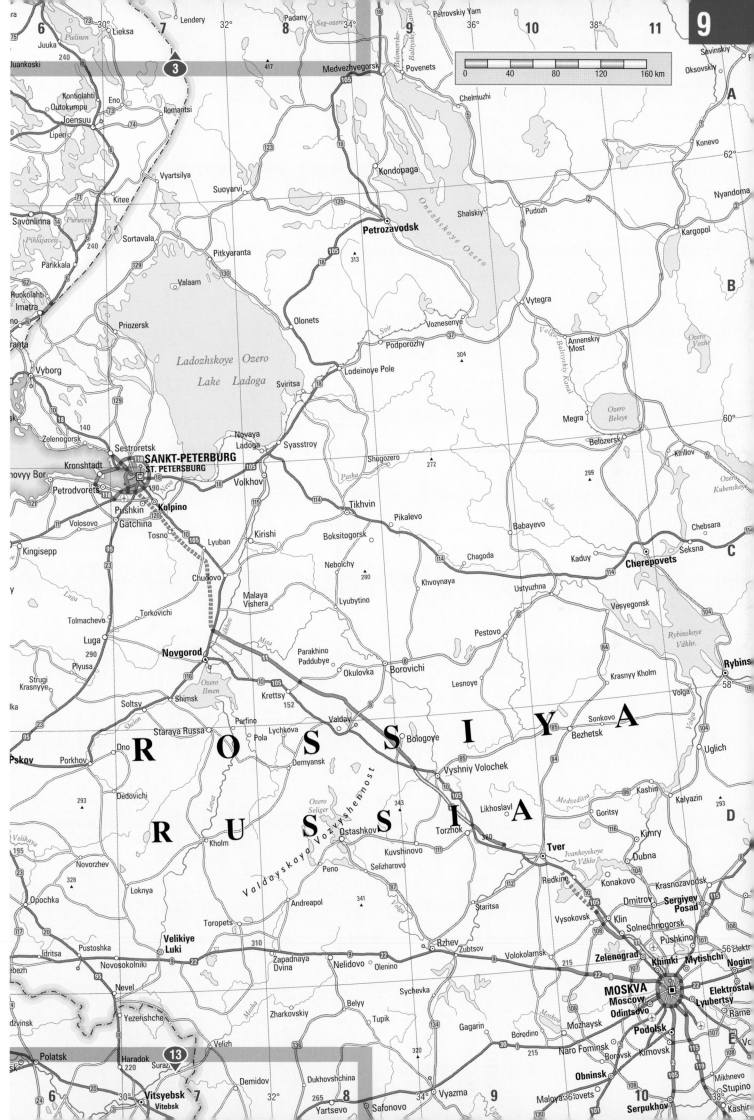

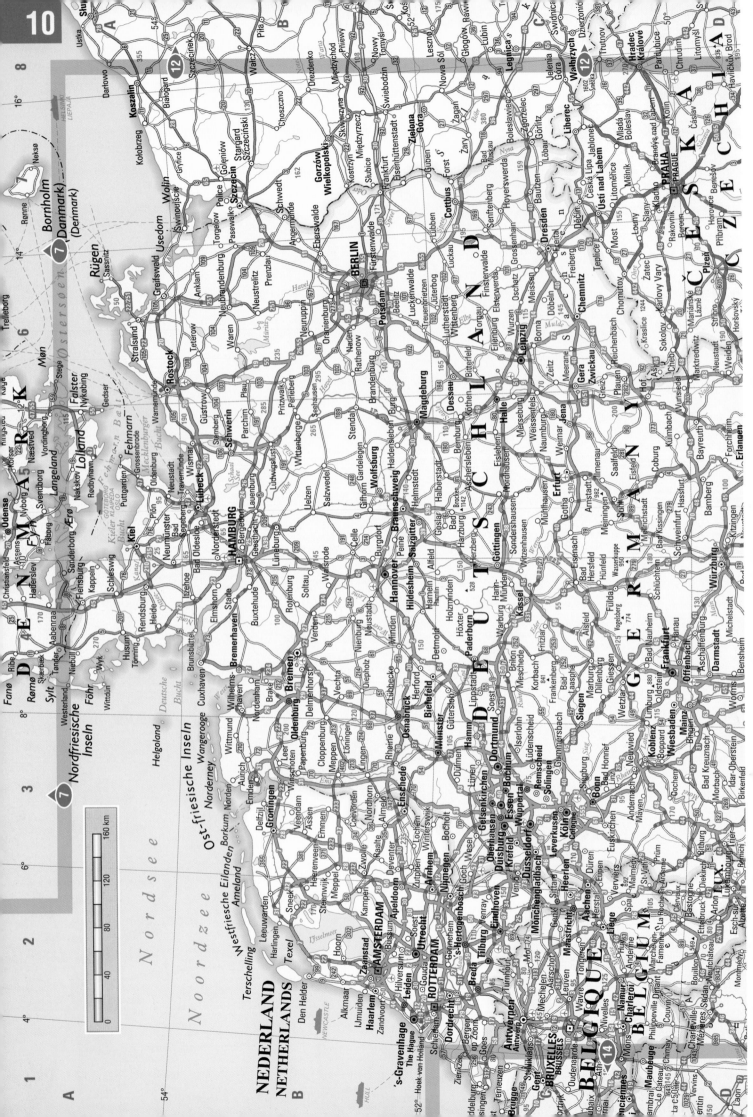

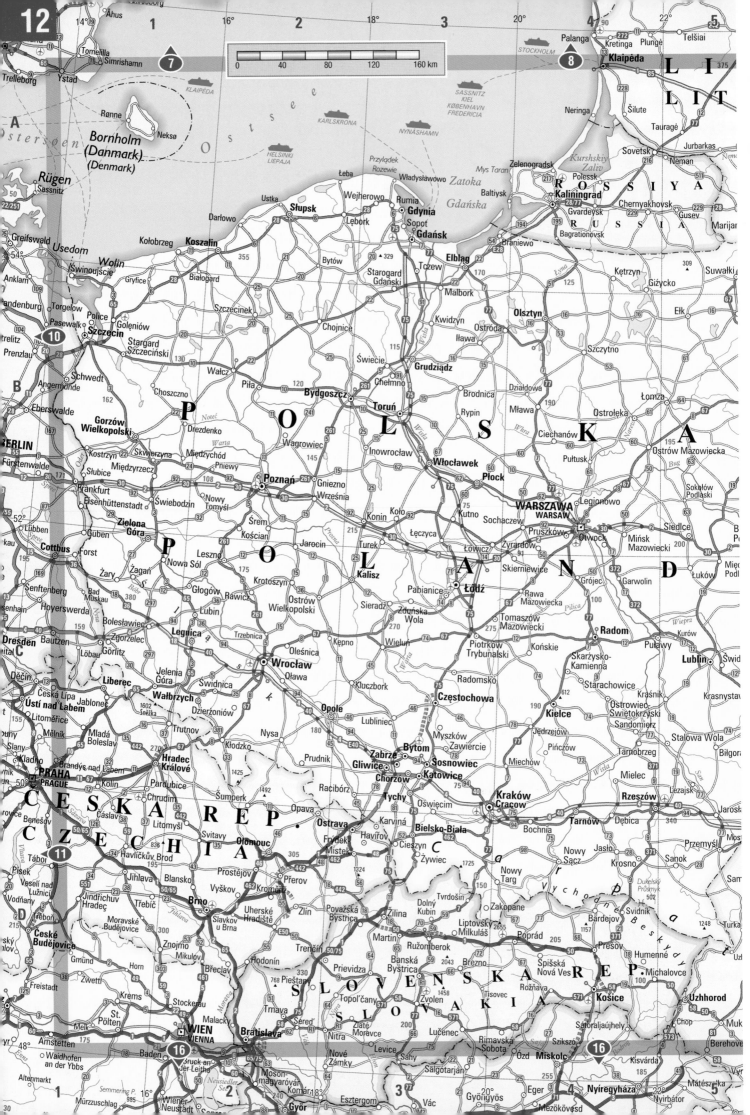

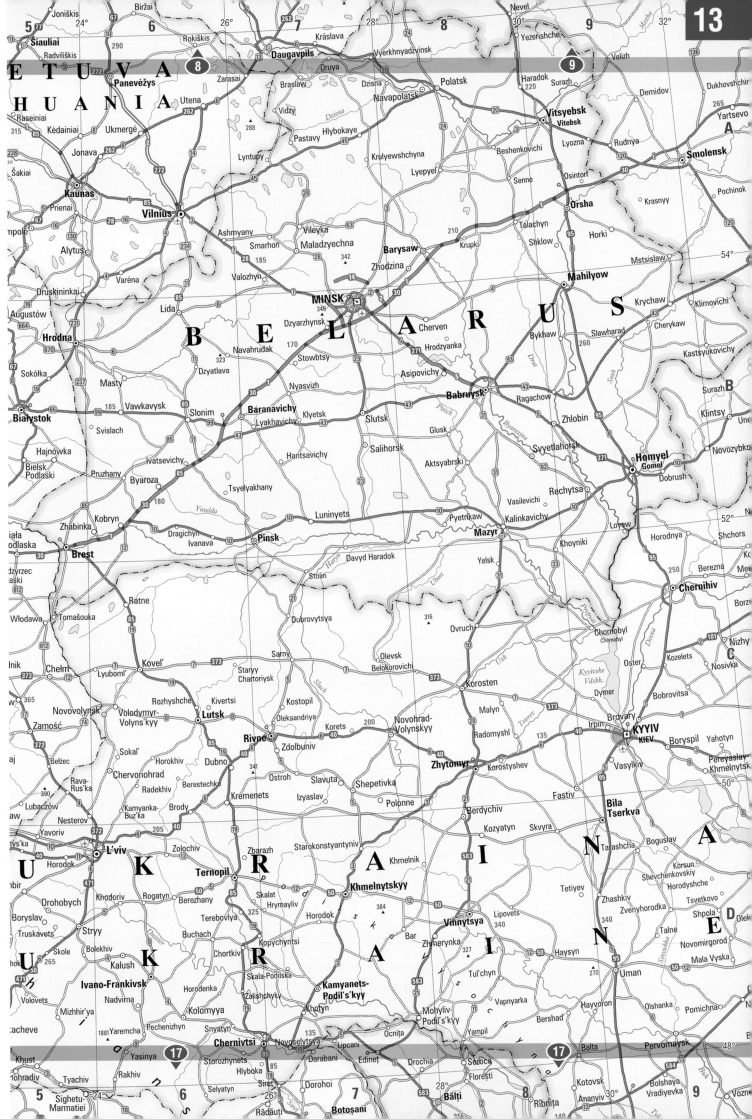

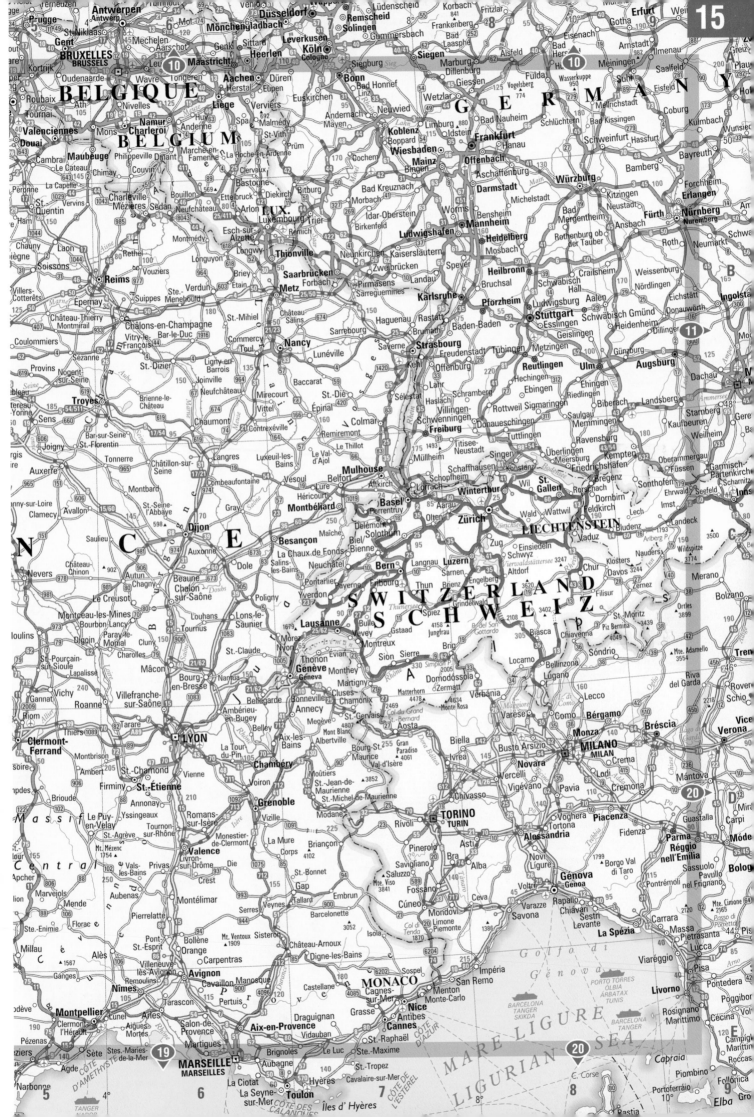

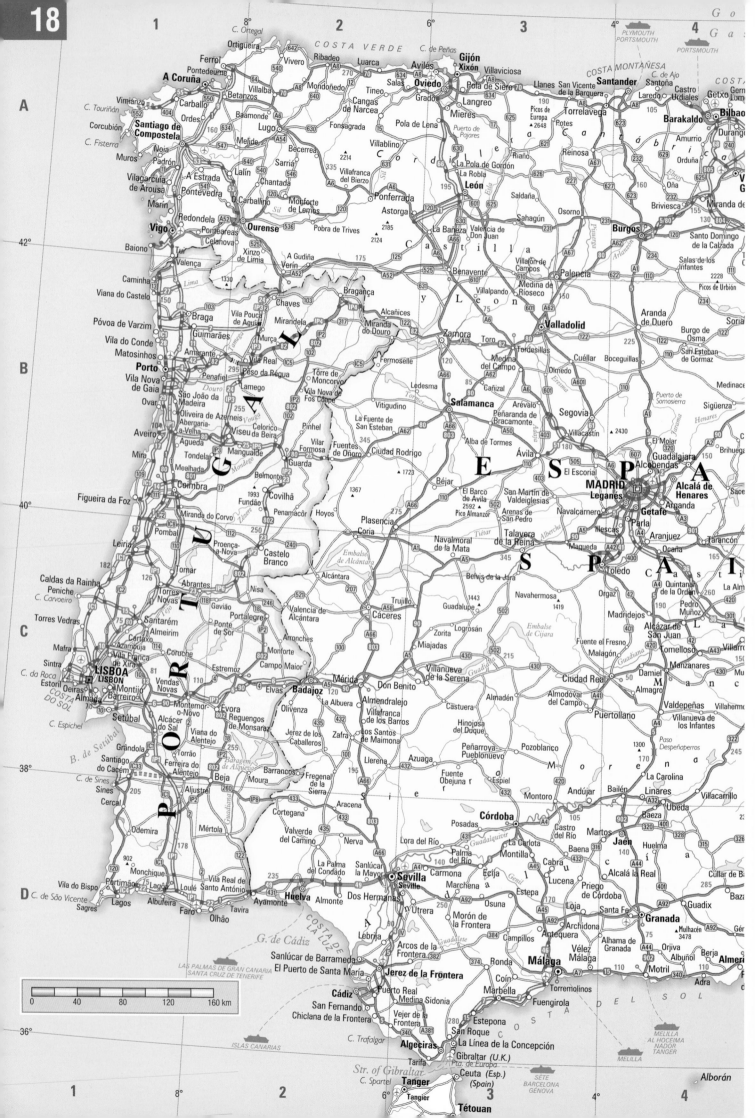

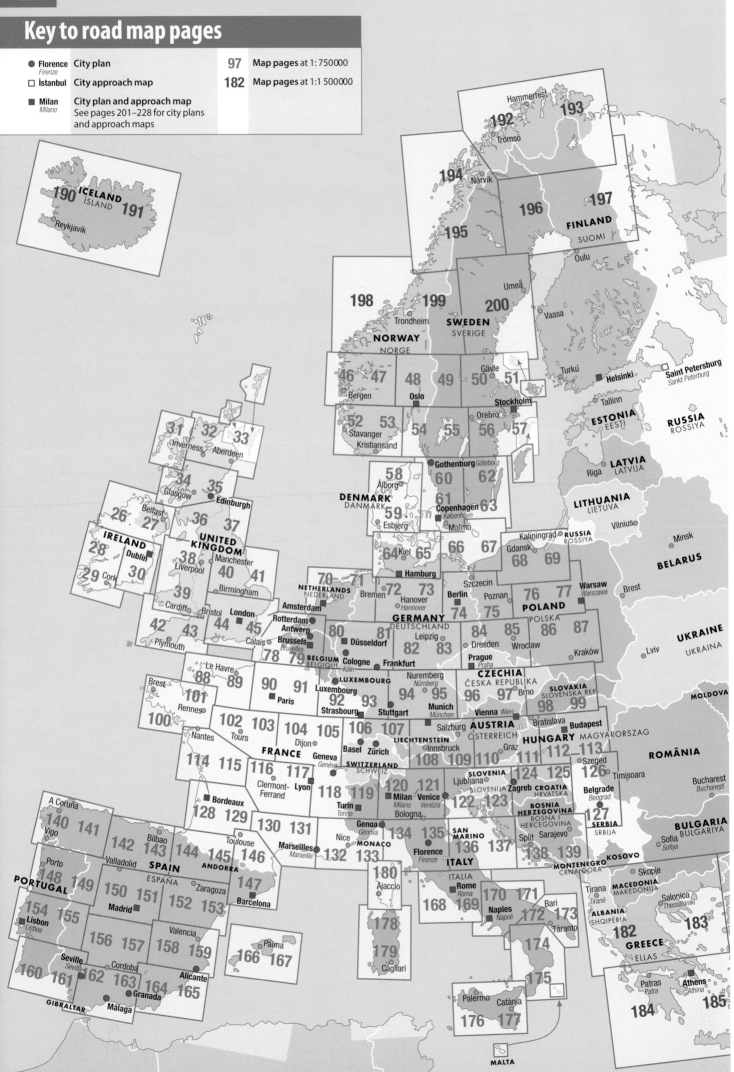

Key to road map pages

● **Florence** **City plan**
Firenze

□ **İstanbul** **City approach map**

■ **Milan** **City plan and approach map**
Milano See pages 201–228 for city plans
and approach maps

97 Map pages at 1:750000

182 Map pages at 1:1 500000

Distance table

Amsterdam

Athina	2945
Barcelona	1505 3192
Bergen	1484 3742 2803
Berlin	650 2412 1863 1309
Bruxelles	197 2895 1308 1586 764
Bucuresti	2245 1219 2644 3037 1707 2181
Budapest	1420 1530 1999 2212 882 1358 852
Calais	367 3100 1269 1783 956 215 2398 1573
Dublin	533 3630 1817 270 1504 763 3021 2196 548
Edinburgh	1093 3826 1995 176 1696 941 3124 2299 726 346
Frankfurt	441 2499 1313 1508 550 383 1804 979 575 1123 1301
Göteborg	1029 3080 2362 819 668 1145 1734 1550 1342 477 176 1067
Hamburg	447 2719 1780 1023 286 563 2014 1189 760 477 1486 485 582
Helsinki	1560 2539 2338 1063 475 1239 1834 1009 1431 1318 1236 1598 505 1113
İstanbul	2756 1145 2990 3653 2223 2706 690 1341 2911 3537 3657 2314 2891 2530 2350
København	965 2782 2090 1103 370 1081 2077 1252 1278 752 479 795 284 518 803 2593
Köln	256 2684 1376 1427 566 198 1983 1158 390 938 1116 180 986 404 1517 2499 714
Lisboa	2331 4460 1268 3723 2869 3141 3917 3222 2069 2617 2795 2400 3282 2700 3817 4342 3014 2339
London	480 3200 1387 458 1074 333 2591 1766 118 430 608 693 122 878 1991 3107 1188 508 2187
Luxembourg	406 2661 1190 1613 749 209 2052 1227 424 972 1150 240 1172 590 1703 2472 900 186 2160 542
Madrid	1790 3809 617 3183 2364 1600 3262 2622 1528 1634 2254 1930 2742 2160 3276 3589 2473 1798 651 1646 1628
Marseille	1210 2683 509 2435 1541 1030 2154 1505 1063 1588 1789 1023 1994 1412 2525 2479 1722 1006 1777 1182 822 1126
Milano	1085 2182 1038 2141 1060 890 1668 992 1072 1620 1798 683 1700 1118 1535 1993 1428 868 2315 1190 679 1655 538
Moskva	2457 2930 3655 2223 1821 2585 1761 2099 2800 3348 3526 2312 1665 2115 1160 2605 2325 2387 4875 2918 2852 4224 3270 3027
München	839 2106 1340 1788 594 789 1497 672 994 1524 1720 398 1347 765 1069 1907 969 580 2545 1094 555 2010 1011 473 2305
Oslo	1347 3372 2680 503 960 1463 2667 1842 1660 773 729 1385 316 900 697 3089 590 1304 3604 1778 1490 3063 2312 2018 1823 1559
Paris	510 2917 988 1922 1051 320 2307 1482 281 829 1007 591 1481 899 2012 2727 1209 495 1821 399 351 1280 782 857 2903 810 1799
Praha	950 2067 1750 1675 345 888 1362 537 1097 1635 1816 512 1013 652 770 1878 715 690 2870 1205 753 2329 1399 853 1853 388 1305 1061
Roma	1691 1140 1385 2706 1502 1520 1904 1263 1678 2226 2404 1289 2265 1683 1977 2237 1993 1474 2653 1796 1285 2002 876 606 3362 918 2583 1389 1309
Sevilla	2347 4223 1031 3736 2894 2150 3709 3010 2078 2626 2804 2344 3295 2713 3826 4034 3023 2318 401 2196 2178 550 1540 2078 4774 2371 3613 1830 2781 2446
Sofia	2206 828 2453 3103 1673 2156 391 790 2361 2891 3087 1764 2341 1980 1800 550 2043 1949 3706 2461 1922 3037 1929 1443 2252 1367 2632 2177 1328 1687 3484
Stockholm	1393 3418 2726 1063 1006 1509 2713 1888 1673 2254 1069 1431 505 946 167 3185 590 1350 3650 1824 1536 3109 2358 2064 1228 1600 530 1845 1351 2629 3659 2679
Warszawa	1256 2128 2366 1909 606 1350 1473 648 1542 2110 2268 1136 1274 886 361 1989 956 1152 3480 1680 1345 2960 2015 1469 1245 996 1506 1677 616 1853 3397 1439 1612
Wien	1168 1772 1856 1970 640 1114 1067 242 1308 1954 2034 731 1308 947 1088 1583 1010 916 3100 1524 993 2473 1353 818 2137 430 1600 1240 295 1126 2876 1033 1646 727
Zürich	816 2426 1030 1938 863 619 1810 985 804 1352 1530 464 1497 915 2164 2323 1433 589 2296 922 410 1647 699 292 2552 303 1815 592 691 898 2061 1173 1861 1307 743

Inset example:

Dublin	548	**Dublin ▶ Göteborg = 477 km**
Edinburgh	726 346	
Frankfurt	575 1123 1301	
Göteborg	1342 477 176 1067	
Hamburg	760 477 1486 485 582	

Distances shown in blue involve at least one ferry journey

km

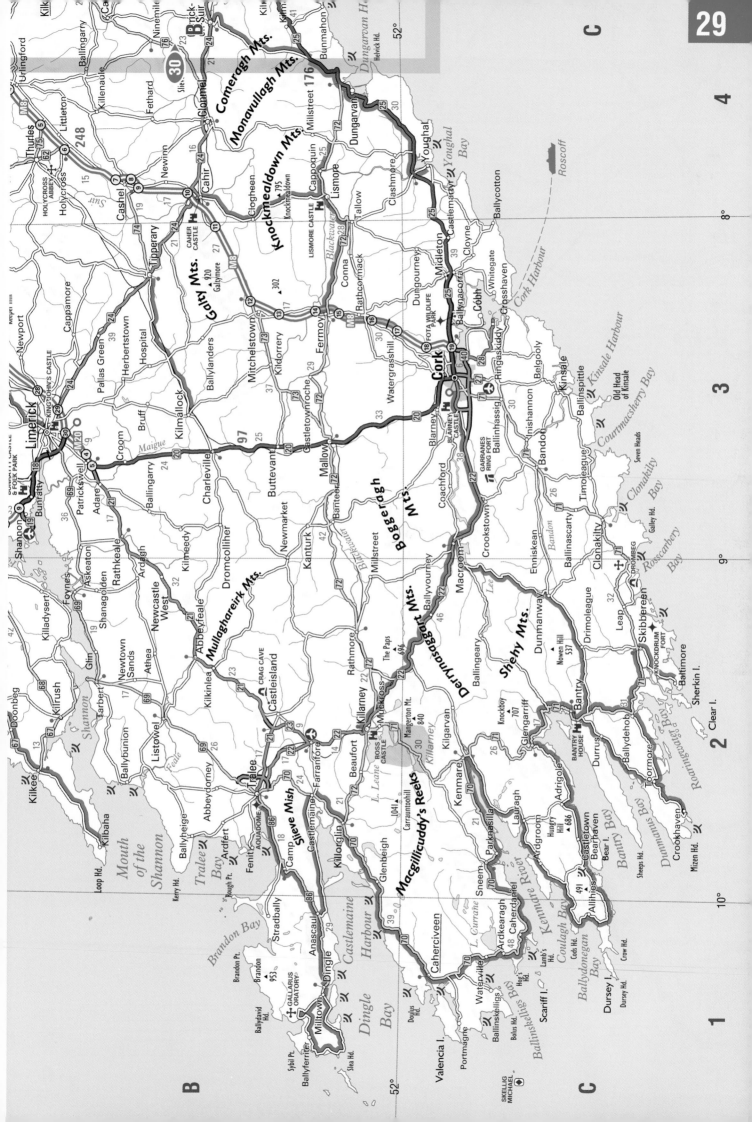

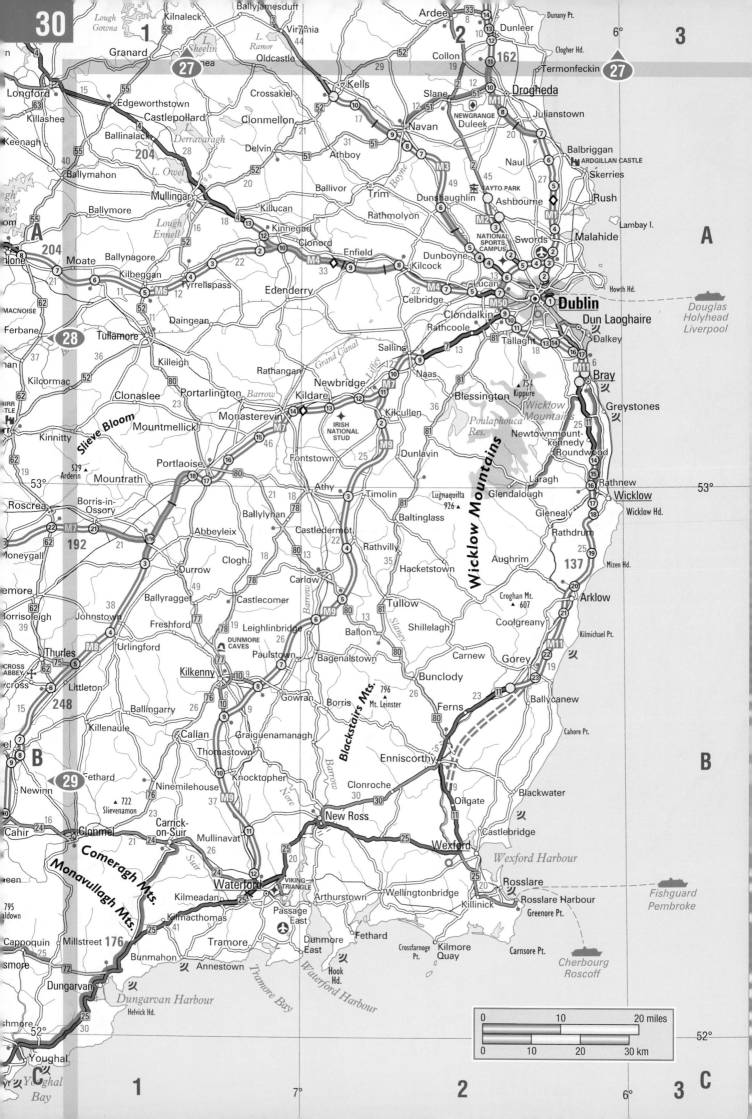

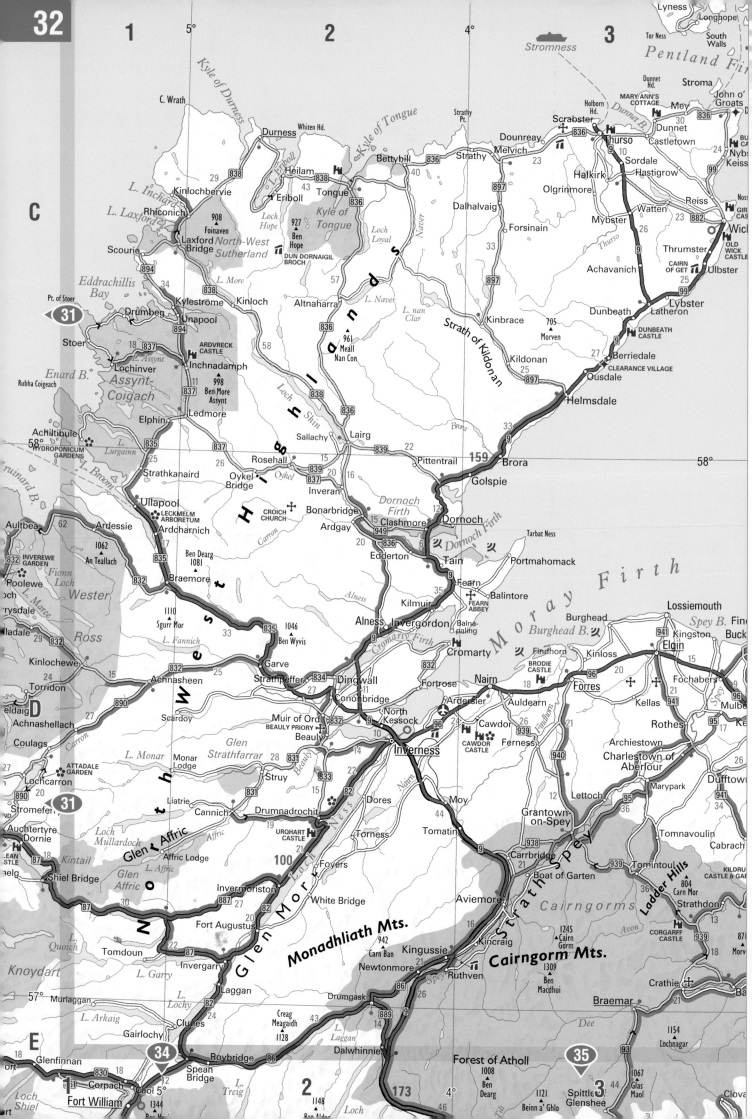

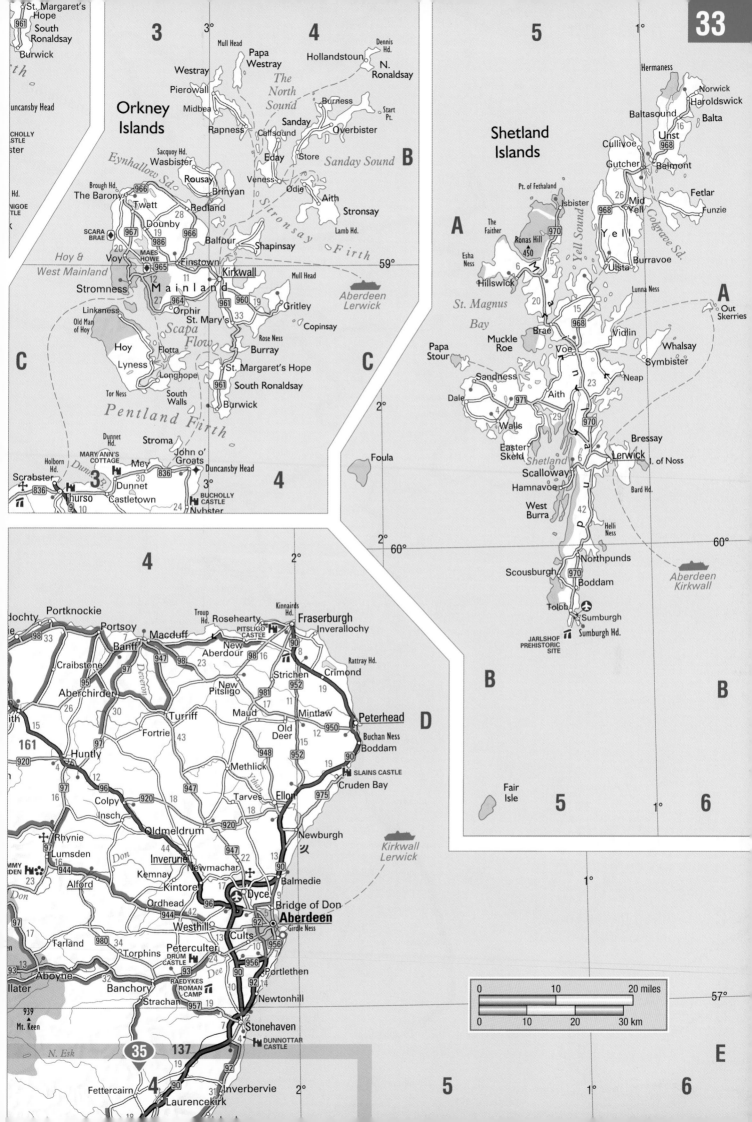

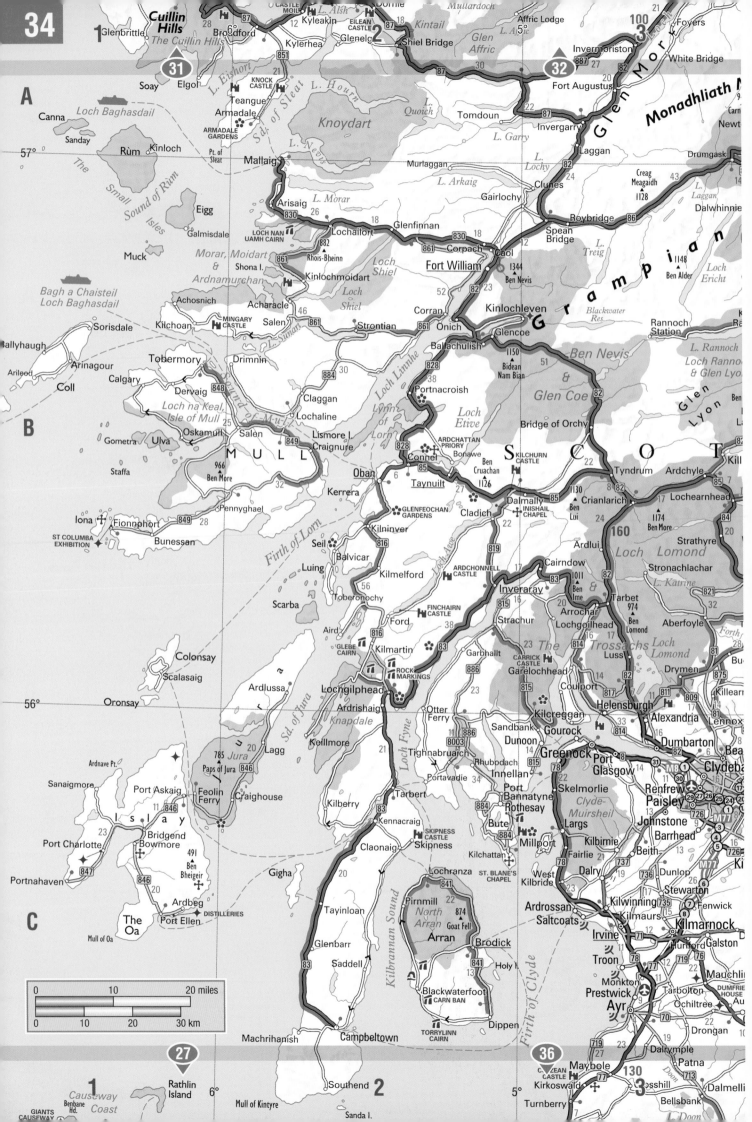

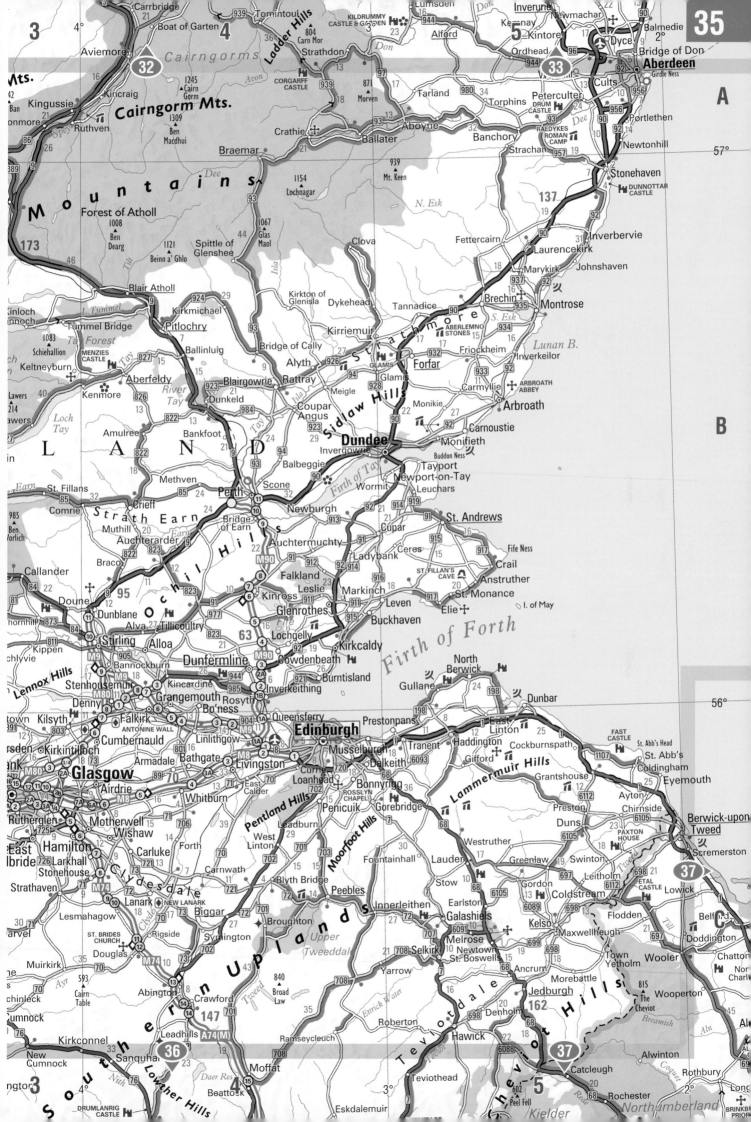

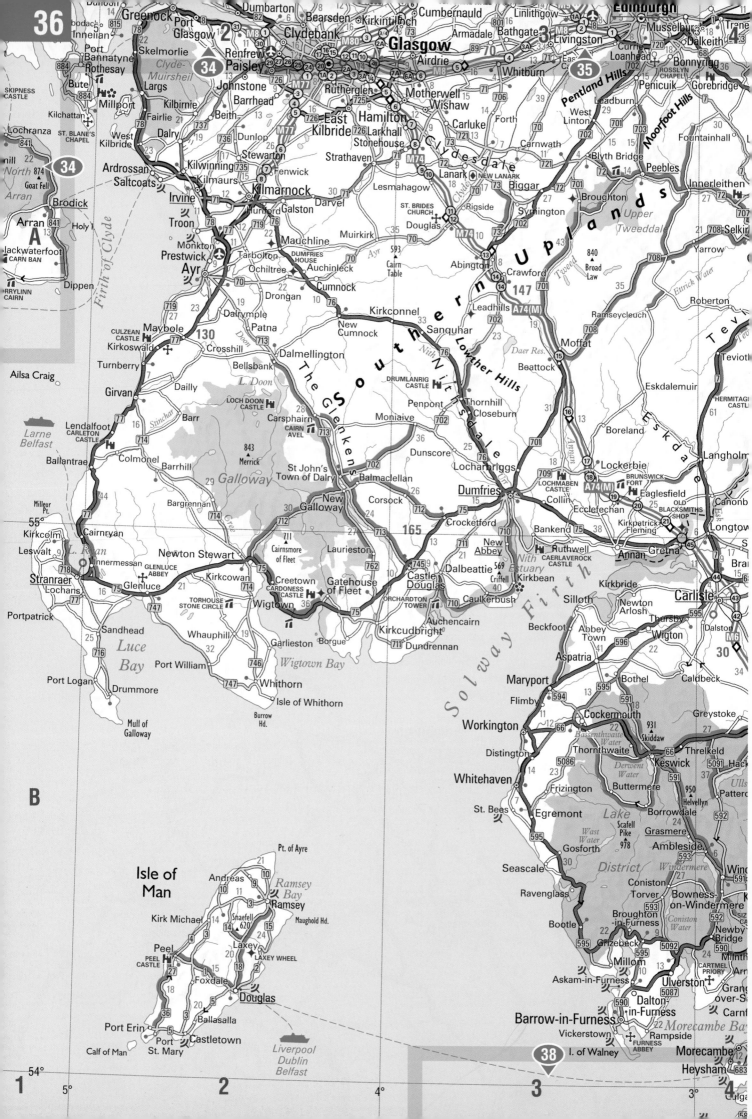

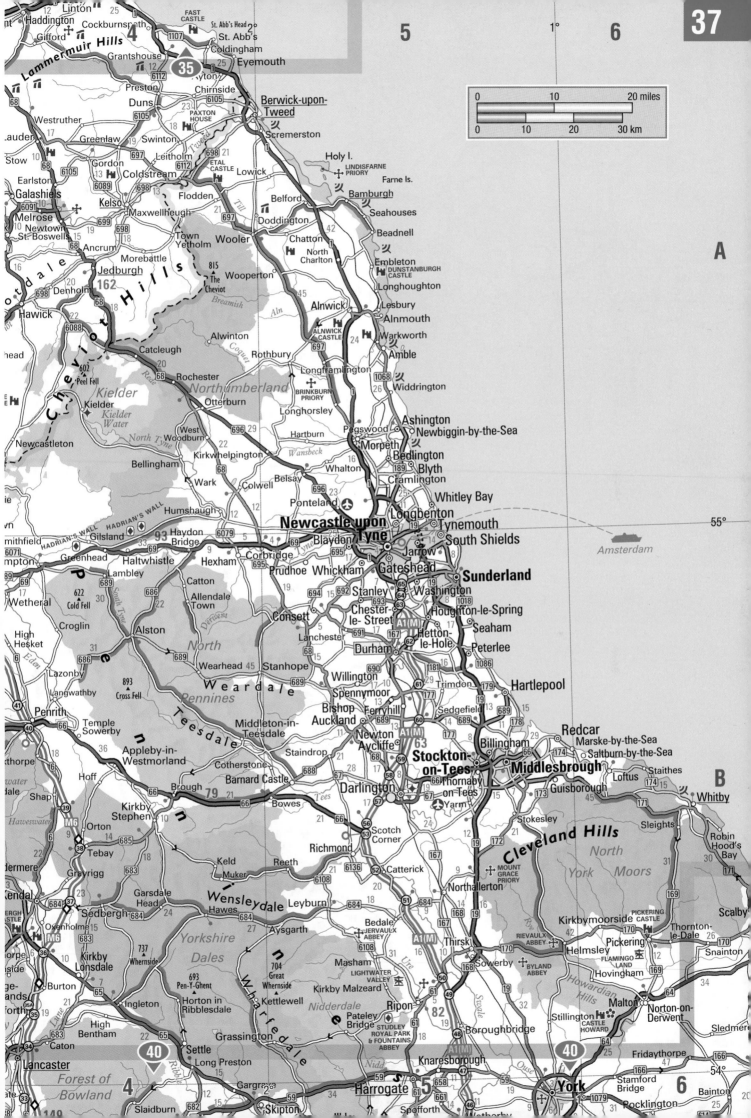

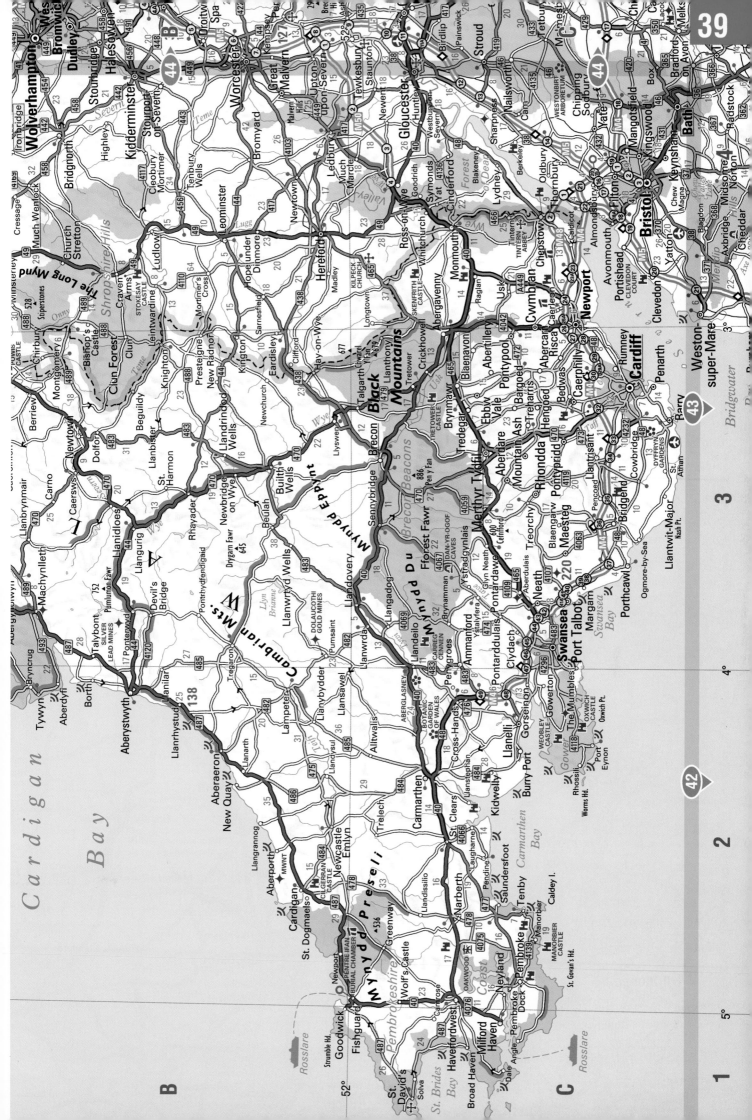

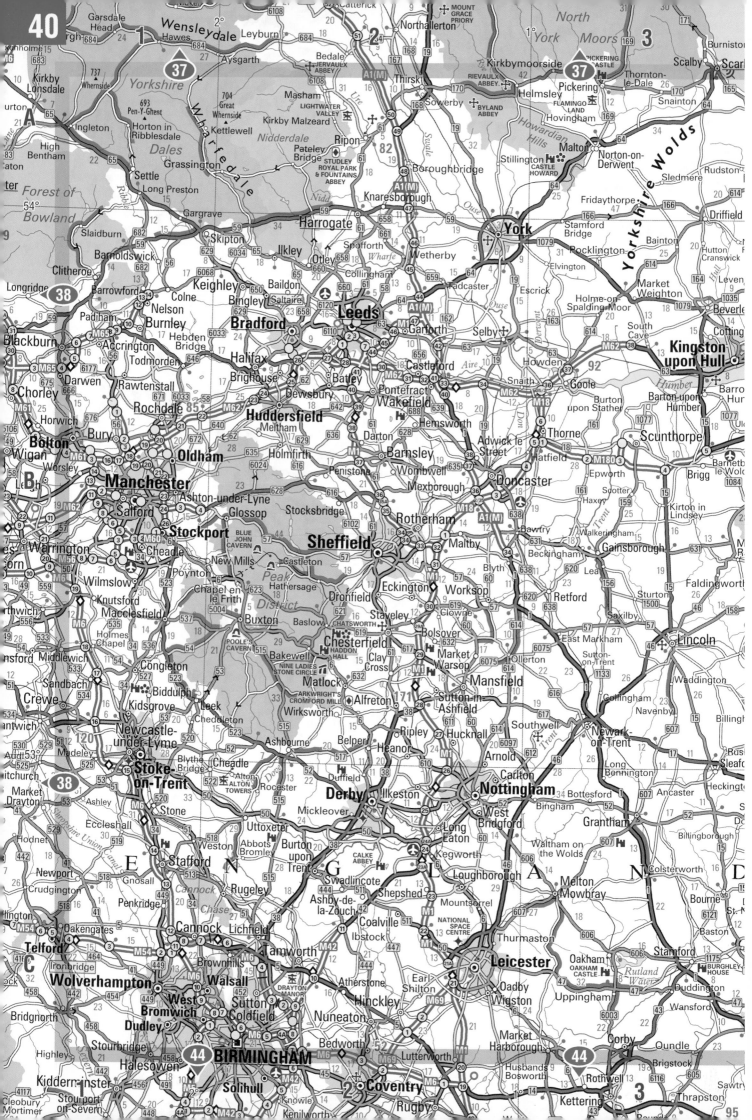

0°

1°

0   10   20 miles

0   10   20   30 km

A

NORTH

SEA

54°

Filey

27

165 Flamborough

Bridlington

Burton
Agnes

Bridlington
Bay

165 Skipsea

North
Frodingham

25 Hornsea

ey

165 19 Aldbrough

ham Sproatley

1033 Hedon

Withernsea

Keyingham

31 1033

ow upon
mber Patrington

Easington

ceby 160 Immingham

Grimsby

Spurn Hd.

180 24

18 Cleethorpes

Laceby Humberston

Rotterdam
Zeebrugge

B

1173 46 1031

Caistor Lincolnshire

16 1031

North
Thoresby North Somercotes

23 41 Saltfleet

Market
asen Binbrook

27

631 ST. JAMES
CHURCH.

Louth 1031

22

157 153 Withern Mablethorpe

Wragby 21 157 Sutton-on-Sea

16 23 1104

Scamblesby 20 1111

158 Alford 26 Huttoft

16 158 1028 52

Bardney Horncastle Partney

Woodhall
Spa 158 16 Burgh le
Marsh

153 Mareham
le Fen Spilsby Skegness

33 155

hay Coningsby 16 Wainfleet All Saints

153 29 34 52

kington Sibsey Wrangle
ord

The Wash

Norfolk Coast

53°

on 17 1121 Benington Brancaster Wells-next- Cley

52 Boston 149 the-Sea Sheringham

Swineshead 12 Kirton Hunstanton 25 Burnham 31 149 148 Cromer

onington Heacham Market HOLKHAM Holt Mundesley

Gosberton 11 Docking HALL Little 148 140

Pinchbeck 17 Long Dersingham Walsingham Saxthorpe 149 North
Walsham

Spalding 151 Sutton SANDRINGHAM 27 Fakenham BICKLING HALL Aylsham

9 149 148 1067 Reepham 34 36 Coltishall

51 20 Holbeach King's 1065 30 DINOSAUR 1151 149 29 C
 ADVENTURE

Deeping 17 20 Lynn Gayton Litcham PARK 1270 Wroxham Martham

Nicholas 14 47 1067 19 1064 Caister-on-Sea

175 32 1101 CASTLE ACRE 25 47 Dereham Drayton Acle
PRIORY 47 47 The

22 Crowland Wisbech 13 Norwich 23 BURGH Broads Great Yarmouth

Market 15 16 Downham 13 1122 Swaffham 1075 CASTLE Gorleston-
Deeping The Market Fincham New Costessey 26 146 on-sea

15 16 Eye Nene Outwell OXBURGH 1065 11 21 Corton

Peterborough 141 March Hilgey HALL Watton Wymondham 16 47

Whittlesey 1101 Methwold 134 Attleborough 45 31 Oulton

16 20 Breckland Bu 45 Oulton Broad

Yaxley 10 19 GRIMES 140 Beccles

16 GRAVES Brandon 1075 146

A1(M) Chatteris 45 Littleport Thetford 69 23 143 5 Lowestoft

15 24 8 Lakenheath 5° Diss Harleston 22 12 Wrentham

Ramsey 141 142 Ely 1101 1065 10 6° Scole 145 27
mersham 50 Mildenhall 1088 Halesworth

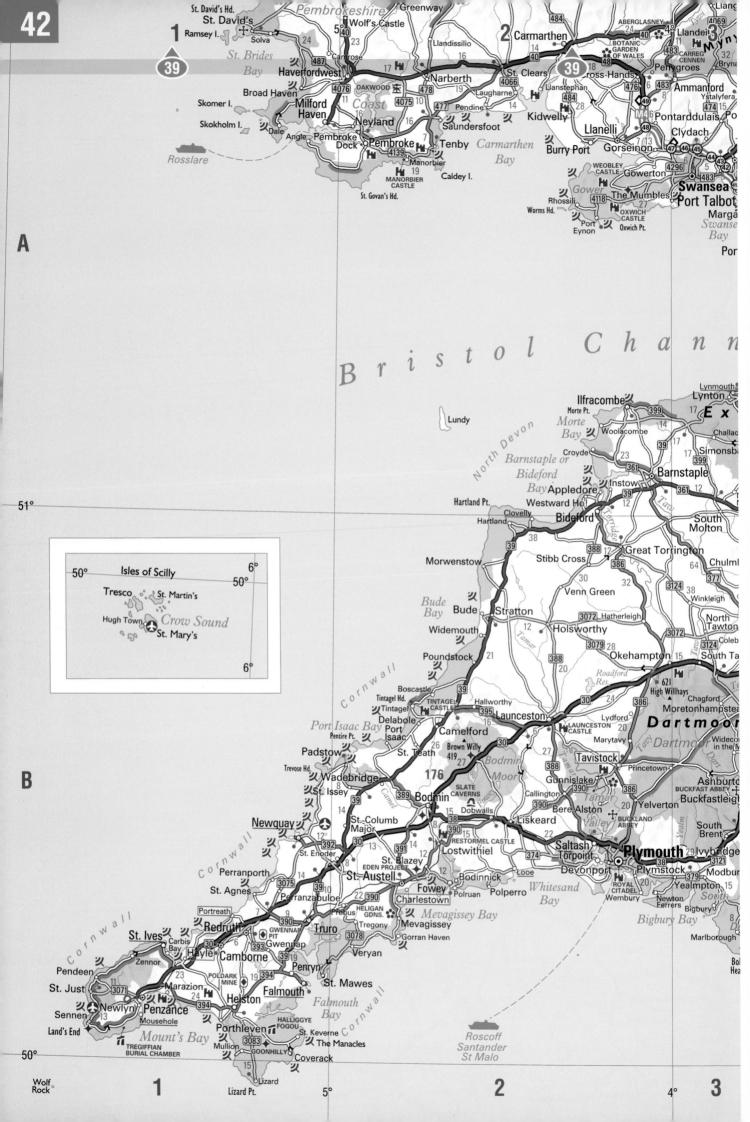

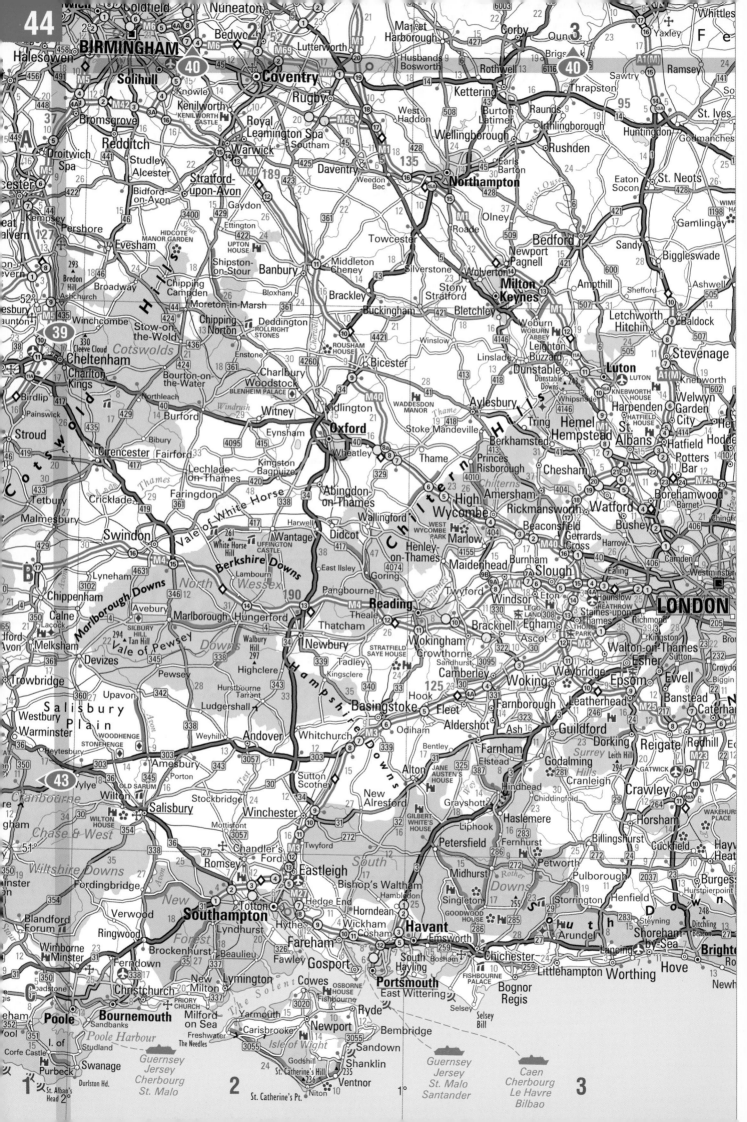

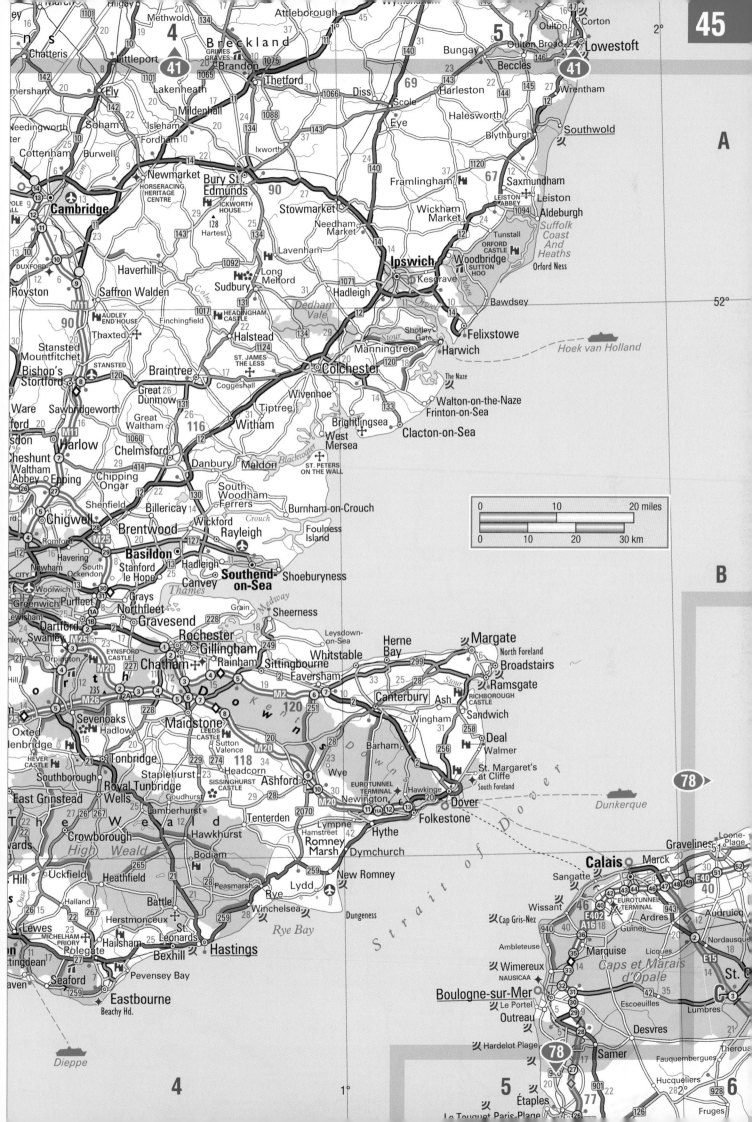

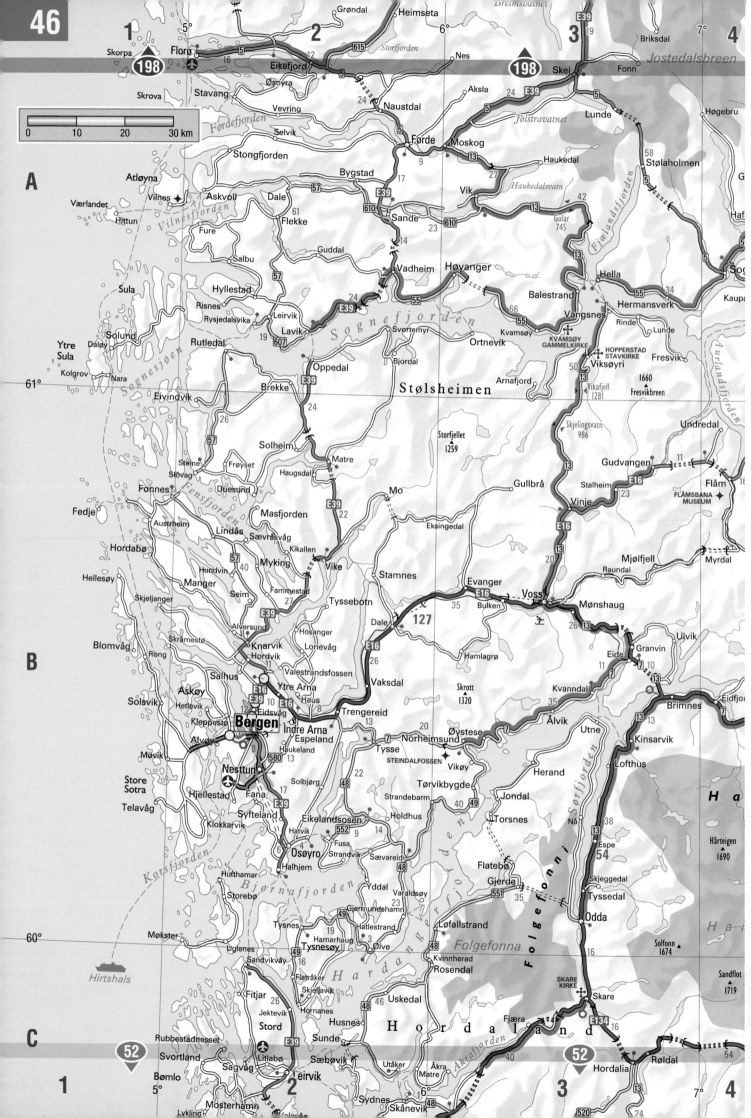

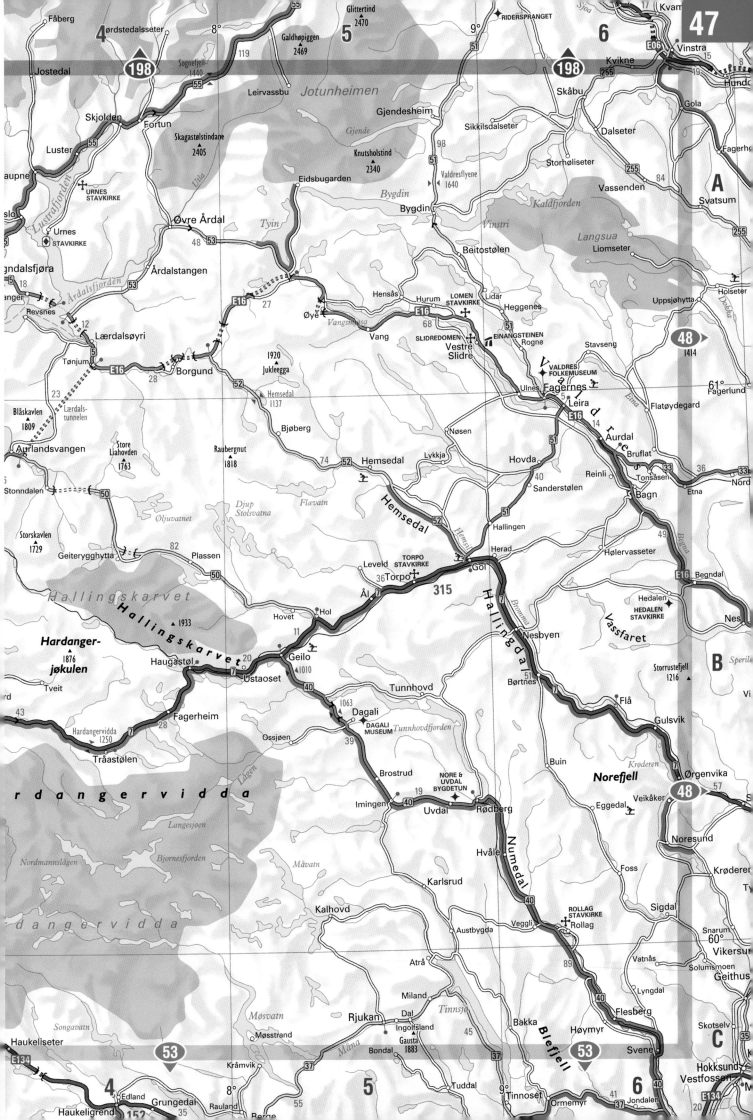

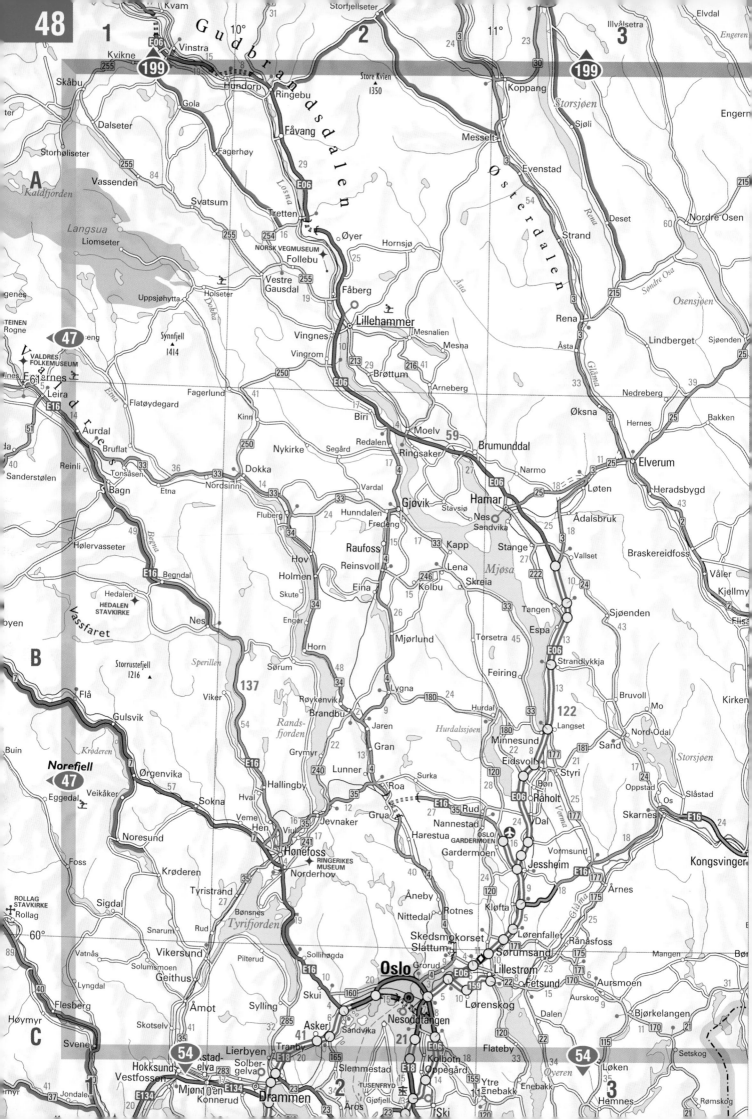

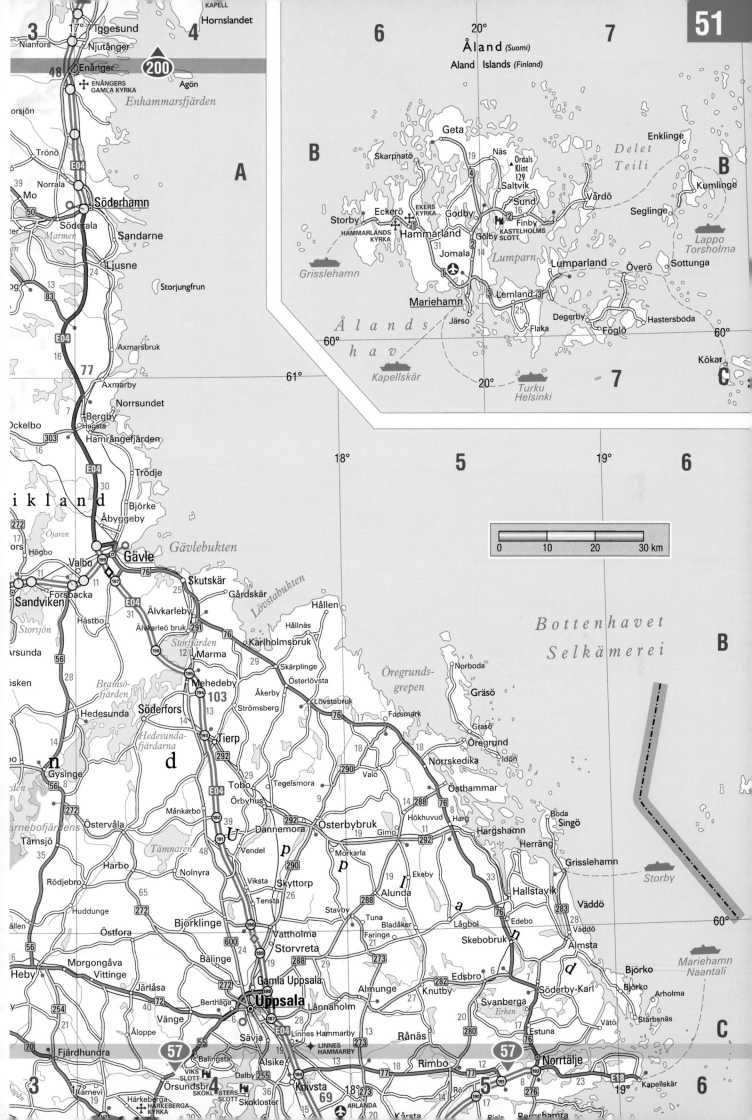

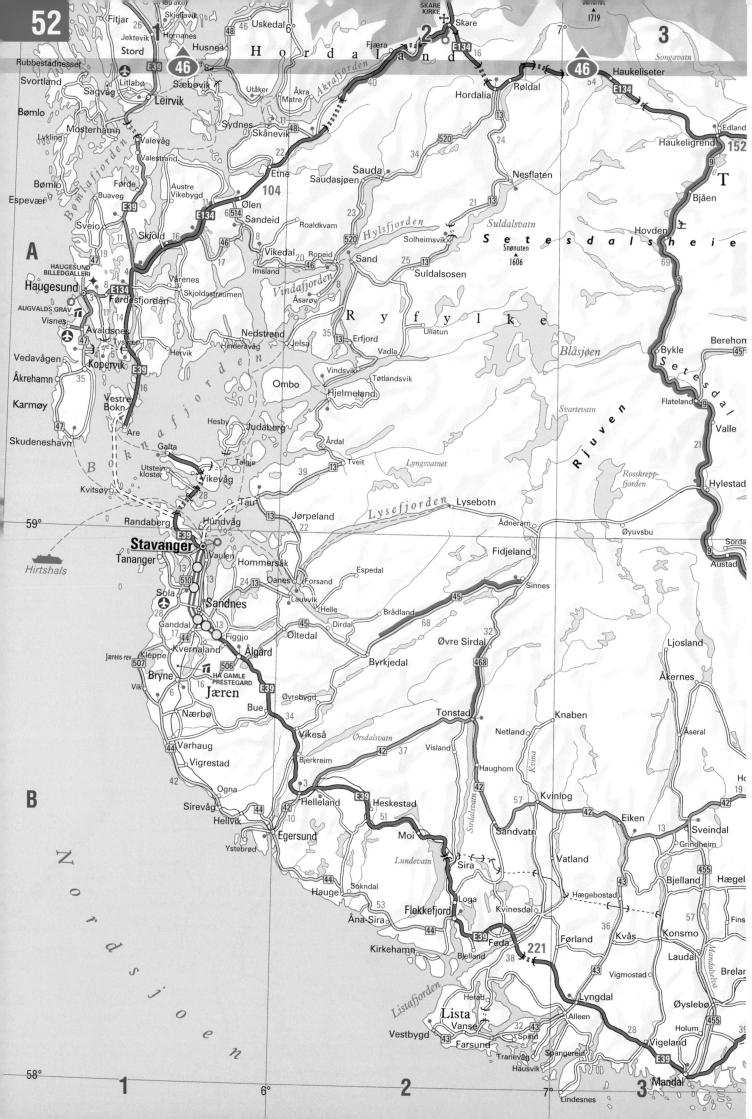

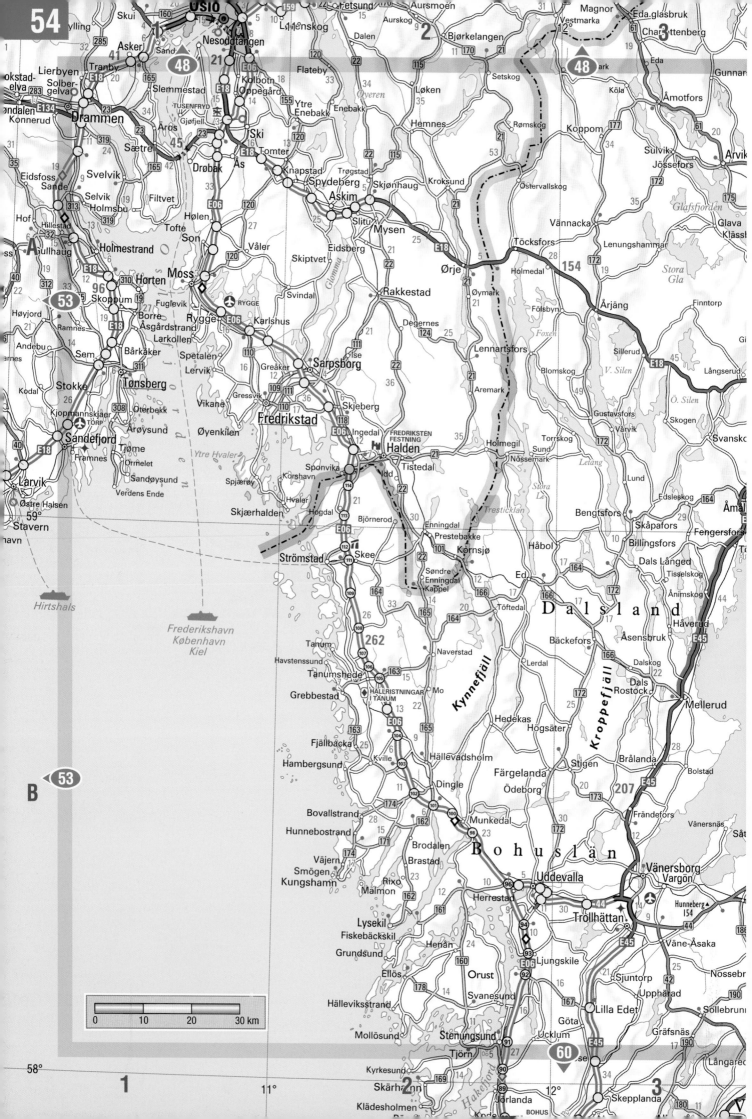

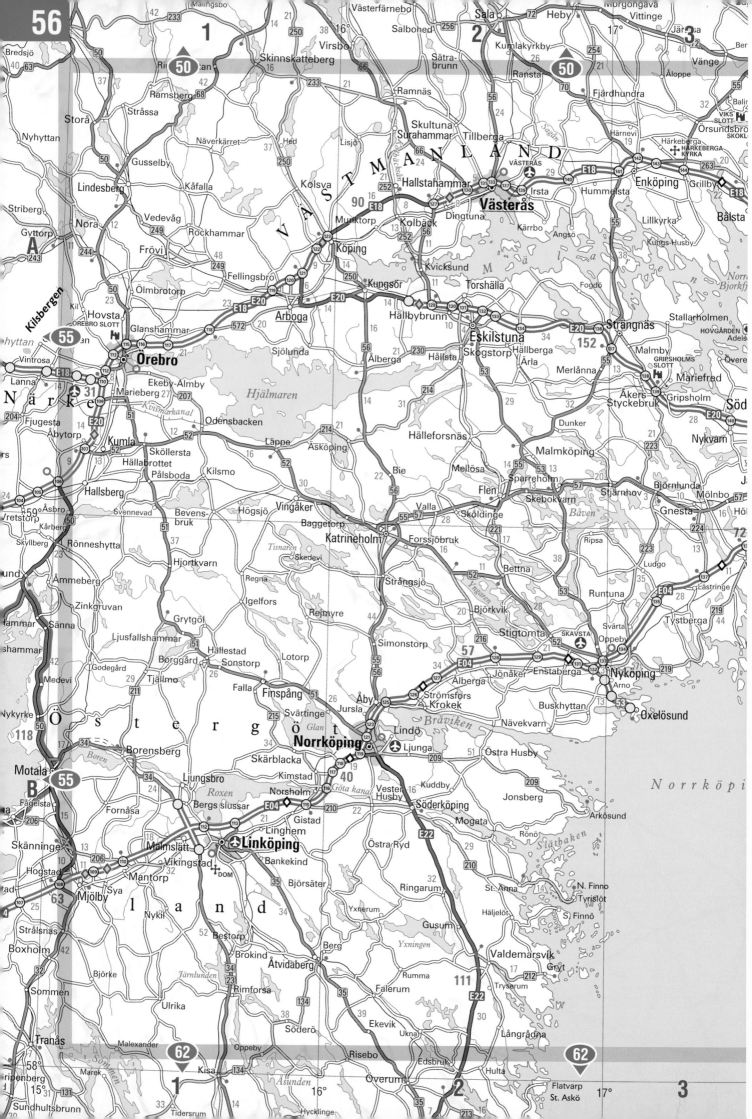

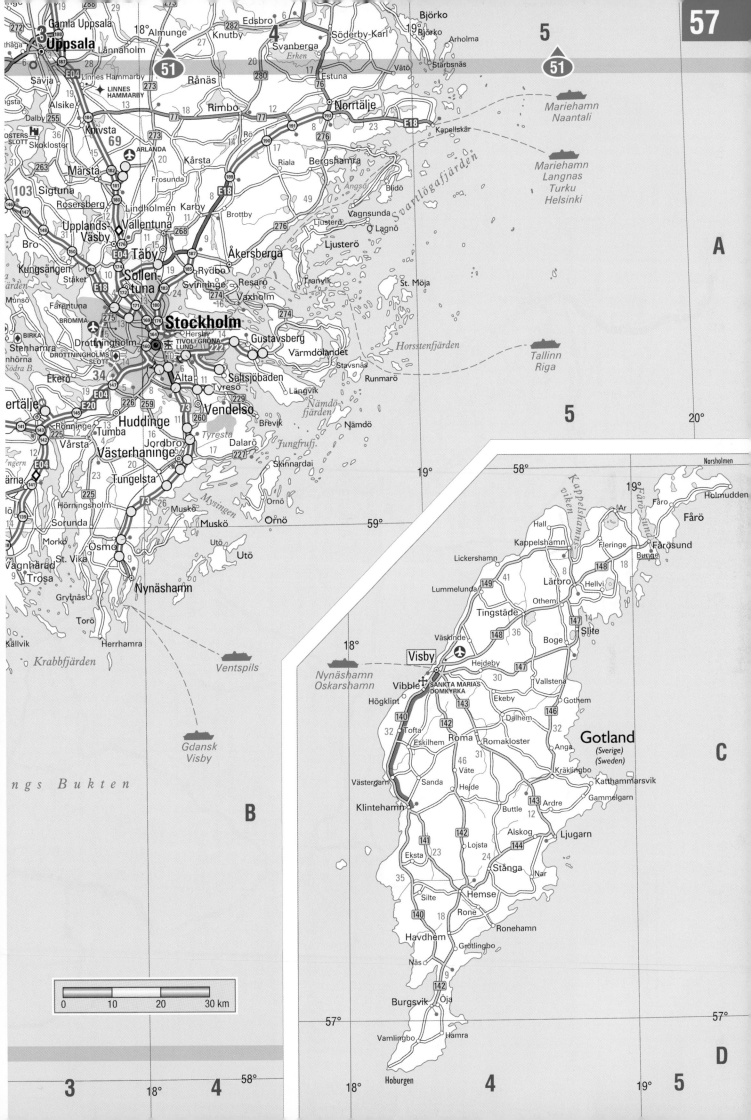

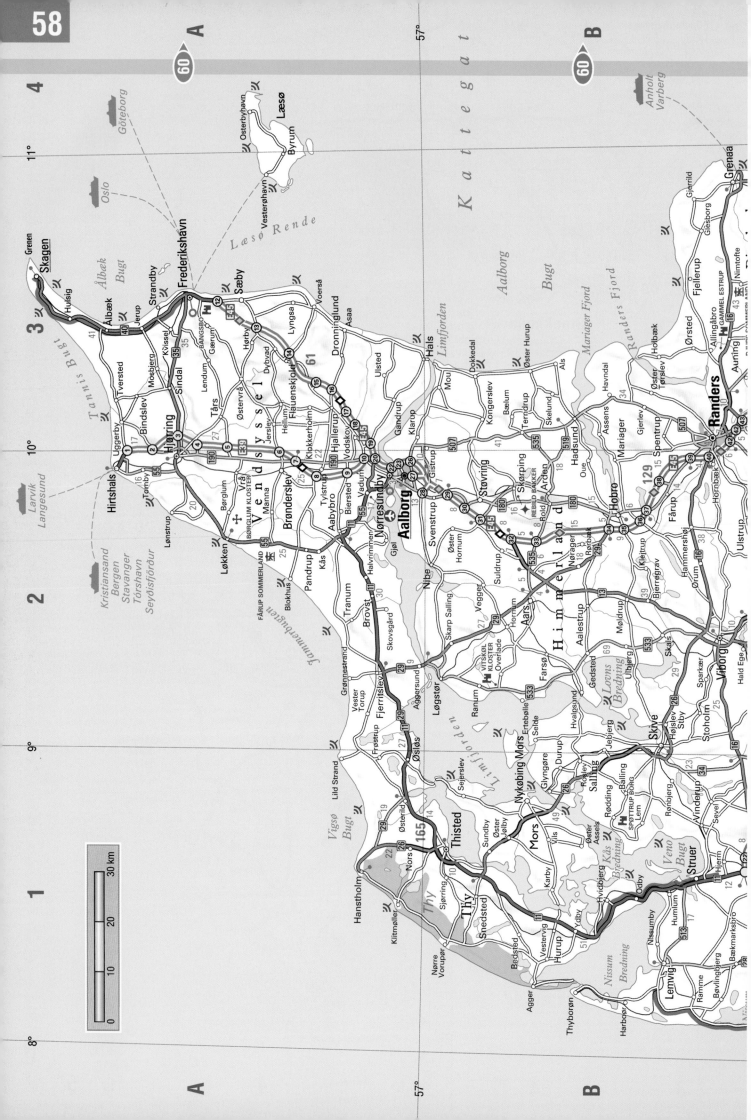

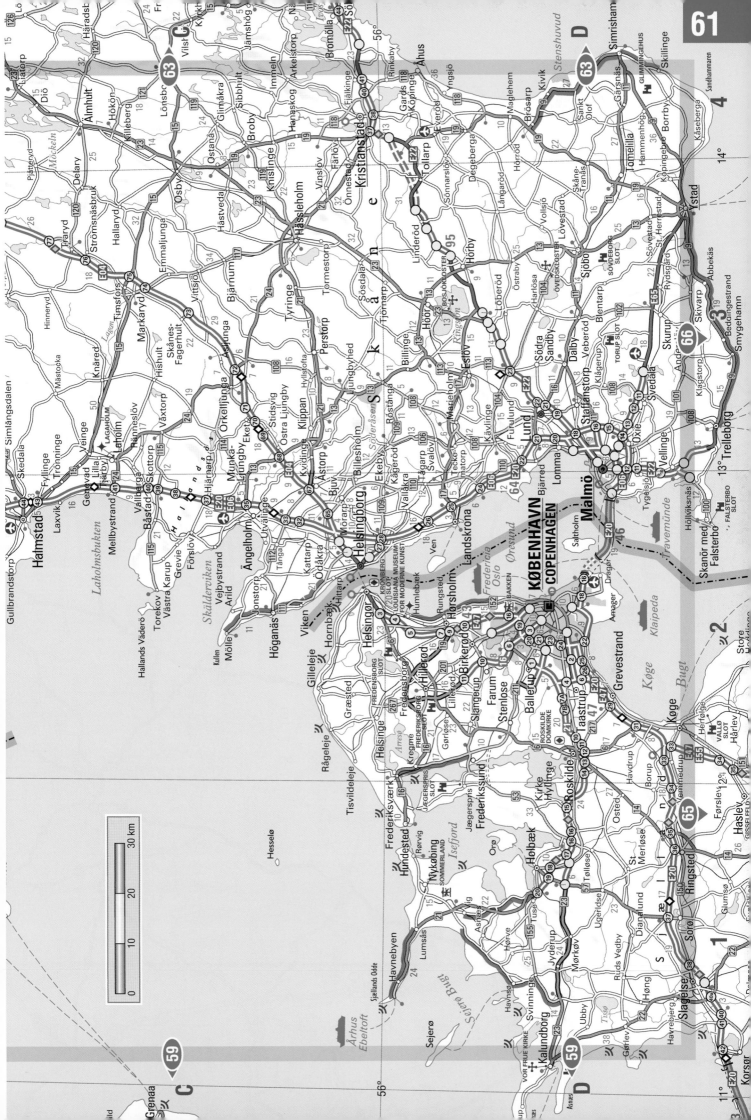

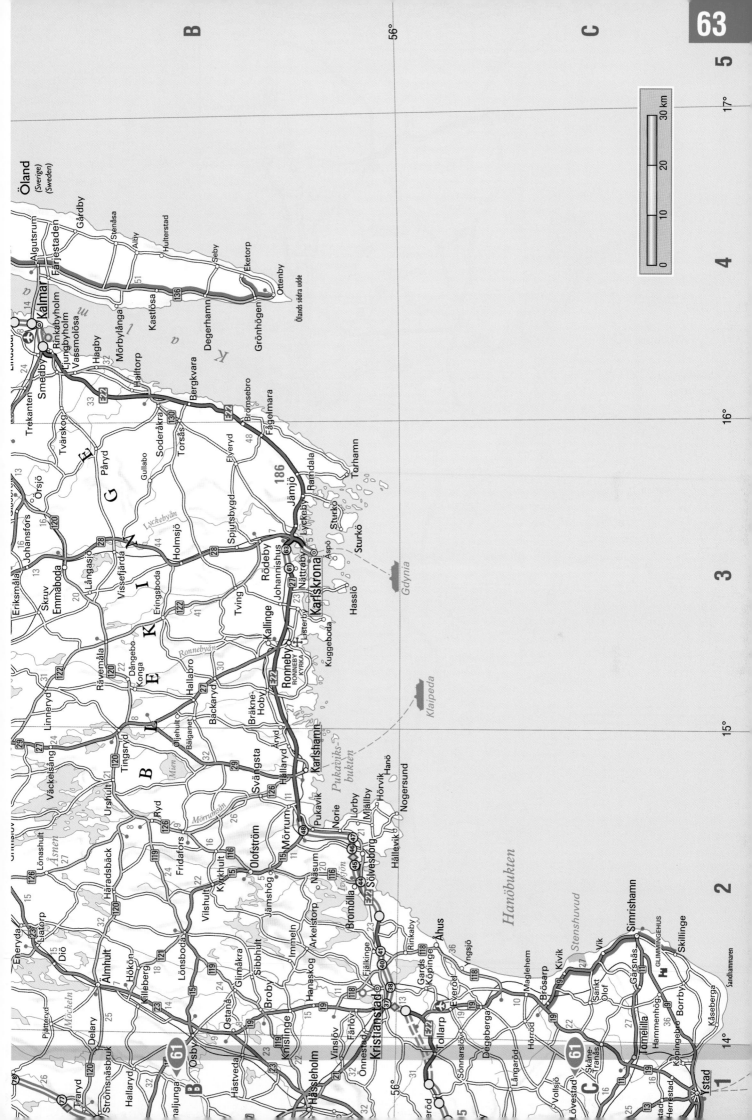

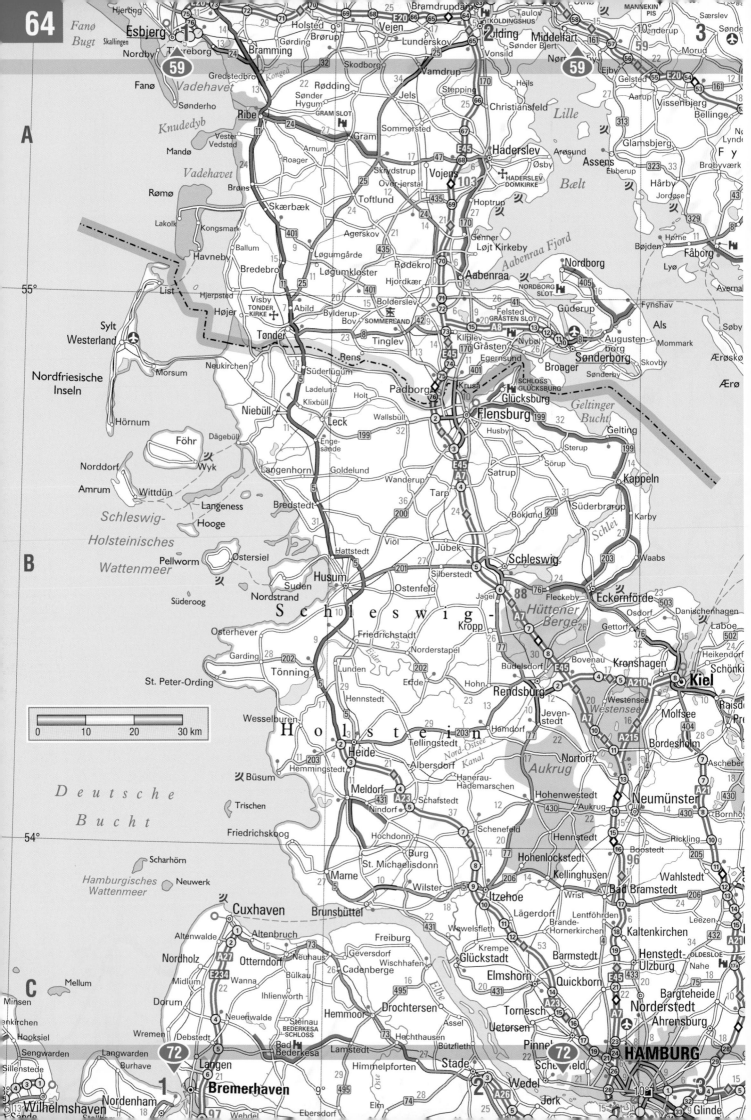

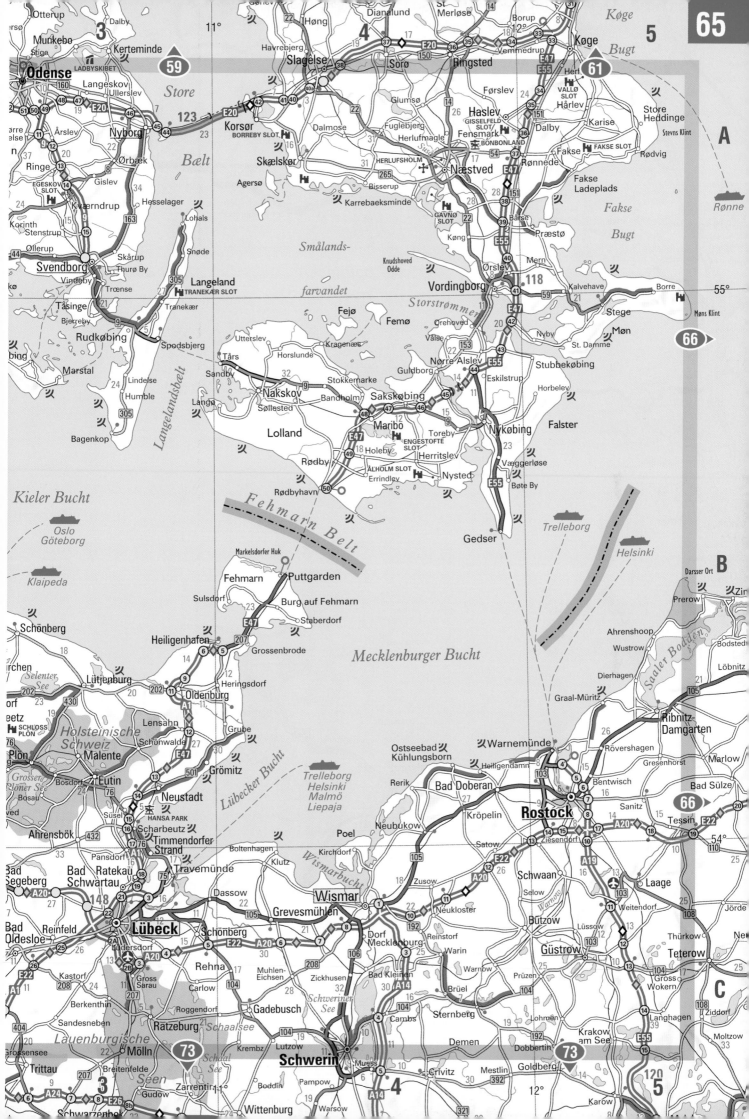

Stenshuvud

Vik

Simrishamn

MINGEHUS

Skillinge

A

holmsgattet

0 10 20 30 km

Hammeren
HAMMARSHUS Sandvig-Allinge
Ertholmene
Tejn
Bornholm
(Danmark)
(Denmark) Rø Gudhjem
Hasle Klemensker
Nyker Svaneke
Øster-
marie
Køge Østermarie
Rønne Nylars 38 Åkirkeby
28 Neksø
Pedersker Snogebaek

55°

Trelleborg
Ystad

Jaroslawiec
J.
B
J. Kopań
203 64 Wieprza
Darłowo Stary
Jaroslaw
MUZEUM
Dąbki DARŁOWO Sławno
68
Łazy J.
Bukowo E28 32 Ostrowiec
203 6
Mielno J. Jamno Lejkowo
Sarbinowo Jamno
Ustronie 42 Koszalin Sianow
Morskie 11 6 206
Kołobrzeg 11 Dobrzyca ZAMEK W Bonin 35 Nacław
Wrzosowo KOSZALINIE
Mrzezyno 5 26 Biesiekierz Manowo Radew
Dygowo 163 Niedalino Rosnowo
Niechorze 102 162 Mostowo
Rewal 21 Gościno Karlino 31 37 11 54°
Pobierowo 102 31 Trzebiatów 166 163
Dziwnów 103 Cerkwica 18 219 Białogard Dargiń Bobolice
Międzywodzie 109 Rega E28 16 19 169
8 Kamień Gorawino 6 163 12 Tychowo 25
Wolinski Pomorski 23 Rymań Sławoborze 167 171
102 32 Kolczewo Swierzno 17 Rzesznikowo Tychówka
Międzyzdroje 105 33 Rabino 17 167 Białowąs 29 Grzmiąca
107 Mechowo Gryfice Żabrowo 162 23 Parsęta 30
3 21 13 23 Resko Sława 167 23 Połczyn- Szczeci
ujście Lubin 108 Gołczewo 20 Płoty 152 Rusinowo Świdwin 21 ZAMEK W Zdrój 18 Barwice
Wolin E65 75 Przybiernów 106 Żabowo 18 Starogard 16° POŁCZYNIE 172
r Haff E28 151 163 24 172
Zalew 3 Radowo 4 Brzeżno Bierzwina 5
Szczeciński 15° Drawski 27 171
Nowe Warpno C

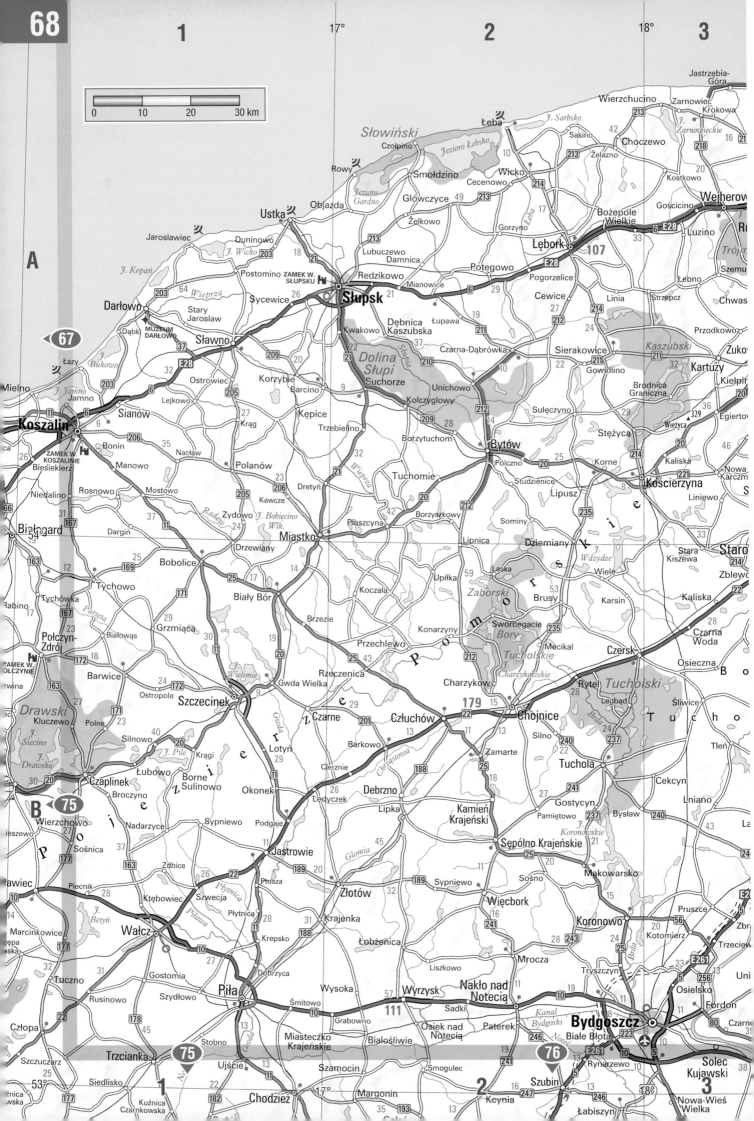

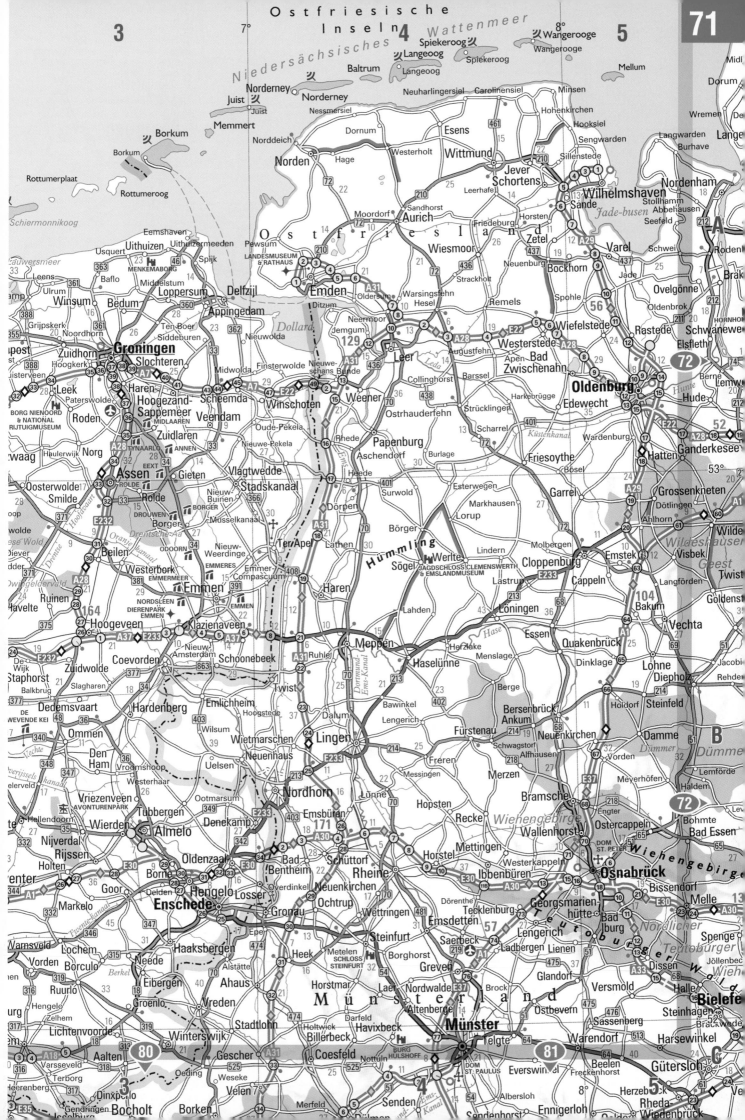

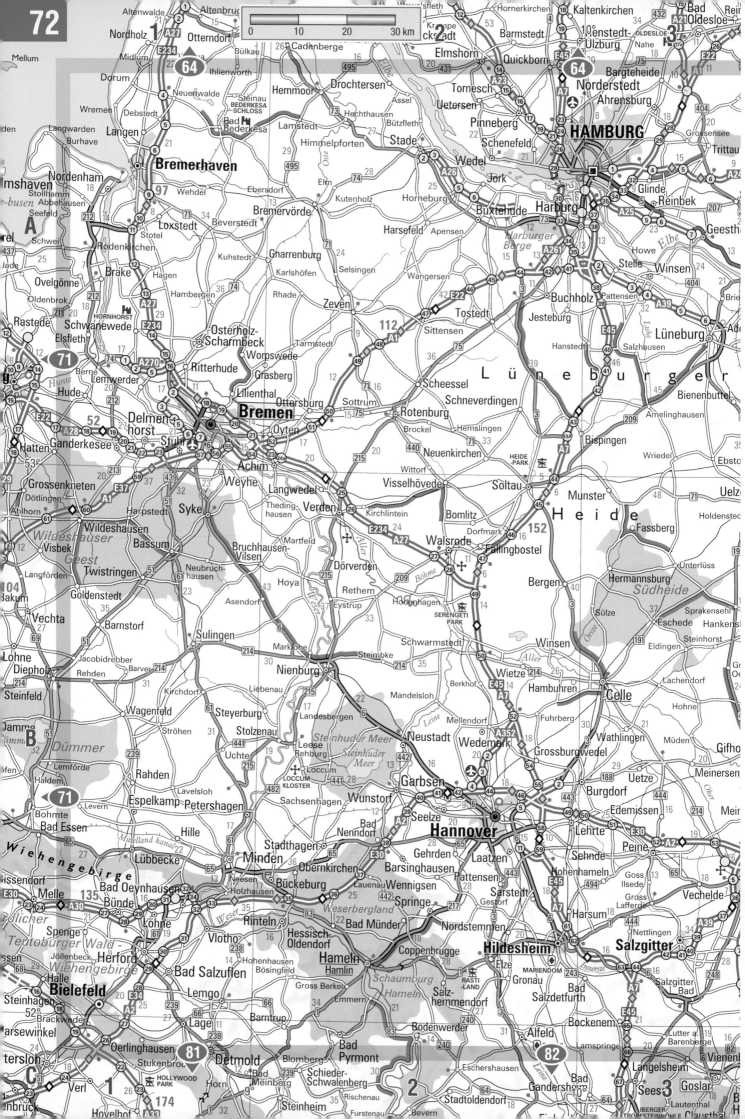

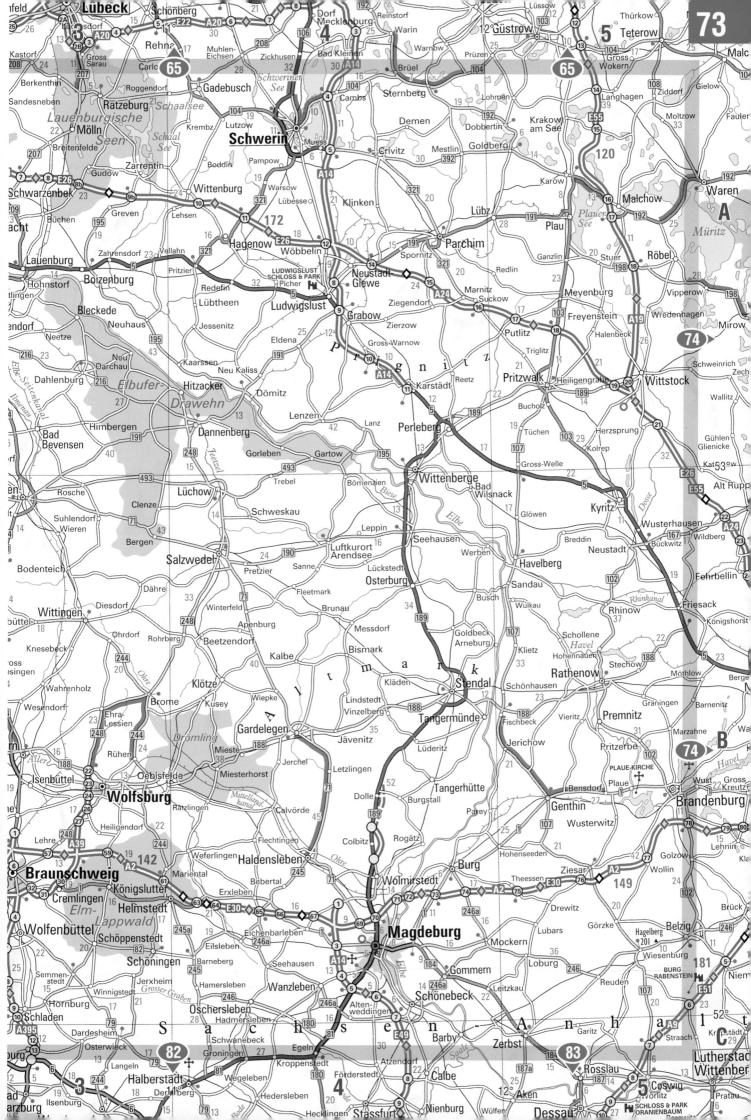

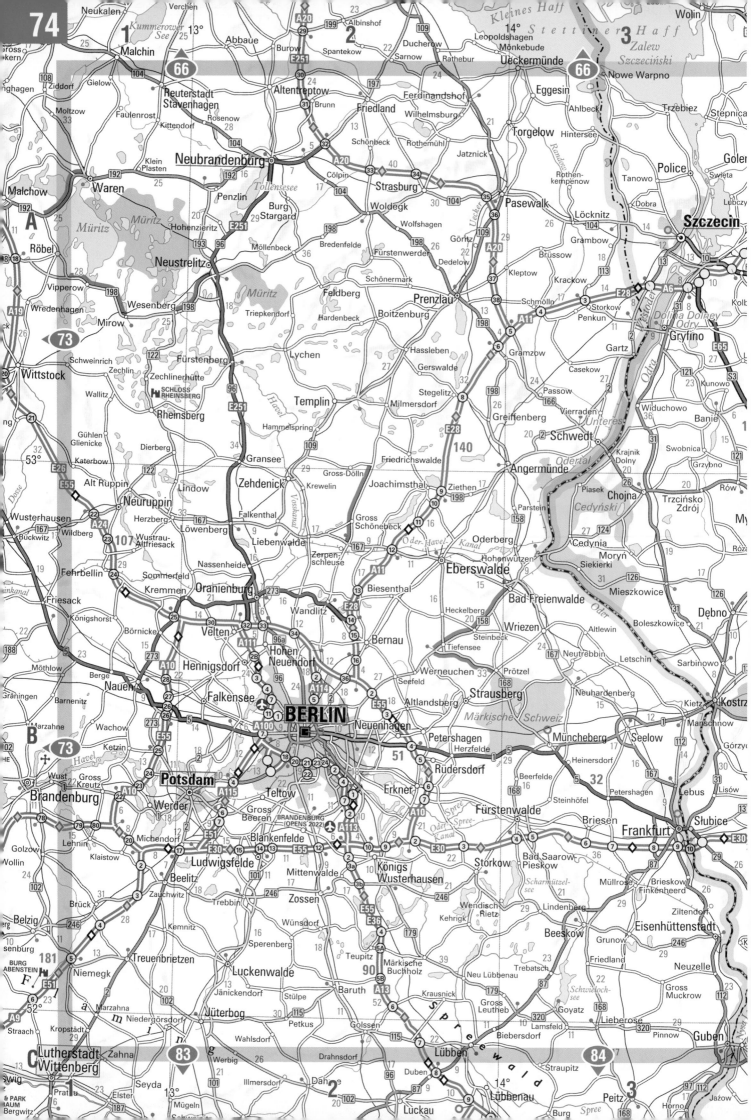

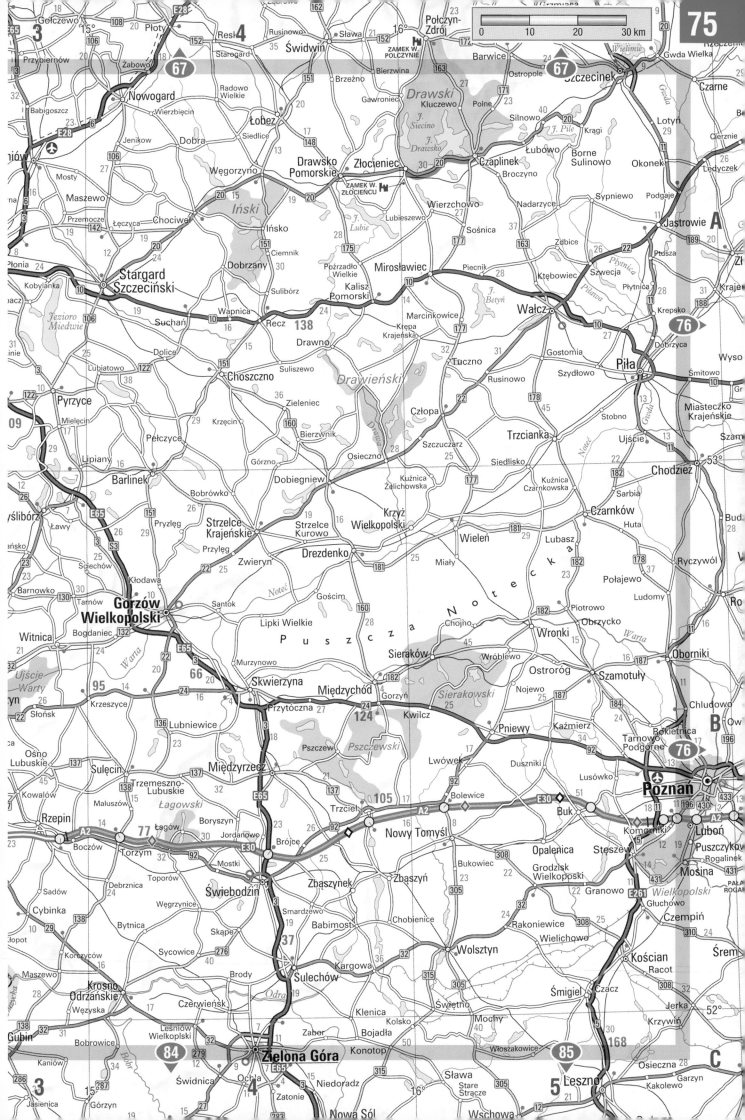

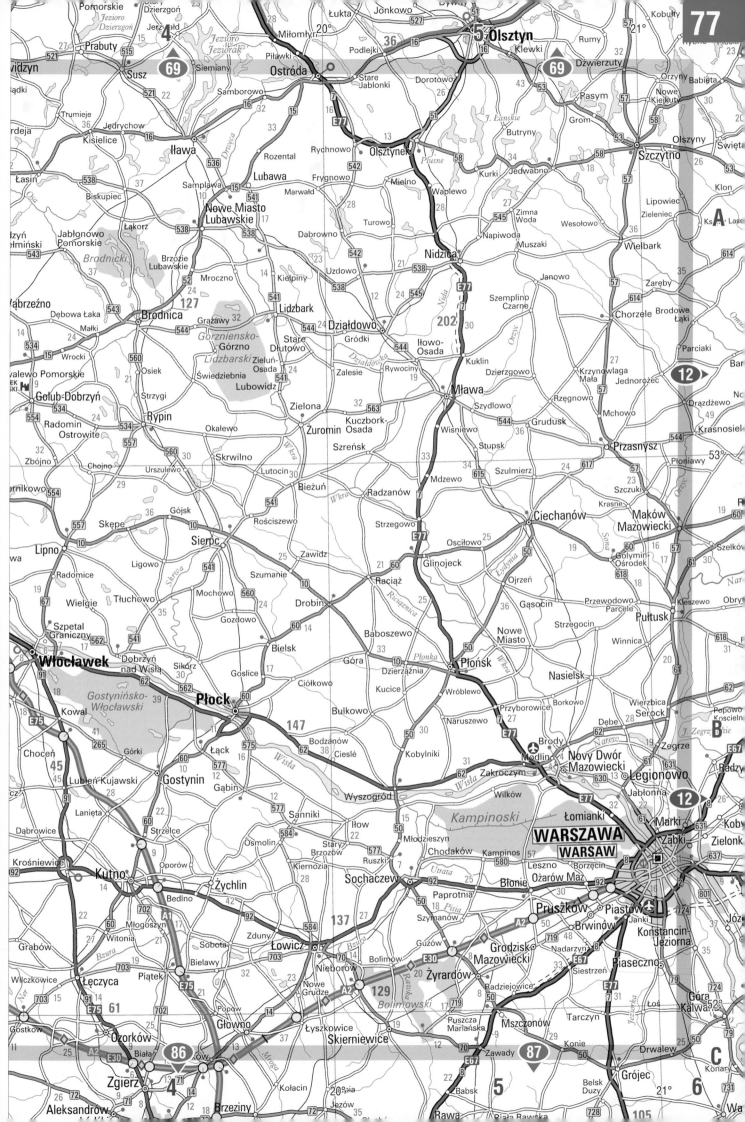

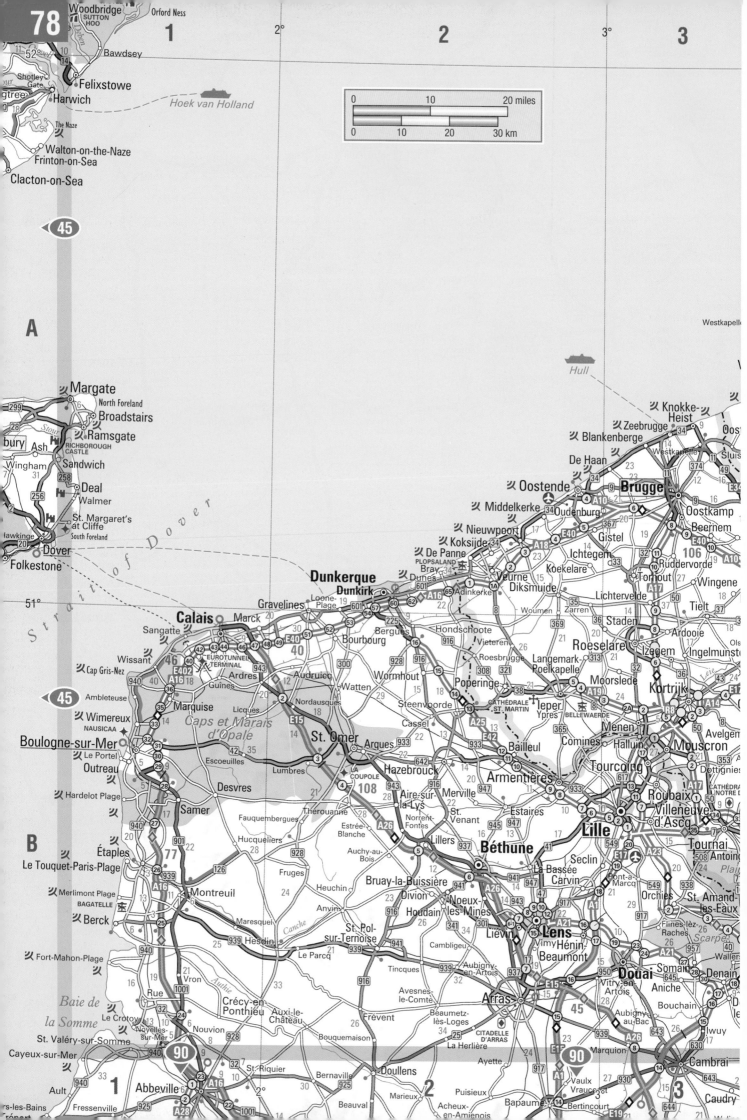

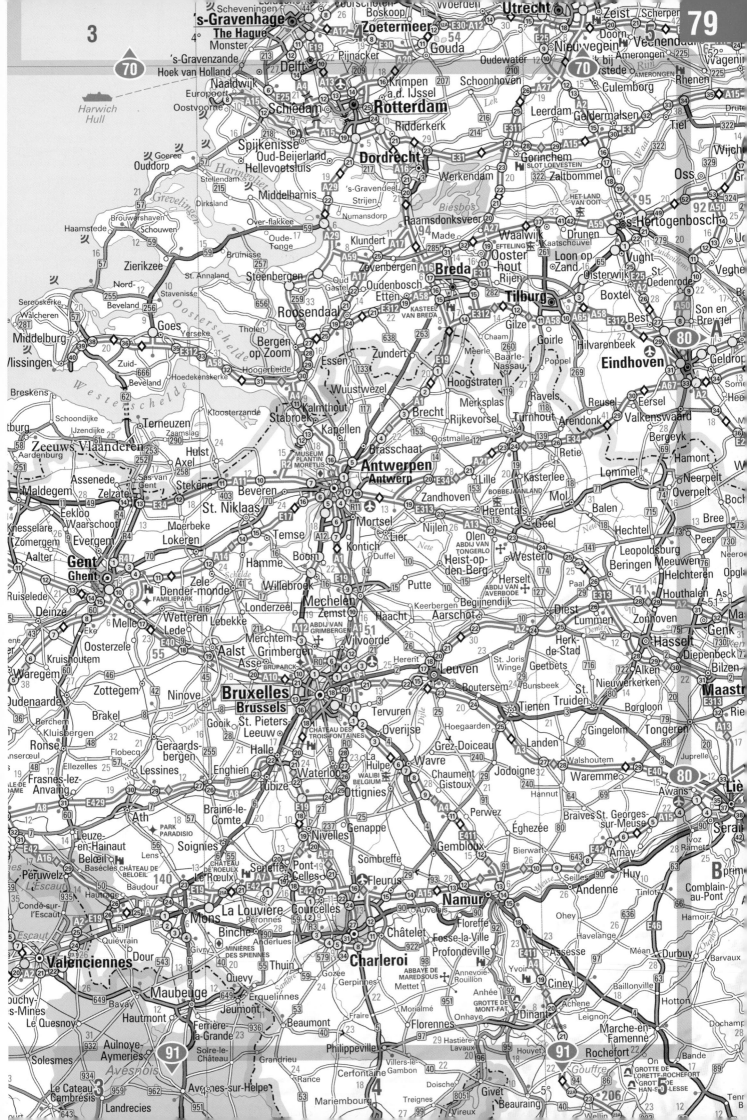

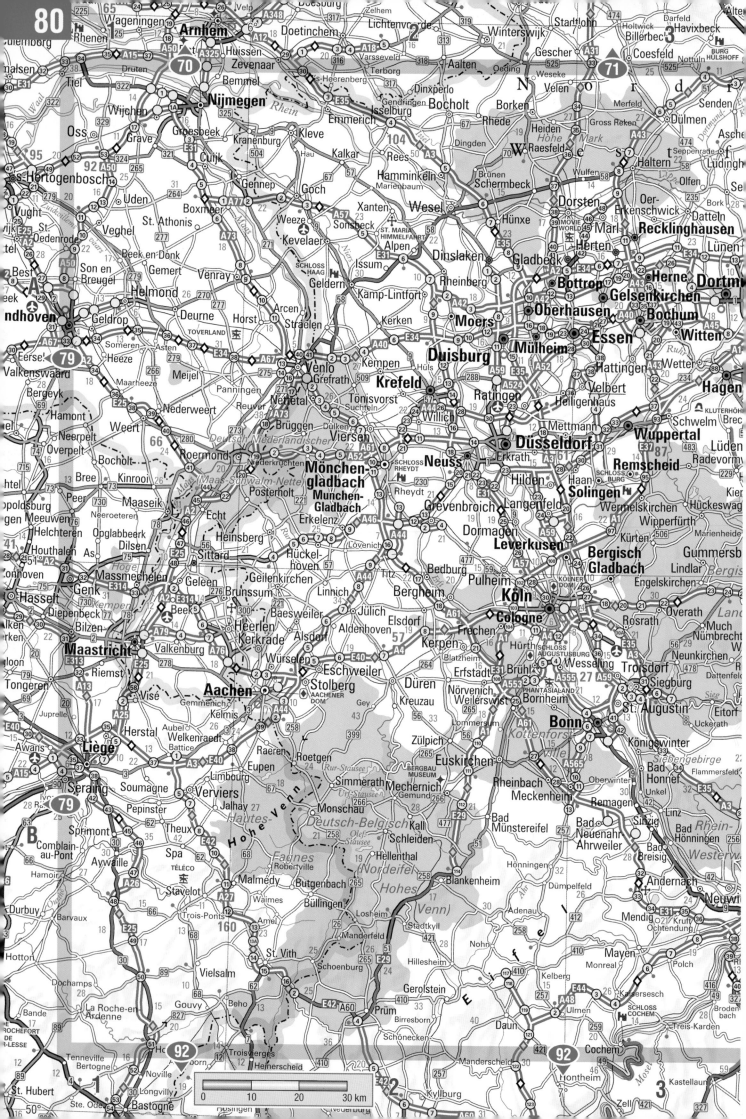

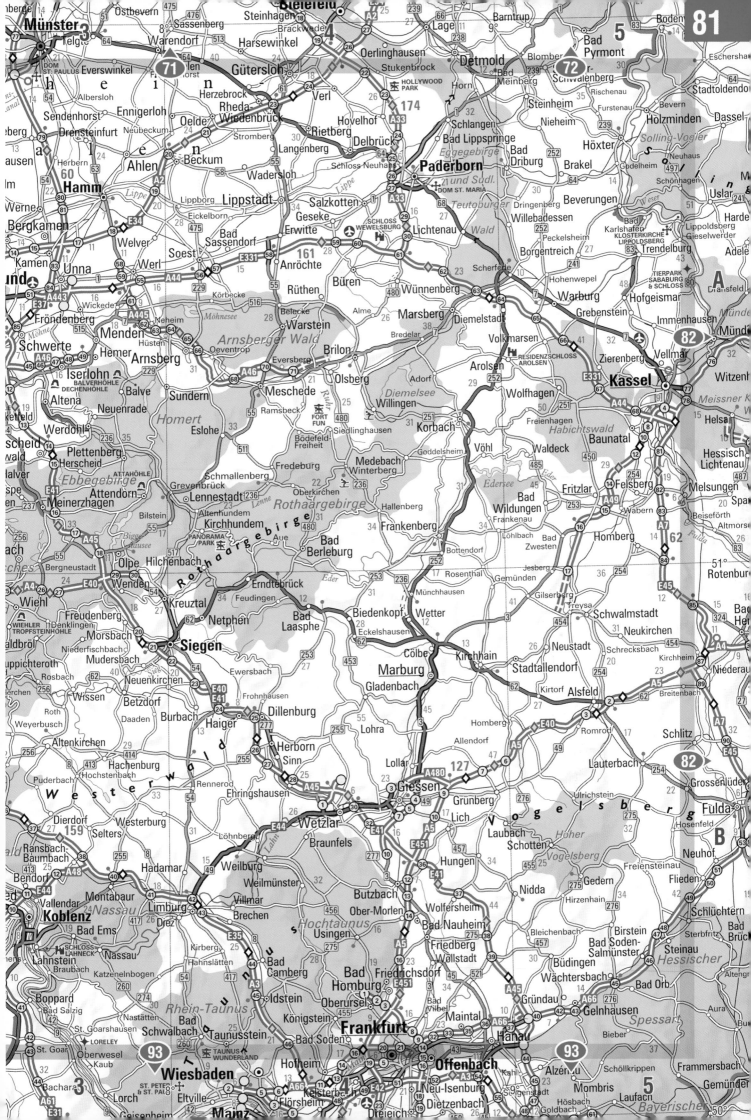

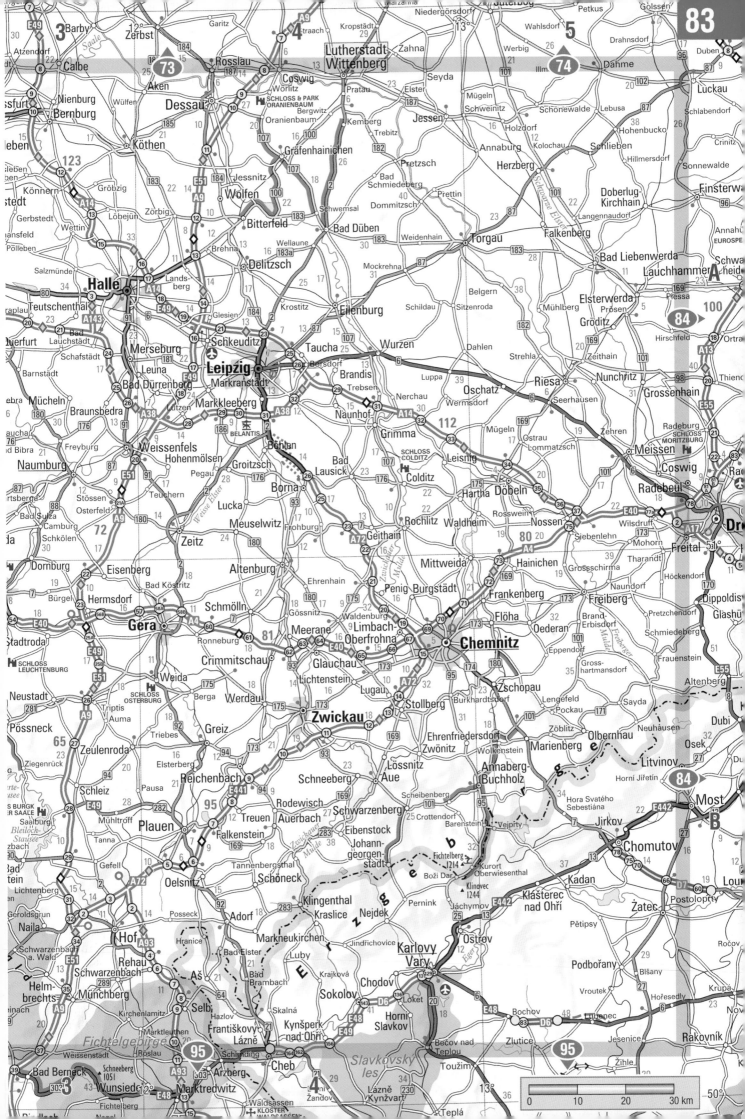

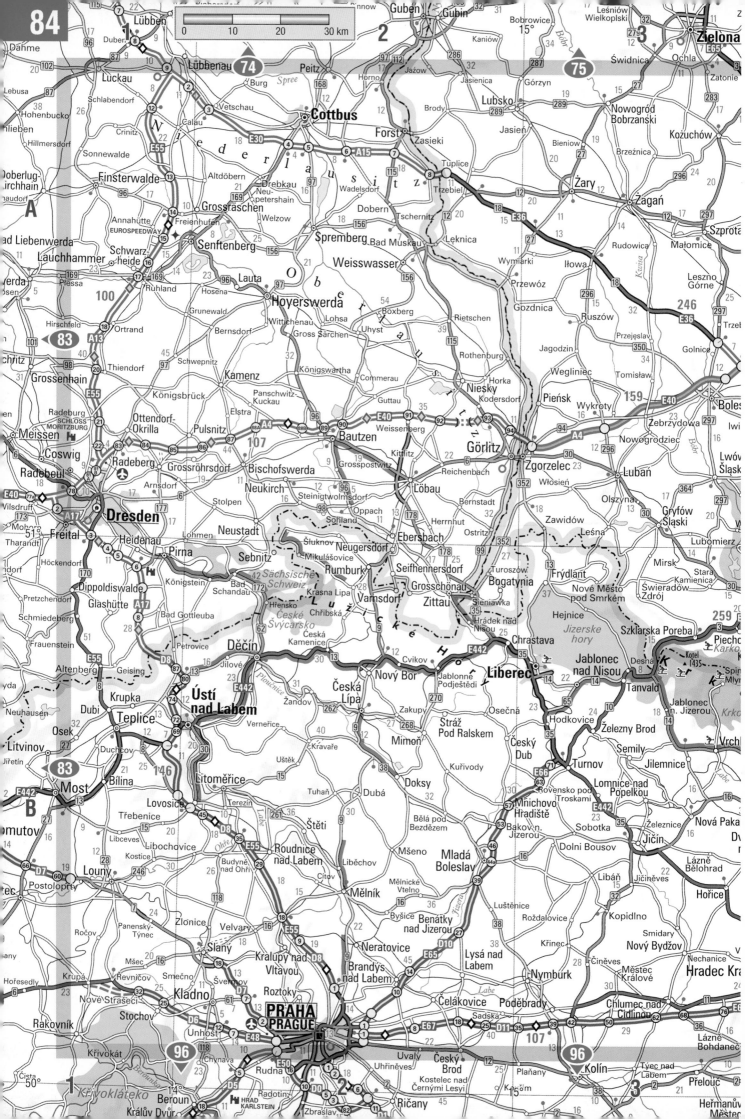

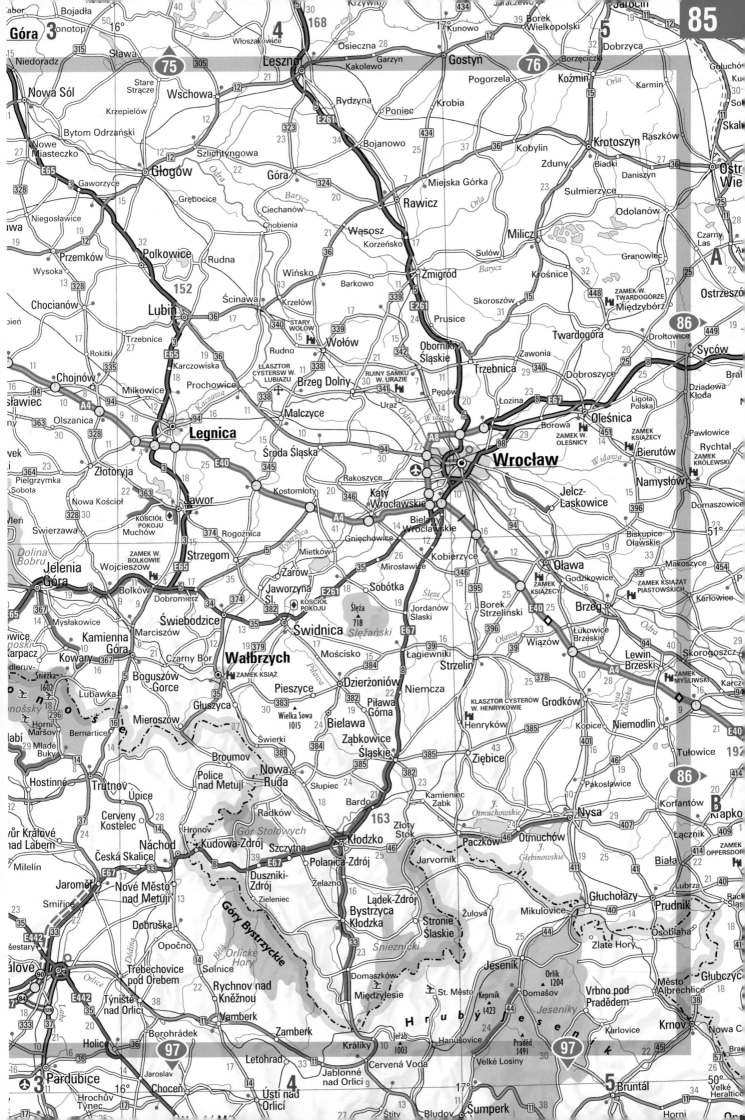

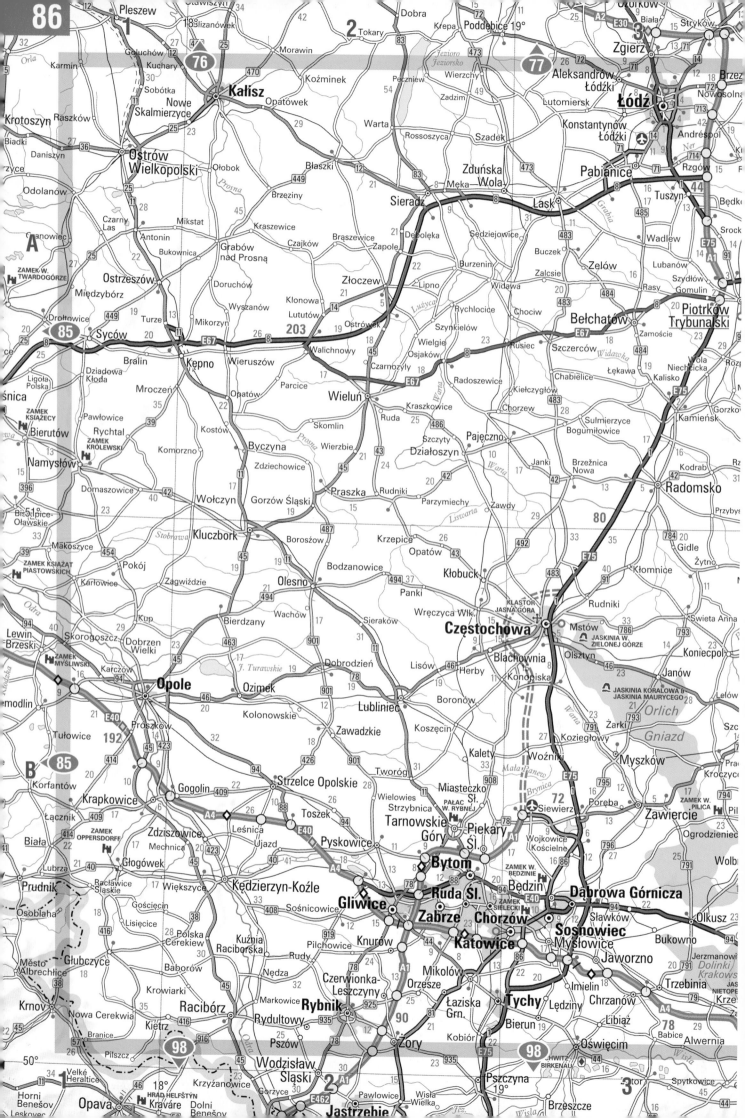

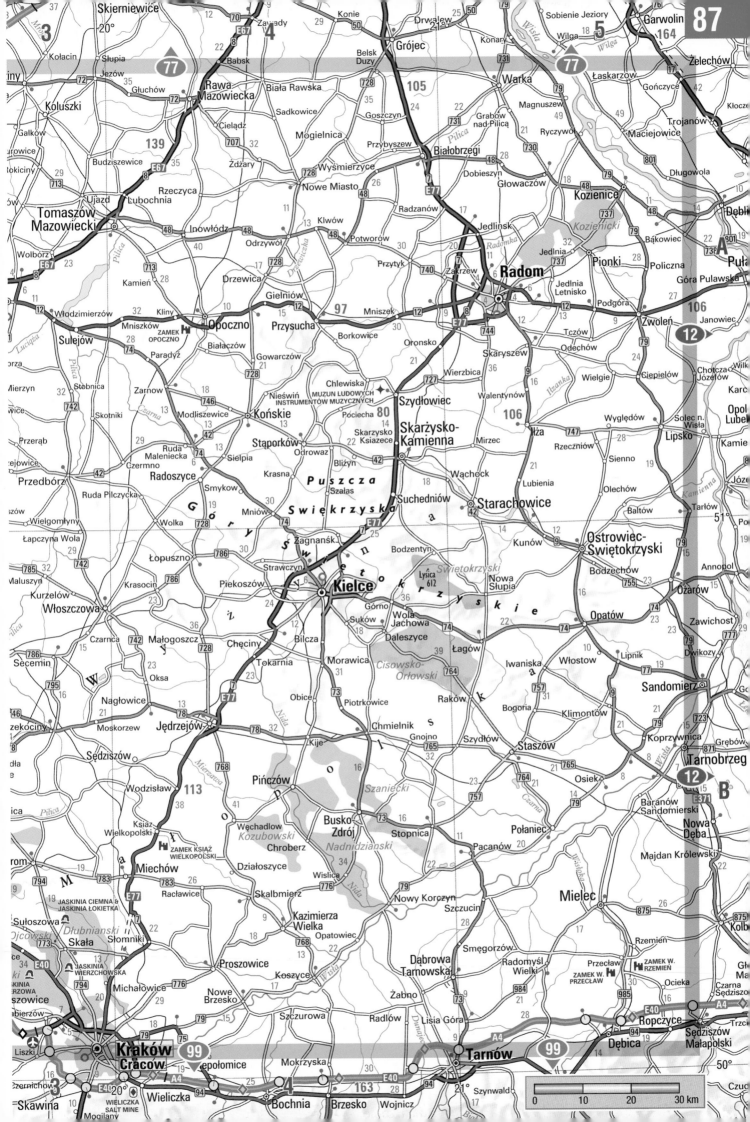

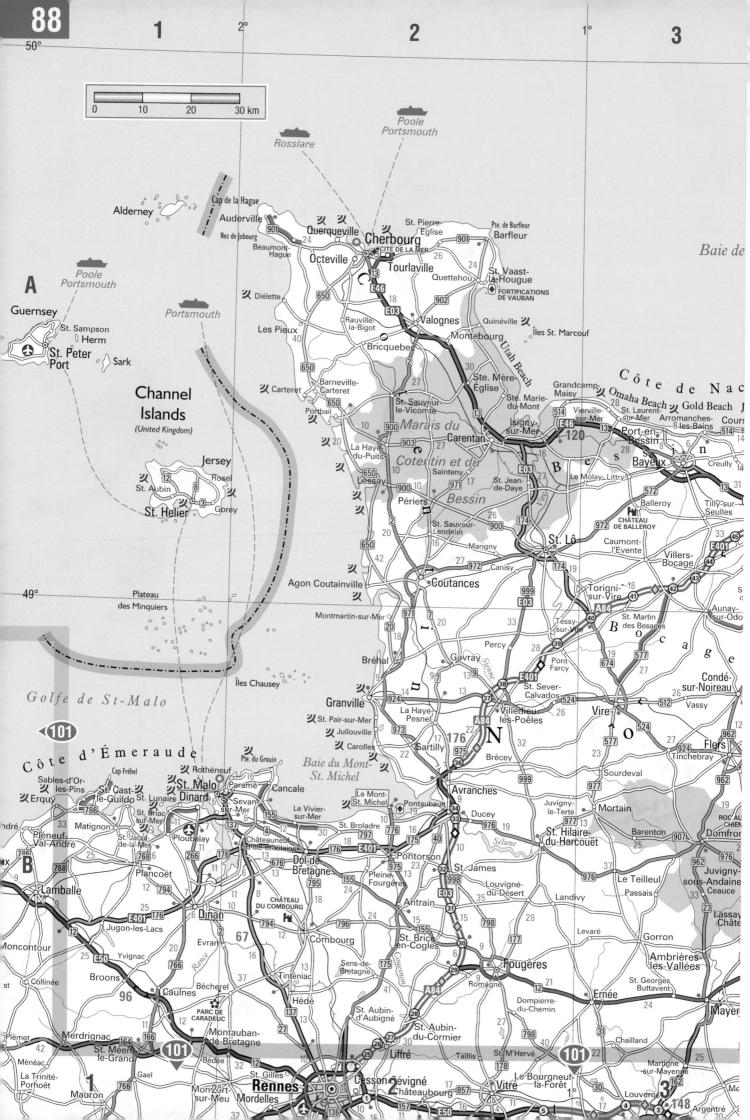

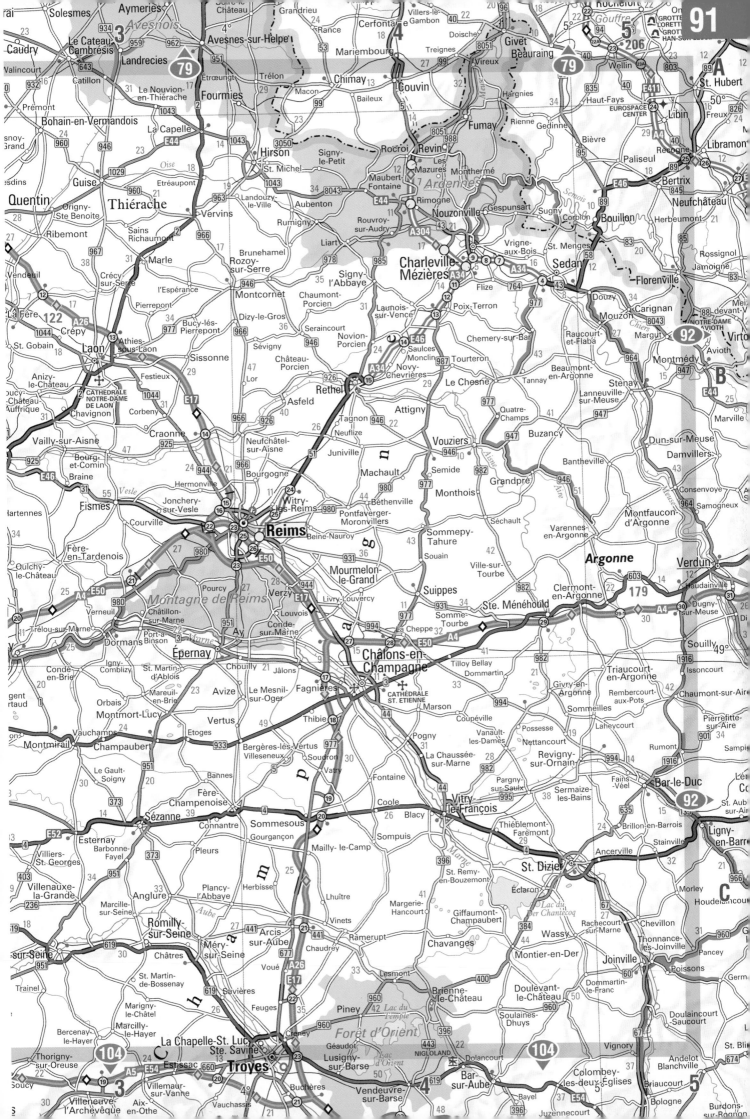

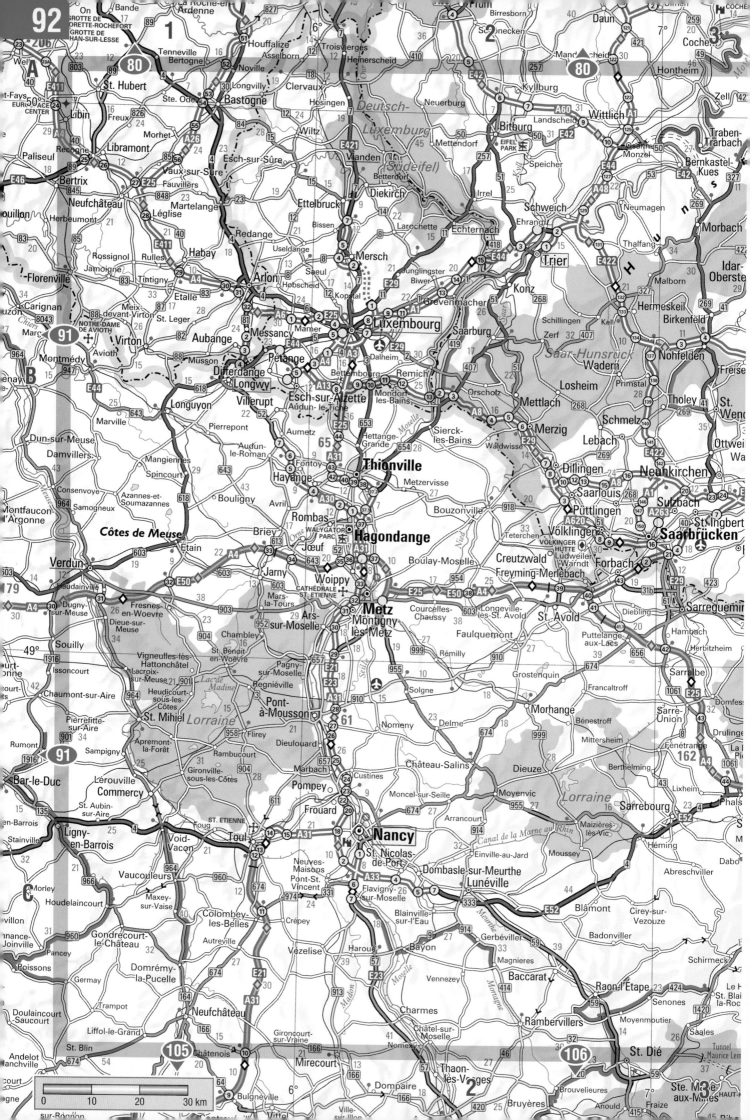

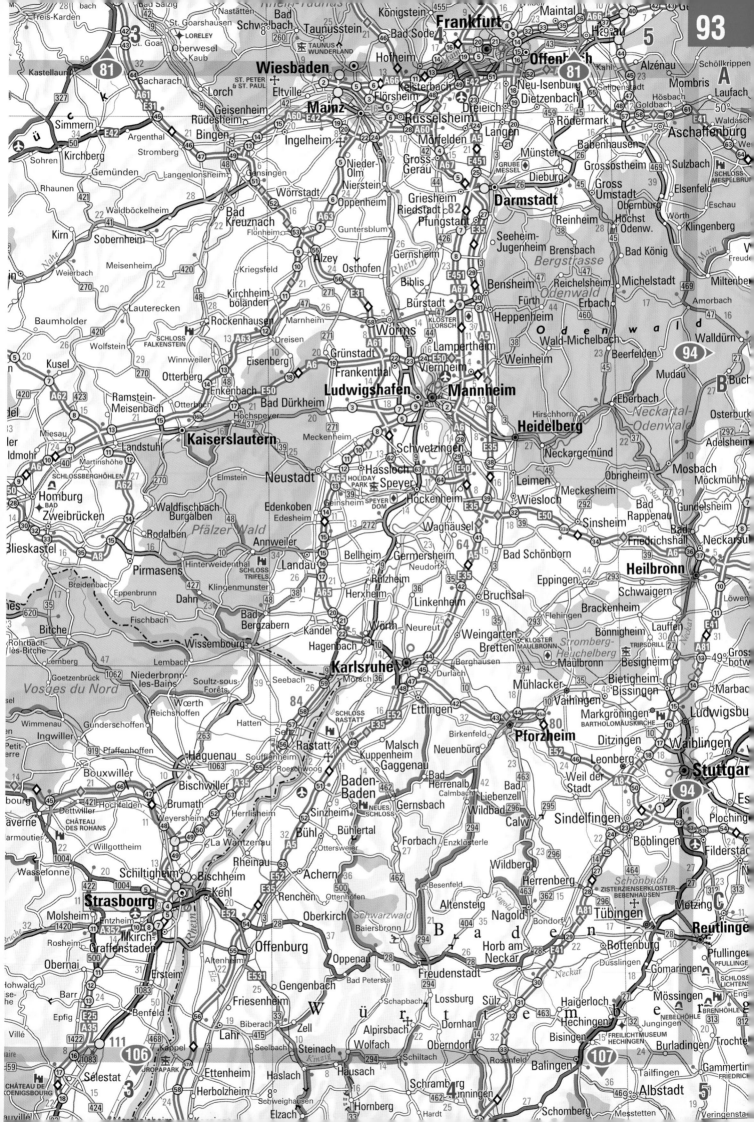

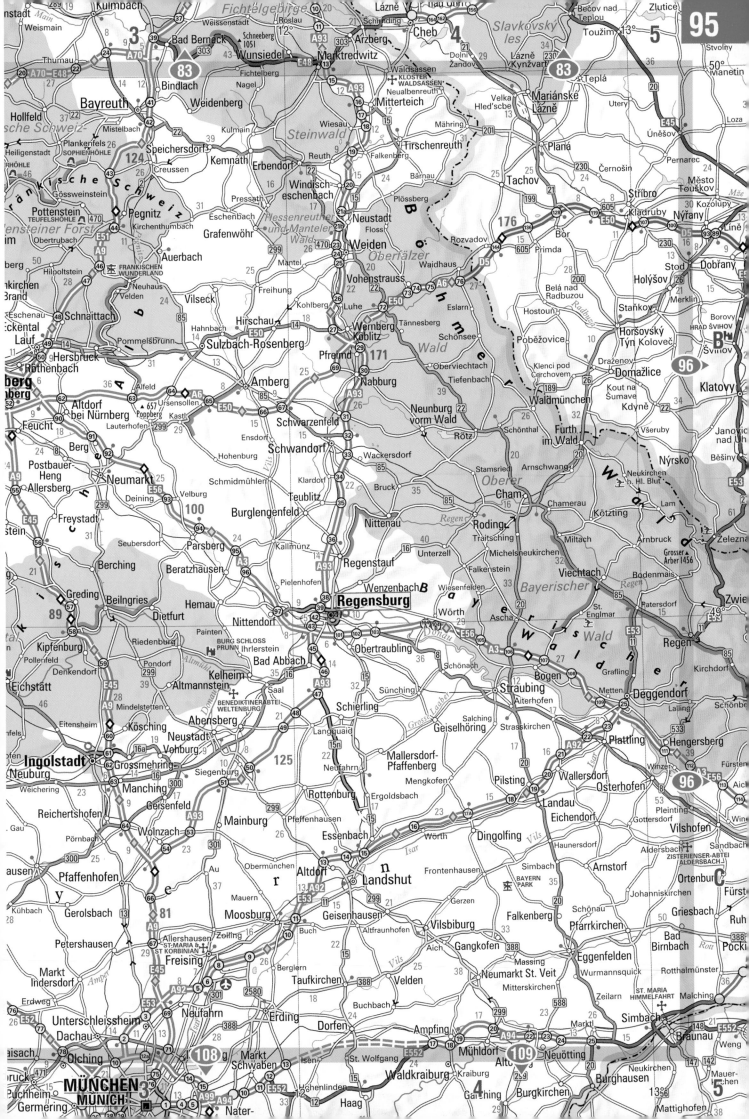

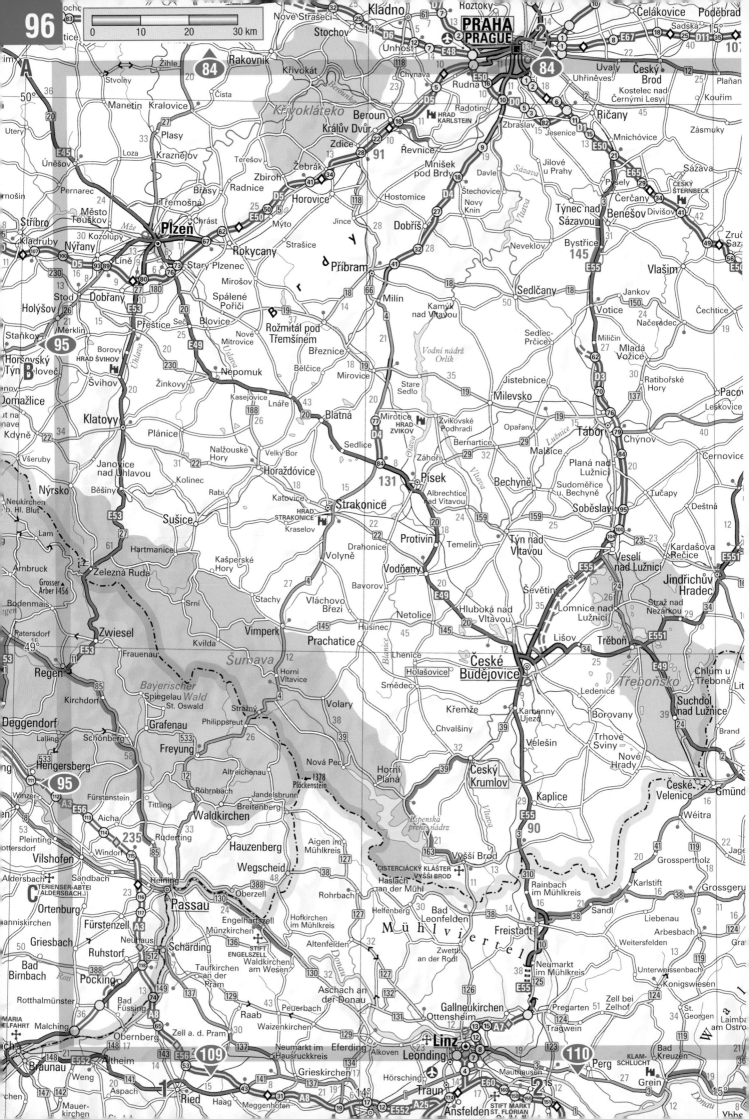

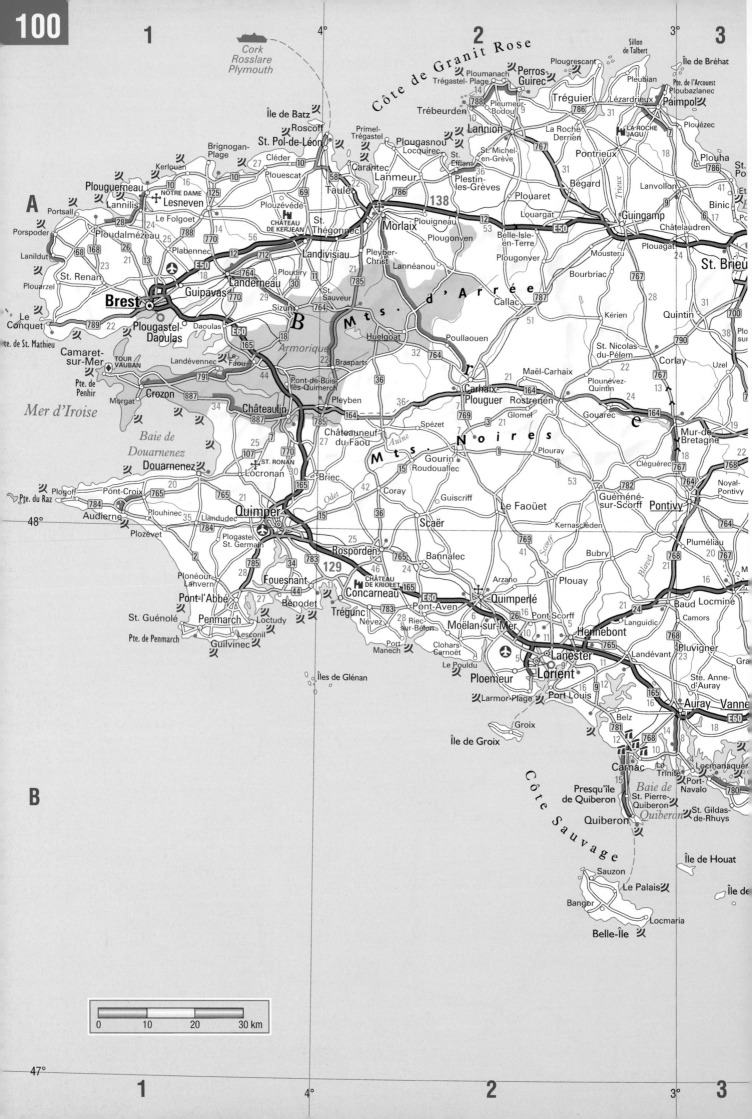

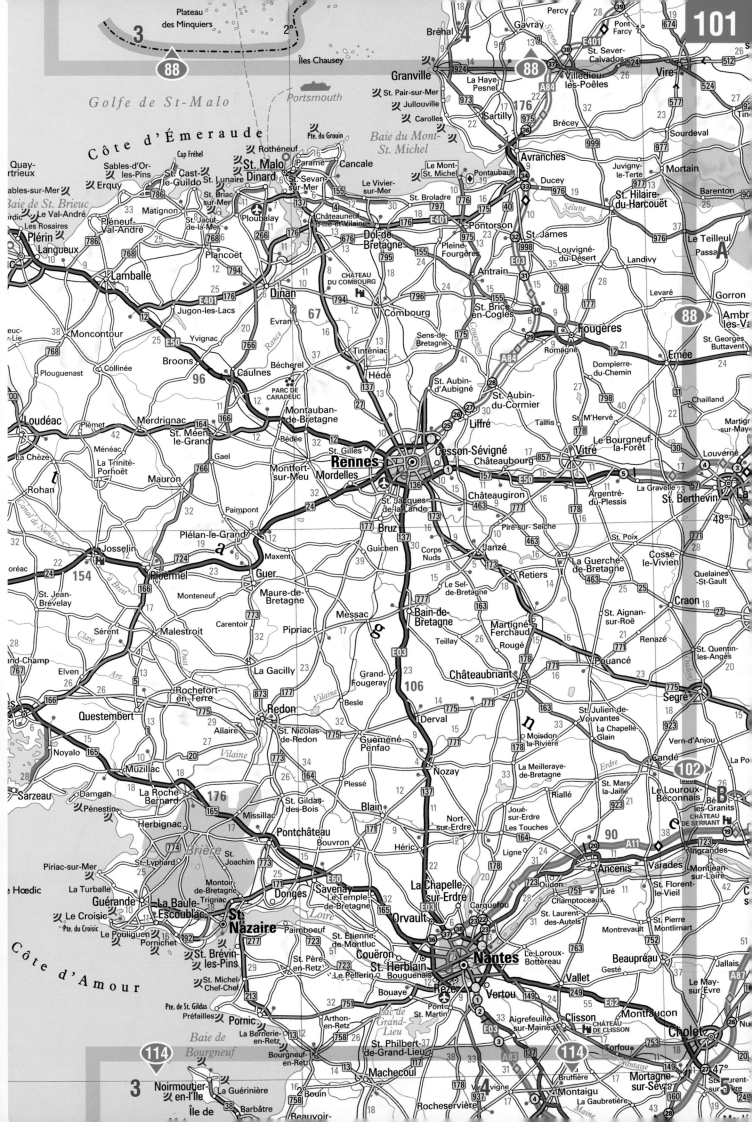

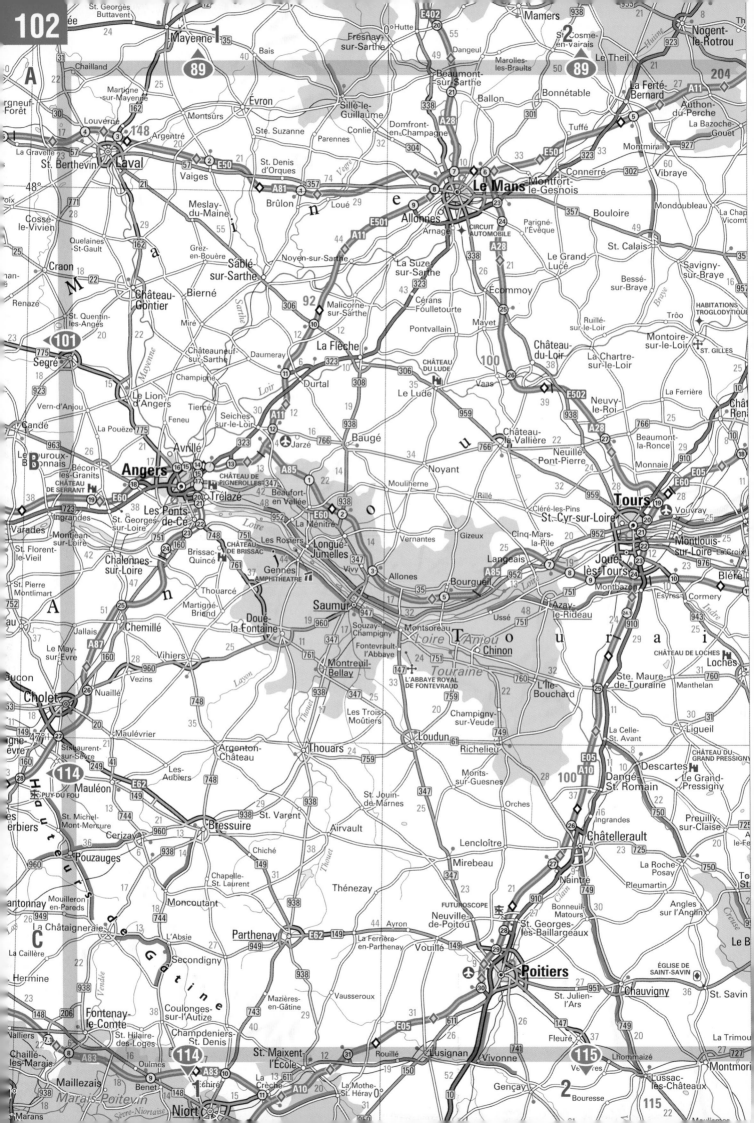

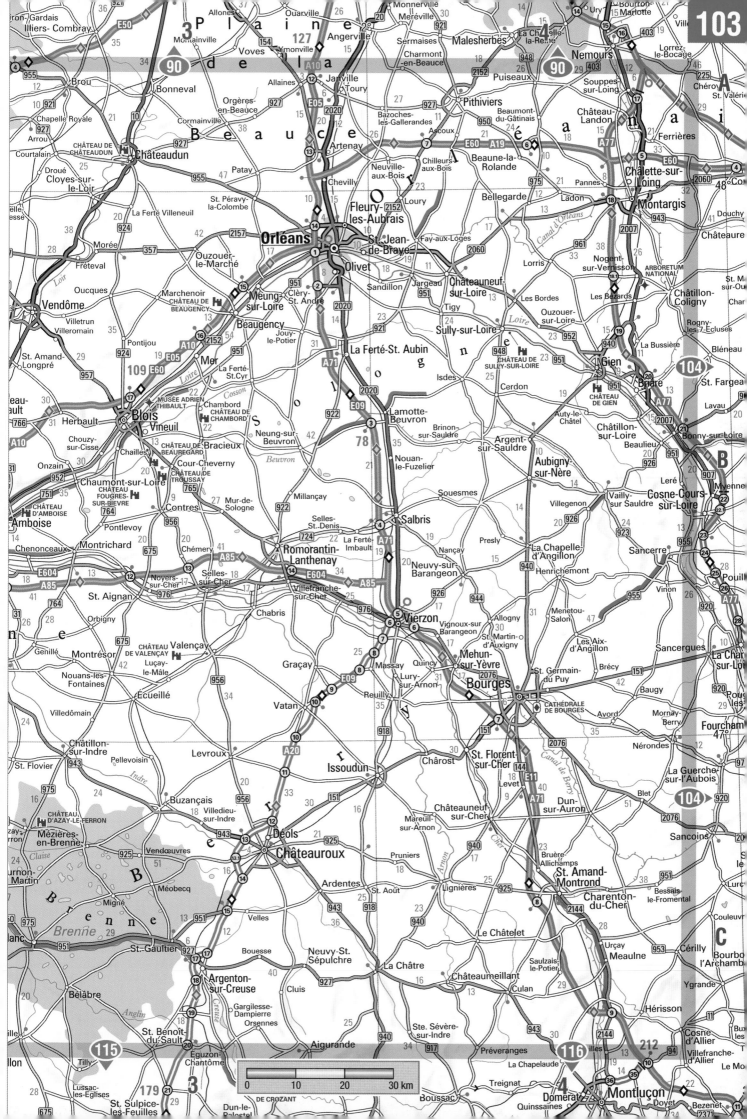

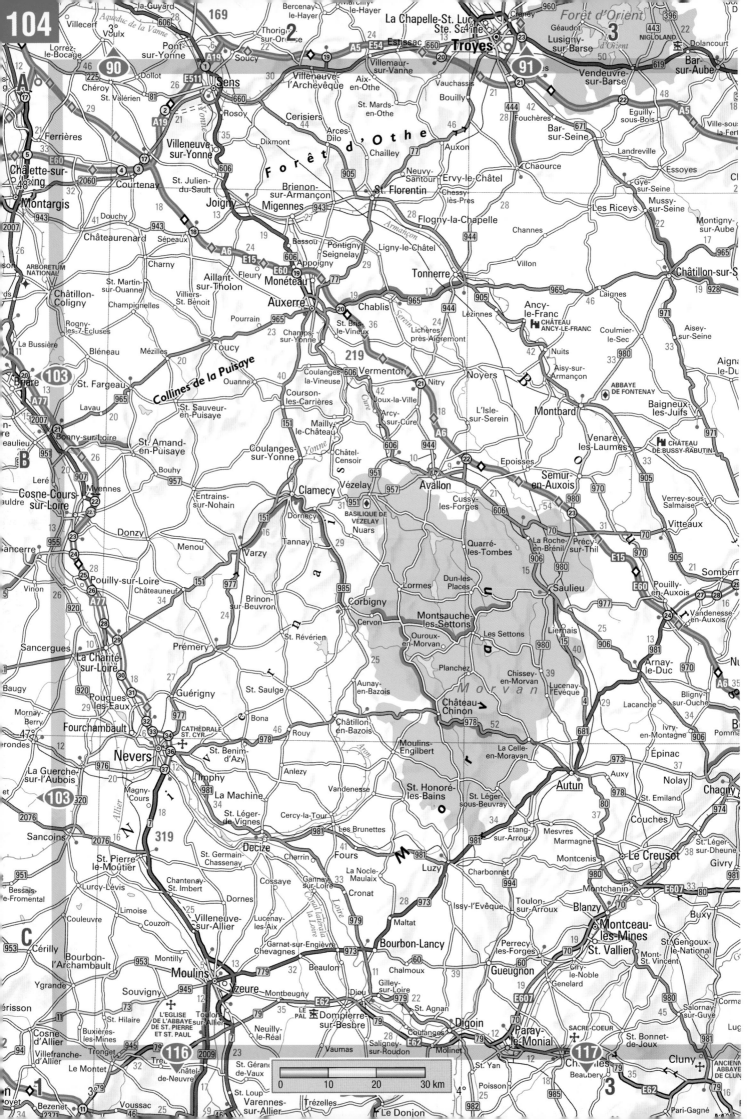

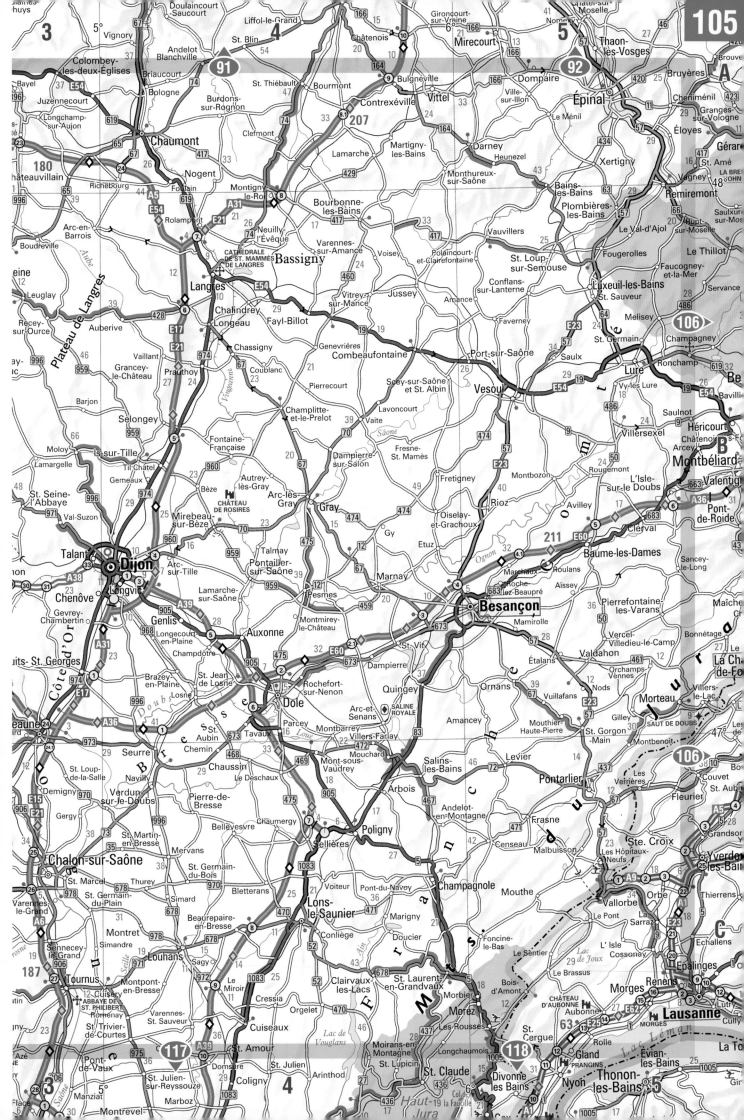

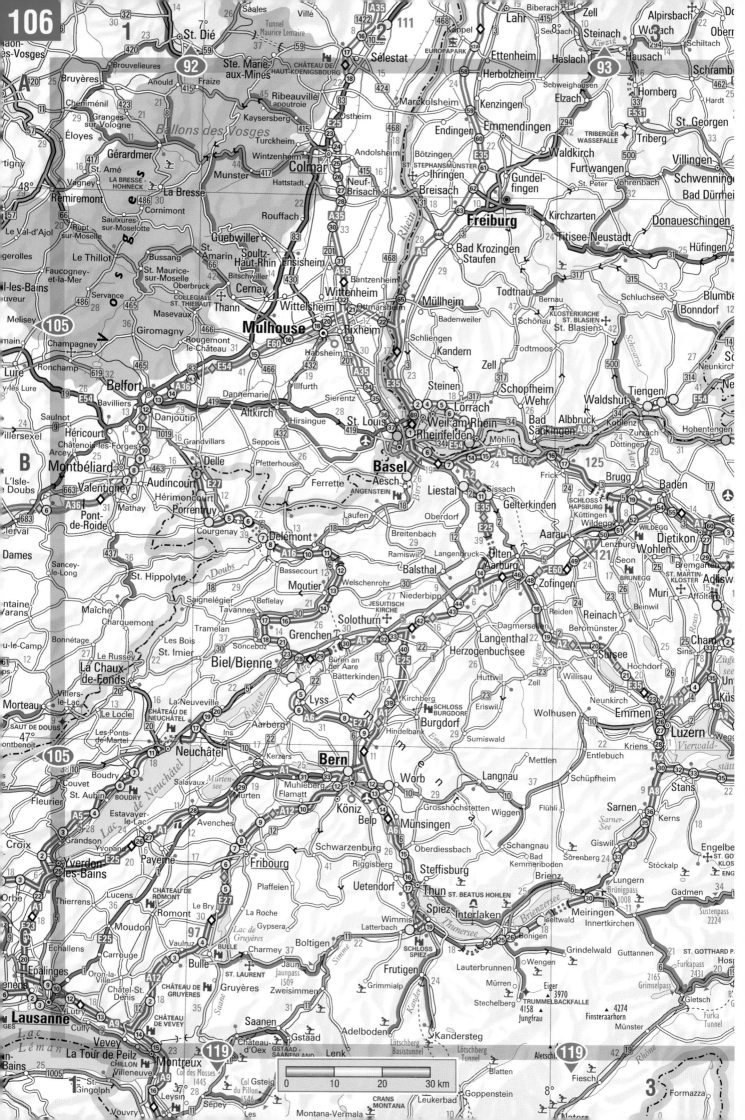

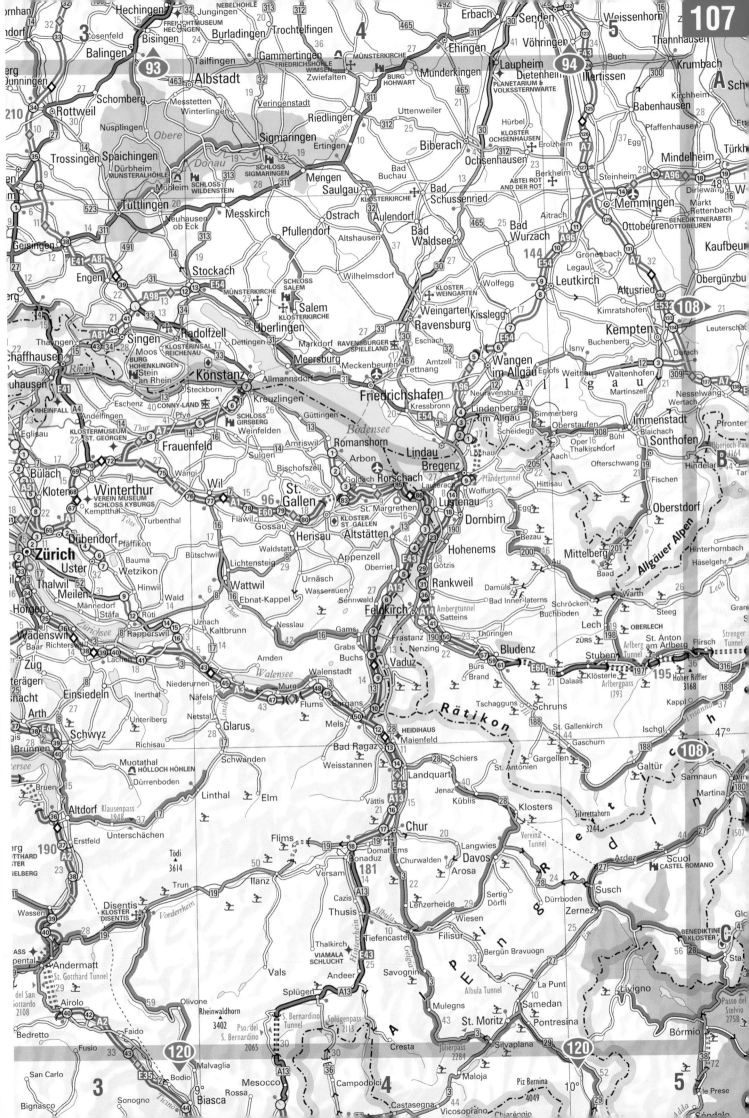

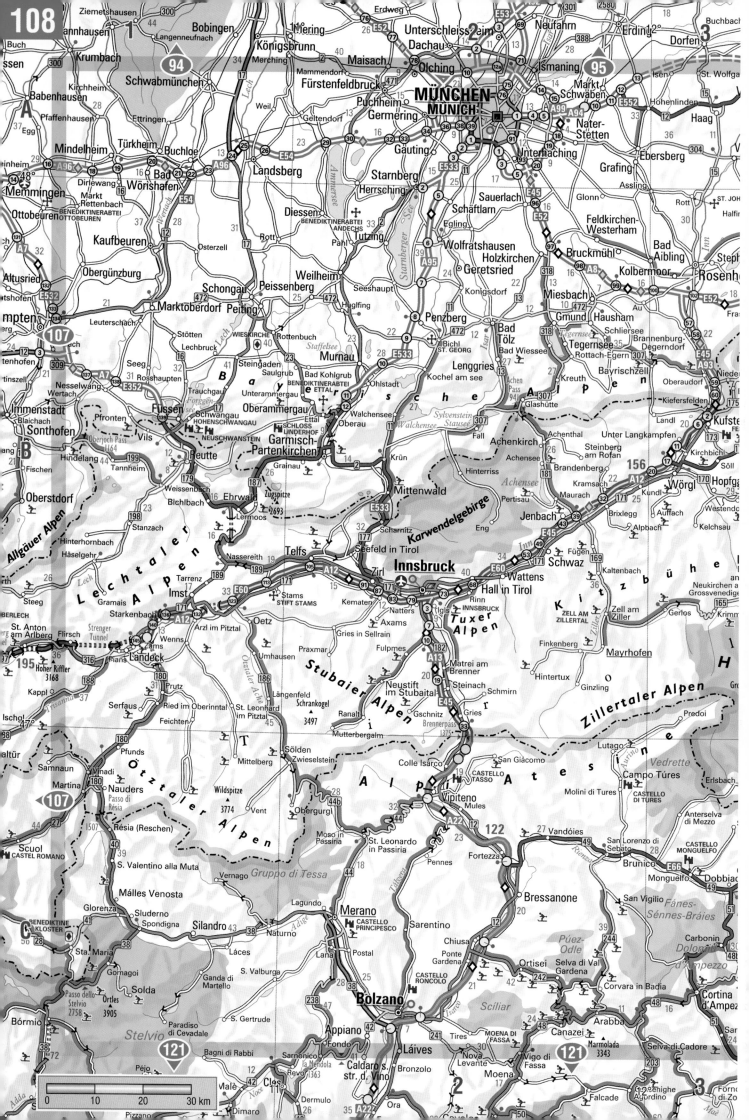

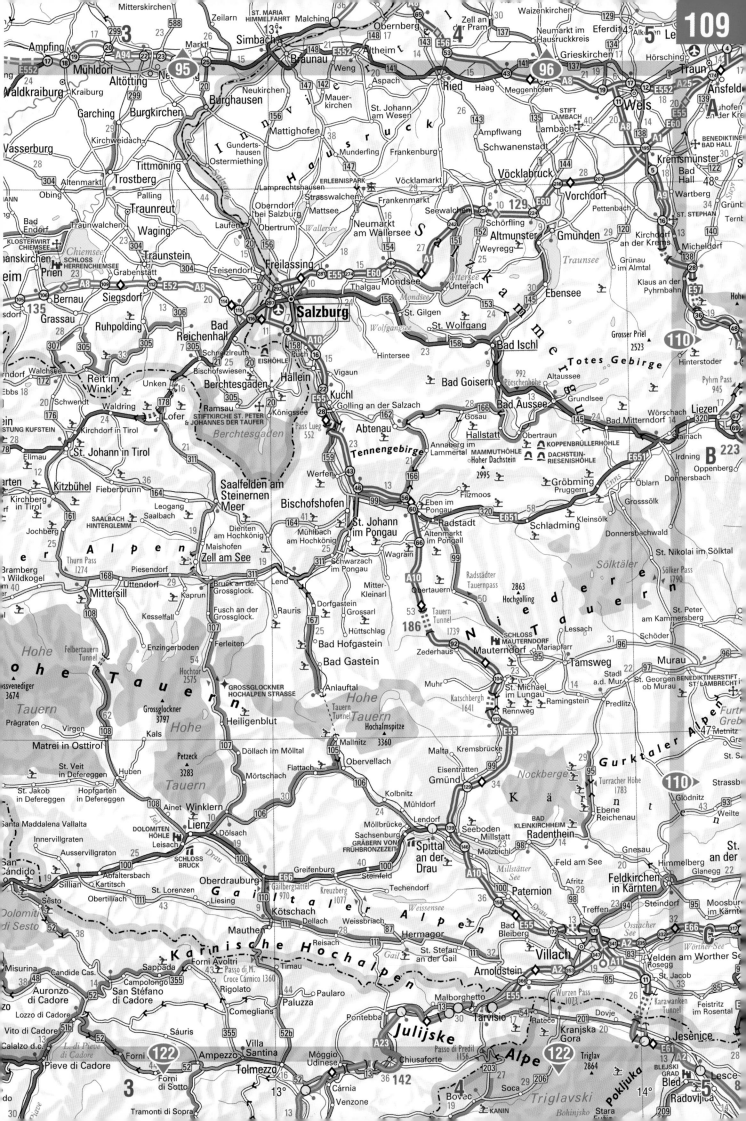

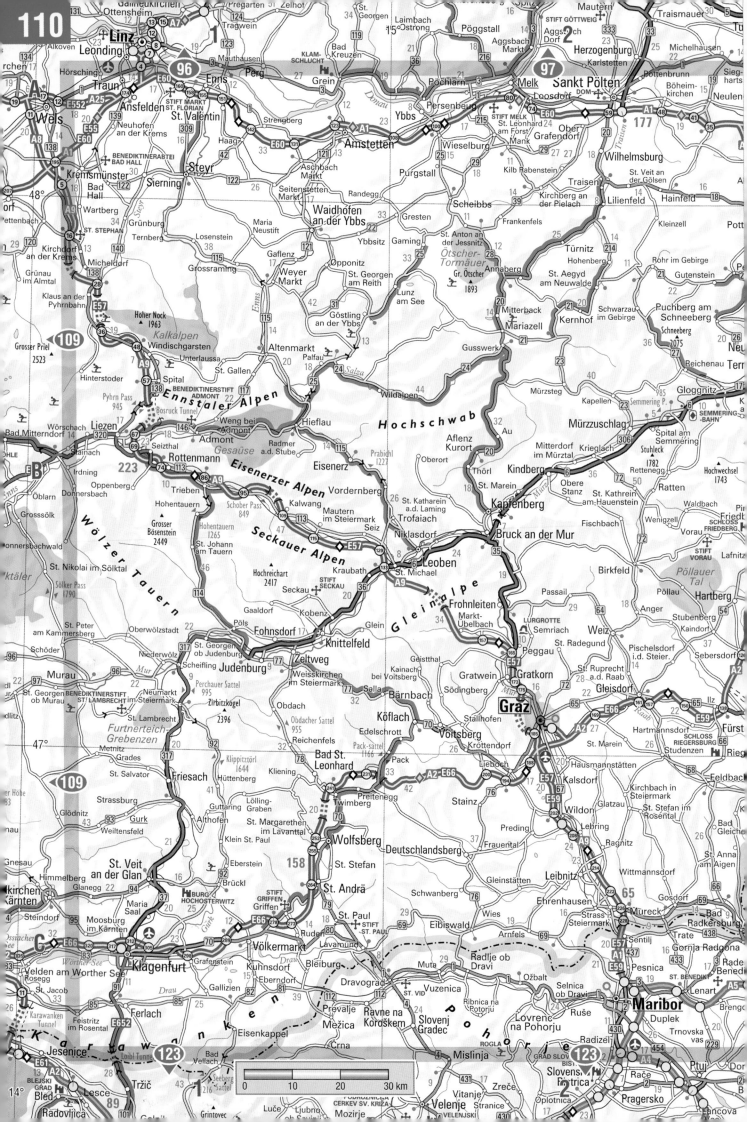

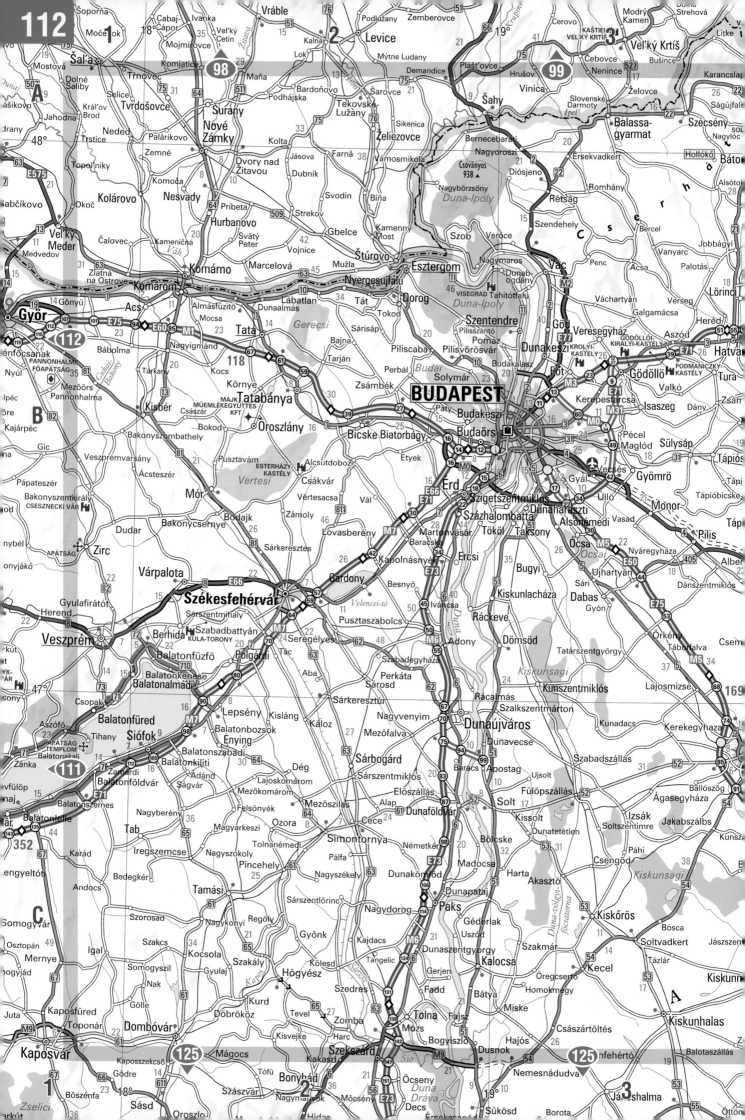

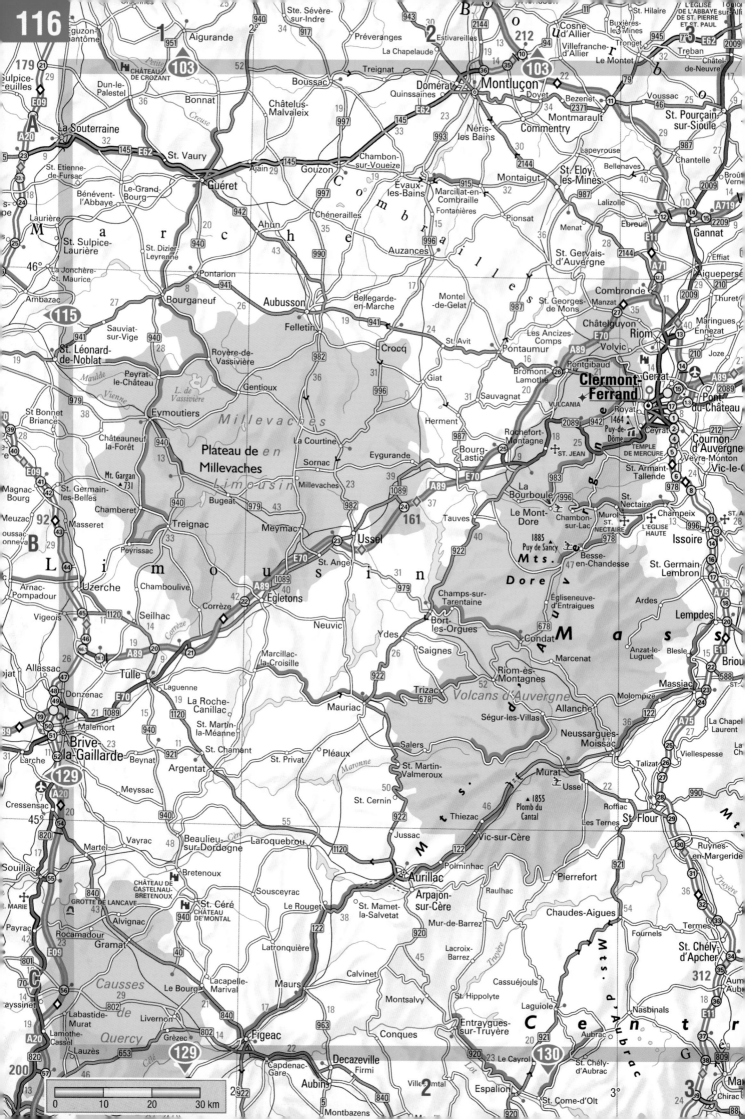

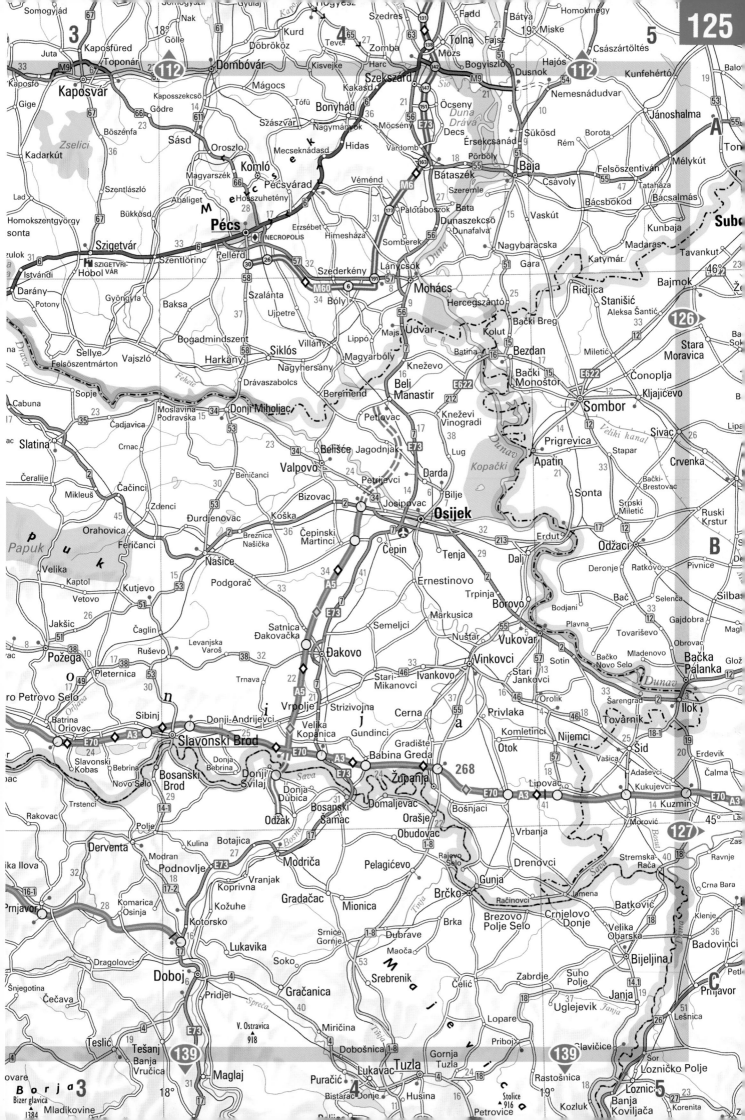

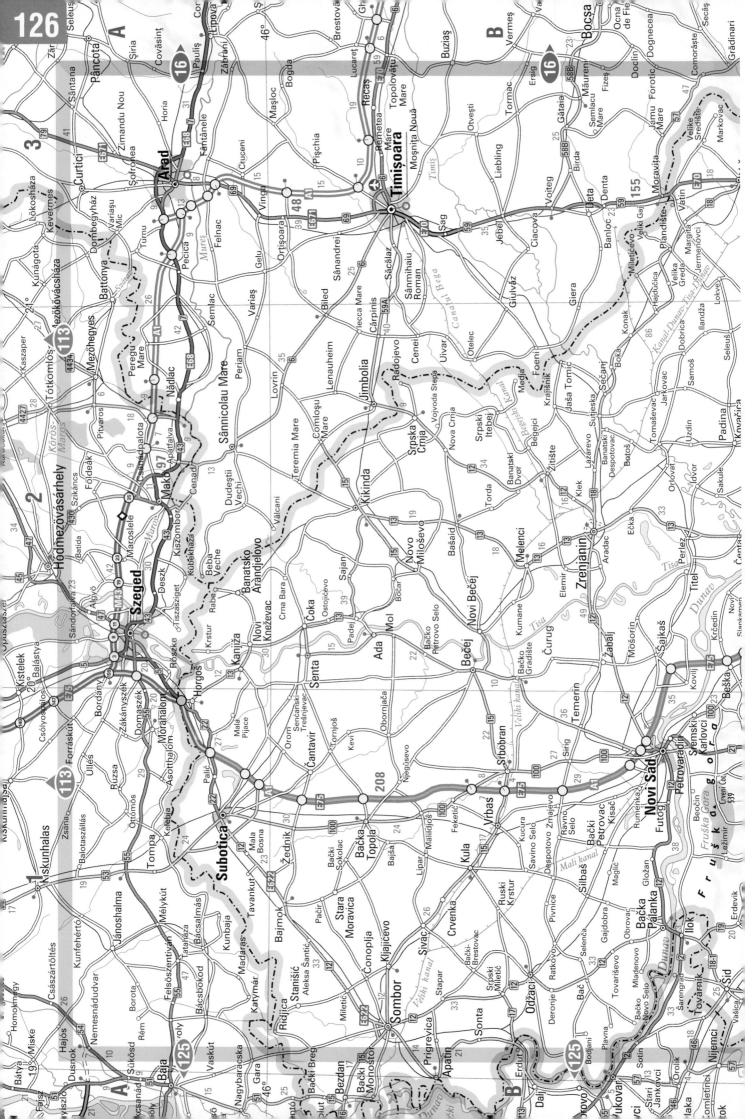

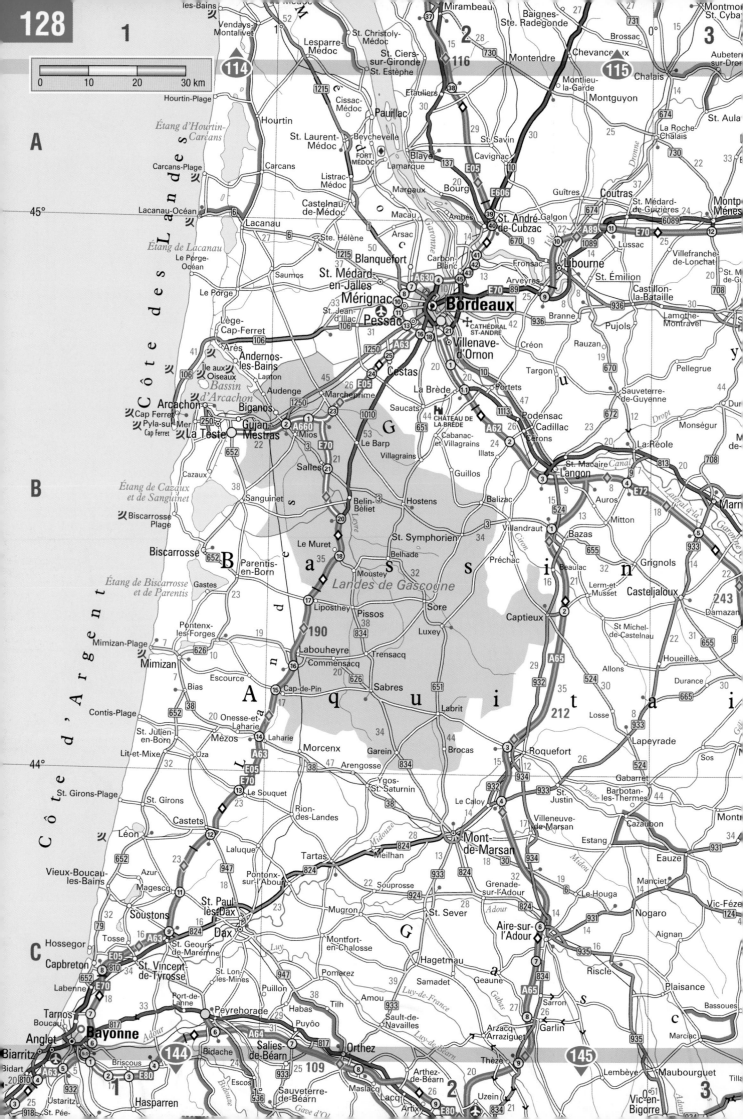

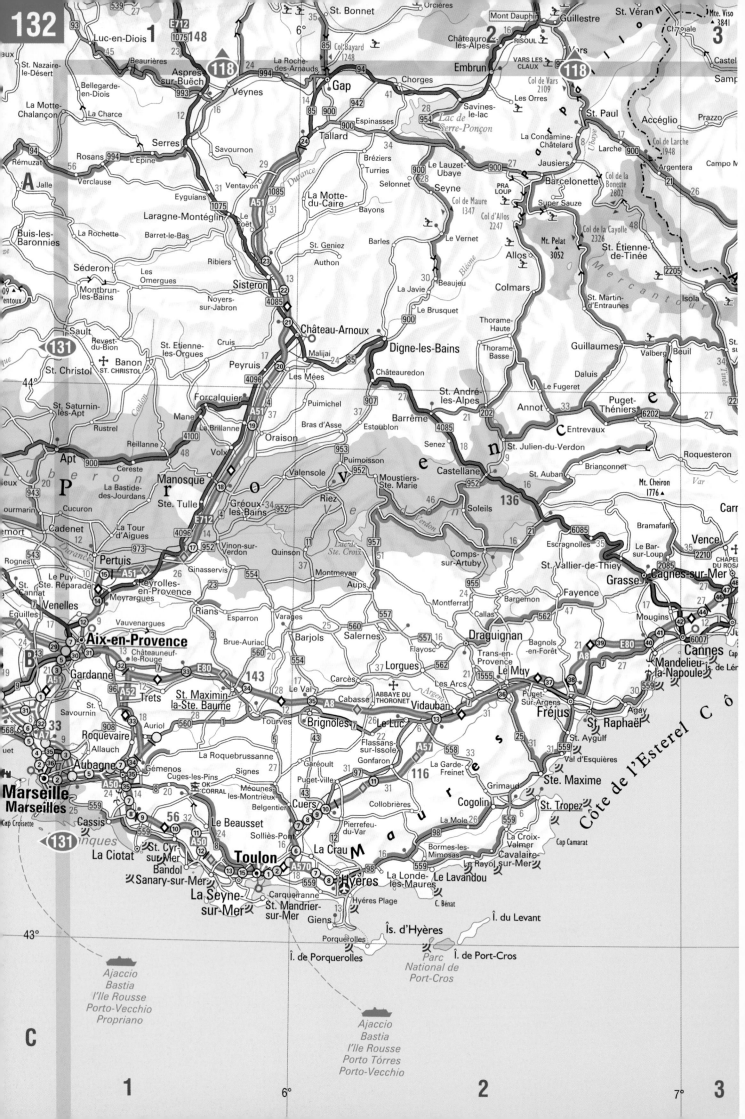

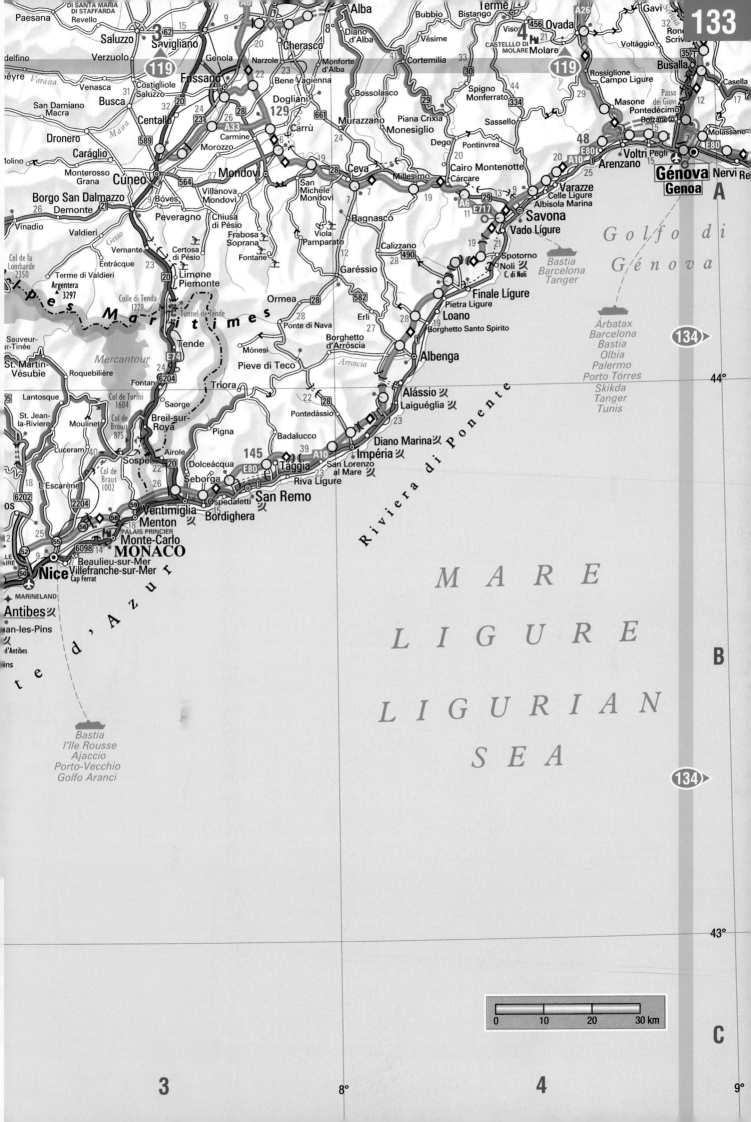

DI SANTA MARIA
DI STAFFARDA
Revello
Paesana
Saluzzo
Savigliano
Verzuolo
Costigliole
Saluzzo
Fossano
Genola
Narzole
Cherasco
Alba
Diano
d'Alba
Bubbio
Bistagno
Terme
Viso
Ovada
Gavi
Voltaggio
Busalla
Casella
Bene Vagienna
Monforte
d'Alba
Cortemilia
Spigno
Monferrato
Rossiglione
Campo Ligure
Pegli
Molassana
Dogliani
Bossolasco
CASTELLO DI
MOLARE Molare
Masone
Pontedécimo
Bolzaneto
Carrù
Murazzano
Monesiglio
Piana Crixia
Sassello
Dronero
Centallo
Carmine
Morozzo
Mondoví
Ceva
Millesimo
Dego
Pontinvrea
Cairo Montenotte
Cárcare
Voltri
Arenzano
GÉNOVA
Genoa
Nervi
Caráglio
Monterosso
Grana
Cúneo
Villanova
Mondoví
San Michéle
Mondoví
Bagnasco
Celle Ligure
Albisola Marina
Savona
Varazze
Borgo San Dalmazzo
Demonte
Bóves
Peveragno
Chiusa
di Pésio
Frabosa
Soprana
Fontane
Viola
Pamparato
Garéssio
Calizzano
Vado Lígure
Golfo di
Génova
Vinadio
Valdieri
Vernante
Certosa
di Pésio
Spotorno
Noli
C. di Noli
Bastia
Barcelona
Tanger
Col de la
Lombarde
2350
Terme di Valdieri
Argentera
3297
Limone
Piemonte
Ormea
Erli
Finale Lígure
Pietra Ligure
Loano
Borghetto Santo Spirito
Árbatax
Barcelona
Bastia
Olbia
Palermo
Porto Tórres
Skikda
Tanger
Tunis
Colle di Tenda
1279
Tunnel de Tende
Ponte di Nava
Borghetto
d'Arróscia
Albenga
Sauveur-
sur-Tinée
Tende
Pieve di Teco
Arroscia
St. Martin-
Vésubie
Mercantour
Roquebilière
Fontan
Triora
Alássio
Laiguéglia
Lantosque
Col de Turini
1604
Saorge
Pontedássio
Moulinet
Col de
Brouis
875
Breil-sur-
Roya
Pigna
Badalucco
Diano Marina
Impéria
St. Jean-
la-Rivière
Airole
Dolceácqua
Mónesi
San Lorenzo
al Mare
Lucéram
Sospel
Seborga
Tággia
Riva Lígure
L'Escarène
Col de
Braus
1002
Ospedaletti
San Remo
Riviera di Ponente
Ventimiglia
Bordighera
Menton
Monte-Carlo
PALAIS PRINCIER
MONACO
Nice
Beaulieu-sur-Mer
Villefranche-sur-Mer
Cap Ferrat
MARINELAND
Côte d'Azur
Antibes
Juan-les-Pins
Cap d'Antibes
Bastia
l'Ile Rousse
Ajaccio
Porto-Vecchio
Golfo Aranci

M A R E
L I G U R E
L I G U R I A N
S E A

44°

43°

0   10   20   30 km

3   8°   4   9°

A

B

C

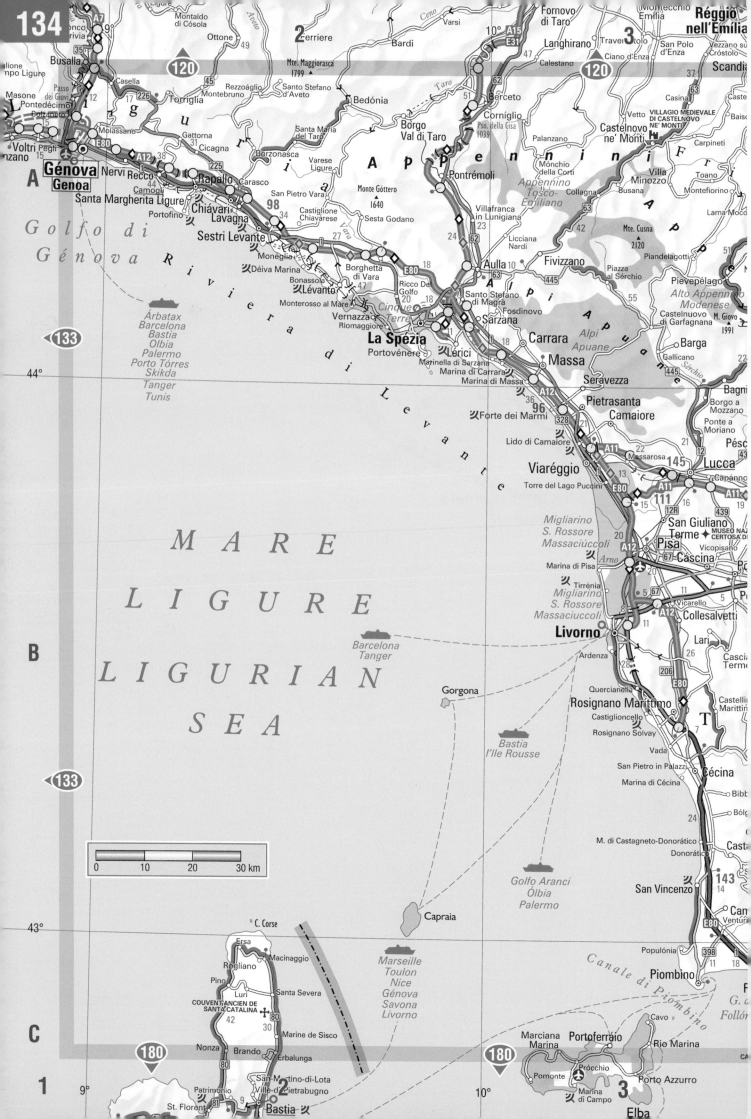

Montecchio
Emília

Réggio
nell'Emília

Fornovo
di Taro

Varsi

10° A15
E31

Langhirano

Travers...tolo

San Polo
d'Enza

Vezzano su...
Cróstolo

Scandia...

Bardi

120

Ottone 49

Montaldo
di Cósola

2 Ferriere

Mte. Maggiorasca
1799

Berceto

120

62

Calestano

Ciano d'Enza

Casina 63

Castel...

A7
9°...rivia

35

Busalla

Casella

226

Torriglia

Montebruno

Rezzóaglio

Santo Stefano
d'Aveto

Bedónia

51

Corníglio

Pso. della Cisa
1039

VILLAGIO MEDIEVALE
DI CASTELNOVO
NE' MONTI

Castelnovo
ne' Monti H

Carpineti

Baiso

Masone

Passo
dei Giovi

Pontedécimo
Bolzaneto

12

17

Casella

45

Gattorna

Cicagna

31

Santa Maria
del Taro

Borgo
Val di Taro

Pontrémoli

Palanzano

Mónchio
della Córti

Collagna

Busana

Villa
Minozzo

Toano

Montefiorino

Lama Mocó...

lione
npo Ligure

Voltri Pégli
nzano 15

Génova
Genoa

E80

Molassano

A12 38

Nervi Recco

Rapallo

225

Carasco

Borzonasca

Varese
Ligure

Appennino

Appennini

Fri

Gottora

1640

Villafranca
in Lunigiana

Licciana
Nardi

42

Mte. Cusna
2120

Pievepélago

Alto Appennino
Modenese

63

Castelnuovo
di Garfagnana

M. Giovo
1991

A

44

Camogli

Santa Margherita Ligure

Chiávari

Portofino

Lavagna

98

34

Castiglione
Chiavarese

Sesta Godano

24 23

62

Aulla 10
63

Fivizzano

Piazza
al Sérchio

55

Appennino
Tosco-Emiliano

L i g u r i a

Golfo di
Génova

Riviera

San Pietro Vara

Moneglia

Déiva Marina

Bonassola

Lévanto

Monterosso al Mare

Vernazza

Riomaggiore

Cinque
Terre

Sestri Levante

Borghetta
di Vara

Ricco Del
Golfo

E80 18

27

Vara

47

18

18

Santo Stefano
di Magra

Fosdinovo

Sarzana

Carrara

Alpi
Apuane

Barga

Gallicano

445 Sérchio

22

Bagni...

B...a

La Spézia

Portovénere

Lérici

Marinella di Sarzana

Marina di Carrara

Marina di Massa

Massa

1 18

Alpi Apuane

Seravezza

445

Árbatax
Barcelona
Bastia
Olbia
Palermo
Porto Tórres
Skikda
Tanger
Tunis

133

44°

A12

36

96

328

Forte dei Marmi

Pietrasanta

Camaiore

21

Ponte a
Moriano

Borgo a
Mozzano

Pésc...

Golfo di Génova

Lido di Camaiore

A11

22

Massarosa

21

145

Lucca

43

Capánno...

Viaréggio

Torre del Lago Puccini

E80

A11

13

A11...

111

16

439

M A R E

15

12R

San Giuliano
Terme

Migliarino
S. Rossore
Massaciúccoli

20

MUSEO NAZ...
CERTOSA DI...

L I G U R E

A12

Pisa

67

Cáscina

Po...

Marina di Pisa

Arno

Vicopisano

L I G U R I A N

Tirrénia

Migliarino
S. Rossore
Massaciuccoli

5

67

Vicarello

4

A12

Collesalvetti

S E A

Livorno

11

11

Lari

Casci...
Term...

B

Barcelona
Tanger

Ardenza

26

Gorgona

Quercianella

Rosignano Maríttimo

Castelli...
Maríttim...

133

Castiglioncello

Rosignano Solvay

T

7

Bastia
l'Ile Rousse

Vada

San Pietro in Palazzi

Cécina

Marina di Cécina

Bibb...

Bólg...

Golfo Aranci
Ólbia
Palermo

24

M. di Castagneto-Donorático

Donorático

Casta...

143

14

San Vincenzo

43°

0   10   20   30 km

C. Corse

Ersa

Macinaggio

Capraia

Marseille
Toulon
Nice
Génova
Savona
Livorno

Populónia

398

18

Piombino

G. d...
Follo...

Rogliano

Pino

Luri

Santa Severa

180

COUVENT ANCIEN DE
SANTA CATALINA

80

Marine de Sisco

30

42

Canale di Piombino

Cavo

Marciana
Marina

Portoferráio

Rio Marina

180

Nonza

Brando

Erbalunga

Pomonte

Prócchio

Porto Azzurro

1

9°

San-Martino-di-Lota

Ville-di-Pietrabugno

2

10°

Marina
di Campo

Elba

3

Patrimonio

81

Bastia

St. Florent

Unije
Nerezine
Klanac
Ličkí
Osik
Jošan
Donj

Čunski
3
Prizna
15°
4
odlapača
Donj

Stara
Novalja
Cesarica
Gospić
7
389
Vrebac
123
Udbina

Pula
Novalja
Karlobag
928
Brušane
29
Bilaj
50
22
Gornja
Ploča
17
1
Kremen
1591
Mazin
218

Mali Lošinj
Veli Lošinj
123
Pag
Metajna
E65
25
Lukovo
Šugorje
Medak
Vaganski
vrh
1757
Raduc
7
Sveti Rok
A1
50
21
Bruvno
33

Susak
Pag
AENONA
Gorica
29
Barič Draga
Tribanj
Kruščica
Paklenica
Starigrad-
Paklenica
26
Gračac
16
A

Silba
Olib
Vir
Povljana
Ražanac
28
A1
27
Velebit
20
27

Premuda
Ist
Molat
Vir
Vrsi
12
E65
Jasenice
54
27
Žrmanja
Kaštel
Žegarski

Virsko
more
Privlaka
Nin
Posedarje
12
Obrovac
16
Ervenik
Mok
Po

AENONA
Policnik
8
Novigrad
27
Medvide

Sestrunj
Petrčane
17
8
10

Božava
Murvica
424
Zemunik Donji
10

Ancona
Zadar
18
56
21
Benkovac
138
BURNUM

Ugljan
Preko
Bibinje
17
ASSERIA
44°

Brbinj
TVRĐAVA SV.
MIHOVILA
Kali
Sukošan
Miranje
21
33
59
Kist

Kukljica
26
27
56
Đevrske
Krka

Dugi Otok
Turanj
Biograd na Moru
Pakoštane
49
MANASTIR
KRKA

Pašman
Pašman
Stankovci
Vransko
Jezero
39
E65
22
Skradin

Zaglav
Sali
Tkon
Žut
8
16
Pirovac
27
138

Telašćica
Kornat
Murter
Tisno
37
Vodice
8
33

Zadar
Kornati
KATEDRALA
SV JAKOVA
Šibenik

Žirje
Zablaće
149
29

Jabucka
Krapanj

Split
Starigrad
Durrës
Trieste
A
D
R
I
A
T
I
C
Primošten

Svetac
Rogoznica
B

43°

el Tronto

S
E
A

0   10   20   30 km

degli Abruzzi
3
15°
4
C

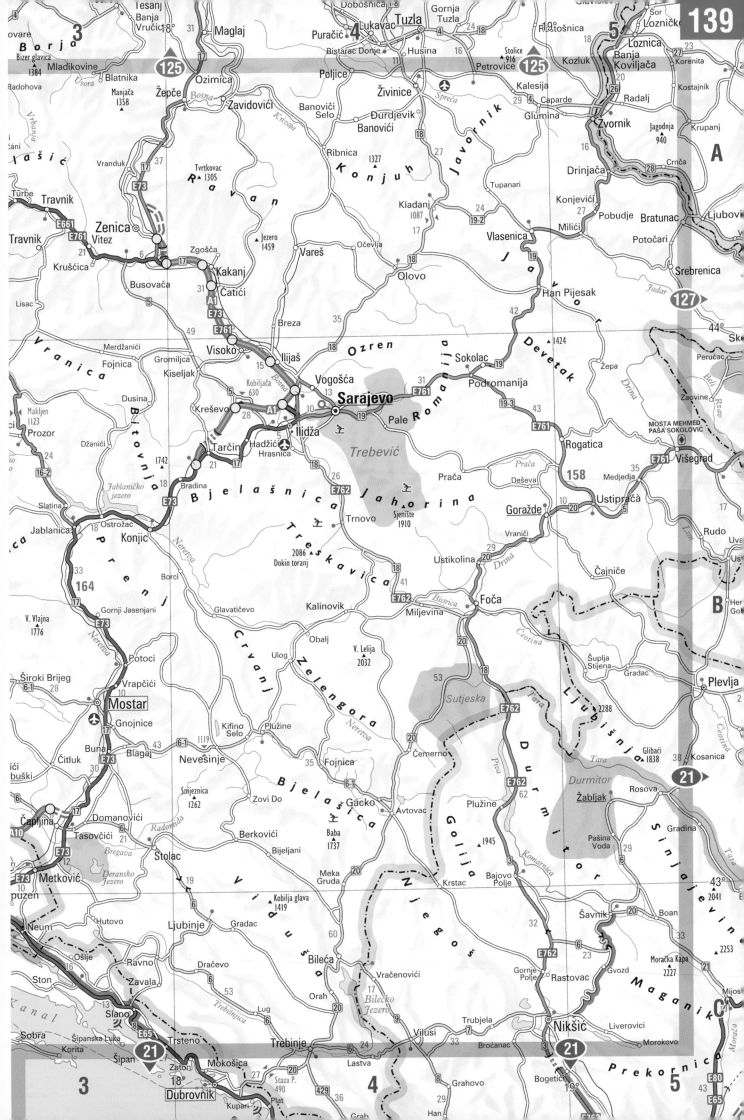

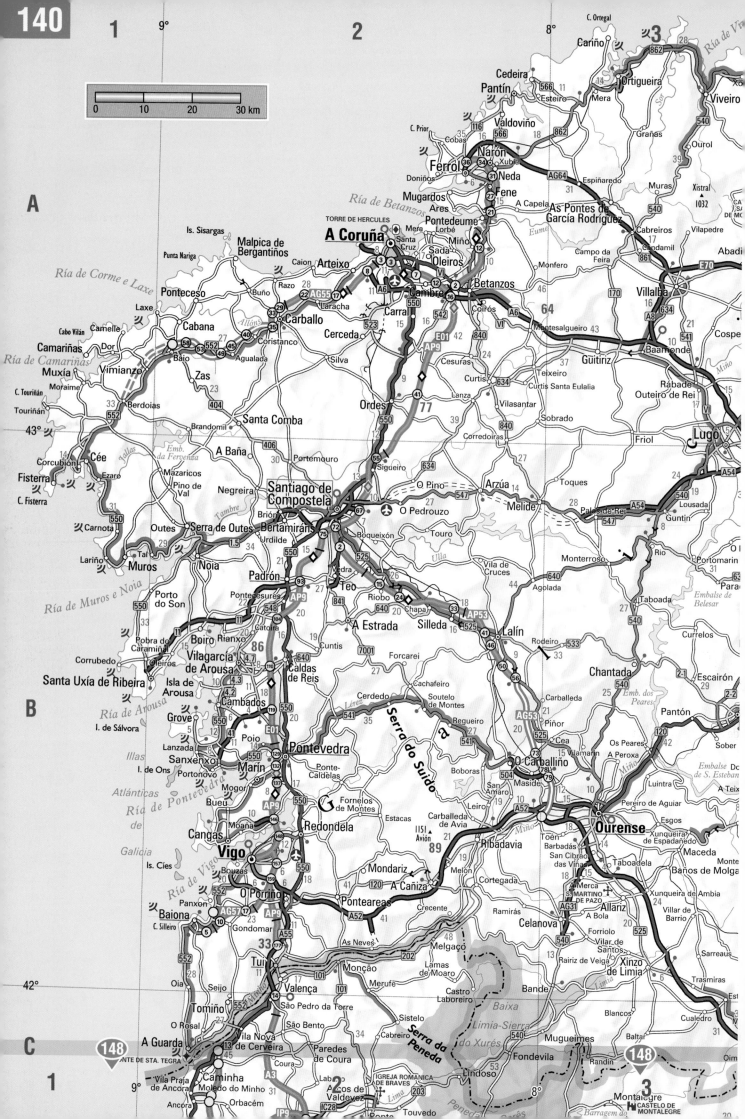

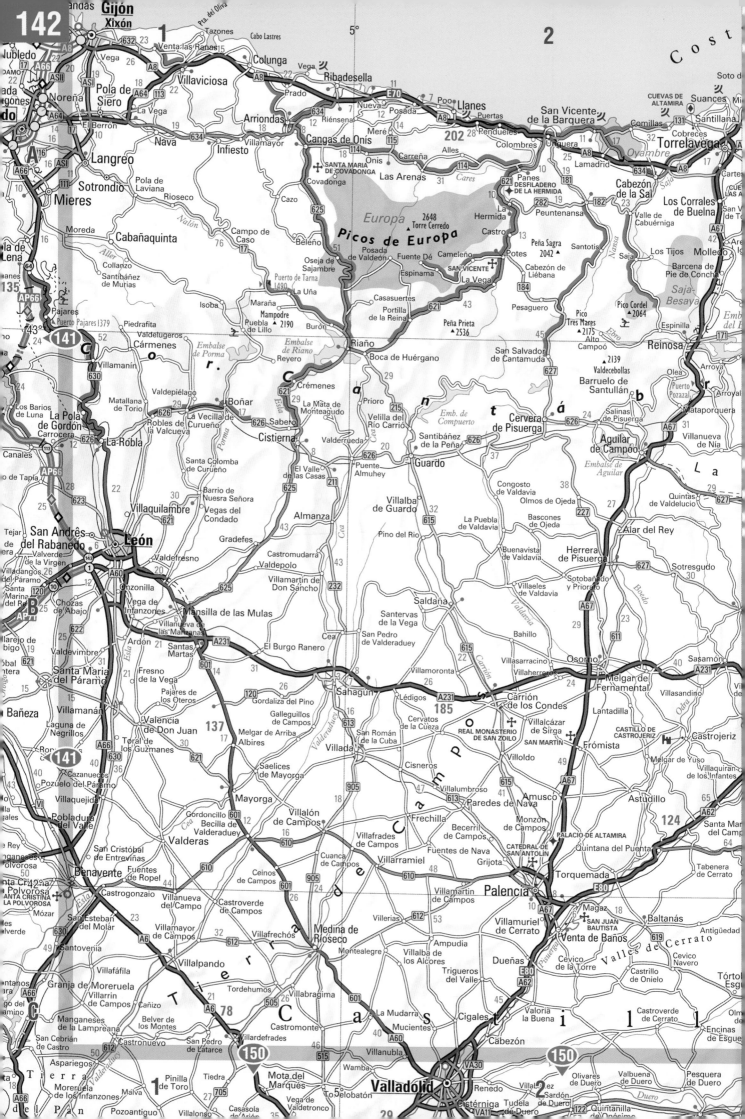

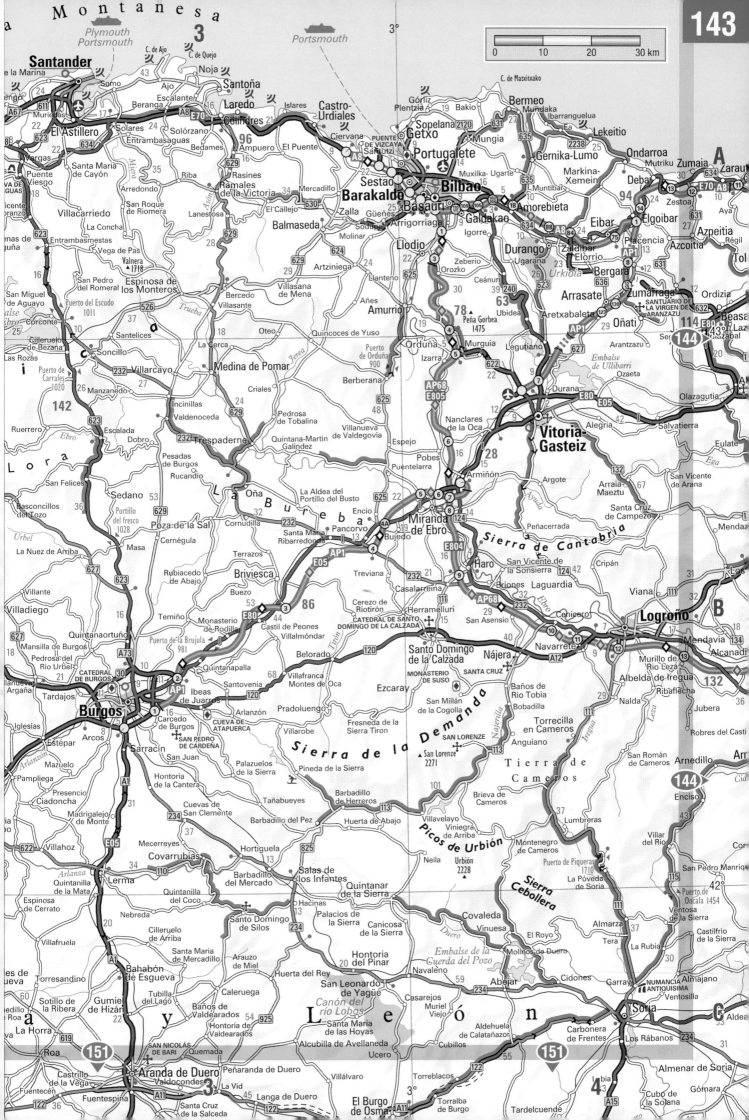

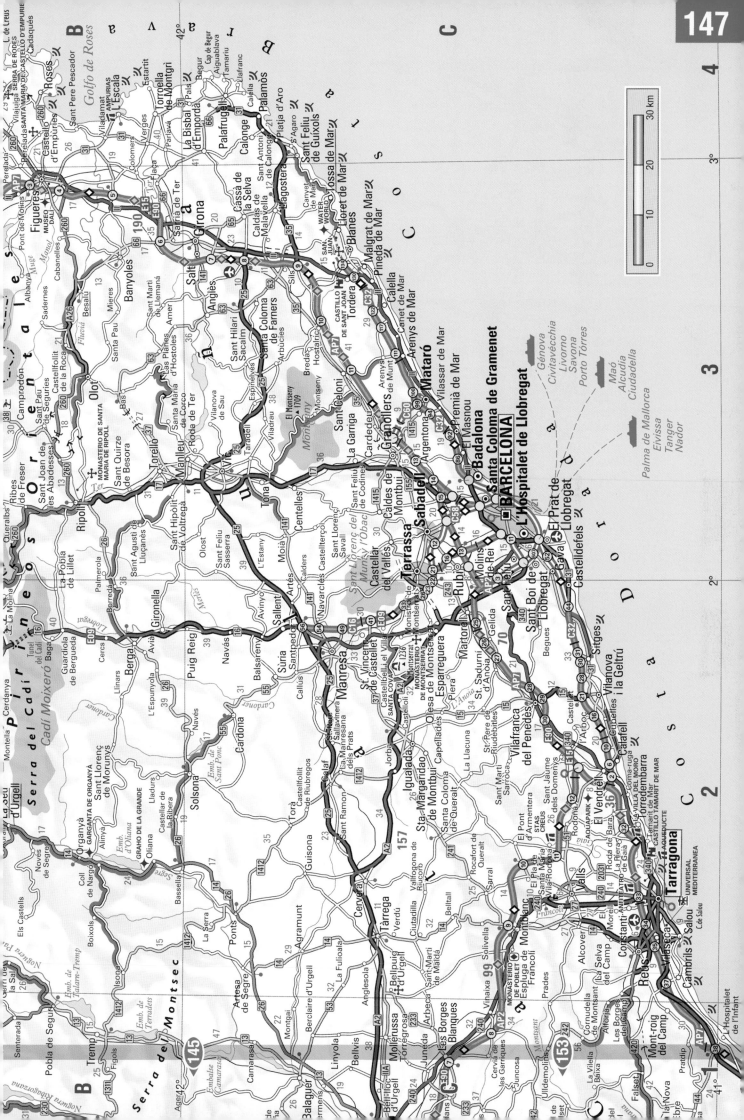

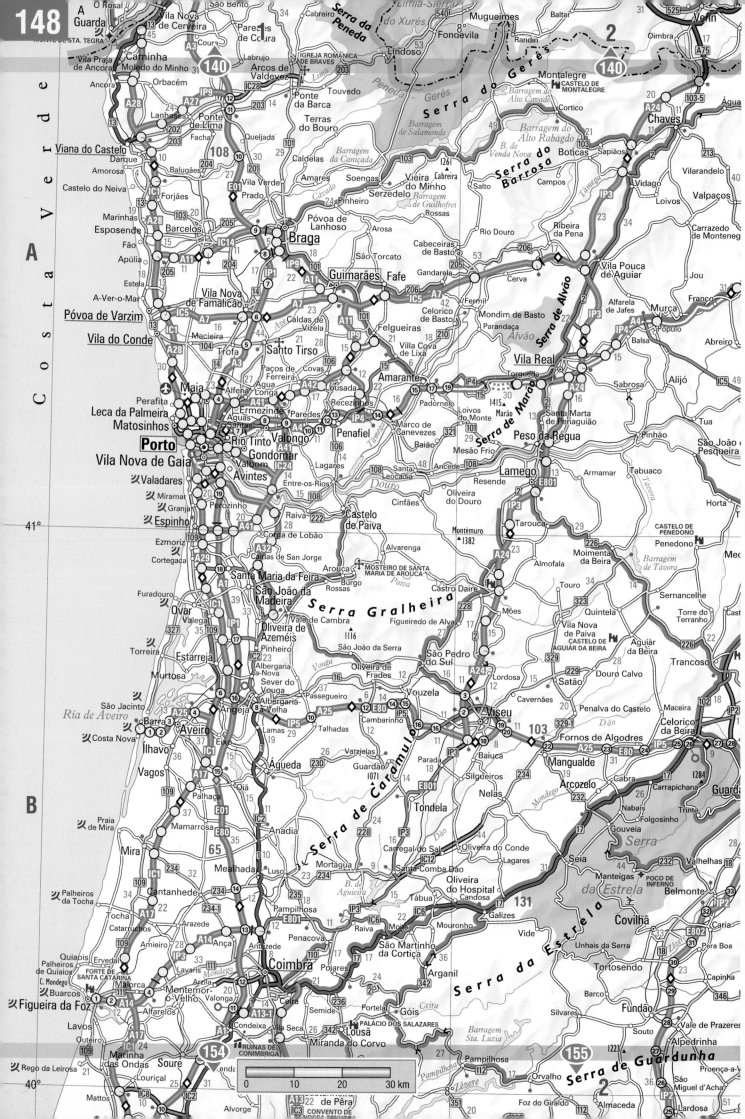

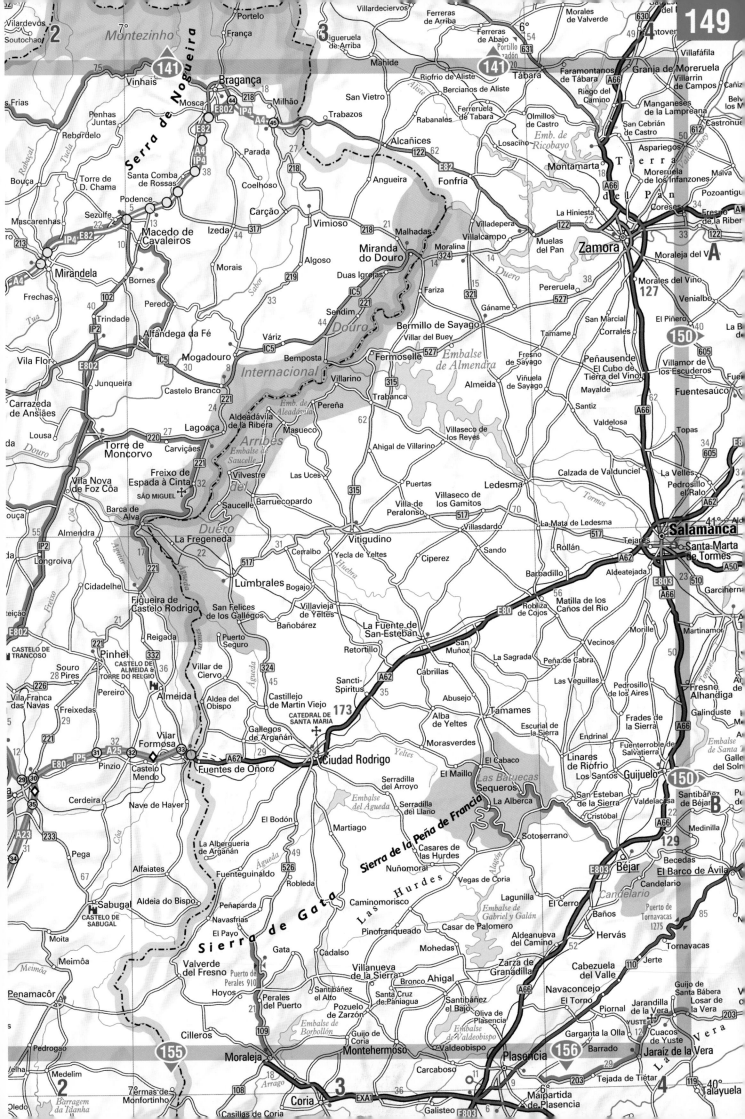

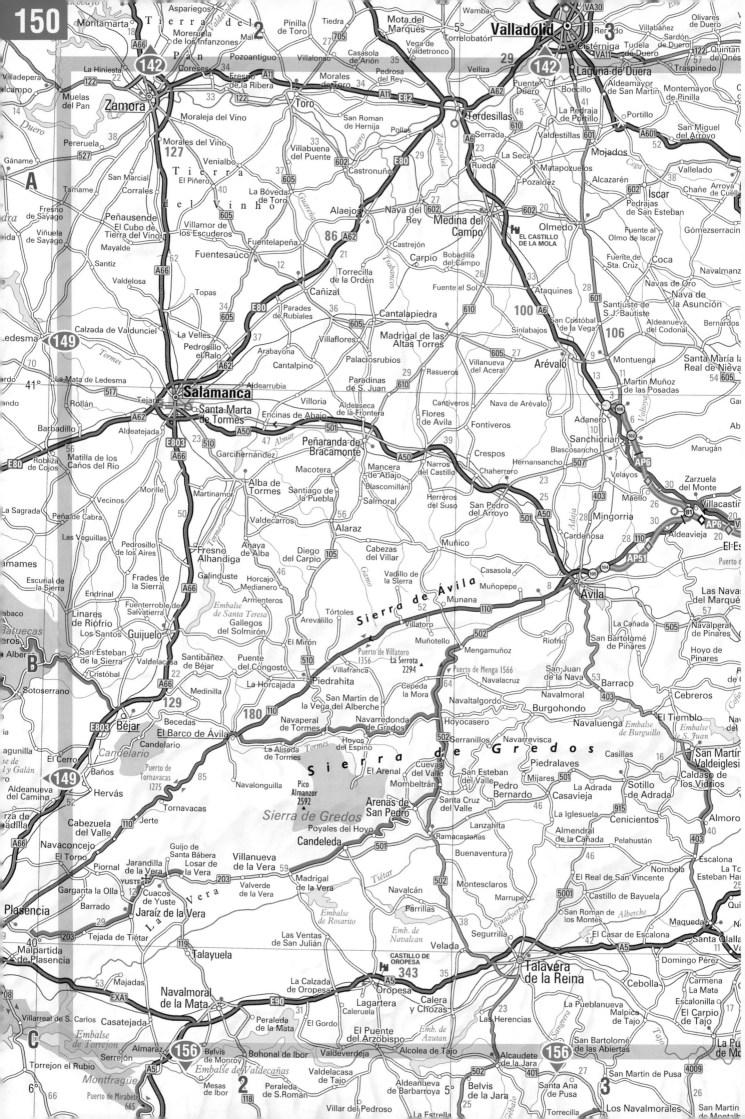

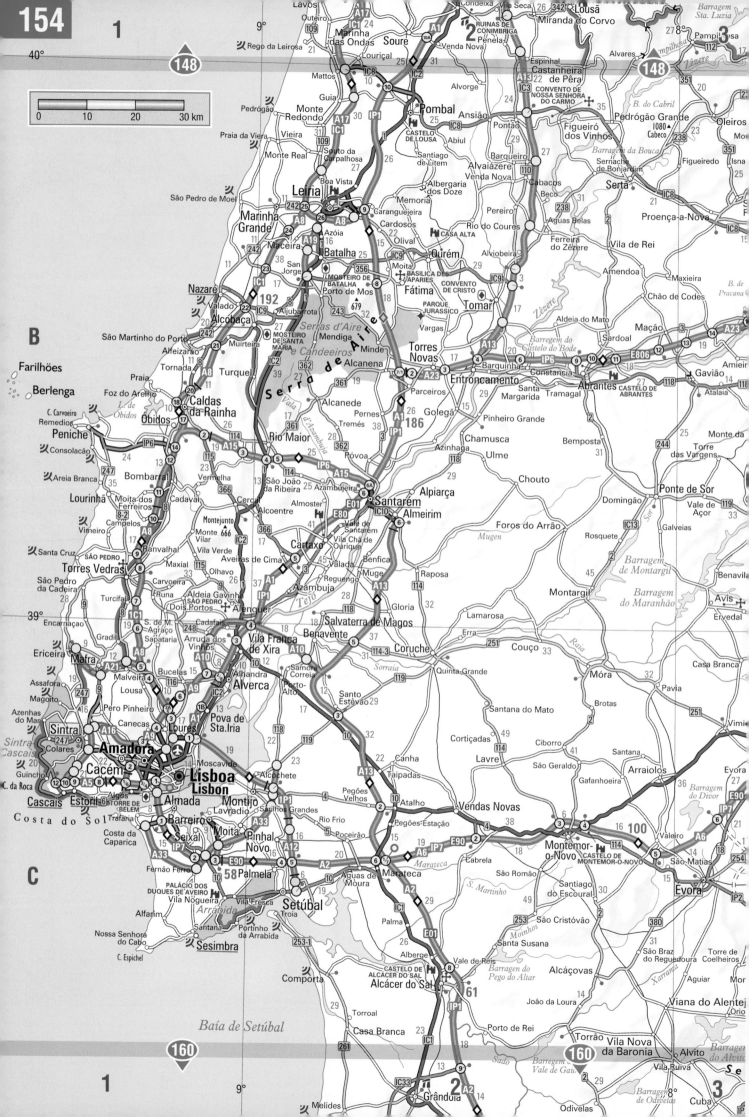

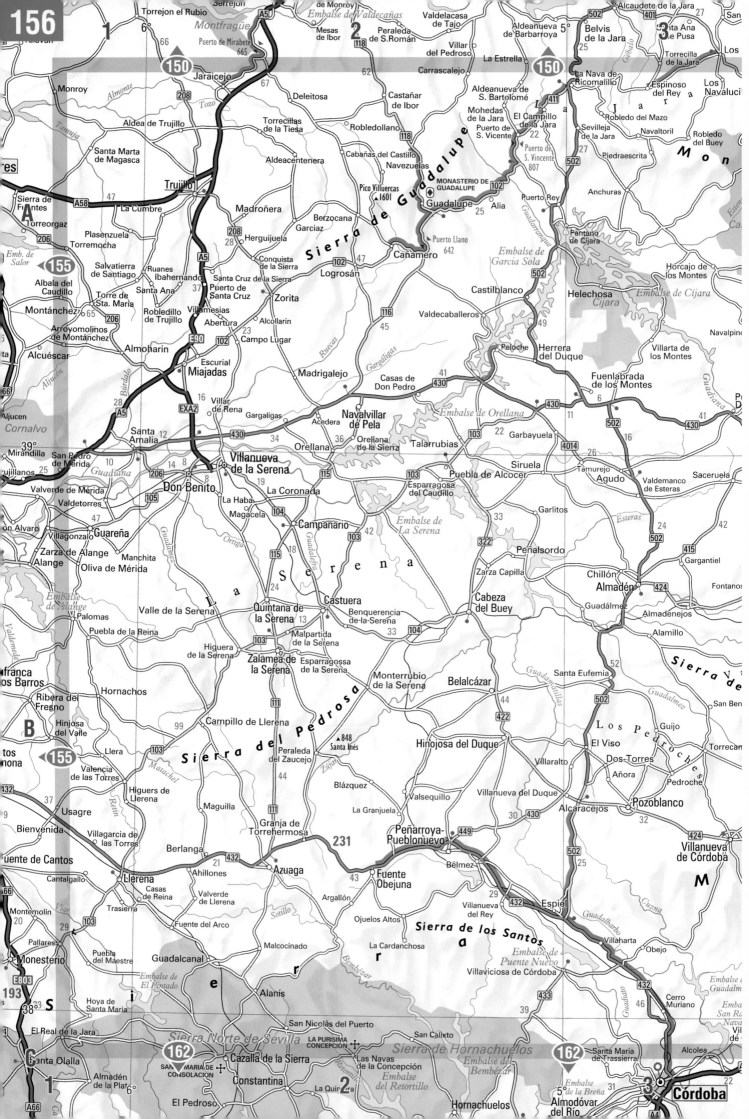

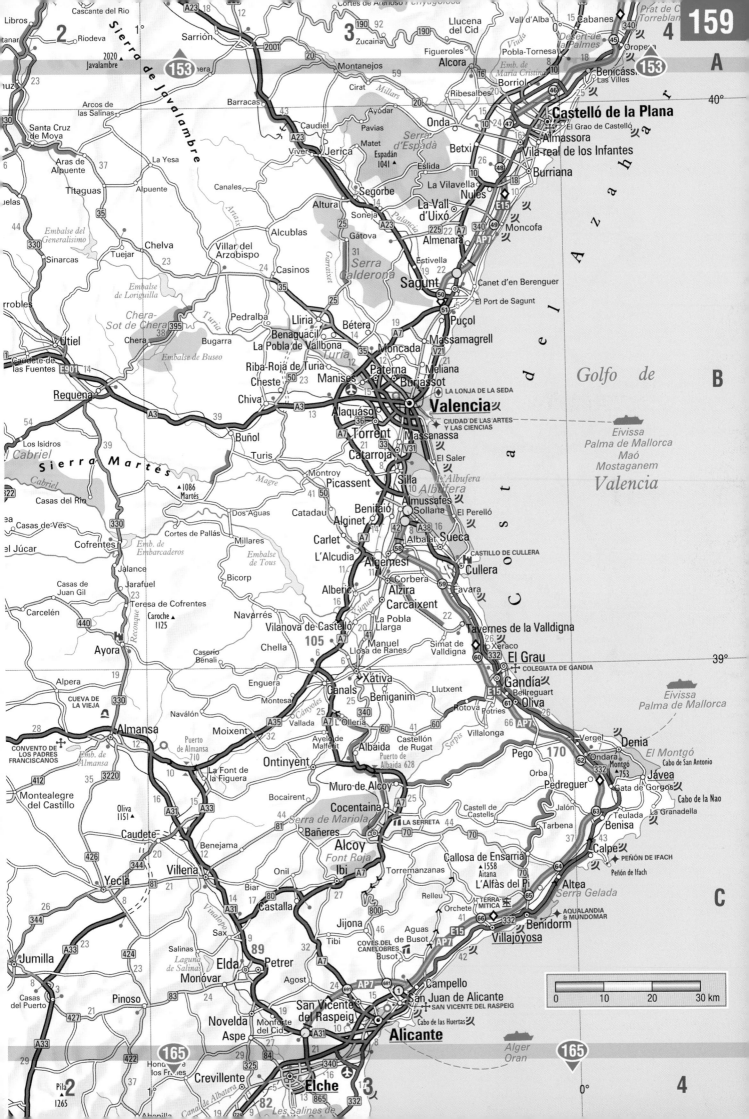

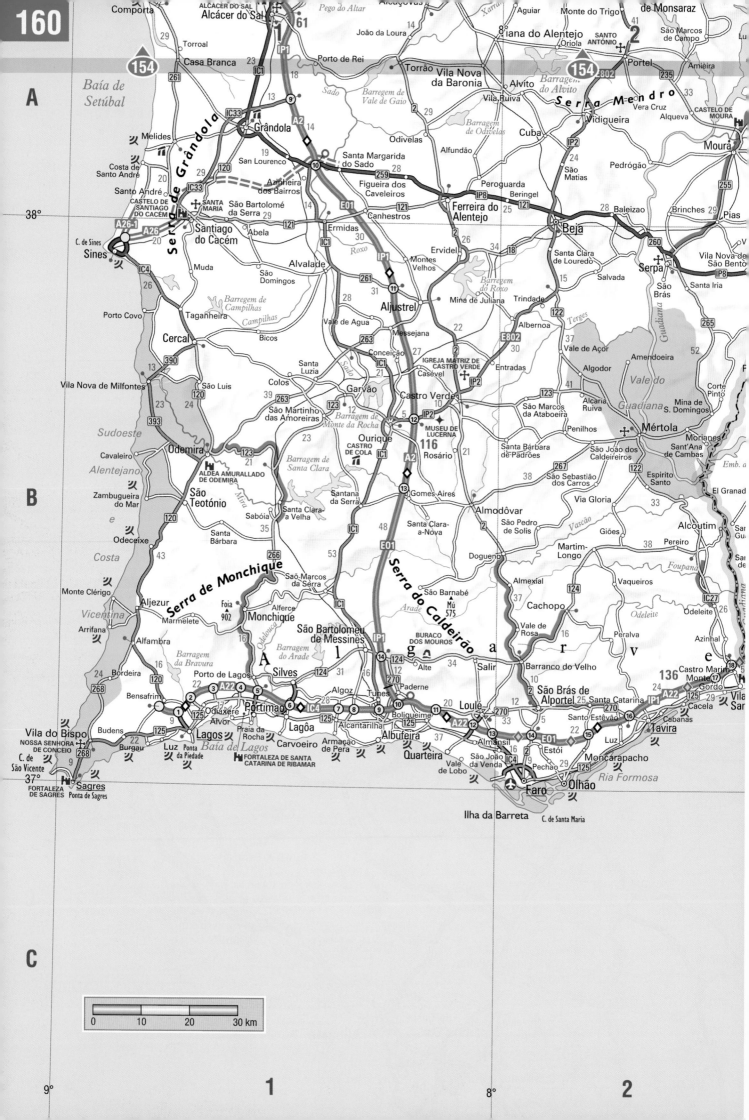

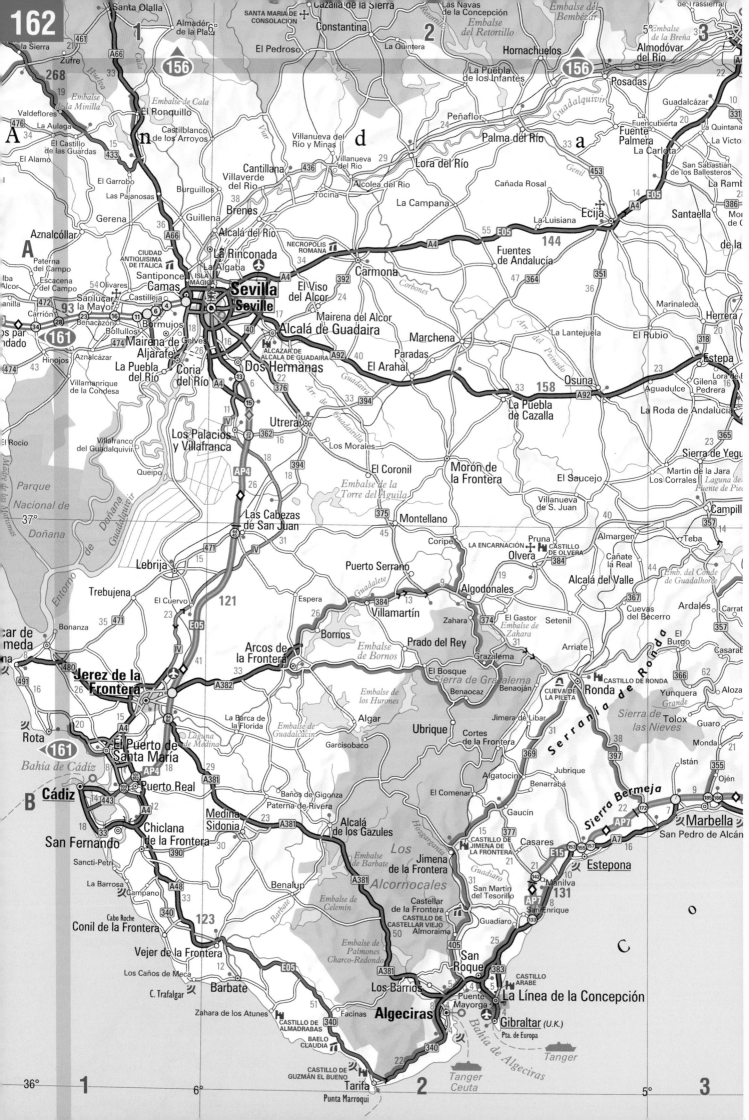

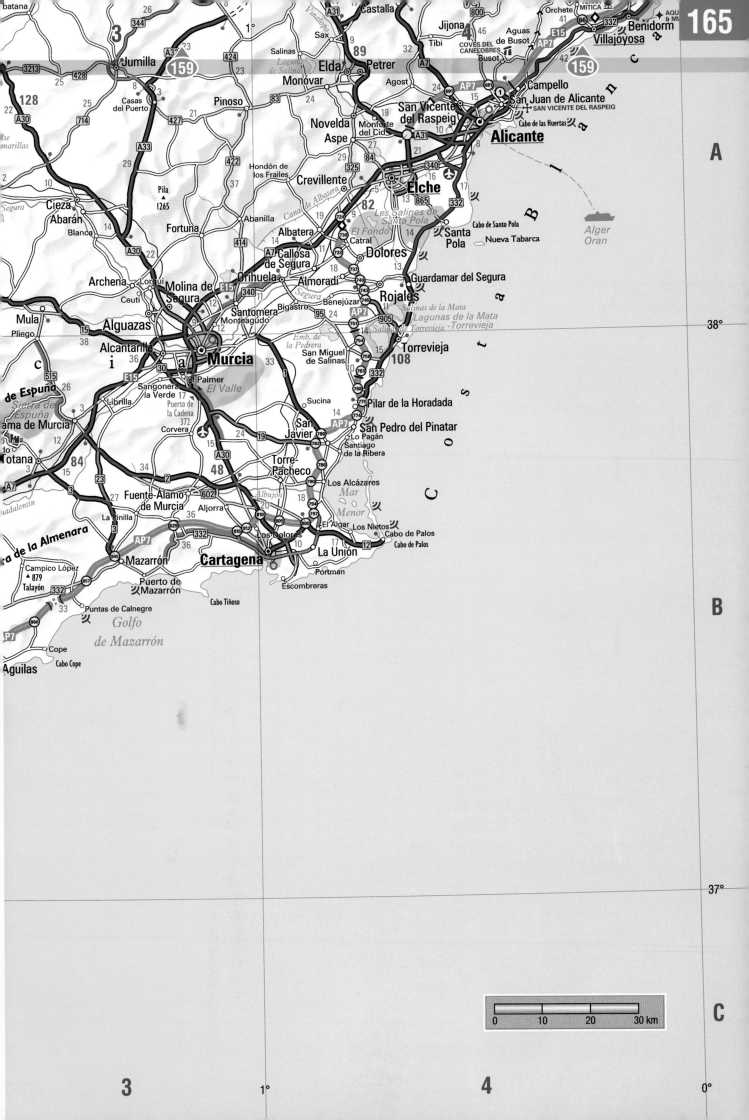

batana
26
3
344
Jumilla
A33
159
3213
128
A30
25
428
424
23
Casas del Puerto
714
3
Pinoso
427
21
Cieza
Abarán
Blanca
10
14
Fortuna
Archena
Lorquí
Ceutí
Mula
Pliego
Alguazas
15
38
Alcantarilla
36
Murcia
c
de Espuña
515
26
Sierra de Espuña
ma de Murcia
Librilla
Sangonera la Verde
El Palmer
El Valle
Puerto de la Cadena
372
Corvera
Totana
84
15
Sucina
A7
2
34
48
24
15
Fuente-Álamo de Murcia
602
La Pinilla
3
Aljorra
Albujón
829
332
P7
36
Mazarrón
Campico López
879
Talayón
332
957
845
33
Puntas de Calnegre
866
Golfo de Mazarrón
de Mazarrón
Cope
Cabo Cope
Aguilas
P7

Castalla
Jijona
800
Orchete
MITICA
46
A31
Sax
9
89
Elda
Petrer
32
A7
Salinas
Monóvar
83
24
Agost
Novelda
Monforte del Cid
Aspe
27
A31
Crevillente
325
84
82
Abanilla
Albatera
730
Catral
Callosa de Segura
A7
11
Dolores
18
737
Orihuela
340
11
Almoradí
Santomera
Monteagudo
Bigastro
Benejúzar
95
24
9
12
740
743
745
Rojales
11
Emb. de la Pedrera
San Miguel de Salinas
905
14
754
108
15
758
763
332
San Javier
San Pedro del Pinatar
768
770
Pilar de la Horadada
14
774
AP7
780
Lo Pagán
782
Santiago de la Ribera
Torre-Pacheco
786
Los Alcázares
Mar Menor
790
18
794
Los Dolores
810
805
797
El Algar
Los Nietos
815 812
800
Cabo de Palos
La Unión
Cartagena
10
17
12
Cabo de Palos
Portmán
Escombreras
Cabo Tiñoso

Aguas de Busot
Busot
41
E15
66
332
4
COVES.DEL CANELOBRES
Villajoyosa
Benidorm
42
AP7
159
691
Campello
15
681
San Juan de Alicante
SAN VICENTE DEL RASPEIG
1
San Vicente del Raspeig
Cabo de las Huertas
Alicante
24
10
C
Elche
340
16
17
865
332
a
Les Salines de Santa Pola
Cabo de Santo Pola
Santa Pola
Nueva Tabarca
Alger Oran
14
Guardamar del Segura
Salinas de la Mata
Lagunas de la Mata -Torrevieja
Salinas de Torrevieja
Torrevieja
B
l
l
a
n
c
a

A
38°
37°
B
C

3
1°
4
0°

0   10   20   30 km

A

1   2°

40°

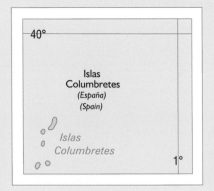

40°

Islas
Columbretes
(España)
(Spain)

*Islas
Columbretes*

1°

ISLAS
BALEARES

BALEARIC
ISLANDS

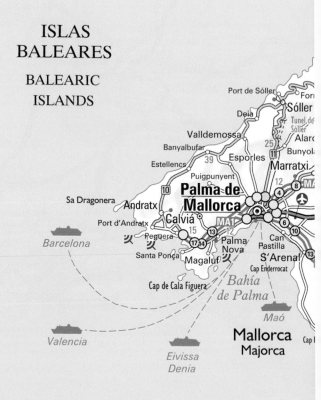

Port de Sóller
Fori
Sóller
Deià
Tunel de
Sóller
Valldemossa
Alar
Banyalbufar
Bunyol
Estellencs   39   Esporles   11   Marratxi
Puigpunyent
Sa Dragonera   10   **Palma de**   12   8   MA
Andratx   **Mallorca**   4
Calvià   MA1   6
Port d'Andratx   15   13   12   10
Reguera   Palma   Can   13
17 14   Nova   Pastilla
Santa Ponça   S'Arenal
Barcelona   Magaluf   Cap Enderrocat
Cap de Cala Figuera   *Bahía
de Palma*
Valencia   *Maó*
*Eivissa   **Mallorca**
Denia*   Majorca   Cap

B

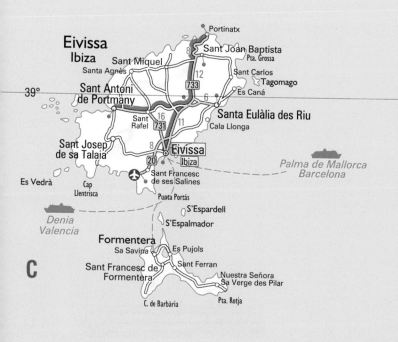

39°

Eivissa
Ibiza   Portinatx
Sant Miquel   Sant Joan Baptista
Santa Agnès   Pta. Grossa
8
12   Sant Carlos
Sant Antoni   733   Tagomago
de Portmany   6   Es Canà
16   Santa Eulàlia des Riu
Sant   731   11
Rafel   Cala Llonga
Sant Josep   8
de sa Talaia   20   Eivissa
Ibiza   *Palma de Mallorca
Barcelona*
Es Vedrà   Cap   Sant Francesc
Llentrisca   de ses Salines
Punta Portàs
*Denia
Valencia*   S'Espardell
S'Espalmador
Formentera   Es Pujols
Sa Savina
Sant Ferran
Sant Francesc de   Nuestra Señora
Formentera   Sa Verge des Pilar
C.de Barbària   Pta. Rotja

C

1   2°   2

2   3°   3   4°   4

A

Barcelona

Capo de Cavalleria

Punta Nati   Cala Morell   Fornells   *Barcelona*

15

19

23   Es   Cap de Favàritx   40°

Ciudadela   Mercadal

de Menorca   Ferreries   358

Toro

Cala   **Alaior**

Galdana   Es Migjorn   20   1

C. de Artrutx   Gran   **Maó**

Son Bou

Cap de Formentor   *Barcelona*   **Menorca**   Sant   **Es Castell**

                             Minorca   Climent   Sant Luis

Port de Pollença   Pta. de s'Esperó

Punta Beca   *B. de Pollença*   Punta Prima

Pollença   14   Cap des Pinar   I. de l'Aire

10   2220   **Alcúdia**

12   2200   10   Es Port d'Alcúdia

39   13

Puig Major   40   *B. d'Alcúdia*

alutx 1445   12   **Sa Pobla**   C'an Picafort

Selva   MA13   12   Cap Ferrutx

Lloseta   30   33   562   Cap des Freu

        Inca   **Muro**   Morey

13A   25   27   **Santa**   **Artà**   9   Cala Ratjada

Sta. Maria   **Margalida**   **Capdepera**

del Camí   17   20   15   CUEVAS DE ARTA

13   Sencelles   **Sineu**   Sant Llorenç   Cap des Pinar

                    des Carctassar   21   **Son Servera**

             Montuïri   Petra   Cala Millor

35   Punta de n'Amer

Algaida   MONASTERIO   18   **Manacor**   B

        DE CORA   14   Porto Cristo

       Porreres   27   CUEVAS DEL DRACH

29

MA19   **Llucmajor**   **Felanitx**   Cales de Mallorca

22   7

26   19   27   SAN SALVADOR   Porto Colom

                 (MONASTERIO)

Campos del Port   Cala d'Or

lanc   Sa Rapita   Ses Salines   Porto Petro

                      Santanyí

Colònia de

Sant Jordi

Cap de ses Salines

I. des Conills

Archipiélago

de Cabrera

Cabrera

39°

C

0   10   20   30 km

42°

Tremiti

Lago di Lésina
Lago di Varano
Chiéuti
Lésina
693
28
Rodi Gargánico
Ischitella
Peschici
27
Vieste
Poggio Imperiale
Sannicandro Gargánico
Vico del Gárgano
Carpino
18
Testa del Gargano
San Páolo di Civitate
Apricena
San Marco in Lámis
Cagnano Varano
Gargano
14
Torremaggiore
89
Mte. Calvo
1055
Pugnochiuso
Báia delle Zágare
Rignano Gargánico
San Giovanni Rotondo
Monte Sant'Ángelo
Mattinata
25
alnuovo terotaro
Castelnuovo della Dáunia
San Severo
19
109
16
25
89
Manfredónia
Lido di Siponto
a Montecorvino
Lucera
A14
36
Golfo di Manfredónia
17
18
7
Améndola
B
Fóggia
59
Zapponeta
Salina di Margherita di Savóia
26 Celone
11
Carapelle
20
159
Margherita di Savóia
Bíccari
Cornacchia
1151
Tróia
22
Giardinetto Vécchio
655
24
Carapelle
13
Orta Nova
110
77
Trinitápoli
18
CANNAE ANTICA
14
Barletta
173
109
Ascoli Satriano
16
13
San Ferdinando di Púglia
16
Trani
Orsara di Púglia
8 90
Castellúccio de' Sáuri
19
20
Stornara
13
7
Cerignola
Canosa di Púglia
93
22
Andria
23
Biscéglie
15
Savignano Irpino
Bovino
27
Deliceto
655
17
E842
14
Ofanto
A14
231
17
E55
27
Molfetta
Giovinazzo
Monteleone di Púglia
Accadía
44
378
16
Corato
22
Santo Spirito
Villanova d. Battista
Sant'Ágata di Púglia
25
Candela
31
Posta Piana
6
13
Minervino Murge
170d
24
Terlizzi
220
21
Bari
12
inarda
Rocchetta S. António
19
9
93
234
CASTEL DEL MONTE
24
234
Ruvo di Púglia
27
Bitonto
96
Modogno
18
ástèl ónia
A16
Lacedónia
658
655
13
Lavello
28
Montemilone
10
Alta Murgia
238
Bitetto
Grumo Áppula
Sannicandro di Bari
Capurso
elfia
Vallata
Bisáccia
15
Aquilónia
Melfi
Rapolla
Venosa
Montescaglioso
Toritto
21
41
303
1326
M. Vúlture
Rionero in Vúlture
168
Palazzo San Gervásio
10
29
230
Gravina in Púglia
238
47
37
Acquaviva delle Fonti
E843
Andretta
Calitri
401
Ofanto
Ripacándida
26
655
L. di Serra di Corvo
12
96
Altamura
271
Cassano delle Murge
100
Sant'Ángelo dei Lombardi
Lioni
7dC
30
Ruvo del Monte
Atella
169
Genzano di Lucánia
24
171
14
Santéramo in Colle
A14
691
91
Teora
Pescopagano
93
31
Forenza
CASTELLO DI LAGOPESOLE
658
169
Acerenza
Brádano
24
99
15
173
18
Laviano
23
San Fele
1136
Pso. d. Crocelle
Bella
Pietragalla
169
Oppido Lucano
Irsina
38
20
Matera
7
11
Muro Lucano
Avigliano
Cancellara
96
41
Laterza
Castellaneta
San Gregorio Magno
Ruoti
93
12
Váglio Basilicata
Tolve
Grassano
L. di S. Giuliano
58
175
Ginosa
Contursi Termi
94d
Picerno
Tricárico
7
Gróttole
Migliónico
Buccino
E847
Potenza
24
407
Salandrella
208
22
407
Pomárico
Montescaglioso
Vietri di Potenza
12
Tito
92
Trivigno
Garaguso
Salandra
Serre
Caggiano
95
GROTTA DELL'ANGELO
Pso. Croce d. Scrivano 1143
E847
24
San Máuro Forte
Ferrandina
Bernalda
407
Mte. Alburno
1742
Auletta
Anzi
Accettura
Brádano
580
Controne
E45
Polla
Brienza
Calvello
Laurenzana
E847
12
Montescaglioso
Roccadáspide
166
San Rufo
Márrico Nuovo
M. Volturino 1836
15
Corleto Perticara
103
Stigliano
25
175
Montalbano Iónico
Felitto
34
Sella d. Corticato 1026
Sala Consilina
598
21
Cirigliano
Craco
36
176
Pisticci
18
Cilento
Teggiano
Viggiano
Montemurro
92
Missanello
Cávone
Roccadáspide
Stio
Laurino
Vallo di Diano
174
Padula
CERTOSA DI SAN LORENZO
103
Spinoso
GRUMENTUM ANTICA
Agri
598
Sáuro
Lido di M
Vallo della Lucánia
1705
Mte. Cervati 1898
Montesano sulla Marcellana
Sella Cessuta 1040
31
San Arcángelo
SANTUARIO MARIA D'A
174
Tursi
Policoro
PARCO METAP
asana
Cinto
M. Sacro o Gelbison
Montano-Antilia
Casalbuono
Moliterno
San Francisco San Chírico Raparo
92
L. di Monte Cotugno
33
653
Scanzano Jónico
Ceraso
Roccanova
Colobraro
Lido di Policoro
Castelsaraceno
Mte. Sirino 1040

16°   3   4

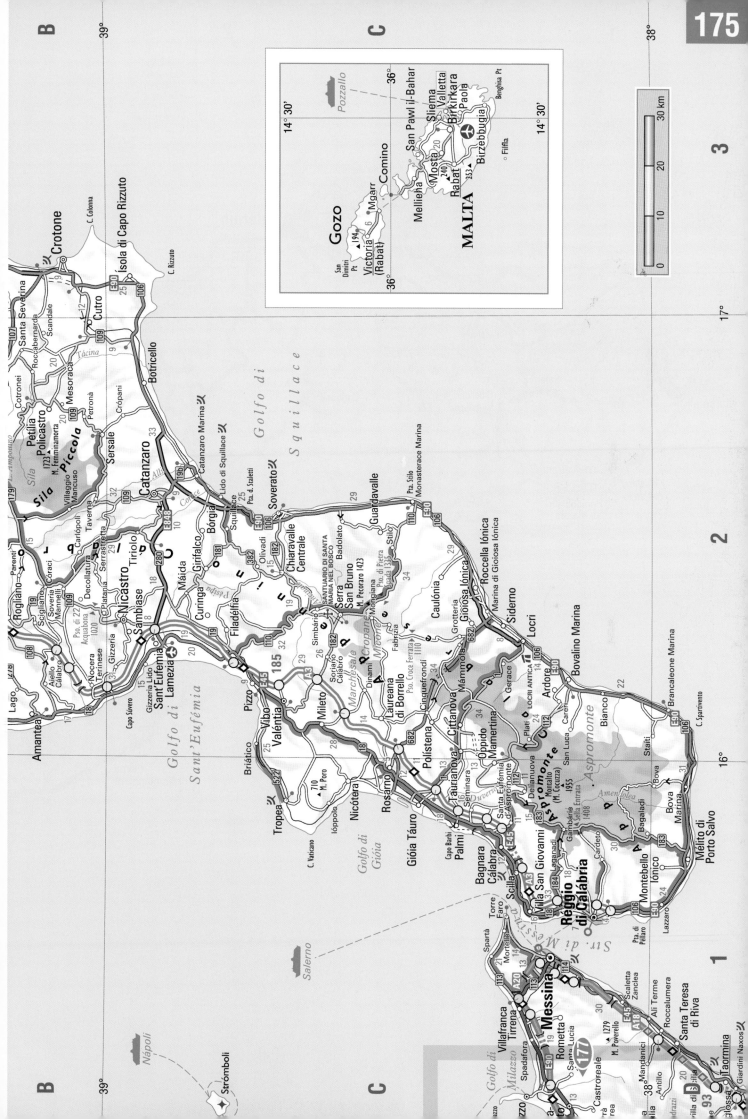

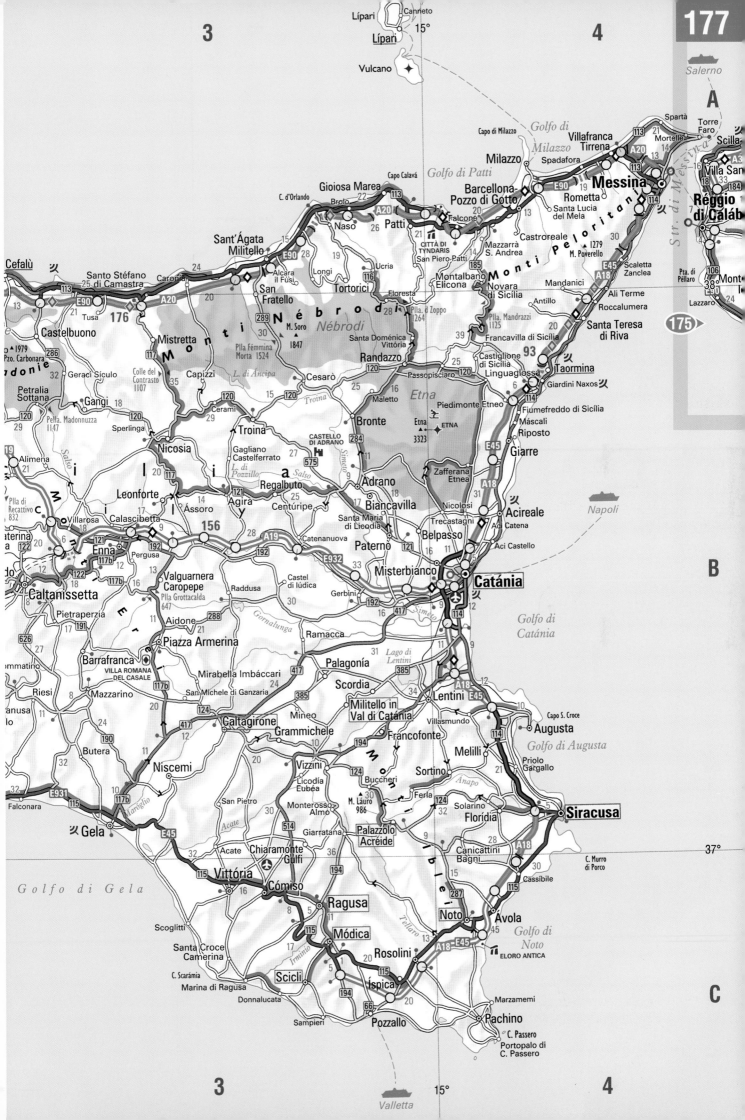

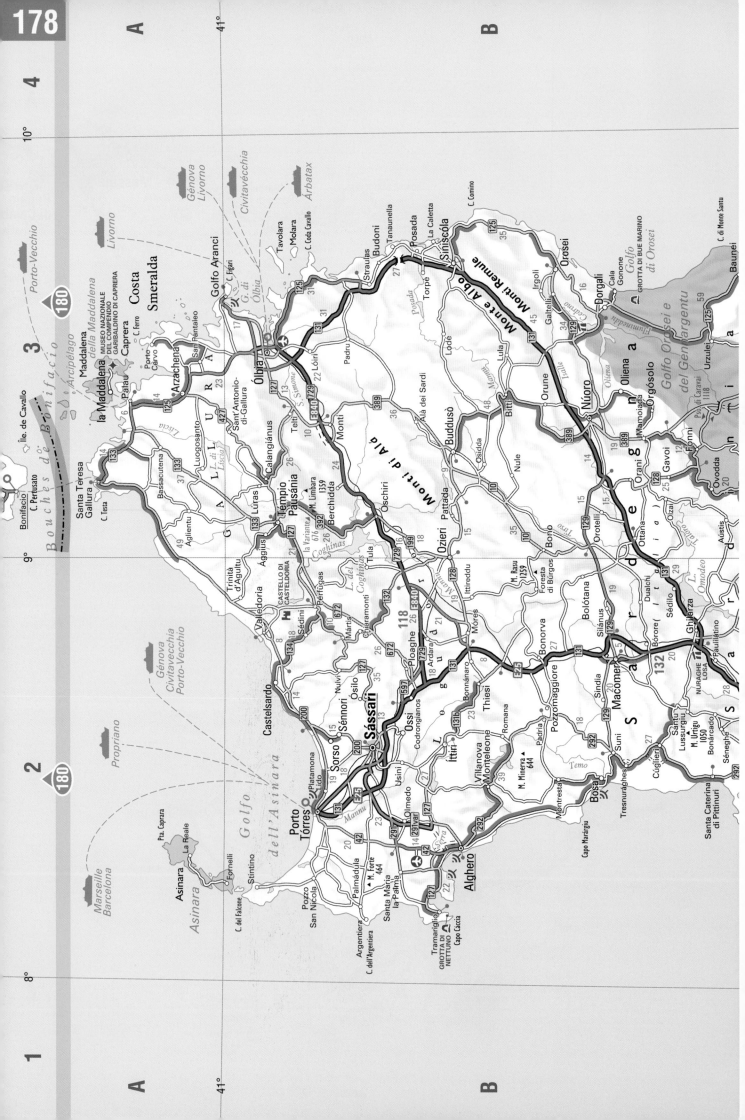

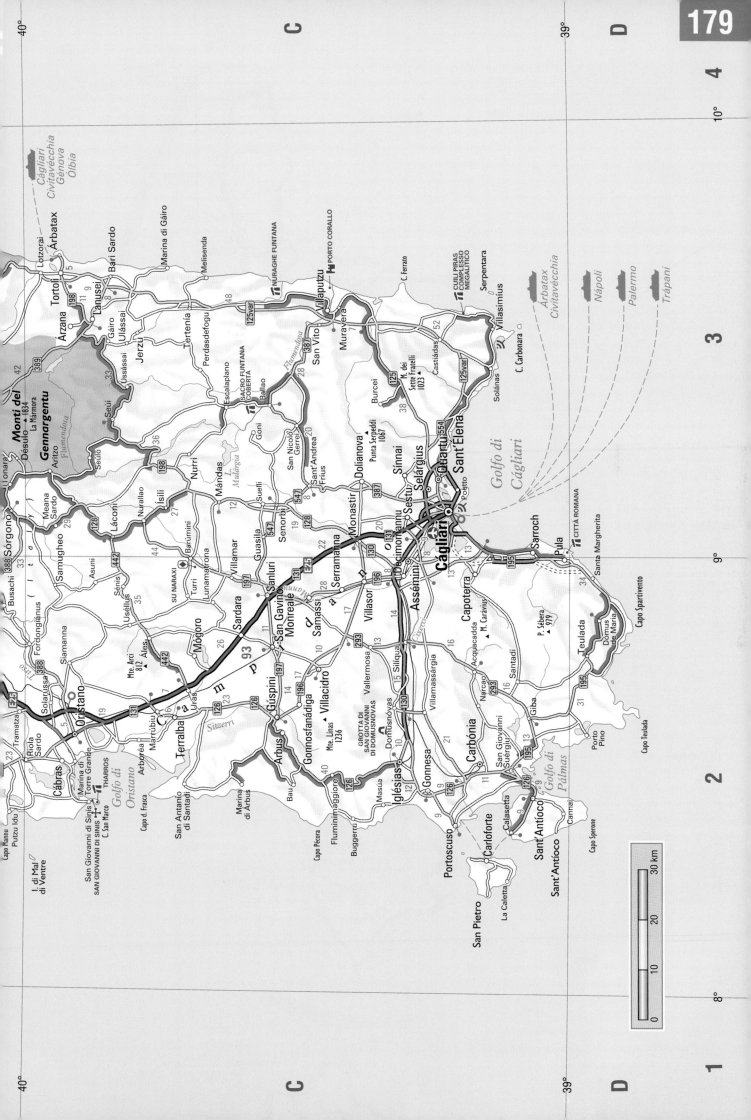

Cágliari
Civitavécchia
Génova
Ólbia

Arbatax
Civitavécchia

Nápoli

Palermo

Trápani

Monti del
Gennargentu

Désulo ▲ 1834
La Mármora

Sórgono

Lotzorai
Arbatax
Tortolì
Árzana
Lanusei
Bari Sardo
Marina di Gáiro
Ussássai
Ulássai
Gáiro
Melisenda
Aritzo
Seúi
Jerzu
Tertenia
Meana Sardo
Seúlo
Perdasdefogu
NURAGHE FUNTANA
Escalaplano
Villaputzu
PORTO CORALLO
SACRO FUNTANA
COBERTA
San Vito
Ballao
Muravera
C. Ferrato

CULI PIRAS
COMPLESSO
MEGALITICO
Serpentara
Villasímius
C. Carbonara

Busachi
Fordongiánus
I. Onara
Samugheo
Láconi
Nurallao
Isili
Nurri
Mándas
Goni
San Nicoló Gerrei
Sant'Andrea
Frius
Dolianova
Punta Serpeddi 1067
Burcei
M. dei Sette Fratelli 1023 ▲
Castiádas
Solánas

Tramatza
Riola Sardo
Cábras
Putzu Idu
Capo Mannu
I. di Mal di Ventre
San Giovanni di Sinis
SAN GIOVANNI DI SINIS
C. San Marco
THARROS
Marina di Torre Grande
Oristano
Solarussa
Siamanna
Asuni
Uséllus
Sénis
Mte. Arci 812 ▲
Áles
Arboréa
Capo d. Frasca
Terralba
Uras
Marrúbiu
San Antonio di Santadi
Marina di Árbus
Capo Pécora
Árbus
Guspini
Gonnosfanádiga
Mte. Línas 1236 ▲
Fluminimaggiore
Buggerrù
Masúa
Bau
GROTTA DI SAN GIOVANNI DI DOMUSNOVAS
Villacidro
Domusnóvas
Iglésias
Gonnesa
Portoscuso
Carloforte
San Pietro
La Caletta
Sant'Antíoco
Calasetta
Cannai
Capo Sperone
Sant'Antíoco
Golfo di Pálmas
Porto Pino
Capo Teulada
Carbónia
San Giovanni Suérgiu
Giba
Narcao
Villamassárgia
Domusnóvas
Vallermosa
Santadi
Villasor
Decimomannu
Assémini
Siliqua
Serramanna
Samassi
San Gavino Monreale
Sanluri
Sardara
Mógoro
Villamar
Lunamatrona
Turri
Villanovafranca
Barúmini
SU NARAXI
Senorbì
Suelli
Guasila
Gesico
Monastir
Sestu
Selárgius
Sinnai
Quartu Sant'Elena
Maracalagonis
Poetto
Cágliari
CITTÀ ROMANA
Sarroch
Pula
Santa Margherita
Capo Spartivento
Domus de Maria
Teulada
P. Sébera 979
M. Caráviu
Acquacadda
Capoterra

Golfo di Oristano

Golfo di Cágliari

SU NARAXI

Golfo di Pálmas

Sitzerri
Campidano

Flumendosa
Flumendosa

Tirso

30 km
20
10
0

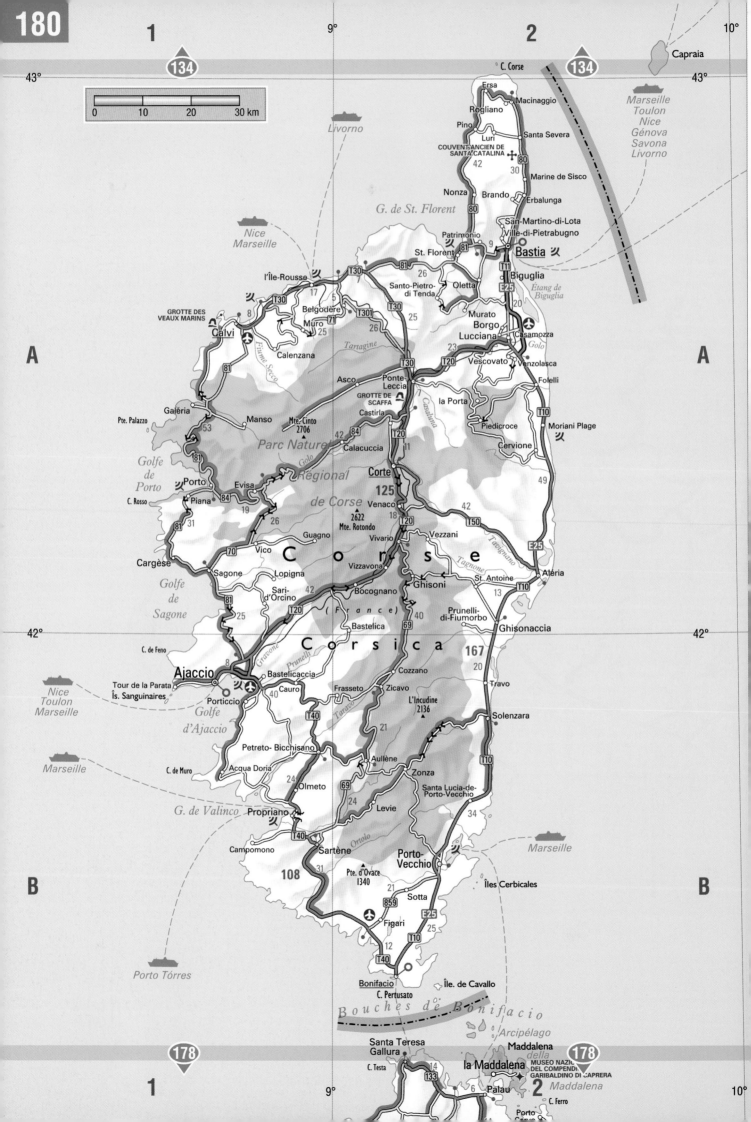

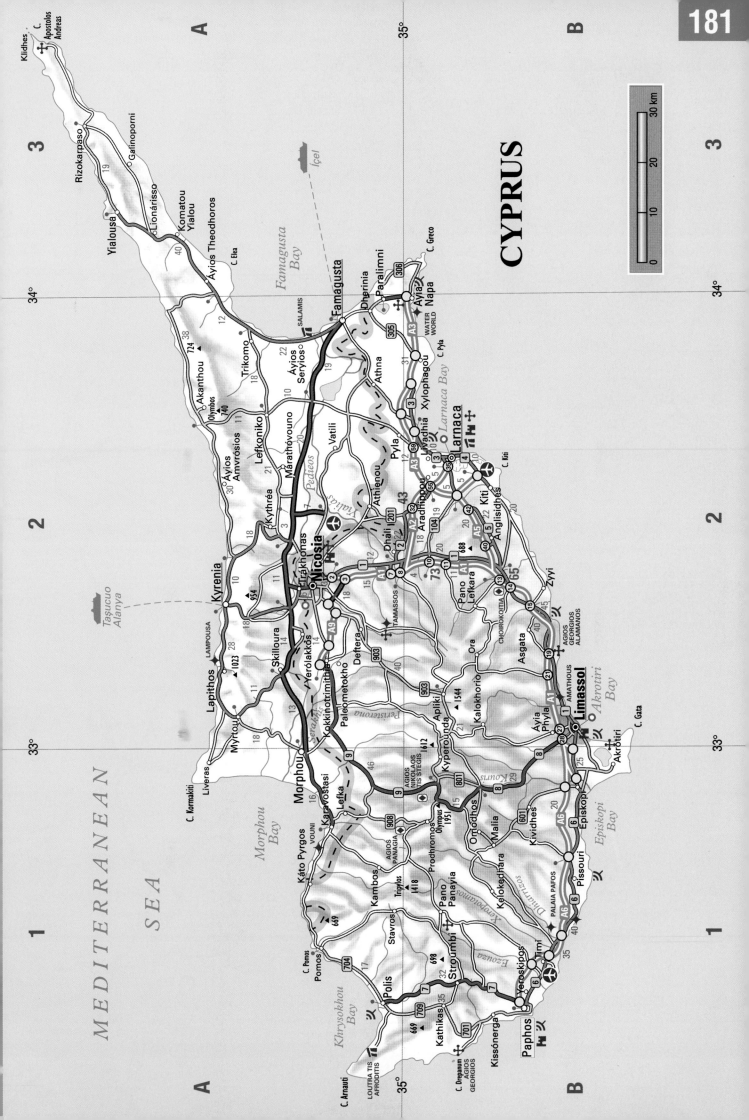

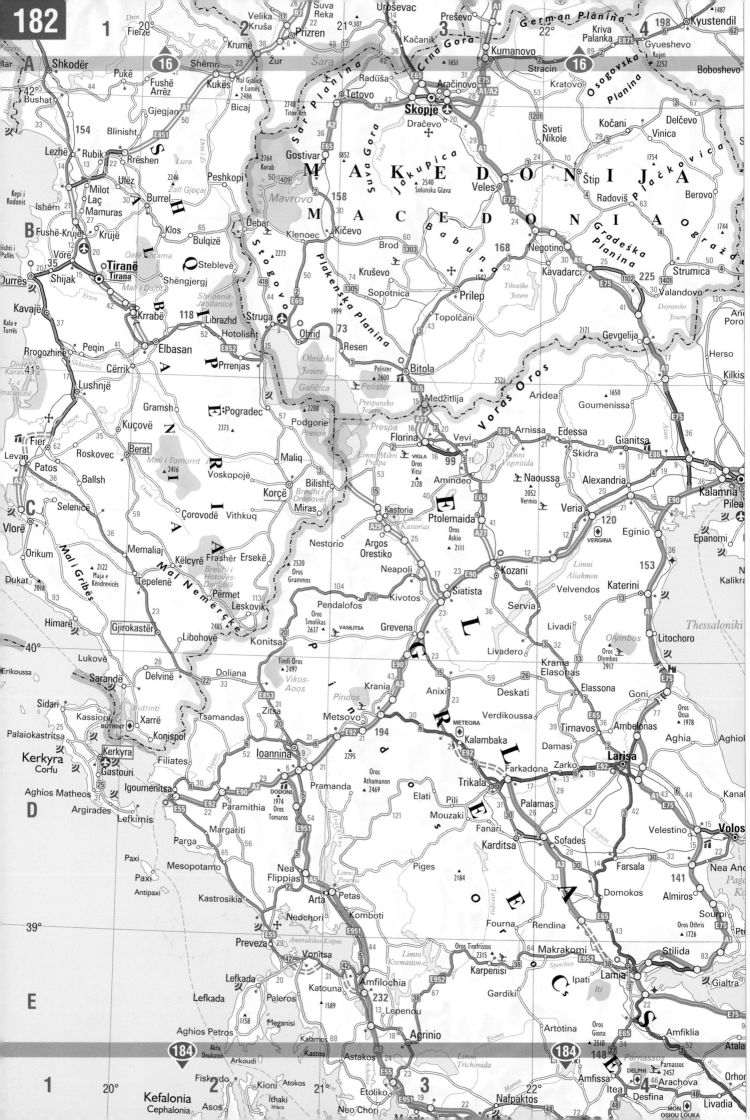

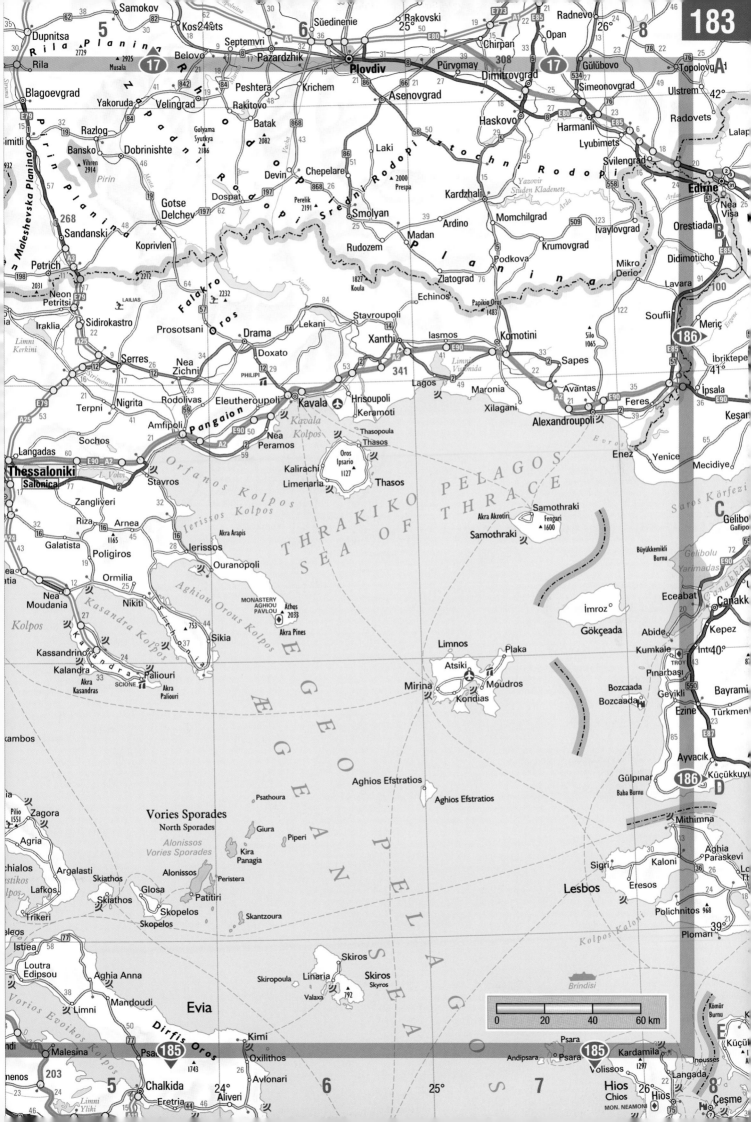

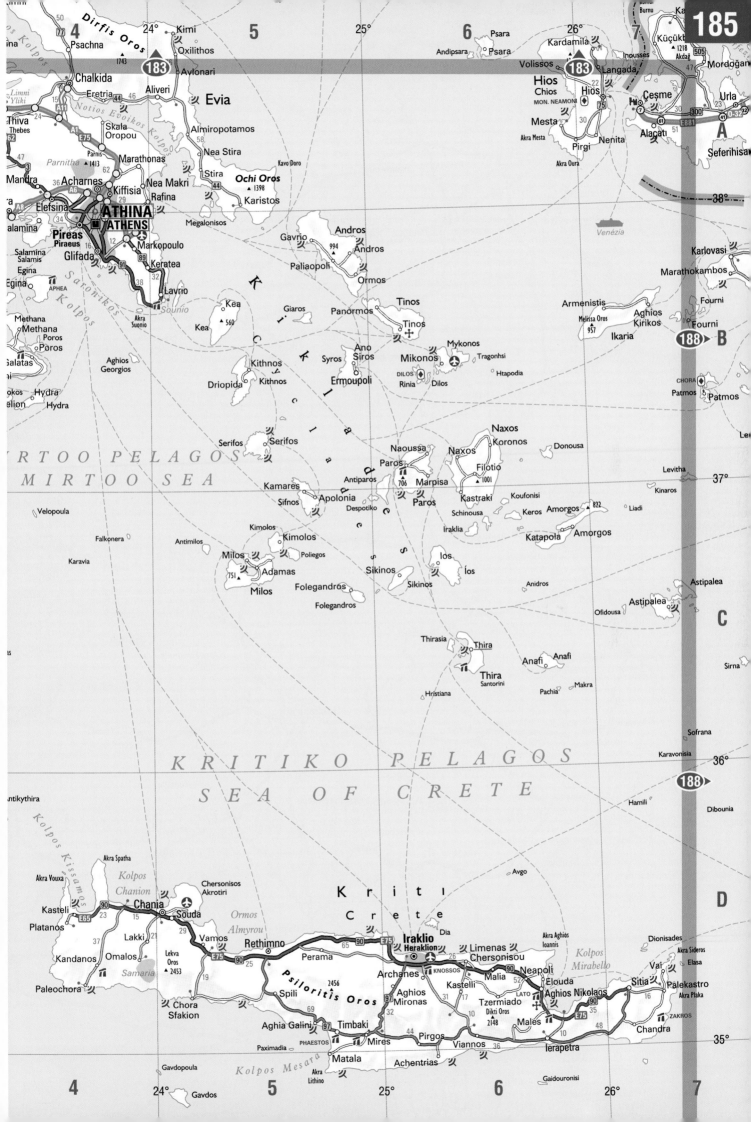

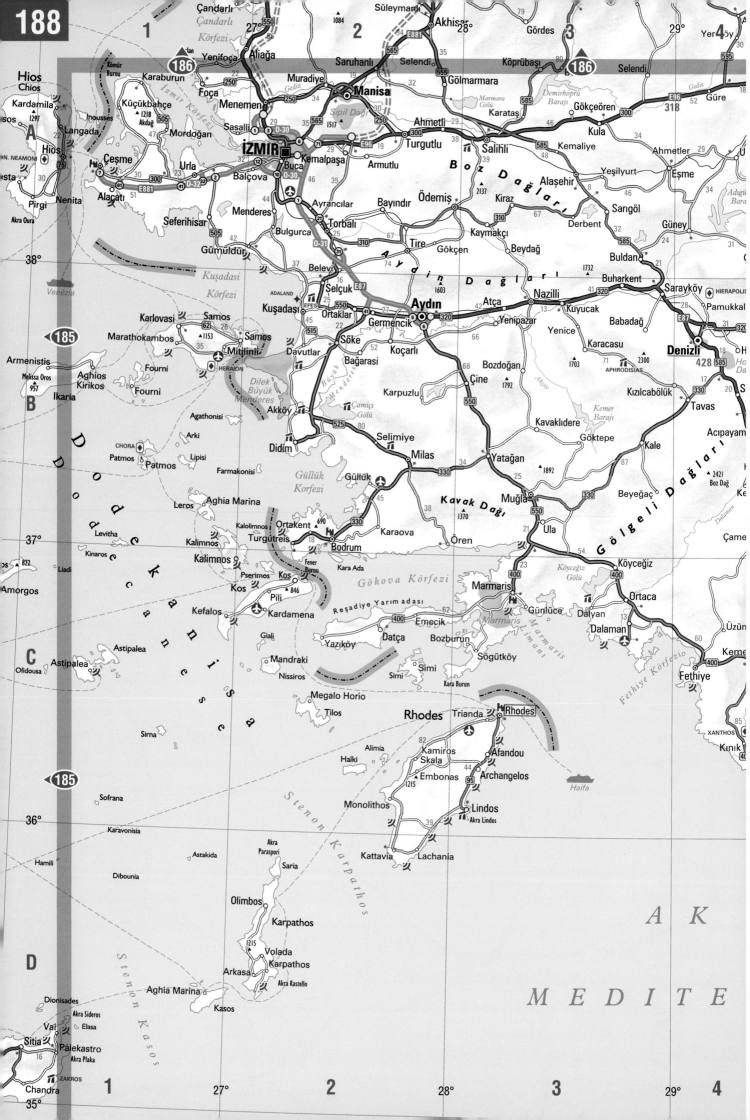

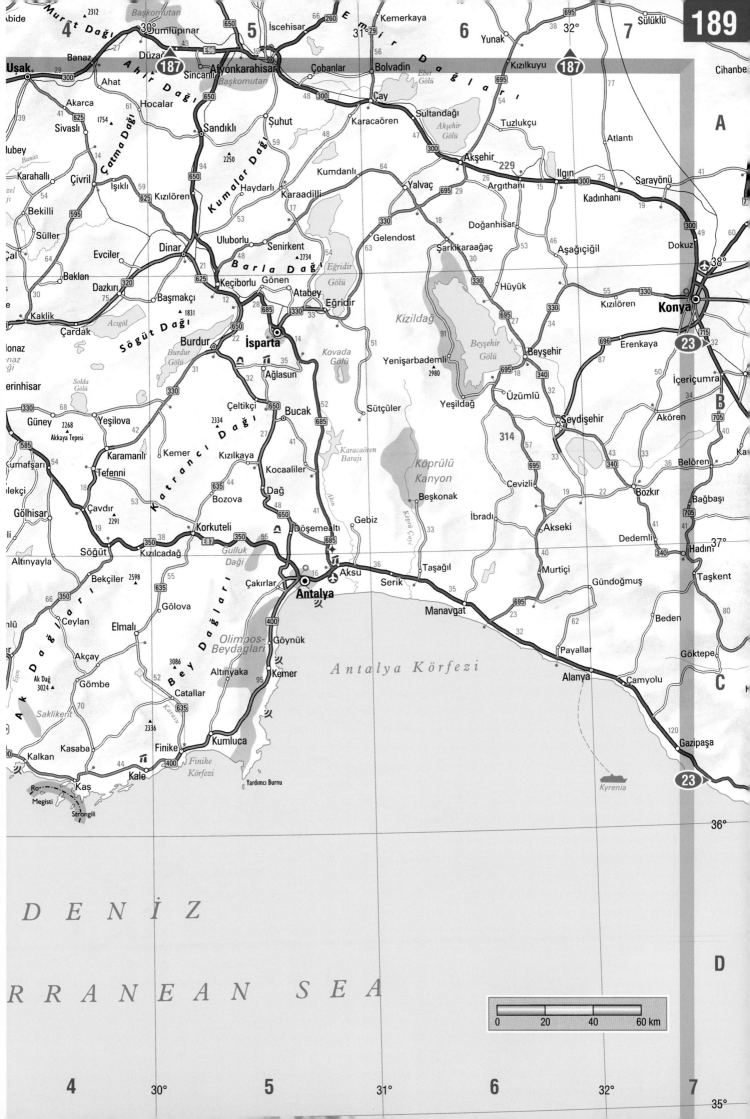

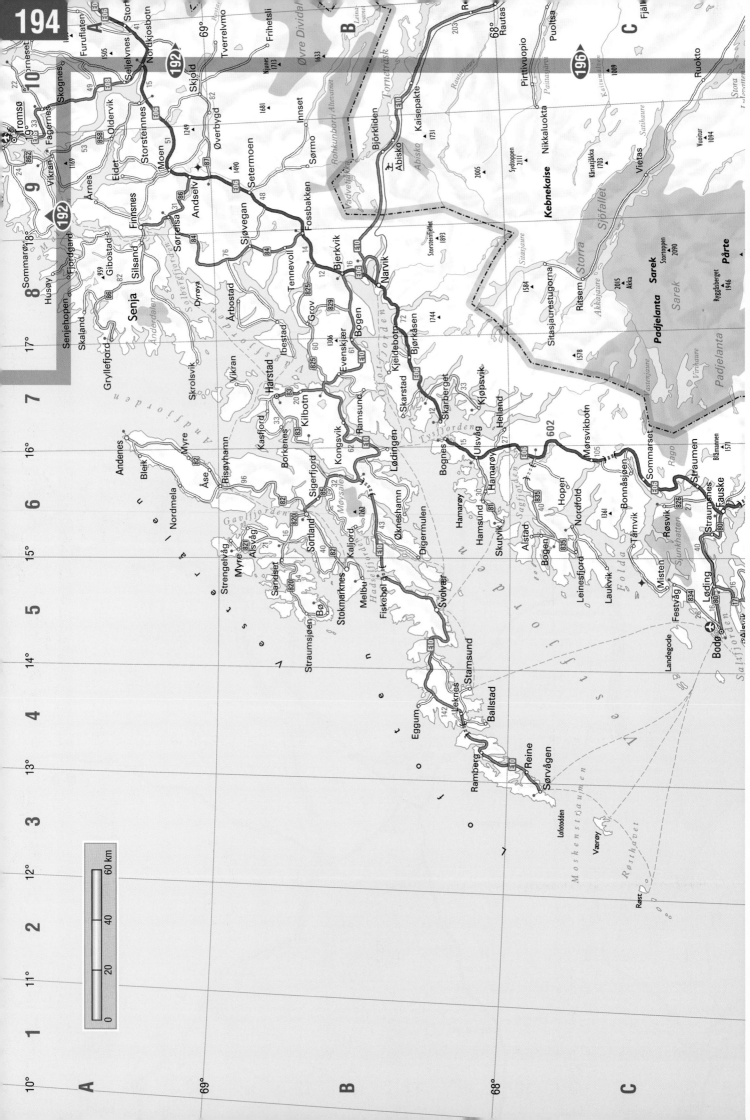

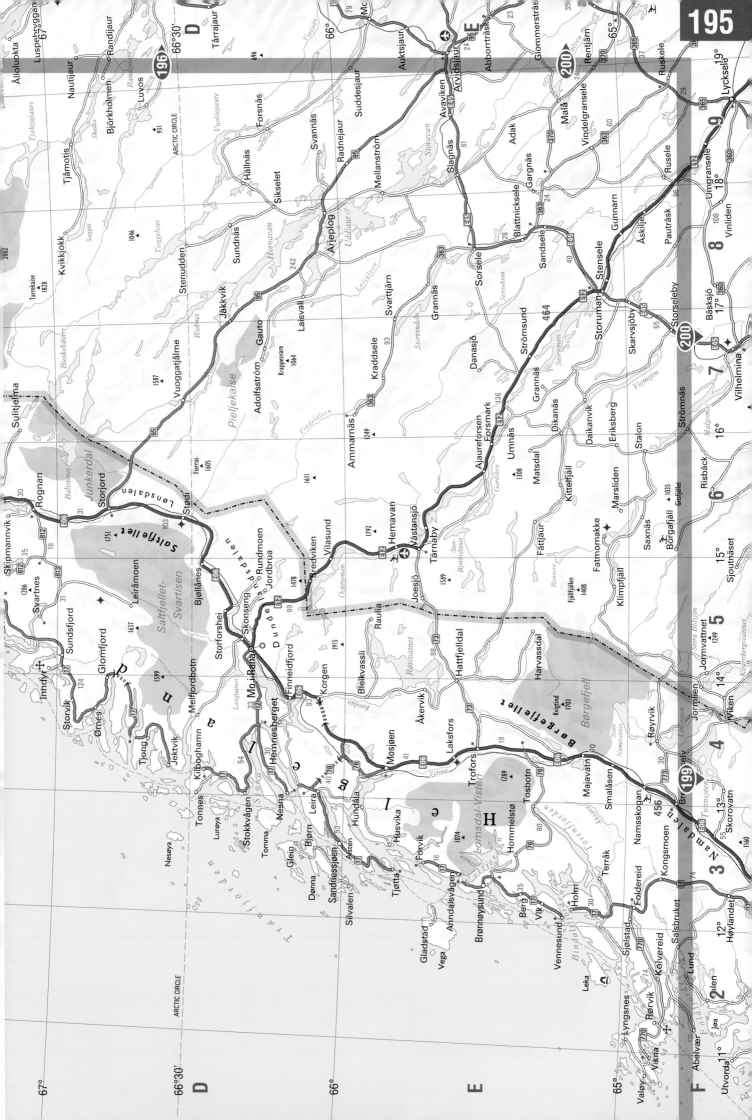

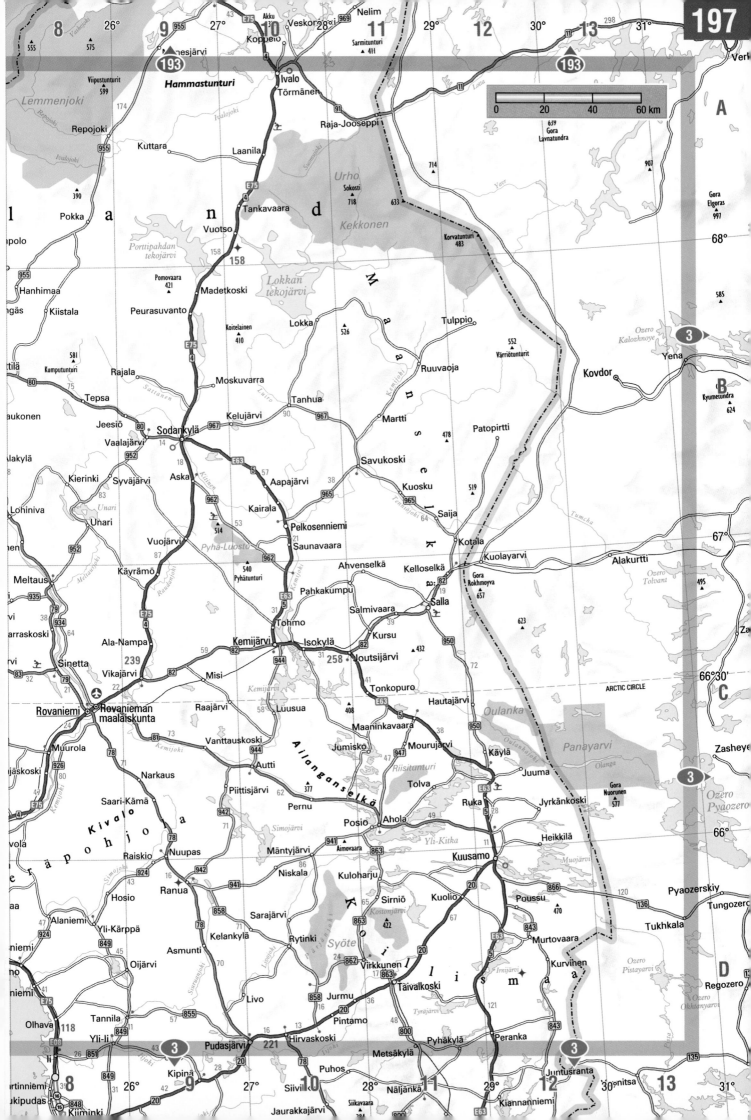

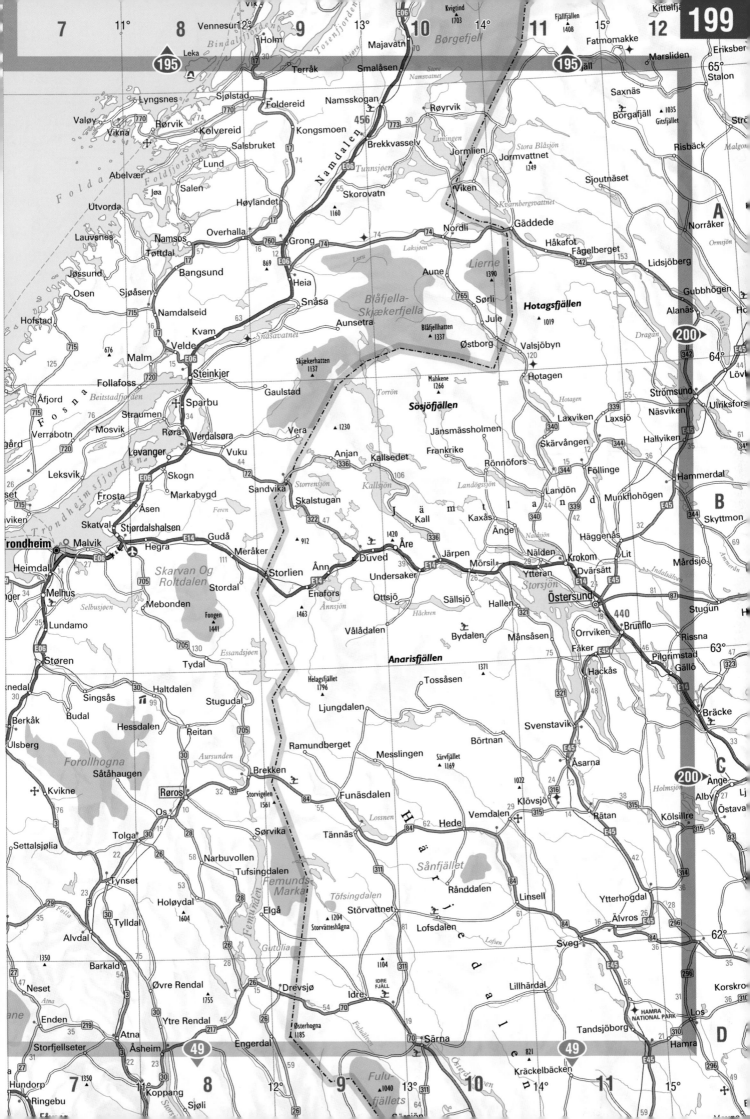

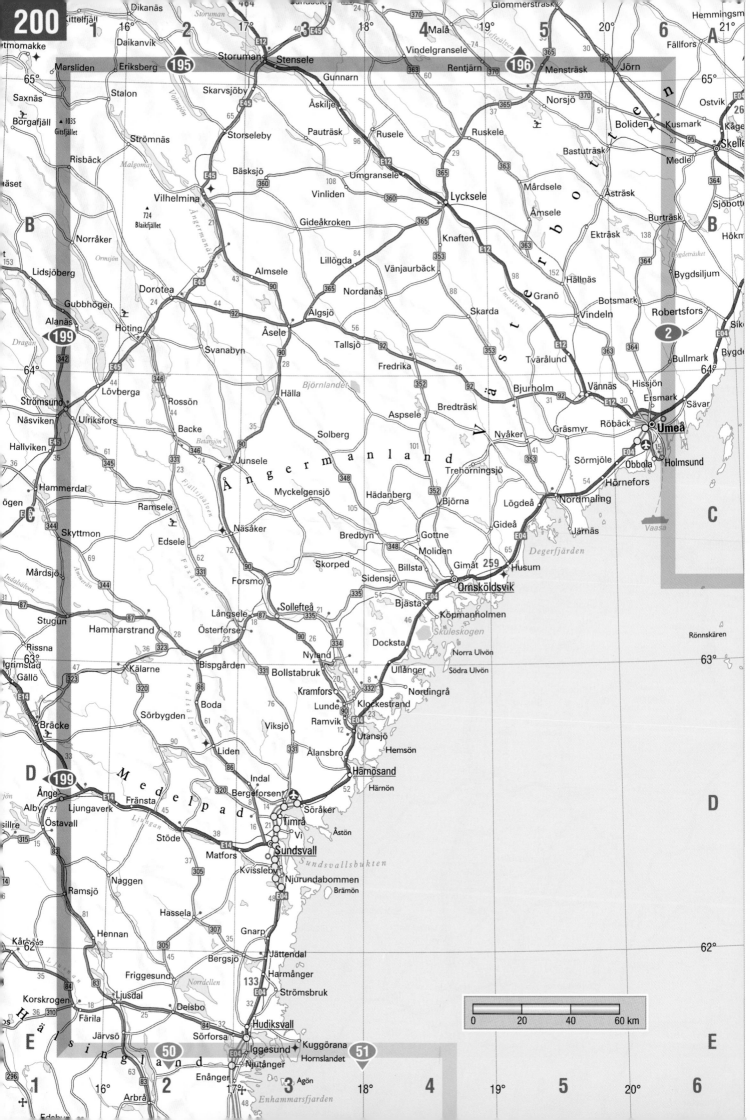

City plans • Plans de villes
Stadtpläne • Piante di città

Motorway	Autoroute
Major through route	Route principale majeur
Through route	Route principale
Secondary road	Route secondaire
Dual carriageway	Chaussées séparées
Other road	Autre route
Tunnel	Tunnel
Limited access / pedestrian road	Rue réglementée / rue piétonne
One-way street	Sens unique
Parking	Parc de stationnement
Motorway number (A7)	Numéro d'autoroute
National road number (447)	Numéro de route nationale
European road number (E45)	Numéro de route européenne
Destination (GENT)	Destination
Car ferry	Bac passant les autos
Railway	Chemin de fer
Rail/bus station	Gare/gare routière
Underground, metro station	Station de métro
Cable car	Téléférique
Abbey, cathedral	Abbaye, cathédrale
Church of interest	Église intéressante
Synagogue	Synagogue
Hospital	Hôpital
Police station (POL)	Police
Post office	Bureau de poste
Tourist information	Office de tourisme
Place of interest (Theatre)	Autre curiosité

Autobahn	Autostrada
Hauptstrecke	Strada di grande communicazione
Schnellstrasse	Strada d'importanza regionale
Nebenstrasse	Strada d'interesse locale
Zweispurig Schnellstrasse	Strada a carreggiate doppie
Nebenstrecke	Altra strada
Tunnel	Galleria stradale
Beschränkter Zugang/ Fussgängerzone	Strada pedonale / a accesso limitato
Einbahnstrasse	Senso unico
Parkplatz	Parcheggio
Autobahnnummer (A7)	Numero di autostrada
Nationalstrassennummer (447)	Numero di strada nazionale
Europäische Strassennummer (E45)	Numero di strada europea
Ziel (GENT)	Destinazione
Autofähre	Traghetto automobili
Eisenbahn	Ferrovia
Bahnhof / Busstation	Stazione ferrovia / pullman
U-Bahnstation	Metropolitano
Drahtseilbahn	Funivia
Abtei, Kloster, Kathedrale	Abbazia, duomo
Interessante Kirche	Chiesa da vedere
Synagoge	Sinagoga
Krankenhaus	Ospedale
Polizeiwache (POL)	Polizia
Postamt	Ufficio postale
Informationsbüro	Ufficio informazioni turistiche
Sonstige Sehenswürdigkeit (Theatre)	Luogo da vedere

Approach maps • Agglomérations
Carte régionale • Regionalkarte

Toll motorway – with motorway number (A10)	Autoroute à péage – avec numéro d'autoroute
Toll-free motorway – with European road number (E51)	Autoroute – avec numéro de route européenne
Pre-pay motorway – vignette required	Autoroute – 'vignette'
Motorway services	Aire de service
Motorway junction – full access, restricted access (24)	Échangeur d'autoroute – accès libre, accès reglémenté
Under construction	En construction
Tunnel	Tunnel
Major route – dual carriageway (14), single carriageway (14)	Route principale – chausées séparées, chausée sans séparation
Secondary route – dual carriageway (96), single carriageway (96)	Route secondaire – chausées séparées, chausée sans séparation
Other road	Autre route
Car ferry	Bac passant les autos
Destination (GIRONA)	Destination
Railway	Chemin de fer
Railway station (Estación Central)	Gare
Height – in metres (234)	Altitude – en mètres
Airport	Aéroport principal
Airfield	Autre aéroport
City plan coverage area	Région de plan de ville

Gebührenpflichtige Autobahn – mit Autobahnnummer (A10)	Autostrada a pedaggio – con numero
Gebührenfreie Autobahn – Europäische Strassennummer (E51)	Autostrada – con numero di strada europea
Autobahn – 'vignette'	Autostrada – 'vignette'
Autobahnservice	Area di servizio autostradale
Autobahnkreuz – voller/begrenzter Zugang (24)	Raccordi autostradali – completo/parziali
Im Bau	In construzione
Tunnel	Galleria stradale
Hauptstrecke – zweispurige (14), Schnellstrasse (14)	Strada di grande communicazione – carreggiata doppia, carreggiata unica
Nebenstrasse – zweispurige (96), Schnellstrasse (96)	Strada d'interesse locale – carreggiata doppia, carreggiata unica
Nebenstrecke	Altra strada
Autofähre	Traghetto automobili
Ziel (GIRONA)	Destinazione
Eisenbahn	Ferrovia
Hauptbahnhof (Estación Central)	Stazione ferrovia
Höhe – über dem Meeresspiegel (234)	Altezza in metri
Flughafen	Aeroporto
Flugplatz	Aerodromo/ campo d'aviazione
Vom Stadtplan abgedecktes Gebiet	Area della pianta della città

Alicante

0 km 0.5

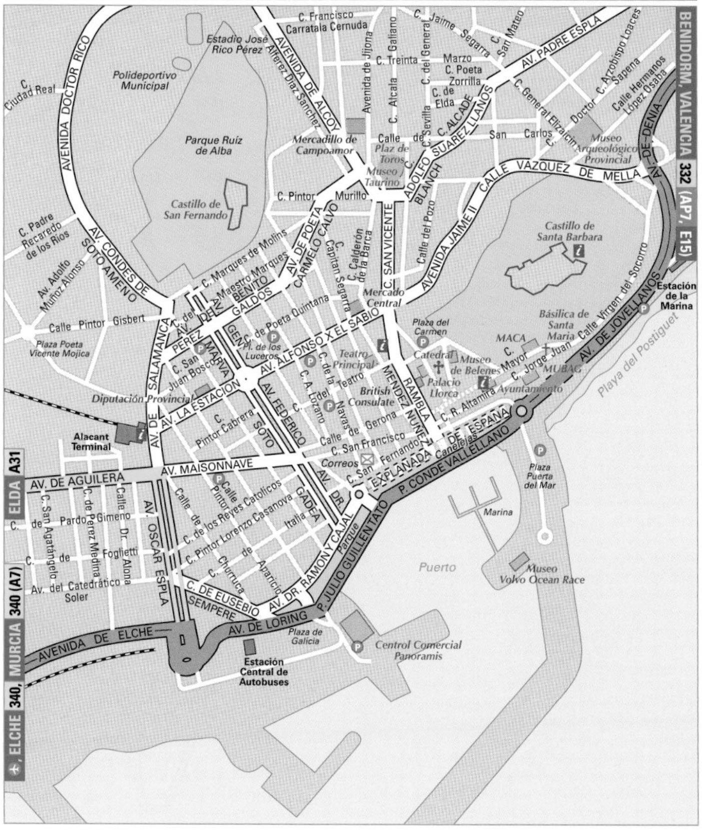

Antwerpen Antwerp

0 km 1

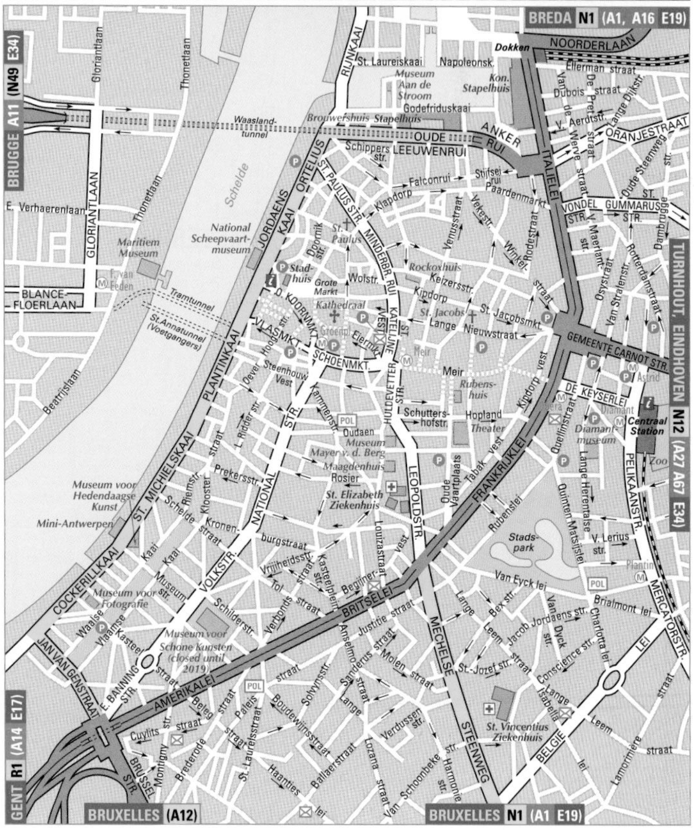

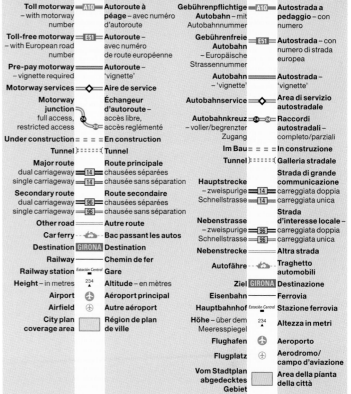

Amsterdam

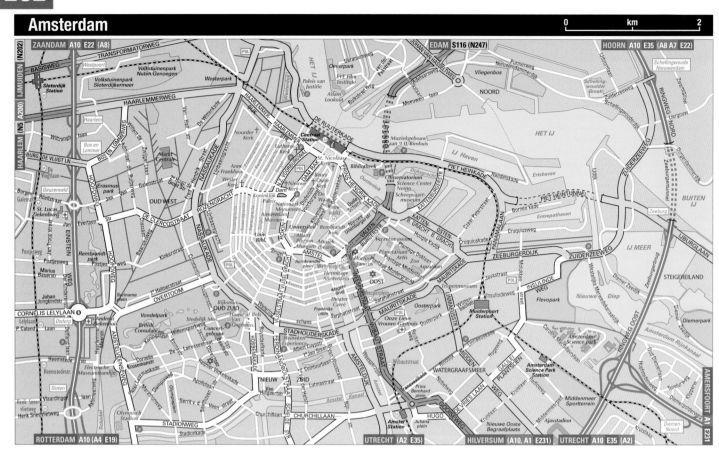

Amsterdam

Athina Athens

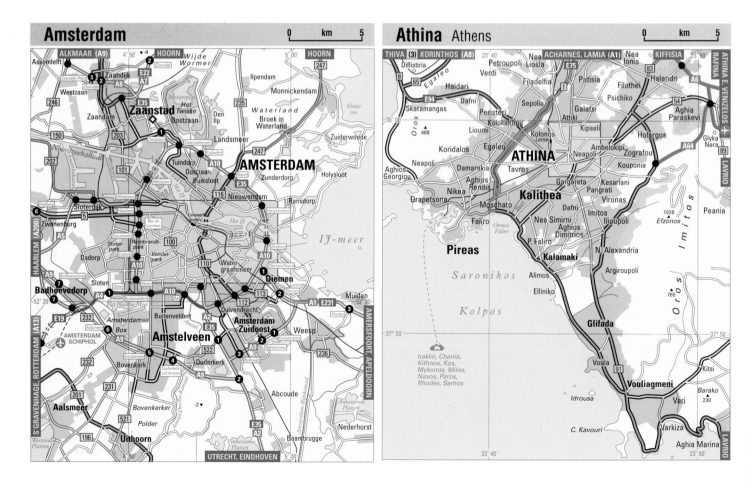

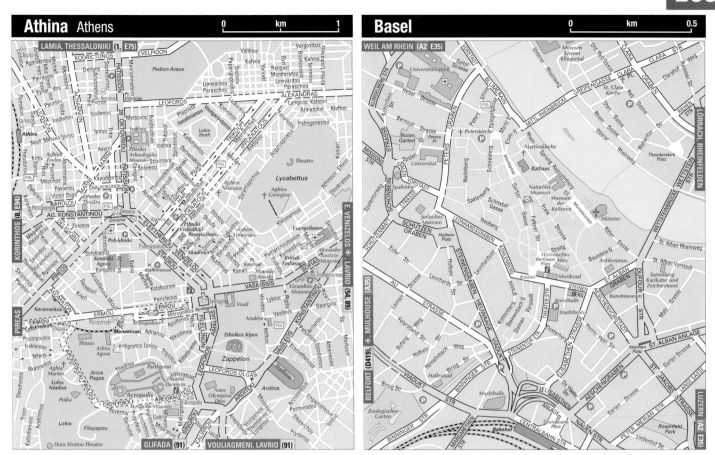

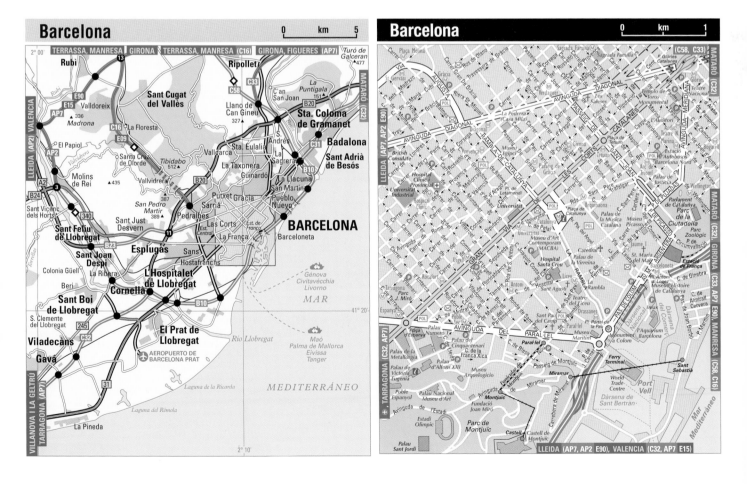

Berlin

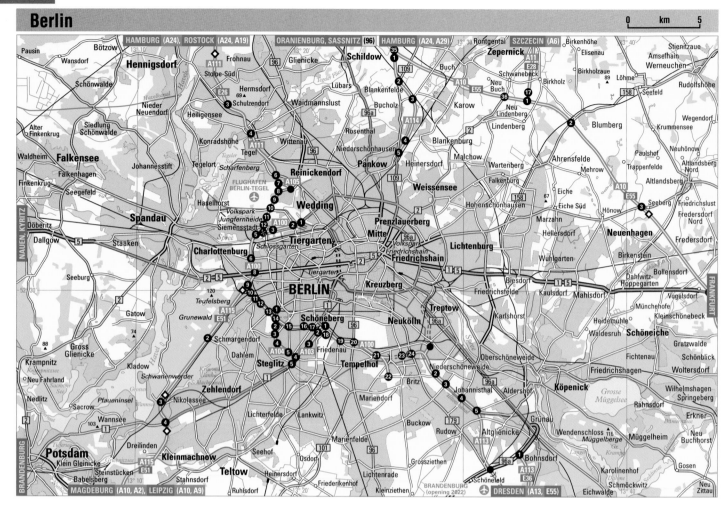

Berlin

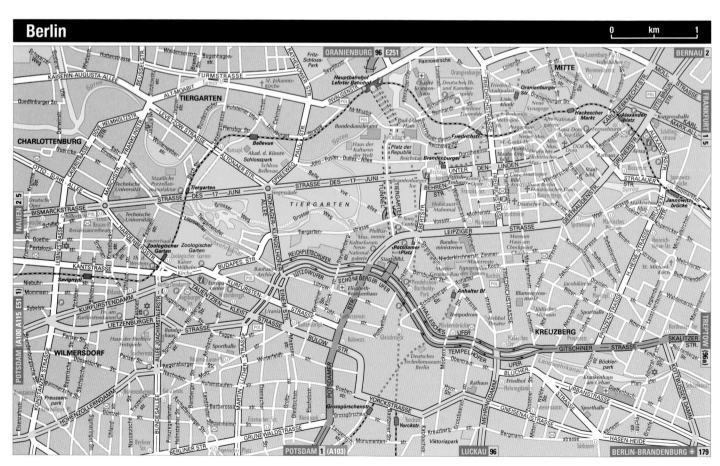

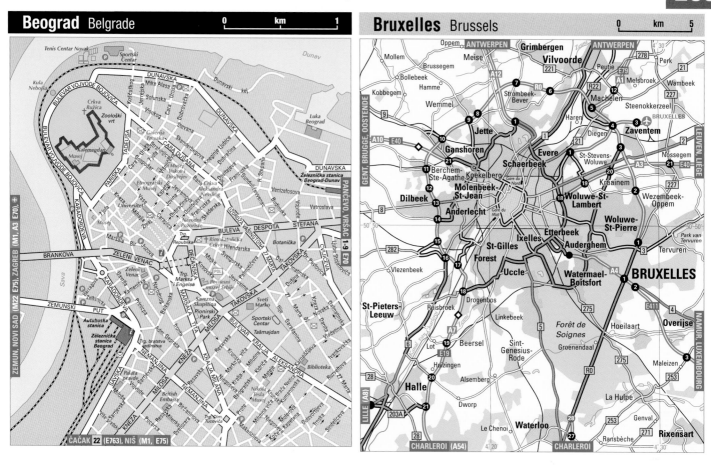

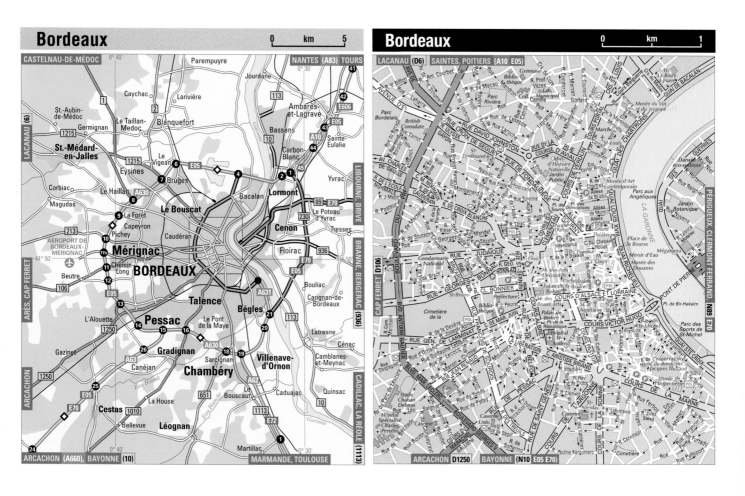

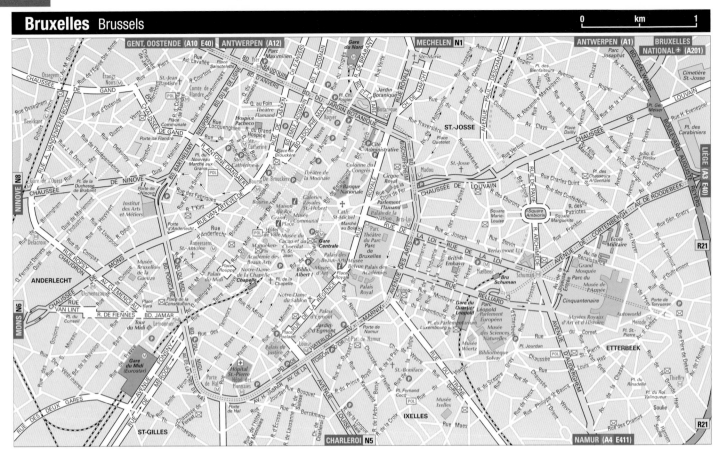

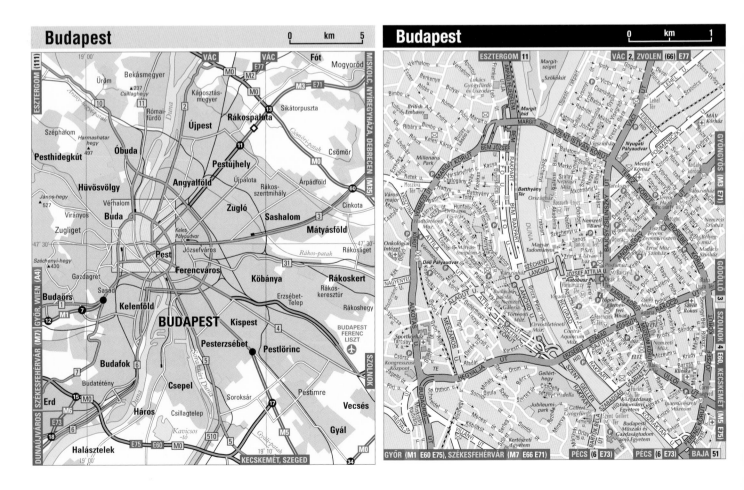

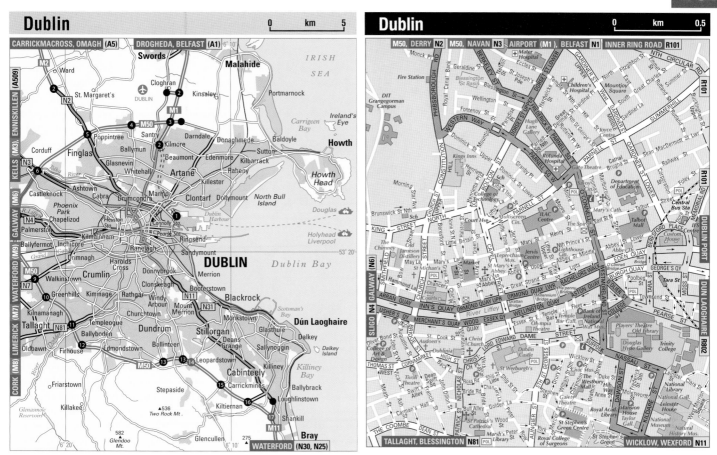

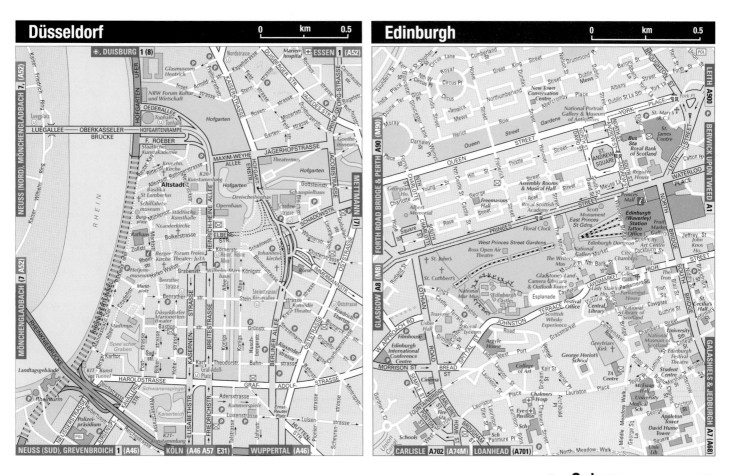

For **Cologne** see page 212

For **Copenhagen** see page 212

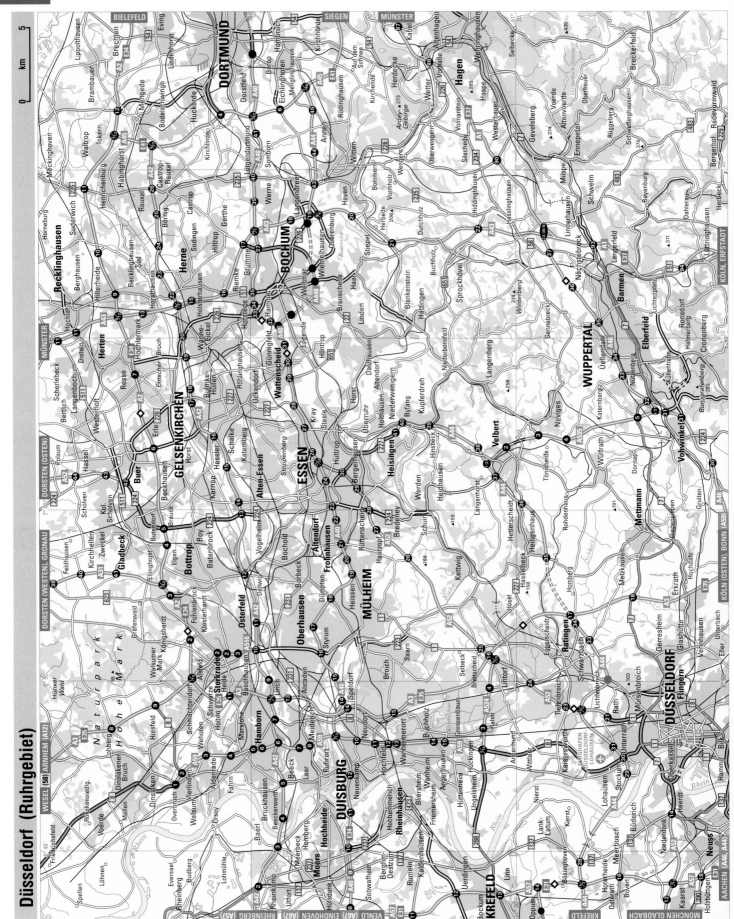

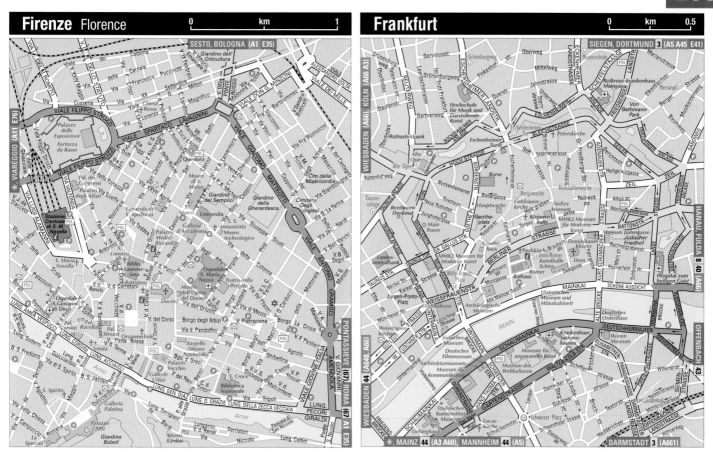

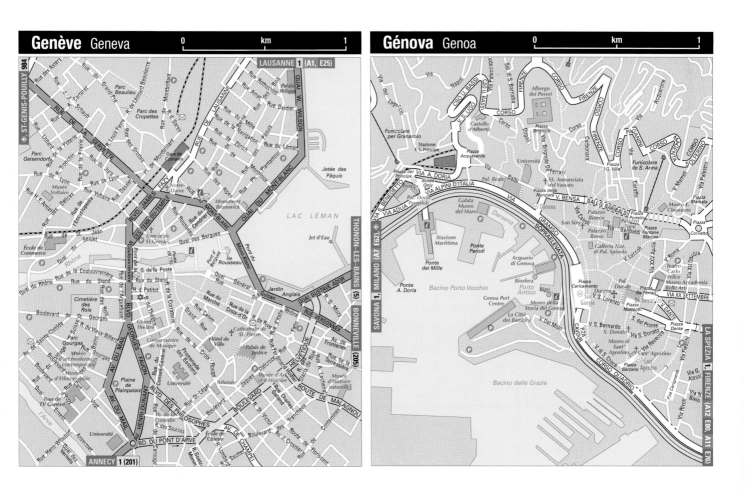

Granada

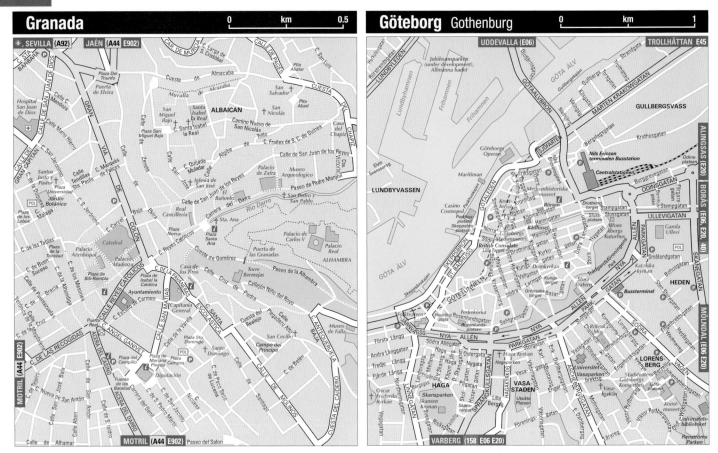

Göteborg Gothenburg

Hamburg

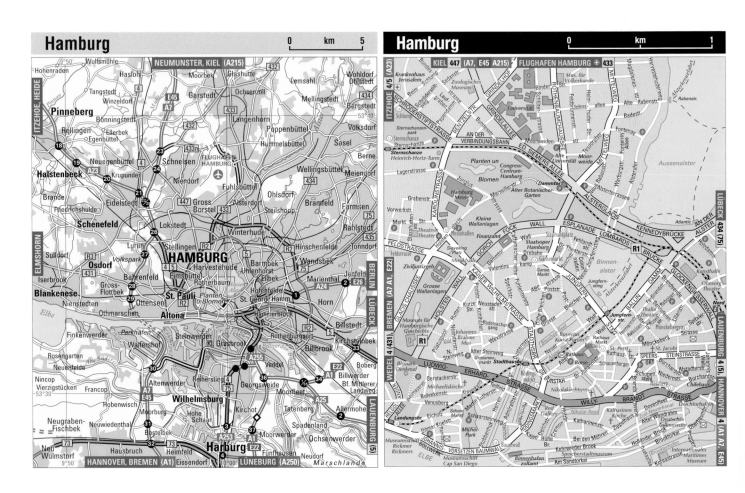

Hamburg

Helsinki

İstanbul

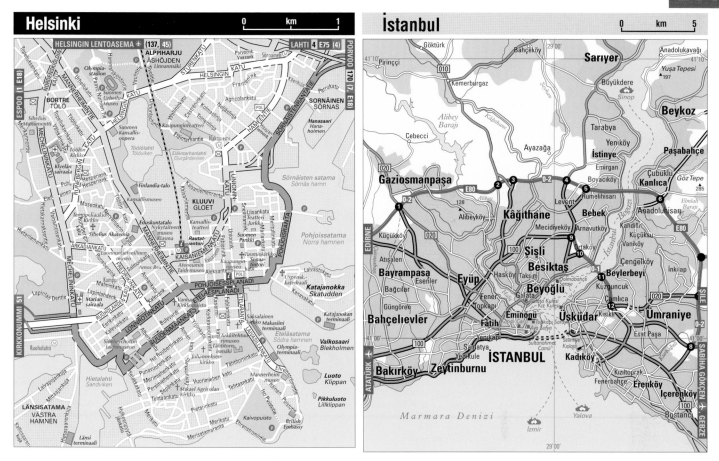

Helsinki

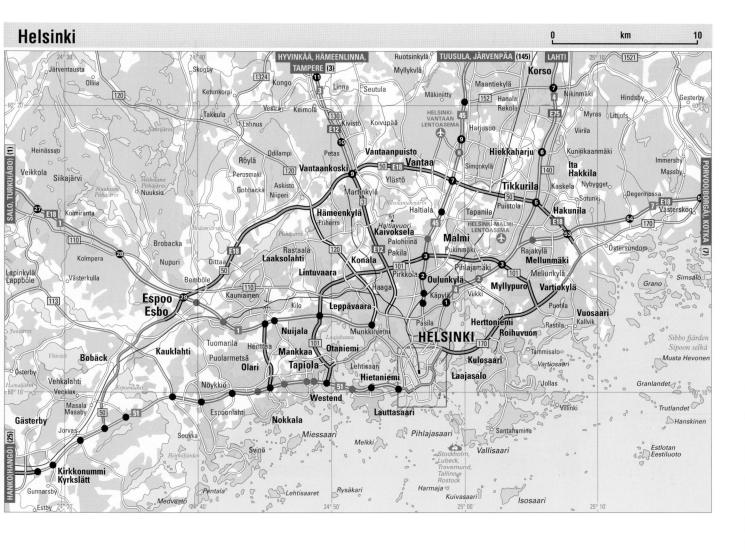

København Copenhagen

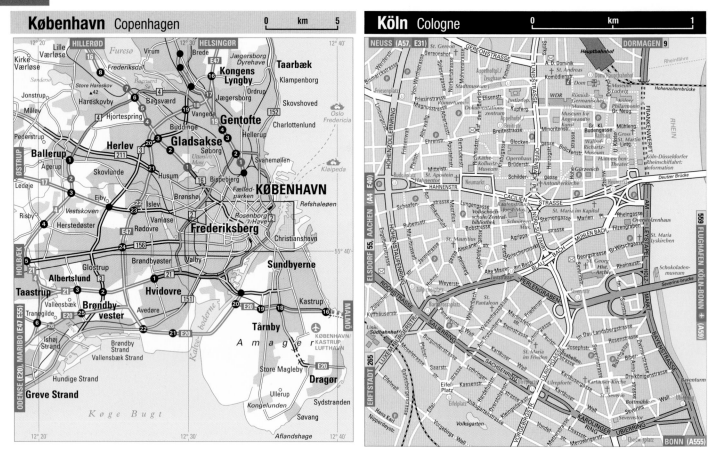

Köln Cologne

København Copenhagen

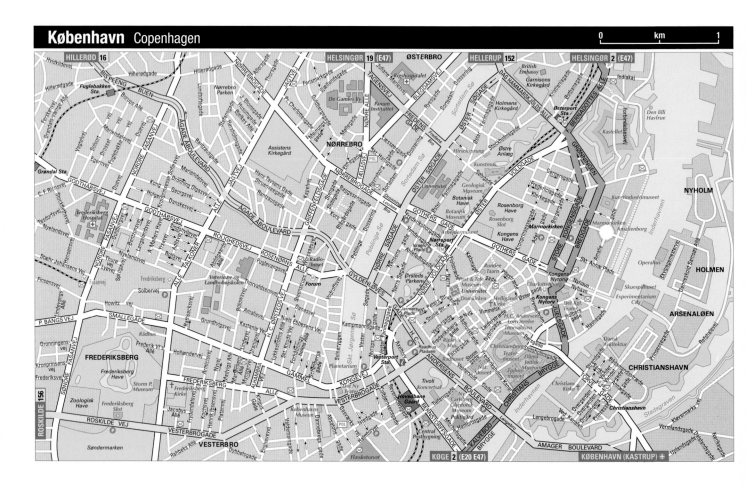

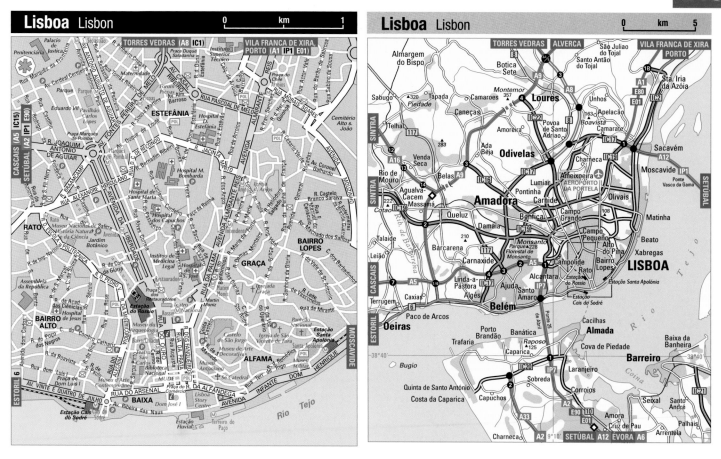

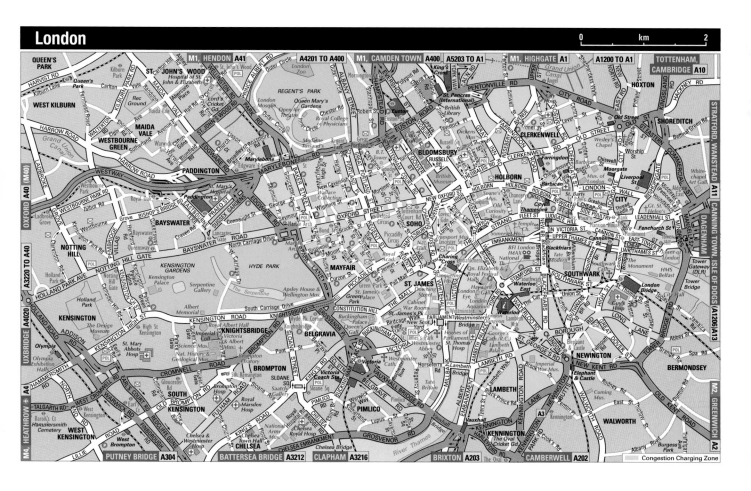

London

London

0   km   10

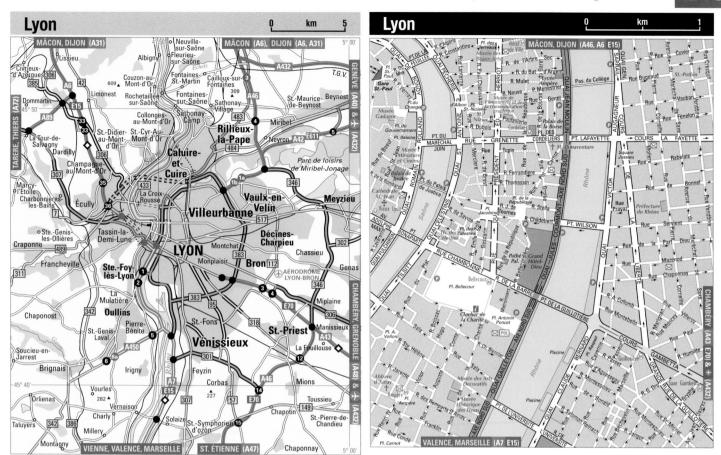

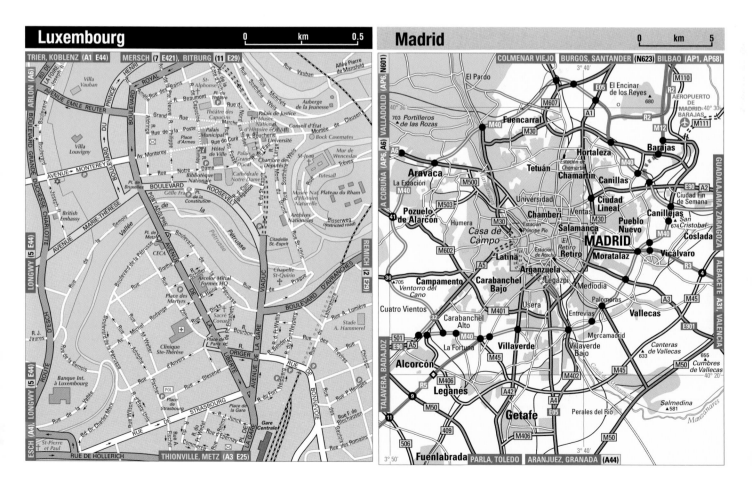

Madrid

0 km 1

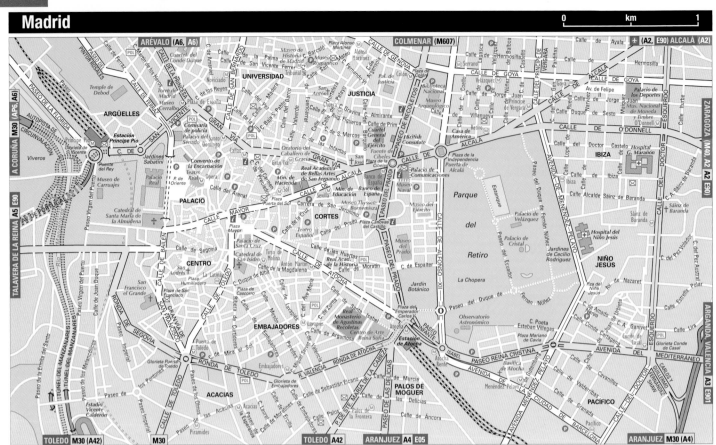

Málaga

0 km 0.5

Marseille / Marseilles

0 km 0.5

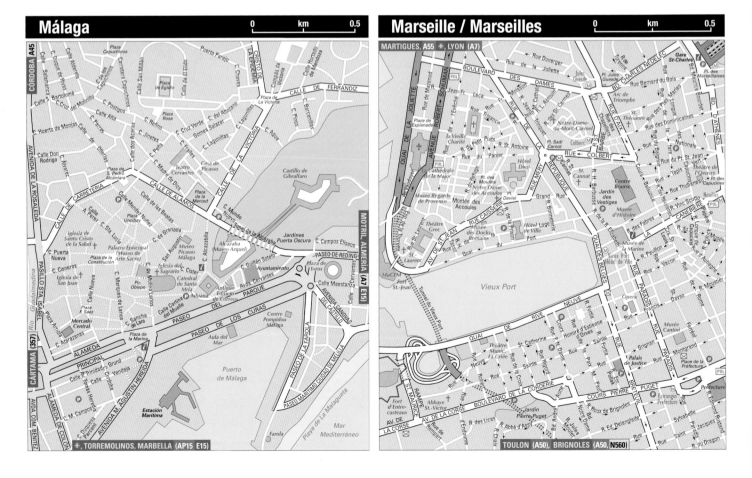

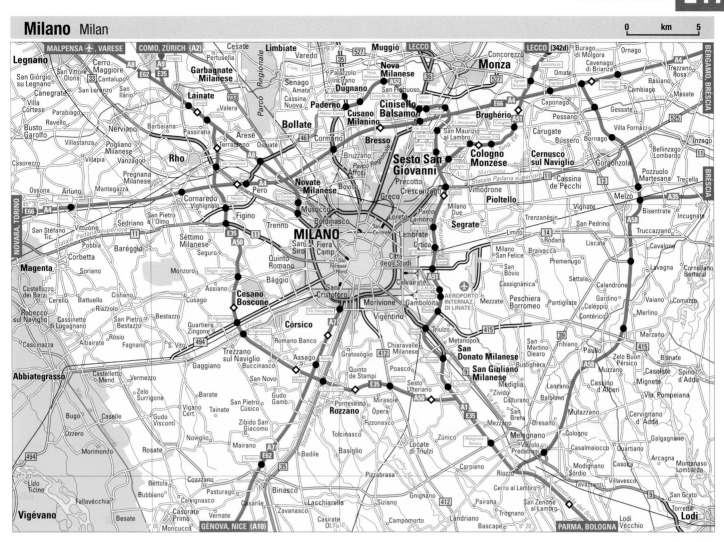

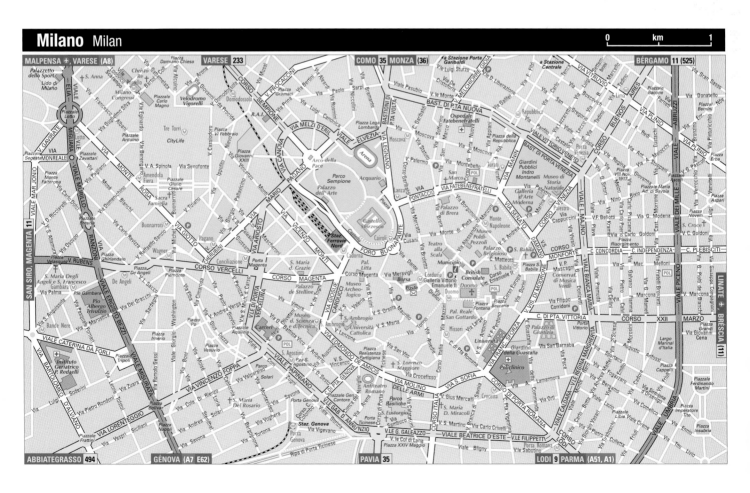

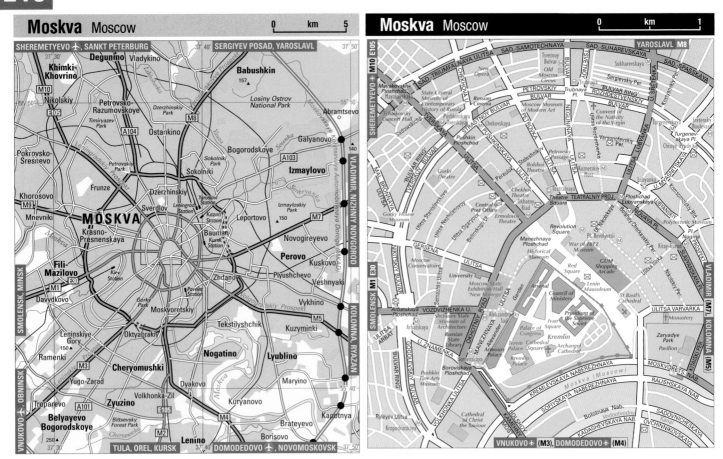

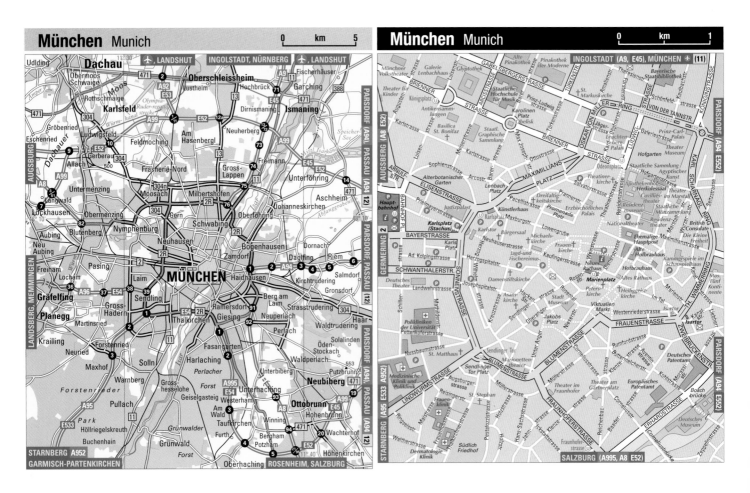

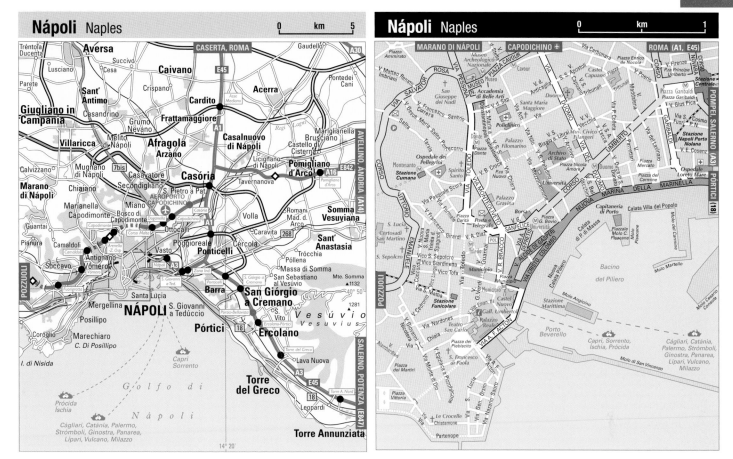

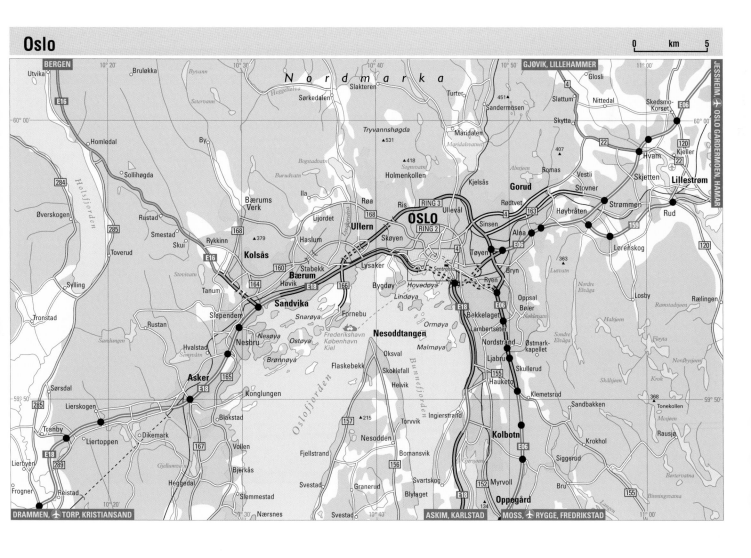

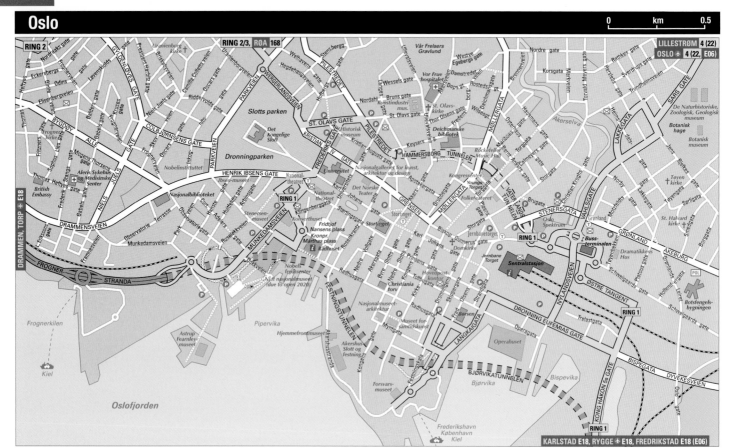

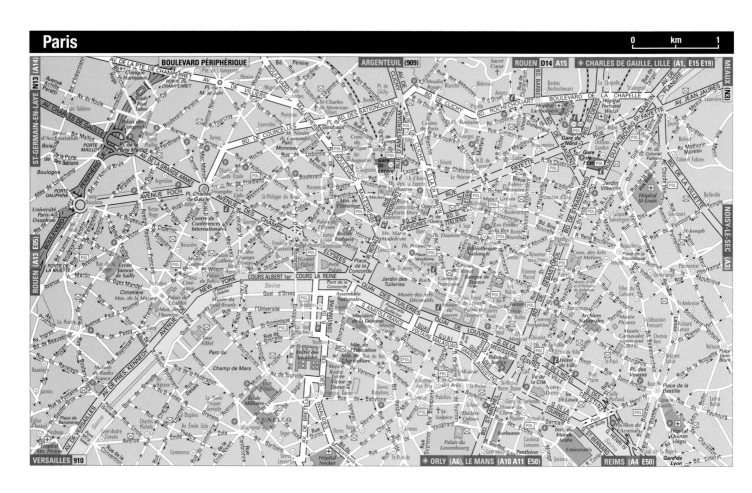

Paris

0 km 5

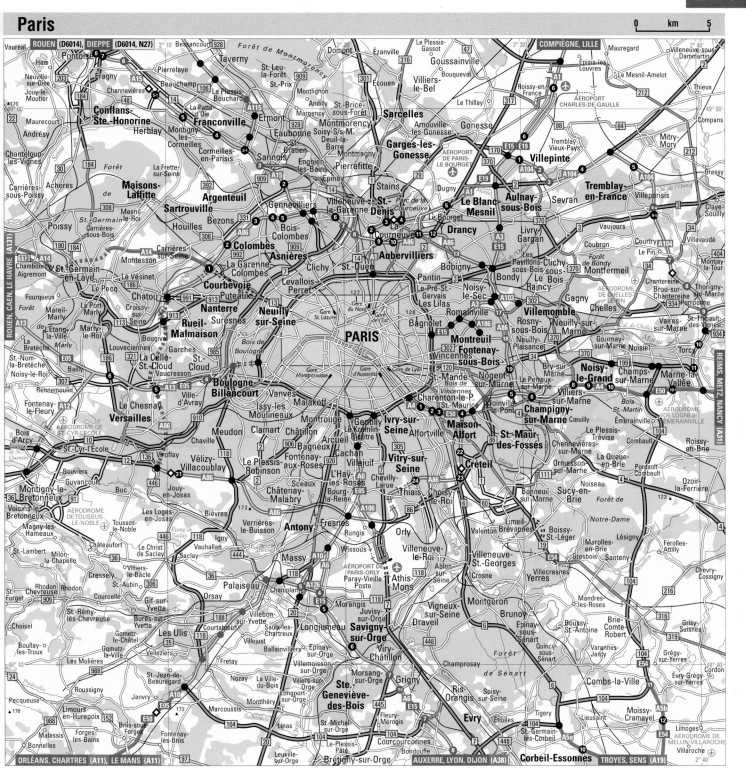

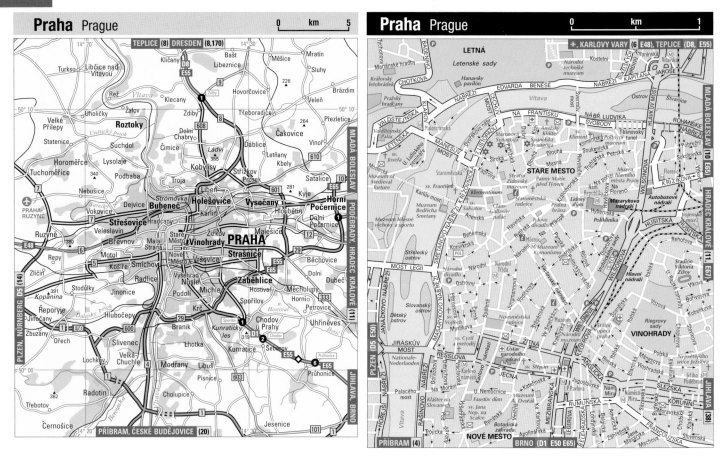

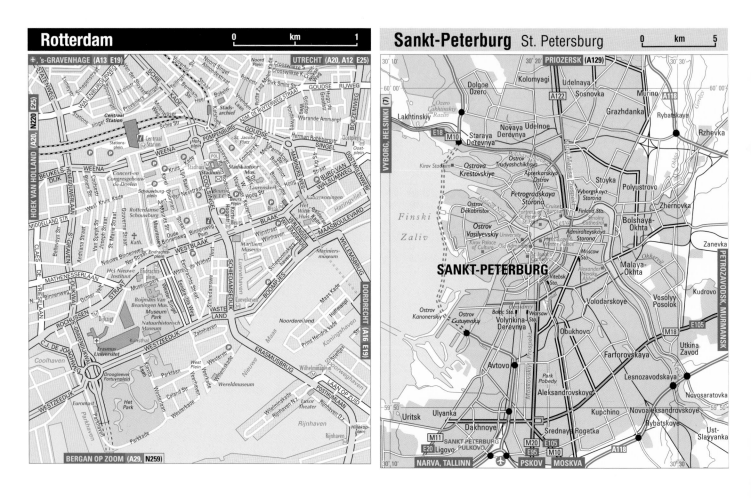

Roma Rome

Roma Rome

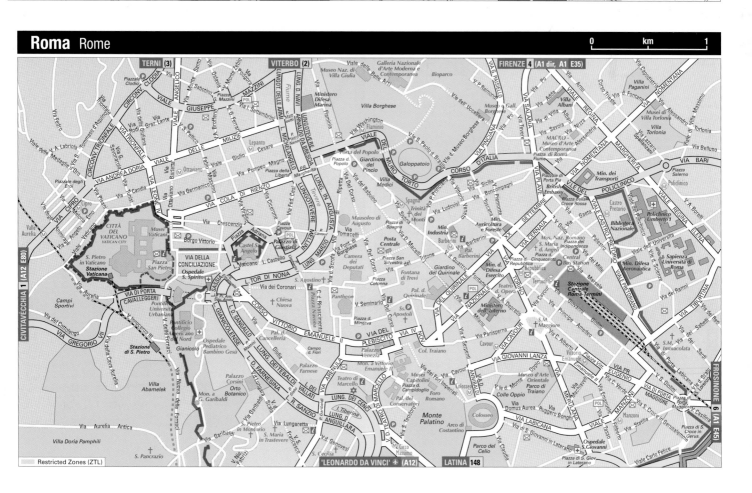

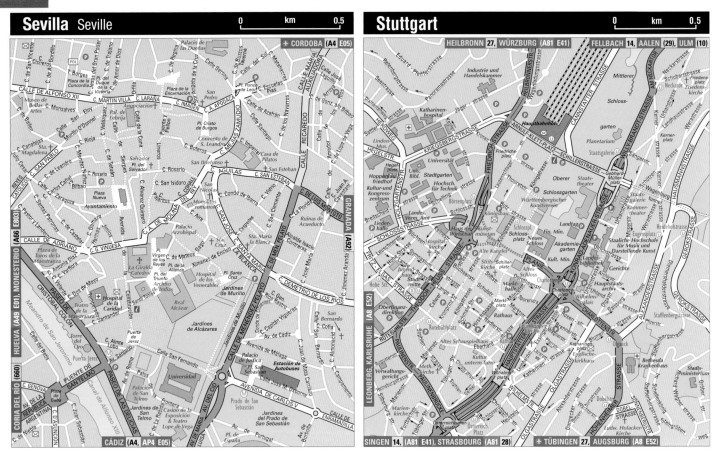

Sevilla Seville

0 km 0.5

✈ CORDOBA (A4) E05

CÁDIZ (A4, AP4 E05)

Stuttgart

0 km 0.5

HEILBRONN 27, WÜRZBURG (A81 E41) | FELLBACH 14, AALEN (29), ULM (10)

SINGEN 14, (A81 E41), STRASBOURG (A81 28) | ✈ TÜBINGEN 27, AUGSBURG (A8 E52)

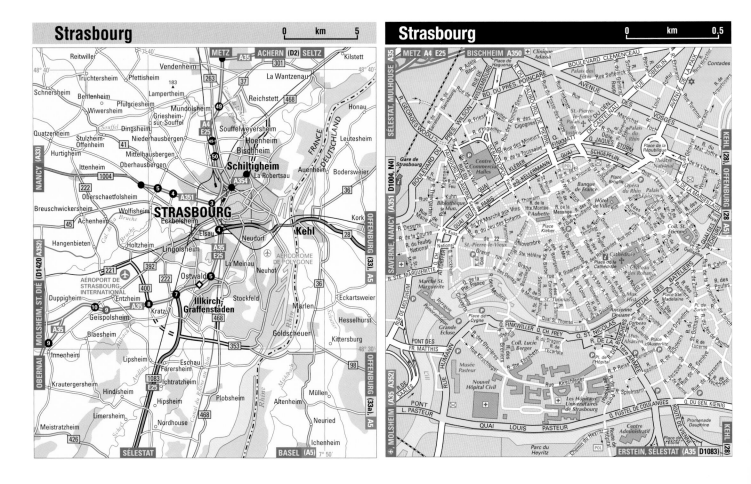

Strasbourg

0 km 5

METZ (A35) ACHERN (D2) SELTZ

STRASBOURG

SÉLESTAT | BASEL (A5) 7° 50'

Strasbourg

0 km 0.5

METZ A4 E25 | BISCHHEIM A350

ERSTEIN, SÉLESTAT (A35) D1083 (28)

Stockholm

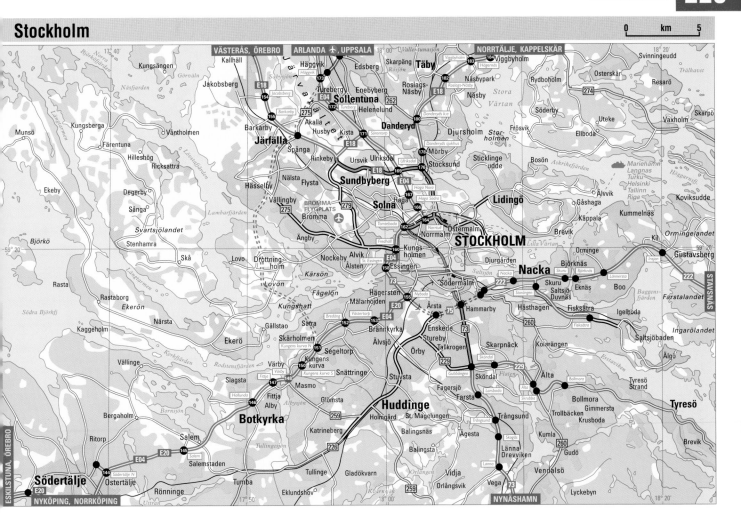

Stockholm

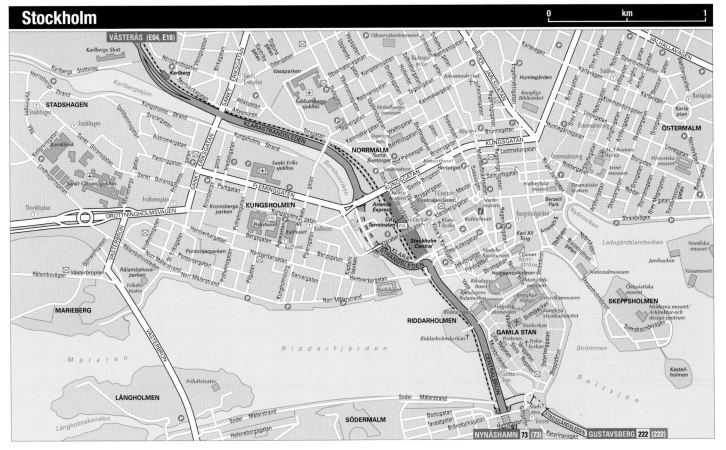

Torino Turin

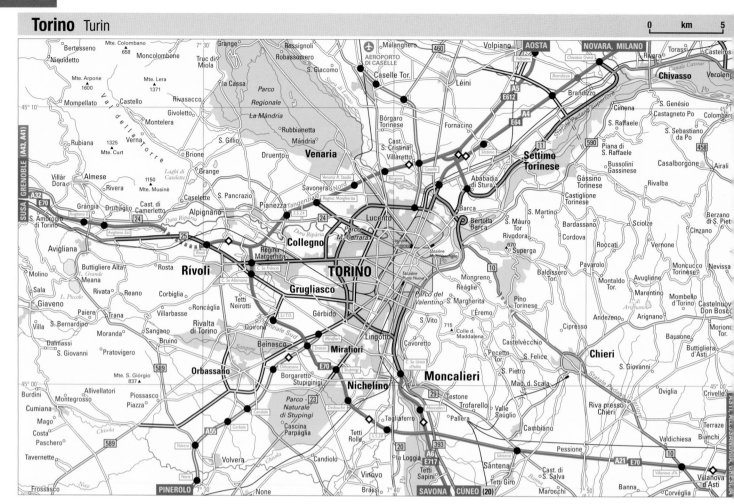

Venézia Venice

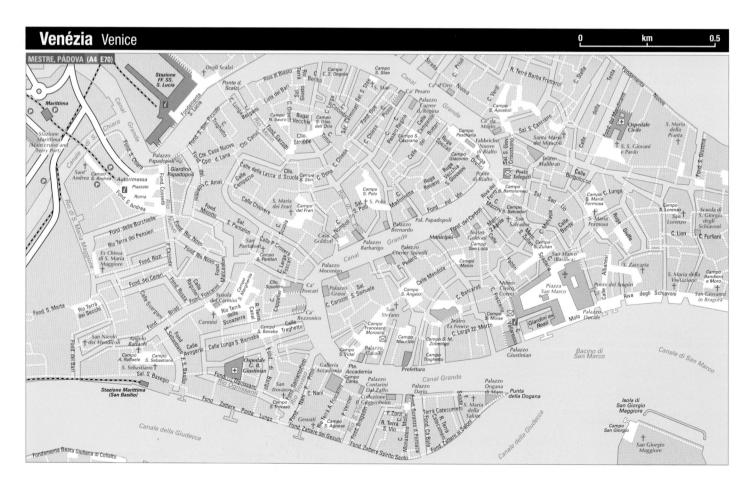

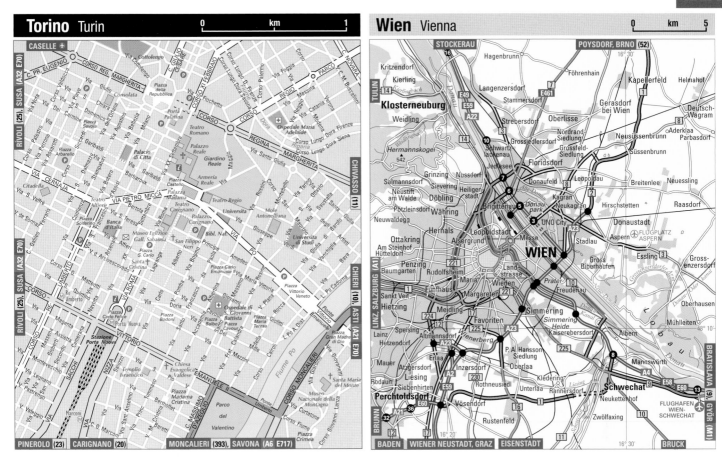

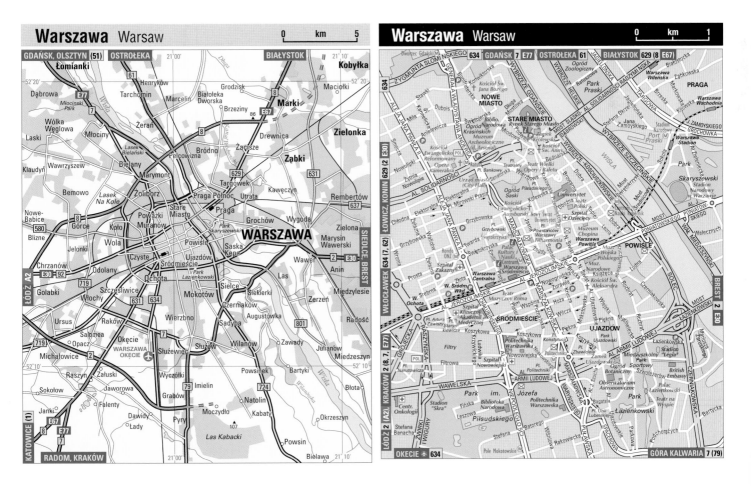

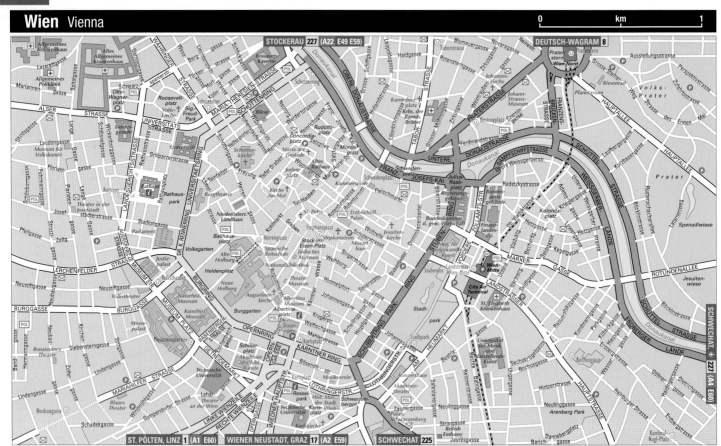

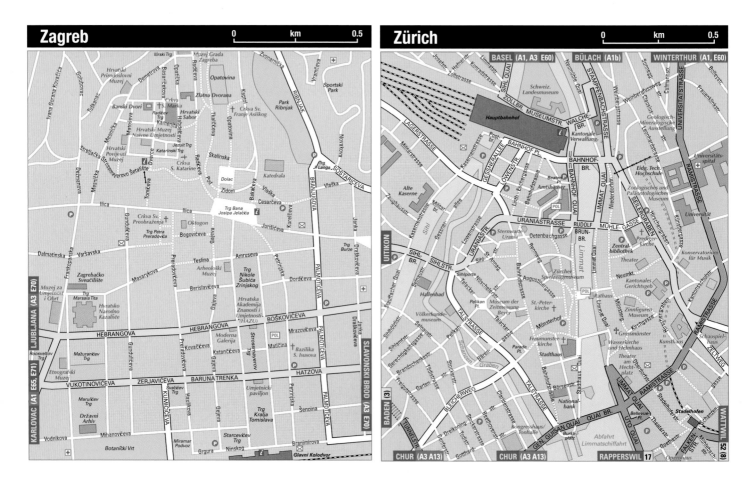

Index

🇬🇧	🇮🇹	⬛	🇮🇹
(A) Austria	Autriche	Österreich	Austria
(AL) Albania	Albanie	Albanien	Albania
(AND) Andorra	Andorre	Andorra	Andorra
(B) Belgium	Belgique	Belgien	Belgio
(BG) Bulgaria	Bulgarie	Bulgarien	Bulgaria
(BIH) Bosnia-Herzegovin	Bosnia-Herzegovine	Bosnien-Herzegowina	Bosnia-Herzogovina
(BY) Belarus	Belarus	Weissrussland	Bielorussia
(CH) Switzerland	Suisse	Schweiz	Svizzera
(CY) Cyprus	Chypre	Zypern	Cipro
(CZ) Czechia	République Tchèque	Tschechische Republik	Repubblica Ceca
(D) Germany	Allemagne	Deutschland	Germania
(DK) Denmark	Danemark	Dänemark	Danimarca
(E) Spain	Espagne	Spanien	Spagna
(EST) Estonia	Estonie	Estland	Estonia
(F) France	France	Frankreich	Francia
(FIN) Finland	Finlande	Finnland	Finlandia
(FL) Liechtenstein	Liechtenstein	Liechtenstein	Liechtenstein
(FO) Faeroe Islands	Îles Féroé	Färöer-Inseln	Isole Faroe
(GB) United Kingdom	Royaume Uni	Grossbritannien und Nordirland	Regno Unito
(GBZ) Gibraltar	Gibraltar	Gibraltar	Gibilterra
(GR) Greece	Grèce	Greichenland	Grecia
(H) Hungary	Hongrie	Ungarn	Ungheria
(HR) Croatia	Croatie	Kroatien	Croazia

🇬🇧	🇮🇹	⬛	🇮🇹
(I) Italy	Italie	Italien	Italia
(IRL) Ireland	Irlande	Irland	Irlanda
(IS) Iceland	Islande	Island	Islanda
(KOS) Kosovo	Kosovo	Kosovo	Kosovo
(L) Luxembourg	Luxembourg	Luxemburg	Lussemburgo
(LT) Lithuania	Lituanie	Litauen	Lituania
(LV) Latvia	Lettonie	Lettland	Lettonia
(M) Malta	Malte	Malta	Malta
(MC) Monaco	Monaco	Monaco	Monaco
(MD) Moldova	Moldavie	Moldawien	Moldavia
(MK) Macedonia	Macédoine	Makedonien	Macedonia
(MNE) Montenegro	Monténégro	Montenegro	Montenegro
(N) Norway	Norvège	Norwegen	Norvegia
(NL) Netherlands	Pays-Bas	Niederlande	Paesi Bassi
(P) Portugal	Portugal	Portugal	Portogallo
(PL) Poland	Pologne	Polen	Polonia
(RO) Romania	Roumanie	Rumänien	Romania
(RSM) San Marino	Saint-Marin	San Marino	San Marino
(RUS) Russia	Russie	Russland	Russia
(S) Sweden	Suède	Schweden	Svezia
(SK) Slovakia	République Slovaque	Slowak Republik	Repubblica Slovacca
(SLO) Slovenia	Slovénie	Slowenien	Slovenia
(SRB) Serbia	Serbie	Serbien	Serbia
(TR) Turkey	Turquie	Türkei	Turchia
(UA) Ukraine	Ukraine	Ukraine	Ucraina

A

Aabenraa DK 64 A2
Aabybro DK 58 A2
Aach D 107 B4
Aachen D 80 B2
Aalborg DK 58 A2
Aalen D 94 C2
Aalestrup DK 58 B2
Aalsmeer NL 70 B1
Aalst B 79 B4
Aalten NL 71 C3
Aalter B 79 A3
Äänekoski FIN 8 A4
Aapajärvi FIN 197 B10
Ağapınar TR 187 C5
Aarau CH 106 B3
Aarberg CH 106 B2
Aarburg CH 106 B2
Aardenburg NL . . . 79 A3
Aars DK 58 B2
Aarschot B 79 B4
Aarup DK 59 C3
Aba H 112 B2
Abádanes E 152 B1
Abades E 151 B3
Abadin E 141 A3
Abádszalók H 113 B4
Abaliget H 125 A4
Abana TR 23 A8
A Baña E 140 B2
Abanilla E 165 A3
Abano Terme I 121 B4
Abarán E 165 A3
Abasár H 113 B4
Abbadia San Salvatore
I 135 C4
Abbaue D 74 A2
Abbehausen D 72 A1
Abbekäs S 66 A2
Abbeville F 90 A1
Abbey IRL 28 A3
Abbeydorney IRL . . 29 B2
Abbeyfeale IRL . . . 29 B2
Abbeyleix IRL 30 B1
Abbey Town GB . . . 36 B3
Abbiategrasso I . . . 120 B1
Abborrträsk S 196 D2
Abbots Bromley GB 40 C2
Abbotsbury GB . . . 43 B4
Abda H 111 B4
Abejar E 143 C4
Abela P 160 B1
Abelvær N 199 A8
Abenberg D 94 B2
Abenójar E 157 B3
Abensberg D 95 C3
Aberaeron GB 39 B2
Abercarn GB 39 C3
Aberchirder GB 33 D4

Aberdare GB 39 C3
Aberdaron GB 38 B2
Aberdeen GB 33 D4
Aberdulais GB 39 C3
Aberdyfi GB 39 B2
Aberfeldy GB 35 B4
Aberffraw GB 38 A2
Aberfoyle GB 34 B3
Abergavenny GB . . 39 C3
Abergele GB 38 A3
Abergynolwyn GB . . 38 B3
Aberporth GB 39 B2
Abersoch GB 38 B2
Abertillery GB 39 C3
Abertura E 156 A2
Aberystwyth GB . . 39 B2
Abetone I 135 A3
Abfaltersbach A . . . 109 C3
Abide
  Çanakkale TR 186 B1
  Kütahya TR 187 D4
Abiego E 145 B3
Abild DK 64 B1
Abingdon-on-Thames
  GB 44 B2
Abington GB 36 A3
Abisko S 194 B9
Abiul P 154 B2
Abla E 164 B2
Ablis F 90 C1
A Bola E 140 B3
Abondance F 118 A3
Abony H 113 B4
Aboyne GB 33 D4
Abrantes P 154 B2
Abreiro P 148 A2
Abreschviller F . . . 92 C3
Abrest F 117 A3
Abriès F 119 C3
Abrud RO 17 B5
Absdorf A 97 C3
Abtenau A 109 B4
Abtsgmünd D 94 C1
Abusejo E 149 B3
Åby
  Kronoberg S 62 A2
  Östergötland S 56 B2
Åbyggeby S 51 B4
Åbytorp S 55 A6
A Cañiza E 140 B2
A Capela E 140 A2
Acate I 177 B3
Accadia I 171 B3
Accéglio I 132 A2
Accettura I 172 B2
Acciaroli I 170 C3
Accous F 145 A3
Accrington GB 40 B1
Accúmoli I 169 A3
Acedera E 156 A2
Acehúche E 155 B4

Acered E 152 A2
Acerenza I 172 B1
Acerno I 170 C3
Acerra I 170 C2
Aceuchal E 155 C4
Acharacle GB 34 B2
Acharnes GR 185 A4
Achavanich GB . . . 32 C3
Achene B 79 B5
Achenkirch A 108 B2
Achensee A 108 B2
Achenthal A 108 B2
Achentrias GR 185 E6
Achern D 93 C4
Acheux-en-Amienois
  F 90 A2
Achiltibuie GB 32 C1
Achim D 72 A2
Achladokambos
  GR 184 B3
Achnasheen GB . . 32 D1
Achnashellach GB . 32 D1
Achosnich GB 34 B1
Aci Castello I 177 B4
Aci Catena I 177 B4
Acilia I 168 B2
Acıpayam TR 189 B4
Acireale I 177 B4
Acle GB 41 C5
A Coruña E 140 A2
Acquacadda I 179 C2
Acqua Doria F . . . 180 B1
Acquanegra sul Chiese
  I 121 B3
Acquapendente I . . 168 A1
Acquasanta Terme
  I 136 C2
Acquasparta I 168 A2
Acquaviva I 135 B4
Acquaviva delle Fonti
  I 171 C4
Acquaviva Picena
  I 136 C2
Acquigny F 89 A5
Ácqui Terme I 119 C5
Acri I 174 B2
Acs H 112 B2
Acsa H 112 B3
Ácsteszér H 112 B1
Acy-en-Multien F . . 90 B2
Ada SRB 126 B2
Adak S 195 E9
Ádalsbruk N 48 B3
Adamas GR 185 C5
Adamsfjord N . . . 193 B10
Adamuz E 157 B3
Adana TR 23 C8
Ádánd H 112 C2
Adanero E 150 B3
Adare IRL 29 B3
Adaševci SRB 125 B5

Adeanueva de Ebro
  E 144 B2
Adelboden CH 106 C2
Adelebsen D 82 A1
Adelmannsfelden D 94 C2
Adelsheim D 94 B1
Adelsö S 57 A3
Ademuz E 152 B2
Adenau D 80 B2
Adendorf D 72 A3
Adinkerke B 78 A2
Adjud RO 17 B7
Adliswil CH 107 B3
Admont A 110 B1
Adneram N 52 A2
Adolfsström S 195 D7
Adony H 112 B2
Adorf
  Hessen D 81 A4
  Sachsen D 83 B4
Adra E 164 C1
Adradas E 152 A1
Adrall E 147 B2
Adrano I 177 B3
Ádria I 121 B5
Adrigole IRL 29 C2
Adwick le Street GB 40 B2
Adzaneta E 153 B3
Aesch CH 106 B2
Afandou GR 188 C3
Áfarnes N 198 C4
Affing D 94 C2
Affoltern CH 106 B3
Affric Lodge GB . . 32 D1
Åfjord N 199 B7
Aflenz Kurort A 110 B2
A Fonsagrada E . . . 141 A3
Afragóla I 170 C2
Afritz A 109 C4
Afyonkarahisar TR 187 D5
Ágasegyháza H . . .112 C3
Agay F 132 B2
Agazzano I 120 C2
Agde F 130 B2
Agdenes N 198 B6
Agen F 129 B3
Ager E 145 C4
Agerbæk DK 59 C1
Agerskov DK 64 A2
Agger DK 58 B1
Aggersund DK 58 A2
Ággius I 178 B3
Aggsbach Dorf A . . 97 C3
Aggsbach Markt A . 97 C3
Aggtelek H 99 C4
Aghalee GB 27 B4
Aghia GR 182 D4
Aghia Anna GR . . . 183 E5
Aghia Galini GR . 185 D5

Aghia Marina GR . . 188 D1
Aghia Paraskevi
  GR 186 C1
Aghia Pelagia GR . . 184 C3
Aghia Triada GR . . 184 B2
Aghiokambos GR . 182 D4
Aghios Efstratios
  I 183 D6
Aghios Kirikos GR 185 B7
Aghios Matheos
  GR 182 D1
Aghios Mironas
  GR 185 D6
Aghios Nikolaos
  GR 185 D6
Aghios Petros GR . 182 E2
Aghio Theodori
  GR 184 B4
Agiči BIH 124 C2
Agira I 177 B3
Aglientu I 178 A3
Agnières F 118 C2
Agno CH 120 B1
Agnone I 170 B2
Agolada E 140 B2
Agon Coutainville F 88 A2
Ágordo I 121 A5
Agost E 165 A4
Agramón E 158 C2
Agramunt E 147 C2
Agreda E 144 C2
Agria GR 183 D5
Agrigento I 176 B2
Agrinio GR 182 E3
Agrón E 163 A4
Agrópoli I 170 C2
Aguadulce
  Almería E 164 C2
  Sevilla E 162 A3
Agualada E 140 A2
Agua Longa P 148 A1
A Guarda E 140 C2
Aguarón E 152 A2
Aguas E 145 B3
Aguas Belas P 154 B2
Aguas de Busot E . 159 C3
Aguas de Moura P . 154 C2
Aguas Frias P 148 A2
Aguas Santas P . . . 148 A1
Aguaviva E 153 B3
Aguaviva de la Vega
  E 152 A1
A Gudiña E 141 B3
Agudo E 156 B3
Águeda P 148 B1
Aguessac F 130 A2
Agugliano I 136 B2
Aguiar P 154 C2
Aguiàr da Beira P . 148 B2
Aguilafuente E . . . 151 A3

Aab–Ail

Aguilar de Campóo
  E 142 B2
Aguilar de la Frontera
  E 163 A3
Aguilas E 164 B3
Agunnaryd S 60 C4
Ahat TR 187 D4
Ahaus D 71 B3
Åheim N 198 C2
Ahigal E 149 B3
Ahigal de Villarino
  E 149 A3
Ahillones E 156 B2
Ahlbeck
  Mecklenburg-
    Vorpommern D . . .66 C3
  Mecklenburg-
    Vorpommern D . . .74 A3
Ahlen D 81 A3
Ahlhorn D 71 B5
Ahmetbey TR 186 A2
Ahmetler TR 188 A4
Ahmetli TR 188 A2
Ahoghill GB 27 B4
Ahola FIN 197 C11
Ahrensbök D 65 B3
Ahrensburg D 72 A3
Ahrenshoop D 66 B1
Ahun F 116 A2
Åhus S 63 C2
Ahvenselkä FIN . . 197 C11
Aibar E 144 B2
Aich D 95 C4
Aicha D 96 C1
Aichach D 94 C3
Aidone I 177 B3
Aiello Cálabro I . . 175 B2
Aigen im Mühlkreis
  A 96 C1
Aigle CH 119 A3
Aignan F 128 C3
Aignay-le-Duc F . . 104 B3
Aigre F 115 C4
Aigrefeuille-d'Aunis
  F 114 B3
Aigrefeuille-sur-Maine
  F 101 B4
Aiguablava E 147 C4
Aiguebelle F 118 B3
Aigueperse F 116 A3
Aigues-Mortes F . . 131 B3
Aigues-Vives F . . . 130 B1
Aiguilles F 119 C3
Aiguillon F 129 B3
Aigurande F 103 C3
Ailefroide F 118 C3
Aillant-sur-Tholon
  F 104 B2

Ailly-sur-Noye F 90 B2
Ailly-sur-Somme F 90 B2
Aimargues F 131 B3
Aime F 118 B3
Ainaži LV 8 D4
Ainet A 109 C3
Ainhoa F 144 A2
Ainsa E 145 B4
Airaines F 90 B1
Aird GB 34 B2
Aird Asaig Tairbeart GB 31 B2
Airdrie GB 35 C4
Aire-sur-l'Adour F 128 C2
Aire-sur-la-Lys F 78 B2
Airole I 133 B3
Airolo CH 107 C3
Airvault F 102 C1
Aisey-sur-Seine F 104 B3
Aïssey F 105 B5
Aisy-sur-Armançon F 104 B3
Aiterhofen D 95 C4
Aith
Orkney GB 33 B4
Shetland GB 33 A5
Aitona E 153 A4
Aitrach D 107 B5
Aiud RO 17 B5
Aix-en-Othe F 104 A2
Aix-en-Provence F 131 B4
Aixe-sur-Vienne F 115 C5
Aix-les-Bains F 118 B2
Aizenay F 114 B2
Aizkraukle LV 8 D4
Aizpute LV 8 D2
Ajac F 146 A3
Ajaccio F 180 B1
Ajain F 116 A1
Ajaureforsen S 195 E6
Ajdovščina SLO 122 B2
Ajka H 111 B4
Ajo E 143 A3
Ajofrin E 157 A4
Ajos FIN 196 D7
Ajuda P 155 C3
Akanthou CY 181 A2
Akarca TR 189 A4
Akasztó H 112 C3
Akçakoca TR 187 A6
Akçaova TR 187 A4
Akçay TR 189 C4
Aken D 83 A4
Åkerby S 51 B4
Åkernes N 52 B3
Åkersberga S 57 A4
Åkers styckebruk S 56 A3
Åkervik N 195 E4
Akhisar TR 186 D2
Åkirkeby DK 67 A3
Akköy TR 188 B2
Akkrum NL 70 A2
Akören TR 189 B7
Åkra N 52 A2
Akranes IS 190 C3
Åkrehamn N 52 A1
Akrotiri CY 181 B1
Aksaray TR 23 B8
Akşehir TR 189 A6
Akseki TR 189 B6
Aksla N 46 A3
Aksu TR 189 C5
Aktsyabrski BY 13 B8
Akureyri IS 191 B7
Åkvåg N 53 B5
Akyazı TR 187 B5
Ål N 47 B5
Ala I 121 B4
Alaca TR 23 A8
Alacaatlı TR 186 C3
Alaçam TR 23 A8
Alaçatı TR 188 A1
Alàdei Sardi I 178 B3
Ala di Stura I 119 B4
Alaejos E 150 A2
Alagna Valsésia I 119 B4
Alagón E 144 C2
Alaior E 167 B4
Alájar E 161 B3
Alakurtti RUS 197 C13
Alakylä FIN 196 B7
Alameda E 163 A3
Alameda de la Sagra E 151 B4
Alamedilla E 163 A4
Alamillo E 156 B3
Alaminos E 151 B5
Ala-Nampa FIN 197 C9
Alanäs S 199 A12
Alandroal P 155 C3
Alange E 156 B1
Alaniemi FIN 197 D8
Alanís E 156 B2
Alanno I 169 A3
Ålansbro S 200 D3
Alanya TR 189 C7
Alap H 112 C2
Alaquàso E 159 B3
Alaraz E 150 B2
Alarcón E 158 B1
Alar del Rey E 142 B2
Alaró E 167 B2
Alaşehir TR 188 A3
Alássio I 133 A4
Ağlasun TR 189 B5
Alatoz E 158 B2
Alatri I 169 B3
Alavus FIN 8 A3
Alba
E 152 B2
I 119 C5
Alba Adriática I 136 C2
Albacete E 158 C2
Alba de Tormes E 150 B2
Alba de Yeltes E 149 B3
Albaida E 159 C3
Alba-Iulia RO 17 B5
Ålbæk DK 58 A3
Albaladejo E 158 C1
Albala del Caudillo E 156 A1
Albalat E 159 B3
Albalate de Cinca E 145 C4
Albalate del Arzobispo E 153 A3
Albalate de las Nogueras E 152 B1
Albalete de Zorita E 151 B5
Alban F 130 B1
Albánchez E 164 B2
Albanchez de Ubeda E 163 A4
Albano Laziale I 168 B2
Albanyà E 147 B3
Albaredo d'Adige I 121 B4
Albares E 151 B4
Albarracín E 152 B2
Albatana E 158 C2
Albatarrec E 153 A4
Albatera E 165 A4
Albbruck D 106 B3
Albedin E 163 A3
Albelda de Iregua E 143 B4
Albenga I 133 A4
Albens F 118 B2
Ålberga
Södermanland S 56 A2
Södermanland S 56 B2
Albergaria-a-Nova P 148 B1
Albergaria-a-Velha P 148 B1
Albergaria dos Doze P 154 B2
Alberge P 154 C2
Alberic E 159 B3
Albernoa P 160 B2
Alberobello I 173 B3
Alberoni I 122 B1
Albersdorf D 64 B2
Albersloh D 81 A3
Albert F 90 A2
Albertirsa H 112 B3
Albertville F 118 B3
Alberuela de Tubo E 145 C3
Albi F 130 B1
Albidona I 174 B2
Albinia I 168 A1
Albino I 120 B2
Albinshof D 66 C2
Albires E 142 B1
Albisola Marina I 133 A4
Albocácer E 153 B4
Albolote E 163 A4
Albondón E 164 C1
Alborea E 158 B2
Albox E 164 B2
Albrechtice nad Vitavou CZ 96 B2
Albstadt D 107 A4
Albufeira P 160 B1
Albuñol E 164 C1
Albuñuelas E 163 B4
Alburquerque E 155 B3
Alby
Öland S 63 B4
Västernorrland S 200 D1
Alcácer do Sal P 154 C2
Alcáçovas P 154 C2
Alcadozo E 158 C2
Alcafoces P 155 B3
Alcains P 155 B3
Alcaláde Guadaira E 162 A2
Alcaláde Gurrea E 144 B3
Alcaláde Henares E 151 B4
Alcaláde la Selva E 153 B3
Alcaládel Júcar E 158 B2
Alcaláde los Gazules E 162 B2
Alcaládel Río E 162 A2
Alcaládel Valle E 162 B2
Alcaláde Xivert E 153 B4
Alcalála Real E 163 A4
Álcamo I 176 B1
Alcampell E 145 C4
Alcanadre E 144 B1
Alcanar E 153 B4
Alcanede P 154 B2
Alcanena P 154 B2
Alcañices E 149 A3
Alcántara E 155 B4
Alcantarilha P 160 B1
Alcantarilla E 165 B3
Alcañiz E 153 A3
Alcaracejos E 156 B3
Alcara il Fusi I 177 A3
Alcaraz E 158 C1
Alcaria Ruiva P 160 B2
Alcarraz E 153 A4
Alcaudete E 163 A3
Alcaudete de la Jara E 150 C3
Alcázar de San Juan E 157 A4
Alcazarén E 150 A3
Alcester GB 44 A2
Alcoba E 157 A3
Alcobaça P 154 B1
Alcobendas E 151 B4
Alcocer E 151 B5
Alcochete P 154 C2
Alcoentre P 154 B2
Alcolea
Almería E 164 C2
Córdoba E 156 C3
Alcolea de Calatrava E 157 B3
Alcolea de Cinca E 145 C4
Alcolea del Pinar E 152 A1
Alcolea del Rio E 162 A2
Alcolea de Tajo E 150 C2
Alcollarin E 156 A2
Alconchel E 155 C3
Alconera E 155 C4
Alcontar E 164 B2
Alcora E 153 B3
Alcorcón E 151 B4
Alcorisa E 153 B3
Alcossebre E 153 B4
Alcoutim P 160 B2
Alcover E 147 C2
Alcoy E 159 C3
Alcsútdoboz H 112 B2
Alcubierre E 145 C3
Alcubilla de Avellaneda E 143 C3
Alcubilla de Nogales E 141 B5
Alcubillas E 157 B4
Alcublas E 159 B3
Alcúdia E 167 B3
Alcudia de Guadix E 164 B1
Alcuéscar E 155 B4
Aldbrough GB 41 B3
Aldeacentenera E 156 A2
Aldeadávila de la Ribera E 149 A3
Aldea del Cano E 155 B4
Aldea del Fresno E 151 B3
Aldea del Obispo E 149 B3
Aldea del Rey E 157 B4
Aldea de Trujillo E 156 A2
Aldealcorvo E 151 A4
Aldealuenga de Santa Maria E 151 A4
Aldeamayor de San Martin E 150 A3
Aldeanueva de Barbarroya E 150 C2
Aldeanueva del Camino E 149 B4
Aldeanueva del Codonal E 150 A3
Aldeanueva de San Bartolomé E 156 A2
Aldeapozo E 144 C1
Aldeaquemada E 157 B4
Aldea Real E 151 A3
Aldearrubia E 150 A2
Aldeaseca de la Frontera E 150 B2
Aldeasoña E 151 A3
Aldeatejada E 150 B2
Aldeavieja E 150 B3
Aldeburgh GB 45 A5
Aldehuela E 152 B2
Aldehuela de Calatañazor E 143 C4
Aldeia da Serra P 155 C3
Aldeia do Bispo P 149 B3
Aldeia do Mato P 154 B2
Aldeia Gavinha P 154 B1
Aldeire E 164 B1
Aldenhoven D 80 B2
Aldersbach D 95 C5
Aldershot GB 44 B3
Aldudes F 144 A2
Åled S 60 C2
Aledo E 165 B3
Alegria E 143 B4
Aleksandrovac SRB 127 C3
Aleksandrów Kujawski PL 76 B3
Aleksandrów Łódźki PL 86 A3
Aleksa Šantić SRB 126 B1
Ålem S 62 B4
Alençon F 89 B4
Alenquer P 154 B1
Alenya F 146 B3
Aléria F 180 A2
Alès F 131 A3
Áles I 179 C2
Alessándria I 120 C1
Alessándria della Rocca I 176 B2
Alessano I 173 C4
Ålesund N 198 C3
Alet-les-Bains F 146 B3
Alexandria
GB 34 C3
Alexandria *continued*
GR 182 C4
RO 17 D6
Alexandroupoli GR 183 C7
Aleyrac F 131 A3
Alézio I 173 B4
Alfacar E 163 A4
Alfaiates P 149 B3
Alfajarin E 153 A3
Alfambra
E 152 B2
P 160 B1
Alfândega da Fé P 149 A3
Alfarela de Jafes P 148 A2
Alfarelos P 148 B1
Alfarim P 154 C1
Alfarnate E 163 B3
Alfaro E 144 B2
Alfarràs E 145 C4
Alfaz del Pi E 159 C3
Alfedena I 169 B4
Alfeizarão P 154 B1
Alfeld
Bayern D 95 B3
Niedersachsen D 72 C2
Alfena P 148 A1
Alferce P 160 B1
Alfhausen D 71 B4
Alfonsine I 135 A5
Alford
Aberdeenshire GB 33 D4
Lincolnshire GB 41 B4
Alforja E 147 C1
Alfoz E 141 A3
Alfreton GB 40 B2
Alfta S 50 A3
Alfundão P 160 A1
Algaida E 167 B2
Algar E 162 B2
Älgarås S 55 B5
Ålgård N 52 B1
Algarinejo E 163 A3
Algarrobo E 163 B3
Algatocin E 162 B2
Algeciras E 162 B2
Algemesí E 159 B3
Algés P 154 C1
Algete E 151 B4
Alghero I 178 B2
Älghult S 62 A3
Alginet E 159 B3
Algodonales E 162 B2
Algodor
E 151 C4
P 160 B2
Algora E 151 B5
Algoso P 149 A3
Algoz P 160 B1
Älgsjö S 200 B3
Alguaire E 145 C4
Alguazas E 165 A3
Algutsrum S 63 B4
Algyö H 126 A2
Alhama de Almería E 164 C2
Alhama de Aragón E 152 A2
Alhama de Granada E 163 B4
Alhama de Murcia E 165 B3
Alhambra E 157 B4
Alhandra P 154 C1
Alhaurin de la Torre E 163 B3
Alhaurín el Grande E 163 B3
Alhendin E 163 A4
Alhóndiga E 151 B5
Alia E 156 A2
Ália I 176 B2
Aliağa TR 186 D1
Aliaga E 153 B3
Alibunar SRB 127 B2
Alicante E 165 A4
Alicún de Ortega E 164 B1
Alife I 170 B2
Alija del Infantado E 141 B5
Alijó P 148 A2
Alimena I 177 B3
Alingsås S 60 B2
Alinyà E 147 B2
Aliseda E 155 B4
Ali Terme I 177 A4
Aliveri GR 185 A5
Alixan F 117 C5
Aljaraque E 161 B2
Aljezur P 160 B1
Aljorra E 165 B3
Aljubarrota P 154 B2
Aljucen E 155 B4
Aljustrel P 160 B1
Alken B 79 B5
Alkmaar NL 70 B1
Alkoven A 96 C2
Allaines F 103 A3
Allaire F 101 B3
Allanche F 116 B2
Alland A 111 A3
Allariz E 140 B3
Allassac F 129 A4
Allauch F 131 B4
Alleen N 52 B3
Allègre F 117 B3
Allemont F 118 B3
Allendale Town GB 37 B4
Allendorf D 81 B4
Allentsteig A 97 C3
Allepuz E 153 B3
Allersberg D 95 B3
Allershausen D 95 C3
Alles E 142 A2
Allevard F 118 B3
Allgunnen S 62 A3
Allihies IRL 29 C1
Allingåbro DK 58 B3
Allmannsdorf D 107 B4
Allo E 144 B1
Alloa GB 35 B4
Allogny F 103 B4
Ålloluokta S 196 B2
Allones
Eure et Loire F 90 C1
Maine-et-Loire F 102 B2
Allonnes F 102 B2
Allons F 128 B2
Allos F 132 A2
Allstedt D 82 A3
Alltwalis GB 39 C2
Allumiere I 168 A1
Almaceda P 155 B3
Almacelles E 145 C4
Almachar E 163 B3
Almada P 154 C1
Almadén E 156 B3
Almadén de la Plata E 161 B3
Almadenejos E 156 B3
Almadrones E 151 B5
Almagro E 157 B4
Almajano E 144 C1
Almansa E 159 C2
Almansil P 160 B1
Almanza E 142 B1
Almaraz E 150 C2
Almargen E 162 B2
Almarza E 143 C4
Almásfüzitő H 112 B2
Almassora E 159 B3
Almazán E 152 A1
Almazul E 152 A1
Alme D 81 A4
Almedina E 158 C1
Almedinilla E 163 A3
Almeida
E 149 A3
P 149 B3
Almeirim P 154 B2
Almelo NL 71 B3
Almenar E 145 C4
Almenara E 159 B3
Almenar de Soria E 152 A1
Almendra P 149 B2
Almendral E 155 C4
Almendral de la Cañada E 150 B3
Almendralejo E 155 C4
Almenno San Bartolomeo I 120 B2
Almere NL 70 B2
Almería E 164 C2
Almerimar E 164 C2
Almese I 119 B4
Almexial P 160 B2
Älmhult S 63 B2
Almiropotamos GR 185 A5
Almiros GR 182 D4
Almodôvar P 160 B1
Almodóvar del Campo E 157 B3
Almodóvar del Pinar E 158 B2
Almodóvar del Río E 162 A2
Almofala P 148 B2
Almogia E 163 B3
Almoharin E 156 A1
Almonacid de la Sierra E 152 A2
Almonacid de Toledo E 157 A4
Almonaster la Real E 161 B3
Almondsbury GB 43 A4
Almonte E 161 B3
Almoradí E 165 A4
Almoraima E 162 B2
Almorox E 150 B3
Almoster P 154 B2
Almsele S 200 B3
Älmsta S 51 C5
Almudena E 164 A3
Almudévar E 145 B3
Almuñécar E 163 B4
Almunge S 51 C5
Almuradiel E 157 B4
Almussafes E 159 B3
Almvik S 62 A4
Alness GB 32 D2
Alnmouth GB 37 A5
Alnwick GB 37 A5
Åloppe S 51 C4
Álora E 163 B3
Alos d'Ensil E 146 B2
Alosno E 161 B2
Alozaina E 162 B3
Alpbach A 108 B2
Alpedrete de la Sierra E 151 B4
Alpedrinha P 148 B2
Alpen D 80 A2
Alpera E 159 C2
Alphen aan de Rijn NL 70 B1
Alpiarça P 154 B2
Alpignano I 119 B4
Alpirsbach D 93 C4
Alpu TR 187 C5
Alpuente E 159 B2
Alqueva P 160 A2
Alquézar E 145 B4
Als DK 58 B3
Alsasua E 144 B1
Alsdorf D 80 B2
Alselv DK 59 C1
Alsfeld D 81 B5
Alsike S 57 A3
Alskog S 57 C4
Alsleben D 83 A3
Alsónémedi H 112 B3
Alsótold H 112 B3
Alsóújlak H 111 B3
Alstad N 194 C6
Alstätte D 71 B3
Alsterbro S 62 B3
Alstermo S 62 B3
Alston GB 37 B4
Alsvåg N 194 B6
Alsvik N 194 C5
Alta N 192 C7
Älta S 57 A4
Altamura I 172 B2
Altarejos E 158 B1
Altaussee A 109 B4
Altavilla Irpina I 170 B2
Altavilla Silentina I 170 C3
Altdöbern D 84 A2
Altdorf
CH 107 C3
D 95 C4
Altdorf bei Nürnberg D 95 B3
Alte P 160 B1
Altea E 159 C3
Altedo I 121 C4
Altena D 81 A3
Altenau D 82 A2
Altenberg D 84 B1
Altenberge D 71 B4
Altenbruch D 64 C1
Altenburg D 83 B4
Altenfelden A 96 C1
Altengronau D 82 B1
Altenheim D 93 C3
Altenhundem D 81 A4
Altenkirchen
Mecklenburg-Vorpommern D 66 B2
Radom D 81 B3
Altenkunstadt D 82 B3
Altenmarkt
A 110 B1
D 109 A3
Altenmarkt im Pongall A 109 B4
Altensteig D 93 C4
Altentreptow D 74 A2
Altenwalde D 64 C1
Alten-weddingen D 73 B4
Alter do Chão P 155 B3
Altfraunhofen D 95 C4
Altheim
A 109 A4
D 94 B1
Althofen A 110 C1
Altınoluk TR 186 C1
Altınova TR 186 C1
Altıntaş TR 187 C5
Altınyaka TR 189 C5
Altınyayla TR 189 B4
Altkirch F 106 B2
Altlandsberg D 74 B2
Altlewin D 74 B3
Altmannstein D 95 C3
Altmorschen D 82 A1
Altmunster A 109 B4
Altnaharra GB 32 C2
Alto Campoó E 142 A2
Altofonte I 176 A2
Altomonte I 174 B2
Alton
Hampshire GB 44 B3
Staffordshire GB 40 C2
Altopáscio I 135 B3
Altötting D 109 A3
Altreichenau D 96 C1
Alt Ruppin D 74 B1
Altshausen D 107 B4
Altstätten CH 107 B4
Altura E 159 B3
Altusried D 107 B5
Alūksne LV 8 D5
Alunda S 51 B5
Alustante E 152 B2
Alva GB 35 B4
Alvaiázere P 154 B2
Alvalade P 160 B1
Älvängen S 60 B2
Alvarenga P 148 B1
Alvares P 154 A2
Alvdal N 199 C7
Älvdalen S 49 A6
Alverca P 154 C1
Alversund N 46 B2
Alvesta S 62 B2
Alvignac F 129 B4
Alvignano I 170 B2
Ålvik N 46 B3

Alvik S	50	B1
Alvimare F	89	A4
Alviobeira P	154	B2
Alvito P	160	A2
Älvkarleby S	51	B4
Älvkarleöbruk S	51	B4
Alvor P	160	B1
Alvorge P	154	B2
Alvøy N	46	B2
Älvros S	199	C11
Alvsbacka S	55	A4
Älvsered S	60	B2
Alwernia PL	86	B3
Alwinton GB	37	A4
Alyth GB	35	B4
Alytus LT	13	A6
Alzénau D	93	A5
Alzey D	93	B4
Alzira E	159	B3
Alzonne F	146	A3
Amadora P	154	C1
Åmål S	55	A3
Amalfi I	170	C2
Amaliada GR	184	B2
Amance F	105	B5
Amancey F	105	B5
Amándola I	136	C2
Amantea I	175	B2
Amarante P	148	A1
Amareleja P	161	A2
Amares P	148	A1
Amaseno I	169	B3
Amasra TR	187	A7
Amatrice I	169	A3
Amay B	79	B5
Ambarnyy RUS	3	D13
Ambazac F	115	C5
Ambelonas GR	182	D4
Amberg D	95	B3
Ambérieu-en-Bugey F	118	B2
Ambérieux-en-Dombes F	117	A4
Ambert F	117	B3
Ambès F	128	A2
Ambjörby S	49	B5
Ambjörnarp S	60	B3
Amble GB	37	A5
Ambleside GB	36	B4
Ambleteuse F	78	B1
Amboise F	102	B2
Ambrières-les-Vallées F	88	B3
Amden CH	107	B4
Amel B	80	B2
Amélia I	168	A2
Amélie-les-Bains-Palalda F	146	B3
Amelinghausen D	72	A3
Amendoa P	154	B2
Amendoeira P	160	B2
Améndola I	171	B3
Amendolara I	174	B2
Amer E	147	B3
A Merca E	140	B3
Amerongen NL	70	B2
Amersfoort NL	70	B2
Amersham GB	44	B3
Amesbury GB	44	B2
Amfíklia GR	182	E4
Amfilochia GR	182	E3
Amfipoli GR	183	C5
Amfissa GR	184	A3
Amièira P	155	C3
Amieira P	154	B3
Amieiro P	148	B1
Amiens F	90	B2
Amindeo GR	182	C3
Åminne S	60	B3
Åmli N	53	B4
Amlwch GB	38	A2
Ammanford GB	39	C3
Ammarnäs S	195	E7
Åmmeberg S	55	B5
Amorbach D	94	B1
Amorebieta E	143	A4
Amorosa I	148	A1
Amorosi I	170	B2
Åmot *Buskerud* N	48	C1
Åmot *Telemark* N	53	A3
Åmot S	50	B3
Åmotfors S	54	A3
Åmotsdal N	53	A4
Amou F	128	C2
Ampezzo I	122	A1
Ampfing D	95	C4
Ampflwang A	109	A4
Amplepuis F	117	B4
Amposta E	153	B4
Ampthill GB	44	A3
Ampudia E	142	C2
Ampuero E	143	A3
Amriswil CH	107	B4
Åmsele S	200	B6
Amstelveen NL	70	B1
Amsterdam NL	70	B1
Amstetten A	110	A1
Amtzell D	107	B4
Amulree GB	35	B4
Amurrio E	143	A4
Amusco E	142	B2
Anacapri I	170	C2
Anadia P	148	B1
Anadon E	152	B2
Anafi GR	185	C6
Anagni I	169	B3
Anamur TR	23	C7
Ananyiv UA	17	B8
Anascaul IRL	29	B1
Anáset S	2	D7
Anastaźewo PL	76	B3
Anaya de Alba E	150	B2
Ança P	148	B1
Ancaster GB	40	C3
Ancede P	148	A1
Ancenis F	101	B4
Ancerville F	91	C5
Anchuras E	156	A3
Ancona I	136	B2
Ancora P	148	A1
Ancrum GB	35	C5
Ancy-le-Franc F	104	B3
Andalo I	121	A3
Åndalsnes N	198	C4
Andance F	117	B4
Andau A	111	B4
Andebu N	53	A6
Andeer CH	107	C4
Andelfingen CH	107	B3
Andelot-Blanchville F	105	A4
Andelot-en-Montagne F	105	C4
Andenes N	194	A7
Andenne B	79	B5
Anderlues B	79	B4
Andermatt CH	107	C3
Andernach D	80	B3
Andernos-les-Bains F	128	B1
Anderslöv S	66	A2
Anderstorp S	60	B3
Andijk NL	70	B2
Andoain E	144	A1
Andocs H	112	C1
Andolsheim F	106	A2
Andorra E	153	B3
Andorra La Vella AND	146	B2
Andosilla E	144	B2
Andover GB	44	B2
Andratx E	166	B2
Andreapol RUS	9	D8
Andreas GB	36	B2
Andréspol PL	86	A3
Andrest F	145	A4
Andretta I	172	B1
Andrezieux-Bouthéon F	117	B4
Ándria I	171	B4
Andrijevica MNE	16	D3
Andritsena GR	184	B2
Andros GR	185	B5
Andrychów PL	99	B3
Andselv N	194	A9
Andújar E	157	B3
Anduze F	131	A2
Åneby N	48	B2
Åneby S	62	A2
Añes E	143	A3
Anet F	90	C1
Anfo I	121	B3
Ang S	62	A2
Anga S	57	C4
Angaïs F	145	A3
Ånge S	199	B11
Änge S	200	D1
Angeja P	148	B1
Ängelholm S	61	C2
Angeli FIN	193	D9
Ängelsberg S	50	C3
Anger A	110	B2
Angera I	120	B1
Angermünde D	74	A3
Angern A	97	C4
Angers F	102	B1
Angerville F	90	C2
Anghiari I	135	B5
Angle GB	39	C1
Anglès E	147	C3
Anglés F	130	B1
Angles F	114	B2
Anglesola E	147	C2
Angles sur l'Anglin F	115	B4
Anglet F	128	C1
Anglisídhes CY	181	B2
Anglure F	91	C3
Angoulême F	115	C4
Angoulins F	114	B2
Angsö S	56	A2
Angueira P	149	A3
Angües E	145	B3
Anguiano E	143	B4
Anguillara Sabazia I	168	A2
Anguillara Véneta I	121	B4
Anhée B	79	B4
Anholt DK	60	C1
Aniane F	130	B2
Aniche F	78	B3
Ånimskog S	54	B3
Anina RO	16	C4
Anixi GR	182	D3
Anizy-le-Château F	91	B3
Anjalankoski FIN	8	B5
Anjan S	199	B9
Ankara TR	187	C7
Ankaran SLO	122	B2
Ankarsrum S	62	A4
Ankerlia N	192	C4
Anklam D	66	C2
Ankum D	71	B4
Anlauftal A	109	B4
Anlezy F	104	C2
Ånn S	199	B9
Annaberg A	110	B2
Annaberg-Buchholz D	83	B5
Annaberg im Lammertal A	109	B4
Annaburg D	83	A5
Annahütte D	84	A1
Annalong GB	27	B5
Annan GB	36	B3
Anndalsvågen N	195	E3
Anneberg *Halland* S	60	B2
Anneberg *Jönköping* S	62	A2
Annecy F	118	B3
Annelund S	60	B3
Annemasse F	118	A3
Annenskiy Most RUS	9	B10
Annerstad S	60	C3
Annestown IRL	30	B1
Annevoie-Rouillon B	79	B4
Annonay F	117	B4
Annot F	132	B2
Annweiler D	93	B3
Ano Poroia GR	183	B5
Ano Siros GR	185	B5
Añora E	156	B3
Anould F	106	A1
Anquela del Ducado E	152	B1
Anröchte D	81	A4
Ans DK	59	B2
Ansager DK	59	C1
Ansbach D	94	B2
Anse F	117	B4
Anseroeul B	79	B3
Ansfelden A	110	A1
Ansião P	154	B2
Ansó E	144	B3
Ansoain E	144	B2
Anstruther GB	35	B5
Antalya TR	189	C5
Antas E	164	B3
Antegnate I	120	B2
Antequera E	163	A3
Anterselva di Mezzo I	108	C3
Antibes F	132	B3
Antigüedad E	142	C2
Antillo I	177	B4
Antirio GR	184	A2
Antnäs S	196	D4
An t-Ob GB	31	B1
Antoing B	79	B3
Antonin PL	86	A1
Antrain F	88	B2
Antrim GB	27	B4
Antrodoco I	169	A3
Antronapiana I	119	A5
Anttis S	196	B5
Antuzede P	148	B1
Antwerp = Antwerpen B	79	A4
Antwerpen = Antwerp B	79	A4
Anversa d'Abruzzi I	169	B3
Anvin F	78	B2
Anzat-le-Luguet F	116	B3
Anzi I	172	B1
Ánzio I	168	B2
Anzola d'Emilia I	135	A4
Anzón E	144	C2
Aoiz E	144	B2
Aosta I	119	B4
Apalhão P	155	B3
Apátfalva H	126	A2
Apatin SRB	125	B5
Apatity RUS	3	C13
Apc H	112	B3
Apécchio I	136	B1
Apeldoorn NL	70	B2
Apen D	71	A4
Apenburg D	73	B4
Apensen D	72	A2
A Peroxa E	140	B3
Apiro I	136	B2
Apli̇ki CY	181	B2
Apolda D	82	A3
Apolonia GR	185	C5
A Pontenova E	141	A3
Apostag H	112	C2
Äppelbo S	49	B6
Appennino I	136	C2
Appenzell CH	107	B4
Appiano I	108	C2
Appingedam NL	71	A3
Appleby-in-Westmorland GB	37	B4
Applecross GB	31	B3
Appledore GB	42	A2
Appoigny F	104	B2
Apremont-la-Forêt F	92	C1
Aprica I	120	A3
Apricena I	171	B3
Aprigliano I	174	B2
Aprília I	168	B2
Apt F	131	B4
Apúlia P	148	A1
Aquiléia I	122	B2
Aquilónia I	172	B1
Aquino I	169	B3
Ar S	57	C4
Arabayona E	150	A2
Arabba I	108	C2
Araç TR	23	A7
Aracena E	161	B3
Arachova GR	184	A3
Aračinovo MK	182	A3
Arad RO	126	A3
Aradac SRB	126	B2
Aradhippou CY	181	B2
Aragnouet F	145	B4
Aragona I	176	B2
Aramits F	144	A3
Aramon F	131	B3
Aranda de Duero E	143	C3
Aranda de Moncayo E	152	A2
Aranjuez E	151	B4
Arantzazu E	143	B4
Aranzueque E	151	B4
Aras de Alpuente E	159	B2
Arazede P	148	B1
Arbas F	145	B4
Árbatax I	179	C3
Arbeca E	147	C1
Arberg D	94	B2
Arbesbach A	96	C2
Arboga S	56	A1
Arbois F	105	C4
Arbon CH	107	B4
Arboréa I	179	C2
Arbório I	119	B5
Årbostad N	194	B8
Arbrå S	50	A3
Arbroath GB	35	B5
Arbúcies E	147	C3
Arbuniel E	163	A4
Arbus I	179	C2
Arcachon F	128	B1
Arce I	169	B3
Arc-en-Barrois F	105	B3
Arces-Dilo F	104	A2
Arc-et-Senans F	105	B4
Arcévia I	136	B1
Arcey F	106	B1
Archanes GR	185	D6
Archangelos GR	188	C3
Archena E	165	A3
Archez E	163	B4
Archiac F	115	C3
Archidona E	163	A3
Archiestown GB	32	D3
Archivel E	164	A3
Arcidosso I	135	C4
Arcille I	135	C4
Arcis-sur-Aube F	91	C4
Arc-lès-Gray F	105	B4
Arco I	121	B3
Arcones E	151	A4
Arcos E	143	B3
Arcos de Jalón E	152	A1
Arcos de la Frontera E	162	B2
Arcos de la Sierra E	152	B1
Arcos de las Salinas E	159	B2
Arcos de Valdevez P	148	A1
Arcozelo P	148	B2
Arc-sur-Tille F	105	B4
Arcusa E	145	B4
Arcy-sur-Cure F	104	B2
Ardagh IRL	29	B2
Årdal N	52	A2
Ardala S	55	B4
Ardales E	162	B3
Årdalstangen N	47	A4
Ardara I	178	B2
Ardara IRL	26	B2
Ardarroch GB	31	B3
Ardbeg GB	34	C1
Ardcharnich GB	32	D1
Ardchyle GB	34	B3
Ardee IRL	27	C4
Arden DK	58	B2
Ardentes F	103	C3
Ardenza I	134	B3
Ardersier GB	32	D2
Ardes F	116	B3
Ardessie GB	32	D1
Ardez CH	107	C5
Ardfert IRL	29	B2
Ardgay GB	32	D2
Ardglass GB	27	B5
Ardgroom IRL	29	C2
Ardhasig GB	31	B2
Ardino BG	183	B7
Ardisa E	144	B3
Ardkearagh IRL	29	C1
Ardlui GB	34	B3
Ardlussa GB	34	B2
Ardón E	142	B1
Ardooie B	78	B3
Ardore I	175	C2
Ardrahan IRL	28	A3
Ardre S	57	C4
Ardres F	78	B1
Ardrishaig GB	34	B2
Ardrossan GB	34	C3
Are N	52	A2
Åre S	199	B10
Areia Branca P	154	B1
Aremark N	54	A2
Arenales de San Gregorio E	157	A4
Arenas E	163	B3
Arenas de Iguña E	142	A2
Arenas del Rey E	163	B4
Arenas de San Juan E	157	A4
Arenas de San Pedro E	150	B2
Arendal N	53	B4
Arendonk B	79	A5
Arengosse F	128	B2
Arentorp S	55	B3
Arenys de Mar E	147	C3
Arenys de Munt E	147	C3
Arenzano I	133	A4
Areo E	146	B2
Areopoli GR	184	C3
Ares E	140	A2
Arès F	128	B1
Ares del Maestrat E	153	B3
Aresvika N	198	B5
Arette F	144	A3
Arévalo E	150	A3
Arez P	155	B3
Arezzo I	135	B4
Arfeuilles F	117	A3
Argalasti GR	183	D5
Argallón E	156	B2
Argamasilla de Alba E	157	A4
Argamasilla de Calatrava E	157	B3
Arganda E	151	B4
Arganil P	148	B1
Argasion GR	184	B1
Argegno I	120	B2
Argelès-Gazost F	145	A3
Argelès-sur-Mer F	146	B4
Argenta I	121	C4
Argentan F	89	B3
Argentat F	116	B1
Argentera I	132	A2
Argenteuil F	90	C2
Argenthal D	93	B3
Argentiera I	178	B2
Argentona E	147	C3
Argenton-Château F	102	C1
Argenton-sur-Creuse F	103	C3
Argentré F	102	A1
Argentré-du-Plessis F	101	A4
Argent-sur-Sauldre F	103	B4
Argirades GR	182	D1
Argithani TR	189	A6
Argos GR	184	B3
Argos Orestiko GR	182	C3
Argostoli GR	184	A1
Argote E	143	B4
Arguedas E	144	B2
Argueil F	90	B1
Arholma S	51	C6
Århus DK	59	B3
Ariano Irpino I	170	B3
Ariano nel Polésine I	121	C5
Aribe E	144	B2
Aridea GR	182	C4
Arienzo I	170	B2
Arild S	61	C2
Arileod GB	34	B1
Arinagour GB	34	B1
Ariño E	153	A3
Arinthod F	118	A2
Arisaig GB	34	B2
Arisgotas E	157	A4
Aritzo I	179	C3
Ariza E	152	A1
Årjäng S	54	A3
Arjeplog S	195	D8
Arjona E	157	C3
Arjonilla E	157	C3
Arkasa GR	188	D2
Arkelstorp S	63	B2
Arklow IRL	30	B2
Arkösund S	56	B3
Ärla S	56	A2
Arlanc F	117	B3
Arlanzón E	143	B3
Arlebosc F	117	B4
Arlena di Castro I	168	A1
Arles F	131	B3
Arles-sur-Tech F	146	B3
Arló H	113	A4
Arlon B	92	B1
Armação de Pera P	160	B1
Armadale *Highland* GB	31	B3
Armadale *West Lothian* GB	35	C4
Armagh GB	27	B4
Armamar P	148	A2
Armenistis GR	185	B7
Armeno I	119	B5
Armenteros E	150	B2
Armentières F	78	B2
Armilla E	163	A4
Armiñón E	143	B4
Armoy GB	27	A4
Armuña de Tajuña E	151	B4
Armutlu *Bursa* TR	186	B3
Armutlu *İzmir* TR	188	A2
Arnac-Pompadour F	115	C5
Arnafjord N	46	A3
Arnage F	102	B2
Arnas F	117	A4
Arnäs S	55	B4
Arnay-le-Duc F	104	B3
Arnborg DK	59	B2
Arnbruck D	95	B4
Arnea GR	183	C5
Arneberg *Hedmark* N	48	A2
Arneberg *Hedmark* N	49	B4
Arneburg D	73	B5
Arnedillo E	144	B1
Arnedo E	144	B1
Arneguy F	144	A2
Arnés E	153	B4
Árnes IS	190	A4
Årnes *Akershus* N	48	B3
Årnes *Troms* N	194	A9
Arnfels A	110	C2
Arnhem NL	70	C2
Arnissa GR	182	C3
Arno S	56	B3
Arnold GB	40	B2
Arnoldstein A	109	C4
Arnsberg D	81	A4
Arnschwang D	95	B4
Arnsdorf D	84	A1
Årnset N	198	B6
Arnside GB	37	B4
Arnstadt D	82	B2
Arnstein D	94	B1
Arnstorf D	95	C4
Arnum DK	59	C1
Aroche E	161	B3
Ároktő H	113	B4
Arolla CH	119	A4
Arolsen D	81	A5
Arona I	119	B5
Äros N	54	A1
Arosa CH	107	C4
Arosa P	148	A1
Ærøskøbing DK	65	B3
Arøsund DK	59	C2
Arouca P	148	B1
Arøysund N	54	A1
Arpajon F	90	C2
Arpajon-sur-Cère F	116	C2
Arpela FIN	196	C7
Arpino I	169	B3
Arquata del Tronto I	136	C2
Arques F	78	B2
Arques-la-Bataille F	89	A5
Arquillos E	157	B4
Arraia-Maeztu E	143	B4
Arraiolos P	154	C2
Arrancourt F	92	C2
Arras F	78	B2
Årre DK	59	C1
Arreau F	145	B4
Arredondo E	143	A3
Arrens-Marsous F	145	A3
Arriondas E	142	A1
Arroba de los Montes E	157	A3
Arrochar GB	34	B3
Arromanches-les-Bains F	88	A3
Arronches P	155	B3
Arroniz E	144	B1
Arrou F	103	A3
Arroya E	142	B2
Arroya de Cuéllar E	150	A3
Arroyal E	142	B2
Arroyo de la Luz E	155	B4
Arroyo del Ojanco E	164	A2
Arroyo de San Servan E	155	C4
Arroyomolinos de León E	161	A3
Arroyomolinos de Montánchez E	156	A1
Arruda dos Vinhos P	154	C1
Arsac F	128	B2
Ars-en-Ré F	114	B2
Arsiè I	121	B4
Arsiero I	121	B4
Årslev DK	59	C3
Ársoli I	169	A3
Ars-sur-Moselle F	92	B2
Årsunda S	50	B3
Artà E	167	B3
Arta GR	182	D3
Artajona E	144	B2
Artegna I	122	A2
Arteixo E	140	A2

Artemare F........118 B2
Arten I.........121 A4
Artena I.........169 B2
Artenay F........103 A3
Artern D.........82 A3
Artés E.........147 C2
Artesa de Segre E. 147 C2
Arth CH.........107 B3
Arthez-de-Béarn F . 145 A2
Arthon-en-Retz F . 101 B4
Arthurstown IRL ... 30 B2
Artieda E.........144 B3
Artix F.........145 A3
Artotina GR......182 E4
Artsyz UA.........17 B8
Artziniega E.......143 A3
A Rúa E.........141 B3
Arudy F.........145 A3
Arundel GB.......44 C3
Arveyres F........128 B2
Arvidsjaur S......196 D2
Arvieux F........118 C3
Arvika S.........54 A3
Åryd
  Blekinge S.......63 B3
  Kronoberg S......62 B2
Arzachena I.......178 A3
Arzacq-Arraziguet
  F.........128 C2
Árzana I.........179 C3
Arzano F.........100 B2
Aržano HR........138 B2
Arzberg D........95 A4
Arzignano I.......121 B4
Arzila P.........148 B1
Arzl im Pitztal A... 108 B1
Arzúa E.........140 B2
As B.........80 A1
Aš CZ.........83 B4
Ås N.........54 A1
Åsa S.........60 B2
Åsaa DK.........58 A3
Aşağıçiğil TR......189 A6
Ašanja SRB......127 C2
Åsarna S.........199 C11
Åsarøy N.........52 A2
Åsarp S.........55 B4
Asasp F.........145 A3
Åsbro S.........55 A6
Åsby S.........60 B2
Asby S.........62 A3
Åsbygri IS.......191 A9
Ascain F.........144 A2
Ascea I.........172 B1
Ascha D.........95 B4
Aschach an der Donau
  A.........96 C2
Aschaffenburg D .. 93 B5
Aschbach Markt A. .110 A1
Ascheberg
  Nordrhein-Westfalen
  D.........81 A3
  Schleswig-Holstein
  D.........65 B3
Aschendorf D 71 A4
Aschersleben D ... 82 A3
Asciano I.........135 B4
Ascó E.........153 A4
Asco F.........180 A2
Áscoli Piceno I ... 136 C2
Áscoli Satriano I .. 171 B3
Ascona CH.......120 A1
Ascot GB.........44 B3
Ascoux F.........103 A4
Åse N.........194 A6
Aseda E.........62 A3
Åsele S.........200 B3
Åsen
  N.........199 B8
  S.........49 A5
Asendorf D.......72 B2
Asenovgrad BG...183 A6
Åsensbruk S.....54 B3
Åseral N.........52 B3
Asfeld F.........91 B4
Åsgårdstrand N... 54 A1
Ásgarður IS......190 B1
Asgate CY.......181 B2
Ash
  Kent GB.......45 B5
  Surrey GB.......44 B3
Ashammar S.....50 B3
Ashbourne
  GB.........40 B2
  IRL.........30 A2
Ashburton GB.... 43 B3
Ashby-de-la-Zouch
  GB.........40 C2
Ashchurch GB.... 44 B1
Asheim N.........199 D8
Ashford GB......45 B4
Ashington GB 37 A5
Ashley GB.......38 B4
Ashmyany BY ... 13 A6
Ashton Under Lyne
  GB.........40 B1
Ashwell GB......44 A3
Asiago I.........121 B4
Asipovichy BY.... 13 B8
Aska FIN.........197 B9
Askam-in-Furness
  GB.........36 B3
Askeaton IRL.... 29 B3
Asker N.........48 C2
Askersund S......55 B5

Åskilje S.........200 B3
Askim N.........54 A2
Askland N.........53 B4
Äsköping S.......56 A2
Askvoll N.........46 A2
Åsljunga S.......61 C3
Asmunti FIN......197 D9
Asnæs DK.......61 D1
As Neves E.......140 B2
As Nogais E.......141 B3
Ásola I.........120 B3
Asolo I.........121 B4
Asos GR.........184 A1
Asotthalom H.....126 A1
Aspach A.........109 A4
Aspang Markt A...111 B3
Aspariegos E.....149 A1
Asparn an der Zaya
  A.........97 C4
Aspatria GB.......36 B3
Aspberg S.......55 A4
Aspe E.........165 A4
Aspet F.........145 A4
Äspö S.........63 B3
As Pontes de García
  Rodríguez E 140 A3
Aspres-sur-Buëch
  F.........132 A1
Aspsele S.......200 C4
Assafora P.......154 C1
Asse B.........79 B4
Assebakte N.....193 C9
Assel D.........72 A2
Asselborn L.......92 A1
Assémini I.......179 C2
Assenede B.......79 A3
Assens
  Aarhus Amt. DK...58 B3
  Fyns Amt. DK....59 C2
Assesse B.........79 B5
Assisi I.........136 B1
Åsskard N.......198 B5
Assling D.........108 B3
Asso I.........120 B2
Asson F.........145 A3
Ássoro I.........177 B3
Assumar P.......155 B3
Asta N.........48 A3
Astaffort F.......129 B3
Astakos GR......184 A2
Asten NL.........80 A1
Asti I.........119 C5
Astipalea GR.....188 C1
Astorga E.......141 B4
Åstorp S.........61 C2
Ástrásk S.......200 B5
Astudillo E.......142 B2
Asuni I.........179 C2
Asványbáró H 111 B4
Aszód H.........112 B3
Aszófö H.........111 C4
Atabey TR.......189 B5
Atalaia P.........154 B3
Atalandi GR.....182 E4
Atalho P.........154 C2
Átány H.........113 B4
Atanzón E........151 B4
Ataquines E......150 A3
Atarfe E.........163 A4
Atça TR.........188 B3
Ateca E.........152 A2
A Teixeira E......141 B3
Atella I.........172 B1
Atessa I.........169 A4
Ath B.........79 B3
Athboy IRL.......30 A2
Athea IRL.......29 B2
Athenry IRL.......28 A3
Athens = Athina
  GR.........185 B4
Atherstone GB ... 40 C2
Athienou CY......181 A2
Athies F.........90 B2
Athies-sous-Laon F 91 B3
Athina = Athens
  GR.........185 B4
Athleague IRL.... 28 A3
Athlone IRL......28 A4
Athna CY.........181 A2
Athy IRL.........30 B2
Atienza E.........151 A5
Atina I.........169 B3
Atkár H.........113 B3
Atlantı TR.......189 A7
Atna N.........199 D7
Åtorp S.........55 A5
Atrá N.........47 C5
Atran S.........60 B2
Atri I.........169 A3
Atripalda I.......170 C2
Atsiki GR.......183 D7
Attendorn D.......81 A3
Attichy F.........90 B3
Attigliano I......168 A2
Attigny F.........91 B4
Attleborough GB....41 C5
Ätvidaberg S.....56 B1
Atzendorf D.......73 C4
Au
  Steiermark A....110 B2
  Vorarlberg A....107 B4
  Bayern D.......95 C3
  Bayern D.......108 B2
Aub D.........94 B2
Aubagne F.......132 B1
Aubange B.......92 B1
Aubel B.........80 B1

Aubenas F........117 C4
Aubenton F.......91 B4
Auberive F........105 B4
Aubeterre-sur-Dronne
  F.........128 A3
Aubiet F.........129 C3
Aubigné F........115 B3
Aubigny F.......114 B2
Aubigny-au-Bac F . 78 B3
Aubigny-en-Artois
  F.........78 B2
Aubigny-sur-Nère
  F.........103 B4
Aubin F.........130 A1
Aubonne CH.....105 C5
Aubrac F.........116 C2
Aubusson F......116 B2
Auch F.........129 C3
Auchencairn GB ... 36 B3
Auchinleck GB ... 36 A2
Auchterarder GB.. 35 B4
Auchtermuchty GB. 35 B4
Auchtertyre GB.... 31 B3
Auchy-au-Bois F... 78 B2
Audenge F.......128 B1
Auderville F......88 A2
Audierne F.......100 A1
Audincourt F......106 B1
Audlem GB.......38 B4
Audruicq F.......78 B2
Audun-le-Roman F . 92 B1
Audun-le-Tiche F . 92 B1
Aue
  Nordrhein-Westfalen
  D.........81 A4
  Sachsen D......83 B4
Auerbach
  Bayern D.......95 B3
  Sachsen D......83 B4
Auffach A.........108 B3
Augher GB.......27 B3
Aughnacloy GB... 27 B4
Aughrim IRL.......30 B2
Augignac F.......115 C4
Augsburg D.......94 C2
Augstfehn D.......71 A4
Augusta I.........177 B4
Augusten-borg DK . 64 B2
Augustów PL.....12 B5
Aukrug D.........64 B2
Auktsjaur S......196 D2
Auldearn GB.....32 D3
Aulendorf D......107 B4
Auletta I.........172 B1
Aulla I.........134 A2
Aullène F.........180 B2
Aulnay F.........115 B3
Aulnoye-Aymeries
  F.........79 B3
Ault F.........90 A1
Aultbea GB.......31 B3
Aulum DK.......59 B1
Aulus-les-Bains F . 146 B2
Auma D.........83 B3
Aumale F.........90 B1
Aumetz F.........92 B1
Aumont-Aubrac F. 116 C3
Aunay-en-Bazois F 104 B2
Aunay-sur-Odon F . 88 A3
Aune N.........199 A10
Auneau F.......90 C1
Auneuil F.........90 B1
Auning DK.......58 B3
Aunsetra N.......199 A9
Aups F.........132 B2
Aura D.........82 B1
Auray F.........100 B3
Aurdal N.........47 B6
Aure N.........198 B5
Aurich D.........71 A4
Aurignac F.......145 A4
Aurillac F.........116 C2
Auriol F.........132 B1
Auritz-Burguette F 144 B2
Aurlandsvangen N . 47 B4
Auronzo di Cadore
  I.........109 C3
Auros F.........128 B2
Auroux F.........117 C3
Aurskog N.......48 C3
Aursmoen N.....48 C3
Ausónia I.........169 B3
Ausservillgraton A 109 C3
Austad N.........52 B3
Austbygda N.....47 B5
Austmarka N.....49 B4
Austre Moland N.. 53 B4
Austre Vikebygd N . 52 A1
Austrheim N.....46 B1
Auterive F.......146 A2
Autheuil-Authouillet
  F.........89 A5
Authon F.........132 A2
Authon-du-Perche
  F.........102 A2
Autol E.........144 B2
Autreville F......92 C1
Autrey-lès-Gray F. 105 B4
Autti FIN.........197 C10
Autun F.........104 C3
Auty-le-Châtel F.. 103 B4
Auvelais B.......79 B4
Auvillar F.........129 B3
Auxerre F.......104 B2
Auxi-le-Château F. 78 B2
Auxon F.........104 A2
Auxonne F.......105 B4

Auxy F.........104 C3
Auzances F......116 A2
Auzon F.........117 B3
Ağva TR.........187 A4
Availles-Limouzine
  F.........115 B4
Availe F.........128 C1
Avallon F.........104 B2
Avantas GR......183 C7
Avaviken S......195 E9
Avebury GB.......44 B2
A Veiga E.......141 B3
Aveiras de Cima P. 154 B2
Aveiro E.........148 A1
Avelgem B.......79 B3
Avellino I.........170 C2
Avenches CH.....106 C2
A-Ver-o-Mar P...148 A1
Aversa I.........170 C2
Avesnes-le-Comte
  F.........78 B2
Avesnes-sur-Helpe
  F.........91 A3
Avesta S.........50 B3
Avetrana I........173 B3
Avezzano I......169 A3
Avià E.........147 B2
Aviano I.........122 A1
Aviemore GB.... 32 D3
Avigliana I.......119 B4
Avigliano I.......172 B1
Avignon F.........131 B3
Ávila E.........150 B3
Avilés E.........141 A5
Avilley F.........105 B5
Avintes P........148 A1
Avinyo E.........147 C2
Ávio I.........121 B3
Avioth F.........92 B1
Avis P.........154 B3
Avize F.........91 C4
Avlonari GR......185 A5
Ávola I.........177 C4
Avon F.........90 C2
Avonmouth GB... 43 A4
Avord F.........103 B4
Avranches F......88 B2
Avril F.........92 B1
Avrillé F.........102 B1
Avtovac BIH.....139 B4
Awans B.........79 B5
Axams A.........108 B2
Axat F.........146 B3
Axbridge GB.... 43 A4
Axel NL.........79 A3
Ax-les-Thermes F . 146 B2
Axmarby S.......51 B4
Axmarsbruk S... 51 A4
Axminster GB.... 43 B3
Axvall S.........55 B4
Ay F.........91 B4
Aya E.........144 A1
Ayamonte E......161 B2
Ayancık TR.......23 A8
Ayaş TR.........187 B7
Aydın TR.........188 B2
Ayelo de Malferit E 159 C3
Ayer CH.........119 A4
Ayerbe E.........144 B3
Ayette F.........78 B2
Ayia Napa CY....181 B2
Áyia Phyla CY....181 B2
Áyios Amvrósios
  CY.........181 A2
Áyios Seryios CY . 181 A2
Áyios Theodoros
  CY.........181 A3
Aykirikçi TR......187 C5
Aylesbury GB.... 44 B3
Ayllón E.........151 A4
Aylsham GB..... 41 C5
Ayna E.........158 C1
Ayódar E.........159 B3
Ayora E.........159 B2
Ayr GB.........36 A2
Ayrancı TR.......23 C7
Ayrancılar TR.... 188 A2
Ayron F.........115 B4
Aysgarth GB..... 37 B4
Ayton GB.........35 C5
Aytos BG.........17 D7
Ayvacık TR......186 C1
Ayvalık TR.......186 C1
Aywaille B.......80 B1
Azaila E.........153 A3
Azambuja P......154 B2
Azambujeira P... 154 B2
Azanja SRB......127 C2
Azannes-et-
  Soumazannes F .. 92 B1
Azaruja P.........155 C3
Azay-le-Ferron F.. 115 B5
Azay-le-Rideau F. 102 B2
Azcoitia E.......143 A4
Azé F.........117 A4
Azeiteiros P......155 B3
Azenhas do Mar P. 154 C1
Azinhaga P......154 B2
Azinhal P.........160 B2
Azinheira dos Bairros
  P.........160 A1
Aznalcázar E.... 161 B3
Aznalcóllar E.... 161 B3
Azóia P.........154 B2
Azpeitia E.......144 A1
Azuaga E.......156 B2
Azuara E.........153 A3

Azuqueca de Henares
  E.........151 B4
Azur F.........128 C1
Azzano Décimo I.. 122 B1

B

Baad A.........107 B5
Baamonde E......140 A3
Baar CH.........107 B3
Baarle-Nassau B .. 79 A4
Baarn NL.........70 B2
Babadağ TR.....188 B3
Babadag RO.....17 C8
Babaeski TR......186 A2
Babayevo RUS ... 9 C9
Babenhausen
  Bayern D.......107 A5
  Hessen D.......93 B4
Babiak PL.........76 B3
Babice PL.........86 B3
Babigoszcz PL.... 75 A3
Babimost PL......75 B4
Babina Greda HR . 125 B4
Babócsa H.......124 A3
Bábolma H.......112 B1
Baborów PL.......86 B1
Baboszewo PL.... 77 B5
Babót H.........111 B4
Babruysk BY.....13 B8
Babsk PL.........87 A4
Bac SRB.........125 B5
Bač SRB.........125 B5
Bacares E.......164 B2
Bacău RO.........17 B7
Baccarat F.......92 C2
Bacharach D.....93 A3
Backa S.........50 B2
Bačka Palanka
  SRB.........126 B1
Backaryd S.......63 B3
Bačka Topola SRB 126 B1
Backe S.........200 C2
Bäckebo S.......62 B4
Bäckefors S......54 B3
Bäckhammar S... 55 A5
Bački Breg SRB.. 125 B4
Bački-Brestovac
  SRB.........126 B1
Bački Monoštor
  SRB.........125 B4
Bački Petrovac
  SRB.........126 B1
Bački Sokolac
  SRB.........126 B1
Bačko Gradište
  SRB.........126 B2
Bačko Novo Selo
  SRB.........125 B5
Bačko Petrovo Selo
  SRB.........126 B2
Bácoli I.........170 C2
Bacqueville-en-Caux
  F.........89 A5
Bácsalmás H.... 126 A1
Bácsbokod H.... 125 A5
Badacsonytomaj
  H.........111 C4
Badajoz E.......155 C4
Badalona E......147 C3
Badalucco I......133 B3
Bad Abbach D.... 95 C4
Bad Aibling D.... 108 B3
Badajóz E.......155 C4
Bad Aussee A.... 109 B4
Bad Bederkesa D . 72 A1
Bad Bentheim D.. 71 B4
Bad Bergzabern D . 93 B3
Bad Berka D......82 B3
Bad Berleburg D.. 81 A4
Bad Berneck D... 95 A3
Bad Bevensen D . 73 A3
Bad Bibra D......82 A3
Bad Birnbach D... 95 C5
Bad Blankenburg D 82 B3
Bad Bleiberg A... 109 C4
Bad Brambach D.. 83 B4
Bad Bramstedt D.. 64 C2
Bad Breisig D.....80 B3
Bad Brückenau D.. 82 B1
Bad Buchau D.... 107 A4
Bad Camberg D.. 81 B4
Badderen N......192 C6
Bad Doberan D... 65 B4
Bad Driburg D.... 81 A5
Bad Düben D......83 A4
Bad Dürkheim D.. 93 B4
Bad Dürrenberg D. 83 A4
Bad Dürrheim D.. 107 A3
Bad Elster D......83 B4
Bad Ems D......81 B3
Baden
  A.........111 A3
  CH.........106 B3
Baden-Baden D... 93 C4
Bad Endorf D.... 109 B3
Badenweiler D.... 106 B2
Baderna HR......122 B2
Bad Essen D......71 B5
Bad Fischau A....111 B3
Bad Frankenhausen
  D.........82 A3
Bad Freienwalde D. 74 B3
Bad Friedrichshall
  D.........93 B5

Bad Füssing D.... 96 C1
Bad Gandersheim D 82 A2
Bad Gastein A.... 109 B4
Bad Gleichenberg
  A.........110 C2
Bad Goisern A.... 109 B4
Bad Gottleuba D.. 84 B1
Bad Grund D......82 A2
Bad Hall A........110 A1
Bad Harzburg D.. 82 A2
Bad Herrenalb D.. 93 C4
Bad Hersfeld D ... 82 B1
Bad Hofgastein A . 109 B4
Bad Homburg D.. 81 B4
Bad Honnef D.... 80 B3
Bad Hönningen D. 80 B3
Badia Calavena I. 121 B4
Badia Polésine I.. 121 B4
Badia Pratáglia I.. 135 B4
Badia Tedalda I... 135 B5
Bad Iburg D......71 B5
Bad Innerlaterns A 107 B4
Bad Ischl A......109 B4
Bad Karlshafen D . 81 A5
Bad Kemmeriboden
  CH.........106 C2
Bądki PL.........69 B3
Bad Kissingen D.. 82 B2
Bad Kleinen D.... 65 C4
Bad Kohlgrub D.. 108 B2
Bad König D......93 B5
Bad Königshofen D 82 B2
Bad Köstritz D.... 83 B4
Badkowo PL.......76 B3
Bad Kreuzen A... 110 A1
Bad Kreuznach D . 93 B3
Bad Krozingen D.. 106 B2
Bad Laasphe D... 81 B4
Bad Langensalza D. 82 A2
Bad Lauchstädt D . 83 A3
Bad Lausick D.... 83 A4
Bad Lauterberg D. 82 A2
Bad Leonfelden A . 96 C2
Bad Liebenwerda D 83 A5
Bad Liebenzell D.. 93 C4
Bad Lippspringe D. 81 A4
Badljevina HR.... 124 B3
Bad Meinberg D.. 81 A4
Bad Mergentheim D 94 B1
Bad Mitterndorf A . 109 B4
Bad Münder D.... 72 B2
Bad Münstereifel D. 80 B2
Bad Muskau D.... 84 A2
Bad Nauheim D... 81 B4
Bad Nenndorf D.. 72 B2
Bad Neuenahr-Ahrweiler
  D.........80 B3
Bad Neustadt D.. 82 B2
Bad Oeynhausen D. 72 B1
Badolato I.........175 C2
Badolatosa E.....163 A3
Bad Oldesloe D.. 65 C3
Badonviller F..... 92 C2
Bad Orb D......81 B5
Badovinci SRB ... 127 C1
Bad Peterstal D... 93 C4
Bad Pyrmont D... 72 C2
Bad Radkersburg
  A.........110 C2
Bad Ragaz CH.... 107 C4
Bad Rappenau D.. 93 B5
Bad Reichenhall D 109 B4
Bad Saarow-Pieskow
  D.........74 B3
Bad Sachsa D.... 82 A2
Bad Säckingen D. 106 B2
Bad Salzdetfurth D. 72 B2
Bad Salzig D.....81 B3
Bad Salzuflen D.. 72 B1
Bad Salzungen D.. 82 B2
Bad Sankt Leonhard
  A.........110 C1
Bad Sassendorf D. 81 A4
Bad Schandau D.. 84 B2
Bad Schmiedeberg
  D.........83 A4
Bad Schönborn D . 93 B4
Bad Schussenried
  D.........107 A4
Bad Schwalbach D. 81 B4
Bad Schwartau D. 65 C3
Bad Segeberg D.. 64 C3
Bad Soden D.....81 B4
Bad Soden-Salmünster
  D.........81 B5
Bad Sooden-Allendorf
  D.........82 A1
Bad Sulza D......83 A3
Bad Sülze D......66 B1
Bad Tatzmannsdorf
  A.........111 B3
Bad Tennstedt D.. 82 A2
Bad Tölz D......108 B2
Badules E.......152 A2
Bad Urach D.....94 C1
Bad Vellach A.... 110 C1
Bad Vilbel D......81 B4
Bad Vöslau A.....111 B3
Bad Waldsee D... 107 B4
Bad Wiessee D... 108 B2
Bad Wildungen D.. 81 A5
Bad Wilsnack D.. 73 B4
Bad Windsheim D. 94 B2
Bad Wörishofen D. 108 A1
Bad Wurzach D.. 107 B4
Bad Zwesten D... 81 A5
Bad Zwischenahn D 71 A5
Baells E.........145 C4

Baena E . . . 163 A3
Baesweiler D . . . 80 B2
Baeza E . . . 157 C4
Baflo NL . . . 71 A3
Baga E . . . 147 B2
Bagaladi I . . . 175 C1
Bagenkop DK . . . 65 B3
Baggetorp S . . . 56 A2
Bagh a Chaisteil GB 31 C1
Bagheria I . . . 176 A2
Bagn N . . . 47 B6
Bagnacavallo I . . . 135 A4
Bagnáia I . . . 168 A2
Bagnara Cálabra I . . 175 C1
Bagnasco I . . . 133 A4
Bagnères-de-Bigorre
  F . . . 145 A4
Bagnères-de-Luchon
  F . . . 145 B4
Bagni del Másino I 120 A2
Bagni di Lucca I . . 135 A3
Bagni di Rabbi I . . . 121 A3
Bagni di Tívoli I . . . 168 B2
Bagno di Romagna
  I . . . 135 B4
Bagnoles-de-l'Orne
  F . . . 89 B3
Bagnoli dei Trigno
  I . . . 170 B2
Bagnoli di Sopra I . 121 B4
Bagnoli Irpino I . . . 170 C3
Bagnolo Mella I . . . 120 B3
Bagnols-en-Forêt
  F . . . 132 B2
Bagnols-sur-Cèze
  F . . . 131 A3
Bagnorégio I . . . 168 A2
Bagolino I . . . 121 B3
Bagrationovsk RUS 12 A4
Bagrdan SRB . . . 127 C3
Báguena E . . . 152 A2
Bahabón de Esgueva
  E . . . 143 C3
Bahillo E . . . 142 B2
Báia delle Zágare
  I . . . 171 B4
Báia Domízia I . . . 169 B3
Baia Mare RO . . . 17 B5
Baiano I . . . 170 C2
Baião P . . . 148 A1
Baiersbronn D . . . 93 C4
Baiersdorf D . . . 94 B3
Baignes-Ste Radegonde
  F . . . 115 C3
Baigneux-les-Juifs
  F . . . 104 B3
Baildon GB . . . 40 B2
Bailén E . . . 157 B4
Baileux B . . . 91 A4
Bailieborough IRL . 27 C4
Bailleul F . . . 78 B2
Baillonville B . . . 79 B5
Bailó E . . . 144 B3
Bain-de-Bretagne
  F . . . 101 B4
Bains F . . . 117 B3
Bains-les-Bains F . 105 A5
Bainton GB . . . 40 B3
Baio E . . . 140 A2
Baiona E . . . 140 B2
Bais F . . . 89 B3
Baiso I . . . 134 A3
Baiuca P . . . 148 B2
Baja H . . . 125 A4
Bajánsenye H . . . 111 C3
Bajina Bašta SRB . 127 D1
Bajmok SRB . . . 126 B1
Bajna H . . . 112 B2
Bajovo Polje MNE . 139 B4
Bajša SRB . . . 126 B1
Bak H . . . 111 C3
Bakar HR . . . 123 B3
Bakewell GB . . . 40 B2
Bakio E . . . 143 A4
Bakka N . . . 47 C6
Bakkafjörður IS . . . 191 A11
Bakkagerði IS . . . 191 B12
Bække DK . . . 59 C2
Bakken N . . . 48 B3
Baklan TR . . . 189 B4
Bækmarksbro DK . 58 B1
Bakonybél H . . . 111 B4
Bakonycsernye H . .112 B2
Bakonyjákó H . . . 111 B4
Bakonyszentkirály
  H . . . 111 B4
Bakonyszombathely
  H . . . 112 B1
Bakov nad Jizerou
  CZ . . . 84 B2
Bąkowice PL . . . 87 A5
Baks H . . . 113 C4
Baksa H . . . 125 B4
Bakum D . . . 71 B5
Bala GB . . . 38 B3
Bâlă RO . . . 23 B7
Balaguer E . . . 145 C4
Balassagyarmat H .112 A3
Balástya H . . . 113 C4
Balatonakali H . . .111 C4
Balatonalmádi H . .112 B2
Balatonboglár H . .111 C4
Balatonbozsok H . 112 C2
Balatonederics H . .111 C4
Balatonfenyves H . 111 C4
Balatonföldvár H . 112 C1
Balatonfüred H . . 112 C1

Balatonfüzfö H . . .112 B2
Balatonkenese H . .112 B2
Balatonkiliti H . . . 112 C2
Balatonlelle H . . . 111 C4
Balatonszabadi H . 112 C2
Balatonszemes H . .111 C4
Balatonszentgyörgy
  H . . . 111 C4
Balazote E . . . 158 C1
Balbeggie GB . . . 35 B4
Balbigny F . . . 117 B4
Balboa E . . . 141 B4
Balbriggan IRL . . . 30 A2
Balchik BG . . . 17 D8
Balçova TR . . . 188 A2
Baldock GB . . . 44 B3
Bale HR . . . 122 B2
Baleira E . . . 141 A3
Baleizao P . . . 160 A2
Balen B . . . 79 A5
Balerma E . . . 164 C2
Balestrand N . . . 46 A3
Balestrate I . . . 176 A2
Balfour GB . . . 33 B4
Bälganet S . . . 63 B3
Balgari BG . . . 17 D7
Balıkesir TR . . . 186 C2
Balıklıçeşme TR . 186 B2
Bälinge S . . . 51 C4
Balingen D . . . 107 A3
Balingsta S . . . 56 A3
Balintore GB . . . 32 D3
Balizac F . . . 128 B2
Balk NL . . . 70 B2
Balkbrug NL . . . 71 B3
Balla IRL . . . 28 A2
Ballachulish GB . . 34 B2
Ballaghaderreen
  IRL . . . 26 C2
Ballancourt-sur-
  Essonne F . . . 90 C2
Ballantrae GB . . . 36 A2
Ballao I . . . 179 C3
Ballasalla GB . . . 36 B2
Ballater GB . . . 32 D3
Ballen DK . . . 59 C3
Ballenstedt D . . . 82 A3
Ballerias E . . . 145 C3
Balleroy F . . . 88 A3
Ballerup DK . . . 61 D2
Ballesteros de Calatrava
  E . . . 157 B4
Ballı TR . . . 186 B2
Ballina IRL . . . 26 B1
Ballinalack IRL . . . 30 A1
Ballinamore IRL . . 26 B3
Ballinascarty IRL . . 29 C3
Ballinasloe IRL . . . 28 A3
Ballindine IRL . . . 28 A3
Balling DK . . . 58 B1
Ballingarry
  Limerick IRL . . . 29 B3
  Tipperary IRL . . . 30 B1
Ballingeary IRL . . . 29 C2
Ballinhassig IRL . . 29 C3
Ballinluig GB . . . 35 B4
Ballino I . . . 121 B3
Ballinrobe IRL . . . 28 A2
Ballinskelligs IRL . 29 C1
Ballinspittle IRL . . 29 C3
Ballintra IRL . . . 26 B2
Ballivor IRL . . . 30 A2
Ballobar E . . . 153 A4
Ballon
  F . . . 102 A2
  IRL . . . 30 B2
Ballószög H . . . 112 C3
Ballsh AL . . . 182 C1
Ballstad N . . . 194 B4
Ballum DK . . . 64 A1
Ballybay IRL . . . 27 B4
Ballybofey IRL . . . 26 B3
Ballybunion IRL . . 29 B2
Ballycanew IRL . . . 30 B2
Ballycarry GB . . . 27 B5
Ballycastle
  GB . . . 27 A4
  IRL . . . 26 B1
Ballyclare GB . . . 27 B5
Ballyconneely IRL . 28 A1
Ballycotton IRL . . . 29 C3
Ballycroy IRL . . . 26 B1
Ballydehob IRL . . . 29 C2
Ballyferriter IRL . . 29 B1
Ballygawley GB . . . 27 B3
Ballygowan GB . . . 27 B5
Ballyhaunis IRL . . . 28 A3
Ballyheige IRL . . . 29 B2
Ballyjamesduff IRL . 27 C3
Ballylanders IRL . . 29 B3
Ballylynan IRL . . . 30 B1
Ballymahon IRL . . . 28 A4
Ballymena GB . . . 27 B4
Ballymoe IRL . . . 28 A3
Ballymoney GB . . . 27 A4
Ballymore IRL . . . 28 A4
Ballymote IRL . . . 26 B2
Ballynacorra IRL . . 29 C3
Ballynagore IRL . . . 30 A1
Ballynahinch GB . . 27 B5
Ballynure GB . . . 27 B5
Ballyragget IRL . . . 30 B1
Ballysadare IRL . . . 26 B2
Ballyshannon IRL . . 26 B2
Ballyvaughan IRL . . 28 A2
Ballyvourney IRL . . 29 C2
Ballywalter GB . . . 27 B5
Balmaclellan GB . . 36 A2

Balmaseda E . . . 143 A3
Balmazújváros H . .113 B5
Balme I . . . 119 B4
Balmedie GB . . . 33 D4
Balmuccia I . . . 119 B5
Balna-paling GB . . 32 D2
Balneario de Panticosa
  E . . . 145 B3
Balotaszállás H . . . 126 A1
Balsa P . . . 148 A2
Balsareny E . . . 147 C2
Balsorano-Nuovo I 169 B3
Bålsta S . . . 57 A3
Balsthal CH . . . 106 B2
Balta UA . . . 17 A8
Baltanás E . . . 142 C2
Baltar E . . . 140 C3
Baltasound GB . . . 33 A6
Bălţi MD . . . 17 B7
Baltimore IRL . . . 29 C2
Baltinglass IRL . . . 30 B2
Baltiysk RUS . . . 69 A4
Bałtów PL . . . 87 A5
Balugães P . . . 148 A1
Bælum DK . . . 58 B3
Balve D . . . 81 A3
Balvi LV . . . 8 D5
Balvicar GB . . . 34 B2
Balya TR . . . 186 C2
Balzo I . . . 136 C2
Bamberg D . . . 94 B2
Bamburgh GB . . . 37 A5
Banatska Palanka
  SRB . . . 127 C3
Banatski Brestovac
  SRB . . . 127 C2
Banatski Despotovac
  SRB . . . 126 B2
Banatski Dvor
  SRB . . . 126 B2
Banatski-Karlovac
  SRB . . . 127 B3
Banatsko Aranđelovo
  SRB . . . 126 A2
Banatsko-Novo Selo
  SRB . . . 127 C2
Banaz TR . . . 187 D4
Banbridge GB . . . 27 B4
Banbury GB . . . 44 A2
Banchory GB . . . 33 D4
Bande
  B . . . 79 B5
  E . . . 140 B3
Bandholm DK . . . 65 B4
Bandırma TR . . . 186 B2
Bandol F . . . 132 B1
Bandon IRL . . . 29 C3
Bañeres E . . . 159 C3
Banff GB . . . 33 D4
Bangor
  F . . . 100 B2
  Down GB . . . 27 B5
  Gwynedd GB . . . 38 A2
  IRL . . . 26 B1
Bangsund N . . . 199 A8
Banie PL . . . 74 A3
Banja Koviljača
  SRB . . . 127 C1
Banjaloka SLO . . . 123 B3
Banja Luka BIH . . . 124 C3
Banjani SRB . . . 127 C1
Banja Vrućica BIH . 125 C3
Banka SK . . . 98 C1
Bankekind S . . . 56 B1
Bankend GB . . . 36 A3
Bankeryd S . . . 62 A2
Bankfoot GB . . . 35 B4
Bankso BG . . . 183 B5
Banloc RO . . . 126 B3
Bannalec F . . . 100 B2
Bannes F . . . 91 C3
Bannockburn GB . . 35 B4
Bañobárez E . . . 149 B3
Bañon E . . . 152 B2
Banon F . . . 132 A1
Baños E . . . 149 B4
Baños de Gigonza
  E . . . 162 B2
Baños de la Encina
  E . . . 157 B4
Baños de Molgas
  E . . . 140 B3
Baños de Rio Tobia
  E . . . 143 B4
Baños de Valdearados
  E . . . 143 C3
Bánov CZ . . . 98 C1
Banova Jaruga HR 124 B2
Bánovce nad Bebravou
  SK . . . 98 C2
Banovići BIH . . . 139 A4
Banovići Selo BIH . 139 A4
Bánréve H . . . 99 C4
Bansin D . . . 66 C3
Banská Belá SK . . . 98 C2
Banská Bystrica
  SK . . . 99 C3
Banská Štiavnica
  SK . . . 98 C2
Bansko BG . . . 183 B5
Banstead GB . . . 44 B3
Banteer IRL . . . 29 B3
Bantheville F . . . 91 B5
Bantry IRL . . . 29 C2
Bantzenheim F . . . 106 B2
Banyalbufar E . . . 166 B2
Banyoles E . . . 147 B3
Banyuls-sur-Mer F 146 B4

Bapaume F . . . 90 A2
Bar
  MNE . . . 16 D3
  UA . . . 13 D7
Barabhas GB . . . 31 A2
Baračići BIH . . . 138 A2
Baracs H . . . 112 C2
Baracska H . . .112 B2
Barahona E . . . 151 A5
Barajas de Melo E . 151 B5
Barakaldo E . . . 143 A4
Baralla E . . . 141 B3
Barañain E . . . 144 B2
Baranello I . . . 170 B2
Baranów Sandomierski
  PL . . . 87 B5
Barão de Melo P . 154 B2
Baraqueville F . . . 130 A1
Barasoain E . . . 144 B2
Barbacena P . . . 155 C3
Barbadás E . . . 140 B3
Barbariga HR . . . 122 C2
Barbaros TR . . . 186 B2
Barbastro E . . . 145 B4
Barbate E . . . 162 B2
Barbatona E . . . 152 A1
Barbâtre F . . . 114 B1
Barbazan F . . . 145 A4
Barbeitos E . . . 141 A3
Barberino di Mugello
  I . . . 135 A4
Barbezieux-St Hilaire
  F . . . 115 C3
Barbonne-Fayel F . 91 C3
Barbotan-les-Thermes
  F . . . 128 C2
Barby D . . . 73 C4
Bárcabo E . . . 145 B4
Barca de Alva P . . 149 A3
Barcarrota E . . . 155 C4
Barcellona-Pozzo di
  Gotto I . . . 177 A4
Barcelona E . . . 147 C3
Barcelonette F . . . 132 A2
Barcelos P . . . 148 A1
Bárcena del Monasterio
  E . . . 141 A4
Barcena de Pie de
  Concha E . . . 142 A2
Barchfeld D . . . 82 B2
Barcin PL . . . 76 B2
Barcino PL . . . 68 A1
Barco P . . . 148 B2
Barcones E . . . 151 A5
Barcs H . . . 124 B3
Barcus F . . . 144 A3
Bardejov SK . . . 12 D4
Bárcis I . . . 122 A1
Bardi I . . . 120 C2
Bardney GB . . . 40 B3
Bardo PL . . . 85 B4
Bardolino I . . . 121 B3
Bardonécchia I . . .118 B3
Bardoňovo SK . . . 112 A2
Barèges F . . . 145 B4
Barenstein D . . . 83 B5
Barentin F . . . 89 A4
Barenton F . . . 88 B3
Barevo BIH . . . 138 A3
Barfleur F . . . 88 A2
Barga I . . . 134 A3
Bargas E . . . 151 C3
Barge I . . . 119 C4
Bargemon F . . . 132 B2
Barghe I . . . 120 B3
Bargoed GB . . . 39 C3
Bargrennan GB . . . 36 A2
Bargteheide D . . . 64 C3
Barham GB . . . 45 B5
Bari I . . . 173 A2
Barič Draga HR . . 137 A4
Barilović HR . . . 123 B4
Bari Sardo I . . . 179 C3
Barisciano I . . . 169 A3
Barjac F . . . 131 A3
Barjols F . . . 132 B1
Barjon F . . . 105 B3
Barkald N . . . 199 D7
Barkowo
  Dolnośląskie PL . .85 A4
  Pomorskie PL . . 68 B2
Bar-le-Duc F . . . 91 C5
Barles F . . . 132 A2
Barletta I . . . 171 B4
Barlinek PL . . . 75 B4
Barmouth GB . . . 38 B2
Barmstedt D . . . 64 C2
Barnard Castle GB . 37 B5
Barnarp S . . . 62 A2
Bârnau D . . . 95 B4
Bärnbach A . . .110 B2
Barneberg D . . . 73 B4

Barnenitz D . . . 74 B1
Barnet GB . . . 44 B3
Barnetby le Wold
  GB . . . 40 B3
Barneveld NL . . . 70 B2
Barneville-Carteret
  F . . . 88 A2
Barnoldswick GB . 40 B1
Barnowko PL . . . 75 B3
Barnsley GB . . . 40 B2
Barnstädt D . . . 83 A3
Barnstaple GB . . . 42 A2
Barnstorf D . . . 72 B1
Barntrup D . . . 72 C2
Baron F . . . 90 B2
Baronissi I . . . 170 C2
Barqueiro P . . . 154 B2
Barquinha P . . . 154 B2
Barr
  F . . . 93 C3
  GB . . . 36 A2
Barra P . . . 148 B1
Barraco E . . . 150 B3
Barracas E . . . 159 A3
Barrado E . . . 150 B2
Barrafranca I . . . 177 B3
Barranco do Velho
  P . . . 160 B2
Barrancos P . . . 161 A3
Barrax E . . . 158 B1
Barrbaar D . . . 94 C2
Barre-des-Cevennes
  F . . . 130 A2
Barreiro P . . . 154 C1
Barreiros E . . . 141 A3
Barrême F . . . 132 B2
Barret-le-Bas F . . 132 A1
Barrhead GB . . . 34 C3
Barrhill GB . . . 36 A2
Barrio de Nuesra
  Señora E . . . 142 B1
Barrowford GB . . 40 B1
Barrow-in-Furness
  GB . . . 36 B3
Barrow upon Humber
  GB . . . 40 B3
Barruecopardo E . 149 A3
Barruelo de Santullán
  E . . . 142 B2
Barruera E . . . 145 B4
Barry GB . . . 39 C3
Bårse DK . . . 65 A4
Barsinghausen D . 72 B2
Barssel D . . . 71 A4
Bartholomä D . . . 94 C1
Bartin TR . . . 187 A7
Barton upon Humber
  GB . . . 40 B3
Barúmini I . . . 179 C2
Baruth D . . . 74 B2
Barvaux B . . . 80 B1
Barver D . . . 72 B1
Barwatd PL . . . 99 B3
Barwice PL . . . 68 B1
Barysaw BY . . . 13 A8
Barzana E . . . 141 A5
Bârzava RO . . . 16 B4
Bárzio I . . . 120 B2
Bas E . . . 147 B3
Bašaid SRB . . . 126 B2
Basaluzzo I . . . 120 C1
Basarabeasca MD . 17 B8
Basauri E . . . 143 A4
Baschi I . . . 168 A2
Baschurch GB . . . 38 B4
Basconcillos del Tozo
  E . . . 143 B3
Bascones de Ojeda
  E . . . 142 B2
Basécles B . . . 79 B3
Basel CH . . . 106 B2
Basélice I . . . 170 B2
Basildon GB . . . 45 B4
Basingstoke GB . . 44 B2
Baška
  CZ . . .98 B2
  HR . . .123 C3
Baška Voda HR . . 138 B2
Bäsksjö S . . . 200 B3
Båsmakçı TR . . . 189 B5
Basovizza I . . . 122 B2
Bassacutena I . . . 178 A3
Bassano del Grappa
  I . . . 121 B4
Bassano Romano I 168 A2
Bassecourt CH . . . 106 B2
Bassella E . . . 147 B2
Bassevuovdde N . . 193 D9
Bassou F . . . 104 B2
Bassoues F . . . 128 C3
Bassum D . . . 72 B1
Båstad S . . . 61 C2
Bastardo I . . . 136 C1
Bastelica F . . . 180 A2
Bastelicaccia F . . 180 B1
Bastia
  F . . . 180 A2
  I . . . 136 B1
Bastogne B . . . 92 A1
Baston GB . . . 40 C3
Bastträsk S . . . 200 B6
Bata H . . . 125 A4
Batajnica SRB . . . 127 C2
Batak BG . . . 183 B6

Batalha P . . . 154 B2
Bátaszék H . . . 125 A4
Batea E . . . 153 A4
Batelov CZ . . . 97 B3
Bath GB . . . 43 A4
Bathgate GB . . . 35 C4
Batida H . . . 126 A2
Batignano I . . . 135 C4
Batina HR . . . 125 B4
Bátka SK . . . 99 C4
Batković BIH . . . 125 C5
Batley GB . . . 40 B2
Batnfjordsøra N . . 198 C4
Batočina SRB . . . 127 C3
Bátonyterenye H . .113 B3
Batrina HR . . . 125 B3
Bátsfjord N . . . 193 B13
Båtskärsnäs S . . . 196 D6
Battaglia Terme I . 121 B4
Bätterkinden CH . . 106 B2
Battice B . . . 80 B1
Battipáglia I . . . 170 C2
Battle GB . . . 45 C4
Battonya H . . . 126 A3
Batuša SRB . . . 127 C3
Bátya H . . . 112 C2
Bau I . . . 179 C2
Baud F . . . 100 B2
Baudour B . . . 79 B3
Baugé F . . . 102 B1
Baugy F . . . 103 B4
Bauma CH . . . 107 B3
Baume-les-Dames
  F . . . 105 B5
Baumholder D . . . 93 B3
Baunatal D . . . 81 A5
Baunei I . . . 178 B3
Bauska LV . . . 8 D4
Bautzen D . . . 84 A2
Bavanište SRB . . . 127 C2
Bavay F . . . 79 B3
Bavilliers F . . . 106 B1
Bavorov CZ . . . 96 B2
Bawdsey GB . . . 45 A5
Bawinkel D . . . 71 B4
Bawtry GB . . . 40 B2
Bayat TR . . . 187 D5
Bayel F . . . 105 A3
Bayeux F . . . 88 A3
Bayındır TR . . . 188 A2
Bayon F . . . 92 C2
Bayonne F . . . 128 C1
Bayons F . . . 132 A2
Bayramiç TR . . . 186 C1
Bayreuth D . . . 95 B3
Bayrischzell D . . .108 B3
Baza E . . . 164 B2
Bazas F . . . 128 B2
Baziege F . . . 146 A2
Bazoches-les-
  Gallerandes F . . 103 A4
Bazoches-sur-Hoëne
  F . . . 89 B4
Bazzano I . . . 135 A4
Beaconsfield GB . . 44 B3
Beade E . . . 140 B2
Beadnell GB . . . 37 A5
Beaminster GB . . . 43 B4
Bearsden GB . . . 34 C3
Beas E . . . 161 B3
Beasain E . . . 144 A1
Beas de Segura E . 164 A2
Beattock GB . . . 36 A3
Beaubery F . . . 117 A4
Beaucaire F . . . 131 B3
Beaufort
  F . . . 118 B3
  IRL . . .29 B2
Beaufort-en Vallée
  F . . . 102 B1
Beaugency F . . . 103 B3
Beaujeu
  Alpes-de-Haute-
  Provence F . . 132 A2
  Rhône F . . . 117 A4
Beaulac F . . . 128 B2
Beaulieu
  F . . . 103 B4
  GB . . . 44 C2
Beaulieu-sous-la-Roche
  F . . . 114 B2
Beaulieu-sur-Dordogne
  F . . . 129 B4
Beaulieu-sur-Mer
  F . . . 133 B3
Beaulon F . . . 104 C2
Beauly GB . . . 32 D2
Beaumaris GB . . . 38 A2
Beaumesnil F . . . 89 A4
Beaumetz-lès-Loges
  F . . . 78 B2
Beaumont
  B . . . 79 B4
  F . . . 129 B3
Beaumont-de-Lomagne
  F . . . 129 C3
Beaumont-du-Gâtinais
  F . . . 103 A4
Beaumont-en-Argonne
  F . . . 91 B5
Beaumont-Hague F. 88 A2
Beaumont-la-Ronce
  F . . . 102 B2
Beaumont-le-Roger
  F . . . 89 A4

Beaumont-sur-Oise F 90 B2
Beaumont-sur-Sarthe F 102 A2
Beaune F 105 B3
Beaune-la-Rolande F 103 A4
Beaupréau F 101 B5
Beauraing B 91 A4
Beaurepaire F 117 B5
Beaurepaire-en-Bresse F 105 C4
Beaurières F 132 A1
Beauvais F 90 B2
Beauval F 90 A2
Beauville F 129 B3
Beauvoir-sur-Mer F 114 B1
Beauvoir-sur-Niort F 114 B3
Beba Veche RO 126 A2
Bebertal D 73 B4
Bebington GB 38 A3
Bebra D 82 B1
Bebrina HR 125 B3
Beccles GB 45 A5
Becedas E 150 B2
Beceite E 153 B4
Bečej SRB 126 B2
Becerreá E 141 B3
Becerril de Campos E 142 B2
Bécherel F 101 A4
Bechhofen D 94 B2
Bechyně CZ 96 B2
Becilla de Valderaduey E 142 B1
Beckfoot GB 36 B3
Beckingham GB 40 B3
Beckum D 81 A4
Beco P 154 B2
Bécon-les-Granits F 102 B1
Bečov nad Teplou CZ 83 B4
Becsehely H 111 C3
Bedale GB 37 B5
Bedames E 143 A3
Bédar E 164 B3
Bédarieux F 130 B2
Bédarrides F 131 A3
Bedburg D 80 B2
Beddgelert GB 38 A2
Beddingestrand S 66 B2
Bédée F 101 A4
Bedegkér H 112 C2
Beden TR 189 C7
Bedford GB 44 A3
Będków PL 87 A3
Bedlington GB 37 A5
Bedlno PL 77 B4
Bedmar E 163 A4
Bédoin F 131 A4
Bedónia I 134 A2
Bedretto CH 107 C3
Bedsted DK 58 B1
Bedum NL 71 A3
Bedwas GB 39 C3
Bedworth GB 40 C2
Będzin PL 86 B3
Beekbergen NL 70 B2
Beek en Donk NL 80 A1
Beelen D 71 C5
Beelitz D 74 B1
Beer GB 43 B3
Beerfelde D 74 B3
Beerfelden D 93 B4
Beernem B 78 A3
Beeskow D 74 B3
Beetsterzwaag NL 70 A3
Beetzendorf D 73 B4
Beflelay CH 106 B2
Begaljica SRB 127 C2
Bégard F 100 A2
Begejci SRB 126 B2
Begijar E 157 C4
Begijnendijk B 79 A4
Begndal N 48 B1
Begues E 147 C2
Beguildy GB 39 B3
Begur E 147 C4
Beho B 80 B1
Behringen D 82 A2
Beilen NL 71 B3
Beilngries D 95 B3
Beine-Nauroy F 91 B4
Beinwil CH 106 B3
Beiseförth D 82 A1
Beith GB 34 C3
Beitostølen N 47 A5
Beiuş RO 16 B5
Beja P 160 A2
Béjar E 149 B4
Bekçiler TR 189 C4
Békés H 113 C5
Békéscsaba H 113 C5
Bekilli TR 189 A4
Bekkarfjord N 193 B11
Bela SK 98 B2
Bélâbre F 115 B5
Bela Crkva SRB 127 C3
Belalcázar E 156 B2
Belánad Radbuzou CZ 95 B4
Belanovica SRB 127 C2
Bélapátfalva H 113 A4
Bělápod Bezdězem CZ 84 B2
Belcaire F 146 B2
Bełchatów PL 86 A3
Belchite E 153 A3
Bělčice CZ 96 B1
Belcoo GB 26 B3
Belecke D 81 A4
Beled H 111 B4
Belej HR 123 C3
Beleño E 142 A1
Bélesta F 146 B2
Belevi TR 188 A2
Belfast GB 27 B5
Belford GB 37 A5
Belfort F 106 B1
Belgentier F 132 B1
Belgern D 83 A5
Belgioioso I 120 B2
Belgodère F 180 A2
Belgooly IRL 29 C3
Belgrade = Beograd SRB 127 C2
Belhade F 128 B2
Belica HR 124 A2
Beli Manastir HR 125 B4
Belin-Bèliet F 128 B2
Belinchón E 151 B4
Belišće HR 125 B4
Bělkovice-Lašťany CZ 98 B1
Bella I 172 B1
Bellac F 115 B5
Bellágio I 120 B2
Bellananagh IRL 27 C3
Bellano I 120 A2
Bellária I 136 A1
Bellavary IRL 26 C1
Belleau F 90 B3
Belleek GB 26 B2
Bellegarde
Gard F 131 B3
Loiret F 103 B4
Bellegarde-en-Diois F 132 A1
Bellegarde-en-Marche F 116 B2
Bellegarde-sur-Valserine F 118 A2
Belle-Isle-en-Terre F 100 A2
Bellême F 89 B4
Bellenaves F 116 A3
Bellentre F 118 B3
Bellevaux F 118 A3
Bellevesvre F 105 C4
Belleville F 117 A4
Belleville-sur-Vie F 114 B2
Bellevue-la-Montagne F 117 B3
Belley F 118 B2
Bellheim D 93 B4
Bellinge DK 59 C3
Bellingham GB 37 A4
Bellinzago Novarese I 120 B1
Bellinzona CH 120 A2
Bell-lloc d'Urgell E 153 A4
Bello E 152 B2
Bellpuig d'Urgell E 147 C2
Bellreguart E 159 C3
Bellsbank GB 36 A2
Belltall E 147 C2
Belluno I 121 A5
Bellver de Cerdanya E 146 B2
Bellvis E 147 C1
Bélmez E 156 B2
Belmez de la Moraleda E 163 A4
Belmont GB 33 A6
Belmont-de-la-Loire F 117 A4
Belmonte
Asturias E 141 A4
Cuenca E 158 B1
P 148 B2
Belmonte de San José E 153 B3
Belmonte de Tajo E 151 B4
Belmont-sur-Rance F 130 B1
Belmullet IRL 26 B1
Belobreşca RO 127 C3
Beloeil B 79 B3
Belogradchik BG 16 D5
Belokorovichi UA 13 C8
Belorado E 143 B3
Belotič SRB 127 C1
Bělotin CZ 98 B1
Belovo BG 183 A6
Belozersk RUS 9 C10
Belp CH 106 C2
Belpasso I 177 B3
Belpech F 146 A2
Belper GB 40 B2
Belsay GB 37 A5
Belsk Duzy PL 87 A4
Beltinci SLO 111 C3
Beltra IRL 26 C1
Belturbet IRL 27 B3
Beluša SK 98 B2
Belvedere Maríttimo I 174 B1
Belver de Cinca E 153 A4
Belver de los Montes E 142 C1
Belvès F 129 B3
Belvezet F 130 A2
Belvis de la Jara E 150 C3
Belvis de Monroy E 150 C2
Belyy RUS 9 E8
Belz F 100 B2
Bełżec PL 13 C5
Belzig D 73 B5
Bembibre E 141 B4
Bembridge GB 44 C2
Bemmel NL 80 A1
Bemposta
Bragança P 149 A3
Santarém P 154 B2
Benabarre E 145 B4
Benacazón E 161 B3
Benaguacil E 159 B3
Benahadux E 164 C2
Benalmádena E 163 B3
Benalúa de Guadix E 164 B1
Benalúa de las Villas E 163 A4
Benalup E 162 B2
Benamargosa E 163 B3
Benamaurel E 164 B2
Benameji E 163 A3
Benamocarra E 163 B3
Benaocaz E 162 B2
Benaoján E 162 B2
Benarrabá E 162 B2
Benasque E 145 B4
Benátky nad Jizerou CZ 84 B2
Benavente
E 142 B1
P 154 C2
Benavides de Órbigo E 141 B5
Benavila P 154 B3
Bendorf D 81 B3
Benedikt SLO 110 C2
Benejama E 159 C3
Benejúzar E 165 A4
Benešov CZ 96 B2
Bénestroff F 92 C2
Benet F 114 B3
Bene Vagienna I 133 A3
Bénévent-l'Abbaye F 116 A1
Benevento I 170 B2
Benfeld F 93 C3
Benfica P 154 B2
Bengtsfors S 54 A3
Bengtsheden S 50 B2
Beničanci HR 125 B4
Benicarló E 153 B4
Benicássim E 153 B4
Benidorm E 159 C3
Benifaió E 159 B3
Beniganim E 159 C3
Benington GB 41 B4
Benisa E 159 C4
Benkovac HR 137 A4
Benllech GB 38 A2
Benneckenstein D 82 A2
Bénodet F 100 B1
Benquerencia de la Serena E 156 B2
Bensafrim P 160 B1
Bensbyn S 196 D5
Bensdorf D 73 B5
Benshausen D 82 B2
Bensheim D 93 B4
Bentley GB 44 B3
Bentwisch D 65 B5
Beočin SRB 126 B1
Beograd = Belgrade SRB 127 C2
Beragh GB 27 B3
Beranga E 143 A3
Berat AL 182 C1
Bérat F 146 A2
Beratzhausen D 95 B3
Bérbaltavár H 111 B3
Berbegal E 145 C3
Berbenno di Valtellina I 120 A2
Berberana E 143 B3
Bercedo E 143 A3
Bercel H 112 B3
Bercenay-le-Hayer F 91 C3
Berceto I 134 A2
Berchem B 79 B3
Berchidda I 178 B3
Berching D 95 B3
Berchtesgaden D 109 B4
Bérchules E 163 B4
Bercianos de Aliste E 149 A3
Berck F 78 B1
Berclaire d'Urgell E 147 C1
Berdoias E 140 A1
Berducedo E 141 A4
Berdún E 144 B3
Berdychiv UA 13 D8
Bere Alston GB 42 B2
Bereguardo I 120 B2
Berehommen N 53 A3
Berehove UA 16 A5
Berek BIH 124 B3
Beremend H 125 B4
Bere Regis GB 43 B4
Berestechko UA 13 C6
Berettyóújfalu H 113 B5
Berezhany UA 13 D6
Berezivka UA 17 B9
Berezna UA 13 C9
Berg
D 95 B3
N 195 E3
S 56 B2
Berga
Sachsen-Anhalt D 82 A3
Thüringen D 83 B4
E 147 B2
S 62 A4
Bergama TR 186 C2
Bérgamo I 120 B2
Bergara E 143 A4
Bergby S 51 B4
Berge
Brandenburg D 74 B1
Niedersachsen D 71 B4
Telemark N 53 A4
Telemark N 53 A4
Bergeforsen S 200 D3
Bergen
Mecklenburg-Vorpommern D 66 B2
Niedersachsen D 72 B2
Niedersachsen D 73 B3
N 46 B2
NL 70 B1
Bergen op Zoom NL 79 A4
Bergerac F 129 B3
Bergères-lés-Vertus F 91 C4
Bergeyk NL 79 A5
Berghausen D 93 C4
Bergheim D 80 B2
Berghem S 60 B2
Berg im Gau D 95 C3
Bergisch Gladbach D 80 B3
Bergkamen D 81 A3
Bergkvara S 63 B4
Berglern D 95 C3
Bergnäset S 196 D5
Bergneustadt D 81 A3
Bergsäng S 49 B5
Bergshamra S 57 A4
Bergsjö S 200 E3
Bergs slussar S 56 B1
Bergsviken S 196 D4
Bergtheim D 94 B2
Bergues F 78 B2
Bergum NL 70 A2
Bergün Bravuogn CH 107 C4
Bergwitz D 83 A4
Berhida H 112 B2
Beringel P 160 A2
Beringen B 79 A5
Berja E 164 C2
Berkåk N 199 C7
Berkeley GB 43 A4
Berkenthin D 65 C3
Berkhamsted GB 44 B3
Berkheim D 107 A5
Berkhof D 72 B2
Berkovići BIH 139 B4
Berkovitsa BG 17 D5
Berlanga E 156 B2
Berlanga de Duero E 151 A5
Berlevåg N 193 B13
Berlikum NL 70 A2
Berlin D 74 B2
Berlstedt D 82 A3
Bermeo E 143 A4
Bermillo de Sayago E 149 A3
Bern CH 106 C2
Bernalda I 174 A2
Bernardos E 150 A3
Bernartice
Jihočeský CZ 96 B2
Vychodočeský CZ 85 B3
Bernau
Baden-Württemberg D 106 B3
Bayern D 109 B3
Brandenburg D 74 B2
Bernaville F 90 A2
Bernay F 89 A4
Bernburg D 83 A3
Berndorf A 111 B3
Berne D 72 A1
Bernecebarati H 112 A2
Bernhardsthal A 97 C4
Bernkastel-Kues D 92 B3
Bernolakovo SK 111 A4
Bernsdorf D 84 A2
Bernstadt D 84 A2
Bernstein A 111 B3
Bernués E 145 B3
Beromünster CH 106 B3
Beroun CZ 96 B2
Berovo MK 182 B4
Berre-l'Etang F 131 B4
Berriedale GB 32 C3
Berriew GB 39 B3
Berrocal E 161 B3
Bersenbrück D 71 B4
Bershad' UA 13 D8
Bertamiráns E 140 B2
Berthåga S 51 C4
Berthelming F 92 C2
Bertincourt F 90 A2
Bertinoro I 135 A5
Bertogne B 92 A1
Bertrix B 91 B5
Berufjörður IS 191 C11
Berville-sur-Mer F 89 A4
Berwick-upon-Tweed GB 37 A4
Berzasca RO 16 C4
Berzence H 124 A3
Berzocana E 156 A2
Besalú E 147 B3
Besançon F 105 B5
Besenfeld D 93 C4
Besenyötelek H 113 B4
Besenyszög H 113 B4
Beshenkovichi BY 13 A8
Besigheim D 93 C5
Běšiny CZ 96 B1
Beška SRB 126 B2
Beşkonak TR 189 B6
Besle F 101 B4
Besnyö H 112 B2
Bessais-le-Fromental F 103 C4
Bessan F 130 B2
Besse-en-Chandesse F 116 B2
Bessèges F 131 A3
Bessé-sur-Braye F 102 B2
Bessines-sur-Gartempe F 115 B5
Best NL 79 A5
Bestorp S 56 B1
Betanzos E 140 A2
Betelu E 144 A2
Bétera E 159 B3
Beteta E 152 B1
Béthenville F 91 B4
Bethesda GB 38 A2
Béthune F 78 B2
Beton-Bazoches F 90 C3
Bettembourg L 92 B2
Betterdorf L 92 B2
Bettna S 56 B2
Béttola I 120 C2
Bettona I 136 B1
Bettyhill GB 32 C2
Betws-y-Coed GB 38 A3
Betxi E 159 B3
Betz F 90 B2
Betzdorf D 81 B3
Beuil F 132 A2
Beulah GB 39 B3
Beuzeville F 89 A4
Bevagna I 136 C1
Bevens-bruk S 56 A1
Beveren B 79 A4
Beverley GB 40 B3
Bevern D 81 A5
Beverstedt D 72 A1
Beverungen D 81 A5
Beverwijk NL 70 B1
Bex CH 119 A4
Bexhill GB 45 C4
Beyazköy TR 186 A2
Beychevelle F 128 A2
Beydağ TR 188 A3
Beyeğaç TR 188 B3
Beykoz TR 186 A4
Beynat F 129 A4
Beyoğlu TR 186 A4
Beypazarı TR 187 B6
Beyşehir TR 189 B6
Bezas E 152 B2
Bezau A 107 B4
Bezdan SRB 125 B4
Bèze F 105 B4
Bezenet F 116 A2
Bezhetsk RUS 9 D10
Béziers F 130 B2
Bezzecca I 121 B3
Biadki PL 85 A5
Biała
Łódzkie PL 77 C4
Opolskie PL 85 B5
Białaczów PL 87 A4
Biała Podlaska PL 13 B5
Biała Rawska PL 87 A4
Biale Błota PL 76 A2
Białobłoty PL 76 B2
Białobrzegi PL 87 A4
Białogard PL 67 C4
Bialośliwie PL 76 A2
Białowąs PL 68 B1
Biały Bór PL 68 B1
Białystok PL 13 B5
Biancavilla I 177 B3
Bianco I 175 C2
Biandrate I 119 B5
Biar E 159 C3
Biarritz F 144 A2
Bias F 128 B1
Biasca CH 120 A1
Biatorbágy H 112 B2
Bibbiena I 135 B4
Bibbona I 134 B3
Biberach
Baden-Württemberg D 93 C4
Baden-Württemberg D 107 A4
Bibinje HR 137 A4
Bibione I 122 B2
Biblis D 93 B4
Bibury GB 44 B2
Bicaj AL 182 B2
Biccari I 171 B3
Bicester GB 44 B2
Bichl D 108 B2
Bichlbach A 108 B1
Bicorp E 159 B3
Bicos P 160 B1
Bicske H 112 B2
Bidache F 128 C1
Bidart F 144 A2
Biddinghuizen NL 70 B2
Biddulph GB 40 B1
Bideford GB 42 A2
Bidford-on-Avon GB 44 A2
Bidjovagge N 192 C6
Bie S 56 A2
Bieber D 81 B5
Biebersdorf D 74 C2
Biedenkopf D 81 B4
Biel E 144 B3
Bielany Wroclawskie PL 85 A4
Bielawa PL 85 B4
Bielawy PL 77 B4
Biel / Bienne CH 106 B2
Bielefeld D 72 B1
Biella I 119 B5
Bielsa E 145 B4
Bielsk PL 77 B4
Bielsko-Biała PL 99 B3
Bielsk Podlaski PL 13 B5
Bienenbuttel D 72 A3
Bieniow PL 84 A3
Bienservida E 158 C1
Bienvenida E 156 B1
Bierdzany PL 86 B2
Bierné F 102 B1
Biersted DK 58 A2
Bierun PL 86 B3
Bierutów PL 85 A5
Bierwart B 79 B5
Bierzwina PL 75 A4
Bierzwnik PL 75 A4
Biescas E 145 B3
Biesenthal D 74 B2
Biesiekierz PL 67 B5
Bietigheim-Bissingen D 93 C5
Bièvre B 91 B5
Bieżuń PL 77 B4
Biga TR 186 B2
Bigadiç TR 186 C3
Biganos F 128 B2
Bigas P 148 B2
Bigastro E 165 A4
Bigbury GB 42 B3
Biggar GB 36 A3
Biggin Hill GB 45 B4
Biggleswade GB 44 A3
Bignasco CH 119 A5
Biguglia F 180 A2
Bihać BIH 124 C1
Biharnagybajom H 113 B5
Bijeljani BIH 139 B4
Bijeljina BIH 125 C5
Bijuesca E 152 A2
Bilaj HR 137 A4
Bila Tserkva UA 13 D9
Bilbao E 143 A4
Bilcza PL 87 B4
Bíldudalur IS 190 B2
Bileća BIH 139 C4
Bilecik TR 187 B4
Biled RO 126 B2
Biłgoraj PL 12 C5
Bilhorod-Dnistrovskyy UA 17 B9
Bilina CZ 84 B1
Bilisht AL 182 C2
Bilje HR 125 B4
Billdal S 60 B1
Billerbeck D 71 C4
Billericay GB 45 B4
Billesholm S 61 C2
Billingborough GB 40 C3
Billinge S 61 D3
Billingham GB 37 B5
Billinghay GB 41 B3
Billingsfors S 54 B3
Billingshurst GB 44 B3
Billom F 116 B3
Billsta S 200 C4
Billund DK 59 C2
Bílovec CZ 98 B2
Bilstein D 81 A4
Bilthoven NL 70 B2
Bilto N 192 C5
Bilzen B 80 B1
Biňa SK 112 B2
Binaced E 145 C4
Binasco I 120 B2
Binbrook GB 41 B3
Binche B 79 B4
Bindlach D 95 B3
Bindslev DK 58 A3
Binefar E 145 C4
Bingen D 93 B3
Bingham GB 40 C3
Bingley GB 40 B2
Bingsjö S 50 A2
Binic F 100 A3
Binz D 66 B2
Biograd na Moru HR 137 B4
Bionaz I 119 B4
Bioska SRB 127 D1
Birda RO 126 B3
Birdlip GB 44 B1
Biri N 48 B2
Birkeland N 53 B4

Birkenfeld
  Baden-Württemberg
  D. 93 C4
  Rheinland-Pfalz D . 92 B3
Birkenhead GB . . . 38 A3
Birkerød DK. 61 D2
Birkfeld A. 110 B2
Birkirkara M. . . . 175 C3
Birmingham GB . . 40 C2
Birr IRL. 28 A4
Birresborn D 80 B2
Birstein D. 81 B5
Biržai LT. 8 D4
Birzebbugia M. . . 175 C3
Bisáccia I. 172 A1
Bisacquino I 176 B2
Bisbal de Falset E. 153 A4
Biscarosse F. . . . 128 B1
Biscarosse Plage
  F. 128 B1
Biscarrués E 144 B3
Biscéglie I 171 B4
Bischheim F 93 C3
Bischofsheim D . . 82 B1
Bischofshofen A . 109 B4
Bischofswerda D . 84 A2
Bischofswiesen D. 109 B3
Bischofszell CH . 107 B4
Bischwiller F 93 C3
Bisenti I 169 A3
Bishop Auckland
  GB 37 B5
Bishop's Castle GB. 39 B4
Bishops Lydeard
  GB 43 A3
Bishop's Stortford
  GB 45 B4
Bishop's Waltham
  GB 44 C2
Bisignano I 174 B2
Bisingen D. 93 C4
Biskupice-Oławskie
  PL. 85 A5
Biskupiec PL. 69 B4
Bismark D 73 B4
Bismo N. 198 D5
Bispgården S . . . 200 C2
Bispingen D. 72 A2
Bissen L. 92 B2
Bissendorf D 71 B5
Bisserup DK. 65 A4
Bistango I 119 C5
Bistarac Donje BIH 139 A4
Bistrica BIH 124 C3
Bistrica ob Sotli
  SLO 123 A4
Bistriţa RO. 17 B6
Bitburg D. 92 B2
Bitche F. 93 B3
Bitetto I 171 B4
Bitola MK. 182 B3
Bitonto I. 171 B4
Bitschwiller F . . . 106 B2
Bitterfeld D 83 A4
Bitti I. 178 B3
Biville-sur-Mer F . 89 A5
Bivona I 176 B2
Biwer L. 92 B2
Bizeljsko SLO . . . 123 A4
Bizovac HR 125 B4
Bjåen N. 52 A3
Bjärnum S 61 C3
Bjärred S 61 D3
Bjästa S 200 C4
Bjelland
  Vest-Agder N 52 B3
  Vest-Agder N 52 B3
Bjelovar HR. 124 B2
Bjerkreim N 52 B2
Bjerkvik N 194 B8
Bjerreby DK. 65 B3
Bjerregrav DK . . . 58 B2
Bjerringbro DK . . 59 B2
Bjøberg N 47 B5
Bjøllånes N 195 D5
Björbo S. 50 B1
Bjordal N 46 A2
Björg IS 191 B8
Bjørkåsen N. . . . 194 B7
Björke
  Gävleborg S. 51 B4
  Östergötland S. . . 56 B1
Bjørkelangen N. . . 48 C3
Björketorp S 60 B2
Björkholmen S . . 196 C2
Björkliden S. . . . 194 B9
Björklinge S. 51 B4
Björko S. 51 C6
Björkö S. 60 B1
Björköby S. 62 A2
Björkvik S 56 B2
Bjørn N. 195 D3
Björna S 200 C4
Bjørnevatn N . . . 193 C13
Björnlunda S. 56 A3
Bjørnstad N 193 C14
Björsäter S 56 B2
Bjurberget S 49 B4
Bjurholm S 200 C5
Bjursås S 50 B2
Bjurtjärn S. 55 A5
Bjuv S 61 C2
Blachownia PL . . . 86 B2
Blackburn GB . . . 38 A4
Blackpool GB . . . 38 A3
Blackstad S. 62 A4

Blackwater IRL 30 B2
Blackwaterfoot GB . 34 C2
Blacy F 91 C4
Bladåker S. 51 B5
Blaenau Ffestiniog
  GB 38 B3
Blaenavon GB. . . . 39 C3
Blaengarw GB 39 C3
Blagaj
  BIH. 124 B2
  BIH. 139 B3
Blagdon GB 43 A4
Blagnac F 129 C4
Blagoevgrad BG. . 183 A5
Blaichach D 107 B5
Blain F. 101 B4
Blainville-sur-l'Eau
  F. 92 C2
Blair Atholl GB . . . 35 B4
Blairgowrie GB . . . 35 B4
Blajan F. 145 A4
Blakeney GB 39 C4
Blakstad N. 53 B4
Blâmont F. 92 C2
Blanca E 165 A3
Blancos E 140 C3
Blandford Forum
  GB 43 B4
Blanes E 147 C3
Blangy-sur-Bresle F 90 B1
Blankaholm S 62 A4
Blankenberge B . . 78 A3
Blankenburg D . . . 82 A2
Blankenfelde D . . . 74 B2
Blankenhain D . . . 82 B3
Blankenheim D . . . 80 B2
Blanquefort F . . . 128 B2
Blansko CZ 97 B4
Blanzac F. 115 C4
Blanzy F. 104 C3
Blaricum NL. 70 B2
Blarney IRL 29 C3
Blascomillán E . . 150 B2
Blascosancho E . . 150 B3
Błaszki PL 86 A2
Blatná CZ. 96 B1
Blatné SK. 111 A4
Blatnice CZ 98 C1
Blatnika BIH. 139 A3
Blato HR. 138 C2
Blato na Cetini HR 138 B2
Blatten CH. 119 A4
Blattnicksele S . . 195 E8
Blatzheim D 80 B2
Blaubeuren D 94 C1
Blaufelden D 94 B1
Blaustein D 94 C1
Blaydon GB 37 B5
Blaye F. 128 A2
Blaye-les-Mines F . 130 A1
Blázquez E 156 B2
Bleckede D 73 A3
Blecua E 145 B3
Bled SLO 123 A3
Bleiburg A 110 C1
Bleichenbach D. . . 81 B5
Bleicherode D. . . . 82 A2
Bleik N. 194 A6
Bleikvassli N . . . 195 E4
Bléneau F 104 B1
Blentarp S 61 D3
Blera I. 168 A2
Blérancourt F 90 B3
Bléré F 102 B2
Blesle F. 116 B3
Blessington IRL. . . 30 A2
Blet F 103 C4
Bletchley GB 44 B3
Bletterans F. 105 C4
Blidö S. 57 A4
Blidsberg S 60 B3
Blieskastel D 92 B3
Bligny-sur-Ouche
  F. 104 B3
Blikstorp S. 55 B5
Blinisht AL 182 B1
Blinja HR 124 B2
Blizanówek PL. . . . 76 C3
Bliżyn PL 87 A4
Blois F 103 B3
Blokhus DK 58 A2
Blokzijl NL 70 B2
Blombacka S. 55 A4
Blomberg D 72 C2
Blomskog S 54 A3
Blomstermåla S . . 62 B4
Błonie PL 77 B5
Blonville-sur-Mer F . 89 A4
Blötberget S 50 B2
Blovice CZ. 96 B1
Bloxham GB 44 A2
Bludenz A. 107 B4
Bludov CZ. 97 B4
Blumberg D 107 B3
Blyberg S. 49 A6
Blyth
  Northumberland
  GB. 37 A5
  Nottinghamshire
  GB. 40 B2
Blyth Bridge GB . . 35 C4
Blythburgh GB . . . 45 A5
Blythe Bridge GB . 40 C1
Bø
  Nordland N. 194 B5

Bø continued
  Telemark N 53 A5
Boal E 141 A4
Boan MNE 139 C5
Boario Terme I. . . . 120 B3
Boat of Garten GB . 32 D3
Boa Vista P 154 B2
Boğazkale TR 23 A8
Boğazliyan TR. . . . 23 B8
Boba H. 111 B4
Bobadilla
  Logroño E 143 B4
  Málaga E 163 A3
Bobadilla del Campo
  E. 150 A2
Bobadilla del Monte
  E. 151 B4
Bóbbio I 120 C2
Bóbbio Pellice I. . . 119 C4
Bobigny F 90 C2
Bobingen D 94 C2
Böblingen D 93 C5
Bobolice PL 68 B1
Boboras E 140 B2
Boboshevo BG . . 182 A4
Bobowa PL 99 B4
Bobrová CZ. 97 B4
Bobrovitsa UA. . . . 13 C9
Bobrowo PL 75 C4
Bobrówko PL. 75 B4
Boca de Huérgano
  E. 142 B2
Bocairent E 159 C3
Bočar SRB. 126 B2
Bocchigliero I . . . 174 B2
Boceguillas E . . . 151 A4
Bochnia PL 99 B4
Bocholt
  B. 80 A1
  D. 80 A2
Bochov CZ. 83 B5
Bochum D 80 A3
Bockara S 62 A4
Bockenem D 72 B3
Bockfliess A. 97 C4
Bockhorn D 71 A5
Bocognano F . . . 180 A2
Boconád H. 113 B4
Bőcs H 113 A4
Boczów PL. 75 B3
Boda S 50 A2
Böda S. 62 A5
Boda
  Stockholm S. 51 B5
  Värmland S 55 A4
  Västernorrland S . 200 D2
Bodafors S 62 A2
Boda Glasbruk S . . 63 B3
Bodajk H. 112 B2
Boddam
  Aberdeenshire
  GB. 33 D5
  Shetland GB 33 B5
Boddin D 73 A4
Bödefeld-Freiheit D 81 A4
Boden S 196 D4
Bodenmais D. 95 B5
Bodenteich D 73 B3
Bodenwerder D. . . 72 C2
Bodiam GB 45 B4
Bodinnick GB 42 B2
Bodio CH 120 A1
Bodjani SRB 125 B5
Bodmin GB 42 B2
Bodø N. 194 C5
Bodrum TR 188 B2
Bodstedt D 66 B1
Bodträskfors S . . . 196 C3
Bodzanów PL. 77 B5
Bodzanowice PL. . . 86 B2
Bodzechów PL . . . 87 B5
Bodzentyn PL 87 B4
Boecillo E 150 A3
Boëge F 118 A3
Boën F 117 B3
Bogács H. 113 B4
Bogadmindszent
  H. 125 B4
Bogajo E 149 B3
Bogarra E 158 C1
Bogarre E 163 A4
Bogatić SRB 127 C1
Bogatynia PL. 84 B2
Bogda RO 126 B3
Bogdaniec PL 75 B4
Boge S 57 C4
Bogen
  D 95 C4
  Nordland N. 194 B7
  Nordland N. 194 C6
  S 49 B4
Bogense DK 59 C3
Bognanco Fonti . . 119 A5
Bognelv N 192 B6
Bognes N 194 B7
Bogno CH 120 A2
Bognor Regis GB . . 44 C3
Bogoria PL. 87 B5
Bogøstrand N . . . 194 B7
Bogojevo SRB . . . 125 B5
Bogomila MK . . . 182 B3
Boguchwaly PL. . . . 69 B5
Bogumiłowice PL. . 86 A3
Boguszów-Gorce
  PL. 85 B4
Bogyiszló H. 112 C2

Bohain-en-Vermandois
  F. 91 B3
Böheimkirchen A. . .110 A2
Bohinjska Bistrica
  SLO 122 A2
Böhlen D 83 A4
Böhmenkirch D . . . 94 C1
Bohmte D. 71 B5
Bohonal de Ibor E. 150 C2
Böhönye H. 124 A3
Bohuňovice CZ . . . 98 B1
Bohuslav UA 13 D9
Boiro E. 140 B2
Bois-d'Amont F . . 105 C5
Boisseron F 131 B3
Boitzenburg D . . . 74 A2
Boixols E 147 B2
Boizenburg D 73 A3
Bojance I 170 B2
Bojanowo PL. 85 A4
Bojano I 170 B2
Bojanowo PL 85 A4
Bojkovice CZ. 98 B1
Bojná SK 98 C2
Bojnice SK. 98 C2
Boka SRB 126 B2
Böklund D 64 B2
Bokod H. 112 B2
Böksholm S. 62 A2
Boksitogorsk RUS . 9 C8
Bol HR. 138 B2
Bolaños de Calatrava
  E. 157 B4
Bolayır TR 186 B1
Bolbec F. 89 A4
Bölcske H 112 C2
Boldog H 113 B3
Boldva H. 113 A4
Böle S 196 D4
Bolea E 145 B3
Bolekhiv UA. 13 D5
Bolesławiec PL. . . . 84 A3
Boleszkowice PL. . . 74 B3
Bolewice PL. 75 B4
Bólgheri I 134 B3
Bolhrad UA 17 C8
Böle I 196 A4
Bolhrad UA 17 C8
Boliden S 200 B6
Bolimów PL 77 B5
Boljevci SRB 127 C2
Boljkovci SRB . . . 127 C2
Bolków PL 85 B4
Bollebygd S 60 B2
Bollène F 131 A3
Bollnäs S 50 A3
Bollstabruk S . . . 200 D3
Bollullos E 161 B3
Bollullos par del
  Condado E 161 B3
Bologna I 135 A4
Bologne F 105 A4
Bolognetta I. 176 B2
Bolognola I 136 C2
Bologoye RUS. . . . 9 D9
Bolótana I 178 B2
Bolsena I 168 A1
Bolshaya Vradiyevka
  UA 17 B9
Bolsover GB 40 B2
Bolstad S 54 B3
Bolsward NL 70 A2
Boltaña E 145 B4
Boltenhagen D . . . 65 C4
Boltigen CH. 106 C2
Bolton GB 38 A4
Bolu TR 187 B6
Bolungarvik IS . . . 190 A2
Bolvadin TR. 187 D6
Bóly H 125 B4
Bolzaneto I 133 A4
Bolzano I 108 C2
Bomba I 169 A4
Bombarral P 154 B1
Bömenzien D 73 B4
Bomlitz D 72 B2
Bømlo N. 52 A1
Bøn N 48 B3
Bona F 104 B2
Bonaduz CH 107 C4
Bonanza E 161 C3
Boñar E 142 B1
Bonarbridge GB . . 32 D2
Bonárcado I 178 B2
Bonares E 161 B3
Bonäs S 50 A1
Bonassola I 134 A2
Bonawe GB 34 B2
Bondal N 53 A4
Bondeno I 121 C4
Bondorf D 93 C4
Bondstorp S 60 B3
Bon-Encontre F. . . 129 B3
Bo'ness GB 35 B4
Bonete E 158 C2
Bonifacio F 180 B2
Bonigen CH. 106 C2
Bonin PL 67 B5
Bonn D. 80 B3
Bonnánaro I 178 B2
Bonnásjøen N . . . 194 C6
Bonnat F 116 A1
Bonndorf D 106 B3
Bonnétable F. . . . 102 A2
Bonneuil-les-Eaux
  F. 90 B2

Bonneuil-Matours
  F. 115 B4
Bonneval F 103 A3
Bonneval-sur-Arc
  F. 119 B4
Bonneville F. 118 A3
Bonnières-sur-Seine
  F. 90 B1
Bonnieux F 131 B4
Bönnigheim D 93 B5
Bonnyrigg GB 35 C4
Bonny-sur-Loire F 103 B4
Bono
  E 145 B4
  I 178 B3
Bonorva I 178 B2
Bønsnes N 48 B2
Bonyhád H. 125 A4
Boom B 79 A4
Boos F 89 A5
Boostedt D 64 B3
Bootle
  Cumbria GB. 36 B3
  Merseyside GB . . . 38 A3
Bopfingen D 94 C2
Boppard D 81 B3
Boqueixón E 140 B2
Bor
  CZ 95 B4
  S 62 A2
  SRB 16 C5
  TR 23 C8
Boran-sur-Oise F . . 90 B2
Borås S 60 B2
Borba P 155 C3
Borbona I. 169 A3
Borča SRB 127 C2
Borci BIH 139 B4
Borculo NL. 71 B3
Bordány H. 126 A1
Bordeaux F 128 B2
Bordeira P 160 B1
Bordesholm D . . . 64 B3
Borðeyri IS 190 B4
Bórdighera I 133 B3
Bording DK 59 B2
Bordón E 153 B3
Bore I 120 C2
Borehamwood GB . 44 B3
Borek Strzeliński
  PL. 85 B5
Borek Wielkopolski
  PL. 76 C2
Boreland GB 36 A3
Borello I 135 A5
Borensberg S 56 B1
Borgafjäll S 199 A12
Borgarnes IS . . . 190 C4
Borghamn S 55 B5
Borghetto d'Arróscia
  I 133 A3
Borghetto Santo Spirito
  I 133 A4
Borgholm S 62 B4
Borghorst D 71 B4
Bórgia I 175 C2
Borgloon B 79 B5
Borglum DK 58 A2
Borgo F 180 A2
Borgo alla Collina
  I 135 B4
Borgo a Mozzano I 134 B3
Borgoforte I 121 B3
Borgofranco d'Ivrea
  I 119 B4
Borgomanero I . . .119 B5
Borgomasino I . . .119 B4
Borgonovo Val Tidone
  I 120 B2
Borgo Pace I 135 B5
Borgorose I 169 A3
Borgo San Dalmazzo
  I 133 A3
Borgo San Lorenzo
  I 135 B4
Borgosésia I. 119 B5
Borgo Val di Taro I 134 A2
Borgo Valsugana I 121 A4
Borgo Vercelli I . . .119 B5
Borgstena S 60 B3
Borgue GB 36 B2
Borgund N 47 A4
Borgvik S 55 A3
Borja E 144 C2
Bork D 80 A3
Borken D 80 A2
Borkenes N 194 B7
Børkop DK 59 C2
Borkowice PL 87 A4
Borkowo PL. 77 B5
Borkum D 71 A4
Borlänge S 50 B2
Borlu TR. 186 D3
Bormes-les-Mimosas
  F. 132 B2
Bórmio I 107 C5
Bormujos E 161 B3
Borna D 83 A4
Borne NL 71 B3
Bornes P 149 A2
Borne Sulinowo PL. 68 B1
Bornheim D 80 B2
Bornhöved D 64 B3

Börnicke D. 74 B1
Bornos E 162 B2
Borobia E 152 A2
Borodino RUS. . . . 9 E9
Borohrádek CZ. . . 85 B4
Boronów PL. 86 B2
Bórore I 178 B2
Boroszów PL. 86 B2
Borota H 126 A1
Boroughbridge GB . 40 A2
Borovany CZ. 96 C2
Borovichi RUS . . . 9 C8
Borovnica SLO . . 123 B3
Borovo HR. 125 B4
Borovsk RUS. . . . 9 E10
Borovy CZ 96 B1
Borowa PL 85 A5
Borox E 151 B4
Borrby S 66 A3
Borre
  DK. 65 B5
  N 54 A1
Borredá E 147 B2
Borrenes E 141 B4
Borriol E 159 A3
Borris
  DK. 59 C1
  IRL. 30 B2
Borris-in-Ossory
  IRL 28 B4
Borrisokane IRL . . 28 B3
Borrisoleigh IRL . . 28 B4
Borrowdale GB . . . 36 B3
Børrud N 49 C4
Borşa RO. 17 B6
Borsdorf D 83 A4
Børselv N 193 B9
Borsfa H. 111 C3
Borský Mikuláš SK . 98 C1
Borsodivánka H . . .113 B4
Borsodnádasd H . .113 A4
Börte N 53 A3
Borth GB 39 B2
Bort-les-Orgues F . .116 B2
Börtnan S 199 C10
Børtnes N 47 B6
Borup DK. 61 D1
Boryslav UA. 13 D5
Boryspil UA 13 C9
Boryszyn PL 75 B4
Borzęciczki PL. . . . 85 A5
Borzęcin PL 77 B5
Borzonasca I 134 A2
Borzyszkowy PL . . 68 A2
Borzytuchom PL . . 68 A2
Bosa I 178 B2
Bošáca SK. 98 C1
Bosanci HR 123 B4
Bosanska Dubica
  BIH. 124 B2
Bosanska Gradiška
  BIH. 124 B3
Bosanska Kostajnica
  BIH. 124 B2
Bosanska Krupa
  BIH. 124 C2
Bosanski Brod BIH 125 B3
Bosanski Novi BIH 124 B2
Bosanski Petrovac
  BIH. 124 C2
Bosanski Šamac
  BIH. 125 B4
Bosansko Grahovo
  BIH. 138 A2
Bošány SK. 98 C2
Bősárkány H. 111 B4
Bosau D. 65 B3
Bósca H 112 C3
Boscastle GB 42 B2
Bosco I 120 C1
Bosco Chiesanuova
  I 121 B4
Bösdorf D 65 B3
Bösel D 71 A4
Bosham GB 44 C3
Bösingfeld D 72 B2
Bosjön S 49 C5
Boskoop NL. 70 B1
Boskovice CZ 97 B4
Bošnjaci HR 125 B4
Bošnjane SRB . . . 127 D3
Bossast E 145 B4
Bossolasco I 133 A4
Boštanj SLO 123 A4
Boston GB 41 C3
Bostrak N 53 A5
Böszénfa H 125 A3
Bot E 153 A4
Botajica BIH 125 C4
Bøte By DK 65 B4
Bothel GB 36 B3
Boticas P 148 A2
Botilsäter S 55 A4
Botngård N 198 B6
Botoš SRB 126 B2
Botoşani RO 17 B7
Botricello I 175 C2
Botsmark S 200 B6
Bottendorf D 81 A4
Bottesford GB . . . 40 C3
Bottnaryd S 60 B3
Bottrop D. 80 A2
Botunje SRB 127 C3
Bötzingen D 106 A2
Bouaye F 101 B4

Bouça P 149 A2
Boucau F 128 C1
Bouchain F 78 B3
Bouchoir F 90 B2
Boudreville F 105 B3
Boudry CH 106 C1
Bouesse F 103 C3
Bouguenais F 101 B4
Bouhy F 104 B2
Bouillargues F 131 B3
Bouillon B 91 B5
Bouilly F 104 A2
Bouin F 114 B2
Boulay-Moselle F 92 B2
Boulazac F 129 A3
Boule-d'Amont F 146 B3
Bouligny F 92 B1
Boulogne-sur-Gesse F 145 A4
Boulogne-sur-Mer F 78 B1
Bouloire F 102 B2
Bouquemaison F 78 B2
Bourbon-Lancy F 104 C2
Bourbon-l'Archambault F 104 C2
Bourbonne-les-Bains F 105 B4
Bourbourg F 78 B2
Bourbriac F 100 A2
Bourcefranc-le-Chapus F 114 C2
Bourdeaux F 131 A4
Bouresse F 115 B4
Bourg F 128 A2
Bourg-Achard F 89 A4
Bourganeuf F 116 B1
Bourg-Argental F 117 B4
Bourg-de-Péage F 117 B5
Bourg-de-Thizy F 117 A4
Bourg-de-Visa F 129 B3
Bourg-en-Bresse F 118 A2
Bourges F 103 B4
Bourg-et-Comin F 91 B3
Bourg-Lastic F 116 B2
Bourg-Madame F 146 B2
Bourgneuf-en-Retz F 114 A2
Bourgogne F 91 B4
Bourgoin-Jallieu F 118 B2
Bourg-St Andéol F 131 A3
Bourg-St Maurice F 119 B3
Bourgtheroulde F 89 A4
Bourgueil F 102 B2
Bourmont F 105 A4
Bourne GB 40 C3
Bournemouth GB 43 B5
Bourneville F 89 A4
Bournezeau F 114 B2
Bourran F 129 B3
Bourret F 129 C4
Bourron-Marlotte F 90 C2
Bourton-on-The-Water GB 44 B2
Boussac F 116 A2
Boussens F 145 A4
Boutersem B 79 B4
Bouttencourt F 90 B1
Bouvières F 131 A4
Bouvron F 101 B4
Bouxwiller F 93 C3
Bouzas E 140 B2
Bouzonville F 92 B2
Bova I 175 D1
Bovalino Marina I 175 C2
Bovallstrand S 54 B2
Bova Marina I 175 D1
Bovec SLO 122 A2
Bóveda E 141 B3
Bóvegno I 120 B3
Bovenau D 64 B2
Bovenden D 82 A1
Bøverdal N 198 D5
Boves F 90 B2
Bóves I 133 A3
Bovey Tracey GB 43 B3
Bovino I 171 B3
Bøvlingbjerg DK 58 B1
Bovolenta I 121 B4
Bovolone I 121 B4
Bowes GB 37 B5
Bowmore GB 34 C1
Bowness-on-Windermere GB 36 B4
Box GB 43 A4
Boxberg
Baden-Württemberg D 94 B1
Sachsen D 84 A2
Boxholm S 55 B6
Boxmeer NL 80 A1
Boxtel NL 79 A5
Boyabat TR 23 A8
Boyalıca TR 187 B4
Boyle IRL 26 C2
Bozan TR 187 C6
Božava HR 137 A3
Bozburun TR 188 C3
Bozcaada TR 186 C1
Bozdoğan TR 188 B3
Božepole Wielkie PL 68 A2
Boževac SRB 127 C3
Božice CZ 97 C4
Boži Dar CZ 83 B4
Bozkır TR 189 B7
Bozouls F 130 A1
Bozova TR 189 B5
Bozüyük TR 187 C5
Bózzolo I 121 B3
Bra I 119 C4
Braås S 62 A3
Brabrand DK 59 B3
Bracadale GB 31 B2
Bracciano I 168 A2
Bracieux F 103 B3
Bräcke S 199 C12
Brackenheim D 93 B5
Brackley GB 44 A2
Bracklin IRL 27 C4
Bracknell GB 44 B3
Brackwede D 72 C1
Braco GB 35 B4
Brad RO 16 B5
Bradford GB 40 B2
Bradford on Avon GB 43 A4
Bradina BIH 139 B4
Brådland N 52 B2
Brædstrup DK 59 C2
Brae GB 33 A5
Braemar GB 32 D3
Braemore GB 32 D1
Braga P 148 A1
Bragança P 149 A3
Brăila RO 17 C7
Braine F 91 B3
Braine-le-Comte B 79 B4
Braintree GB 45 B4
Braives B 79 B5
Brake D 72 A1
Brakel
B 79 B3
D 81 A5
Bräkne-Hoby S 63 B3
Brålanda S 54 B3
Bralin PL 86 A1
Brallo di Pregola I 120 C2
Bram F 146 A3
Bramafan F 132 B2
Bramberg am Wildkogel A 109 B3
Bramdrupdam DK 59 C2
Bramming DK 59 C1
Brampton GB 37 B4
Bramsche D 71 B4
Branca I 136 B1
Brancaleone Marina I 175 D2
Brancaster GB 41 C4
Brand
Nieder Östereich A 96 C3
Vorarlberg A 107 B4
Brandbu N 48 B2
Brande DK 59 C2
Brande-Hornerkirchen D 64 C2
Brandenberg A 108 B2
Brandenburg D 73 B5
Brand-Erbisdorf D 83 B5
Brandis D 83 A4
Brando F 180 A2
Brandomil E 140 A2
Brandon GB 45 A4
Brandshagen D 66 B2
Brandval N 49 B4
Brandýs nad Labem CZ 84 B2
Branice PL 98 A1
Braničevo SRB 127 C3
Braniewo PL 69 A4
Branik SLO 122 B2
Brankovina SRB 127 C1
Branky CZ 98 B1
Branne F 128 B2
Brannenburg-Degerndorf D 108 B3
Brantôme F 115 C4
Branzi I 120 A2
Bras d'Asse F 132 B2
Braskereidfoss N 48 B3
Braslaw BY 13 A7
Braşov RO 17 C6
Brasparts F 100 A2
Brassac F 130 B1
Brassac-les-Mines F 116 B3
Brasschaat B 79 A4
Brastad S 54 B2
Břasy CZ 96 B1
Brąszewice PL 86 A2
Bratislava SK 111 A4
Brattfors S 55 A5
Brattvåg N 198 C3
Bratunac BIH 127 C1
Braubach D 81 B3
Braunau A 95 C5
Braunfels D 81 B4
Braunlage D 82 A2
Braunsbedra D 83 A3
Braunschweig D 73 B3
Bray IRL 30 A2
Bray Dunes F 78 A2
Bray-sur-Seine F 90 C3
Bray-sur-Somme F 90 B2
Brazatortas E 157 B3
Brazey-en-Plaine F 105 B4
Brbinj HR 137 A4
Brčko BIH 125 C4
Brdani SRB 127 D2
Brdów PL 76 B3
Brea de Tajo E 151 B4
Brécey F 88 B2
Brechen D 81 B4
Brechin GB 35 B5
Brecht B 79 A4
Brecketfeld D 80 A3
Břeclav CZ 97 C4
Brecon GB 39 C3
Brécy F 103 B4
Breda
E 147 C3
NL 79 A4
Bredaryd S 60 B3
Bredbyn S 200 C4
Breddin D 73 B5
Bredebro DK 64 A1
Bredelar D 81 A4
Bredenfelde D 74 A2
Bredsjö S 50 C1
Bredstedt D 64 B1
Bredsten DK 59 C2
Bredträsk S 200 C4
Bredviken S 195 D5
Bree B 80 A1
Bregana HR 123 B4
Breganze I 121 B4
Bregenz A 107 B4
Bréhal F 88 B2
Brehna D 83 A4
Breiðdalsvík IS 191 C11
Breidenbach F 93 B3
Breil-sur-Roya F 133 B3
Breisach D 106 A2
Breitenbach
CH 106 B2
D 81 B5
Breitenberg D 96 C1
Breitenfelde D 73 A3
Breitengussbach D 94 B2
Breivikbotn N 192 B6
Brejning DK 59 C2
Brekke N 46 A2
Brekken N 199 C8
Brekkestø N 53 B4
Brekkvasselv N 199 A10
Brekstad N 198 B6
Breland N 53 B3
Bremanger N 198 D1
Bremen D 72 A1
Bremerhaven D 72 A1
Bremervörde D 72 A2
Bremgarten CH 106 B3
Bremsnes N 198 B4
Brem-sur-Mer F 114 B2
Brenderup DK 59 C2
Brenes E 162 A2
Brengova SLO 110 C2
Brenna PL 98 B2
Breno I 120 B3
Brénod F 118 A2
Brensbach D 93 B4
Brentwood GB 45 B4
Brescello I 121 C3
Bréscia I 120 B3
Breskens NL 79 A3
Bresles F 90 B2
Bresnica SRB 127 D2
Bressana I 120 B2
Bressanone I 108 C2
Bressuire F 102 C1
Brest
BY 13 B5
F 100 A1
HR 122 B2
Brestač SRB 127 C1
Brestanica SLO 123 A4
Brestova HR 123 B3
Brestovac HR 125 B3
Bretenoux F 129 B4
Breteuil
Eure F 89 B4
Oise F 90 B2
Brétigny-sur-Orge F 90 C2
Bretten D 93 B4
Bretteville-sur-Laize F 89 A3
Brettheim D 94 B2
Breuil-Cervinia I 119 B4
Breukelen NL 70 B2
Brevik
N 53 A5
Stockholm S 57 A4
Västra Götaland S 55 B5
Breza BIH 139 A4
Brežice SLO 123 B4
Bréziers F 132 A2
Breznica HR 124 A2
Breznica Našička HR 125 B4
Březnice CZ 96 B1
Brezno SK 99 C3
Brezolles F 89 B5
Březovánad Svitavou CZ 97 B4
Brezovápod Bradlom SK 98 C1
Brezovica
SK 99 B4
SLO 123 A3
Brezovo Polje Selo BIH 125 C4
Briançon F 118 C3
Brianconnet F 132 B2
Briare F 103 B4
Briatexte F 129 C4
Briático I 175 C2
Briaucourt F 105 A4
Bribir HR 123 B3
Bricquebec F 88 A2
Bridgend
Argyll & Bute GB 34 C1
Bridgend GB 39 C3
Bridge of Cally GB 35 B4
Bridge of Don GB 33 D4
Bridge of Earn GB 35 B4
Bridge of Orchy GB 34 B3
Bridgnorth GB 39 B4
Bridgwater GB 43 A4
Břidličná CZ 98 B1
Bridlington GB 41 A3
Bridport GB 43 B4
Briec F 100 A1
Brie-Comte-Robert F 90 C2
Brienne-le-Château F 91 C4
Brienon-sur-Armançon F 104 B2
Brienz CH 106 C3
Brienza I 172 B1
Briesen D 74 B3
Brieskow Finkenheerd D 74 B3
Brietlingen D 72 A3
Brieva de Cameros E 143 B4
Briey F 92 B1
Brig CH 119 A5
Brigg GB 40 B3
Brighouse GB 40 B2
Brightlingsea GB 45 B5
Brighton GB 44 C3
Brignogan-Plage F 100 A1
Brignoles F 132 B2
Brigstock GB 40 C3
Brihuega E 151 B5
Brijuni HR 122 C2
Brillon-en-Barrois F 91 C5
Brilon D 81 A4
Brimnes N 46 B3
Brinches P 160 A2
Brindisi I 173 B3
Brinje HR 123 B4
Brinon-sur-Beuvron F 104 B2
Brinon-sur-Sauldre F 103 B4
Brinyan GB 33 B3
Brión E 140 B2
Briones E 143 B4
Brionne F 89 A4
Brioude F 117 B3
Brioux-sur-Boutonne F 115 B3
Briouze F 89 B3
Briscous F 144 A2
Brisighella I 135 A4
Brissac-Quincé F 102 B1
Brissago CH 120 A1
Bristol GB 43 A4
Brive-la-Gaillarde F 129 A4
Briviesca E 143 B3
Brixham GB 43 B3
Brixlegg A 108 B2
Brjánslækur IS 190 B2
Brka BIH 125 C4
Brnaze HR 138 B2
Brněnec CZ 97 B4
Brno CZ 97 B4
Bro S 57 A3
Broadclyst GB 43 B3
Broadford
GB 31 B3
IRL 28 B3
Broad Haven GB 39 C1
Broadstairs GB 45 B5
Broadstone GB 43 B4
Broadway GB 44 A2
Broager DK 64 B2
Broaryd S 60 B3
Broby S 61 C4
Brobyværk DK 59 C3
Bročanac BIH 138 B3
Brocas F 128 B2
Brock D 71 B4
Brockel D 72 A2
Brockenhurst GB 44 C2
Broczyno PL 75 A5
Brod MK 182 B3
Brodalen S 54 B2
Broddbo S 50 C3
Brodek u Přerova CZ 98 B1
Broden-bach D 80 B3
Brodick GB 34 C2
Brod na Kupi HR 123 B3
Brodnica PL 69 B4
Brodnica Graniczna PL 68 A3
Brodowe Łąki PL 77 A6
Brody
Lubuskie PL 75 B4
Lubuskie PL 84 A2
Mazowieckie PL 77 B5
UA 13 C6
Broglie F 89 B4
Brójce PL 75 B4
Brokind S 56 B1
Brolo I 177 A3
Brome D 73 B3
Bromley GB 45 B4
Bromölla S 63 B2
Bromont-Lamothe F 116 B2
Brömsebro S 63 B3
Bromsgrove GB 44 A1
Bromyard GB 39 B4
Bronchales E 152 B2
Bronco E 149 B3
Brønderslev DK 58 A2
Broni I 120 B2
Brønnøysund N 195 E3
Brøns DK 59 C1
Bronte I 177 B3
Bronzani Mejdan BIH 124 C2
Bronzolo I 121 A4
Broons F 101 A3
Broquies F 130 A1
Brora GB 32 C3
Brørup DK 59 C2
Brösarp S 63 C2
Brossac F 115 C3
Brostrud N 47 B5
Brotas P 154 C2
Brötjärna S 50 B2
Broto E 145 B3
Brottby S 57 A4
Brøttum N 48 A2
Brou F 103 A3
Brouage F 114 C2
Brough GB 37 B4
Broughshane GB 27 B4
Broughton GB 35 C4
Broughton-in-Furness GB 36 B3
Broumov CZ 85 B4
Broût-Vernet F 116 A3
Brouvelieures F 106 A1
Brouwershaven NL 79 A3
Brovary UA 13 C9
Brovst DK 58 A2
Brownhills GB 40 C2
Brozas E 155 B4
Brozzo I 120 B3
Brtnice CZ 97 B3
Brtonigla HR 122 B2
Bruay-la-Buissière F 78 B2
Bruchhausen-Vilsen D 72 B2
Bruchsal D 93 B4
Bruck D 95 B4
Brück D 74 B1
Bruck an der Grossglocknerstrasse A 109 B3
Bruck an der Leitha A 111 A3
Bruck an der Mur A 110 B2
Brückl A 110 C1
Bruckmühl D 108 B2
Brue-Auriac F 132 B1
Brüel D 65 C4
Bruen CH 107 C3
Bruère-Allichamps F 103 C4
Bruff IRL 29 B3
Bruflat N 47 B6
Brugg CH 106 B3
Brugge B 78 A3
Brüggen D 80 A2
Brühl D 80 B2
Bruinisse NL 79 A4
Brûlon F 102 B1
Brumano I 120 B2
Brumath F 93 C3
Brummen NL 70 B3
Brumov-Bylnice CZ 98 B2
Brumunddal N 48 B2
Brunau D 73 B4
Brunehamel F 91 B4
Brünen D 80 A2
Brunete E 151 B3
Brunflo S 199 B11
Brunico I 108 C2
Brunkeberg N 53 A4
Brunn D 74 A2
Brunnen CH 107 C3
Brunsbüttel D 64 C2
Brunssum NL 80 B1
Bruntál CZ 98 B1
Brušane HR 137 A4
Brusasco I 119 B5
Brusio CH 120 A3
Brusno SK 99 C3
Brusque F 130 B1
Brussels = Bruxelles B 79 B4
Brusson I 119 B4
Brüssow D 74 A3
Brusy PL 68 B2
Bruton GB 43 A4
Bruvno HR 138 A1
Bruvoll N 48 B3
Bruxelles = Brussels B 79 B4
Bruyères F 106 A1
Bruz F 101 A4
Bruzaholm S 62 A3
Brwinów PL 77 B5
Brynamman GB 39 C3
Bryncrug GB 39 B2
Bryne N 52 B1
Brynmawr GB 39 C3
Bryrup DK 59 B2
Brzeg PL 85 B5
Brzeg Dolny PL 85 A4
Brześć Kujawski PL 76 B3
Brzesko PL 99 B4
Brzeszcze PL 99 B3
Brzezie PL 68 B1
Brzeziny
Łódzkie PL 87 A3
Wielkopolskie PL 86 A2
Brzeźnica PL 84 A3
Brzeźnica Nowa PL 86 A3
Brzeżno PL 75 A4
Brzotin SK 99 C4
Brzozie Lubawskie PL 69 B4
Bua S 60 B2
Buarcos P 148 B1
Buaveg N 52 A1
Bubbio I 119 C5
Bubry F 100 B2
Buca TR 188 A2
Bucak TR 189 B5
Bučany SK 98 C1
Buccheri I 177 B3
Buccino I 172 B1
Bucelas P 154 C1
Buch
Bayern D 94 C2
Bayern D 95 C4
Buchach UA 13 D6
Bucharest = Bucureşti RO 17 C7
Buchbach D 95 C4
Buchboden A 107 B4
Buchen D 94 B1
Büchen D 73 A3
Buchenberg D 107 B5
Buchères F 104 A3
Buchholz D 72 A2
Buchloe D 108 A1
Buchlovice CZ 98 B1
Buchlyvie GB 34 B3
Bucholz D 73 A5
Buchs CH 107 B4
Buchy F 89 A5
Bückeburg D 72 B2
Buckfastleigh GB 42 B3
Buckhaven GB 35 B4
Buckie GB 33 D4
Buckingham GB 44 A3
Buckley GB 38 A3
Bückwitz D 73 B5
Bučovice CZ 97 B5
Bucsa H 113 B5
Bucureşti = Bucharest RO 17 C7
Bucy-lés-Pierrepont F 91 B3
Buczek PL 86 A3
Bud N 198 C3
Budakalasz H 112 B3
Budakeszi H 112 B2
Budal N 199 C7
Budaörs H 112 B2
Budapest H 112 B3
Búðardalur IS 190 B4
Budča SK 99 C3
Buddusò I 178 B3
Bude GB 42 B2
Budeč CZ 97 B3
Büdelsdorf D 64 B2
Budens P 160 B1
Budia E 151 B5
Budimlić-Japra BIH 124 C2
Büdingen D 81 B5
Budinšćina HR 124 A2
Budišov CZ 98 B1
Budleigh Salterton GB 43 B3
Budmerice SK 98 C1
Budoni I 178 B3
Búdrio I 135 A4
Budva MNE 16 D3
Budyněnad Ohří CZ 84 B2
Budziszewice PL 87 A3
Budzyń PL 76 B1
Bue N 52 B1
Bueña E 152 B2
Buenache de Alarcón E 158 B1
Buenache de la Sierra E 152 B2
Buenaventura E 150 B3
Buenavista de Valdavia E 142 B2
Buendia E 151 B5
Bueu E 140 B2
Buezo E 143 B3
Bugac H 112 C3
Bugarra E 159 B3
Bugeat F 116 B1
Buggerru I 179 C2
Bugojno BIH 138 A3
Bugøyfjord N 193 C13
Bugøynes N 193 C13
Bugyi H 112 B3
Buharkent TR 188 B3
Bühl
Baden-Württemberg D 93 C4
Bayern D 107 B5
Bühlertal D 93 C4
Bühlertann D 94 B1
Buia I 122 A2
Builth Wells GB 39 B3
Buin N 47 B6
Buis-les-Baronnies F 131 A4
Buitenpost NL 70 A3
Buitrago del Lozoya E 151 B4
Bujalance E 157 C3

Bujaraloz E 153 A3
Buje HR 122 B2
Bujedo E 143 B3
Bük H 111 B3
Buk PL 75 B5
Bükkösd H 125 A3
Bükkzsérc H 113 B4
Bukovci SLO 124 A1
Bukowiec PL 75 B5
Bukowina Tatrzańska
  PL. 99 B4
Bukownica PL. 86 A2
Bukowno PL 86 B3
Bülach CH 107 B3
Búland IS 191 D7
Buldan TR 188 A3
Bulgnéville F 105 A4
Bulgurca TR 188 A2
Bülkau D 64 C1
Bulken N 46 B3
Bulkowo PL 77 B5
Bullas E 164 A3
Bulle CH 106 C2
Büllingen B 80 B2
Bullmark S 200 B6
Bulqizë AL 182 B2
Buna BIH 139 B3
Bunahowen IRL . . . 26 B1
Bunbeg IRL 26 A2
Bunclody IRL. 30 B2
Buncrana IRL. 27 A3
Bunde D 71 A4
Bünde D 72 B1
Bundoran IRL 26 B2
Bunessan GB 34 B1
Bungay GB 45 A5
Bunge S 57 C5
Bunić HR 123 C4
Bunmahon IRL 30 B1
Bunnyconnellan
  IRL 26 B1
Buño E 140 A2
Buñol E 159 B3
Bunratty IRL 29 B3
Bunsbeek B 79 B4
Buñuel E 144 C2
Bunyola E 166 B2
Buonabitácolo I . . . 172 B1
Buonalbergo I 170 B2
Buonconvento I . . . 135 B4
Buonvicino I 174 B1
Burano I 122 B1
Burbach D 81 B4
Burcei I 179 C3
Burdons-sur-Rognon
  F. 105 A4
Burdur TR 189 B5
Bureå S 2 D7
Burela E 141 A3
Büren D 81 A4
Büren an der Aare
  CH 106 B2
Burford GB 44 B2
Burg
  Cottbus D. 84 A2
  Magdeburg D. . .73 B4
  Schleswig-Holstein
  D. 64 C2
Burgas BG 17 D7
Burgau
  A. 111 B3
  D 94 C2
  P. 160 B1
Burg auf Fehmarn
  D 65 B4
Burgbernheim D . . . 94 B2
Burgdorf
  CH 106 B2
  D 72 B3
Burgebrach D 94 B2
Bürgel D 83 B3
Burgess Hill GB. . . . 44 C3
Burghaslach D 94 B2
Burghausen D 109 A3
Burghead GB. 32 D3
Burgheim D 94 C3
Burgh le Marsh GB . . 41 B4
Búrgio I 176 B2
Burgkirchen D 109 A3
Burgkunstadt D. . . . 82 B3
Burglengenfeld D . . 95 B4
Burgo P 148 B1
Burgoberbach D . . . 94 B2
Burgohondo E 150 B3
Burgos E 143 B3
Burgsinn D 82 B1
Burgstädt D 83 B4
Burgstall D 73 B4
Burg Stargard D . . . 74 A2
Burgsvik S 57 C4
Burgui E 144 B3
Burguillos E 162 A2
Burguillos del Cerro
  E. 155 C4
Burguillos de Toledo
  E. 151 C4
Burhaniye TR 186 C1
Burhave D 71 A5
Burie F 114 C3
Burjassot E 159 B3
Burk D 94 B2
Burkhardtsdorf D . . 83 B4
Burlada E 144 B2
Burladingen D 107 A4
Burness GB 33 B4
Burnham GB 44 B3

Burnham Market
  GB 41 C4
Burnham-on-Crouch
  GB 45 B4
Burnham-on-Sea
  GB 43 A4
Burniston GB 40 A3
Burnley GB 40 B1
Burntisland GB . . . 35 B4
Burón E 142 A1
Buronzo I 119 B5
Burovac SRB. 127 C3
Burow D. 74 A2
Burravoe GB 33 A5
Burrel AL 182 B2
Burret F 146 B2
Burriana E 159 B3
Burry Port GB 39 C2
Bürs A 107 B4
Bursa TR 186 B4
Burseryd S 60 B3
Bürstadt D 93 B4
Burton GB 37 B4
Burton Agnes GB . . 41 A3
Burton Bradstock
  GB 43 B4
Burton Latimer GB . 44 A3
Burton upon Stather
  GB 40 B3
Burton upon Trent
  GB 40 C2
Burträsk S 200 B6
Burujón E 151 C3
Burwell GB 45 A4
Burwick GB 33 C4
Bury GB. 40 B1
Bury St Edmunds
  GB 45 A4
Burzenin PL. 86 A2
Busachi I 179 B2
Busalla I 134 A1
Busana I 134 A3
Busano I 119 B4
Busca I 133 A3
Busch D 73 B4
Bušévec HR. 124 B2
Bushat AL 182 B1
Bushey GB 44 B3
Bushmills GB 27 A4
Bušince SK 112 A3
Buskhyttan S 56 B2
Busko-Zdrój PL. . . . 87 B4
Busot E 159 C3
Busovača BIH 139 A3
Busquistar E 163 B4
Bussang F. 106 B1
Busseto I 120 C3
Bussière-Badil F . . 115 C4
Bussière-Poitevine
  F. 115 B4
Bussolengo I 121 B3
Bussoleno I 119 B4
Bussum NL 70 B2
Busto Arsízio I 120 B1
Büsum D 64 B1
Butera I 177 B3
Butgenbach B 80 B2
Butler's Bridge IRL . 27 B3
Butryny PL. 77 A5
Bütschwil CH 107 B4
Buttermere GB 36 B3
Buttevant IRL. 29 B3
Buttle GB 57 C4
Buttstädt D 82 A3
Butzbach D 81 B4
Bützfleth D 72 A2
Bützow D. 65 C4
Buxières-les-Mines
  F. 104 C1
Buxtehude D 72 A2
Buxton GB. 40 B2
Buxy F 104 C3
Büyükçekmece
  TR 186 A3
Büyükkariştiran
  TR 186 A2
Büyükorhan TR . . . 186 C3
Buzançais F. 103 C3
Buzancy F 91 B4
Buzău RO 17 C7
Buzet HR 122 B2
Buziaş RO 126 B3
Buzsák H 111 C4
Buzy F 145 A3
By S 50 B3
Byala BG 17 D6
Byaroza BY 13 B6
Byczyna PL 86 A2
Bydalen S 199 B10
Bydgoszcz PL. 76 A3
Bygdin N 47 A5
Bygdsiljum S. 200 B6
Bygland N 53 B3
Bygstad N 46 A2
Bykhaw BY 13 B9
Bykle N 52 A3
Bylderup-Bov DK . . 64 B2
Byrkjedal N 52 B2
Byrkjelo N 198 D3
Byrum DK 58 A3
Byšice CZ 84 B2
Byske S 2 D7
Býškovice CZ 98 B1
Bysław PL 76 A2
Bystré CZ. 97 B4
Bystřice CZ 96 B2
Bystrice CZ 98 B2

Bystřice nad
  Pernštejnem CZ . . 97 B4
Bystřice pod Hostýnem
  CZ 98 B1
Bystrzyca Kłodzka
  PL. 85 B4
Bytča SK 98 B2
Bytnica PL. 75 B4
Bytom PL 86 B2
Bytom Odrzański
  PL. 85 A3
Bytów PL 68 A2
Byxelkrok S. 62 A5
Bzenec CZ. 98 C1
Bzince SK 98 C1

C

Çağa TR. 187 B7
Cabacos P 154 B2
Cabaj-Čápor SK . . . 98 C2
Cabana E 140 A2
Cabanac-et-Villagrains
  F. 128 B2
Cabañaquinta E . . 142 A1
Cabanas P 160 B2
Cabañas del Castillo
  E. 156 A2
Cabañas de Yepes
  E. 151 C4
Cabanelles E 147 B3
Cabanes E 153 B4
Cabanillas E 144 B2
Čabar HR 123 B3
Cabasse F 132 B2
Cabdella E 146 B2
Cabeceiras de Basto
  P. 148 A1
Cabeço de Vide P . 155 B3
Cabella Ligure I. . . 120 C2
Cabeza del Buey E 156 B2
Cabeza la Vaca E . 161 A3
Cabezamesada E . 151 C4
Cabezarados I . . . 157 B3
Cabezarrubias del
  Puerto E 157 B3
Cabezas del Villar
  E. 150 B2
Cabezas Rubias E. 161 B2
Cabezón E 142 C2
Cabezón de la Sal
  E. 142 A2
Cabezón de Liébana
  E. 142 A2
Cabezuela E 151 A4
Cabezuela del Valle
  E. 149 B4
Cabo de Gata E . . 164 C2
Cabo de Palos E . . 165 B4
Cabolafuente E . . . 152 A1
Cabourg F 89 A3
Cabra
  E. 163 A3
  P. 148 B2
Cabrach GB 32 D3
Cabra del Santo Cristo
  E. 163 A4
Cábras I 179 C2
Cabreiro P 140 C2
Cabreiros E 140 A3
Cabrejas E 152 B1
Cabrela P. 154 C2
Cabrillas E 149 B3
Cabuna HR 125 B3
Čačak SRB. 127 D2
Cáccamo I 176 B2
Caccuri I 174 B2
Cacela P. 160 B2
Cacém P 154 C1
Cáceres E 155 B4
Cachafeiro E 140 B2
Cáchopo P 160 B2
Cachtice SK. 98 C1
Cacin E 163 A4
Čačinci HR. 125 B3
Cadafais P. 154 C1
Cadalen F 129 C5
Cadalso E 149 B3
Cadaqués E 147 B4
Cadaval P. 154 B1
Cadavedo E 141 A4
Čadavica BIH. 138 A2
Cadéac F 145 B4
Cadelbosco di Sopra
  I 121 C3
Cadenazzo CH. . . . 120 A1
Cadenberge D. 64 C2
Cadenet F. 131 B4
Cadeuil F 114 C3
Cádiar E 164 C1
Cadillac F. 128 B2
Cádiz E 162 B1
Čadjavica HR 125 B3
Cadouin F 129 B3
Cadours F 129 C4
Cadrete E 152 A3
Caen F 89 A3
Caerleon GB 39 C4
Caernarfon GB 38 A2
Caerphilly GB 39 C3
Caersws GB. 39 B3
Cafede P 155 B3
Caggiano I 172 B1
Cagli I 136 B1
Cágliari I 179 C3

Čaglin HR 125 B3
Cagnano Varano I . 171 B3
Cagnes-sur-Mer F . 132 B3
Caher IRL. 29 B4
Caherciveen IRL. . . 29 C1
Caherdaniel IRL. . . 29 C1
Cahors F 129 B4
Cahul MD. 17 C8
Caiazzo I 170 B2
Caion E 140 A2
Cairndow GB 34 B3
Cairnryan GB. 36 B1
Cairo Montenotte I 133 A4
Caister-on-Sea GB . 41 C5
Caistor GB 41 B3
Caivano I 170 C2
Cajarc F 129 B4
Čajniče BIH 139 B5
Çakırlar TR. 189 C5
Çakmak TR 187 C6
Cakovec HR. 124 A2
Çal TR 189 A4
Cala E. 161 B3
Calabritto I 172 B1
Calaceite E 153 B4
Calacuccia F 180 A2
Cala d'Or E 167 B3
Calaf E 147 C2
Calafat RO 17 C5
Calafell E 147 C2
Cala Galdana E . . 167 B3
Cala Gonone I . . . 178 B3
Calahonda
  Granada E 163 B4
  Málaga E 163 B3
Calahorra E 144 B2
Calais F 78 B1
Cala Llonga E . . . 166 C1
Calalzo di Cadore I 109 C3
Cala Millor E 167 B3
Calamocha E 152 B2
Calamonaci I 176 B2
Calanais GB. 31 A2
Calañas E 161 B3
Calanda E 153 B3
Calangianus I 178 B3
Călăraşi RO 17 C7
Cala Ratjada E . . . 167 B3
Calascibetta I 177 B3
Calasetta I 179 C2
Calasparra E 164 A3
Calatafimi I 176 B1
Calatayud E 152 A2
Calatorao E 152 A2
Calau D 84 A1
Calbe D 73 C4
Calcena E 152 A2
Calcinelli I 136 B1
Calco I 120 B2
Caldara I 172 B1
Caldaro sulla strada del
  Vino I 121 A4
Caldas da Rainha
  P. 154 B1
Caldas de Bo i E . . 145 B4
Caldas de Malavella
  E. 147 C3
Caldas de Reis E . 140 B2
Caldas de San Jorge
  P. 148 B1
Caldas de Vizela P 148 A1
Caldaso de los Vidrios
  E. 150 B3
Caldbeck GB 36 B3
Caldearenas E . . . 145 B3
Caldelas P 148 A1
Calders E 147 C2
Caldes de Montbui
  E. 147 C3
Caldicot GB 39 C4
Caldirola I 120 C2
Caledon GB 27 B4
Calella
  Barcelona E 147 C3
  Girona E 147 C4
Calenzana F 180 A1
Calera de León E . 161 A3
Calera y Chozas E . 150 C3
Caleruega E 143 C3
Caleruela E 150 C2
Cales de Mallorca
  E. 167 B3
Calestano I 134 A3
Calfsound GB 33 B4
Calgary GB 34 B1
Calimera I 173 B4
Calitri I 172 B1
Calizzano I 133 A4
Callac F 100 A2
Callan IRL 30 B1
Callander GB. 35 B3
Callas F 132 B2
Calliano
  Piemonte I 119 B5
  Trentino Alto Adige
  I 121 B4
Callington GB 42 B2
Callosa de Ensarriá
  E. 159 C3
Callosa de Segura
  E. 165 A4
Callús E 147 C2
Calmbach D 93 C4
Calne GB 43 A5
Calolziocorte I . . . 120 B2
Calonge E 147 C4

Čalovec SK 112 B1
Calpe E 159 C4
Caltabellotta I 176 B2
Caltagirone I 177 B3
Caltanissetta I . . . 177 B3
Caltavuturo I 176 B2
Çaltılıbük TR 186 C3
Caltojar E 151 A5
Caluire-et-Cuire F .117 B4
Caluso I 119 B4
Calvello I 172 B1
Calvi F 180 A1
Calviá E 166 B2
Calvinet F 116 C2
Calvisson F 131 B3
Calvörde D. 73 B4
Calw D 93 C4
Calzada de Calatrava
  E. 157 B4
Calzada de Valdunciel
  E. 150 A2
Calzadilla de los Barros
  E. 155 C4
Cam GB 43 A4
Camaiore I 134 B3
Camarasa E 145 C4
Camarena E 151 B3
Camarès F 130 B1
Camaret-sur-Aigues
  F. 131 A3
Camaret-sur-Mer F 100 A1
Camarillas E 153 B3
Camariñas E 140 A1
Camarma E 151 B4
Camarzana de Tera
  E. 141 B4
Camas E 162 A1
Camastra I 176 B2
Cambados E 140 B2
Cambarinho P. . . . 148 B1
Camberley GB. . . . 44 B3
Cambil E 163 A4
Cambligeu F 78 B2
Camborne GB 42 B1
Cambrai F. 78 B3
Cambre E 140 A2
Cambridge GB. . . . 45 A4
Cambrils E 147 C2
Cambs D 65 C4
Camburg D 83 A3
Camden GB 44 B3
Cameleño E 142 A2
Camelford GB 42 B2
Camerano I 136 B2
Camerino I 136 B2
Camerota I 172 B1
Camigliatello Silano
  I 174 B2
Caminha P. 148 A1
Caminomorisco E . 149 B3
Caminreal E 152 B2
Camisano Vicentino
  I 121 B4
Camlıdere TR 187 B7
Cammarata I 176 B2
Camogli I 134 A2
Camp IRL 29 B2
Campagna I 172 B1
Campagnano di Roma
  I 168 A2
Campagnático I . . . 135 C4
Campan F 145 A4
Campana I 174 B2
Campanario E 156 B2
Campanillas E . . . 163 B3
Campano E 162 B1
Campaspero E . . . 151 A3
Campbeltown GB . . 34 C2
Campello
  E. 165 A4
  P. 154 B1
Campelos P 154 B1
Campi Bisénzio I . . 135 B4
Campico López E . 165 B3
Campíglia Maríttima
  I 134 B3
Campillo de Altobuey
  E. 158 B2
Campillo de Aragón
  E. 152 A2
Campillo de Arenas
  E. 163 A4
Campillo de Llerena
  E. 156 B2
Campillos E 162 A3
Campo da Feira E . 140 A3
Campodársego I . . 121 B4
Campo de Bacerros
  E. 141 B3
Campo de Caso E . 142 A1
Campo de Criptana
  E. 157 A4
Campodolcino I . . . 120 A2
Campofelice di Roccella
  I 176 B2
Campofiorito I 176 B2

Campofórmido I . . . 122 A2
Campofranco I . . . 176 B2
Campofrío E 161 B3
Campogalliano I . . 121 C3
Campo Ligure I . . . 133 A4
Campolongo I 109 C3
Campo Lugar E . . . 156 A2
Campo Maior P . . . 155 B3
Campomanes E . . 141 A5
Campomarino I . . . 170 B3
Campo Molino I . . . 133 A3
Campomono F . . . 180 B1
Campo Real E . . . 151 B4
Camporeale I 176 B2
Camporeggiano I . . 136 B1
Camporrells E . . . 145 C4
Camporrobles E . . 158 B2
Campos P 148 A2
Camposampiero I . 121 B4
Camposanto I 121 C4
Campos del Port E 167 B3
Camposines E . . . 153 A4
Campotéjar E 163 A4
Campotosto I. 169 A3
Campo Túres I . . . 108 C2
Camprodón E 147 B3
Campsegret F 129 B3
Camrose GB 39 C1
Camuñas E 157 A4
Çamyolu TR 189 C7
Çan TR 186 B2
Cana I 135 C4
Cañada del Hoyo
  E. 158 B2
Cañadajuncosa E . 158 B1
Cañada Rosal E . . 162 A2
Čanak HR. 123 C4
Çanakkale TR 186 B1
Canale I 119 C4
Canales
  Asturias E 141 B5
  Castellón de la Plana
  E. 159 B3
Canals E 159 C3
Canal San Bovo I . 121 A4
Cañamares E 152 B1
Cañamero E 156 A2
Cañar E 163 B4
Cañate la Real E . . 162 B2
Cañaveral E 155 B4
Cañaveral de León
  E. 161 A3
Cañaveras E 152 B1
Cañaveruelas E . . 151 B5
Canazei I 108 C2
Cancale F 88 B2
Cancellara I 172 B1
Cancello ed Arnone
  I 170 B2
Cancon F 129 B3
Canda E 141 B4
Candamil E 140 A3
Candanchu E 145 B3
Candarlı TR 186 D1
Candas E 141 A5
Candasnos E 153 A4
Candé F 101 B4
Candela I 172 A1
Candelario E 150 B2
Candeleda E 150 B2
Candide Casamazzago
  I 109 C3
Candin E 141 B4
Candosa P 148 B2
Canecas P 154 C1
Canelli I 119 C5
Canena E 157 B4
Canencia E 151 B4
Canero E 141 A4
Canet F 130 B2
Canet de Mar E . . 147 C3
Canet d'en Berenguer
  E. 159 B3
Cañete E 158 B2
Cañete de las Torres
  E. 163 A3
Canet-Plage F 146 B4
Canfranc E 145 B3
Cangas
  Lugo E 141 A3
  Pontevedra E 140 B2
Cangas de Narcea
  E. 141 A4
Cangas de Onís E . 142 A1
Canha P 154 C2
Canhestros P. 160 A1
Canicatì I 176 B2
Canicattini Bagni I 177 B4
Canicosa de la Sierra
  E. 143 C3
Caniles E 164 B2
Canillas de Aceituno
  E. 163 B3
Canino I 168 A1
Canisy F 88 A2
Cañizal E 150 A2
Cañizo E 142 C1
Canjáyar E 164 C2
Çankırı TR 23 A7
Cannai I 179 C2
Cannara I 136 B1
Cánnero Riviera I . 120 A1
Cannes F 132 B3

Canneto
  Sicilia I 177 A3
  Toscana I 135 B3
Canneto sull'Oglio
  I 120 B3
Cannich GB 32 D2
Cannóbio I 120 A1
Cannock GB 40 C1
Canonbie GB 36 A4
Canosa di Púglia I . 171 B4
Can Pastilla E 166 B2
C'an Picafort E . . . 167 B3
Cantalapiedra E . . . 150 A2
Cantalejo E 151 A4
Cantalgallo E 161 A3
Cantalice I 169 A2
Cantalpino E 150 A2
Cantalupo in Sabina
  I 168 A2
Cantanhede P 148 B1
Cantavieja E 153 B3
Čantavir SRB . . . 126 B1
Canterbury GB 45 B5
Cantiano I 136 B1
Cantillana E 162 A2
Cantiveros E 150 B3
Cantoria E 164 B2
Cantù I 120 B2
Canvey GB 45 B4
Cany-Barville F . . . 89 A4
Canyet de Mar E . . 147 C3
Caol GB 34 B2
Cáorle I 122 B1
Caorso I 120 B2
Capáccio I 172 B1
Capaci I 176 A2
Capálbio I 168 A1
Capánnori I 134 B3
Caparde BIH . . . 139 A4
Caparroso E 144 B2
Capbreton F 128 C1
Capdenac-Gare F . 116 C2
Cap-de-Pin F 128 B2
Capdepera E 167 B3
Capel Curig GB . . . 38 A3
Capellades E 147 C2
Capena I 168 A2
Capendu F 146 A3
Capestang F 130 B2
Capestrano I 169 A3
Cap Ferret F 128 B1
Capileira E 163 B4
Capinha P 148 B2
Ca'Pisani I 122 C1
Capistrello I 169 B3
Capizzi I 177 B3
Caplje BIH 124 C2
Čapljina BIH . . . 139 B3
Capo di Ponte I . . 120 A3
Caposile I 122 B1
Capoterra I 179 C2
Cappamore IRL . . . 29 B3
Cappeln D 71 B5
Cappoquin IRL . . . 29 B4
Capracotta I 169 B4
Capránica E 168 A2
Caprarola I 168 A2
Capretta I 135 C5
Capri I 170 C2
Capriati a Volturno
  I 170 B2
Caprino Veronese
  I 121 B3
Captieux F 128 B2
Cápua I 170 B2
Capurso I 173 A2
Capvern F 145 A4
Carabaña E 151 B4
Carabias E 151 A4
Caracal RO . . . 17 C6
Caracenilla E . . . 152 B1
Caráglio I 133 A3
Caraman F 146 A2
Caramánico Terme
  I 169 A4
Caranga E 141 A4
Caranguejeira P . . 154 B2
Caransebeş RO . . . 16 C5
Carantec F 100 A2
Carapelle I 171 B3
Carasco I 134 A2
Carate Brianza I . . . 120 B2
Caravaca de la Cruz
  E 164 A3
Caravággio I 120 B2
Carbajal E 163 B3
Carbajo E 155 B3
Carballeda E 140 B3
Carballeda de Avia
  E 140 B2
Carballo E 140 A2
Carbis Bay GB 42 B1
Carbon-Blanc F . . . 128 B2
Carbonera de Frentes
  E 143 C4
Carboneras E 164 C3
Carboneras de
  Guadazaón E . 158 B2
Carbonero el Mayor
  E 151 A3
Carboneros E 157 B4
Carbónia I 179 C2
Carbonin I 108 C3
Carbonne F 146 A2

Carbost
  Highland GB 31 B2
  Highland GB 31 B2
Carcaboso E 149 B3
Carcabuey E 163 A3
Carcaixent E 159 B3
Carcans F 128 A1
Carcans-Plage F . . 128 A1
Carção P 149 A3
Carcar E 144 B2
Cárcare I 133 A4
Carcassonne F . . 146 A3
Carcastillo E 144 B2
Carcedo de Burgos
  E 143 B3
Carcelén E 159 B2
Carcès F 132 B2
Carchelejo E 163 A4
Çardak
  Çanakkale TR . . . 186 B1
  Denizli TR 189 B4
Cardedeu E 147 C3
Cardeña E 157 B3
Cardenete E 158 B2
Cardeñosa E 150 B3
Cardeto I 175 C1
Cardiff GB 39 C3
Cardigan GB 39 B2
Cardona E 147 C2
Cardosos P 154 B2
Carei RO . . . 16 B5
Carentan F 88 A2
Carentoir F 101 B3
Careri I 175 C2
Carevdar HR . . 124 A2
Cargèse F 180 A1
Carhaix-Plouguer
  F 100 A2
Caria P 148 B2
Cariati I 174 B2
Carignan F 91 B5
Carignano I 119 C4
Cariñena E 152 A2
Carini I 176 A2
Cariño E 140 A3
Carinola I 170 B1
Carisbrooke GB . . 44 C2
Carlabhagh GB . . 31 A2
Carlepont F 90 B3
Carlet E 159 B3
Carlingford IRL . . 27 B4
Carlisle GB 36 B4
Carloforte I 179 C2
Carlópoli I 175 B2
Carlow
  D 65 C3
  IRL 30 B2
Carlton GB 40 C2
Carluke GB 35 C4
Carmagnola I . . . 119 C4
Carmarthen GB . . . 39 C2
Carmaux F 130 A1
Carmena E 150 C3
Cármenes E 142 B1
Carmine I 133 A3
Carmona E 162 A2
Carmonita E 155 B4
Carmyllie GB 35 B5
Carnac F 100 B2
Carndonagh IRL . . 27 A3
Carnew IRL 30 B2
Carnforth GB 37 B4
Cárnia I 122 A2
Carnlough GB . . . 27 B5
Carno GB 39 B3
Carnon Plage F . . . 131 B2
Carnota E 140 B1
Carnoustie GB . . . 35 B5
Carnwath GB 35 C4
Carolei I 174 B2
Carolinensiel D . . . 71 A4
Carolles F 88 B2
Carona I 120 A2
Caronía I 177 A3
Carovigno I 173 B3
Carovilli I 170 B2
Carpaneto Piacentino
  I 120 C2
Carpegna I 135 B5
Carpenédolo I . . . 121 B3
Carpentras F 131 A4
Carpi I 121 C3
Carpignano Sésia
  I 119 B5
Carpineti I 134 A3
Carpineto Romano
  I 169 B3
Cărpinis RO . . . 126 B2
Carpino I 171 B3
Carpinone I 170 B2
Carpio E 150 A2
Carquefou F 101 B4
Carqueiranne F . . 132 B2
Carral E 140 A2
Carranque E 151 B4
Carrapichana P . . . 148 B2
Carrara I 134 A3
Carraroe IRL . . 28 A2
Carrascalejo E 156 A2
Carrascosa del Campo
  E 151 B5
Carratraca E 162 B3
Carrazeda de Ansiães
  P 148 A2
Carrazedo de
  Montenegro P . . 148 A2
Carrbridge GB 32 D3
Carregal do Sal P . 148 B1

Carreña E 142 A2
Carrick IRL . . . 26 B2
Carrickart IRL . . . 26 A3
Carrickfergus GB . . 27 B5
Carrickmacross IRL 27 C4
Carrick-on-Shannon
  IRL 26 C2
Carrick-on-Suir IRL . 30 B1
Carrigallen IRL . . . 27 C3
Carrión E 161 B3
Carrión de Calatrava
  E 157 A4
Carrión de los Condes
  E 142 B2
Carrizo de la Ribera
  E 141 B5
Carrizosa E 157 B5
Carro F 131 B4
Carrocera E 142 B1
Carrouge CH . . . 106 C1
Carrouges F 89 B3
Carrù I 133 A3
Carryduff GB 27 B5
Carry-le-Rouet F . . 131 B4
Carsóli I 169 A3
Carsphairn GB . . . 36 A2
Cartagena E 165 B4
Cártama E 163 B3
Cartaxo P 154 B2
Cartaya E 161 B2
Carteret F 88 A2
Cartes E 142 A2
Carúncho I 170 B2
Carviçães P 149 A3
Carvin F 78 B2
Carvoeira P 154 B1
Carvoeiro P 160 B1
Casabermeja E . . . 163 B3
Casa Branca
  Portalegre P 154 C3
  Setúbal P 154 C2
Casacalenda I . . . 170 B2
Casa Castalda I . . . 136 B1
Casaio E 141 B4
Casa l'Abate I . . 173 B4
Casalarreina E . . 143 B4
Casalbordino I . . . 169 A4
Casalborgone I . . . 119 B4
Casalbuttano ed Uniti
  I 174 A1
Casàl di Principe I . 170 B2
Casalécchio di Reno
  I 135 A4
Casale Monferrato
  I 119 B5
Casalina I 136 C1
Casalmaggiore I . . 121 C3
Casalnuovo
  Monterotaro I . . 170 B3
Casaloldo I 121 B3
Casalpusterlengo I 120 B2
Casamássima I . . . 173 B2
Casamicciola Terme
  I 170 C1
Casamozza F 180 A2
Casarabonela E . . 162 B3
Casarano I 173 B4
Casar de Cáceres
  E 155 B4
Casar de Palomero
  E 149 B3
Casarejos E 143 C3
Casares E 162 B2
Casares de las Hurdes
  E 149 B3
Casariche E 163 A3
Casarrubios del Monte
  E 151 B3
Casas de Don Pedro
  E 156 A2
Casas de Fernando
  Alonso E 158 B1
Casas de Haro E . . 158 B1
Casas de Juan Gil
  E 159 B2
Casas del Juan Núñez
  E 158 B2
Casas del Puerto
  E 159 C2
Casas del Río E . . 159 B2
Casas de Millán E . 155 B4
Casas de Reina E . . 156 B2
Casas de Ves E . . 159 B2
Casas-Ibáñez E . . 158 B2
Casasimarro E . . 158 B1
Casas Nuevas E . . 164 B3
Casasola E 150 B3
Casasola de Arión
  E 150 A2
Casasuertes E 142 A2
Casatejada E . . 150 C2
Casavieja E . . 150 B3
Casazza I 120 B2
Cascais P 154 C1
Cascante E 144 C2
Cascante del Rio E 152 B2
Cáscia I 169 A3
Casciana Terme I . . 134 B3
Cáscina I 134 B3
Cáseda E 144 B2
Casekow D 74 A3
Casella I 134 A2
Caselle Torinese I . 119 B4
Casemurate I . . . 135 A5
Casenove I 136 C1
Caseres E 153 A4

Caserío Benali E . . 159 B3
Caserta I 170 B2
Casével P 160 B1
Cashel IRL . . . 29 B4
Casillas E 150 B3
Casillas de Coria E 155 B4
Casina I 134 A3
Casinos E 159 B3
Čáslav CZ . . . 97 B3
Cásola Valsénio I . 135 A4
Cásole d'Elsa I . . 135 B4
Casória I 170 C2
Caspe E 153 A3
Cassàde la Selva
  E 147 C3
Cassagnas F 130 A2
Cassagnes-Bégonhès
  F 130 A1
Cassano allo Iónio
  I 174 B2
Cassano d'Adda I . 120 B2
Cassano delle Murge
  I 171 C4
Cassano Magnago
  I 120 B1
Cassano Spinola I . 120 C1
Cassel F 78 B2
Cassibile I 177 C4
Cassine I 119 C5
Cassino I 169 B3
Cassis F 132 B1
Cassolnovo I 120 B1
Cassuéjouls F . . . 116 C2
Častá SK 98 C1
Castagnaro I 121 B4
Castagneto Carducci
  I 134 B3
Castagnola CH . . . 120 A1
Castalla E 159 C3
Castañar de Ibor E 156 A2
Castasegna CH . . . 120 A2
Cástano Primo I . . . 120 B1
Castéggio I 120 B2
Casteição P 148 B2
Castejón E 144 B2
Castejón de Monegros
  E 153 A3
Castejón de Sos E 145 B4
Castejón de Valdejasa
  E 144 C3
Castèl Baronia I . . . 172 A1
Castel Bolognese I 135 A4
Castelbuono I . . . 177 B3
Casteldáccia I . . . 176 A2
Castel d'Aiano I . . 135 A3
Castel d'Ario I . . . 121 B3
Castel de Cabra E 153 B3
Casteldelfino I . . . 132 A3
Castél del Monte I 169 A3
Castel del Piano I . 135 C4
Castèl di Iúdica I . . 177 B3
Castel di Rio I . . . 135 A4
Castèl di Sangro I . 169 B4
Castél di Tora I . . . 169 A2
Casteldidardo I . . . 136 B2
Castelfidardo I . . . 136 B2
Castelfiorentino I . 135 B3
Castelforte I 169 B3
Castelfranco Emilia
  I 121 C4
Castelfranco in Miscano
  I 170 B3
Castelfranco Véneto
  I 121 B4
Castèl Frentano I . 169 A4
Casteljaloux F 128 B3
Castellabate I 170 C2
Castellammare del Golfo
  I 176 A1
Castellammare di Stábia
  I 170 C2
Castellamonte I . . . 119 B4
Castellana Grotte I 173 B3
Castellane F 132 B2
Castellaneta I . . . 173 B2
Castellaneta Marina
  I 173 B2
Castellar E 157 B4
Castellarano I . . . 135 A3
Castellar de la Frontera
  E 162 B2
Castellar de la Ribera
  E 147 B2
Castellar del Vallès
  E 147 C3
Castellar de Santiago
  E 157 B4
Castelldans E 153 A4
Castell de Cabres
  E 153 B4
Castell de Castells
  E 159 C3
Castelldefels E . . . 147 C2
Castell de Ferro E 163 B4
Castelleone I . . . 120 B2
Castellet E 147 C2
Castelletto di Brenzone
  I 121 B3
Castellfollit de la Roca
  E 147 B3
Castellfollit de
  Riubregos E 147 C2

Castellfort E 153 B3
Castellina in Chianti
  I 135 B4
Castellina Marittima
  I 134 B3
Castellóde Farfaña
  E 145 C4
Castellóde la Plana
  E 159 B3
Castello d'Empúries
  E 147 B4
Castello di Fiemme
  I 121 A4
Castelloli E 147 C2
Castellón de Rugat
  E 159 C3
Castellote I 153 B3
Castello Tesino I . . 121 A4
Castellterçol E . . . 147 C3
Castellúcchio I . . . 121 B3
Castellúccio de'Sáuri
  I 171 B3
Castelluccio Inferiore
  I 174 B1
Castelmassa I . . . 121 B4
Castelmáuro I . . . 170 B2
Castelmoron-sur-Lot
  F 129 B3
Castelnaudary F . 146 A2
Castelnau-de-Médoc
  F 128 A2
Castelnau-de-Montmirail
  F 129 C4
Castelnau-Magnoac
  F 145 A4
Castelnau-Montratier
  F 129 B4
Castelnou E 153 A3
Castelnovo ne'Monti
  I 134 A3
Castelnuovo
  Berardenga I . . . 135 B4
Castelnuovo della
  Dáunia I 170 B3
Castelnuovo di
  Garfagnana I . . . 134 A3
Castelnuovo di Val di
  Cécina I 135 B3
Castelnuovo Don Bosco
  I 119 B4
Castelnuovo Scrivia
  I 120 C1
Castelo Branco
  Bragança P 149 A3
  Castelo Branco P . . 155 B3
Castelo de Paiva P 148 A1
Castelo de Vide P . 155 B3
Castelo do Neiva P 148 A1
Castelo Mendo P . . 149 B3
Castelraimondo I . 136 B2
Castel San Gimignano
  I 135 B4
Castèl San Giovanni
  I 120 B2
Castèl San Pietro Terme
  I 135 A4
Castelsantángelo
  I 136 C2
Castél Sant'Elia I . 168 A2
Castelsaraceno I . . 174 A1
Castelsardo I . . . 178 B2
Castelserás E . . . 153 B3
Casteltérmini I . . . 176 B2
Castelvecchio Subéquo
  I 169 A3
Castelvetrano I . . . 176 B1
Castél Volturno I . . 170 B1
Castenédolo I . . . 120 B3
Castets F 128 C1
Castiádas I 179 C3
Castiglioncello I . . 134 B3
Castiglione I . . . 169 A3
Castiglione Chiavarese
  I 134 A2
Castiglione d'Adda
  I 120 B2
Castiglione dei Pepoli
  I 135 A4
Castiglione del Lago
  I 135 B5
Castiglione della
  Pescáia I 135 C3
Castiglione delle
  Stiviere I 121 B3
Castiglione di Sicilia
  I 177 B4
Castiglione d'Órcia
  I 135 B4
Castiglione Messer
  Marino I 170 B2
Castiglione Messer
  Raimondo I 169 A3
Castiglion Fibocchi
  I 135 B4
Castiglion Fiorentino
  I 135 B4
Castilblanco E . . . 156 A2
Castilblanco de los
  Arroyos E 161 B4
Castil de Peones E 143 B3
Castilfrio de la Sierra
  E 144 C1
Castilgaleu E . . . 145 B4
Castiliscar E . . . 144 B2
Castilleja E 161 B3
Castillejar E 164 B2

Castillejo de Martin
  Viejo E 149 B3
Castillejo de Mesleón
  E 151 A4
Castillejo de Robledo
  E 151 A4
Castillo de Bayuela
  E 150 B3
Castillo de Locubín
  E 163 A4
Castillonès F . . . 129 B3
Castillon-la-Bataille
  F 128 B2
Castillon-Len-
  Couserans F 146 B2
Castilruiz E 144 C1
Castione CH . . . 120 A2
Castions di Strada
  I 122 B2
Castirla F 180 A2
Castlebar IRL . . . 28 A2
Castlebellingham
  IRL 27 C4
Castleblaney IRL . . . 27 B4
Castlebridge IRL . . 30 B2
Castle Cary GB . . . 43 A4
Castlecomer IRL . . 30 B1
Castlederg GB . . . 27 B3
Castledermot IRL . . 30 B2
Castle Douglas GB 36 B3
Castleford GB . . . 40 B2
Castleisland IRL . . . 29 B2
Castlemaine IRL . . . 29 B2
Castlemartyr IRL . . . 29 C3
Castlepollard IRL . . 30 A1
Castlerea IRL . . . 28 A3
Castleton GB . . . 40 B2
Castletown
  Highland GB 32 C3
  Isle of Man GB 36 B2
Castletown Bearhaven
  IRL 29 C2
Castletownroche
  IRL 29 B3
Castlewellan GB . . . 27 B5
Casto I 120 B3
Castrejón E 150 A2
Castrelo del Valle
  E 141 B3
Castres F 130 B1
Castricum NL 70 B1
Castries F 131 B2
Castrignano del Capo
  I 173 C4
Castril E 164 B2
Castrillo de Duero
  E 151 A4
Castrillo de la Vega
  E 143 C3
Castrillo de Onielo
  E 142 C2
Castro
  E 142 A2
  I 173 B4
Castrocabón E . . . 141 B5
Castro-Caldelas E . 141 B3
Castrocaro Terme
  I 135 A4
Castrocontrigo E . 141 B4
Castro Daire P . . . 148 B2
Castro dei Volsci I . 169 B3
Castro del Rio E . . 163 A3
Castro de Rey E . . 141 A3
Castrofilippo I . . . 176 B2
Castrogonzaio E . . 142 B1
Castrojeriz E 142 B2
Castro Laboreiro P 140 B2
Castro Marim P . . . 160 B2
Castromonte E . . . 142 C1
Castromudarra E . 142 B1
Castronuevo E . . . 142 C1
Castronuño E . . . 150 A2
Castropol E 141 A3
Castroreale I 177 A4
Castroserracín E . . 151 A4
Castro-Urdiales E . 143 A3
Castroverde E . . . 141 A3
Castro Verde P . . . 160 B1
Castroverde de Campos
  E 142 C1
Castroverde de Cerrato
  E 142 C2
Castrovillari I 174 B2
Castuera E 156 B2
Catadau E 159 B3
Catáeggio I 120 A2
Çatalca TR 186 A3
Catallar TR 189 C5
Çatalzeytin TR . . 23 A8
Catánia I 177 B4
Catanzaro I 175 C2
Catanzaro Marina I 175 C2
Catarroja E 159 B3
Catarruchos P . . . 148 B1
Catcleugh GB . . . 37 A4
Catenanuova I 177 B3
Caterham GB 44 B3
Cati E 153 B4
Čatići BIH 139 A4
Catignano I 169 A3
Catillon F 91 A3
Catoira E 140 B2
Caton GB 37 B4
Catral E 165 A4
Catterick GB 37 B5
Cáttolica I 136 B1
Cáttolica Eraclea I . 176 B2

Catton GB 37 B4
Caudebec-en-Caux F 89 A4
Caudete E 159 C3
Caudete de las Fuentes E 159 B2
Caudiel E 159 B3
Caudiès-de-Fenouillèdes F 146 B3
Caudry F 91 A3
Caulkerbush GB 36 B3
Caulnes F 101 A3
Caulónia I 175 C2
Caumont-l'Evente F 88 A3
Caunes-Minervois F 146 A3
Cauro F 180 B1
Caussade F 129 B4
Causse-de-la-Selle F 130 B2
Cauterets F 145 B3
Cava de Tirreni I 170 C2
Cavaglia I 119 B5
Cavaillon F 131 B4
Cavalaire-sur-Mer F 132 B2
Cavaleiro P 160 B1
Cavalese I 121 A4
Cavallermaggiore I 119 C4
Cavallino I 122 B1
Cavan IRL 27 C3
Cavárzere I 121 B5
Çavdarhisar TR 187 C4
Çavdır TR 189 B4
Cavernães P 148 B2
Cavezzo I 121 C4
Cavignac F 128 A2
Čavle HR 123 B3
Cavo I 134 C3
Cavour I 119 C4
Cawdor GB 32 D3
Çay TR 187 D6
Çaycuma TR 187 A7
Cayeux-sur-Mer F 78 B1
Cayıralan TR 23 B8
Çayırhan TR 187 B6
Caylus F 129 B4
Cayres F 117 C3
Cazalilla E 157 C4
Cazalla de la Sierra E 156 C2
Cazals F 129 B4
Cazanuecos E 142 B1
Cazaubon F 128 C2
Cazaux F 128 B1
Cazavet F 146 A2
Cazères F 146 A2
Cazin BIH 124 C1
Cazis CH 107 C4
Čazma HR 124 B2
Cazo E 142 A1
Cazorla E 164 B2
Cazouls-lès-Béziers F 130 B2
Cea
León E 142 B1
Orense E 140 B3
Ceánuri E 143 A4
Ceauce F 88 B3
Cebolla E 150 C3
Čebovce SK 112 A3
Cebreros E 150 B3
Čečava BIH 125 C3
Ceccano I 169 B3
Cece H 112 C2
Cecenowo PL 68 A2
Čechtice CZ 96 B3
Čechtín CZ 97 B3
Cécina I 134 B3
Ceclavín E 155 B4
Cedégolo I 120 A3
Cedeira E 140 A2
Cedillo E 155 B3
Cedillo del Condado E 151 B4
Cedrillas E 153 B3
Cedynia PL 74 B3
Cée E 140 B1
Cefalù I 177 A3
Céggia I 122 B1
Cegléd H 113 B3
Ceglédbercel H 112 B3
Céglie Messápica I 173 B3
Cehegín E 164 A3
Ceilhes-et-Rocozels F 130 B2
Ceinos de Campos E 142 B1
Ceira P 148 B1
Čejč CZ 97 C4
Cekcyn PL 76 A3
Čela BIH 124 C2
Čelákovice CZ 84 B2
Celano I 169 A3
Celanova E 140 B3
Celbridge IRL 30 A2
Čelebič BIH 138 B2
Celenza Valfortore I 170 B2
Čelić BIH 125 C4
Čelinac BIH 124 C3
Celje SLO 123 A4
Cella E 152 B2
Celldömölk H 111 B4
Celle D 72 B3
Celle Ligure I 133 A4
Celles B 79 B4
Celles-sur-Belle F 115 B3
Cellino San Marco I 173 B3
Celorico da Beira P 148 B2
Celorico de Basto P 148 A1
Çeltik TR 187 C6
Çeltikçi TR 189 B5
Cemaes GB 38 A2
Cembra I 121 A4
Čemerno BIH 139 B4
Cenad RO 126 A2
Cencenighe Agordino I 121 A4
Cenei RO 126 B2
Ceneselli I 121 B4
Cenicero E 143 B4
Cenicientos E 150 B3
Censeau F 105 C5
Čenta SRB 126 B2
Centallo I 133 A3
Centelles E 147 C3
Cento I 121 C4
Centúripe I 177 B3
Cepeda la Mora E 150 B2
Cépet F 129 C4
Čepin HR 125 B4
Čepinski Martinci HR 125 B4
Cepovan SLO 122 A2
Ceprano I 169 B3
Čeralije HR 125 B3
Cerami I 177 B3
Cerano I 120 B1
Cérans Foulletourte F 102 B2
Ceraso I 172 B1
Cerbaia I 135 B4
Cerbère F 146 B4
Cercadillo E 151 A5
Cercal
Lisboa P 154 B1
Setúbal P 160 B1
Čerčany CZ 96 B2
Cerceda E 151 B4
Cercedilla E 151 B3
Cercemaggiore I 170 B2
Cercs E 147 B2
Cercy-la-Tour F 104 C2
Cerda I 176 B2
Cerdedo E 140 B2
Cerdeira P 149 B2
Cerdon F 103 B4
Cerea I 121 B4
Ceres
GB 35 B5
I 119 B4
Cerese I 121 B3
Ceresole-Reale I 119 B4
Cereste F 132 B1
Céret F 146 B3
Cerezo de Abajo E 151 A4
Cerezo de Riotirón E 143 B3
Cerfontaine B 79 B4
Cergy F 90 B2
Cerignola I 171 B3
Cérilly F 103 C4
Cerisiers F 104 A2
Cerizay F 114 B3
Çerkeş TR 23 A7
Çerkezköy TR 186 A3
Cerkije SLO 123 A3
Cerknica SLO 123 B3
Cerkno SLO 122 A2
Cerkwica PL 67 B4
Cerna HR 125 B4
Černá Hora CZ 97 B4
Cernavodă RO 17 C8
Cernay F 106 B2
Cerne Abbas GB 43 B4
Cernégula E 143 B3
Cernik HR 124 B3
Cernóbbio I 120 B2
Černošin CZ 95 B4
Cernovice CZ 96 B2
Cérons F 128 B2
Cerovlje HR 123 B3
Cerovo SK 99 C3
Cerqueto I 135 C5
Cerralbo E 149 B3
Cerreto d'Esi I 136 B1
Cerreto Sannita I 170 B2
Cerrigydrudion GB 38 A3
Cërrik AL 182 B1
Cerro Muriano E 156 B3
Certaldo I 135 B4
Certosa di Pésio I 133 A3
Cerva P 148 A2
Cervaro I 169 B3
Cervatos de la Cueza E 142 B2
Červena Řečice CZ 97 B3
Červená-Skala SK 99 C4
Cervená Voda CZ 97 A4
Cerveny Kostelec CZ 85 B4
Cervera E 147 C2
Cervera de la Cañada E 152 A2
Cervera del Llano E 158 B1
Cervera del Río Alhama E 144 B2
Cervera de Pisuerga E 142 B2
Cervéteri I 168 B2
Cérvia I 135 A5
Cerviáde les Garriques E 147 C1
Cervignano del Friuli I 122 B2
Cervinara I 170 B2
Cervione F 180 A2
Cervo E 141 A3
Cervon F 104 B2
Cesana Torinese I 119 C3
Cesarica HR 137 A4
Cesarò I 177 B3
Cesena I 135 A5
Cesenático I 135 A5
Cēsis LV 8 D4
Česká Belá CZ 97 B3
Česká Kamenice CZ 84 B2
Česká Lípa CZ 84 B2
Česká Skalice CZ 85 B4
Česká Třebová CZ 97 B4
České Budějovice CZ 96 C2
České Velenice CZ 96 C2
Český Brod CZ 96 A2
Český Dub CZ 84 B2
Český Krumlov CZ 96 C2
Český Těšín CZ 98 B2
Češljeva Bara SRB 127 C3
Çeşme TR 188 A1
Cessenon F 130 B2
Cesson-Sévigné F 101 A4
Cestas F 128 B2
Čestobrodica SRB 127 D2
Cesuras E 140 A2
Cetina E 152 A2
Cetin Grad HR 123 B4
Cetinje MNE 16 D3
Cetraro I 174 B1
Ceuti E 165 A3
Ceva I 133 A4
Cevico de la Torre E 142 C2
Cevico Navero E 142 C2
Cevins F 118 B3
Cévio CH 119 A5
Cevizli TR 189 B6
Cewice PL 68 A2
Ceylan TR 189 C4
Ceyrat F 116 B3
Ceyzériat F 118 A2
Chaam NL 79 A4
Chabanais F 115 C4
Chabeuil F 117 C5
Chabielice PL 86 A3
Chablis F 104 B2
Châbons F 118 B2
Chabówka PL 99 B3
Chabreloche F 117 B3
Chabris F 103 B3
Chagford GB 42 B3
Chagny F 105 C3
Chagoda RUS 9 C9
Chaherrero E 150 B3
Chailland F 88 B3
Chaillé-les-Marais F 114 B2
Chailles F 103 B3
Chailley F 104 A2
Chalabre F 146 B3
Chalais F 128 A3
Chalamont F 118 B2
Châlette-sur-Loing F 103 A4
Chalindrey F 105 B4
Chalkida GR 185 A4
Challacombe GB 42 A3
Challans F 114 B2
Challes-les-Eaux F 118 B2
Chalmazel F 117 B3
Chalmoux F 104 C2
Chalonnes-sur-Loire F 102 B1
Châlons-en-Champagne F 91 C4
Chalon-sur-Saône F 105 C3
Chalupy PL 69 A3
Châlus F 115 C4
Cham
CH 106 B3
D 95 B4
Chamberet F 116 B1
Chambéry F 118 B2
Chambilly F 117 A4
Chambley F 92 B1
Chambly F 90 B2
Chambois F 89 B4
Chambon-sur-Lac F 116 B2
Chambon-sur-Voueize F 116 A2
Chambord F 103 B3
Chamborigaud F 131 A2
Chamboulive F 116 B1
Chamerau D 95 B4
Chamonix-Mont Blanc F 119 B3
Chamoux-sur-Gelon F 118 B3
Champagnac-le-Vieux F 117 B3
Champagney F 106 B1
Champagnole F 105 C4
Champagny-Mouton F 115 B4
Champaubert F 91 C3
Champdeniers-St Denis F 114 B3
Champdieu F 117 B4
Champdôtre F 105 B4
Champeix F 116 B3
Champéry CH 119 A3
Champigne F 102 B1
Champignelles F 104 B2
Champigny-sur-Veude F 102 B2
Champlitte-et-le-Prelot F 105 B4
Champoluc I 119 B4
Champoly F 117 B3
Champorcher I 119 B4
Champrond-en-Gâtine F 89 B5
Champs-sur-Tarentaine F 116 B2
Champs-sur-Yonne F 104 B2
Champtoceaux F 101 B4
Chamrousse F 118 B2
Chamusca P 154 B2
Chanac F 130 A2
Chanaleilles F 117 C3
Chandler's Ford GB 44 C2
Chandra GR 185 D7
Chandrexa de Queixa E 141 B3
Chañe E 150 A3
Changy F 117 A3
Chania GR 185 D5
Channes F 104 B3
Chantada E 140 B3
Chantelle F 116 A3
Chantenay-St Imbert F 104 C2
Chanteuges F 117 B3
Chantilly F 90 B2
Chantonnay F 114 B2
Chão de Codes P 154 B2
Chaource F 104 A3
Chapa E 140 B2
Chapareillan F 118 B2
Chapel en le Frith GB 40 B2
Chapelle Royale F 103 A3
Chapelle-St Laurent F 102 C1
Charbonnat F 104 C3
Chard GB 43 B4
Charenton-du-Cher F 103 C4
Charlbury GB 44 B2
Charleroi B 79 B4
Charlestown
GB 42 B2
IRL 26 C2
Charlestown of Aberlour GB 32 D3
Charleville IRL 29 B3
Charleville-Mézières F 91 B4
Charlieu F 117 A4
Charlottenberg S 49 C4
Charlton Kings GB 44 B1
Charly F 90 C3
Charmes F 92 C2
Charmes-sur-Rhône F 117 C4
Charmey CH 106 C2
Charminster GB 43 B4
Charmont-en-Beauce F 103 A4
Charny F 104 B2
Charolles F 117 A4
Chârost F 103 C4
Charquemont F 106 B1
Charrin F 104 C2
Charroux F 115 B4
Chartres F 90 C1
Charzykow PL 68 B2
Chasseneuil-sur-Bonnieure F 115 C4
Chassigny F 105 B4
Château-Arnoux F 132 A2
Châteaubernard F 115 C3
Châteaubourg F 101 A4
Châteaubriant F 101 B4
Château-Chinon F 104 B2
Château-d'Oex CH 106 C2
Château-d'Olonne F 114 B2
Château-du-Loir F 102 B2
Châteaudun F 103 A3
Châteaugiron F 101 A4
Château-Gontier F 102 B1
Château-Landon F 103 A4
Château-la-Vallière F 102 B2
Château-l'Evêque F 129 A3
Châteaulin F 100 A1
Châteaumeillant F 103 C4
Châteauneuf
Nièvre F 104 B2
Saône-et-Loire F 117 A4
Châteauneuf-de-Randon F 117 C3
Châteauneuf-d'Ille-et-Vilaine F 88 B2
Châteauneuf-du-Faou F 100 A2
Châteauneuf-du-Pape F 131 A3
Châteauneuf-en-Thymerais F 89 B5
Châteauneuf la-Forêt F 116 B1
Châteauneuf-le-Rouge F 132 B1
Châteauneuf-sur-Charente F 115 C3
Châteauneuf-sur-Cher F 103 C4
Châteauneuf-sur-Loire F 103 B4
Châteauneuf-sur-Sarthe F 102 B1
Châteauponsac F 115 B5
Château-Porcien F 91 B4
Châteauredon F 132 A2
Châteaurenard
Bouches du Rhône F 131 B3
Loiret F 104 B1
Château-Renault F 102 B2
Châteauroux F 103 C3
Châteauroux-les-Alpes F 118 C3
Château-Salins F 92 C2
Château-Thierry F 91 B3
Châteauvillain F 105 A3
Châtel F 119 A3
Châtelaillon-Plage F 114 B2
Châtelaudren F 100 A3
Châtel-Censoir F 104 B2
Châtel-de-Neuvre F 116 A3
Châtelet B 79 B4
Châtelguyon F 116 B3
Châtellerault F 115 B4
Châtel-Montagne F 117 A3
Châtel-St Denis CH 106 C1
Châtel-sur-Moselle F 92 C2
Châtelus-Malvaleix F 116 A2
Châtenois F 105 A4
Châtenois-les-Forges F 106 B1
Chatham GB 45 B4
Châtillon I 119 B4
Châtillon-Coligny F 103 B4
Châtillon-en-Bazois F 104 B2
Châtillon-en-Diois F 118 C2
Châtillon-sur Chalaronne F 117 A4
Châtillon-sur-Indre F 103 C3
Châtillon-sur-Loire F 103 B4
Châtillon-sur-Marne F 91 B3
Châtillon-sur-Seine F 104 B3
Châtres F 91 C3
Chatteris GB 45 A4
Chatton GB 37 A5
Chauchina E 163 A4
Chaudes-Aigues F 116 C3
Chaudrey F 91 C4
Chauffailles F 117 A4
Chaulnes F 90 B2
Chaument Gistoux B 79 B4
Chaumergy F 105 C4
Chaumont F 105 A4
Chaumont-en-Vexin F 90 B1
Chaumont-Porcien F 91 B4
Chaumont-sur-Aire F 91 C5
Chaumont-sur-Loire F 103 B3
Chaunay F 115 B4
Chauny F 90 B3
Chaussin F 105 C4
Chauvigny F 115 B4
Chavagnes-en-Paillers F 114 B2
Chavanges F 91 C4
Chaves P 148 A2
Chavignon F 91 B3
Chazelles-sur-Lyon F 117 B4
Chazey-Bons F 118 B2
Cheadle
Greater Manchester GB 40 B1
Staffordshire GB 40 C2
Cheb CZ 83 B4
Chebsara RUS 9 C11
Checa E 152 B2
Chęciny PL 87 B4
Cheddar GB 43 A4
Cheddleton GB 40 B1
Chef-Boutonne F 115 B3
Cheles E 155 C3
Chella E 159 B3
Chelles F 90 C2
Chełm PL 13 C5
Chełmno
Kujawsko-Pomorskie PL 76 A3
Wielkopolskie PL 76 B3
Chelmsford GB 45 B4
Chelmuzhi RUS 9 A9
Chełmża PL 76 A3
Cheltenham GB 44 B1
Chelva E 159 B2
Chémery F 103 B3
Chemery-sur-Bar F 91 B4
Chemillé F 102 B1
Chemin F 105 C4
Chemnitz D 83 B4
Chénerailles F 116 A2
Cheniménil F 105 A5
Chenonceaux F 103 B3
Chenôve F 105 B3
Chepelare BG 183 B6
Chepstow GB 39 C4
Chera E 159 B3
Cherasco I 119 C4
Cherbonnières F 115 C3
Cherbourg F 88 A2
Cherchiara di Calábria I 174 B2
Cherepovets RUS 9 C10
Chernihiv UA 13 C9
Chernivtsi UA 17 A6
Chernobyl = Chornobyl UA 13 C9
Chernyakhovsk RUS 12 A4
Chéroy F 104 A1
Cherven BY 13 B8
Chervonohrad UA 13 C6
Cherykaw BY 13 B9
Chesham GB 44 B3
Cheshunt GB 44 B3
Chessy-lès-Pres F 104 A2
Cheste E 159 B3
Chester GB 38 A4
Chesterfield GB 40 B2
Chester-le-Street GB 37 B5
Chevagnes F 104 C2
Chevanceaux F 115 C3
Chevillon F 91 C5
Chevilly F 103 A3
Chew Magna GB 43 A4
Chézery-Forens F 118 A2
Chialamberto I 119 B4
Chiampo I 121 B4
Chianale I 119 C4
Chianciano Terme I 135 B4
Chiaramonte Gulfi I 177 B3
Chiaramonti I 178 B2
Chiaravalle I 136 B2
Chiaravalle Centrale I 175 C2
Chiaréggio I 120 A2
Chiari I 120 B2
Chiaromonte I 174 A2
Chiasso CH 120 B2
Chiávari I 134 A2
Chiavenna I 120 A2
Chiché F 102 C1
Chichester GB 44 C3
Chiclana de la Frontera E 162 B1
Chiclana de Segura E 164 A1
Chiddingfold GB 44 B3
Chieri I 119 B4
Chiesa in Valmalenco I 120 A2
Chieti I 169 A4
Chieti Scalo I 169 A4
Chiéuti I 171 B3
Chigwell GB 45 B4
Chiliomodi GR 184 B3
Chillarón de Cuenca E 152 B1
Chillarón del Rey E 151 B5
Chilleurs-aux-Bois F 103 A4
Chillón E 156 B3
Chilluevar E 164 B1
Chiloeches E 151 B4
Chimay B 91 A4
Chimeneas E 163 A4
Chinchilla de Monte Aragón E 158 C2
Chinchón E 151 B4
Chingford GB 45 B4
Chinon F 102 B2
Chióggia I 122 B1
Chiomonte I 119 B3
Chipiona E 161 C3
Chippenham GB 43 A4
Chipping Campden GB 44 A2
Chipping Norton GB 44 B2
Chipping Ongar GB 45 B4
Chipping Sodbury GB 43 A4
Chirac F 130 A2
Chirbury GB 39 B3
Chirens F 118 B2
Chirivel E 164 B2
Chirk GB 38 B3
Chirnside GB 35 C5
Chişinău = Khisinev MD 17 B8
Chişineu Criş RO 113 C5
Chissey-en-Morvan F 104 B3

Chiusa I 108 C2
Chiusa di Pésio I . . 133 A3
Chiusaforte I 122 A2
Chiusa Scláfani I . . 176 B2
Chiusi I 135 B4
Chiva E 159 B3
Chivasso I 119 B4
Chlewiska PL 87 A4
Chludowo PL 75 B5
Chlumec nad Cidlinou
CZ 84 B3
Chlum u Třeboně
CZ 96 C2
Chmielnik PL 87 B4
Chobienia PL 85 A4
Chobienice PL 75 B4
Choceň CZ 97 A4
Choceň PL 77 B4
Chochołow PL 99 B3
Chocianów PL 85 A3
Chociw PL 86 A3
Chociwel PL 75 A4
Choczewo PL 68 A2
Chodaków PL 77 B5
Chodecz PL 77 B4
Chodov CZ 83 B4
Chodzież PL 75 B5
Chojna PL 74 B3
Chojnice PL 68 B2
Chojno
Kujawsko-Pomorskie
PL 77 B4
Wielkopolskie PL . .75 B5
Chojnów PL 85 A3
Cholet F 114 A3
Chomérac F 117 C4
Chomutov CZ 83 B5
Chop UA. 12 D5
Chora GR. 184 B2
Chora Sfakion GR . 185 D5
Chorges F 132 A2
Choristanco E 140 A2
Chorley GB 38 A4
Chornobyl = Chernobyl
UA 13 C9
Chortkiv UA. 13 D6
Chorzele PL 77 A5
Chorzew PL 86 A2
Chorzów PL 86 B2
Choszczno PL 75 A4
Chotěboř CZ 97 B3
Chouilly F 91 B4
Chouto P 154 B2
Chouzy-sur-Cisse
F 103 B3
Chozas de Abajo E 142 B1
Chrast CZ 97 B3
Chrást CZ 96 B1
Chrastava CZ 84 B2
Chřibská CZ 84 B2
Christchurch GB. . . 44 C2
Christiansfeld DK . . 59 C2
Chroberz PL 87 B4
Chropyně CZ. 98 B1
Chrudim CZ 97 B3
Chrzanów PL. 86 B3
Chtelnica SK 98 C1
Chudovo RUS 9 C7
Chueca E 157 A4
Chulmleigh GB . . . 42 B3
Chur CH 107 C4
Churriana E 163 B3
Churwalden CH. . . 107 C4
Chvalšiny CZ. 96 C2
Chwaszczyno PL. . . 68 A3
Chynava CZ. 96 A2
Chýnov CZ 96 B2
Ciacova RO 126 B3
Ciadîr-Lunga MD. . . 17 B8
Ciadoncha E 143 B3
Cianciana I 176 B2
Ciano d'Enza I 134 A3
Ciążeń PL 76 B2
Cibakháza H 113 C4
Ciborro P 154 C2
Cicagna I 134 A2
Cicciano I 170 C2
Ciciliano I 169 B2
Cicognolo I 120 B3
Cidadelhe P 149 B2
Cide TR 23 A7
Cidones E 143 C4
Ciechanów
Dolnośląskie PL. . . .85 A4
Mazowieckie PL. . . .77 B5
Ciechocinek PL . . . 76 B3
Cieląd PL 87 A4
Ciemnik PL 75 A4
Ciempozuelos E . . 151 B4
Ciepielów PL 87 A5
Cierny Balog SK . . 99 C3
Cierp-Gaud F 145 B4
Cierpice PL 76 B3
Ciervana E 143 A3
Cierznie PL 68 B2
Cieslé PL 77 B5
Cieszyn PL 98 B2
Cieutat F 145 A4
Cieza E 165 A3
Cifer SK 98 C1
Çifteler TR 187 C6
Cifuentes E 151 B5
Cigales E 142 C2
Cigliano I 119 B5

Cihanbeyli TR 23 B7
Cillas E 152 B2
Cilleros E 149 B3
Cilleruelo de Arriba
E 143 C3
Cilleruelo de Bezana
E 143 B3
Cimalmotto CH . . .119 A5
Cimanes del Tejar
E 141 B5
Ciminna I 176 B2
Cimişlia MD 17 B8
Cimoláis I 122 A1
Cîmpulung RO 17 C6
Çınarcık TR 186 B4
Cinctorres E 153 B3
Cinderford GB. . . . 39 C4
Çine TR 188 B3
Činěves CZ 84 B3
Ciney B 79 B5
Cinfães P 148 A1
Cingia de Botti I . . . 120 B3
Cíngoli I 136 B2
Cinigiano I 135 C4
Cinobaňa SK 99 C3
Cinq-Mars-la-Pile
F 102 B2
Cinquefrondi I 175 C2
Cintegabelle F 146 A2
Cintruénigo E 144 B2
Ciółkowo PL 77 B4
Ciperez E 149 B3
Cirat E 153 B3
Cirella I 174 B1
Cirencester GB . . . 44 B2
Cirey-sur-Vezouze
F 92 C2
Ciria E 152 A2
Ciriè I 119 B4
Cirigliano I 174 A2
Cirò I 174 B3
Cirò Marina I 174 B3
Ciry-le-Noble F . . . 104 C3
Cislău RO 17 C7
Cismon del Grappa
I 121 B4
Cisneros E 142 B2
Cissac-Médoc F . . 128 A2
Cista CZ 96 A1
Cisterna di Latina I 169 B2
Cistérniga E 150 A3
Cisternino I 173 B3
Cistierna E 142 B1
Cítov CZ. 84 B2
Cittadella I 121 B4
Città della Pieve I . 135 C5
Cittádel Vaticano =
Vatican City I . . . 168 B2
Città di Castello I . 135 B5
Cittaducale I 169 A2
Cittanova I 175 C2
Città Sant'Angelo
I 169 A4
Ciudadela de Menorca
E 167 B3
Ciudad Real E 157 B4
Ciudad Rodrigo E . 149 B3
Ciutadilla E 147 C2
Cividale del Friuli I 122 A2
Civita I 169 A3
Civita Castellana I . 168 A2
Civitanova Alta I . . 136 B2
Civitanova Marche
I 136 B2
Civitavécchia I . . . 168 A1
Civitella di Romagna
I 135 A4
Civitella di Tronto
I 136 C2
Civitella Roveto I . . 169 B3
Civray F 115 B4
Çivril TR. 189 A4
Cizur Mayor E 144 B2
Clabhach GB 34 B1
Clachan GB 31 B2
Clachan na Luib GB 31 B1
Clacton-on-Sea GB. 45 B5
Cladich GB 34 B2
Claggan GB 34 B2
Clairvaux-les-Lacs
F 105 C4
Clamecy F 104 B2
Claonaig GB 34 C2
Clarecastle IRL . . . 28 B3
Claregalway IRL . . . 28 A3
Claremorris IRL. . . . 28 A2
Clarinbridge IRL . . . 28 A3
Clashmore
GB 32 D2
IRL 29 B4
Claudy GB 27 B3
Clausthal-Zellerfeld
D 82 A2
Cláut I 122 A1
Clay Cross GB. . . . 40 B2
Claye-Souilly F . . . 90 C2
Cléder F 100 A1
Cleethorpes GB. . . 41 B3
Clefmont F 105 A4
Cléguérec F 100 A2
Clelles F 118 C2
Clenze D 73 B3
Cleobury Mortimer
GB 39 B4
Cléon-d'Andran F . 117 C4
Cléré-les-Pins F . . 102 B2
Clères F 89 A5

Clermont F 90 B2
Clermont-en-Argonne
F 91 B5
Clermont-Ferrand
F 116 B3
Clermont-l'Hérault
F 130 B2
Clerval F 105 B5
Clervaux L 92 A2
Clèry-St André F . . 103 B3
Cles I 121 A4
Clevedon GB 43 A4
Cleveleys GB 38 A3
Cley GB 41 C5
Clifden IRL 28 A1
Clifford GB. 39 B3
Clisson F 101 B4
Clitheroe GB 40 B1
Clogh IRL. 30 B1
Cloghan
Donegal IRL. 26 B3
Offaly IRL. 28 A4
Clogheen IRL. 29 B4
Clogher GB 27 B3
Cloghjordan IRL . . . 28 B3
Clohars-Carnoët F 100 B2
Clonakilty IRL 29 C3
Clonaslee IRL 30 A1
Clondalkin IRL. . . . 30 A2
Clones IRL. 27 B3
Clonmany IRL 27 A3
Clonmel IRL. 29 B4
Clonmellon IRL . . . 30 A1
Clonord IRL. 30 A1
Clonroche IRL. . . . 30 B2
Cloone IRL. 26 C3
Cloppenburg D . . . 71 B5
Closeburn GB 36 A3
Clough GB 27 B5
Clova GB 35 B4
Clovelly GB 42 B2
Clowne GB 40 B2
Cloyes-sur-le-Loir
F 103 B3
Cloyne IRL 29 C3
Cluis F 103 C3
Cluj-Napoca RO . . 17 B5
Clun GB 39 B3
Clunes GB 34 B3
Cluny F 117 A4
Cluses F 118 A3
Clusone I 120 B2
Clydach GB 39 C3
Clydebank GB 34 C3
Coachford IRL 29 C3
Coagh GB 27 B4
Coalisland GB 27 B4
Coalville GB. 40 C2
Coaña E 141 A4
Çobanlar TR 187 D5
Cobas E 140 A2
Cobertelade E 151 A5
Cobeta E 152 B1
Cóbh IRL 29 C3
Cobreces E 142 A2
Coburg D 82 B2
Coca E 150 A3
Cocentaina E. 159 C3
Cochem D 80 B3
Codigoro I 121 C5
Codogno I 120 B2
Codos E 152 A2
Codróipo I 122 B1
Codrongianos I . . . 178 B2
Coelhoso P 149 A3
Coesfeld D 71 C4
Coevorden NL. . . . 71 B3
Cofrentes E 159 B2
Cogeces del Monte
E 150 A3
Coggeshall GB . . . 45 B4
Cognac F 115 C3
Cogne I 119 B4
Cognin F 118 B2
Cogolin F 132 B2
Cogollos de Guadix
E 164 B1
Cogollos-Vega E . . 163 A4
Cogolludo E 151 B4
Coimbra P 148 B1
Coín E 163 B3
Coirós E 140 A2
Čoka SRB 126 B2
Col SLO 123 B3
Colares P 154 C1
Cölbe D 81 B4
Colbitz D 73 B4
Colchester GB. . . . 45 B4
Coldingham GB. . . 35 C5
Colditz D 83 A4
Coldstream GB . . . 35 C5
Colebrooke GB . . . 43 B3
Colera E 146 B4
Coleraine GB. 27 A4
Colfiorito I 136 B1
Cólico I 120 A2
Coligny F 118 A2
Colindres E 143 A3
Collado-Mediano E 151 B3
Collado Villalba E . 151 B4
Collagna I 134 A3
Collanzo E 142 A1
Collat F 117 B3
Coll de Nargó E . . 147 B2
Collécchio I 120 C3
Colledimezzo I . . . 169 B4

Colle di Val d'Elsa
I 135 B4
Colleferro I 169 B3
Colle Isarco I 108 C2
Collelongo I 169 B3
Collepasso I 173 B4
Collepepe I 136 C1
Collesalvetti I 134 B3
Colle Sannita I . . . 170 B2
Collesano I 176 B2
Colli a Volturno I . . 169 B4
Collin GB 36 A3
Collinée F 101 A3
Collingham
Nottinghamshire
GB 40 B2
West Yorkshire GB .40 B3
Collinghorst D. . . . 71 A4
Cóllio I 120 B3
Collobrières F 132 B2
Colmar F 106 A2
Colmars F 132 A2
Colmenar E 163 B3
Colmenar de la Sierra
E 151 A4
Colmenar de Oreja
E 151 B4
Colmenar Viejo E . 151 B4
Colmonel GB 36 A2
Colne GB 40 B1
Colobraro I 174 A2
Cologna Véneta I . . 121 B4
Cologne = Köln D . . 80 B2
Cologne F 129 C3
Cologne al Serio I . 120 B2
Colombey-les-Belles
F 92 C1
Colombey-les-deux-
Églises F 105 A3
Colombres E 142 A2
Colomera E 163 A4
Colomers E 147 B3
Colomiers F 129 C4
Colònia de Sant Jordi
E 167 B3
Colorno I 120 C3
Colos P 160 B1
Cölpin D 74 A2
Colpy GB 33 D4
Colsterworth GB . . 40 C3
Coltishall GB. 41 C5
Colunga E 142 A1
Colwell GB 37 A4
Colwyn Bay GB . . . 38 A3
Colyford GB. 43 B3
Comácchio I 121 C5
Coma-ruga E 147 C2
Combarros E 141 B4
Combeaufontaine
F 105 B4
Comber GB 27 B5
Comblain-au-Pont B 80 B1
Combloux F 118 B3
Combourg F 88 B2
Combronde F 116 B3
Comeglians I 109 C3
Comillas E 142 A2
Comines F 78 B3
Cómiso I 177 C3
Comloşu Mare RO . 126 B2
Commensacq F. . . 128 B2
Commentry F 116 A2
Commerau D 84 A2
Commercy F 92 C1
Como I 120 B2
Cómpeta E 163 B4
Comps-sur-Artuby
F 132 B2
Comrat MD 17 B8
Comrie GB 35 B4
Comunanza I 136 C2
Cona
Emilia Romagna
I 121 C4
Veneto I 121 B5
Concarneau F 100 B2
Conceição P 160 B1
Conches-en-Ouche
F 89 B4
Concordia Sagittária
I 122 B1
Concordia sulla Sécchia
I 121 C3
Concots F 129 B4
Condat F 116 B2
Condé-en-Brie F . . 91 C3
Condeixa P 148 B1
Condemios de Abajo
E 151 A4
Condemios de Arriba
E 151 A4
Condé-sur-l'Escaut
F 79 B3
Conde-sur-Marne F 91 B4
Condé-sur-Noireau
F 88 B3
Condino I 121 B3
Condom F 129 C3
Condove I 119 B4
Condrieu F 117 B4
Conegliano I 122 B1
Conflans-sur-Lanterne
F 105 B5
Confolens F 115 B4

Conforto E 141 A3
Cong IRL 28 A2
Congleton GB 40 B1
Congosto E 141 B4
Congosto de Valdavia
E 142 B2
Congostrina E 151 A4
Conil de la Frontera
E 162 B1
Coningsby GB. . . . 41 B3
Coniston GB 36 B3
Conlie F 102 A1
Conliège F 105 C4
Conna IRL 29 B3
Connah's Quay GB . 38 A3
Connantre F 91 C3
Connaugh IRL 28 B3
Connaux F 131 A3
Connel GB. 34 B2
Connerré F 102 A2
Cononbridge GB . . 32 D2
Conoplja SRB 126 B1
Conques F 116 C2
Conques-sur-Orbiel
F 146 A3
Conquista E 157 B3
Conquista de la Sierra
E 156 A2
Consándolo I 121 C4
Consélice I 135 A4
Conselve I 121 B4
Consenvoye F 91 B5
Consett GB 37 B5
Consolação P 154 B1
Constancia P 154 B2
Constanța RO 17 C8
Constanti E 147 C2
Constantina E 162 A2
Consuegra E 157 A4
Consuma I 135 B4
Contarina I 122 B1
Contay F 90 B2
Conthey CH. 119 A4
Contigliano I 168 A2
Contis-Plage F . . . 128 B1
Contrada I 170 C2
Contres F 103 B3
Contrexéville F . . . 105 A4
Controne I 172 B1
Contursi Termi I . . 172 B1
Conty F 90 B2
Conversano I 173 B3
Conwy GB 38 A3
Cookstown GB . . . 27 B4
Coole F 91 C4
Coolgreany IRL. . . 30 B2
Cooneen GB 27 B3
Cootehill IRL 27 B3
Cope E 165 B3
Copenhagen =
København DK . . 61 D2
Copertino I 173 B4
Copparo I 121 C4
Coppenbrugge D . . 72 B2
Corabia RO 17 D6
Córaci I 175 B2
Coralići BIH 124 C1
Corato I 171 B4
Coray F 100 A2
Corbeil-Essonnes F 90 C2
Corbeny F 91 B3
Corbera E 159 B3
Corbie F 90 B2
Corbigny F 104 B2
Corbion B 91 B4
Corbridge GB. 37 B4
Corby GB. 40 C3
Corconte E 143 A3
Corcubión E 140 B1
Corcumello I 169 A3
Cordenòns I. 122 B1
Cordes-sur-Ciel F . 129 B4
Córdoba E 156 C3
Cordobilla de Lácara
E 155 B4
Cordovado I. 122 B1
Corella E 144 B2
Coreses E 150 A2
Corfe Castle GB . . 43 B4
Corga de Lobão P . 148 B1
Cori I 169 B2
Coria E 155 B4
Coria del Río E . . . 162 A1
Corigliano Cálabro
I 174 B2
Corinaldo I 136 B1
Corinth = Korinthos
GR 184 B3
Cório I 119 B4
Coripe E 162 B2
Corlay F 100 A2
Corleone I 176 B2
Corleto Monforte I . 172 B1
Corleto Perticara I . 174 A2
Çorlu TR. 186 A2
Cormainville F 103 A3
Cormatin F 104 C3
Cormeilles F 89 A4
Cormery F 102 B2
Cormòns I 122 B2
Cormoz F 118 A2
Cornago I 144 B1
Cornberg D 82 A1
Cornellana E 141 A4
Corneşti MD 17 B8
Corníglio I 134 A3
Cornimont F 106 B1

Corniolo I 135 B4
Cornuda I 121 B5
Cornudella de Montsant
E 147 C1
Cornudilla E 143 B3
Cornus F 130 B2
Corod RO 17 B7
Çorovodë AL 182 C2
Corpach GB 34 B2
Corps F 118 C2
Corps Nuds F 101 B4
Corral de Almaguer
E 157 A4
Corral de Ayllon E . 151 A4
Corral de Calatrava
E 157 B3
Corrales E 149 A4
Corral-Rubio E . . . 158 C2
Corran GB 34 B2
Corredoiras E 140 A2
Corréggio I 121 C3
Corrèze F 116 B1
Corridónia I 136 B2
Corris GB. 38 B3
Corrubedo E 140 B1
Corte F 180 A2
Corteconceptión
E 161 B3
Corte de Peleas E . 155 C4
Cortegaca P. 148 B1
Cortegada E 140 B2
Cortegana E 161 B3
Cortemaggiore I . . 120 B2
Cortemília I 133 A4
Corte Pinto P 160 B2
Cortes E 144 C2
Cortes de Aragón
E 153 B3
Cortes de Arenoso
E 153 B3
Cortes de Baza E . 164 B2
Cortes de la Frontera
E 162 B2
Cortes de Pallás E 159 B3
Cortiçadas P 154 C2
Cortico P 148 A2
Cortijo de Arriba E 157 A3
Cortijos Nuevos E . 164 A2
Cortina d'Ampezzo
I 108 C3
Corton GB 41 C5
Cortona I 135 B4
Coruche P 154 C2
Corullón E 141 B4
Çorum TR 23 A8
Corvara in Badia I . 108 C2
Corvera E 165 B3
Corwen GB 38 B3
Cosenza I 174 B2
Cosham GB. 44 C2
Coslada E 151 B4
Cosne-Cours-sur-Loire
F 104 B1
Cosne d'Allier F . . 103 C4
Cospeito E 140 A3
Cossato I. 119 B5
Cossaye F 104 C2
Cossé-le-Vivien F . 101 B5
Cossonay CH 105 C5
Costa da Caparica
P 154 C1
Costa de Santo André
P 160 A1
Costalpino I 135 B4
Costa Nova P. 148 B1
Costaros F 117 C3
Costeşti RO 17 C6
Costigliole d'Asti I 119 C5
Costigliole Saluzzo
I 133 A3
Coswig
Sachsen D 83 A5
Sachsen-Anhalt D . .83 A4
Cotherstone GB . . 37 B5
Cotronei I 175 B2
Cottbus D 84 A2
Cottenham GB. . . . 45 A4
Cottingham GB . . . 40 B3
Coublanc F 105 B4
Couches F 104 C3
Couço P 154 C2
Coucouron F 117 C3
Coucy-le-Château-
Auffrique F 90 B3
Couëron F 101 B4
Couflens F 146 B2
Couhé F 115 B4
Couiza F 146 B3
Coulags GB 31 B3
Coulanges F 104 C2
Coulanges-la-Vineuse
F 104 B2
Coulanges-sur-Yonne
F 104 B2
Couleuvre F 104 C1
Coulmier-le-Sec F . 104 B3
Coulommiers F . . . 90 C3
Coulonges-sur-l'Autize
F 114 B3
Coulounieix-Chamiers
F 129 A3
Coulport GB 34 B3
Coupar Angus GB . 35 B4
Coupéville F 91 C4
Couptrain F 89 B3
Coura P 140 C2
Courcelles B 79 B4

Courcelles-Chaussy
F. 92 B2
Courchevel F. . . .118 B3
Cour-Cheverny F . 103 B3
Courçon F 114 B3
Cour-et-Buis F. . . .117 B4
Courgenay CH . . . 106 B2
Courmayeur I 119 B3
Courniou F 130 B1
Cournon-d'Auvergne
F. 116 B3
Cournonterral F . . 130 B2
Courpière F 117 B3
Coursan F 130 B2
Courseulles-sur-Mer
F. 89 A3
Cours-la-Ville F . . .117 A4
Courson-les-Carrières
F. 104 B2
Courtalain F 103 A3
Courtenay F. 104 A2
Courtomer F 89 B4
Courville
Eure-et-Loire F. . .89 B5
Marne F 91 B3
Coussac-Bonneval
F. 115 C5
Coutances F 88 A2
Couterne F 89 B3
Coutras F 128 A2
Couvet CH 106 C1
Couvin B 91 A4
Couzon F 104 C2
Covadonga E. . . . 142 A1
Covaleda E. 143 C4
Covarrubias E . . . 143 B3
Covas P 148 A1
Cove GB 31 B3
Coventry GB 44 A2
Coverack GB 42 B1
Covigliáio I 135 A4
Covilhã E 148 B2
Cowbridge GB . . . 39 C3
Cowdenbeath GB . 35 B4
Cowes GB 44 C2
Cox F 129 C4
Cózar E 157 B4
Cozes F 114 C3
Cozzano F 180 B2
Craco I 174 A2
Cracow = Kraków
PL. 99 A3
Craibstone GB. . . . 33 D4
Craighouse GB . . . 34 C2
Craignure GB 34 B2
Crail GB 35 B5
Crailsheim D 94 B2
Craiova RO 17 C5
Cramlington GB . . . 37 A5
Cranleigh GB. 44 B3
Craon F 101 B5
Craonne F 91 B3
Craponne F 117 B4
Craponne-sur-Arzon
F. 117 B3
Crathie GB. 32 D3
Crato P. 155 B3
Craughwell IRL . . . 28 A3
Craven Arms GB . . 39 B4
Crawford GB 36 A3
Crawinkel D. 82 B2
Crawley GB 44 B3
Creag Ghoraidh GB 31 B1
Crecente E 140 B2
Crèches-sur-Saône
F. 117 A4
Crécy-en-Ponthieu
F. 78 B1
Crécy-la-Chapelle F 90 C2
Crécy-sur-Serre F . 91 B3
Crediton GB 43 B3
Creeslough IRL . . . 26 A3
Creetown GB. 36 B2
Creeve GB 27 B4
Creglingen D 94 B2
Creil F 90 B2
Creissels F 130 A2
Crema I 120 B2
Crémenes E. 142 B1
Crémieu F 118 B2
Cremlingen D 73 B3
Cremona I 120 B3
Creney F 91 C4
Črenšovci SLO 111 C3
Créon F 128 B2
Crepaja SRB 127 B2
Crépey F 92 C1
Crépy F 91 B3
Crépy-en-Valois F . 90 B2
Cres HR 123 C3
Crescentino I. 119 B5
Crespino I 121 C4
Crespos E 150 B3
Cressage GB 39 B4
Cressensac F 129 A4
Cressia F 105 C4
Crest F 117 C5
Cresta CH 107 C4
Créteil F 90 C2
Creully F 88 A3
Creussen D 95 B3
Creutzwald F 92 B2
Creuzburg D 82 A2
Crevalcore I 121 C4
Crèvecoeur-le-Grand
F. 90 B2

Crevillente E 165 A4
Crévola d'Ossola I . .119 A5
Crewkerne GB 43 B4
Crewe GB. 38 A4
Criales E 143 B3
Crianlarich GB. . . . 34 B3
Criccieth GB 38 B2
Crickhowell GB. . . . 39 C3
Cricklade GB 44 B2
Crieff GB 35 B4
Criel-sur-Mer F . . . 90 A1
Crikvenica HR 123 B3
Crillon F. 90 B1
Crimmitschau D . . . 83 B4
Crimond GB 33 D5
Crinitz D. 84 A1
Cripán E 143 B4
Criquetot-l'Esneval
F. 89 A4
Crispiano I 173 B3
Crissolo I 119 C4
Cristóbal E. 149 B4
Crivitz D. 73 A4
Črna SLO 110 C1
Crna Bara
Srbija SRB. 127 C1
Vojvodina SRB. . . 126 B2
Crnac HR 125 B3
Crnča SRB. 127 C1
Crni Lug
BIH. 138 A2
HR. 123 B3
Črni Vrh SLO 123 B3
Crnjelovo Donje
BIH. 125 C5
Črnomelj SLO 123 B4
Crocketford GB. . . . 36 A3
Crocq F. 116 B2
Crodo I. 119 A5
Croglin GB. 37 B4
Crolly IRL. 26 A2
Cromarty GB 32 D2
Cromer GB. 41 C5
Cronat F. 104 C2
Crookhaven IRL . . . 29 C2
Crookstown IRL . . . 29 C3
Croom IRL 29 B3
Cropalati I 174 B2
Crópani I 175 C2
Crosbost GB 31 A2
Crosby GB. 38 A3
Crosia I 174 B2
Crossakiel IRL 27 C3
Cross-Hands GB . . 39 C2
Crosshaven IRL. . . 29 C3
Crosshill GB 36 A2
Crossmolina IRL . . 26 B1
Crotone I 175 B3
Crottendorf D 83 B4
Crouy F 90 B3
Crowborough GB . . 45 B4
Crowland GB. 41 C3
Crowthorne GB . . . 44 B3
Croyde GB 42 A2
Croydon GB. 44 B3
Crozon F 100 A1
Cruas F 117 C4
Cruceni RO 126 A3
Crúcoli I 174 B3
Cruden Bay GB . . . 33 D5
Crudgington GB . . . 38 B4
Cruis F 132 A1
Crumlin GB 27 B4
Cruseilles F 118 A3
Crusheen IRL. 28 B3
Cruz de Incio E . . . 141 B3
Crvenka SRB 126 B1
Črveny Kamen SK . 98 B2
Csabacsüd H 113 C4
Csabrendek H 111 B4
Csákánydoroszló
H. 111 C3
Csákvár H 112 B2
Csanádapáca H . . .113 C4
Csanádpalota H . . 126 A2
Csány H. 113 B3
Csanytelek H 113 C4
Csapod H. 111 B3
Császár H 112 B2
Császártöltés H. . . .112 C3
Csávoly H 125 A5
Csemö H 113 B3
Csengöd H 112 C3
Csépa H 113 C4
Csepreg H. 111 B3
Cserkeszölö H. 113 C4
Csernely H 113 A4
Csesztreg H. 111 C3
Csökmö H 113 B5
Csököly H. 124 A3
Csokonyavisonta
H. 124 A3
Csólyospálos H. . . .113 C3
Csongrád H 113 C4
Csopak H. 112 C1
Csorna H. 111 B4
Csorvás H 113 C4
Cuacos de Yuste E 150 B2
Cualedro E. 140 C3
Cuanca de Campos
E. 142 B1
Cuba E 160 A2
Cubel E. 152 A2
Cubelles E 147 C2
Cubillos E 143 C4
Cubillos del Sil E . . 141 B4
Cubjac F 129 A3

Cubo de la Solana
E. 152 A1
Çubuk TR. 23 A7
Cuckfield GB 44 B3
Cucuron F 131 B4
Cudillero E 141 A4
Cuéllar E 151 A3
Cuenca E 152 B1
Cuers F 132 B2
Cuerva E 157 A3
Cueva de Agreda
E. 144 C2
Cuevas Bajas E. . . 163 A3
Cuevas del Almanzora
E. 164 B3
Cuevas del Becerro
E. 162 B2
Cuevas del Campo
E. 164 B2
Cuevas del Valle E 150 B2
Cuevas de San
Clemente E 143 B3
Cuevas de San Marcos
E. 163 A3
Cuges-les-Pins F . 132 B1
Cúglieri I 178 B2
Cugnaux F. 129 C4
Cuijk NL 80 A1
Cuinzier F 117 A4
Cuiseaux F 105 C4
Cuisery F 105 C4
Culan F 103 C4
Culemborg NL. . . . 79 A5
Cúllar E 164 B2
Cullaville GB 27 B4
Cullera E 159 B3
Cullivoe GB 33 A5
Cullompton GB . . . 43 B3
Cults GB 33 D4
Cumbernauld GB . . 35 C4
Cumbres de San
Bartolomé E 161 A3
Cumbres Mayores
E. 161 A3
Cumiana I 119 C4
Çumra TR. 23 C7
Cúneo I 133 A3
Cunlhat F. 117 B3
Čunski HR 123 C3
Cuntis E 140 B2
Cuorgnè I. 119 B4
Cupar GB 35 B4
Cupello I 170 A2
Cupra Marittima I . 136 B2
Cupramontana I . . 136 B2
Ćuprija SRB. 127 D3
Curcani RO 17 C7
Curelos E 140 B3
Currie GB 35 C4
Curtea de Argeş
RO 17 C6
Curtici RO 126 A3
Curtis E 140 A2
Curtis Santa Eulalia
E. 140 A2
Čurug SRB. 126 B2
Cusano Mutri I . . . 170 B2
Cushendall GB . . . 27 A4
Cusset F 117 A3
Cussy-les-Forges
F. 104 B3
Custines F 92 C2
Cutanda E 152 B2
Cutro I 175 B2
Cutrofiano I 173 B4
Cuts F 90 B3
Cuvilly F 90 B2
Cuxhaven D. 64 C1
Cvikov CZ 84 B2
Cwmbran GB 39 C3
Cybinka PL 75 B3
Czacz PL. 75 B5
Czajków PL. 86 A2
Czaplinek PL 75 A5
Czarlin PL 69 A3
Czarna-Dąbrówka
PL. 68 A2
Czarna Woda PL . . 68 B3
Czarnca PL 87 B3
Czarne PL 68 B1
Czarnków PL 75 B5
Czarnowo PL 76 A3
Czarnozyly PL. . . . 86 A2
Czarny Bór PL 85 B4
Czarny Las PL. . . . 86 A1
Czchow PL. 99 B4
Czechowice-Dziedzice
PL. 98 B2
Czempiń PL 75 B5
Czermno PL 87 A4
Czernichow PL 99 B3
Czernikowo PL. . . . 76 B3
Czersk PL. 68 B2
Czerwieńsk PL. . . . 75 B4
Czerwionka-Leszczyny
PL. 86 B2
Częstochowa PL. . . 86 B3
Czeszewo PL. 76 B2
Człopa PL. 75 A5
Człuchów PL 68 B2
Czołpino PL. 68 A2

D

Dağ TR 189 B5
Daaden D. 81 B3
Dabas H. 112 B3
Dąbie PL. 76 B3
Dąbki PL. 67 B5
Dabo F 92 C3
Dabrowa PL. 76 B2
Dąbrowa Górnicza
PL. 86 B3
Dąbrowa Tarnowska
PL. 87 B4
Dąbrowice PL 77 B4
Dąbrowno PL. 77 A5
Dachau D. 108 A2
Dačice CZ 97 B3
Daday TR. 23 A7
Dagali N. 47 B5
Dägebüll D 64 B1
Dagmersellen CH . 106 B2
Dahlen D. 83 A4
Dahlenburg D 73 A3
Dahme D. 83 A5
Dahn D 93 B3
Dähre D 73 B3
Daikanvik S 195 E7
Dail bho Dheas GB . 31 A2
Dailly GB 36 A2
Daimiel E 157 A4
Dakovica KOS . . . 16 D4
Đakovo HR 125 B4
Dal
Akershus N 48 B3
Telemark N 47 C5
Dalaas A 107 B5
Dalabrog GB 31 B1
Dala-Floda S 50 B1
Dala-Husby S 50 B2
Dala-Järna S 50 B1
Dalaman TR 188 C3
Dalarö S. 57 A4
Dalbeattie GB 36 B3
Dalby
DK 59 C3
Skåne S 61 D3
Uppsala S. 57 A3
Värmland S 49 B4
Dale
Pembrokeshire
GB. 39 C1
Shetland GB. 33 A5
Hordaland N. 46 B2
Sogn og Fjordane
N. 46 A2
Dalen
Akershus N 48 C3
Telemark N 53 A4
Daleszyce PL. 87 B4
Dalhalvaig GB 32 C3
Dalheim L. 92 B2
Dalhem S 57 C4
Dalias E 164 C2
Dalj HR. 125 B4
Dalkeith GB 35 C4
Dalkey IRL 30 A2
Dalmally GB. 34 B3
Dalmellington GB . . 36 A2
Dalmose DK. 65 A4
Dalry
Dumfries & Galloway
GB. 36 A3
North Ayrshire GB . 36 A2
Dalrymple GB 36 A2
Dalseter N. 47 A6
Dalsjöfors S. 60 B3
Dalskog S 54 B3
Dals Långed S. . . . 54 B3
Dals Rostock S . . . 54 B3
Dalston GB 36 B4
Dalstorp S 60 B3
Dalton-in-Furness
GB 36 B3
Daluis F 132 A2
Dalum
D 71 B4
S 60 B3
Dalvík IS. 191 B7
Dalwhinnie GB . . . 32 E2
Dalyan TR 188 C3
Damasi GR 182 D4
Damasławek PL. . . 76 B2
Damazan F. 129 B3
Damgan F 101 B3
Dammarie-les-Lys F 90 C2
Dammartin-en-Goële
F. 90 B2
Damme D. 71 B5
Damnica PL. 68 A2
Dampierre F 105 B4
Dampierre-sur-Salon
F. 105 B4
Damüls A 107 B4
Damville F 89 B5
Damvillers F 92 B1
Damwoude NL. . . . 70 A2
Danasjö S 195 E7
Danbury GB 45 B4
Dångebo S 63 B3
Dangers F 89 B5
Dangé-St Romain
F. 102 C2
Dangeul F. 89 B4
Danilovgrad MNE . 16 D3
Danischenhagen D . 64 B3

Daniszyn PL. 85 A5
Danjoutin F 106 B1
Dannas S 60 B3
Dannemarie F 106 B2
Dannenberg D 51 B4
Dannenberg D 73 A4
Dánszentmiklós H. .112 B3
Dány H 112 B3
Daoulas F 100 A1
Darabani RO 17 A7
Darány H 125 B3
Darda HR 125 B4
Dardesheim D 73 C3
Darfeld D 71 B4
Darfo I 120 B3
Dargiń PL. 68 A1
Dargun D 66 C1
Darlington GB 37 B5
Darłowo PL. 68 A1
Darmstadt D 93 B4
Darney F 105 A5
Daroca E 152 A2
Darque P 148 A1
Darragh IRL 28 B2
Dartford GB 45 B4
Dartington GB 43 B3
Dartmouth GB 43 B3
Darton GB 40 B2
Daruvar HR 124 B3
Darvel GB 36 A2
Darwen GB 38 A4
Dassel D. 82 A1
Dassow D 65 C3
Datça TR 188 C2
Datteln D. 80 A3
Dattenfeld D 81 B3
Daugard DK 59 C2
Daugavpils LV 8 E5
Daumeray F 102 B1
Daun D. 80 B2
Daventry GB 44 A2
Davle CZ 96 B2
Davor HR 124 B3
Davos CH 107 C4
Davutlar TR 188 B2
Davyd Haradok BY . 13 B7
Dawlish GB 43 B3
Dax F 128 C1
Dazkırı TR 189 B4
Deal GB 45 B5
Deauville F. 89 A4
Deba E 143 A4
Debar MK 182 B2
Dębe PL 77 B5
Dębica PL. 87 B5
Dębnica Kaszubska
PL. 68 A2
Dębno PL. 74 B3
Dębołeka PL 86 A2
Dębowa Łąka PL. . . 69 B4
Debrc SRB. 127 C1
Debrecen H 113 B5
Debrznica PL. 75 B4
Debrzno PL. 68 B2
Debstedt D. 72 A1
Decazeville F 130 A1
Dechtice SK 98 C1
Decima I 168 B2
Decimomannu I. . . 179 C2
Děčín CZ 84 B2
Decize F. 104 C2
De Cocksdorp NL . . 70 A1
Decollatura I 175 B2
Decs H 125 A4
Deddington GB . . . 44 B2
Dedeler TR. 187 B5
Dedelow D 74 A2
Dedemli TR 189 B7
Dedemsvaart NL. . . 71 B3
Dédestapolcsány
H 113 A4
Dedovichi RUS . . . 9 D6
Deeping St Nicholas
GB 41 C3
Deftera CY 181 A2
Dég H 112 C2
Degaña E 141 B4
Degeberga S 61 D4
Degerby FIN 51 B7
Degerfors S 55 A5
Degerhamn S 63 B4
Degernes N 54 A2
Deggendorf D 95 C4
Deggingen D 94 C1
Dego I 133 A4
Degolados P 155 B3
De Haan B 78 A3
Dehesas de Guadix
E. 164 B1
Dehesas Viejas E . 163 A4
Deia E 166 B2
Deining D 95 B3
Deinze B. 79 B3
Déiva Marina I . . . 134 A2
Dej RO 17 B5
Deje S 55 A4
De Koog NL 70 A1
Delabole GB 42 B2
Delary S. 61 C3
Delbrück D. 81 A4
Delčevo MK 182 B4
Delden NL 71 B3
Deleitosa E 156 A2
Delekovec HR . . . 124 A2
Delémont CH 106 B2
Delft NL 70 B1
Delfzijl NL. 71 A3

Délia I 176 B2
Delianuova I 175 C1
Deliblato SRB 127 C3
Delice TR. 23 B7
Deliceto I 171 B3
Delitzsch D 83 A4
Dellach A 109 C4
Delle F 106 B2
Delme F 92 C2
Delmen-horst D. . . 72 A1
Delnice HR. 123 B3
Delsbo S 200 E2
Delvin IRL 30 A1
Delvinë AL 182 D2
Demandice SK. . . .112 A2
Demen D 73 A4
Demidov RUS 13 A9
Demigny F 105 C3
Demirci TR. 186 C3
Demirköy TR. 186 A2
Demirtaş TR. 186 B4
Demmin D 66 C2
Demonte I 133 A3
Demyansk RUS . . . 9 D8
Denain F. 78 B3
Denbigh GB. 38 A3
Den Burg NL 70 A1
Dender-monde B. . . 79 A4
Denekamp NL 71 B4
Den Ham NL. 71 B3
Den Helder NL . . . 70 B1
Denholm GB 35 C5
Denia E 159 C4
Denizli TR 188 B4
Denkendorf D 95 C3
Denklingen D. 81 B3
Denny GB 35 B4
Den Oever NL 70 B2
Denta RO. 126 B3
Déols F 103 C3
De Panne B 78 A2
Derby GB. 40 C2
Derecske H. 113 B5
Dereköy TR 186 A2
Derenberg D 82 A2
Derinkuyu TR 23 B8
Dermbach D 82 B2
Dermulo I 121 A4
Deronje SRB 125 B5
Derrygonnelly GB . 26 B3
Derrylin GB 27 B3
Derry/Londonderry
GB 27 B3
Dersingham GB. . . 41 C4
Deruta I 136 C1
Derval F 101 B4
Derveni GR 184 A3
Derventa BIH 125 C3
Dervock GB 27 A4
Desana I 119 B5
Descartes F. 102 C2
Desenzano del Garda
I 121 B3
Deset N 48 A3
Deševa BIH 139 B4
Desfina GR 184 A3
Desimirovac SRB . 127 C2
Désio I 120 B2
Deskati GR 182 D3
Deskle SLO 122 A2
Desná CZ. 84 B3
Dešov CZ. 97 C3
Despotovac SRB. . 127 C3
Despotovo SRB. . . 126 B1
Dessau D. 83 A4
Deszk H 126 A2
Destriana E 141 B4
Désulo I 179 B3
Desvres F 78 B1
Deszk H 126 A2
Deta RO 126 B3
Detmold D 72 C1
Dětřichov CZ. 98 B1
Dettelbach D 94 B2
Dettingen
Baden-Württemberg
D. 94 C1
Baden-Württemberg
D. 107 B4
Dettwiller F 93 C3
Detva SK 99 C3
Deurne NL 80 A1
Deutschkreutz A . . .111 B3
Deutschlandsberg
A. 110 C2
Deutsch Wagram
A. 111 A3
Deva RO. 16 C5
Dévaványa H. 113 B5
Deveci konağı TR. . 186 C3
Devecser H. 111 B4
Develi TR 23 B8
Deventer NL 70 B3
Devil's Bridge GB . 39 B3
Devin BG 183 B6
Devinska Nova Ves
SK. 111 A3
Devizes GB 43 A5
Devonport GB 42 B2
Devrek TR 187 A6
Devrekâni TR. 23 A7
Ðevrske HR 137 B4
De Wijk NL 71 B3

Dewsbury GB 40 B2
Deza E 152 A1
Dežanovac HR . . 124 B3
Dezzo I 120 B3
Dhali CY 181 A2
Dherinia CY 181 A2
Diamante I 174 B1
Dianalund DK 61 D1
Diano d'Alba I 119 C5
Diano Marina I 133 B4
Dicomano I 135 B4
Didcot GB 44 B2
Didim TR 188 B2
Didimoticho GR . . 186 A1
Die F 118 C2
Diebling F 92 B2
Dieburg D 93 B4
Diego del Carpio E 150 B2
Diekirch L 92 B2
Diélette F 88 A2
Diemelstadt D 81 A5
Diémoz F 118 B2
Dienten am Hochkönig
  A. 109 B3
Diepenbeck B 79 B5
Diepholz D 71 B5
Dieppe F 89 A5
Dierberg D 74 A1
Dierdorf D 81 B3
Dieren NL 70 B3
Dierhagen D 66 B1
Diesdorf D 73 B4
Diessen D 108 B2
Diest B 79 B5
Dietenheim D 94 C2
Dietfurt D 95 B3
Dietikon CH 106 B3
Dietzenbach D 93 A4
Dieue-sur-Meuse F 92 B1
Dieulefit F 131 A4
Dieulouard F 92 C2
Dieuze F 92 C2
Diever NL 71 B3
Diez D 81 B4
Diezma E 163 A4
Differdange L 92 B1
Digermulen N 194 B6
Dignac F 115 C4
Dignano I 122 A1
Digne-les-Bains F . 132 A2
Digny F 89 B5
Digoin F 104 C2
Dijon F 105 B4
Dikanäs S 195 E7
Dikili TR 186 C1
Diksmuide B 78 A2
Dilar E 163 A4
Dillenburg D 81 B4
Dillingen
  Bayern D 94 C2
  Saarland D 92 B2
Dilsen B 80 A1
Dimaro I 121 A3
Dimitrovgrad BG . . 183 A7
Dimitsana GR 184 B3
Dinami I 175 C2
Dinan F 101 A3
Dinant B 79 B4
Dinar TR 189 A5
Dinard F 101 A3
Dinek TR 187 C6
Dingden D 80 A2
Dingelstädt D 82 A2
Dingle
  IRL 29 B1
  S 54 B2
Dingolfing D 95 C4
Dingtuna S 56 A2
Dingwall GB 32 D2
Dinkelsbühl D 94 B2
Dinkelscherben D . 94 C2
Dinklage D 71 B5
Dinslaken D 80 A2
Dinxperlo NL 80 A2
Diö S 63 B2
Diósgyőr H 113 A4
Diósjeno H 112 B3
Diou F 104 C2
Dippen GB 34 C2
Dipperz D 82 B1
Dippoldiswalde D . 84 B1
Dirdal N 52 B2
Dirksland NL 79 A4
Dirlewang D 108 B1
Dischingen D 94 C2
Disentis CH 107 C3
Diso I 173 B4
Diss GB 45 A5
Dissen D 71 B5
Distington GB 36 B3
Ditzingen D 93 C5
Ditzum D 71 A4
Divača SLO 122 B2
Dives-sur-Mer F . . 89 A3
Divin SK 99 C3
Divion F 78 B2
Divišov CZ 96 B2
Divonne les Bains
  F. 118 A3
Dixmont F 104 A2
Dizy-le-Gros F . . . 91 B4
Djúpivogur IS . . . 191 C11
Djupvasshytta N . 198 C4
Djura S 50 B1
Djurås S 50 B2

Djurmo S 50 B2
Djursdala S 62 A3
Dlouhá Loucka CZ . 98 B1
Długowola PL 87 A5
Dmitrov RUS 9 D10
Dno RUS 9 D6
Doade E 141 B3
Doğanhisar TR . . . 189 A6
Dobanovci SRB . . 127 C2
Dobbertin D 73 A5
Dobbiaco I 108 C3
Dobczyce PL 99 B4
Dobele LV 8 D3
Döbeln D 83 A5
Doberlug-Kirchhain
  D 83 A5
Dobern D 84 A2
Dobersberg A 97 C3
Dobiegniew PL . . . 75 B4
Dobieszyn PL 87 A5
Doboj BIH 125 C4
Dobošnica BIH . . . 125 C4
Doboz H 113 C5
Dobrá CZ 98 B2
Dobra
  Wielkopolskie PL . 76 C3
  Zachodnio-Pomorskie
  PL 74 A3
  Zachodnio-Pomorskie
  PL 75 A4
Dobrá Niva SK . . . 99 C3
Dobřany CZ 96 B1
Dobre PL 76 B3
Dobre Miasto PL . . 69 B5
Dobreta-Turnu-Severin
  RO 16 C5
Dobri H 111 C3
Dobrica SRB 126 B2
Dobrich BG 17 D7
Dobrinishte BG . . 183 B5
Dobříš CZ 96 B2
Dobro E 143 B3
Dobrodzień PL . . . 86 B2
Dobromierz PL . . . 85 B4
Dobrosołowo PL . . 76 B3
Dobroszyce PL . . . 85 A5
Dobrovnik SLO . . . 111 C3
Dobrush BY 13 B9
Dobruška CZ 85 B4
Dobrzany PL 75 A4
Dobrzen Wielki PL . 86 B1
Dobrzyca
  Wielkopolskie PL . 75 A5
  Wielkopolskie PL . 85 A5
  Zachodnio-Pomorskie
  PL 67 B4
Dobrzyńnad Wisłą
  PL 77 B4
Dobšiná SK 99 C4
Dobwalls GB 42 B2
Dochamps B 80 B1
Docking GB 41 C4
Docksta S 200 C4
Doddington GB . . . 37 A4
Döderhult S 62 A4
Doesburg NL 70 B3
Doetinchem NL . . . 71 C3
Dogliani I 133 A3
Dogueno P 160 B2
Doische B 91 A4
Dois Portos P . . . 154 B1
Dojč SK 98 C1
Dokka N 48 B2
Dokkedal DK 58 B3
Dokkum NL 70 A2
Dokležovje SLO . . 111 C3
Doksy CZ 84 B2
Dokuz TR 189 A7
Dolancourt F 104 A3
Dolceácqua I 133 B3
Dol-de-Bretagne F . 88 B2
Dole F 105 B4
Dølemo N 53 B4
Dolenja vas SLO . . 123 B3
Dolenjske Toplice
  SLO 123 B4
Dolfor GB 39 B3
Dolgarrog GB 38 A3
Dolgellau GB 38 B3
Doliana GR 182 D2
Dolianova I 179 C3
Dolice PL 75 A4
Doljani HR 138 A2
Döllach im Mölltal
  A. 109 C3
Dolle D 73 B4
Dollnstein D 94 C3
Dollot F 104 A2
Döllstadt D 82 A2
Dolný Kubín SK . . 99 B3
Dolo I 121 B5
Dolores E 165 A4
Dolovo SRB 127 C2
Dölsach A 109 C3
Dolsk PL 76 B2
Dolwyddelan GB . . 38 A3
Domaljevac BIH. . . 125 B4
Domanič TR 187 C4
Domaniža SK 98 B2

Domanovići BIH . . 139 B3
Domašov CZ 85 B5
Domaszék H 126 A1
Domaszków PL . . . 85 B4
Domaszowice PL . . 86 A1
Domat-Ems CH . . . 107 C4
Domažlice CZ 95 B4
Dombås N 198 C6
Dombegyház H . . 126 A3
Dombóvár H 112 C2
Domène F 118 B2
Domérat F 116 A2
Domfessel F 92 C3
Domfront F 88 B3
Domfront-en-
  Champagne F . . 102 A2
Domingão P 154 B2
Domingo Pérez
  Granada E 163 A4
  Toledo E 150 C3
Dömitz D 73 A4
Dommartin F 91 C4
Dommartin-le-Franc
  F. 91 C4
Domme F 129 B4
Dommitzsch D . . . 83 A4
Domodóssola I . . . 119 A5
Domokos GR 182 D4
Domoszló H 113 B4
Dompaire F 105 A5
Dompierre-du-Chemin
  F. 88 B2
Dompierre-sur-Besbre
  F. 104 C2
Dompierre-sur-Mer
  F. 114 B2
Domrémy-la-Pucelle
  F. 92 C1
Dömsöd H 112 B3
Domsure F 118 A2
Dómus de Maria I . 179 D2
Domusnóvas I . . . 179 C2
Domvena GR 184 A3
Domžale SLO 123 A3
Donado E 141 B4
Donaghadee GB . . 27 B5
Don Alvaro E 155 C4
Doña Mencía E . . 163 A3
Donaueschingen
  D 106 B3
Donauwörth D. . . . 94 C2
Don Benito E 156 B2
Doncaster GB 40 B2
Donegal IRL 26 B2
Donestebe-Santesteban
  E. 144 A2
Donges F 101 B3
Dongo I 120 A2
Donington GB 41 C3
Doniños E 140 A2
Donja Bebrina F . . 125 B4
Donja Brela HR . . 138 B2
Donja Dubica BIH . 125 B4
Donja Dubrava HR 124 A2
Donja Kupčina HR 123 B4
Donja Šatornja
  SRB 127 C2
Donja Stubica HR . 124 B1
Donje Brišnik BIH . 138 B3
Donje Stative HR . 123 B4
Donji-Andrijevci
  HR 125 B4
Donji Kazanci BIH . 138 B2
Donji Koričani BIH 138 A3
Donji Lapac HR . . 124 C1
Donji Malovan BIH 138 B3
Donji Miholjac HR . 125 B4
Donji Mosti HR . . 124 A2
Donji Poloj HR . . . 123 B4
Donji-Rujani BIH . 138 B2
Donji Srb HR 138 A2
Donji Svilaj BIH . . 125 B4
Donji Tovarnik
  SRB 127 C1
Donji Vakuf BIH . . 138 A3
Donnalucata I . . . 177 C3
Donnemarie-Dontilly
  F. 90 C3
Donnersbach A . . 110 B1
Donnersbachwald
  A. 109 B5
Donnerskirchen A . 111 B3
Donorático I 134 B3
Donostia-San Sebastián
  E. 144 A2
Donovaly SK 99 C3
Donzac F 129 A4
Donzère F 131 A3
Donzy F 104 B2
Doonbeg IRL 29 B2
Doorn NL 70 B2
Dor E 140 A1
Dorchester GB . . . 43 B4
Dørdal N 53 B5
Dordrecht NL 79 A4
Dörenthe D 71 B4
Dores GB 32 D2
Dorfen D 95 C4
Dorfgastein A. . . . 109 B4
Dorfmark D 72 B2
Dorf Mecklenburg D 65 C4
Dorgali I 178 B3
Dorking GB 44 B3
Dormagen D 80 A2
Dormánd H 113 B4
Dormans F 91 B3

Dornava SLO 124 A1
Dornbirn A 107 B4
Dornburg D 83 A3
Dorndorf D 82 B2
Dornecy F 104 B2
Dornes F 104 C2
Dornhan D 93 C4
Dornie GB 31 B3
Dornoch GB 32 D2
Dornum D 71 A4
Dorog H 112 B2
Dorohoi RO 17 B7
Dorotea S. 200 B2
Dorotowo PL 69 B5
Dörpen D 71 B4
Dorsten D 80 A2
Dortan F 118 A2
Dortmund D 80 A3
Doruchów PL 86 A2
Dorum D 64 C1
Dörverden D 72 B2
Dörzbach D 94 B1
Dos Aguas E 159 B3
Dosbarrios E 151 C4
Dos Hermanas E . 162 A2
Dospat BG 183 B6
Dos-Torres E 156 B3
Dötlingen D 72 B1
Dottignies B. 78 B3
Döttingen CH. . . . 106 B3
Douai F 78 B3
Douarnenez F . . . 100 A1
Douchy F 104 B2
Douchy-les-Mines F 78 B3
Doucier F 105 C4
Doudeville F 89 A4
Doué-la-Fontaine
  F. 102 B1
Doulaincourt-Saucourt
  F. 91 C5
Doulevant-le-Château
  F. 91 C4
Doullens F 90 A2
Dounby GB 33 B3
Doune GB 35 B3
Dounreay GB 32 C3
Dour B 79 B3
Dourdan F 90 C2
Dourgne F 146 A3
Dournazac F 115 C4
Douro Calvo P . . . 148 B2
Douvaine F 118 A3
Douvres-la-Délivrande
  F. 89 A3
Douzy F 91 B5
Dover GB 45 B5
Dovje SLO 109 C4
Dovre N 198 D6
Downham Market
  GB 41 C4
Downhill GB 27 A4
Downpatrick GB . . 27 B5
Dowra IRL 26 B2
Doxato GR 183 B6
Doyet F 116 A2
Dozule F 89 A3
Drača SRB 127 C2
Dračevo
  BIH. 139 C4
  MK 182 B3
Drachten NL 70 A3
Draga SLO 123 B3
Drăgăşani RO . . . 17 C6
Dragatuš SLO . . . 123 B4
Dragichyn BY 13 B6
Draginja SRB. . . . 127 C1
Dragocvet SRB . . 127 D3
Dragolovci BIH . . . 125 C3
Dragoni I 170 B2
Drągowina PL . . . 84 A3
Dragør DK 61 D2
Dragotina HR 124 B2
Dragotinja BIH . . . 124 B2
Dragozetići HR . . 123 B3
Draguignan F . . . 132 B2
Drahnsdorf D 74 C2
Drahonice CZ 96 B1
Drahovce SK 98 C1
Drama GR 183 B6
Drammen N 54 A1
Drangedal N 53 A5
Drangsnes IS . . . 190 B4
Dransfeld D 82 A1
Dranske D 66 B2
Draperstown GB . . 27 B4
Drasenhofen A . . . 97 C4
Drassburg A 111 B3
Drávaszabolcs H . 125 B4
Dravograd SLO . . 110 C2
Drawno PL 75 A4
Drawsko Pomorskie
  PL 75 A4
Drayton GB 41 C5
Drążdżewo PL . . . 77 A6
Draženov CZ 95 B4
Draževac SRB . . . 127 C2
Dražice HR 123 B3
Drebkau D 84 A2
Dreieich D 93 A4
Dreisen D 93 B4
Drenovci HR 125 C4
Drensteinfurt D . . . 81 A3
Dresden D 84 A1
Dretyń PL 68 A1
Dreux F 89 B5

Dřevohostice CZ . . 98 B1
Drevsjø N 199 D9
Drewitz D 73 B5
Drezdenko PL 75 B4
Drežnica HR 123 B4
Drežnik-Grad HR . 123 C4
Drietona SK 98 C1
Driffield GB 40 A3
Drimmin GB 34 B2
Drimoleague IRL . . 29 C2
Dringenberg D . . . 81 A5
Drinić BIH 138 A2
Drinjača BIH 139 A5
Drinovci BIH 138 B3
Driopida GR 185 B5
Drivstua N 198 C6
Drlače SRB 127 C1
Drnholec CZ 97 C4
Drniš HR 138 B2
Drnje HR 124 A2
Drnovice CZ 97 B4
Dro I 121 B3
Drøbak N 54 A1
Drobin PL 77 B5
Drochia MD 17 A7
Drochtersen D . . . 64 C2
Drogheda IRL . . . 30 A2
Drohobych UA . . . 13 D5
Droitwich Spa GB . 44 A1
Drołtowice PL . . . 85 A5
Dromahair IRL . . . 26 B2
Dromcolliher IRL . 29 B3
Dromore
  Down GB 27 B4
  Tyrone GB 27 B3
Dromore West IRL . 26 B2
Dronero I 133 A3
Dronfield GB 40 B2
Drongan GB 36 A2
Dronninglund DK . . 58 A3
Dronrijp NL 70 A2
Dronten NL 70 B2
Drosendorf A 97 C3
Drösing A 97 C4
Drottningholm S . . 57 A3
Droué F 103 A3
Drulingen F 92 C3
Drumbeg GB 32 C1
Drumcliff IRL 26 B2
Drumgask GB . . . 32 D2
Drumkeeran IRL . . 26 B2
Drummore GB . . . 36 B2
Drumnadrochit GB 32 D2
Drumquin GB 27 B3
Drumshanbo IRL . 26 B2
Drumsna IRL 26 C2
Drunen NL 79 A5
Druskininkai LT . . 13 A5
Druten NL 80 A1
Druya BY 13 A7
Družetići SRB . . . 127 C2
Drvar BIH 138 A2
Drvenik HR 138 B3
Drwalew PL 77 C6
Drymen GB 34 B3
Drynoch GB 31 B2
Drzewce PL 76 B2
Drzewiany PL 68 B1
Drzewica PL 87 A4
Dualchi I 178 B2
Duas Igrejas P . . 149 A3
Dub SRB 127 D1
Dubá CZ 84 B2
Dubăsari MD 17 B8
Duben D 74 C2
Dübendorf CH . . . 107 B3
Dubi CZ 84 B1
Dubică HR 124 B2
Dublin IRL 30 A2
Dubna RUS 9 D10
Dubňany CZ 98 C1
Dubnica nad Váhom
  SK 98 C2
Dubnik SK 112 B2
Dubno UA 13 C6
Dubodiel SK 98 C2
Dubona SRB 127 C2
Dubovac SRB . . . 127 C3
Dubovic BIH 124 C2
Dubranec HR 124 B1
Dubrava
  HR 123 B4
  SRB 127 C3
Dubrave BIH 125 C4
Dubravica
  HR 123 B4
  SRB 127 C3
Dubrovnik HR . . . 139 C4
Dubrovytsya UA . . 13 C7
Ducey F 88 B2
Duchcov CZ 84 B1
Ducherow D 74 A2
Dučina SRB 127 C2
Duclair F 89 A4
Dudar H 112 B1
Duddington GB . . 40 C3
Duderstadt D 82 A2
Dudeştii Vechi RO. 126 A2
Dudley GB 40 C1
Dueñas E 142 C2
Duesund N 46 B2
Dueville I 121 B4
Duffel B 79 A4
Duffield GB 40 C2
Dufftown GB 32 D3
Duga Resa HR . . . 123 B4
Dugi Rat HR 138 B2
Dugny-sur-Meuse F 92 B1
Dugopolje HR . . . 138 B2
Dugo Selo HR . . . 124 B2

Duino I 122 B2
Duisburg D 80 A2
Dukat AL. 182 C1
Dukovany CZ. . . . 97 B4
Duleek IRL 30 A2
Dülken D 80 A2
Dülmen D. 80 A3
Dulovo BG 17 D7
Dulpetorpet N . . . 49 B4
Dulverton GB 43 A3
Dumbarton GB . . . 34 C3
Dümerek TR 187 C6
Dumfries GB 36 A3
Dumlupınar TR . . 187 D4
Dümpelfeld D 80 B2
Dunaalmás H 112 B2
Dunabogdány H . .112 B3
Dunafalva H 125 A4
Dunaföldvár H . . .112 C2
Dunaharaszti H . .112 B3
Dunajská Streda
  SK 111 B4
Dunakeszi H 112 B3
Dunakiliti H 111 B4
Dunakömlöd H . . .112 C2
Dunapataj H. 112 C2
Dunaszekcsö H . . 125 A4
Dunaszentgyorgy
  H 112 C2
Dunatetétlen H . . .112 C3
Dunaújváros H . . .112 C2
Dunavecse H 112 C2
Dunbar GB 35 B5
Dunbeath GB 32 C3
Dunblane GB 35 B4
Dunboyne IRL . . . 30 A2
Dundalk IRL. 27 B4
Dundee GB 35 B5
Dundrennan GB . . 36 B3
Dundrum GB 27 B5
Dunfanaghy IRL . . 26 A3
Dunfermline GB . . 35 B4
Dungannon GB . . 27 B4
Dungarvan IRL . . . 29 B4
Dungiven GB 27 B4
Dunglow IRL 26 B2
Dungourney IRL . . 29 C3
Duninowo PL 68 A2
Dunkeld GB 35 B4
Dunker S 56 A2
Dunkerque = Dunkirk
  F. 78 A2
Dunkineely IRL . . . 26 B2
Dunkirk = Dunkerque
  F. 78 A2
Dun Laoghaire IRL . 30 A2
Dunlavin IRL 30 A2
Dunleer IRL 27 B4
Dun-le-Palestel F. .116 A1
Dun-les-Places F . 104 B3
Dunlop GB 36 A2
Dunloy GB 27 A4
Dunmanway IRL . . 29 C2
Dunmore IRL 28 A3
Dunmore East IRL . 30 B2
Dunmurry GB 27 B4
Dunnet GB 32 C3
Dunningen D 107 A3
Dunoon GB 34 C3
Duns GB 35 C5
Dunscore GB 36 A3
Dunsford GB 43 B3
Dunshaughlin IRL . 30 A2
Dunstable GB . . . 44 B3
Dunster GB 43 A3
Dun-sur-Auron F . 103 C4
Dun-sur-Meuse F . 91 B5
Dunvegan GB . . . 31 B2
Duplek SLO 110 C2
Dupnitsa BG 17 D5
Durağan TR 23 A8
Durach D 107 B5
Durak TR 186 C3
Durana E 143 B4
Durance F 128 B3
Durango E 143 A4
Durankulak BG . . 17 D8
Duras F 128 B3
Durban-Corbières
  F. 146 B3
Dürbheim D 107 A3
Durbuy B 79 B5
Dúrcal E 163 B4
Ðurdjenovac HR . . 125 B4
Ðurdjevac HR . . . 124 A3
Ðurdjevik BIH . . . 139 A4
Düren D 80 B2
Durham GB 37 B5
Ðurinci SRB. 127 C2
Durlach D 93 C4
Ðurmanec HR . . . 124 A1
Durness GB 32 C2
Dürnkrut A 97 C4
Dürrboden CH . . . 107 C4
Dürrenboden CH. . 107 C3
Durrës AL. 182 B1
Durrow IRL 30 B1
Durrus IRL 29 C2
Dursunbey TR . . . 186 C3
Durtal F 102 B1
Durup DK 58 B1
Durusu TR 186 A3
Dusina BIH. 139 B3
Dusnok H 112 C2
Dusocin PL 69 B3
Düsseldorf D 80 A2
Dusslingen D 93 C5
Duszniki PL 75 B5

Duszniki-Zdrój PL . . 85 B4
Dutovlje SLO 122 B2
Duvebo S 55 B5
Duved S 199 B9
Düzağac TR 187 D5
Düzce TR 187 B6
Dvärsätt S 199 B11
Dvor HR 124 B2
Dvorce CZ 98 B1
Dvorníky SK 98 C1
Dvory nad Žitavou
 SK 112 B2
Dvůr Králové nad Labem
 CZ 85 B3
Dybvad DK 58 A3
Dyce GB 33 D4
Dygowo PL 67 B4
Dykehead GB 35 B4
Dymchurch GB . . . 45 B5
Dymer UA 13 C9
Dyrnes N 198 B4
Dywity PL 69 B5
Džanići BIH 139 B3
Dziadowa Kłoda PL . 86 A1
Działdowo PL 77 A5
Działoszyce PL . . . 87 B4
Działoszyn PL . . . 86 A2
Dziemiany PL 68 A2
Dzierzążnia PL . . . 77 B5
Dzierzgoń PL 69 B4
Dzierzgowo PL . . . 77 A5
Dzierżoniów PL . . . 85 B4
Dzisna BY 13 A8
Dziwnów PL 67 B3
Dźwierzuty PL . . . 77 A5
Dzyarzhynsk BY . . 13 B7
Dzyatlava BY 13 B6

E

Ea E 143 A4
Eaglesfield GB . . . 36 A3
Ealing GB 44 B3
Eardisley GB 39 B3
Earls Barton GB . . . 44 A3
Earl Shilton GB . . . 40 C2
Earlston GB 35 C5
Easington GB 41 B4
Easky IRL 26 B2
Eastbourne GB . . . 45 C4
East Calder GB . . . 35 C4
East Dereham GB . . 41 C4
Easter Skeld GB . . 33 A5
East Grinstead GB . 45 B4
East Ilsley GB 44 B2
East Kilbride GB . . . 36 A2
Eastleigh GB 44 C2
East Linton GB . . . 35 C5
East Markham GB . . 40 B3
Easton GB 43 B4
East Wittering GB . . 44 C3
Eaton Socon GB . . 44 A3
Eaux-Bonnes F . . . 145 B3
Eauze F 128 C3
Ebberup DK 59 C2
Ebbs A 108 B3
Ebbw Vale GB . . . 39 C3
Ebeleben D 82 A2
Ebeltoft DK 59 B3
Ebene Reichenau
 A 109 C4
Eben im Pongau A . 109 B4
Ebensee A 109 B4
Ebensfeld D 94 A2
Eberbach D 93 B4
Ebergötzen D 82 A2
Ebermann-Stadt D . 94 B3
Ebern D 82 B2
Eberndorf A 110 C1
Ebersbach D 84 A2
Ebersberg D 108 A2
Ebersdorf
 Bayern D 82 B3
 Niedersachsen D . .72 A2
Eberstein A 110 C1
Eberswalde D 74 B2
Ebnat-Kappel CH . 107 B4
Éboli I 170 C3
Ebrach D 94 B2
Ebreichsdorf A . . . 111 B3
Ebreuil F 116 A3
Ebstorf D 72 A3
Ecclefechan GB . . . 36 A3
Eccleshall GB 40 C1
Eceabat TR 186 B1
Echallens CH 106 C1
Echauri E 144 B2
Echinos GR 183 B7
Echiré F 114 B3
Échirolles F 118 B2
Echourgnac F . . . 128 A3
Echt NL 80 A1
Echte D 82 A2
Echternach L 92 B2
Ecija E 162 A2
Ečka SRB 126 B2
Eckartsberga D . . . 82 A3
Eckelshausen D . . 81 B4
Eckental D 94 B3
Eckernförde D . . . 64 B2
Eckington GB 40 B2
Éclaron F 91 C4
Écommoy F 102 B2
Écouché F 89 B3
Ecouis F 90 B1
Ecsed H 113 B3

Ecsegfalva H 113 B4
Écueillé F 103 B3
Ed S 54 B2
Eda S 49 C4
Eda glasbruk S . . . 49 C4
Edam NL 70 B2
Edderton GB 32 D2
Ede NL 70 B2
Edebäck S 49 B5
Edebo S 51 B5
Edelschrott A 110 B2
Edelsfeld D 95 B3
Edemissen D 72 B3
Edenbridge GB . . . 45 B4
Edenderry IRL . . . 30 A1
Edenkoben D 93 B4
Edesheim D 93 B4
Edessa GR 182 C4
Edewecht D 71 A4
Edgeworthstown
 IRL 30 A1
Edinburgh GB 35 C4
Edineţ MD 17 A7
Edirne TR 186 A1
Edland N 52 A3
Edolo I 120 A3
Edøy N 198 B5
Edremit TR 186 C2
Edsbro S 51 C5
Edsbruk S 56 B2
Edsbyn S 50 A2
Edsele S 200 C2
Edsleskog S 54 A3
Edsvalla S 55 A4
Eekloo B 79 A3
Eemshaven NL . . . 71 A3
Eerbeek NL 70 B3
Eersel NL 79 A5
Eferding A 96 C2
Effiat F 116 A3
Eftelot N 53 A5
Egeln D 73 C4
Eger H 113 B4
Egerbakta H 113 B4
Egernsund DK . . . 64 B2
Egersund N 52 B2
Egerszólát H 113 B4
Egervár H 111 C3
Egg
 A 107 B4
 D 107 A5
Eggby S 55 B4
Eggedal N 47 B6
Eggenburg A 97 C3
Eggenfelden D . . . 95 C4
Eggesin D 74 A3
Eggum N 194 B4
Éghezée B 79 B4
Egiertowo PL 68 A3
Egilsstaðir IS 191 B11
Egina GR 185 B4
Eginio GR 182 C4
Egio GR 184 A3
Égletons F 116 B2
Egling D 108 B2
Eglinton GB 27 A3
Eglisau CH 107 B3
Égliseneuve-
 d'Entraigues F . .116 B2
Eglofs D 107 B4
Egmond aan Zee NL 70 B1
Egna I 121 A4
Egosthena GR . . . 184 A4
Egremont GB 36 B3
Egtved DK 59 C2
Eguilles F 131 B4
Eguilly-sous-Bois
 F 104 A3
Éguzon-Chantôme
 F 103 C3
Egyek H 113 B4
Egyházasrádóc H . .111 B3
Ehekirchen D 94 C3
Ehingen D 94 C1
Ehra-Lessien D . . . 73 B3
Ehrang D 92 B2
Ehrenfriedersdorf D 83 B4
Ehrenhain D 83 B4
Ehrenhausen A . . . 110 C2
Ehringshausen D . . 81 B4
Ehrwald A 108 B1
Eibar E 143 A4
Eibelstadt D 94 B2
Eibenstock D 83 B4
Eibergen NL 71 B3
Eibiswald A 110 C2
Eichenbarleben D . . 73 B4
Eichendorf D 95 C4
Eichstätt D 95 C3
Eickelborn D 81 A4
Eide
 Hordaland N 46 B3
 Møre og Romsdal
 N 198 C4
Eidet N 194 A9
Eidfjord N 46 B3
Eidsberg N 54 A2
Eidsbugarden N . . . 47 A5
Eidsdal N 198 C4
Eidsfoss N 53 A6
Eidskog N 49 B4
Eidsvåg
 Hordaland N 46 B2
 Møre og Romsdal
 N 198 C5
Eidsvoll N 48 B3

Eikefjord N 46 A2
Eikelandsosen N . . 46 B2
Eikesdal N 198 C5
Eikstrand N 53 A5
Eilenburg D 83 A4
Eilsleben D 73 B4
Eina N 48 B2
Einbeck D 82 A1
Eindhoven NL 79 A5
Einsiedeln CH . . . 107 B3
Einville-au-Jard F . . 92 C2
Eisenach D 82 B2
Eisenberg
 Rheinland-Pfalz D . 93 B4
 Thüringen D 83 B3
Eisenerz A 110 B1
Eisenhüttenstadt D . 74 B3
Eisenkappel A . . . 110 C1
Eisenstadt A 111 B3
Eisentratten A . . . 109 C4
Eisfeld D 82 B2
Eisleben D 82 A3
Eitensheim D 95 C3
Eiterfeld D 82 B1
Eitorf D 80 B3
Eivindvik N 46 A2
Eivissa = Ibiza E . . 166 C1
Eixo P 148 B1
Ejby DK 59 C2
Ejea de los Caballeros
 E 144 B2
Ejstrupholm DK . . . 59 C2
Ejulve E 153 B3
Eke B 79 B3
Ekeby
 Gotland S 57 C4
 Skåne S 61 D2
 Uppsala S 51 B5
Ekeby-Almby S . . . 56 A1
Ekenäs S 55 B4
Ekenässjön S 62 A3
Ekerö S 57 A3
Eket S 61 C3
Eketorp S 63 B4
Ekevik S 56 B2
Ekkerøy N 193 B14
Ekshärad S 49 B5
Eksingedal N 46 B2
Eksjö S 62 A2
Eksta S 57 C4
Ekträsk S 200 B5
El Alamo
 Madrid E 151 B4
 Sevilla E 161 B3
El Algar E 165 B4
El Almendro E . . . 161 B2
El Alquián E 164 C2
Élancourt F 90 C1
El Arahal E 162 A2
El Arenal E 150 B2
El Arguellite E . . . 164 A2
Elassona GR 182 D4
El Astillero E 143 A3
Elati GR 182 D3
Żelazno PL 85 B4
El Ballestero E . . . 158 C1
El Barco de Ávila
 E 150 B2
Elbasan AL 182 B2
El Berrón E 142 A1
El Berrueco E . . . 151 B4
Elbeuf F 89 A4
Elbingerode D 82 A2
Elbląg PL 69 A4
El Bodón E 149 B3
El Bonillo E 158 C1
El Bosque E 162 B2
El Bullaque E 157 A3
Elburg NL 70 B2
El Burgo E 162 B3
El Burgo de Ebro
 E 153 A3
El Burgo de Osma
 E 151 A4
El Burgo Ranero E 142 B1
El Buste E 144 C2
El Cabaco E 149 B3
El Callejo E 143 A3
El Campillo E 161 B3
El Campillo de la Jara
 E 156 A2
El Cañavete E . . . 158 B1
El Carpio E 157 C3
El Carpio de Tajo
 E 150 C3
El Casar E 151 B4
El Casar de Escalona
 E 150 B3
El Castillo de las
 Guardas E 161 B3
El Centenillo E . . . 157 B4
El Cerro E 149 B4
El Cerro de Andévalo
 E 161 B3
Elche E 165 A4
Elche de la Sierra
 E 158 C1
Elchingen D 94 C2
El Comenar E . . . 162 B2
El Coronil E 162 A2
El Crucero E 141 A4
El Cubo de Tierra del
 Vino E 149 A4
El Cuervo E 162 B1
Elda E 159 C3
Eldena D 73 A4

Eldingen D 72 B3
Elefsina GR 185 A4
El Ejido E 164 C2
Elek H 113 C5
Elemir SRB 126 B2
El Escorial E 151 B3
El Espinar E 151 B3
Eleutheroupoli GR 183 C6
El Frago E 144 B3
El Frasno E 152 A2
Elgå N 199 C8
El Garrobo E 161 B3
El Gastor E 162 B2
Elgin GB 32 D3
El Gordo E 150 C2
El Grado E 145 B4
El Granado E 161 B2
El Grao de Castelló
 E 159 B4
El Grau E 159 C3
Elgshøa N 49 A4
El Higuera E 163 A3
El Hijate E 164 B2
El Hontanar E . . . 152 B2
El Hoyo E 157 B4
Elie GB 35 B5
El Madroño E 161 B3
El Maillo E 149 B3
Elmalı TR 189 C4
El Masnou E 147 C3
El Mirón E 150 B2
El Molar E 151 B4
El Molinillo E 157 A3
El Morell E 147 C2
Elmshorn D 64 C2
Elmstein D 93 B3
El Muyo E 151 A4
Elne F 146 B3
Elnesvågen N . . . 198 C4
Elorrio E 143 A4
El Palo E 163 B3
El Pardo E 151 B4
El Payo E 149 B3
El Pedernoso E . . . 158 B1
El Pedroso E 162 A2
El Peral E 158 B2
El Perelló
 Tarragona E . . . 153 B4
 Valencia E 159 B3
Elphin GB 32 C1
El Picazo E 158 B1
El Pinell de Bray E 153 A4
El Piñero E 150 A2
El Pla de Santa Maria
 E 147 C2
El Pobo E 153 B3
El Pobo de Dueñas
 E 152 B2
El Pont d'Armentera
 E 147 C2
El Port de la Selva
 E 147 A4
El Port de Llança
 E 146 B4
El Port de Sagunt
 E 159 B3
El Prat de Llobregat
 E 147 C3
El Provencio E . . . 158 B1
El Puente del Arzobispo
 E 150 C2
El Puerto E 141 A4
El Puerto de Santa María
 E 162 B1
El Real de la Jara
 E 161 B3
El Real de San Vicente
 E 150 B3
El Robledo E 157 A3
El Rocio E 161 B3
El Rompido E 161 B2
El Ronquillo E . . . 161 B3
El Royo E 143 C4
El Rubio E 162 A3
El Sabinar E 164 A2
El Saler E 159 B3
El Salobral E 158 C2
El Saucejo E 162 A2
Els Castells E . . . 147 B2
Elsdorf D 80 B2
Elsenfeld D 93 B5
El Serrat AND . . . 146 B2
Elsfleth D 72 A1

Elspeet NL 70 B2
Elst NL 70 C2
Elstead GB 44 B3
Elster D 83 A4
Elsterberg D 83 B4
Elsterwerda D . . . 83 A5
Elstra D 84 A2
El Temple E 144 C3
El Tiemblo E 150 B3
Eltmann D 94 B2
El Toboso E 157 A5
El Tormillo E 145 C3
El Torno E 149 B4
Eltville D 93 A4
El Valle de las Casas
 E 142 B1
Elvas P 155 C3
Elvebakken N . . . 192 C7
El Vellón E 151 B4
Elven F 101 B3
El Vendrell E 147 C2
El Villar de Arnedo
 E 144 B1
Elvington GB 40 B3
El Viso E 156 B3
El Viso del Alcor E 162 A2
Elxleben D 82 A2
Ely GB 45 A4
Elzach D 106 A3
Elze D 72 B2
Emådalen S 50 A1
Embleton GB 37 A5
Embonas GR . . . 188 C2
Embrun F 132 C2
Embún E 144 B3
Emden D 71 A4
Emecík TR 188 C2
Emet TR 186 C4
Emirdağ TR 187 C6
Emlichheim D . . . 71 B3
Emmaboda S . . . 63 B3
Emmaljunga S . . . 61 C3
Emmeloord NL . . . 70 B2
Emmen
 CH 106 B3
 NL 71 B3
Emmendingen D . . 106 A2
Emmer-Compascuum
 NL 71 B4
Emmerich D 80 A2
Emmern D 72 B2
Emöd H 113 B4
Émpoli I 135 B3
Emsbüren D 71 B4
Emsdetten D 71 B4
Emsfors S 62 A4
Emskirchen D . . . 94 B2
Emstek D 71 B5
Emsworth GB . . . 44 C3
Emyvale IRL 27 B4
Enafors S 199 B9
Enänger S 51 A4
Encamp AND . . . 146 B2
Encarnaçao P . . . 154 C1
Encinas de Abajo
 E 150 B2
Encinas de Esgueva
 E 142 C2
Encinasola E 161 A3
Encinas Reales E . 163 A3
Encio E 143 B3
Enciso E 144 B1
Enden N 199 D7
Endingen D 106 A2
Endrinal E 149 B4
Endröd H 113 C4
Enebakk N 54 A2
Eneryda S 63 B2
Enese H 111 B4
Enez TR 183 C8
Enfield IRL 30 A2
Eng A 108 B2
Engelberg CH . . . 106 C3
Engelhartszell A . . 96 C1
Engelskirchen D . . 80 B3
Engen D 107 B3
Enger N 48 B2
Engerdal N 199 D8
Enge-sande D . . . 64 B1
Engesvang DK . . . 59 B2
Enghien B 79 B4
Engstingen D 94 C1
Engter D 71 B5
Enguera E 159 C3
Enguidanos E . . . 158 B2
Enkenbach D 93 B3
Enkhuizen NL . . . 70 B2
Enklinge FIN 51 B7
Enköping S 56 A3
Enna I 177 B3
Ennezat F 116 B3
Ennigerloh D 81 A4
Enningdal N 54 B2
Ennis IRL 28 B3
Enniscorthy IRL . . 30 B2
Enniskean IRL . . . 29 C3
Enniskillen GB . . . 27 B3
Ennistimon IRL . . . 28 B2
Enns A 110 A1
Eno FIN 9 A7
Enontekiö FIN . . . 196 A6
Ens NL 70 B2
Enschede NL 71 B3
Ensdorf D 95 B3
Ensisheim F 106 B2
Enstaberga S 56 B2

Enstone GB 44 B2
Entlebuch CH . . . 106 B3
Entrácque I 133 A3
Entradas P 160 B1
Entrains-sur-Nohain
 F 104 B2
Entrambasaguas E 143 A3
Entrambasmestas
 E 143 A3
Entraygues-sur-Truyère
 F 116 C2
Entre-os-Rios P . . 148 A1
Entrevaux F 132 B2
Entrín Bajo E 155 C4
Entroncamento P . 154 B2
Entzheim F 93 C3
Envermeu F 89 A5
Enviken S 50 B2
Enying H 112 C2
Enzingerboden A . . 109 B3
Enzklösterle D . . . 93 C4
Épagny F 90 B3
Epalinges CH . . . 106 C1
Epannes F 114 B3
Epanomi GR 182 C4
Epe
 D 71 B4
 NL 70 B2
Épernay F 91 B3
Épernon F 90 C1
Epfig F 93 C3
Epierre F 118 B3
Épila E 152 A2
Épinac F 104 C3
Épinal F 105 A5
Episcopia I 174 A2
Episkopi CY 181 B1
Epitalio GR 184 B2
Epoisses F 104 B3
Eppenbrunn D . . . 93 B3
Eppendorf D 83 B5
Epping GB 45 B4
Eppingen D 93 B4
Epsom GB 44 B3
Epworth GB 40 B3
Eraclea I 122 B1
Eraclea Mare I . . . 122 B1
Erba I 120 B2
Erbach
 Baden-Württemberg
 D 94 C1
 Hessen D 93 B4
Erbalunga F 180 A2
Erbendorf D 95 B4
Erchie I 173 B3
Ercolano I 170 C2
Ercsi H 112 B2
Érd H 112 B2
Erdek TR 186 B2
Erdemli TR 23 C8
Erdevik SRB 126 B1
Erding D 95 C3
Erdötelek H 113 B4
Erdut HR 125 B5
Erdweg D 95 C3
Eregli
 Konya TR 23 C8
 Zonguldak TR . . 187 A6
Erenkaya TR 189 B7
Eresfjord N 198 C5
Eresos GR 183 D7
Eretria GR 185 A4
Erfde D 64 B2
Erfjord N 52 A2
Erftstadt D 80 B2
Erfurt D 82 B3
Ergli LV 8 D4
Ergoldsbach D . . . 95 C4
Eriboll GB 32 C2
Érice I 176 A1
Ericeira P 154 C1
Eğridir TR 189 B5
Eriksberg S 195 E6
Eriksmåla S 62 B3
Eringsboda S 63 B3
Eriswil CH 106 B2
Erithres GR 185 A4
Erkelenz D 80 A2
Erkner D 74 B2
Erkrath D 80 A2
Erla E 144 B3
Erlangen D 94 B3
Erli I 133 A4
Erlsbach A 109 C3
Ermelo NL 70 B2
Ermenak TR 23 C7
Ermenonville F . . . 90 B2
Ermezinde P 148 A1
Ermidas P 160 A1
Ermioni GR 184 B4
Ermoupoli GR . . . 185 B5
Ermsleben D 82 A3
Erndtebrück D . . . 81 B4
Ernée F 88 B3
Ernestinovo HR . . 125 B4
Ernstbrunn A 97 C4
Erolzheim D 107 A5
Erquelinnes B . . . 79 B4
Erquy F 101 A3
Erra P 154 C2
Erratzu E 144 A2
Errindlev DK 65 B4
Erro E 144 B2
Ersa F 180 A2
Érsekcsanád H . . 125 A4

Ersekë AL 182 C2
Érsekvadkert H 112 B3
Ersmark S 200 C6
Erstein F 93 C3
Erstfeld CH 107 C3
Ertebølle DK 58 B2
Ertingen D 107 A4
Ervedal
  Coimbra P 148 B1
  Portalegre P 154 B3
Ervenik HR 138 A1
Ervidel P 160 B1
Ervy-le-Châtel F . . 104 A2
Erwitte D 81 A4
Erxleben D 73 B4
Erzsébet H 125 A4
Esbjerg DK 59 C1
Esbly F 90 C2
Escacena del Campo
  E 161 B3
Escairón E 140 B3
Escalada E 143 B3
Escalante E 143 A3
Escalaplano I 179 C3
Escalona E 150 B3
Escalona del Prado
  E 151 A3
Escalonilla E 150 C3
Escalos de Baixo
  P 155 B3
Escalos de Cima P 155 B3
Escamilla E 152 B1
Es Caná E 166 B1
Escañuela E 157 C3
Es Castell E 167 B4
Escatrón E 153 A3
Eschach D 107 B4
Eschau D 94 B1
Eschede D 72 B3
Eschenau D 95 B3
Eschenbach D 95 B3
Eschenz CH 107 B3
Eschershausen D . 72 C2
Esch-sur-Alzette L . 92 B1
Esch-sur-Sûre L . . 92 B1
Eschwege D 82 A2
Eschweiler D 80 B2
Escobasa de Almazán
  E 152 A1
Escoeuilles F 78 B1
Escombreras E . . . 165 B4
Escos F 144 A2
Escource F 128 B1
Escragnolles F . . . 132 B2
Escrick GB 40 B2
Escurial E 156 A2
Escurial de la Sierra
  E 149 B4
Esens D 71 A4
Esgos E 140 B3
Esher GB 44 B3
Eskdalemuir GB . . . 36 A3
Eskifjörður IS . . . 191 B12
Eskilhem S 57 C4
Eskilsäter S 55 B4
Eskilstrup DK 65 B4
Eskilstuna S 56 A2
Eskipazar TR 187 B7
Eskişehir TR 187 C5
Eslarn D 95 B4
Eslava E 144 B2
Eslida E 159 B3
Eslohe D 81 A4
Eslöv S 61 D3
Eşme TR 188 A3
Es Mercadal E . . . 167 B4
Es Migjorn Gran E. 167 B4
Espa N 48 B3
Espalion F 130 A1
Esparragalejo E . . 155 C4
Esparragosa del
  Caudillo E 156 B2
Esparragossa de la
  Serena E 156 B2
Esparreguera E . . 147 C2
Esparron F 132 B1
Espe N 46 B3
Espedal N 52 B2
Espejo
  Alava E 143 B3
  Córdoba E 163 A3
Espeland N 46 B2
Espelkamp D 72 B1
Espeluche F 131 A3
Espeluy E 157 B4
Espera E 162 B2
Esperança P 155 B3
Espéraza F 146 B3
Espéria I 169 B3
Espevær N 52 A1
Espiel E 156 B2
Espinama E 142 A2
Espiñaredo E 140 A3
Espinasses F 132 A2
Espinelves E 147 C3
Espinhal P 154 A2
Espinho P 148 A1
Espinilla E 142 A2
Espinosa de Cerrato
  E 143 C3
Espinosa de los
  Monteros E 143 A3
Espinoso del Rey
  E 156 A3
Espírito Santo P . . 160 B2

Espluga de Francolí
  E 147 C2
Esplús E 145 C4
Espolla E 146 B3
Espoo FIN 8 B4
Esporles E 166 B2
Es Port d'Alcúdia
  E 167 B3
Esposende P 148 A1
Espot E 146 B2
Es Pujols E 166 C1
Esquedas E 145 B3
Esquivias E 151 B4
Essay F 89 B4
Essen
  B 79 A4
  Niedersachsen D . .71 B4
  Nordrhein-Westfalen
   D 80 A3
Essenbach D 95 C4
Essertaux F 90 B2
Essingen D 94 C2
Esslingen D 94 C1
Es Soleràs E 153 A4
Essoyes F 104 A3
Estacas E 140 B2
Estadilla E 145 B4
Estagel F 146 B3
Estaires F 78 B2
Estang F 128 C2
Estarreja P 148 B1
Estartit E 147 B4
Estavayer-le-Lac
  CH 106 C1
Este I 121 B4
Esteiro E 140 A2
Estela P 148 A1
Estella E 144 B1
Estellencs E 166 B2
Estepa E 162 A3
Estépar E 143 B3
Estepona E 162 B2
Esternay F 91 C3
Esterri d'Aneu E . . 146 B2
Esterwegen D 71 B4
Estissac F 104 A2
Estivadas E 140 B3
Estivareilles F 116 A2
Estivella E 159 B3
Estói P 160 B2
Estopiñán E 145 C4
Estoril P 154 C1
Estoublon F 132 B2
Estrela P 155 C3
Estremera E 151 B4
Estremoz P 155 C3
Estuna S 51 C5
Esyres F 102 B2
Esztergom H 112 B2
Étables-sur-Mer F . 100 A3
Étain F 92 B1
Étalans F 105 B5
Étalle B 92 B1
Étampes F 90 C2
Etang-sur-Arroux
  F 104 C3
Étaples F 78 B1
Etauliers F 128 A2
Etili TR 186 C1
Etna N 48 B1
Etne N 52 A1
Etoges F 91 C3
Etoliko GR 184 A2
Eton GB 44 B3
Étréaupont F 91 B3
Étréchy F 90 C2
Étrépagny F 90 B1
Étretat F 89 A4
Étroeungt F 91 A3
Étroubles I 119 B3
Ettal D 108 B2
Ettelbruck L 92 B2
Etten NL 79 A4
Ettenheim D 106 A2
Ettington GB 44 A2
Ettlingen D 93 C4
Ettringen D 108 A1
Etuz F 105 B4
Etxarri-Aranatz E . 144 B1
Etyek H 112 B2
Eu F 90 A1
Euerdorf D 82 B2
Eulate E 144 B1
Eupen B 80 B2
Europoort NL 79 A4
Euskirchen D 80 B2
Eutin D 65 B3
Evanger N 46 B3
Évaux-les-Bains F . 116 A2
Evciler
  Afyon TR 189 A4
  Çanakkale TR . . .186 C1
Evenskjær N 194 B7
Evenstad N 48 A3
Evercreech GB 43 A4
Evergem B 79 A3
Everöd S 61 D4
Eversberg D 81 A4
Everswinkel D 71 C4
Evertsberg S 49 A5
Evesham GB 44 A2
Évian-les-Bains F . .118 A3
Evisa F 180 A1
Evje N 53 B3
Evolène CH 119 A4
Évora P 154 C3

Evoramonte P 155 C3
Evran F 101 A4
Évrecy F 89 A3
Évreux F 89 A5
Évron F 102 A1
Évry F 90 C2
Ewell GB 44 B3
Ewersbach D 81 B4
Excideuil F 115 C5
Exeter GB 43 B3
Exmes F 89 B4
Exminster GB 43 B3
Exmouth GB 43 B3
Eydehamn N 53 B4
Eye
  Peterborough GB . .41 C3
  Suffolk GB 45 A5
Eyemouth GB 35 C5
Eyguians F 132 A1
Eyguières F 131 B4
Eygurande F 116 B2
Eylie F 145 B4
Eymet F 129 B3
Eymoutiers F 116 B1
Eynsham GB 44 B2
Eyrarbakki IS 190 D4
Eystrup D 72 B2
Ezaro E 140 B1
Ezcaray E 143 B4
Ezcároz E 144 B2
Ezine TR 186 C1
Ezmoriz P 148 B1

F

Fabara E 153 A4
Fábbrico I 121 C3
Fåberg N 48 A2
Fabero E 141 B4
Fábiánsebestyén
  H 113 C4
Fåborg DK 64 A3
Fabrègues F 130 B2
Fabriano I 136 B1
Fabrizia I 175 C2
Facha P 148 A1
Facinas E 162 B2
Fačkov SK 98 B2
Fadagosa P 155 B3
Fadd H 112 C2
Faédis I 122 A2
Faenza I 135 A4
Fafe P 148 A1
Fagagna I 122 A2
Făgăraş RO 17 C6
Fågelberget S . . .199 A11
Fågelfors S 62 A3
Fågelmara S 63 B3
Fågelsta S 55 B6
Fagerås S 55 A4
Fagerheim N 47 B4
Fagerhøy N 48 A1
Fagerhult S 62 A3
Fagerlund N 48 B2
Fagernes
  Oppland N 47 B6
  Troms N 192 C3
Fagersanna S 55 B5
Fagersta S 50 B2
Fåglavik S 55 B4
Fagnano Castello I 174 B2
Fagnières F 91 C4
Faido CH 107 C3
Fains-Véel F 91 C5
Fairford GB 44 B2
Fairlie GB 34 C3
Fajsz H 112 C2
Fakenham GB 41 C4
Fåker S 199 B11
Fakse DK 65 A5
Fakse Ladeplads
  DK 65 A5
Falaise F 89 B3
Falcade I 121 A4
Falcarragh IRL 26 A2
Falces E 144 B2
Fălciu RO 17 B7
Falconara I 177 B3
Falconara Marittima
  I 136 B2
Falcone I 177 A4
Faldingworth GB . . 40 B3
Falerum S 56 B2
Fălesti MD 17 B7
Falkenberg
  Bayern D 95 B4
  Bayern D 95 C4
  Brandenburg D . . .83 A5
  S 60 C2
Falkensee D 74 B2
Falkenstein
  Bayern D 95 B4
  Sachsen D 83 B4
Falkirk GB 35 B4
Falkland GB 35 B4
Falköping S 55 B4
Fall D 108 B2
Falla S 56 B1
Fallingbostel D 72 B2
Falmouth GB 42 B1
Falset E 147 C1
Fălticeni RO 17 B7
Falun S 50 B2
Famagusta CY . . . 181 A2
Fammestad N 46 B2
Fana N 46 B2

Fanano I 135 A3
Fanari GR 182 D3
Fanjeaux F 146 A3
Fano I 136 B2
Fântânele RO 126 A3
Fão P 148 A1
Fara in Sabina I . . 168 A2
Faramontanos de
  Tábara E 149 A4
Fara Novarese I . . .119 B5
Farasdues E 144 B2
Fárbo S 62 A4
Fareham GB 44 C2
Färentuna S 57 A3
Färgelanda S 54 B2
Färila S 200 E1
Faringdon GB 44 B2
Faringe S 51 C5
Farini I 120 C2
Fariza E 149 A3
Färjestaden S 63 B4
Farkadona GR 182 D4
Farkasfa H 111 C3
Farlete E 153 A3
Färlöv S 61 C4
Farmos H 113 B3
Farnă SK 112 B2
Farnborough GB . . . 44 B3
Farnese I 168 A1
Farnham GB 44 B3
Farnroda D 82 B2
Faro P 160 B2
Fåro S 57 C5
Fårösund S 57 C5
Farra d'Alpago I . . 122 A1
Farranfore IRL 29 B2
Farre DK 59 B2
Farsala GR 182 D4
Farsø DK 58 B2
Farsund N 52 B2
Farum DK 61 D2
Fårup DK 58 B2
Fasana I 172 B1
Fasano I 173 B3
Fáskrúðsfjörður
  IS 191 C11
Fassberg D 72 B3
Fastiv UA 13 C8
Fastnäs S 49 B5
Fátima P 154 B2
Fatmomakke S . . . 195 E6
Fättjaur S 195 E6
Faucogney-et-la-Mer
  F 105 B5
Fauguerolles F . . . 128 B3
Faulenrost D 74 A1
Faulquemont F 92 B2
Fauquembergues F 78 B2
Fauske N 194 C6
Fauville-en-Caux F . 89 A4
Fauvillers B 92 B1
Fåvang N 48 A2
Favara
  E 159 B3
  I 176 B2
Faverges F 118 B3
Faverney F 105 B5
Faversham GB 45 B4
Favignana I 176 B1
Fawley GB 44 C2
Fay-aux-Loges F . . 103 B4
Fayence F 132 B2
Fayet F 130 B1
Fayl-Billot F 105 B4
Fayón E 153 A4
Fearn GB 32 D3
Fécamp F 89 A4
Feda N 52 B2
Fedje N 46 B1
Feeny IRL 27 B3
Fegen S 60 B3
Fegyvernek H 113 B4
Fehrbellin D 74 B1
Fehring A 111 C3
Feichten A 108 B1
Feiring N 48 B3
Feistritz im Rosental
  A 110 C1
Feketić SRB 126 B1
Felanitx E 167 B3
Feld am See A . . . 109 C4
Feldbach A 110 C2
Feldberg D 74 A2
Feldkirch A 107 B4
Feldkirchen in Kärnten
  A 109 C5
Feldkirchen-Westerham
  D 108 B2
Felgueiras P 148 A1
Felitto I 172 B1
Félix E 164 C2
Ficulle I 135 C5
Fidenza I 120 C3
Felixstowe GB 45 B5
Felizzano I 119 C5
Felletin F 116 B2
Fellbach D 94 C1
Fellingsbro S 56 A1
Felnac RO 126 A3
Felnémet H 113 B4
Felpéc H 111 B4
Fels am Wagram A . 97 C3
Felsberg D 81 A5
Felsőnyék H 112 C2
Felsőszentiván H . 126 A1
Felsőszentmárton
  H 125 B3
Felsőzsolca H 113 A4
Felsted DK 64 B2
Feltre I 121 A4

Femsjö S 60 C3
Fenagh IRL 26 B3
Fene E 140 A2
Fenestrelle I 119 B4
Fénétrange F 92 C3
Feneu F 102 B1
Fengersfors S 54 B3
Fenit IRL 29 B2
Fensmark DK 65 A4
Fenwick GB 36 A2
Feolin Ferry GB . . . 34 C1
Ferbane IRL 28 A4
Ferdinandovac HR 124 A3
Ferdinandshof D . . 74 A2
Fère-Champenoise
  F 91 C3
Fère-en-Tardenois
  F 91 B3
Ferentillo I 168 A2
Ferentino I 169 B3
Feres GR 183 C8
Feria E 155 C4
Feričanci HR 125 B3
Ferizli TR 187 B5
Ferla I 177 B3
Ferlach A 110 C1
Ferleiten A 109 B3
Fermil P 148 A2
Fermo I 136 B2
Fermoselle E 149 A3
Fermoy IRL 29 B3
Fernán Nuñéz E . . 163 A3
Fernán Peréz E . . . 164 C2
Fernão Ferro P . . . 154 C1
Fernay-Voltaire F . .118 A3
Ferndown GB 43 B5
Ferness GB 32 D3
Fernhurst GB 44 B3
Ferns IRL 30 B2
Ferpécle CH 119 A4
Ferrals-les-Corbières
  F 146 A3
Ferrandina I 172 B2
Ferrara I 121 C4
Ferrara di Monte Baldo
  I 121 B3
Ferreira E 141 A3
Ferreira do Alentejo
  P 160 A1
Ferreira do Zêzere
  P 154 B2
Ferreras de Abajo
  E 141 C4
Ferreras de Arriba
  E 141 C4
Ferreries E 167 B4
Ferreruela E 152 A2
Ferreruela de Tabara
  E 149 A3
Ferret CH 119 B4
Ferrette F 106 B2
Ferriere I 120 C2
Ferrière-la-Grande
  F 79 B3
Ferrières
  Hautes-Pyrénées
   F 145 A3
  Loiret F 103 A4
  Oise F 90 B2
Ferrières-sur-Sichon
  F 117 A3
Ferrol E 140 A2
Ferryhill GB 37 B5
Fertörakos H 111 B3
Fertöszentmiklós
  H 111 B3
Ferwerd NL 70 A2
Festieux F 91 B3
Festøy N 198 C3
Festvåg N 194 C5
Feteşti RO 17 C7
Fethard
  Tipperary IRL 29 B4
  Wexford IRL 30 B2
Fethiye TR 188 C4
Fetsund N 48 B3
Fettercairn GB 35 B5
Feucht D 95 B3
Feuchtwangen D . . 94 B2
Feudingen D 81 B4
Feuges F 91 C4
Feuquières F 90 B1
Feurs F 117 B4
Fevik N 53 B4
Ffestiniog GB 38 B3
Fiamignano I 169 A3
Fiano I 119 B4
Ficarazzi I 176 A2
Ficarolo I 121 C4
Fichtelberg D 95 A3
Fidjeland N 52 B2
Fieberbrunn A 109 B3
Fier AL 182 C1
Fiera di Primiero I . 121 A4
Fiesch CH 119 A5
Fiesso Umbertiano
  I 121 C4
Figari F 180 B2
Figeac F 116 C2
Figeholm S 62 A4
Figgjo N 52 B1
Figline Valdarno I . 135 B4
Figols E 145 B4
Figueira da Foz P . 148 B1

Figueira de Castelo
  Rodrigo P 149 B3
Figueira dos Caveleiros
  P 160 A1
Figueiredo P 154 B3
Figueiredo de Alva
  P 148 B2
Figueiródos Vinhos
  P 154 B2
Figueres E 147 B3
Figueroles E 153 B3
Figueruela de Arriba
  E 141 C4
Filadélfia I 175 C2
Fil'akovo SK 99 C3
Filderstadt D 94 C1
Filey GB 41 A3
Filiaşi RO 17 C5
Filiates GR 182 D2
Filiatra GR 184 B2
Filipstad S 55 A5
Filisur CH 107 C4
Fillan N 198 B5
Filotio GR 185 B6
Filottrano I 136 B2
Filskov DK 59 C2
Filton GB 43 A4
Filtvet N 54 A1
Filzmoos A 109 B4
Finale Emília I 121 C4
Finale Lígure I 133 A4
Fiñana E 164 B2
Finby FIN 51 B7
Fincham GB 41 C4
Finchingfield GB . . 45 B4
Findhorn GB 32 D3
Findochty GB 33 D4
Finike TR 189 C5
Finkenberg A 108 B2
Finnea IRL 27 C3
Finneidfjord N . . . 195 D4
Finnerödja S 55 B5
Finnsnes N 194 A9
Finntorp S 54 A3
Finócchio I 168 B2
Finsjö S 62 A4
Finsland N 52 B3
Finspång S 56 B1
Finsterwalde D . . . 84 A1
Finsterwolde NL . . 71 A4
Finstown GB 33 B3
Fintona GB 27 B3
Fionnphort GB 34 B1
Fiorenzuola d'Arda
  I 120 C2
Firenze = Florence
  I 135 B4
Firenzuola I 135 A4
Firmi F 130 A1
Firminy F 117 B4
Firmo I 174 B2
Fischamend Markt
  A 111 A3
Fischbach
  A 110 B2
  D 93 B3
Fischbeck D 73 B5
Fischen D 107 B5
Fishbourne GB 44 C2
Fishguard GB 39 C2
Fiskardo GR 184 A1
Fiskebäckskil S . . . 54 B2
Fiskebøl N 194 B5
Fismes F 91 B3
Fisterra E 140 B1
Fitero E 144 B2
Fitjar N 46 C2
Fiuggi I 169 B3
Fiumata I 169 A3
Fiumefreddo Brúzio
  I 174 B2
Fiumefreddo di Sicília
  I 177 B4
Fiumicino I 168 B2
Fivemiletown GB . . 27 B3
Fivizzano I 134 A3
Fjälkinge S 63 B2
Fjällåsen S 196 B3
Fjällbacka S 54 B2
Fjæra N 46 C3
Fjärdhundra S 56 A2
Fjellerup DK 58 B3
Fjerritslev DK 58 A2
Fjordgard N 194 A8
Fjugesta S 55 A5
Flå N 47 B6
Flåbygd N 53 A4
Flaça E 147 B3
Flace F 117 A4
Fladungen D 82 B2
Flaine F 118 A3
Flaka FIN 51 B7
Flåm N 46 B4
Flamatt CH 106 C2
Flamborough GB . . 41 A3
Flammersfeld D . . . 81 B3
Flassans-sur-Issole
  F 132 B2
Flatdal N 53 A4
Flatebø N 46 B3
Flateby N 48 C3
Flateland N 52 A3
Flateyri IS 190 A2
Flatøydegard N . . . 47 B6
Flatråker N 46 C2
Flattach A 109 C4
Flatvarp S 62 A4

Flauenskjold DK 58 A3
Flavigny-sur-Moselle F 92 C2
Flavy-le-Martel F 90 B3
Flawil CH 107 B4
Flayosc F 132 B2
Flechtingen D 73 B4
Fleckeby D 64 B2
Fleet GB 44 B3
Fleetmark D 73 B4
Fleetwood GB 38 A3
Flehingen D 93 B4
Flekke N 46 A2
Flekkefjord N 52 B2
Flen S 56 A2
Flensburg D 64 B2
Fleringe S 57 C4
Flerohopp S 62 B3
Flers F 88 B3
Flesberg N 47 C6
Fleurance F 129 C3
Fleuré F 115 B4
Fleurier CH 105 C5
Fleurus B 79 B4
Fleury
Hérault F 130 B2
Yonne F 104 B2
Fleury-les-Aubrais F 103 B3
Fleury-sur-Andelle F 89 A5
Fleury-sur-Orne F 89 A3
Flieden D 81 B5
Flimby GB 36 B3
Flims CH 107 C4
Flines-lèz-Raches F 78 B3
Flint GB 38 A3
Flirey F 92 C1
Flirsch A 108 B1
Flisa N 49 B4
Flisby S 62 A2
Fliseryd S 62 A4
Flix E 153 A4
Flixecourt F 90 A2
Flize F 91 B4
Flobecq B 79 B3
Floby S 55 B4
Floda S 60 B2
Flodden GB 37 A4
Flogny-la-Chapelle F 104 B2
Flöha D 83 B5
Flonheim D 93 B4
Florac F 130 A2
Floreffe B 79 B4
Florence = Firenze I 135 B4
Florennes B 79 B4
Florensac F 130 B2
Florentin F 129 C5
Florenville B 91 B5
Flores de Avila E 150 B2
Floresta I 177 B3
Floreşti MD 17 B8
Florídia I 177 B4
Florina GR 182 C3
Florø N 46 A2
Flörsheim D 93 A4
Floss D 95 B4
Fluberg N 48 B2
Flúðir IS 190 C5
Flühli CH 106 C3
Flumet F 118 B3
Fluminimaggiore I 179 C2
Flums CH 107 B4
Flyeryd S 63 B3
Flygsfors S 62 B3
Foča BIH 139 B4
Foça TR 186 D1
Fochabers GB 32 D3
Focşani RO 17 C7
Foel GB 38 B3
Foeni RO 126 B2
Fogdö S 56 A2
Fóggia I 171 B3
Foglianise I 170 B2
Föglö FIN 51 B7
Fohnsdorf A 110 B1
Foiano della Chiana I 135 B4
Foix F 146 B2
Fojnica
BIH 139 B3
BIH 139 B4
Fokstua N 198 C6
Földeák H 126 A2
Foldereid N 199 A9
Főldes H 113 B5
Folegandros GR 185 C5
Folelli F 180 A2
Folgaria I 121 B4
Folgosinho P 148 B2
Folgoso de la Ribera E 141 B4
Folgoso do Courel E 141 B3
Foligno I 136 C1
Folkärna S 50 B3
Folkestad N 198 C3
Folkestone GB 45 B5
Follafoss N 199 B8
Folldal N 198 C6
Follebu N 48 A2
Follina I 121 B5
Föllinge S 199 B11
Follónica I 135 C3
Fölsbyn S 54 A3
Foncebadón E 141 B4
Foncine-le-Bas F 105 C5
Fondevila E 140 C2
Fondi I 169 B3
Fondo I 121 A4
Fonelas E 164 B1
Fonfría
Teruel E 152 B2
Zamora E 149 A3
Fonn N 46 A3
Fonnes N 46 B1
Fonni I 178 B3
Fontaine F 91 C4
Fontainebleau F 90 C2
Fontaine de Vaucluse F 131 B4
Fontaine-Française F 105 B4
Fontaine-le-Dun F 89 A4
Fontan F 133 A3
Fontanarejo E 157 A3
Fontane I 133 A3
Fontanélice I 135 A4
Fontanières F 116 A2
Fontanosas E 157 B3
Fonteblanda I 168 A1
Fontenay-le-Comte F 114 B3
Fontenay-Trésigny F 90 C2
Fontevrault-l'Abbaye F 102 B2
Fontiveros E 150 B3
Fontoy F 92 B1
Fontpédrouse F 146 B3
Font-Romeu F 146 B3
Fontstown IRL 30 A2
Fonyód H 111 C4
Fonz E 145 B4
Fonzaso I 121 A4
Fóppolo I 120 A2
Föra S 62 A4
Forbach
D 93 C4
F 92 B2
Forcall E 153 B3
Forcalquier F 132 B1
Forcarei E 140 B2
Forchheim D 94 B3
Forchtenau A 111 B3
Forchtenberg D 94 B1
Ford GB 34 B2
Førde
Hordaland N 52 A1
Sogn og Fjordane N 46 A2
Förderstedt D 83 A3
Førdesfjorden N 52 A1
Fordham GB 45 A4
Fordingbridge GB 44 C2
Fordon PL 76 A3
Fordongiánus I 179 C2
Forenza I 172 B1
Foresta di Búrgos I 178 B2
Forfar GB 35 B5
Forges-les-Eaux F 90 B1
Foria I 172 B1
Forío I 170 C1
Forjães P 148 A1
Førland N 52 B3
Forlì I 135 A5
Forlimpopoli I 135 A5
Formazza I 119 A5
Formby GB 38 A3
Formerie F 90 B1
Fórmia I 169 B3
Formígine I 135 A3
Formigliana I 119 B5
Formiguères F 146 B3
Fornalutx E 166 B2
Fornåsa S 56 B1
Fornelli I 178 B2
Fornells E 167 A4
Fornelos de Montes E 140 B2
Fornes E 163 B4
Forneset N 192 C3
Forni Avoltri I 109 C3
Forni di Sopra I 122 A1
Forni di Sotto I 122 A1
Forno
Piemonte I 119 B4
Piemonte I 119 B5
Forno Alpi-Gráie I 119 B4
Forno di Zoldo I 121 A5
Fornos de Algodres P 148 B2
Fornovo di Taro I 120 C3
Foros do Arrão P 154 B2
Forráskút H 126 A1
Forres GB 32 D3
Forriolo E 140 B3
Fors S 50 B3
Forsand N 52 B2
Forsbacka S 51 B3
Forserum S 62 A2
Forshaga S 55 A4
Forsheda S 60 B3
Forsinain GB 32 C3
Førslev DK 65 A4
Förslöv S 61 C2
Forsmark
Uppsala S 51 B5
Västerbotten S 195 E6
Forsmo S 200 C3
Forsnäs S 195 D9
Forsnes N 198 B5
Forssa FIN 8 B3
Forssjöbruk S 56 B2
Forst D 84 A2
Forsvik S 55 B5
Fortanete E 153 B3
Fort Augustus GB 32 D2
Forte dei Marmi I 134 B3
Fortezza I 108 C2
Forth GB 35 C4
Fort-Mahon-Plage F 78 B1
Fortrie GB 33 D4
Fortrose GB 32 D2
Fortun N 47 A4
Fortuna E 165 A3
Fortuneswell GB 43 B4
Fort William GB 34 B2
Forvik N 195 E3
Fos F 145 B4
Fosdinovo I 134 A3
Foss N 47 B6
Fossacésia I 169 A4
Fossano I 133 A3
Fossato di Vico I 136 B1
Fossbakken N 194 B8
Fosse-la-Ville B 79 B4
Fossombrone I 136 B1
Fos-sur-Mer F 131 B3
Fot H 112 B3
Fouchères F 104 A3
Fouesnant F 100 B1
Foug F 92 C1
Fougères F 88 B2
Fougerolles F 105 B5
Foulain F 105 A4
Fountainhall GB 35 C5
Fouras F 114 C2
Fourchambault F 104 B2
Fourmies F 91 A4
Fourna GR 182 D3
Fournels F 116 C3
Fourni GR 188 B1
Fournols F 117 B3
Fourques F 146 B3
Fourquevaux F 146 A2
Fours F 104 C2
Fowey GB 42 B2
Foxdale GB 36 B2
Foxford IRL 26 C1
Foyers GB 32 D2
Foynes IRL 29 B2
Foz E 141 A3
Foza I 121 B4
Foz do Arelho P 154 B1
Foz do Giraldo P 155 B3
Frabosa Soprana I 133 A3
Frades de la Sierra E 149 B4
Fraga E 153 A4
Fragagnano I 173 B3
Frailes E 163 A4
Fraire B 79 B4
Fraize F 106 A1
Framlingham GB 45 A5
Frammersbach D 94 A1
Framnes N 54 A1
França P 141 C4
Francaltroff F 92 C2
Francavilla al Mare I 169 A4
Francavilla di Sicília I 177 B4
Francavilla Fontana I 173 B3
Francavilla in Sinni I 174 A2
Francescas F 129 B3
Franco P 148 A2
Francofonte I 177 B3
Francos E 151 A4
Frändefors S 54 B3
Franeker NL 70 A2
Frangy F 118 A2
Frankenau D 81 A4
Frankenberg
Hessen D 81 A4
Sachsen D 83 B5
Frankenburg A 109 A4
Frankenfels A 110 B2
Frankenmarkt A 109 B4
Frankenthal D 93 B4
Frankfurt
Brandenburg D 74 B3
Hessen D 81 B4
Frankrike S 199 B10
Fränsta S 200 D2
Františkovy Lázně CZ 83 B4
Franzburg D 66 B1
Frascati I 168 B2
Frasdorf D 109 B3
Fraserburgh GB 33 D4
Frashër AL 182 C2
Frasne F 105 C5
Frasnes-lez-Anvaing B 79 B3
Frasseto F 180 B2
Frastanz A 107 B4
Fratel P 155 B3
Fratta Todina I 135 C5
Frauenau D 96 C1
Frauenfeld CH 107 B3
Frauenkirchen A 111 B3
Frauenstein D 83 B5
Frauental A 110 C2
Frayssinet F 129 B4
Frayssinet-le-Gélat F 129 B4
Frechas P 149 A2
Frechen D 80 B2
Frechilla E 142 B2
Freckenhorst D 71 C4
Fredeburg D 81 A4
Fredelsloh D 82 A1
Fredeng N 48 B2
Fredensborg DK 61 D2
Fredericia DK 59 C2
Frederiks DK 59 B2
Frederikshavn DK 58 A3
Frederikssund DK 61 D2
Frederiksværk DK 61 D2
Fredrika S 200 B4
Fredriksberg S 50 B1
Fredriksdal S 62 A2
Fredrikstad N 54 A1
Fregenal de la Sierra E 161 A3
Fregene I 168 B2
Freiberg D 83 B5
Freiburg
Baden-Württemberg D 106 B2
Niedersachsen D 64 C2
Freienhagen D 81 A5
Freienhufen D 84 A1
Freiensteinau D 81 B5
Freihung D 95 B3
Freilassing D 109 B3
Freisen D 92 B3
Freising D 95 C3
Freistadt A 96 C2
Freital D 84 A1
Freixedas P 149 B2
Freixo de Espada à Cinta P 149 A3
Fréjus F 132 B2
Fremdingen D 94 C2
Frenštát pod Radhoštěm CZ 98 B2
Freren D 71 B4
Freshford IRL 30 B1
Freshwater GB 44 C2
Fresnay-sur-Sarthe F 89 B4
Fresneda de la Sierra E 152 B1
Fresneda de la Sierra Tiron E 143 B3
Fresnedillas E 151 B3
Fresnes-en-Woevre F 92 B1
Fresne-St Mamès F 105 B4
Fresno Alhandiga E 150 B2
Fresno de la Ribera E 150 A2
Fresno de la Vega E 142 B1
Fresno de Sayago E 149 A4
Fresnoy-Folny F 90 B1
Fresnoy-le-Grand F 91 B3
Fressenville F 90 A1
Fresvik N 46 A3
Fréteval F 103 B3
Fretigney F 105 B4
Freudenberg
Baden-Württemberg D 94 B1
Nordrhein-Westfalen D 81 B3
Freudenstadt D 93 C4
Freux B 92 B1
Frévent F 78 B2
Freyburg D 83 A3
Freyenstein D 73 A5
Freyming-Merlebach F 92 B2
Freystadt D 95 B3
Freyung D 96 C1
Frias de Albarracin E 152 B2
Fribourg CH 106 C2
Frick CH 106 B3
Fridafors S 63 B2
Fridaythorpe GB 40 A3
Friedberg
A 111 B3
Bayern D 94 C2
Hessen D 81 B4
Friedeburg D 71 A4
Friedewald D 82 B1
Friedland
Brandenburg D 74 B3
Mecklenburg-Vorpommern D 74 A2
Niedersachsen D 82 A1
Friedrichroda D 82 B2
Friedrichsdorf D 81 B4
Friedrichshafen D 107 B4
Friedrichskoog D 64 B1
Friedrichstadt D 64 B2
Friedrichswalde D 74 A2
Friesach A 110 C1
Friesack D 73 B5
Friesenheim D 93 C3
Friesoythe D 71 A4
Friggesund S 200 E2
Frigiliana E 163 B4
Frihetsli N 192 D3
Frillesås S 60 B2
Frinnaryd S 62 A2
Frinton-on-Sea GB 45 B5
Friockheim GB 35 B5
Friol E 140 A3
Fristad S 60 B2
Fritsla S 60 B2
Fritzlar D 81 A5
Frizington GB 36 B3
Frödinge S 62 A4
Froges F 118 B2
Frohburg D 83 A4
Frohnhausen D 81 B4
Frohnleiten A 110 B2
Froissy F 90 B2
Frombork PL 69 A4
Frome GB 43 A4
Frómista E 142 B2
Fröndenberg D 81 A3
Fronsac F 128 B2
Front I 119 B4
Fronteira P 155 B3
Frontenay-Rohan-Rohan F 114 B3
Frontenhausen D 95 C4
Frontignan F 130 B2
Fronton F 129 C4
Fröseke S 62 B3
Frosinone I 169 B3
Frosolone I 170 B2
Frosta N 199 B7
Frøstrup DK 58 A1
Frosunda S 57 A4
Frouard F 92 C2
Frövi S 56 A1
Frøyset N 46 B2
Fruges F 78 B2
Frutigen CH 106 C2
Frýdek-Místek CZ 98 B2
Frýdlant CZ 84 B3
Frydlant nad Ostravicí CZ 98 B2
Frygnowo PL 77 A5
Fryšták CZ 98 B1
Fucécchio I 135 B3
Fuencaliente
Ciudad Real E 157 A4
Ciudad Real E 157 B3
Fuencemillán E 151 B4
Fuendejalón E 144 C2
Fuengirola E 163 B3
Fuenlabrada E 151 B4
Fuenlabrada de los Montes E 156 A3
Fuensalida E 151 B3
Fuensanta E 164 B3
Fuensanta de Martos E 163 A4
Fuente-Alamo E 158 C2
Fuente-Álamo de Murcia E 165 B3
Fuentealbilla E 158 B2
Fuente al Olmo de Iscar E 150 A3
Fuentecén E 151 A4
Fuente Dé E 142 A2
Fuente de Cantos E 155 C4
Fuente del Arco E 156 B2
Fuente del Conde E 163 A3
Fuente del Maestre E 155 C4
Fuente de Santa Cruz E 150 A3
Fuente el Fresno E 157 A4
Fuente el Saz de Jarama E 151 B4
Fuente el Sol E 150 A3
Fuenteguinaldo E 149 B3
Fuentelapeña E 150 A2
Fuentelcésped E 151 A4
Fuentelespino de Haro E 158 B1
Fuentelespino de Moya E 158 B2
Fuentenovilla E 151 B4
Fuente Obejuna E 156 B2
Fuente Palmera E 162 A2
Fuentepelayo E 151 A3
Fuentepinilla E 151 A5
Fuenterroble de Salvatierra E 150 B2
Fuenterrobles E 158 B2
Fuentes E 158 B1
Fuentesauco E 151 A3
Fuentesaúco E 150 A2
Fuentes de Andalucía E 162 A2
Fuentes de Ebro E 153 A3
Fuentes de Jiloca E 152 A2
Fuentes de la Alcarria E 151 B5
Fuentes de León E 161 A3
Fuentes de Nava E 142 B2
Fuentes de Oñoro E 149 B3
Fuentes de Ropel E 142 B1
Fuentespalda E 153 B4
Fuentespina E 151 A4
Fuente-Tójar E 163 A3
Fuente Vaqueros E 163 A4
Fuentidueña E 151 A4
Fuentidueña de Tajo E 151 B4
Fuerte del Rey E 157 C4
Fügen A 108 B2
Fuglebjerg DK 65 A4
Fuglevik N 54 A1
Fuhrberg D 72 B2
Fulda D 82 B1
Fulgatore I 176 B1
Fully CH 119 A4
Fulnek CZ 98 B1
Fülöpszállás H 112 C3
Fulpmes A 108 B2
Fulunäs S 49 A5
Fumay F 91 B4
Fumel F 129 B3
Funäsdalen S 199 C9
Fundão P 148 B2
Funzie GB 33 A6
Furadouro P 148 B1
Fure N 46 A2
Fürstenau D 71 B4
Furstenau D 81 A5
Fürstenberg D 74 A2
Fürstenfeld A 111 B3
Fürstenfeldbruck D 108 A2
Fürstenstein D 96 C1
Fürstenwalde D 74 B3
Fürstenwerder D 74 A2
Fürstenzell D 96 C1
Furta H 113 B5
Fürth
Bayern D 94 B2
Hessen D 93 B4
Furth im Wald D 95 B4
Furtwangen D 106 A3
Furuby S 62 B3
Furudal S 50 A2
Furuflaten N 192 C4
Furulund S 61 D3
Furusjö S 60 B3
Fusa N 46 B2
Fuscaldo I 174 B2
Fusch an der Grossglocknerstrasse A 109 B3
Fushë Arrëz AL 182 A2
Fushë-Krujë AL 182 B1
Fusina I 122 B1
Fusio CH 107 C3
Füssen D 108 B1
Fustiñana E 144 B2
Futog SRB 126 B1
Futrikelv N 192 C3
Füzesabony H 113 B4
Füzesgyarmat H 113 B5
Fužine HR 123 B3
Fyllinge S 61 C2
Fynshav DK 64 B2
Fyresdal N 53 A4

G

Gaaldorf A 110 B1
Gabaldón E 158 B2
Gabarret F 128 C2
Gabčíkovo SK 111 B4
Gąbin PL 77 B4
Gabriac F 130 A1
Gabrovo BG 17 D6
Gaby I 119 B4
Gacé F 89 B4
Gacko BIH 139 B4
Gäddede S 199 A11
Gadebusch D 65 C4
Gadmen CH 106 C3
Gádor E 164 C2
Gádoros H 113 C4
Gael F 101 A3
Găeşti RO 17 C6
Gaeta I 169 B3
Gafanhoeira P 154 C2
Gaflenz A 110 B1
Gagarin RUS 9 E9
Gaggenau D 93 C4
Gagliano Castelferrato I 177 B3
Gagliano del Capo I 173 C4
Gagnet S 50 B2
Gaibanella I 121 C4
Gaildorf D 94 B1
Gaillac F 129 C4
Gaillefontaine F 90 B1
Gaillon F 89 A5
Gainsborough GB 40 B3
Gairloch GB 31 B3
Gairlochy GB 34 B3
Gáiro I 179 C3
Gaj
HR 124 B3
SRB 127 C3
Gaja-la-Selve F 146 A2
Gajanejos E 151 B5
Gajary SK 97 C4
Gajdobra SRB 126 B1
Galan F 145 A4
Galanta SK 111 A4
Galapagar E 151 B3
Galápagos E 151 B4
Galaroza E 161 B3
Galashiels GB 35 C5
Galatas GR 185 B4
Galaţi RO 17 C8
Galatina I 173 B4
Galatista GR 183 C5
Galátone I 173 B4
Galaxidi GR 184 A3
Galdakao E 143 A4
Galeata I 135 B4
Galende E 141 B4

Galera E 164 B2
Galéria F 180 A1
Galgamácsa H . . 112 B3
Galgate GB 38 A4
Galgon F 128 B2
Galinduste E 150 B2
Galinoporni CY . . 181 A3
Galisteo E 155 B4
Galizes P 148 B2
Galków PL 87 A3
Gallarate I 120 B1
Gallardon F 90 C1
Gallegos de Argañán
E 149 B3
Gallegos del Solmirón
E 150 B2
Galleguillos de Campos
E 142 B1
Galleno I 135 B3
Galliate I 120 B1
Gallicano I 134 A3
Gállio I 121 B4
Gallipoli = Gelibolu
TR 186 B1
Gallípoli I 173 B3
Gällivare S 196 B3
Gallizien A 110 C1
Gallneukirchen A . . 96 C2
Gällö S 199 C12
Gallocanta E 152 B2
Gällstad S 60 B3
Gallur E 144 C2
Galmisdale GB . . . 31 C2
Galmpton GB 43 B3
Galston GB 36 A2
Galta N 52 A1
Galtelli I 178 B3
Galten DK 59 B2
Galtür A 107 C5
Galve de Sorbe E . 151 A4
Galveias P 154 B2
Gálvez E 157 A3
Galway IRL 28 A2
Gamaches F 90 B1
Gámbara I 120 B3
Gambárie I 175 C1
Gambassi Terme I . 135 B3
Gambatesa I 170 B2
Gambolò I 120 B1
Gaming A 110 B2
Gamla Uppsala S . 51 C4
Gamleby S 62 A4
Gamlingay GB 44 A3
Gammelgarn S . . . 57 C4
Gammelstad S . . . 196 D5
Gammertingen D . . 107 A4
Gams CH 107 B4
Gamvik
Finnmark N 192 B6
Finnmark N 193 A12
Gan F 145 A3
Gáname E 149 A3
Ganda di Martello I 108 C1
Gandarela P 148 A1
Ganddal N 52 B1
Ganderkesee D . . . 72 A1
Gandesa E 153 A4
Gandía E 159 C3
Gandino I 120 B2
Gandrup DK 58 A3
Ganges F 130 B2
Gånghester S 60 B3
Gangi I 177 B3
Gangkofen D 95 C4
Gannat F 116 A3
Gannay-sur-Loire
F 104 C2
Gänserdorf A 97 C4
Ganzlin D 73 A5
Gap F 132 A2
Gara H 125 A5
Garaballa E 158 B2
Garaguso I 172 B2
Garbayuela E 156 A2
Garbhallt GB 34 B2
Garbsen D 72 B2
Garching D 109 A3
Garciaz E 156 A2
Garcihernández E . 150 B2
Garcillán E 151 B3
Garcinarro E 151 B5
Garcisobaco E . . . 162 B2
Garda I 121 B3
Gardanne F 131 B4
Gårdås S 49 B5
Gårdby S 63 B4
Gardeja PL 69 B3
Gardelegen D 73 B4
Gardermoen N . . . 48 B3
Gardiki GR 182 E3
Garding D 64 B1
Gardone Riviera I . 121 B3
Gardone Val Trómpia
I 120 B3
Gárdony H 112 B2
Gardouch F 146 A2
Gårdsjö S 55 B5
Gårdskär S 51 B4
Gards Köpinge S . . 63 C2
Garein F 128 B2
Garelochhead GB . 34 B3
Garéoult F 132 B2
Garešnica HR . . . 124 B2
Garéssio I 133 A4
Garforth GB 40 B2

Gargaliani GR 184 B2
Gargaligas E 156 A2
Gargallo E 153 B3
Garganta la Olla E . 150 B2
Gargantiel E 156 B3
Gargellen A 107 C4
Gargilesse-Dampierre
F 103 C3
Gargnano I 121 B3
Gárgnäs S 195 E8
Gárgoles de Abajo
E 152 B1
Gargrave GB 40 B1
Garitz D 73 C5
Garlasco I 120 B1
Garlieston GB 36 B2
Garlin F 128 C2
Garliestle GB 94 C1
Garmisch-Partenkirchen
D 108 B2
Garnat-sur-Engièvre
F 104 C2
Garpenberg S 50 B3
Garphyttan S 55 A5
Garray E 143 C4
Garrel D 71 B5
Garriguella E 146 B4
Garrison GB 26 B2
Garrovillas E 155 B4
Garrucha E 164 B3
Gars-am-Kamp A . . 97 C3
Garsås S 50 B1
Garsdale Head GB . 37 B4
Gärsnäs S 63 C2
Garstang GB 38 A4
Gartow D 73 A4
Gartz D 74 A3
Gærum DK 58 A3
Garvagh GB 27 B4
Garvão P 160 B1
Garve GB 32 D2
Garwolin PL 12 C4
Garz D 66 B2
Garzyn PL 85 A4
Gąsawa PL 76 B2
Gaschurn A 107 C5
Gascueña E 152 B1
Gasny F 90 B1
Gąsocin PL 77 B5
Gastes F 128 B1
Gastouni GR 184 B2
Gastouri GR 182 D1
Gata
E 149 B3
HR 138 B2
Gata de Gorgos E . 159 C4
Gătaia RO 126 B3
Gatehouse of Fleet
GB 36 B2
Gáter H 113 C3
Gateshead GB 37 B5
Gátova E 159 B3
Gattendorf A 111 A3
Gatteo a Mare I . . 136 A1
Gattinara I 119 B5
Gattorna I 134 A2
Gaucín E 162 B2
Gaulstad N 199 B9
Gaupne N 47 A4
Gautefall N 53 A4
Gauting D 108 A2
Gauto S 195 D7
Gava E 147 C3
Gávavencsello H . . 113 A5
Gavi I 120 C1
Gavião P 154 B3
Gavirate I 120 B1
Gavoi I 178 B3
Gavorrano I 135 C3
Gavray F 88 B2
Gavrio GR 185 B5
Gávunda S 49 B6
Gaweinstal A 97 C4
Gaworzyce PL 85 A4
Gawroniec PL 75 A5
Gaydon GB 44 A2
Gayton GB 41 C4
Gazipaşa TR 189 C7
Gazoldo degli Ippoliti
I 121 B3
Gazzuolo I 121 B3
Gbelce SK 112 B2
Gdańsk PL 69 A3
Gdinj HR 138 B2
Gdov RUS 8 C5
Gdów PL 99 B4
Gdynia PL 69 A3
Gea de Albarracin
E 152 B2
Geary GB 31 B2
Géaudot F 91 C4
Gebesee D 82 A2
Gebiz TR 189 B5
Gebze TR 187 B4
Géderlak H 112 C2
Gedern D 81 B5
Gedinne B 91 B4
Gediz TR 187 D4
Gèdre F 145 B4
Gedser DK 65 B4
Gedsted DK 58 B2
Geel B 79 A4

Geesthacht D 72 A3
Geetbets B 79 B5
Gefell D 83 B3
Gehrden D 72 B2
Gehren D 82 B3
Geilenkirchen D . . 80 B2
Geilo N 47 B5
Geinsheim D 93 B4
Geisa D 82 B1
Geiselhöring D . . . 95 C4
Geiselwind D 94 B2
Geisenfeld D 95 C3
Geisenhausen D . . 95 C4
Geisenheim D . . . 93 B4
Geising D 84 B1
Geisingen D 107 B3
Geislingen D 94 C1
Geistthal A 110 B2
Geiterygghytta N . . 47 B4
Geithain D 83 A4
Geithus N 48 C1
Gela I 177 B3
Geldermalsen NL . . 79 A5
Geldern D 80 A2
Geldrop NL 80 A1
Geleen NL 80 B1
Gelembe TR 186 C2
Gelendost TR 189 A6
Gelibolu = Gallipoli
TR 186 B1
Gelida E 147 C2
Gelnhausen D 81 B5
Gelnica SK 99 C4
Gelsa E 153 A3
Gelse H 111 C3
Gelsenkirchen D . . 80 A3
Gelsted DK 59 C2
Gelterkinden CH . . 106 B2
Gelting D 64 B2
Gelu RO 126 A3
Gelves E 162 A1
Gembloux B 79 B4
Gemeaux F 105 B4
Gémenos F 132 B1
Gemerská Poloma
SK 99 C4
Gemerská Ves SK . . 99 C4
Gemert NL 80 A1
Gemla S 62 B2
Gemlik TR 186 B4
Gemmenich D 80 B1
Gemona del Friuli I 122 A2
Gémozac F 114 C3
Gemund D 80 B2
Gemünden
Bayern D 94 A1
Hessen D 81 B4
Rheinland-Pfalz D . 93 B3
Genappe B 79 B4
Génave E 164 A2
Genazzano I 169 B2
Gençay F 115 B4
Gencsapáti H 111 B3
Gendringen NL . . . 80 A2
Genelard F 104 C3
Genemuiden NL . . . 70 B3
Generalski Stol HR 123 B4
Geneva = Genève
CH 118 A3
Genevad S 61 C3
Genève = Geneva
CH 118 A3
Geneviéres F 105 B4
Gengenbach D . . . 93 C4
Genillé F 103 B3
Genk B 80 B1
Genlis F 105 B4
Gennep NL 80 A1
Genner DK 64 A2
Gennes F 102 B1
Genoa = Génova I . 134 A1
Genola I 133 A3
Génova = Genoa I . 134 A1
Genowefa PL 76 B3
Gensingen D 93 B3
Gent = Ghent B . . . 79 A3
Genthin D 73 B5
Gentioux F 116 B1
Genzano di Lucánia
I 172 B2
Genzano di Roma I 168 B2
Georgenthal D . . . 82 B2
Georgsmarienhütte
D 71 B5
Gera D 83 B4
Geraards-bergen B . 79 B3
Gerace I 175 C2
Geraci Sículo I . . . 177 B3
Geraki GR 184 C3
Gérardmer F 106 A1
Geras A 97 C3
Gerbéviller F 92 C2
Gerbini I 177 B3
Gerði IS 191 C9
Gerede TR 187 B7
Gerena E 161 B3
Geretsried D 108 B2
Gérgal E 164 B2
Gergy F 105 C3
Gerindote E 150 C3
Gerjen H 112 C2
Gerlos A 108 B3
Germay F 92 C1
Germencik TR 188 B2
Germering D 108 A2
Germersheim D . . . 93 B4

Gernika-Lumo E . . 143 A4
Gernrode D 82 A3
Gernsbach D 93 C4
Gernsheim D 93 B4
Geroda D 82 B1
Gerola Alta I 120 A2
Geroldsgrun D . . . 83 B3
Gerolstein D 80 B2
Gerolzhofen D . . . 94 B2
Gerovo HR 123 B3
Gerpinnes B 79 B4
Gerrards Cross GB . 44 B3
Gerri de la Sal E . 147 B2
Gersfeld D 82 B1
Gerstetten D 94 C2
Gersthofen D 94 C2
Gerstungen D 82 B2
Gerswalde D 74 A2
Gerzat F 116 B3
Gerze TR 23 A8
Gerzen D 95 C4
Gescher D 71 C4
Geseke D 81 A4
Geslau D 94 B2
Gespunsart F 91 B4
Gesté F 101 B4
Gestorf D 72 B2
Gesualda I 170 C3
Gesztely H 113 A4
Geta FIN 51 B6
Getafe E 151 B4
Getinge S 60 C2
Getxo E 143 A4
Geversdorf D 64 C2
Gevgelija MK 182 B4
Gevora del Caudillo
E 155 C4
Gevrey-Chambertin
F 105 B3
Gex F 118 A3
Gey D 80 B2
Geyikli TR 186 C1
Geysir IS 190 C5
Geyve TR 187 B5
Gföhl A 97 C3
Ghedi I 120 B3
Ghent = Gent B . . . 79 A3
Gheorgheni RO . . . 17 B6
Ghigo I 119 C4
Ghilarza I 178 B2
Ghisonaccia F . . . 180 A2
Ghisoni F 180 A2
Gialtra GR 182 E4
Gianitsa GR 182 C4
Giardinetto Vécchio
I 171 B3
Giardini Naxos I . . 177 B4
Giarratana I 177 B3
Giarre I 177 B4
Giat F 116 B2
Giaveno I 119 B4
Giazza I 121 B4
Giba I 179 C2
Gibellina Nuova I . . 176 B1
Gibostad N 194 A9
Gibraleón E 161 B3
Gibraltar GBZ 162 B2
Gic H 111 B4
Gideå S 200 C5
Gideåkroken S . . . 200 B3
Gidle PL 86 B3
Giebelstadt D 94 B1
Gieboldehausen D . 82 A2
Gielniów PL 87 A4
Gielow D 74 A1
Gien F 103 B4
Giengen D 94 C2
Giens F 132 B2
Giera RO 126 B2
Gieselwerder D . . . 81 A5
Giessen D 81 B4
Gieten NL 71 A3
Giethoorn NL 70 B3
Giffaumont-
Champaubert F . . 91 C4
Gifford GB 35 C5
Gifhorn D 73 B3
Gige H 125 A3
Gignac F 130 B2
Gijón = Xixón E . . 142 A1
Gilena E 162 A3
Gilford GB 27 B4
Gilleleje DK 61 C2
Gilley F 105 B5
Gilley-sur-Loire F . 104 C2
Gillingham
Dorset GB 43 A4
Medway GB 45 B4
Gilocourt F 90 B2
Gilserberg D 81 B5
Gilsland GB 37 B4
Gilze NL 79 A4
Gimåt S 200 C4
Gimo S 51 B5
Gimont F 129 C3
Ginasservis F 132 B1
Gingelom B 79 B5
Gingst D 66 B2
Ginosa I 171 C4
Ginzling A 108 B2
Giões P 160 B2
Gióia dei Marsi I . . 169 B3
Gióia del Colle I . . 173 B2
Gióia Sannitica I . . 170 B2
Gióia Táuro I 175 C1

Gioiosa Iónica I . . . 175 C2
Gioiosa Marea I . . . 177 A3
Giosla GB 31 A2
Giovinazzo I 171 B4
Girifalco I 175 C2
Giromagny F 106 B1
Girona E 147 C3
Gironcourt-sur-Vraine
F 92 C1
Gironella E 147 B2
Gironville-sous-les-
Côtes F 92 C1
Girvan GB 36 A2
Gislaved S 60 B3
Gislev DK 59 C3
Gislinge DK 61 D1
Gisors F 90 B1
Gissi I 170 A2
Gistad S 56 B1
Gistel B 78 A2
Gistrup DK 58 B3
Giswil CH 106 C3
Githio GR 184 C3
Giugliano in Campania
I 170 C2
Giulianova I 136 C2
Giulvăz RO 126 B2
Giurgiu RO 17 D6
Give DK 59 C2
Givet F 91 A4
Givors F 117 B4
Givry
B 79 B4
F 104 C3
Givry-en-Argonne F 91 C4
Givskud DK 59 C2
Giżałki PL 76 B2
Gizeux F 102 B2
Giżycko PL 12 A4
Gizzeria I 175 C2
Gizzeria Lido I . . . 175 C2
Gjedved DK 59 C2
Gjegjan AL 182 B2
Gjendesheim N . . . 47 A5
Gjerde N 46 B3
Gjerlev DK 58 B3
Gjermundshamn N . 46 B2
Gjerrild DK 58 B3
Gjerstad N 53 B5
Gjesås N 49 B4
Gjesvær N 193 A9
Gjirokastër AL . . . 182 C2
Gjøfjell N 54 A1
Gjøl DK 58 A2
Gjøra N 198 C6
Gjøvik N 48 B2
Gladbeck D 80 A2
Gladenbach D 81 B4
Gladstad N 195 E2
Glamis GB 35 B4
Glamoč BIH 138 A2
Glamsbjerg DK . . . 59 C3
Gland CH 105 C5
Glandorf D 71 B4
Glanegg A 110 C1
Glanshammar S . . 56 A1
Glarus CH 107 B4
Glasgow GB 35 C3
Glashütte
Bayern D 108 B2
Sachsen D 84 B1
Glastonbury GB . . . 43 A4
Glatzau A 110 C2
Glauchau D 83 B4
Glava S 54 A3
Glavatičevo BIH . . 139 B4
Glavičice BIH 127 C1
Glavnik SRB 127 A3
Glein
A 110 B1
N 195 D3
Gleinstätten A . . . 110 C2
Gleisdorf A 110 B2
Glenamoy IRL 26 B1
Glenarm GB 27 B5
Glenavy GB 27 B4
Glenbarr GB 34 C2
Glenbeigh IRL . . . 29 B2
Glencoe GB 34 B2
Glencolumbkille IRL 26 B2
Glendalough IRL . . 30 A2
Glenealy IRL 30 B2
Glenelg GB 31 B3
Glenfinnan GB . . . 34 B2
Glengarriff IRL . . . 29 C2
Glenluce GB 36 B2
Glenmaddy IRL . . . 28 A3
Glenrothes GB . . . 35 B4
Glenties IRL 26 B2
Glesborg DK 58 B3
Glesien D 83 A4
Gletsch CH 106 C3
Glewitz D 66 B1
Glifada GR 185 B4
Glimåkra S 63 B2
Glin IRL 29 B2
Glina HR 124 B2
Glinde D 72 A3
Glinojeck PL 77 B5
Glinsk IRL 28 A2
Gliwice PL 86 B2
Glödnitz A 109 C5
Gloggnitz A 110 B2
Głogoczów PL 99 B3
Glogonj SRB 127 C2
Głogów PL 85 A4
Głogówek PL 86 B1

Glomel F 100 A2
Glomfjord N 195 D4
Glommen S 60 C2
Glommersträsk S . 196 D2
Glonn D 108 B2
Glorenza I 108 C1
Gloria P 154 B2
Glosa P 183 D5
Glossop GB 40 B2
Gloucester GB 39 C4
Głowaczów PL . . . 87 A5
Glówczyce PL 68 A2
Glöwen D 73 B5
Glowno PL 77 C4
Głożan SRB 126 B1
Głubczyce PL 86 B1
Głuchołazy PL 85 B5
Głuchów PL 87 A4
Głuchowo PL 75 B5
Glücksburg D 64 B2
Glückstadt D 64 C2
Glumina BIH 139 A5
Glumsø DK 65 A4
Glušci SRB 127 C1
Glusk BY 13 B8
Glusk BY 13 B8
Glyn Neath GB . . . 39 C3
Gmünd
Kärnten A 109 C4
Nieder Österreich A . 96 C2
Gmund D 108 B2
Gmunden A 109 B4
Gnarp S 200 D3
Gnarrenburg D . . . 72 A2
Gnesau A 109 C4
Gnesta S 56 A3
Gnięchowice PL . . 85 A4
Gniew PL 69 B3
Gniewkowo PL . . . 76 B3
Gniezno PL 76 B2
Gnoien D 66 C1
Gnojnice BIH 139 B3
Gnojno PL 87 B4
Gnosall GB 40 C1
Gnosjö S 60 B3
Göbel TR 186 B3
Goch D 80 A2
Gochsheim D 94 A2
Göd H 112 B3
Godalming GB 44 B3
Godby FIN 51 B6
Goðdalir IS 190 B6
Goddelsheim D . . . 81 A4
Gódega di Sant'Urbano
I 122 B1
Godegård S 56 B1
Godelheim D 81 A5
Goderville F 89 A4
Godiasco I 120 C2
Godič SLO 123 A3
Godkowo PL 69 A4
Godmanchester GB 44 A3
Gödöllő H 112 B3
Gödre H 125 A3
Godshill GB 44 C2
Godzikowice PL . . 85 B5
Godziszewo PL . . . 69 A3
Goes NL 79 A3
Goetzenbrück F . . 93 C3
Góglio I 119 A5
Gogolin PL 86 B2
Göhren D 66 B2
Goirle NL 79 A5
Góis P 148 B1
Góito I 121 B3
Goizueta E 144 A2
Gojna Gora SRB . . 127 D2
Gójsk PL 77 B4
Gökçedağ TR 186 C3
Gökçen TR 188 A2
Gökçeören TR . . . 188 A3
Gökçeyazı TR 186 C2
Göktepe TR 188 B3
Gol N 47 B5
Gola
HR 124 A3
N 48 A1
Gołańcz PL 76 B2
Gölbaşı TR 23 B7
Gölby FIN 51 B6
Gölcük
Kocaeli TR 187 B4
Niğde TR 23 B8
Golčův Jenikov CZ . 97 B3
Gołczewo PL 67 C3
Goldach CH 107 B4
Goldbach D 93 A5
Goldbeck D 73 B4
Goldberg D 73 A5
Goldelund D 64 B2
Goldenstedt D . . . 72 B1
Golegã P 154 B2
Goleniów PL 75 A3
Golfo Aranci I 178 B3
Gölhisar TR 189 B4
Golina PL 76 B3
Gölle H 112 C2
Göllersdorf A 97 C4
Golling an der Salzach
A 109 B4
Gölmarmara TR . . 186 D2
Golnice PL 84 A3
Golnik SLO 123 A3
Gölova TR 189 C5
Gölpazarı TR 187 B5

Gols A. 111 B3
Golspie GB 32 D3
Golssen D 74 C2
Golub-Dobrzyń PL . 77 A4
Golubinci SRB. . . 127 C2
Goluchów PL. 86 A1
Golymin-Ośrodek
PL. 77 B5
Golzow D 73 B5
Gomagoi I 108 C1
Gómara E. 152 A1
Gomaringen D. . . 93 C5
Gömbe TR 189 C4
Gömeç TR 186 C1
Gomel = Homyel BY 13 B9
Gomes Aires P . . 160 B1
Gómezserracin E . 150 A3
Gommern D. 73 B4
Gomulin PL 86 A3
Gonäs S. 50 B2
Goncelin F 118 B2
Gończyce PL 87 A5
Gondomar
E 140 B2
P. 148 A1
Gondrecourt-le-Château
F. 92 C1
Gondrin F 128 C3
Gönen
Balıkesir TR. . .186 B2
İsparta TR 189 B5
Gonfaron F 132 B2
Goñi E 144 B2
Goni
GR. 182 D4
I. 179 C3
Gonnesa I 179 C2
Gonnosfanádiga I . 179 C2
Gönyü H. 111 B4
Gonzaga I 121 C3
Goodrich GB . . . 39 C4
Goodwick GB . . . 39 B1
Gooik B 79 B4
Goole GB 40 B3
Goor NL 71 B3
Göpfritz an der Wild
A. 97 C3
Goppenstein CH . .119 A4
Göppingen D. . . . 94 C1
Gor E 164 B2
Góra
Dolnośląskie PL. . . 85 A4
Mazowieckie PL. . . 77 B5
Gorafe E. 164 B1
Gorawino PL 67 C4
Goražde BIH . . . 139 B4
Görbeháza H 113 B5
Gordaliza del Pino
E. 142 B1
Gördes TR 186 D3
Gørding DK 59 C1
Górdola CH 120 A1
Gordon GB 35 C5
Gordoncillo E . . . 142 B1
Gorebridge GB . . 35 C4
Gorenja Vas SLO . 123 A3
Gorenje Jelenje
HR 123 B3
Gorey
GB 88 A1
IRL 30 B2
Gorgonzola I . . . 120 B2
Gorica HR 137 A4
Gorican HR 124 A2
Gorinchem NL . . . 79 A4
Goring GB 44 B2
Goritsy RUS 9 D10
Göritz D 74 A2
Gorízia I 122 B2
Górki PL. 77 B4
Gorleben D 73 A4
Gorleston-on-sea
GB 41 C5
Gørlev DK 61 D1
Görlitz D 84 A2
Görliz E 143 A4
Görmin D 66 C2
Górna Grupa PL . 69 B3
Gorna Oryahovitsa
BG 17 D6
Gornja Gorevnica
SRB 127 D2
Gornja Ploča HR . 137 A4
Gornja Radgona
SLO 110 C2
Gornja Sabanta
SRB 127 D3
Gornja Trešnjevica
SRB 127 C2
Gornja Tuzla BIH . 125 C4
Gornje Polje MNE . 139 C4
Gornje Ratkovo
BIH 124 C2
Gornji Grad SLO . 123 A3
Gornji Humac HR . 138 B2
Gornji Jasenjani
BIH. 139 B3
Gornji Kamengrad
BIH. 124 C2
Gornji Kneginec
HR 124 A2
Gornji Kosinj HR. 123 C4
Gornji Milanovac
SRB 127 C2
Gornji Podgradci
BIH. 124 B3
Gornji Ravno BIH . 138 B3
Gornji Sjenicak HR 124 B1

Gornji Vakuf BIH . 138 B3
Górno PL 87 B4
Görömböly H. . . .113 A4
Górowo Iławeckie
PL. 69 A5
Gorran Haven GB . 42 B2
Gorredijk NL 70 A3
Gorron F 88 B3
Gorseinon GB . . . 39 C2
Gort IRL 28 A3
Gortin GB. 27 B3
Görzke D 73 B5
Gorzkowice PL . . 86 A3
Górzno
Kujawsko-Pomorskie
PL. 77 A4
Zachodnio-Pomorskie
PL. 75 A4
Gorzów Śląski PL . 86 A2
Gorzów Wielkopolski
PL. 75 B4
Gorzyca PL 74 B3
Gorzyce PL 98 B2
Górzyn PL 84 A2
Gorzyń PL 75 B4
Gorzyno PL 68 A2
Gosaldo I 121 A4
Gosau A. 109 B4
Gosberton GB . . 41 C3
Gościcino PL . . . 68 A3
Gościęcin PL . . . 86 B2
Gościm PL 75 B4
Gościno PL 67 B4
Gosdorf A. 110 C2
Gosforth GB . . . 36 B3
Goslar D. 82 A2
Goślice PL 77 B4
Gospič HR 137 A4
Gosport GB . . . 44 C2
Gössäter S. . . . 55 B4
Gossau CH . . . 107 B4
Goss Ilsede D . . 72 B3
Gössnitz D. . . . 83 B4
Gossweinstein D. . 95 B3
Gostivar MK. . . 182 B2
Gostkow PL . . . 77 C4
Göstling an der Ybbs
A. 110 B1
Gostomia PL . . . 75 A5
Gostycyn PL . . . 76 A2
Gostyń PL 85 A5
Gostynin PL. . . 77 B4
Goszczyn PL . . . 87 A4
Göta S 54 B3
Göteborg = Gothenburg
S. 60 B1
Götene S 55 B4
Gotha D 82 B2
Gothem S. . . . 57 C4
Gothenburg = Göteborg
S. 60 B1
Gotse Delchev BG. 183 B5
Gottesdorf D . . . 95 C4
Göttingen D. . . . 82 A1
Gottne S 200 C4
Götzis A 107 B4
Gouarec F . . . 100 A2
Gouda NL 70 B1
Goudhurst GB . . 45 B4
Goumenissa GR . 182 C4
Goura GR. . . . 184 B3
Gourdon F . . . 129 B4
Gourgançon F . . 91 C4
Gourin F 100 A2
Gournay-en-Bray F. 90 B1
Gourock GB . . . 34 C3
Gouveia P 148 B2
Gouvy B 80 B1
Gouzeacourt F . . 90 A3
Gouzon F 116 A2
Govedari HR . . 138 C3
Govérnolo I . . . 121 B3
Gowarczów PL . . 87 A4
Gowerton GB . . 39 C2
Gowidlino PL . . . 68 A2
Gowran IRL . . . 30 B1
Goyatz D 74 B3
Göynük
TR 187 B5
Antalya TR. . . 189 C5
Gozdnica PL . . . 84 A3
Gozdowo PL . . . 77 B4
Gozee B 79 B4
Graal-Müritz D . . 65 B5
Grabenstätt D . . 109 B3
Grabhair GB . . . 31 A2
Grábo S 60 B2
Grabovac
HR 138 B2
SRB 127 C2
Grabovci SRB . . 127 C1
Grabow D. . . . 73 A4
Grabów PL. . . . 77 B4
Grabów nad Pilicą
PL. 87 A5
Grabowno PL. . . 76 A2
Grabs CH 107 B4
Gračac HR . . . 138 A1
Gračanica BIH . . 125 C4
Graçay F 103 B3
Grad SLO 111 C3
Gradac
BIH 139 C4
HR 138 B3
MNE 139 B5
Gradačac BIH . . 125 C4

Gradec HR . . . 124 B2
Gradefes E. . . . 142 B1
Grades A 110 C1
Gradil P 154 C1
Gradina
HR 124 B3
MNE. 139 B5
Gradisca d'Isonzo
I. 122 B2
Gradište HR. . . 125 B4
Grado
E 141 A4
I. 122 B2
Grafenau D . . . 96 C1
Gräfenberg D. . . 95 B3
Gräfenhainichen D . 83 A4
Grafenschlag A . . 97 C3
Grafenstein A. . . 110 C1
Gräfenthal D . . . 82 B3
Grafentonna D. . . 82 A2
Grafenwöhr D . . 95 B3
Grafing D 108 A2
Grafling D 95 C4
Gräfsnäs S. . . . 54 B3
Gragnano I . . . 170 C2
Grahovo SLO . . . 122 A2
Graiguenamanagh
IRL 30 B2
Grain GB 45 B4
Grainau D 108 B2
Graja de Iniesta E . 158 B2
Grajera E 151 A4
Gram DK 59 C2
Gramais A . . . 108 B1
Gramat F 129 B4
Gramatneusiedl A . .111 A3
Grambow D . . . 74 A3
Grammichele I . . 177 B3
Gramsh AL. . . . 182 C2
Gramzow D . . . 74 A3
Gran N 48 B2
Granada E . . . 163 A4
Granard IRL . . . 27 C3
Grañas E 140 A3
Granátula de Calatrava
E 157 B4
Grancey-le-Château
F. 105 B4
Grandas de Salime
E 141 A4
Grandcamp-Maisy F 88 A2
Grand-Champ F . 100 B3
Grand Couronne F . 89 A5
Grand-Fougeray F 101 B4
Grândola P. . . . 160 A1
Grandpré F . . . 91 B4
Grandrieu
B 79 B4
F. 117 C3
Grandson CH . . 106 C1
Grandvillars F . . 106 B1
Grandvilliers F . . 90 B1
Grañén E 145 C3
Grangärde S . . . 50 B1
Grange IRL . . . 26 B2
Grangemouth GB . 35 B4
Grange-over-Sands
GB 36 B4
Grängesberg S . . 50 B1
Granges-de-Crouhens
F. 145 B4
Granges-sur-Vologne
F. 106 A1
Gräningen D . . . 73 B5
Granitola-Torretta
I. 176 B1
Granja
Évora P 155 C3
Porto P 148 A1
Granja de Moreruela
E 142 C1
Granja de Torrehermosa
E 156 B2
Gränna S 55 B5
Grannäs
Västerbotten S. . .195 E7
Västerbotten S. . .195 E8
Granö S 200 B5
Granollers E . . . 147 C3
Granowiec PL . . 85 A5
Granowo PL . . . 75 B5
Gransee D 74 A2
Gransherad N . . 53 A5
Grantham GB . . 40 C3
Grantown-on-Spey
GB 32 D3
Grantshouse GB . 35 C5
Granville F 88 B2
Granvin N 46 B3
Grærup Strand DK . 59 C1
Gräsås S 60 C2
Grasbakken N . . 193 B12
Grasberg D . . . 72 A2
Grasmere GB. . . 36 B3
Grasse F 132 B2
Grassington GB . 40 A2
Græsted DK . . . 61 C2
Grästen DK . . . 64 B2
Grästorp S. . . . 54 B3
Gratkorn A. . . . 110 B2
Gråträsk S . . . 196 D2
Gratwein A. . . . 110 B2
Graulhet F . . . 129 C4
Graus E 145 B4

Grávalos E. . . . 144 B2
Gravberget N. . . 49 B4
Grave NL 80 A1
Gravedona I . . . 120 A2
Gravelines F . . . 78 A2
Gravellona Toce I . .119 B5
Gravendal S. . . . 50 B1
Gravens DK . . . 59 C2
Gravesend GB. . . 45 B4
Graveson F . . . 131 B3
Gravina in Púglia I 172 B2
Gray F 105 B4
Grayrigg GB . . . 37 B4
Grays GB 45 B4
Grayshott GB . . 44 B3
Graz A. 110 B2
Grazalema E . . . 162 B2
Grązawy PL . . . 69 B4
Grazzano Visconti
I. 120 C2
Greåker N. . . . 54 A1
Great Dunmow GB . 45 B4
Great Malvern GB . 39 B4
Great Torrington
GB 42 B2
Great Waltham GB . 45 B4
Great Yarmouth GB. 41 C5
Grebbestad S . . 54 B1
Grebenstein D . . 81 A5
Grębocice PL. . . 85 A4
Grębocin PL. . . 76 A3
Greding D 95 B3
Gredstedbro DK . 59 C1
Greencastle IRL. . 27 A3
Greenhead GB. . 37 B4
Greenisland GB. . 27 B5
Greenlaw GB . . 35 C5
Greenock GB . . 34 C3
Greenway GB . . 39 C2
Greenwich GB. . 45 B4
Grefrath D . . . 80 A2
Greifenburg A . . 109 C4
Greiffenberg D . . 74 A2
Greifswald D . . 66 B2
Grein A. 110 A1
Greipstad N. . . 53 B3
Greiz D 83 B4
Grenaa DK . . . 58 B3
Grenade F . . . 129 C4
Grenade-sur-l'Adour
F. 128 C2
Grenchen CH. . . 106 B2
Grendi N 53 B3
Grenivik IS . . . 191 B7
Grenoble F. 118 B2
Gréoux-les-Bains
F. 132 B1
Gresenhorst D. . . 66 B1
Gressoney-la-Trinité
I. 119 B4
Gressoney-St.-Jean
I. 119 B4
Gressthal D . . . 82 B2
Gressvik N . . . 54 A1
Gresten A. 110 B2
Greussen D. . . . 82 A2
Greve in Chianti I . 135 B4
Greven
Mecklenburg-
Vorpommern D. . .73 A3
Nordrhein-Westfalen
D. 71 B4
Grevena GR. . . 182 C3
Grevenbroich D. . 80 A2
Grevenbrück D . . 81 A4
Grevenmacher L . 92 B2
Grevesmühlen D . 65 C4
Grevestrand DK . 61 D2
Grevie S. 61 C2
Greystoke GB . . 36 B4
Greystones IRL. . 30 A2
Grez-Doiceau B . 79 B4
Grèzec F 129 B4
Grez-en-Bouère F . 102 B1
Grezzana I . . . 121 B4
Grgar SLO . . . 122 A2
Grgurevci SRB . . 127 B1
Gries A 108 B2
Griesbach D . . . 96 C1
Griesheim D . . . 93 B4
Gries in Sellrain A . 108 B2
Grieskirchen A. . . 109 A4
Griffen A. 110 C1
Grignan F. . . . 131 A3
Grignano I . . . 122 B2
Grigno I 121 A4
Grignols F . . . 128 B2
Grignon F 118 B3
Grijota E. 142 B2
Grijpskerk NL . . 71 A3
Grillby S. 56 A3
Grimaud F . . . 132 B2
Grimbergen B . . 79 B4
Grimma D 83 A4
Grimmen D . . . 66 B2
Grímmialp CH . . 106 C2
Grimsås S 60 B3
Grimsby GB. . . 41 B3
Grimslöv S. . . . 62 B2
Grímsstaðir IS . . 191 B9
Grimstad N . . . 53 B4
Grindavik IS . . . 190 D3
Grindelwald CH. . 106 C3
Grindheim N. . . 52 B3
Grindsted DK. . . 59 C1
Griñón E 151 B4

Gripenberg S. . . 62 A2
Gripsholm S . . . 56 A3
Grisolles F . . . 129 C4
Grisslehamn S . . 51 B5
Gritley GB . . . 33 C4
Grizebeck GB . . 36 B3
Grndina BIH. . . 124 C2
Gröbming A . . . 109 B4
Gröbzig D 83 A3
Grocka SRB. . . 127 C2
Gröditz D 83 A5
Gródki PL. . . . 77 A5
Grodków PL. . . 85 B5
Grodziec PL. . . 76 B3
Grodzisk Mazowiecki
PL. 77 B5
Grodzisk Wielkoposki
PL. 75 B5
Groenlo NL . . . 71 B3
Groesbeek NL . . 80 A1
Grohote HR . . . 138 B2
Groitzsch D . . . 83 A4
Groix F 100 B2
Grójec PL 77 C5
Grom PL. 77 A5
Gromiljca BIH . . 139 B4
Grömitz D 65 B3
Gromnik PL . . . 99 B4
Gromo I 120 B2
Gronau
Niedersachsen D. . .72 B2
Nordrhein-Westfalen
D. 71 B4
Grønbjerg DK . . 59 B1
Grönenbach D. . . 107 B5
Grong N 199 A9
Grönhögen S . . 63 B4
Groningen
D 73 C4
NL 71 A3
Grønnestrand DK . 58 A2
Grono CH. . . . 120 A2
Grönskåra S . . . 62 A3
Grorud N 48 C2
Grósio I 120 A3
Grošnica SRB . . 127 D2
Grossalmerode D . . 82 A1
Grossarl A . . . 109 B4
Gross Beeren D . . 74 B2
Gross Berkel D . . 72 B2
Grossbodungen D . 82 A2
Gross-botwar D. . 94 C1
Grossburgwedel D . 72 B2
Grosschönau D . . 84 B2
Gross-Dölln D . . 74 A2
Grossenbrode D . . 65 B4
Grossenehrich D. . 82 A2
Grossengottern D . 82 A2
Grossenhain D . . 83 A5
Grossenkneten D . 71 B5
Grossenlüder D . . 81 B5
Grossensee D . . 72 A3
Grossenzersdorf A .111 A3
Grosseto I . . . 135 C4
Gross-Gerau D . . 93 B4
Grossgerungs A . . 96 C2
Grossglobnitz A . . 97 C3
Grosshabersdorf D . 94 B2
Grossharras A . . 97 C4
Grosshartmansdorf
D 83 B5
Grosshöchstetten
CH 106 C2
Gross Kreutz D. . 74 B1
Grosskrut A . . . 97 C4
Gross Lafferde D. . 72 B3
Gross Leutheb D. . 74 B3
Grosslohra D. . . 82 A2
Grossmehring D . . 95 C3
Gross Muckrow D . 74 B3
Gross Oesingen D . 72 B3
Grossostheim D . . 93 B5
Grosspertholz A . . 96 C2
Grosspetersdorf A .111 B3
Grosspostwitz D. . 84 A2
Grossraming A . . .110 B1
Grossräschen D . . 84 A2
Gross Reken D . . 80 A2
Grossrinderfeld D. . 94 B1
Grossröhrsdorf D . 84 A2
Gross Sarau D. . 65 C3
Gross Särchen D . 84 A2
Grossschirma D . . 83 B5
Gross Schönebeck
D 74 B2
Grosssschweinbarth
A 97 C4
Grosssieghartts A . 97 C3
Grosssölk A . . . 109 B4
Gross Umstadt D . 93 B4
Gross Warnow D. . 73 A4
Gross-Weikersdorf
A. 97 C3
Gross-Welle D . . 73 A5
Grosswilfersdorf A .110 B2
Gross Wokern D . 65 C5
Grostenquin F . . 92 C2
Grosuplje SLO . . 123 B3
Grotli N 198 C4
Grötlingbo S . . . 57 C4
Grottáglie I . . . 173 B3
Grottaminarda I . . 170 B3
Grottammare I . . 136 C2
Grotte di Castro I . 168 A1
Grotteria I . . . 175 C2

Gróttole I 172 B2
Grouw NL. . . . 70 A2
Grov N 194 B8
Grova N 53 A4
Grove E 140 B2
Grua N 48 B2
Grube D 65 B4
Grubišno Polje HR 124 B3
Grude BIH . . . 138 B3
Grudusk PL . . . 77 A5
Grudziądz PL . . 69 B3
Grue N 49 B4
Gruissan F . . . 130 B2
Grullos E 141 A4
Grumo Áppula I. . 171 B4
Grums S 55 A4
Grünau im Almtal
A. 109 B4
Grünberg D . . . 81 B4
Grünburg A 110 B1
Grundarfjörður IS . 190 C2
Gründau D . . . 81 B5
Gründelhardt D . . 94 B1
Grundforsen S . . 49 A4
Grundlsee A . . . 109 B4
Grundsund S . . 54 B2
Grunewald D . . 84 A1
Grungedal N . . 53 A3
Grunow D . . . 74 B3
Grünstadt D . . . 93 B4
Gruvberget S . . 50 A3
Gruyères CH . . 106 C2
Gruža SRB . . . 127 D2
Grybów PL . . . 99 B4
Grycksbo S . . . 50 B2
Gryfice PL . . . 67 C4
Gryfino PL . . . 74 A3
Gryfów Śląski PL. 84 A3
Gryllefjord N . . 194 A8
Grymyr N . . . 48 B2
Gryt S. 56 B2
Grytgöl S 56 B1
Grythyttan S . . 55 A5
Grytnäs S. . . . 57 B3
Grzmiąca PL . . 68 B1
Grzybno PL . . . 74 A3
Grzywna PL . . . 76 A3
Gschnitz A . . . 108 B2
Gschwend D . . . 94 C1
Gstaad CH . . . 106 C2
Gsteig CH 119 A4
Guadahortuna E . 163 A4
Guadalajara E . . 151 B4
Guadalaviar E . . 152 B2
Guadalcanal E . . 156 B2
Guadalcázar E . . 162 A3
Guadalix de la Sierra
E. 151 B4
Guadálmez E . . 156 B3
Guadalupe E . . 156 A2
Guadamur E . . 151 C3
Guadarrama E . . 151 B3
Guadiaro E . . . 162 B2
Guadix E 164 B1
Guagnano I . . . 173 B3
Guagno F 180 A1
Guajar-Faragüit E . 163 B4
Gualchos E . . . 163 B4
Gualdo Tadino I. . 136 B1
Gualtieri I 121 C3
Guarcino I . . . 169 B3
Guarda P 149 B2
Guardamar del Segura
E. 165 A4
Guardão P. . . . 148 B1
Guardavalle I . . 175 C2
Guardea I 168 A2
Guárdia I 172 B1
Guardiagrele I . . 169 A4
Guardiarégia I . . 170 B2
Guárdia Sanframondi
I. 170 B2
Guardias Viejas E . 164 C2
Guardiola de Berguedá
E. 147 B2
Guardo E 142 B2
Guareña E . . . 156 B1
Guaro E 162 B3
Guarromán E . . 157 B4
Guasila I 179 C3
Guastalla I . . . 121 C3
Gubbhögen S . . 199 A12
Gúbbio I 136 B1
Guben D 74 C3
Gubin PL 74 C3
Gudå N. 199 B8
Gudavac BIH . . 124 C2
Guddal N . . . 46 A2
Güderup DK. . . 64 B2
Gudhem S . . . 55 B4
Gudhjem DK . . 67 A3
Gudovac HR . . 124 B2
Gudow D 73 A3
Güdül TR . . . 187 B7
Gudvangen N . . 46 B3
Guebwiller F . . 106 B2
Guéjar-Sierra E . 163 A4
Guémené-Penfao
F. 101 B4
Guémené-sur-Scorff
F. 100 A2
Güeñes E . . . 143 A3
Guer F 101 B3
Guérande F . . . 101 B3
Guéret F 116 A1

Guérigny F 104 B2
Guesa E 144 B2
Gueugnon F 104 C3
Guglionesi I 170 B2
Gühlen Glienicke D 74 A1
Guia P 154 B2
Guichen F 101 B4
Guidizzolo I 121 B3
Guidónia-Montecélio I 168 B2
Guiglia I 135 A3
Guignes F 90 C2
Guijo E 156 B3
Guijo de Coria E 149 B3
Guijo de Santa Bábera E 150 B2
Guijuelo E 150 B2
Guildford GB 44 B3
Guillaumes F 132 A2
Guillena E 162 A1
Guillestre F 118 C3
Guillos F 128 B2
Guilsfield GB 38 B3
Guilvinec F 100 B1
Guimarães P 148 A1
Guincho P 154 C1
Guînes F 78 B1
Guingamp F 100 A2
Guipavas F 100 A1
Guisborough GB 37 B5
Guiscard F 90 B3
Guiscriff F 100 A2
Guise F 91 B3
Guisona E 147 C2
Guitiriz E 140 A3
Guîtres F 128 A2
Gujan-Mestras F 128 B1
Gulbene LV 8 D5
Gulçayır TR 187 C6
Guldborg DK 65 B4
Gullabo S 63 B3
Gullane GB 35 B5
Gullbrå N 46 B3
Gullbrandstorp S 61 C2
Gulleråsen S 50 A2
Gullhaug N 53 A6
Gullringen S 62 A3
Gullspång S 55 B5
Gullstein N 198 B5
Güllük TR 188 B2
Gülnar TR 23 C7
Gülpınar TR 186 C1
Gülşehir TR 23 B8
Gulsvik N 48 B1
Gumiel de Hizán E 143 C3
Gummersbach D 81 A3
Gümüldür TR 188 A2
Gümüşhaciköy TR 23 A8
Gümüşova TR 187 B5
Gundelfingen D 94 C2
Gundel-fingen D 106 A2
Gundelsheim D 93 B5
Gunderschoffen F 93 C3
Gundertshausen A 109 A3
Gundinci HR 125 B4
Gündoğmuş TR 189 C7
Güney
Burdur TR 189 B4
Denizli TR 188 A4
Gunja HR 125 C4
Günlüce TR 188 C3
Gunnarn S 195 E8
Gunnarsbyn S 196 C4
Gunnarskog S 49 C4
Gunnebo S 62 A4
Gunnislake GB 42 B2
Günselsdorf A 111 B3
Guntersblum D 93 B4
Guntersdorf A 97 C4
Guntín E 140 B3
Günyüzü TR 187 C6
Günzburg D 94 C2
Gunzenhausen D 94 B2
Güre
Balıkesir TR 186 C1
Uşak TR 186 D4
Gurk A 110 C1
Gurrea de Gállego E 144 B3
Gürsu TR 186 B4
Gušće HR 124 B2
Gusev RUS 12 A5
Gúspini I 179 C2
Gusselby S 56 A1
Güssing A 111 B3
Gusswerk A 110 B2
Gustav Adolf S 49 B5
Gustavsberg S 57 A4
Gustavsfors S 54 A3
Güstrow D 65 C5
Gusum S 56 B2
Gutcher GB 33 A5
Gutenstein A 110 B2
Gütersloh D 81 A4
Guttannen CH 106 C3
Guttaring A 110 C1
Guttau D 84 A2
Güttingen CH 107 B4
Gützkow D 66 C2
Guzów PL 77 B5
Gvardeysk RUS 12 A4
Gvarv N 53 A5
Gvozd MNE 139 C5
Gvozdansko HR 124 B2
Gwda Wielka PL 68 B1
Gwennap GB 42 B1
Gy F 105 B4
Gyál H 112 B3
Gyarmat H 111 B4
Gyékényes H 124 A3
Gyé-sur-Seine F 104 A3
Gyljen S 196 C5
Gylling DK 59 C3
Gyoma H 113 C4
Gyömöre H 111 B4
Gyömrő H 112 B3
Gyón H 112 B3
Gyöngyfa H 125 B3
Gyöngyös H 113 B3
Gyöngyöspata H 113 B3
Gyönk H 112 C2
Györ H 111 B4
Györszemere H 111 B4
Gypsera CH 106 C2
Gysinge S 51 B3
Gyttorp S 55 A5
Gyula H 113 C5
Gyulafirátót H 112 B1
Gyulaj H 112 C2

H

Haacht B 79 B4
Haag
Nieder Östereich A 110 A1
Ober Östereich A 109 A4
D 108 A3
Haaksbergen NL 71 B3
Haamstede NL 79 A3
Haan D 80 A3
Haapajärvi FIN 3 E9
Haapsalu EST 8 C3
Haarlem NL 70 B1
Habas F 128 C2
Habay B 92 B1
Habo S 62 A2
Håbol S 54 B3
Habry CZ 97 B3
Habsheim F 106 B2
Hachenburg D 81 B3
Hacıbektaş TR 23 B8
Hacılar TR 23 B8
Hacinas E 143 C3
Hackås S 199 C11
Hacketstown IRL 30 B2
Hackthorpe GB 37 B4
Hadamar D 81 B4
Hädanberg S 200 C4
Haddington GB 35 C5
Hadersdorf am Kamp A 97 C3
Haderslev DK 59 C2
Haderup DK 59 B1
Hadım TR 23 C7
Hadleigh
Essex GB 45 B4
Suffolk GB 45 A4
Hadlow GB 45 B4
Hadmersleben D 73 B4
Hadsten DK 59 B3
Hadsund DK 58 B3
Hadžići BIH 139 B4
Hafnarfjörður IS 190 C4
Hafnir IS 190 D3
Hafslo N 47 A4
Haganj HR 124 B2
Hagby S 63 B4
Hage D 71 A4
Hægebostad N 52 B3
Hægeland N 53 B3
Hagen
Niedersachsen D 72 A1
Nordrhein-Westfalen D 80 A3
Hagenbach D 93 B4
Hagenow D 73 A4
Hagetmau F 128 C2
Hagfors S 49 B5
Häggenås S 199 B11
Hagondange F 92 B2
Hagsta S 51 B4
Haguenau F 93 C3
Hahnbach D 95 B3
Hahnslätten D 81 B4
Hahót H 111 C3
Haiger D 81 B4
Haigerloch D 93 C4
Hailsham GB 45 C4
Hainburg A 111 A3
Hainfeld A 110 A2
Hainichen D 83 B5
Hajdúböszörmény H 113 B5
Hajdučica SRB 126 B2
Hajdúdorog H 113 B5
Hajdúnánás H 113 B5
Hajdúszoboszló H 113 B5
Hajnáčka SK 113 A3
Hajnówka PL 13 B5
Hajós H 112 C3
Håkafot S 199 A11
Hakkas S 196 C4
Håksberg S 50 B2
Halaszi H 111 B4
Halberstadt D 82 A3
Halberton GB 43 B3
Hald Ege DK 58 B2
Haldem D 71 B5
Halden N 54 A2
Haldensleben D 73 B4
Halenbeck D 73 A5
Halesowen GB 40 C1
Halesworth GB 45 A5
Halfing D 109 B3
Halhjem N 46 B2
Håliden S 49 B5
Halifax GB 40 B2
Häljelöt S 56 B2
Halkirk GB 32 C3
Hall S 57 C4
Hälla S 200 C3
Hallabro S 63 B3
Hällabrottet S 56 A1
Halland GB 45 C4
Hällaryd S 63 B2
Hallaryd S 61 C3
Hällberga S 56 A2
Hällbybrunn S 56 A2
Halle
B 79 B4
Nordrhein-Westfalen D 72 B1
Sachsen-Anhalt D 83 A3
Hålleberga S 62 B3
Hällefors S 55 A5
Hälleforsnäs S 56 A2
Hallein A 109 B4
Hällekis S 55 B4
Hallen S 199 B11
Hållen S 51 B4
Hallenberg D 81 A4
Hällestad S 56 B1
Hällevadsholm S 54 B2
Hällevik S 63 B2
Hälleviksstrand S 54 B2
Hallingby N 48 B2
Hallingeberg S 62 A4
Hallingen N 47 B6
Hall in Tirol A 108 B2
Hällnäs S 195 D9
Hållnäs S 51 B4
Hällnäs S 200 B5
Hallormsstaður IS 191 B11
Hallsberg S 56 A1
Hållsta S 56 A2
Hallstahammar S 56 A2
Hallstatt A 109 B4
Hallstavik S 51 B5
Halltorp S 63 B4
Halluin F 78 B3
Hallviken S 199 B12
Hallworthy GB 42 B2
Halmstad S 61 C2
Hals DK 58 A3
Halsa N 198 B5
Halstead GB 45 B4
Haltdalen N 199 C8
Haltern D 80 A3
Haltwhistle GB 37 B4
Halvarsgårdarna S 50 B2
Halver D 80 A3
Halvrimmen DK 58 A2
Ham F 90 B3
Hamar N 48 B3
Hamarhaug N 46 B2
Hamarøy N 194 B6
Hambach F 92 B3
Hambergen D 72 A1
Hambergsund S 54 B2
Hambledon GB 44 C2
Hambuhren D 72 B2
Hamburg D 72 A3
Hamdibey TR 186 C2
Hamdorf D 64 B2
Hämeenlinna FIN 8 B4
Hameln = Hamlin D 72 B2
Hamersleben D 73 B4
Hamidiye TR 187 C5
Hamilton GB 36 A2
Hamina FIN 8 B5
Hamlagrø N 46 B3
Hamlin = Hameln D 72 B2
Hamm D 81 A3
Hammar S 55 B5
Hammarland FIN 51 B6
Hammarö S 55 A4
Hammarstrand S 200 C2
Hamme B 79 A4
Hammel DK 59 B2
Hammelburg D 82 B1
Hammelspring D 74 A2
Hammenhög S 66 A3
Hammerdal S 199 B12
Hammerfest N 192 B7
Hammershøj DK 58 B2
Hammerum DK 59 B2
Hamminkeln D 80 A2
Hamnavoe GB 33 A5
Hamneda S 60 C3
Hamningberg N 193 B14
Hamoir B 80 B1
Hamont B 80 A1
Hámor H 113 A4
Hamra
Gävleborg S 199 D12
Gotland S 57 D4
Hamrångefjärden S 51 B4
Hamstreet GB 45 B4
Hamsund N 194 B6
Han TR 187 C5
Hanaskog S 61 C4
Hanau D 81 B4
Händelöp S 62 A4
Handlová SK 98 C2
Hanerau-Hademarschen D 64 B2
Hånger S 60 B3
Hanhimaa FIN 197 B8
Hanken S 55 B5
Hankensbüttel D 73 B3
Han Knežica BIH 124 B2
Hanko FIN 8 C3
Hannover D 72 B2
Hannut B 79 B5
Han Pijesak BIH 139 A4
Hansnes N 192 C3
Hanstedt D 72 A3
Hanstholm DK 58 A1
Hantsavichy BY 13 B7
Hanušovice CZ 85 B4
Haparanda S 196 D7
Haradok BY 13 A8
Harads S 196 C4
Häradsbäck S 63 B2
Häradsbygden S 50 B2
Harbo S 51 B4
Harboør DK 58 B1
Harburg
Bayern D 94 C2
Hamburg D 72 A2
Hårby DK 59 C3
Harc H 112 C2
Hardegarijp NL 70 A2
Hardegsen D 82 A1
Hardelot Plage F 78 B1
Hardenbeck D 74 A2
Hardenberg NL 71 B3
Harderwijk NL 70 B2
Hardheim D 94 B1
Hardt D 106 A3
Hareid N 198 C3
Haren
D 71 B4
NL 71 A3
Harestua N 48 B2
Harfleur F 89 A4
Harg S 51 B5
Hargicourt F 90 B3
Hargnies F 91 A4
Hargshamn S 51 B5
Härja S 55 B4
Harkány H 125 B4
Härkeberga S 56 A3
Harkebrügge D 71 A4
Harlech GB 38 B2
Harleston GB 45 A5
Hårlev DK 65 A5
Harlingen NL 70 A2
Harlösa S 61 D3
Harlow GB 45 B4
Harmancık TR 186 C4
Harmånger S 200 E3
Harmanli BG 183 B7
Härnevi S 56 A3
Härnösand S 200 D3
Haro E 143 B4
Haroldswick GB 33 A6
Háromfa H 124 A3
Haroué F 92 C2
Harpenden GB 44 B3
Harplinge S 60 C2
Harpstedt D 72 B1
Harrogate GB 40 A2
Harrow GB 44 B3
Härryda S 60 B2
Harsefeld D 72 A2
Harsewinkel D 71 C5
Hârşova 17 C7
Harstad N 194 B7
Harsum D 72 B2
Harsvik N 199 A7
Harta H 112 C3
Hartberg A 110 B2
Hartburn GB 37 A5
Hartennes F 90 B3
Hartest GB 45 A4
Hartha D 83 A4
Hartland GB 42 B2
Hartlepool GB 37 B5
Hartmanice CZ 96 B1
Hartmannsdorf A 110 B2
Harvassdal N 195 E5
Harwell GB 44 B2
Harwich GB 45 B5
Harzgerode D 82 A3
Häselgehr A 108 B1
Haselünne D 71 B4
Haskovo BG 183 B7
Hasköy TR 186 A1
Haslach D 106 A3
Haslach an der Mühl A 96 C2
Hasle DK 67 A3
Haslemere GB 44 B3
Haslev DK 65 A4
Hasloch D 94 B1
Hasparren F 144 A2
Hassela S 200 D2
Hasselfelde D 82 A2
Hasselfors S 55 A5
Hasselt
B 79 B5
NL 70 B3
Hassfurt D 94 A2
Hassleben D 74 A2
Hässleholm S 61 C3
Hasslö S 63 B3
Hassloch D 93 B4
Hästbo S 51 B4
Hastersboda FIN 51 B7
Hästholmen S 55 B5
Hastière-Lavaux B 79 B4
Hastigrow GB 32 C3
Hastings GB 45 C4
Hästveda S 61 C3
Hasvik N 192 B6
Hatfield
Hertfordshire GB 44 B3
South Yorkshire GB 40 B3
Hatherleigh GB 42 B2
Hathersage GB 40 B2
Hatlestrand N 46 B2
Hattem NL 70 B3
Hatten
D 71 A5
F 93 C3
Hattfjelldal N 195 E4
Hatting DK 59 C2
Hattingen D 80 A3
Hattstadt F 106 A2
Hattstedt D 64 B2
Hatvan H 112 B3
Hatvik N 46 B2
Hau D 80 A2
Haudainville F 92 B1
Hauganes IS 191 B7
Haugastøl N 47 B4
Hauge N 52 B2
Haugesund N 52 A1
Haughom N 52 B2
Haugsdal N 46 B2
Haugsdorf A 97 C4
Haukedal N 46 A3
Haukeland N 46 B2
Haukeligrend N 52 A3
Haukeliseter N 52 A3
Haukipudas FIN 3 D9
Haulerwijk NL 71 A3
Haunersdorf D 95 C4
Haus N 46 B2
Hausach D 106 A3
Hausham D 108 B2
Hausmannstätten A 110 C2
Hausvik N 52 B2
Hautajärvi FIN 197 C12
Hautefort F 129 A4
Hauterives F 117 B5
Hauteville-Lompnès F 118 B2
Haut-Fays B 91 A5
Hautmont F 79 B3
Hautrage B 79 B3
Hauzenberg D 96 C1
Havant GB 44 C3
Havdhem S 57 C4
Havdrup DK 61 D2
Havelange B 79 B5
Havelberg D 73 B5
Havelte NL 70 B3
Haverfordwest GB 39 C2
Haverhill GB 45 A4
Havering GB 45 B4
Håverud S 54 B3
Havířov CZ 98 B2
Havixbeck D 71 C4
Havlíčkův Brod CZ 97 B3
Havndal DK 58 B3
Havneby DK 64 A1
Havnebyen DK 61 D1
Havnsø DK 61 D1
Havøysund N 193 A8
Havran TR 186 C2
Havrebjerg DK 61 D1
Havsa TR 186 A1
Havstenssund S 54 B2
Havza TR 23 A8
Hawes GB 37 B4
Hawick GB 35 C5
Hawkhurst GB 45 B4
Hawkinge GB 45 B5
Haxey GB 40 B3
Hayange F 92 B2
Haydarlı TR 189 A5
Haydon Bridge GB 37 B4
Hayle GB 42 B1
Haymana TR 187 C7
Hay-on-Wye GB 39 B3
Hayrabolu TR 186 A2
Haysyn UA 13 D8
Hayvoron UA 13 D8
Haywards Heath GB 44 C3
Hazebrouck F 78 B2
Hazlov CZ 83 B4
Heacham GB 41 C4
Headcorn GB 45 B4
Headford IRL 28 A2
Heanor GB 40 B2
Héas F 145 B4
Heathfield GB 45 C4
Hebden Bridge GB 40 B1
Heberg S 60 C2
Heby S 51 C3
Hechingen D 93 C4
Hechlingen D 94 C2
Hecho E 144 B3
Hechtel B 79 A5
Hechthausen D 72 A2
Heckelberg D 74 B2
Heckington GB 41 C3
Hecklingen D 82 A3
Hed S 56 A1
Hedalen N 48 B1
Hedared S 60 B2
Heddal N 53 A5
Hédé F 101 A4
Hede S 199 C10
Hedekas S 54 B2
Hedemora S 50 B2
Hedenäset S 196 C6
Hedensted DK 59 C2
Hedersleben D 82 A3
Hedesunda S 51 B4
Hedge End GB 44 C2
Hedon GB 41 B3
Heede D 71 B4
Heek D 71 B4
Heemstede NL 70 B1
Heerde NL 70 B3
Heerenveen NL 70 B2
Heerhugowaard NL 70 B1
Heerlen NL 80 B1
Heeze NL 80 A1
Heggenes N 47 A6
Hegra N 199 B8
Hegyeshalom H 111 B4
Hegyközség H 111 B3
Heia N 199 A9
Heide D 64 B2
Heidelberg D 93 B4
Heiden D 80 A2
Heidenau D 84 B1
Heidenheim D 94 C2
Heidenreichstein A 97 C3
Heikendorf D 64 B3
Heikkilä FIN 197 C12
Heilam GB 32 C2
Heiland N 53 B4
Heilbad Heiligenstadt D 82 A2
Heilbronn D 93 B5
Heiligenblut A 109 B3
Heiligendamn D 65 B4
Heiligendorf D 73 B3
Heiligengrabe D 73 A5
Heiligenhafen D 65 B3
Heiligenhaus D 80 A2
Heiligenkreuz A 111 C3
Heiligenstadt D 94 B3
Heiloo NL 70 B1
Heilsbronn D 94 B2
Heim N 198 B6
Heimburg D 82 A2
Heimdal N 199 B7
Heinerscheid L 92 A2
Heinersdorf D 74 B3
Heining D 96 C1
Heiningen D 94 C1
Heinola FIN 8 B5
Heinsberg D 80 A2
Heist-op-den-Berg B 79 A4
Hejde S 57 C4
Hejdeby S 57 C4
Hejls DK 59 C2
Hejnice CZ 84 B3
Hel PL 69 A3
Helchteren B 79 A5
Heldburg D 82 B2
Heldrungen D 82 A3
Helechosa E 156 A3
Helensburgh GB 34 B3
Helfenberg A 96 C2
Helgen N 53 A5
Helgeroa N 53 B5
Hella
IS 190 D5
N 46 A3
Helland N 194 B7
Hellas S 55 B3
Helle N 52 B2
Helleland N 52 B2
Hellendoorn NL 71 B3
Hellenthal D 80 B2
Hellesøy N 46 B1
Hellesylt N 198 C3
Hellevoetsluis NL 79 A4
Helligskogen N 192 C4
Hellín E 158 C2
Hellissandur IS 190 C2
Hellnar IS 190 C2
Hellum DK 58 A3
Hellvi S 57 C4
Hellvik N 52 B1
Helm-brechts D 83 B3
Helmond NL 80 A1
Helmsdale GB 32 C3
Helmsley GB 37 B5
Helmstedt D 73 B3
Hel'pa SK 99 C3
Helsa D 82 A1
Helsby GB 38 A4
Helsingborg S 61 C2
Helsinge DK 61 C2
Helsingør DK 61 C2
Helsinki FIN 8 B4
Helston GB 42 B1
Hemau D 95 B3
Hemavan S 195 E6
Hemel Hempstead GB 44 B3
Hemer D 81 A3
Héming F 92 C2
Hemmet DK 59 C1
Hemmingstedt D 64 B2
Hemmoor D 64 C2
Hemnes N 54 A2
Hemnesberget N 195 D4
Hemse S 57 C4
Hemsedal N 47 B5
Hemslingen D 72 A2
Hemsworth GB 40 B2
Hen N 48 B2
Henån S 54 B2
Hendaye F 144 A2
Hendek TR 187 B5
Hendungen D 82 B2
Henfield GB 44 C3
Hengelo
Gelderland NL 71 B3
Overijssel NL 71 B3
Hengersberg D 95 C5

Hengoed GB 39 C3
Hénin-Beaumont F . 78 B2
Henley-on-Thames
GB 44 B3
Hennan S 200 D1
Henneberg D 82 B2
Hennebont F 100 B2
Henne Strand DK . 59 C1
Hennigsdorf D 74 B2
Hennset N 198 B5
Hennstedt
Schleswig-Holstein
D. 64 B2
Schleswig-Holstein
D. 64 B2
Henrichemont F . 103 B4
Henryków PL 85 B5
Henrykowo PL 69 A5
Hensås N 47 A5
Henstedt-Ulzburg D 64 C2
Heppenheim D . . . 93 B4
Herad
Buskerud N 47 B6
Vest-Agder N 52 B2
Heradsbygd N 48 B3
Heraklion = Iraklio
GR 185 D6
Herálec CZ 97 B4
Herand N 46 B3
Herbault F 103 B3
Herbern D 81 A3
Herbertstown IRL . 29 B3
Herbeumont B 91 B5
Herbignac F 101 B3
Herbisse F 91 C4
Herbitzheim F 92 B3
Herbolzheim D . . . 106 A2
Herborn D 81 B4
Herbrechtingen D . 94 C2
Herby PL 86 B2
Herceg-Novi MNE . 16 D3
Hercegovać HR . . 124 B3
Hercegszántó H . . 125 B4
Herchen D 80 B3
Heréd H 112 B3
Hereford GB 39 B4
Herefoss N 53 B4
Hereke TR 187 B4
Herencia E 157 A4
Herend H 111 B4
Herent B 79 B4
Herentals B 79 A4
Hérépian F 130 B2
Herfølge DK 61 D2
Herford D 72 B1
Herguijuela E 156 A2
Héric F 101 B4
Héricourt F 106 B1
Héricourt-en-Caux
F. 89 A4
Hérimoncourt F . . 106 B1
Heringsdorf D . . . 65 B4
Herisau CH 107 B4
Hérisson F 103 C4
Herk-de-Stad B . . 79 B5
Herlufmagle DK . . 65 A4
Hermagor A 109 C4
Hermannsburg D . 72 B3
Hermansverk N . . 46 A3
Heřmanův Městec
CZ 97 B3
Herment F 116 B2
Hermeskeil D 92 B2
Hermisende E . . . 141 C4
Hermonville F 91 B3
Hermsdorf D 83 B3
Hernani E 144 A2
Hernansancho E . . 150 B3
Herne D 80 A3
Herne Bay GB . . . 45 B5
Hernes N 48 B3
Herning DK 59 B1
Herøya N 53 A5
Herramelluri E . . . 143 B3
Herräng S 51 B5
Herre N 53 A5
Herrenberg D 93 C4
Herrera E 162 A3
Herrera de Alcántara
E. 155 B3
Herrera del Duque
E. 156 A2
Herrera de los Navarros
E. 152 A2
Herrera de Pisuerga
E. 142 B2
Herreros del Suso
E. 150 B2
Herrestad S 54 B2
Herrhamra S 57 B3
Herritslev DK 65 B4
Herrlisheim F 93 C3
Herrljunga S 55 B4
Herrnhut D 84 A2
Herrsching D 108 A2
Hersbruck D 95 B3
Hersby S 57 A4
Herscheid D 81 A3
Herselt B 79 A4
Herso GR 182 B4
Herstal B 80 B1
Herstmonceux GB . 45 C4
Herten D 80 A3
Hertford GB 44 B3
Hervás E 149 B4
Hervik N 52 A1
Herxheim D 93 B4

Herzberg
Brandenburg D . . . 74 B1
Brandenburg D . . . 83 A5
Niedersachsen D . . 82 A2
Herzbrock D 81 A4
Herzfelde D 74 B2
Herzlake D 71 B4
Herzogenaurach D . 94 B2
Herzogenbuchsee
CH 106 B2
Herzogenburg A . . 110 A2
Herzsprung D 73 A5
Hesby N 52 A1
Hesdin F 78 B2
Hesel D 71 A4
Heskestad N 52 B2
Hessdalen N 199 C8
Hesselager DK . . . 65 A3
Hesseng N 193 C13
Hessisch Lichtenau
D 82 A1
Hessisch-Oldendorf
D 72 B2
Hestra S 60 B3
Heswall GB 38 A3
Hetlevik N 46 B2
Hettange-Grande F . 92 B2
Hetton-le-Hole GB . 37 B5
Hettstedt D 82 A3
Heuchin F 78 B2
Heudicourt-sous-les-
Côtes 92 C1
Heunezel F 105 A5
Heuqueville F 89 A4
Heves H 113 B4
Héviz H 111 C4
Hexham GB 37 B4
Heysham GB 36 B4
Heytesbury GB . . . 43 A4
Hidas H 125 A4
Hieflau A 110 B1
Hiendelaencina E . 151 A5
Hiersac F 115 C4
High Bentham GB . 37 B4
Highclere GB 44 B2
High Hesket GB . . 37 B4
Highley GB 39 B4
High Wycombe GB . 44 B3
Higuera de Arjona
E. 157 C4
Higuera de Calatrava
E. 163 A3
Higuera de la Serena
E. 156 B2
Higuera de la Sierra
E. 161 B3
Higuera de Vargas
E. 155 C4
Higuera la Real E . 161 A3
Higuers de Llerena
E. 156 B1
Higueruela E 158 C2
Híjar E 153 A3
Hilchenbach D . . . 81 A4
Hildburghausen D . 82 B2
Hilden D 80 A2
Hilders D 82 B1
Hildesheim D 72 B2
Hilgay GB 41 C4
Hillared S 60 B3
Hille D 72 B1
Hillegom NL 70 B1
Hillerød DK 61 D2
Hillerstorp S 60 B3
Hillesheim D 80 B2
Hillestad N 53 A6
Hillmersdorf D . . . 83 A5
Hillsborough GB . . 27 B4
Hillswick GB 33 A5
Hilpoltstein D 95 B3
Hiltpoltstein D . . . 94 B3
Hilvarenbeek NL . . 79 A5
Hilversum NL 70 B2
Himarë AL 182 C1
Himbergen D 73 A3
Himeshaza H 125 A4
Himmelberg A . . . 109 C5
Himmelpforten D . . 72 A2
Himód H 111 B4
Hinckley GB 40 C2
Hindås S 60 B2
Hindelang D 108 B1
Hindelbank CH . . 106 B2
Hinderavåg N 52 A1
Hindhead GB 44 B3
Hinjosa del Valle E 156 B1
Hinnerup DK 59 B3
Hinneryd S 61 C3
Hinojal E 155 B4
Hinojales E 161 B3
Hinojos E 161 B3
Hinojosa del Duque
E. 156 B2
Hinojosas de Calatrava
E. 157 B3
Hinterhornbach A . 108 B1
Hinterriss A 108 B2
Hintersee
A. 109 B4
D. 74 A3
Hinterstoder A . . . 110 B1
Hintertux A 108 B2
Hinterweidenthal D . 93 B3
Hinwil CH 107 B3
Hios GR 185 A7
Hippolytushoef NL . 70 B1
Hirschaid D 94 B2
Hirschau D 95 B3

Hirschfeld D 83 A5
Hirschhorn D 93 B4
Hirsingue F 106 B2
Hirson F 91 B4
Hirtshals DK 58 A2
Hirvaskoski FIN . 197 D10
Hirzenhain D 81 B5
Hisarcik TR 186 C4
Hishult S 61 C3
Hissjön S 200 C6
Hitchin GB 44 B3
Hitra N 198 B5
Hittarp S 61 C2
Hittisau A 107 B4
Hittun N 46 A1
Hitzacker D 73 A4
Hjallerup DK 58 A3
Hjällstad S 49 B5
Hjältevad S 62 A3
Hjärnarp S 61 C2
Hjartdal N 53 A4
Hjellestad N 46 B2
Hjelmeland N 52 A2
Hjelset N 198 C4
Hjerkinn N 198 C6
Hjerm DK 58 B1
Hjerpsted DK 64 A1
Hjerting DK 59 C1
Hjo S 55 B5
Hjordkær DK 64 A2
Hjørring DK 58 A2
Hjorted S 62 A4
Hjortkvarn S 56 B1
Hjortnäs S 50 B1
Hjortsberga S . . . 62 B2
Hjukse N 53 A5
Hjuksebø N 53 A5
Hjulsjö S 55 A5
Hlinsko CZ 97 B3
Hlío IS 191 A10
Hlohovec SK 98 C1
Hlubokánad Vltavou
CZ 96 B2
Hlučín CZ 98 B2
Hlyboka UA 17 A6
Hlybokaye BY . . . 13 A7
Hniezdne SK 99 B4
Hnilec SK 99 C4
Hnúšťa SK 99 C3
Hobol H 125 A3
Hobro DK 58 B2
Hobscheid L 92 B1
Hocalar TR 189 A4
Hochdonn D 64 B2
Hochdorf CH . . . 106 B3
Hochfelden F 93 C3
Hochspeyer D . . . 93 B3
Höchstadt D 94 B2
Höchstädt D 94 C2
Hochstenbach D . . 81 B3
Höchst im Odenwald
D 93 B5
Höckendorf D . . . 83 B5
Hockenheim D . . . 93 B4
Hoddesdon GB . . . 44 B3
Hodejov SK 99 C3
Hodenhagen D . . . 72 B2
Hodkovice CZ . . . 84 B3
Hódmezővásárhely
H 113 C4
Hodnet GB 38 B4
Hodonín CZ 98 C1
Hodslavice CZ . . . 98 B2
Hoedekenskerke NL 79 A3
Hoegaarden B . . . 79 B4
Hoek van Holland
NL. 79 A4
Hoenderlo NL . . . 70 B2
Hof
D 83 B3
N 53 A6
Hofbieber D 82 B1
Hoff GB 37 B4
Hofgeismar D . . . 81 A5
Hofheim
Bayern D 82 B2
Hessen D 93 A4
Hofkirchen im Mühlkreis
A. 96 C1
Höfn IS 191 C10
Hofors S 50 B3
Hofsós IS 190 B6
Hofstad N 199 A7
Höganäs S 61 C2
Høgebru N 46 A4
Høgfors S 50 B3
Hogdal S 54 A2
Høgebru N 46 A4
Høgsäter S 54 B3
Högsby S 62 A4
Högsjö S 56 A1
Hogstad S 55 B6
Högyész H 112 C2
Hohenau D 97 C4
Hohenberg A 110 B2
Hohenbucko D . . . 83 A5
Hohenburg D 95 B3
Hohendorf D 66 B1
Hohenems A . . . 107 B4
Hohenhameln D . . 72 B3
Hohenhausen D . . 72 B1
Hohenkirchen D . . 71 A4
Hohenlinden D . . 108 A2
Hohenlockstedt D . 64 C2
Hohenmölsen D . . 83 A4

Hohennauen D . . . 73 B5
Hohen Neuendorf D 74 B2
Hohenseeden D . . 73 B5
Hohentauern A . . .110 B1
Hohentengen D . . 106 B3
Hohenwepel D . . . 81 A5
Hohenwestedt D . . 64 B2
Hohenwutzen D . . 74 B3
Hohenzieritz D . . . 74 A2
Hohn D 64 B2
Hohne D 72 B3
Hohnstorf D 73 A3
Højer DK 64 B1
Højslev Stby DK . . 58 B2
Hok S 62 A2
Hökerum S 60 B3
Hökhuvud S 51 B5
Hokksund N 53 A5
Hökön S 63 B2
Hol N 47 B5
Hólar IS 190 B6
Holašovice CZ . . . 96 C2
Holbæk
Aarhus Amt. DK . .58 B3
Vestsjællands Amt.
DK. 61 D1
Holbeach GB 41 C4
Holdenstedt D . . . 73 B3
Holdhus N 46 B2
Holdorf D 71 B5
Holeby DK 65 B4
Hølen N 54 A1
Hølervasseter N . . 47 B6
Holešov CZ 98 B1
Holguera E 155 B4
Holíč SK 98 C1
Holice
CZ 97 A3
SK 111 B4
Höljes S 49 B4
Hollabrunn A 97 C4
Hollandstoun GB . 33 B4
Høllen N 53 B3
Hollfeld D 95 B3
Hollókő H 112 B3
Hollstadt D 82 B2
Hollum NL 70 A2
Höllviksnäs S . . . 66 A1
Holm N 195 E3
Hólmavík IS . . . 190 B4
Holmbukt N . . . 192 B5
Holmedal S 54 A2
Holmegil N 54 A2
Holmen N 48 B2
Holme-on-Spalding-
Moor GB 40 B3
Holmes Chapel GB . 38 A4
Holmestrand N . . 54 A1
Holmfirth GB 40 B2
Holmfoss N . . . 193 C14
Holmsbu N 54 A1
Holmsjö S 63 B3
Holmsund S . . . 200 C6
Holmsveden S . . 50 A3
Holmudden S . . . 57 C5
Holö S 57 A3
Holøydal N 199 C8
Holsbybrunn S . . 62 A3
Holseter N 48 A1
Holsljunga S 60 B2
Holstebro DK 59 B1
Holsted DK 59 C1
Holsworthy GB . . . 42 B2
Holt
D 64 B2
Norfolk GB 41 C5
Wrexham GB 38 A4
IS 190 D6
N 53 B4
Holten NL 71 B3
Holtwick D 71 B4
Holum N 52 B3
Holwerd NL 70 A2
Holycross IRL . . . 29 B4
Holyhead GB 38 A2
Holýšov CZ 95 B5
Holywell GB 38 A3
Holywood GB . . . 27 B5
Holzdorf D 83 A5
Holzhausen D . . . 72 B1
Holzheim D 94 C2
Holzkirchen D . . . 108 B2
Holzminden D . . . 81 A5
Holzthaleben D . . 82 A2
Homberg
Hessen D 81 A5
Hessen D 81 B5
Homburg D 93 B3
Hommelstø N . . . 195 E3
Hommersåk N . . . 52 B1
Homokmegy H . . 112 C3
Homokszentgyörgy
H 124 A3
Homyel = Gomel BY 13 B9
Honaz TR 188 B4
Hondarribia E . . . 144 A2
Hondón de los Frailes
E. 165 A4
Hondschoote F . . . 78 B2
Hönebach D 82 B1
Hønefoss N 48 B2
Honfleur F 89 A4
Høng DK 61 D1
Honington GB . . . 40 C3
Höningen D 93 B4
Honningsvåg N . . 193 B9
Hönö S 60 B1
Honrubia E 158 B1

Hontalbilla E . . . 151 A3
Hontheim D 92 A2
Hontianske-Nemce
SK 98 C2
Hontoria de la Cantera
E. 143 B3
Hontoria del Pinar
E. 143 C3
Hontoria de
Valdearados E . . 143 C3
Hoofddorp NL . . . 70 B1
Hoogerheide NL . . 79 A4
Hoogeveen NL . . . 71 B3
Hoogezand-Sappemeer
NL. 71 A3
Hoogkarspel NL . . 70 B2
Hoogkerk NL 71 A3
Hoogstede D 71 B3
Hoogstraten B . . . 79 A4
Hook GB 44 B3
Hooksiel D 71 A5
Höör S 61 D3
Hoorn NL 70 B2
Hope GB 38 A3
Hopen N 194 C6
Hope under Dinmore
GB 39 B4
Hopfgarten A . . . 108 B3
Hopfgarten in
Defereggen A . . 109 C3
Hopseidet N 193 B11
Hopsten D 71 B4
Hoptrup DK 59 C2
Hora Svatého
Sebastiána CZ . . 83 B5
Horaždovice CZ . . 96 B1
Horb am Neckar D . 93 C4
Horbelev DK 65 B5
Hørby DK 58 A3
Hörby S 61 D3
Horcajada de la Torre
E. 158 A1
Horcajo de los Montes
E. 156 A3
Horcajo de Santiago
E. 151 C4
Horcajo-Medianero
E. 150 B2
Horche E 151 B4
Horda S 62 A2
Hordabø N 46 B1
Hordalia N 52 A2
Hordvik N 46 B2
Hořesedly CZ . . . 83 B5
Horezu RO 17 C6
Horgen CH 107 B3
Horgoš SRB 126 A1
Horia RO 126 A3
Hořice CZ 84 B3
Horjul SLO 123 A3
Horka D 84 A2
Hörken S 50 B1
Horki BY 13 A9
Hörle S 60 B4
Horn
A. 97 C3
D 81 A4
N 48 B2
S 62 A3
Horna E 158 C2
Hornachos E . . . 156 B1
Hornachuelos E . . 162 A2
Horná Maríková SK. 98 B2
Hornanes N 46 C2
Horná Streda SK . . 98 C1
Horná Štrubna SK . 98 C2
Horná Súča SK . . 98 C1
Hornbæk
Aarhus Amt. DK . .58 B2
Frederiksværk DK .61 C2
Hornberg D 106 A3
Hornburg D 73 B3
Horncastle GB . . . 41 B3
Horndal S 50 B3
Horndean GB 44 C2
Horne
Fyns Amt. DK . . . 64 A3
Ribe Amt. DK . . .59 C1
Hörnebo S 55 B5
Horneburg D 72 A2
Hörnefors S 200 C5
Horní Bečva CZ . . 98 B2
Horní Cerekev CZ . 97 B3
Horní Jiřetín CZ . . 83 B5
Horní Lomná CZ . . 98 B2
Horní Maršov CZ . . 85 B3
Hornindal N 198 D3
Hørning DK 59 B3
Hörningsholm S . . 57 A3
Horní Planá CZ . . 96 C2
Horni Slavkov CZ . 83 B4
Horní Vltavice CZ . 96 C1
Hornnes N 53 B3
Hornos E 164 A2
Hornoy-le-Bourg F . 90 B1
Hornsea GB 41 B3
Hornsjø N 48 A2
Hornslet DK 59 B3
Hornstein A 111 B3
Hörnum D 64 B1
Horný Tisovnik SK . 99 C3
Horodenka UA . . . 13 D6
Horodnya UA 13 C9
Horodok
Khmelnytskyy UA . .13 D7

Horodok *continued*
Lviv UA. 13 D5
Horokhiv UA 13 C6
Horovice CZ 96 B1
Horred S 60 B2
Hörröd S 61 D4
Hörsching A. 110 A1
Horsens DK 59 C2
Horsham GB 44 B3
Hørsholm DK 61 D2
Horslunde DK . . . 65 B4
Horšovský Týn CZ . 95 B4
Horst N 80 A2
Horstel D 71 B4
Horsten D 71 A4
Horstmar D 71 B4
Hort H 113 B3
Horta P 148 A2
Horten N 54 A1
Hortezuela E . . . 151 A5
Hortiguela E . . . 143 B3
Hortobágy H 113 B5
Horton in Ribblesdale
GB 37 B4
Hørve DK 61 D1
Hörvik S 63 B2
Horwich GB 38 A4
Hosanger N 46 B2
Hösbach D 93 A5
Hosena D 84 A2
Hosenfeld D 81 B5
Hosingen L 92 A2
Hosio FIN 197 D8
Hospental CH . . . 107 C3
Hospital IRL 29 B3
Hossegor F 128 C1
Hosszuhétény H . . 125 A4
Hostal de Ipiés E . 145 B3
Hošťálková CZ . . . 98 B1
Hostalric E 147 C3
Hostens F 128 B2
Hostěradice CZ . . 97 C4
Hostinné CZ 85 B3
Hostomice CZ . . . 96 B2
Hostouň CZ 95 B4
Hotagen S 199 B11
Hoting S 200 B2
Hotolisht AL . . . 182 B2
Hotton B 79 B5
Houdain F 78 B2
Houdan F 90 C1
Houdelaincourt F . . 92 C1
Houeillès F 128 B3
Houffalize B 92 A1
Houghton-le-Spring
GB 37 B5
Houlberg DK 59 B2
Houlgate F 89 A3
Hounslow GB . . . 44 B3
Hourtin F 128 A1
Hourtin-Plage F . . 128 A1
Houthalen B 79 A5
Houyet B 79 B4
Hov
DK 59 C3
N 48 B2
Hova S 55 B5
Høvåg N 53 B4
Hovborg DK 59 C1
Hovda N 47 B6
Hovden N 52 A3
Hove GB 44 C3
Hovedgård DK . . . 59 C2
Hovelhof D 81 A4
Hoven DK 59 C1
Hovet N 47 B5
Hovingham GB . . 40 A3
Hovmantorp S . . . 62 B3
Hovsta S 56 A1
Howden GB 40 B3
Howe D 72 A3
Höxter D 81 A5
Hoya D 72 B2
Hoya de Santa Maria
E. 161 B3
Hoya-Gonzalo E . 158 C2
Høyanger N 46 A3
Hoyerswerda D . . 84 A2
Høyjord N 53 A6
Hoylake GB 38 A3
Høylandet N . . . 199 A9
Hoym D 82 A3
Høymyr N 47 C6
Hoyocasero E . . . 150 B3
Hoyo de Manzanares
E. 151 B4
Hoyo de Pinares E 150 B3
Hoyos E 149 B3
Hoyos del Espino
E. 150 B2
Hrabušice SK . . . 99 C4
Hradec Králové CZ . 85 B3
Hradec nad Moravicí
CZ 98 B1
Hrádek CZ 97 C4
Hrádek nad Nisou
CZ 84 B2
Hradište SK 98 C2
Hrafnagil IS . . . 191 B7
Hrafnseyri IS . . . 190 B2
Hranice
Severomoravsky
CZ 98 B1
Západočeský CZ . .83 B4
Hranovnica SK . . . 99 C4

Hrasnica BIH 139 B4
Hrastnik SLO 123 A4
Hřensko CZ 84 B2
Hriňová SK 99 C3
Hrisoupoli GR 183 C6
Hrochov CZ 97 B4
Hrochův Tynec CZ . 97 B3
Hrodna BY 13 B5
Hrodzyanka BY . . . 13 B8
Hronov CZ 85 B4
Hronský Beňadik
  SK 98 C2
Hrotovice CZ 97 B4
Hrtkovci SRB 127 C1
Hrun IS 190 A5
Hrušov SK 112 A3
Hrušovany nad
  Jevišovkou CZ . . 97 C4
Hřuštin SK 99 B3
Hrvaćani BIH 124 C3
Hrvace HR 138 B2
Hrymayliv UA. 13 D7
Huben A 109 C3
Hückel-hoven D . . . 80 A2
Hückeswagen D . . . 80 A3
Hucknall GB 40 B2
Hucqueliers F 78 B1
Huddersfield GB . . 40 B2
Huddinge S 57 A3
Huddunge S 51 B3
Hude D 72 A1
Hudiksvall S 200 E3
Huélago E 163 A4
Huélamo E 152 B2
Huelgoat F 100 A2
Huelma E 163 A4
Huelva E 161 B3
Huéneja E 164 B2
Huércal de Almeria
  E 164 C2
Huércal-Overa E . 164 B3
Huerta de Abajo E . 143 B3
Huerta del Rey E . 143 C3
Huerta de
  Valdecarabanos
  E 151 C4
Huertahernando E 152 B1
Huesa E 164 B1
Huesca E 145 B3
Huéscar E 164 B2
Huete E 151 B5
Huétor Tájar E . . . 163 A3
Hüfingen D 106 B3
Hufthamar N 46 B2
Hugh Town GB . . . 42 B1
Huglfing D 108 B2
Huissen NL 70 C2
Huittinen FIN. 8 B3
Huizen NL 70 B2
Hulín CZ 98 B1
Hüls D 80 A2
Hulsig DK 58 A3
Hulst NL 79 A4
Hult S 62 A3
Hulta S 56 B2
Hulteby S 55 A5
Hulterstad S 63 B4
Hultsfred S 62 A3
Humanes E 151 B4
Humberston GB . . . 41 B3
Humble DK 65 B3
Humilladero E . . . 163 A3
Humlebæk DK 61 D2
Humlum DK 58 B1
Hummelsta S 56 A2
Humpolec CZ 97 B3
Humshaugh GB . . . 37 A4
Hundåla N 195 E3
Hundested DK 61 D1
Hundorp N 48 A1
Hundvåg N 52 A1
Hundvin N 46 B2
Hunedoara RO . . . 17 C5
Hünfeld D. 82 B1
Hungen D. 81 B4
Hungerford GB . . . 44 B2
Hunndalen N 48 B2
Hunnebostrand S . . 54 B2
Hunstanton GB . . . 41 C4
Huntingdon GB . . . 44 A3
Huntley GB 39 C4
Huntly GB 33 D4
Hünxe D 80 A2
Hurbanovo SK. . . .112 B2
Hürbel D. 107 A4
Hurdal N 48 B3
Hurezani RO 17 C5
Hurlford GB 36 A2
Hurstbourne Tarrant
  GB 44 B2
Hurstpierpoint GB. . 44 C3
Hürth D 80 B2
Hurum N 47 A5
Hurup DK. 58 B1
Húsafell IS 190 C5
Húsavík IS 191 A8
Husbands Bosworth
  GB 44 A2
Husby
  D 64 B2
  DK 59 B1
Husey IS 191 B11
Huşi RO 17 B8
Husina BIH 139 A4

Husinec CZ 96 B1
Husinish GB 31 B1
Huskvarna S 62 A2
Husnes N 46 C2
Husøy N 194 A8
Hustad N 198 C4
Hüsten D 81 A3
Hustopeče CZ 97 C3
Hustopeče nad Bečvou
  CZ 98 B1
Husum
  D 64 B2
  S 200 C5
Husvika N 195 E3
Huta PL 75 B5
Hutovo BIH 139 C3
Hüttenberg A 110 C1
Hüttlingen D 94 C2
Huttoft GB 41 B4
Hutton Cranswick
  GB 40 B3
Hüttschlag A 109 B4
Huttwil CH 106 B2
Huy B 79 B5
Hval N 48 B2
Hvåle N 47 B6
Hvaler N 54 A2
Hvalpsund DK 58 B2
Hvammstangi IS . . 190 B5
Hvammur IS. 190 B6
Hvanneyri IS 190 C4
Hvar HR 138 B2
Hveragerði IS . . . 190 D4
Hvidbjerg DK. 58 B1
Hvide Sande DK . . . 59 C1
Hvittingfoss N 53 A6
Hvolsvöllur IS . . . 190 D5
Hybe SK. 99 B3
Hycklinge S 62 A3
Hydra GR 185 B4
Hyen N 198 D2
Hyères F 132 B2
Hyères Plage F . . . 132 B2
Hylestad N 52 A3
Hylke DK 59 C2
Hyllestad N 46 A2
Hyllinge S 61 C3
Hyltebruk S 60 B3
Hynnekleiv N 53 B4
Hythe
  Hampshire GB . . .44 C2
  Kent GB 45 B5
Hyvinkää FIN 8 B4

I
Iam RO 127 B3
Iaşi RO 17 B7
Iasmos GR. 183 B7
Ibahernando E . . . 156 A2
Ibarranguelua E . . 143 A4
Ibbenbüren D 71 B4
Ibeas de Juarros E 143 B3
Ibestad N 194 B8
Ibi E 159 C3
Ibiza = Eivissa E . 166 C1
İbradı TR 189 B6
İbriktepe TR. 186 A1
Ibros E 157 B4
Ibstock GB. 40 C2
İçel TR 23 C8
Ichenhausen D . . . 94 C2
Ichtegem B 78 A3
Ichtershausen D . . 82 B2
Idanha-a-Novo P . . 155 B3
Idar-Oberstein D . . 93 B3
Idd N. 54 A2
Idiazábal E 144 B1
Idivuoma S 196 A4
Idön S. 51 B5
Idre S 199 D9
Idrija SLO 123 A3
Idritsa RUS 9 D6
Idstein D 81 B4
Idvor SRB 126 B2
Iecca Mare RO . . . 126 B2
Ielsi I. 170 B2
Ieper = Ypres B . . . 78 B2
Ierapetra GR 185 D6
Ierissos GR 183 C5
Ifjord N. 193 B11
Ig SLO 123 B3
Igal H 112 C1
Igea E 144 B1
Igea Marina I 136 A1
Igelfors S 56 B1
Igersheim D 94 B1
Iggesund S 200 E3
Iglesias E 143 B3
Iglésias I 179 C2
Igny-Comblizy F . . 91 B3
Igorre E 143 A4
Igoumenitsa GR . . 182 D2
Igries E 145 B3
Igualada E 147 C2
Igüeña E 141 B4
Iharosberény H . . . 124 A3
Ihl'any SK 99 B4
Ihlienworth D 64 C1
Ihringen D 106 A2
Ihrlerstein D 95 C3
İhsaniye TR 187 C5

Ii FIN 197 D8
Iijärvi FIN 193 C11
Iisalmi FIN 3 E10
IJmuiden NL 70 B1
IJsselmuiden NL . . 70 B2
IJzendijke NL 79 A3
Ikast DK 59 B2
Ikervár H 111 B3
Ilandža SRB 126 B2
Ilanz CH 107 C4
Ilava SK 98 C2
Iława PL 69 B4
il Castagno I 135 B3
Ilche E 145 C4
Ilchester GB. 43 B4
Ilfeld D 82 A2
Ilfracombe GB 42 A2
Ilgaz TR 23 A7
İlgın TR. 189 A6
Ílhavo P 148 B1
Ilica TR 186 C2
Ilidža BIH 139 B4
Ilijaš BIH. 139 B4
Ilirska Bistrica
  SLO 123 B3
Ilkeston GB 40 C2
Ilkley GB 40 B2
Illana E 151 B5
Illano E 141 A4
Illar E 164 C2
Illas E 141 A5
Illats F 128 B2
Illescas E 151 B4
Ille-sur-Têt F 146 B3
Illfurth F. 106 B2
Illiers-Combray F . . 89 B5
Illkirch-Graffenstaden
  F. 93 C3
Illmersdorf D 74 C2
Illmitz A 111 B3
Íllora E 163 A4
Illueca E 152 A2
Ilmajoki FIN 8 A3
Ilmenau D 82 B2
Ilminster GB 43 B4
Ilok HR 126 B1
Ilomantsi FIN. 9 A7
Iłow PL 77 B5
Iłowa PL 84 A3
Iłowo-Osada PL . . 77 A5
Ilsenburg D 82 A2
Ilshofen D 94 B1
Ilz A 110 B2
Iłża PL. 87 A5
Imatra FIN 9 B6
Imielin PL 86 B3
Imingen N 47 B5
Immeln S 63 B2
Immenhausen D . . 81 A5
Immingham GB . . . 41 B3
Immenstadt D . . . 107 B5
Ímola I 135 A4
Imon E 151 A5
Imotski HR. 138 B3
Impéria I 133 B4
Imphy F 104 C2
Imroz TR 183 C7
Imsland N 52 A1
Imst A 108 B1
Inagh IRL 28 B2
Inari FIN 193 D10
Inca E 167 B2
Inchnadamph GB . . 32 C2
Incinillas E 143 B3
Indal S 200 D3
Indjija SRB 127 B2
Indre Arna N 46 B2
Indre Billefjord N. . 193 B9
Indre Brenna N . . 193 B9
Inndyr N 195 C5
İnebolu TR 23 A7
İnegöl TR 187 B4
Inerthal CH 107 B3
Infiesto E 142 A1
Ingatorp S 62 A3
Ingedal N 54 A2
Ingelheim D 93 B4
Ingelmunster B . . . 78 B3
Ingelstad S 62 B2
Ingleton GB 37 B4
Ingolfsland N 47 C5
Ingolstadt D 95 C3
Ingrandes
  Maine-et-Loire F . .101 B5
  Vienne F 102 C2
Ingwiller F 93 C3
Inhisar TR 187 B5
Iniesta E 158 B2
Inishannon IRL . . . 29 C3
Inishcrone IRL 26 B1
Inke H. 124 A3
Innfjord N 198 C4
Innellan GB 34 C3
Innerleithen GB. . . 35 C4
Innermessan GB . . 36 B2
Innertkirchen CH. . 106 C3
Innervillgraten A . . 109 C3
Innset N 194 B9
Innsbruck A 108 B2
Innvik N 198 D3
İnönü TR 187 C5
Inowłódz PL. 87 A4
Inowrocław PL. . . . 76 B3
Ins CH 106 B2
Insch GB 33 D4

Insjön S 50 B2
Ińsko PL 75 A4
Instow GB 42 A2
İntepe TR 186 B1
Interlaken CH . . . 106 C2
Intragna CH 120 A1
Introbio I 120 B2
Inveran
  GB 32 D2
  IRL 28 A2
Inveraray GB 34 B2
Inverbervie GB . . . 35 B5
Invergarry GB 32 D2
Invergordon GB . . . 32 D2
Invergowrie GB . . . 35 B4
Inverkeilor GB 35 B5
Inverkeithing GB . . 35 B4
Invermoriston GB . . 32 D2
Inverness GB. 32 D2
Inveruno I 120 B1
Inverurie GB 33 D4
Ioannina GR 182 D2
Iolanda di Savoia I 121 C4
Ion Corvin RO . . . 17 C7
Ioppolo I. 175 C1
Ios GR 185 C6
Ipati GR 182 E4
İpsala TR 186 B1
Ipswich GB 45 A5
Iraklia GR. 183 B5
Iraklio = Heraklion
  GR 185 D6
Irdning A 110 B1
Iregszemcse H . . . 112 C2
Irgoli I 178 B3
Irig SRB 127 B1
Ironbridge GB 39 B4
Irpin UA 13 C9
Irrel D 92 B2
Irsina I 172 B2
Irsta S 56 A2
Irthlingborough GB. 44 A3
Iruela E 141 B4
Irún E 144 A2
Irurita E 144 A2
Irurzun E 144 B2
Irvine GB 36 A2
Irvinestown GB . . . 27 B3
Isaba E 144 B3
Isabela E 157 B4
Ísafjörður IS 190 A2
Isane N 198 D2
Isaszeg H 112 B3
Isbister GB 33 A5
Íscar E 150 A3
İscehisar TR 187 D5
Ischgl A 107 B5
İschia I 170 C1
Ischia di Castro I . . 168 A1
Ischitella I 171 B3
Isdes F 103 B4
Ise N 54 A2
Iselle I 119 A5
Iseltwald CH 106 C2
Isen D 108 A3
Isenbüttel D 73 B3
Iseo I 120 B3
Iserlohn D 81 A3
Isérnia I 170 B2
Isfjorden N 198 C4
Ishëm AL 182 B1
Isigny-sur-Mer F . . 88 A2
Işıklı TR 189 A4
Isili I 179 C3
İskilip TR 23 A8
Isla Canela E . . . 161 B2
Isla Cristina E . . . 161 B2
Islares E 143 A3
Isleham GB 45 A4
Isle of Whithorn GB 36 B2
Ismaning D 108 A2
Isna P 154 B3
Isnestoften N 192 B6
Isny D. 107 B5
Isoba E 142 A1
Isokylä
  FIN 197 C10
  S 196 B5
Isola F 132 A3
Isola d'Asti I 119 C5
Isola del Gran Sasso
  d'Itália I 169 A3
Ísola della Scala I . 121 B4
Isola delle Fémmine
  I 176 A2
Ísola del Liri I 169 B3
İsola di Capo Rizzuto
  I 175 C3
Isona E 147 B2
Ispagnac F 130 A2
İsparta TR 189 B5
Isperih BG 17 D7
İspica I 177 C3
Isselburg D 80 A2
Issigeac F 129 B3
Íssime I 119 B4
Issogne I 119 B4
Issoire F 116 B3
Issoncourt F 91 C5
Issoudun F 103 C4
Issum D 80 A2
Is-sur-Tille F 105 B4
Issy-l'Evêque F . . . 104 C2
İstán E 162 B3
İstanbul TR 186 A3
İstebna PL 98 B2
Ístia d'Ombrone I . 135 C4
Istiea GR 183 E5

Istres F 131 B3
Istvándi H 125 A3
Itea GR. 184 A3
Ithaki GR 184 A1
Itoiz E 144 B2
İtrabo E 163 B4
Itri I 169 B3
Ittireddu I 178 B2
Íttiri I 178 B2
Itzehoe D 64 C2
Ivalo FIN. 193 D11
Iván H 111 B3
Ivanava BY 13 B6
Ivančice CZ 97 B4
Ivančna Gorica
  SLO 123 B3
Ivanec HR 124 A2
Ivanić Grad HR . . . 124 B2
Ivanjska BIH 124 C3
Ivanka SK 98 C2
Ivankovo HR 125 B4
Ivano-Frankivsk UA 13 D6
Ivanovice na Hané
  CZ 98 B1
Ivanska HR 124 B2
Ivatsevichy BY . . . 13 B6
Ivaylovgrad BG . . 183 B8
Iveland N 53 B3
Ivoz Ramet B 79 B5
Ivrea I 119 B4
İvrindi TR 186 C2
Ivry-en-Montagne
  F 104 B3
Ivry-la-Bataille F . . 90 C1
Ivybridge GB 42 B3
Iwaniska PL 87 B5
Iwiny PL 85 A3
Iwuy F 78 B3
Ixworth GB. 45 A4
Izarra E 143 B4
Izbica Kujawska PL. 76 B3
Izbište SRB 127 B3
Izeda P 149 A3
Izegem B 78 B3
Izernore F 118 A2
İzmail UA 17 C8
İzmir TR 188 A2
İzmit = Kocaeli TR . 187 B4
İznájar E 163 A3
İznalloz E 163 A4
İznatoraf E 164 A1
İznik TR 187 B4
Izola SLO 122 B2
Izsák H 112 C3
Izsófalva H 99 C4
Izyaslav UA 13 C7

J
Jabalquinto E 157 B4
Jablanac HR 123 C3
Jablanica BIH 139 B3
Jablonec nad Jizerou
  CZ 84 B3
Jablonec nad Nisou
  CZ 84 B3
Jablonica SK 98 C1
Jablonka PL. 99 B3
Jabłonna PL. 77 B5
Jablonné Podještědí
  CZ 84 B2
Jablonov nad Turňou
  SK 99 C4
Jabłonowo Pomorskie
  PL. 69 B4
Jablůnka CZ 98 B1
Jablunkov CZ 98 B2
Jabučje SRB 127 C2
Jabugo E 161 B3
Jabuka SRB 127 C2
Jabukovac HR . . . 124 B2
Jaca E 145 B3
Jáchymov CZ 83 B4
Jacobidrebber D . . 72 B1
Jade D 71 A5
Jäderfors S 50 B3
Jädraås S 50 B3
Jadraque E 151 B5
Jaén E 163 A4
Jagare BIH 124 C3
Jagel D 64 B2
Jagenbach A 96 C3
Jagodina SRB . . . 127 D3
Jagodnjak HR . . . 125 B4
Jagodzin PL. 84 A3
Jagstheim D 94 B2
Jagstzell D 94 B2
Jahodna SK 111 A4
Jajce BIH 138 A3
Ják H 111 B3
Jakabszálbs H . . . 112 C3
Jäkkvik S 195 D8
Jakobsnes N . . . 193 C14
Jakovlje HR 124 B1
Jakšic HR 125 B3
Jakubany SK 99 B4
Jalance E 159 B2
Jalasjärvi FIN 8 A3
Jalhay B 80 B1
Jaligny-sur-Besbre
  F 117 A3
Jallais F 102 B1
Jalón E 159 C3

Jâlons F 91 C4
Jamena SRB 125 C5
Jamilena E 163 A4
Jämjö S 63 B3
Jamnička Kiselica
  HR 124 B1
Jamno PL 67 B5
Jamoigne B 92 B1
Jämsä FIN 8 B4
Jämshög S 63 B2
Jamu Mare RO. . . 126 B3
Janakkala FIN 8 B4
Jandelsbrunn D . . 96 C1
Jänickendorf D . . . 74 B2
Janikowo PL 76 B3
Janja BIH 125 C5
Janjina HR 138 C3
Janki
  Łódzkie PL. 86 A3
  Mazowieckie PL. . . 77 B5
Jankov CZ 96 B2
Jankowo Dolne PL . 76 B2
Jánoshalma H . . . 126 A1
Jánosháza H 111 B4
Jánoshida H 113 B4
Jánossomorja H . . .111 B4
Janovice nad Uhlavou
  CZ 96 B1
Janów PL. 86 B3
Janowiec Wielkopolski
  PL. 76 B2
Janowo PL. 77 A5
Jänsmässholmen
  S 199 B10
Janville F 103 A3
Janzé F 101 B4
Jarabá SK 99 C3
Jaraczewo PL 76 C2
Jarafuel E 159 B2
Jaraicejo E 156 A2
Jaraíz de la Vera E. 150 B2
Jarandilla de la Vera
  E 150 B2
Jaray E 152 A1
Järbo S 50 B3
Jard-sur-Mer F . . .114 B2
Jaren N 48 B2
Jargeau F 103 B4
Jarkovac SRB . . . 126 B2
Järlåsa S 51 C4
Jarmen D 66 C2
Järna S. 57 A3
Jarnac F 115 C3
Järnforsen S 62 A3
Jarny F. 92 B1
Jarocin PL 76 C2
Jaroměř CZ 85 B3
Jaroměřice nad
  Rokytnou CZ. . . . 97 B3
Jaroslav CZ 97 A4
Jaroslavice CZ . . . 97 C4
Jarosław PL. 12 C5
Jarosławiec PL . . . 68 A1
Jarošov nad Nežarkou
  CZ 96 B3
Järpås S 55 B3
Järpen S 199 B10
Jarrow GB 37 B5
Järso FIN 51 B6
Järvenpää FIN 8 B4
Jarvornik CZ 85 B4
Järvsö S. 200 E2
Jarzé F 102 B1
Jaša Tomic SRB . . 126 B2
Jasenak HR 123 B4
Jasenica BIH 124 C2
Jasenice HR 137 A4
Jasenovac HR . . . 124 B2
Jasenovo SRB. . . . 127 C3
Jasień PL. 84 A3
Jasienica PL 84 A2
Jasło PL. 12 D4
Jásova SK 112 B2
Jasseron F. 118 A2
Jastarnia PL. 69 A3
Jastrebarsko HR. . . 123 B4
Jastrowie PL 68 B1
Jastrzębia-Góra PL. 68 A3
Jastrzębie Zdrój PL. 98 B2
Jászals-Lószentgyörgy
  H 113 B4
Jászapáti H 113 B4
Jászárokszállás
  H 113 B3
Jászberény H 113 B3
Jászdózsa H 113 B4
Jászfényszaru H . .113 B3
Jászkáhalma H . . .113 B4
Jászkarajenő H . . .113 B3
Jászkisér H 113 B4
Jászladány H 113 B4
Jászszentlászló
  H 113 C3
Jásztelek H 113 B4
Játar E 163 B4
Jättendal S 200 E3
Jatznick D 74 A2
Jaun CH 106 C2
Jausiers F 132 A2
Jávea E 159 C4
Jävenitz D 73 B4
Javerlhac F 115 C4
Javier E 144 B2
Javorani BIH 124 C3
Javorina SK 99 B4
Javron F. 89 B3

Jawor PL 85 A4
Jaworzno PL 86 B3
Jaworzyna Śl. PL . . 85 B4
Jayena E 163 B4
Jażów PL 84 A2
Jebel RO 126 B3
Jebjerg DK 58 B2
Jedburgh GB 35 C5
Jedlinsk PL 87 A5
Jedlnia PL 87 A5
Jedlnia Letnisko PL 87 A5
Jednorożec PL 77 A6
Jedovnice CZ 97 B4
Jędrychow PL 69 B4
Jędrzejów PL 87 B4
Jedwabno PL 77 A5
Jeesiö FIN 197 B9
Jegłownik PL 69 A4
Jegun F 129 C3
Jēkabpils LV 8 D4
Jektevik N 46 C2
Jektvik N 195 D4
Jelcz-Laskowice PL 85 A5
Jelenec SK 98 C2
Jelenia Góra PL . . . 85 B3
Jelgava LV 8 D3
Jelka SK 111 A4
Jelling DK 59 C2
Jels DK 59 C2
Jelsa
  HR 138 B2
  N 52 A2
Jelšava SK 99 C4
Jemgum D 71 A4
Jemnice CZ 97 B3
Jena D 82 B3
Jenaz CH 107 C4
Jenbach A 108 B2
Jenikow PL 75 A4
Jennersdorf A . . . 111 C3
Jenny S 62 A4
Jerchel D 73 B4
Jeres del Marquesado
  E 164 B1
Jerez de la Frontera
  E 162 B1
Jerez de los Caballeros
  E 155 C4
Jerica E 159 B3
Jerichow D 73 B5
Jerka PL 75 B5
Jermenovci SRB . . 126 B3
Jerslev DK 58 A3
Jerte E 150 B2
Jerup DK 58 A3
Jerxheim D 73 B3
Jerzmanowice PL . . 87 B3
Jerzu I 179 C3
Jerzwałd PL 69 B4
Jesberg D 81 B5
Jesenice
  Středočeský CZ . . 83 B5
  Středočeský CZ . . 96 B2
  SLO 109 C5
Jeseník CZ 85 B5
Jesenké SK 99 C4
Jesi I 136 B2
Jésolo I 122 B1
Jessen D 83 A4
Jessheim N 48 B3
Jessnitz D 83 A4
Jesteburg D 72 A2
Jeumont F 79 B4
Jeven-stedt D 64 B2
Jever D 71 A4
Jevičko CZ 97 B4
Jevišovice CZ 97 C3
Jevnaker N 48 B2
Jezerane HR 123 B4
Jezero
  BIH 138 A3
  HR 123 B4
Jeżów PL 87 A3
Jičín CZ 84 B3
Jičiněves CZ 84 B3
Jihlava CZ 97 B3
Jijona E 159 C3
Jilemnice CZ 84 B3
Jílové CZ 84 B2
Jílové u Prahy CZ . . 96 B2
Jimbolia RO 126 B2
Jimena E 163 A4
Jimena de la Frontera
  E 162 B2
Jimera de Líbar E . 162 B2
Jimramov CZ 97 B4
Jince CZ 96 B1
Jindřichovice CZ . . 83 B4
Jindřichův Hradec
  CZ 96 B3
Jirkov CZ 83 B5
Jistebnice CZ 96 B2
Joachimsthal D . . . 74 B2
João da Loura P . . 154 C2
Jobbágyi H 112 B3
Jochberg A 109 B3
Jockfall S 196 C5
Jódar E 163 A4
Jodoigne B 79 B4
Joensuu FIN 9 A6
Joesjö S 195 E5
Jœuf F 92 B1
Jõgeva EST 8 C5
Johanngeorgenstadt
  D 83 B4
Johannishus S . . . 63 B3
Johanniskirchen D . 95 C4

Johansfors S 63 B3
John o'Groats GB . . 32 C3
Johnshaven GB . . . 35 B5
Johnstone GB 34 C3
Johnstown IRL . . . 30 B1
Jõhvi EST 8 C5
Joigny F 104 B2
Joinville F 91 C5
Jokkmokk S 196 C2
Jöllenbeck D 72 B1
Jomala FIN 51 B6
Jonava LT 13 A6
Jonchery-sur-Vesle
  F 91 B3
Jondal N 46 B3
Jondalen N 53 A5
Joniškis LT 8 D3
Jönköping S 62 A2
Jonkowo PL 69 B5
Jønnbu N 53 A5
Jonsberg S 56 B2
Jonsered S 60 B2
Jonstorp S 61 C2
Jonzac F 114 C3
Jorba E 147 C2
Jordanów PL 99 B3
Jordanowo PL 75 B4
Jordanów Śląski PL 85 B4
Jordbro S 57 A4
Jordbrua N 195 D5
Jördenstorf D 66 C1
Jordet N 49 A4
Jordøse DK 59 C3
Jork D 72 A2
Jörlanda S 60 B1
Jormlien S 199 A10
Jormvattnet S . . . 199 A11
Jörn S 200 A6
Jørpeland N 52 A2
Jorquera E 158 B2
Jošan HR 123 C4
Jošavka BIH 124 C3
Josipdol HR 123 B4
Josipovac HR 125 B4
Jössefors S 54 A3
Josselin F 101 B3
Jøssund N 199 A7
Jostedal N 47 A4
Jósvafő H 99 C4
Jou P 148 A2
Jouarre F 90 C3
Joué-lès-Tours F . . 102 B2
Joué-sur-Erdre F . . 101 B4
Joure NL 70 B2
Joutseno FIN 9 B6
Joutsijärvi FIN . . 197 C10
Joux-la-Ville F . . . 104 B2
Jouy F 90 C1
Jouy-le-Châtel F . . 90 C3
Jouy-le-Potier F . . 103 B3
Joyeuse F 131 A3
Joze F 116 B3
Juankoski FIN 8 A6
Juan-les-Pins F . . 132 B3
Jübek D 64 B2
Jubera E 144 B1
Jubrique E 162 B2
Jüchsen D 82 B2
Judaberg N 52 A1
Judenburg A 110 B1
Juelsminde DK . . . 59 C3
Jugon-les-Lacs F . . 101 A3
Juillac F 129 A4
Juillan F 145 A4
Juist D 71 A4
Jukkasjärvi S 196 B3
Jule N 199 A10
Julianadorp NL . . . 70 B1
Julianstown IRL . . 30 A2
Jülich D 80 B2
Jullouville F 88 B2
Jumeaux F 117 B3
Jumièges F 89 A4
Jumilhac-le-Grand
  F 115 C5
Jumilla E 159 C2
Jumisko FIN . . . 197 C11
Juncosa E 153 A4
Juneda E 147 C1
Jung S 55 B4
Jungingen D 93 C5
Junglingster L . . . 92 B2
Juniville F 91 B4
Junosuando S . . . 196 B5
Junsele S 200 C2
Juoksengi S 196 C6
Juoksenki FIN . . . 196 C6
Juprelle B 80 B1
Jurata PL 69 A3
Jurbarkas LT 12 A5
Jurjevo HR 123 C3
Jūrmala LV 8 D3
Jurmu FIN 197 D10
Juromenha P . . . 155 C3
Jursla S 56 B2
Jussac F 116 C2
Jussey F 105 B4
Jussy F 90 B3
Juta H 125 A3
Jüterbog D 74 C2
Juuka FIN 3 E11
Juuma FIN 197 C12
Juvigny-le-Terte F . 88 B2
Juvigny-sous-Andaine
  F 89 B3
Juzennecourt F . . 105 A3

Jyderup DK 61 D1
Jyrkänkoski FIN . 197 C12
Jyväskylä FIN 8 A4

K

Kaamanen FIN . . 193 C11
Kaamasmukka
  FIN 193 C10
Kaaresuvanto FIN . 192 D6
Kaarssen D 73 A4
Kaatscheuvel NL . . 79 A5
Kaba H 113 B5
Kåbdalis S 196 C3
Kačarevo SRB . . . 127 C2
Kács H 113 B4
Kadan CZ 83 B5
Kadarkút H 125 A3
Kadınhanı TR . . . 189 A7
Kaduy RUS 9 C10
Kåfalla S 56 A1
Kåfjord N 192 C7
Kåfjordbotn N . . . 192 C4
Kågeröd S 61 D3
Kahl D 93 A5
Kahla D 82 B3
Kainach bei Voitsberg
  A 110 B2
Kaindorf A 110 B2
Kainulasjärvi S . . 196 C5
Kairala FIN 197 B10
Kaisepakte S 192 D3
Kaisersesch D 80 B3
Kaiserslautern D . . 93 B3
Kaisheim D 94 C2
Kajaani FIN 3 D10
Kajárpéc H 111 B4
Kajdacs H 112 C2
Kakanj BIH 139 A4
Kakasd H 125 A4
Kaklik TR 189 B4
Kakolewo PL 85 A4
Kál H 113 B4
Kalajoki FIN 3 D8
Kalak N 193 B11
Kalamata GR . . . 184 B3
Kalambaka GR . . 182 D3
Kalamria GR 182 C4
Kalandra GR . . . 183 D5
Kälarne S 200 D2
Kalavrita GR . . . 184 A3
Kalbe D 73 B4
Kalce SLO 123 B3
Kald H 111 B4
Kale
  Antalya TR . . . 189 C4
  Denizli TR 188 B3
Kalecik TR 23 A7
Kalefeld D 82 A2
Kalesija BIH 139 A4
Kalety PL 86 B2
Kalevala RUS . . . 3 D12
Kalhovd N 47 B5
Kali HR 137 A4
Kalimnos GR . . . 188 C2
Kaliningrad RUS . . 69 A5
Kalinkavichy BY . . 13 B8
Kalinovac HR . . . 124 A3
Kalinovik BIH . . . 139 B4
Kalinovo SK 99 C3
Kalirachi GR 183 C6
Kaliska
  Pomorskie PL . . 68 A3
  Pomorskie PL . . 68 B3
Kalisko PL 86 A3
Kalisz PL 86 A2
Kalisz Pomorski PL . 75 A4
Kaljord N 194 B6
Kalkan TR 189 C4
Kalkar D 80 A2
Kalkım TR 186 C2
Kall
  D 80 B2
  S 199 B10
Källby S 55 B4
Kållered S 60 B2
Kållerstad S 60 B3
Kallinge S 63 B3
Kallmünz D 95 B3
Kallo FIN 196 B7
Kallsedet S 199 B9
Källvik S 56 B3
Kalmar S 63 B4
Kalmthout B 79 A4
Kalná SK 112 A2
Kalocsa H 112 C2
Kalokhorio CY . . . 181 B2
Kalo Nero GR . . . 184 B2
Kaloni GR 186 C1
Káloz H 112 C2
Kals A 109 B3
Kalsdorf A 110 C2
Kaltbrunn CH . . . 107 B4
Kaltenbach A . . . 108 B2
Kaltenkirchen D . . 64 C2
Kaltennordheim D . 82 B2
Kalundborg DK . . . 61 D1
Kalush UA 13 D6
Kalvåg N 198 D1
Kalvehave DK . . . 65 A5
Kalwang A 110 B1
Kalwaria-Zebrzydowska
  PL 99 B3
Kalyazin RUS . . . 9 D10
Kam H 111 B3
Kaman TR 23 B7

Kamares GR . . . 185 C5
Kambos CY 181 A1
Kamen D 81 A3
Kamenice CZ 97 B3
Kamenice nad Lipou
  CZ 96 B3
Kameničná SK . . . 112 B2
Kamenný Most SK . 112 B2
Kamenny Ujezd CZ . 96 C2
Kamensko HR . . . 138 B2
Kamenz D 84 A2
Kamičak BIH . . . 124 C2
Kamień PL 87 A4
Kamieniec Ząbk. PL . 85 B4
Kamienka SK 99 B4
Kamień Krajeński
  PL 76 A2
Kamienna Góra PL . 85 B4
Kamień Pomorski
  PL 67 C3
Kamieńsk PL 86 A3
Kamiros Skala GR . 188 C2
Kamnik SLO 123 A3
Kampen NL 70 B2
Kampinos PL 77 B5
Kamp-Lintfort D . . 80 A2
Kampor HR 123 C3
Kamyanets-
  Podil's'kyy UA . . 13 D7
Kamyanka-Buz'ka
  UA 13 C6
Kamýk nad Vltavou
  CZ 96 B2
Kanal SLO 122 A2
Kanalia GR 182 D4
Kandalaksha RUS . 3 C13
Kandanos GR . . . 185 D4
Kandel D 93 B4
Kandern D 106 B2
Kandersteg CH . . 106 C2
Kandila GR 184 B3
Kandıra TR 187 A5
Kandy TR 69 A5
Kanfanar HR . . . 122 B2
Kangasala FIN 8 B4
Kangos S 196 B5
Kangosjärvi FIN . . 196 B6
Kaniów PL 75 C3
Kanjiža SRB . . . 126 A2
Kankaanpää FIN . . 8 B3
Kannus FIN 3 E8
Kanturk IRL 29 B3
Kapaklı TR 186 A2
Kapellen
  A 110 B2
  B 79 A4
Kapellskär S 57 A5
Kapfenberg A . . . 110 B2
Kapfenstein A . . . 110 C2
Kaplice CZ 96 C2
Kapljuh BIH 124 C2
Kápolna H 113 B4
Kaposfő H 125 A3
Kaposfüred H . . . 125 A3
Kaposszekcsö H . . 125 A4
Kaposvár H 125 A3
Kapp N 48 B2
Kappel D 93 C3
Kappeln D 64 B2
Kappelshamn S . . 57 C4
Kappl A 107 B5
Kappstad S 55 A4
Kaprun A 109 B3
Kaptol HR 125 B3
Kapuvár H 111 B4
Karaadilli TR . . . 189 A5
Karabiğa TR 186 B2
Karabük TR 187 A7
Karaburun TR . . . 186 D1
Karacabey TR . . . 186 B3
Karacaköy TR . . . 186 A3
Karacasu TR 188 B3
Karácsond H 113 B4
Karád H 112 C1
Karahallı TR 189 A4
Karaisali TR 23 C8
Karaman
  Balıkesir TR . . . 186 C3
  Karaman TR 23 C7
Karamanlı TR . . . 189 A4
Karamürsel TR . . 187 B4
Karan SRB 127 D1
Karancslapujto H . 113 A3
Karapınar TR 23 C7
Karasjok N 193 C9
Karasu TR 187 A5
Karataş
  Adana TR 23 C8
  Manisa TR 188 A3
Karavostasi CY . . 181 A1
Karben D 81 B4
Karbenning S . . . 50 B3
Kårböle S 199 D12
Karby
  D 64 B2
  DK 58 B1
  S 57 A4
Karbyd S 62 A4
Karcag H 113 B4
Karczów PL 86 B1
Karczowiska PL . . 85 A4
Kardamena GR . . 188 C2
Kardamila GR . . . 185 A7

Kardamili GR . . . 184 C3
Kardašova Rečice
  CZ 96 B2
Kardis S 196 C6
Karditsa GR 182 D3
Kärdla EST 8 C3
Kardoskút H 113 C4
Kardzhali BG . . . 183 B7
Karesuando S . . . 192 D6
Kargı TR 23 A8
Kargopol RUS . . . 9 B11
Kargowa PL 75 B4
Karigasniemi FIN . 193 C9
Karise DK 65 A5
Karistos GR 185 A5
Karkkila FIN 8 B4
Karlholmsbruk S . . 51 B4
Karlino PL 67 B4
Karlobag HR 137 A4
Karlovac HR 123 B4
Karlovasi GR . . . 188 B1
Karlovčic SRB . . . 127 C2
Karlovice CZ 85 B5
Karlovo BG 17 D6
Karlovy Vary CZ . . 83 B4
Karłowice PL 86 B1
Karlsborg S 55 B5
Karlshamn S 63 B2
Karlshöfen D 72 A2
Karlshus N 54 A1
Karlskoga S 55 A5
Karlskrona S 63 B3
Karlsrud N 47 B5
Karlsruhe D 93 B4
Karlstad S 55 A4
Karlstadt D 94 B1
Karlstetten A 110 A2
Karlstift A 96 C2
Karlstorp S 62 A3
Karmacs H 111 C4
Kärna S 60 B1
Karmin PL 85 A5
Karnobat BG 17 D7
Karojba HR 122 B2
Karow D 73 A5
Karpacz PL 85 B3
Karpathos GR . . . 188 D2
Karpenisi GR . . . 182 E3
Karpuzlu TR 188 B2
Kärrbo S 56 A2
Karrebaeksminde
  DK 65 A4
Karshult S 60 B3
Karsin PL 68 B2
Kårsta S 57 A4
Karstädt D 73 A4
Kartal TR 186 B4
Kartitsch A 109 C3
Kartuzy PL 68 A3
Karungi S 196 C6
Karunki FIN 196 C7
Karup DK 59 B2
Karviná CZ 98 B2
Kås DK 58 A2
Kaş TR 189 C4
Kasaba TR 189 C4
Kašava CZ 98 B1
Kåsberga S 66 A3
Kasejovice CZ . . . 96 B1
Kashin RUS 9 D10
Kašina HR 124 B2
Kasina-Wielka PL . 99 B4
Kaskinen FIN 8 A2
Kašperské Hory CZ . 96 B1
Kassandrino GR . . 183 C5
Kassel D 81 A5
Kassiopi GR . . . 182 D1
Kastamonu TR . . . 23 A7
Kastav HR 123 B3
Kasteli GR 185 D4
Kastellaun D 93 A3
Kastelli GR 185 D6
Kaštel-Stari HR . . 138 B2
Kaštel Zegarski
  HR 138 A1
Kasterlee B 79 A4
Kastl D 95 B3
Kastlösa S 63 B4
Kastorf D 65 C3
Kastoria GR 182 C3
Kastorio GR 184 B3
Kastraki GR 185 C6
Kastrosikia GR . . 182 D2
Kastsyukovichy
  BY 13 B10
Kaszaper H 113 C4
Katakolo GR . . . 184 B2
Katapola GR . . . 185 C6
Katastari GR . . . 184 B1
Katerbow D 74 B1
Katerini GR 182 C4
Kathikas CY 181 B1
Kätkesuando S . . 196 A6
Katlenburg-Lindau
  D 82 A2
Kato Achaia GR . . 184 A2
Katouna GR 182 E3
Káto Pyrgos CY . . 181 A1
Katowice PL 86 B3
Katrineberg S . . . 50 A3
Katrineholm S . . . 56 B2
Kattarp S 61 C2
Kattavia GR 188 D2
Katthammarsvik S . 57 C4
Kattilstorp S 55 B4
Katwijk NL 70 B1

Katymár H 125 A5
Kąty Wrocławskie
  PL 85 A4
Katzenelnbogen D . 81 B3
Katzhütte D 82 B3
Kaub D 93 A3
Kaufbeuren D . . . 108 B1
Kauhajoki FIN 8 A3
Kauhava FIN 8 A3
Kaukonen FIN . . . 196 B7
Kauliranta FIN . . . 196 C6
Kaulsdorf D 82 B3
Kaunas LT 13 A5
Kaunisvaara S . . . 196 B6
Kaupanger N 47 A4
Kautokeino N . . . 192 C7
Kautzen A 97 C3
Kavadarci MK . . . 182 B4
Kavajë AL 182 B1
Kavakköy TR . . . 186 B1
Kavaklı TR 186 A2
Kavaklıdere TR . . 188 B3
Kavala GR 183 C6
Kavarna BG 17 D8
Kävlinge S 61 D3
Kawcze PL 68 A1
Kaxås S 199 B10
Kaxholmen S . . . 62 A2
Käylä FIN 197 C12
Kaymakçı TR . . . 188 A3
Kaymaz TR 187 C6
Kaynarca TR 187 A5
Käyrämö FIN . . . 197 C9
Kayseri TR 23 B8
Kaysersberg F . . . 106 A2
Kazanlak BG 17 D6
Kazár H 113 A3
Kazimierza Wielka
  PL 87 B4
Kazincbarcika H . . 113 A4
Kaźmierz PL 75 B5
Kcynia PL 76 A2
Kdyně CZ 95 B5
Kea GR 185 B5
Keadew IRL 26 B2
Keady GB 27 B4
Kecel H 112 C3
Keçiborlu TR . . . 189 B5
Kecskemét H . . . 113 C3
Kėdainiai LT 13 A5
Kędzierzyn-Koźle
  PL 86 B2
Keel IRL 28 A1
Keenagh IRL 28 A4
Keerbergen B . . . 79 A4
Kefalos GR 188 C1
Kefken TR 187 A5
Keflavík IS 190 C3
Kegworth GB . . . 40 C2
Kehl D 93 C3
Kehrigk D 74 B2
Keighley GB 40 B2
Keila EST 8 C4
Keillmore GB . . . 34 C2
Keiss GB 32 C3
Keith GB 33 D4
Kelankylä FIN . . 197 D10
Kelberg D 80 B2
Kelbra D 82 A3
Kelč CZ 98 B1
Kelchsau A 108 B3
Këlcyrë AL 182 C2
Keld GB 37 B4
Kelebia H 126 A1
Kelheim D 95 C3
Kella D 82 A2
Kellas GB 32 D3
Kellinghusen D . . 64 C2
Kelloselkä FIN . . 197 C11
Kells
  GB 27 B4
  IRL 27 C4
Kelmis B 80 B2
Kelottijärvi FIN . . 192 D6
Kelsall GB 38 A4
Kelso GB 35 C5
Kelsterbach D . . . 93 A4
Keltneyburn GB . . 35 B3
Kelujärvi FIN . . . 197 B10
Kemaliye TR 23 B8
Kemalpaşa TR . . . 188 A2
Kematen A 108 B2
Kemberg D 83 A4
Kemer
  Antalya TR . . . 189 C5
  Burdur TR 189 B5
  Muğla TR 189 C4
Kemerkaya TR . . 187 D6
Kemi FIN 196 D7
Kemijärvi FIN . . . 197 C10
Keminmaa FIN . . . 196 D7
Kemnath D 95 B3
Kemnay GB 33 D4
Kemnitz
  Brandenburg D . . 74 B1
  Mecklenburg-
  Vorpommern D . . 66 B2
Kempen D 80 A2
Kempsey GB 39 B4
Kempten D 107 B5

Kemptthal CH 107 B3
Kendal GB 37 B4
Kenderes H 113 B4
Kengyel H 113 B4
Kenilworth GB 44 A2
Kenmare IRL 29 C2
Kenmore GB 35 B4
Kennacraig GB 34 C2
Kenyeri H 111 B4
Kenzingen D 106 A2
Kepez TR 186 B1
Kępice PL 68 A1
Kępno PL 86 A2
Kepsut TR 186 C3
Keramoti GR 183 C6
Keräntöjärvi S 196 B6
Keratea GR 185 B4
Kerava FIN 8 B4
Kerecsend H 113 B4
Kerekegyhaza H . . . 112 C3
Kerepestarcsa H . . .112 B3
Keri GR 184 B1
Kérien F 100 A2
Kerkafalva H 111 C3
Kerken D 80 A2
Kerkrade NL 80 B2
Kerkyra GR 182 D1
Kerlouan F 100 A1
Kernascléden F . . . 100 A2
Kernhof A 110 B2
Kerns CH 106 C3
Kerpen D 80 B2
Kerrysdale GB 31 B3
Kerta H 111 B4
Kerzers CH 106 C2
Keşan TR 186 B1
Kesgrave GB 45 A5
Kesh GB 26 B3
Keskin TR 23 B7
Kesselfall A 109 B3
Kestenga RUS 3 D12
Keswick GB 36 B3
Keszthely H 111 C4
Kétegyháza H 113 C5
Kéthely H 111 C4
Kętrzyn PL 12 A4
Kettering GB 44 A3
Kettlewell GB 40 A1
Kęty PL 99 B3
Ketzin D 74 B1
Keula D 82 A2
Keuruu FIN 8 A4
Kevelaer D 80 A2
Kevermes H 113 C5
Kevi SRB 126 B1
Keyingham GB 41 B3
Keynsham GB 43 A4
Kežmarok SK 99 B4
Khimki RUS 9 E10
Khisinev = Chişinău
MD 17 B8
Khmelnik UA 13 D7
Khmelnytskyy UA . . 13 D7
Khodoriv UA 13 D6
Kholm RUS 9 D7
Khotyn UA 13 D7
Khoyniki BY 13 C8
Khust UA 17 A5
Khvoynaya RUS . . . 9 C9
Kiato GR 184 A3
Kibæk DK 59 B1
Kiberg N 193 B14
Kicasalih TR 186 A1
Kičevo MK 182 B2
Kidderminster GB . . 39 B4
Kidlington GB 44 B2
Kidsgrove GB 40 B1
Kidwelly GB 39 C2
Kiefersfelden D 108 B3
Kiel D 64 B3
Kielce PL 87 B4
Kiełczygłów PL 86 A3
Kielder GB 37 A4
Kiełpino PL 68 A3
Kiełpiny PL 77 A4
Kierinki FIN 197 B8
Kiernozia PL 77 B4
Kierspe D 81 A3
Kietrz PL 86 B2
Kietz D 74 B3
Kiev = Kyyiv UA . . . 13 C9
Kiezmark PL 69 A3
Kiffisia GR 185 A4
Kifino Selo BIH . . . 139 B4
Kihlanki
FIN 196 B6
S 196 B6
Kiistala FIN 197 B8
Kije PL 87 B4
Kijevo HR 138 B2
Kikallen N 46 B2
Kikinda SRB 126 B2
Kil
N 53 B5
Örebro S 55 A6
Värmland S 55 A4
Kila S 55 A3
Kilafors S 50 A3
Kilbaha IRL 29 B2
Kilbeggan IRL 30 A1
Kilberry GB 34 C2
Kilbirnie GB 34 C3
Kilboghamn N 195 D4
Kilbotn N 194 B7
Kilb Rabenstein A . .110 A2
Kilchattan GB 34 C2
Kilchoan GB 34 B1
Kilcock IRL 30 A2
Kilconnell IRL 28 A3
Kilcormac IRL 28 A4
Kilcreggan GB 34 C3
Kilcullen IRL 30 A2
Kilcurry IRL 27 B4
Kildare IRL 30 A2
Kildinstroy RUS . . . 3 B13
Kildonan GB 32 C3
Kildorrery IRL 29 B3
Kilegrend N 53 A4
Kilen N 53 A4
Kilgarvan IRL 29 C2
Kilkee IRL 29 B2
Kilkeel GB 27 B4
Kilkelly IRL 26 C2
Kilkenny IRL 30 B1
Kilkieran IRL 28 A2
Kilkinlea IRL 29 B2
Kilkis GR 182 B4
Killadysert IRL 29 B2
Killala IRL 26 B1
Killaloe IRL 28 B3
Killarney IRL 29 B2
Killashandra IRL . . . 27 B3
Killashee IRL 28 A4
Killearn GB 34 B3
Killeberg S 61 C4
Killeigh IRL 30 A1
Killenaule IRL 29 B4
Killimor IRL 28 A3
Killin GB 34 B3
Killinaboy IRL 28 B2
Killinge S 196 B3
Killinick IRL 30 B2
Killorglin IRL 29 B2
Killucan IRL 30 A1
Killybegs IRL 26 B2
Killyleagh GB 27 B5
Kilmacrenan IRL . . . 26 A3
Kilmacthomas IRL . . 30 B1
Kilmaine IRL 28 A2
Kilmallock IRL 29 B3
Kilmarnock GB 36 A2
Kilmartin GB 34 B2
Kilmaurs GB 36 A2
Kilmeadan IRL 30 B1
Kilmeedy IRL 29 B3
Kilmelford GB 34 B2
Kilmore Quay IRL . . 30 B2
Kilmuir GB 32 D2
Kilnaleck IRL 27 C3
Kilninver GB 34 B2
Kilpisjärvi FIN 192 C4
Kilrea GB 27 B4
Kilrush IRL 29 B2
Kilsmo S 56 A1
Kilsyth GB 35 C3
Kiltoom IRL 28 A3
Kilwinning GB 36 A2
Kimasozero RUS . . 3 D13
Kimi GR 185 A5
Kimolos GR 185 C5
Kimovsk RUS 9 E10
Kimratshofen D . . . 107 B5
Kimry RUS 9 D10
Kimstad S 56 B1
Kinbrace GB 32 C3
Kincardine GB 35 B4
Kincraig GB 32 D3
Kindberg A 110 B2
Kindelbruck D 82 A3
Kingarrow IRL 26 B2
Kingisepp RUS 9 C6
Kingsbridge GB . . . 43 B3
Kingsclere GB 44 B2
Kingscourt IRL 27 C4
King's Lynn GB . . . 41 C4
Kingsteignton GB . . 43 B3
Kingston
Greater London
GB 44 B3
Moray GB 32 D3
Kingston Bagpuize
GB 44 B2
Kingston upon Hull
GB 40 B3
Kingswear GB 43 B3
Kingswood GB 43 A4
Kington GB 39 B3
Kingussie GB 32 D2
Kınık
Antalya TR 188 C4
İzmir TR 186 C2
Kinloch
Highland GB 31 B2
Highland GB 32 C2
Kinlochbervie GB . . 32 C1
Kinlochewe GB . . . 32 D1
Kinlochleven GB . . 34 B3
Kinlochmoidart GB . 34 B2
Kinloch Rannoch
GB 35 B3
Kinloss GB 32 D3
Kinlough IRL 26 B2
Kinn N 48 B2
Kinna S 60 B2
Kinnared S 60 B3
Kinnarp S 55 B4
Kinnegad IRL 30 A1
Kinne-Kleva S 55 B4
Kinnitty IRL 28 A4
Kinrooi B 80 A1
Kinross GB 35 B4
Kinsale IRL 29 C3
Kinsarvik N 46 B3
Kintarvie GB 31 A2
Kintore GB 33 D4
Kinvarra IRL 28 A3
Kioni GR 184 A1
Kiparissia GR 184 B2
Kipfenburg D 95 C3
Kippen GB 35 B3
Kiraz TR 188 A3
Kirazlı TR 186 B1
Kirberg D 81 B4
Kirchbach in Steiermark
A 110 C2
Kirchberg
CH 106 B2
Baden-Württemberg
D 94 B1
Rheinland-Pfalz D . 93 B3
Kirchberg am Wechsel
A 110 B2
Kirchberg an der
Pielach A 110 A2
Kirchberg in Tirol
A 109 B3
Kirchbichl A 108 B3
Kirchdorf
Bayern D 96 C1
Mecklenburg-
Vorpommern D . .65 C4
Niedersachsen D . .72 B1
Kirchdorf an der Krems
A 109 B5
Kirchdorf in Tirol
A 109 B3
Kirchenlamitz D . . . 83 B3
Kirchenthumbach D 95 B3
Kirchhain D 81 B4
Kirchheim
Baden-Württemberg
D 94 C1
Bayern D 108 A1
Hessen D 81 B5
Kirchheimbolanden
D 93 B4
Kirchhundem D . . . 81 A4
Kirchlintein D 72 B2
Kirchschlag A 111 B3
Kirchweidach D . . . 109 A3
Kirchzarten D 106 B2
Kircubbin GB 27 B5
Kireç TR 186 C3
Kırıkkale TR 23 B7
Kirillov RUS 9 C11
Kirishi RUS 9 C8
Kırka TR 187 C5
Kırkağaç TR 186 C2
Kirkbean GB 36 B3
Kirkbride GB 36 B3
Kirkby GB 38 A4
Kirkby Lonsdale GB 37 B4
Kirkby Malzeard GB 40 A2
Kirkbymoorside GB 37 B6
Kirkby Stephen GB . 37 B4
Kirkcaldy GB 35 B4
Kirkcolm GB 36 B1
Kirkconnel GB 36 A2
Kirkcowan GB 36 B2
Kirkcudbright GB . . 36 B2
Kirkehamn N 52 B2
Kirke Hyllinge DK . . 61 D1
Kirkenær N 49 B4
Kirkenes N 193 C14
Kirkham GB 38 A4
Kirkintilloch GB . . . 35 C3
Kirkjubæjarklaustur
IS 191 D7
Kirkkonummi FIN . . 8 B4
Kırklareli TR 186 A2
Kirkmichael GB . . . 35 B4
Kirk Michael GB . . . 36 B2
Kirkoswald GB 36 A2
Kirkpatrick Fleming
GB 36 A3
Kirkton of Glenisla
GB 35 B4
Kirkwall GB 33 C4
Kirkwhelpington GB 37 A5
Kirn D 93 B3
Kirovsk RUS 3 C13
Kirriemuir GB 35 B5
Kırşehir TR 23 B8
Kirton GB 41 C3
Kirton in Lindsey
GB 40 B3
Kirtorf D 81 B5
Kiruna S 196 B3
Kisa S 62 A3
Kisač SRB 126 B1
Kisbér H 112 B2
Kiseljak BIH 139 B4
Kisielice PL 69 B4
Kisköre H 113 B4
Kiskőrös H 112 C3
Kiskunfélegyháza
H 113 C3
Kiskunhalas H 112 C3
Kiskunlacháza H . . .112 B2
Kiskunmajsa H . . . 113 C3
Kisláng H 112 C2
Kisslegg D 107 B4
Kissolt H 112 C3
Kissónerga CY . . . 181 B1
Kist D 94 B1
Kistanje HR 138 B1
Kistelek H 113 C3
Kisterenye H 113 A3
Kisújszállás H 113 B4
Kisvárda H 16 A5
Kisvejke H 112 C2
Kiszkowo H 76 B2
Kiszombor H 126 A2
Kitee FIN 9 A7
Kithnos GR 185 B5
Kiti CY 181 B2
Kitkiöjärvi S 196 B6
Kitkiöjoki S 196 B6
Kittelfjäll S 195 E6
Kittendorf D 74 A1
Kittilä FIN 196 B7
Kittlitz D 84 A2
Kittsee A 111 A4
Kitzbühel A 109 B3
Kitzingen D 94 B2
Kiuruvesi FIN 3 E10
Kivertsi UA 13 C6
Kividhes CY 181 B1
Kivik S 63 C2
Kivotos GR 182 C3
Kıyıköy TR 186 A3
Kızılcabölük TR . . . 188 B4
Kızılcadağ TR 189 B4
Kızılcahamam TR . . 23 A7
Kızılırmak TR 23 A7
Kızılkaya TR 189 B5
Kızılkuyu TR 187 D6
Kızılören
Afyon TR 189 A5
Konya TR 189 B7
Kjeldebotn N 194 B7
Kjellerup DK 59 B2
Kjellmyra N 49 B4
Kjøllefjord N 193 B11
Kjopmannskjaer N . 54 A1
Kjøpsvik N 194 B7
Kl'ačno SK 98 C2
Kladanj BIH 139 A4
Kläden D 73 B4
Klädesholmen S . . . 60 B1
Kladnice HR 138 B2
Kladno CZ 84 B2
Kladruby CZ 95 B4
Klagenfurt A 110 C1
Klågerup S 61 D3
Klagstorp S 66 A2
Klaipéda LT 8 E2
Klaistow D 74 B1
Klaksvík FO 4 A3
Klana HR 123 B3
Klanac HR 123 C4
Klanjec HR 123 A4
Klardorf D 95 B4
Klarup DK 58 A3
Klašnice BIH 124 C3
Klässbol S 55 A3
Klášterec nad Ohří
CZ 83 B5
Kláštor pod Znievom
SK 98 C2
Klatovy CZ 96 B1
Klaus an der Pyhrnbahn
A 110 B1
Klazienaveen NL . . 71 B3
Kłecko PL 76 B2
Kleczew PL 76 B3
Klein Plasten D . . . 74 A2
Klein Sankt Paul A . 110 C1
Kleinsölk A 109 B4
Kleinzell A 110 B2
Klejtrup DK 58 B2
Klek SRB 126 B2
Klemensker DK . . . 67 A3
Klenak SRB 127 C1
Klenci pod Cerchovem
CZ 95 B4
Klenica PL 75 C4
Klenje SRB 127 C1
Klenoec MK 182 B2
Klenovec SK 99 C3
Klenovica HR 123 B3
Klenovnik HR 124 A2
Kleppe N 52 B1
Kleppestø N 46 B2
Kleptow D 74 A2
Kleszewo PL 77 B6
Kleve D 80 A2
Klevshult S 60 B4
Klewki PL 77 A5
Kličevac SRB 127 C3
Kliening A 110 C1
Klietz D 73 B5
Klikuszowa PL 99 B3
Klimkovice CZ 98 B2
Klimontów PL 87 B5
Klimovichi BY 13 B9
Klimpfjäll S 195 E5
Klin RUS 9 D10
Klinča Sela HR . . . 123 B4
Klingenbach A 111 B3
Klingenberg D 93 B5
Klingenmunster D . . 93 B4
Klingenthal D 83 B4
Klinkhamn S 57 C4
Klintehamn S 57 C4
Kliny PL 87 A4
Klipan S 61 C3
Klippav DK 64 B2
Klippan S 61 C3
Klis HR 138 B2
Klitmøller DK 58 A1
Klitten D 49 A6
Klixbüll D 64 B1
Kljajićevo SRB . . . 126 B1
Ključ BIH 138 A2
Klobouky CZ 97 C4
Kłobuck PL 86 B2
Klockestrand S . . . 200 D3
Kłodawa
Lubuskie PL 75 B4
Wielkopolskie PL . .76 B3
Kłodzko PL 85 B4
Kløfta N 48 B3
Klokkarvik N 46 B2
Klokkerholm DK . . . 58 A3
Klokočov SK 98 B2
Kłomnice PL 86 B3
Klonowa PL 86 A2
Kloosterzande NL . . 79 A4
Kłopot PL 74 B3
Klos AL 182 B2
Kloštar Ivanić HR . . 124 B2
Kloster
D 66 B2
DK 59 B1
Klösterle A 107 B5
Klostermansfeld D . 82 A3
Klosterneuburg A . . 97 C4
Klosters CH 107 C4
Kloten CH 107 B3
Klötze D 73 B4
Klöverträsk S 196 D4
Klövsjö S 199 C11
Kluczbork PL 86 B2
Kluczewo PL 75 A5
Kluisbergen B 79 B3
Klundert NL 79 A4
Klutz D 65 C4
Klyetsk BY 13 B7
Knaben N 52 B2
Knaften S 200 B4
Knapstad N 54 A2
Knäred S 61 C3
Knaresborough GB . 40 A2
Knarvik N 46 B2
Knebel D 59 B3
Knebworth GB 44 B3
Knesebeck D 73 B3
Knesselare B 78 A3
Knežak SLO 123 B3
Kneževi Vinogradi
HR 125 B4
Kneževo HR 125 B4
Knić SRB 127 C2
Knighton GB 39 B3
Knin HR 138 A2
Knislinge S 61 C4
Knittelfeld A 110 B1
Knivsta S 57 A3
Knock IRL 28 A3
Knocktopher IRL . . 30 B1
Knokke-Heist B . . . 78 A3
Knowle GB 44 A2
Knurów PL 86 B2
Knutby S 51 C5
Knutsford GB 38 A4
Kobarid SLO 122 A2
København =
Copenhagen DK . 61 D2
Kobenz A 110 B1
Kobersdorf A 111 B3
Kobiernice PL 99 B3
Kobierzyce PL 85 B4
Kobilje SLO 111 C3
Kobiór PL 86 B2
Koblenz
CH 106 B3
D 81 B3
Kobryn BY 13 B6
Kobylanka PL 75 A4
Kobylin PL 85 A5
Kobylniki PL 77 B5
Kocaali TR 187 A5
Kocaaliler TR 189 B5
Kocaeli = İzmit TR . 187 B4
Koçani MK 182 B4
Koçarlı TR 188 B2
Koceljevo SRB . . . 127 C1
Kočerin BIH 138 B3
Kočevje SLO 123 B3
Kočevska Reka
SLO 123 B3
Kochel am see D . . 108 B2
Kocs H 112 B2
Kocsér H 113 B3
Kocsola H 112 C2
Koczala PL 68 B2
Kodal N 53 A6
Kode S 60 B1
Kodersdorf D 84 A2
Kodrab PL 86 A3
Koekelare B 78 A2
Kofçaz TR 186 A2
Köflach A 110 B2
Køge DK 61 D2
Kohlberg D 95 B4
Kohtla-Järve EST . . 8 C5
Köinge S 60 B2
Kojetin CZ 98 B1
Kökar FIN 51 C7
Kokava SK 99 C3
Kokkinotrimithia . . . 181 A2
Kokkola FIN 3 E8
Kokori BIH 124 C3
Kokoski PL 69 A3
Koksijde B 78 A2
Kola
BIH 124 C3
RUS 3 B13
Køla S 54 A3
Kolari FIN 196 B6
Kolárovo SK 112 B1
Kołacin PL 87 A3
Kolašin MNE 16 D3
Kolbäck S 56 A2
Kolbacz PL 75 A3
Kolbeinsstaðir IS . . 190 C3
Kolbermoor D 108 B3
Kolbnitz A 109 C4
Kolbotn N 54 A1
Kolbu N 48 B2
Kolby Kås DK 59 C3
Kolczewo PL 67 C3
Kolczyglowy PL . . . 68 A2
Kolding DK 59 C2
Kölesd H 112 C2
Kolgrov N 46 A1
Kolín CZ 97 A3
Kolind DK 59 B3
Kolinec CZ 96 B1
Koljane HR 138 B2
Kølkær DK 59 B2
Kölleda D 82 A3
Kollum NL 70 A3
Köln = Cologne D . . 80 B2
Koło PL 76 B3
Kołobrzeg PL 67 B4
Kolochau D 83 A5
Kolomyya UA 13 D6
Kolonowskie PL . . . 86 B2
Koloveč CZ 95 B5
Kolpino RUS 9 C7
Kolrep D 73 A5
Kölsillre S 199 C12
Kolsko PL 75 C4
Kolsva S 56 A1
Kolta SK 112 A2
Kolunić BIH 138 A2
Koluszki PL 87 A3
Kolut SRB 125 B4
Kolvereid N 199 A8
Kølvrå D 59 B2
Komadi H 113 B5
Komagvær N 193 B14
Komarica BIH 125 C3
Komárno SK 112 B2
Komárom H 112 B2
Komatou Yialou
CY 181 A3
Komboti GR 182 D3
Komen SLO 122 B2
Komin HR 138 B3
Komiža HR 138 B2
Komjáti H 99 C4
Komjatice SK 112 A2
Komletinci HR 125 B4
Komló H 125 A4
Kömlo H 113 B4
Komoča SK 112 B2
Komorniki PL 75 B5
Komorzno PL 86 A2
Komotini GR 183 B7
Konak SRB 126 B2
Konakovo RUS . . . 9 D10
Konarzyny PL 68 B2
Kondias GR 183 D7
Kondopaga RUS . . 9 A9
Kondorfa H 111 C3
Kondoros H 113 C4
Konevo RUS 9 A11
Køng DK 65 A4
Konga S 63 B3
Köngäs FIN 196 B7
Kongerslev DK . . . 58 B3
Kongsberg N 53 A5
Kongshamn N 53 B4
Kongsmark DK . . . 64 A1
Kongsmoen N 199 A9
Kongsvik N 194 B7
Kongsvinger N 48 B3
Konice CZ 97 B4
Konie PL 77 C5
Koniecpol PL 86 B3
Königsberg D 82 B2
Königsbronn D . . . 94 C2
Königsbrück D 84 A1
Königsbrunn D . . . 94 C2
Konigsdorf D 108 B2
Königsee D 82 B3
Königshorst D 74 B1
Königslutter D 73 B3
Königssee D 109 B3
Königstein
Hessen D 81 B4
Sachsen D 84 B2
Königstetten A 97 C4
Königswartha D . . . 84 A2
Konigswiesen A . . . 96 C2
Königswinter D . . . 80 B3
Königs Wusterhausen
D 74 B2
Konin PL 76 B3
Konispol AL 182 D2
Konitsa GR 182 C2
Köniz CH 106 C2
Konjevići BIH 139 A5
Konjevrate HR 138 B2
Konjic BIH 139 B3
Konjščina HR 124 A2
Könnern D 83 A3
Konnerud N 53 A6
Konopiska PL 86 B2
Konotop PL 75 C4
Końskie PL 87 A4
Konsmo N 52 B3
Konstancin-Jeziorna
PL 77 B6
Konstantynów Łódzki
PL 86 A3
Konstanz D 107 B4
Kontich B 79 A4
Kontiolahti FIN 9 A6
Konya TR 189 B7

Konz D 92 B2
Kópasker IS 191 A9
Kópavogur IS 190 C4
Kopčany SK. 98 C1
Koper SLO 122 B2
Kopervik N. 52 A1
Kópháza H 111 B3
Kopice PL 85 B5
Kopidlno CZ 84 B3
Köping S 56 A1
Köpingebro S 66 A2
Köpingsvik S 62 B4
Köpmanholmen S . . 200 C4
Koppang N 48 A3
Koppangen N 192 C4
Kopparberg S 50 C1
Koppelo FIN 193 D11
Koppom S 54 A3
Koprivlen BG. 183 B5
Koprivna BIH. 125 C4
Koprivnica HR. . . . 124 A2
Kopřivnice CZ 98 B2
Köprübaşı TR 186 D3
Koprzywnica PL . . . 87 B5
Kopstal L 92 B2
Kopychyntsi UA 13 D6
Kopytkowo PL. 69 B3
Korbach D 81 A4
Körbecke D 81 A4
Korçe AL 182 C2
Korčula HR 138 C3
Korczyców PL 75 B3
Korenita SRB. 127 C1
Korets UA 13 C7
Korfantów PL. 85 B5
Körfez TR. 187 B4
Korgen N 195 D4
Korinth DK 64 A3
Korinthos = Corinth
    GR 184 B3
Korita
    BIH 138 A2
    HR 139 C3
Korithi GR 184 B1
Korkuteli TR 189 B5
Körmend H 111 B3
Korne PL 68 A2
Korneuburg A 97 C4
Kornevo RUS 69 A5
Kórnik PL. 76 B2
Kornsjø N 54 B2
Környe H 112 B2
Koromačno HR . . . 123 C3
Koroni GR 184 C2
Koronos GR 185 B6
Koronowo PL. 76 A2
Körösladány H 113 C5
Köröstarcsa H. 113 C5
Korosten UA 13 C8
Korostyshev UA . . . 13 C8
Korpikå S 196 D6
Korpikylä FIN 196 C6
Korpilombolo S . . . 196 C6
Korsberga
    Jönköping S 62 A3
    Skaraborg S 55 B5
Korshavn N 54 A1
Korskrogen S . . . 200 E1
Korsnäs S 50 B2
Korsør DK 65 A4
Korsun
    Shevchenkovskiy
    UA 13 D9
Korträsk S 196 D3
Kortrijk B 78 B3
Korucu TR 186 C2
Koryčany CZ 98 B1
Korzeńsko PL 85 A4
Korzybie PL. 68 A1
Kos GR 188 C2
Kosakowo PL. 69 A3
Kosanica MNE. . . . 139 B5
Kösching D 95 C3
Kościan PL 75 B5
Kościelec PL 76 B3
Kościerzyna PL. . . . 68 A2
Koserow D 66 B2
Košetice CZ. 97 B3
Košice SK 12 D4
Kosjerić SRB 127 D1
Koška HR 125 B4
Koskullskulle S . . . 196 B3
Kosovska Mitrovica
    KOS 16 D4
Kosta S 62 B3
Kostajnica HR . . . 124 B2
Kostajnik SRB. . . . 127 C1
Kostanjevica SLO . 123 B4
Kostelec nad Černými
    Lesy CZ 96 B2
Kostelec na Hané
    CZ 97 B5
Kostice CZ. 84 B1
Kostkowo PL. 68 A3
Kostojevići SRB . . 127 C1
Kostolac SRB 127 C3
Kostomłoty PL. 85 A4
Kostopil UA 13 C7
Kostów PL. 86 A2
Kostrzyn
    Lubuskie PL. 74 B3
    Wielkopolskie PL . . 76 B2
Koszalin PL 67 B5
Koszęcin PL. 86 B2
Köszeg H 111 B3
Koszwaly PL 69 A3
Koszyce PL 87 B4
Kot SLO 123 B4

Kotala FIN 197 B11
Kötelek H 113 B4
Köthen D 83 A3
Kotka FIN. 8 B5
Kotomierz PL. 76 A3
Kotor MNE. 16 D3
Kotoriba HR. 124 A2
Kotorsko BIH. 125 C4
Kotor Varoš BIH . . 124 C3
Kotovsk UA 17 B8
Kotronas GR 184 C3
Kötschach A 109 C3
Kötzting D 95 B4
Koudum NL 70 B2
Kouřim CZ 96 A2
Kout na Šumave CZ 95 B5
Kouvola FIN. 8 B5
Kovačevac SRB . . 127 C2
Kovačica SRB 126 B2
Kovdor RUS 197 B13
Kovel' UA 13 C6
Kovilj SRB 126 B2
Kovin SRB. 127 C2
Kowal PL 77 B4
Kowalewo Pomorskie
    PL. 69 B3
Kowalów PL. 75 B3
Kowary PL. 85 B3
Köyceğiz TR. 188 C3
Kozani GR 182 C3
Kozarac
    BIH 124 C2
    HR 124 B1
Kozárovce SK 98 C2
Kozelets UA. 13 C9
Kozica HR 138 B3
Koziegłowy PL. 86 B3
Kozienice PL 87 A5
Kozina SLO 122 B2
Kozje SLO 123 A4
Kozlu TR 187 A6
Kozluk BIH 139 A5
Koźmin PL. 85 A5
Koźminek PL. 86 A2
Kozolupy CZ 96 B1
Kožuchów PL. 84 A3
Kožuhe BIH 125 C4
Kozyatyn UA 13 D8
Kozyürük TR 186 A1
Kräckelbräken S . . 49 A6
Krackow D 74 A3
Kraddsele S 195 E7
Kråg D. 68 A1
Kragenæs DK 65 B4
Kragerø N 53 B5
Krągi PL. 68 B1
Kragujevac SRB . . 127 C2
Kraiburg D 109 A3
Krajenka PL. 68 B1
Krajišnik SRB 126 B2
Krajková CZ 83 B4
Krajné SK. 98 C1
Krajnik Dolny PL. . . 74 A3
Krakača BIH 124 B1
Kräklingbo S 57 C4
Kraków = Cracow
    PL. 99 A3
Krakow am See D . 73 A5
Králíky CZ 85 B4
Kraljevica HR 123 B3
Kraljevo SRB 16 D4
Kral'ovany SK. 99 B3
Král'ov Brod SK . . .111 A4
Kralovice CZ 96 B1
Kralupy nad Vltavou
    CZ 84 B2
Králův Dvůr CZ . . . 96 B2
Kramfors S 200 D3
Kramsach A 108 B2
Kramsk PL 76 B3
Kråmvik N 53 A4
Kranenburg D 80 A2
Krania GR 182 D3
Krania Elasonas
    GR 182 D4
Kranichfeld D 82 B3
Kranidi GR 184 B4
Kranj SLO 123 A3
Kranjska Gora
    SLO 109 C4
Krapanj HR 138 B1
Krapina HR 124 A1
Krapje HR 124 B2
Krapkowice PL. . . . 86 B1
Kraselov CZ. 96 B1
Krašić HR 123 B4
Kräslava LV 8 E5
Kraslice CZ 83 B4
Krasna PL 87 A4
Krasna Lipa CZ . . . 84 B2
Krasne PL 77 B5
Kraśnik PL. 12 C5
Krašnja SLO 123 A3
Krásno SK 98 B2
Krásnohorské
    Podhradie SK . . . 99 C4
Krasno Polje HR . . 123 C4
Krasnozavodsk
    RUS 9 D11
Krasnystaw PL 13 C5
Krasnyy RUS. 13 A9
Krasnyy Kholm
    RUS 9 C10
Krasocin PL 87 B4
Kraszewice PL. . . . 86 A2
Kraszkowice PL. . . 86 A2
Kratigos GR. 186 C1
Kratovo MK 182 A4

Kraubath A. 110 B1
Krausnick D. 74 B2
Krautheim D 94 B1
Kravaře CZ 84 B2
Kraváre CZ 98 B2
Kravarsko HR 124 B2
Kraznějov CZ. 96 B1
Krčedin SRB 126 B2
Kŭrdzhali BG. 183 B7
Krefeld D 80 A2
Kregme DK 61 D2
Krembz D 73 A4
Kremenets UA 13 C6
Kremmen D 74 B2
Kremna SRB 127 D1
Kremnica SK 98 C2
Krempe D 64 C2
Krems A 97 C3
Kremsbrücke A . . . 109 C4
Kremsmünster A . . .110 A1
Křemže CZ 96 C2
Křenov CZ 97 B4
Krepa PL 76 C3
Krępa Krajeńska PL 75 A5
Krepsko PL 68 B1
Kreševo BIH 139 B4
Kressbronn D 107 B4
Krestena GR 184 B2
Kretinga LT 8 E2
Kreuzau D 80 B2
Kreuzlingen CH. . . 107 B4
Kreuztal D 81 B3
Krewelin D 74 B2
Krezluk BIH 138 A3
Krichem BG. 183 A6
Krieglach A 110 B2
Kriegsfeld D 93 B3
Kriens CH 106 B3
Krimml A 108 B3
Krimpen aan de IJssel
    NL. 79 A4
Křinec CZ. 84 B3
Kristdala S 62 A4
Kristiansand N 53 B4
Kristianstad S 61 C4
Kristiansund N . . . 198 B4
Kristiinankaupunki
    FIN 8 A2
Kristinefors S 49 B4
Kristinehamn S . . . 55 A5
Kriváň SK. 99 C3
Kriva Palanka MK . 182 A4
Křivoklát CZ 96 A1
Kriz HR 124 B2
Křižanov CZ. 97 B4
Križevci HR 124 A2
Krk HR 123 B3
Krka SLO 123 B3
Krnjača SRB 127 C2
Krnjak HR 123 B4
Krnjeuša BIH 124 C2
Krnjevo SRB 127 C3
Krnov CZ 98 A1
Krobia PL. 85 A4
Kroczyce PL 86 B3
Krøderen N 48 B1
Krokees GR. 184 C3
Krokek S 56 B2
Krokom S 199 B11
Krokowa PL 68 A3
Krokstad-elva N . . . 53 A5
Kroksund N. 54 A2
Kroměříž CZ 98 B1
Krommenie NL 70 B1
Krompachy SK . . . 99 C4
Kronach D. 82 B3
Kronshagen D 64 B3
Kronshtadt RUS . . . 9 C6
Kröpelin D 65 B4
Kropp D 64 B2
Kroppenstedt D . . . 73 C4
Kropstädt D 74 C1
Krościenko nad
    Dunajcem PL . . . 99 B4
Kröslin D 66 B2
Krośnice PL. 85 A5
Krośniewice PL. . . . 77 B4
Krosno PL. 12 D4
Krosno Odrzańskie
    PL. 75 B4
Krostitz D 83 A4
Krotoszyn PL. 85 A5
Krottendorf A. 110 B2
Krouna CZ 97 B4
Krowiarki PL 86 B2
Krrabë AL. 182 B1
Kršan HR 123 B3
Krško SLO 123 B4
Krstac MNE 139 B4
Krstur SRB 126 A2
Křtiny CZ 97 B4
Kruft D 80 B3
Kruishoutem B 79 B3
Krujë AL 182 B1
Krumbach
    A. 111 B3
    D 94 C2
Krumovgrad BG . . 183 B7
Krün D 108 B2
Krupá CZ 84 B1
Krupa na Vrbasu
    BIH 124 C3
Krupanj SRB 127 C1
Krupina SK 99 C3
Kup
    H 111 B4
    PL. 86 B1

Krupki BY. 13 A8
Kruså DK 64 B2
Kruščica BIH 139 A3
Kruševac SRB 16 D4
Kruševo MK. 182 B3
Kruszwica PL. 76 B3
Kruszyn PL. 77 B4
Krychaw BY. 13 B9
Krynica PL. 99 B4
Krynica Morska PL . 69 A4
Krzęcin PL. 75 A4
Krzelów PL. 85 A4
Krzepice PL. 86 B2
Krzepielów PL. 85 A4
Krzeszowice PL. . . 86 B3
Krzeszyce PL. 75 B4
Krzynowlaga Mała
    PL. 77 A5
Krzywiń PL. 75 C5
Krzyżanowice PL. . 98 B2
Krzyżowa PL 99 B3
Krzyż Wielkopolski
    PL. 75 B5
Ksiaz Wielkopolski
    PL. 87 B4
Książ Wielkopolski
    PL. 76 B2
Ktębowiec PL 75 A5
Kübekháza H 126 A2
Küblis CH 107 C4
Kuchary PL 86 A1
Kuchl A. 109 B4
Kucice PL. 77 B5
Kuciste HR 138 C3
Kuçovë AL 182 C1
Küçükbahçe TR. . . 188 A1
Küçükköy TR. 186 C1
Küçükkuyu TR. . . . 186 C1
Kucura SRB. 126 B1
Kuddby S. 56 B2
Kudowa-Zdrój PL . . 85 B4
Kufstein A. 108 B3
Kuggeboda S 63 B3
Kuggören S 200 E3
Kühbach D. 95 C3
Kuhmo FIN. 3 D11
Kuhmoinen FIN. . . . 8 B4
Kuhnsdorf A 110 C1
Kuhstedt D 72 A1
Kuinre NL. 70 B2
Kuivaniemi FIN . . . 197 D8
Kuivastu EST. 8 C3
Kukës AL 182 A2
Kuklin PL 77 A5
Kukljica HR 137 A4
Kukujevci SRB . . . 127 B1
Kula
    Srbija SRB. 127 C3
    Vojvodina SRB. . . 126 B1
    TR 188 A3
Kuldīga LV 8 D2
Kulen Vakuf BIH . . 124 C2
Kulina BIH 125 C4
Kullstedt D. 82 A2
Kulmain D 95 B3
Kulmbach D. 82 B3
Kuloharju FIN . . . 197 D11
Kulu TR 23 B7
Kumafşarı TR . . . 189 B4
Kumane SRB. 126 B2
Kumanovo MK. . . . 182 A3
Kumbağ TR 186 B2
Kumdanlı TR 189 A5
Kumkale TR. 186 C1
Kumla S 56 A1
Kumlakyrkby S . . . 50 C3
Kumlinge FIN 51 B7
Kumluca TR. 189 C5
Kumrovec HR 123 A4
Kunadacs H. 112 C3
Kunágota H 113 C5
Kunbaja H 126 A1
Kunda EST. 8 C5
Kundl A 108 B2
Kunes N 193 B10
Kunfehértó H 126 A1
Kungälv S 60 B1
Kungsängen S 57 A3
Kungsäter S 60 B2
Kungsbacka S. . . . 60 B2
Kungsgården S. . . . 50 B3
Kungshamn S 54 B2
Kungs-Husby S . . . 56 A3
Kungsör S 56 A2
Kunhegyes H. 113 B4
Kunmadaras H . . . 113 B4
Kunovice CZ 98 B1
Kunów PL 87 B5
Kunowo
    Wielkopolskie PL. . 76 C2
    Zachodnio-Pomorskie
    PL. 74 A3
Kunštát CZ 97 B4
Kunszállás H 113 C3
Kunszentmárton
    H 113 C4
Kunszentmiklós H .112 B3
Kunžak CZ. 97 B3
Künzelsau D 94 B1
Kuolayarvi RUS. . . 197 C12
Kuolio FIN. 197 D11
Kuopio FIN 8 A5
Kuosku FIN 197 B11

Kupferzell D. 94 B1
Kupinec HR 123 B4
Kupinečki Kraljevac
    HR 124 B1
Kupinovo SRB. . . . 127 C2
Kupirovo HR 138 A2
Kupjak HR 123 B3
Kuppenheim D 93 C4
Kupres BIH 138 B3
Küps D 82 B3
Kurd H 112 C2
Küre TR 23 A7
Kuressaare EST . . . 8 C3
Kurikka FIN 8 A3
Kuřim CZ 97 B4
Kuřivody CZ 84 B2
Kurki PL. 77 A5
Kurort Oberwiesenthal
    D 83 B4
Kurort Schmalkalden
    D 82 B2
Kurort Stolberg D . . 82 A2
Kurort Wippra D . . . 82 A3
Kurów PL. 12 C5
Kurowice PL 86 A3
Kurravaara S 196 B3
Kursu FIN 197 C11
Kurşunlu
    Bursa TR. 187 B4
    Çankırı TR. 23 A7
Kurtakko FIN 196 B7
Kürten D 80 A3
Kurucaşile TR. . . . 187 A7
Kurvinen FIN 197 D12
Kurzelów PL 87 B3
Kusadak SRB 127 C2
Kuşadası TR 188 B2
Kusel D 93 B3
Kusey D 73 B4
Küsnacht CH. 106 B3
Kütahya TR 187 C4
Kutenholz D 72 A2
Kutina HR 124 B2
Kutjevo HR 125 B3
Kutná Hora CZ. . . . 97 B3
Kutno PL 77 B4
Kuttara FIN 193 D10
Küttingen CH 106 B3
Kúty SK 98 C1
Kuusamo FIN 197 D12
Kuusankoski FIN . . 8 B5
Kuvshinovo RUS . . 9 D9
Kuyucak TR 188 B3
Kuzmin SRB 127 B1
Kuźnia Raciborska
    PL. 86 B2
Kuźnica Czarnkowska
    PL. 75 B5
Kuźnica Żelichowska
    PL. 75 B5
Kvåløyvestia N . . . 192 C2
Kvalsund N 192 B7
Kvam
    Nord-Trøndelag
    N. 199 A8
    Oppland N 198 D6
Kvamsøy N 46 A3
Kvanndal N. 46 A3
Kvänum S 55 B4
Kværndrup DK. . . . 59 C3
Kvås N. 52 B3
Kvasice CZ 98 B1
Kvelde N 53 A5
Kvenna N 198 C5
Kvernaland N 52 B1
Kvibille S 60 C2
Kvicksund S 56 A2
Kvidinge S 61 C3
Kvikkjokk S 195 D8
Kvikne
    Hedmark N. 199 C7
    Oppland N 47 A6
Kville S 54 B2
Kvillsfors S 62 A3
Kvinesdal N 52 B2
Kvinlog N 52 B2
Kvinnherad N 46 C3
Kvissel DK. 58 A3
Kvissleby S 200 D3
Kviteseid N 53 A4
Kvitsøy N 52 A1
Kwakowo PL 68 A2
Kwidzyn PL. 69 B3
Kwilcz PL. 75 B5
Kyjov CZ 98 C1
Kyleakin GB. 31 B3
Kyle of Lochalsh
    GB 31 B3
Kylerhea GB 31 B3
Kylestrome GB . . . 32 C1
Kyllburg D 80 B2
Kyllini GR 184 B2
Kynsperk nad Ohří
    CZ 83 B4
Kyperounda CY. . . 181 B1
Kyrenia CY. 181 A2
Kyritz D 73 B5
Kyrkesund S 60 A1
Kyrkhult S 63 B2
Kyrksæterøra N. . . 198 B6
Kysucké Nové Mesto
    SK 98 B2
Kythira GR. 184 C3
Kythréa CY 181 A2
Kyustendil BG. . . . 16 D5
Kyyiv = Kiev UA. . . 13 C9

Kyyjärvi FIN 8 A4

L

Laa an der Thaya A . 97 C4
La Adrada E 150 B3
Laage D 65 C5
La Alameda E 157 B4
La Alberca E 149 B3
La Alberca de Zàncara
    E. 158 B1
La Albergueria de
    Argañán E 149 B3
La Albuera E 155 C4
La Aldea del Portillo del
    Busto E 143 B3
La Algaba E 162 A1
La Aliseda de Tormes
    E. 150 B2
La Almarcha E 158 B1
La Almolda E 153 A3
La Almunia de Doña
    Godina E 152 A2
Laanila FIN 193 D11
La Antillas E 161 B2
La Arena E 141 A4
Laatzen D 72 B2
La Aulaga E 161 B3
La Balme-de-Sillingy
    F. 118 B3
La Bañeza E 141 B5
La Barca de la Florida
    E. 162 B2
La Barre-de-Monts
    F. 114 B1
La Barre-en-Ouche
    F. 89 B4
La Barrosa E 162 B1
La Barthe-de-Neste
    F. 145 A4
La Bassée F 78 B2
La Bastide-de-Sèrou
    F. 146 A2
La Bastide-des-
    Jourdans F 132 B1
Labastide-Murat F . 129 B4
La Bastide-Puylaurent
    F. 117 C3
Labastide-Rouairoux
    F. 130 B1
Labastide-St Pierre
    F. 129 C4
La Bathie F 118 B3
Lábatlan H 112 B2
La Baule-Escoublac
    F. 101 B3
La Bazoche-Gouet
    F. 102 A2
La Bégude-de-Mazenc
    F. 131 A3
Labenne F 128 C1
La Bernerie-en-Retz
    F. 114 A1
Labin HR 123 B3
La Bisbal d'Empordà
    E. 147 C4
Łabiszyn PL. 76 B2
Lablachère F 131 A3
Lábod H 124 A3
Laboe D. 64 B3
La Boissière F 89 A4
Labouheyre F 128 B2
La Bourboule F . . .116 B2
La Bóveda de Toro
    E. 150 A2
Łabowa PL. 99 B4
La Brède F 128 B2
La Bresse F 106 A1
La Bridoire F 118 B2
La Brillanne F 132 B1
Labrit F 128 B2
Labros E 152 A2
La Bruffière F 114 A2
Labruguière F 130 B1
Labrujo P. 148 A1
L'Absie F 114 B3
La Bussière F 103 B4
Laç AL 182 B1
La Caillère F 114 B3
Lacalahorra E 164 B1
La Caletta
    Cágliari I. 179 C2
    Núoro I. 178 B3
La Calmette F 131 B3
La Calzada de Oropesa
    E. 150 C2
La Campana E 162 A2
La Cañada E 150 B3
Lacanau F 128 B1
Lacanau-Océan F . 128 A1
Lacanche F 104 B3
La Canourgue F . . 130 A2
La Capelle F. 91 B3
Lacapelle-Marival
    F. 129 B4
Lácara SRB 127 B1
La Cardanchosa E 156 B2
La Caridad E 141 A4
La Carlota E 162 A3
La Carolina E 157 B4
La Cava E 153 B4
La Cavalerie F . . . 130 A2
Laceby GB 41 B3

Lacedónia I 172 A1
La Celle-en-Moravan
  F. 104 B3
La Celle-St Avant
  F. 102 B2
La Cerca E 143 B3
Láces I 108 C1
La Chaise-Dieu F. . .117 C2
La Chaize-Giraud
  F. 114 B2
La Chaize-le-Vicomte
  F. 114 B2
La Chambre F 118 B3
Lachania GR 188 D2
La Chapelaude F . .116 A2
La Chapelle-d'Angillon
  F. 103 B4
La Chapelle-en-
  Aalgaudémar F. . 118 C3
La Chapelle-en-Vercors
  F. 118 C2
La Chapelle-Glain
  F. 101 B4
La Chapelle-la-Reine
  F. 90 C2
La Chapelle-Laurent
  F. 116 B3
La Chapelle-St Luc
  F. 91 C4
La Chapelle-sur-Erdre
  F. 101 B4
La Chapelle-Vicomtesse
  F. 103 B3
La Charce F 132 A1
La Charité-sur-Loire
  F. 104 B2
La Chartre-sur-le-Loir
  F. 102 B2
La Châtaigneraie
  F. 114 B3
La Châtre F 103 C3
La Chaussée-sur-Marne
  F. 91 C4
La Chaux-de-Fonds
  CH 106 B1
Lachen CH. 107 B3
Lachendorf D 72 B3
La Cheppe F 91 B4
La Chèze F 101 A3
Lachowice PL 99 B3
La Ciotat F 132 B1
Łąck PL 77 B4
Läckeby S 62 B4
Läckö S 55 B4
La Clayette F 117 A4
La Clusaz F 118 B3
Lacock GB 43 A4
La Codosera E 155 B3
La Concha E 143 A3
La Condamine-
  Châtelard F. 132 A2
Láconi I 179 C3
La Contienda E . . . 161 A3
La Coquille F 115 C4
La Coronada E . . . 156 B2
La Côte-St André
  F. 118 B2
La Cotinière F 114 C2
La Courtine F 116 B2
Lacq F 145 A3
La Crau F 132 B2
La Crèche F 115 B3
La Croix F 102 B2
Lacroix-Barrez F. . . 116 C2
Lacroix-St Ouen F . . 90 B2
Lacroix-sur-Meuse
  F. 92 C1
La Croix-Valmer F . 132 B2
La Cumbre E 156 A2
Łącznik PL 86 B1
Lad H 125 A3
Ladbergen D 71 B4
Lądek-Zdrój PL 85 B4
Ladelund D 64 B2
Ladendorf A. 97 C4
Ladignac-le-Long
  F. 115 C5
Ladíspoli I 168 B2
Ladoeiro P 155 B3
Ladon F 103 B4
La Douze F. 129 A3
Ladushkin RUS. . . . 69 A5
Ladybank GB. 35 B4
Laer D 71 B4
La Espina E 141 A4
La Estrella E 156 A2
La Farga de Moles
  E. 146 B2
La Fatarella E 153 A4
La Felipa E 158 B2
La Fère F 90 B3
La Ferrière
  Indre-et-Loire F . .102 B2
  Vendée F 114 B2
La Ferrière-en-
  Parthenay F. 115 B3
La-Ferté-Alais F . . . 90 C2
La-Ferté-Bernard
  F. 102 A2
La Ferté-Frênel F. . . 89 B4
La Ferté-Gaucher F. 90 C3
La Ferté-Imbault F. 103 B3
La Ferté-Macé F . . . 89 B3
La Ferté-Milon F . . . 90 B3

La Ferté-sous-Jouarre
  F. 90 C3
La Ferté-St-Aubin
  F. 103 B3
La Ferté-St-Cyr F. . 103 B3
La Ferté-Vidame F. . 89 B4
La Ferté Villeneuil
  F. 103 B3
La Feuillie F 90 B1
Lafkos GR 183 D5
La Flèche F 102 B1
La Flotte F 114 B2
Lafnitz A. 111 B3
La Font de la Figuera
  E. 159 C3
La Fouillade F 130 A1
Lafrançaise F 129 B4
La Fregeneda E. . . 149 B3
La Fresneda E. . . . 153 B4
La Fuencubierta E. 162 A3
La Fuente de San
  Esteban E 149 B3
La Fulioala E 147 C2
La Gacilly F 101 B3
La Galera E 153 B4
Lagan S 60 C3
Laganadi I 175 C1
Lagarde F 146 A2
La Garde-Freinet F 132 B2
Lagares
  Coimbra P 148 B2
  Porto P 148 A1
La Garnache F. 114 B2
Lagaro I 135 A4
La Garriga E 147 C3
La Garrovilla E . . . 155 C4
Lagartera E 150 C2
La Gaubretière F. . .114 B2
Lågbol S 51 B5
Lage D 72 C1
Lägerdorf D 64 C2
Lagg GB. 34 C2
Laggan GB. 32 D2
Laggartorp S 55 A5
Łagiewniki PL 85 B4
La Gineta E 158 B1
Láglio I. 120 B2
Lagnieu F 118 B2
Lagny-sur-Marne F . 90 C2
Lago
  Calabria I 175 B2
  Veneto I 121 B5
Lagôa P 160 B1
Lagoaça P 149 A3
Lagonegro I. 174 A1
Lagos
  GR 183 B7
  P. 160 B1
Lagosanto I 121 C5
Łagów
  Lubuskie PL 75 B4
  Świętokrzyskie PL . 87 B5
La Granadella
  Alicante E 159 C4
  Lleida E 153 A4
La Grand-Combe F 131 A3
La Grande-Croix F .117 B4
La Grande-Motte F 131 B3
La Granja d'Escarp
  E. 153 A4
La Granjuela E . . . 156 B2
Lagrasse F 146 A3
La Grave F 118 B3
La Gravelle F 101 A4
Laguardia E 143 B4
La Guardia E 151 C4
La Guardia de Jaén
  E. 163 A4
Laguarres E 145 B4
Laguenne F 116 B1
Laguépie F 129 B4
La Guerche-de-Bretagne
  F. 101 B4
La Guerche-sur-l'Aubois
  F. 104 C1
La Guérinière F . . .114 B1
Laguiole F 116 C2
Laguna de Duera
  E. 150 A3
Laguna del Marquesado
  E. 152 B2
Laguna de Negrillos
  E. 142 B1
Lagundo I 108 C2
Lagunilla E 149 B3
La Haba E 156 B2
Laharie F 128 B1
La Haye-du-Puits F . 88 A2
La Haye-Pesnel F . . 88 B2
Lahden D 71 B4
La Herlière F 78 B2
La Hermida E 142 A2
La Herrera E 158 C1
Laheycourt F 91 C5
La Higuera E 158 C2
La Hiniesta E 149 A4
Lahnstein D 81 B3
Laholm S 61 C3
La Horcajada E . . . 150 B2
La Horra E 143 C3
Lahr D 93 C3
Lahti FIN 8 B4
La Hulpe B 79 B4
La Hutte F 89 B4
Laichingen D 94 C1
L'Aigle F. 89 B4
La Iglesuela E 150 B3

La Iglesuela del Cid
  E. 153 B3
Laignes F. 104 B3
Laiguéglia I 133 B4
L'Aiguillon-sur-Mer
  F. 114 B2
Laimbach am Ostrong
  A. 97 C3
Laina E. 152 A1
Lainio S 196 B5
Lairg GB. 32 C2
La Iruela E 164 B2
Laissac F 130 A1
Laisvall S 195 D8
Láives I 121 A4
La Javie F 132 A2
Lajkovac SRB 127 C2
La Jonchère-St Maurice
  F. 116 A1
La Jonquera E 146 B3
Lajoskomárom H . . 112 C2
Lajosmizse H. 112 B3
Lak H 99 C4
Lakenheath GB 45 A4
Laki BG 183 B6
Lakitelek H. 113 C4
Lakki GR 185 D4
Lakolk DK 64 A1
Łąkorz PL 69 B4
Lakšárska Nová Ves
  SK 98 C1
Lakselv N. 193 B8
Laksfors N 195 E4
Laktaši BIH 124 C3
La Lantejuela E . . . 162 A2
Lalapaşa TR. 186 A1
L'Albagès E 153 A4
Lalbenque F 129 B4
L'Alcudia E 159 B3
L'Aldea E 153 B4
Lalín E 140 B2
Lalinde F 129 B3
La Línea de la
  Concepción E . . . 162 B2
Lalizolle F 116 A3
La Llacuna E 147 C2
Lalley F 118 C2
Lalling D 95 C5
Lalm N 198 D6
La Londe-les-Maures
  F. 132 B2
La Loupe F. 89 B5
La Louvière B 79 B4
L'Alpe-d'Huez F . . .118 B3
La Luisiana E. 162 A2
Laluque F 128 C1
Lam D 95 B5
La Machine F 104 C2
la Maddalena I 178 A3
Lama dei Peligni I . 169 A4
Lamadrid E 142 A2
Lamagistère F 129 B3
La Mailleraye-sur-Seine
  F. 89 A4
La Malène F 130 A2
Lama Mocogno I . . 135 A3
La Mamola E 163 B4
La Manresana dels Prats
  E. 147 C2
Lamarche F 105 A4
Lamarche-sur-Saône
  F. 105 B4
Lamargelle F 105 B3
Lamarosa P 154 B2
Lamarque F 128 A2
Lamas P. 148 B1
La Masadera E. . . . 145 C3
Lamas de Moaro P 140 B2
Lamastre F 117 C4
La Mata E 150 C3
La Mata de Ledesma
  E. 149 A4
La Mata de Monteagudo
  E. 142 B1
Lambach A. 109 A4
Lamballe F 101 A3
Lamberhurst GB . . . 45 B4
Lambesc F 131 B4
Lambia GR. 184 B2
Lambley GB. 37 B4
Lambourn GB 44 B2
Lamego P. 148 A2
La Meilleraye-de-
  Bretagne F 101 B4
La Ménitré F 102 B1
L'Ametlla de Mar E 153 B4
Lamia GR. 182 E4
Lammhult S. 62 A2
La Mojonera E 164 C2
La Mole F 132 B2
La Molina E 147 B2
La Monnerie-le-Montel
  F. 117 B3
La Morera E 155 C4
La Mothe-Achard
  F. 114 B2
Lamothe-Cassel F. 129 B4
Lamothe-Montravel
  F. 128 B3
La Mothe-St Héray
  F. 115 B3
Lamotte-Beuvron
  F. 103 B4
La Motte-Chalançon
  F. 131 A4
La Motte-du-Caire
  F. 132 A2

La Motte-Servolex
  F. 118 B2
Lampertheim D 93 B4
Lampeter GB 39 B2
L'Ampolla E 153 B4
Lamprechtshausen
  A. 109 B3
Lamsfeld D 74 C3
Lamspringe D 72 C3
Lamstedt D 72 A2
La Mudarra E. 142 C2
La Muela E 152 A2
La Mure F 118 C2
Lamure-sur-Azergues
  F. 117 A4
Lana I 108 C2
Lanaja E 145 C3
Lanarce F 117 C3
Lanark GB 36 A3
La Nava E 161 B3
La Nava de Ricomalillo
  E. 156 A3
La Nava de Santiago
  E. 155 B4
Lancaster GB 37 B4
Lanchester GB 37 B5
Lanciano I 169 A4
Lancing GB 44 C3
Lançon-Provence
  F. 131 B4
Lancova Vas SLO . 124 A1
Landau
  Bayern D 95 C4
  Rheinland-Pfalz D . 93 B4
Landeck A 108 B1
Landen B 79 B5
Landerneau F 100 A1
Landeryd S 60 B3
Landesbergen D . . . 72 B2
Landete E 158 B2
Landévant F 100 B2
Landévennec F . . . 100 A1
Landeyjahöfn 190 D5
Landivisiau F 100 A1
Landivy F 88 B2
Landl A 108 B3
Landön S 199 B11
Landos F 117 C3
Landouzy-le-Ville F . 91 B4
Landquart CH 107 C4
Landrecies F 91 A3
Landreville F 104 A3
Landriano I 120 B2
Landsberg D 108 A1
Lands-berg D 83 A4
Landsbro S 62 A2
Landscheid D 92 B2
Landshut D 95 C4
Landskrona S 61 D2
Landstuhl D. 93 B3
Lanesborough IRL . . 28 A4
Lanester F 100 B2
Lanestosa E 143 A3
La Neuve-Lyre F . . . 89 B4
La Neuveville CH. . 106 B2
Langå DK. 59 B2
Langada GR 185 A7
Langadas GR 183 C5
Langa de Duero E . 151 A4
Langadia GR 184 B3
Langangen N 53 A5
Långared S 60 A2
Långaröd S 61 D3
Långaryd S 60 B3
Långås S 60 C2
Långasjö S 63 B3
Langau A 97 C3
Langeac F 117 B3
Langeais F 102 B2
Langedijk NL 70 B1
Langeln D 73 C3
Langelsheim D 72 C3
Langemark-Poelkapelle
  B. 78 B2
Langen
  Hessen D 93 B4
  Niedersachsen D . 72 A1
Langenau D 94 C2
Langenberg D 81 A4
Langenbruck CH. . . 106 B2
Langenburg D 94 B1
Längenfeld A 108 B1
Langenfeld D. 80 A2
Langenhorn D 64 B1
Langenlois A. 97 C3
Langenlonsheim D . 93 B3
Langennaudorf D . . 83 A5
Langenneufnach D . 94 C2
Langenthal CH . . . 106 B2
Langenzenn D 94 B2
Langeoog D 71 A4
Langeskov DK. 59 C3
Langesund N 53 A5
Langewiesen D 82 B2
Långflon S 49 A4
Langförden D 71 B5
Langhagen D 73 A5
Länghem S 60 B3
Langhirano I 120 C3
Langholm GB 36 A4
Langholt IS 191 D7
Långlöt S 62 B4
Langnau CH 106 C2
Langø DK. 65 B4
Langogne F 117 C3
Langon F 128 B2
Langquaid D 95 C4
Långrådna S 56 B2

Langreo E 142 A1
Langres F 105 B4
Långsele S. 200 C3
Långserud S 54 A3
Langset N 48 B3
Långshyttan S. 50 B3
Langstrand N 192 B7
Långträsk S 196 D3
Langueux F 101 A3
Langvassdal N 195 E4
Längvik S 57 A4
Langwarden D. 71 A5
Langwathby GB 37 B4
Langwedel D 72 B2
Langweid D 94 C2
Langwies CH 107 C4
Lanheses P 148 A1
Lanięta PL 77 B4
Lanildut F 100 A1
Lanjarón E 163 B4
Lanmeur F 100 A2
Lanna
  Jönköping S. 60 B3
  Örebro S 55 A5
Lännaholm S 51 C4
Lannavaara S 196 A4
Lannéanou F 100 A2
Lannemezan F . . . 145 A4
Lanneuville-sur-Meuse
  F. 91 B5
Lannilis F 100 A1
Lannion F 100 A2
La Nocle-Maulaix
  F. 104 C2
Lanouaille F 115 C5
Lansjärv S 196 C5
Lanškroun CZ 97 B4
Lanslebourg-Mont-
  Cenis F 119 B3
Lanta F 129 C4
Lantadilla E 142 B2
Lanton F 128 B1
Lantosque F 133 B3
La Nuez de Arriba
  E. 143 B3
Lanusei I 179 C3
Lanúvio I 168 B2
Lanvollon F 100 A3
Lány CZ 96 A4
Lánycsók H 125 A4
Lanz D 73 A4
Lanza E 140 A2
Lanzada E 140 B2
Lanzahíta E 150 B3
Lanžhot CZ. 97 C4
Lanzo Torinese I . . .119 B4
Laole SRB 127 C3
Laon F 91 B3
Laons F 89 B5
La Paca E 164 B3
La Pacaudière F . . .117 A3
Lapalisse F 117 A3
La Palma d'Ebre E 153 A4
La Palma del Condado
  E. 161 B3
La Palme F 146 B4
La Palmyre F 114 C2
La Parra E 155 C4
Łapczyna Wola PL. . 87 B3
La Pedraja de Portillo
  E. 150 A3
La Peraleja E 152 B1
La Petit-Pierre F . . . 93 C3
Lapeyrade F 128 B2
Lapeyrouse F 116 A2
Lapford GB 42 B3
La Pinilla E 165 B3
Lapithos CY. 181 A2
La Plagne F 118 B3
La Plaza E 141 A4
Laplume F 129 B3
La Pobla de Lillet
  E. 147 B2
La Pobla de Vallbona
  E. 159 B3
La Pobla Llarga E . 159 B3
La Pola de Gordón
  E. 142 B1
la Porta F 180 A2
La Pouëze F 102 B1
Lapoutroie F 106 A2
La Póveda de Soria
  E. 143 B4
Lapovo SRB 127 C3
Läppe S 56 A1
Lappeenranta FIN . . 8 B6
Lappoluobbal N . . . 192 C7
Lappträsk S 196 C6
La Preste F 146 B3
La Primaube F 130 A1
Lapseki TR. 186 B1
Lapua FIN 8 A3
La Puebla de Almoradie
  E. 157 A4
La Puebla de Cazalla
  E. 162 A2
La Puebla de los
  Infantes E 162 A2
La Puebla del Río
  E. 162 A1
La Puebla de Montalbán
  E. 150 C3
La Puebla de Roda
  E. 145 B4
La Puebla de Valdavia
  E. 142 B2
La Puebla de Valverde
  E. 152 B3
La Pueblanueva E. 150 C3

La Puerta de Segura
  E. 164 A2
La Punt CH 107 C4
L'Áquila I 169 A3
La Quintana E 162 A3
La Quintera E 162 A2
La Rábita
  Granada E 164 C1
  Jaén E 163 A3
Laracha E 140 A2
Laragh IRL 30 A2
Laragne-Montéglin
  F. 132 A1
La Rambla E 163 A3
l'Arboç E 147 C2
L'Arbresle F. 117 B4
Lärbro S. 57 C4
Larceveau F 144 A2
Larche
  Alpes-de-Haute-
   Provence F. 132 A2
  Corrèze F 129 A4
Lårdal N 53 A4
Lærdalsøyri N 47 A4
Lardosa P 155 B3
La Reale I 178 A2
Laredo E 143 A3
La Redondela E . . . 161 B2
La Réole F 128 B2
Largentière F 131 A3
L'Argentière-la-Bessée
  F. 118 C3
Largs GB 34 C3
Lari I 134 B3
La Riera E 141 A4
La Riera de Gaià E 147 C2
La Rinconada E. . . 162 A1
Lariño E 140 B1
Larino I. 170 B2
Larisa GR. 182 D4
La Rivière-Thibouville
  F. 89 A4
Larkhall GB 36 A3
Larkollen N 54 A1
Larmor-Plage F . . . 100 B2
Larnaca CY 181 B2
Larne GB 27 B5
La Robla E 142 B1
La Roche F 106 C2
La Rochebeaucourt-
  Argentine F 115 C4
La Roche-Bernard
  F. 101 B3
La Roche-Canillac
  F. 116 B1
La Roche-Chalais
  F. 128 A3
La Roche Derrien
  F. 100 A2
La Roche-des-Arnauds
  F. 132 A1
La Roche-en-Ardenne
  B. 80 B1
La Roche-en-Brénil
  F. 104 B3
La Rochefoucauld
  F. 115 C4
La Roche-Guyon F . 90 B1
La Rochelle F 114 B2
La Roche-Posay F . 115 B4
La Roche-sur-Foron
  F. 118 A3
La Roche-sur-Yon
  F. 114 B2
Larochette L 92 B2
La Rochette F 131 A4
La Roda
  Albacete E 158 B1
  Oviedo E 141 A4
La Roda de Andalucía
  E. 162 A3
Laroquebrou F . . . 116 C2
La Roquebrussanne
  F. 132 B1
Laroque d'Olmes
  F. 146 B2
La Roque-Gageac
  F. 129 B4
La Roque-Ste
  Marguerite F. . . . 130 A2
Laroque-Timbaut
  F. 129 B3
Larouco E 141 B3
Larraga E 144 B2
Larrau F 144 A3
Larrazet F 129 C4
Larsnes N 198 C2
La Rubia E 143 C4
Laruns F 145 A3
Larva E 164 B1
Larvik N 53 A6
La Sagrada E 149 B3
La Salceda E 151 A4
Lasalle F 131 A2
La Salle F 118 C3
la Salute di Livenza
  I 122 B1
La Salvetat-Peyralès
  F. 130 A1
La Salvetat-sur-Agout
  F. 130 B1
Las Arenas E 142 A2
La Sarraz CH 105 C5
Lasarte E 144 A1
Låsby DK 59 B2
Las Cabezadas E . 151 A4

Las Cabezas de San
  Juan E 162 B2
Las Corredéras E . 157 B4
Las Cuevas de Cañart
  E 153 B3
La Seca E 150 A3
La Selva del Camp
  E 147 C2
La Senia E 153 B4
La Serra E 147 C2
La Seu d'Urgell E . 146 B2
La Seyne-sur-Mer
  F 132 B1
Las Gabias E 163 A4
Las Herencias E . . 150 C3
Las Herrerías E . . . 161 B2
Łasin PL 69 B4
Lask PL 86 A3
Laska PL 68 B2
Łaskarzow PL 87 A5
Laško SLO 123 A4
Laskowice PL 76 A3
Las Labores E 157 A4
Las Mesas E 158 B1
Las Minas E 164 A3
Las Navas E 163 A3
Las Navas de la
  Concepción E . . . 156 C2
Las Navas del Marqués
  E 150 B3
Las Navillas E 157 A3
Las Negras E 164 C3
La Solana E 157 B4
La Souterraine F . . .116 A1
Las Pajanosas E . . 161 B3
Laspaules E 145 B4
Las Pedroñas E . . . 158 B1
La Spézia I 134 A2
Las Planes d'Hostoles
  E 147 B3
Laspuña E 145 B4
Las Rozas
  Cantabria E 142 B2
  Madrid E 151 B4
Lassan D 66 C2
Lassay-les-Châteaux
  F 89 B3
Lasseube F 145 A3
Lassigny F 90 B2
La Storta I 168 B2
Lastovo HR 138 C2
Lastras de Cuéllar
  E 151 A3
Lästringe S 56 B3
Lastrup D 71 B4
Las Uces E 149 A3
La Suze-sur-Sarthe
  F 102 B2
Las Veguillas E . . . 149 B4
Las Ventas con Peña
  Aguilera E 157 A3
Las Ventas de San
  Julián E 150 B2
Las Villes E 153 B4
Latasa E 144 B2
Látera I 168 A1
Laterza I 171 C4
La Teste F 128 B1
Lathen D 71 B4
Latheron GB 32 C3
La Thuile I 119 B3
Latiano I 173 B3
Latina I 169 B2
Latisana I 122 B2
Látky SK 99 C3
La Toba E 152 B2
La Toledana E 157 A3
La Torre de Cabdella
  E 146 B1
La Torre de Esteban
  Hambrán E 151 B3
La Torre del l'Espanyol
  E 153 A4
La Torresaviñán E . 152 B1
La Tour d'Aigues
  F 132 B1
La Tour de Peilz
  CH 106 C1
La Tour-du-Pin F . . .118 B2
La Tranche-sur-Mer
  F 114 B2
La Tremblade F . . . 114 C2
La Trimouille F 115 B5
La Trinité F 100 B2
La Trinité-Porhoët
  F 101 A3
Latrónico I 174 A2
Latronquière F 116 C2
Latterbach CH 106 C2
La Turballe F 101 B3
Laubach D 81 B4
Laubert F 117 C3
Laucha D 83 A3
Lauchhammer D . . . 84 A1
Lauchheim D 94 C2
Lauda-Königshofen
  D 94 B1
Laudal N 52 B3
Lauder GB 35 C5
Lauenau D 72 B2
Lauenburg D 73 A3
Lauf D 95 B3
Laufach D 94 A1
Laufen
  CH 106 B2
  D 109 B3
Lauffen D 93 B5
Laugar IS 191 B8

Laugarás IS 190 C5
Laugarbakki IS 190 B5
Laugarvatn IS 190 C5
Laugharne GB 39 C2
Lauingen D 94 C2
Laujar de Andarax
  E 164 C2
Laukaa FIN 8 A4
Lauker S 196 D2
Laukvik N 194 C5
La Uña E 142 A1
Launceston GB . . . 42 B2
La Unión E 165 B4
Launois-sur-Vence
  F 91 B4
Laupheim D 94 C1
Lauragh IRL 29 C2
Laureana di Borrello
  I 175 C2
Laurencekirk GB . . . 35 B5
Laurencetown IRL . . 28 A3
Laurenzana I 172 B1
Lauria I 174 A1
Laurière F 116 A1
Laurieston GB 36 B2
Laurino I 172 B1
Lausanne CH 106 C1
Laussonne F 117 C4
Lauta D 84 A2
Lautenthal D 82 A2
Lauterach A 107 B4
Lauterbach D 81 B5
Lauterbrunnen CH 106 C2
Lauterecken D 93 B3
Lauterhofen D 95 B3
Lautrec F 130 B1
Lauvsnes N 199 A7
Lauvvlk N 52 B2
Lavagna I 134 A2
Laval F 102 A1
La Vall d'Uixó E . . . 159 B3
Lavamünd A 110 C1
Lavara GR 186 A1
Lavardac F 129 B3
Lavaris P 148 B1
Lavarone I 121 B4
Lavau F 104 B1
Lavaur F 129 C4
La Vecilla de Curueño
  E 142 B1
La Vega
  Asturias E 141 A5
  Asturias E 142 A1
  Cantabria E 142 A2
Lavelanet F 146 B2
La Velilla E 151 A4
La Velles E 150 A2
Lavello I 172 A1
Lavelsloh D 72 B1
Lavenham GB 45 A4
Laveno I 120 B1
La Ventosa E 152 B1
Lavezzola I 135 A4
Laviano I 172 B1
La Victoria E 162 A3
La Vid E 151 A4
Lavik N 46 A2
La Vilavella E 159 B3
La Vilella Baixa E . 147 C1
La Villa de Don Fadrique
  E 157 A4
Lavilledieu F 131 A3
La Villedieu F 115 B3
La Ville Dieu-du-Temple
  F 129 B4
Lavinio-Lido di Enea
  I 168 B2
Lav is I 121 A4
Lavit F 129 C3
Lavoncourt F 105 B4
Lavos P 148 B1
La Voulte-sur-Rhône
  F 117 C4
Lavoûte-Chilhac F .117 B3
Lavradio P 154 C1
Lavre P 154 C2
Lavrio GR 185 B5
La Wantzenau F . . . 93 C3
Lawers GB 35 B3
Ławy PL 75 B3
Laxá S 55 B5
Laxamýri IS 191 B8
Laxe E 140 A2
Laxey GB 36 B2
Laxford Bridge GB . 32 C1
Laxhall S 55 B4
Laxsjö S 199 B11
Laxtjarn S 49 B6
Laxvik S 61 C2
Laxviken S 199 B11
La Yesa E 159 B3
Laza E 141 B3
Lazarevac SRB . . . 127 C2
Lazarevo SRB 126 B2
Lazise I 121 B3
Łaziska Grn. PL. . . . 86 B2
Lazkao E 144 A1
Lázně Bělohrad CZ. 84 B3
Lázně Bohdaneč
  CZ 97 A3
Lázně Kynžvart CZ . 95 A4
Lazonby GB. 37 B4
La Zubia E 163 A4
Łazy PL 67 B5
Lazzaro I 175 D1

Lea GB 40 B3
Leadburn GB 35 C4
Leadhills GB 36 A3
Leap IRL 29 C2
Leatherhead GB . . 44 B3
Łeba PL 68 A2
Lebach D 92 B2
Le Barp F 128 B2
Le Bar-sur-Loup F . 132 B2
Le Béage F 117 C4
Le Beausset F 132 B1
Lebekke B 79 A4
Lébény H 111 B4
Le Bessat F 117 B4
Le Blanc F 115 B5
Le Bleymard F 130 A2
Łebno PL 68 A3
Leboreiro E 140 B3
Łebork PL 68 A2
Le Boullay-Mivoye
  F 89 B5
Le Boulou F 146 B3
Le Bourg F 129 B4
Le Bourg-d'Oisans
  F 118 B3
Le Bourget-du-Lac
  F 118 B2
Le Bourgneuf-la-Forêt
  F 101 A5
Le Bousquet d'Orb
  F 130 B2
Le Brassus CH 105 C5
Le Breuil F 117 A3
Le Breuil-en-Auge F 89 A4
Lebrija E 162 B1
Lebring A 110 C2
Le Brusquet F 132 A2
Le Bry CH 106 C2
Le Bugue F 129 B3
Le Buisson F 129 B3
Lebus D 74 B3
Lebusa D 83 A5
Leca da Palmeira
  P. 148 A1
Le Caloy F 128 C2
Le Cap d'Agde F . . 130 B2
Le Cateau Cambrésis
  F 91 A3
Le Caylar F 130 B2
Le Cayrol F 116 C2
Lecce I 173 B4
Lecco I 120 B2
Lécera E 153 A3
Lećevica HR 138 B2
Lech A 107 B5
Le Chambon-
  Feugerolles F 117 B4
Le Chambon-sur-Lignon
  F 117 B4
Le Château d'Oléron
  F 114 C2
Le Châtelard F 118 B3
Le Châtelet F 103 C4
Le Chatelet-en-Brie
  F 90 C2
Lechbruck D 108 B1
Lechena GR 184 B2
Le Chesne F 91 B4
Le Cheylard F 117 C4
Lechlade GB 44 B2
Lechovice CZ 97 C4
Leciñena E 145 C3
Leck D 64 B1
Le Collet-de-Deze
  F 131 A2
Le Conquet F 100 A1
Le Creusot F 104 C3
Le Croisic F 101 B3
Le Crotoy F 78 B1
Lectoure F 129 C3
Łęczyca
  Łódzkie PL. 77 B4
  Zachodnio-Pomorskie
  PL. 75 A4
Ledaña E 158 B2
Ledbury GB 39 B4
Lede B 79 B3
Ledečnad Sazavou
  CZ 97 B3
Ledenice CZ 96 C2
Lédergues F 130 A1
Lédigos E 142 B2
Ledmore GB 32 C2
Lednice CZ 97 C4
Lednicke-Rovné SK 98 B2
Le Donjon F 117 A3
Le Dorat F 115 B5
Lędyczek PL 68 B1
Lędziny PL 86 B3
Leeds GB 40 B2
Leek
  GB 40 B1
  NL 71 A3
Leenaun IRL 28 A2
Leens NL 71 A3
Leer D 71 A4
Leerdam NL. 79 A5
Leerhafe D 71 A4
Leese D 72 B2
Leeuwarden NL . . . 70 A2
Leezen D 64 C3
Le Faou F 100 A1
Le Faoüet F 100 A2
Lefka CY 181 A1
Lefkada GR 182 E2
Lefkimis GR 182 D2

Lefkoniko CY. 181 A2
Le Folgoet F 100 A1
Le Fossat F 146 A2
Le Fousseret F . . . 146 A2
Le Fugeret F 132 A2
Leganés E 151 B4
Legau D 107 B5
Le Gault-Soigny F . 91 C3
Legbąd PL 68 B2
Legé F 114 B2
Lège-Cap-Ferret F . 128 B1
Legionowo PL 77 B5
Léglise B 92 B1
Legnago I 121 B4
Legnano I 120 B1
Legnaro I 121 B4
Legnica PL 85 A4
Łęgowo PL 69 A3
Legrad HR 124 A2
Le Grand-Bornand
  F 118 B3
Le-Grand-Bourg F .116 A1
Le Grand-Lucé F . . 102 B2
Le Grand-Pressigny
  F 102 C2
Le Grand-Quevilly F 89 A4
Le Grau-du-Roi F . 131 B3
Léguevin F 129 C4
Legutiano E 143 B4
Le Havre F 89 A4
Lehesten D 82 B3
Lehnice SK 111 A4
Lehnin D 74 B1
Le Hohwald F 93 C3
Le Houga F 128 C2
Lehrberg D 94 B2
Lehre D 73 B3
Lehrte D 72 B2
Lehsen D 73 A4
Leibnitz A 110 C2
Leicester GB 40 C2
Leiden NL. 70 B1
Leidschendam NL . 70 B1
Leigh GB 38 A4
Leighlinbridge IRL . 30 B2
Leighton Buzzard
  GB 44 B3
Leignon B 79 B5
Leikanger N 198 C2
Leimen D 93 B4
Leinefelde D 82 A2
Leinesfjord N 194 C6
Leintwardine GB . . 39 B4
Leipojärvi S 196 B4
Leipzig D 83 A4
Leira
  Nordland N 195 D4
  Oppland N 47 B6
Leiråmoen N 195 D5
Leiria P 154 B2
Leirvassbu N 47 A5
Leirvik
  Hordaland N 52 A1
  Sogn og Fjordane
  N. 46 A2
Leisach A 109 C3
Leisnig D 83 A4
Leiston GB. 45 A5
Leitholm GB 35 C5
Leitrim IRL 26 C2
Leitza E 144 A2
Leitzkau D 73 B4
Lejkowo PL 68 A1
Lekani GR 183 B6
Lekawa PL 86 A3
Łekawica PL 99 B3
Lekeitio E 143 A4
Lekenik HR 124 B2
Lekeryd S 62 A2
Leknes N 194 B4
Łęknica PL. 84 A2
Leksand S 50 B1
Leksvik N 199 B7
Lekunberri E 144 A2
Lekvattnet S 49 B4
Le Lardin-St Lazare
  F 129 A4
Le Lauzet-Ubaye F 132 A2
Le Lavandou F 132 B2
Le Lion-d'Angers
  F 102 B1
Lelkowo PL 69 A5
Le Locle CH 106 B1
Le Loroux-Bottereau
  F 101 B5
Le Louroux-Béconnais
  F 101 B5
Lelów PL 86 B3
Le Luc F 132 B2
Le Lude F 102 B2
Lelystad NL 70 B2
Lem
  Ringkøbing DK 59 B1
  Viborg Amt. DK 58 B1
Le Malzieu-Ville F . 116 C3
Le Mans F 102 A2
Le Mas-d'Azil F . . . 146 A2
Le Massegros F . . . 130 A2
Le Mayet-de-Montagne
  F 117 A3
Le May-sur-Evre F. 101 B5
Lembach F 93 B3
Lemberg F 93 B3
Lembèye F 145 A3
Lemelerveld NL . . . 71 B3
Le Mêle-sur-Sarthe
  F 89 B4
Le Ménil F 105 A5

Le Merlerault F 89 B4
Le Mesnil-sur-Oger
  F 91 C4
Lemförde D 71 B5
Lemgo D 72 B1
Le Miroir F 105 C4
Lemland FIN 51 B7
Lemmer NL 70 B2
Le Molay-Littry F . . 88 A3
Le Monastier-sur-
  Gazeille F 117 C3
Le Monêtier-les-Bains
  F 118 C3
Le Mont-Dore F . . .116 B2
Le Montet F 116 A3
Le Mont-St Michel F 88 B2
Lempdes F 116 B3
Le Muret F 128 B2
Le Muy F 132 B2
Lemvig DK 58 B1
Lemwerder D 72 A1
Lena N 48 B2
Lénárd SLO 110 C2
Lenartovce SK. . . . 99 C4
Lenauheim RO 126 B2
Lencloître F 102 C2
Lend A 109 B4
Lendalfoot GB 36 A2
Lendava SLO 111 C3
Lendinara I 121 B4
Lendorf A 109 C4
Lendum DK 58 A3
Le Neubourg F . . . 89 A4
Lengefeld D 83 B5
Lengerich
  Niedersachsen D . .71 B4
  Nordrhein-Westfalen
  D. 71 B4
Lenggries D 108 B2
Lengyeltóti H. 111 C4
Lenhovda S 62 B3
Lenk CH 106 C2
Lennartsfors S 54 A2
Lennestadt D 81 A4
Lennoxtown GB . . . 35 C3
Leno I 120 B3
Lénola I 169 B3
Le Nouvion-en-
  Thiérache F 91 A3
Lens
  B 79 B3
  F 78 B2
Lensahn D 65 B3
Lens Lestang F . . .117 B5
Lensvik N 198 B6
Lentellais E 141 B3
Lentföhrden D 64 C2
Lenti I 111 C3
Lentini I 177 B3
Lenungshammar S . 54 A3
Lenzburg CH 106 B3
Lenzen D 73 A4
Lenzerheide CH . . . 107 C4
Leoben A 110 B2
Leogang A 109 B3
Leominster GB . . . 39 B4
León E 142 B1
Léon F 128 C1
Leonberg D 93 C5
Léoncel F 118 C2
Leonding A 96 C2
Leonessa I 169 A2
Leonforte I 177 B3
Leonidio GR 184 B3
Leopoldsburg B . . . 79 A5
Leopoldsdorf im
  Marchfeld A. 111 A3
Leopoldshagen D . . 74 A2
Leova MD. 17 B8
Le Palais F 100 B2
Le Parcq F 78 B2
Lepe E 161 B2
Le Péage-de-Roussillon
  F 117 B4
Le Pellerin F 101 B4
Lepenou GR 182 E3
Le Perthus F 146 B3
Le Pertuis F 117 B4
Le Petit-Bornand F .118 B3
Lephin GB 31 B2
L'Epine F 132 A1
Le Poët F 132 A1
Lepoglava HR 124 A2
Le Poirè-sur-Vie F .114 B2
Le Pont CH 105 C5
Le Pont-de-Montvert
  F 130 A2
Le Porge F 128 B1
Le Porge-Océan F . 128 B1
Le Portel F 78 B1
Le Pouldu F 100 B2
Le Pouliguen F . . . 101 B3
Leppäjärvi FIN 192 D7
Leppävirta FIN. 8 A5
Leppin D 73 B4
le Prese I 120 A3
Lepsény FIN 112 C2
Le Puy-en-Velay F .117 B3
Le Puy-Ste Réparade
  F 131 B4
Le Quesnoy F 79 B3
Léquile I 173 B4
Le Rayol F 132 B2
Lercara Friddi I . . . 176 B2
Lerdal S 54 B2
Leré F 103 B4
Lerici I 134 A2

Lerin E 144 B2
Lerma E 143 B3
Lerm-et-Musset F . 128 B2
Lermoos A 108 B1
Le Roeulx B 79 B4
Le Rouget F 116 C2
Lérouville F 92 C1
Le Rozier F 130 A2
Lerum S 60 B2
Le Russey F 106 B1
Lervik N 54 A1
Lerwick GB 33 A5
Lés E 145 B4
Les Abrets F 118 B2
Les Aix-d'Angillon
  F 103 B4
Lesaka E 144 A2
Les Ancizes-Comps
  F 116 B2
Les Andelys F 90 B1
Les Arcs
  Savoie F 119 B3
  Var F 132 B2
Les-Aubiers F 102 C1
Les Baux-de-Provence
  F 131 B3
Les Bézards F 103 B4
Les Bois CH 106 B1
Les Bordes F 103 B4
Les Borges Blanques
  E 147 C1
Les Borges del Camp
  E 147 C2
Les Brunettes F . . . 104 C2
Lesbury GB 37 A5
Les Cabannes F . . 146 B2
L'Escala E 147 B4
Lescar F 145 A3
L'Escarène F 133 B3
Lesce SLO 123 A3
Lescheraines F . . .118 B3
Lesconil F 100 B1
Les Contamines-
  Montjoie F 118 B3
les Coves de Vinroma
  E 153 B4
Les Déserts F 118 B3
Les Deux-Alpes F .118 C3
Les Diablerets CH . .119 A4
Lesdins F 90 B3
Le Sel-de-Bretagne
  F 101 B4
Le Sentier CH 105 C5
Les Escaldes AND. 146 B2
Les Essarts F 114 B2
Les Estables F . . . 117 C4
Les Eyzies-de-Tayac
  F 129 B4
Les Gets F 118 A3
Les Grandes-Ventes
  F 89 A5
Les Haudères F . . .119 A4
Les Herbiers F 114 B2
Les Hôpitaux-Neufs
  F 105 C5
Lesično SLO 123 A4
Lésina I 171 B3
Lesjaskog N 198 C5
Lesjöfors S 49 C6
Leskovac SRB 16 D4
Leskova Dolina
  SLO 123 B3
Leskovec
  CZ 98 B1
  SLO 123 B4
Leskovice CZ 97 B3
Leskovik AL. 182 C2
Leslie GB. 35 B4
Les Lucs-sur-Boulogne
  F 114 B2
Les Mages F 131 A3
Lesmahagow GB . . 36 A3
Les Mazures F 91 B4
Les Mées F 132 A1
Lesmont F 91 C4
Les Mureaux F 90 C1
Leśna PL 84 A3
Lesneven F 100 A1
Leśnica PL. 86 B2
Leśnica SRB 127 C1
Leśniów Wielkopolski
  PL. 75 C4
Lesnoye RUS 9 C9
Les Omergues F . . 132 A1
Les Ormes-sur-Voulzie
  F 90 C2
Les Orres F 132 A2
Le Souquet F 128 C1
Lesparre-Médoc F . 128 A2
l'Espérance F 91 B3
l'Esperou F 130 A2
Les Pieux F 88 A2
Lesponne F 145 A4
Les Ponts-de-Cé F 102 B1
Les Ponts-de-Martel
  CH 106 C1
Les Praz F 119 B3
L'Espunyola E 147 B2
Les Riceys F 104 B3
Les Roches F 117 B4
Les Rosaires F 101 A3
Les Rosiers F 102 B1
Les Rousses F 105 C5

Les Sables-d'Olonne
F 114 B2
Lessach A 109 B4
Lessay F 88 A2
Lessebo S 62 B3
Les Settons F 104 B3
Lessines B 79 B3
L'Estany E 147 C3
Les Ternes F 116 B2
Lesterps F 115 B4
Les Thilliers en-Vexin
F 90 B1
Les Touches F 101 B4
Les Trois Moûtiers
F 102 B2
Les Vans F 131 A3
Les Verrières CH . . 105 C5
Les Vignes F 130 A2
Leswalt GB 36 B1
Leszno
Mazowieckie PL . . .77 B5
Wielkopolskie PL . .85 A4
Leszno Górne PL . . 84 A3
Letchworth GB 44 B3
Le Teil F 131 A3
Le Teilleul F 88 B3
Le Temple-de-Bretagne
F 101 B4
Letenye H 111 C3
Le Theil F 89 B4
Le Thillot F 106 B1
Letino I 170 B2
Letohrad CZ 97 A4
Le Touquet-Paris-Plage
F 78 B1
Le Touvet F 118 B2
Letovice CZ 97 B4
Le Translay F 90 B1
Le Tréport F 90 A1
Letschin D 74 B3
Letterfrack IRL 28 A2
Letterkenny IRL . . . 26 B3
Lettermacaward IRL 26 B2
Lettoch GB 32 D3
Letur E 164 A2
Letux E 153 A3
Letzlingen D 73 B4
Leucate F 146 B4
Leuchars GB 35 B5
Leuglay F 105 B3
Leuk CH 119 A4
Leukerbad CH 119 A4
Leumrabhagh GB . . 31 A2
Leuna D 83 A4
Leusden NL 70 B2
Leutenberg D 82 B3
Leuterschach D . . . 108 B1
Leutershausen D . . 94 B2
Leutkirch D 107 B5
Leuven B 79 B4
Leuze-en-Hainaut B 79 B3
Le Val F 132 B2
Le Val-André F 101 A3
Le Val-d'Ajol F 105 B5
Levan AL 182 C1
Levanger N 199 B8
Levanjska Varoš
HR 125 B4
Lévanto I 134 A2
Levaré F 88 B3
Levata I 120 B3
Leveld N 47 B5
Leven
East Yorkshire
GB 41 B3
Fife GB 35 B5
Leverano I 173 B3
Le Verdon-sur-Mer
F 114 C2
Leverkusen D 80 A2
Levern D 72 B1
Le Vernet F 132 A2
Levet F 103 C4
Levice SK 112 A2
Lévico Terme I 121 A4
Levie F 180 B2
Levier F 105 C5
Le Vigan F 130 B2
Lévignen F 90 B2
le Ville I 135 B5
Levinovac HR 124 B3
Le Vivier-sur-Mer F . 88 B2
Levoča SK 99 B4
Levroux F 103 C3
Lewes GB 45 C4
Lewin Brzeski PL . . 85 B5
Lewisham GB 44 B3
Leyburn GB 37 B5
Leyland GB 38 A4
Leysdown-on-Sea
GB 45 B4
Leysin CH 119 A4
Lezajsk PL 12 C5
Lézardrieux F 100 A2
Lézat-sur-Léze F . . 146 A2
Lezay F 115 B3
Lezhë AL 182 B1
Lézignan-Corbières
F 130 B1
Lezignan-la-Cèbe
F 130 B2
Ležimir SRB 126 B1
Lézinnes F 104 B3
Lezoux F 117 B3
Lezuza E 158 C1

Lhenice CZ 96 C2
Lherm F 146 A2
Lhommaizé F 115 B4
L'Hospitalet F 146 B2
L'Hospitalet de l'Infant
E 147 D1
L'Hospitalet de
Llobregat E 147 C3
L'Hospitalet-du-Larzac
F 130 B2
Lhuître F 91 C4
Liancourt F 90 B2
Liart F 91 B4
Liatorp S 63 B2
Liatrie GB 32 D2
Libáň CZ 84 B3
Libceves CZ 84 B1
Libčchov CZ 84 B2
Liber E 141 B3
Liberec CZ 84 B3
Libiąż PL 86 B3
Libina CZ 98 B1
Libochovice CZ . . . 84 B2
Libohovë AL 182 C2
Libourne F 128 B2
Libramont B 92 B1
Librazhd AL 182 B2
Librilla E 165 B3
Libros E 152 B2
Licata I 176 B2
Licciana Nardi I . . . 134 A3
Licenza I 169 A2
Liceros E 151 A4
Lich D 81 B4
Lichères-près-
Aigremont F 104 B2
Lichfield GB 40 C2
Lichtenau
A 97 C3
D 81 A4
Lichtenberg D 83 B3
Lichtenfels D 82 B3
Lichtensteig CH . . . 107 B4
Lichtenstein D 83 B4
Lichtenvoorde NL . . 71 C3
Lichtervelde B 78 A3
Lička Jesenica HR . 123 B4
Lickershamn S 57 C4
Lički Osik HR 123 C4
Ličko Lešce HR . . . 123 C4
Licodía Eubéa I . . . 177 B3
Licques F 78 B1
Lida BY 13 B6
Lidar N 47 A6
Lidečko CZ 98 B2
Liden S 200 D2
Lidhult S 60 C3
Lidköping S 55 B4
Lido I 122 B1
Lido Azzurro I 173 B3
Lido degli Estensi
I 122 C1
Lido degli Scacchi
I 122 C1
Lido della Nazioni
I 122 C1
Lido di Camaiore I . 134 B3
Lido di Casalbordino
I 169 A4
Lido di Castél Fusano
I 168 B2
Lido di Cincinnato
I 168 B2
Lido di Classe I . . . 135 A5
Lido di Fermo I . . . 136 B2
Lido di Fondi I 169 B3
Lido di Jésolo I . . . 122 B1
Lido di Licola I 170 C2
Lido di Metaponto
I 174 A2
Lido di Óstia I 168 B2
Lido di Policoro I . . 174 A2
Lido di Pomposa I . 122 C1
Lido di Savio I 135 A5
Lido di Scanzano I . 174 A2
Lido di Siponto I . . 171 B3
Lido di Squillace I . 175 C2
Lido di Volano I . . . 122 C1
Lido Riccio I 169 A4
Lidoriki GR 184 A3
Lido Silvana I 173 B3
Lidsjöberg S 199 A12
Lidzbark PL 77 A4
Lidzbark Warmiński
PL 69 A5
Liebenau
A 96 C2
D 72 B2
Liebenwalde D 74 B2
Lieberose D 74 C3
Liebling RO 126 B3
Lieboch A 110 C2
Liège B 80 B1
Lieksa FIN 3 E12
Lienen D 71 B4
Lienz A 109 C3
Liepāja LV 8 D2
Lier B 79 A4
Lierbyen N 54 A1
Liernais F 104 B3
Liesing A 109 C3
Liestal CH 106 B2
Liétor E 158 C2
Lieurac F 146 B2
Lieurey F 89 A4
Liévin F 78 B2
Liezen A 110 B1
Liffol-le-Grand F . . . 92 C1

Lifford IRL 27 B3
Liffré F 101 A4
Ligardes F 129 B3
Lignano Sabbiadoro
I 122 B2
Ligne F 101 B4
Lignières F 103 C4
Ligny-en-Barrois F . 92 C1
Ligny-le-Châtel F . . 104 B2
Ligoła Polska PL . . . 85 A5
Ligourio GR 184 B4
Ligowo PL 77 B4
Ligueil F 102 B2
Likavka SK 99 B3
Likenäs S 49 B5
Likhoslavl RUS 9 D9
Lild Strand DK 58 A1
L'Île-Bouchard F . . 102 B2
l'Île-Rousse F 180 A1
Lilienfeld A 110 A2
Lilienthal D 72 A1
Lilla Edet S 54 B3
Lilla Tjärby S 61 C3
Lille
B 79 A4
F 78 B3
Lillebonne F 89 A4
Lillehammer N 48 A2
Lillerød DK 61 D2
Lillers F 78 B2
Lillesand N 53 B4
Lillestrøm N 48 C3
Lillhärdal S 199 D11
Lillkyrka S 56 A3
Lillo E 157 A4
Lillögda S 200 B3
Lillpite S 196 D4
Lima S 49 B5
Limanowa PL 99 B4
Limassol CY 181 B2
Limavady GB 27 A4
Limbach-Oberfrohna
D 83 B4
Limbaži LV 8 D4
Limbourg B 80 B1
Limburg D 81 B4
Lime DK 58 B3
Limedsforsen S . . . 49 B5
Limenaria GR 183 C6
Limenas Chersonisou
GR 185 D6
Limerick IRL 29 B3
Limes I 121 B3
Limésy F 89 A4
Limmared S 60 B3
Limni GR 183 E5
Limoges F 115 C5
Limogne-en-Quercy
F 129 B4
Limoise F 104 C2
Limone Piemonte I . 133 A3
Limone sul Garda I . 121 B3
Limons F 117 B3
Limours F 90 C2
Limoux F 146 A3
Linares E 157 B4
Linares de Mora E . 153 B3
Linares de Riofrio
E 149 B4
Linaria GR 183 E6
Linas de Broto E . . 145 B3
Lincoln GB 40 B3
Lind DK 59 B1
Lindås N 46 B2
Lindau D 107 B4
Lindberget N 48 A3
Lindelse DK 65 B3
Lindenberg D 74 B3
Lindenberg im Allgäu
D 107 B4
Lindern D 71 B4
Linderöd S 61 D3
Lindesberg S 56 A1
Lindesnäs S 50 B1
Lindesnes N 52 C3
Lindholmen S 57 A4
Lindknud DK 59 C2
Lindlar D 80 A3
Lindö S 56 B2
Lindome S 60 B2
Lindos GR 188 C3
Lindoso P 148 A1
Lindow D 74 B1
Lindsdal S 62 B4
Lindshammar S . . . 62 A3
Lindstedt D 73 B4
Lindved DK 59 C2
Lině CZ 96 B1
Lingbo S 50 A3
Linge F 101 B4
Lingen D 71 B4
Linghed S 50 B2
Linghem S 56 B1
Linguaglossa I 177 B4
Linia PL 68 A2
Linie PL 74 A3
Liniewo PL 68 A3
Linkenheim D 93 B4
Linköping S 56 B1
Linksness GB 33 C3
Linlithgow GB 35 C4
Linneryd S 63 B3
Linnes Hammarby
S 51 C4
Linnich D 80 B2
Linsell S 199 C10
Linslade GB 44 B3
Linthal CH 107 C4
Linyola E 147 C1

Linz
A 96 C2
D 80 B3
Liomseter N 47 A6
Lionárisso CY 181 A3
Lioni I 172 B1
Lion-sur-Mer F 89 A3
Lipany SK 99 B4
Lipar SRB 126 B1
Lípari I 177 A3
Lipcani MD 17 A7
Liperi FIN 9 A6
Liphook GB 44 B3
Lipiany PL 75 A3
Lipik HR 124 B3
Lipka PL 68 B2
Lipki Wielkie PL . . . 75 B4
Lipnica PL 68 B2
Lipnica Murowana
PL 99 B4
Lipnik PL 87 B5
Lipník nad Bečvou
CZ 98 B1
Lipno
Kujawsko-Pomorskie
PL 77 B4
Łódzkie PL 86 A2
Liposthey F 128 B2
Lipovac HR 125 B5
Lipovec CZ 97 B4
Lipovets UA 13 D8
Lipovljani HR 124 B2
Lipowiec PL 77 A6
Lipowina PL 69 A4
Lippborg D 81 A4
Lippó H 125 B4
Lippoldsberg D 81 A5
Lippstadt D 81 A4
Lipsko PL 87 A5
Liptál CZ 98 B1
Liptovská-Lúžna
SK 99 C3
Liptovská Osada
SK 99 C3
Liptovská-Teplička
SK 99 C4
Liptovský Hrádok
SK 99 B3
Liptovský Milkuláš
SK 99 B3
Lipusz PL 68 A2
Lipůvka CZ 97 B4
Liré F 101 B4
Lisac BIH 139 A3
Lisbellaw GB 27 B3
Lisboa = Lisbon P . 154 C1
Lisbon = Lisboa P . 154 C1
Lisburn GB 27 B4
Liscannor IRL 28 B2
Lisdoonvarna IRL . . 28 A2
Lisewo PL 69 B3
Lisia Góra PL 87 B5
Lisięcice PL 86 B1
Lisieux F 89 A4
Lisjö S 56 A2
Liskeard GB 42 B2
L'Isle CH 105 C5
L'Isle-Adam F 90 B2
L'Isle-de-Noé F . . . 129 C3
L'Isle-en-Dodon F . 145 A4
L'Isle-Jourdain
Gers F 129 C4
Vienne F 115 B4
L'Isle-sur-la-Sorgue
F 131 B4
L'Isle-sur-le-Doubs
F 105 B5
L'Isle-sur-Serein F . 104 B3
Lisle-sur-Tarn F . . . 129 C4
Lismore IRL 29 B4
Lisnaskea GB 27 B3
Lišov CZ 96 B2
Lisów
Lubuskie PL 74 B3
Śląskie PL 86 B2
Lisse NL 70 B1
Lissycasey IRL 28 B2
List D 64 A1
Listerby S 63 B3
Listowel IRL 29 B2
Listrac-Médoc F . . . 128 A2
Lit S 199 B11
Litava SK 99 C3
Litcham GB 41 C4
Lit-et-Mixe F 128 B1
Litija SLO 123 A3
Litke H 112 A3
Litlabø N 52 A1
Litochoro GR 182 C4
Litoměřice CZ 84 B2
Litomyšl CZ 97 B4
Litovel CZ 98 B1
Litschau A 96 C3
Littlehampton GB . . 44 C3
Littleport GB 45 A4
Littleton IRL 29 B4
Little Walsingham
GB 41 C4
Litvinov CZ 83 B5
Livadero GR 182 C3
Livadhia CY 181 B2
Livadi GR 182 C4
Livadia GR 184 A3
Livarot F 89 B4
Liveras CY 181 A1
Livernon F 129 B4

Liverovici MNE . . . 139 C5
Liverpool GB 38 A4
Livigno I 107 C5
Living ston GB 35 C4
Livno BIH 138 B2
Livo FIN 197 D9
Livold SLO 123 B3
Livorno I 134 B3
Livorno Ferraris I . .119 B5
Livron-sur-Drôme
F 117 C4
Livry-Louvercy F . . 91 B4
Lixheim F 92 C3
Lixouri GR 184 A1
Lizard GB 42 C1
Lizy-sur-Ourcq F . . 90 B3
Lizzano I 173 B3
Lizzano in Belvedere
I 135 A3
Ljig SRB 127 C2
Ljørdalen N 49 A4
Ljosland N 52 B3
Ljubija BIH 124 C2
Ljubinje BIH 139 C4
Ljubljana SLO 123 A3
Ljubno ob Savinji
SLO 123 A3
Ljubovija SRB 127 C1
Ljubuški BIH 138 B3
Ljugarn S 57 C4
Ljung S 60 B3
Ljunga S 56 B2
Ljungaverk S 200 D2
Ljungby S 60 C3
Ljungbyhed S 61 C3
Ljungbyholm S 63 B4
Ljungdalen S 199 C9
Ljungsarp S 60 B3
Ljungsbro S 56 B1
Ljungskile S 54 B2
Ljusdal S 200 E2
Ljusfallshammar S . 56 B1
Ljusne S 51 A4
Ljusterö S 57 A4
Ljutomer SLO 111 C3
Lüki BG 183 B6
Lladurs E 147 B2
Llafranc E 147 C4
Llagostera E 147 C3
Llanaelhaiarn GB . . 38 B2
Llanarth GB 39 B2
Llanbedr GB 38 B2
Llanbedrog GB 38 B2
Llanberis GB 38 A2
Llanbister GB 39 B3
Llanbrynmair GB . . 39 B3
Llançà E 146 B4
Llandeilo GB 39 C3
Llandissilio GB 39 C2
Llandovery GB 39 C3
Llandrillo GB 38 B3
Llandrindod Wells
GB 39 B3
Llandudec F 100 A1
Llandudno GB 38 A3
Llandysul GB 39 B2
Llanelli GB 39 C2
Llanerchymedd GB . 38 A2
Llanes E 142 A2
Llanfair Caereinion
GB 39 B3
Llanfairfechan GB . . 38 A3
Llanfyllin GB 38 B3
Llangadog GB 39 C3
Llangefni GB 38 A2
Llangollen GB 38 B3
Llangrannog GB . . . 39 B2
Llangurig GB 39 B3
Llanidloes GB 39 B3
Llanilar GB 39 B2
Llanrhystud GB . . . 39 B2
Llanrwst GB 38 A3
Llansannan GB 38 A3
Llansawel GB 39 B2
Llanstephan GB . . . 39 C2
Llanteno E 143 A3
Llanthony GB 39 C3
Llantrisant GB 39 C3
Llantwit-Major GB . . 38 B3
Llanuwchllyn GB . . 38 B3
Llanwddyn GB 38 B3
Llanwrda GB 39 C3
Llanwrtyd Wells GB . 39 B3
Llanybydder GB . . . 39 B2
Llanymynech GB . . 38 B3
Llavorsi E 146 B2
Lleida E 153 A4
Llera E 156 B1
Llerena E 156 B1
Lles E 146 B2
Llessui E 146 B2
Llinars E 147 B2
Lliria E 159 B3
Llivia E 146 B2
Llodio E 143 A4
Lloret de Mar E . . . 147 C3
Llosa de Ranes E . . 159 B3
Lloseta E 167 B2
Llucena del Cid E . . 153 B3
Llucmajor E 167 B2
Llutxent E 159 C3
Llwyngwril GB 38 B2
Llyswen GB 39 B3
Lnáře CZ 96 B1
Lniano PL 76 A3
Loanhead GB 35 C4
Loano I 133 A4
Loarre E 145 B3

Löbau D 84 A2
Löbejün D 83 A3
Löberöd S 61 D3
Łobez PL 75 A4
Löbnitz D 66 B1
Lobón E 155 C4
Loburg D 73 B5
Łobżenica PL 76 A2
Locana I 119 B4
Locarno CH 120 A1
Loccum D 72 B2
Loče SLO 123 A4
Lochailort GB 34 B2
Lochaline GB 34 B2
Lochans GB 36 B1
Locharbriggs GB . . 36 A3
Lochau A 107 B4
Loch Baghasdail
GB 31 B1
Lochcarron GB 31 B3
Lochearnhead GB . . 34 B3
Lochem NL 71 B3
Loches F 102 B2
Lochgelly GB 35 B4
Lochgilphead GB . . 34 B2
Lochgoilhead GB . . 34 B3
Lochinver GB 32 C1
Loch nam Madadh
GB 31 B1
Lochranza GB 34 C2
Ločika SRB 127 D3
Lockenhaus A 111 B3
Lockerbie GB 36 A3
Löcknitz D 74 A3
Locmaria F 100 B2
Locmariaquer F . . . 100 B3
Locminé F 100 B3
Locorotondo I 173 B3
Locquirec F 100 A2
Locri I 175 C2
Locronan F 100 A1
Loctudy F 100 B1
Lodares de Osma
E 151 A5
Lodé F 178 B3
Lodève F 130 B2
Lodi I 120 B2
Løding N 194 C5
Lødingen N 194 B6
Lodosa E 144 B1
Lödöse S 54 B3
Łódź PL 86 A3
Loeches E 151 B4
Løfallstrand N 46 B3
Lofer A 109 B3
Lofsdalen S 199 C10
Loftahammar S 62 A4
Lofthus N 46 B3
Loftus GB 37 B6
Loga N 52 B2
Logatec SLO 123 B3
Lögdeå S 200 C5
Lograto I 120 B3
Logroño E 143 B4
Logrosán E 156 A2
Løgstør DK 58 B2
Løgumgårde DK . . . 64 A1
Løgumkloster DK . . 64 A1
Lohals DK 65 A3
Lohiniva FIN 197 B8
Lohja FIN 8 B4
Löhlbach D 81 A4
Lohmen
Mecklenburg-
Vorpommern D 65 C5
Sachsen D 84 B2
Löhnberg D 81 B4
Lohne D 71 B5
Löhne D 72 B1
Lohr D 94 B1
Lohra D 81 B4
Lohsa D 84 A2
Loiano I 135 A4
Loimaa FIN 8 B3
Lóiri I 178 B3
Loitz D 66 C2
Loivos P 148 A2
Loivos do Monte P . 148 A2
Loja E 163 A3
Lojanice SRB 127 C1
Lojsta S 57 C4
Løjt Kirkeby DK . . . 64 A2
Lok SK 112 A2
Lokca SK 99 B3
Løken N 54 A2
Lokeren B 79 A3
Loket CZ 83 B4
Lokka FIN 197 B10
Løkken
DK 58 A2
N 198 B6
Loknya RUS 9 D7
Lökosháza H 113 C5
Lokve SRB 126 B3
Lollar D 81 B4
L'Olleria E 159 C3
Lölling-Graben A . . .110 C1
Lom
BG 17 D5
N 198 D5
SK 99 C3
Lombez F 146 A1
Lomello I 120 B1
Łomianki PL 77 B5
Lomma S 61 D3
Lommaryd S 62 A2
Lommatzsch D 83 A5

Lommel B 79 A5
Lommersum D 80 B2
Lomnice CZ 97 B4
Lomnice nad Lužnici
CZ 96 B2
Lomnice-nad Popelkou
CZ 84 B3
Lompolo FIN . . 196 A7
Łomza PL 12 B5
Lönashult S 63 B2
Lønborg DK 59 C1
Londerzeel B 79 A4
Londinières F 89 A5
London GB 44 B3
Lonevåg N 46 B2
Longa GR 184 C2
Longare I 121 B4
Longares E 152 A2
Longarone I 122 A1
Longastrino I 135 A5
Long Bennington
GB 40 C3
Longbenton GB . . . 37 A5
Longchamp-sur-Aujon
F 105 A3
Longchaumois F . . . 118 A2
Long Eaton GB . . . 40 C2
Longeau F 105 B4
Longecourt-en-Plaine
F 105 B4
Longeville-les-St Avold
F 92 B2
Longeville-sur-Mer
F 114 B2
Longford IRL 28 A4
Longframlington
GB 37 A5
Longhope GB . . . 33 C3
Longhorsley GB . . 37 A5
Longhoughton GB . 37 A5
Longi I 177 A3
Long Melford GB . . 45 A4
Longny-au-Perche
F 89 B4
Longobucco I 174 B2
Long Preston GB . . 40 A1
Longré F 115 B3
Longridge GB 38 A4
Longroiva P 149 B2
Long Sutton GB . . 41 C4
Longtown
Cumbria GB 36 A4
Herefordshire GB . . 39 C4
Longueau F 90 B2
Longué-Jumelles
F 102 B1
Longuyon F 92 B1
Longvic F 105 B4
Longvilly B 92 A1
Longwy F 92 B1
Lonigo I 121 B4
Löningen D 71 B4
Lonja HR 124 B2
Lönneberga S 62 A3
Lönsboda S 63 B2
Lønset N 198 C6
Lons-le-Saunier F . 105 C4
Lønstrup DK 58 A2
Looe GB 42 B2
Loone-Plage F . . . 78 A2
Loon op Zand NL . . 79 A5
Loosdorf A 110 A2
Lo Pagán E 165 B4
Lopar HR 123 C3
Lopare BIH 125 C4
Lopera E 157 C3
Lopigna F 180 A1
Loppersum NL . . . 71 A3
Łopuszna PL 99 B4
Łopuszno PL 87 B4
Lor F 91 B4
Lora F 198 C5
Lora de Estepa E . 162 A3
Lora del Río E . . . 162 A2
Loranca del Campo
E 151 B5
Lorbé E 140 A2
Lörby S 63 B2
Lorca E 164 B3
Lorch D 93 A3
Lørenfallet N 48 B3
Lørenskog N 48 C2
Loreo I 122 B1
Loreto I 136 B2
Lorgues F 132 B2
Lorica I 174 B2
Lorient F 100 B2
Lörinci H 112 B3
Loriol-sur-Drôme
F 117 C4
Lormes F 104 B2
Loro Ciuffenna I . . 135 B4
Lorqui E 165 A3
Lörrach D 106 B2
Lorrez-le-Bocage
F 103 A4
Lorris F 103 B4
Lorup D 71 B4
Łoś PL 77 C5
Los S 199 D12
Losacino E 149 A3
Los Alcázares E . . 165 B4
Los Arcos E 144 B1
Losar de la Vera E . 150 B2
Los Barios de Luna
E 141 B5
Los Barrios E . . . 162 B2

Los Caños de Meca
E 162 B1
Los Cerricos E . . . 164 B2
Los Corrales E . . . 162 A3
Los Corrales de Buelna
E 142 A2
Los Dolores E . . . 165 B3
Losenstein A 110 B1
Los Gallardos E . . 164 B3
Losheim
Nordrhein-Westfalen
D 80 B2
Saarland D 92 B2
Los Hinojosos E . . 158 B1
Los Isidros E 159 B2
Los Molinos E . . . 151 B3
Los Morales E . . . 162 A2
Los Navalmorales
E 156 A3
Los Navalucillos E . 156 A3
Losne F 105 B4
Los Nietos E 165 B4
Løsning DK 59 C2
Los Palacios y
Villafranca E 162 A2
Los Pozuelos de
Calatrava E 157 B3
Los Rábanos E . . . 143 C4
Los Santos E 149 B4
Los Santos de la
Humosa E 151 B4
Los Santos de Maimona
E 155 C4
Lossburg D 93 C4
Losse F 128 B2
Losser NL 71 B4
Lossiemouth GB . . 32 D3
Lössnitz D 83 B4
Loštice CZ 97 B4
Los Tijos E 142 A2
Lostwithiel GB . . . 42 B2
Los Villares E . . . 163 A4
Los Yébenes E . . . 157 A4
Løten N 48 B3
Lotorp S 56 B1
Lottefors S 50 A3
Löttorp S 62 A5
Lotyn PL 68 B1
Lotzorai I 179 C3
Louargat F 100 A2
Loudéac F 101 A3
Loudun F 102 B2
Loué F 102 B1
Loughborough GB . 40 C2
Loughbrickland GB . 27 B4
Loughrea IRL 28 A3
Louhans F 105 C4
Louisburgh IRL . . . 28 A2
Loukhi RUS 3 C13
Loulay F 114 B3
Loulé P 160 B1
Louny CZ 84 B1
Lourdes F 145 A3
Lourenzá E 141 A3
Loures P 154 C1
Loures-Barousse
F 145 A4
Louriçal P 154 A2
Lourinhã P 154 B1
Lourmarin F 131 B4
Loury F 103 B4
Lousa
Bragança P 149 A2
Castelo Branco P . 155 B3
Lousã P 148 B1
Lousa P 154 C1
Lousada
E 140 B3
P 148 A1
Louth GB 41 B3
Loutra Edipsou
GR 183 E5
Loutraki GR 184 B3
Loutropoli Thermis
GR 186 C1
Louverné F 102 A1
Louvie-Juzon F . . 145 A3
Louviers F 89 A5
Louvigné-du-Désert
F 88 B2
Louvois F 91 B4
Lova I 121 B5
Lovasberény H . . . 112 B2
Lövåsen S 49 C5
Lovászpatona H . . 111 B4
Lövberga S 200 C1
Lovech BG 17 D6
Lovenich D 80 A2
Lóvere I 120 B3
Lövestad S 61 D3
Loviisa FIN 8 B5
Lovikka S 196 B5
Lovinobaňa SK . . . 99 C3
Loviste HR 138 B3
Lovke HR 123 B3
Lovnäs S 49 A5
Lövö H 111 B3
Lovosice CZ 84 B2
Lovozero RUS . . . 3 C14
Lovran HR 123 B3
Lovreć HR 138 B2
Lovrenc na Pohorju
SLO 110 C2
Lovrin RO 126 B2
Lövstabruk S 51 B4
Löwenberg D 74 B2
Löwenstein D 94 B1
Lowestoft GB 41 C5

Lowick GB 37 A5
Łowicz PL 77 B4
Loxstedt D 72 A1
Loyew BY 13 C9
Lož SLO 123 B3
Loza CZ 96 B1
Lozance SRB . . . 127 C1
Lozničko Polje
SRB 127 C1
Lozorno SK 111 A4
Lozovik SRB 127 C3
Lozoya E 151 B4
Lozoyuela E 151 B4
Lozzo di Cadore I . 109 C3
Luanco E 141 A5
Luarca E 141 A4
Lubaczów PL 13 C5
Lubań PL 84 A3
Lubanie PL 76 B3
Lubanów PL 86 A3
Lubars D 73 B5
Lubasz PL 75 B5
Lubawa PL 69 B4
Lubawka PL 85 B4
Lübbecke D 72 B1
Lübben D 74 C2
Lübbenau D 84 A1
Lubczyna PL 74 A3
Lübeck D 65 C3
Lubenec CZ 83 B5
Lubersac F 115 C5
Lübesse D 73 A4
Lubia E 152 A1
Lubian E 141 B4
Lubiatowo PL 75 A4
Lubichowo PL 69 B3
Lubicz Dolny PL . . 76 A3
Lubień PL 99 B3
Lubienia PL 87 A5
Lubień Kujawski PL 77 B4
Lubieszewo PL . . . 75 A4
Lubin
Dolnośląskie PL . . 85 A4
Zachodnio-Pomorskie
PL 67 C3
Lublin PL 12 C5
Lubliniec PL 86 B2
Lubmin D 66 B2
Lubniewice PL . . . 75 B4
Lubochnia PL 87 A4
Lubomierz
Dolnośląskie PL . . 84 A3
Małopolskie PL . . . 99 B4
Lubomino PL 69 A5
Luboń PL 76 B1
L'ubotín SK 99 B4
Lubowidz PL 77 A4
Łubowo
Wielkopolskie PL . 76 B2
Zachodnio-Pomorskie
PL 68 B1
Lubraniec PL 76 B3
Lubrin E 164 B2
Lubrza PL 85 B5
Lubsko PL 84 A2
Lübtheen D 73 A4
Lubuczewo PL . . . 68 A2
Luby CZ 83 B4
Lübz D 73 A5
Luc F 117 C3
Lucainena de las Torres
E 164 B2
Lucan IRL 30 A2
Lučani SRB 127 D2
Lúcar E 164 B2
Luçay-le-Mâle F . . 103 B3
Lucca I 134 B3
Lucciana F 180 A2
Lucé F 90 C1
Luče SLO 123 A3
Lucena
Córdoba E 163 A3
Huelva E 161 B3
Lucenay-les-Aix F . 104 C2
Lucenay-l'Evêque
F 104 B3
Luc-en-Diois F . . . 118 C2
Lučenec SK 99 C3
Luceni E 144 C2
Lucens CH 106 C1
Lucera I 171 B3
Luceram F 133 B3
Lüchow D 73 B4
Luciana E 157 B3
Lucignano I 135 B4
Lucija SLO 122 B2
Lucka D 83 A4
Luckau D 84 A1
Luckenwalde D . . . 74 B2
Lückstedt D 73 B4
Luco dei Marsi I . . 169 B3
Luçon F 114 B2
Luc-sur-Mer F . . . 89 A3
Ludanice SK 98 C2
Ludbreg HR 124 A2
Lüdenscheid D . . . 81 A3
Lüderitz D 73 B4
Lüdersdorf D 65 C3
Ludgershall GB . . . 44 B2
Ludgo S 56 B3
Ludlow GB 39 B4
Ludomy PL 75 B5
Ludvika S 50 B2
Ludweiler Warndt D 92 B2
Ludwigsburg D . . . 94 C1
Ludwigsfelde D . . . 74 B2

Ludwigshafen D . . 93 B4
Ludwigslust D . . . 73 A4
Ludwigsstadt D . . . 82 B3
Ludza LV 8 D5
Luesia E 144 B2
Luftkurort Arendsee
D 73 B4
Lug
BIH 139 C4
HR 125 B4
Luga RUS 9 C6
Lugagnano Val d'Arda
I 120 C2
Lugano CH 120 A1
Lugau D 83 B4
Lugny F 105 C3
Lugo
E 140 A3
I 135 A4
Lugoj RO 16 C4
Lugones E 141 A5
Lugros E 163 A4
Luhačovice CZ . . . 98 B1
Luhe D 95 B4
Luino I 120 B1
Luintra E 140 B3
Lújar E 163 B4
Luka nad Jihlavou
CZ 97 B3
Lukavac BIH . . . 125 C4
Lukavika BIH . . . 125 C4
Lukovë AL 182 D1
Lukovica SLO . . . 123 A3
Lukovit BG 17 D6
Lukovo HR 123 C3
Lukovo Šugorje
HR 137 A4
Łuków PL 12 C5
Łukowice Brzeskie
PL 85 B5
Luksefjell N 53 A5
Łukta PL 69 B5
Luleå S 196 D5
Lüleburgaz TR . . . 186 A2
Lumbarda HR . . . 138 C3
Lumbier E 144 B2
Lumbrales E 149 B3
Lumbreras E 143 B4
Lumbres F 78 B2
Lummelunda S . . . 57 C4
Lummen B 79 B5
Lumparland FIN . . 51 B7
Lumpiaque E 152 A2
Lumsås DK 61 D1
Lumsden GB 33 D4
Lumsheden S 50 B3
Lun HR 123 C3
Luna E 144 B3
Lunamatrona I . . . 179 C2
Lunano I 136 B1
Lunas F 130 B2
Lund
N 199 A8
Skåne S 61 D3
Västra Götaland S . 54 A3
Lundamo N 199 B7
Lunde
DK 59 C1
Sogn og Fjordane
N 46 A3
Sogn og Fjordane
N 46 A3
Telemark N 53 A5
S 200 D3
Lundebyvollen N . . 49 B4
Lunden D 64 B2
Lunderseter N . . . 49 B4
Lunderskov DK . . . 59 C2
Lundsberg S 55 A5
Lüneburg D 72 A3
Lunel F 131 B3
Lünen D 81 A3
Lunéville F 92 C2
Lungern CH 106 C3
Lungro I 174 B2
Luninyets BY 13 B7
Lünne D 71 B4
Lunner N 48 B2
Lunteren NL 70 B2
Lunz am See A . . 110 B2
Luogosanto I 178 A3
Łupawa PL 68 A2
Lupión E 157 B4
Lupoglav HR 123 B3
Luppa D 83 A4
Luque E 163 A3
Lurago d'Erba I . . 120 B2
Lúras I 178 B3
Lurcy-Lévis F . . . 104 C1
Lure F 105 B5
Lurgan GB 27 B4
Luri F 180 A2
Lury-sur-Arnon F . 103 B4
Lusanger F 101 B4
Lusevera I 122 A2
Lushnjë AL 182 C1
Lusignan F 115 B4
Lusigny-sur-Barse
F 104 A3
Lusk IRL 30 A2
Lušnić BIH 138 B2
Luso P 148 B1
Lusówko PL 75 B5
Luspebryggan S . . 196 B2
Luss GB 34 B3
Lussac F 128 B2

Lussac-les-Châteaux
F 115 B4
Lussac-les-Eglises
F 115 B5
Lussan F 131 A3
Lüssow D 65 C5
Lustenau A 107 B4
Luštěnice CZ 84 B2
Luster N 47 A4
Lutago I 108 C2
Lutherstadt Wittenberg
D 83 A4
Lütjenburg D 65 B3
Lutnes N 49 A4
Lutocin PL 77 B4
Lutomiersk PL . . . 86 A3
Luton GB 44 B3
Lutry CH 106 C1
Lutsk UA 13 C6
Lutter am Barenberge
D 72 C3
Lutterworth GB . . . 40 C2
Lututów PL 86 A2
Lützen D 83 A4
Lutzow D 73 A4
Luusua FIN 197 C10
Luvos S 196 C1
Luxembourg L 92 B2
Luxeuil-les-Bains
F 105 B5
Luxey F 128 B2
Luz
Évora P 155 C3
Faro P 160 B1
Faro P 160 B2
Luzarches F 90 B2
Luže CZ 97 B4
Luzech F 129 B4
Luzern CH 106 B3
Luzino PL 68 A3
Luz-St Sauveur F . 145 B3
Luzy F 104 C2
Luzzi I 174 B2
L'viv UA 13 D6
Lwówek PL 75 B5
Lwówek Śląski PL . 84 A3
Lyakhavichy BY . . 13 B7
Lybster GB 32 C3
Lychen D 74 A2
Lychkova RUS 9 D8
Lyckeby S 63 B3
Lycksele S 200 B4
Lydd GB 45 C4
Lydford GB 42 B2
Lydney GB 39 C4
Lyepyel BY 13 A8
Lygna N 48 B2
Lykke N 47 B5
Lykling N 52 A1
Lyme Regis GB . . 43 B4
Lymington GB . . . 44 C2
Lympne GB 45 B5
Lyndhurst GB . . . 44 C2
Lyneham GB 43 A5
Lyness GB 33 C3
Lyngdal
Buskerud N 47 C6
Vest-Agder N 52 B3
Lyngør N 53 B5
Lyngsa DK 58 A3
Lyngseidet N 192 C4
Lyngsnes N 199 A8
Lynmouth GB . . . 42 A3
Lynton GB 42 A3
Lyntupy BY 13 A7
Lyon F 117 B4
Lyons-la-Forêt F . . 90 B1
Lyozna BY 13 A9
Lyrestad S 55 B5
Lysánad Labem CZ 84 B2
Lysápod Makytou
SK 98 B2
Lysebotn N 52 A2
Lysekil S 54 B2
Lysice CZ 97 B4
Lysomice PL 76 A3
Lysøysund N . . . 198 B6
Lyss CH 106 B2
Lystrup DK 59 B3
Lysvik S 49 B5
Łyszkowice PL . . . 77 C4
Lytham St Anne's
GB 38 A3

Ludwigshafen D . . 93 B4

Macduff GB 33 D4
Maceda E 140 B3
Macedo de Cavaleiros
P 149 A3
Maceira
Guarda P 148 B2
Leiria P 154 B2
Macelj HR 124 A1
Macerata I 136 B2
Macerata Féltria I . 136 B1
Machault F 91 B4
Machecoul F 114 B2
Mchowo PL 77 A5
Machrihanish GB . . 34 C2
Machynlleth GB . . 39 B3
Macieira P 148 B1
Maciejowice PL . . . 87 A5
Macinaggio F . . . 180 A2
Mackenrode D . . . 82 A2
Mačkovci SLO . . . 111 C3
Macomer I 178 B2
Macon B 91 A4
Mâcon F 117 A4
Macotera E 150 B2
Macroom IRL 29 C3
Macugnaga I 119 B4
Madan BG 183 B6
Mädängsholm S . . 55 B4
Madaras H 126 A1
Made NL 79 A4
Madeley GB 38 B4
Maderuelo E 151 A4
Madetkoski FIN . . 197 B9
Madley GB 39 B4
Madocsa H 112 C2
Madona LV 8 D5
Madonna di Campíglio
I 121 A3
Madrid E 151 B4
Madridejos E 157 A4
Madrigal de las Altas
Torres E 150 A2
Madrigal de la Vera
E 150 B2
Madrigalejo E . . . 156 A2
Madrigalejo de Monte
E 143 B3
Madriguera E . . . 151 A4
Madrigueras E . . . 158 B2
Madroñera E . . . 156 A2
Maël-Carhaix F . . 100 A2
Maella E 153 A4
Maello E 150 B3
Maesteg GB 39 C3
Mafra P 154 C1
Magacela E 156 B2
Magallon E 144 C2
Magaluf E 166 B2
Magaña E 151 C4
Magasa I 121 B3
Magaz E 142 C2
Magdeburg D 73 B4
Magenta I 120 B1
Magescq F 128 C1
Maghera GB 27 B4
Magherafelt GB . . 27 B4
Maghull GB 38 A4
Magilligan GB 27 A4
Magione I 135 B5
Magioto P 154 C1
Maglaj BIH 125 C4
Maglehem S 63 C2
Magliano de'Marsi
I 169 A3
Magliano in Toscana
I 168 A1
Magliano Sabina I . 168 A2
Maglić SRB 126 B1
Máglie I 173 B4
Maglód H 112 B3
Magnac-Bourg F . . 115 C5
Magnac-Laval F . . 115 B5
Magnieres F 92 C2
Magnor N 49 C4
Magnuszew PL . . . 87 A5
Magny-Cours F . . 104 C2
Magny-en-Vexin F . 90 B1
Mágocs H 125 A4
Maguilla E 156 B2
Maguiresbridge GB. 27 B3
Magyarbóly H . . . 125 B4
Magyarkeszi H . . . 112 C2
Magyarszék H . . . 125 A4
Mahide E 141 C4
Mahilyow BY 13 B9
Mahmudiye TR . . . 187 C5
Mahora E 158 B2
Mahovo HR 124 B2
Mähring D 95 B4
Maia
E 144 A2
P 148 A1
Maiaelrayo E . . . 151 A4
Maials E 153 A4
Maîche F 106 B1
Máida I 175 C2
Maiden Bradley GB. 43 A4
Maidenhead GB . . 44 B3
Maiden Newton GB. 43 B4
Maidstone GB . . . 45 B4
Maienfeld CH . . . 107 B4
Maignelay Montigny
F 90 B2

Maijanen FIN 197 B8
Maillezais F 114 B3
Mailly-le-Camp F . . 91 C4
Mailly-le-Château
  F. 104 B2
Mainar E. 152 A2
Mainbernheim D . . 94 B2
Mainburg D 95 C3
Mainhardt D. 94 B1
Maintal D 81 B4
Maintenon F 90 C1
Mainvilliers F. 90 C1
Mainz D 93 A4
Maiorca P. 148 B1
Mairena de Aljarafe
  E. 162 A1
Mairena del Alcor
  E. 162 A2
Maisach D 108 A2
Maishofen A. 109 B3
Maison-Rouge F . . 90 C3
Maissau A 97 C3
Maisse F 90 C2
Maizières-lès-Vic F . 92 C2
Maja HR 124 B2
Majadahonda E . . 151 B4
Majadas E 150 C2
Majavatn N. 195 E4
Majs H 125 B4
Majšperk SLO . . . 123 A4
Makarska HR 138 B3
Makkum NL 70 A2
Maklár H. 113 B4
Makó H. 126 A2
Makoszyce PL 85 B5
Makov SK. 98 B2
Mąkowarsko PL. . . 76 A2
Maków Mazowiecki
  PL. 77 B6
Maków Podhalański
  PL. 99 B3
Makrakomi GR . . 182 E4
Maksniemi FIN . . 196 D7
Malå S 195 E9
Mala Bosna SRB . . 126 A1
Malacky SK 97 C5
Maladzyechna BY . . 13 A7
Málaga E 163 B3
Malagón E 157 A4
Malaguilla E 151 B4
Malahide IRL 30 A2
Mala Kladuša BIH . 124 B1
Mala Krsna SRB . . 127 C3
Malalbergo I. 121 C4
Malá Lehota SK . . 98 C2
Malanów PL. 76 C3
Mala Pijace SRB . . 126 A1
Mala Subotica HR . 124 A2
Malaucène F 131 A4
Malaunay F 89 A5
Malaya Vishera RUS . 9 C8
Malborghetto I . . . 109 C4
Malbork PL. 69 A4
Malborn D 92 B2
Malbuisson F. . . . 105 C5
Malcésine I 121 B3
Malchin D. 74 A1
Malching D 96 C1
Malchow D. 73 A5
Malcocinado E . . . 156 B2
Malczyce PL. 85 A4
Maldegem B. 79 A3
Maldon GB. 45 B4
Małdyty PL. 69 B4
Malè I 121 A3
Malemort F 129 A4
Malente D. 65 B3
Måleräs S. 62 B3
Males GR 185 D6
Malesherbes F. . . . 90 C2
Malesina GR 183 E5
Malestroit F 101 B3
Maletto I. 177 B3
Malexander S 56 B1
Malgrat de Mar E . 147 C3
Malhadas P 149 A3
Malia
  CY 181 B1
  GR 185 D6
Malicorne-sur-Sarthe
  F. 102 B1
Malijai F 132 A2
Malildjoš SRB . . . 126 B1
Málilla S. 62 A3
Mali Lošinj HR . . 137 A3
Malin IRL 27 A3
Málinec SK 99 C3
Malingsbo S 50 C2
Maliniec PL 76 B3
Malinska HR 123 B3
Maliq AL. 182 C2
Maljevac HR 123 B4
Malkara TR. 186 B1
Małki PL. 69 B4
Malko Tarnovo BG . 17 D7
Mallaig GB 34 A2
Mallaranny IRL . . . 28 A2
Mallemort F 131 B4
Mallén E. 144 C2
Malléon F. 146 A2
Mallersdorf-Pfaffenberg
  D 95 C4
Málles Venosta I . . 108 C1
Malling DK. 59 B3
Mallnitz A. 109 C4
Mallow IRL. 29 B3
Mallwyd GB. 38 B3
Malm N. 199 A8
Malmbäck S. 62 A2
Malmberget S . . . 196 B3
Malmby S. 56 A3
Malmédy B. 80 B2
Malmesbury GB . . 43 A4
Malmköping S . . . 56 A2
Malmö S. 61 D3
Malmon S. 54 B2
Malmslätt S 56 B1
Malnate I 120 B1
Malo I 121 B4
Małogoszcz PL . . . 87 B4
Maloja CH 120 A2
Małomice PL 84 A3
Måløy N 198 D2
Malpartida E 155 B4
Malpartida de la Serena
  E. 156 B2
Malpartida de Plasencia
  E. 150 C1
Malpas
  E 145 B4
  GB 38 A4
Malpica P. 155 B3
Malpica de Bergantiños
  E. 140 A2
Malpica de Tajo E . 150 C3
Malsch D 93 C4
Malšice CZ. 96 B2
Malta A 109 C4
Maltat F 104 C2
Maltby GB 40 B2
Malung S 49 B5
Malungsfors S. . . . 49 B5
Maluszów PL. 75 B4
Maluszyn PL 87 B3
Malva E. 142 C1
Malvaglia CH . . . 120 A1
Malveira P 154 C1
Malvik N. 199 B7
Malyn UA 13 C8
Mamarrosa P. . . . 148 B1
Mamer L 92 B2
Mamers F. 89 B4
Mamirolle F 105 B5
Mammendorf D . . 108 A2
Mámmola I 175 C2
Mamoiada I 178 B3
Mamonovo RUS . . 69 A4
Mamuras AL. . . . 182 B1
Maña SK. 112 A2
Manacor E 167 B3
Manavgat TR. . . . 189 C6
Mancera de Abajo
  E. 150 B2
Mancha Real E . . 163 A4
Manchester GB . . . 40 B1
Manching D 95 C3
Manchita E. 156 B1
Manciano I 168 A1
Manciet F. 128 C3
Mandal N 52 B3
Mandanici I 177 A4
Mándas I 179 C3
Mandatoríccio I . . 174 B2
Mandayona E . . . 151 B5
Mandelieu-la-Napoule
  F. 132 B2
Mandello del Lário
  I 120 B2
Mandelsloh D 72 B2
Manderfeld B. . . . 80 B2
Manderscheid D . . 80 B2
Mandino Selo BIH . 138 B3
Mandoudi GR . . . 183 E5
Mandra GR 185 A4
Mandraki GR . . . 188 C2
Mandúria I 173 B3
Mane
  Alpes-de-Haute-
    Provence F. . . . 132 B1
  Haute-Garonne F. . 145 A4
Manérbio I 120 B3
Mañeru E 144 B2
Manetin CZ 96 B1
Manfredónia I . . . 171 B3
Mangalia RO 17 D8
Manganeses de la
  Lampreana E . . 149 A4
Manganeses de la
  Polvorosa E . . . 141 B5
Mangen N. 48 C3
Manger N. 46 B2
Mangiennes F . . . 92 B1
Mangotsfield GB. . . 43 A4
Mångsbodarna S. . 49 A5
Mangualde P 148 B2
Maniago I 122 A1
Manilva E. 162 B2
Manisa TR. 186 D2
Manises E 159 B3
Mank A 110 A2
Månkarbo S 51 B4
Manlleu E. 147 C3
Manna DK 58 A2
Männedorf CH . . 107 B3
Mannersdorf am
  Leithagebirge A. .111 B3
Mannheim D 93 B4
Manningtree GB . . 45 B5
Manoppello I 169 A4
Manorbier GB . . . 39 C2
Manorhamilton IRL . 26 B2
Manosque F 132 B1
Manowo PL 67 B5

Manresa E 147 C2
Mânsarp S 62 A2
Månsåsen S. . . .199 B11
Manschnow D 74 B3
Mansfeld D 82 A3
Mansfield GB. 40 B2
Mansilla de Burgos
  E. 143 B3
Mansilla de las Mulas
  E. 142 B1
Manskog S. 55 A3
Mansle F 115 C4
Manso F. 180 A1
Manteigas P. 148 B2
Mantel D. 95 B4
Mantes-la-Jolie F . . 90 C1
Mantes-la-Ville F. . 90 C1
Manthelan F. 102 B2
Mantorp S 56 B1
Mántova I. 121 B3
Mänttä FIN 8 A4
Mäntyjärvi FIN. . 197 C10
Manuel E 159 B3
Manyas TR. 186 B2
Manzanal de Arriba
  E. 141 B4
Manzanares E . . . 157 A4
Manzanares el Real
  E. 151 B4
Manzaneda
  León E. 141 B4
  Orense E 141 B3
Manzanedo E. . . . 143 B3
Manzaneque E. . . 157 A4
Manzanera E 153 B3
Manzanilla E 161 B3
Manzat F. 116 B2
Manziana I 168 A2
Manziat F. 117 A4
Maó I 167 B4
Maoča BIH 125 C4
Maqueda E. 150 B3
Mara E 152 A2
Maramaraereğlisi
  TR 186 B2
Maraña E 142 A1
Maranchón E 152 A1
Maranello I 135 A3
Marano I. 170 C2
Marano Lagunare I . 122 B2
Marans F. 114 B2
Maratea I 174 B1
Marateca P. 154 C2
Marathókambos
  GR 188 B1
Marathonas GR . . 185 A4
Marathóvouno CY . 181 A2
Marazion GB 42 B1
Marbach
  Baden-Württemberg
    D. 94 C1
  Hessen D. 82 B1
  F. 92 C2
Marbäck S 60 B3
Mårbacka S. 55 A4
Marbella E 162 B3
Marboz F 118 A2
Marburg D 81 B4
Marcali H. 111 C4
Marčana HR. 122 C2
Marcaria I 121 B3
Marcelová SK 112 B2
Marcenat F. 116 B2
March GB. 41 C4
Marchamalo E . . . 151 B4
Marchaux F 105 B5
Marche-en-Famenne
  B. 79 B5
Marchegg A 111 A3
Marchena E 162 A2
Marchenoir F . . . 103 B3
Marcheprime F . . 128 B2
Marciac F 128 C3
Marciana Marina I . 134 C3
Marcianise I 170 B2
Marcigny F. 117 A4
Marcilla E 144 B2
Marcillac-la-Croisille
  F. 116 B2
Marcillac-Vallon F . 130 A1
Marcillat-en-Combraille
  F. 116 A2
Marcille-sur-Seine F . 91 C3
Marcilloles F 118 B2
Marcilly-le-Hayer F . 91 C3
Marcinkowice PL. . . 75 A5
Marck F 78 B1
Marckolsheim F . . 106 A2
Marco de Canevezes
  P. 148 A1
Mårdsele S. 200 B5
Mårdsjö S 200 C1
Mareham le Fen GB . 41 B3
Marek S 62 A3
Marennes F 114 C2
Maresquel F. 78 B1
Mareuil F 115 C4
Mareuil-en-Brie F . 91 C3
Mareuil-sur-Arnon
  F. 103 C4
Mareuil-sur-Lay F . .114 B2
Mareuil-sur-Ourcq F . 90 B3
Margam GB 39 C3
Margariti GR . . . 182 D2
Margate GB. 45 B5
Margaux F 128 A2

Margerie-Hancourt
  F. 91 C4
Margès F. 117 B5
Margherita di Savóia
  I 171 B4
Margone I. 119 B4
Margonin PL 76 B2
Marguerittes F . . . 131 B3
Margut F 91 B5
Maria E. 164 B2
Mariager DK. 58 B2
Mariana E. 152 B1
Mariannelund S. . . 62 A3
Marianópoli I . . . 176 B2
Mariánské Lázně
  CZ 95 B4
Maria Saal A 110 C1
Mariazell A. 110 B2
Maribo DK 65 B4
Maribor SLO 110 C2
Marieberg S. 56 A1
Mariefred S 56 A3
Mariehamn FIN . . . 51 B6
Marieholm S 61 D3
Mariembourg B . . 91 A4
Marienbaum D. . . 80 A2
Marienberg D. . . . 83 B5
Marienheide D. . . 81 A3
Mariental D 73 B3
Mariestad S 55 B4
Marieux F. 90 A2
Marigliano I 170 C2
Marignane F 131 B4
Marigny
  Jura F. 105 C4
  Manche F. 88 A2
Marigny-le-Châtel F . 91 C3
Marija Bistrica HR . 124 A2
Marijampolė LT . . . 13 A5
Marín E 140 B2
Marina HR 138 B2
Marina del Cantone
  I 170 C2
Marina di Acquappesa
  I 174 B1
Marina di Alberese
  I 168 A1
Marina di Amendolara
  I 174 B2
Marina di Campo I. 134 C3
Marina di Carrara I . 134 A3
Marina di Castagneto-
  Donorático I . . . 134 B3
Marina di Cécina I . 134 B3
Marina di Gáiro I . . 179 C3
Marina di Ginosa I. 173 B2
Marina di Gioiosa Iónica
  I 175 C2
Marina di Grosseto
  I 135 C3
Marina di Léuca I. . 173 C4
Marina di Massa I . 134 A3
Marina di Nováglie
  I 173 C4
Marina di Pisa I . . 134 B3
Marina di Ragusa I . 177 C3
Marina di Ravenna
  I 135 A5
Marina di Torre Grande
  I 179 C2
Marinaleda E 162 A3
Marina Romea I . . 135 A5
Marine di Sisco F . 180 A2
Marinella I 176 B1
Marinella di Sarzana
  I 134 A3
Marineo I 176 B2
Marines F 90 B1
Maringues F 116 B3
Marinha das Ondas
  P. 154 A2
Marinha Grande P. 154 B2
Marinhas P. 148 A1
Marino I 168 B2
Marjaliza E 157 A4
Markabygd N 199 B8
Markaryd S 61 C3
Markdorf D. 107 B4
Markelo NL. 71 B3
Market Deeping GB. 40 C3
Market Drayton GB . 38 B4
Market Harborough
  GB 40 C3
Markethill GB. . . . 27 B4
Market Rasen GB . . 40 B3
Market Warsop GB . 40 B2
Market Weighton
  GB 40 B3
Markgröningen D . . 93 C5
Markhausen D . . . 71 B4
Marki PL. 77 B6
Markina-Xemein E. 143 A4
Markinch GB 35 B4
Markitta S 196 B4
Markkleeberg D. . . 83 A4
Marklohe D 72 B2
Marknesse NL. . . . 70 B2
Markneukirchen D . 83 B4
Markopoulo GR . . 185 B4
Markovac
  Srbija SRB. 127 C3
  Vojvodina SRB. . . 126 B2

Markowice PL 86 B2
Markranstädt D . . . 83 A4
Marksuhl D 82 B2
Markt Allhau A. . . .111 B3
Markt Bibart D . . . 94 B2
Marktbreit D. 94 B2
Markt Erlbach D . . 94 B2
Markt-heidenfeld D . 94 B1
Markt Indersdorf D . 95 C3
Marktl D. 95 C4
Marktleuthen D . . . 83 B3
Marktoberdorf D . . 108 B1
Marktredwitz D . . . 95 A4
Markt Rettenbach
  D 108 B1
Markt Schwaben D . 108 A2
Markt-Übelbach A . .110 B2
Marl D. 80 A3
Marlborough
  Devon GB 42 B3
  Wiltshire GB. 44 B2
Marle F. 91 B3
Marlieux F 117 A5
Marlow
  D 66 B1
  GB 44 B3
Marma S. 51 B4
Marmagne F 104 C3
Marmande F 128 B3
Marmara TR 186 B2
Marmaris TR 188 C3
Marmelete P. . . . 160 B1
Marmolejo E 157 B3
Marmoutier F. . . . 93 C3
Marnay F 105 B4
Marne D 64 C2
Marnheim D. 93 B4
Marnitz D. 73 A4
Maroldsweisach D . 82 B2
Marolles-les-Braults
  F. 89 B4
Maromme F 89 A5
Marone I. 120 B3
Maronia GR 183 C7
Maroslele H 126 A2
Maróstica I 121 B4
Marotta I 136 B2
Marpisa GR 185 B6
Marquion F. 78 B3
Marquise F. 78 B1
Marradi I. 135 A4
Marrasjärvi FIN . . 197 C8
Marraskoski FIN . . 197 C8
Marratxi E 166 B2
Marrúbiu I 179 C2
Marrum NL. 70 A2
Marrupe E 150 B3
Marsac F 129 C5
Marsac-en-Livradois
  F. 117 B3
Marság lia I 120 C2
Marsala I 176 B1
Marsberg D 81 A4
Marsciano I 135 C5
Marseillan F. 130 B2
Marseille = Marseilles
  F. 131 B4
Marseille en Beauvaisis
  F. 90 B1
Marseilles = Marseille
  F. 131 B4
Mársico Nuovo I. . 172 B1
Marske-by-the-Sea
  GB 37 B5
Mars-la-Tours F . . 92 B1
Marsliden S 195 E6
Marson F 91 C4
Märsta S. 57 A3
Marstal DK. 65 B3
Marstrand S 60 B1
Marta I 168 A1
Martano I 173 B4
Martel F 129 B4
Martelange B. . . . 92 B1
Martfeld D 72 B2
Martfü H. 113 B4
Martham GB 41 C5
Marthon F 115 C4
Martiago E 149 B3
Martigné-Briand F. 102 B1
Martigné-Ferchaud
  F. 101 B4
Martigne-sur-Mayenne
  F. 102 A1
Martigny CH 119 A4
Martigny-les-Bains
  F. 105 A4
Martigues F 131 B4
Martim-Longo P . . 160 B2
Martin SK 98 B2
Martina CH. 108 C1
Martina Franca I . . 173 B3
Martinamor E. . . . 150 B2
Martin de la Jara E . 162 A3
Martin Muñoz de las
  Posadas E. . . . 150 A3
Martinsberg A . . . 97 C3
Martinšćica HR . . 123 C3
Martinshöhe D . . . 93 B3
Martinsicuro I . . . 136 C2
Martinszell D . . . 107 B5
Martofte DK 59 C3
Martonvásár H. . . .112 B2
Martorell E 147 C2

Martos E 163 A4
Martres Tolosane
  F. 146 A1
Martti FIN 197 B11
Marugán E. 150 B3
Marúggio I 173 B3
Marvão P. 155 B3
Marvejols F. 130 A2
Marville F 92 B1
Marwałd PL 77 A4
Marykirk GB. 35 B5
Marypark GB 32 D3
Maryport GB 36 B3
Marytavy GB 42 B2
Marzabotto I . . . 135 A4
Marzahna D. 74 C1
Marzahne D 73 B5
Marzamemi I 177 C4
Marzocca I 136 B2
Masa E 143 B3
Mas-Cabardès F . . 146 A3
Máscali I. 177 B4
Mascaraque E . . . 157 A4
Mascarenhas P . . 149 A2
Mascioni I 169 A3
Mas de Barberáns
  E. 153 B4
Mas de las Matas
  E. 153 B3
Masegoso E. 158 C1
Masegoso de Tajuña
  E. 151 B5
Masera I 119 A5
Masevaux F 106 B1
Masfjorden N. . . . 46 B2
Masham GB. 37 B5
Masi N 192 C7
Maside E 140 B2
Maslacq F 144 A3
Maslinica HR . . . 138 B2
Maşloc RO. 126 B3
Maslovare BIH . . 138 A3
Masone I 133 A4
Massa I. 134 A3
Massa Fiscáglia I. 121 C5
Massafra I 173 B3
Massa Lombarda I 135 A4
Massa Lubrense I . 170 C2
Massamagrell E . . 159 B3
Massa Marittima I . 135 B3
Massa Martana I . 136 C1
Massanassa E. . . 159 B3
Massarosa I 134 B3
Massat F 146 B2
Massay F 103 B3
Massbach D 82 B2
Masseret F 116 B1
Masseube F 145 A4
Massiac F. 116 B3
Massignac F 115 C4
Massing D 95 C4
Massmechelen B. . 80 B1
Masterud N 49 B4
Mästocka S 61 C3
Masty BY 13 B6
Masúa I 179 C2
Masueco E. 149 A3
Masugnsbyn S . . . 196 B5
Mašun SLO 123 B3
Maszewo
  Lubuskie PL. 75 B3
  Zachodnio-Pomorskie
    PL. 75 A4
Mata de Alcántara
  E. 155 B4
Matala GR 185 E5
Matalebreras E . . 144 C1
Matallana de Torio
  E. 142 B1
Matamala E 151 A5
Mataporquera E . . 142 B2
Matapozuelos E . . 150 A3
Mataró E 147 C3
Matarocco I 176 B1
Matélica I 136 B2
Matera I 172 B2
Mátészalka H. . . . 16 B5
Matet E 159 B3
Matfors S 200 D3
Matha F 115 C3
Mathay F 106 B1
Matignon F 101 A3
Matilla de los Caños del
  Rio E 149 B4
Matlock GB 40 B2
Matosinhos P . . . 148 A1
Matour F 117 A4
Mátrafüred H 113 B3
Mátraterenye H . . .113 A3
Matre
  Hordaland N. 46 B2
  Hordaland N. 52 A1
Matrei am Brenner
  A. 108 B2
Matrei in Osttirol A 109 B3
Matrice I 170 B2
Matsdal S. 195 E6
Mattarello I 121 A4
Mattersburg A. . . .111 B3
Mattighofen A . . . 109 A4
Mattinata I 171 B4
Mattos P. 154 B2
Mattsee A 109 B4
Mattsmyra S 50 A2
Måttsund S 196 D5
Matulji HR 123 B3
Maubert-Fontaine F . 91 B4
Maubeuge F 79 B3

Maubourguet F . . . 145 A4
Mauchline GB 36 A2
Maud GB 33 D4
Mauer-kirchen A . . 109 A4
Mauern D. 95 C3
Mauguio F 131 B3
Maulbronn D 93 C4
Maule F 90 C1
Mauléon F 114 B3
Mauléon-Barousse
  F. 145 B4
Mauléon-Licharre
  F. 144 A3
Maulévrier F 114 A3
Maum IRL 28 A2
Maurach A 108 B2
Maure-de-Bretagne
  F. 101 B4
Maureilhan F . . . 130 B2
Mǎureni RO 126 B3
Mauriac F. 116 B2
Mauron F 101 A3
Maurs F 116 C2
Maury F 146 B3
Maussane-les-Alpilles
  F. 131 B3
Mautern A 97 C3
Mauterndorf A . . . 109 B4
Mautern im Steiermark
  A. 110 B1
Mauthausen A 110 A1
Mauthen A 109 C3
Mauvezin F 129 C3
Mauzé-sur-le-Mignon
  F. 114 B3
Maxent F 101 B3
Maxey-sur-Vaise F . 92 C1
Maxial P 154 B2
Maxieira P 154 B2
Maxwellheugh GB . . 35 C5
Mayalde E 149 A4
Maybole GB 36 A2
Mayen D 80 B3
Mayenne F 88 B3
Mayet F 102 B2
Mayorga E 142 B1
Mayres F 117 C4
Mayrhofen A 108 B2
Mazagón E 161 B3
Mazaleón E 153 A4
Mazamet F 130 B1
Mazan F 131 A4
Mazara del Vallo I . 176 B1
Mazarambroz E . . . 157 A3
Mazarete E 152 B1
Mazaricos E 140 B2
Mazarrón E 165 B3
Mažeikiai LT 8 D3
Mazères F 146 A2
Mazères-sur-Salat
  F. 145 A4
Mazières-en-Gâtine
  F. 115 B3
Mazin HR 138 A1
Mazuelo E 143 B3
Mazyr BY 13 B8
Mazzarino I 177 B3
Mazzarrà Sant'Andrea
  I 177 A4
Mazzo di Valtellina
  I 120 A3
Mdzewo PL 77 B5
Mealabost GB 31 A2
Mealhada P 148 B1
Méan B 79 B5
Meana Sardo I . . . 179 C3
Meaulne F 103 C4
Meaux F 90 C2
Mebonden N 199 B8
Mecerreyes E 143 B3
Mechelen B 79 A4
Mechernich D 80 B2
Mechnica PL 86 B2
Mechowo PL 67 C4
Mechterstädt D . . . 82 B2
Mecidiye TR 186 B1
Mecikal PL 68 B2
Mecina-Bombarón
  E. 164 C1
Mecitözü TR. 23 A8
Meckenbeuren D . . 107 B4
Meckenheim
  Rheinland-Pfalz D . . 80 B3
  Rheinland-Pfalz D . . 93 B4
Meckesheim D 93 B4
Mecseknádasd H . . 125 A4
Meda
  I 120 B2
  P. 149 B2
Medak HR 137 A4
Mede I 120 B1
Medebach D 81 A4
Medelim P 155 A3
Medemblik NL 70 B2
Medena Selista
  BIH 138 A2
Medesano I 120 C3
Medevi S 55 B5
Medgidia RO 17 C8
Medgyesháza H. . . 113 C5
Medhamn S 55 A4
Mediaş RO 17 B6
Medicina I 135 A4
Medinaceli E 152 A1
Medina de las Torres
  E. 155 C4
Medina del Campo
  E. 150 A3

Medina de Pomar
  E. 143 B3
Medina de Ríoseco
  E. 142 C1
Medina Sidonia E . 162 B2
Medinilla E. 150 B2
Medja SRB 126 B2
Medjedja BIH 139 B5
Medulin HR 122 C2
Meduno I 122 A1
Medveda SRB 127 C3
Medvedov SK. 111 B4
Medvezhyegorsk
  RUS 9 A9
Medvide HR. 137 A4
Medvode SLO 123 A3
Medzev SK. 99 C4
Medžitlija MK 182 C3
Meerane D 83 B4
Meerle B. 79 A4
Meersburg D 107 B4
Meeuwen B 79 A5
Megala Horio GR . . 188 C2
Megalopoli GR . . . 184 B3
Megara GR. 185 A4
Megève F 118 B3
Meggenhofen A . . . 109 A4
Megra RUS 9 B10
Megyaszó H. 113 A5
Mehamn N 193 A11
Mehedeby S. 51 B4
Méhkerék H 113 C5
Mehun-sur-Yèvre
  F. 103 B4
Meigle GB 35 B4
Meijel NL 80 A1
Meilen CH 107 B3
Meilhan F 128 C2
Meimôa P. 149 B2
Meina I 119 B5
Meine D 73 B3
Meinersen D 72 B3
Meinerzhagen D . . . 81 A3
Meiningen D 82 B2
Meira E 141 A3
Meiringen CH 106 C3
Meisenheim D 93 B3
Meissen D 83 A5
Meitingen D 94 C2
Meix-devant-Virton
  B. 92 B1
Męka PL 86 A2
Meka Gruda BIH . . 139 B4
Mel I 121 A5
Melbu N 194 B5
Melč CZ 98 B1
Meldal N. 198 B6
Méldola I 135 A5
Meldorf D. 64 B2
Melegnano I 120 B2
Melenci SRB 126 B2
Melendugno I 173 B4
Melfi I 172 B1
Melfjordbotn N . . . 195 D4
Melgaço P. 140 B2
Melgar de Arriba E 142 B1
Melgar de Fernamental
  E. 142 B2
Melgar de Yuso E . 142 B2
Melhus N 199 B7
Melide
  CH 120 B1
  E 140 B2
Melides P 160 A1
Meligales GR. 184 B2
Melilli I 177 B4
Melinovac HR 124 C1
Melisenda I 179 C3
Melisey F 105 B5
Mélito di Porto Salvo
  I 175 D1
Melk A. 110 A2
Melksham GB 43 A4
Mellakoski FIN . . . 196 C7
Mellanström S . . . 195 E9
Mellbystrand S . . . 61 C2
Melle
  B 79 A3
  D 71 B5
  F. 115 B3
Mellendorf D 72 B2
Mellerud S 54 B3
Mellieha M 175 C3
Mellrichstadt D . . . 82 B2
Melnice CZ. 84 B2
Mělnické Vtelno CZ. 84 B2
Mělník CZ. 84 B2
Melón E 140 B2
Melrose GB 35 C5
Mels CH 107 B4
Melsungen D 82 A1
Meltaus FIN 197 C8
Meltham GB. 40 B2
Melton Mowbray
  GB 40 C3
Meltosjärvi FIN . . . 196 C7
Melun F 90 C2
Melvaig GB 31 B3
Melvich GB 32 C3
Mélykút H. 126 A1
Melzo I 120 B2
Memaliaj AL. 182 C1
Membrilla E 157 B4
Membrio E. 155 B3
Memer F. 129 B4
Memmelsdorf D. . . . 94 B2
Memmingen D 107 B5

Memoria P 154 B2
Menággio I. 120 A2
Menai Bridge GB . . 38 A2
Menasalbas E 157 A3
Menat F 116 A2
Mendavia E 144 B1
Mendaza E 144 B1
Mende F 130 A2
Menden D. 81 A3
Menderes TR. 188 A2
Mendig D 80 B3
Mendiga P 154 B2
Mendrisio CH 120 B1
Ménéac F 101 A3
Menemen TR. 188 A2
Menen B 78 B3
Menesjärvi FIN . . . 193 D10
Menetou-Salon F. . 103 B4
Menfi I 176 B1
Ménföcsanak H . . .111 B4
Mengamuñoz E . . . 150 B3
Mengen
  D 107 A4
  TR 187 B7
Mengeš SLO 123 A3
Mengíbar E 157 C4
Mengkofen D 95 C4
Menou F 104 B2
Mens F 118 C2
Menslage D 71 B4
Menstrásk S 200 A5
Mentana I 168 A2
Menton F 133 B3
Méntrida E 151 B3
Méobecq F 115 B5
Méounes-les-Montrieux
  F. 132 B1
Meppel NL 70 B3
Meppen D 71 B4
Mequinenza E 153 A4
Mer F 103 B3
Mera
  Coruña E 140 A2
  Coruña E 140 A3
Meråker N 199 B8
Merano I 108 C2
Merate I 120 B2
Mercadillo E 143 A3
Mercatale I 135 B5
Mercatino Conca I . 136 B1
Mercato San Severino
  I 170 C2
Mercato Saraceno
  I 135 B5
Merching D 108 A1
Merchtem B 79 B4
Merdrignac F 101 A3
Merdžanići BIH . . . 139 B3
Meré E 142 A2
Mere GB 43 A4
Meréville F 90 C2
Merfeld D 80 A3
Méribel F 118 B3
Méribel Motraret F. .118 B3
Meriç TR. 186 A1
Mérida E 155 C4
Mérignac F 128 B2
Měřín CZ 97 B3
Mering D 94 C2
Merkendorf D 94 B2
Merklin CZ. 96 B1
Merksplas B. 79 A4
Merlánna S 56 A2
Merlimont Plage F . 78 B1
Mern DK. 65 A5
Mernye H 111 C4
Mersch L 92 B2
Merseburg D 83 A3
Mers-les-Bains F . . 90 A1
Mertyr Tydfil GB . . 39 C3
Mertingen D. 94 C2
Mértola P 160 B2
Méru F 90 B2
Merufe P 140 B2
Mervans F 105 C4
Merville F 78 B2
Méry-sur-Seine F . . 91 C3
Merzen D 71 B4
Merzifon TR 23 A8
Merzig D 92 B2
Mesagne I 173 B3
Mesão Frio P 148 A2
Mesas de Ibor E . . 156 A2
Meschede D. 81 A4
Meschers-sur-Gironde
  F. 114 C3
Meslay-du-Maine F 102 B1
Mesna N. 48 A2
Mesnalien N. 48 A2
Mesocco CH 120 A2
Mésola I 122 C1
Mesologi GR 184 A2
Mesopotamo GR . . 182 D2
Mesoraca I 175 B2
Messac F 101 B4
Messancy B 92 B1
Messdorf D 73 B4
Messei F 88 B3
Messejana P 160 B1
Messelt N 48 A3
Messina I 177 A4
Messingen D 71 B4
Messini GR 184 B3
Messkirch D 107 B4
Messlingen S 199 C9
Messstetten D 107 A3
Mesta GR 185 A6
Mestanza E 157 B3

Městec Králové CZ . 84 B3
Mestlin D 73 A4
Město Albrechtice
  CZ. 85 B5
Město Libavá CZ . . 98 B1
Město Touškov CZ . 96 B1
Mestre I 122 B1
Mesvres F 104 C3
Meszna PL 87 B4
Mesztegnyő H 111 C4
Meta I 170 C2
Metajna HR 137 A4
Metelen D 71 B4
Methana GR. 185 B4
Methlick GB. 33 D4
Methven GB. 35 B4
Methwold GB. 41 C4
Metković HR 139 B3
Metlika SLO 123 B4
Metnitz A 110 C1
Metsäkylä FIN . . . 197 D11
Metslawier NL 70 A3
Metsovo GR. 182 D3
Metten D 95 C4
Mettendorf D 92 B2
Mettet B 79 B4
Mettingen D 71 B4
Mettlach D 92 B2
Mettlen CH 106 C2
Mettmann D 80 A2
Metz F 92 B2
Metzervisse F 92 B2
Metzingen D 94 C1
Meulan F 90 B1
Meung-sur-Loire F 103 B3
Meuselwitz D. 83 A4
Meuzac F 115 C5
Mevagissey GB. . . . 42 B2
Mexborough GB . . . 40 B2
Meximieux F 118 B2
Mey GB 32 C3
Meyenburg D. 73 A5
Meyerhöfen D 71 B5
Meylan F 118 B2
Meymac F 116 B2
Meyrargues F 132 B1
Meyrueis F 130 A2
Meyssac F 129 A4
Meyzieu F 117 B4
Mèze F 130 B2
Mézériat F 117 A5
Mézidon-Canon F . . 89 A3
Mézières-en-Brenne
  F. 115 B5
Mézières-sur-Issoire
  F. 115 B4
Mézilhac F 117 C4
Mézilles F 104 B2
Mézin F 128 B3
Mezöberény H 113 C5
Mezöcsát H 113 B4
Mezöfalva H 112 C2
Mezöhegyes H . . . 126 A2
Mezökeresztes H. . 113 B4
Mezökomárom H . . 112 C2
Mezökövácsháza
  H 113 C4
Mezökövesd H. . . . 113 B4
Mezöörs H 111 B4
Mezöszilas H 112 C2
Mezötúr H 113 B4
Mezquita de Jarque
  E. 153 B3
Mezzano
  Emilia Romagna
  I 135 A5
  Trentino Alto Adige
  I 121 A4
Mezzojuso I 176 B2
Mezzoldo I 120 A2
Mezzolombardo I . 121 A4
Mgarr M 175 C3
Miajadas E 156 A2
Miały PL 75 B5
Mianowice PL 68 A2
Miasteczko Krajeńskie
  PL. 76 A2
Miasteczko Śl. PL . 86 B2
Miastko PL. 68 A1
Michalovce SK 12 D4
Michałowice PL. . . . 87 B3
Michelau D. 94 B2
Micheldorf A 110 B1
Michelhausen A . . .110 A2
Michelsneukirchen
  D 95 B4
Michelstadt D 93 B5
Michendorf D. 74 B2
Mickleover GB. . . . 40 C2
Mickleton GB. 37 B5
Midbea GB. 33 B4
Middelburg NL. . . . 79 A3
Middelfart DK 59 C2
Middelharnis NL . . 79 A4
Middelkerke B 78 A2
Middelstum NL . . . 71 A3
Middlesbrough GB . 37 B5
Middleton Cheney
  GB 44 A2
Middleton-in-Teesdale
  GB 37 B4
Middletown GB . . . 27 B4
Middlewich GB . . . 38 A4
Middlezoy GB 43 A4
Midhurst GB 44 C3
Midleton IRL 29 C3

Midlum D 64 C1
Midsomer Norton
  GB 43 A4
Midtgulen N 198 D2
Midtskogberget N . 49 A4
Midwolda NL 71 A4
Mid Yell GB 33 A5
Miedes de Aragón
  E. 152 A2
Miedes de Atienza
  E. 151 A4
Międzybodzie Bielskie
  PL. 99 B3
Międzybórz PL. . . . 85 A5
Międzychód PL . . . 75 B4
Międzylesie PL . . . 85 B4
Międzyrzec Podlaski
  PL. 12 C5
Międzyrzecz PL . . . 75 B4
Międzyzdroje PL . . 67 C3
Miejska Górka PL . 85 A4
Mielan F 145 A4
Mielec PL 87 B5
Mielęcin PL 75 A3
Mielno
  Warmińsko-Mazurskie
  PL. 77 A5
  Zachodnio-Pomorskie
  PL. 67 B5
Mieraslompolo
  FIN 193 C11
Miercurea Ciuc RO . 17 B6
Mieres
  Asturias E 141 A5
  Girona E. 147 B3
Mieroszów PL 85 B4
Mierzyn PL. 86 A3
Miesau D 93 B3
Miesbach D 108 B2
Mieścisko PL 76 B2
Mieste D. 73 B4
Mieszków PL 76 B2
Mieszkowice PL. . . 74 B3
Mietków PL 85 B4
Migennes F 104 B2
Migliánico I 169 A4
Migliarino I. 121 C4
Migliónico I. 172 B2
Mignano Monte Lungo
  I 169 B3
Migné F 115 B5
Miguel Esteban E . 157 A4
Miguelturra E 157 B4
Mihajlovac SRB. . . 127 C2
Miháld H. 111 C4
Mihalgazi TR 187 B5
Mihaliççik TR. 187 C6
Mihla D. 82 A2
Miholjsko HR 123 B4
Mihovljan HR. 124 A1
Mijares E 150 B3
Mijas E 163 B3
Mike H 124 A3
Mikines GR 184 B3
Mikkeli FIN. 8 B5
Mikkelvik N 192 B3
Mikleuš HR 125 B3
Mikołajki Pomorskie
  PL. 69 B4
Mikolów PL 86 B2
Mikorzyn PL. 86 A2
Mikro Derio GR . . . 183 B8
Mikstat PL 86 A1
Mikulášovice CZ . . 84 B2
Mikulov CZ. 97 C4
Mikulovice CZ 85 B5
Milagro E 144 B2
Miłakowo PL 69 A5
Milan = Milano I . . 120 B2
Miland N. 47 C5
Milano = Milan I . . 120 B2
Milano Marittima I . 135 A5
Milas TR. 188 B2
Milazzo I 177 A4
Mildenhall GB 45 A4
Milejewo PL 69 A4
Milelín CZ. 85 B3
Mileto I 175 C2
Milevsko CZ. 96 B2
Milford IRL 26 A3
Milford Haven GB . 39 C1
Milford on Sea GB . 44 C2
Milhão P 149 A3
Milići BIH 139 A5
Miličin CZ. 96 B2
Milicz PL. 85 A5
Milín CZ 96 B2
Militello in Val di
  Catánia I 177 B3
Miljevina BIH 139 B4
Milkowice PL 85 A4
Millançay F 103 B3
Millares E 159 B3
Millas F 146 B3
Millau F 130 A2
Millesimo I 133 A4
Millevaches F 116 B2
Millom GB 36 B3

Millport GB 34 C3
Millstatt A 109 C4
Millstreet
  Cork IRL. 29 B2
  Waterford IRL. . . . 29 B4
Milltown
  Galway IRL 28 A3
  Kerry IRL 29 B1
Milltown Malbay IRL 28 B2
Milly-la-Forêt F . . . 90 C2
Milmarcos E 152 A2
Milmersdorf D 74 A2
Milna HR 138 B2
Milnthorpe GB 37 B4
Milogórze PL 69 A5
Miłomłyn PL. 69 B4
Milos GR 185 C5
Miloševo SRB . . . 127 C3
Miłosław P 76 B2
Milot AL 182 B1
Miłówka PL 99 B3
Miltach D 95 B4
Miltenberg D 94 B1
Milton Keynes GB . 44 B3
Miltzow D. 66 B2
Milverton GB 43 A3
Milzyn PL 76 B3
Mimice HR 138 B2
Mimizan F 128 B1
Mimizan-Plage F . . 128 B1
Mimoň CZ 84 B2
Mina de Juliana P . 160 B1
Mina de São Domingos
  P. 160 B2
Minas de Riotinto
  E. 161 B3
Minateda E 158 C2
Minaya E 158 B1
Minde P. 154 B2
Mindelheim D 108 A1
Mindelstetten D. . . 95 C3
Minden D 72 B1
Mindszent H 113 C4
Minehead GB 43 A3
Mineo I 177 B3
Minerbe I 121 B4
Minérbio I. 121 C4
Minervino Murge I. 171 B4
Minglanilla E 158 B2
Mingorria E 150 B3
Minnesund N 48 B3
Miño E 140 A2
Miño de San Esteban
  E. 151 A4
Minsen D 71 A4
Minsk BY 13 B7
Mińsk Mazowiecki
  PL. 12 B4
Minsterley GB 39 B4
Mintlaw GB 33 D4
Minturno I 169 B3
Mionica
  BIH. 125 C4
  SRB 127 C2
Mios F 128 B2
Mira
  E 158 B2
  I 121 B5
  P. 148 B1
Mirabel E 155 B4
Mirabel-aux-Baronnies
  F. 131 A4
Mirabella Eclano I . 170 B3
Mirabella Imbáccari
  I 177 B3
Mirabello I 121 C4
Miradoux F 129 B3
Miraflores de la Sierra
  E. 151 B4
Miralrio E 151 B5
Miramar P 148 A1
Miramare I 136 A1
Miramas F 131 B3
Mirambeau F 114 C3
Miramont-de-Guyenne
  F. 129 B3
Miranda de Arga E 144 B2
Miranda de Ebro E 143 B4
Miranda do Corvo
  P. 148 B1
Miranda do Douro
  P. 149 A3
Mirande F. 129 C3
Mirandela P 149 A2
Mirandilla E 155 C4
Mirándola I 121 C4
Miranje HR 137 A4
Mirano I 121 B5
Miras AL 182 C2
Miravet E 153 A4
Miré F 102 B1
Mirebeau F 102 C2
Mirebeau-sur-Bèze
  F. 105 B4
Mirecourt F 105 A5
Mirepoix F 146 A2
Mires GR 185 D5
Miribel F 117 B4
Miriĉina BIH 125 C4
Mirina GR 183 D7
Miroslav CZ 97 C4
Miroševce SRB . . . 85 B4
Mirosławiec PL . . . 75 A5
Mirošov CZ 96 B1

Mirotice CZ 96 B2
Mirovice CZ 96 B2
Mirow D 74 A1
Mirsk PL 84 B3
Mirzec PL 87 A5
Misi FIN 197 C9
Misilmeri I 176 A2
Miske H 112 C3
Miskolc H 113 A4
Mislinja SLO 110 C2
Missanello I 174 A2
Missillac F 101 B3
Mistelbach
A 97 C4
D 95 B3
Misten N 194 C5
Misterbianco I 177 B4
Misterhult S 62 A4
Mistretta I 177 B3
Misurina I 109 C3
Mitchelstown IRL 29 B3
Mithimna GR 186 C1
Mithoni GR 184 C2
Mitilini GR 186 C1
Mitilinii GR 188 B1
Mittelberg
Tirol A 108 C1
Vorarlberg A 107 B5
Mittenwald D 108 B2
Mittenwalde D 74 B2
Mitterback A 110 B2
Mitterdorf im Mürztal
A 110 B2
Mitter-Kleinarl A 109 B4
Mittersheim F 92 C2
Mittersill A 109 B3
Mitterskirchen D 95 C4
Mitterteich D 95 B4
Mitton F 128 B2
Mittweida D 83 B4
Mitwitz D 82 B3
Mizhhir'ya UA 13 D5
Mjällby S 63 B2
Mjåvatn N 53 B4
Mjöbäck S 60 B2
Mjölby S 56 B1
Mjølfjell N 46 B3
Mjøndalen N 53 A6
Mjørlund N 48 B2
Mladá Boleslav CZ 84 B2
Mladá Vožice CZ 96 B2
Mladé Buky CZ 85 B3
Mladenovac SRB 127 C2
Mladenovo SRB 126 B1
Mladikovine BIH 139 A3
Mława PL 77 A5
Mlinište BIH 138 A2
Młodzieszyn PL 77 B5
Młogoszyn PL 77 B4
Młynary PL 69 A4
Mnichóvice CZ 96 B2
Mnichovo Hradiště
CZ 84 B2
Mniów PL 87 A4
Mnisek nad Hnilcom
SK 99 C4
Mníšek pod Brdy
CZ 96 B2
Mniszek PL 87 A4
Mniszków PL 87 A4
Mo
Hedmark N 48 B3
Hordaland N 46 B2
Møre og Romsdal
N 198 C5
Telemark N 53 A3
Gävleborg S 51 A3
Västra Götaland S 54 B2
Moaña E 140 B2
Moate IRL 28 A4
Mocejón E 151 C4
Močenok SK 111 A4
Mochales E 152 A1
Mochowo PL 77 B4
Mochy PL 75 B5
Mockern D 73 B4
Mockfjärd S 50 B1
Möckmühl D 94 B1
Mockrehna D 83 A4
Moclin E 163 A4
Mocsa H 112 B2
Möcsény H 125 A4
Modane F 118 B3
Modbury GB 42 B3
Módena I 121 C3
Módica I 177 C3
Modigliana I 135 A4
Modlin PL 77 B5
Mödling A 111 A3
Modliszewice PL 87 A4
Modliszewko PL 76 B2
Modogno I 171 B4
Modra SK 98 C1
Modran BIH 125 C3
Modriča BIH 125 C4
Möðrudalur IS 191 B10
Modrý Kamen SK 99 C3
Moëlan-sur-Mer F 100 B2
Moelfre GB 38 A2
Moelv N 48 B2
Moen N 194 A9
Moena I 121 A4
Moerbeke B 79 A3
Moers D 80 A2
Móes P 148 B2
Moffat GB 36 A3
Mogadouro P 149 A3
Mogata S 56 B2
Móggio Udinese I 122 A2
Mogielnica PL 87 A4
Mogilany PL 99 B3
Mogilno PL 76 B2
Mogliano I 136 B2
Mogliano Véneto I 122 B1
Mogor E 140 B2
Mógoro I 179 C2
Moguer E 161 B3
Mohács H 125 B4
Moheda S 62 A2
Mohedas E 149 B3
Mohedas de la Jara
E 156 A2
Mohelnice CZ 97 B4
Mohill IRL 26 C3
Möhlin CH 106 B2
Moholm S 55 B5
Mohorn D 83 A5
Mohyliv-Podil's'kyy
UA 13 D7
Moi N 52 B2
Moià E 147 C3
Móie I 136 B2
Moimenta da Beira
P 148 B2
Mo i Rana N 195 D5
Moirans F 118 B2
Moirans-en-Montagne
F 118 A2
Moisaküla EST 8 C4
Moisdon-la-Rivière
F 101 B4
Moissac F 129 B4
Moita
Coimbra P 148 B1
Guarda P 149 B2
Santarém P 154 B2
Setúbal P 154 C1
Moita dos Ferreiros
P 154 B1
Moixent E 159 C3
Mojacar E 164 B3
Mojados E 150 A3
Mojmírovce SK 112 A2
Mojtin SK 98 C2
Möklinta S 50 B3
Mokošica HR 139 C4
Mokronog SLO 123 B4
Mokro Polje HR 138 A2
Mokrzyska PL 99 A4
Møkster N 46 B2
Mol
B 79 A5
SRB 126 B2
Mola di Bari I 173 A3
Molai GR 184 C3
Molare I 133 A4
Molaretto I 119 B4
Molas F 145 A4
Molassano I 134 A1
Molbergen D 71 B4
Mold GB 38 A3
Molde N 198 C4
Møldrup DK 58 B2
Moledo do Minho
P 148 A1
Molfetta I 171 B4
Molfsee D 64 B3
Moliden S 200 C4
Molières F 129 B4
Molina de Aragón
E 152 B2
Molina de Segura
E 165 A3
Molinar E 143 A3
Molinaseca E 141 B4
Molinella I 121 C4
Molinet F 104 C2
Molinicos E 158 C1
Molini di Tures I 108 C2
Molinos de Duero
E 143 C4
Molins de Rei E 147 C3
Moliterno I 174 A1
Molkom S 55 A4
Möllbrücke A 109 C4
Mölle S 61 C2
Molledo E 142 A2
Möllenbeck D 74 A2
Mollerussa E 147 C1
Mollet de Perelada
E 146 B3
Mollina E 163 A3
Mölln D 73 A3
Molló E 146 B3
Mollösund S 54 B2
Mölltorp S 55 B5
Mölnbo S 56 A3
Mölndal S 60 B2
Mölnlycke S 60 B2
Molompize F 116 B3
Moloy F 105 B3
Molsheim F 93 C3
Moltzow D 73 A5
Molve HR 124 A3
Molveno I 121 A3
Molvizar E 163 B4
Molzbichl A 109 C4
Mombaróccio I 136 B1
Mombeltrán E 150 B2
Mombris D 93 A5
Mombuey E 141 B4
Momchilgrad BG 183 B7
Mommark DK 64 B3
Momo I 119 B5
Monaghan IRL 27 B4
Monar Lodge GB 32 D2
Monasterace Marina
I 175 C2
Monasterevin IRL 30 A1
Monasterio de Rodilla
E 143 B3
Monastir I 179 C3
Monbahus F 129 B3
Monbazillac F 129 B3
Moncada E 159 B3
Moncalieri I 119 B4
Moncalvo I 119 B5
Monção P 140 B2
Moncarapacho P 160 B2
Moncel-sur-Seille F 92 C2
Monchegorsk RUS 3 C13
Mönchengladbach =
Munchen-Gladbach
D 80 A2
Mónchio della Corti
I 134 A3
Monchique P 160 B1
Monclar-de-Quercy
F 129 C4
Moncofa E 159 B3
Moncontour F 101 A3
Moncoutant F 114 B3
Monda E 162 B3
Mondariz E 140 B2
Mondavio I 136 B1
Mondéjar E 151 B4
Mondello I 176 A2
Mondim de Basto
P 148 A2
Mondolfo I 136 B2
Mondoñedo E 141 A3
Mondorf-les-Bains
L 92 B2
Mondoubleau F 102 B2
Mondov i I 133 A3
Mondragon F 131 A3
Mondragone I 170 B1
Mondsee A 109 B4
Monéglia I 134 A2
Monegrillo E 153 A3
Monein F 145 A3
Monemvasia GR 184 C4
Mónesi I 133 A3
Monesiglio I 133 A4
Monesterio E 161 A3
Monestier-de-Clermont
F 118 C2
Monestiés F 130 A1
Monéteau F 104 B2
Moneygall IRL 28 B4
Moneymore GB 27 B4
Monfalcone I 122 B2
Monfero E 140 A2
Monflanquin F 129 B3
Monflorite E 145 B3
Monforte P 155 B3
Monforte da Beira
E 155 B3
P 155 B3
Monforte d'Alba I 133 A3
Monforte del Cid E 165 A4
Monforte de Lemos
E 140 B3
Monforte de Moyuela
E 152 A2
Monghidoro I 135 A4
Mongiana I 175 C2
Monguelfo I 108 C3
Monheim D 94 C2
Moniaive GB 36 A3
Monifieth GB 35 B5
Monikie GB 35 B5
Monistrol-d'Allier
F 117 C3
Monistrol de Montserrat
E 147 C2
Monistrol-sur-Loire
F 117 B4
Mönkebude D 74 A2
Monkton GB 36 A2
Monmouth GB 39 C4
Monnaie F 102 B2
Monnerville F 90 C2
Monnickendam NL 70 B2
Monolithos GR 188 C2
Monópoli I 173 B3
Monor H 112 B3
Monóvar E 159 C3
Monpazier F 129 B3
Monreal
D 80 B3
E 144 B2
Monreal del Campo
E 152 B2
Monreale I 176 A2
Monroy E 155 B4
Monroyo E 153 B3
Mons B 79 B3
Monsaraz P 155 C3
Monschau D 80 B2
Monségur F 128 B3
Monsélice I 121 B4
Mønshaug N 46 B3
Monster NL 70 B1
Mönsterås S 62 A4
Monsummano Terme
I 135 B3
Montabaur D 81 B3
Montafia I 119 C5
Montagnac F 130 B2
Montagnana I 121 B4
Montaigu F 114 B2
Montaigu-de-Quercy
F 129 B4
Montaiguët-en-Forez
F 117 A3
Montaigut F 116 A2
Montaigut-sur-Save
F 129 C4
Montainville F 90 C1
Montalbán E 153 B3
Montalbán de Córdoba
E 163 A3
Montalbano Elicona
I 177 A4
Montalbano Iónico
I 174 A2
Montalbo E 158 B1
Montalcino I 135 B4
Montaldo di Cósola
I 120 C2
Montalegre P 148 A2
Montalieu-Vercieu
F 118 B2
Montalivet-les-Bains
F 114 C2
Montallegro I 176 B2
Montalto delle Marche
I 136 C2
Montalto di Castro
I 168 A1
Montalto Pavese I 120 C2
Montalto Uffugo I 174 B2
Montalvão P 155 B3
Montamarta E 149 A4
Montana BG 17 D5
Montana-Vermala
CH 119 A4
Montánchez E 156 A1
Montanejos E 153 B3
Montano Antilia I 172 B1
Montans F 129 C4
Montargil P 154 B2
Montargis F 103 B4
Montastruc-la-
Conseillère F 129 C4
Montauban F 129 B4
Montauban-de-Bretagne
F 101 A3
Montbard F 104 B3
Montbarrey F 105 B4
Montbazens F 130 A1
Montbazon F 102 B2
Montbéliard F 106 B1
Montbenoit F 105 C5
Montbeugny F 104 C2
Montblanc E 147 C2
Montbozon F 105 B5
Montbrison F 117 B4
Montbron F 115 C4
Montbrun-les-Bains
F 131 A4
Montceau-les-Mines
F 104 C3
Montcenis F 104 C3
Montchanin F 104 C3
Montcornet F 91 B4
Montcuq F 129 B4
Montdardier F 130 B2
Mont-de-Marsan F 128 C2
Montdidier F 90 B2
Monteagudo E 165 A3
Monteagudo de las
Vicarias E 152 A1
Montealegre E 142 C2
Montealegre del Castillo
E 159 C2
Montebello Iónico
I 175 D1
Montebello Vicentino
I 121 B4
Montebelluna I 121 B5
Montebourg F 88 A2
Montebruno I 134 A2
Monte-Carlo MC 133 B3
Montecarotto I 136 B2
Montecassiano I 136 B2
Montecastrilli I 168 A2
Montecatini Terme
I 135 B3
Montécchio I 136 B1
Montécchio Emilia
I 121 C3
Montécchio Maggiore
I 121 B4
Montech F 129 C4
Montechiaro d'Asti
I 119 B5
Monte Clara P 155 B3
Monte Clérigo P 160 B1
Montecórice I 170 C2
Montecorvino Rovella
I 170 C2
Monte da Pedra P 155 B3
Monte de Goula P 155 B3
Montederramo E 141 B3
Montedoro I 176 B2
Monte do Trigo P 155 C3
Montefalco I 136 C1
Montefalcone di Val
Fortore I 170 B3
Montefalcone nel
Sánnio I 170 B2
Montefano I 136 B2
Montefiascone I 168 A2
Montefiorino I 134 A3
Montefortino I 136 C2
Montefranco I 168 A2
Montefrío E 163 A4
Montegiordano Marina
I 174 A2
Montegiórgio I 136 B2
Monte Gordo P 160 B2
Montegranaro I 136 B2
Montehermoso E 149 B3
Montejicar E 163 A4
Montejo de la Sierra
E 151 A4
Montejo de Tiermes
E 151 A4
Monte Juntos P 155 C3
Montel-de-Gelat F 116 B2
Monteleone di Púglia
I 171 B3
Monteleone di Spoleto
I 169 A2
Monteleone d'Orvieto
I 135 C5
Montelepre I 176 A2
Montelibretti I 168 A2
Montelier F 117 C5
Montélimar F 131 A3
Montella
E 146 B2
I 170 C3
Montellano E 162 A2
Montelupo Fiorentino
I 135 B4
Montemaggiore Belsito
I 176 B2
Montemagno I 119 C5
Montemayor E 163 A3
Montemayor de Pinilla
E 150 A3
Montemésola I 173 B3
Montemilleto I 170 B2
Montemilone I 172 A1
Montemolin E 161 A3
Montemónaco I 136 C2
Montemor-o-Novo
P 154 C2
Montemor-o-Velho
P 148 B1
Montemurro I 174 A1
Montendre F 128 A2
Montenegro de Cameros
E 143 B4
Montenero di Bisáccia
I 170 B2
Monteneuf F 101 B3
Monteparano I 173 B3
Montepescali I 135 C4
Montepiano I 135 A4
Monte Porzio I 136 B2
Montepulciano I 135 B4
Monte Real P 154 B2
Montereale I 169 A3
Montereale Valcellina
I 122 A1
Montereau-Faut-Yonne
F 90 C2
Monte Redondo P 154 B2
Monterénzio I 135 A4
Monte Romano I 168 A1
Monteroni d'Arbia
I 135 B4
Monteroni di Lecce
I 173 B4
Monterosso al Mare
I 134 A2
Monterosso Almo I 177 B3
Monterosso Grana
I 133 A3
Monterotondo I 168 A2
Monterotondo Marittimo
I 135 B3
Monterrey E 141 C3
Monterroso E 140 B3
Monterrubio de la
Serena E 156 B2
Monterubbiano I 136 B2
Montesa E 159 C3
Montesalgueiro E 140 A2
Monte San Giovanni
Campano I 169 B3
Montesano sulla
Marcellana I 174 A1
Monte San Savino
I 135 B4
Monte Sant'Angelo
I 171 B3
Montesárchio I 170 B2
Montescaglioso I 171 C4
Montesclaros E 150 B3
Montesilvano I 169 A4
Montespértoli I 135 B4
Montesquieu-Volvestre
F 146 A2
Montesquiou F 129 C3
Montestruc-sur-Gers
F 129 C3
Montes Velhos P 160 B1
Montevarchi I 135 B4
Montevéglio I 135 A4
Monte Vilar P 154 B1
Montfaucon F 101 B4
Montfaucon-d'Argonne
F 91 B5
Montfaucon-en-Velay
F 117 B4
Montferrat
Isère F 118 B2
Var F 132 B2
Montfort-en-Chalosse
F 128 C2
Montfort-l'Amaury
F 90 C1
Montfort-le-Gesnois
F 102 A2
Montfort-sur-Meu
F 101 A4
Montfort-sur-Risle F 89 A4
Montgai E 147 C1
Montgaillard F 145 A4
Montgenèvre F 118 C3
Montgiscard F 146 A2
Montgomery GB 39 B3
Montguyon F 128 A2
Monthermé F 91 B4
Monthey CH 119 A3
Monthois F 91 B4
Monthureux-sur-Saône
F 105 A4
Monti I 178 B3
Monticelli d'Ongina
I 120 B2
Montichiari I 120 B3
Monticiano I 135 B4
Montiel E 158 C1
Montier-en-Der F 91 C4
Montieri I 135 B4
Montiglio I 119 B5
Montignac F 129 A4
Montigny-le-Roi F 105 B4
Montigny-lès-Metz
F 92 B2
Montigny-sur-Aube
F 105 B3
Montijo
E 155 C4
P 154 C2
Montilla E 163 A3
Montillana E 163 A4
Montilly F 104 C2
Montivilliers F 89 A4
Montjaux F 130 A1
Montjean-sur-Loire
F 102 B1
Montlhéry F 90 C2
Montlieu-la-Garde
F 128 A2
Mont-Louis F 146 B3
Montlouis-sur-Loire
F 102 B2
Montluçon F 116 A2
Montluel F 117 B5
Montmarault F 116 A2
Montmartin-sur-Mer
F 88 B2
Montmédy F 92 B1
Montmélian F 118 B3
Montmeyan F 132 B2
Montmeyran F 117 C4
Montmirail
Marne F 91 C3
Sarthe F 102 A2
Montmiral F 118 B2
Montmirat F 131 B3
Montmirey-le-Château
F 105 B4
Montmoreau-St Cybard
F 115 C4
Montmorency F 90 C2
Montmorillon F 115 B4
Montmort-Lucy F 91 C3
Montoir-de-Bretagne
F 101 B3
Montoire-sur-le-Loir
F 102 B2
Montoito P 155 C3
Montolieu F 146 A3
Montório al Vomano
I 169 A3
Montoro E 157 B3
Montpellier F 131 B2
Montpezat-de-Quercy
F 129 B4
Montpezat-sous-Bouzon
F 117 C4
Montpon-Ménestérol
F 128 A3
Montpont-en-Bresse
F 105 C4
Montréal
Aude F 146 A3
Gers F 128 C3
Montredon-Labessonnié
F 130 B1
Montréjeau F 145 A4
Montrésor F 103 B3
Montresta I 178 B2
Montret F 105 C4
Montreuil
Pas de Calais F 78 B1
Seine St Denis F 90 C2
Montreuil-aux-Lions
F 90 B3
Montreuil-Bellay F 102 B1
Montreux CH 106 C1
Montrevault F 101 B4
Montrevel-en-Bresse
F 118 A2
Montrichard F 103 B3
Montricoux F 129 B4
Mont-roig del Camp
E 147 C1
Montrond-les-Bains
F 117 B4
Montrose GB 35 B5
Montroy E 159 B3
Montsalvy F 116 C2
Montsauche-les-Settons
F 104 B3
Montseny E 147 C3
Montsoreau F 102 B2

Mont-sous-Vaudrey F 105 C4
Monts-sur-Guesnes F 102 C2
Mont-St Aignan F 89 A5
Mont-St Vincent F 104 C3
Montsûrs F 102 A1
Montuenga E 150 A3
Montuïri E 167 B3
Monturque E 163 A3
Monza I 120 B2
Monzón E 145 C4
Monzón de Campos E 142 B2
Moorbad Lobenstein D 83 B3
Moordorf D 71 A4
Moorslede B 78 B3
Moos D 107 B3
Moosburg D 95 C3
Moosburg im Kärnten A 110 C1
Mór H 112 B2
Mora E 157 A4
Móra P 154 C2
Mora S 50 A1
Moraby S 50 B2
Mòra d'Ebre E 153 A4
Mora de Rubielos E 153 B3
Moradillo de Roa E 151 A4
Morąg PL 69 B4
Mórahalom H 126 A1
Moraime E 140 A1
Morais P 149 A3
Mòra la Nova E 153 A4
Moral de Calatrava E 157 B4
Moraleda de Zafayona E 163 A4
Moraleja E 149 B3
Moraleja del Vino E 150 A2
Morales del Vino E 150 A2
Morales de Toro E 150 A2
Morales de Valverde E 141 C5
Moralina E 149 A3
Morano Cálabro I 174 B2
Mörarp S 61 C2
Morasverdes E 149 B3
Morata de Jalón E 152 A2
Morata de Jiloca E 152 A2
Morata de Tajuña E 151 B4
Moratalla E 164 A3
Moravče SLO 123 A3
Moravec CZ 97 B4
Moraviţa RO 126 B3
Morávka CZ 98 B2
Moravská Třebová CZ 97 B4
Moravské Budějovice CZ 97 B3
Moravské Lieskové SK 98 C1
Moravske Toplice SLO 111 C3
Moravský-Beroun CZ 98 B1
Moravský Krumlov CZ 97 B4
Moravský Svätý Ján SK 98 C1
Morawica PL 87 B4
Morawin PL 86 A2
Morbach D 92 B3
Morbegno I 120 A2
Morbier F 105 C5
Mörbisch am See A 111 B3
Mörbylånga S 63 B4
Morcenx F 128 B2
Morciano di Romagna I 136 B1
Morcone I 170 B2
Morcuera E 151 A4
Mordelles F 101 A4
Mordoğan TR 188 A1
Moréac F 100 B3
Morebattle GB 35 C5
Morecambe GB 36 B4
Moreda
Granada E 163 A4
Oviedo E 142 A1
Morée F 103 B3
Moreles de Rey E 141 B5
Morella E 153 B3
Moreruela de los Infanzones E 149 A4
Morés E 152 A2
Móres I 178 B2
Morestel F 118 B2
Moretonhampstead GB 43 B3
Moreton-in-Marsh GB 44 B2
Moret-sur-Loing F 90 C2
Moretta I 119 C4
Moreuil F 90 B2
Morez F 105 C5
Mörfelden D 93 B4
Morgat F 100 A1
Morges CH 105 C5
Morgex I 119 B4
Morgongåva S 51 C3
Morhange F 92 C2
Morhet B 92 B1
Mori I 121 B3
Morialmé B 79 B4
Morianes P 160 B2
Moriani Plage F 180 A2
Móricháida H 111 B4
Moriles E 163 A3
Morille E 150 B2
Moringen D 82 A1
Morjärv S 196 C5
Morkarla S 51 B4
Mørke DK 59 B3
Mørkøv DK 61 D1
Morkovice-Slížany CZ 98 B1
Morlaàs F 145 A3
Morlaix F 100 A2
Morley F 91 C5
Mörlunda S 62 A3
Mormanno I 174 B1
Mormant F 90 C2
Mornant F 117 B4
Mornay-Berry F 103 B4
Morón de Almazán E 152 A1
Morón de la Frontera E 162 A2
Morović SRB 125 B5
Morozzo I 133 A3
Morpeth GB 37 A5
Morphou CY 181 A1
Mörrum S 63 B2
Morsbach D 81 B3
Mörsch D 93 C4
Mörsil S 199 B10
Morsum D 64 B1
Mørsvikbotn N 194 C6
Mortagne-au-Perche F 89 B4
Mortagne-sur-Gironde F 114 C3
Mortagne-sur-Sèvre F 114 B3
Mortágua P 148 B1
Mortain F 88 B3
Mortara I 120 B1
Morteau F 105 B5
Mortegliano I 122 B2
Mortelle I 177 A4
Mortemart F 115 B4
Mortimer's Cross GB 39 B4
Mortrée F 89 B4
Mörtschach A 109 C3
Mortsel B 79 A4
Morud DK 59 C3
Morwenstow GB 42 B2
Moryń PL 74 B3
Morzeszczyn PL 69 B3
Morzewo PL 69 B4
Morzine F 118 A3
Mosbach D 93 B5
Mosbjerg DK 58 A3
Mosby N 53 B3
Mosca P 149 A3
Moscavide P 154 C1
Moščenica HR 124 B2
Mošćenice HR 123 B3
Moščenicka Draga HR 123 B3
Mosciano Sant'Ángelo I 136 C2
Mościsko PL 85 B4
Moscow = Moskva RUS 9 E10
Mosina PL 75 B5
Mosjøen N 195 E4
Moskog N 46 A3
Moskorzew PL 87 B3
Moskosel S 196 D2
Moskuvarra FIN 197 B9
Moskva = Moscow RUS 9 E10
Moslavina Podravska HR 125 B3
Moşniţa Nouă RO 126 B3
Moso in Passíria I 108 C2
Mosonmagyaróvár H 111 B4
Mošorin SRB 126 B2
Mošovce SK 98 C2
Mosqueruela E 153 B3
Moss N 54 A1
Mossfellsbær IS 190 C4
Mössingen D 93 C5
Møsstrand N 47 C5
Most CZ 83 B5
Mosta M 175 C3
Mostar BIH 139 B3
Mosterhamn N 52 A1
Mostki PL 75 B4
Most na Soči SLO 122 A2
Móstoles E 151 B4
Mostová SK 111 A4
Mostowo PL 68 A1
Mostuéjouls F 130 A2
Mosty PL 75 A3
Mostys'ka UA 13 D5
Mosvik N 199 B7
Mota del Cuervo E 158 B1
Mota del Marqués E 150 A2
Motala S 55 B6
Motherwell GB 35 C4
Möthlow D 74 B1
Motilla del Palancar E 158 B2
Motnik SLO 123 A3
Motovun HR 122 B2
Motril E 163 B4
Motta I 121 B4
Motta di Livenza I 122 B1
Motta Montecorvino I 170 B3
Motta Visconti I 120 B1
Mottisfont GB 44 B2
Móttola I 173 B3
Mou DK 58 B3
Mouchard F 105 C4
Moudon CH 106 C1
Moudros GR 183 D7
Mougins F 132 B2
Mouilleron en-Pareds F 114 B3
Mouliherne F 102 B2
Moulinet F 133 B3
Moulins F 104 C2
Moulins-Engilbert F 104 C2
Moulins-la-Marche F 89 B4
Moulismes F 115 B4
Moult F 89 A3
Mountain Ash GB 39 C3
Mountbellew IRL 28 A3
Mountfield GB 27 B3
Mountmellick IRL 30 A1
Mountrath IRL 30 A1
Mountsorrel GB 40 C2
Moura P 160 A2
Mourão P 155 C3
Mourenx F 145 A3
Mouriés F 131 B3
Mourmelon-le-Grand F 91 B4
Mouronho P 148 B1
Mourujärvi FIN 197 C11
Mouscron B 78 B3
Mousehole GB 42 B1
Moussac F 131 B3
Moussey F 92 C2
Mousteru F 100 A2
Moustey F 128 B2
Moustiers-Ste Marie F 132 B2
Mouthe F 105 C5
Mouthier-Haute-Pierre F 105 B5
Mouthoumet F 146 B3
Moutier CH 106 B2
Moûtiers F 118 B3
Moutiers-les-Mauxfaits F 114 B2
Mouy F 90 B2
Mouzaki GR 182 D3
Mouzon F 91 B5
Møvik N 46 B2
Moville IRL 27 A3
Moy
Highland GB 32 D2
Tyrone GB 27 B4
Moycullen IRL 28 A2
Moyenmoutier F 92 C2
Moyenvic F 92 C2
Moylough IRL 28 A3
Mózar E 141 C5
Mozhaysk RUS 9 E10
Mozirje SLO 123 A3
Mözs H 112 C2
Mozzanica I 120 B2
Mramorak SRB 127 C2
Mrčajevci SRB 127 D2
Mrkonjić Grad BIH 138 A3
Mrkopalj HR 123 B3
Mrocza PL 76 A2
Mroczeń PL 86 A1
Mroczno PL 69 B4
Mrzezyno PL 67 B4
Mšec CZ 84 B1
Mšeno CZ 84 B2
Mstów PL 86 B3
Mstsislaw BY 13 A9
Mszana Dolna PL 99 B4
Mszczonów PL 77 C5
Muć HR 138 B2
Múccia I 136 B2
Much D 80 B3
Mücheln D 83 A3
Much Marcle GB 39 C4
Muchów PL 85 A4
Much Wenlock GB 39 B4
Mucientes E 142 C2
Muckross IRL 29 B2
Mucur TR 23 B8
Muda P 160 B1
Mudanya TR 186 B3
Mudau D 93 B5
Müden D 72 B3
Mudersbach D 81 B3
Mudurnu TR 187 B6
Muel E 152 A2
Muelas del Pan E 149 A4
Muess D 73 A4
Muff IRL 27 A3
Mugardos E 140 A2
Muge P 154 B2
Mügeln
Sachsen D 83 A5
Sachsen-Anhalt D 83 A5
Múggia I 122 B2
Mugnano I 135 B5
Mugron F 128 C2
Mugueimes E 140 C3
Muhi H 113 B4
Mühlacker D 93 C4
Mühlbach am Hochkönig A 109 B4
Mühlberg
Brandenburg D 83 A5
Thüringen D 82 B2
Mühldorf
A 109 C4
D 95 C4
Muhleberg CH 106 C2
Mühleim D 107 A3
Muhlen-Eichsen D 65 C4
Mühlhausen
Bayern D 94 B2
Thüringen D 82 A2
Mühltroff D 83 B3
Muhos FIN 3 D10
Muhr A 109 B4
Muine Bheag IRL 30 B2
Muirkirk GB 36 A2
Muir of Ord GB 32 D2
Muirteira P 154 B1
Mukacheve UA 12 D5
Muker GB 37 B4
Mula E 165 A3
Muğla TR 188 B3
Mulben GB 32 D3
Mulegns CH 107 C4
Mules I 108 C2
Mülheim D 80 A2
Mulhouse F 106 B2
Muljava SLO 123 B3
Mullanys Cross IRL 26 B2
Müllheim D 106 B2
Mullhyttan S 55 A5
Mullinavat IRL 30 B1
Mullingar IRL 30 A1
Mullion GB 42 B1
Müllrose D 74 B3
Mullsjö S 60 B3
Mulseryd S 60 B3
Munaðarnes IS 190 A4
Munana E 150 B2
Muñás E 141 A4
Münchberg D 83 B3
Müncheberg D 74 B3
München = Munich D 108 A2
Munchen-Gladbach = Mönchengladbach D 80 A2
Münchhausen D 81 B4
Mundaka E 143 A4
Münden D 82 A1
Munderfing A 109 A4
Munderkingen D 107 A4
Mundesley GB 41 C5
Munera E 158 B1
Mungia E 143 A4
Munich = München D 108 A2
Muñico E 150 B2
Muniesa E 153 A3
Munka-Ljungby S 61 C2
Munkebo DK 59 C3
Munkedal S 54 B2
Munkflohögen S 199 B11
Munkfors S 49 C5
Munktorp S 56 A2
Münnerstadt D 82 B2
Muñopepe E 150 B3
Muñotello E 150 B2
Münsingen
CH 106 C2
D 94 C1
Munsö S 57 A3
Münster
CH 106 C3
Hessen D 93 B4
Munster D 72 B3
Münster D 71 C4
Munster F 106 A2
Muntibar E 143 A4
Münzkirchen A 96 C1
Muodoslompolo S 196 B6
Muonio FIN 196 B6
Muotathal CH 107 C3
Muradiye TR 186 D2
Murakeresztúr H 124 A2
Murán SK 99 C4
Murano I 122 B1
Muras E 140 A3
Murat F 116 B2
Muratlı TR 186 A2
Murato F 180 A2
Murat-sur-Vèbre F 130 B1
Murau A 109 B5
Muravera I 179 C3
Murazzano I 133 A4
Murça P 148 A2
Murchante E 144 B2
Murchin D 66 C2
Murcia E 165 B3
Murczyn PL 76 B2
Mur-de-Barrez F 116 C2
Mur-de-Bretagne F 100 A2
Mur-de-Sologne F 103 B3
Mureck A 110 C2
Mürefte TR 186 B2
Muret F 146 A2
Murg CH 107 B4
Murguia E 143 B4
Muri CH 106 B3
Murias de Paredes E 141 B4
Muriedas E 143 A3
Muriel Viejo E 143 C4
Murillo de Rio Leza E 143 B4
Murillo el Fruto E 144 B2
Murjek S 196 C3
Murlaggan GB 34 B2
Murmansk RUS 3 B13
Murmashi RUS 3 B13
Murnau D 108 B2
Muro
E 167 B3
F 180 A1
Muro de Alcoy E 159 C3
Murol F 116 B2
Muro Lucano I 172 B1
Muron F 114 B3
Muros E 140 B1
Muros de Nalón E 141 A4
Murowana Goślina PL 76 B2
Mürren CH 106 C2
Murrhardt D 94 C1
Murska Sobota SLO 111 C3
Mursko Središce HR 111 C3
Murtas E 164 C1
Murten CH 106 C2
Murter HR 137 B4
Murtiçi TR 189 C6
Murtosa P 148 B1
Murtovaara FIN 197 D12
Murvica HR 137 A4
Murviel-lès-Béziers F 130 B2
Mürzsteg A 110 B2
Murzynowo PL 75 B4
Mürzzuschlag A 110 B2
Musculdy F 144 A3
Muskö S 57 A4
Mušov CZ 97 C4
Musselburgh GB 35 C4
Musselkanaal NL 71 B4
Mussidan F 129 A3
Mussomeli I 176 B2
Musson B 92 B1
Mussy-sur-Seine F 104 B3
Mustafakemalpaşa TR 186 B3
Muszaki PL 77 A5
Muszyna PL 99 B4
Mut TR 23 C7
Muta SLO 110 C2
Muthill GB 35 B4
Mutné SK 99 B3
Mutriku E 143 A4
Muttalip TR 187 C5
Mutterbergalm A 108 B2
Muurola FIN 197 C8
Muxía E 140 A1
Muxilka-Ugarte E 143 A4
Muzillac F 101 B3
Mužla SK 112 B2
Muzzano del Turgnano I 122 B2
Mybster GB 32 C3
Myckelgensjö S 200 C3
Myennes F 104 B1
Myjava SK 98 C1
Myking N 46 B2
Mykland N 53 B4
Myra N 53 B5
Myrdal N 46 B4
Myre
Nordland N 194 A6
Nordland N 194 B6
Myresjö S 62 A2
Mýri IS 191 B8
Myrtou CY 181 A2
Mysen N 54 A2
Mysłakowice PL 85 B3
Myślenice PL 99 B3
Myślibórz PL 75 B3
Mysłowice PL 86 B3
Myszków PL 86 B3
Mytishchi RUS 9 E10
Mýtna SK 99 C3
Mýtne Ludany SK 112 A2
Mýto CZ 96 B1

N

Nå N 46 B3
Naaldwijk NL 79 A4
Naantali FIN 8 B2
Naas IRL 30 A2
Nabais P 148 B2
Nabbelund S 62 A5
Nabburg D 95 B4
Načeradec CZ 96 B2
Náchod CZ 85 B4
Nacław PL 68 A1
Nadarzyce PL 75 A5
Nadarzyn PL 77 B5
Nádasd H 111 C3
Nădlac RO 126 A2
Nádudvar H 113 B5
Nadvirna UA 13 D6
Näfels CH 107 B4
Nafpaktos GR 184 A2
Nafplio GR 184 B3
Nagel D 95 B3
Nagele NL 70 B2
Naggen S 200 D2
Nagłowice PL 87 B4
Nagold D 93 C4
Nagore E 144 B2
Nagyatád H 124 A3
Nagybajom H 124 A3
Nagybaracska H 125 A4
Nagybátony H 113 B3
Nagyberény H 112 C2
Nagybörzsöny H 112 B2
Nagycenk H 111 B3
Nagycserkesz H 113 B5
Nagydorog H 112 C2
Nagyfüged H 113 B4
Nagyhersány H 125 B4
Nagyigmánd H 112 B2
Nagyiván H 113 B4
Nagykanizsa H 111 C3
Nagykáta H 113 B3
Nagykonyi H 112 C2
Nagykörös H 113 B3
Nagykörü H 113 B4
Nagylóc H 112 A3
Nagymágocs H 113 C4
Nagymányok H 125 A4
Nagymaros H 112 B2
Nagyoroszi H 112 A3
Nagyrábé H 113 B5
Nagyréde H 113 B3
Nagyszékely H 112 C2
Nagyszénás H 113 C4
Nagyszokoly H 112 C2
Nagytöke H 113 C4
Nagyvázsony H 111 C4
Nagyvenyim H 112 C2
Naharros E 152 B1
Nahe D 64 C3
Naila D 83 B3
Nailloux F 146 A2
Nailsworth GB 43 A4
Naintré F 115 B4
Nairn GB 32 D3
Najac F 129 B4
Nájera E 143 B4
Nak H 112 C2
Nakksjø N 53 A5
Nakło nad Notecią PL 76 A2
Nakskov DK 65 B4
Nalda E 143 B4
Nälden S 199 B11
Nálepkovo SK 99 C4
Nalliers F 114 B2
Nallıhan TR 187 B6
Nalzen F 146 B2
Nalžouské Hory CZ 96 B1
Namdalseid N 199 A8
Náměšť nad Oslavou CZ 97 B4
Námestovo SK 99 B3
Namnå N 49 B4
Namsos N 199 A8
Namsskogan N 199 A10
Namur B 79 B4
Namysłów PL 86 A1
Nançay F 103 B4
Nanclares de la Oca E 143 B4
Nancy F 92 C2
Nangis F 90 C3
Nannestad N 48 B3
Nant F 130 A2
Nanterre F 90 C2
Nantes F 101 B4
Nanteuil-le-Haudouin F 90 B2
Nantiat F 115 B5
Nantua F 118 A2
Nantwich GB 38 A4
Naoussa
Cyclades GR 185 B6
Imathia GR 182 C4
Napajedla CZ 98 B1
Napiwoda PL 77 A5
Naples = Nápoli I 170 C2
Nápoli = Naples I 170 C2
Nar S 57 C4
Nara N 46 A1
Naraval E 141 A4
Narberth GB 39 C2
Nærbø N 52 B1
Narbonne F 130 B1
Narbonne-Plage F 130 B2
Narbuvollen N 199 C8
Narcao I 179 C2
Nardò I 173 B4
Narkaus FIN 197 C9
Narken S 196 C5
Narmo N 48 B3
Narni I 168 A2
Naro I 176 B2
Naro Fominsk RUS 9 E10
Narón E 140 A2
Narros del Castillo E 150 B2
Narta HR 124 B2
Naruszewo PL 77 B5
Narva EST 8 C6
Narvik N 194 B8
Narzole I 133 A3
Näs FIN 51 B7
Nås S 50 B1
Näs S 57 C4
Näsåker S 200 C2
Năsăud RO 17 B6
Nasavrky CZ 97 B3
Nasbinals F 116 C3
Næsbjerg DK 59 C1
Näshull S 62 A3
Našice HR 125 B4
Nasielsk PL 77 B5
Naso I 177 A3
Nassau D 81 B3
Nassenfels D 95 C3

Nassenheide D 74 B2
Nassereith A 108 B1
Nässjö S 62 A2
Nastätten D 81 B3
Næstved DK 65 A4
Näsum S 63 B2
Näsviken S 199 B12
Natalinci SRB ... 127 C2
Naters CH 119 A5
Nater-Stetten D ... 108 A2
Natters A 108 B2
Nattheim D..... 94 C2
Nättraby S 63 B3
Naturno I 108 C1
Naucelle F 130 A1
Nauders A 108 C1
Nauen D........ 74 B1
Naul IRL 30 A2
Naumburg D 83 A3
Naundorf D 83 B5
Naunhof D 83 A4
Naustdal N..... 46 A2
Nautijaur S 196 C2
Nautsi RUS ... 193 D13
Nava E 142 A1
Navacerrada E .. 151 B3
Navaconcejo E .. 149 B4
Nava de Arévalo E. 150 B3
Nava de la Asunción
    E..... 150 A3
Nava del Rey E .. 150 A2
Navafriá E 151 A4
Navahermosa E.. 157 A3
Navahrudak BY... 13 B6
Naval E 145 B4
Navalacruz E 150 B3
Navalcán E 150 B2
Navalcarnero E .. 151 B3
Navaleno E 143 C3
Navalmanzano E.. 151 A3
Navalmoral E.... 150 B3
Navalmoral de la Mata
    E..... 150 C2
Navalón E 159 C3
Navalonguilla E .. 150 B2
Navalperal de Pinares
    E..... 150 B3
Navalpino E 157 A3
Navaltalgordo E .. 150 B3
Navaltoril E 156 A3
Navaluenga E .. 150 B3
Navalvillar de Pela
    E..... 156 A2
Navan IRL 30 A2
Navaperal de Tormes
    E..... 150 B2
Navapolatsk BY... 13 A8
Navarclés E 147 C2
Navarredonda de
  Gredos E.... 150 B2
Navarrenx F..... 144 A3
Navarrés E 159 B3
Navarrete E 143 B4
Navarrevisca E .. 150 B3
Navás E 147 C2
Navascués E 144 B2
Navas del Madroño
    E..... 155 B4
Navas del Rey E .. 151 B3
Navas del Sepillar
    E..... 163 A3
Navas de Oro E .. 150 A3
Navas de San Juan
    E..... 157 B4
Navasfrias E 149 B3
Nave I........ 120 B3
Nave de Haver P .. 149 B3
Nävekvarn S 56 B2
Navelli I 169 A3
Navenby GB 40 B3
Näverkärret S 56 A1
Naverstad S..... 54 B2
Navés E 147 C2
Navezuelas E.... 156 A2
Navia E 141 A4
Navia de Suarna E 141 B4
Navilly F..... 105 C4
Năvodari RO 17 C8
Naxos GR 185 B6
Nay F 145 A3
Nazaré P..... 154 B1
Nazarje SLO..... 123 A3
Nazilli TR 188 B3
Nazza D 82 A2
Nea Anchialos GR. 182 D4
Nea Epidavros GR. 184 B4
Nea Flippias GR . 182 D2
Nea Kalikratia GR. 183 C5
Nea Makri GR ... 185 A4
Nea Moudania GR. 183 C5
Neap GB..... 33 A5
Nea Peramos GR. 183 C6
Neapoli
  Kozani GR...182 C3
  Kriti GR.....185 D6
  Lakonia GR...184 C4
Nea Stira GR 185 A5
Neath GB 39 C3
Nea Visa GR ... 186 A1
Nea Zichni GR... 183 B5
Nebljusi HR..... 124 C1
Neblo SLO..... 122 A2
Nebolchy RUS... 9 C8
Nebra D 82 A3

Nebreda E 143 C3
Nechanice CZ 84 B3
Neckargemünd D . 93 B4
Neckarsulm D 94 B1
Neda E 140 A2
Nedelišće HR.... 124 A2
Nederweert NL.... 80 A1
Nedreberg N..... 48 B3
Nedre Gärdsjö S .. 50 B2
Nedre Soppero S . 196 A4
Nedstrand N..... 52 A1
Nedvědice CZ.... 97 B4
Nędza PL..... 86 B2
Neede NL..... 71 B3
Needham Market
    GB..... 45 A5
Needingworth GB.. 44 A3
Neermoor D..... 71 A4
Neeroeteren B.... 80 A1
Neerpelt B 79 A5
Neesen D 72 B1
Neetze D 73 A3
Nefyn GB 38 B2
Negotin SRB 16 C5
Negotino MK.... 182 B4
Negrar I 121 B3
Negredo E 151 A5
Negreira E 140 B2
Nègrepelisse F .. 129 B4
Negru Vodă RO .. 17 D8
Negueira de Muñiz
    E..... 141 A4
Neheim D..... 81 A3
Neila E 143 B4
Néive I 119 C5
Nejdek CZ 83 B4
Nekla PL..... 76 B2
Neksø DK..... 67 A4
Nelas I 148 B2
Nelaug N 53 B4
Nelidovo RUS ... 9 D8
Nelim FIN ... 193 D12
Nellingen D 94 C1
Nelson GB 40 B1
Neman RUS ... 12 A5
Nemea GR 184 B3
Nemesgörzsöny
    H.....111 B4
Nemeskér H.....111 B4
Nemesnádudvar H. 125 A5
Nemesszalók H.....111 B4
Németkér H ... 112 C2
Nemours F..... 103 A4
Nempomuk CZ ... 96 B1
Nérac F 129 B3
Neratovice CZ.... 84 B2
Nerchau D 83 A4
Néré F 115 C3
Neresheim D 94 C2
Nereto I 136 C2
Nerezine HR 123 C3
Nerežišća HR. ... 138 B2
Neringa LT..... 12 A4
Néris-les Bains F.. 116 A2
Nerito I 169 A3
Nerja E 163 B4
Néronde F 117 B4
Nérondes F 103 C4
Nerpio E 164 A2
Nersingen D 94 C2
Nerva E 161 B3
Nervesa della Battáglia
    I..... 121 B5
Nervi I 134 A2
Nes
  Buskerud N....48 B1
  Hedmark N....48 B2
  NL.....70 A2
  Sogn og Fjordane
    N.....46 A3
  Sør-Trøndelag N .198 B6
Nesbyen N 47 B6
Neset N 199 D7
Nesflaten N 52 A2
Nesjahverfi IS . 191 C10
Neskaupstaður IS 191 B12
Nesland N 53 A4
Neslandsvatn N... 53 B5
Nesle F 90 B2
Nesna N 195 D4
Nesoddtangen N.. 48 C2
Nesovice CZ..... 98 B1
Nesselwang D ... 108 B1
Nesslau CH..... 107 B4
Nessmersiel D ... 71 A4
Nesso I 120 B2
Nesterov UA 13 C5
Nestorio GR..... 182 C3
Nestun N..... 46 B2
Nesvady SK.....112 B2
Nesvatnstemmen N 53 B4
Nether Stowey GB. 43 A3
Netland N..... 52 B2
Netolice CZ 96 B2
Netphen D 81 B4
Netstal CH..... 107 B4
Nettancourt F.... 91 C4

Nettetal D........ 80 A2
Nettlingen D 72 B3
Nettuno I..... 168 B2
Neualbenreuth D.. 95 B4
Neubeckum D.... 81 A4
Neubrandenburg D. 74 A2
Neubukow D 65 B4
Neuburg D 94 C3
Neu Darchau D ... 73 A3
Neudau A.....111 B3
Neudietendorf D .. 82 B2
Neudorf D 93 B4
Neuenbürg D 93 C4
Neuenburg D 71 A4
Neuendorf D 66 B2
Neuenhagen D ... 74 B2
Neuenhaus D 71 B3
Neuenkirchen
  Niedersachsen D...71 B5
  Niedersachsen D...72 A2
  Nordrhein-Westfalen
    D.....71 B4
  Nordrhein-Westfalen
    D.....81 B3
Neuenrade D 81 A3
Neuenwalde D.... 64 C1
Neuerburg D 92 A2
Neufahrn
  Bayern D....95 C3
  Bayern D....95 C4
Neuf-Brisach D .. 106 A2
Neufchâteau
  B.....92 B1
  F.....92 C1
Neufchâtel-en-Bray
    F.....90 B1
Neufchâtel-sur-Aisne
    F.....91 B4
Neuflize F 91 B4
Neugersdorf D.... 84 B2
Neuhardenberg D . 74 B3
Neuharlingersiel D . 71 A4
Neuhaus
  Bayern D....95 B3
  Bayern D....96 C1
  Niedersachsen D..64 C2
  Niedersachsen D..73 A3
  Niedersachsen D..81 A5
Neuhaus a Rennweg
    D.....82 B3
Neuhausen
  CH.....107 B3
  D.....83 B5
Neuhausen ob Eck
    D.....107 B3
Neuhof
  Bayern D....94 B2
  Hessen D....81 B5
Neuhofen an der Krems
    A.....110 A1
Neuillé-Pont-Pierre
    F.....102 B2
Neuilly-en-Thelle F. 90 B2
Neuilly-le-Réal F .. 104 C2
Neuilly-l'Évêque F. 105 B4
Neuilly-St Front F .. 90 B3
Neu-Isenburg D .. 93 A4
Neukalen D 66 C1
Neu Kaliss D 73 A4
Neukirch D..... 84 A2
Neukirchen
  A.....109 A4
  Hessen D....81 B5
  Schleswig-Holstein
    D.....64 B1
Neukirchen am
  Grossvenediger
    A.....109 B3
Neukirchen bei Heiligen
  Blut D..... 95 B4
Neukloster D 65 C4
Neulengbach A....110 A2
Neulise F.....117 B4
Neu Lübbenau D .. 74 B2
Neum BIH..... 139 C3
Neumagen D 92 B2
Neumarkt D 95 B3
Neumarkt am Wallersee
    A.....109 B4
Neumarkt im
  Hausruckkreis A. 109 A4
Neumarkt im Mühlkreis
    A.....96 C2
Neumarkt im Steiermark
    A.....110 B1
Neumarkt Sankt Veit
    D.....95 C4
Neumünster D ... 64 B2
Neunburg vorm Wald
    D.....95 B4
Neung-sur-Beuvron
    F.....103 B3
Neunkirch
  Luzern CH....106 B3
  Schaffhausen CH..107 B3
Neunkirchen
  A.....111 B3
  Nordrhein-Westfalen
    D.....80 B3
  Saarland D....92 B3
Neunkirchen am Brand
    D.....94 B3
Neuötting D 95 C4
Neupetershain D.. 84 A2
Neuravensburg D. 107 B4
Neureut D 93 B4

Neuruppin D 74 B1
Neusäss D 94 C2
Neusiedl A.....111 B3
Neuss D 80 A2
Neussargues-Moissac
  F.....116 B2
Neustadt
  Bayern D....94 B2
  Bayern D....95 B4
  Bayern D....95 C3
  Brandenburg D ...73 B5
  Hessen D....81 B5
  Niedersachsen D..72 B2
  Rheinland-Pfalz D.93 B4
  Sachsen D....84 A2
  Schleswig-Holstein
    D.....65 B3
  Thüringen D....82 B3
  Thüringen D....83 B3
Neustadt-Glewe D. 73 A4
Neustift im Stubaital
    A.....108 B2
Neustrelitz D 74 A2
Neutal A.....111 B3
Neutrebbin D 74 B3
Neu-Ulm D 94 C2
Neuves-Maisons F. 92 C2
Neuvic
  Corrèze F....116 B2
  Dordogne F...129 A3
Neuville-aux-Bois
  F.....103 A4
Neuville-de-Poitou
  F.....115 B4
Neuville-les-Dames
  F.....117 A5
Neuville-sur-Saône
  F.....117 B4
Neuvy-le-Roi F... 102 B2
Neuvy-Santour F.. 104 A2
Neuvy-St Sépulchre
  F.....103 C3
Neuvy-sur-Barangeon
  F.....103 B4
Neuwied D 80 B3
Neuzelle D 74 B3
Névache F 118 B3
Neveklov CZ 96 B2
Nevel RUS 9 D6
Neverfjord N 192 B7
Nevers F 104 C2
Nevesinje BIH.... 139 B4
Névez F 100 B2
Nevlunghavn N ... 53 B5
Nevşehir TR..... 23 B8
New Abbey GB ... 36 B3
New Aberdour GB. 33 D4
New Alresford GB. 44 B2
Newark-on-Trent
  GB.....40 B3
Newbiggin-by-the-Sea
  GB.....37 A5
Newbliss IRL 27 B3
Newborough GB.. 38 A2
Newbridge IRL.... 30 A2
Newbridge on Wye
  GB.....39 B3
Newburgh
  Aberdeenshire
  GB.....33 D4
  Fife GB.....35 B4
Newbury GB 44 B2
Newby Bridge GB. 36 B4
Newcastle GB ... 27 B5
Newcastle Emlyn
  GB.....39 B2
Newcastleton GB. 37 A4
Newcastle-under-Lyme
  GB.....40 B1
Newcastle upon Tyne
  GB.....37 B5
Newcastle West IRL 29 B2
Newchurch GB... 39 B3
New Costessey GB. 41 C5
New Cumnock GB. 36 A2
Newent GB..... 39 C4
New Galloway GB. 36 A2
Newham GB..... 45 C4
Newhaven GB ... 45 C4
Newington GB... 45 B5
Newinn IRL..... 29 B4
Newlyn GB..... 42 B1
Newmachar GB .. 33 D4
Newmarket
  Suffolk GB....45 A4
  Western Isles GB..31 A2
  IRL.....29 B3
Newmarket-on-Fergus
  IRL.....28 B3
New Mills GB.... 40 B2
New Milton GB... 44 C2
New Pitsligo GB.. 33 D4
Newport
  Isle of Wight GB..44 C2
  Newport GB....39 C4
  Pembrokeshire GB.39 B2
  Telford & Wrekin
  GB.....38 B4
  Mayo IRL....28 A2
  Tipperary IRL...29 B3
Newport-on-Tay GB 35 B5
Newport Pagnell GB 44 A3
Newquay GB 42 B1
New Quay GB ... 39 B2
New Radnor GB .. 39 B3
New Romney GB. 45 C4
New Ross IRL ... 30 B2
Newry GB..... 27 B4

New Scone GB 35 B4
Newton Abbot GB. 43 B3
Newton Arlosh GB. 36 B3
Newton Aycliffe GB. 37 B5
Newton Ferrers GB. 42 B2
Newtonhill GB.... 33 D4
Newtonmore GB .. 32 D2
Newton Stewart GB. 36 B2
Newtown
  Herefordshire GB..39 B4
  Powys GB.....39 B3
Newtownabbey GB. 27 B5
Newtownards GB.. 27 B5
Newtownbutler GB. 27 B3
Newtown Cunningham
  IRL.....27 B3
Newtownhamilton
  GB.....27 B4
Newtownmountkennedy
  IRL.....30 A2
Newtown St Boswells
  GB.....35 C5
Newtown Sands IRL 29 B2
Newtownstewart
  GB.....27 B3
Nexon F 115 C5
Neyland GB 39 C2
Nibbiano I 120 C2
Nibe DK 58 B2
Nicastro I 175 C2
Niccone I 135 B5
Nice F 133 B3
Nickelsdorf A.....111 B4
Nicolosi I 177 B4
Nicosia
  CY.....181 A2
  I.....177 B3
Nicótera I 175 C1
Nidda D 81 B5
Niğde TR 23 C8
Nidzica PL..... 77 A5
Niebüll D 64 B1
Niechanowo PL... 76 B2
Niechorze PL..... 67 B4
Niedalino PL..... 67 B5
Niederaula D 82 B1
Niederbipp CH.... 106 B2
Niederbronn-les-Bains
  F.....93 C3
Niederfischbach D. 81 B3
Niedergörsdorf D .. 74 C1
Niederkrüchten D . 80 A2
Niederndorf A 108 B3
Nieder-Olm D 93 B4
Niedersachswerfen
  D.....82 A2
Niederstetten D.... 94 B1
Niederurnen CH .. 107 B4
Niederwölz A.....110 B1
Niedoradz PL..... 85 A3
Niedzica PL..... 99 B4
Niegosławice PL... 85 A3
Nieheim D 81 A5
Niemcza PL..... 85 B4
Niemegk D..... 74 B1
Niemisel S 196 C5
Niemodlin PL..... 85 B5
Nienburg
  Niedersachsen D..72 B2
  Sachsen-Anhalt D. 83 A3
Niepołomice PL... 99 A4
Nierstein D 93 B4
Niesky D 84 A2
Niestronno PL.... 76 B2
Nieświń PL..... 87 A4
Nieszawa PL..... 76 B3
Nieul-le-Dolent F.. 114 B2
Nieul-sur-Mer F.. 114 B2
Nieuw-Amsterdam
  NL.....71 B3
Nieuw-Buinen NL. 71 B3
Nieuwegein NL... 70 B2
Nieuwe Niedorp NL. 70 B1
Nieuwe-Pekela NL. 71 A3
Nieuwerkerken B.. 79 B4
Nieuwe-schans NL. 71 A4
Nieuwolda NL ... 71 A3
Nieuwpoort B ... 78 A2
Nieuw-Weerdinge
  NL.....71 B3
Nigrita GR..... 183 C5
Nigüelas E 163 B4
Níjar E 164 C2
Nijemci HR..... 125 B5
Nijkerk NL 70 B2
Nijlen B 79 A4
Nijmegen NL 80 A1
Nijverdal NL..... 71 B3
Nikel RUS ... 193 C14
Nikinci SRB..... 127 C1
Nikiti GR 183 C5
Nikitsch A.....111 B3
Nikkaluokta S ... 196 B2
Nikla H.....111 C4
Niklasdorf A.....110 B2
Nikšić MNE 139 C4
Nilivaara S 196 B4
Nîmes F 131 B3
Nimis I 122 A2
Nimtofte DK..... 58 B3
Nin HR 137 A4
Nindorf D 64 B2
Ninemilehouse IRL. 30 B1
Ninove B 79 B4
Niort F 114 B3
Niš SRB 16 D4

Nisa P..... 155 B3
Niscemi I 177 B3
Niskala FIN ... 197 D10
Nissafors S 60 B3
Nissan-lez-Enséruine
  F.....130 B2
Nissedal N 53 A4
Nissumby DK 58 B1
Nisterud N 53 A5
Niton GB 44 C2
Nitra SK 98 C2
Nitrianske-Pravno
  SK.....98 C2
Nitrianske Rudno
  SK.....98 C2
Nitry F 104 B2
Nittedal N..... 48 B2
Nittenau D 95 B4
Nittendorf D 95 B3
Nivala FIN 3 E9
Nivelles B 79 B4
Nivnice CZ..... 98 C1
Nižná SK 99 B3
Nižná Boca SK.... 99 C3
Nižne Repaše SK... 99 B3
Nizza Monferrato I. 119 C5
Njarðvík IS 190 D3
Njegoševo SRB .. 126 B1
Njivice HR 123 B3
Njurundabommen
  S.....200 D3
Njutånger S 200 E3
Noailles F..... 90 B2
Noain E 144 B2
Noale I 121 B5
Noalejo E 163 A4
Noblejas E 151 C4
Noceda E 141 B4
Nocera Inferiore I.. 170 C2
Nocera Terinese I. 175 C2
Nocera Umbra I... 136 B1
Noceto I 120 C3
Noci I 173 B3
Nociglia I 173 B4
Nodeland N 53 B3
Nödinge S 60 B2
Nods F 105 B5
Noé F 146 A2
Noépoli I 174 A2
Noeux-les-Mines F. 78 B2
Noez E 157 A3
Nogales E 155 C4
Nogara I 121 B4
Nogarejas E 141 B4
Nogaro F 128 C2
Nogent F 105 A4
Nogent l'Artaud F. 90 C3
Nogent-le-Roi F... 90 C1
Nogent-le-Rotrou F. 89 B4
Nogent-sur-Seine F 91 C3
Nogent-sur-Vernisson
  F.....103 B4
Nogersund S 63 B2
Noguera E 152 B2
Noguerones E 163 A3
Nohfelden D 92 B3
Nohn D 80 B2
Noia E 140 B2
Noicáttaro I 173 A2
Noirétable F..... 117 B3
Noirmoutier-en-l'Île
  F.....114 A1
Noja E 143 A3
Nojewo PL..... 75 B5
Nokia FIN 8 B3
Nol S 60 B2
Nola I 170 C2
Nolay F 104 C3
Noli I 133 A4
Nolnyra S 51 B4
Nombela E 150 B3
Nomeny F 92 C2
Nomexy F 92 C2
Nonancourt F 89 B5
Nonant-le-Pin F .. 89 B4
Nonántola I 121 C4
Nonaspe E 153 A4
None I 119 C4
Nontron F 115 C4
Nonza F 180 A2
Noordhorn NL.... 71 A3
Noordwijk NL..... 70 B1
Noordwijkerhout NL. 70 B1
Noordwolde NL... 70 B3
Noppikoski S 50 A1
Nora S 55 A6
Nørager DK 58 B2
Norberg S 50 B2
Norboda S 51 B5
Nórcia I 136 C2
Nordagutu N 53 A5
Nordanås S 200 B4
Nordausques F .. 78 B2
Nordborg DK 64 A2
Nordby
  Aarhus Amt. DK..59 C3
  Ribe Amt. DK.....59 C1
Norddeich D 71 A4
Norddorf D 64 B1
Norden D 71 A4
Nordenham D ... 72 A1
Norderhov N 48 B2
Norderney D 71 A4
Norderstapel D ... 64 B2
Norderstedt D ... 64 C3
Nordfjord N ... 193 B14
Nordfjordeid N .. 198 D3
Nordfold N 194 C6

Nordhalben D 82 B3
Nordhausen D 82 A2
Nordheim vor der Rhön D 82 B2
Nordholz D 64 C1
Nordhorn D 71 B4
Nordingrå S 200 D4
Nordkjosbotn N 192 C3
Nordli N 199 A10
Nördlingen D 94 C2
Nordmaling S 200 C5
Nordmark S 49 C6
Nordmela N 194 A6
Nord-Odal N 48 B3
Nordre Osen N 48 A3
Nordsinni N 48 B1
Nørdstedalsseter N 198 D4
Nordstemmen D 72 B2
Nordvågen N 193 B10
Nordwalde D 71 B4
Noreña E 142 A1
Noresund N 48 B1
Norg NL 71 A3
Norheimsund N 46 B3
Norie S 63 B2
Norma I 169 B2
Nornäs S 49 A5
Norrahammar S 62 A2
Norråker S 200 B1
Norrala S 51 A3
Norra Vi S 62 A3
Nørre Aaby DK 59 C2
Nørre Alslev DK 65 B4
Nørre Lyndelse DK 59 C3
Nørre Nebel DK 59 C1
Norrent-Fontes F 78 B2
Nørre Snede DK 59 C2
Nørresundby DK 58 A2
Nørre Vorupør DK 58 B1
Norrfjärden S 196 D4
Norrhed S 196 C3
Norrhult Klavreström S 62 A3
Norrköping S 56 B2
Norrskedika S 51 B5
Norrsundet S 51 B4
Norrtälje S 57 A4
Nors DK 58 A1
Norsbron S 55 A4
Norsholm S 56 B1
Norsjö S 200 B5
Nörten-Hardenberg D 82 A1
Northallerton GB 37 B5
Northampton GB 44 A3
North Berwick GB 35 B5
North Charlton GB 37 A5
Northeim D 82 A2
Northfleet GB 45 B4
North Frodingham GB 40 B3
North Kessock GB 32 D2
Northleach GB 44 B2
North Molton GB 42 A3
North Petherton GB 43 A3
Northpunds GB 33 B5
North Somercotes GB 41 B4
North Tawton GB 42 B3
North Thoresby GB 41 B3
North Walsham GB 41 C5
Northwich GB 38 A4
Norton GB 40 A3
Nortorf D 64 B2
Nort-sur-Erdre F 101 B4
Nörvenich D 80 B2
Norwich GB 41 C5
Norwick GB 33 A6
Nøsen N 47 B5
Nossa Senhora do Cabo P 154 C1
Nossebro S 55 B3
Nössemark S 54 A2
Nossen D 83 A5
Notaresco I 169 A3
Noto I 177 C4
Notodden N 53 A5
Nottingham GB 40 C2
Nottuln D 71 C4
Nouan-le-Fuzelier F 103 B4
Nouans-les-Fontaines F 103 B3
Nougaroulet F 129 C3
Nouvion F 78 B1
Nouzonville F 91 B4
Nova H 111 C3
Nová Baňa SK 98 C2
Nová Bystrica SK 99 B3
Nová Bystřice CZ 97 B3
Nova Crnja SRB 126 B2
Novaféltria I 135 B5
Nova Gorica SLO 122 B2
Nova Gradiška HR 124 B3
Nováky SK 98 C2
Novalaise F 118 B2
Novales E 145 B3
Nova Levante I 108 C2
Novalja HR 137 A3
Nová Paka CZ 84 B3
Nova Pazova SRB 127 C2
Nová Pec CZ 96 C1
Novara I 120 B1
Novara di Sicília I 177 A4
Nova Siri I 174 A2
Novate Mezzola I 120 A2
Nova Topola BIH 124 B3
Novaya Ladoga RUS 9 B8
Nova Zagora BG 17 D6
Nové Hrady CZ 96 C2
Novelda E 165 A4
Novellara I 121 C3
Nové Město SK 98 C1
Nové Město nad Metují CZ 85 B4
Nové Město na Moravě CZ 97 B4
Nové Město pod Smrkem CZ 84 B3
Nové Mitrovice CZ 96 B1
Noventa di Piave I 122 B1
Noventa Vicentina I 121 B4
Novés E 151 B3
Noves F 131 B3
Nové Sady SK 98 C1
Novés de Segre E 147 B2
Nové Strašeci CZ 84 B1
Nové Zámky SK 112 B2
Novgorod RUS 9 C7
Novi Bečej SRB 126 B2
Novi di Módena I 121 C3
Novigrad
Istarska HR 122 B2
Zadarsko-Kninska HR 137 A4
Novigrad Podravski HR 124 A2
Novi Kneževac SRB 126 A2
Novi Lígure I 120 C1
Noville B 92 A1
Novi Marof HR 124 A2
Novion-Porcien F 91 B4
Novi Pazar
BG 17 D7
SRB 16 D4
Novi Sad SRB 126 B1
Novi Slankamen SRB 126 B2
Novi Travnik BIH 139 A3
Novi Vinodolski HR 123 B3
Novohrad-Volynskyy UA 13 C7
Novo Mesto SLO 123 B4
Novo Miloševo SRB 126 B2
Novorzhev RUS 9 D6
Novo Selo BIH 125 B3
Novoselytsya UA 17 A7
Novosokolniki RUS 9 D6
Novoveská Huta SK 99 C4
Novovolynsk UA 13 C6
Novska HR 124 B2
Nový Bor CZ 84 B2
Nový Bydžov CZ 84 B3
Novy-Chevrières F 91 B4
Novy Dwór Mazowiecki PL 77 B5
Nový-Hrozenkov CZ 98 B2
Nový Jičín CZ 98 B2
Novy Knin CZ 96 B2
Nowa Cerekwia PL 86 B1
Nowa Dęba PL 87 B5
Nowa Karczma PL 68 A3
Nowa Kościoł PL 85 A3
Nowa Ruda PL 85 B4
Nowa Słupia PL 87 B5
Nowa Sól PL 85 A3
Nowa Wieś PL 69 B4
Nowa-Wieś Wielka PL 76 B3
Nowe PL 69 B3
Nowe Brzesko PL 87 B4
Nowe Grudze PL 77 B4
Nowe Kiejkuty PL 77 A6
Nowe Miasteczko PL 85 A3
Nowe Miasto
Mazowieckie PL 77 B5
Mazowieckie PL 87 A4
Nowe Miasto Lubawskie PL 69 B4
Nowe Miasto nad Wartą PL 76 B2
Nowe Skalmierzyce PL 86 A2
Nowe Warpno PL 74 A3
Nowica PL 69 A4
Nowogard PL 75 A4
Nowogród Bobrzanski PL 84 A3
Nowogrodziec PL 84 A3
Nowosolna PL 86 A3
Nowy Dwór Gdański PL 69 A4
Nowy Korczyn PL 87 B4
Nowy Sącz PL 99 B4
Nowy Staw PL 69 A4
Nowy Targ PL 99 B4
Nowy Tomyśl PL 75 B5
Nowy Wiśnicz PL 99 B4
Noyalo F 101 B3
Noyal-Pontivy F 100 A3
Noyant F 102 B2
Noyelles-sur-Mer F 78 B1
Noyen-sur-Sarthe F 102 B1
Noyers F 104 B2
Noyers-sur-Cher F 103 B3
Noyers-sur-Jabron F 132 A1
Noyon F 90 B2
Nozay F 101 B4
Nuaillé F 102 B1
Nuaillé-d'Aunis F 114 B3
Nuars F 104 B2
Nubledo E 141 A5
Nuéno E 145 B3
Nuestra Señora Sa Verge des Pilar E 166 C1
Nueva E 142 A2
Nueva Carteya E 163 A3
Nuevalos E 152 A2
Nuits F 104 B3
Nuits-St Georges F 105 B3
Nule I 178 B3
Nules E 159 B3
Nulvi I 178 B2
Numana I 136 B2
Numansdorp NL 79 A4
Nümbrecht D 81 B3
Nunchritz D 83 A5
Nuneaton GB 40 C2
Nunnanen FIN 196 A7
N Unnaryd S 60 B3
Nuñomoral E 149 B3
Nunspeet NL 70 B2
Nuorgam FIN 193 B11
Núoro I 178 B3
Nurallao I 179 C3
Nuremberg = Nürnberg D 94 B3
Nurmes FIN 3 E11
Nürnberg = Nuremberg D 94 B3
Nurri I 179 C3
Nürtingen D 94 C1
Nus I 119 B4
Nusnäs S 50 B1
Nusplingen D 107 A3
Nuštar HR 125 B4
Nuupas FIN 197 C9
Nyåker S 200 C5
Nyáregyháza H 112 B3
Nyarlörinc H 113 C3
Nyasvizh BY 13 B7
Nybble S 55 A5
Nybergsund N 49 A4
Nybøl DK 64 B2
Nyborg
DK 59 C3
S 196 D6
Nybro S 62 B3
Nybster GB 32 C3
Nyby DK 65 B5
Nye S 62 A3
Nyékládháza H 113 B4
Nyergesujfalu H 112 B2
Nyhammar S 50 B1
Nyhyttan S 55 A5
Nyirád H 111 B4
Nyirbátor H 16 B5
Nyíregyháza H 16 B4
Nyker DK 67 A3
Nykil S 56 B1
Nykirke N 48 B2
Nykøbing
Falster DK 65 B4
Vestsjællands Amt. DK 61 D1
Nykøbing Mors DK 58 B1
Nyköping S 56 B3
Nykroppa S 55 A5
Nykvarn S 56 A3
Nykyrke S 55 B5
Nyland S 200 C3
Nylars DK 67 A3
Nymburk CZ 84 B3
Nynäshamn S 57 B3
Nyon CH 118 A3
Nyons F 131 A4
Nýřany CZ 96 B1
Nýrsko CZ 95 B5
Nyrud N 193 C13
Nysa PL 85 B5
Nysäter S 55 A3
Nyseter N 198 C5
Nyskoga S 49 B4
Nysted DK 65 B4
Nystrand N 53 A5
Nyúl H 111 B4
Nyvoll N 192 B7

O

Oadby GB 40 C2
Oakengates GB 38 B4
Oakham GB 40 C3
Oanes N 52 B2
Obalj BIH 139 B4
Oban GB 34 B2
O Barco E 141 B4
Obbola S 200 C6
Obdach A 110 B1
Obejo E 156 B3
Oberammergau D 108 B2
Oberasbach D 94 B2
Oberau D 108 B2
Oberaudorf D 108 B3
Oberbruck F 106 B1
Oberdiessbach CH 106 C2
Oberdorf CH 106 B2
Oberdrauburg A 109 C3
Oberelsbach D 82 B2
Obere Stanz A 110 B2
Ober Grafendorf A 110 A2
Obergünzburg D 108 B1
Obergurgl A 108 C2
Oberhausen D 80 A2
Oberhof D 82 B2
Oberkirch D 93 C4
Oberkirchen D 81 A4
Oberkochen D 94 C2
Obermassfeld-Grimmenthal D 82 B2
Ober-Morlen D 81 B4
Obermünchen D 95 C3
Obernai F 93 C3
Obernberg A 96 C1
Obernburg D 93 B5
Oberndorf D 93 C4
Oberndorf bei Salzburg A 109 B3
Obernkirchen D 72 B2
Oberort A 110 B2
Oberpullendorf A 111 B3
Oberriet CH 107 B4
Oberröblingen D 82 A3
Oberrot D 94 B1
Oberstaufen D 107 B5
Oberstdorf D 107 B5
Obertauern A 109 B4
Obertilliach A 109 C3
Obertraubling D 95 C4
Obertraun A 109 B4
Obertrubach D 95 B3
Obertrum A 109 B4
Oberursel D 81 B4
Obervellach A 109 C4
Oberviechtach D 95 B4
Oberwart A 111 B3
Oberwesel D 93 A3
Oberwinter D 80 B3
Oberwölzstadt A 110 B1
Oberzell D 96 C1
Obice PL 87 B4
Óbidos P 154 B1
Obing D 109 B3
Objat F 129 A4
Objazda PL 68 A2
Öblarn A 109 B5
Obninsk RUS 9 E10
O Bolo E 141 B3
Oborniki PL 75 B5
Oborniki Śląskie PL 85 A4
Obornjača SRB 126 B1
Obrenovac SRB 127 C2
Obrež SRB 127 C1
Obrigheim D 93 B5
Obrov SLO 123 B3
Obrovac
HR 137 A4
SRB 126 B1
Obrovac Sinjski HR 138 B2
Obruk TR 23 B7
Obrzycko PL 75 B5
Obudovac BIH 125 C4
Ocaña E 151 C4
O Carballiño E 140 B2
Occhiobello I 121 C4
Occimiano I 119 B5
Očevlja BIH 139 A4
Ochagavía E 144 B2
Ochiltree GB 36 A2
Ochla PL 84 A3
Ochotnica-Dolna PL 99 B4
Ochotnica-Górna PL 99 B4
Ochsenfurt D 94 B2
Ochsenhausen D 107 A4
Ochtendung D 80 B3
Ochtrup D 71 B4
Ocieka PL 87 B5
Ockelbo S 50 B3
Öckerö S 60 B1
Ocniţa MD 17 A7
O Corgo E 141 B3
Očová SK 99 C3
Ócsa H 112 B3
Öcseny H 125 A4
Öcsöd H 113 C4
Octeville F 88 A2
Ocypel PL 69 B3
Ödåkra S 61 C2
Odby DK 58 B1
Odda N 46 B3
Odder DK 59 C3
Ödeborg S 54 B2
Odeceixe P 160 B1
Odechów PL 87 A5
Odeleite P 160 B2
Odemira P 160 B1
Ödemiş TR 188 A2
Ödensbacken S 56 A1
Odense DK 59 C3
Odensjö
Jönköping S 62 A2
Kronoberg S 60 C3
Oderberg D 74 B3
Oderzo I 122 B1
Odesa = Odessa UA 17 B9
Ödeshög S 55 B5
Odessa = Odesa UA 17 B9
Odiáxere P 160 B1
Odie GB 33 B4
Odiham GB 44 B3
Odintsovo RUS 9 E10
Odivelas P 160 A1
Odolanów PL 85 A5
Odón E 152 B2
Odorheiu Secuiesc RO 17 B6
Odrowąz PL 87 A4
Odry CZ 98 B1
Odrzywół PL 87 A4
Ødsted DK 59 C2
Odžaci SRB 126 B1
Odžak BIH 125 B4
Oebisfelde D 73 B3
Oederan D 83 B5
Oeding D 71 C3
Oegstgeest NL 70 B1
Oelde D 81 A4
Oelsnitz D 83 B4
Oer-Erkenschwick D 80 A3
Oerlinghausen D 72 C1
Oettingen D 94 C2
Oetz A 108 B1
Oeventrop D 81 A4
Offanengo I 120 B2
Offenbach D 81 B4
Offenburg D 93 C3
Offida I 136 C2
Offingen D 94 C2
Offranville F 89 A5
Ofte N 53 A4
Ofterschwang D 107 B5
Oggiono I 120 B2
Ogihares E 163 A4
Ogliastro Cilento I 170 C3
Ogliastro Marina I 170 C2
Ogmore-by-Sea GB 39 C3
Ogna N 52 B1
Ogre LV 8 D4
Ogrodzieniec PL 86 B3
Ogulin HR 123 B4
Ögur IS 190 A3
Ohanes E 164 B2
Ohey B 79 B5
Ohlstadt D 108 B2
Ohrdorf D 73 B3
Ohrdruf D 82 B2
Ohrid MK 182 B2
Öhringen D 94 B1
Oia E 140 B2
Oiã P 148 B1
Oiartzun E 144 A2
Oijärvi FIN 197 D8
Oilgate IRL 30 B2
Oimbra E 148 A2
Oiselay-et-Grachoux F 105 B4
Oisemont F 90 B1
Oisterwijk NL 79 A5
Öja S 57 C4
Öje S 49 B5
Ojén E 162 B3
Ojrzeń PL 77 B5
Ojuelos Altos E 156 B2
Okalewo PL 77 A4
Okány H 113 C5
Okehampton GB 42 B2
Oklaj HR 138 B2
Økneshamn N 194 B6
Okoč SK 111 B4
Okoličné SK 99 B3
Okonek PL 68 B1
Okonin PL 69 B3
Okřisky CZ 97 B3
Oksa PL 87 B4
Oksbøl DK 59 C1
Oksby DK 59 C1
Øksfjord N 192 B6
Øksna N 48 B3
Okučani HR 124 B3
Okulovka RUS 9 C8
Ólafsfjörður IS 191 A7
Ólafsvík IS 190 C2
ÖLagnö S 57 A4
Olagüe E 144 B2
Oland N 53 B4
Olargues F 130 B1
Oława PL 85 B5
Olazagutia E 144 B1
Olbernhau D 83 B5
Ólbia I 178 B3
Olching D 108 A2
Oldbury GB 43 A4
Oldcastle IRL 27 C3
Old Deer GB 33 D4
Oldeberkoop NL 70 B3
Oldeboorn NL 70 A2
Olden N 198 D3
Oldenbrok D 71 A5
Oldenburg
Niedersachsen D 71 A5
Schleswig-Holstein D 65 B3
Oldenzaal NL 71 B3
Olderdalen N 192 C4
Olderfjord N 193 B9
Oldersum D 71 A4
Oldervik N 192 C2
Oldham GB 40 B1
Oldisleben D 82 A3
Oldmeldrum GB 33 D4
Olea E 142 B2
Oleby S 49 B5
Olechów PL 87 A5
Oledo P 155 B3
Oléggio I 120 B1
Oleiros
Coruña E 140 A2
Coruña E 140 B1
P 154 B3
Oleksandriya UA 13 C7
Olen B 79 A4
Ølen N 52 A1
Olenegorsk RUS 3 B13
Olenino RUS 9 D8
Olesa de Montserrat E 147 C2
Oleśnica PL 85 A5
Olešnice CZ 97 B4
Olesno PL 86 B2
Oletta F 180 A2
Olette F 146 B3
Olevsk UA 13 C7
Olfen D 80 A3
Olgiate Comasco I 120 B1
Olginate I 120 B2
Ølgod DK 59 C1
Olgrinmore GB 32 C3
Olhão P 160 B2
Olhava FIN 197 D8
Olhavo P 154 B1
Oliana E 147 B2
Olias del Rey E 151 C4
Oliena I 178 B3
Oliete E 153 B3
Olimbos GR 188 D2
Olite E 144 B2
Oliva E 159 C3
Oliva de la Frontera E 155 C4
Oliva de Mérida E 156 B1
Oliva de Plasencia E 149 B3
Olivadi I 175 C2
Olival P 154 B2
Olivar E 163 B4
Olivares E 161 B3
Olivares de Duero E 142 C2
Olivares de Júcar E 158 B1
Oliveira de Azeméis P 148 B1
Oliveira de Frades P 148 B1
Oliveira do Conde P 148 B2
Oliveira do Douro P 148 A1
Oliveira do Hospital P 148 B2
Olivenza E 155 C3
Olivet F 103 B3
Olivone CH 107 C3
Öljehult S 63 B3
Olkusz PL 86 B3
Ollerton GB 40 B2
Ollerup DK 65 A3
Olliergues F 117 B3
Ölmbrottorp S 56 A1
Ölme S 55 A4
Olmedilla de Alarcón E 158 B1
Olmedillo de Roa E 143 C3
Olmedo
E 150 A3
I 178 B2
Olmeto F 180 B1
Olmillos de Castro E 149 A3
Olmos de Ojeda E 142 B2
Olney GB 44 A3
Ołobok PL 86 A2
Olocau del Rey E 153 B3
Olofström S 63 B2
Olomouc CZ 98 B1
Olonets RUS 9 B8
Olonne-sur-Mer F 114 B2
Olonzac F 130 B1
Oloron-Ste Marie F 145 A3
Olost E 147 C3
Olot E 147 B3
Olovo BIH 139 A4
Olpe D 81 A3
Olsberg D 81 A4
Olsene B 79 B3
Olserud S 55 A4
Olshammar S 55 B5
Olshanka UA 13 D9
Olszanica PL 85 A3
Olsztyn
Śląskie PL 86 B3
Warmińsko-Mazurskie PL 69 B5
Olsztynek PL 77 A5
Olszyna PL 84 A3
Olszyny PL 77 A6
Oltedal N 52 B2
Olten CH 106 B2
Olteniţa RO 17 C7
Olula del Rio E 164 B2
Ølve N 46 B2
Olvega E 144 C2
Olvera E 162 B2
Olympia GR 184 B2
Olzai I 178 B3
Omagh GB 27 B3
Omalos GR 185 D4
Omegna I 119 B5
Omiš HR 138 B2
Omišalj HR 123 B3
Ommen NL 71 B3
Omodhos CY 181 B1
Omoljica SRB 127 C2
On B 79 B5
Oña E 143 B3
Onano I 168 A1
O Näsberg S 49 B5
Oñati E 143 A4

Onda E . . . 159 B3
Ondara E . . . 159 C4
Ondarroa E . . . 143 A4
Onesse-et-Laharie
F . . . 128 B1
Oneşti RO . . . 17 B7
Onhaye B . . . 79 B4
Onich GB . . . 34 B2
Onil E . . . 159 C3
Onis E . . . 142 A2
Önnestad S . . . 61 C4
Onsala S . . . 60 B2
Ontinyent E . . . 159 C3
Ontur E . . . 158 C2
Onzain F . . . 103 B3
Onzonilla E . . . 142 B1
Oostburg NL . . . 79 A3
Oostende B . . . 78 A2
Oosterend NL . . . 70 A2
Oosterhout NL . . . 79 A4
Oosterwolde NL . . . 71 B3
Oosterzele B . . . 79 B3
Oosthuizen NL . . . 70 B2
Oostkamp B . . . 78 A3
Oostmalle B . . . 79 A4
Oost-Vlieland NL . . . 70 A2
Oostvoorne NL . . . 79 A4
Ootmarsum NL . . . 71 B3
Opalenica PL . . . 75 B5
O Páramo E . . . 140 B3
Opařany CZ . . . 96 B2
Opatija HR . . . 123 B3
Opatów
Śląskie PL . . . 86 B2
Świętokrzyskie PL . . . 87 B5
Wielkopolskie PL . . . 86 A2
Opatówek PL . . . 86 A2
Opatowiec PL . . . 87 B4
Opava CZ . . . 98 B1
O Pedrouzo E . . . 140 B2
Opeinde NL . . . 70 A3
Oper Thalkirchdorf
D . . . 107 B5
Opglabbeerk B . . . 80 A1
Opicina I . . . 122 B2
O Pino E . . . 140 B2
Oplotnica SLO . . . 123 A4
Opmeer NL . . . 70 B1
Opochka RUS . . . 9 D6
Opočno CZ . . . 85 B4
Opoczno PL . . . 87 A4
Opole PL . . . 86 B1
Oporów PL . . . 77 B4
O Porriño E . . . 140 B2
Opovo SRB . . . 127 B2
Oppach D . . . 84 A2
Oppdal N . . . 198 C6
Oppeby
Östergötland S . . . 56 B1
Södermanland S . . . 56 B2
Oppedal N . . . 46 A2
Oppegård N . . . 54 A1
Oppenau D . . . 93 C4
Oppenberg A . . . 110 B1
Oppenheim D . . . 93 B4
Óppido Lucano I . . . 172 B1
Óppido Mamertina
I . . . 175 C1
Opponitz A . . . 110 B1
Oppstad N . . . 48 B3
Oprtalj HR . . . 122 B2
Opsaheden S . . . 49 B5
Ópusztaszer H . . . 113 C4
Opuzen HR . . . 138 B3
Ora
CY . . . 181 B2
I . . . 121 A4
Orada P . . . 155 C3
Oradea RO . . . 16 B4
Oradour-sur-Glane
F . . . 115 C5
Oradour-sur-Vayres
F . . . 115 C4
Oragonja SLO . . . 122 B2
Orah BIH . . . 139 C4
Orahova BIH . . . 138 A3
Orahovica HR . . . 125 B3
Orahovo BIH . . . 124 B3
Oraison F . . . 132 B1
Orajärvi FIN . . . 196 C7
Orange F . . . 131 A3
Orani I . . . 178 B3
Oranienbaum D . . . 83 A4
Oranienburg D . . . 74 B2
Oranmore IRL . . . 28 A3
Orašac SRB . . . 127 C2
Orašje BIH . . . 125 B4
Oravská Lesná SK . . . 99 B3
Oravská Polhora
SK . . . 99 B3
Oravské Veselé SK . . . 99 B3
Oravsky-Podzámok
SK . . . 99 B3
Orba E . . . 159 C3
Orbacém P . . . 148 A1
Orbais F . . . 91 C3
Ørbæk DK . . . 59 C3
Orbassano I . . . 119 B4
Orbe CH . . . 105 C5
Orbec F . . . 89 A4
Orbetello I . . . 168 A1
Orbetello Scalo I . . . 168 A1
Orbigny F . . . 103 B3
Ørby DK . . . 59 B3
Örbyhus S . . . 51 B4

Orce E . . . 164 B2
Orcera E . . . 164 A2
Orchamps-Vennes
F . . . 105 B5
Orches F . . . 102 C2
Orchete E . . . 159 C3
Orchies F . . . 78 B3
Orchowo PL . . . 76 B3
Orcières F . . . 118 C3
Ordes E . . . 140 A2
Ordhead GB . . . 33 D4
Ordino AND . . . 146 B2
Ordizia E . . . 144 A1
Orduña E . . . 143 B4
Orea E . . . 152 B2
Orebić HR . . . 138 C3
Örebro S . . . 56 A1
Öregcsertő H . . . 112 C3
Öregrund S . . . 51 B5
Orehoved DK . . . 65 B4
Orellana E . . . 156 A2
Orellana de la Sierra
E . . . 156 A2
Ören TR . . . 188 B2
Örencik TR . . . 187 C4
Orestiada GR . . . 186 A1
Organyà E . . . 147 B2
Orgaz E . . . 157 A4
Orgelet F . . . 105 C4
Ørgenvika N . . . 48 B1
Orgères-en-Beauce
F . . . 103 A3
Orgibet F . . . 145 B4
Orgnac-l'Aven F . . . 131 A3
Orgon F . . . 131 B4
Orgósolo I . . . 178 B3
Orhaneli TR . . . 186 C3
Orhangazi TR . . . 187 B4
Orhei MD . . . 17 B8
Orhomenos GR . . . 184 A3
Oria E . . . 164 B2
Oria I . . . 173 B3
Origny-Ste Benoite
F . . . 91 B3
Orihuela E . . . 165 A4
Orihuela del Tremedal
E . . . 152 B2
Orikum AL . . . 182 C1
Oriola P . . . 154 C3
Oriolo I . . . 174 A2
Oriovac HR . . . 125 B3
Orissaare EST . . . 8 C3
Oristano I . . . 179 C2
Öriszentpéter H . . . 111 C3
Ørje N . . . 54 A2
Orjiva E . . . 163 B4
Orkanger N . . . 198 B6
Örkelljunga S . . . 61 C3
Örkény H . . . 112 B3
Orlamünde D . . . 82 B3
Orléans F . . . 103 B3
Orlová CZ . . . 98 B2
Orlovat SRB . . . 126 B2
Ormea I . . . 133 A3
Ormelet N . . . 54 A1
Ormemyr N . . . 53 A5
Ormília GR . . . 183 C5
Ormos GR . . . 185 B5
Ormož SLO . . . 124 A2
Ormskirk GB . . . 38 A4
Ornans F . . . 105 B5
Ornäs S . . . 50 B2
Ørnes N . . . 195 D4
Örnsköldsvik S . . . 200 C4
Orolik HR . . . 125 B4
Orom SRB . . . 126 B1
Oron-la-Ville CH . . . 106 C1
Oronsko PL . . . 87 A4
Oropa I . . . 119 B4
Oropesa
Castellón de la Plana
E . . . 153 B4
Toledo E . . . 150 C2
O Rosal E . . . 140 C2
Orosei I . . . 178 B3
Orosháza H . . . 113 C4
Oroslavje HR . . . 124 B1
Oroszlány H . . . 112 B2
Oroszlo H . . . 125 A4
Orotelli I . . . 178 B3
Orozko E . . . 143 A4
Orphir GB . . . 33 C3
Orpington GB . . . 45 B4
Orreaga-Roncesvalles
E . . . 144 A2
Orrefors S . . . 62 B3
Orriven S . . . 199 B11
Orsa S . . . 50 A1
Orsara di Púglia I . . . 171 B3
Orsay F . . . 90 C2
Orscholz D . . . 92 B2
Orsennes F . . . 103 C3
Orserum S . . . 55 B5
Orsha BY . . . 13 A9
Orsières CH . . . 119 A4
Örsjö S . . . 63 B3
Ørslev DK . . . 65 A4
Örslösa S . . . 55 B3
Orsogna I . . . 169 A4
Orsomarso I . . . 174 B1
Orşova RO . . . 16 C5
Ørsta N . . . 198 C3
Ørsted DK . . . 58 B3
Örsundsbro S . . . 56 A3

Ortaca TR . . . 188 C3
Ortakent TR . . . 188 B2
Ortaklar TR . . . 188 B2
Ortaköy TR . . . 23 B8
Orta Nova I . . . 171 B3
Orte I . . . 168 A2
Ortenburg D . . . 96 C1
Orth A . . . 111 A3
Orthez F . . . 128 C2
Ortigueira E . . . 140 A3
Ortilla E . . . 145 B3
Ortisei I . . . 108 C2
Ortişoara RO . . . 126 B3
Ortnevik N . . . 46 A3
Orton GB . . . 37 B4
Ortona I . . . 169 A4
Ortrand D . . . 84 A1
Órum DK . . . 58 B2
Orune I . . . 178 B3
Orusco E . . . 151 B4
Orvalho P . . . 155 A3
Orvault F . . . 101 B4
Ørvella N . . . 53 A5
Orvieto I . . . 168 A2
Orvínio I . . . 169 A2
Oryahovo BG . . . 17 D5
Orzesze PL . . . 86 B2
Orzinuovi I . . . 120 B2
Orzivécchi I . . . 120 B2
Orzyny PL . . . 77 A6
Os
Hedmark N . . . 48 B3
Hedmark N . . . 199 C8
Osann-Monzel D . . . 92 B2
Osbruk S . . . 62 A2
Øsby DK . . . 59 C2
Osby S . . . 61 C3
Oščadnica SK . . . 98 B2
Oschatz D . . . 83 A5
Oschersleben D . . . 73 B4
Óschiri I . . . 178 B3
Osciłowo PL . . . 77 B5
Osdorf D . . . 64 B3
Osečina SRB . . . 127 C1
Osečná CZ . . . 84 B2
Oseja de Sajambre
E . . . 142 A1
Osek CZ . . . 84 B1
Osen N . . . 199 A7
Osera de Ebro E . . . 153 A3
Osidda I . . . 178 B3
Osie PL . . . 69 B3
Osieczna
Pomorskie PL . . . 68 B3
Wielkopolskie PL . . . 75 C5
Osieczno PL . . . 75 A4
Osiek
Kujawsko-Pomorskie
PL . . . 76 B3
Kujawsko-Pomorskie
PL . . . 77 A4
Pomorskie PL . . . 69 B3
Świętokrzyskie PL . . . 87 B5
Osiek nad Notecią
PL . . . 76 A2
Osielsko PL . . . 76 A3
Osijek HR . . . 125 B4
Osilnica SLO . . . 123 B3
Ósilo I . . . 178 B2
Ósimo I . . . 136 B2
Osinja BIH . . . 125 C3
Osintorf BY . . . 13 A9
Osipaonica SRB . . . 127 C3
Osjaków PL . . . 86 A2
Oskamull GB . . . 34 B1
Oskarshamn S . . . 62 A4
Oskarström S . . . 60 C2
Oslany SK . . . 98 C2
Oslavany CZ . . . 97 B4
Óslje HR . . . 139 C3
Oslo N . . . 48 C2
Øsløs DK . . . 58 A1
Osmancık TR . . . 23 A8
Osmaneli TR . . . 187 B4
Ösmo S . . . 57 B3
Osmolin PL . . . 77 B4
Osnabrück D . . . 71 B5
Ośno Lubuskie PL . . . 75 B3
Osoblaha CZ . . . 85 B5
Osor HR . . . 123 C3
Osorno E . . . 142 B2
Øsoyra N . . . 46 A2
Øsøyro N . . . 46 B2
Óspakseyri IS . . . 190 B4
Os Peares E . . . 140 B3
Ospedaletti I . . . 133 B3
Ospitaletto I . . . 120 B3
Oss NL . . . 80 A1
Ossa de Montiel E . . . 158 C1
Ossi I . . . 178 B2
Ossjøen N . . . 47 B5
Ossun F . . . 145 A3
Ostaná S . . . 61 C4
Ostanvik S . . . 50 A2
Ostashkov RUS . . . 9 D8
Óstavall S . . . 200 D1
Ostbevern D . . . 71 B4
Østborg N . . . 199 A10
Østby N . . . 49 A4
Ostenfeld D . . . 64 B2
Øster Assels DK . . . 58 B1
Osterburg D . . . 73 B4
Osterburken D . . . 94 B1
Österbybruk S . . . 51 B4
Østerbyhavn DK . . . 58 B2

Österbymo S . . . 62 A3
Ostercappeln D . . . 71 B5
Österfärnebo S . . . 51 B3
Osterfeld D . . . 83 A3
Österforse S . . . 200 C3
Osterhever D . . . 64 B1
Osterhofen D . . . 95 C5
Osterholz-Scharmbeck
D . . . 72 A1
Øster Hornum DK . . . 58 B2
Øster Hurup DK . . . 58 B3
Østerild DK . . . 58 A1
Øster Jølby DK . . . 58 B1
Österlövsta S . . . 51 B4
Øster-marie DK . . . 67 A4
Ostermiething A . . . 109 A3
Osterode am Harz D . . . 82 A2
Ostersiel D . . . 64 B1
Östersund S . . . 199 B11
Øster Tørslev DK . . . 58 B3
Östervåla S . . . 51 B4
Östervallskog S . . . 54 A2
Østervrå DK . . . 58 A3
Osterwieck D . . . 73 C3
Osterzell D . . . 108 B1
Ostffyasszonyfa H . . . 111 B4
Östfora S . . . 51 C4
Ostheim F . . . 106 A2
Ostheim vor der Rhön
D . . . 82 B2
Osthofen D . . . 93 B4
Ostiano I . . . 120 B3
Ostíglia I . . . 121 B4
Ostiz E . . . 144 B2
Östmark S . . . 49 B4
Östnor S . . . 50 A1
Ostojićevo SRB . . . 126 B2
Ostra I . . . 136 B2
Östra Amtervik S . . . 55 A4
Östraby S . . . 61 D3
Ostrach D . . . 107 B4
Östra Husby S . . . 56 B2
Östra Ljungby S . . . 61 C3
Östra Ryd S . . . 56 B2
Ostrau D . . . 83 A5
Ostrava CZ . . . 98 B2
Østre Halsen N . . . 53 A6
Ostrhauderfehn D . . . 71 A4
Ostritz D . . . 84 A2
Ostróda PL . . . 69 B4
Ostroh UA . . . 13 C7
Ostrołęka PL . . . 12 B4
Ostropole PL . . . 68 B1
Ostrorog PL . . . 75 B5
Ostrošovac BIH . . . 124 C1
Ostrov
CZ . . . 83 B4
RUS . . . 8 D6
Ostrov nad Oslavou
CZ . . . 97 B3
Ostrówek PL . . . 86 A2
Ostrowiec PL . . . 68 A1
Ostrowiec-Świętokrzyski
PL . . . 87 B5
Ostrowite PL . . . 77 A4
Ostrów Mazowiecka
PL . . . 12 B4
Ostrowo PL . . . 76 B3
Ostrów Wielkopolski
PL . . . 86 A1
Ostrožac BIH . . . 139 B3
Ostrzeszów PL . . . 86 A1
Ostseebad
Kühlungsborn D . . . 65 B4
Ostuni I . . . 173 B3
Osuna E . . . 162 A2
Osvětimany CZ . . . 98 B1
Oswestry GB . . . 38 B3
Oświęcim PL . . . 86 B3
Osztopán H . . . 111 C4
Oteiza E . . . 144 B2
Otelec RO . . . 126 B2
Oteo E . . . 143 A3
Oterbekk N . . . 54 A1
Otero de Herreros
E . . . 151 B3
Otero de O Bodas
E . . . 141 C4
Othem S . . . 57 C4
Otley GB . . . 40 B2
Otmuchów PL . . . 85 B5
Otočac HR . . . 123 C4
Otok
Splitsko-Dalmatinska
HR . . . 138 B2
Vukovarsko-Srijemska
HR . . . 125 B4
Otoka BIH . . . 124 C2
Otranto I . . . 173 B4
Otrić HR . . . 138 A2
Otríčoli I . . . 168 A2
Otrokovice CZ . . . 98 B1
Otta N . . . 198 D6
Ottana I . . . 178 B3
Ottaviano I . . . 170 C2
Ottenby S . . . 63 B4
Ottendorf-Okrilla D . . . 84 A1
Ottenhöfen D . . . 93 C4
Ottenschlag A . . . 97 C3
Ottensheim A . . . 96 C2
Otterbach D . . . 93 B3
Otterbäcken S . . . 55 B5
Otterberg D . . . 93 B3
Otter Ferry GB . . . 34 B2
Otterndorf D . . . 64 C1
Ottersburg D . . . 72 B2

Ottersweier D . . . 93 C4
Otterup DK . . . 59 C3
Ottery St Mary GB . . . 43 B3
Ottignies B . . . 79 B4
Ottmarsheim F . . . 106 B2
Ottobeuren D . . . 107 B5
Öttömös H . . . 126 A1
Ottone I . . . 120 C2
Ottsjö S . . . 199 B10
Ottweiler D . . . 92 B3
Otvešti RO . . . 126 B3
Ötvöskónyi H . . . 124 A3
Otwock PL . . . 12 B4
Ouanne F . . . 104 B2
Ouarville F . . . 90 C1
Oucques F . . . 103 B3
Oud-Beijerland NL . . . 79 A4
Ouddorp NL . . . 79 A3
Oudemirdum NL . . . 70 B2
Oudenaarde B . . . 79 B3
Oudenbosch NL . . . 79 A4
Oudenburg B . . . 78 A3
Oude-Pekela NL . . . 71 A4
Oude-Tonge NL . . . 79 A4
Oudewater NL . . . 70 B1
Oud Gastel NL . . . 79 A4
Oudon F . . . 101 B4
Oue DK . . . 58 B2
Oughterard IRL . . . 28 A2
Ouguela P . . . 155 B3
Ouistreham F . . . 89 A3
Oulainen FIN . . . 3 D9
Oulchy-le-Château
F . . . 91 B3
Oullins F . . . 117 B4
Oulmes F . . . 114 B3
Oulton GB . . . 41 C5
Oulton Broad GB . . . 41 C5
Oulu FIN . . . 3 D9
Oulx I . . . 119 B3
Oundle GB . . . 40 C3
Ouranópoli GR . . . 183 C6
Ourém P . . . 154 B2
Ourense E . . . 140 B3
Ourique P . . . 160 B1
Ourol E . . . 140 A3
Ouroux-en-Morvan
F . . . 104 B2
Ousdale GB . . . 32 C3
Oust F . . . 146 B2
Outakoski FIN . . . 193 C10
Outeiro P . . . 148 B1
Outeiro de Rei E . . . 140 A3
Outes E . . . 140 B2
Outokumpu FIN . . . 9 A6
Outreau F . . . 78 B1
Outwell GB . . . 41 C4
Ouzouer-le-Marché
F . . . 103 B3
Ouzouer-sur-Loire
F . . . 103 B4
Ovada I . . . 133 A4
Ovar P . . . 148 B1
Ovelgönne D . . . 72 A1
Overath D . . . 80 B3
Overbister GB . . . 33 B4
Överbygd N . . . 192 D3
Overdinkel NL . . . 71 B4
Överenhörna S . . . 56 A3
Overhalla N . . . 199 A8
Overijse B . . . 79 B4
Over-jerstal DK . . . 59 C2
Overlade DK . . . 58 B2
Överlida S . . . 60 B2
Överö FIN . . . 51 B7
Overpelt B . . . 79 A5
Overton GB . . . 38 B4
Övertorneå S . . . 196 C6
Överum S . . . 62 A4
Ovidiopol UA . . . 17 B9
Oviedo E . . . 141 A5
Oviglio I . . . 119 C5
Ovindoli I . . . 169 A3
Ovodda I . . . 178 B3
Øvre Årdal N . . . 47 A4
Øvrebygd N . . . 52 B2
Øvre Rendal N . . . 199 D8
Øvre Sirdal N . . . 52 B2
Övre Soppero S . . . 196 A4
Övre Ullerud S . . . 55 A4
Ovruch UA . . . 13 C8
Öxabäck S . . . 60 B2
Oxberg S . . . 49 A6
Oxelösund S . . . 56 B3
Oxenholme GB . . . 37 B4
Oxford GB . . . 44 B2
Oxie S . . . 61 D3
Oxilithos GR . . . 185 A5
Oxted GB . . . 45 B4
Oyaca TR . . . 187 C7
Øye N . . . 47 A5
Øyenkilen N . . . 54 A1
Øyer N . . . 48 A2
Øyeren N . . . 49 B4
Oyfiell N . . . 53 A4
Øygårdslia N . . . 53 B4
Oykel Bridge GB . . . 32 D2
Øymark N . . . 54 A2
Oyonnax F . . . 118 A2
Øyslebø N . . . 52 B3
Øystese N . . . 46 B3
Oyten D . . . 72 A2
Øyuvsbu N . . . 52 B3
Ozaeta E . . . 143 B4
Ozalj HR . . . 123 B4
Ożarów PL . . . 87 B5

Ożarów Maz PL . . . 77 B5
Ožbalt SLO . . . 110 C2
Ózd H . . . 113 A4
Ožd'any SK . . . 99 C3
Ozieri I . . . 178 B3
Ozimek PL . . . 86 B2
Ozimica BIH . . . 139 A4
Ozora H . . . 112 C2
Ozorków PL . . . 77 C4
Ozzano Monferrato
I . . . 119 B5

P

Paakkola FIN . . . 196 D7
Paal B . . . 79 A5
Pabianice PL . . . 86 A3
Pacanów PL . . . 87 B5
Paceco I . . . 176 B1
Pachino I . . . 177 C4
Pačir SRB . . . 126 B1
Pack A . . . 110 B2
Paços de Ferreira
P . . . 148 A1
Pacov CZ . . . 96 B3
Pacsa H . . . 111 C4
Pacy-sur-Eure F . . . 89 A5
Paczków PL . . . 85 B5
Padany RUS . . . 3 E13
Padborg DK . . . 64 B2
Padej SRB . . . 126 B2
Padene HR . . . 138 A2
Paderborn D . . . 81 A4
Paderne P . . . 160 B1
Padiham GB . . . 40 B1
Padina SRB . . . 126 B2
Padinska Skela
SRB . . . 127 C2
Padornelo P . . . 148 A1
Pádova I . . . 121 B4
Padragkút H . . . 111 B4
Padria I . . . 178 B2
Padrón E . . . 140 B2
Padru I . . . 178 B3
Padstow GB . . . 42 B2
Padul E . . . 163 A4
Padula I . . . 172 B1
Paduli I . . . 170 B2
Paesana I . . . 119 C4
Paese I . . . 121 B5
Pag HR . . . 137 A4
Pagani I . . . 170 C2
Pagánica I . . . 169 A3
Pagánico I . . . 135 C4
Pagl ieta I . . . 169 A4
Pagny-sur-Moselle
F . . . 92 C2
Páhi H . . . 112 C3
Pahkakumpu FIN . . . 197 C11
Pahl D . . . 108 B2
Paide EST . . . 8 C4
Paignton GB . . . 43 B3
Pailhès F . . . 146 A2
Paimboeuf F . . . 101 B3
Paimpol F . . . 100 A2
Paimpont F . . . 101 A3
Painswick GB . . . 43 A4
Painten D . . . 95 C3
Paisley GB . . . 34 C3
Pajala S . . . 196 B6
Pajares E . . . 141 A5
Pajares de los Oteros
E . . . 142 B1
Pajęczno PL . . . 86 A2
Páka H . . . 111 C3
Pakość PL . . . 76 B3
Pakosławice PL . . . 85 B5
Pakostane HR . . . 137 B4
Pakrac HR . . . 124 B3
Paks H . . . 112 C2
Palacios de la Sierra
E . . . 143 C3
Palacios de la
Valduerna E . . . 141 B5
Palacios del Sil E . . . 141 B4
Palacios de Sanabria
E . . . 141 B4
Palaciosrubios E . . . 150 A2
Palafrugell E . . . 147 C4
Palagiano I . . . 173 B3
Palagonía I . . . 177 B3
Paláia I . . . 135 B3
Palaiokastritsa GR . . . 182 D1
Palaiseau F . . . 90 C2
Palamas GR . . . 182 D4
Palamós E . . . 147 C4
Påläng S . . . 196 D5
Palanga LT . . . 8 E2
Palanzano I . . . 134 A3
Palárikovo SK . . . 112 A2
Palas de Rei E . . . 140 B3
Palata I . . . 170 B2
Palau I . . . 178 A3
Palavas-les-Flots
F . . . 131 B2
Palazuelos de la Sierra
E . . . 143 B3
Palazzo Adriano I . . . 176 B2
Palazzo del Pero I . . . 135 B4
Palazzolo Acréide
I . . . 177 B3
Palazzolo sull Oglio
I . . . 120 B2
Palazzo San Gervásio
I . . . 172 B1
Palazzuolo sul Senio
I . . . 135 A4

Paldiski EST 8 C4
Pale BIH 139 B4
Palekastro GR 185 D7
Palena I 169 B4
Palencia E 142 B2
Palenciana E 163 A3
Paleochora GR . . . 185 D4
Paleometokho CY . 181 A2
Palermo I 176 A2
Paleros GR 182 E2
Palestrina I 169 B2
Pálfa H 112 C2
Palfau A 110 B1
Palhaça P 148 B1
Palheiros da Tocha
P 148 B1
Palheiros de Quiaios
P 148 B1
Paliaopoli GR 185 B5
Palić SRB 126 A1
Palidoro I 168 B2
Palinuro I 172 B1
Paliouri GR 183 D5
Paliseul B 91 B5
Pallanza I 119 B5
Pallares E 161 A3
Pallaruelo de Monegros
E 153 A3
Pallas Green IRL . . . 29 B3
Pallerols E 146 B2
Palling D 109 A3
Palluau F 114 B2
Palma P 154 C2
Palma Campània I . 170 C2
Palma del Río E . . . 162 A2
Palma de Mallorca
E 166 B2
Palma di Montechiaro
I 176 B2
Palmádula I 178 B2
Palmanova I 122 B2
Palma Nova E 166 B2
Palmela P 154 C2
Palmerola E 147 B3
Palmi I 175 C1
Pälmonostora H . . 113 C3
Palo del Colle I . . . 171 B4
Palojärvi FIN 192 D7
Palojoensuu FIN . . 196 A6
Palomares E 164 B3
Palomares del Campo
E 158 B1
Palomas E 156 B1
Palombara Sabina
I 168 A2
Palos de la Frontera
E 161 B3
Palotaboszok H . . . 125 A4
Palotás H 112 B3
Pals E 147 C4
Pålsboda S 56 A1
Paluzza I 109 C4
Pamhagen A 111 B3
Pamiers F 146 A2
Pamiętowo PL 76 A2
Pampaneira E 163 B4
Pamparato I 133 A3
Pampilhosa
Aveiro P 148 B1
Coimbra P 148 B2
Pampliega E 143 B3
Pamplona E 144 B2
Pampow D 73 A4
Pamukçu TR 186 C2
Pamukkale TR 188 B4
Pamukova TR 187 B5
Panagyurishte BG . . 17 D6
Pancalieri I 119 C4
Pančevo SRB 127 C2
Pancey F 91 C5
Pancorvo E 143 B3
Pancrudo E 152 B2
Pandino I 120 B2
Pandrup DK 58 A2
Panenský-Týnec
CZ 84 B1
Panes E 142 A2
Panevėžys LT 8 E4
Pangbourne GB . . . 44 B2
Panissières F 117 B4
Panki PL 86 B2
Pannes F 103 A4
Panningen NL 80 A1
Pannonhalma H . . .111 B4
Pano Lefkara CY . . 181 B2
Pano Panayia CY . 181 B1
Panormos GR 185 B6
Panschwitz-Kuckau
D 84 A2
Pansdorf D 65 C3
Pantano de Cíjara
E 156 A3
Panticosa E 145 B3
Pantín E 140 A2
Pantoja E 151 B4
Pantón E 140 B3
Panxon E 140 B2
Páola I 174 B2
Paola M 175 C3
Pápa H 111 B4
Papasídero I 174 B1
Pápateszér H 111 B4
Papenburg D 71 A4
Paphos CY 181 B1
Pappenheim D 94 C2
Paprotnia PL 77 B5
Parábita I 173 B4
Paraćin SRB 127 D3
Parád H 113 B4
Parada
Bragança P 149 A3
Viseu P 148 B1
Paradas E 162 A2
Paradela E 140 B3
Parades de Rubiales
E 150 A2
Paradinas de San Juan
E 150 B2
Paradiso di Cevadale
I 108 C1
Paradyż PL 87 A4
Parainen FIN 8 B3
Parakhino Paddubye
RUS 9 C8
Parakka S 196 B4
Paralimni CY 181 A2
Parallo Astros GR . 184 B3
Paramé F 88 B2
Paramithia GR 182 D2
Páramo E 141 A4
Páramo del Sil E . . 141 B4
Parandaça P 148 A2
Paravadella E 141 A3
Paray-le-Monial F . 104 C3
Parceiros P 154 B2
Parcey F 105 B4
Parchim D 73 A4
Parciaki PL 77 A6
Parcice PL 86 A2
Pardilla E 151 A4
Pardubice CZ 97 A3
Paredes
E 151 B5
P 148 A1
Paredes de Coura
P 140 C2
Paredes de Nava E 142 B2
Paredes de Siguenza
E 151 A5
Pareja E 151 B5
Parennes F 102 A1
Parenti I 175 B2
Parentis-en-Born F 128 B1
Parey D 73 B4
Parfino RUS 9 D7
Parga GR 182 D2
Pargny-sur-Saulx F. 91 C4
Pari-Gagné F 117 A4
Parigné-l'Évêque
F 102 B2
Parikkala FIN 9 B6
Paris F 90 C2
Parisot F 129 B4
Parkalompolo S . . 196 B5
Parkano FIN 8 A3
Parknasilla IRL 29 C2
Parla E 151 B4
Parlavá E 147 B4
Parma I 120 C3
Parndorf A 111 B3
Párnica SK 99 B3
Parnu EST 8 C4
Parolis E 164 A2
Paros GR 185 B6
Parrillas E 150 B2
Parsberg D 95 B3
Parstein D 74 B3
Partakko FIN 193 C11
Partanna I 176 B1
Parthenay F 102 C1
Partinico I 176 A2
Partizani SRB 127 C2
Partizánske SK 98 C2
Partney GB 41 B4
Påryd S 63 B3
Parzymiechy PL . . . 86 A2
Paşcani RO 17 B7
Pasewalk D 74 A2
Pašina Voda MNE . 139 B5
Påskallavik S 62 A4
Pasłęk PL 69 A4
Pašman HR 137 B4
Passage East IRL . . 30 B2
Passail A 110 B2
Passais F 88 B3
Passau D 96 C1
Passegueiro P 148 B1
Passignano sul
Trasimeno I 135 B5
Passo di Tréia I . . . 136 B2
Passopisciaro I . . . 177 B4
Passow D 74 A3
Passy F 118 B3
Pastavy BY 13 A7
Pástena I 170 B2
Pastrana E 151 B5
Pastrengo I 121 B3
Pasym PL 77 A5
Pásztó H 113 B3
Pata SK 98 C1
Patay F 103 A3
Pateley Bridge GB . . 40 A2
Paterek PL 76 A2
Paterna E 159 B3
Paterna del Campo
E 161 B3
Paterna del Madera
E 158 C1
Paterna de Rivera
E 162 B2
Paternion A 109 C4
Paternò I 177 B3
Paternópoli I 170 C3
Patersdorf D 95 B4
Paterswolde NL 71 A3
Patitiri GR 183 D5
Patmos GR 188 B1
Patna GB 36 A2
Pątnow PL 76 B3
Patoniva FIN 193 C11
Patopirtti FIN 197 B12
Patos AL 182 C1
Patra = Patras GR . 184 A2
Patras = Patra GR . 184 A2
Patreksfjörður IS . . 190 B2
Patrickswell IRL . . . 29 B3
Patrimonio F 180 A2
Patrington GB 41 B3
Pattada I 178 B3
Pattensen
Niedersachsen D . . . 72 A3
Niedersachsen D . . . 72 B2
Patterdale GB 36 B4
Patti I 177 A3
Páty H 112 B2
Pau F 145 A3
Pauillac F 128 A2
Paularo I 109 C4
Paulhaguet F 117 B3
Paulhan F 130 B2
Paulilátino I 178 B2
Paulistrom S 62 A3
Paullo I 120 B2
Paulstown IRL 30 B1
Pausa D 83 B3
Pauträsk S 200 B3
Pavia
I 120 B2
P 154 C2
Pavias E 159 B3
Pavilly F 89 A4
Pāvilosta LV 8 D2
Pavullo nel Frignano
I 135 A3
Pawłowice PL 86 A1
Pawlowice PL 98 B2
Paxi GR 182 D2
Payallar TR 189 C6
Payerne CH 106 C1
Paymogo E 161 B2
Payrac F 129 B4
Pazardzhik BG 183 A6
Pazaryeri TR 187 B4
Pazin HR 122 B2
Paziols F 146 B3
Pčelić HR 124 B3
Peal de Becerro E . 164 B1
Peasmarsh GB 45 C4
Peć KOS 16 D4
Péccioli I 135 B3
Pécel H 112 B3
Pechao P 160 B2
Pechenga RUS 3 B12
Pechenizhyn UA . . . 13 D6
Pecica RO 126 A3
Pećinci SRB 127 C1
Pecka SRB 127 C1
Peckelsheim D 81 A5
Pečory RUS 8 D5
Pécs H 125 A4
Pécsvárad H 125 A4
Peczniew PL 86 A2
Pedaso I 136 B2
Pedavena I 121 A4
Pedérobba I 121 B4
Pedersker DK 67 A3
Pedescala I 121 B4
Pedrafita E 141 B3
Pedrajas de San
Esteban E 150 A3
Pedralba E 159 B3
Pedralba de la Praderia
E 141 B4
Pedraza E 151 A4
Pedreguer E 159 C4
Pedrera E 162 A3
Pedro Abad E 157 C3
Pedro Bernardo E . 150 B3
Pedroche E 156 B3
Pedrógão P 160 A2
Pedrogao P 149 B2
Pedrógão P 154 B2
Pedrógão Grande
P 154 B2
Pedrola E 144 C2
Pedro-Martinez E . 164 B1
Pedro Muñoz E . . . 158 B1
Pedrosa del Rey E 150 A2
Pedrosa del Rio Urbel
E 143 B3
Pedrosa de Tobalina
E 143 B3
Pedrosillo de los Aires
E 150 B2
Pedrosillo el Ralo
E 150 A2
Pędzewo PL 76 A3
Peebles GB 35 C4
Peel GB 36 B2
Peenemünde D 66 B2
Peer B 79 A5
Pega P 149 B2
Pegalajar E 163 A4
Pegau D 83 A4
Peggau A 110 B2
Pegli I 133 A4
Pegnitz D 95 B3
Pego E 159 C3
Pegões-Estação
P 154 C2
Pegões Velhos P . . 154 C2
Pęgów PL 85 A4
Pegswood GB 37 A5
Peguera E 166 B2
Pehlıvanköy TR . . . 186 A1
Peine D 72 B3
Peisey-Nancroix F .118 B3
Peissenberg D 108 B2
Peiting D 108 B1
Peitz D 84 A2
Péjo I 121 A3
Pelagićevo BIH . . . 125 C4
Pelahustán E 150 B3
Pełczyce PL 75 A4
Pelhřimov CZ 97 B3
Pélissanne F 131 B4
Pelkosenniemi
FIN 197 B10
Pellegrino Parmense
I 120 C2
Pellegrue F 128 B3
Pellérd H 125 A4
Pellestrina I 122 B1
Pellevoisin F 103 C3
Pellizzano I 121 A3
Pello
FIN 196 C7
S 196 C6
Peloche E 156 A2
Pelplin PL 69 B3
Pelussin F 117 B4
Pély H 113 B4
Pembroke GB 39 C2
Pembroke Dock GB 39 C2
Peñacerrada E 143 B4
Penacova P 148 B1
Peña de Cabra E . . 149 B4
Peñafiel E 151 A3
Penafiel P 148 A1
Peñaflor E 162 A2
Peñalba de Santiago
E 141 B4
Peñalsordo E 156 B2
Penalva do Castelo
P 148 B2
Penamacôr P 149 B2
Peñaparda E 149 B3
Peñaranda de
Bracamonte E . . . 150 B2
Peñaranda de Duero
E 143 C3
Peñarroya de Tastavins
E 153 B4
Peñarroya-Pueblonuevo
E 156 B2
Peñarrubla E 141 B3
Penarth GB 39 C3
Peñascosa E 158 C1
Peñas de San Pedro
E 158 C2
Peñausende E 149 A4
Penc H 112 B3
Pencoed GB 39 C3
Pendalofos GR . . . 182 C3
Pendeen GB 42 B1
Pendine GB 39 C2
Pendueles E 142 A2
Penedono P 148 B2
Penela P 154 A2
Pénestin F 101 B3
Penhas Juntas P . . 149 A2
Peniche P 154 B1
Penicuik GB 35 C4
Penig D 83 B4
Penilhos P 160 B2
Peñíscola E 153 B4
Penistone GB 40 B2
Penkridge GB 40 C1
Penkun D 74 A3
Penmarch F 100 B1
Pennabilli I 135 B5
Penne I 169 A3
Penne-d'Agenais F 129 B3
Pennes I 108 C2
Pennyghael GB 34 B1
Peno RUS 9 D8
Penpont GB 36 A3
Penrhyndeudraeth
GB 38 B2
Penrith GB 37 B4
Penryn GB 42 B1
Pentraeth GB 38 A2
Penybontfawr GB . . 38 B3
Penygroes
Carmarthenshire
GB 39 C2
Gwynedd GB 38 A2
Penzance GB 42 B1
Penzberg D 108 B2
Penzlin D 74 A2
Pepinster B 80 B1
Peqin AL 182 B1
Pér H 111 B4
Pera Boa P 148 B2
Perachora GR 184 A3
Perafita P 148 A1
Peraleda de la Mata
E 150 C2
Peraleda del Zaucejo
E 156 B2
Peraleda de San Román
E 156 A2
Perales de Alfambra
E 152 B2
Perales del Puerto
E 149 B3
Perales de Tajuña
E 151 B4
Peralta E 144 B2
Peralta de la Sal E 145 C4
Peralva P 160 B2
Peralveche E 152 B1
Perama GR 185 D5
Peranka FIN 197 D12
Perbál H 112 B2
Perchtoldsdorf A . . .111 A3
Percy F 88 B2
Perdasdefogu I . . . 179 C3
Perdiguera E 145 C3
Peredo P 149 A3
Peregu Mare RO . . 126 A2
Pereiro
Faro P 160 B2
Guarda P 149 B2
Santarém P 154 B2
Pereiro de Aguiar
E 140 B3
Perelada E 147 B4
Perelejos de las Truchas
E 152 B2
Pereña E 149 A3
Pereruela E 149 A4
Pérfugas I 178 B2
Perg A 110 A1
Pérgine Valsugana
I 121 A4
Pérgola I 136 B1
Pergusa I 177 B3
Periam RO 126 A2
Periana E 163 B3
Périers F 88 A2
Périgueux F 129 A3
Perino I 120 C2
Perjasica HR 123 B4
Perkáta H 112 B2
Perković HR 138 B2
Perleberg D 73 A4
Perlez SRB 126 B2
Përmet AL 182 C2
Pernarec CZ 95 B5
Pernek SK 98 C1
Pernes P 154 B2
Pernes-les-Fontaines
F 131 A4
Pernik BG 17 D5
Pernink CZ 83 B4
Pernitz A 110 B2
Pernu FIN 197 C10
Peroguarda P 160 A1
Pérols F 131 B2
Péronne F 90 B2
Péronnes B 79 B4
Pero Pinheiro P . . . 154 C1
Perorrubio E 151 A4
Perosa Argentina I 119 C4
Perozinho P 148 A1
Perpignan F 146 B3
Perranporth GB 42 B1
Perranzabuloe GB . . 42 B1
Perrecy-les-Forges
F 104 C3
Perrero I 119 C4
Perrignier F 118 A3
Perros-Guirec F . . 100 A2
Persan F 90 B2
Persberg S 55 A5
Persenbeug A 110 A2
Pershore GB 44 A1
Persön S 196 D5
Perstorp S 61 C3
Perth GB 35 B4
Pertisau A 108 B2
Pertoča SLO 111 C3
Pertuis F 131 B4
Perućac SRB 127 D1
Perúgia I 136 B1
Perušić HR 123 C4
Péruwelz B 79 B3
Pervomaysk UA 13 D9
Perwez B 79 B4
Pesadas de Burgos
E 143 B3
Pesaguero E 142 A2
Pésaro I 136 B1
Pescantina I 121 B3
Pescara I 169 A4
Pescasséroli I 169 B3
Peschici I 171 B4
Peschiera del Garda
I 121 B3
Péscia I 135 B3
Pescina I 169 A3
Pescocostanzo I . . 169 B4
Pescopagano I . . . 172 B1
Pesco Sannita I . . . 170 B2
Peshkopi AL 182 B2
Peshtera BG 183 A6
Pesmes F 105 B4
Pesnica SLO 110 C2
Peso da Régua P . . 148 A2
Pesquera de Duero
E 142 C2
Pessac F 128 B2
Pestovo RUS 9 C9
Petäjäskoski FIN . . 197 C8
Petalidi GR 184 C2
Pétange L 92 B1
Petas GR 182 D3
Peteranec HR 124 A2
Peterborough GB . . 41 C3
Peterculter GB 33 D4
Peterhead GB 33 D5
Peterlee GB 37 B5
Petersfield GB 44 B3
Petershagen
Brandenburg D 74 B2
Brandenburg D 74 B3
Nordrhein-Westfalen
D 72 B1
Petershausen D . . . 95 C3
Peterswell IRL 28 A3
Pétervására H 113 A4
Petilia Policastro I. 175 B2
Petín E 141 B3
Pětipsy CZ 83 B5
Petkus D 74 C2
Petlovac HR 125 B4
Petlovača SRB . . . 127 C1
Petőfiszallás H . . . 113 C3
Petra E 167 B3
Petralia Sottana I . . 177 B3
Petrčane HR 137 A4
Petrella Tifernina I. 170 B2
Petrer E 159 C3
Petreto-Bicchisano
F 180 B1
Petrich BG 183 B5
Petrijevci HR 125 B4
Petrinja HR 124 B2
Petrodvorets RUS . . . 9 C6
Pétrola E 158 C2
Petronà I 175 B2
Petronell A 111 A3
Petroşani RO 17 C5
Petrovac SRB 127 C3
Petrovaradin SRB . 126 B1
Petrovice
BIH 139 A4
CZ 84 B1
Petrovo RUS 69 A5
Petrozavodsk RUS . . 9 B9
Pettenbach A 109 B5
Pettigo IRL 26 B3
Petworth GB 44 C3
Peuerbach A 96 C1
Peuntenansa E 142 A2
Peurasuvanto FIN . 197 B9
Pevensey Bay GB . . 45 C4
Peveragno I 133 A3
Pewsey GB 44 B2
Pewsum D 71 A4
Peyrat-le-Château
F 116 B1
Peyrehorade F 128 C1
Peyriac-Minervois
F 146 A3
Peyrins F 117 B5
Peyrissac F 116 B1
Peyrolles-en-Provence
F 132 B1
Peyruis F 132 A1
Pézarches F 90 C2
Pézenas F 130 B2
Pezinok SK 111 A4
Pezuls F 129 B3
Pfaffenhausen D . . 108 A1
Pfaffenhofen
Bayern D 94 C2
Bayern D 95 C3
Pfaffenhoffen F 93 C3
Pfäffikon CH 107 B3
Pfarrkirchen D 95 C4
Pfeffenhausen D . . . 95 C3
Pfetterhouse F . . . 106 B2
Pforzheim D 93 C4
Pfreimd D 95 B4
Pfronten D 108 B1
Pfullendorf D 107 B4
Pfullingen D 94 C1
Pfunds A 108 C1
Pfungstadt D 93 B4
Pfyn CH 107 B3
Phalsbourg F 92 C3
Philippeville B 79 B4
Philippsreut D 96 C1
Philippsthal D 82 B1
Piacenza I 120 B2
Piacenza d'Adige I 121 B4
Piádena I 120 B3
Piana F 180 A1
Piana Crixia I 133 A4
Piana degli Albanesi
I 176 B2
Piana di Monte Verna
I 170 B2
Piancastagnáio I . . 135 C4
Piandelagotti I 134 A3
Pianella
Abruzzi I 169 A4
Toscana I 135 B4
Pianello Val Tidone
I 120 C2
Pianoro I 135 A4
Pians A 108 B1
Pías E 141 B4
Pias P 160 A2
Piaseczno PL 77 B6
Piasek PL 74 B3
Piaski PL 69 A4
Piastów PL 77 B5
Piaszcyna PL 68 A2
Piątek PL 77 B4
Piatra Neamț RO . . . 17 B7
Piazza al Sérchio I . 134 A3
Piazza Armerina I . 177 B3
Piazza Brembana I 120 B2
Piazze I 135 C4
Piazzola sul Brenta
I 121 B4
Picassent E 159 B3
Piccione I 136 B1
Picerno I 172 B1
Picher D 73 A4
Pickering GB 40 A3
Pico I 169 B3

Picón E 157 A3
Picquigny F . . . 90 B2
Piechowice PL . . . 84 B3
Piecnik PL . . . 75 A5
Piedicavallo I . . . 119 B4
Piedicroce F . . . 180 A2
Piedimonte Etneo I . 177 B4
Piedimonte Matese
I 170 B2
Piedimulera I . . . 119 A5
Piedipaterno I . . . 136 C1
Piedrabuena E . . . 157 A3
Piedraescrita E . . . 156 A3
Piedrafita E . . . 142 A1
Piedrahita E . . . 150 B2
Piedralaves E . . . 150 B3
Piedras Albas E . . . 155 B4
Piedras Blancas E . 141 A5
Piegaro I . . . 135 C5
Piekary Śl. PL . . . 86 B2
Piekoszów PL . . . 87 B4
Pieksämäki FIN . . 8 A5
Pielenhofen D . . . 95 B3
Pielgrzymka PL . . . 85 A3
Pieniężno PL . . . 69 A5
Pieńsk PL . . . 84 A3
Pienza I . . . 135 B4
Piera E . . . 147 C2
Pieranie PL . . . 76 B3
Pierowall GB . . . 33 B4
Pierre-Buffière F . 115 C5
Pierrecourt F . . . 105 B4
Pierre-de-Bresse F 105 C4
Pierrefeu-du-Var F 132 B2
Pierrefitte-Nestalas
F 145 B3
Pierrefitte-sur-Aire
F 92 C1
Pierrefonds F . . . 90 B2
Pierrefontaine-les-
Varans F . . . 105 B5
Pierrefort F . . . 116 C2
Pierrelatte F . . . 131 A3
Pierrepont
Aisne F . . . 91 B3
Meurthe-et-Moselle
F 92 B1
Piesendorf A . . . 109 B3
Pieštany SK . . . 98 C1
Pieszkowo PL . . . 69 A5
Pieszyce PL . . . 85 B4
Pietarsaari FIN . . . 3 E8
Pietragalla I . . . 172 B1
Pietra Ligure I . . . 133 A4
Pietralunga I . . . 136 B1
Pietramelara I . . . 170 B2
Pietraperzia I . . . 177 B3
Pietrasanta I . . . 134 B3
Pietravairano I . . . 170 B2
Pieve del Cáiro I . . 120 B1
Pieve di Bono I . . . 121 B3
Pieve di Cadore I . . 122 A1
Pieve di Cento I . . 121 C4
Pieve di Solígo I . . 121 B5
Pieve di Teco I . . . 133 A3
Pievepélago I . . . 134 A3
Pieve Santo Stefano
I 135 B5
Pieve Torina I . . . 136 B2
Piges GR . . . 182 D3
Píglio I . . . 169 B3
Pigna I . . . 133 B3
Pignan F . . . 130 B2
Pignataro Maggiore
I 170 B2
Piittisjärvi FIN . . 197 C9
Pijnacker NL . . . 70 B1
Pikalevo RUS . . . 9 C9
Piła PL . . . 75 A5
Pilar de la Horadada
E 165 B4
Pilas E . . . 161 B3
Pilastri I . . . 121 C4
Piława Górna PL . . 85 B4
Piławki PL . . . 69 B4
Pilchowice PL . . . 86 B2
Pilea GR . . . 183 C5
Pilgrimstad S . . . 199 C12
Pili
Dodekanisa GR . 188 C2
Trikala GR . . . 182 D3
Pilica PL . . . 86 B3
Pilis H . . . 112 B3
Piliscaba H . . . 112 B2
Pilisszántó H . . . 112 B2
Pilisvörösvár H . . . 112 B2
Pilos GR . . . 184 C2
Pilsting D . . . 95 C4
Pilszcz PL . . . 98 A1
Pilterud N . . . 48 C2
Pilu RO . . . 113 C5
Pina de Ebro E . . . 153 A3
Piñar E . . . 163 A4
Pınarbaşı TR . . . 186 C1
Pınarhisar TR . . . 186 A2
Pinas F . . . 145 A4
Pincehely H . . . 112 C2
Pinchbeck GB . . . 41 C3
Pińczów PL . . . 87 B4
Pineda de la Sierra
E 143 B3
Pineda de Mar E . . 147 C3
Pinerella I . . . 135 A5
Pinerolo I . . . 119 C4
Pineta Grande I . . 170 C1

Pineto I . . . 169 A4
Piney F . . . 91 C4
Pinggau A . . . 111 B3
Pinhal Novo P . . . 154 C2
Pinhão P . . . 148 A2
Pinheiro
Aveiro P . . . 148 A1
Aveiro P . . . 148 B1
Pinheiro Grande P 154 B2
Pinhel P . . . 149 B2
Pinhoe GB . . . 43 B3
Pinilla E . . . 158 C2
Pinilla de Toro E . . 150 A2
Pinkafeld A . . . 111 B3
Pinneberg D . . . 72 A2
Pinnow D . . . 74 C3
Pino F . . . 180 A2
Pino del Rio E . . . 142 B2
Pino de Val E . . . 140 B2
Pinofranqueado E . 149 B3
Pinols F . . . 117 B3
Piñor E . . . 140 B2
Pinos del Valle E . . 163 B4
Pinoso E . . . 159 C2
Pinos Puente E . . . 163 A4
Pinsk BY . . . 13 B7
Pintamo FIN . . . 197 D10
Pinto E . . . 151 B4
Pinzano al Tagliamento
I 122 A1
Pinzio P . . . 149 B2
Pinzolo I . . . 121 A3
Pióbbico I . . . 136 B1
Piombino I . . . 134 C3
Pionki PL . . . 87 A5
Pionsat F . . . 116 A2
Pióraco I . . . 136 B1
Piornal E . . . 150 B2
Piotrkowice PL . . . 87 B4
Piotrków-Kujawski
PL 76 B3
Piotrków Trybunalski
PL 86 A3
Piotrowo PL . . . 75 B5
Piove di Sacco I . . 121 B5
Piovene I . . . 121 B4
Piperskärr S . . . 62 A4
Pipriac F . . . 101 B4
Piraeus = Pireas
GR 185 B4
Piran SLO . . . 122 B2
Pireas = Piraeus
GR 185 B4
Piré-sur-Seiche F . 101 A4
Pirgi GR . . . 185 A6
Pirgos
Ilia GR . . . 184 B2
Kriti GR . . . 185 D6
Piriac-sur-Mer F . . 101 B3
Piringsdorf A . . . 111 B3
Pirmasens D . . . 93 B3
Pirna D . . . 84 B1
Pirnmill GB . . . 34 C2
Pirot SRB . . . 16 D5
Pirovac HR . . . 137 B4
Pirttivuopio S . . . 196 B2
Pisa I . . . 134 B3
Pisany F . . . 114 C3
Pisarovina HR . . . 124 B1
Pischelsdorf in der
Steiermark A . . 110 B2
Pişchia RO . . . 126 B3
Pisciotta I . . . 172 B1
Písek CZ . . . 96 B2
Pisogne I . . . 120 B3
Pissos F . . . 128 B2
Pissouri CY . . . 181 B1
Pisticci I . . . 174 A2
Pistóia I . . . 135 B3
Piteå S . . . 196 D4
Piteşti RO . . . 17 C6
Pithiviers F . . . 103 A4
Pitigliano I . . . 168 A1
Pitkyaranta RUS . . 9 B7
Pitlochry GB . . . 35 B4
Pitomača HR . . . 124 B3
Pitres E . . . 163 B4
Pittentrail GB . . . 32 D2
Pitvaros H . . . 126 A2
Pivka SLO . . . 123 B3
Pivnice SRB . . . 126 B1
Piwniczna PL . . . 99 B4
Pizarra E . . . 163 B3
Pizzano I . . . 121 A3
Pizzighettone I . . . 120 B2
Pizzo I . . . 175 C2
Pizzoli I . . . 169 A3
Pizzolungo I . . . 176 A1
Pjätteryd S . . . 61 C4
Plabennec F . . . 100 A1
Placencia E . . . 143 A4
Plaffeien CH . . . 106 C2
Plaisance
Gers F . . . 128 C3
Haute-Garonne F . 129 C4
Tarn F . . . 130 B1
Plaka GR . . . 183 D7
Plan E . . . 145 B4
Planá CZ . . . 95 B4
Planánad Lužnicí
CZ 96 B2
Plaňany CZ . . . 96 A3
Planchez F . . . 104 B3
Plancoët F . . . 101 A3
Plancy-l'Abbaye F . 91 C3
Plan-de-Baix F . . . 118 C2
Plandište SRB . . . 126 B3
Plan-d'Orgon F . . . 131 B3

Plánice CZ . . . 96 B1
Planina
SLO 123 A4
SLO 123 B3
Plankenfels D . . . 95 B3
Plasencia E . . . 149 B3
Plasenzuela E . . . 156 A1
Plaški HR . . . 123 B4
Plassen
Buskerud N . . . 47 B4
Hedmark N . . . 49 A4
Plášťovce SK . . . 112 A3
Plasy CZ . . . 96 B1
Platamona Lido I . . 178 B2
Platania I . . . 175 B2
Platanos GR . . . 185 D4
Plati I . . . 175 C2
Platičevo SRB . . . 127 C1
Platja d'Aro E . . . 147 C4
Plattling D . . . 95 C4
Plau D . . . 73 A5
Plaue
Brandenburg D . . 73 B5
Thüringen D . . . 82 B2
Plauen D . . . 83 B4
Plavecký Mikuláš
SK 98 C1
Plavinas LV . . . 8 D4
Plavna SRB . . . 125 B5
Plavnica SK . . . 99 B4
Plavno HR . . . 138 A2
Pléaux F . . . 116 B2
Pleine-Fougères F . 88 B2
Pleinfeld D . . . 94 B2
Pleinting D . . . 95 C5
Plélan-le-Grand F . 101 B3
Plémet F . . . 101 A3
Pléneuf-Val-André
F 101 A3
Plentzia E . . . 143 A4
Plérin F . . . 101 A3
Plešivec SK . . . 99 C4
Plessa D . . . 83 A5
Plessé F . . . 101 B4
Plestin-les-Grèves
F 100 A2
Pleszew PL . . . 76 C2
Pleternica HR . . . 125 B3
Plettenberg D . . . 81 A3
Pleubian F . . . 100 A2
Pleumartin F . . . 115 B4
Pleumeur-Bodou F 100 A2
Pleurs F . . . 91 C3
Pleven BG . . . 17 D6
Plevnik-Drienové
SK 98 B2
Pleyben F . . . 100 A2
Pleyber-Christ F . . 100 A2
Pliego E . . . 165 B3
Pliešovce SK . . . 99 C3
Plitvička Jezera
HR 123 C4
Plitvički Ljeskovac
HR 123 C4
Ploaghe I . . . 178 B2
Ploče HR . . . 138 B3
Plochingen D . . . 94 C1
Płock PL . . . 77 B4
Ploemeur F . . . 100 B2
Ploërmel F . . . 101 B3
Ploeuc-sur-Lie F . . 101 A3
Plogastel St Germain
F 100 B1
Plogoff F . . . 100 A1
Ploiești RO . . . 17 C7
Plomari GR . . . 186 D1
Plombières-les-Bains
F 105 B5
Plomin HR . . . 123 B3
Plön D . . . 65 B3
Plonéour-Lanvern
F 100 B1
Płonia PL . . . 74 A3
Płoniawy PL . . . 77 B6
Płońsk PL . . . 77 B5
Płoskinia PL . . . 69 A4
Plössberg D . . . 95 B4
Płoty PL . . . 67 C4
Plouagat F . . . 100 A2
Plouaret F . . . 100 A2
Plouarzel F . . . 100 A1
Plouay F . . . 100 B2
Ploubalay F . . . 101 A3
Ploubazlanec F . . . 100 A2
Ploudalmézeau F . 100 A1
Ploudiry F . . . 100 A1
Plouescat F . . . 100 A1
Plouézec F . . . 100 A3
Plougasnou F . . . 100 A2
Plougastel-Daoulas
F 100 A1
Plougonven F . . . 100 A2
Plougonver F . . . 100 A2
Plougrescant F . . . 100 A2
Plouguenast F . . . 101 A3
Plouguerneau F . . 100 A1
Plouha F . . . 100 A3
Plouhinec F . . . 100 A1
Plouigneau F . . . 100 A2
Ploumanach F . . . 100 A2
Plounévez-Quintin
F 100 A2
Plouray F . . . 100 A2
Plouzévédé F . . . 100 A1
Plovdiv BG . . . 183 A6
Plozévet F . . . 100 B1
Plumbridge GB . . 27 B3
Pluméliau F . . . 100 B3

Plumlov CZ . . . 97 B5
Plungė LT . . . 8 E2
Pluty PL . . . 69 A5
Pluvigner F . . . 100 B3
Plužine
BIH 139 B4
MNE 139 B4
Płużnica PL . . . 69 B3
Plymouth GB . . . 42 B2
Plymstock GB . . . 42 B2
Plytnica PL . . . 68 B1
Plyusa RUS . . . 9 C6
Plzeň CZ . . . 96 B1
Pniewy PL . . . 75 B5
Pobes E . . . 143 B4
Poběžovice CZ . . 95 B4
Pobiedziska PL . . . 76 B2
Pobierowo PL . . . 67 B3
Pobla de Segur E . 145 B4
Pobladura del Valle
E 142 B1
Pobla-Tornesa E . . 153 B4
Pobra de Trives E . 141 B3
Pobra do Brollón
E 141 B3
Pobra do Caramiñal
E 140 B2
Pobudje BIH . . . 139 A5
Počátky CZ . . . 97 B3
Poceirão P . . . 154 C2
Pöchlarn A . . . 110 A2
Pociecha PL . . . 87 A4
Pockau D . . . 83 B5
Pocking D . . . 96 C1
Pocklington GB . . 40 B3
Podbořany CZ . . . 83 B5
Podbrdo SLO . . . 122 A2
Podbrezová SK . . . 99 C3
Podčetrtek SLO . . 123 A4
Poděbrady CZ . . . 84 B3
Poddębice HR . . . 76 C3
Podence P . . . 149 A3
Podensac F . . . 128 B2
Podenzano I . . . 120 C2
Podersdorf am See
A 111 B3
Podgaje PL . . . 68 B1
Podgora HR . . . 138 B3
Podgóra PL . . . 87 A5
Podgorač HR . . . 125 B4
Podgorica MNE . . 16 D3
Podgorie AL . . . 182 C2
Podgrad SLO . . . 123 B3
Podhájska SK . . . 112 A2
Podkova BG . . . 183 B7
Podlapača HR . . . 123 C4
Podlejki PL . . . 69 B5
Podlužany SK . . . 98 C2
Podnovlje BIH . . . 125 C4
Podolie SK . . . 98 C1
Podolínec SK . . . 99 B4
Podolsk RUS . . . 9 E10
Podporozhy RUS . . 9 B9
Podromanija BIH . . 139 B4
Podturen HR . . . 111 C3
Podvín CZ . . . 97 C4
Podwilk PL . . . 99 B3
Poetto I . . . 179 C3
Poggendorf D . . . 66 B2
Poggiardo I . . . 173 B4
Poggibonsi I . . . 135 B4
Póggio a Caiano I . 135 B4
Póggio Imperiale I . 171 B3
Póggio Mirteto I . . 168 A2
Póggio Moiano I . . 169 A2
Póggio Renatico I . 121 C4
Póggio Rusco I . . . 121 C4
Pöggstall A . . . 97 C3
Pogny F . . . 91 C4
Pogorzela PL . . . 85 A5
Pogorzelice PL . . . 68 A2
Pogradec AL . . . 182 C2
Pogrodzie PL . . . 69 A4
Pohorelá SK . . . 99 C4
Pohořelice CZ . . . 97 C4
Pohronská Polhora
SK 99 C3
Poiares P . . . 148 B1
Poio E . . . 140 B2
Poirino I . . . 119 C4
Poisson F . . . 117 A4
Poissons F . . . 91 C5
Poissy F . . . 90 C2
Poitiers F . . . 115 B4
Poix-de-Picardie F . 90 B1
Poix-Terron F . . . 91 B4
Pokka FIN . . . 197 A8
Pokój PL . . . 86 B1
Pokupsko HR . . . 124 B1
Pol E . . . 141 A3
Pola RUS . . . 9 D7
Pol a Charra GB . . 31 B1
Pola de Allande E . 141 A4
Pola de Laviana E . 142 A1
Pola de Lena E . . . 141 A5
Pola de Siero E . . . 142 A1
Pola de Somiedo E 141 A4
Polaincourt-et-
Clairefontaine F . 105 B5
Połajewo PL . . . 75 B5
Polán E . . . 151 C3
Polanica-Zdrój PL . 85 B4
Połaniec PL . . . 87 B5
Polanów PL . . . 68 A1
Polati TR . . . 187 C7
Polatsk BY . . . 13 A8
Polch D . . . 80 B3
Polcirkeln S . . . 196 C4

Pólczno PL . . . 68 A2
Połczyn-Zdrój PL . 67 C5
Polegate GB . . . 45 C4
Poleñino E . . . 145 C3
Polesella I . . . 121 C4
Polessk RUS . . . 12 A4
Polgár H . . . 113 B5
Polgárdi H . . . 112 B2
Polhov Gradec
SLO 123 A3
Police CZ . . . 74 A3
Police nad Metují
CZ 85 B4
Polichnitos GR . . . 186 C1
Polička CZ . . . 97 B4
Poličnik HR . . . 137 A4
Policoro I . . . 174 A2
Policzna PL . . . 87 A5
Poligiros GR . . . 183 C5
Polignano a Mare I 173 B3
Poligny F . . . 105 C4
Polis CY . . . 181 A1
Polístena I . . . 175 C2
Polizzi Generosa I . 176 B3
Poljana SRB . . . 127 C3
Poljanák HR . . . 123 C4
Poljčane SLO . . . 123 A4
Polje BIH . . . 125 C3
Poljice
BIH 138 A2
BIH 139 A4
Polkowice PL . . . 85 A4
Polla I . . . 172 B1
Pollas E . . . 150 A2
Pöllau A . . . 110 B2
Polleben D . . . 82 A3
Pollença E . . . 167 B3
Pollenfeld D . . . 95 C3
Pollfoss N . . . 198 D4
Póllica I . . . 170 C3
Polminhac F . . . 116 C2
Polná CZ . . . 97 B3
Polna RUS . . . 8 C6
Polne PL . . . 75 A5
Polomka SK . . . 99 C3
Polonne UA . . . 13 C7
Polperro GB . . . 42 B2
Polruan GB . . . 42 B2
Pöls A . . . 110 B1
Polska Cerekiew PL 86 B2
Poltár SK . . . 99 C3
Põltsamaa EST . . 8 C4
Polyarny RUS . . . 3 B13
Polyarnyye Zori
RUS 3 C13
Polzela SLO . . . 123 A4
Pomarance I . . . 135 B3
Pomarez F . . . 128 C2
Pomárico I . . . 172 B2
Pomáz H . . . 112 B3
Pombal P . . . 154 B2
Pomézia I . . . 168 B2
Pommard F . . . 105 B3
Pommelsbrunn D . 95 B3
Pomonte I . . . 134 C3
Pomorie BG . . . 17 D7
Pomos CY . . . 181 A1
Pompei I . . . 170 C2
Pompey F . . . 92 C2
Pomposa I . . . 122 C1
Poncin F . . . 118 A2
Pondorf D . . . 95 C3
Ponferrada E . . . 141 B4
Poniec PL . . . 85 A4
Ponikva SLO . . . 123 A4
Poniky SK . . . 99 C3
Pons F . . . 114 C3
Ponsacco I . . . 134 B3
Pont I . . . 119 B4
Pont-a-Celles B . . 79 B4
Pontacq F . . . 145 A3
Pontailler-sur-Saône
F 105 B4
Pont-a-Marcq F . . 78 B3
Pont-à-Mousson F . 92 C2
Pontão P . . . 154 B2
Pontardawe GB . . 39 C3
Pontarddulais GB . 39 C2
Pontarion F . . . 116 B1
Pontarlier F . . . 105 C5
Pontassieve I . . . 135 B4
Pontaubault F . . . 88 B2
Pontaumur F . . . 116 B2
Pont-Audemer F . . 89 A4
Pont-Aven F . . . 100 B2
Pont Canavese I . . 119 B4
Pontcharra F . . . 118 B3
Pontcharra-sur-Turdine
F 117 B4
Pontchâteau F . . . 101 B3
Pont-Croix F . . . 100 A1
Pont-d'Ain F . . . 118 A2
Pont-de-Beauvoisin
F 118 B2
Pont-de-Buis-lès-
Quimerch F . . . 100 A1
Pont-de-Chéruy F . 118 B2
Pont de Dore F . . . 117 B3
Pont-de-Labeaume
F 117 C4
Pont de Molins E . 147 B3
Pont-de-Roide F . . 106 B1
Pont-de-Salars F . . 130 A1
Pont-d'Espagne F . 145 B3
Pont de Suert E . . 145 B4
Pont-de-Vaux F . . 117 A4

Pont-de-Veyle F . . 117 A4
Pont d'Ouilly F . . . 89 B3
Pont-du-Château
F 116 B3
Pont-du-Navoy F . . 105 C4
Ponte a Moriano I . 134 B3
Ponte Arche I . . . 121 A3
Pontebba I . . . 109 C4
Ponte Cáffaro I . . . 121 B3
Pontecagnano I . . 170 C2
Ponte-Caldelas E . 140 B2
Ponteceso E . . . 140 A2
Pontecesures E . . 140 B2
Pontecorvo I . . . 169 B3
Ponte da Barca P . 148 A1
Pontedássio I . . . 133 B4
Pontedécimo I . . . 133 A4
Ponte de Lima P . . 148 A1
Ponte dell'Ólio I . . 120 C2
Pontedera I . . . 134 B3
Ponte de Sor P . . . 154 B2
Pontedeume E . . . 140 A2
Ponte di Barbarano
I 121 B4
Ponte di Legno I . . 121 A3
Ponte di Nava I . . . 133 A3
Ponte di Piave I . . 122 B1
Ponte Felcino I . . . 136 B1
Pontefract GB . . . 40 B2
Ponte Gardena I . . 108 C2
Pontegniori I . . . 135 B3
Pontelagoscuro I . . 121 C4
Ponteland GB . . . 37 A5
Pontelandolfo I . . . 170 B2
Ponte-Leccia F . . . 180 A2
Pontelongo I . . . 121 B5
Ponte nelle Alpi I . 122 A1
Pont-en-Royans F . 118 B2
Pontenure I . . . 120 C2
Pontenx-les-Forges
F 128 B1
Ponterwyd GB . . . 39 B3
Ponte San Giovanni
I 136 B1
Ponte San Pietro I . 120 B2
Pontevedra E . . . 140 B2
Pontevico I . . . 120 B3
Pont Farcy F . . . 88 B2
Pontfaverger-
Moronvillers F . . 91 B4
Pontgibaud F . . . 116 B2
Ponticino I . . . 135 B4
Pontigny F . . . 104 B2
Pontijou F . . . 103 B3
Pontínia I . . . 169 B3
Pontinvrea I . . . 133 A4
Pontivy F . . . 100 A3
Pont-l'Abbé F . . . 100 B1
Pont-l'Évêque F . . 89 A4
Pontlevoy F . . . 103 B3
Pontoise F . . . 90 B2
Pontones E . . . 164 A2
Pontonx-sur-l'Abour
F 128 C2
Pontoon IRL . . . 26 C1
Pontorson F . . . 88 B2
Pontrémoli I . . . 134 A2
Pont-Remy F . . . 90 A1
Pontresina CH . . . 107 C4
Pontrhydfendigaid
GB 39 B3
Pontrieux F . . . 100 A2
Ponts E . . . 147 C2
Ponts-aux-Dames F 90 C2
Pont Scorff F . . . 100 B2
Pöntsö FIN . . . 196 B7
Pont-Ste Maxence F 90 B2
Pont-St Esprit F . . 131 A3
Pont-St Martin
F 101 B4
I 119 B4
Pont-St Vincent F . 92 C2
Pont-sur-Yonne F . 104 A2
Pontvallain F . . . 102 B2
Pontypool GB . . . 39 C3
Pontypridd GB . . . 39 C3
Ponza I . . . 169 C2
Poo E . . . 142 A2
Poole GB . . . 43 B5
Poolewe GB . . . 31 B3
Poperinge B . . . 78 B2
Pópoli I . . . 169 A3
Popovac SRB . . . 127 D3
Popovača HR . . . 124 B2
Popow PL . . . 77 B4
Poppel B . . . 79 A5
Poppenhausen
Bayern D . . . 82 B2
Hessen D . . . 82 B1
Poppi I . . . 135 B4
Poprad SK . . . 99 B4
Popučke SRB . . . 127 C1
Pópulo P . . . 148 A2
Populónia I . . . 134 C3
Pörböly H . . . 125 A4
Porcuna E . . . 163 A3
Pordenone I . . . 122 B1
Pordic F . . . 100 A3
Poręba PL . . . 86 B3
Poreč HR . . . 122 B2
Pori FIN . . . 8 B2
Porjus S . . . 196 C2
Porkhov RUS . . . 9 D6
Porlezza I . . . 120 A2
Porlock GB . . . 43 A3
Pörnbach D . . . 95 C3

Pornic F 101 B3
Pornichet F 101 B3
Porodin SRB 127 C3
Poronin PL 99 B3
Poros
Attiki GR 185 B4
Kefalonia GR 184 A1
Poroszló H 113 B4
Porozina HR 123 B3
Porquerolles F 132 C2
Porrentruy CH 106 B2
Porreres E 167 B3
Porretta Terme I 135 A3
Porsgrunn N 53 A5
Porspoder F 100 A1
Port-a-Binson F 91 B3
Portacloy IRL 26 B1
Portadown GB 27 B4
Portaferry GB 27 B5
Portaje E 155 B4
Portalegre P 155 B3
Portarlington IRL 30 A1
Port Askaig GB 34 C1
Portavadie GB 34 C2
Portavogie GB 27 B5
Portbail F 88 A2
Port Bannatyne GB 34 C2
Port-Barcarès F 146 B4
Portbou E 146 B4
Port-Camargue F 131 B3
Port Charlotte GB 34 C1
Port d'Andratx E 166 B2
Port-de-Bouc F 131 B3
Port-de-Lanne F 128 C1
Port de Pollença E 167 B3
Port-des-Barques
F 114 C2
Port de Sóller E 166 B2
Portegrandi I 122 B1
Portel P 155 C3
Portela P 148 B1
Port Ellen GB 34 C1
Portelo P 141 C4
Portemouro E 140 B2
Port-en-Bessin F 88 A3
Port'Ercole I 168 A1
Port Erin GB 36 B2
Portes-lès-Valence
F 117 C4
Portets F 128 B2
Port Eynon GB 39 C2
Portezuelo E 155 B4
Port Glasgow GB 34 C3
Portglenone GB 27 B4
Porthcawl GB 39 C3
Port Henderson GB 31 B3
Porthleven GB 42 B1
Porthmadog GB 38 B2
Porticcio F 180 B1
Portici I 170 C2
Portico di Romagna
I 135 A4
Portilla de la Reina
E 142 A2
Portillo E 150 A3
Portimao P 160 B1
Portinatx E 166 B1
Portinho da Arrabida
P 154 C1
Port Isaac GB 42 B2
Portishead GB 43 A4
Port-Joinville F 114 B1
Portknockie GB 33 D4
Port-la-Nouvelle F 130 B2
Portlaoise IRL 30 A1
Portlethen GB 33 D4
Port Logan GB 36 B2
Port Louis F 100 B2
Portmagne IRL 29 C1
Portmahomack GB 32 D3
Portman E 165 B4
Port Manech F 100 B2
Portnacroish GB 34 B2
Portnahaven GB 34 C1
Port Nan Giuran GB 31 A2
Port-Navalo F 100 B3
Port Nis GB 31 A2
Porto
F 180 A1
P 148 A1
Porto-Alto P 154 C2
Porto Azzurro I 134 C3
Portocannone I 170 B3
Porto Cerésio I 120 B1
Porto Cervo I 178 A3
Porto Cesáreo I 173 B3
Porto Colom E 167 B3
Porto Covo P 160 B1
Porto Cristo E 167 B3
Porto d'Áscoli I 136 C2
Porto de Lagos P 160 B1
Porto de Mos P 154 B2
Porto de Rei P 154 C2
Porto do Son E 140 B2
Porto Empédocle I 176 B2
Portoferráio I 134 C3
Portofino I 134 A2
Porto Garibaldi I 122 C1
Portogruaro I 122 B1
Portokhelion GR 184 B4
Portomaggiore I 121 C4
Portomarin E 140 B3
Porton GB 44 B2
Portonovo E 140 B2
Portopalo di Capo
Passero I 177 C4
Porto Petro E 167 B3
Porto Pino I 179 D2
Porto Potenza Picena
I 136 B2
Portør N 53 B5
Porto Recanati I 136 B2
Porto San Giórgio
I 136 B2
Porto Sant'Elpídio
I 136 B2
Porto Santo Stéfano
I 168 A1
Portoscuso I 179 C2
Porto Tolle I 122 C1
Porto Tórres I 178 B2
Porto-Vecchio F 180 B2
Portovénere I 134 A2
Portpatrick GB 36 B1
Portreath GB 42 B1
Portree GB 31 B2
Portroe IRL 28 B3
Portrush GB 27 A4
Port St Mary GB 36 B2
Portsall F 100 A1
Portsmouth GB 44 C2
Portsoy GB 33 D4
Port-Ste Marie F 129 B3
Portstewart GB 27 A4
Port-St-Louis-du-Rhône
F 131 B3
Port-sur-Saône F 105 B5
Port Talbot GB 39 C3
Portugalete E 143 A4
Portumna IRL 28 A3
Port-Vendres F 146 B4
Port William GB 36 B2
Porvoo FIN 8 B4
Porzuna E 157 A3
Posada
Oviedo E 141 A5
Oviedo E 142 A2
I 178 B3
Posada de Valdeón
E 142 A2
Posadas E 162 A2
Poschiavo CH 120 A3
Posedarje HR 137 A4
Posio FIN 197 C11
Positano I 170 C2
Possagno I 121 B4
Posseck D 83 B4
Possesse F 91 C4
Pössneck D 83 B3
Posta I 169 A3
Postal I 108 C2
Posta Piana I 172 A1
Postbauer-Heng D 95 B3
Posterholt NL 80 A2
Postioma I 121 B5
Postira HR 138 B2
Postojna SLO 123 B3
Postolprty CZ 84 B1
Postomino PL 68 A1
Posušje BIH 138 B3
Potamos
Attiki GR 184 C3
Attiki GR 184 D4
Potegowo PL 68 A2
Potenza I 172 B1
Potenza Picena I 136 B2
Potes E 142 A2
Potigny F 89 B3
Potočari BIH 127 C1
Potoci
BIH 138 A2
BIH 139 B3
Potony H 125 B3
Potries E 159 C3
Potsdam D 74 B2
Potštát CZ 98 B1
Pottenbrunn A 110 A2
Pottendorf A 111 B3
Pottenstein
A 111 B3
D 95 B3
Potters Bar GB 44 B3
Pöttmes D 94 C3
Pöttsching A 111 B3
Potworów PL 87 A4
Pouancé F 101 B4
Pougues-les-Eaux
F 104 B2
Pouilly-en-Auxois
F 104 B3
Pouilly-sous Charlieu
F 117 A4
Pouilly-sur-Loire F 104 B1
Poujol-sur-Orb F 130 B2
Poullaouen F 100 A2
Poulton-le-Fylde GB 38 A4
Poundstock GB 42 B2
Pourcy F 91 B3
Pourrain F 104 B2
Poussu FIN 197 D12
Pouyastruc F 145 A4
Pouy-de-Touges F 146 A2
Pouzauges F 114 B3
Pova de Santa Iria
P 154 C1
Považská Bystrica
SK 98 B2
Povedilla E 158 C1
Povenets RUS 9 A9
Povlja HR 138 B2
Povljana HR 137 A4
Póvoa
Beja P 161 A2
Santarém P 154 B2
Póvoa de Lanhoso
P 148 A1
Póvoa de Varzim
P 148 A1
Póvoa e Meadas P 155 B3
Powidz PL 76 B2
Poyales del Hoyo
E 150 B2
Poynton GB 40 B1
Poyntz Pass GB 27 B4
Poysdorf A 97 C4
Poza de la Sal E 143 B3
Pozaldez E 150 A3
Pozán de Vero E 145 B4
Pozanti TR 23 C8
Požarevac SRB 127 C3
Požega
HR 125 B3
SRB 127 D2
Poznań PL 76 B1
Pozo Alcón E 164 B2
Pozoantiguo E 150 A2
Pozoblanco E 156 B3
Pozo Cañada E 158 C2
Pozo de Guadalajara
E 151 B4
Pozo de la Serna E 157 B4
Pozohondo E 158 C2
Pozondón E 152 B2
Poźrzadło Wielkie
PL 75 A4
Pozuel del Campo
E 152 B2
Pozuelo de Alarcón
E 151 B4
Pozuelo de Calatrava
E 157 B4
Pozuelo del Páramo
E 142 B1
Pozuelo de Zarzón
E 149 B3
Pozzallo I 177 C3
Pozzomaggiore I 178 B2
Pozzo San Nicola I 178 B2
Pozzuoli I 170 C2
Pozzuolo I 135 B4
Prabuty PL 69 B4
Prača BIH 139 B4
Prachatice CZ 96 B1
Prada E 141 B3
Pradelle F 118 C2
Pradelles F 117 C3
Prades
E 147 C1
F 146 B3
Pradła PL 86 B3
Prado
E 142 A1
P 148 A1
Prado del Rey E 162 B2
Pradoluengo E 143 B3
Pragelato I 119 B3
Pragersko SLO 123 A4
Prägraten A 109 B3
Prague = Praha CZ 84 B2
Praha = Prague CZ 84 B2
Prahecq F 115 B3
Praia P 154 B1
Práia a Mare I 174 B1
Praia da Rocha P 160 B1
Praia da Viera P 154 B2
Praia de Mira P 148 B1
Praiano I 170 C2
Pralboino I 120 B3
Pralognan-la-Vanoise
F 118 B3
Pramanda GR 182 D3
Pranjani SRB 127 C2
Prapatnica HR 138 B2
Præstø DK 65 A5
Praszka PL 86 A2
Prat F 146 A1
Prata I 135 B3
Prata di Pordenone
I 122 B1
Pratau D 83 A4
Prat de Compte E 153 B4
Pratdip E 147 C1
Pratella I 170 B2
Prato I 135 B4
Prátola Peligna I 169 A3
Pratola Serra I 170 C2
Prats-de-Mollo-la-Preste
F 146 B3
Prauthoy F 105 B4
Pravia E 141 A4
Praxmar A 108 B2
Prayssac F 129 B4
Prazzo I 132 A3
Prebold SLO 123 A4
Préchac F 128 B2
Précy-sur-Thil F 104 B3
Predáppio I 135 A4
Predazzo I 121 A4
Předin CZ 97 B3
Preding A 110 C2
Predjame SLO 123 B3
Predlitz A 109 B4
Predmeja SLO 122 B2
Predoi I 108 B3
Pré-en-Pail F 89 B3
Prees GB 38 B4
Preetz D 64 B3
Préfailles F 101 B3
Pregarten A 96 C2
Pregrada HR 123 A4
Preignan F 129 C3
Preiļi LV 8 D5
Preitenegg A 110 C1
Prekaja BIH 138 A2
Preko HR 137 A4
Preljina SRB 127 D2
Prelog HR 124 A2
Prelošćica HR 124 B2
Přelouč CZ 97 A3
Prem SLO 123 B3
Premantura HR 122 C2
Prémery F 104 B2
Prémia I 119 A5
Premiàde Mar E 147 C3
Premnitz D 73 B5
Prémont F 91 A3
Prenzlau D 74 A2
Preodac BIH 138 A2
Přerov CZ 98 B1
Prerow D 66 B1
Presencio E 143 B3
Presicce I 173 C4
Presly F 103 B4
Prešov SK 12 D4
Pressac F 115 B4
Pressath D 95 B3
Pressbaum A 111 A3
Prestatyn GB 38 A3
Prestebakke N 54 B2
Presteigne GB 39 B3
Přeštice CZ 96 B1
Preston
Lancashire GB 38 A4
Scottish Borders
GB 35 C5
Prestonpans GB 35 C5
Prestwick GB 36 A2
Prettin D 83 A4
Preturo I 169 A3
Pretzchendorf D 83 B5
Pretzier D 73 B4
Pretzsch D 83 A4
Preuilly-sur-Claise
F 115 B4
Prevalje SLO 110 C1
Prevenchères F 131 A2
Préveranges F 116 A2
Preveza GR 182 E2
Prevršac HR 124 B2
Prezid HR 123 B3
Priaranza del Bierzo
E 141 B4
Priay F 118 A2
Pribeta SK 112 B2
Priboj
BIH 125 C4
SRB 16 D3
Příbor CZ 98 B2
Příbram CZ 96 B2
Pribylina SK 99 B3
Přibyslav CZ 97 B3
Pričević SRB 127 C1
Pridjel BIH 125 C4
Priego E 152 B1
Priego de Córdoba
E 163 A3
Priekule LV 8 D2
Prien D 109 B3
Prienai LT 13 A5
Prievidza SK 98 C2
Prigradica HR 138 C2
Prigrevica SRB 125 B5
Prijeboj HR 123 C4
Prijedor BIH 124 C2
Prijepolje SRB 16 D3
Prilep MK 182 B3
Priluka BIH 138 B2
Primda CZ 95 B4
Primel-Trégastel F 100 A2
Primišje HR 123 B4
Primorsk
Kaliningrad RUS 69 A5
Severo-Zapadnyy
RUS 9 B6
Primošten HR 138 B1
Primstal D 92 B2
Princes Risborough
GB 44 B3
Princetown GB 42 B2
Principina a Mare I 135 C4
Priolo Gargallo I 177 B4
Prioro E 142 B2
Priozersk RUS 9 B7
Prirechnyy RUS 193 C14
Prisoje BIH 138 B3
Priština KOS 16 D4
Pritzerbe D 73 B5
Pritzier D 73 A4
Pritzwalk D 73 A5
Privas F 117 C4
Priverno I 169 B3
Privlaka
Vukovarsko-Srijemska
HR 125 B4
Zadarska HR 137 A4
Prizna HR 123 C3
Prizren KOS 16 D4
Prizzi I 176 B2
Prnjavor
BIH 125 C3
HR 124 B1
SRB 127 C1
Proaza E 141 A4
Probstzella D 82 B3
Probus GB 42 B2
Prócchio I 134 C3
Prochowice PL 85 A4
Prócida I 170 C2
Prodhromos CY 181 B1
Prodo I 135 C5
Proença-a-Nova P 154 B3
Proença-a-Velha P 155 A3
Profondeville B 79 B4
Prokuplje SRB 16 D4
Propriano F 180 B1
Prosec CZ 97 B4
Prösen D 83 A5
Prosenjakovci
SLO 111 C3
Prosotsani GR 183 B5
Prostějov CZ 98 B1
Prószków PL 86 B1
Proszowice PL 87 B4
Protić BIH 138 A2
Protivanov CZ 97 B4
Protivín CZ 96 B2
Prötzel D 74 B2
Provins F 90 C3
Prozor BIH 139 B3
Prrenjas AL 182 B2
Prudhoe GB 37 B5
Prudnik PL 85 B5
Pruggern A 109 B4
Průgy H 113 A5
Prüm D 80 B2
Pruna E 162 B2
Prunelli-di-Fiumorbo
F 180 A2
Prunetta I 135 A3
Pruniers F 103 C4
Prusice PL 85 A4
Pruské SK 98 B2
Pruszce PL 76 A3
Pruszcz Gdański PL 69 A3
Pruszków PL 77 B5
Prutz A 108 B1
Prüzen D 65 C5
Pruzhany BY 13 B6
Pružina SK 98 B2
Pŭrvomay BG 183 A7
Pryzlęg PL 75 B4
Przasnysz PL 77 A5
Przechlewo PL 68 B2
Przecław PL 87 B5
Przedbórz PL 87 A3
Przedecz PL 76 B3
Przejęslav PL 84 A3
Przemków PL 85 A3
Przemocze PL 75 A3
Przemyśl PL 12 D5
Przerąb PL 87 A3
Przewodnik PL 69 B3
Przewodowo Parcele
PL 77 B5
Przewóz PL 84 A2
Przezmark PL 69 B4
Przodkowo PL 68 A3
Przybiernów PL 75 A3
Przyborowice PL 77 B5
Przybyszew PL 87 A4
Przybyszów PL 86 A3
Przylęg PL 75 B4
Przysucha PL 87 A4
Przytóczna PL 75 B4
Przytyk PL 87 A4
Przywidz PL 68 A3
Psachna GR 185 A4
Psara GR 185 A6
Psary PL 76 C3
Pskov RUS 8 D6
Pszczew PL 75 B4
Pszczółki PL 69 A3
Pszczyna PL 98 B2
Pszów PL 86 B2
Pteleos GR 182 D4
Ptolemaida GR 182 C3
Ptuj SLO 124 A1
Ptusza PL 68 B1
Puch A 109 B4
Puchberg am
Schneeberg A 110 B2
Puchevillers F 90 A2
Puchheim D 108 A2
Púchov SK 98 B2
Pučišća HR 138 B2
Puck PL 69 A3
Puçol E 159 B3
Puconci SLO 111 C3
Pudasjärvi FIN 197 D10
Puderbach D 81 B3
Pudozh RUS 9 B10
Puebla de Albortón
E 153 A3
Puebla de Alcocer
E 156 B2
Puebla de Beleña
E 151 B4
Puebla de Don Fadrique
E 164 B2
Puebla de Don Rodrigo
E 156 A3
Puebla de Guzmán
E 161 B2
Puebla de la Calzada
E 155 C4
Puebla de la Reina
E 156 B1
Puebla de Lillo E 142 A1
Puebla del Maestre
E 161 A3
Puebla del Principe
E 158 C1
Puebla de Obando
E 155 B4
Puebla de Sanabria
E 141 B4
Puebla de Sancho Pérez
E 155 C4
Puente Almuhey E 142 B2
Puente de Domingo
Flórez E 141 B4
Puente de Génave
E 164 A2
Puente del Congosto
E 150 B2
Puente de Montañana
E 145 B4
Puente Duero E 150 A3
Puente-Genil E 162 A3
Puente la Reina E 144 B2
Puente la Reina de Jaca
E 144 B3
Puentelarra E 143 B3
Puente Mayorga E 162 B2
Puente Viesgo E 143 A3
Puertas
Asturias E 142 A2
Salamanca E 149 A3
Puerto de Mazarrón
E 165 B3
Puerto de Santa Cruz
E 156 A2
Puerto de San Vicente
E 156 A2
Puerto-Lápice E 157 A4
Puertollano E 157 B3
Puerto Lumbreras
E 164 B3
Puerto Moral E 161 B3
Puerto Real E 162 B1
Puerto Rey E 156 A2
Puerto Seguro E 149 B3
Puerto Serrano E 162 B2
Puget-Sur-Argens
F 132 B2
Puget-Théniers F 132 B2
Puget-ville F 132 B2
Pugnochiuso I 171 B4
Puigcerdà E 146 B2
Puigpunyent E 166 B2
Puig Reig E 147 C2
Puillon F 128 C2
Puimichel F 132 B2
Puimoisson F 132 B2
Puiseaux F 103 A4
Puisieux F 90 A2
Puisserguier F 130 B2
Puivert F 146 B3
Pujols F 128 B2
Pukanec SK 98 C2
Pukavik S 63 B2
Pukë AL 182 A1
Pula
HR 122 C2
I 179 C2
Puławy PL 12 C4
Pulborough GB 44 C3
Pulfero I 122 A2
Pulgar E 157 A3
Pulheim D 80 A2
Pulkau A 97 C3
Pulpi E 164 B3
Pulsano I 173 B3
Pulsnitz D 84 A2
Pułtusk PL 77 B6
Pumpsaint GB 39 B3
Punat HR 123 B3
Punta Marina I 135 A5
Punta Prima E 167 B4
Punta Sabbioni I 122 B1
Puntas de Calnegre
E 165 B3
Punta Umbria E 161 B3
Puolanka FIN 3 D10
Puoltikasvaara S 196 B4
Puoltsa S 196 B2
Puračić BIH 125 C4
Purbach am Neusiedler
See A 111 B3
Purchena E 164 B2
Purfleet GB 45 B4
Purgstall A 110 A2
Purkersdorf A 111 A3
Purmerend NL 70 B1
Purullena E 164 B1
Pushkin RUS 9 C7
Pushkino RUS 9 D10
Püspökladány H 113 B5
Pusté Ulany SK 111 A4
Pustoshka RUS 9 D6
Puszcza Mariańska
PL 77 C5
Puszczykowo PL 76 B1
Pusztamagyaród
H 111 C3
Pusztamonostor H 113 B3
Pusztaszabolcs H 112 B2
Pusztavám H 112 B2
Putanges-Pont-Ecrepin
F 89 B3
Putbus D 66 B2
Putignano I 173 B3
Putlitz D 73 A5
Putnok H 99 C4
Putte B 79 A4
Puttelange-aux-Lacs
F 92 B2
Putten NL 70 B2
Puttgarden D 65 B4
Püttlingen D 92 B2
Putzu Idu I 179 B2
Puy-Guillaume F 117 B3
Puylaroque F 129 B4
Puylaurens F 146 A3

Puy-l'Évêque F . . . 129 B4
Puymirol F . . . 129 B3
Puyôo F . . . 128 C2
Puyrolland F . . .114 B3
Pwllheli GB 38 B2
Pyetrikaw BY . . . 13 B8
Pyhäjärvi FIN 3 E9
Pyhäkylä FIN . . . 197 D11
Pyla CY . . . 181 A2
Pyla-sur-Mer F . . . 128 B1
Pyrzyce PL. . . . 75 A3
Pysely CZ 96 B2
Pyskowice PL . . . 86 B2
Pytalovo RUS 8 D5
Pyzdry PL. 76 B2

Q

Quakenbrück D 71 B4
Quargnento I 119 C5
Quarré-les-Tombes F. 104 B2
Quarteira P . . . 160 B1
Quartu Sant'Elena I 179 C3
Quatre-Champs F . . 91 B4
Quedlinburg D. 82 A3
Queensferry
 Edinburgh GB 35 C4
 Flintshire GB 38 A3
Queige F 118 B3
Queipo E 161 B3
Queixans E . . . 146 B2
Quel E 144 B1
Quelaines-St-Gault F. 102 B1
Queljada P . . . 148 A1
Quemada E . . . 143 C3
Queralbs E . . . 147 B3
Quercianella I . . . 134 B3
Querfurt D 82 A3
Quérigut F . . . 146 B3
Quero
 E 157 A4
 I 121 B4
Querqueville F. . . . 88 A2
Quesada E . . . 164 B1
Questembert F . . 101 B3
Quettehou F 88 A2
Quevauvillers F. . . 90 B2
Quevy B 79 B4
Quiaios P. . . . 148 B1
Quiberon F . . . 100 B2
Quiberville F . . . 89 A4
Quickborn D . . . 64 C2
Quiévrain B 79 B3
Quillan F 146 B3
Quillebeuf F. 89 A4
Quimper F . . . 100 A1
Quimperlé F 100 B2
Quincampoix F . . . 89 A5
Quincoces de Yuso E 143 B3
Quincy F 103 B4
Quinéville F 88 A2
Quingey F . . . 105 B4
Quinson F . . . 132 B2
Quinssaines F. . .116 A2
Quinta-Grande P . 154 C2
Quintana de la Serena E 156 B2
Quintana del Castillo E 141 B4
Quintana del Marco E 141 B5
Quintana del Puenta E 142 B2
Quintana-Martin Galindez E. 143 B3
Quintanaortuño E . 143 B3
Quintanapalla E . . 143 B3
Quintanar de la Orden E 157 A4
Quintanar de la Sierra E 143 C3
Quintanar del Rey E 158 B2
Quintanilla de la Mata E 143 C3
Quintanilla del Coco E 143 C3
Quintanilla de Onésimo E 150 A3
Quintanilla de Somoza E 141 B4
Quintas de Valdelucio E 142 B2
Quintela P . . . 148 B2
Quintin F 100 A3
Quinto E 153 A3
Quinzano d'Oglio I . 120 B3
Quiroga E 141 B3
Quismondo E . . . 150 B3
Quissac F 131 B2
Quistello I . . . 121 B3

R

Raab A 96 C1
Raabs an der Thaya A. 97 C3
Raahe FIN 3 D9
Raajärvi FIN . . . 197 C9

Raalte NL. 71 B3
Raamsdonksveer NL. 79 A4
Raanujarvi FIN . . . 196 C7
Raattama FIN. . . 196 A7
Rab HR. 123 C3
Rábade E 140 A3
Rábafüzes H 111 C3
Rábahidvég H 111 B3
Rábanales E . . . 149 A3
Rábapatona H 111 B4
Rabapordány H 111 B4
Rabastens F . . . 129 C4
Rabastens-de-Bigorre F. 145 A4
Rabat = Victoria M. 175 C3
Rabat M 175 C3
Rabča SK 99 B3
Rabe SRB 126 A2
Rabi CZ 96 B1
Rabino PL 67 C4
Rabka PL 99 B3
Rabrovo SRB. . . . 127 C3
Rača SRB. 127 C3
Rácale I 173 C4
Rácalmás H 112 B2
Racalmuto I . . . 176 B2
Racconigi I . . . 119 C4
Rače SLO 123 A4
Rachecourt-sur-Marne F. 91 C5
Raciąż PL. 77 B5
Racibórz PL. . . . 86 B2
Račinovci HR . . . 125 C4
Ráckeve H 112 B2
Racławice PL 87 B4
Racławice Śląskie PL. 86 B1
Racot PL 75 B5
Råda
 Skaraborg S. . . . 55 B4
 Värmland S 49 B5
Radalj SRB . . . 127 C1
Rădăuți RO 17 B6
Radda in Chianti I . 135 B4
Raddusa I 177 B3
Radeberg D 84 A1
Radebeul D 84 A1
Radeburg D 84 A1
Radeče SLO . . . 123 A4
Radekhiv UA 13 C6
Radenci SLO 111 C3
Radenthein A . . . 109 C4
Radevormwald D . . 80 A3
Radicófani I . . . 135 C4
Radicóndoli I 135 B4
Radišići BIH . . . 138 B3
Radizel SLO . . . 110 C2
Radków PL. 85 B4
Radlje ob Dravi SLO 110 C2
Radłów PL 87 B4
Radmer an der Stube A. 110 B1
Radnejaur S . . . 195 E9
Radnice CZ 96 B1
Radohova BIH . . . 138 A3
Radojevo SRB. . . 126 B2
Radolfzell D. . . . 107 B3
Radom PL 87 A5
Radomice PL . . . 77 B4
Radomin PL 77 A4
Radomsko PL . . . 86 A3
Radomyshl UA . . . 13 C8
Radomyśl Wielki PL 87 B5
Radošina SK 98 C1
Radošovce SK. . . . 98 C1
Radoszewice PL . . 86 A2
Radoszyce PL . . . 87 A4
Radotin CZ 96 B2
Radovets BG . . . 186 A1
Radoviš MK . . . 182 B4
Radovljica SLO . . . 123 A3
Radowo Wielkie PL. 75 A4
Radstadt A 109 B4
Radstock GB 43 A4
Raduša MK . . . 182 A3
Radviliškis LT 8 E3
Radzanów
 Mazowieckie PL. . .77 B5
 Mazowieckie PL. . .87 A4
Radziejów PL . . . 76 B3
Radziejowice PL . . 77 B5
Radzovce SK. 113 A3
Radzyń Chełmiński PL. 69 B3
Raeren B 80 B2
Raesfeld D 80 A2
Raffadali I 176 B2
Rafina GR 185 A4
Rafsbotn N . . . 192 B7
Ragachow BY . . . 13 B9
Ragály H 99 C4
Rågeleje DK 61 C2
Raglan GB 39 C4
Ragnitz A 110 C2
Ragusa I 177 C3
Rahden D 72 B1
Råholt N 48 B3
Raiano I 169 A3
Raigada E 141 B3
Rain D 94 C2
Rainbach im Mühlkreis A. 96 C2
Rainham GB 45 B4
Rairiz de Veiga E . . 140 B3

Raisdorf D 64 B3
Raisio FIN. 8 B3
Raiskio FIN . . . 197 D9
Raiva
 Aveiro P. 148 A1
 Coimbra P. 148 B1
Raja-Jooseppi FIN. 193 D12
Rajala FIN 197 B9
Rajcza PL 99 B3
Rajec SK 98 B2
Rájec-Jestřebi CZ . 97 B4
Rajecké Teplice SK . 98 B2
Rajevo Selo HR . . 125 C4
Rajhrad CZ 97 B4
Rajić HR. 124 B3
Rajka H 111 B4
Rakaca H 99 C4
Rakamaz H 113 A5
Rakek SLO 123 B3
Rakitovo BG . . . 183 B6
Rakkestad N 54 A2
Rákóczifalva H . . .113 B4
Rakoniewice PL . . . 75 B5
Raková SK 98 B2
Rakovac BIH . . . 125 B3
Rakovica HR . . . 123 C4
Rakovník CZ 96 A1
Rakow D 66 B2
Raków PL. 87 B5
Rakvere EST. 8 C5
Ralja SRB. 127 C2
Rälla S. 62 B4
Ramacastañas E . . 150 B2
Ramacca I 177 B3
Ramales de la Victoria E 143 A3
Ramberg N . . . 194 B4
Rambervillers F . . . 92 C2
Rambouillet F . . . 90 C1
Rambucourt F . . . 92 C1
Ramdala S 63 B3
Ramerupt F 91 C4
Ramingstein A . . . 109 B4
Ramirás E 140 B2
Ramiswil CH . . . 106 B2
Ramkvilla S 62 A2
Ramme DK 58 B1
Rämmen S 49 B6
Ramnäs S 56 A2
Ramnes N 54 A1
Râmnicu Vâlcea RO 17 C6
Ramonville-St Agne F. 129 C4
Rampside GB 36 B3
Ramsau D 109 B3
Ramsbeck D 81 A4
Ramsberg S 56 A1
Ramsele S 200 C2
Ramsey
 Cambridgeshire GB. 44 A3
 Isle of Man GB. . . .36 B2
Ramseycleuch GB . . 36 A3
Ramsgate GB 45 B5
Ramsjö S 200 D1
Ramstein-Meisenbach D 93 B3
Ramsund N . . . 194 B7
Ramundberget S. . 199 C9
Ramvik S 200 D3
Ranalt A 108 B2
Rånäs S 51 C5
Rånåsfoss N 48 B3
Rance F 91 A4
Ránchio I 135 B5
Randaberg N 52 A1
Randalstown GB . . . 27 B4
Randan F 117 A3
Randazzo I 177 B3
Rånddalen S . . . 199 C10
Randegg A. 110 A1
Randers DK 58 B3
Randijaur S . . . 196 C2
Randin E 140 C3
Randsverk N . . . 198 D6
Råneå S 196 D5
Rânes F 89 B3
Rångedala S 60 B3
Ranis D 82 B3
Rankweil A 107 B4
Rånnäväg S 60 B3
Rännelöv S 61 C3
Rannoch Station GB 34 B3
Ranovac SRB . . . 127 C3
Ransäter S 55 A4
Ransbach-Baumbach D 81 B3
Ransta S 56 A2
Ranttila FIN . . . 193 C9
Ranua FIN 197 D9
Ranum DK 58 B2
Ranvalhal P . . . 154 B1
Raon-l'Étape F . . . 92 C2
Ráossi I 121 B4
Rapallo I 134 A2
Rapla EST. 8 C4
Rapness GB 33 B4
Rapolano Terme I . 135 B4
Rapolla I 172 B1
Raposa P 154 B2
Rapperswil CH . . . 107 B3
Raša HR. 123 B3

Rasal E 145 B3
Rascafria E 151 B4
Rasdorf D 82 B1
Raseiniai LT 13 A5
Rašica SLO 123 B3
Rasines E 143 A3
Rasquera E . . . 153 A4
Rássina I 135 B4
Rastatt D 93 C4
Rastede D 71 A5
Rastenberg D 82 A3
Rastošnica BIH . . 125 C4
Rastovac MNE . . . 139 C4
Rasueros E . . . 150 A2
Rasy PL 86 A3
Raszków PL 86 A2
Rätan S 199 C11
Rateče SLO 109 C4
Ratekau D 65 C3
Ratež SLO 123 B4
Rathangan IRL . . . 30 A2
Rathcoole IRL . . . 30 A2
Rathcormack IRL . . 29 B3
Rathdrum IRL . . . 30 B2
Rathebur D 74 A2
Rathenow D. 73 B5
Rathfriland GB . . . 27 B4
Rathkeale IRL . . . 29 B3
Rathmelton IRL . . . 27 A3
Rathmolyon IRL . . . 30 A2
Rathmore IRL . . . 29 B2
Rathmullan IRL . . . 27 A3
Rathnew IRL 30 B2
Rathvilly IRL 30 B2
Ratibořské Hory CZ 96 B2
Ratingen D 80 A2
Ratková SK 99 C4
Ratkovo SRB . . . 126 B1
Ratne UA 13 C6
Rattelsdorf D 94 A2
Ratten A 110 B2
Rattosjärvi FIN . . . 196 C7
Rattray GB 35 B4
Rättvik S 50 B2
Ratvika N 199 B7
Rätzlingen D 73 B4
Raucourt-et-Flaba F 91 B4
Raudeberg N . . . 198 D2
Raufarhöfn IS . . . 191 A10
Raufoss N 48 B2
Rauhala FIN . . . 196 B7
Rauland N 53 A4
Raulhac F 116 C2
Raulia N 195 E5
Rauma FIN. 8 B2
Raundal N 46 B3
Raunds GB 44 A3
Rauris A 109 B4
Rautas S 196 B2
Rautavaara FIN. . . .3 E11
Rauville-la-Bigot F . . 88 A2
Rauzan F 128 B2
Ravanusa I 176 B2
Rava-Rus'ka UA . . 13 C5
Ravča HR 138 B3
Ravels B 79 A4
Ravenglass GB . . . 36 B3
Ravenna I 135 A5
Ravensburg D . . . 107 B4
Rävemåla S 63 B3
Rävlanda S 60 B2
Ravna Gora HR . . 123 B3
Ravne na Koroškem SLO 110 C1
Ravnje SRB . . . 127 C1
Ravno BIH . . . 139 C3
Ravno Selo SRB . . 126 B1
Rawa Mazowiecka PL 87 A4
Rawicz PL 85 A4
Rawtenstall GB . . . 40 B1
Rayleigh GB 45 B4
Ražana SRB . . . 127 C1
Ražanac HR . . . 137 A4
Razboj BIH 124 B3
Razes F 115 B5
Razgrad BG 17 D7
Razkrižje SLO 111 C3
Razlog BG 183 B5
Razo E 140 A2
Reading GB 44 B3
Réalmont F . . . 130 B1
Rebais F 90 C3
Reboly RUS 3 E12
Rebordelo P. . . . 149 A2
Recanati I 136 B2
Recas E 151 B4
Recco I 134 A2
Recess IRL. 28 A2
Recey-sur-Ource F 105 B3
Recezinhos P . . . 148 A1
Rechnitz A 111 A1
Rechytsa BY 13 B9
Recke D 71 B4
Recklinghausen D . 80 A3
Recoaro Terme I . . 121 B4
Recogne B 92 B1
Recoules-Prévinquières F. 130 A1
Recz PL 75 A4
Reda PL 69 A3
Redalen N 48 B2
Redange L 92 B1
Redcar GB 37 B5
Redditch GB 44 A2

Redefin D 73 A4
Redhill GB 44 B3
Redics H 111 C3
Redkino RUS 9 D10
Redland GB 33 B3
Redlin D 73 A5
Red Point GB 31 B3
Redruth GB 42 B1
Redzikowo PL . . . 68 A2
Reepham GB 41 C5
Rees D 80 A2
Reeth GB 37 B5
Reetz D 73 A4
Reftele S 60 B3
Regalbuto I . . . 177 B3
Regen D 95 C5
Regensburg D . . . 95 B4
Regenstauf D 95 B4
Reggello I 135 B4
Réggio di Calábria I 175 C1
Réggio nell'Emília I 121 C3
Reghin RO 17 B6
Régil E 144 A1
Regna S 56 B1
Regniéville F 92 C1
Regny F 117 B4
Rego da Leirosa P. 154 A2
Regöly H 112 C2
Regueiro E . . . 140 B2
Reguengo
 Portalegre P. . . 155 B3
 Santarém P . . . 154 B2
Reguengos de Monsaraz P . . . 155 C3
Rehau D 83 B4
Rehburg D 72 B2
Rehden D 72 B1
Rehna D 65 C4
Reichelsheim D . . . 93 B4
Reichelshofen D . . 94 B2
Reichenau A 110 B2
Reichenbach
 Sachsen D 83 B4
 Sachsen D. 84 A2
Reichenfels A 110 B1
Reichensachsen D. 82 A2
Reichertshofen D . . 95 C3
Reichshoffen F . . . 93 C3
Reiden CH 106 B2
Reigada
 E. 141 A4
 P. 149 B3
Reigate GB 44 B3
Reillanne F 132 B1
Reillo E 158 B2
Reims F 91 B4
Reinach CH . . . 106 B3
Reinbek D 72 A3
Reinberg D 66 B2
Reine N 194 C4
Reinfeld D 65 C3
Reinheim D 93 B4
Reinli N 47 B6
Reinosa E 142 A2
Reinstorf D 65 C4
Reinsvoll N 48 B2
Reisach A 109 C4
Reiss GB 32 C3
Reitan N 199 C8
Reit im Winkl D . . 109 B3
Rejmyre S 56 B1
Rekavice BIH . . . 124 C3
Rekovac SRB . . . 127 D3
Relleu E 159 C3
Rém H 125 A5
Remagen D 80 B3
Rémalard F 89 B4
Rembercourt-aux-Pots F. 91 C5
Remedios P . . . 154 B1
Remels D 71 A4
Remetea Mare RO. 126 B3
Remich L 92 B2
Rémilly F 92 B2
Remiremont F . . . 105 A5
Remolinos E . . . 144 C2
Remoulins F . . . 131 B3
Remscheid D 80 A3
Rémuzat F 131 A4
Rena N 48 A3
Renaison F 117 A3
Renazé F 101 B4
Renchen D 93 C4
Rencurel F 118 B2
Rende I 174 B2
Rendina GR . . . 182 D3
Rendsburg D 64 B2
Renedo E 150 A3
Renens CH . . . 105 C5
Renfrew GB 34 C3
Rengsjö S 50 A3
Reni UA 17 C8
Rennebu N . . . 198 C6
Rennerod D 81 B4
Rennertshofen D . . 94 C3
Rennes F 101 A4
Rennes-les-Bains F. 146 B3
Rennweg A 109 B4
Rens DK 64 B2
Rensjön S 196 A2
Rentería E 144 A2

Rentjärn S 200 A4
Répcelak H 111 B4
Repojoki FIN . . . 193 D9
Repvåg N 193 B9
Requena E 159 B2
Réquista F 130 A1
Rerik D 65 B4
Resana I 121 B4
Resarö S 57 A4
Reschen = Résia I. 108 C1
Resen MK 182 B3
Resende P 148 A2
Résia = Reschen I. 108 C1
Reşiţa
 RO. 16 C4
 RO 126 B3
Resko PL 67 C4
Resnik SRB . . . 127 C2
Ressons-sur-Matz F 90 B2
Restábal E 163 B4
Resuttano I . . . 177 B3
Retamal E 155 C4
Retford GB. 40 B3
Rethel F 91 B4
Rethem D 72 B2
Rethimno GR. . . . 185 D5
Retie B 79 A5
Retiers F 101 B4
Retortillo E 149 B3
Retortillo de Soria E 151 A4
Retournac F. 117 B4
Rétság H 112 B3
Rettenegg A 110 B2
Retuerta del Bullaque E. 157 A3
Retz A 97 C3
Retzbach D 94 B1
Reuden D 73 B5
Reuilly F 103 B4
Reus E 147 C2
Reusel NL 79 A5
Reuterstadt Stavenhagen D . . . 74 A1
Reuth D 95 B4
Reutlingen D 94 C1
Reutte A 108 B1
Reuver NL 80 A2
Revel F 146 A2
Revello I 119 C4
Revenga E 151 B3
Revest-du-Bion F . 132 A1
Révfülöp H 111 C4
Revigny-sur-Ornain F. 91 C4
Revin F 91 B4
Řevnice CZ 96 B2
Řevničov CZ 84 B1
Revo I 121 A4
Revsnes N 47 A4
Revúca SK 99 C4
Rewa PL 69 A3
Rewal PL 67 B4
Rexbo S 50 B2
Reyðarfjörður IS . .191 B11
Reyero E 142 B1
Reykhólar IS . . . 190 B3
Reykholt
 Árnessýsla IS . . .190 C5
 Borgarfjarðarsýsla IS. 190 C4
Reykjahlið IS . . . 191 B9
Reykjavík IS. . . . 190 C4
Rezé F 101 B4
Rēzekne LV 8 D5
Rezovo BG 17 E8
Rezzato I 120 B3
Rhade D 72 A2
Rhaunen D 93 B3
Rhayader GB 39 B3
Rheda-Wiedenbrück D 81 A4
Rhede
 Niedersachsen D . .71 A4
 Nordrhein-Westfalen D. 80 A2
Rheinau D 93 C3
Rheinbach D 80 B2
Rheinberg D 80 A2
Rheine D 71 B4
Rheinfelden D . . . 106 B2
Rheinsberg D 74 A1
Rhêmes-Notre-Dame I. 119 B4
Rhenen NL 70 C2
Rhens D 81 B3
Rheydt D 80 A2
Rhiconich GB 32 C2
Rhinow D 73 B5
Rhiw GB 38 B2
Rho I 120 B2
Rhodes GR . . . 188 C3
Rhondda GB 39 C3
Rhosllanerchrugog GB 38 A3
Rhosneigr GB . . . 38 A2
Rhossili GB 39 C2
Rhubodach GB . . . 34 C2
Rhuddlan GB 38 A3
Rhyl GB 38 A3
Rhynie GB 33 D4
Riala S 57 A4
Riallé F 101 B4
Riaño E 142 B1
Riano I 168 A2
Rians F 132 B1
Rianxo E 140 B2

Riaza E 151 A4
Riba E 143 A3
Ribadavia E 140 B2
Ribadeo E 141 A3
Riba de Saelices E 152 B1
Ribadesella E . . . 142 A1
Ribaflecha E 143 B4
Ribaforada E 144 C2
Ribare SRB 127 C3
Riba-roja d'Ebre E . 153 A4
Riba-Roja de Turia
  E 159 B3
Ribe DK 59 C1
Ribeauvillé F 106 A2
Ribécourt-Dreslincourt
  F 90 B2
Ribeira da Pena P . 148 B2
Ribeira de Piquín
  E 141 A3
Ribemont F 91 B3
Ribera I 176 B2
Ribérac F 129 A3
Ribera de Cardós
  E 146 B2
Ribera del Fresno
  E 156 B1
Ribesalbes E 159 A3
Ribes de Freser E . 147 B3
Ribiers F 132 A1
Ribnica
  BIH 139 A4
  SLO 123 B3
Ribnica na Potorju
  SLO 110 C2
Ribnik HR 123 B4
Ribniţa MD 17 B8
Ribnitz-Damgarten
  D 66 B1
Ribolla I 135 C4
Říčany CZ 97 B4
Ričany CZ 96 B2
Riccia I 170 B2
Riccione I 136 A1
Ricco Del Golfo I . . 134 A2
Richebourg F 105 A4
Richelieu F 102 B2
Richisau CH 107 B3
Richmond
  Greater London
  GB 44 B3
  North Yorkshire GB . 37 B5
Richtenberg D 66 B1
Richterswil CH . . . 107 B3
Rickling D 64 B3
Rickmansworth GB . 44 B3
Ricla E 152 A2
Riddarhyttan S . . . 50 C2
Ridderkerk NL 79 A4
Riddes CH 119 A4
Ridjica SRB 125 B5
Riec-sur-Bélon F . . 100 B2
Ried A 109 A4
Riedenburg D 95 C3
Ried im Oberinntal
  A 108 B1
Riedlingen D 107 A4
Riedstadt D 93 B4
Riegersburg A . . . 110 C2
Riego de la Vega E 141 B5
Riego del Camino
  E 149 A4
Riello E 141 B5
Riemst B 80 B1
Rienne B 91 B4
Riénsena E 142 A2
Riesa D 83 A5
Riese Pio X I 121 B4
Riesi I 177 B3
Riestedt D 82 A3
Rietberg D 81 A4
Rieti I 169 A2
Rietschen D 84 A2
Rieumes F 146 A2
Rieupeyroux F 130 A1
Rieux-Volvestre F . 146 A2
Riez F 132 B2
Rīga LV 8 D4
Riggisberg CH . . . 106 C2
Rignac F 130 A1
Rignano Gargánico
  I 171 B3
Rigolato I 109 C3
Rigside GB 36 A3
Rigutino I 135 B4
Riihimäki FIN 8 B4
Rijeka HR 123 B3
Rijen NL 79 A4
Rijkevorsel B 79 A4
Rijssen NL 71 B3
Rila BG 183 A5
Rilić BIH 138 B3
Rilievo I 176 B1
Rillé F 102 B2
Rillo de Gallo E . . 152 B2
Rimavská Baňa SK . 99 C3
Rimavská Seč SK . 99 C4
Rimavská Sobota
  SK 99 C4
Rimbo S 57 A4
Rimforsa S 56 B1
Rímini I 136 A1
Rîmnicu Sărat RO . . 17 C7
Rimogne F 91 B4
Rimpar D 94 B1
Rimske Toplice
  SLO 123 A4
Rincón de la Victoria
  E 163 B3

Rincón de Soto E . 144 B2
Rindal N 198 B6
Rinde N 46 A3
Ringarum S 56 B2
Ringaskiddy IRL . . 29 C3
Ringe DK 59 C3
Ringebu N 48 A2
Ringkøbing DK . . . 59 B1
Ringsaker N 48 B2
Ringsted DK 61 D1
Ringwood GB 44 C2
Rinkaby S 63 C2
Rinkabyholm S . . . 63 B4
Rinlo E 141 A3
Rinn A 108 B2
Rinteln D 72 B2
Rio E 140 B3
Riobo E 140 B2
Riodeva E 152 B2
Rio do Coures P . . 154 B2
Rio Douro P 148 A2
Riofrio E 150 B3
Riofrio de Aliste E . 149 A3
Rio frio de Riaza E 151 A4
Riogordo E 163 B3
Rioja E 164 C2
Riola I 135 A4
Riola Sardo I 179 C2
Riolobos E 155 B4
Riom F 116 B3
Riomaggiore I 134 A2
Rio Maior P 154 B2
Rio Marina I 134 C3
Riom-ès-Montagnes
  F 116 B2
Rion-des-Landes
  F 128 C2
Rionegro del Puente
  E 141 B4
Rionero in Vúlture
  I 172 B1
Riopar E 158 C1
Riós E 141 C3
Rioseco E 142 A1
Rioseco de Tapia
  E 141 B5
Rio Tinto P 148 A1
Riotord F 117 B4
Riotorto E 141 A3
Rioz F 105 B5
Ripač BIH 124 C1
Ripacándida I 172 B1
Ripanj SRB 127 C2
Ripatransone I 136 C2
Ripley GB 40 B2
Ripoll E 147 B3
Ripon GB 40 A2
Riposto I 177 B4
Ripsa S 56 B2
Risan MNE 16 D3
Risbäck S 200 B1
Risca GB 39 C3
Rischenau D 81 A5
Riscle F 128 C2
Risnes N 46 A2
Rišňovce SK 98 C1
Risør N 53 B5
Risøyhamn N 194 B6
Rissna S 199 B12
Ritsem S 194 C8
Ritterhude D 72 A1
Riutula FIN 193 D10
Riva del Garda I . . 121 B3
Riva Ligure I 133 B3
Rivanazzano I 120 C2
Rivarolo Canavese
  I 119 B4
Rivarolo Mantovano
  I 121 B3
Rive-de-Gier F . . . 117 B4
Rivedoux-Plage F . 114 B2
Rivello I 174 A1
Rivergaro I 120 C2
Rives F 118 B2
Rivesaltes F 146 B3
Rivignano I 122 B2
Rivne UA 13 C7
Rívoli I 119 B4
Rivolta d'Adda I . . 120 B2
Rixheim F 106 B2
Rixo S 54 B2
Riza GR 183 C5
Rizokarpaso CY . . 181 A3
Rjukan N 47 C5
Rø DK 67 A3
Rö S 57 A4
Roa
  E 143 C3
  N 48 B2
Roade GB 44 A3
Roager DK 59 C1
Roaldkvam N 52 A2
Roanne F 117 A4
Röbäck S 200 C6
Robakowo PL 69 B3
Róbbio I 120 B1
Röbel D 73 A5
Roberton GB 35 C5
Robertsfors S . . . 200 B6
Robertville B 80 B2
Robin Hood's Bay
  GB 37 B6
Robleda E 149 B3
Robledillo de Trujillo
  E 156 A2

Robledo
  Albacete E 158 C1
  Orense E 141 B4
Robledo de Chavela
  E 151 B3
Robledo del Buey
  E 156 A3
Robledo del Mazo
  E 156 A3
Robledollano E . . . 156 A2
Robles de la Valcueva
  E 142 B1
Robliza de Cojos E 149 B4
Robres E 145 C3
Robres del Castillo
  E 144 B1
Rocafort de Queralt
  E 147 C2
Rocamadour F . . . 129 B4
Roccabernarda I . . 175 B2
Roccabianca I 120 B3
Roccadáspide I . . . 172 B1
Rocca di Mezzo I . . 169 A3
Rocca di Papa I . . . 168 B2
Roccagorga I 169 B3
Rocca Imperiale I . . 174 A2
Roccalbegna I 135 C4
Roccalumera I 177 B4
Roccamena I 176 B2
Roccamonfina I . . . 170 B1
Roccanova I 174 A2
Roccapalumba I . . . 176 B2
Roccapassa I 169 A3
Rocca Priora I 136 B2
Roccaraso I 169 B4
Rocca San Casciano
  I 135 A4
Roccasecca I 169 B3
Rocca Sinibalda I . 169 A2
Roccastrada I 135 B4
Roccatederighi I . . 135 B4
Roccella Iónica I . . 175 C2
Rocchetta Sant'António
  I 172 A1
Rocester GB 40 C2
Rochdale GB 40 B1
Rochechouart F . . 115 C4
Rochefort
  B 79 B5
  F 114 C3
Rochefort-en-Terre
  F 101 B3
Rochefort-Montagne
  F 116 B2
Rochefort-sur-Nenon
  F 105 B4
Roche-lez-Beaupré
  F 105 B5
Rochemaure F . . . 131 A3
Rocheservière F . . 114 B2
Rochester
  Medway GB 45 B4
  Northumberland
  GB 37 A4
Rochlitz D 83 A4
Rociana del Condado
  E 161 B3
Rockenhausen D . . 93 B3
Rockhammar S . . . 56 A1
Rockneby S 62 B4
Ročko Polje HR . . . 123 B3
Ročov CZ 84 B1
Rocroi F 91 B4
Rodach D 82 B2
Roda de Bara E . . 147 C2
Roda de Ter E . . . 147 C3
Rodalben D 93 B3
Rødberg N 47 B5
Rødby DK 65 B4
Rødbyhavn DK . . . 65 B4
Rødding
  Sonderjyllands Amt.
  DK 59 C2
  Viborg Amt. DK . . 58 B1
Rödeby S 63 B3
Rodeiro E 140 B3
Rødekro DK 64 A2
Roden NL 71 A3
Ródenas E 152 B2
Rodenkirchen D . . 72 A1
Rödental D 82 B3
Rödermark D 93 B4
Rodewisch D 83 B4
Rodez F 130 A1
Rodi Gargánico I . . 171 B3
Roding D 95 B4
Rödjebro S 51 B4
Rødkærsbro DK . . 59 B2
Rodolivas GR 183 C5
Rodoñá E 147 C2
Rødvig DK 65 A5
Roermond NL 80 A1
Roesbrugge B 78 B2
Roeschwoog F . . . 93 C4
Roeselare B 78 B3
Roetgen D 80 B2
Roffiac F 116 B3
Röfors S 55 B5
Rofrano I 172 B1
Rogač HR 138 B2
Rogačica SRB . . . 127 C1
Rogaška Slatina
  SLO 123 A4
Rogatec SLO 123 A4
Rogatica BIH 139 B5
Rogatyn UA 13 D6
Rogätz D 73 B4

Roggendorf D 65 C4
Roggiano Gravina
  I 174 B2
Roghadal GB 31 B2
Rogliano
  F 180 A2
  I 175 B2
Rognan N 195 C6
Rogne N 47 A6
Rognes F 131 B4
Rogny-les-7-Ecluses
  F 103 B4
Rogowo PL 76 B2
Roggznica HR . . . 138 B1
Rogoźnica PL 85 A4
Rogoźno PL 76 B2
Rohan F 101 A3
Röhlingen D 94 C2
Rohožník SK 98 C1
Rohr D 82 B2
Rohrbach-lès-Bitche
  F 92 B3
Rohrberg D 73 B4
Rohr im Gebirge A. 110 B2
Rohrnbach D 96 C1
Roisel F 90 B3
Roja LV 8 D3
Rojales E 165 A4
Rojewo PL 76 B3
Rokiciny PL 87 A3
Rokietnica PL 75 B5
Rokiškis LT 8 E4
Rokitki PL 85 A3
Rokycany CZ 96 B1
Rolampont F 105 B4
Rold DK 58 B2
Røldal N 52 A2
Rolde NL 71 B3
Rolfs S 196 D6
Rollag N 47 B6
Rollán E 149 B4
Rolle CH 105 C5
Roma = Roma I . . . 168 B2
Roma S 57 C4
Romagnano Sésia
  I 119 B5
Romagné F 88 B2
Romakloster S . . . 57 C4
Roman RO 17 B7
Romana I 178 B2
Romanèche-Thorins
  F 117 A4
Romano di Lombardia
  I 120 B2
Romanshorn CH . . 107 B4
Romans-sur-Isère
  F 118 B2
Rombas F 92 B2
Rome = Roma I . . . 168 B2
Romeán E 141 B3
Romenay F 105 C4
Romeral E 157 A4
Römerstein D 94 C1
Rometta I 177 A4
Romford GB 45 B4
Romhány H 112 B3
Römhild D 82 B2
Romilly-sur-Seine F 91 C3
Romont CH 106 C1
Romorantin-Lanthenay
  F 103 B3
Romrod D 81 B5
Romsey GB 44 C2
Rømskog N 54 A2
Rønbjerg DK 58 B1
Roncal E 144 B3
Ronce-les-Bains F . 114 C2
Ronchamp F 106 B1
Ronchi dei Legionari
  I 122 B2
Ronciglione I 168 A2
Ronco Canavese I . 119 B4
Ronco Scrivia I . . . 120 C1
Ronda E 162 B2
Rønde DK 59 B3
Rone S 57 C4
Ronehamn S 57 C4
Rong N 46 B1
Rönnäng S 60 B1
Ronneburg D 83 B4
Ronneby S 63 B3
Rönneshytta S . . . 55 B6
Rönninge S 57 A3
Rönnöfors S 199 B10
Rönö S 56 B2
Ronov nad Doubravou
  CZ 97 B3
Ronse B 79 B3
Roosendaal NL . . . 79 A4
Roosky IRL 26 C3
Ropczyce PL 87 B5
Ropeid N 52 A2
Ropinsalmi FIN . . 192 D5
Ropuelos del Páramo
  E 141 B5
Roquebilière F . . . 133 A3
Roquebrun F 130 B2
Roquecourbe F . . . 130 B1
Roquefort F 128 B2
Roquemaure F . . . 131 A3
Roquesteron F . . . 132 B3
Roquetas de Mar
  E 164 C2
Roquetes E 153 B4
Roquevaire F 132 B1

Røra N 199 B8
Rörbäcksnäs S . . . 49 A4
Rørbæk DK 58 B2
Rore BIH 138 A2
Røro S 60 B1
Røros N 199 C8
Rørvig DK 61 D1
Rørvik N 199 A8
Rörvik S 62 A2
Rosà I 121 B4
Rosal de la Frontera
  E 161 B2
Rosalina Mare I . . 122 B1
Rosa Marina I 173 B3
Rosans F 132 A1
Rosário P 160 B1
Rosarno I 175 C1
Rosbach D 81 B3
Rosche D 73 B3
Rościszewo PL . . . 77 B4
Roscoff F 100 A2
Roscommon IRL . . 28 A3
Roscrea IRL 28 B4
Rosdorf D 82 A1
Rose I 174 B2
Rosegg A 109 C5
Rosehall GB 32 D2
Rosehearty GB . . . 33 D4
Rosel GB 88 A1
Rosell E 153 B4
Roselló E 153 A4
Rosendal N 46 C3
Rosenfeld D 93 C4
Rosenforsa S 62 A3
Rosenheim D 108 B3
Rosenow D 74 A2
Rosenthal D 81 A4
Rosersberg S 57 A3
Roses E 147 B4
Roseto degli Abruzzi
  I 169 A4
Roseto Valfortore I 170 B2
Rosheim F 93 C3
Rosia I 135 B4
Rosice CZ 97 B4
Rosières-en-Santerre
  F 90 B2
Rosignano Maríttimo
  I 134 B3
Rosignano Solvay
  I 134 B3
Roşiori-de-Vede RO 17 C6
Roskhill GB 31 B2
Roskilde DK 61 D2
Roskovec AL 182 C1
Röslau D 83 B3
Roslev DK 58 B1
Rosmaninhal P . . . 155 B3
Rosnowo PL 67 B5
Rosolini I 177 C3
Rosova MNE 139 B5
Rosoy F 104 A2
Rosporden F 100 B2
Rosquete P 154 B2
Rosrath D 80 B3
Rossa CH 120 A2
Rossano I 174 B2
Rossas
  Aveiro P 148 B1
  Braga P 148 A1
Rossdorf D 82 B2
Rossett GB 38 A4
Rosshaupten D . . . 108 B1
Rossiglione I 133 A4
Rossignol B 92 B1
Rossla D 82 A3
Rosslare IRL 30 B2
Rosslare Harbour
  IRL 30 B2
Rosslau D 83 A4
Rosslea GB 27 B3
Rossleben D 82 A3
Rossön S 200 C2
Ross-on-Wye GB . . 39 C4
Rossoszyca PL . . . 86 A2
Rosswein D 83 A5
Röstånga S 61 C3
Roštár SK 99 C4
Rostock D 65 B5
Rostrenen F 100 A2
Røsvik N 194 C6
Rosvik S 196 D4
Rosyth GB 35 B4
Röszke H 126 A2
Rot S 49 A6
Rota E 161 C3
Rota Greca I 174 B2
Rot am See D 94 B2
Rotberget N 49 B4
Rotella I 136 C2
Rotenburg
  Hessen D 82 B1
  Niedersachsen D . 72 A2
Roth
  Bayern D 94 B3
  Rheinland-Pfalz D . 81 B3
Rothbury GB 37 A5
Rothemühl D 74 A2
Röthenbach D 95 B3
Rothenburg D 84 A2
Rothenburg ob der
  Tauber D 94 B2
Rothéneuf F 88 B2
Rothenklempenow
  D 74 A3
Rothenstein D 94 C3
Rotherham GB . . . 40 B2

Ria–Ruc 269

Rothes GB 32 D3
Rothesay GB 34 C2
Rothwell GB 44 A3
Rotnes N 48 B2
Rotonda I 174 B2
Rotondella I 174 A2
Rotova E 159 C3
Rott
  Bayern D 108 B1
  Bayern D 108 B3
Rottach-Egern D . . 108 B2
Röttenbach D 94 B3
Rottenbach D 108 B3
Rottenburg
  Baden-Württemberg
  D 93 C4
  Bayern D 95 C4
Rottenmann A . . . 110 B1
Rotterdam NL 79 A4
Rotthalmünster D . 96 C1
Rottingdean GB . . 44 C3
Röttingen D 94 B1
Rottleberode D . . . 82 A2
Rottne S 62 A2
Rottneros S 55 A4
Rottofreno I 120 B2
Rottweil D 107 A3
Rötz D 95 B4
Roubaix F 78 B3
Roudnice nad Labem
  CZ 84 B2
Roudouallec F . . . 100 A2
Rouen F 89 A5
Rouffach F 106 B2
Rougé F 101 B4
Rougemont F . . . 105 B5
Rougemont le-Château
  F 106 B1
Rouillac F 115 C3
Rouillé F 115 B4
Roujan F 130 B2
Roulans F 105 B5
Roundwood IRL . . 30 A2
Rousínov CZ 97 B4
Roussac F 115 B5
Roussennac F . . . 130 A1
Rousses F 130 A2
Roussillon F 117 B4
Rouvroy-sur-Audry
  F 91 B4
Rouy F 104 B2
Rovaniemi
  maalaiskunta FIN 197 C8
Rovaniemi FIN. . . 197 C8
Rovato I 120 B2
Rovensko pod Troskami
  CZ 84 B3
Roverbella I 121 B3
Rovereto I 121 B4
Rövershagen D . . . 65 B5
Roverud N 49 B4
Rovigo I 121 B4
Rovinj HR 122 B2
Rovišce HR 124 B2
Rów PL 74 B3
Rowy PL 68 A2
Royal Leamington Spa
  GB 44 A2
Royal Tunbridge Wells
  GB 45 B4
Royan F 114 C2
Royat F 116 B3
Roybon F 118 B2
Roybridge GB 34 B3
Roye F 90 B2
Royère-de-Vassivière
  F 116 B1
Røykenvik N 48 B2
Royos E 164 B2
Røyrvik N 199 A10
Royston GB 44 A3
Rozadas E 141 A4
Rozalén del Monte
  E 151 C5
Rózańsko PL 75 B3
Rozay-en-Brie F . . 90 C2
Roždalovice CZ . . 84 B3
Rozdilna UA 17 B9
Rozental PL 69 B4
Rozhyshche UA . . 13 C6
Rožmitál pod
  Třemšínem CZ . . 96 B1
Rožňava SK 99 C4
Rožnov pod Radhoštěm
  CZ 98 B2
Rozoy-sur-Serre F . 91 B4
Rozprza PL 86 A3
Roztoky CZ 84 B2
Rozvadov CZ 95 B4
Rozzano I 120 B2
Rrëshen AL 182 B1
Rrogozhine AL . . . 182 B1
Ruanes E 156 A2
Rubbestadnesset N 46 C2
Rubi E 147 C3
Rubiá E 141 B4
Rubiacedo de Abajo
  E 143 B3
Rubielos Bajos E . 158 B1
Rubielos de Mora
  E 153 B3
Rubiera I 121 C3
Rubik AL 182 B1
Rucandio E 143 B3

270 Rud–St J

Rud
Akershus N 48 B3
Buskerud N 48 B2
Ruda
PL 86 A2
S 62 A4
Rudabánya H 99 C4
Ruda Maleniecka
PL 87 A4
Ruda Pilczycka PL 87 A4
Ruda Śl. PL 86 B2
Ruddervorde B 78 A3
Ruden A 110 C1
Rudersberg D 94 C1
Rudersdorf A 111 B3
Rüdersdorf D 74 B2
Ruderting D 96 C1
Rüdesheim D 93 B3
Rudkøbing DK 65 B3
Rudmanns A 97 C3
Rudna
CZ 96 A2
PL 85 A4
Rudnik SRB 127 C2
Rudniki
Opolskie PL 86 A2
Śląskie PL 86 B3
Rudno
Dolnośląskie PL 85 A4
Pomorskie PL 69 B3
Rudnya RUS 13 A9
Rudolstadt D 82 B3
Rudowica PL 84 A3
Rudozem BG 183 B6
Rudskoga S 55 A5
Rudston GB 40 A3
Ruds Vedby DK 61 D1
Rudy PL 86 B2
Rue F 78 B1
Rueda E 150 A3
Rueda de Jalón E 152 A2
Ruelle-sur-Touvre
F 115 C4
Ruerrero E 143 B3
Ruffano I 173 C4
Ruffec F 115 B4
Rufina I 135 B4
Rugby GB 44 A2
Rugeley GB 40 C2
Ruggstrop S 62 B4
Rugles F 89 B4
Rugozero RUS 3 D13
Rühen D 73 B3
Ruhla D 82 B2
Ruhland D 84 A1
Ruhle D 71 B4
Ruhpolding D 109 B3
Ruhstorf D 96 C1
Ruidera E 158 C1
Ruillé-sur-le-Loir F 102 B2
Ruinen NL 71 B3
Ruiselede B 78 A3
Ruka FIN 197 C12
Rulles B 92 B1
Rülzheim D 93 B4
Rum H 111 B3
Ruma SRB 127 B1
Rumboci BIH 138 B3
Rumburk CZ 84 B2
Rumenka SRB 126 B1
Rumia PL 69 A3
Rumigny F 91 B4
Rumilly F 118 B2
Rumma S 56 B2
Rumney GB 39 C3
Rumont F 91 C5
Runa P 154 B1
Runcorn GB 38 A4
Rundmoen N 195 D5
Rungsted DK 61 D2
Runhällen S 51 B3
Runowo PL 69 A5
Runtuna S 56 B3
Ruokojärvi FIN 196 B7
Ruokolahti FIN 9 B6
Ruokto S 196 B2
Ruoms F 131 A3
Ruoti I 172 B1
Rupa HR 123 B3
Ruppichteroth D 80 B3
Rupt-sur-Moselle
F 106 B1
Rus E 157 B4
Ruse BG 17 D7
Ruše SLO 110 C2
Rusele S 200 B4
Ruševo HR 125 B4
Rush IRL 30 A2
Rushden GB 44 A3
Rusiec PL 86 A2
Rusinowo
Zachodnio-Pomorskie
PL 67 C4
Zachodnio-Pomorskie
PL 75 A5
Ruskele S 200 B4
Ruski Krstur SRB 126 B1
Ruskington GB 40 B3
Rusovce SK 111 A4
Rüsselsheim D 93 B4
Russelv N 192 C4
Russi I 135 A5
Rust A 111 B3
Rustefjelbma N 193 B12
Rustrel F 131 B4
Ruszki PL 77 B5
Ruszów PL 84 A3
Rute E 163 A3
Rüthen D 81 A4
Rutherglen GB 35 C3
Ruthin GB 38 A3
Ruthven GB 32 D2
Ruthwell GB 36 B3
Rüti CH 107 B3
Rutigliano I 173 A3
Rutledal N 46 A2
Rutvik S 196 D5
Ruurlo NL 71 B3
Ruuvaoja FIN 197 B11
Ruvo del Monte I 172 B1
Ruvo di Púglia I 171 B4
Ruynes-en-Margeride
F 116 C3
Ružic HR 138 B2
Ružomberok SK 99 B3
Ruzsa H 126 A1
Ry DK 59 B2
Rybany SK 98 C2
Rybina PL 69 A4
Rybnik PL 86 B2
Rychliki PL 69 B4
Rychlocice PL 86 A2
Rychnov nad Kněžnou
CZ 85 B4
Rychnowo PL 77 A5
Rychtal PL 86 A1
Rychwał PL 76 B3
Ryczywół PL 87 A5
Ryczywól PL 75 B5
Ryd S 63 B2
Rydaholm S 62 B2
Rydal S 60 B2
Rydbo S 57 A4
Rydboholm S 60 B2
Ryde GB 44 C2
Rydöbruk S 60 C3
Rydsgård S 66 A2
Rydsnäs S 62 A3
Rydultowy PL 86 B2
Rydzyna PL 85 A4
Rye GB 45 C4
Rygge N 54 A1
Ryjewo PL 69 B3
Rykene N 53 B4
Rymań PL 67 C4
Rýmařov CZ 98 B1
Rynarzewo PL 76 A2
Ryomgård DK 59 B3
Rypefjord N 192 B7
Rypin PL 77 A4
Rysjedalsvika N 46 A2
Ryssby S 60 C4
Rytel PL 68 B2
Rytinki FIN 197 D10
Rytro PL 99 B4
Rywociny PL 77 A5
Rzeczenica PL 68 B2
Rzeczniów PL 87 A5
Rzeczyca PL 87 A4
Rzęgnowo PL 77 A5
Rzejowice PL 87 A3
Rzemień PL 87 B5
Rzepin PL 75 B3
Rzesznikowo PL 67 C4
Rzeszów PL 12 C4
Rzgów PL 86 A3
Rzhev RUS 9 D9

S

Saal
Bayern D 82 B2
Bayern D 95 C3
Saalbach A 109 B3
Saalburg D 83 B3
Saales F 92 C3
Saalfeld D 82 B3
Saalfelden am
Steinernen Meer
A 109 B3
Saanen CH 106 C2
Saarbrücken D 92 B2
Saarburg D 92 B2
Saarijärvi FIN 8 A4
Saari-Kämä FIN 197 C9
Saarlouis D 92 B2
Saas-Fee CH 119 A4
Šabac SRB 127 C1
Sabadell E 147 C3
Sabáudia I 169 B3
Sabbioneta I 121 C3
Sabero E 142 B1
Sabiñánigo E 145 B3
Sabiote E 157 B4
Sables-d'Or-les-Pins
F 101 A3
Sablé-sur-Sarthe F 102 B1
Sabóia P 160 B1
Saborsko HR 123 B4
Sæbøvik N 52 A1
Sabres F 128 B2
Sabrosa P 148 A2
Sabugal P 149 B2
Sabuncu TR 187 C5
Sæby DK 58 A3
Săcălaz RO 126 B3
Sacecorbo E 152 B1
Saceda del Rio E 151 B5
Sacedón E 151 B5
Săcele RO 17 C6
Saceruela E 156 B3
Sachsenburg A 109 C4
Sachsenhagen D 72 B2
Sacile I 122 B1
Sacramenia E 151 A4
Sada E 140 A2
Sádaba E 144 B2
Saddell GB 34 C2
Sadernes E 147 B3
Sadki PL 76 A2
Sadkowice PL 87 A4
Sadlinki PL 69 B3
Sadów PL 75 B3
Sadská CZ 84 B2
Saelices E 151 C5
Saelices de Mayorga
E 142 B1
Saerbeck D 71 B4
Saeul L 92 B1
Safaalan TR 186 A3
Safara P 161 A2
Säffle S 55 A3
Saffron Walden GB 45 A4
Safranbolu TR 187 A7
Säfsnäs S 50 B1
Şag RO 126 B3
Sagard D 66 B2
S'Agaro E 147 C4
Sågmyra S 50 B2
Sagone F 180 A1
Sagres P 160 C1
Ságújfalu H 113 A3
Sagunt E 159 B3
Sagvåg N 52 A1
Ságvár H 112 C2
Sagy F 105 C4
Sahagún E 142 B1
Šahy SK 112 A2
Saignelégier CH 106 B1
Saignes F 116 B2
Saija FIN 197 B11
Saillagouse F 146 B3
Saillans F 118 C2
Sains Richaumont
F 91 B3
St Abb's GB 35 C5
St Affrique F 130 B1
St Agnan F 104 C2
St Agnant F 114 C3
St Agnes GB 42 B1
St Agrève F 117 B4
St Aignan F 103 B3
St Aignan-sur-Roë
F 101 B4
St Albans GB 44 B3
St Alban-sur-Limagnole
F 117 C3
St Amand-en-Puisaye
F 104 B2
St Amand-les-Eaux
F 79 B3
St Amand-Longpré
F 103 B3
St Amand-Montrond
F 103 C4
St Amans F 117 C3
St Amans-Soult F 130 B1
St Amant-Roche-Savine
F 117 B3
St Amarin F 106 B1
St Ambroix F 131 A3
St Amé F 106 A1
St Amour F 118 A2
St André-de-Corcy
F 117 B4
St André-de-Cubzac
F 128 B2
St André-de-l'Eure
F 89 B5
St André-de-
Roquepertuis F 131 A3
St André-de-Sangonis
F 130 B2
St Andre-de-Valborgne
F 130 A2
St André-les-Alpes
F 132 B2
St Andrews GB 35 B5
St Angel F 116 B2
St Anthème F 117 B3
St Antoine F 180 A2
St Antoine-de-Ficalba
F 129 B3
St Antönien CH 107 C4
St Antonin-Noble-Val
F 129 B4
St Août F 103 C3
St Armant-Tallende
F 116 B3
St Arnoult F 90 C1
St Asaph GB 38 A3
St Astier F 129 A3
St Athan GB 39 C3
St Auban F 132 B2
St Aubin
CH 106 C1
F 105 B4
GB 88 A1
St Aubin-d'Aubigne
F 101 A4
St Aubin-du-Cormier
F 101 A4
St Aubin-sur-Aire F 92 C1
St Aubin-sur-Mer F 89 A3
St Aulaye F 128 A3
St Austell GB 42 B2
St Avit F 116 B2
St Avold F 92 B2
St Aygulf F 132 B2
St Bauzille-de-Putois
F 130 B2
St Béat F 145 B4
St Beauzély F 130 A1
St Bees GB 36 B3
St Benim-d'Azy F 104 C2
St Benoît-du-Sault
F 115 B5
St Benoit-en-Woëvre
F 92 C1
St Berthevin F 102 A1
St Blaise-la-Roche
F 92 C3
St Blazey GB 42 B2
St Blin F 105 A4
St Bonnet F 118 C3
St Bonnet Briance
F 115 C5
St Bonnet-de-Joux
F 104 C3
St Bonnet-le-Château
F 117 B4
St Bonnet-le-Froid
F 117 B4
St Brévin-les-Pins
F 101 B3
St Briac-sur-Mer F 101 A3
St Brice-en-Coglès
F 88 B2
St Brieuc F 101 A3
St Bris-le-Vineux F 104 B2
St Broladre F 88 B2
St Calais F 102 B2
St Cannat F 131 B4
St Cast-le-Guildo F 101 A3
St Céré F 129 B4
St Cergue CH 118 A3
St Cergues F 118 A3
St Cernin F 116 B2
St Chamant F 116 B1
St Chamas F 131 B4
St Chamond F 117 B4
St Chély-d'Apcher
F 116 C3
St Chély-d'Aubrac
F 116 C2
St Chinian F 130 B1
St Christol F 131 A4
St Christol-lès-Alès
F 131 A3
St Christoly-Médoc
F 114 C3
St Christophe-du-
Ligneron F 114 B2
St Christophe-en-
Brionnais F 117 A4
St Ciers-sur-Gironde
F 128 A2
St Clair-sur-Epte F 90 B1
St Clar F 129 C3
St Claud F 115 C4
St Claude F 118 A2
St Clears GB 39 C2
St Columb Major
GB 42 B2
St Come-d'Olt F 130 A1
St Cosme-en-Vairais
F 89 B4
St Cyprien
Dordogne F 129 B4
Pyrenées-Orientales
F 146 B4
St Cyr-sur-Loire F 102 B2
St Cyr-sur-Mer F 132 B1
St Cyr-sur-Methon
F 117 A4
St David's GB 39 C1
St Denis F 90 C2
St Denis-d'Oléron
F 114 B2
St Denis d'Orques
F 102 A1
St Didier F 117 A4
St Didier-en-Velay
F 117 B4
St Dié F 92 C2
St Dier-d'Auvergne
F 117 B3
St Dizier F 91 C4
St Dizier-Leyrenne
F 116 A1
St Dogmaels GB 39 B2
Ste Adresse F 89 A4
Ste Anne F 89 B4
Ste Anne-d'Auray
F 100 B3
Ste Croix CH 105 C5
Ste Croix-Volvestre
F 146 A2
Ste Engrâce F 144 A3
Ste Enimie F 130 A2
St Efflam F 100 A2
Ste Foy-de-Peyrolières
F 146 A2
Ste Foy-la-Grande
F 128 B3
Ste Foy l'Argentiere
F 117 B4
Ste Gauburge-Ste
Colombe F 89 B4
Ste Gemme la Plaine
F 114 B2
Ste Geneviève F 90 B2
St Égrève F 118 B2
Ste Hélène F 128 B2
Ste Hélène-sur-Isère
F 118 B3
Ste Hermine F 114 B2
Ste Jalle F 131 A4
Ste Livrade-sur-Lot
F 129 B3
St Eloy-les-Mines
F 116 A2
Ste Marie-aux-Mines
F 106 A2
Ste Marie-du-Mont
F 88 A2
Ste Maure-de-Touraine
F 102 B2
Ste Maxime F 132 B2
Ste Ménéhould F 91 B4
Ste Mère-Église F 88 A2
St Emiland F 104 C3
St Émilion F 128 B2
St Enoder GB 42 B2
Sainteny F 88 A2
Ste Ode B 92 A1
Saintes F 114 C3
Ste Savine F 91 C4
Ste Sévère-sur-Indre
F 103 C4
Ste Sigolène F 117 B4
St Esteben F 144 A2
St Estèphe F 128 A2
Ste Suzanne F 102 A1
St Étienne F 117 B4
St Etienne-de-Baigorry
F 144 A2
St Étienne-de-Cuines
F 118 B3
St Etienne-de-Fursac
F 116 A1
St Etienne-de-Montluc
F 101 B4
St Etienne-de-St Geoirs
F 118 B2
St Étienne-de-Tinée
F 132 A2
St Étienne-du-Bois
F 118 A2
St Étienne-du-Rouvray
F 89 A5
St Etienne-les-Orgues
F 132 A1
Ste Tulle F 132 B1
St Fargeau F 104 B2
St Félicien F 117 B4
St Felix-de-Sorgues
F 130 B1
St Félix-Lauragais
F 146 A2
Saintfield GB 27 B5
St Fillans GB 35 B3
St Firmin F 118 C3
St Florent F 180 A2
St Florentin F 104 B2
St Florent-le-Vieil
F 101 B4
St Florent-sur-Cher
F 103 C4
St Flour F 116 B3
St Flovier F 103 C3
St Fort-sur-le-Né F 115 C3
St Fulgent F 114 B2
St Galmier F 117 B4
St Gaudens F 145 A4
St Gaultier F 115 B5
St Gély-du-Fesc F 130 B2
St Genest-Malifaux
F 117 B4
St Gengoux-le-National
F 104 C3
St Geniez F 132 A2
St Geniez-d'Olt F 130 A1
St Genis-de-Saintonge
F 114 C3
St Genis-Pouilly F 118 A3
St Genix-sur-Guiers
F 118 B2
St Georges Buttavent
F 88 B3
St Georges-d'Aurac
F 117 B3
St Georges-de-
Commiers F 118 B2
St Georges-de-Didonne
F 114 C3
St Georges-de-
Luzençon F 130 A1
St Georges-de Mons
F 116 B2
St Georges-de-Reneins
F 117 A4
St Georges d'Oléron
F 114 C2
St Georges-en-Couzan
F 117 B3
St Georges-lès-
Baillargeaux F 115 B4
St Georges-sur-Loire
F 102 B1
St Georges-sur-Meuse
B 79 B5
St Geours-de-Maremne
F 128 C1
St Gérand-de-Vaux
F 117 A3
St Gérand-le-Puy
F 117 A3
St Germain F 105 B5
St Germain-Chassenay
F 104 C2
St Germain-de-Calberte
F 130 A2
St Germain-de-
Confolens F 115 B4
St Germain-de-Joux
F 118 A2
St Germain-des-Fossés
F 117 A3
St Germain-du-Bois
F 105 C4
St Germain-du-Plain
F 105 C3
St Germain-du Puy
F 103 B4
St Germain-en-Laye
F 90 C2
St Germain-Laval
F 117 B4
St Germain-Lembron
F 116 B3
St Germain-les-Belles
F 116 B1
St Germain-Lespinasse
F 117 A3
St Germain-l'Herm
F 117 B3
St Gervais-d'Auvergne
F 116 A2
St Gervais-les-Bains
F 118 B3
St Gervais-sur-Mare
F 130 B2
St Gildas-de-Rhuys
F 100 B3
St Gildas-des-Bois
F 101 B3
St Gilles
Gard F 131 B3
Ille-et-Vilaine F 101 A4
St Gilles-Croix-de-Vie
F 114 B2
St Gingolph F 119 A3
St Girons
Ariège F 146 B2
Landes F 128 C1
St Girons-Plage F 128 C1
St Gobain F 91 B3
St Gorgon-Main F 105 B5
St Guénolé F 100 B1
St Harmon GB 39 B3
St Helens GB 38 A4
St Helier GB 88 A1
St Herblain F 101 B4
St Hilaire
Allier F 104 C2
Aude F 146 A3
St Hilaire-de-Riez
F 114 B2
St Hilaire-des-Loges
F 114 B3
St Hilaire-de-
Villefranche F 114 C3
St Hilaire-du-Harcouët
F 88 B2
St Hilaire-du-Rosier
F 118 B2
St Hippolyte
Aveyron F 116 C2
Doubs F 106 B1
St Hippolyte-du-Fort
F 130 B2
St Honoré-les-Bains
F 104 C2
St Hubert B 92 A1
St Imier CH 106 B2
St Issey GB 42 B2
St Ives
Cambridgeshire
GB 44 A3
Cornwall GB 42 B1
St Izaire F 130 B1
St Jacques-de-la-Lande
F 101 A4
St Jacut-de-la-Mer
F 101 A3
St James F 88 B2
St Jaume d'Enveja
E 153 B4
St Jean-Brévelay
F 101 B3
St Jean-d'Angély
F 114 C3
St Jean-de-Belleville
F 118 B3
St Jean-de-Bournay
F 118 B2
St Jean-de-Braye
F 103 B3
St Jean-de-Côle F 115 C4
St Jean-de-Daye F 88 A2
St Jean de Losne
F 105 B4
St Jean-de-Luz F 144 A2
St Jean-de-Maurienne
F 118 B3
St Jean-de-Monts
F 114 B1
St Jean-d'Illac F 128 B2
St Jean-du-Bruel F 130 A2
St Jean-du-Gard F 131 A2
St Jean-en-Royans
F 118 B2
St Jean-la-Riviere
F 133 B3
St Jean-Pied-de-Port
F 144 A2
St Jean-Poutge F 129 C3
St Jeoire F 118 A3
St Joachim F 101 B3
St Johnstown IRL 27 B3
St Jorioz F 118 B3
St Joris Winge B 79 B4

St Jouin-de-Marnes
F 102 C1
St Juéry F 130 B1
St Julien F 118 A2
St Julien-Chapteuil
F 117 B4
St Julien-de-Vouvantes
F 101 B4
St Julien-du-Sault
F 104 A2
St Julien-du-Verdon
F 132 B2
St Julien-en-Born
F 128 B1
St Julien-en-Genevois
F 118 A3
St Julien-l'Ars F . . . 115 B4
St Julien la-Vêtre
F 117 B3
St Julien-Mont-Denis
F 118 B3
St Julien-sur-Reyssouze
F 118 A2
St Junien F 115 C4
St Just
F 131 A4
GB 42 B1
St Just-en-Chaussée
F 90 B2
St Just-en-Chevalet
F 117 B3
St Justin F 128 C2
St Just-St Rambert
F 117 B4
St Keverne GB 42 B1
St Lary-Soulan F . . 145 B4
St Laurent-d'Aigouze
F 131 B3
St Laurent-de-
  Chamousset F . . . 117 B4
St Laurent-de-Condel
F 89 A3
St Laurent-de-la-
  Cabrerisse F 146 A3
St Laurent-de-la-
  Salanque F 146 B3
St Laurent-des-Autels
F 101 B4
St Laurent-du-Pont
F 118 B2
St Laurent-en-Caux
F 89 A4
St Laurent-en-
  Grandvaux F . . . 105 C4
St Laurent-Médoc
F 128 A2
St Laurent-sur-Gorre
F 115 C4
St Laurent-sur-Mer
F 88 A3
St Laurent-sur-Sèvre
F 114 B3
St Leger B 92 B1
St Léger-de-Vignes
F 104 C2
St Léger-sous-Beuvray
F 104 C3
St Léger-sur-Dheune
F 104 C3
St Léonard-de-Noblat
F 116 B1
St Leonards GB 45 C4
St Lô F 88 A2
St Lon-les-Mines F . 128 C1
St Louis F 106 B2
St Loup F 117 A3
St Loup-de-la-Salle
F 105 C3
St Loup-sur-Semouse
F 105 B5
St Lunaire F 101 A3
St Lupicin F 118 A2
St Lyphard F 101 B3
St Lys F 146 A2
St Macaire F 128 B2
St Maclou F 89 A4
St Maixent-l'École
F 115 B3
St Malo F 88 B1
St Mamet-la-Salvetat
F 116 C2
St Mandrier-sur-Mer
F 132 B1
St Marcel
Drôme F 117 C4
Saône-et-Loire F . . 105 C3
St Marcellin F 118 B2
St Marcellin sur Loire
F 117 B4
St Marcet F 145 A4
St Mards-en-Othe
F 104 A2
St Margaret's-at-Cliffe
GB 45 B5
St Margaret's Hope
GB 33 C4
St Mars-la-Jaille F . 101 B4
St Martin-d'Ablois F 91 C3
St Martin-d'Auxigny
F 103 B4
St Martin-de-Belleville
F 118 B3
St Martin-de-Bossenay
F 91 C3
St Martin-de-Crau
F 131 B3
St Martin-de-Londres
F 130 B2

St Martin-d'Entraunes
F 132 A2
St Martin-de-Queyrières
F 118 C3
St Martin-de-Ré F . . 114 B2
St Martin des Besaces
F 88 A3
St Martin-d'Estreaux
F 117 A3
St Martin-de-Valamas
F 117 C4
St Martin-d'Hères
F 118 B2
St Martin-du-Frêne
F 118 A2
St Martin-en-Bresse
F 105 C4
St Martin-en-Haut
F 117 B4
St Martin-la-Méanne
F 116 B1
St Martin-Osmonville
F 90 B1
St Martin-sur-Ouanne
F 104 B2
St Martin-Valmeroux
F 116 B2
St Martin-Vésubie
F 133 A3
St Martory F 145 A4
St Mary's GB 33 C4
St Mathieu F 115 C4
St Mathieu-de-Tréviers
F 131 B2
St Maurice CH 119 A3
St Maurice-Navacelles
F 130 B2
St Maurice-sur-Moselle
F 106 B1
St Mawes GB 42 B1
St Maximin-la-Ste
  Baume F 132 B1
St Méard-de-Gurçon
F 128 B3
St Médard-de-Guizières
F 128 A2
St Médard-en-Jalles
F 128 B2
St Méen-le-Grand
F 101 A3
St Menges F 91 B4
St Merløse DK 61 D1
St Město CZ 85 B4
St M'Hervé F 101 A4
St Michel
Aisne F 91 B4
Gers F 145 A4
St Michel-Chef-Chef
F 101 B3
St Michel-de-Castelnau
F 128 B2
St Michel-de-Maurienne
F 118 B3
St Michel-en-Grève
F 100 A2
St Michel-enl'Herm
F 114 B2
St Michel-Mont-Mercure
F 114 B3
St Mihiel F 92 C1
St Monance GB 35 B5
St Montant F 131 A3
St Moritz CH 107 C4
St Nazaire F 101 B3
St Nazaire-en-Royans
F 118 B2
St Nazaire-le-Désert
F 131 A4
St Nectaire F 116 B2
St Neots GB 44 A3
St Nicolas-de-Port
F 92 C2
St Nicolas-de-Redon
F 101 B3
St Nicolas-du-Pélem
F 100 A2
St Niklaas B 79 A4
St Omer F 78 B2
St Pair-sur-Mer F . . 88 B2
St Palais F 144 A2
St Palais-sur-Mer
F 114 C2
St Pardoux-la-Rivière
F 115 C4
St Paul-Cap-de-Joux
F 129 C4
St Paul-de-Fenouillet
F 146 B3
St Paul-de-Varax F .118 A2
St Paulien F 117 B3
St Paul-le-Jeune F . 131 A3
St Paul-lès-Dax F . 128 C2
St Paul-Trois-Châteaux
F 131 A3
St Pée-sur-Nivelle
F 144 A2
St Péravy-la-Colombe
F 103 B3
St Péray F 117 C4
St Père-en-Retz F . 101 B3
St Peter Port GB . . 88 A1
St Petersburg = Sankt-
  Peterburg RUS . . . 9 C7
St Philbert-de-Grand-
  Lieu F 114 A2
St Pierre F 130 B1

St Pierre-d'Albigny
F 118 B3
St Pierre-d'Allevard
F 118 B3
St Pierre-de-Chartreuse
F 118 B2
St Pierre-de-Chignac
F 129 A3
St Pierre-de-la-Fage
F 130 B2
St Pierre-d'Entremont
F 118 B2
St Pierre-d'Oléron
F 114 C2
St Pierre-Eglise F . 88 A2
St Pierre-en-Port F . 89 A4
St Pierre-le-Moûtier
F 104 C2
St Pierre Montlimart
F 101 B4
St Pierre-Quiberon
F 100 B2
St Pierre-sur-Dives
F 89 A3
St Pierreville F . . 117 C4
St Pieters-Leeuw B . 79 B4
St Plancard F 145 A4
St Poix F 101 B4
St Pol-de-Léon F . . 100 A2
St Polgues F . . .117 B3
St Pol-sur-Ternoise
F 78 B2
St Pons-de-Thomières
F 130 B1
St Porchaire F 114 C3
St Pourçain-sur-Sioule
F 116 A3
St Priest F 117 B4
St Privat F 116 B2
St Quay-Portrieux
F 100 A3
St Quentin F 90 B3
St Quentin-la-Poterie
F 131 A3
St Quentin-les-Anges
F 102 B1
St Rambert-d'Albon
F 117 B4
St Rambert-en-Bugey
F 118 B2
St Raphaël F 132 B2
St Rémy-de-Provence
F 131 B3
St Rémy-du-Val F . 89 B4
St Remy-en-Bouzemont
F 91 C4
St Renan F 100 A1
St Révérien F 104 B2
St Riquier F 90 A1
St Romain-de-Colbosc
F 89 A4
St Rome-de-Cernon
F 130 A1
St Rome-de-Tarn F . 130 A1
St Sadurní-d'Anoia
E 147 C2
St Saëns F 89 A5
St Sampson GB 88 A1
St Samson-la-Poterie
F 90 B1
St Saturnin-de-Lenne
F 130 A2
St Saturnin-lès-Apt
F 131 B4
St Sauflieu F 90 B2
St Saulge F 104 B2
St Sauveur
Finistère F 100 A2
Haute-Saône F . . 105 B5
St Sauveur-de-Montagut
F 117 C4
St Sauveur-en-Puisaye
F 104 B2
St Sauveur-en-Rue
F 117 B4
St Sauveur-Lendelin
F 88 A2
St Sauveur-le-Vicomte
F 88 A2
St Sauveur-sur-Tinée
F 132 A3
St Savin
Gironde F 128 A2
Vienne F 115 B4
St Savinien F 114 C3
St Savournin F . . . 131 B4
St Seine-l'Abbaye
F 105 B3
St Sernin-sur-Rance
F 130 B1
St Sevan-sur-Mer F . 88 B1
St Sever F 128 C2
St Sever-Calvados
F 88 B2
St Sorlin-d'Arves F 118 B3
St Soupplets F 90 B2
St Sulpice F 129 C4
St Sulpice-Laurière
F 116 A1
St Sulpice-les-Feuilles
F 115 B5
St Symphorien F . 128 B2
St Symphoriende-Lay
F 117 B4
St Symphorien d'Ozon
F 117 B4
St Symphoriensur-Coise
F 117 B4

St Teath GB 42 B2
St Thégonnec F . . . 100 A2
St Thiébault F 105 A4
St Trivier-de-Courtes
F 114 C2
St Trivier sur-Moignans
F 117 A4
St Trojan-les-Bains
F 114 C2
St Tropez F 132 B2
St Truiden B 79 B5
St Vaast-la-Hougue
F 88 A2
St Valérien F 104 A2
St Valery-en-Caux F 89 A4
St Valéry-sur-Somme
F 78 B1
St Vallier
Drôme F 117 B4
Saône-et-Loire F . 104 C3
St Vallier-de-Thiey
F 132 B2
St Varent F 102 C1
St Vaury F 116 A1
St Venant F 78 B2
St Véran F 119 C3
St Vincent I 119 B4
St Vincent-de-Tyrosse
F 128 C1
St Vit F 117 A4
St Vith B 80 B2
St Vivien-de-Médoc
F 114 C2
St Yan F 117 A4
St Ybars F 146 A2
St Yorre F 117 A3
St Yrieix-la-Perche
F 115 C5
Saissac F 146 A3
Saja E 142 A2
Sajan SRB 126 B2
Šajkaš SRB 126 B2
Sajókaza H 99 C4
Sajószentpéter H . .113 A4
Sajóvámos H 113 A4
Sakarya TR 187 B5
Šakiai LT 13 A5
Sakskøbing DK 65 B4
Sakule SRB 126 B2
Sala S 50 C3
Šal'a SK 111 A4
Sala Baganza I . . . 120 C3
Sala Consilina I . . . 172 B1
Salakovac SRB . . . 127 C3
Salamanca E 150 B2
Salamina GR 185 B4
Salandra I 172 B2
Salaparuta I 176 B1
Salar E 163 A3
Salardú E 145 B4
Salas E 141 A4
Salas de los Infantes
E 143 B3
Salau F 146 B2
Salavaux CH 106 C2
Salbertrand I . . .119 B3
Salbohed S 50 C3
Salbris F 103 B4
Salbu N 46 A2
Salce E 141 B4
Salching D 95 C4
Salcombe GB 43 B3
Saldaña E 142 B2
Saldus LV 8 D3
Sale I 120 C1
Saleby S 55 B4
Salem D 107 B4
Salemi I 176 B1
Salen
Argyll & Bute GB . .34 B2
Highland GB 34 B2
N 199 A8
Sälen S 49 A5
Salernes F 132 B2
Salerno I 170 C2
Salers F 116 B2
Salford GB 40 B1
Salgótarján H . . .113 A3
Salgueiro P 155 B3
Salhus N 46 B2
Sali HR 137 B4
Sálice Salentino I . 173 B3
Salientes E 141 B4
Salies-de-Béarn F . 144 A3
Salies-du-Salat F . 145 A4
Salignac-Eyvigues
F 129 B4
Saligney-sur-Roudon
F 104 C2
Salihli TR 188 A3
Salihorsk BY 13 B7
Salinas
Alicante E 159 C3
Huesca E 145 A4
Salinas de Medinaceli
E 152 A1
Salinas de Pisuerga
E 142 B2
Salindres F 131 A3
Saline di Volterra I . 135 B3
Salins-les-Bains F . 105 C4
Salir P 160 B1
Salisbury GB 44 B2
Salla
A 110 B1
FIN 197 C11
Sallachy GB 32 C2
Sallanches F 118 B3

Sallent E 147 C2
Sallent de Gállego
E 145 B3
Salles F 128 B2
Salles-Curan F . . . 130 A1
Salles-sur-l'Hers F . 146 A2
Sallins IRL 30 A2
Sällsjö S 199 B10
Salmerón E 152 B1
Salmiech F 130 A1
Salmivaara FIN . . 197 C11
Salmoral E 150 B2
Salo FIN 8 B3
Salò I 121 B3
Salobreña E 163 B4
Salon-de-Provence
F 131 B4
Salonica = Thessaloniki
GR 182 C4
Salonta RO 16 B4
Salorino E 155 B3
Salornay-sur-Guye
F 104 C3
Salorno I 121 A4
Salou E 147 C2
Šalovci SLO 111 C3
Salsbruket N 199 A8
Salses-le-Chateau
F 146 B3
Salsomaggiore Terme
I 120 C2
Salt E 147 C3
Saltaire GB 40 B2
Saltara I 136 B1
Saltash GB 42 B2
Saltburn-by-the-Sea
GB 37 B6
Saltcoats GB 34 C3
Saltfleet GB 41 B4
Salto P 148 A2
Saltrød N 53 B4
Saltsjöbaden S . . 57 A4
Saltvik
FIN 51 B7
S 62 A4
Saludécio I 136 B1
Salussola I 119 B5
Saluzzo I 119 C4
Salvacañete E . . 152 B2
Salvada P 160 B2
Salvagnac F 129 C4
Salvaleon E 155 C4
Salvaterra de Magos
P 154 B2
Salvaterra do Extremo
P 155 B4
Salvatierra
Avila E 143 B4
Badajoz E 155 C4
Salvatierra de Santiago
E 156 A1
Salviac F 129 B4
Salzburg A 109 B4
Salzgitter D 72 B3
Salzgitter Bad D . . 72 B3
Salzhausen D 72 A3
Salzhemmendorf D . 72 B2
Salzkotten D 81 A4
Salzmünde D 83 A3
Salzwedel D 73 B4
Samadet F 128 C2
Samandıra TR . . . 186 B4
Samassi I 179 C2
Samatan F 146 A1
Sambiase I 175 C2
Sambir UA 13 D5
Samborowo PL . . . 69 B4
Sambuca di Sicília
I 176 B2
Samedan CH 107 C4
Samer F 78 B1
Sami GR 184 A1
Şamlı TR 186 C2
Sammichele di Bari
I 173 B2
Samnaun CH 107 C5
Samobor HR 123 B4
Samoëns F 118 A3
Samogneux F 92 B1
Samokov BG 17 D5
Samora Correia P . 154 C2
Samorín SK 111 A4
Samos
E 141 B3
GR 188 B1
Šamoš SRB 126 B2
Samothraki GR . . 183 C7
Samper de Calanda
E 153 A3
Sampéyre I 133 A3
Sampieri I 177 C3
Sampigny F 92 C1
Samplawa PL 69 B4
Samproniano I . . . 168 A1
Samtens D 66 B2
Samugheo I 179 C2
San Adrián E 144 B2
San Agustín E 164 C2
San Agustin de
  Guadalix E 151 B4
Sanaigmore GB . . . 34 C1
San Alberto I 135 A5
San Amaro E 140 B2
San Andrés del
  Rabanedo E 142 B1
San Antanio di Santadi
I 179 C2

San Antolín de Ibias
E 141 A4
San Arcángelo I . . 174 A2
Sanary-sur-Mer F . 132 B1
San Asensio E 143 B4
San Bartoloméde las
  Abiertas E 150 C3
San Bartoloméde la
  Torre E 161 B2
San Bartoloméde
  Pinares E 150 B3
San Bartolomeo in
  Galdo I 170 B3
San Benedetto del
  Tronto I 136 C2
San Benedetto in Alpe
I 135 B4
San Benedetto Po
I 121 B3
San Benito E 156 B3
San Benito de la
  Contienda E 155 C3
San Biágio Plátani
I 176 B2
San Biágio Saracinisco
I 169 B3
San Bonifacio I . . 121 B4
San Calixto E 156 C2
San Cándido I 109 C3
San Carlo
CH 119 A5
I 176 B2
San Carlos del Valle
E 157 B4
San Casciano dei Bagni
I 135 C4
San Casciano in Val di
  Pesa I 135 B4
San Cataldo
Puglia I 173 B4
Sicília I 176 B2
San Cebrián de Castro
E 149 A4
Sancergues F 104 B1
Sancerre F 103 B4
San Cesário di Lecce
I 173 B4
Sancey-le-Long F . 105 B5
Sanchiorian E 150 B3
San Chírico Raparo
I 174 A2
Sanchonuño E . . . 151 A3
San Cibrao das Viñas
E 140 B3
San Cipirello I . . 176 B2
San Ciprián E 141 A3
San Clemente E . . 158 B1
San Clodio E 141 B3
Sancoins F 104 C1
San Colombano al
  Lambro I 120 B2
San Costanzo I . . 136 B2
San Crisóbal de
  Entreviñas E . . . 142 B1
San Cristóbal de la
  Polantera E 141 B5
San Cristóbal de la
  Vega E 150 A3
San Cristovo E . . 141 C3
Sancti-Petri E 162 B1
Sancti-Spíritus E . 149 B3
Sand
Hedmark N 48 B3
Rogaland N 52 A2
Sanda S 57 C4
San Damiano d'Asti
I 119 C5
San Damiano Macra
I 133 A3
Sandane N 198 D3
San Daniele del Friuli
I 122 A2
Sandanski BG 183 B5
Sandared S 60 B2
Sandarne S 51 A4
Sandau D 73 B5
Sandbach
D 96 C1
GB 38 A4
Sandbank GB 34 C3
Sandbanks GB 43 B5
Sandbukt N 192 C5
Sandby DK 65 B4
Sande
D 71 A5
Sogn og Fjordane
  N 46 A2
Vestfold N 54 A1
Sandefjord N 54 A1
Sandeid N 52 A1
San Demétrio Corone
I 174 B2
San Demétrio né Vestini
I 169 A3
Sandersleben D . . 82 A3
Sanderstølen N . . 47 B6
Sandes N 53 B3
Sandesneben D . . 65 C3
Sandhead GB 36 B2
Sandhem S 60 B3
Sandhorst D 71 A4
Sandhurst GB 44 B3
Sandıklı TR 189 A5
Sandillon F 103 B4
Sandl A 96 C2

Sandnes N 52 B1
Sandness GB 33 A5
Sandnessjøen N . . 195 D3
Sando E 149 B3
Sandomierz PL 87 B5
San Dónaci I 173 B3
San Donàdi Piave
  I 122 B1
San Donato Val di
  Comino I 169 B3
Sándorfalva H 126 A2
Sandown GB 44 C2
Sandøysund N 54 A1
Sandrigo I 121 B4
Sandsele S 195 E8
Sandset N 194 B5
Sandsjöfors S 62 A2
Sandstad N 198 B6
Sandvatn N 52 B2
Sandvig-Allinge DK 67 A3
Sandvika
  Akershus N 48 C2
  Hedmark N 48 B3
  Nord-Trøndelag N . 199 B9
Sandviken S 51 B3
Sandvikvåy N 46 C2
Sandwich GB. 45 B5
Sandy GB. 44 A3
San Emiliano E . . 141 B5
San Enrique E 162 B2
San Esteban E. . . . 141 A4
San Esteban de Gormaz
  E. 151 A4
San Esteban de la Sierra
  E. 149 B4
San Esteban de Litera
  E. 145 C4
San Esteban del Molar
  E. 142 C1
San Esteban del Valle
  E. 150 B3
San Esteban de
  Valdueza E 141 B4
San Fele I 172 B1
San Felice Circeo I 169 B3
San Felices E. 143 B3
San Felices de los
  Gallégos E. 149 B3
San Felice sul Panaro
  I 121 C4
San Ferdinando di
  Púglia I 171 B4
San Fernando E . . 162 B1
San Fernando de
  Henares E 151 B4
San Fili I 174 B2
San Foca I 173 B4
San Fratello I 177 B3
Sangatte F 78 B1
San Gavino Monreale
  I 179 C2
San Gémini Fonte
  I 168 A2
Sangerhausen D . . 82 A3
San Germano Vercellese
  I 119 B5
San Giácomo
  Trentino Alto Adige
    I 108 C2
  Umbria I 136 C1
San Gimignano I . . 135 B4
San Ginésio I 136 B2
Sangineto Lido I . . 174 B1
San Giórgio a Liri
  I 169 B3
San Giórgio della
  Richinvelda I 122 A1
San Giórgio del Sánnio
  I 170 B2
San Giórgio di
  Lomellina I 120 B1
San Giórgio di Nogaro
  I 122 B2
San Giorgio di Piano
  I 121 C4
San Giórgio Iónico
  I 173 B3
San Giovanni a Piro
  I 172 B1
San Giovanni Bianco
  I 120 B2
San Giovanni di Sinis
  I 179 C2
San Giovanni in Croce
  I 120 B3
San Giovanni in Fiore
  I 174 B2
San Giovanni in
  Persiceto I 121 C4
San Giovanni Reatino
  I 169 A2
San Giovanni Rotondo
  I 171 B3
San Giovanni Suérgiu
  I 179 C2
San Giovanni Valdarno
  I 135 B4
Sangis S 196 D6
San Giuliano Terme
  I 134 B3
San Giustino I 135 B5
San Godenzo I 135 B4
Sangonera la Verde
  E. 165 B3

San Gregorio Magno
  I 172 B1
Sangüesa E 144 B2
Sanguinet F 128 B1
San Guiseppe Jato
  I 176 B2
Sanica BIH 124 C2
Sanitz D 65 B5
San Javier E 165 B4
San Jorge P 154 B2
San José E 164 C2
San Juan E 143 B3
San Juan de Alicante
  E. 165 A4
San Juan de la Nava
  E. 150 B3
San Justo de la Vega
  E. 141 B4
Sankt Aegyd am
  Neuwalde A 110 B2
Sankt Andrä A . . . 110 C1
Sankt Andreasberg
  D 82 A2
Sankt Anna S 56 B2
Sankt Anna am Aigen
  A. 110 C2
Sankt Anton am Arlberg
  A. 107 B5
Sankt Anton an der
  Jessnitz A 110 B2
Sankt Augustin D . . 80 B3
Sankt Blasien D . . 106 B3
Sankt Englmar D . . 95 B4
Sankt Gallen
  A. 110 B1
  CH 107 B4
Sankt Gallenkirch
  A. 107 B4
Sankt Georgen
  A. 96 C2
  D 106 A3
Sankt Georgen am Reith
  A. 110 B1
Sankt Georgen ob
  Judenburg A 110 B1
Sankt Georgen ob
  Murau A 109 B5
Sankt Gilgen A. . . . 109 B4
Sankt Goar D 81 B3
Sankt Goarshausen
  D 81 B3
Sankt Ingbert D . . . 92 B3
Sankt Jacob A 109 C5
Sankt Jakob in
  Defereggen A . . . 109 C3
Sankt Johann am
  Tauern A 110 B1
Sankt Johann am
  Wesen A 109 A4
Sankt Johann im
  Pongau A 109 B4
Sankt Johann in Tirol
  A. 109 B3
Sankt Katharein an der
  Laming A. 110 B2
Sankt Kathrein am
  Hauenstein A. . . . 110 B2
Sankt Lambrecht
  A. 110 B1
Sankt Leonhard am
  Forst A 110 A2
Sankt Leonhard im
  Pitztal A. 108 B1
Sankt Lorenzen A . 109 C3
Sankt Marein
  Steiermark A 110 B2
  Steiermark A 110 B2
Sankt Margarethen im
  Lavanttal A 110 C1
Sankt Margrethen
  CH 107 B4
Sankt Michael A. . . 110 B2
Sankt Michael im
  Burgenland A . . . 111 B3
Sankt Michael im
  Lungau A. 109 B4
Sankt Michaelisdonn
  D 64 C2
Sankt Niklaus CH . 119 A4
Sankt Nikolai im Sölktal
  A. 109 B5
Sankt Olof S 63 C2
Sankt Oswald D. . . 96 C1
Sankt Paul
  A. 110 C1
  F. 132 A2
Sankt Peter D 106 A3
Sankt Peter am
  Kammersberg A . 110 B1
Sankt-Peterburg = St
  Petersburg RUS . . 9 C7
Sankt Peter-Ording
  D 64 B1
Sankt Pölten A. . . 110 A2
Sankt Radegund A . 110 B2
Sankt Ruprecht an der
  Raab A 110 B2
Sankt Salvator A . . 110 C1
Sankt Stefan A . . . 110 C1
Sankt Stefan an der Gail
  A. 109 C4
Sankt Stefan im
  Rosental A. 110 C2
Sankt Valentin A . . 110 A1
Sankt Veit an der Glan
  A. 110 C1
Sankt Veit an der
  Gölsen A 110 A2

Sankt Veit in
  Defereggen A . . . 109 C3
Sankt Wendel D. . . 92 B3
Sankt Wolfgang
  A. 109 B4
  D 108 A3
San Lazzaro di Sávena
  I 135 A4
San Leo I 135 B5
San Leonardo de Yagüe
  E. 143 C3
San Leonardo in
  Passiria I 108 C2
San Lorenzo al Mare
  I 133 B3
San Lorenzo a Merse
  I 135 B4
San Lorenzo Bellizzi
  I 174 B2
San Lorenzo de
  Calatrava E 157 B4
San Lorenzo de El
  Escorial E 151 B3
San Lorenzo de la
  Parrilla E 158 B1
San Lorenzo di Sebato
  I 108 C2
San Lorenzo in Campo
  I 136 B1
San Lorenzo Nuovo
  I 168 A1
San Lourenço P . . 160 A1
San Luca I 175 C2
Sanlúcar de Barrameda
  E. 161 C3
Sanlúcar de Guadiana
  E. 160 B2
Sanlúcar la Mayor
  E. 161 B3
San Lúcido I 174 B2
Sanluri I 179 C2
San Marcello I . . . 136 B2
San Marcello Pistoiese
  I 135 A3
San Marcial E 149 A4
San Marco I 170 C2
San Marco Argentano
  I 174 B2
San Marco dei Cavoti
  I 170 B2
San Marco in Lámis
  I 171 B3
San Marino RSM . . 136 B1
San Martin de
  Castañeda E 141 B4
San Martín de la Vega
  E. 151 B4
San Martín de la Vega
  del Alberche E . . 150 B2
San Martín del Tesorillo
  E. 162 B2
San Martin de Luiña
  E. 141 A4
San Martin de
  Montalbán E 157 A3
San Martin de Oscos
  E. 141 A4
San Martin de Pusa
  E. 150 C3
San Martin de Unx
  E. 144 B2
San Martin de
  Valdeiglesias E . . 150 B3
San Martino di
  Campagna I 122 A1
San Martino di
  Castrozza I 121 A4
San-Martino-di-Lota
  F. 180 A2
San Martino in Pénsilis
  I 170 B3
San Mateo de Gallego
  E. 144 C3
San Máuro Forte I . 172 B2
San Michele all'Adige
  I 121 A4
San Michele di Ganzaria
  I 177 B3
San Michele Mondov í
  I 133 A3
San Miguel de Aguayo
  E. 142 A2
San Miguel de Bernuy
  E. 151 A4
San Miguel del Arroyo
  E. 150 A3
San Miguel de Salinas
  E. 165 B4
Sânmihaiu Roman
  RO 126 B3
San Millán de la Cogolla
  E. 143 B4
San Miniato I 135 B3
San Muñoz E 149 B3
Sänna S 55 B5
Sannazzaro de'Burgondi
  I 120 B1
Sanne D 73 B4
Sannicandro di Bari
  I 171 B4
Sannicandro Gargánico
  I 171 B3
San Nicola del'Alto
  I 174 B2
San Nicolás del Puerto
  E. 156 C2
Sânnicolau Mare
  RO 126 A2

San Nicolò I 121 C4
San Nicolò Gerrei
  I 179 C3
Sannidal N 53 B5
Sanniki PL 77 B4
Sanok PL 12 D5
San Pablo de los
  Montes E 157 A3
San Pancrázio
  Salentino I 173 B3
San Pantaleo I . . . 178 A3
San Páolo di Civitate
  I 171 B3
San Pawl il-Baħar
  M 175 C3
San Pedro
  Albacete E 158 C1
  Oviedo E 141 A4
San Pedro de Alcántara
  E. 162 B3
San Pedro de Ceque
  E. 141 B4
San Pedro del Arroyo
  E. 150 B3
San Pedro de Latarce
  E. 142 C1
San Pedro del Pinatar
  E. 165 B4
San Pedro del Romeral
  E. 143 A3
San Pedro de Merida
  E. 156 B1
San Pedro de
  Valderaduey E . . . 142 B2
San Pedro Manrique
  E. 144 B1
San Pellegrino Terme
  I 120 B2
San Piero a Sieve I 135 B4
San Piero in Bagno
  I 135 B4
San Piero Patti I . . 177 A3
San Pietro I 177 B3
San Pietro in Casale
  I 121 C4
San Pietro in Gu I . 121 B4
San Pietro in Palazzi
  I 134 B3
San Pietro in Volta
  I 122 B1
San Pietro Vara I . . 134 A2
San Pietro Vernótico
  I 173 B3
San Polo d'Enza I . 121 C3
Sanquhar GB. 36 A3
San Quírico d'Órcia
  I 135 B4
San Rafael del Rio
  E. 153 B4
San Remo I 133 B3
San Román de Cameros
  E. 143 B4
San Roman de Hernija
  E. 150 A2
San Román de la Cuba
  E. 142 B2
San Roman de los
  Montes E 150 B3
San Romao P. 155 C3
San Roque E 162 B2
San Roque de Riomera
  E. 143 A3
San Rufo I 172 B1
San Sebastián de los
  Ballesteros E . . . 162 A3
San Salvador de
  Cantamuda E . . . 142 B2
San Salvo I 170 A2
San Salvo Marina I 170 A2
San Sebastián de los
  Reyes E 151 B4
San Sebastiano Curone
  I 120 C2
San Secondo Parmense
  I 120 C3
Sansepolcro I 135 B5
San Serverino Marche
  I 136 B2
San Severino Lucano
  I 174 A2
San Severo I 171 B3
San Silvestre de
  Guzmán E 161 B2
Sanski Most BIH . . 124 C2
San Sosti I 174 B2
San Stéfano di Cadore
  I 109 C3
San Stino di Livenza
  I 122 B1
Santa Agnès E . . . 166 B1
Santa Amalia E . . . 156 A1
Santa Ana
  Cáceres E 156 A2
  Jaén E 163 A4
Santa Ana de Pusa
  E. 150 C3
Santa Barbara E . . 153 B4
Santa Barbara P . . 160 B2
Santa Barbara de Casa
  E. 161 B2
Santa Bárbara de
  Padrões P 160 B2
Santacara E 144 B2
Santa Catarina P . . 160 B2
Santa Caterina di
  Pittinuri I 178 B2
Santa Caterina
  Villarmosa I 177 B3

Santa Cesárea Terme
  I 173 B4
Santa Clara-a-Nova
  P 160 B1
Santa Clara-a-Velha
  P 160 B1
Santa Clara de Louredo
  P 160 B2
Santa Coloma de
  Farners E 147 C3
Santa Coloma de
  Gramenet E 147 C3
Santa Coloma de
  Queralt E 147 C2
Santa Colomba de
  Curueño E 142 B1
Santa Colomba de
  Somoza E 141 B4
Santa Comba E . . . 140 A2
Santa Comba Dáo
  P 148 B1
Santa Comba de Rossas
  P 149 A3
Santa Cristina I . . . 120 B2
Santa Cristina de la
  Polvorosa E 141 B5
Santa Croce Camerina
  I 177 C3
Santa Croce di Magliano
  I 170 B2
Santa Cruz
  E 140 A2
  P 154 B1
Santa Cruz de Alhama
  E 163 A4
Santa Cruz de Campezo
  E 143 B4
Santa Cruz de Grio
  E 152 A2
Santa Cruz de la
  Salceda E 151 A4
Santa Cruz de la Sierra
  E 156 A2
Santa Cruz de la Zarza
  E 151 C4
Santa Cruz del Retamar
  E 151 B3
Santa Cruz del Valle
  E 150 B2
Santa Cruz de Moya
  E 159 B2
Santa Cruz de Mudela
  E 157 B4
Santa Cruz de Paniagua
  E 149 B3
Santadi I 179 C2
Santa Doménica Talao
  I 174 B1
Santa Doménica
  Vittória I 177 B3
Santa Elena E 157 B4
Santa Elena de Jamuz
  E 141 B5
Santaella E 162 A3
Santa Eufemia E . . 156 B3
Santa Eufémia
  d'Aspromonte I . . 175 C1
Santa Eulália E . . . 152 B2
Santa Eulália P . . . 155 C3
Santa Eulalia de Oscos
  E 141 A3
Santa Eulàlia des Riu
  E 166 C1
Santa Fe E 163 A4
Santa Fiora I 135 C4
Sant'Ágata dei Goti
  I 170 B2
Sant'Ágata di Ésaro
  I 174 B1
Sant'Ágata di Puglia
  I 171 B3
Sant'Agata Feltria
  I 135 B5
Sant'Ágata Militello
  I 177 A3
Santa Gertrude I . . 108 C1
Santa Giustina I . . 121 A5
Sant Agust íde Lluçanès
  E 147 B3
Santa Iria P 160 B2
Santa Leocadia P . 148 A1
Santa Lucia del Mela
  I 177 A4
Santa Lucia-de-Porto-
  Vecchio F 180 B2
Santa Luzia P 160 B1
Santa Maddalena
  Vallalta I 108 C3
Santa Magdalena de
  Polpis E 153 B4
Santa Margalida E . 167 B3
Santa Margarida P 154 B2
Santa Margarida do
  Sado P 160 A1
Santa Margaridao de
  Montbui E 147 C2
Santa Margherita I . 179 D2
Santa Margherita di
  Belice I 176 B2
Santa Margherita Ligure
  I 134 A2
Santa Maria
  CH 108 C1
  I 144 B3
Santa Maria al Bagno
  I 173 B3
Santa Maria Cápua
  Vétere I 170 B2

Santa Maria da Feira
  P 148 B1
Santa Maria de Cayón
  E 143 A3
Santa Maria de Corco
  E 147 B3
Santa Maria de Huerta
  E 152 A1
Santa Maria de la
  Alameda E 151 B3
Santa Maria de las
  Hoyas E 143 C3
Santa Maria del Camí
  E 167 B2
Santa Maria del Campo
  E 143 B3
Santa Maria del Campo
  Rus E 158 B1
Santa Maria della Versa
  I 120 C2
Santa Maria del Páramo
  E 142 B1
Santa Maria del Taro
  I 134 A2
Santa Maria de
  Mercadillo E 143 C3
Santa Maria de Nieva
  E 164 B3
Santa Maria de
  Trassierra E 156 C3
Santa Maria di Licodia
  I 177 B3
Santa Maria-di-
  Rispéscia I 168 A1
Santa Maria la Palma
  I 178 B2
Santa Maria la Real de
  Nieva E 150 A3
Santa Maria Maggiore
  I 119 A5
Santa Maria
  Ribarredonda E . 143 B3
Santa Marina del Rey
  E 141 B5
Santa Marinella I . . 168 A1
Santa Marta
  Albacete E 158 B1
  Badajoz E 155 C4
Santa Marta de Magasca
  E 156 A1
Santa Marta de
  Penaguião P 148 A2
Santa Marta de Tormes
  E 150 B2
Santana
  Évora P 154 C2
  Setúbal P 154 C1
Sântana RO 126 A3
Santana da Serra
  P 160 B1
Sant'Ana de Cambas
  P 160 B2
Santana do Mato P 154 C2
Sant'Anastasia I . . 170 C2
Santander E 143 A3
Sant'Andrea Frius
  I 179 C3
Sant'Ángelo dei
  Lombardi I 172 B1
Sant'Angelo in Vado
  I 136 B1
Sant'Angelo Lodigiano
  I 120 B2
Santa Ninfa I 176 B1
Sant'Antíoco I 179 C2
Sant Antoni de Calonge
  E 147 C4
Sant Antoni de
  Portmany E 166 C1
Sant'Antonio-di-Gallura
  I 178 B3
Santanyí E 167 B3
Santa Olalla
  Huelva E 161 B3
  Toledo E 150 B3
Santa Pau E 147 B3
Santa Pola E 165 A4
Santa Ponça E . . . 166 B2
Santarcángelo di
  Romagna I 136 A1
Santarém P 154 B2
Santa Severa
  F 180 A2
  I 168 A1
Santa Severina I . . 175 B2
Santas Martas E . . 142 B1
Santa Sofia I 135 B4
Santa Susana P . . 154 C2
Santa Suzana P . . 155 C3
Santa Teresa di Riva
  I 177 B4
Santa Teresa Gallura
  I 178 A3
Santa Uxía E 140 B2
Santa Valburga I . . 108 C1
Santa Vittória in
  Matenano I 136 B2
Sant Boi de Llobregat
  E 147 C3
Sant Carles de la Ràpita
  E 153 B4
Sant Carlos E 166 B1
Sant'Caterina I . . . 135 C4
Sant Celoni E 147 C3
Sant Climent E . . . 167 B4
Santed E 152 A2
Sant'Egídio alla Vibrata
  I 136 C2

Sant'Elia a Pianisi
I 170 B2
Sant'Elia Fiumerapido
I 169 B3
Santelices E 143 A3
San Telmo E 161 B3
Sant'Elpidio a Mare
I 136 B2
Santéramo in Colle
I 171 C4
Santervas de la Vega
E 142 B2
Sant' Eufemia
Lamezia 175 C2
Sant Feliu E 147 C3
Sant Feliu de Codines
E 147 C3
Sant Feliu de Guíxols
E 147 C4
Sant Feliu Sasserra
E 147 C3
Sant Ferran E 166 C1
Sant Francesc de
Formentera E . . . 166 C1
Sant Francesc de ses
Salines E 166 C1
Santhià I 119 B5
Sant Hilari Sacalm
E 147 C3
Sant Hipòlit de Voltregà
E 147 B3
Santiago de Alcántara
E 155 B3
Santiago de Calatrava
E 163 A3
Santiago de Compostela
E 140 B2
Santiago de la Espade
E 164 A2
Santiago de la Puebla
E 150 B2
Santiago de la Ribera
E 165 B4
Santiago del Campo
E 155 B4
Santiago de Litem
P 154 B2
Santiago do Cacém
P 160 B1
Santiago do Escoural
P 154 C2
Santiago Maior P . . 155 C3
Santibáñez de Béjar
E 150 B2
Santibáñez de la Peña
E 142 B2
Santibáñez de Murias
E 142 A1
Santibáñez de Vidriales
E 141 B4
Santibáñez el Alto
E 149 B3
Santibáñez el Bajo
E 149 B3
Santillana E 142 A2
Santiponce E 162 A1
San Tirso de Abres
E 141 A3
Santisteban del Puerto
E 157 B4
Santiuste de San Juan
Bautiste E 150 A3
Santiz E 149 A4
Sant Jaume dels
Domenys E 147 C2
Sant Joan Baptista
E 166 B1
Sant Joan de les
Abadesses E 147 B3
Sant Jordi E 153 B4
Sant Josep de sa Talaia
E 166 C1
Sant Juliáde Loria
AND 146 B2
Sant'Ilario d'Enza I 121 C3
Sant Llorençde Morunys
E 147 B2
Sant Llorençdes
Carctassar E 167 B3
Sant Llorenç Savall
E 147 C3
Sant Luis E 167 B4
Sant Mart ide Llemaná
E 147 B3
Sant Marti de Maldá
E 147 C2
Sant Marti Sarroca
E 147 C2
Sant Mateu E 153 B4
Sant Miquel E 166 B1
Santo Aleixo P . . . 161 A2
Santo Amado P . . . 161 A2
Santo Amaro P . . . 155 C3
Santo André P . . . 160 A1
Santo Domingo E . . 155 C3
Santo Domingo de la
Calzada E 143 B4
Santo Domingo de Silos
E 143 C3
Santo Estêvão
Faro P 160 B2
Santarém P 154 C2
Santok PL 75 B4
Santomera E 165 A3
Santoña E 143 A3
Santo-Pietro-di Tenda
F 180 A2
Sant'Oreste I 168 A2

Santo Spirito I 171 B4
Santo Stefano d'Aveto
I 134 A2
Santo Stéfano di
Camastra I 177 A3
Santo Stefano di Magra
I 134 A2
Santo Stéfano
Quisquina I 176 B2
Santo Tirso P 148 A1
Santotis E 142 A2
Santo Tomé E 164 A1
Santovenia
Burgos E 143 B3
Zamora E 142 C1
Sant Pau de Seguries
E 147 B3
Santpedor E 147 C2
Sant Pere de Riudebitles
E 147 C2
Sant Pere Pescador
E 147 B4
Sant Pere Sallavinera
E 147 C2
Sant Quirze de Besora
E 147 B3
Sant Rafel E 166 C1
Sant Ramon E 147 C2
Santu Lussurgiu I . . 178 B2
Santutzi E 143 A3
Sant Vincençde
Castellet E 147 C2
San Valentino alla Muta
I 108 C1
San Venanzo I 135 C5
San Vicente de
Alcántara E 155 B3
San Vicente de Arana
E 144 B1
San Vicente de la
Barquera E 142 A2
San Vicente de la
Sonsierra E 143 B4
San Vicente de Toranzo
E 143 A3
San Vietro E 149 A3
San Vigilio I 108 C2
San Vicente del
Raspeig E 165 A4
San Vincenzo I 134 B3
San Vito I 179 C3
San Vito al Tagliamento
I 122 B1
San Vito Chietino I . 169 A4
San Vito dei Normanni
I 173 B3
San Vito di Cadore
I 108 C3
San Vito lo Capo I . 176 A1
San Vito Romano I . 169 B2
Sanxenxo E 140 B2
Sanza I 172 B1
São Aleixo P 155 C3
São Barnabé P . . . 160 B1
São Bartoloméda Serra
P 160 A1
São Bartolomeu de
Messines P 160 B1
São Bento P 140 C2
São Brás P 160 B2
São Brás do
Reguedoura P . . 154 C2
São Cristóvão P . . 154 C2
São Domingos P . . 160 B1
São Geraldo P . . . 154 C2
São Jacinto P 148 B1
São João da Madeira
P 148 B1
São João da Pesqueira
P 148 A2
São João da Ribeira
P 154 B2
São João da Serra
P 148 B1
São João da Venda
P 160 B2
São João dos
Caldeireiros P . . . 160 B2
São Julião P 155 B3
São Leonardo P . . . 155 C3
São Luis P 160 B1
São Manços P 155 C3
São Marcos da
Ataboeira P 160 B2
Saõ Marcos da Serra
P 160 B1
São Marcos de Campo
P 155 C3
São Martinho da Cortiça
P 148 B1
São Martinho das
Amoreiras P 160 B1
São Martinho do Porto
P 154 B1
São Matias
Beja P 160 A2
Évora P 154 C2
São Miguel d'Acha
P 155 A3
São Miguel de Machede
P 155 C3
São Pedro da Torre
P 140 C2
São Pedro de Cadeira
P 154 B1

São Pedro de Moel
P 154 B1
São Pedro de Solis
P 160 B2
São Pedro do Sul
P 148 B1
Saorge F 133 B3
São Romão P 154 C2
São Sebastião dos
Carros P 160 B2
São Teotónio P . . . 160 B1
São Torcato P 148 A1
Sapataria P 154 C1
Sapes GR 183 B7
Sapiãos P 148 A2
Sa Pobla E 167 B3
Sappada I 109 C3
Sappen N 192 C5
Sapri I 174 A1
Sarajärvi FIN . . . 197 D10
Sarajevo BIH 139 B4
Saramon F 129 C3
Sarandë AL 182 D2
Saranovo SRB . . . 127 C2
Saraorci SRB 127 C3
Sa Rapita E 167 B3
Saray TR 186 A2
Saraycık TR 187 C4
Sarayköy TR 188 B3
Saraylar TR 186 B2
Sarayönü TR 189 A7
Sarbia PL 75 B5
Sarbinowo
Zachodnio-Pomorskie
PL 67 B4
Zachodnio-Pomorskie
PL 74 B3
Sárbogárd H 112 C2
Sarcelles F 90 B2
Sarche I 121 A4
Sardara I 179 C2
Sardoal P 154 B2
Sardón de Duero
E 150 A3
Sare F 144 A2
S'Arenal E 166 B2
Šarengrad HR 125 B5
Sarentino I 108 C2
Sarezzo I 120 B3
Sargans CH 107 B4
Sári H 112 B3
Saríbeyler TR 186 C2
Sarıcakaya TR . . . 187 B5
Sari-d'Orcino F . . . 180 A1
Sarıgöl TR 188 A3
Sarıkaya TR 23 B8
Sarıköy TR 186 B2
Sarilhos Grandes
P 154 C2
Sariñena E 145 C3
Sarıoba TR 187 C7
Sariyer TR 186 A4
Sarkad H 113 C5
Sárkeresztes H . . .112 B2
Sárkeresztúr H . . .112 B2
Särkijärvi FIN . . . 196 B6
Şarkikaraağaç TR . 189 A6
Şarköy TR 186 B2
Sarlat-la-Canéda F 129 B4
Sarliac-sur-l'Isle F . 129 A3
Sármellék H 111 C4
Särna S 199 D10
Sarnadas P 155 B3
Sarnano I 136 B2
Sarnen CH 106 C3
Sarnesfield GB 39 B4
Sárnico I 120 B2
Sarno I 170 C2
Sarnonico I 121 A4
Sarnow D 74 A2
Sarny UA 13 C7
Saronno I 120 B2
Sárosd H 112 B2
Šarovce SK 112 A2
Sarpoil F 117 B3
Sarpsborg N 54 A2
Sarracín E 143 B3
Sarral E 147 C2
Sarralbe F 92 B3
Sarrancolin F 145 B4
Sarras F 117 B4
Sarre I 119 B4
Sarreaus E 140 B3
Sarrebourg F 92 C3
Sarreguemines F . . 92 B3
Sárrétudvari H 113 B5
Sarre-Union F 92 C3
Sarria E 141 B3
Sarriàde Ter E . . . 147 B3
Sarrión E 153 B3
Sarroca de Lleida
E 153 A4
Sarroch I 179 C3
Sarron F 128 C2
Sársina I 135 B5
Særslev DK 59 C3
Sarstedt D 72 B2
Sárszentlőrinc H . .112 C2
Sárszentmihaly H .112 B2
Sárszentmiklós H . .112 C2
Sarteano I 135 C4
Sartène F 180 B1
Sartilly F 88 B2
Sartirana Lomellina
I 120 B1
Saruhanlı TR 186 D2

Sárvár H 111 B3
Sarvisvaara S 196 C4
Sarzana I 134 A2
Sarzeau F 101 B3
Sarzedas P 155 B3
Sasalli TR 188 A1
Sasamón E 142 B2
Sa Savina E 166 C1
Sásd H 125 A4
Sasino PL 68 A2
Sássari I 178 B2
Sassello I 133 A4
Sassenberg D 71 C5
Sassetta I 134 B3
Sassnitz D 66 B2
Sasso d'Ombrone
I 135 C4
Sassoferrato I 136 B1
Sassoleone I 135 A4
Sasso Marconi I . . 135 A4
Sassuolo I 135 A3
Sástago E 153 A3
Šaštinske Stráže
SK 98 C1
Sas van Gent NL . . 79 A3
Sâtåhaugen N 199 C7
Satão P 148 B2
Sátenäs S 55 B3
Säter S 50 B2
Sätila S 60 B2
Satillieu F 117 B4
Satnica Đakovačka
HR 125 B4
Sátoraljaújhely H . . 16 A4
Satow D 65 C4
Sätra-brunn S 50 C3
Sætre N 54 A1
Satrup D 64 B2
Satteins A 107 B4
Satu Mare RO 17 B5
Saturnia I 168 A1
Saucats F 128 B2
Saucelle E 149 A3
Sauda N 52 A2
Sauðárkrókur IS . . 190 B6
Saudasjøen N 52 A2
Sauerlach D 108 B2
Saugues F 117 C3
Sauherad N 53 A5
Saujon F 114 C3
Sauland N 53 A4
Saulces Monclin F . 91 B4
Saulgau D 107 A4
Saulgrub D 108 B2
Saulieu F 104 B3
Saulnot F 106 B1
Sault F 131 A4
Sault-Brénaz F 118 B2
Sault-de-Navailles
F 128 C2
Saulx F 105 B5
Saulxures-sur-Moselotte
F 106 B1
Saulzais-le-Potier
F 103 C4
Saumos F 128 B1
Saumur F 102 B1
Saunavaara FIN . . 197 B10
Saundersfoot GB . . 39 C2
Saurat F 146 B2
Saurbær
Borgarfjarðarsýsla
IS 190 C4
Dalasýsla IS 190 B4
Eyjafjarðarsýsla
IS 191 B7
Sáuris I 109 C3
Sausset-les-Pins F 131 B4
Sauteyrargues F . . 131 B2
Sauvagnat F 116 B2
Sauve F 131 B2
Sauveterre-de-Béarn
F 144 A3
Sauveterre-de-Guyenne
F 128 B2
Sauviat-sur-Vige F .116 B1
Sauxillanges F 117 B3
Sauzet
Drôme F 117 C4
Lot F 129 B4
Sauzé-Vaussais F .115 B4
Sauzon F 100 B2
Sava I 173 B3
Sävar S 200 C6
Sævareid N 46 B2
Savarsin RO 16 B5
Sävast S 196 D4
Säve S 60 B1
Savelletri I 173 B3
Savelli I 174 B2
Savenay F 101 B4
Saverdun F 146 A2
Saverne F 93 C3
Savières F 91 C3
Savigliano I 119 C4
Savignac-les-Eglises
F 129 A3
Savignano Irpino I . 171 B3
Savignano sul Rubicone
I 136 A1
Savigny-sur-Braye
F 102 B2
Savines-le-lac F . . 132 A2
Savino Selo SRB . . 126 B1

Savio I 135 A5
Sävja S 51 C4
Šavnik MNE 139 C5
Savognin CH 107 C4
Savona I 133 A4
Savonlinna FIN 9 B6
Savournon F 132 A1
Sævråsvåg N 46 B2
Sävsjö S 62 A2
Sävsjön S 50 C1
Sävsjöström S 62 A3
Savudrija HR 122 B2
Savukoski FIN 197 B11
Sawbridgeworth GB 45 B4
Sawtry GB 44 A3
Sax E 159 C3
Saxdalen S 50 B1
Saxilby GB 40 B3
Saxmundham GB . . 45 A5
Saxnäs S 195 F6
Saxthorpe GB 41 C5
Sayalonga E 163 B3
Sayatón E 151 B5
Sayda D 83 B5
Säytsjärvi FIN . . . 193 C11
Šazava CZ 97 B3
Sázava CZ 96 B2
Scaër F 100 A2
Scafa I 169 A4
Scalasaig GB 34 B1
Scalby GB 40 A3
Scalea I 174 B1
Scaletta Zanclea I . 177 A4
Scalloway GB 33 A5
Scamblesby GB . . . 41 B3
Scandale I 175 B2
Scandiano I 121 C3
Scandicci I 135 B4
Scandolara Ravara
I 120 B3
Scanno I 169 B3
Scansano I 168 A1
Scanzano Jónico I . 174 A2
Scarborough GB . . . 40 A3
Scardovari I 122 C1
Scardoy GB 32 D2
Scarperia I 135 B4
Scarriff IRL 28 B3
Scey-sur-Saône et St
Albin F 105 B4
Schachendorf A . . .111 B3
Schaffhausen CH . 107 B3
Schafstädt D 83 A3
Schafstedt D 64 B2
Schäftlarn D 108 B2
Schagen NL 70 B1
Schalkau D 82 B3
Schangnau CH . . . 106 C2
Schapbach D 93 C4
Scharbeutz D 65 B3
Schärding A 96 C1
Scharnitz A 108 B2
Scharrel D 71 A4
Schattendorf A 111 B3
Scheemda NL 71 A3
Scheessel D 72 A2
Schéggia I 136 B1
Scheibbs A 110 A2
Scheibenberg D . . . 83 B4
Scheidegg D 107 B4
Scheifling A 110 B1
Scheinfeld D 94 B2
Schelklingen D . . . 94 C1
Schenefeld
Schleswig-Holstein
D 64 B2
Schleswig-Holstein
D 72 A2
Schenklengsfeld D . 82 B1
Scherfede D 81 A5
Schermbeck D 80 A2
Scherpenzeel NL . . 70 B2
Schesslitz D 94 B3
Scheveningen NL . . 70 B1
Schiedam NL 79 A4
Schieder-Schwalenberg
D 72 C2
Schierling D 95 C4
Schiers CH 107 C4
Schildau D 83 A4
Schillingen D 92 B2
Schillingsfürst D . . 94 B2
Schilpário I 120 A3
Schiltach D 93 C4
Schiltigheim F 93 C3
Schio I 121 B4
Schirmeck F 92 C3
Schirnding D 83 B4
Schkeuditz D 83 A4
Schkölen D 83 A3
Schlabendorf D . . . 84 A1
Schladen D 73 B3
Schladming A 109 B4
Schlangen D 81 A4
Schleiden D 80 B2
Schleiz D 83 B3
Schleswig D 64 B2
Schleusingen D . . . 82 B2
Schlieben D 83 A5
Schliengen D 106 B2
Schliersee D 108 B2
Schlitz D 81 B5
Schloss Neuhaus D 81 A4
Schlotheim D 82 A2
Schluchsee D 106 B3
Schlüchtern D 81 B5
Schmallenberg D . . 81 A4

San–Sch 273

Schmelz D 92 B2
Schmidmühlen D . . 95 B3
Schmiedeberg D . . 84 B1
Schmiedefeld D . . . 82 B2
Schmirn A 108 B2
Schmölln
Brandenburg D . . .74 A3
Sachsen D 83 B4
Schnaittach D 95 B3
Schneeberg D 83 B4
Schneizlreuth D . . 109 B3
Schneverdingen D . 72 A2
Schöder A 109 B5
Schoenburg B 80 B2
Schollene D 73 B5
Schöllkrippen D . . . 81 B5
Schomberg D 107 A3
Schönach D 95 C4
Schönau
Baden-Württemberg
D 106 B2
Bayern D 95 C4
Schönbeck D 74 A2
Schönberg
Bayern D 96 C1
Mecklenburg-
Vorpommern D . . .65 C3
Schleswig-Holstein
D 65 B3
Schönebeck D 73 B4
Schöneck D 83 B4
Schönecken- D . . . 80 B2
Schönermark D . . . 74 A2
Schönewalde D . . . 83 A5
Schongau D 108 B1
Schöngrabern A . . . 97 C4
Schönhagen D 81 A5
Schönhausen D . . . 73 B5
Schöningen D 73 B3
Schönkirchen D . . . 64 B3
Schönsee D 95 B4
Schöntal D 94 B1
Schönthal D 95 B4
Schonungen D 94 A2
Schönwalde D 65 B3
Schoondijke NL . . . 79 A3
Schoonebeek NL . . 71 B3
Schoonhoven NL . . 79 A4
Schopfheim D 106 B2
Schöppenstedt D . . 73 B3
Schörfling A 109 B4
Schorndorf D 94 C1
Schortens D 71 A4
Schotten D 81 B5
Schramberg D . . . 106 A3
Schraplau D 83 A3
Schrattenberg A . . . 97 C4
Schrecksbach D . . . 81 B5
Schrems A 96 C3
Schrobenhausen D . 95 C3
Schröcken A 107 B5
Schröder D 94 B1
Schruns A 107 B4
Schüpfheim CH . . . 106 C3
Schüttorf D 71 B4
Schwaan D 65 C5
Schwabach D 94 B3
Schwäbisch Gmünd
D 94 C1
Schwäbisch Hall D . 94 B1
Schwabmünchen
D 108 A1
Schwadorf A 111 A3
Schwagstorf D 71 B4
Schwaigern D 93 B5
Schwalmstadt D . . . 81 B5
Schwanberg A 110 C2
Schwanden CH . . . 107 C4
Schwandorf D 95 B4
Schwanebeck D . . . 73 C4
Schwanenstadt A . 109 A4
Schwanewede D . . 72 A1
Schwanfeld D 94 B2
Schwangau D 108 B1
Schwarmstedt D . . . 72 B2
Schwarza D 82 B2
Schwarzach im Pongau
A 109 B4
Schwarzau im Gebirge
A 110 B2
Schwarzenau A . . . 97 C3
Schwarzenbach D . . 83 B3
Schwarzenbach am
Wald D 83 B3
Schwarzenbek D . . 72 A3
Schwarzenberg D . . 83 B4
Schwarzenburg
CH 106 C2
Schwarzenfeld D . . 95 B4
Schwarz-heide D . . 84 A1
Schwaz A 108 B2
Schwechat A 111 A3
Schwedt D 74 A3
Schwei D 71 A5
Schweich D 92 B2
Schweighausen D . 106 A2
Schweinfurt D 94 A2
Schweinitz D 83 A5
Schweinrich D 74 A1
Schwelm D 80 A3
Schwemsal D 83 A4
Schwendt A 109 B3
Schwenningen D . . 107 A3
Schwerin D 73 A4

Schwerte D 81 A3
Schweskau D 73 B4
Schwetzingen D . . . 93 B4
Schwyz CH 107 B3
Sciacca I 176 B2
Scicli I 177 C3
Ściechów PL 75 B3
Scigliano I 175 B2
Scilla I 175 C1
Ścinawa PL 85 A4
Scionzier F 118 A3
Scoglitti I 177 C3
Scole GB 45 A5
Sconser GB 31 B2
Scopello
  Piemonte I 119 B5
  Sicilia I 176 A1
Scordia I 177 B3
Scorzè I 121 B5
Scotch Corner GB . . 37 B5
Scotter GB 40 B3
Scourie GB 32 C1
Scousburgh GB . . . 33 B5
Scrabster GB 32 C3
Screeb IRL 28 A2
Scremerston GB . . . 37 A5
Scritto I 136 B1
Scunthorpe GB 40 B3
Scuol CH 107 C5
Scúrcola Marsicana
  I 169 A3
Seaford GB 45 C4
Seaham GB 37 B5
Seahouses GB 37 A5
Seascale GB 36 B3
Seaton GB 43 B3
Sebazac-Concourès
  F 130 A1
Seben TR 187 B6
Sebersdorf A 110 B2
Sebezh RUS 8 D6
Sebnitz D 84 B2
Seborga I 133 B3
Seby S 63 B4
Seč
  Vychodočeský
    CZ 97 B3
  Západočeský CZ . . . 96 B1
Sečanj SRB 126 B2
Secemin PL 87 B3
Séchault F 91 B4
Seckau A 110 B1
Seclin F 78 B3
Secondigny F 114 B3
Seda P 155 B3
Sedan F 91 B4
Sedano E 143 B3
Sedbergh GB 37 B4
Sedella E 163 B3
Séderon F 131 A4
Sedgefield GB 37 B5
Sedico I 121 A5
Sédilo I 178 B2
Sédini I 178 B2
Sedlarica HR 124 B3
Sedlčany CZ 96 B2
Sedlec-Prčice CZ . . 96 B2
Sedlice CZ 96 B1
Sędziejowice PL . . 86 A3
Sędziszów PL 87 B4
Sędziszów Małopolski
  PL 87 B5
Seebach F 93 C3
Seeboden A 109 C4
Seefeld
  Brandenburg D . . 74 B2
  Niedersachsen D . .71 A5
Seefeld in Tirol A . . 108 B2
Seeg D 108 B1
Seehausen
  Sachsen-Anhalt D . .73 B4
  Sachsen-Anhalt D . .73 B4
Seeheim-Jugenheim
  D 93 B4
Seelbach D 93 C3
Seelow D 74 B3
Seelze D 72 B2
Seerhausen D 83 A5
Sées F 89 B4
Seesen D 82 A2
Seeshaupt D 108 B2
Seewalchen A 109 B4
Seferihisar TR 188 A1
Sefkerin SRB 127 B2
Segård N 48 B2
Segerstad S 55 A4
Segesd H 124 A3
Seglinge FIN 51 B7
Segmon S 55 A4
Segonzac F 115 C3
Segorbe E 159 B3
Segovia E 151 B3
Segré F 101 B5
Segura
  E 144 B1
  P 155 B3
Segura de León E . 161 A3
Segura de los Baños
  E 152 B3
Ségur-les-Villas F . .116 B2
Segurrilla E 150 B3
Sehnde D 72 B2
Seia P 148 B2
Seiches-sur-le-Loir
  F 102 B1

Seifhennersdorf D . 84 B2
Seignelay F 104 B2
Seijo E 140 C2
Seilhac F 116 B1
Seilles B 79 B5
Seim N 46 B2
Seinäjoki FIN 8 A3
Seissan F 145 A4
Seitenstetten Markt
  A 110 A1
Seixal P 154 C1
Seiz A 110 B1
Seizthal A 110 B1
Sejerslev DK 58 B1
Seksna RUS 9 C11
Selárdalur IS 190 B1
Selárgius I 179 C3
Selb D 83 B4
Selby GB 40 B2
Selca HR 138 B2
Selce HR 123 B3
Selçuk TR 188 B2
Selde DK 58 B2
Selenča SRB 126 B1
Selendi
  Manisa TR 186 D2
  Manisa TR 186 D3
Selenicë AL 182 C1
Sélestat F 106 A2
Seleuš SRB 126 B2
Selevac SRB 127 C2
Selfoss IS 190 D5
Selgua E 145 C4
Selice SK 112 A1
Seligenstadt D 93 A4
Seligenthal D 82 B2
Selimiye TR 188 B2
Selizharovo RUS . . . 9 D8
Selja S 50 A1
Selje N 198 C2
Seljelvnes N 192 C3
Seljord N 53 A4
Selkirk GB 35 C5
Sellano I 136 C1
Selles-St Denis F . . 103 B3
Selles-sur-Cher F . . 103 B3
Sellières F 105 C4
Sellin D 66 B2
Sellye H 125 B3
Selm D 80 A3
Selnica ob Dravi
  SLO 110 C2
Selongey F 105 B4
Selonnet F 132 A2
Selow D 65 C4
Selsey GB 44 C3
Selsingen D 72 A2
Selters D 81 B3
Seltz F 93 C4
Selva E 167 B2
Selva di Cadore I . . 108 C3
Selva di Val Gardena
  I 108 C2
Selvik
  Sogn og Fjordane
    N 46 A2
  Vestfold N 54 A1
Selvino I 120 B2
Selyatyn UA 17 B6
Sem N 54 A1
Semeljci HR 125 B4
Semič SLO 123 B4
Semide
  F 91 B4
  P 148 B1
Semily CZ 84 B3
Seminara I 175 C1
Semlac RO 126 A2
Semlacu Mare RO . 126 B3
Semmen-stedt D . . 73 B3
Šempeter SLO 123 A4
Semriach A 110 B2
Semur-en-Auxois
  F 104 B3
Sena E 145 C3
Sena de Luna E . . . 141 B5
Senarpont F 90 B1
Sénas F 131 B4
Senćanski Trešnjevac
  SRB 126 B1
Sencelles E 167 B2
Senčur SLO 123 A3
Senden
  Bayern D 94 C2
  Nordrhein-Westfalen
    D 80 A3
Sendenhorst D 81 A3
Sendim P 149 A3
Senec SK 111 A4
Seneffe B 79 B4
Séneghe I 178 B2
Senés E 164 B2
Senez F 132 B2
Senftenberg D 84 A1
Sengouagnet F . . . 145 B4
Sengwarden D 71 A5
Senica SK 98 C1
Senice na Hané CZ . 98 B1
Senigállia I 136 B2
Senirkent TR 189 A5
Sénis I 179 C2
Senise I 174 A2
Senj HR 123 C3
Senje SRB 127 D3
Senjehopen N 194 A8
Senjski Rudnik
  SRB 127 D3
Senlis F 90 B2

Sennan S 60 C2
Sennecey-le-Grand
  F 105 C3
Sennen GB 42 B1
Senno BY 13 A8
Sénnori I 178 B2
Sennwald CH 107 B4
Sennybridge GB . . . 39 C3
Senohrad SK 99 C3
Senonches F 89 B5
Senones F 92 C2
Senorbì I 179 C3
Senovo SLO 123 A4
Senožeče SLO . . . 123 B3
Senožeti SLO 123 A3
Sens F 104 A2
Sens-de-Bretagne
  F 101 A4
Senta SRB 126 B2
Senterada E 145 B4
Sentilj SLO 110 C2
Šentjernej SLO . . . 123 B4
Šentjur SLO 123 A4
Senumstad N 53 B4
Seoane E 141 B3
Seon CH 106 B3
Sépeaux F 104 B2
Sépey CH 119 A4
Sepino I 170 B2
Sępólno Krajeńskie
  PL 76 A2
Seppenrade D 80 A3
Seppois F 106 B2
Septemvri BG 183 A6
Septeuil F 90 C1
Sepúlveda E 151 A4
Sequals I 122 A1
Sequeros E 149 B3
Seraincourt F 91 B4
Seraing B 80 B1
Seravezza I 134 B3
Seredka RUS 8 C6
Seregélyes H 112 B2
Seregno I 120 B2
Sérent F 101 B3
Serfaus A 108 B1
Sergiyev Posad
  RUS 9 D11
Seriate I 120 B2
Sérifontaine F 90 B1
Serifos GR 185 B5
Sérignan F 130 B2
Serik TR 189 C6
Serina I 120 B2
Serinhisar TR 188 B4
Sermaises F 90 C2
Sermaize-les-Bains
  F 91 C4
Sérmide I 121 C4
Sermoneta I 169 B2
Sernache de Bonjardim
  P 154 B2
Sernancelhe P 148 B2
Serock PL 77 B6
Serón E 164 B2
Serón de Najima E 152 A1
Serooskerke NL . . . 79 A3
Seròs E 153 A4
Serpa P 160 B2
Serracapriola I 171 B3
Serrada E 150 A3
Serradifalco I 176 B2
Serradilla E 155 B4
Serradilla del Arroyo
  E 149 B3
Serradilla del Llano
  E 149 B3
Serramanna I 179 C2
Serramazzoni I . . . 135 A3
Serranillos E 150 B3
Serrapetrona I 136 B2
Serra San Bruno I . 175 C2
Serra San Quírico I 136 B2
Serrastretta I 175 B2
Serravalle
  Piemonte I 119 B5
  Umbria I 136 C2
Serravalle di Chienti
  I 136 B1
Serravalle Scrívia I 120 C1
Serre I 172 B1
Serrejón E 150 C2
Serres
  F 132 A1
  GR 183 B5
Serrières F 117 B4
Serrières-de-Briord
  F 118 B2
Sersale I 175 B2
Sertã P 154 B2
Sertig Dörfli CH . . . 107 C4
Servance F 106 B1
Serverette F 117 C3
Servia GR 182 C4
Servian F 130 B2
Serviers F 131 A3
Servigliano I 136 B2
Serzedelo P 148 A1
Seseña Nuevo E . . 151 B4
Sesimbra P 154 C1
Seskarö S 196 D6
Seskinore GB 27 B3
Sesma E 144 B1
Sessa Aurunca I . . 170 B1
Ses Salines E 167 B3

Sesta Godano I . . . 134 A2
Šestanovac HR . . . 138 B2
Sestao E 143 A4
Sestino I 135 B5
Sesto I 109 C3
Sesto Calende I . . . 120 B1
Sesto Fiorentino I . 135 B4
Séstola I 135 A3
Sesto San Giovanni
  I 120 B2
Sestriere I 119 C3
Sestri Levante I . . . 134 A2
Sestroretsk RUS . . . 9 B7
Sestu I 179 C3
Sesvete HR 124 B2
Setcases E 146 B3
Sète F 130 B2
Setenil E 162 B2
Setermoen N 194 B9
Šetonje SRB 127 C3
Setskog N 54 A2
Settalsjølia N 199 C7
Séttimo Torinese I .119 B4
Séttimo Vittone I . . .119 B4
Settle GB 40 A1
Setúbal P 154 C2
Seubersdorf D 95 B3
Seúi I 179 C3
Seúlo I 179 C3
Seurre F 105 C4
Sevel DK 58 B1
Sevenoaks GB 45 B4
Sévérac-le-Château
  F 130 A2
Sever do Vouga P . 148 B1
Severin HR 123 B4
Severomorsk RUS . 3 B13
Séveso I 120 B2
Ševětín CZ 96 B2
Sevettijärvi FIN . . . 193 C12
Sévigny F 91 B4
Sevilla E 162 A2
Sevilla la Nueva E . 151 B3
Seville = Sevilla E . 162 A2
Sevilleja de la Jara
  E 156 A3
Sevlievo BG 17 D6
Sevnica SLO 123 A4
Sevojno SRB 127 D1
Sevrier F 118 B3
Sexdrega S 60 B3
Seyches F 129 B3
Seyda D 83 A4
Seydişehir TR 189 B6
Seyðisfjörður IS . 191 B12
Seyitgazi TR 187 C5
Seyitömer TR 187 C4
Seymen TR 186 A2
Seyne F 132 A2
Seynes F 131 A3
Seyssel F 118 B2
Sezana SLO 122 B2
Sézanne F 91 C3
Sezulfe P 149 A2
Sezze I 169 B3
Sfântu Gheorghe
  RO 17 C6
Sforzacosta I 136 B2
Sgarsta Mhor GB . . 31 B1
's-Gravendeel NL . . 79 A4
's-Gravenhage = The
  Hague NL 70 B1
's-Gravenzande NL . 79 A4
Shaftesbury GB . . . 43 A4
Shaldon GB 43 B3
Shalskiy RUS 9 B9
Shanagolden IRL . . 29 B2
Shanklin GB 44 C2
Shap GB 37 B4
Sharpness GB 43 A4
Shawbury GB 38 B4
's-Heerenberg NL . . 80 A2
Sheerness GB 45 B4
Sheffield GB 40 B2
Shefford GB 44 A3
Shëmri AL 182 A2
Shenfield GB 45 B4
Shëngjergj AL 182 B2
Shepetivka UA 13 C7
Shepshed GB 40 C2
Shepton Mallet GB . 43 A4
Sherborne GB 43 B4
Shercock IRL 27 C4
Sheringham GB . . . 41 C5
's-Hertogenbosch
  NL 79 A5
Shiel Bridge GB . . . 32 D1
Shieldaig GB 31 B3
Shijak AL 182 B1
Shillelagh IRL 30 B2
Shimsk RUS 9 C7
Shipston-on-Stour
  GB 44 A2
Shklow BY 13 A9
Shkodër AL 182 B1
Shoeburyness GB . . 45 B4
Shoreham-by-Sea
  GB 44 C3
Shotley Gate GB . . 45 B5
Shrewsbury GB . . . 38 B4
Shugozero RUS 9 C9
Shumen BG 17 D7
Sianów PL 67 B5
Siátista GR 182 C3
Siauges-St Romain
  F 117 B3

Šiauliai LT 8 E3
Sibari I 174 B2
Sibbhult S 63 B2
Šibenik HR 138 B1
Siberstedt D 64 B2
Sibinj HR 125 B3
Sibiu RO 17 C6
Sibnica SRB 127 C2
Sibsey GB 41 B4
Siculiana I 176 B2
Šid SRB 125 B5
Sidari GR 182 D1
Siddeburen NL . . . 71 A3
Sidensjö S 200 C4
Siderno I 175 C2
Sidirokastro GR . . . 183 B5
Sidmouth GB 43 B3
Sidzina PL 99 B3
Siebe N 192 D7
Siebenlehn D 83 A5
Siedlce PL 12 B5
Siedlice PL 75 A4
Siedlinghausen D . . 81 A4
Siedlisko PL 75 B5
Siegburg D 80 B3
Siegen D 81 B4
Siegenburg D 95 C3
Sieghartskirchen
  A 111 A3
Siegsdorf D 109 B3
Siekierki PL 74 B3
Sielpia PL 87 A4
Siemiany PL 69 B4
Siena I 135 B4
Sieniawka PL 84 B2
Sienno PL 87 A5
Sieppijärvi FIN . . . 196 B7
Sieradz PL 86 A2
Sieraków
  Śląskie PL 86 B2
  Wielkopolskie PL . .75 B5
Sierakowice PL . . . 68 A2
Sierck-les-Bains F . 92 B2
Sierentz F 106 B2
Sierning A 110 A1
Sierpc PL 77 B4
Sierra de Fuentes
  E 155 B4
Sierra de Luna E . . 144 B3
Sierra de Yeguas
  E 162 A3
Sierre CH 119 A4
Siestrzeń PL 77 B5
Sietamo E 145 B3
Siewierz PL 86 B3
Sigdal N 48 B1
Sigean F 130 B1
Sigerfjord N 194 B6
Sighetu-Marmatiei
  RO 17 B5
Sighişoara RO 17 B6
Sigillo I 136 B1
Siglufjörður IS . . . 191 A7
Sigmaringen D . . . 107 A4
Signa I 135 B4
Signes F 132 B1
Signy-l'Abbaye F . . 91 B4
Signy-le-Petit F . . . 91 B4
Sigogne F 115 C3
Sigri GR 183 D7
Sigtuna S 57 A3
Sigueiro E 140 B2
Sigüenza E 151 A5
Sigües E 144 B2
Sigulda LV 8 D4
Siilinjärvi FIN 8 A5
Sikenica SK 112 A2
Sikfors S 196 D4
Sikia GR 183 C5
Sikinos GR 185 C6
Sikkilsdalseter N . . 47 A6
Siklós H 125 B4
Sikórz PL 77 B4
Sikselet S 195 D8
Silandro I 108 C1
Silánus I 178 B2
Silba HR 137 A3
Silbaš SRB 126 B1
Şile TR 187 A4
Siles E 164 A2
Silgueiros P 148 B2
Silifke TR 23 C7
Silíqua I 179 C2
Silistra BG 17 C7
Silivri TR 186 A3
Siljan N 53 A5
Siljansnäs S 50 B1
Silkeborg DK 59 B2
Silla E 159 B3
Sillamäe EST 8 C5
Silleda E 140 B2
Sillé-le-Guillaume
  F 102 A1
Sillenstede D 71 A4
Sillerud S 54 A3
Sillian A 109 C3
Silloth GB 36 B3
Silno PL 68 B2
Silnowo PL 68 B1
Silo HR 123 B3
Sils E 147 C3
Silsand N 194 A8
Silte S 57 C4
Šilute LT 12 A4
Silvalen N 195 E3
Silvaplana CH 107 C4
Silvares P 148 B2
Silverberg S 50 B2

Silvermines IRL . . . 28 B3
Silverstone GB . . . 44 A2
Silverton GB 43 B3
Silves P 160 B1
Silvi Marina I 169 A4
Simandre F 105 C3
Šimanovci SRB . . . 127 C2
Simard F 105 C4
Simat de Valldigna
  E 159 B3
Simav TR 186 C3
Simbach
  Bayern D 95 C4
  Bayern D 95 C5
Simbário I 175 C2
Simeonovgrad BG . 183 A7
Simeria RO 17 C5
Simi GR 188 C2
Simićevo SRB 127 C3
Simitli BG 183 B5
Simlångsdalen S . . 60 C3
Simmerath D 80 B2
Simmerberg D . . . 107 B4
Simmern D 93 B3
Simo FIN 197 D8
Šimonovce SK 99 C4
Simonsbath GB . . . 43 A3
Simonstorp S 56 B2
Simontornya H 112 C2
Simplon CH 119 A5
Simrishamn S 63 C2
Sinaia RO 17 C6
Sinalunga I 135 B4
Sinarcas E 159 B2
Sincan TR 187 C7
Sincanlı TR 187 D5
Sindal DK 58 A3
Sindelfingen D . . . 93 C5
Sindia I 178 B2
Sındırgı TR 186 C3
Sinekli TR 186 A3
Sines P 160 B1
Sinetta FIN 197 C8
Sineu E 167 B3
Singen D 107 B3
Singleton GB 44 C3
Singsås N 199 C7
Siniscóla I 178 B3
Sinj HR 138 B2
Sinlabajos E 150 A3
Sinn D 81 B4
Sínnai I 179 C3
Sinnes N 52 B2
Sinop TR 23 A8
Sins CH 106 B3
Sinsheim D 93 B4
Sint Annaland NL . . 79 A4
Sint Annaparochie
  NL 70 A2
Sint Athonis NL . . . 80 A1
Sint Nicolaasga NL . 70 B2
Sint Oedenrode NL . 79 A5
Sintra P 154 C1
Sinzheim D 93 C4
Sinzig D 80 B3
Siófok H 112 C2
Sion CH 119 A4
Sion Mills GB 27 B3
Siorac-en-Périgord
  F 129 B3
Šipanska Luka HR 139 C3
Šipovo BIH 138 A3
Sira N 52 B2
Siracusa I 177 B4
Siret RO 17 B7
Sirevåg N 52 B1
Sirig SRB 126 B1
Sirkka FIN 196 B7
Sirmione I 121 B3
Sirniö FIN 197 D11
Sirok H 113 B4
Široké SK 99 C4
Široki Brijeg BIH . . 139 B3
Sirolo I 136 B2
Siruela E 156 B2
Sisak HR 124 B2
Sisante E 158 B1
Šišljavić HR 123 B4
Sissach CH 106 B2
Sissonne F 91 B3
Sistelo P 140 C2
Sisteron F 132 A1
Sistiana I 122 B2
Sistranda N 198 B5
Sitasjaurestugorna
  S 194 C8
Sitges E 147 C2
Sitia GR 185 D7
Sittard NL 80 A1
Sittensen D 72 A2
Sittingbourne GB . . 45 B4
Sitzenroda D 83 A4
Sivac SRB 126 B1
Sivaslı TR 189 A4
Siverić HR 138 B2
Sivrihisar TR 187 C6
Sixt-Fer-á-Cheval
  F 119 A3
Siziano I 120 B2
Sizun F 100 A1
Sjenica SRB 16 D3
Sjoa N 198 D6
Sjøåsen N 199 A8
Sjöbo S 61 D3
Sjøenden
  Hedmark N 48 A3
  Hedmark N 48 B3
Sjøholt N 198 C3

Sjøli N 48 A3
Sjølstad N 199 A9
Sjölunda S 56 A1
Sjømarken S 60 B2
Sjørring DK 58 B1
Sjötofta S 60 B3
Sjötorp S 55 B4
Sjoutnäset S . . .199 A11
Sjøvegan N 194 B8
Sjuntorp S 54 B3
Skåbu N 47 A6
Skafså N 53 A4
Skaftafell IS 191 D9
Skagaströnd IS . 190 B5
Skagen DK. 58 A3
Skagersvik S 55 B5
Skaiå N 53 B3
Skaidi N 193 B8
Skala GR 184 A1
Skała PL 87 B3
Skaland N 194 A8
Skala Oropou GR . 185 A4
Skala-Podilska UA . 13 D7
Skalat UA. 13 D6
Skalbmierz PL 87 B4
Skålevik N 53 B4
Skalica SK 98 C1
Skalité SK 98 B2
Skällinge S 60 B2
Skalná CZ 83 B4
Skals DK 58 B2
Skælskør DK 65 A4
Skalstugan S 199 B9
Skanderborg DK . . 59 B2
Skånes-Fagerhult S 61 C3
Skåne-Tranås S. . . 61 D3
Skånevik N 52 A1
Skänninge S 55 B6
Skanör med Falsterbo
S. 66 A1
Skåpafors S. 54 A3
Skąpe PL 75 B4
Skara S 55 B4
Skærbæk DK 64 A1
Skärberget N 194 B7
Skärblacka S 56 B1
Skarð IS 190 B3
Skarda S 200 B4
Skare N 46 C3
Skåre N 55 A4
Skärhamn S. 60 B1
Skarnes N 48 B3
Skärplinge S 51 B4
Skarpnatö FIN 51 B6
Skarp Salling DK. . 58 B2
Skarrild DK 59 C1
Skarstad N 194 B7
Skärstad S 62 A2
Skarsvåg N 193 A9
Skarszewy PL 69 A3
Skårup DK 65 A3
Skärvången S 199 B11
Skarvsjöby S. 195 F8
Skaryszew PL 87 A5
Skarżysko-Kamienna
PL. 87 A4
Skarzysko Ksiazece
PL. 87 A4
Skatøy N 53 B5
Skattkärr S 55 A4
Skattungbyn S 50 A1
Skatval N 199 B7
Skaulo S 196 B4
Skave DK 59 B1
Skawina PL 99 B3
Skebobruk S 51 C5
Skebokvarn S 56 A2
Skedala S. 61 C2
Skedevi S. 56 B1
Skedsmokorset N . 48 B3
Skee S 54 B2
Skegness GB. 41 B4
Skei N. 46 A3
Skela SRB 127 C2
Skelani BIH 127 D1
Skellefteå S 2 D7
Skelleftehamn S . . . 2 D7
Skelmersdale GB . . 38 A4
Skelmorlie GB 34 C3
Skelund DK 58 B3
Skender Vakuf BIH 138 A3
Skene S 60 B2
Skępe PL 77 B4
Skepplanda S 60 B2
Skeppshult S 60 B3
Skerries IRL. 30 A2
Ski N 54 A1
Skiathos GR 183 D5
Skibbereen IRL . . . 29 C2
Skibotn N. 192 C4
Skidra GR 182 C4
Skien N 53 A5
Skierniewice PL. . . 77 C5
Skillingaryd S 60 B4
Skillinge S 63 C2
Skillingmark S 49 C4
Skilloura CY. 181 A2
Skinnardai S 57 A4
Skinnskatteberg S . 50 C2
Skipmannvik N . . . 195 C6
Skipness GB 34 C2
Skipsea GB 41 B3
Skipton GB 40 B1
Skiptvet N 54 A2
Skiros GR 183 E6
Skivarp S 66 A2
Skive DK 58 B2
Skjånes N 193 B12

Skjærhalden N 54 A2
Skjeberg N. 54 A2
Skjeggedal N 46 B3
Skjeljanger N. 46 B1
Skjeljavik N 46 C2
Skjern DK. 59 C1
Skjervøy N 192 B4
Skjold
Rogaland N. 52 A1
Troms N 192 C3
Skjolden N 47 A4
Skjoldastraumen N. 52 A1
Skjøtningsberg N .193 A11
Škocjan SLO 123 B4
Skoczów PL. 98 B2
Skodborg DK. 59 C2
Škofja Loka SLO . . 123 A3
Škofljica SLO. 123 B3
Skog S 51 A3
Skoganvarre N . . . 193 C9
Skogen S 54 A3
Skogfoss N 193 C13
Skoghall S 55 A4
Skogly N 193 C13
Skogn N 199 B8
Skognes N 192 C3
Skogstorp
Halland S 60 C2
Södermanland S. . 56 A2
Skoki PL. 76 B2
Skokloster S 57 A3
Sköldinge S 56 A2
Skole UA 13 D5
Skollenborg N 53 A5
Sköllersta S 56 A1
Skomlin PL 86 A2
Skonseng N 195 D5
Skopelos GR 183 D5
Skopje MK 182 A3
Skoppum N 54 A1
Skórcz PL. 69 B3
Skorogoszcz PL . . . 86 B1
Skoroszów PL 85 A5
Skorovatn N 199 A10
Skorped S 200 C3
Skørping DK 58 B2
Skotfoss N 53 A5
Skotniki PL 87 A3
Skotselv N 48 C1
Skotterud N 49 C4
Skottorp S 61 C2
Skovby DK 64 B2
Skövde S 55 B4
Skovsgård DK 58 A2
Skrad HR 123 B3
Skradin HR 138 B1
Skradnik HR 123 B4
Skråmestø N 46 B1
Škrdlovice CZ 97 B3
Skrea S 60 C2
Skreia N. 48 B2
Skrolsvik N 194 A7
Skruv S 63 B3
Skrwilno PL 77 A4
Skrydstrup DK. . . . 59 C2
Skucani BIH. 138 B2
Skudeneshavn N. . . 52 A1
Skui N 48 C2
Skulsk PL 76 B3
Skultorp S 55 B4
Skultuna S 56 A2
Skuodas LT 8 D2
Skurup S 66 A2
Skute N 48 B2
Skuteč CZ 97 B3
Skutskär S 51 B4
Skutvik N 194 B6
Skvyra UA 13 D8
Skwierzyna PL. . . . 75 B4
Skýcov SK. 98 C2
Skyllberg S 55 B5
Skyttmon S 200 C1
Skyttorp S 51 B4
Sládkovičovo SK. . .111 A4
Slagelse DK. 61 D1
Slagharen NL. 71 B3
Slagnäs S 195 E9
Slaidburn GB. 40 B1
Slane IRL. 30 A2
Slangerup DK. 61 D2
Slano HR 139 C3
Slantsy RUS. 8 C6
Slaný CZ 84 B2
Šlapanice CZ. 97 B4
Slåstad N 48 B3
Slatina
BIH. 139 B3
HR 125 B3
RO 17 C6
Slatina CZ 97 B3
Slatinice CZ. 98 B1
Slättberg S. 50 A1
Slattum S 48 C2
Slavičín CZ 98 B1
Slavkov CZ 98 C1
Slavkovica SRB. . . 127 C2
Slavkov u Brna CZ . 97 B4
Slavonice CZ. 97 B3
Slavonski Brod HR 125 B4
Slavonski Kobas
HR 125 B3
Slavošovce SK . . . 99 C4
Slavskoye RUS . . . 69 A5
Slavuta UA. 13 C7
Sława
Lubuskie PL 85 A4

Sława continued
Zachodnio-Pomorskie
PL. 67 C4
Slawharad BY 13 B9
Sławków PL. 86 B3
Sławno
Wielkopolskie PL . . .76 B2
Zachodnio-Pomorskie
PL. 68 A1
Sławoborze PL 67 C4
Sl'ažany SK 98 C2
Sleaford GB 40 C3
Sleðbrjótur IS 191 B11
Sledmere GB. 40 A3
Sleights GB. 37 B6
Slemmestad N. . . . 54 A1
Ślesin PL 76 B3
Sliač SK 99 C3
Sliema M 175 C3
Sligo IRL 26 B2
Slite S 57 C4
Slitu N 54 A2
Sliven BG. 17 D7
Śliwice PL 68 B3
Slobozia RO 17 C7
Slochteren NL 71 A3
Slöinge S 60 C2
Słomniki PL. 87 B4
Slonim BY 13 B6
Słonowice PL. 87 B4
Słońsk PL 75 B3
Slootdorp NL. 70 B1
Slottsbron S 55 A4
Slough GB 44 B3
Slövag N 46 B2
Slovenj Gradec
SLO 110 C2
Slovenska Bistrica
SLO 123 A4
Slovenská L'upča
SK 99 C3
Slovenská-Ves SK. 99 B4
Slovenské Darmoty
SK 112 A3
Slovenske Konjice
SLO 123 A4
Słubice PL. 74 B3
Sluderno I 108 C1
Sluis NL 78 A3
Šluknov CZ 84 A2
Slunj HR. 123 B4
Słupca PL. 76 B2
Słupia PL 87 A3
Słupiec PL. 85 B4
Słupsk PL. 68 A2
Slutsk BY 13 B7
Smålandsstenar S . 60 B3
Smalåsen N. 195 E4
Smardzewo PL . . . 75 B4
Smarhon BY 13 A7
Smarje SLO 123 A4
Šmarjeta SLO 123 B4
Šmartno SLO. 123 A3
Smečno CZ 84 B2
Smedby S 63 B4
Smědec CZ 96 C2
Smederevo SRB . . 127 C2
Smederevska Palanka
SRB 127 C2
Smedjebacken S . . 50 B2
Smęgorzów PL . . . 87 B5
Smeland N 53 B4
Smidary CZ 84 B3
Śmigiel PL. 75 B5
Smilde NL 71 B3
Smiřice CZ. 85 B3
Smithfield GB 36 B4
Śmitowo PL. 75 A5
Smögen S 54 B2
Smogulec PL 76 A2
Smołdzino PL 68 A2
Smolenice SK 98 C1
Smolensk RUS . . . 13 A10
Smolník SK 99 C4
Smolyan BG 183 B6
Smuka SLO 123 B3
Smygehamn S 66 A2
Smykow PL 87 A4
Snainton GB 40 A3
Snaith GB 40 B2
Snaptun DK 59 C3
Snarby N 192 C3
Snarum N 48 B1
Snåsa N 199 A9
Snedsted DK 58 B1
Sneek NL 70 A2
Sneem IRL 29 C2
Snejbjerg DK 59 B1
Snillfjord N 198 B6
Šnjegotina BIH . . . 125 C3
Snøde DK. 65 A3
Snøfjord N 193 B8
Snogebæk DK 67 A4
Snyatyn UA. 13 D6
Soave I 121 B4
Sober E 140 B3
Sobernheim D 93 B3
Soběslav CZ 96 B2
Sobota
Dolnośląskie PL. . .85 A3
Łódzkie PL 77 B4
Sobotište SK 98 C1
Sobotka CZ 84 B3
Sobótka
Dolnośląskie PL. . .85 B4
Wielkopolskie PL. . .86 A1
Sobra HR 139 C3
Sobrado
Coruña E 140 A2

Sobrado continued
Lugo E 141 B3
Sobral da Adica P . 161 A2
Sobral de Monte Agraço
P. 154 C1
Sobreira Formosa
P. 154 B3
Soca SLO 122 A2
Sochaczew PL. . . . 77 B5
Sochos GR 183 C5
Socodor RO. 113 C5
Socol RO 127 C3
Socovos E 164 A3
Socuéllamos E . . . 158 B1
Sodankylä FIN. . . . 197 B9
Söderåkra S 63 B4
Söderala S 51 A3
Söderås S 50 B2
Söderbärke S 50 B2
Söderby-Karl S . . . 51 C5
Söderfors S 51 B4
Söderhamn S 51 A4
Söderköping S 56 B2
Söderö S 56 B1
Södertälje S 57 A3
Södingberg A 110 B2
Södra Finnö S 56 B2
Södra Ny S 55 A4
Södra Råda S 55 A5
Södra Sandby S . . 61 D3
Södra Vi S 62 A3
Sodražica SLO . . . 123 B3
Sodupe E 143 A3
Soengas P 148 A1
Soest
D 81 A4
NL 70 B2
Sofades GR 182 D4
Sofia BG. 17 D5
Sofikon GR 184 B4
Şofronea RO 126 A3
Sögel D 71 B4
Sogliano al Rubicone
I 135 A5
Sogndalsfjøra N . . 46 A4
Søgne N. 53 B3
Söğütköy TR 188 C3
Soham GB 45 A4
Sohland D 84 A2
Sohren D 93 B3
Soignies B 79 B4
Soissons F 90 B3
Söjtör H 111 C3
Sokal' UA 13 C6
Söke TR 188 B2
Sokna N 48 B1
Sokndal N 52 B2
Soknedal N 199 C7
Soko BIH 125 C4
Sokolac BIH. 139 B4
Sokolov CZ 83 B4
Sokołowo PL 76 B3
Sokołów Podlaski
PL. 12 B5
Sola N 52 B1
Solana de los Barros
E 155 C4
Solana del Pino E . 157 B3
Solánas I 179 C3
Solares E 143 A3
Solarino I 177 B4
Solarussa I 179 C2
Solas GB 31 B1
Solberg S 200 C3
Solberga S 62 A2
Solber-gelva N . . . 53 A6
Solbjørg N 46 B2
Solčany SK 98 C2
Solčava SLO 123 A3
Solda I 108 C1
Sölden A 108 C2
Solec Kujawski PL . 76 A3
Soleils I. 132 B2
Solenzara F 180 B2
Solera E 163 A4
Soleto I. 173 B4
Solgne F 92 C2
Solheim N 46 B2
Solheimsvik N 52 A2
Solignac F 115 C5
Solihull GB 44 A2
Solin HR. 138 B2
Solingen D. 80 A3
Solivella E 147 C2
Solkan SLO 122 B2
Söll A 108 B3
Sollana E 159 B3
Sollebrunn S 54 B3
Sollefteå S 200 C3
Sollenau A 111 B3
Sollen-tuna S 57 A3
Sollerön S 50 B1
Søllested DK 65 B4
Solliès-Pont F 132 B2
Sollihøgda N 48 C2
Solnechnogorsk
RUS 9 D10
Solnice CZ. 85 B4
Solofra I 170 C2
Sologne F 129 C3
Solopaca I 170 B2
Solórzano E 143 A3
Solre-le-Château F . 79 B4

Solsona E 147 C2
Solsvik N 46 B1
Solt H 112 C3
Soltau D. 72 B2
Soltsy RUS 9 C7
Soltszentimre H . . . 112 C3
Soltvadkert H 112 C3
Solumsmoen N . . . 48 C1
Solund N 46 A1
Solva E 39 C1
Sölvesborg S 63 B2
Solymár H 112 B2
Soma TR 186 C2
Somain F 78 B3
Somberek H. 125 A4
Sombernon F 104 B3
Sombor SRB 125 B5
Sombreffe B 79 B4
Someren NL 80 A1
Somero FIN 8 B3
Somersham GB. . . 44 A3
Somerton GB 43 A4
Sominy PL. 68 A2
Somma Lombardo
I 120 B1
Sommariva del Bosco
I 119 C4
Sommarøy N 192 C2
Sommarset N 194 C6
Sommatino I 176 B2
Sommeilles F 91 C4
Sommen S 55 B5
Sommepy-Tahure F 91 B4
Sömmerda D 82 A3
Sommerfeld D 74 B2
Sommersted DK . . 59 C2
Sommesous F 91 C4
Somme-Tourbe F . . 91 B4
Sommières F 131 B3
Sommières-du-Clain
F. 115 B4
Somo E 143 A3
Somogyfajsz H . . .111 C4
Somogysámson H .111 C4
Somogysárd H . . . 125 A3
Somogyszil H 112 C2
Somogyszob H . . . 124 A3
Somogyvár H 111 C4
Somontin E 164 B2
Somosierra E 151 A4
Somoskőújifalu H . .113 A3
Sompolno PL 76 B3
Sompuis F. 91 C4
Son N 54 A1
Son Bou E 167 B4
Sonceboz CH 106 B2
Soncillo E 143 B3
Soncino I 120 B2
Søndeled N 53 B5
Sønder Bjert DK . . 59 C2
Sønderby DK 64 B2
Sønder Felding DK . 59 C1
Sønderho DK 59 C1
Sønder Hygum DK . 59 C1
Sønder Omme DK . 59 C1
Sondershausen D . . 82 A2
Søndersø DK 59 C3
Søndervig DK 59 B1
Søndre Enningdal
Kappel N 54 B2
Sóndrio I 120 A2
Soneja E 159 B3
Son en Breugel NL . 80 A1
Songe N 53 B5
Songeons F 90 B1
Sonkamuotka FIN . 196 A6
Sonkovo RUS 9 D10
Sönnarslöv S 61 D4
Sonneberg D 82 B3
Sonnefeld D 82 B3
Sonnewalde D 84 A1
Sonnino I 169 B3
Sonogno CH 120 A1
Sonsbeck D 80 A2
Sonseca E 157 A4
Son Servera E . . . 167 B3
Sønsterud N 49 B4
Sonstorp S 56 B1
Sonta SRB 125 B5
Sontheim D 94 C2
Sonthofen D 107 B5
Sontra D. 82 A1
Sopelana E 143 A4
Sopje HR 125 B3
Šoporňa SK 111 A4
Sopot
PL. 69 A3
SRB. 127 C2
Sopotnica MK 182 B3
Sopron H 111 B3
Šor SRB 127 C1
Sora I 169 B3
Soragna I 120 C2
Söråker S 200 D3
Sorano I 168 A1
Sorbara I 121 C4
Sorbas E 164 B2
Sórbolo I. 121 C3
Sörbygden S 200 D2
Sordal N 52 B3
Sordale GB 32 C3
Sore F 128 B2
Sörenberg CH . . . 106 C3
Soresina I 120 B2
Sørfjorden N 194 B7
Sörforsa S 200 E3
Sorges F 115 C4
Sórgono I. 179 B3
Sorgues F 131 A3
Sorgun TR 23 B8
Soria E 143 C4
Soriano Cálabro I . 175 C2
Soriano nel Cimino
I 168 A2
Sorihuela del
Guadalimar E . . . 164 A1
Sorisdale GB 34 B1
Sørkjosen N 192 C4
Sørli N 199 A10
Sormás H. 111 C3
Sörmjöle S 200 C6
Sørmo N 194 B9
Sornac F 116 B2
Sorø DK 61 D1
Soroca MD 17 A8
Sørreisa N 194 A9
Sorrento I 170 C2
Sörsjön S 49 A5
Sorso I 178 B2
Sort E 146 B2
Sortavala RUS. 9 B7
Sortino I 177 B4
Sortland N 194 B6
Sørum N. 48 B2
Sørumsand N 48 C3
Sorunda S 57 A3
Sörup D 64 B2
Sørvågen N 194 C3
Sørvær N 192 B6
Sorvik S 50 B2
Sörvika S 199 C8
Sos F 128 B3
Sösdala S 61 C3
Sos del Rey Católico
E 144 B2
Sošice HR 123 B4
Sośnica PL. 75 A5
Sośnicowice PL. . . 86 B2
Sośno PL 76 A2
Sosnovyy Bor RUS . 9 C6
Sosnowiec PL 86 B3
Sospel F. 133 B3
Šoštanj SLO 123 A4
Sotaseter N 198 D4
Sotillo de Adrada
E 150 B3
Sotillo de la Ribera
E 143 C3
Sotin HR 125 B5
Sotkamo FIN 3 D11
Sotobañado y Priorato
E 142 B2
Soto de la Marina
E 143 A3
Soto del Barco E . . 141 A4
Soto de los Infantes
E 141 A4
Soto de Real E . . . 151 B4
Soto de Ribera E . . 141 A5
Sotoserrano E . . . 149 B3
Soto y Amío E . . . 141 B5
Sotresgudo E 142 B2
Sotrondio E 142 A1
Sotta F 180 B2
Sottomarina I 122 B1
Sottrum D 72 A2
Sottunga FIN 51 B7
Sotuelamos E 158 B1
Souain F 91 B4
Soual F 146 A3
Soucy F 104 A2
Souda GR 185 D5
Soudron F 91 C4
Souesmes F 103 B4
Soufflenheim F . . . 93 C3
Soufli GR 186 A1
Souillac F 129 B4
Souilly F. 91 B5
Soulac-sur-Mer F . 114 C2
Soulaines-Dhuys F . 91 C4
Soulatgé F 146 B3
Soultz-Haut-Rhin F 106 B2
Soultz-sous-Forêts
F. 93 C3
Soumagne B 80 B1
Soumoulou F 145 A3
Souppes-sur-Loing
F. 103 A4
Souprosse F 128 C2
Sourdeval F 88 B3
Soure P 154 A2
Sournia F 146 B3
Souro Pires P 149 B2
Sourpi GR 182 D4
Sours F 90 C1
Sousceyrac F 116 C2
Sousel P. 155 C3
Soustons F 128 C1
Söğüt
Bilecik TR. 187 B5
Burdur TR 189 B4
Soutelo de Montes
E 140 B2
Southam GB 44 A2
Southampton GB . . 44 C2
Southborough GB . 45 B4
South Brent GB. . . 42 B3
South Cave GB . . . 40 B3
Southend GB. 34 C2

Southend-on-Sea
GB 45 B4
South Hayling GB . . 44 C3
South Molton GB. . . 42 A3
South Ockendon
GB 45 B4
South Petherton GB 43 B4
Southport GB 38 A3
South Shields GB . . 37 B5
South Tawton GB . . 42 B3
Southwell GB 40 B3
Southwold GB 45 A5
South Woodham Ferrers
GB 45 B4
Söğütlu TR. 187 B5
Souto P 148 B2
Soutochao E 141 C3
Souto da Carpalhosa
P. 154 B2
Souvigny F 104 C2
Souzay-Champigny
F. 102 B1
Soverato I 175 C2
Soveria Mannelli I . 175 B2
Sövestad S 66 A2
Sovetsk RUS 12 A4
Sovići BIH 138 B3
Sovicille I 135 B4
Søvik N 198 C3
Sowerby GB 37 B5
Soyaux F 115 C4
Sozopol BG 17 D7
Spa B 80 B1
Spadafora I 177 A4
Spaichingen D. . . 107 A3
Spakenburg NL . . 70 B2
Spalding GB 41 C3
Spálené Poříčí CZ . 96 B1
Spalt D 94 B2
Spangenberg D . . 82 A1
Spangereid N . . . 52 B3
Spantekow D . . . 74 A2
Sparanise I 170 B2
Sparbu N 199 B8
Sparkær DK 58 B2
Sparkford GB . . . 43 A4
Sparreholm S . . . 56 A2
Sparta = Sparti GR 184 B3
Spartà I 177 A4
Sparti = Sparta GR 184 B3
Spean Bridge GB . 34 B3
Speicher D. 92 B2
Speichersdorf D . . 95 B3
Speke GB. 38 A4
Spello I 136 C1
Spenge D. 72 B1
Spennymoor GB . . 37 B5
Spentrup DK 58 B3
Sperenberg D . . . 74 B2
Sperlinga I 177 B3
Sperlonga I 169 B3
Spetalen N 54 A1
Spetses GR 184 B4
Speyer D 93 B4
Spézet F 100 A2
Spezzano Albanese
I 174 B2
Spezzano della Sila
I 174 B2
Spiddle IRL 28 A2
Spiegelau D 96 C1
Spiekeroog D . . . 71 A4
Spiez CH 106 C2
Spigno Monferrato
I 133 A4
Spijk NL 71 A3
Spijkenisse NL . . . 79 A4
Spilamberto I . . . 135 A4
Spili GR 185 D5
Spilimbergo I . . . 122 A1
Spilsby GB. 41 B4
Spinazzola I . . . 172 B2
Spincourt F 92 B1
Spind N 52 B2
Spindleruv-Mlyn CZ 84 B3
Spinoso I 174 A1
Špišjć Bukovica
HR 124 B3
Spišská Belá SK . . 99 B4
Spišská Nová Ves
SK 99 C4
Spišská Stará Ves
SK 99 B4
Spišské-Hanušovce
SK 99 B4
Spišské Podhradie
SK 99 C4
Spišské Vlachy SK . 99 C4
Spišský-Štvrtok SK. 99 C4
Spital A 110 B1
Spital am Semmering
A 110 B2
Spittal an der Drau
A 109 C4
Spittle of Glenshee
GB 35 B4
Spitz A 97 C3
Spjald DK 59 B1
Spjærøy N 54 A1
Spjelkavik N . . . 198 C3
Split HR 138 B2
Splügen CH 107 C4
Spodsbjerg DK . . 65 B3
Spofforth GB . . . 40 B2
Spohle D 71 A5
Spoleto I 136 C1
Spoltore I 169 A4
Spondigna I . . . 108 C1
Sponvika N 54 A2
Spornitz D 73 A4
Spotorno I 133 A4
Spraitbach D . . . 94 C1
Sprakensehl D . . 72 B3
Sprecowo PL. . . 69 B5
Spremberg D . . . 84 A2
Spresiano I . . . 122 B1
Sprimont B 80 B1
Springe D. 72 B2
Sproatley GB . . . 41 B3
Spydeberg N . . . 54 A2
Spytkowice PL. . 99 B3
Squillace I . . . 175 C2
Squinzano I . . . 173 B4
Sračinec HR . . . 124 A2
Srbac BIH. 124 B3
Srbobran SRB . . 126 B1
Srebrenica BIH . . 127 C1
Srebrenik BIH . . 125 C4
Sredets BG 17 D7
Središče SLO . . . 124 A2
Šrem PL 76 B2
Sremska Mitrovica
SRB 127 C1
Sremski Karlovci
SRB 126 B1
Srní CZ. 96 B1
Srnice Gornje BIH. 125 C4
Srock PL 86 A3
Środa Śląska PL . 85 A4
Środa Wielkopolski
PL. 76 B2
Srpska Crnja SRB. 126 B2
Srpski Itebej SRB . 126 B2
Srpski Miletić SRB 125 B5
Staatz A 97 C4
Stabbursnes N . . 193 B8
Staberdorf D . . . 65 B4
Stabroek B. 79 A4
Stachy CZ 96 B1
Staðarfell IS . . . 190 B3
Stade D 72 A2
Staden B 78 B3
Stadl an der Mur A. 109 B4
Stadskanaal NL . . 71 B3
Stadtallendorf D . 81 B5
Stadthagen D . . . 72 B2
Stadtilm D 82 B3
Stadtkyll D 80 B2
Stadtlauringen D . 82 B2
Stadtlengsfeld D . 82 B2
Stadtlohn D . . . 71 C3
Stadtoldendorf D . 82 A1
Stadtroda D . . . 83 B3
Stadtsteinach D . 82 B3
Stäfa CH 107 B3
Staffanstorp S . . 61 D3
Staffelstein D . . 82 B2
Staffin GB 31 B2
Stafford GB . . . 40 C1
Stainach A . . . 110 B1
Staindrop GB. . . 37 B5
Staines-upon-Thames
GB 44 B3
Stainville F . . . 91 C5
Stainz A 110 C2
Staithes GB . . . 37 B6
Staití I 175 D2
Stäket S 57 A3
Stakroge DK . . . 59 C1
Štalcerji SLO . . . 123 B3
Stalden CH . . . 119 A4
Stalham GB . . . 41 C5
Stalheim N . . . 46 B3
Stallarholmen S . 56 A3
Ställberg S. . . . 50 C1
Ställdalen S. . . . 50 C1
Stallhofen A . . . 110 B2
Stalon S 195 F6
Stalowa Wola PL. 12 C5
Stamford GB . . . 40 C3
Stamford Bridge GB 40 B3
Stamnes N 46 B2
Stams A 108 B1
Stamsried D. . . . 95 B4
Stamsund N . . . 194 B5
Stanford le Hope
GB 45 B4
Stånga S 57 C4
Stange N 48 B3
Stanghella I . . . 121 B4
Stanhope GB . . . 37 B4
Stanišić SRB . . . 125 B5
Staňkov CZ 95 B5
Stankovci HR . . . 137 B4
Stanley GB. 37 B5
Stans CH 106 C3
Stansted Mountfitchet
GB 45 B4
Stanzach A. . . . 108 B1
Stapar SRB . . . 125 B5
Staphorst NL . . . 70 B3
Staplehurst GB . . 45 B4
Stąporków PL . . 87 A4
Stara Baška HR. . 123 C3
Starachowice PL. . 87 A5
Stara Fužina SLO . 122 A2
Stara Kamienica PL 84 B3
Stara Kiszewa PL . 68 B3
Stará L'ubovňa SK . 99 B4
Stara Moravica
SRB 126 B1
Stara Novalja HR. . 137 A3
Stara Pazova SRB . 127 C2
Stará Turá SK . . 98 C1
Staraya Russa RUS . 9 D7
Stara Zagora BG . . 17 D6
Stärbsnäs S. . . . 51 C6
Starčevo SRB . . 127 C2
Stare Dłutowo PL. 77 A4
Staré Hamry CZ. . 98 B2
Stare Jablonki PL . 69 B5
Staré Město CZ . . 98 B1
Stare Pole PL. . . 69 A4
Stare Sedlo CZ . . 96 B2
Stare Strącze PL. . 85 A4
Stargard Szczeciński
PL. 75 A4
Stårheim N . . . 198 D2
Starigrad
Ličko-Senjska
HR 123 C3
Splitsko-Dalmatinska
HR 138 B2
Stari Gradac HR. . 124 B3
Starigrad-Paklenica
HR 137 A4
Stari Jankovci HR. 125 B4
Stari Majdan BIH . 124 C2
Stari-Mikanovci
HR 125 B4
Štěpánov CZ . . . 98 B1
Staritsa RUS . . . 9 D9
Starkenbach A. . . 108 B1
Starnberg D . . . 108 B2
Starogard PL . . . 75 A4
Starogard Gdański
PL. 69 B3
Starokonstyantyniv
UA 13 D7
Staro Petrovo Selo
HR 124 B3
Staro Selo
HR 124 B1
SRB 127 C3
Stary Brzozów PL. 77 B5
Stary Dzierzgoń PL. 69 B4
Starý Hrozenkov
CZ 98 C1
Stary Jaroslaw PL. 68 A1
Stary Plzenec CZ. . 96 B1
Stary Sącz PL . . 99 B4
Starý Smokovec SK 99 B4
Staryy Chartoriysk
UA 13 C6
Staškov SK . . . 98 B2
Stassfurt D . . . 82 A3
Staszów PL . . . 87 B5
Stathelle N. . . . 53 A5
Staufen D. . . . 106 B2
Staunton GB . . 39 C4
Stavang N . . . 46 A2
Stavanger N. . . 52 B1
Stavåsnäs S . . . 49 B4
Stavby S 51 B5
Staveley GB. . . 40 B2
Stavelot B 80 B1
Stavenisse NL . . 79 A4
Stavern N 53 B6
Stavoren NL . . . 70 B2
Stavros
CY 181 A1
GR 183 C5
Stavroupoli GR . . 183 B6
Stavseng N . . . 47 A6
Stavsjø N 48 B2
Stavsnäs S 57 A4
Steane N 53 A4
Steblevë AL . . . 182 B2
Stechelberg CH. . 106 C2
Štěchovice CZ. . . 96 B2
Stechow D . . . 73 B5
Steckborn CH . . 107 B3
Stede Broek NL . 70 B2
Steeg A 107 B5
Steenbergen NL . 79 A4
Steenvoorde F . . 78 B2
Steenwijk NL . . 70 B3
Štefanje HR . . . 124 B2
Steffisburg CH . . 106 C2
Stegaurach D . . 94 B2
Stege DK 65 B5
Stegelitz D . . . 74 A2
Stegersbach A. . .111 B3
Stegna PL 69 A4
Steimbke D . . . 72 B2
Stein
GB. 31 B2
Steinach
A. 108 B2
Baden-Württemberg
D. 106 A3
Bayern D 82 B2
Thüringen D 82 B2
Stein an Rhein CH. 107 B3
Steinau
Bayern D 81 B5
Niedersachsen D . .64 C1
Steinbeck D . . . 74 B2
Steinberg am Rofan
A. 108 B2
Steindorf A . . . 109 C5
Steine N 46 B2
Steinen D 106 B2
Steinfeld
A. 109 C4
D 71 B5
Steinfurt D . . . 71 B4
Steingaden D . . 108 B1
Steinhagen D . . 72 B1
Stara Baška HR. . 123 C3
Steinheid D . . . 82 B3
Steinheim
Bayern D 107 A5
Nordrhein-Westfalen
D 81 A5
Steinhöfel D . . . 74 B3
Steinhorst D . . . 72 B3
Steinigtwolmsdorf
D 84 A2
Steinkjer N . . . 199 A8
Steinsholt N . . . 53 A5
Stekene B 79 A4
Stelle D 72 A3
Stellendam NL . . 79 A4
Stenåsa S 63 B4
Stenberga S. . . . 62 A3
Stendal D 73 B4
Stenhammar S . . 55 B4
Stenhamra S . . . 57 A3
Stenhousemuir GB . 35 B4
Stenlose DK. . . . 61 D2
Stensätra S . . . 50 B3
Stensele S . . . 195 E8
Stenstorp S . . . 55 B4
Stenstrup DK. . . 65 A3
Stenudden S . . . 195 D8
Stenungsund S . . 54 B2
Štěpánov CZ . . . 98 B1
Stephanskirchen
D 108 B3
Stepnica PL . . . 74 A3
Stepojevac SRB . 127 C2
Stepping DK . . . 59 C2
Sterbfritz D . . . 82 B1
Sternberg D . . . 65 C4
Šternberk CZ . . . 98 B1
Sterup D. 64 B2
Stes Maries-de-la-Mer
F 131 B3
Stevenage GB . . 44 B3
Stewarton GB . . 36 A2
Steyerburg D . . 72 B2
Steyning GB . . . 44 C3
Steyr A 110 A1
Stężyca PL . . . 68 A2
Stezzano I . . . 120 B2
Stia I 135 B4
Stibb Cross GB . . 42 B2
Sticciano Scalo I . 135 C4
Stidsvig S 61 C3
Stiens NL 70 A2
Stige DK. 59 C3
Stigen S 54 B3
Stigliano I . . . 174 A2
Stigtomta S . . . 56 B2
Stilida GR 182 E4
Stilla N 192 C7
Stillington GB . . 40 A2
Stilo I 175 C2
Stintino I . . . 178 B2
Štip MK 182 B4
Stira GR 185 A5
Stirling GB . . . 35 B4
Stjärnhov S . . . 56 A3
Stjärnsund S . . 50 B3
Stjørdalshalsen N . 199 B7
Stobnica PL . . . 87 A3
Stobno PL 75 A5
Stobreč HR . . . 138 B2
Stochov CZ . . . 84 B1
Stockach D . . . 107 B4
Stöckalp CH . . . 106 C3
Stockaryd S . . . 62 A2
Stockbridge GB. . 44 B2
Stockerau A . . . 97 C4
Stockheim D . . . 82 B3
Stockholm S . . . 57 A4
Stockport GB . . 40 B1
Stocksbridge GB. . 40 B2
Stockton-on-Tees
GB 37 B5
Stod CZ 96 B1
Stöde S 200 D2
Stødi N 195 D6
Stöðvarfjörður
IS 191 C12
Stoer GB 32 C1
Stoholm DK . . . 58 B2
Stoke Ferry GB . . 41 C4
Stoke Fleming GB. 43 B3
Stoke Mandeville
GB 44 B3
Stoke-on-Trent GB 40 B1
Stokesley GB. . . 37 B5
Stokke N 54 A1
Stokkemarke DK. . 65 B4
Stokken N 53 B4
Stokkseyri IS. . . 190 D4
Stokkvågen N . . 195 D4
Stokmarknes N . . 194 B5
Štoky CZ 97 B3
Stolac BIH 139 B3
Stølaholmen N . . 46 A3
Stolberg D 80 B2
Stolin BY 13 C7
Stollberg D . . . 83 B4
Stöllet S 49 B5
Stolno PL 76 A3
Stolpen D 84 A2
Stolzenau D . . . 72 B2
Stompetoren NL . 70 B1
Ston HR 139 C3
Stonařov CZ . . . 97 B3
Stone GB 40 C1
Stonehaven GB . . 33 E4
Stonehouse GB . . 36 A3
Stongfjorden N . . 46 A2
Stonndalen N . . 47 B4
Stony Stratford GB . 44 A3
Stopnica PL . . . 87 B4
Storå S 56 A1
Storås N 198 B6
Storby FIN . . . 51 B6
Stordal
Møre og Romsdal
N 198 C4
Nord-Trøndelag N . 199 B8
Store GB 33 B4
Storebø N 46 B2
Storebro S . . . 62 A3
Store Damme DK. . 65 B5
Store Heddinge DK. 65 A5
Store Herrestad S . 66 A2
Store Levene S . . 55 B3
Store Molvik N . . 193 B12
Store Skedvi S . . 50 B2
Store Vika S. . . 57 B3
Storfjellseter N . . 199 D7
Storfjord N . . . 192 C3
Storfjorden N . . 198 C3
Storfors S 55 A5
Storforshei N . . 195 D5
Storhøliseter N . . 47 A6
Storjord N . . . 195 D6
Storkow
Brandenburg D . . 74 B2
Mecklenburg-
Vorpommern D . . 74 A3
Storli N 198 C6
Storlien S . . . 199 B9
Stornara I . . . 171 B3
Stornoway GB . . 31 A2
Storo I 121 B3
Storozhynets UA. . 17 A6
Storrington GB . . 44 C3
Storseleby S . . . 200 B2
Storsjön S 50 A3
Storslett N . . . 192 C5
Storsteinnes N . . 192 C3
Storsund S . . . 196 D3
Storuman S . . . 195 E8
Störvattnet S . . 199 C9
Storvik
N 195 D4
S 50 B3
Storvreta S . . . 51 C4
Štos SK 99 C4
Stössen D 83 A3
Stotel D 72 A1
Stötten D 108 B1
Stotternheim D . . 82 A3
Stouby DK 59 C2
Stourbridge GB . . 40 C1
Stourport-on-Severn
GB 39 B4
Støvring DK . . . 58 B2
Stow GB 35 C5
Stowbtsy BY . . . 13 B7
Stowmarket GB . . 45 A5
Stow-on-the-Wold
GB 44 B2
Straach D. 73 C5
Strabane GB . . . 27 B3
Strachan GB . . . 33 D4
Strachur GB. . . . 34 B2
Stracin MK. . . . 182 A4
Strackholt D . . . 71 A4
Stradbally IRL . . 29 B1
Stradella I . . . 120 B2
Straelen D 80 A2
Stragari SRB . . . 127 C2
Strakonice CZ . . 96 B1
Strålsnäs S . . . 55 B6
Stralsund D . . . 66 B2
Strand N 48 A3
Stranda N . . . 198 C3
Strandby DK . . . 58 A3
Strandebarm N . . 46 B3
Strandhill IRL . . 26 B2
Strandlykkja N . . 48 B3
Strandvik N . . . 46 B2
Strangford GB . . 27 B5
Strängnäs S . . . 56 A3
Strångsjö S . . . 56 B2
Stráni CZ 98 C1
Stranice SLO . . . 123 A4
Stranorlar IRL . . 26 B3
Stranraer GB . . . 36 B1
Strasatti I . . . 176 B1
Strasbourg F . . . 93 C3
Strasburg D . . . 74 A2
Strašice CZ . . . 96 B1
Strass im Steiermark
A 110 C2
Strasskirchen D . . 95 C4
Strasswalchen A . 109 B4
Stratford-upon-Avon
GB 44 A2
Strathaven GB. . . 36 A2
Strathdon GB . . 32 D3
Strathkanaird GB . 32 D1
Strathpeffer GB. . 32 D2
Strathy GB . . . 32 C3
Strathyre GB . . . 34 B3
Stratinska BIH . . 124 C2
Stratton GB . . . 42 B2
Straubing D . . . 95 C4
Straulas I 178 B3
Straume N 53 A5
Straumen
Nordland N. 194 C6
Nord-Trøndelag N . 199 B8
Straumsjøen N . . 194 B5
Straumsnes N . . 194 C6
Straupitz D . . . 74 C3
Strausberg D . . . 74 B2
Straussfurt D . . 82 A3
Strawczyn PL. . . 87 B4
Straža
SLO 123 B4
SRB 127 C3
Stražnad Nezárkou
CZ 96 B2
Strážnice CZ . . . 98 C1
Strážný CZ 96 C1
Stráž Pod Ralskem
CZ 84 B2
Štrbské Pleso SK . 99 B4
Strečno SK 98 B2
Street GB 43 A4
Strehla D 83 A5
Strekov SK. . . . 112 B2
Strem A 111 B3
Stremska-Rača
SRB 127 C1
Strengberg A. . . .110 A1
Strengelvåg N . . 194 B6
Stresa I 119 B5
Streufdorf D . . . 82 B2
Strib DK 59 C2
Striberg S 55 A5
Stříbro CZ . . . 95 B4
Strichen GB . . . 33 D4
Strigno I 121 A4
Štrigova HR . . . 111 C3
Strijen NL 79 A4
Strizivojna HR . . 125 B4
Strmica HR . . . 138 A2
Strmilov CZ . . . 97 B3
Ströhen D 72 B1
Strokestown IRL . 28 A3
Stromberg
Nordrhein-Westfalen
D 81 A4
Rheinland-Pfalz D . 93 B3
Stromeferry GB . . 31 B3
Strömnäs S . . . 200 B2
Stromness GB . . 33 C3
Strömsberg S . . 51 B4
Strömsbruk S . . 200 E3
Strömsfors S . . 56 B2
Strömsnäsbruk S . 61 C3
Strömstad S . . . 54 B2
Strömsund
Jämtland S. 199 B12
Västerbotten S . . 195 E7
Stronachlachar GB . 34 B3
Stróngoli I . . . 174 B3
Stronie Ślaskie PL. . 85 B4
Strontian GB . . . 34 B2
Stroppiana I . . . 119 B5
Stroud GB 43 A4
Stroumbi CY . . . 181 B1
Stróża PL 99 B3
Strücklingen D . . 71 A4
Struer DK 58 B1
Struga MK . . . 182 B2
Strugi Krasnyye RUS 9 C6
Strumica MK . . . 182 B4
Strumien PL. . . . 98 B2
Struy GB 32 D2
Stružec HR . . . 124 B2
Stryków PL . . . 77 C4
Stryn N 198 D3
Stryy UA. 13 D5
Strzałkowo PL . . 76 B2
Strzegocin PL . . 77 B5
Strzegom PL . . . 85 B4
Strzegowo PL . . 77 B5
Strzelce PL. . . . 77 B4
Strzelce Krajeńskie
PL. 75 B4
Strzelce Kurowo PL 75 B4
Strzelce Opolskie
PL. 86 B2
Strzelin PL . . . 85 B5
Strzelno PL . . . 76 B3
Strzepcz PL . . . 68 A3
Strzybnica PL . . 86 B2
Strzyegi PL . . . 77 A4
Stubbekøbing DK . 65 B5
Stuben A 107 B5
Stubenberg A. . . .110 B2
Stubline SRB . . . 127 C2
Studená CZ . . . 97 B3
Studenci HR . . . 138 B3
Studenka CZ . . . 98 B2
Studenzen A . . .110 B2
Studienka SK. . . 98 C1
Studland GB . . . 43 B5
Studley GB . . . 44 A2
Studzienice PL . . 68 A2
Stuer D 73 A5
Stugudal N . . . 199 C8
Stugun S 200 C1
Stuhr D 72 A1
Stukenbrock D . . 81 A4
Stülpe D 74 B2
Stupava SK 111 A4
Stupnik HR . . . 124 B1
Stupsk PL 77 A5
Sturkö S 63 B3

Sturminster Newton
GB 43 B4
Šťúrovo SK 112 B2
Sturton GB. 40 B3
Stuttgart D 94 C1
Stvolny CZ. 96 A1
Stykkishólmur IS . 190 B3
Styri N 48 B3
Stysö S 60 B1
Suances E 142 A2
Subbiano I 135 B4
Subiaco I 169 B3
Subotica SRB 126 A1
Subotište SRB. . . 127 C1
Sučany SK. 98 B2
Suceava RO. 17 B7
Sucha-Beskidzka
PL. 99 B3
Suchacz PL 69 A4
Suchań PL 75 A4
Suchdol nad Lužnice
CZ 96 C2
Suchedniów PL. . . . 87 A4
Suchorze PL 68 A2
Suchteln D. 80 A2
Sucina E 165 B4
Suckow D 73 A4
Sućuraj HR 138 B3
Súðavík IS 190 A3
Sudbury GB. 45 A4
Suddesjaur S. . . . 195 E10
Suden D 64 B1
Süderbrarup D 64 B2
Süderlügum D 64 B1
Sudoměřice u Bechyně
CZ 96 B2
Sudovec HR 124 A2
Suðureyri IS 190 A2
Sueca E 159 B3
Suelli I 179 C3
Sugenheim D. 94 B2
Sugères F 117 B3
Sugny B 91 B4
Suhl D 82 B2
Suhlendorf D 73 B3
Suho Polje BIH . . . 125 C5
Şuhut TR 189 A5
Šuica BIH. 138 B3
Suippes F 91 B4
Sukošan HR 137 A4
Sükösd H. 125 A4
Suków PL 87 B4
Šul’a SK 99 C3
Suldalsosen N. 52 A2
Suldrup DK 58 B2
Sulechów PL 75 B4
Sulęcin PL 75 B4
Sulęczyno PL. 68 A2
Sulejów PL. 87 A3
Süleymanlı TR . . . 186 D2
Sulgen CH 107 B4
Sulibórz PL 75 A4
Sulina RO 17 C8
Sulingen D. 72 B1
Suliszewo PL. 75 A4
Sulitjelma N 195 C7
Sułkowice PL. 99 B3
Süller TR 189 A4
Sully-sur-Loire F . . 103 B4
Sulmierzyce
Łódzkie PL. 86 A3
Wielkopolskie PL . . 85 A5
Sulmona I 169 A3
Süloğlu TR. 186 A1
Sułoszowa PL 87 B3
Sulów PL 85 A5
Sulsdorf D 65 B4
Sultandağı TR 189 A6
Sülüklü TR 187 D7
Suluova TR 23 A8
Sulvik S 54 A3
Sülysáp H 112 B3
Sülz D 93 C4
Sulzbach
Baden-Württemberg
D. 94 B1
Baden-Württemberg
D. 94 C1
Bayern D 93 B5
Saarland D. 92 B3
Sulzbach-Rosenberg
D 95 B3
Sülze D. 72 B3
Sulzfeld D 82 B2
Sumartin HR 138 B2
Sumburgh GB 33 B5
Sümeg H 111 C4
Sumiswald CH. . . . 106 B2
Šumná CZ 97 C3
Šumperk CZ 97 B4
Šumvald CZ. 98 B1
Sunbilla E 144 A2
Sünching D 95 C4
Sund
FIN 51 B7
S 54 A2
Sundborn S 50 B2
Sundby DK 58 B1
Sunde N 46 C2
Sunde bru N 53 B5
Sunderland GB . . . 37 B5
Sundern D 81 A4
Sundhultsbrunn S . 62 A2
Sundnäs S. 195 D8
Sundom S 196 D5
Sunds DK. 59 B2
Sundsfjord N. 195 D5

Sundsvall S 200 D3
Sungurlu TR 23 A8
Suni I 178 B2
Sunja HR 124 B2
Sunnansjö S 50 B1
Sunnaryd S 60 B3
Sunne S 49 C5
Sunnemo S 49 C5
Sunnersberg S . . . 55 B4
Suolovuopmio N . . 192 C7
Suomussalmi FIN . 3 D11
Suoyarvi RUS 9 A8
Super Sauze F . . . 132 A2
Supetar HR 138 B2
Supetarska Draga
HR 123 C3
Supino I 169 B3
Šuplja Stijena MNE 139 B5
Surahammar S 56 A2
Šurany SK 112 A2
Surazh BY 13 A9
Surbo I 173 B4
Surčin SRB 127 C2
Surgères F. 114 B3
Surhuisterveen NL . 70 A3
Sùria E 147 C2
Surin F 115 B4
Surka N 48 B2
Surnadalsøra N . . . 198 C5
Sursee CH 106 B3
Surte S 60 B2
Surwold D 71 B4
Sury-le-Comtal F . .117 B4
Susa I 119 B4
Šušara SRB 127 C3
Susch CH. 107 C5
Susegana I 122 B1
Süsel D 65 B3
Sušice CZ 96 B1
Šušnjevica HR. . . . 123 B3
Sussen D 94 C1
Susurluk TR 186 C3
Susz PL 69 B4
Sütçüler TR 189 B5
Sutivan HR 138 B2
Sutjeska SRB 126 B2
Sutri I 168 A2
Sutton GB 44 B3
Sutton Coldfield GB 40 C2
Sutton-in-Ashfield
GB 40 B2
Sutton-on-Sea GB . 41 B4
Sutton-on-Trent GB 40 B3
Sutton Scotney GB . 44 B2
Sutton Valence GB . 45 B4
Suvaja BIH. 124 C2
Suvereto I 135 B3
Suwałki PL 12 A5
Suze-la-Rousse F . 131 A3
Suzzara I 121 C3
Svabensverk S . . . 50 A2
Svalbard IS 191 A10
Svalöv S 61 D3
Svanabyn S 200 B2
Svanberga S 51 C5
Svaneke DK. 67 A4
Svanesund S 54 B2
Svängsta S 63 B2
Svannäs S 195 D9
Svanskog S 54 A3
Svanstein S 196 C6
Svappavaara S . . . 196 B4
Svärdsjö S 50 B2
Svarstad N 53 A5
Svartå S 55 A5
Svärta S 56 B3
Svartå S 55 A4
Svartbyn S 196 C5
Svärtinge S 56 B2
Svartlå S 196 D4
Svartnäs S 50 B3
Svartnes N. 195 C5
Svärttjärn S 195 E7
Svatsum N. 48 A1
Svätý Jur SK 111 A4
Svätý Peter SK . . .112 B2
Svedala S. 61 D3
Sveg S 199 C11
Sveindal N 52 B3
Sveio N 52 A1
Svejbæk DK. 59 B2
Svelgen N 198 D2
Svelvik N 54 A1
Svendborg DK. . . . 65 A3
Svene N 53 A5
Svenljunga S 60 B3
Svennevad S 56 A1
Svenstavik S 199 C11
Svenstrup DK 58 B2
Švermov CZ. 84 B2
Sveti Ivan Zabno
HR 124 B2
Sveti Ivan Zelina
HR 124 B2
Sveti Nikole MK . . 182 B3
Sveti Rok HR 137 A4
Světlá nad Sázavou
CZ 97 B3
Svetlyy RUS 69 A5
Svetvinčenat HR . . 122 B2
Švica HR 123 C4
Svidník SK. 12 D4
Švihov CZ 96 B1
Svilajnac SRB 127 C3
Svilengrad BG . . . 183 B8
Svindal N 54 A2
Svinhult S 62 A3

Svinna SK 98 C2
Svinninge
DK 61 D1
S 57 A4
Sviritsa RUS 9 B8
Svishtov BG 17 D6
Svislach BY 13 B6
Svit SK. 99 B4
Svitavy CZ. 97 B4
Svodin SK. 112 B2
Svolvær N 194 B5
Svortemyr N 46 A2
Svortland N. 52 A1
Svratka CZ. 97 B4
Svrčinovec SK. 98 B2
Svullrya N 49 B4
Svyetlahorsk BY . . 13 B8
Swadlincote GB . . . 40 C2
Swaffham GB 41 C4
Swanage GB 43 B5
Swanley GB 45 B4
Swanlinbar IRL . . . 26 B3
Swansea GB 39 C3
Swarzędz PL 76 B2
Swatragh GB 27 B4
Świątki PL 69 B5
Świdnica
Dolnośląskie PL. . . 85 B4
Lubuskie PL 84 A3
Świdnik PL 12 C5
Świdwin PL 67 C4
Świebodzice PL. . . 85 B4
Świebodzin PL . . . 75 B4
Świecie PL 76 A3
Świedziebnia PL . . 77 A4
Świeradów Zdrój
PL 84 B3
Świerki PL 85 B4
Świerzawa PL 85 A3
Świerzno PL 67 C3
Święta PL 74 A3
Swieta Anna PL. . . 86 B3
Świętno PL 75 B5
Szydłów
Łódzkie PL. 86 A3
Świętokrzyskie PL . 87 B5
Szydłowiec PL 87 A4
Szydłowo PL 77 A5
Szydłowo PL 75 A5
Szymanów PL. 77 B5
Szynkielów PL. . . . 86 A2

Szemplino Czarne
PL. 77 A5
Szemud PL. 68 A3
Szendehely H 112 B3
Szendrő H 99 C4
Szentendre H. 112 B3
Szentes H 113 C4
Szentgotthárd H . .111 C3
Szentlászló H 125 A3
Szentlőrinc H. 125 A3
Szentmártonkáta
H 113 B3
Szenyér H 111 C4
Szeremle H 125 A4
Szerencs H 113 A5
Szerep H 113 B5
Szigetszentmiklós
H 112 B3
Szigetvár H 125 A3
Szikáncs H. 126 A2
Szikszó H. 113 A4
Szil H 111 B4
Szilvásvárad H 113 A4
Szklarska Poreba
PL. 84 B3
Szlichtyngowa PL. . 85 A4
Szob H. 112 B2
Szolnok H 113 B4
Szombathely H 111 B3
Szorosad H 112 C2
Szpetal Graniczny
PL. 77 B4
Szprotawa PL 84 A3
Szreńsk PL. 77 A5
Sztum PL 69 B4
Sztutowo PL 69 A4
Szubin PL 76 A2
Szücsi H. 113 B3
Szulmierz PL 77 B5
Szulok H 124 A3
Szumanie PL. 77 B4
Szwecja PL 75 A5
Szydłów
Łódzkie PL. 86 A3
Świętokrzyskie PL . 87 B5
Szydłowiec PL 87 A4
Szydłowo PL 77 A5
Szydłowo PL 75 A5
Szymanów PL. 77 B5
Szynkielów PL. . . . 86 A2

T

Taastrup DK. 61 D2
Tab H. 112 C2
Tabanera la Luenga
E. 151 A3
Tabaqueros E 158 B2
Tábara E 149 A4
Tabenera de Cerrato
E. 142 B2
Taberg S. 62 A2
Tabernas E. 164 B2
Tabiano Bagni I . . . 120 C3
Taboada E 140 B3
Taboadela E. 140 B3
Tábor CZ 96 B2
Táborfalva H 112 B3
Taborište HR 124 B2
Tábua P 148 B1
Tabuaco P 148 A2
Tabuenca E 152 A2
Tabuyo del Monte
E. 141 B4
Täby S 57 A4
Tac H 112 B2
Tachov CZ. 95 B4
Tadcaster GB. 40 B2
Tadley GB 44 B2
Tafalla E 144 B2
Tafjord N 198 C4
Taganheira P 160 B1
Tågarp S 61 D2
Tággia I 133 B3
Tagliacozzo I 169 A3
Táglio di Po I 121 B5
Tagnon F 91 B4
Tahal E 164 B2
Tahitótfalu H 112 B3
Tahtaköprü TR. . . . 187 C4
Tailfingen D 107 A4
Taillis F 101 A4
Tain GB 32 D2
Tain-l'Hermitage F . .117 B4
Taipadas P 154 C2
Taivalkoski FIN . . . 197 D11
Taivassalo FIN . . . 8 B2
Takene S 55 A4
Takovo SRB 127 C2
Taksony H 112 B3
Tal E 140 B2
Talachyn BY. 13 A8
Talamello I 135 B5
Talamone I 168 A1
Talant F 105 B3
Talarrubias E 156 A2
Talaván E. 155 B4
Talavera de la Reina
E. 150 C3
Talavera la Real E . 155 C4
Talayuela E 150 C2
Talayuelas E 159 B3
Talgarth GB 39 C3
Talgje N 52 A1
Talhadas P 148 B1
Táliga E 155 C3
Talizat F 116 B3
Tálknafjörður IS . . 190 B2

Talla I 135 B4
Talladale GB 31 B3
Tallaght IRL 30 A2
Tallard F. 132 A2
Tällberg S 50 B1
Tallberg S. 196 C5
Tallinn EST 8 C4
Talloires F 118 B3
Tallow IRL 29 B3
Tällsjö S 200 B4
Tallvik S 196 C5
Talmay F 105 B4
Talmont-St Hilaire
F. 114 B2
Talmont-sur-Gironde
F. 114 C3
Talne UA. 13 D9
Talsano I 173 B3
Talsi LV. 8 D3
Talvik N 192 B6
Talybont GB. 39 B3
Tal-Y-Llyn GB. 38 B3
Tamajón E 151 B4
Tamame E 149 A4
Tamames E 149 B3
Tamarit de Mar E . . 147 C2
Tamarite de Litera
E. 145 C4
Tamariu E 147 C4
Tamási H 112 C2
Tambach-Dietharz
D 82 B2
Tameza E 141 A4
Tammisaari FIN . . . 8 B3
Tampere FIN 8 B3
Tamsweg A 109 B4
Tamurejo E 156 B3
Tañabueyes E . . . 143 B3
Tanakajd H. 111 B3
Tananger N 52 B1
Tanaunella I 178 B3
Tancarville F 89 A4
Tandsjöborg S. . . . 199 D11
Tånga S 61 C2
Tangelic H 112 C2
Tangen N 48 B3
Tangerhütte D 73 B4
Tangermünde D. . . 73 B4
Tanhua FIN 197 B10
Taningés F 118 A3
Tankavaara FIN . . . 197 A10
Tann D 82 B2
Tanna D 83 B3
Tannadice GB 35 B5
Tännäker S. 60 C3
Tännäs S 199 C9
Tannay
Ardennes F 91 B4
Nièvre F 104 B2
Tannenbergsthal D . 83 B4
Tännesberg D 95 B4
Tannheim A 108 B1
Tannila FIN. 197 D8
Tanowo PL 74 A3
Tanum S. 54 B2
Tanumshede S . . . 54 B2
Tanus F 130 A1
Tanvald CZ. 84 B3
Taormina I 177 B4
Tapa EST 8 C4
Tapfheim D 94 C2
Tapia de Casariego
E. 141 A4
Tapio F 146 A2
Tápióbicske H 112 B3
Tápiógyörgye H . . . 113 B3
Tápióság H 112 B3
Tápiószecsö H 112 B3
Tápiószele H 113 B3
Tápiószentmárton
H. 113 B3
Tapolca H 111 C4
Tapolcafö H 111 B4
Tar HR 122 B2
Tarabo S. 60 B2
Taradell E. 147 C3
Taraklı TR. 187 B5
Taramundi E 141 A3
Tarancón E 151 B4
Táranto I 173 B3
Tarare F 117 B4
Tarascon F 131 B3
Tarascon-sur-Ariège
F. 146 B2
Tarashcha UA 13 D9
Tarazona E 144 C2
Tarazona de la Mancha
E. 158 B2
Tarbena E 159 C3
Tarbert
GB 34 C2
IRL 29 B2
Tarbes F 145 A4
Tarbolton GB. 36 A2
Tarcento I. 122 A2
Tarčin BIH 139 B4
Tarczyn PL. 77 C5
Tardajos E 143 B3
Tardelcuende E . . 151 A5
Tardets-Sorholus
F. 144 A3
Tardienta E 145 C3
Tärendö S 196 B5
Targon F. 128 B2
Targovishte BG . . . 17 D7

Târgovişte RO. . . . 17 C6
Târgu-Jiu RO. 17 C5
Târgu Mureş RO . . 17 B6
Târgu Ocna RO . . . 17 B7
Târgu Secuiesc RO. 17 C7
Tarifa E. 162 B2
Tariquejas E. 161 B2
Tarján H 112 B2
Tárkany H 112 B2
Tarland GB. 33 D4
Tarłów PL. 87 A5
Tarm DK 59 C1
Tarmstedt D. 72 A2
Tärnaby S 195 E6
Tarnalelesz H. 113 A4
Tarnaörs H. 113 B4
Târnăveni RO 17 B6
Tårnet N 193 C14
Tarnobrzeg PL. . . . 87 B5
Tarnos F. 128 C1
Tarnów
Lubuskie PL. 75 B3
Małopolskie PL. . . . 87 B4
Tarnowo Podgórne
PL. 75 B5
Tarnowskie Góry
PL. 86 B2
Tärnsjö S 51 B3
Tårnvik N 194 C6
Tarouca P. 148 A2
Tarp D 64 B2
Tarquínia I 168 A1
Tarquinia Lido I . . . 168 A1
Tarragona E 147 C2
Tårrajaur S 196 C2
Tàrrega E 147 C2
Tarrenz A 108 B1
Tårs
Nordjyllands DK. . . 58 A3
Storstrøms DK . . . 65 B4
Tarsia I 174 B2
Tarsus TR 23 C8
Tartas F 128 C2
Tartu EST. 8 C5
Tarves GB 33 D4
Tarvísio I 109 C4
Taşağıl TR 189 C6
Täsch CH. 119 A4
Taşköprü TR 23 A8
Tasov CZ 97 B4
Tasovčići BIH. 139 B3
Taşucuo TR 23 C7
Tát H. 112 B2
Tata H. 112 B2
Tatabánya H. 112 B2
Tataháza H. 126 A1
Tatarbunary UA. . . 17 C8
Tatárszentgyörgy
H 112 B3
Tatranská-Lomnica
SK 99 B4
Tau N. 52 A1
Tauberbischofsheim
D 94 B1
Taucha D 83 A4
Taufkirchen D 95 C4
Taufkirchen an der Pram
A. 96 C1
Taulé E 100 A2
Taulignan F 131 A3
Taulov DK. 59 C2
Taunton GB 43 A3
Taunusstein D 81 B4
Tauragė LT. 12 A5
Taurianova I 175 C2
Taurisano I 173 C4
Tauste E 144 C2
Tauves F. 116 B2
Tavankut SRB 126 A1
Tavannes CH. 106 B2
Tavarnelle val di Pesa
I 135 B4
Tavas TR 188 B4
Tavaux F. 105 B4
Tävelsås S. 62 B2
Taverna I 175 B2
Taverne CH 120 A1
Tavernelle I 135 B5
Taverines de la Valldigna
E. 159 B3
Tavérnola Bergamasca
I 120 B3
Taverny F. 90 B2
Tavescan E 146 B2
Taviano I 173 C4
Tavira P 160 B2
Tavistock GB. 42 B2
Tavşanlı TR 187 C4
Tayinloan GB. 34 C2
Taynuilt GB. 34 B2
Tayport GB. 35 B5
Tazones E 142 A1
Tczew PL 69 A3
Tczów PL. 87 A5
Teangue GB 31 B3
Teano I 170 B2
Teba E 162 B3
Tebay GB 37 B4
Techendorf A 109 C4
Tecklenburg D 71 B4
Tecko-matorp S . . . 61 D3
Tecuci RO 17 C7
Tefenni TR 189 B4
Tegelsmora S 51 B4

Tegernsee D 108 B2
Teggiano I 172 B1
Tegoleto I 135 B4
Teichel D 82 B3
Teignmouth GB 43 B3
Teillay F 101 B4
Teillet F 130 B1
Teisendorf D 109 B3
Teistungen D 82 A2
Teixeiro E. 140 A2
Tejada de Tiétar E . 150 B2
Tejado E. 152 A1
Tejares E 150 B2
Tejn DK 67 A3
Teke TR 187 A4
Tekirdağ TR 186 B2
Tekovské-Lužany
  SK 112 A2
Telavåg N. 46 B1
Telč CZ. 97 B3
Telese Terme I 170 B2
Telford GB 38 B4
Telfs A. 108 B2
Telgárt SK 99 C4
Telgte D 71 C4
Tellingstedt D 64 B2
Telšiai LT 8 E3
Telti I. 178 B3
Teltow D. 74 B2
Tembleque E 157 A4
Temelin CZ. 96 B2
Temerin SRB 126 B1
Temiño E 143 B3
Témpio Pausánia
  I 178 B3
Templederry IRL . . . 28 B3
Templemore IRL . . . 28 B4
Temple Sowerby
  GB 37 B4
Templin D. 74 A2
Temse B 79 A4
Tenay F 118 B2
Ten Boer NL. 71 A3
Tenbury Wells GB . . 39 B4
Tenby GB. 39 C2
Tence F 117 B4
Tende F 133 A3
Tenhult S 62 A2
Tenja HR 125 B4
Tenneville B. 92 A1
Tennevoll N 194 B8
Tensta S. 51 B4
Tenterden GB 45 B4
Teo E 140 B2
Teora I 172 B1
Tepasto FIN 196 B7
Tepelenë AL. 182 C2
Teplá CZ. 95 B4
Teplice CZ 84 B1
Teplička nad Váhom
  SK 98 B2
Tepsa FIN. 197 B8
Tera E. 143 C4
Téramo I. 169 A3
Ter Apel NL 71 B4
Terborg NL. 71 C3
Terchová SK 99 B3
Terebovlya UA. 13 D6
Teremia Mare RO . 126 B2
Terena P. 155 C3
Teresa de Cofrentes
  E. 159 B2
Terešov CZ 96 B1
Terezín CZ 84 B2
Terezino Polje HR . 124 B3
Tergnier F 90 B3
Teriberka RUS 3 B14
Terlizzi I 171 B4
Termas de Monfortinho
  P. 155 A4
Terme di Súio I 169 B3
Terme di Valdieri I. . 133 A3
Termens E 145 C4
Termes F 116 C3
Términi Imerese I . . 176 B2
Terminillo I. 169 A2
Térmoli I. 170 B3
Termonfeckin IRL . . 27 C4
Ternberg A. 110 B1
Terndrup DK 58 B3
Terneuzen NL 79 A3
Terni I 168 A2
Ternitz A. 111 B3
Ternopil UA 13 D6
Terpni GR. 183 C5
Terracina I 169 B3
Terråk N 195 E3
Terralba I 179 C2
Terranova di Pollino
  I 174 B2
Terranova di Sibari
  I 174 B2
Terras do Bouro P. . 148 A1
Terrasini I 176 A2
Terrassa E 147 C3
Terrasson-Lavilledieu
  F. 129 A4
Terrazos E 143 B3
Terriente E. 152 B2
Terrugem P 155 C3
Tertenía E 179 C3
Teruel E 152 B2
Tervola FIN 196 C7
Tervuren B. 79 B4
Terzaga E. 152 B2

Tešanj BIH 125 C3
Tesáske-Mlyňany
  SK 98 C2
Teslić BIH. 125 C3
Tessin D 66 B1
Tessy-sur-Vire F . . . 88 B2
Tét H. 111 B4
Teterchen F 92 B2
Teterow D. 65 C5
Teteven BG 17 D6
Tetovo MK 182 A2
Tettau D 82 B3
Tettnang D 107 B4
Teublitz D 95 B4
Teuchern D 83 A4
Teulada
  E 159 C4
  I 179 D2
Teupitz D 74 B2
Teurajärvi S 196 C5
Teutschenthal D . . . 83 A3
Tevel H 112 C2
Teviothead GB. . . . 36 A4
Tewkesbury GB. . . . 39 C4
Thale D. 82 A3
Thalfang D 92 B2
Thalgau A. 109 B4
Thalkirch CH 107 C4
Thalmässing D 95 B3
Thalwil CH 107 B3
Thame GB 44 B3
Thann F 106 B2
Thannhausen D. . . . 94 C2
Thaon-les-Vosges
  F. 105 A5
Tharandt D. 83 B5
Tharsis E. 161 B2
Thasos GR. 183 C6
Thatcham GB 44 B2
Thaxted GB 45 B4
Thayngen CH 107 B3
Theale GB 44 B2
The Barony GB 33 B3
Thebes = Thiva
  GR 185 A4
Theding-hausen D . . 72 B2
Theessen D 73 B5
The Hague = 's-
  Gravenhage NL. . . 70 B1
Themar D. 82 B2
The Mumbles GB. . . 39 C3
Thénezay F 102 C1
Thenon F 129 A4
Therouanne F 78 B2
Thessaloniki = Salonica
  GR 182 C4
Thetford GB. 45 A4
Theux B 80 B1
Thézar-les-Corbières
  F. 146 A3
Thèze F 145 A3
Thiberville F 89 A4
Thibie F 91 C4
Thiéblemont-Farémont
  F. 91 C4
Thiendorf D 84 A1
Thiene I 121 B4
Thierrens CH 106 C1
Thiers F. 117 B3
Thiesi I 178 B2
Thiessow D 66 B2
Thiezac F 116 B2
Þingeyri IS 190 B2
Þingvellir IS 190 C4
Thionville F 92 B2
Thira GR 185 C6
Thiron-Gardais F. . . 89 B4
Thirsk GB. 37 B5
Thisted DK 58 B1
Thiva = Thebes
  GR 185 A4
Thivars F 90 C1
Thiviers F. 115 C4
Thizy F 117 A4
Tholen NL 79 A4
Tholey D 92 B3
Thomas Street IRL . 28 A3
Thomastown IRL. . . 30 B1
Thônes F 118 B3
Thonnance-les-Joinville
  F. 91 C5
Thonon-les-Bains
  F. 118 A3
Thorame-Basse F . . 132 A2
Thorame-Haute F . . 132 A2
Thorens-Glières F . . 118 A3
Thorigny-sur-Oreuse
  F. 91 C3
Þórl A 110 B2
Þorlákshöfn IS 190 D4
Thornaby on Tees
  GB 37 B5
Thornbury GB. 43 A4
Thorne GB 40 B3
Thornhill
  Dumfries & Galloway
  GB 36 A3
  Stirling GB. 35 B3
Thornthwaite GB. . . 36 B3
Thornton-le-Dale
  GB 40 A3
Þórshöfn IS 191 A10
Thouarcé F 102 B1
Thouars F 102 C1
Thrapston GB 44 A3
Threlkeld GB 36 B3

Thrumster GB 32 C3
Thueyts F. 117 C4
Thuin B 79 B4
Thuir F 146 B3
Thumau D 95 A3
Thun CH. 106 C2
Thuret F. 116 B3
Thurey F 105 C4
Thüringen A. 107 B4
Thurins F 117 B4
Thürkow D. 65 C5
Thurles IRL 29 B4
Thurmaston GB. . . . 40 C2
Thurø By DK 65 A3
Thursby GB 36 B3
Thurso GB 32 C3
Thury-Harcourt F . . 89 B3
Thusis CH 107 C4
Thyborøn DK. 58 B1
Þykkvibær IS 190 D5
Þyregod DK 59 C2
Tibi E 159 C3
Tibro S 55 B5
Tidaholm S 55 B4
Tidan S. 55 B5
Tidersrum S. 62 A3
Tiedra E 150 A2
Tiefenbach D 95 B4
Tiefencastel CH. . . . 107 C4
Tiefenort D 82 B2
Tiefensee D 74 B2
Tiel NL 79 A5
Tielmes E. 151 B4
Tielt B. 78 A3
Tienen B. 79 B4
Tiengen D 106 B3
Tiercé F 102 B1
Tierga E 152 A2
Tiermas E. 144 B2
Tierp S 51 B4
Tierrantona E. 145 B4
Tighina MD 17 B8
Tighnabruaich GB. . 34 C2
Tignes F 119 B3
Tigy F 103 B4
Tihany H. 112 C1
Tijnje NL 70 A2
Tijola E 164 B2
Tikhvin RUS. 9 C8
Til Châtel F 105 B4
Tilh F 128 C2
Tillac F 145 A4
Tillberga S 56 A2
Tille F 90 B2
Tillicoultry GB 35 B4
Tilloy Bellay F 91 B4
Tilly F 115 B5
Tilly-sur-Seulles F . 88 A3
Tim DK. 59 B1
Timau I. 109 C4
Timbaki GR 185 D5
Timi CY 181 B1
Timişoara RO 126 B3
Timmele S 60 B3
Timmendorfer Strand
  D 65 C3
Timmernabben S . . 62 B4
Timmersdala S 55 B4
Timoleague IRL . . . 29 C3
Timolin IRL 30 B2
Timrå S. 200 D3
Timsfors S. 61 C3
Timsgearraidh GB. . 31 A1
Tinajas E 152 B1
Tinalhas P 155 B3
Tinchebray F 88 B3
Tincques F. 78 B2
Tineo E. 141 A4
Tinglev DK 64 B2
Tingsryd S 63 B2
Tingstäde S 57 C4
Tingvoll N 198 C5
Tinlot B. 79 B5
Tinnoset N 53 A5
Tinos GR 185 B6
Tintagel GB 42 B2
Tinténiac F. 101 A4
Tintern GB. 39 C4
Tintigny B 92 B1
Tione di Trento I . . . 121 A3
Tipperary IRL. 29 B3
Tiptree GB 45 B4
Tirana = Tiranë AL. . 182 B1
Tiranë= Tirana AL. . 182 B1
Tirano I. 120 A3
Tiraspol MD 17 B8
Tire TR 188 A2
Tires I 108 C2
Tiriez E. 158 C1
Tirig E. 153 B4
Tiriolo I. 175 C2
Tirnavos GR 182 D4
Tirrénia I. 134 B3
Tirschenreuth D . . . 95 B4
Tisno HR 137 B4
Tisovec SK 99 C3
Tisselskog S 54 B3
Tistedal N. 54 A2
Tistrup DK 59 C1
Tisvildeleje DK 61 C2
Tiszaalpár H 113 C3
Tiszabő H 113 B4
Tiszacsége H. 113 B5
Tiszadorogma H . . 113 B4

Tiszaföldvár H 113 C4
Tiszafüred H 113 B4
Tiszajenő H 113 B4
Tiszakécske H. 113 C4
Tiszakeszi H 113 B4
Tiszakürt H 113 C4
Tiszalök H 113 A5
Tiszalúc H 113 A5
Tiszanána H. 113 B4
Tiszaörs H 113 B4
Tiszaroff H. 113 B4
Tiszasüly H 113 B4
Tiszasziget H 126 A2
Tiszaszőlős H 113 B4
Tiszaújváros H 113 B5
Tiszavasvári H. 113 B5
Titaguas E 159 B2
Titel SRB 126 B2
Titisee-Neustadt D 106 B3
Tito I 172 B1
Titova Korenica
  HR 123 C4
Titran N 198 B5
Tittling D 96 C1
Tittmoning D 109 A3
Titz D 80 A2
Tiurajärvi FIN. 196 B7
Tived S. 55 B5
Tiverton GB 43 B3
Tivisa E 153 A4
Tívoli I 168 B2
Tizsadob H. 113 A5
Tjällmo S 56 B1
Tjåmotis S 195 D9
Tjæreborg DK 59 C1
Tjautjas S. 196 B3
Tjøme N 54 A1
Tjong N 195 D4
Tjonnefoss N. 53 B4
Tjörn IS 190 B5
Tjörnarp S 61 D3
Tjørn IS. 190 B5
Tjøtta N 195 E3
Tkon HR. 137 B4
Tleň PL 68 B3
Tlmače SK 98 C2
Tłuchowo PL 77 B4
Tlumačov CZ. 98 B1
Tłuszcz PL 77 B6
Toamna H. 112 B3
Toano I 134 A3
Toba D 82 A2
Tobarra E 158 C2
Tobermore GB 27 B4
Tobermory GB. 34 B1
Toberonochy GB. . . 34 B2
Tobha Mor GB 31 B1
Tobo S 51 B4
Tocane-St Apre F . . 129 A3
Tocha P 148 B1
Tocina E. 162 A2
Töcksfors S 54 A2
Tocón E. 163 A4
Todal N 198 C5
Todi I 136 C1
Todmorden GB 40 B1
Todorici BIH. 138 A3
Todtmoos D 106 B3
Todtnau D 106 B2
Toén E 140 B3
Tofta
  Gotland S. 57 C4
  Skaraborg S 55 B4
Toftbyn S. 50 B2
Tofte N 54 A1
Töftedal S 54 B2
Tofterup DK. 59 C1
Toftlund DK 59 C2
Tófü H. 125 A4
Tohmo FIN. 197 C10
Tokaj H. 113 A5
Tokarnia PL 87 B4
Tokary PL. 76 C3
Tokod H 112 B2
Tököl H 112 B2
Tolastadh bho Thuath
  GB 31 A2
Toledo E 151 C3
Tolentino I 136 B2
Tolfa I 168 A1
Tolg S 62 A2
Tolga N 199 C8
Tolkmicko PL. 69 A4
Tollarp S 61 D3
Tollered S 60 B2
Tølløse DK 61 D1
Tolmachevo RUS . . 9 C6
Tolmezzo I 122 A2
Tolmin SLO 122 A2
Tolna H 112 C2
Tolnanémedi H 112 C2
Tolob GB 33 B5
Tolosa
  E 144 A1
  P. 155 B3
Tolox E. 162 B3
Tolpuddle GB. 43 B4
Tolva
  E 145 B4
  FIN 197 C11
Tolve I. 172 B2
Tomar P 154 B2
Tomaševac SRB . . . 126 B2
Tomašica BIH 124 C2
Tomašikovo SK. . . . 111 A4
Tomášouka BY 13 C5
Tomášovce SK 99 C3
Tomaszów Mazowiecki
  PL. 87 A4
Tomatin GB 32 D3

Tombeboeuf F 129 B3
Tomdoun GB 32 D1
Tomelilla S 66 C2
Tomellosa E 151 B5
Tomelloso E. 157 A4
Tomiño E 140 C2
Tomintoul GB 32 D3
Tomislavgrad BIH . . 138 B3
Tomisław PL 84 A3
Tomisława PL. 76 B3
Tomnavoulin GB . . 32 D3
Tompa H. 126 A1
Tompaládony H . . . 111 B3
Tomra N 198 C3
Tona E 147 C3
Tonara I 179 B3
Tonbridge GB 45 B4
Tondela P. 148 B1
Tønder DK 64 B1
Tongeren B 79 B5
Tongue GB. 32 C2
Tönisvorst D 80 A2
Tønjum N 47 A4
Tonkopuro FIN . . 197 C11
Tonnay-Boutonne
  F. 114 C3
Tonnay-Charente
  F. 114 C3
Tonneins F 129 B3
Tonnerre F 104 B2
Tonnes N 195 D4
Tönning D 64 B1
Tonsåsen N 47 B6
Tonstad N 52 B2
Toomyvara IRL 28 B3
Toormore IRL. 29 C2
Topares E 164 B2
Topas E 150 A2
Topliţa RO 17 B6
Topola SRB 127 C2
Topolčani MK. 182 B3
Topol'čany SK 98 C2
Topol'čianky SK . . . 98 C2
Topolje HR. 124 B2
Topólka PL 76 B3
Topol'niky SK 111 B4
Topolovăţu Mare
  RO 126 B3
Toponár H 125 A3
Toporów PL 75 B4
Topsham GB 43 B3
Topusko HR. 124 B1
Torà E. 147 C2
Toral de los Guzmanes
  E 142 B1
Toral de los Vados
  E 141 B4
Torbalı TR 188 A2
Torbjörntorp S. 55 B4
Torbole I. 121 B3
Torchiarolo I 173 B4
Torcross GB 43 B3
Torcy-le-Petit F . . . 89 A5
Torda SRB 126 B2
Tordehumos E. 142 C1
Tordera E 147 C3
Tordesillas E 150 A2
Tordesilos E 152 B2
Töre S 196 D5
Töreboda S 55 B5
Toreby DK 65 B4
Torekov S. 61 C2
Torella dei Lombardi
  I 170 C3
Torella del Sánnio
  I 170 B2
Toreno E 141 B4
Torfou F 114 A2
Torgau D 83 A5
Torgelow D 74 A3
Torgueda P 148 A2
Torhamn S 63 B3
Torhop N 193 B11
Torhout B. 78 A3
Torigni-sur-Vire F . . 88 A3
Toril E. 152 B2
Torino = Turin I 119 B4
Toritto I 171 C4
Torla E 145 B3
Tormac RO 126 B3
Törmänen FIN . . 193 D11
Tormestorp S 61 C3
Tórmini I 121 B3
Tornada P. 154 B1
Tornavacas E. 150 B2
Tornby DK 58 A2
Tornesch D 72 A2
Torness GB 32 D2
Torniella I 135 B4
Torninparte I 169 A3
Torning DK. 59 B2
Tornio FIN 196 D7
Tornjoš SRB 126 B1
Tornos E. 152 B2
Toro E 150 A2
Törökszentmiklós
  H 113 B4
Toropets RUS 9 D7
Torpa S 61 C3
Torpè I 178 B3
Torphins GB 33 D4
Torpo N 47 B5

Torpoint GB. 42 B2
Torpsbruk S. 62 A2
Torquay GB 43 B3
Torquemada E 142 B2
Torralba de Burgo
  E 151 A5
Torralba de Calatrava
  E 157 A4
Torrão P. 154 C2
Torre Annunziata I. . 170 C2
Torreblacos E 143 C4
Torreblanca E 153 B4
Torreblascopedro
  E 157 B4
Torrecaballeros E. . 151 A3
Torrecampo E 156 B3
Torre Canne I. 173 B3
Torre Cardela E . . . 163 A4
Torrecilla E 152 B1
Torrecilla de la Jara
  E. 156 A3
Torrecilla de la Orden
  E. 150 A2
Torrecilla del Pinar
  E. 151 A3
Torrecilla en Cameros
  E. 143 B4
Torrecillas de la Tiesa
  E. 156 A2
Torre das Vargens
  P. 154 B3
Torre de Coelheiros
  P. 154 C3
Torre de Dom Chama
  P. 149 A2
Torre de Juan Abad
  E. 157 B4
Torre de la Higuera
  E. 161 B3
Torre del Bierzo E. 141 B4
Torre del Burgo E . 151 B4
Torre del Campo E 163 A4
Torre del Greco I . . 170 C2
Torre del Lago Puccini
  I 134 B3
Torre dell'Orso I . . . 173 B4
Torredembarra E . . 147 C2
Torre de Miguel
  Sesmero E 155 C4
Torre de Moncorvo
  P. 149 A2
Torre de Santa Maria
  E. 156 A1
Torredonjimeno E. 163 A4
Torre do Terranho
  P. 148 B2
Torre Faro I 177 A4
Torregamones E. . . 149 A3
Torregrossa E 147 C1
Torreira P 148 B1
Torrejoncillo E. . . . 155 B4
Torrejón de Ardoz
  E. 151 B4
Torrejón de la Calzada
  E. 151 B4
Torrejón del Rey E 151 B4
Torrejon el Rubio
  E. 156 A1
Torrelaguna E 151 B4
Torrelapaja E 152 A2
Torre la Ribera E . . 145 B4
Torrelavega E 142 A2
Torrelobatón E 150 A2
Torrelodones E 151 B4
Torre los Negros E 152 B2
Torremaggiore I. . . . 171 B3
Torremanzanas E . . 159 C3
Torremayor E. 155 C4
Torremezzo di
  Falconara I 174 B2
Torremocha E 156 A1
Torremolinos E 163 B3
Torrenieri I. 135 B4
Torrenostra I 153 B4
Torrenova I 168 B2
Torrent E 159 B3
Torrente de Cinca
  E. 153 A4
Torrenueva
  Ciudad Real E . . . 157 B4
  Granada E 163 B4
Torreorgaz E 155 B4
Torre Orsáia I. 172 B1
Torre-Pacheco E . . 165 B4
Torre Péllice I 119 C4
Torreperogil E 157 B4
Torres E 163 A4
Torresandino E 143 C3
Torre Santa Susanna
  I 173 B3
Torres-Cabrera E. . 163 A3
Torres de la Alameda
  E. 151 B4
Torres Novas P. . . . 154 B2
Torres Vedras P. . . . 154 B1
Torrevieja E 165 B4
Torricella I. 173 B3
Torri del Benaco I . 121 B3
Torridon GB. 31 B3
Torríglia I. 134 A2
Torrijos E 151 C3
Tørring DK. 59 C2
Torríti di Siena I . . . 135 B4
Torroal P 154 C2
Torroella de Montgrì
  E. 147 B4
Torrox E. 163 B4
Torrskog S. 54 A3

Torsåker S 50 B3
Torsang S 50 B2
Torsås S 63 B4
Torsby S 49 B4
Torshälla S 56 A2
Tórshavn FO 4 A3
Torslanda S 60 B1
Torsminde DK 59 B1
Torsnes N 46 B3
Törtel H 113 B3
Tórtoles E 150 B2
Tórtoles de Esgueva
   E 142 C2
Tortol i I 179 C3
Tortona I 120 C1
Tórtora I 174 B1
Tortoreto Lido I . . . 136 C2
Tortorici I 177 A3
Tortosa E 153 B4
Tortosendo P. 148 B2
Tortuera E 152 B2
Tortuero E 151 B4
Toruń PL 76 A3
Torup S 60 C3
Tor Vaiánica I 168 B2
Torver GB 36 B3
Tørvikbygde N 46 B3
Torvisción S 163 B4
Torzhok RUS 9 D9
Torzym PL 75 B4
Tosbotn N 195 E3
Toscolano-Maderno
   I 121 B3
Tosno RUS. 9 C7
Tossa de Mar E . . . 147 C3
Tossåsen S 199 C10
Tosse F 128 C1
Tösse S 54 B3
Tossícia I 169 A3
Tostedt D 72 A2
Tosya TR 23 A8
Tószeg H 113 B4
Toszek PL 86 B2
Totana E 165 B3
Totebo S. 62 A4
Tôtes F 89 A5
Tótkomlós H 113 C4
Totland N 198 D2
Tøtlandsvik N 52 A2
Totnes GB 43 B3
Tótszerdahely H . . 124 A2
Tøttdal N 199 A8
Totton GB. 44 C2
Touça P 149 A2
Toucy F 104 B2
Toul F 92 C1
Toulon F 132 B1
Toulon-sur-Allier F 104 C2
Toulon-sur-Arroux
   F 104 C3
Toulouse F 129 C4
Tourcoing F 78 B3
Tour de la Parata F 180 B1
Tourlaville F. 88 A2
Tournai B 78 B3
Tournan-en-Brie F . 90 C2
Tournay F 145 A4
Tournon-d'Agenais
   F 129 B3
Tournon-St Martin
   F 115 B4
Tournon-sur-Rhône
   F 117 B4
Tournus F 105 C3
Touro
   E 140 B2
   P 148 B2
Tourouvre F. 89 B4
Tourriers F 115 C4
Tours F. 102 B2
Tourteron F 91 B4
Tourves F 132 B1
Toury F 103 A3
Touvedo P 148 A1
Touvois F 114 B2
Toužim CZ 83 B4
Tovačov CZ 98 B1
Tovariševo SRB. . . 126 B1
Tovarnik HR. 125 B5
Tovdal N. 53 B4
Towcester GB 44 A3
Town Yetholm GB . . 35 C5
Tråastølen N 47 B4
Trabada E 141 A3
Trabadelo E 141 B4
Trabanca E 149 A3
Trabazos E 149 A3
Traben-Trarbach D . 92 B3
Trabia I 176 B2
Tradate I 120 B1
Trädet S 60 B3
Trafaria P 154 C1
Tragacete E 152 B2
Tragwein A. 96 C2
Traiguera E 153 B4
Trainel F 91 C3
Traisen A 110 A2
Traismauer A 97 C3
Traitsching D. 95 B4
Trákhonas CY 181 A2
Tralee IRL. 29 B2
Tramacastilla de Tena
   E 145 B3
Tramagal P. 154 B2
Tramariglio I 178 B2
Tramatza I 179 B2
Tramelan CH 106 B2

Tramonti di Sopra
   I 122 A1
Tramore IRL 30 B1
Trampot F 92 C1
Trana I 119 B4
Tranås S 55 B5
Tranbjerg DK 59 B3
Tranby N 54 A1
Trancoso P 148 B2
Tranebjerg DK 59 C3
Tranekær DK 65 B3
Tranemo S. 60 B3
Tranent GB 35 C5
Tranevåg N 52 B2
Trängslet S 49 A5
Tranhult S 60 B3
Trani I 171 B4
Trans-en-Provence
   F. 132 B2
Transtrand S 49 A5
Tranum DK. 58 A2
Tranvik S 57 A4
Trápani I. 176 A1
Trappes F. 90 C2
Traryd S 61 C3
Trasacco I 169 B3
Trasierra E 156 B1
Traspinedo E 150 A3
Trasmiras E 140 B3
Traspinedo E 150 A3
Trate SLO. 110 C2
Trauchgau D 108 B1
Traun A. 110 A1
Traunreut D 109 B3
Traunstein D 109 B3
Traunwalchen D . 109 B3
Tråvad S 55 B4
Travemünde D. 65 C3
Traversétolo I 120 C3
Travnik
   BIH. 139 A3
   SLO. 123 B3
Travo
   F. 180 B2
   I 120 C2
Trawsfynydd GB . . 38 B3
Trbovlje SLO. 123 A4
Trbušani SRB 127 D2
Treban F. 116 A3
Třebařov CZ 97 B4
Trebatsch D 74 B3
Trebbin D 74 B2
Třebechovice pod
   Orebem CZ 85 B3
Trebel D 73 B4
Třebenice CZ. 84 B1
Trébeurden F. 100 A2
Třebíč CZ. 97 B3
Trebinje BIH 139 C4
Trebisacce I. 174 B2
Trebitz D 83 A4
Trebnje SLO. 123 B4
Třeboň CZ 96 B2
Třebovice CZ. 97 B4
Trebsen D 83 A4
Trebujena E 161 C3
Trecastagni I 177 B4
Trecate I. 120 B1
Trecenta I 121 B4
Tredegar GB 39 C3
Tredózio I 135 A4
Treffen A. 109 C4
Treffort F 118 A2
Treffurt D 82 A2
Trefnant GB 38 A3
Tregaron GB 39 B3
Trégastel-Plage F . 100 A2
Tregnago I 121 B4
Tregony GB 42 B2
Tréguier F 100 A2
Trégunc F 100 B2
Treharris GB 39 C3
Trehörningsjö S . . 200 C4
Tréia I 136 B2
Treignac F 116 B1
Treignat F 116 A2
Treignes B 91 A4
Treis-Karden D . . . 80 B3
Trekanten S 63 B4
Trélazé F 102 B1
Trélech GB. 39 C2
Trélissac F 129 A3
Trelleborg S 66 A2
Trélon F 91 A4
Trélou-sur-Marne F. 91 B3
Tremblay-le-Vicomte
   F. 89 B5
Tremés P 154 B2
Tremezzo I 120 B2
Tremošná CZ. 96 B1
Tremp F 145 B4
Trenčianska Stankovce
   SK 98 C1
Trenčianska Turná
   SK 98 C2
Trenčianske Teplá
   SK 98 C2
Trenčianske Teplice
   SK 98 C2
Trenčín SK. 98 C2
Trendelburg D 81 A5
Trengereid N 46 B2
Trensacq F. 128 B2
Trent D 66 B2
Trento I 121 A4
Treorchy GB 39 C3
Trept F 118 B2
Trepuzzi I 173 B4

Trescore Balneário
   I 120 B2
Tresenda I 120 A3
Tresfjord N. 198 C4
Tresigallo I 121 C4
Trešnjevica SRB . . 127 D3
Tresnuràghes I . . . 178 B2
Trespaderne E. . . . 143 B3
Třešt CZ. 97 B3
Trestina I 135 B5
Tretower GB 39 C3
Trets F 132 B1
Tretten N 48 A2
Treuchtlingen D . . . 94 C2
Treuen D 83 B4
Treuenbrietzen D . . 74 B1
Treungen N 53 A4
Trevelez E 163 B4
Trevi I 136 C1
Treviana E 143 B3
Treviglio I 120 B2
Trevignano Romano
   I. 168 A2
Trevi nel Lázio I . . . 169 B3
Treviso I 122 B1
Trévoux F. 117 B4
Treysa D. 81 B5
Trézelles F 117 A3
Trezzo sull'Adda I . 120 B2
Trhová Kamenice
   CZ 97 B3
Trhové Sviny CZ . . 96 C2
Triacastela E 141 B3
Triaize F 114 B2
Trianda GR 188 C3
Triaucourt-en-Argonne
   F 91 C5
Tribanj Krušcica
   HR. 137 A4
Triberg D 106 A3
Tribsees D 66 B1
Tribuče SLO. 123 B4
Tricárico I 172 B2
Tricase I 173 C4
Tricésimo I. 122 A2
Trieben A 110 B1
Triebes D 83 B4
Triepkendorf D . . . 74 A2
Trier D 92 B2
Trieste I 122 B2
Trie-sur-Baïse F . . 145 A4
Triggiano I 173 A2
Triglitz D 73 A5
Trignac F 101 B3
Trigueros E 161 B3
Trigueros del Valle
   E. 142 C2
Trikala GR 182 D3
Trikeri GR 183 D5
Trikomo CY 181 A2
Trilj HR 138 B2
Trillo E 152 B1
Trilport F 90 C2
Trim IRL 30 A2
Trimdon GB 37 B5
Tring GB. 44 B3
Trinità d'Agultu I . . 178 B2
Trinitápoli I 171 B4
Trino I. 119 B5
Trinta P. 148 B2
Triora I 133 B3
Tripoli GR 184 B3
Triponzo I 136 C1
Triptis D 83 B3
Triste I. 144 B3
Trittau D 72 A3
Trivento I 170 B2
Trivero I 119 B5
Trivigno I 172 B1
Trn BIH 124 C3
Trnava
   HR. 125 B4
   SK. 98 C1
Trnovec SK. 112 A1
Trnovo BIH. 139 B4
Trnovska vas SLO. 110 C2
Troarn F. 89 A3
Trochtelfingen D . . 94 C1
Trödje S 51 B4
Troense DK 65 A3
Trofa P 148 A1
Trofaiach A. 110 B2
Trofors N 195 E4
Trogir HR 138 B2
Trøgstad N 54 A2
Tróia I 171 B3
Troia P 154 C2
Troina I. 177 B3
Troisdorf D 80 B3
Trois-Ponts B 80 B1
Troisvierges L 92 A2
Trojane SLO. 123 A3
Troldhede DK 59 C1
Trollhättan S 54 B3
Trolog BIH 138 B2
Tromello I. 120 B1
Tromøy N 53 B4
Tromsø N. 192 C3
Trondheim N 199 B7
Tronget F 116 A3
Trönninge S 61 C2
Trönningeby S. . . . 60 B2
Trönö S 51 A3

Tronzano-Vercellese
   I 119 B5
Trôo F. 102 B2
Troon GB 36 A2
Tropea I 175 C1
Tropy Sztumskie PL 69 B4
Trosa S 57 B3
Trösken S 50 B3
Trosly-Breuil F 90 B3
Trossingen D. 107 A3
Trostberg D 109 A3
Trouville-sur-Mer F . 89 A4
Trowbridge GB 43 A4
Troyes F 104 A3
Trpanj HR 138 B3
Trpinja HR. 125 B4
Trščce HR 123 B3
Tršice CZ. 98 B1
Trstená SK. 99 B3
Trstenci BIH. 125 B3
Trsteno HR 139 C3
Trstice SK. 111 A4
Trstin SK 98 C1
Trubia E 141 A5
Trubjela MNE. 139 C4
Truchas E 141 B4
Trujillanos E 155 C4
Trujillo E 156 A2
Trumieje PL 69 B4
Trun
   CH 107 C3
   F. 89 B4
Truro GB 42 B1
Trusetal D 82 B2
Truskavets' UA . . . 13 D5
Trustrup DK 59 B3
Trutnov CZ. 85 B3
Tryserum S 56 B2
Trysil N 49 A4
Tryszczyn PL 76 A2
Trzcianka PL 75 A5
Trzciel PL. 75 B4
Trzcińsko Zdrój PL . 74 B3
Trzebiatów PL 67 B4
Trzebiel D. 84 A2
Trzebielino PL 68 A2
Trzebień PL. 84 A3
Trzebiez PL 74 A3
Trzebinia PL. 86 B3
Trzebnica PL. 85 A4
Trzeciewiec PL . . . 76 A3
Trzemeszno PL . . . 76 B2
Trzemeszno-Lubuskie
   PL. 75 B4
Trzetrzewina PL. . . 99 B4
Tržič SLO. 123 A3
Tsamandás GR . . . 182 D2
Tschagguns A 107 B4
Tschernitz D 84 A2
Tsebrykove UA. . . . 17 B9
Tselyakhany BY. . . 13 B6
Tua P 148 A2
Tuam IRL 28 A3
Tubbercurry IRL . . 26 B2
Tubbergen NL 71 B3
Tubilla del Lago E . 143 C3
Tübingen D 93 C5
Tubize B 79 B4
Tučapy CZ 96 B2
Tučepi HR 138 B3
Tuchan F 146 B3
Tüchen D 73 A5
Tuchola PL. 76 A2
Tuchomie PL 68 A2
Tuchów PL 99 B5
Tuczno PL 75 A5
Tuddal N. 53 A4
Tudela E. 144 B2
Tudela de Duero E. 150 A3
Tudweiliog GB. . . . 38 B2
Tuejar E 159 B2
Tuffé F 102 A2
Tufsingdalen N . . . 199 C8
Tuhaň CZ 84 B2
Tui E 140 B2
Tukhkala RUS . . . 197 D13
Tukums LV 8 D3
Tula I 178 B2
Tulcea RO 17 C8
Tul'chyn UA. 13 D8
Tulette F. 131 A3
Tulla IRL. 28 B3
Tullamore IRL 30 A1
Tulle F 116 B1
Tullins F 118 B2
Tulln A 97 C4
Tullow IRL 30 B2
Tułowice PL. 85 B5
Tulppio FIN 197 B12
Tulsk IRL. 28 A3
Tumba S 57 A3
Tummel Bridge GB . 35 B3
Tuna
   Kalmar S. 62 A4
   Uppsala S 51 B5
Tuna Hästberg S . . 50 B2
Tunçbilek TR 187 C4
Tunes P 160 B1
Tungelsta S 57 A4
Tunnerstad S. 55 B5
Tunnhovd N 47 B5
Tunstall GB 45 A5
Tuohikotti FIN 8 B5
Tuoro sul Trasimeno
   I 135 B5

Tupadły PL. 76 B3
Tupanari BIH 139 A4
Tupik RUS 9 E8
Tuplice PL 84 A2
Tura H. 112 B3
Turanj HR. 137 B4
Turany SK 99 B3
Turbe BIH. 139 A3
Turbenthal CH 107 B3
Turcia E 141 B5
Turčianske Teplice
   SK 98 C2
Turcifal P 154 B1
Turckheim F. 106 A2
Turda RO. 17 B5
Turégano E 151 A4
Turek PL. 76 B3
Turgutlu TR 188 A2
Turgutreis TR 188 B2
Turi I 173 B3
Turin = Torino I 119 B4
Turis E 159 B3
Türje H 111 C4
Turka UA 12 D5
Túrkeve H 113 B4
Türkheim D 108 A1
Türkmenli TR 186 C1
Turku FIN 8 B3
Turleque E 157 A4
Turňa nad Bodvou
   SK 99 C4
Turnberry GB. 36 A2
Turnhout B. 79 A4
Türnitz A. 110 B2
Turnov CZ 84 B3
Turnu RO 126 A3
Turnu Măgurele RO. 17 D6
Turón E 164 C1
Turoszów PL 84 B2
Turowo PL 77 A5
Turquel P 154 B1
Turri I 179 C2
Turries F. 132 A2
Turriff GB 33 D4
Tursi I 174 A2
Turtmann CH 119 A4
Turtola FIN 196 C6
Turze PL 86 A1
Turzovka SK 98 B2
Tusa I 177 B3
Tuscánia I 168 A1
Tuse DK 61 D1
Tušilovic HR 123 B4
Tutin SRB 126 C2
Tutow D 66 C2
Tutrakan BG. 17 C7
Tuttlingen D. 107 B3
Tutzing D 108 B2
Tuzla
   BIH. 125 C4
   TR. 23 C8
Tuzlukçu TR. 189 A6
Tvååker S 60 B2
Tväralund S 200 B5
Tvärskog S 63 B4
Tvedestrand N. . . . 53 B4
Tveit
   Hordaland N. 47 B4
   Rogaland N 52 A2
Tver RUS 9 D9
Tverrelvmo N. 192 D3
Tversted DK. 58 A3
Tving S 63 B3
Tvrdošin SK. 99 B3
Tvrdošovce SK . . .112 A2
Twardogóra PL . . . 85 A5
Twatt GB 33 B3
Twello NL. 70 B3
Twimberg A 110 C1
Twist D. 71 B4
Twistringen D 72 B1
Tworóg PL 86 B2
Twyford
   Hampshire GB 44 B2
   Wokingham GB . . . 44 B3
Tyachiv UA. 17 A5
Tychówka PL 67 C5
Tychowo PL 67 C5
Tychy PL 86 B2
Tydal N 199 B8
Týec nad Labem CZ 97 A3
Tyfors S 49 B6
Tygelsjö S 61 D2
Tylldal N 199 C7
Tylstrup DK 58 A2
Tymbark PL 99 B4
Tymowa PL 99 B4
Tyndrum GB 34 B3
Týnec nad Sázavou
   CZ 96 B2
Tynemouth GB . . . 37 A5
Tyngsjö S 49 B6
Týništěnad Orlicí CZ 85 B4
Týn nad Vltavou CZ 96 B2
Tynset N 199 C7
Tyresö S 57 A4
Tyringe
   S. 61 C3
Tyrislöt S 56 B2
Tyristrand N. 48 B2
Tyrrellspass IRL . . 30 A1
Tysnes N 46 B2
Tysse N 46 B2
Tyssebotn N. 46 B2
Tyssedal N 46 B3
Tystberga S 56 B3
Tysvær N 52 A1
Tywyn GB. 39 B2
Tzermiado GR 185 D6

Tzummarum NL. . . . 70 A2

U

Ub SRB 127 C2
Ubby DK. 61 D1
Úbeda E 157 B4
Überlingen D. 107 B4
Ubidea E 143 A4
Ubli HR. 138 C2
Ubrique E. 162 B2
Ucero E 143 C3
Uchaud F 131 B3
Uchte D 72 B1
Uckerath D. 80 B3
Uckfield GB 45 C4
Ucklum S 54 B2
Uclés E 151 C5
Ucria I 177 A3
Udbina HR. 137 A4
Uddebo S. 60 B3
Uddeholm S. 49 B5
Uddevalla S 54 B2
Uddheden S 49 C4
Uden NL. 80 A1
Uder D 82 A2
Udiča SK. 98 B2
Údine I. 122 A2
Udvar H 125 B4
Ueckermünde D . . 74 A3
Uelsen D. 71 B3
Uelzen D 73 B3
Uetendorf CH. . . . 106 C2
Uetersen D. 72 A2
Uetze D 72 B3
Uffculme GB 43 B3
Uffenheim D 94 B2
Ugarana E 143 A4
Ugento I. 173 C4
Ugerløse DK 61 D1
Uggerby DK 58 A3
Uggerslev DK 59 C3
Uggiano la Chiesa
   I 173 B4
Ugijar E 164 C1
Ugine F 118 B3
Uglejevik BIH 125 C5
Uglenes N 46 B2
Uglich RUS 9 D11
Ugljane HR 138 B2
Ugod H 111 B4
Uherské Hradiště
   CZ 98 B1
Uherský Brod CZ . 98 B1
Uherský Ostroh CZ. 98 C1
Uhingen D 94 C1
Uhliřské-Janovice
   CZ 96 B3
Uhřiněves CZ 96 A2
Uhyst D 84 A2
Uig GB 31 B2
Uitgeest NL 70 B1
Uithoorn NL. 70 B1
Uithuizen NL 71 A3
Uithuizermeeden
   NL. 71 A3
Uivar RO 126 B2
Ujazd
   Łódzkie PL. 87 A3
   Opolskie PL 86 B2
Ujezd u Brna CZ . . 97 B4
Ujhartyán H 112 B3
Újkígyós H 113 C5
Ujpetre H. 125 B4
Ujście PL 75 A5
Ujsolt H 112 C3
Ujszász H. 113 B4
Ujszentmargita H .113 B5
Ujué E 144 B2
Ukanc SLO. 122 A2
Ukmergè LT 13 A6
Ukna S 56 B2
Ula TR 188 B3
Ul'anka SK. 99 C3
Ulaş TR 186 A2
Ulássai I 179 C3
Ulbjerg DK. 58 B2
Ulbster GB 32 C3
Ulceby GB 40 B3
Ulcinj MNE. 16 E3
Uldum DK 59 C2
Ulefoss N 53 A5
Uleila del Campo E 164 B2
Ulëz AL. 182 B1
Ulfborg DK. 59 B1
Uljma SRB 127 B3
Ullånger S 200 C4
Ullapool GB. 32 D1
Ullared S 60 B2
Ullatti S 196 B4
Ullatun N 52 A2
Ulldecona E 153 B4
Ulldemolins E 147 C1
Ullerslev DK. 59 C3
Ullervad S 55 B4
Üllés H 126 A1
Üllő H 112 B3
Ulm D 94 C1
Ulme P 154 B2
Ulmen D 80 B2
Ulnes N 47 B6
Ulog BIH. 139 B4
Ulrichstein D 81 B5
Ulricehamn S 60 B3

Ulrika S 56 B1
Ulriksfors S 200 C1
Ulrum NL 71 A3
Ulsta GB. 33 A5
Ulsted DK. 58 A3
Ulsteinvik N. 198 C2
Ulstrup
  Vestsjællands Amt.
  DK 59 C3
  Viborg Amt. DK 59 B2
Ulsvåg N. 194 B6
Ulubey TR 188 A4
Uluborlu TR 189 A5
Ulukışla TR 23 C8
Ulverston GB. 36 B3
Ulvik N. 46 B3
Umag HR 122 B2
Uman UA 13 D9
Umba RUS 3 C14
Umbértide I 135 B5
Umbriático I 174 B2
Umčari SRB. 127 C2
Umeå S 200 C6
Umgransele S 200 B4
Umhausen A 108 B1
Umka SRB 127 C2
Umljanovic HR . . . 138 B2
Umnäs S 195 E7
Umurbey TR 186 B1
Unaðsdalur IS . . . 190 A3
Unapool GB 32 C1
Unari FIN 197 B8
Unbyn S 196 D4
Uncastillo E 144 B2
Undenäs S 55 B5
Undersaker S . . . 199 B10
Undredal N 46 B4
Unešić HR 138 B2
Úněšov CZ 96 B1
Ungheni MD 17 B7
Unhais da Serra P . 148 B2
Unhošt CZ 84 B2
Unichowo PL 68 A2
Uničov CZ 98 B1
Uniejów PL 76 C3
Unisław PL 76 A3
Unkel D 80 B3
Unken A 109 B3
Unna D 81 A3
Unnaryd S 60 C3
Unquera E 142 A2
Unterach A 109 B4
Unterägeri CH . . . 107 B3
Unterammergau D . 108 B2
Unterhaching D . . . 108 A2
Unteriberg CH . . . 107 B3
Unterkochen D . . . 94 C2
Unter Langkampfen
  A. 108 B3
Unterlaussa A . . . 110 B1
Unterlüss D 72 B3
Untermünkheim D . 94 B1
Unterschächen
  CH 107 C3
Unterschleissheim
  D 95 C3
Unterschwaningen
  D 94 B2
Untersiemau D . . . 82 B2
Unter-steinbach D . 94 B2
Unterweissenbach
  A. 96 C2
Unterzell D. 95 B4
Upavon GB 44 B2
Úpice CZ 85 B4
Upiłka PL 68 B2
Upphärad S 54 B3
Uppingham GB . . . 40 C3
Uppsala S 51 C4
Upplands-Väsby S . 57 A3
Uppsjøhytta N . . . 48 A1
Upton-upon-Severn
  GB 39 B4
Ur F 146 B2
Uras I 179 C2
Uraz PL 85 A4
Urbánia I 136 B1
Urbino I 136 B1
Urçay F 103 C4
Urda E 157 A4
Urdax E 144 A2
Urdilde E 140 B2
Urdos F 145 B3
Urk NL 70 B2
Úrkút H. 111 B4
Urla TR 188 A1
Urlingford IRL . . . 30 B1
Urnäsch CH 107 B4
Urnes N 47 A4
Uroševac KOS. . . 16 D4
Urracal E 164 B2
Urries E 144 B2
Urroz E 144 B2
Ursensollen D . . . 95 B3
Urshult S 63 B2
Uršna Sela SLO. . 123 B4
Urszulewo PL . . . 77 B4
Ury F 90 C2
Urziceni RO 17 C7
Urzulei I 178 B3
Usagre E 156 B1
Uşak TR 187 D4
Usedom D 66 C2
Useldange L. 92 B1

Uséllus I 179 C2
Ushakovo RUS . . . 69 A5
Usingen D 81 B4
Usini I 178 B2
Usk GB. 39 C4
Uskedal N 46 C2
Üsküdar TR 186 A4
Uslar D. 82 A1
Úsov CZ. 97 B5
Usquert NL. 71 A3
Ussássai I 179 C3
Ussé F 102 B2
Usséglio I. 119 B4
Ussel
  Cantal F 116 B2
  Corrèze F 116 B2
Usson-du-Poitou F 115 B4
Usson-en-Forez F .117 B3
Usson-les-Bains F 146 B3
Ustaoset N 47 B5
Ustaritz F 144 A2
Uštěk CZ 84 B2
Uster CH 107 B3
Ústí CZ. 98 B1
Ustikolina BIH . . . 139 B4
Ústínad Labem CZ . 84 B2
Ústínad Orlící CZ. . 97 B4
Ustiprača BIH . . . 139 B5
Ustka PL. 68 A1
Ust Luga RUS . . . 8 C6
Ustroń PL. 98 B2
Ustronie Morskie
  PL. 67 B4
Ustyuzhna RUS. . . 9 C10
Uszód H 112 C2
Utåker N. 52 A1
Utansjö S. 200 D3
Utebo E 152 A3
Utena LT. 13 A6
Utery CZ. 95 B5
Uthaug N 198 B6
Utiel E 159 B2
Utne N 46 B3
Utö S 57 B4
Utrecht NL. 70 B2
Utrera E 162 A2
Utrillas E 153 B3
Utsjoki FIN 193 C11
Utstein kloster N . . 52 A1
Uttendorf A 109 B3
Uttenweiler D. . . . 107 A4
Utterslev DK 65 B4
Uttoxeter GB 40 C2
Utvälinge S 61 C2
Utvorda N 199 A7
Uusikaarlepyy FIN . 3 E8
Uusikaupunki FIN . 8 B2
Uvaly CZ 96 A2
Uvdal N 47 B5
Uza F 128 B1
Uzdin SRB 126 B2
Uzdowo PL 77 A5
Uzel F 100 A3
Uzerche F 116 B1
Uzès F 131 A3
Uzhhorod UA. . . . 12 D5
Uzhok UA. 12 D5
Užice SRB 127 D1
Üzümlü
  Konya TR. 189 B6
  Muğla TR. 188 C4
Uzunköprü TR. . . 186 A1

V

Vaalajärvi FIN . . . 197 B9
Vaas F 102 B2
Vaasa FIN 8 A2
Vaasen NL 70 B2
Vabre F 130 B1
Vác H 112 B3
Vacha D 82 B2
Váchartyán H. . . . 112 B3
Väckelsång S . . . 63 B2
Vacqueyras F . . . 131 A3
Vad S 50 B2
Vada I 134 B3
Vadillo de la Sierra
  E. 150 B2
Vadillos E 152 B1
Vadla N. 52 A2
Vado I 135 A4
Vado Lígure I . . . 133 A4
Vadsø N 193 B13
Vadstena S 55 B5
Vadum DK 58 A2
Vaduz FL 107 B4
Vafos N 53 B5
Vág H 111 B4
Vågåmo N 198 D6
Væggerløse DK . . 65 B4
Vaggeryd S 62 A2
Vaghia GR 184 A4
Váglio Basilicata I . 172 B1
Vagney F 106 A1
Vagnhärad S 57 B3
Vagnsunda S . . . 57 A4
Vagos P 148 B1
Vai GR 185 D7
Vaiano I 135 B4
Vaiges F 102 A1

Vaihingen D 93 C4
Vaillant F 105 B4
Vailly-sur-Aisne F . 91 B3
Vailly-sur Sauldre
  F. 103 B4
Vairano Scalo I . . 170 B2
Vaite F 105 B4
Väjern S 54 B2
Vajszló H 125 B3
Vaksdal N 46 B2
Vál H 112 B2
Valaam RUS. 9 B7
Valada P. 154 B2
Vålådalen S . . . 199 B10
Valadares P 148 A1
Valado P. 154 B1
Valandovo MK . . . 182 B4
Valaská SK. 99 C3
Valaská Belá SK . . 98 C2
Valaská Dubová
  SK 99 B3
Valašská Polanka
  CZ 98 B1
Valašské Klobouky
  CZ 98 B2
Valašské Meziříčí
  CZ 98 B1
Valberg F 132 A2
Vålberg S 55 A4
Valbo S 51 B4
Valbom P 148 A1
Valbondione I . . . 120 A3
Valbonnais F . . . 118 C2
Valbuena de Duero
  E. 142 C2
Vălcani RO. 126 B2
Valdagno I 121 B4
Valdahon F 105 B5
Valdaracete E . . . 151 B4
Valday RUS 9 D8
Valdealgorfa E . . . 153 B3
Valdecaballeros E . 156 A2
Valdecabras E . . . 152 B1
Valdecarros E . . . 150 B2
Valdeconcha E . . . 151 B5
Valdeflores E . . . 161 B3
Valdefresno E . . . 142 B1
Valdelacasa E . . . 150 B2
Valdelacasa de Tajo
  E. 156 A2
Valdelarco E 161 B3
Valdelosa E 149 A4
Valdeltormo E . . . 153 B4
Valdelugueros E . . 142 B1
Valdemanco de Esteras
  E. 156 B3
Valdemarsvik S . . 56 B2
Valdemorillo E . . . 151 B3
Valdemoro E 151 B4
Valdemoro Sierra
  E. 152 B2
Valdenoceda E . . . 143 B3
Valdeobispo E . . . 149 B3
Valdeolivas E . . . 152 B1
Valdepeñas E . . . 157 B4
Valdepeñas de Jaén
  E. 163 A4
Valdepiélago E . . . 142 B1
Valdepolo E 142 B1
Valderas E 142 B1
Valderice I 176 A1
Valderrobres E . . . 153 B4
Valderrueda E . . . 142 B2
Val de San Lorenzo
  E. 141 B4
Val de Santo Domingo
  E. 150 B3
Val d'Esquières F . 132 B2
Valdestillas E . . . 150 A3
Valdetorres E . . . 156 B1
Valdetorres de Jarama
  E. 151 B4
Valdeverdeja E . . . 150 C2
Valdevimbre E . . . 142 B1
Valdieri I 133 A3
Valdilecha E 151 B4
Val-d'Isère F 119 B3
Valdobbiádene I . . 121 B4
Valdocondes E . . . 143 C3
Valdoviño E 140 A2
Valea lui Mihai RO. 16 B5
Vale de Açor
  Beja P. 160 B2
  Portalegre P. . . 154 B3
Vale de Agua P . . 160 B1
Vale de Cambra P . 148 B1
Vale de Lobo P . . 160 B1
Vale de Prazeres P 148 B2
Vale de Reis P . . 154 C2
Vale de Rosa P . . 160 B2
Vale de Santarém
  P. 154 B2
Vale de Vargo P . . 160 B2
Vale do Peso P . . 155 B3
Valega P. 148 B1
Valéggio sul Mincio
  I. 121 B3
Valeiro P. 154 C2
Valença P. 140 B2
Valençay F. 103 B3
Valence
  Charente F 115 C4
  Drôme F. 117 C4
Valence d'Agen F . 129 B3

Valence d'Albigeois
  F. 130 A1
Valence-sur-Baise
  F. 129 C3
Valencia E 159 B3
Valencia de Alcántara
  E. 155 B3
Valencia de Don Juan
  E. 142 B1
Valencia de las Torres
  E. 156 B1
Valencia del Ventoso
  E. 161 A3
Valencia de Mombuey
  E. 161 A2
Valenciennes F . . 79 B3
Valensole F 132 B1
Valentano I 168 A1
Valentigney F . . . 106 B1
Valentine F 145 A4
Valenza I 120 B1
Valenzuela E . . . 163 A3
Valenzuela de Calatrava
  E. 157 B4
Våler
  Hedmark N. . . . 48 B3
  Østfold N. 54 A1
Valera de Abajo E . 158 B1
Valeria E 158 B1
Valestrand N . . . 52 A1
Valestrandsfossen
  N 46 B2
Valevåg N. 52 A1
Valfabbrica I 136 B1
Valflaunes F 131 B2
Valga EST 8 D5
Valgorge F 131 A3
Valgrisenche I . . .119 B4
Valguarnera Caropepe
  I. 177 B3
Valhelhas P 148 B2
Valhermoso E . . . 152 B1
Valjevo SRB. . . . 127 C1
Valka LV. 8 D4
Valkeakoski FIN . . 8 B4
Valkenburg NL . . . 80 B1
Valkenswaard NL . 79 A5
Valkó H. 112 B3
Valla S 56 A2
Vallada E 159 C3
Valladolid E 150 A3
Vallåkra S 61 D2
Vallata I 172 A1
Vallberga S 61 C3
Vall d'Alba E . . . 153 B3
Valldemossa E . . . 166 B2
Valle N 52 A3
Valle Castellana I . 136 C2
Valle de Abdalajís
  E. 163 B3
Valle de Cabuérniga
  E. 142 A2
Valle de la Serena
  E. 156 B2
Valle de Matamoros
  E. 155 C4
Valle de Santa Ana
  E. 155 C4
Valledolmo I. . . . 176 B2
Valledoria I 178 B2
Vallelado E 150 A3
Vallelunga Pratameno
  I. 176 B2
Valle Mosso I. . . .119 B5
Vallendar D 81 B3
Vallentuna S 57 A4
Valleraugue F . . . 130 A2
Vallermosa I. . . . 179 C2
Vallet F 101 B4
Valletta M 175 C3
Valley GB 38 A2
Vallfogona de Riucorb
  E. 147 C2
Valli del Pasúbio I . 121 B4
Vallo della Lucánia
  I. 172 B1
Valloire F 118 B3
Vallombrosa I . . . 135 B4
Vallon-Pont-d'Arc
  F. 131 A3
Vallorbe CH 105 C5
Vallouise F 118 C3
Valls E 147 C2
Vallset N 48 B3
Vallsta S 50 A3
Vallstena S 57 C4
Valmadrid E 153 A3
Valmiera LV 8 D4
Valmojado E 151 B3
Valmont F 89 A4
Valmontone I . . . 169 B2
Valö S 51 B5
Valognes F 88 A2
Valongo P. 148 A1
Válor E 164 C1
Valoria la Buena E. 142 C2
Væløy N. 199 A7
Valozhyn BY 13 A7
Valpaços P 148 A2
Valpelline I 119 B4
Valpiana I 135 B3
Valpovo HR 125 B4
Valras-Plage F . . 130 B2
Valréas F 131 A3
Vals CH 107 C4
Valsavarenche I . .119 B4

Vålse DK 65 B4
Valsequillo E 156 B2
Valsjöbyn S 199 A11
Vals-les-Bains F . 117 C4
Valsonne F. 117 B4
Valstagna I. 121 B4
Val-Suzon F 105 B3
Valtablado del Rio
  E. 152 B1
Valþjofsstaður IS .191 B11
Val Thorens F 118 B3
Valtice CZ 97 C3
Valtiendas E 151 A4
Valtierra E 144 B2
Valtopina I 136 B1
Valtorta I 120 B2
Valtournenche I . . .119 B4
Valverde E 144 C2
Valverde de Burguillos
  E. 155 C4
Valverde de Júcar
  E. 158 B1
Valverde de la Vera
  E. 150 B2
Valverde de la Virgen
  E. 142 B1
Valverde del Camino
  E. 161 B3
Valverde del Fresno
  E. 149 B3
Valverde de Llerena
  E. 156 B2
Valverde de Mérida
  E. 156 B1
Valvträsk S 196 C4
Vamberk CZ 85 B4
Vamdrup DK 59 C2
Våmhus S 50 A1
Vamlingbo S 57 D4
Vammala FIN 8 B3
Vámosmikola H. . .112 B2
Vámosszabadi H . .111 B4
Vamos GR 185 D5
Vanault-les-Dames
  F. 91 C4
Vandel DK 59 C2
Vandenesse F . . . 104 C2
Vandenesse-en-Auxois
  F. 104 B3
Vandóies I 108 C2
Väne-Åsaka S . . . 54 B3
Vänersborg S . . . 54 B3
Vänersnäs S 54 B3
Vang N 47 A5
Vänge S 51 C4
Vangsnes N. . . . 46 A3
Vänjaurbäck S. . . 200 B4
Vännacka S 54 A3
Vannareid N . . . 192 B3
Vännäs S 200 C5
Vannes F 101 B3
Vannsätter S 51 A3
Vannvåg N 192 B3
Vansbro S 49 B6
Vanse N 52 B2
Vantaa FIN 8 B4
Vanttauskoski FIN 197 C9
Vanviken N 199 B7
Vanyarc H 112 B3
Vaour F 129 B4
Vapnyarka UA . . . 13 D8
Vaprio d'Adda I . . 120 B2
Vaqueiros P. . . . 160 B2
Vara S 55 B3
Varacieux F. 118 B2
Varades F 101 B4
Varages F 132 B1
Varaldsøy N. . . . 46 B2
Varallo I 119 B5
Varangerbotn N. . 193 B12
Varano de'Melegari
  I. 120 C3
Varaždin HR. . . . 124 A2
Varaždinske Toplice
  HR 124 A2
Varazze I 133 A4
Varberg S 60 B2
Vardal N 48 B2
Varde DK 59 C1
Vårdö FIN 51 B7
Vardø N. 193 B15
Vardomb I 125 A4
Varejoki FIN. . . . 196 C7
Varel D 71 A5
Vårenna LT. 13 A6
Vårenes N 52 A1
Varengeville-sur-Mer
  F. 89 A4
Varenna I 120 A2
Varennes-en-Argonne
  F. 91 B5
Varennes-le-Grand
  F. 105 C3
Varennes-St Sauveur
  F. 105 C4
Varennes-sur-Allier
  F. 117 A3
Varennes-sur-Amance
  F. 105 B4
Vareš BIH 139 A4
Varese I 120 B1
Varese Ligure I . . 134 A2
Vârfurile RO. . . . 16 B5
Vårgårda S 60 A2

Varhaug N 52 B1
Variaş RO. 126 A2
Variaşu Mic RO . . 126 A3
Varilhes F 146 A2
Varin SK 98 B2
Väring S 55 B4
Váriz P 149 A3
Varkaus FIN. 8 A5
Varmahlíð IS . . . 190 B6
Varmaland IS . . . 190 C4
Värmlands Bro S . 55 A4
Värmskog S 55 A3
Varna
  BG 17 D7
  SRB 127 C1
Värnamo S 60 B4
Varnhem S 55 B4
Varnsdorf CZ . . . 84 B2
Värö S 60 B2
Varoška Rijeka
  BIH. 124 B2
Városlöd H. 111 B4
Várpalota H 112 B2
Varreddes F 90 C2
Vars F 118 C3
Varsi I 120 C2
Varsseveld NL . . . 71 C3
Vårsta S 57 A3
Vartdal N 198 C3
Vartofta S 55 B4
Vårvik N 54 A3
Várvölgy H. 111 C4
Varzi I 120 C2
Varzjelas P. 148 B1
Varzo I 119 A5
Varzy F 104 B2
Vasad H 112 B3
Väse S 55 A4
Vašica SRB 125 B5
Vasilevichi BY . . . 13 B8
Vasilikó GR 185 A4
Vaskút H. 125 A4
Vaslui RO. 17 B7
Vassbotn N 53 B4
Vassenden N . . . 47 A6
Vassieux-en-Vercors
  F. 118 C2
Vassmolösa S . . . 63 B4
Vassy F 88 B3
Västansjö S 195 E6
Västanvik S 50 B1
Västerås S 56 A2
Västerby S 50 B2
Västerfärnebo S . . 50 C3
Västergarn S . . . 57 C4
Västerhaninge S . 57 A4
Västervik S 62 A4
Vasto I 170 A2
Västra Ämtervik S . 55 A4
Västra-Bodarne S . 60 B2
Västra Karup S . . 61 C2
Vasvár H. 111 B3
Vasylkiv UA 13 C9
Vát H 111 B3
Vatan F 103 B3
Vathia GR. 184 C3
Vatican City = Cittàdel
  Vaticano I 168 B2
Vatili CY 181 A2
Vatin SRB 126 B3
Vatland N 52 B3
Vatnar N 53 A5
Vatnås N 48 C1
Vatne N 53 B3
Vatnestrøm N . . . 53 B4
Vatra-Dornei RO . 17 B6
Vatry F 91 C4
Vattholma S 51 B4
Vättis CH 107 C4
Vauchamps F . . . 91 C3
Vauchassis F. . . . 104 A2
Vaucouleurs F . . . 92 C1
Vaudoy-en-Brie F . 90 C3
Vaulen N 52 B1
Vaulruz CH. 106 C1
Vaulx Vraucourt F . 90 A2
Vaumas F 104 C2
Vausseroux F 115 B3
Vauvenargues F . . 132 B1
Vauvert F 131 B3
Vauvillers F 105 B5
Vaux-sur-Sure B . . 92 B1
Vawkavysk BY . . . 13 B6
Vaxholm S 57 A4
Växjö S. 62 B2
Våxtorp S 61 C3
Vayrac F 129 B4
Važec SK 99 B3
Veberöd S 61 D3
Vechelde D 72 B3
Vechta D 71 B5
Vecinos E 149 B4
Vecsés H 112 B3
Vedavågen N . . . 52 A1
Veddige S 60 B2
Vedersø DK 59 B1
Vedeseta I 120 B2
Vedevåg S 56 A1
Vedra E 140 B2
Vedum S 55 B3
Veendam NL 71 A3
Veenendaal NL . . 70 B2
Vega
  Asturias E 142 A1
  Asturias E 142 A1

Vega de Espinareda E. 141 B4
Vega de Infanzones E. 142 B1
Vegadeo E. 141 A3
Vega de Pas E . . . 143 A3
Vega de Valcarce E. 141 B4
Vega de Valdetronco E. 150 A2
Vegårshei N 53 B4
Vegas de Coria E. . 149 B3
Vegas del Condado E. 142 B1
Vegby S 60 B3
Vegger DK 58 B2
Veggli N 47 B6
Veghel NL 80 A1
Veglast D 66 B1
Véglie I 173 B3
Veguillas E 151 B4
Vegusdal N 53 B4
Veidholmen N . . . 198 B4
Veidnes N 193 B10
Veikåker N 48 B1
Veinge S 61 C3
Vejbystrand S 61 C2
Vejen DK 59 C2
Vejer de la Frontera E. 162 B2
Vejle DK 59 C2
Vejprty CZ 83 B5
Velada E. 150 B3
Vela Luka HR 138 C2
Velayos E. 150 B3
Velbert D 80 A3
Velburg D 95 B3
Velde N. 199 A8
Velden
Bayern D 95 B3
Bayern D 95 C4
Velden am Worther See A. 109 C5
Velefique E 164 B2
Velen D. 80 A2
Velenje SLO 123 A4
Veles MK 182 B3
Velesevec HR 124 B2
Velešín CZ 96 C2
Velestino GR 182 D4
Velez Blanco E . . . 164 B2
Vélez de Benaudalla E. 163 B4
Vélez-Málaga E . . . 163 B3
Vélez Rubio E 164 B2
Veliiki Radinci SRB 127 B1
Velika HR 125 B3
Velika Gorica HR . . 124 B2
Velika Grdevac HR . 124 B2
Velika Greda SRB . 126 B3
Velika Ilova BIH . . . 125 C3
Velika Kladuša BIH 124 B1
Velika Kopanica HR 125 B4
Velika Krsna SRB . 127 C2
Velika Obarska BIH 125 C5
Velika Pisanica HR 124 B3
Velika Plana SRB. . 127 C3
Velika Zdenci HR. . 124 B3
Velike Lašče SLO . 123 B3
Velike Središte SRB 126 B3
Veliki Gaj SRB 126 B3
Veliki Popović SRB 127 C3
Velikiye Luki RUS . . . 9 D7
Veliko Gradište SRB 127 C3
Veliko Orašje SRB. 127 C3
Veliko Selo SRB . . 127 C3
Veliko Tarnovo BG . 17 D6
Velilla del Río Carrió E. 142 B2
Velilla de San Antonio E. 151 B4
Veli Lošinj HR 137 A3
Velingrad BG 183 A5
Velizh RUS. 9 E7
Veljun HR. 123 B4
Velká Bíteš CZ. . . . 97 B4
Velká Hled'scbe CZ. 95 B4
Velká Lomnica SK. . 99 B4
Velkánad Veličkou CZ 98 C1
Velké Bystřice CZ. . 98 B1
Velké Heraltice CZ. . 98 B1
Velké Karlovice CZ. 98 B2
Vel'ke'Kostol'any SK 98 C1
Vel'ké Leváre SK. . . 97 C5
Velké Losiny CZ . . . 98 A1
Velké Meziříčí CZ. . 97 B4
Velké Pavlovice CZ. 97 C4
Vel'ké Rovné SK. . . 98 B2
Vel'ké Uherce SK. . . 98 C2
Vel'ké Zálužie SK. . . 98 C1
Vel'ký Blahovo SK. . 99 C4
Velky Bor CZ. 96 B1
Vel'ký Cetin SK . . .112 A2
Vel'ký Krtíš SK. . . . 112 A3
Vel'ký Meder SK. . .111 B4
Velky Ujezd CZ 98 B1
Vellahn D 73 A3
Vellberg D 94 B1
Velles F 103 C3

Velletri I 168 B2
Vellinge S. 66 A2
Vellisca E 151 B5
Velliza E 150 A3
Vellmar D 81 A5
Velp NL. 70 B2
Velten D 74 B2
Velvary CZ. 84 B2
Velvendos GR 182 C4
Vemb DK 59 B1
Vemdalen S 199 C10
Veme N. 48 B2
Véménd H 125 A4
Vemmedrup DK . . . 61 D2
Vena S 62 A3
Venaco F 180 A2
Venafro I 169 B4
Venarey-les-Laumes F. 104 B3
Venaría I. 119 B4
Venasca I 133 A3
Venčane SRB. 127 C2
Vence F 132 B3
Venda Nova
Coimbra P 154 A2
Leiria P 154 B2
Vendas Novas P . . 154 C2
Vendays-Montalivet F. 114 C2
Vendel S. 51 B4
Vendelso S 57 A4
Vendeuil F 91 B3
Vendeuvre-sur-Barse F. 104 A3
Vendoeuvres F 115 B5
Vendôme F 103 B3
Venelles F 131 B4
Veness GB 33 B4
Venézia = Venice I. 122 B1
Venialbo E 150 A2
Venice = Venézia I. 122 B1
Vénissieux F 117 B4
Venjan S. 49 B5
Venlo NL. 80 A2
Vennesla N 53 B3
Vennesund N 195 E3
Vennezey F 92 C2
Venn Green GB . . . 42 B2
Venosa I 172 B1
Venray NL 80 A1
Vent A. 108 C1
Venta de Baños E . . 142 C2
Venta del Moro E . . 158 B2
Venta de los Santos E. 157 B4
Venta las Ranas E. 142 A1
Ventanueva E 141 A4
Ventas de Huelma E. 163 A4
Ventas de Zafarraya E. 163 B3
Ventavon F 132 A1
Ventimíglia I. 133 B3
Ventnor GB 44 C2
Ventosa de la Sierra E. 143 C4
Ventosilla E 143 C4
Ventspils LV. 8 D2
Venturina I 134 B3
Venzolasca F. 180 A2
Venzone I 122 A2
Vép H 111 B3
Vera
E. 164 B3
N 199 B9
Vera Cruz P 160 A2
Vera de Bidasoa E. 144 A2
Vera de Moncayo E. 144 C2
Verbánia I. 119 B5
Verberie F 90 B2
Verbicaro I 174 B1
Verbier CH. 119 A4
Vercelli I. 119 B5
Vercel-Villedieu-le-Camp F. 105 B5
Verchen D 66 C1
Vercheny F 118 C2
Verclause F 131 A4
Verdalsøra N 199 B8
Verden D 72 B2
Verdens Ende N . . . 54 A1
Verdikoussa GR . . 182 D3
Verdille F. 115 C3
Verdú E 147 C2
Verdun F 92 B1
Verdun-sur-Garonne F. 129 C4
Verdun-sur-le-Doubs F. 105 C4
Veresegyház H . . .112 B3
Verfeil F 129 C4
Vergato I 135 A4
Vergel E 159 C4
Vergeletto CH 120 A1
Verges E 147 B4
Vergiate I 120 B1
Vergt F 129 A3
Veria GR 182 C4
Verin E 141 C3
Veringenstadt D . . 107 A4
Verl D 81 A4
Verma N. 198 C5
Vermand F 90 B3
Vermelha P 154 B1
Vermenton F 104 B2
Vernago I 108 C1
Vernante I 133 A3

Vernantes F 102 B2
Vernár SK. 99 C4
Vernasca I 120 C2
Vernayaz CH 119 A4
Vernazza I 134 A2
Vern-d'Anjou F . . . 102 B1
Vernet F 146 A2
Vernet-les-Bains F 146 B3
Verneuil F 91 B3
Verneuil-sur-Avre F. 89 B4
Vernier CH 118 A3
Vérnio I 135 A4
Vérnole I 173 B4
Vernon F 90 B1
Vernoux-en-Vivarais F. 117 C4
Veróce H 112 B3
Verolanuova I 120 B3
Véroli I 169 B3
Verona I 121 B4
Verpelét H 113 B4
Verrabotn N 199 B7
Verrès I 119 B4
Verrey-sous-Salmaise F. 104 B3
Verrières F 115 B4
Versailles F 90 C2
Versam CH. 107 C4
Verseg H 112 B3
Versmold D 71 B5
Versoix CH. 118 A3
Verteillac F 115 C4
Vértesacsa H 112 B2
Vertou F 101 B4
Vertus F 91 C3
Verviers B 80 B1
Vervins F 91 B3
Verwood GB 43 B5
Veryan GB 42 B2
Veržej SLO. 111 C3
Verzuolo I. 133 A3
Verzy F 91 B4
Vescovato F. 180 A2
Vése H 124 A3
Veselie BG 17 D7
Veselínad Lužnicí CZ 96 B2
Veselínad Moravou CZ 98 C1
Vésime I. 119 C5
Veskoniemi FIN . . 193 D11
Vesoul F 105 B5
Vespolate I. 120 B1
Vessigebro S 60 C2
Vestbygd N 52 B2
Vestenanova I . . . 121 B4
Vester Husby S . . . 56 B2
Vester Nebel DK . . 59 C2
Vesterøhavn DK . . 58 A3
Vester Torup DK . . 58 A2
Vester Vedsted DK . 59 C1
Vestervig DK 58 B1
Vestfossen N 53 A5
Vestmannaeyjar IS 190 D5
Vestmarka N 48 C3
Vestnes N 198 C4
Vestone I. 120 B3
Vestre Gausdal N . 48 A2
Vestre Jakobselv N 193 B13
Vestre Slidre N . . . 47 A5
Vesyegonsk RUS . . 9 C10
Vetanda S 62 A3
Vetovo HR 125 B3
Vetralla I. 168 A2
Větrný Jeníkov CZ . 97 B3
Vétroz CH 119 A4
Vetschau D 84 A2
Vettasjärvi S 196 B4
Vetto I. 134 A3
Vetulónia I 135 A4
Veules-les-Roses F. 89 A4
Veulettes-sur-Mer F 89 A4
Veum N 53 A4
Veurne B 78 A2
Veverská Bítýška CZ 97 B4
Vevey CH. 106 C1
Vevi GR 182 C3
Vevring N. 46 A2
Vex CH 119 A4
Veynes F 132 A1
Veyre-Monton F . .116 B3
Veyrier F 118 B3
Vézelay F 104 B2
Vézelise F 92 C2
Vézenobres F 131 A3
Vezins F 102 B1
Vézins-de-Lévézou F. 130 A1
Vezirhan TR. 187 B5
Vezirköprü TR . . . 23 A8
Vezza di Óglio I . . 120 A3
Vezzani F 180 A2
Vezzano I 121 A4
Vezzano sul Cróstolo I 121 C3
Vi S 200 D3
Viadana I 121 C3
Via Gloria P 160 B2
Viana P 143 B4
Viana do Alentejo P. 154 C2

Viana do Bolo E. . . 141 B3
Viana do Castelo P . 148 B2
Vianden L. 92 B2
Viannos GR 185 D6
Viaréggio I 134 B3
Viator E 164 C2
Vibble S 57 C4
Viborg DK 58 B2
Vibo Valéntia I . . . 175 C2
Vibraye F 102 A2
Vic E. 147 C3
Vícar E 164 C2
Vicchio I 135 B4
Vicdessos F 146 B2
Vic-en-Bigorre F . . 145 A4
Vicenza I 121 B4
Vic-Fézensac F . . . 129 C3
Vichy F. 117 A3
Vickan S. 60 B2
Vickerstown GB . . . 36 B3
Vic-le-Comte F. . . .116 B3
Vico F. 180 A1
Vico del Gargano I 171 B3
Vico Equense I . . . 170 C2
Vicopisano I. 134 B3
Vicosoprano CH . . 120 A2
Vicovaro I. 169 A2
Vic-sur-Aisne F . . . 90 B3
Vic-sur-Cère F 116 C2
Victoria = Rabat M. 175 C3
Vidago P 148 A2
Viduaban F 132 B2
Vide P. 148 B2
Videbæk DK. 59 B1
Videm SLO. 123 B3
Videseter N 198 D4
Vidigueira P. 160 A2
Vidin BG. 16 D5
Vidlin GB 33 A5
Vidsel S 196 D3
Vidzy BY. 13 A7
Viechtach D. 95 B4
Vieille-Brioude F . .117 B3
Vieira P. 154 B2
Vieira do Minho P . 148 A1
Vieiros P 155 C3
Vielha E 145 B4
Vielle-Aure F 145 B4
Viellespesse F 116 B3
Viellevigne F 114 B2
Vielmur-sur-Agout F. 130 B1
Vielsalm B 80 B1
Viels Maison F 91 C3
Vienenburg D 73 C3
Vienna = Wien A . . .111 A3
Vienne F. 117 B4
Vieritz D 73 B5
Viernheim D 93 B4
Vierraden D 74 A3
Viersen D. 80 A2
Vierville-sur-Mer F . 88 A3
Vierzon F 103 B4
Vieselbach D 82 B3
Vieste I. 171 B4
Vietas S 194 C9
Vieteren B 78 B2
Vietri di Potenza I . 172 B1
Vietri sul Mare I . . 170 C2
Vieux-Boucau-les-Bains F. 128 C1
Vif F 118 B2
Vig DK 61 D1
Vigásio I 121 B3
Vigaun A. 109 B4
Vigeland N 52 B3
Vigeois F 116 B1
Vigévano I 120 B1
Viggianello I. 174 B2
Viggiano I 174 A1
Vigliano I 169 A3
Vigmostad N 52 B3
Vignale I. 119 B5
Vignanello I 168 A2
Vigneulles-lès-Hattonchâtel F . . 92 C1
Vignevieille F. 146 B3
Vignola I 135 A4
Vignory F. 105 A4
Vignoux-sur Barangeon F. 103 B4
Vigo E 140 B2
Vigo di Fassa I . . . 121 A4
Vigone I. 119 C4
Vigrestad N 52 B1
Vihiers F 102 B1
Viitasaari FIN. 8 A4
Vik IS 190 D6
Vik
Nordland N. 195 E3
Rogaland N 52 B1
Sogn og Fjordane N. 46 A3
S. 63 C2
Vika S 50 B2
Vikajärvi FIN 197 C9
Vikane N 54 A1
Vikarbyn S. 50 B2
Vike N. 46 B2
Vikedal N. 52 A1
Vikeland N 53 B3
Viken
Jämtland S. 199 A10
Skåne N. 61 C2
Viker N 48 B2
Vikersund N 48 C1

Villadecanes E. . . . 141 B4
Villa del Prado E . . 150 B3
Villa del Rio E . . . 157 C3
Villadepera E. 149 A3
Villa de Peralonso E. 149 A3
Villa di Chiavenna I. 120 A2
Villadiego E 142 B2
Villadompardo E . . 163 A3
Villadóssola I. 119 A5
Villaeles de Valdavia E. 142 B2
Villaescusa de Haro E. 158 B1
Villafáfila E. 142 C1
Villafeliche E 152 A2
Villaflores E 150 A2
Villafrades de Campos E. 142 B2
Villafranca
Avila E 150 B2
Navarra E 144 B2
Villafranca de Córdoba E. 157 C3
Villafranca del Bierzo E. 141 B4
Villafranca de los Barros E. 155 C4
Villafranca de los Caballeros E 157 A4
Villafranca di Verona I 121 B3
Villafranca in Lunigiana I 134 A2
Villafranca-Montes de Oca E. 143 B3
Villafranca Tirrena I 177 A4
Villafranco del Campo E. 152 B2
Villafranco del Guadalquivir E . . 161 B3
Villafrati I 176 B2
Villafrechós E 142 C1
Villafruela E 143 C3
Villagarcia de las Torres E. 156 B1
Villaggio Mancuso I 175 B2
Villagonzalo E 156 B1
Villagotón E 141 B4
Villagrains F 128 B2
Villaharta E 156 B3
Villahermosa E . . . 158 C1
Villaherreros E . . . 142 B2
Villahoz E. 143 B3
Villaines-la-Juhel F . 89 B3
Villajoyosa E 159 C3
Villalago I. 169 B3
Villalba
E 140 A3
I 176 B2
Villalba de Calatrava E. 157 B4
Villalba de Guardo E. 142 B2
Villalba del Alcor E 161 B3
Villalba de la Sierra E. 152 B1
Villalba de los Alcores E. 142 C2
Villalba de los Barros E. 155 C4
Villalba del Rey E . 151 B5
Villalcampo E 149 A3
Villalcázar de Sirga E. 142 B2
Villalengua E 152 A2
Villalgordo del Júcar E. 158 B1
Villalgordo del Marquesado E. . . 158 B1
Villalmóndar E. . . . 143 B3
Villalón de Campos E. 142 B1
Villalonga E 159 C3
Villalonso E 150 A2
Villalpando E 142 C1
Villaluenga E 151 B4
Villalumbroso E. . . 142 B2
Villálvaro E 143 C3
Villamalea E. 158 B2
Villamanán E 142 B1
Villamanín E 142 B1
Villamanrique E . . 157 B5
Villamanrique de la Condesa E. 161 B3
Villamanta E 151 B3
Villamantilla E . . . 151 B3
Villamar I 179 C2
Villamartín E 162 B2
Villamartín de Campos E. 142 B2
Villamartín de Don Sancho E. 142 B1
Villamassárgia I. . . 179 C2
Villamayor E 142 A1
Villamayor de Calatrava E. 157 B3
Villamayor de Campos E. 142 B1
Villamayor de Santiago E. 157 A5
Villamblard F 129 A3

Villamejil E 141 B4
Villamesias E. . . . 156 A2
Villaminaya E. . . . 157 A4
Villa Minozzo I 134 A3
Villamor de los
Escuderos E 150 A2
Villamoronta E 142 B2
Villamuelas E. 151 C4
Villamuriel de Cerrato
E. 142 C2
Villandraut F 128 B2
Villanova I 173 B3
Villanova d'Asti I . . . 119 C4
Villanova del Battista
I 171 B3
Villanova Mondovì
I 133 A3
Villanova Monteleone
I 178 B2
Villante E 143 B3
Villantério I 120 B2
Villanubla E 142 C2
Villanueva de Alcardete
E. 157 A4
Villanueva de Alcorón
E. 152 B1
Villanueva de Algaidas
E. 163 A3
Villanueva de Argaña
E. 143 B3
Villanueva de Bogas
E. 157 A4
Villanueva de Córdoba
E. 156 B3
Villanueva de Gállego
E. 144 C3
Villanueva del Aceral
E. 150 A3
Villanueva de la
Concepcion E . . . 163 B3
Villanueva de la Fuente
E. 158 C1
Villanueva de la Jara
E. 158 B2
Villanueva de la Reina
E. 157 B4
Villanueva del
Arzobispo E 164 A2
Villanueva de la Serena
E. 156 B2
Villanueva de la Sierra
E. 149 B3
Villanueva de las
Manzanas E. 142 B1
Villanueva de las Peras
E. 141 C5
Villanueva de las Torres
E. 164 B1
Villanueva de la Vera
E. 150 B2
Villanueva del Campo
E. 142 C1
Villanueva del Duque
E. 156 B3
Villanueva del Fresno
E. 155 C3
Villanueva del Huerva
E. 152 A2
Villanueva de los
Castillejos E 161 B2
Villanueva de los
Infantes E 157 B5
Villanueva del Rey
E. 156 B2
Villanueva del Rio
E. 162 A2
Villanueva del Rio y
Minas E 162 A2
Villanueva del Rosario
E. 163 B3
Villanueva del Trabuco
E. 163 A3
Villanueva de Mesia
E. 163 A4
Villanueva de Nía
E. 142 B2
Villanueva de Oscos
E. 141 A4
Villanueva de San
Carlos E. 157 B4
Villanueva de San Juan
E. 162 A2
Villanueva de Tapia
E. 163 A3
Villanueva de
Valdegovia E 143 B3
Villány H. 125 B4
Villaputzu I 179 C3
Villaquejida E 142 B1
Villaquilambre E . . . 142 B1
Villaquiran de los
Infantes E 142 B2
Villaralto E 156 B3
Villarcayo E 143 B3
Villard-de-Lans F. . 118 B2
Villar de Barrio E . . 140 B3
Villar de Cañas E . . 158 B1
Villar de Chinchilla
E. 158 C2
Villar de Ciervo E . . 149 B3
Villardeciervos E . . 141 C4
Villar de Domingo
Garcia E 152 B1
Villardefrades E. . . 142 C1

Villar del Arzobispo
E. 159 B3
Villar del Buey E . . 149 A3
Villar del Cobo E . . 152 B2
Villar del Humo E . 158 B2
Villar de los Navarros
E. 152 A2
Villar del Pedroso
E. 156 A2
Villar del Rey E . . . 155 B4
Villar del Rio E. . . . 143 B4
Villar del Saz de
Navalón E 152 B1
Villar de Rena E. . . 156 A2
Villarejo E 151 A4
Villarejo de Fuentes
E. 158 B1
Villarejo de Orbigo
E. 141 B5
Villarejo de Salvanes
E. 151 B4
Villarejo-Periesteban
E. 158 B1
Villares del Saz E . . 158 B1
Villaretto I 119 B4
Villargordo del Cabriel
E. 158 B2
Villarino E 149 A3
Villarino de Conso
E. 141 B3
Villarluengo E 153 B3
Villarobe E 143 B3
Villarosa I. 177 B3
Villar Perosa I 119 C4
Villarramiel E 142 B2
Villarrasa E 161 B3
Villarreal de San Carlos
E. 150 C1
Villarrin de Campos
E. 142 C1
Villarrobledo E 158 B1
Villarroya de la Sierra
E. 152 A2
Villarroya de los Pinares
E. 153 B3
Villarrubia de los Ojos
E. 157 A4
Villarrubia de Santiago
E. 151 C4
Villarrubio E 151 C5
Villars-les-Dombes
F. 117 A5
Villarta E 158 B2
Villarta de los Montes
E. 156 A3
Villarta de San Juan
E. 157 A4
Villasana de Mena
E. 143 A3
Villasandino E 142 B2
Villa San Giovanni
I 175 C1
Villa Santa Maria I . 169 B4
Villasante E 143 A3
Villa Santina I 122 A1
Villasarracino E. . . . 142 B2
Villasayas E 151 A5
Villasdardo E 149 A3
Villaseca de Henares
E. 151 B5
Villaseca de Laciana
E. 141 B4
Villaseca de la Sagra
E. 151 C4
Villaseco de los
Gamitos E 149 A3
Villaseco de los Reyes
E. 149 A3
Villasequilla de Yepes
E. 151 C4
Villasimíus I 179 C3
Villasmundo I 177 B4
Villasor I. 179 C2
Villastar E 152 B2
Villastellone I. 119 C4
Villatobas E 151 C4
Villatorp E 150 B2
Villatoya E 158 B2
Villavaliente E 158 B2
Villavelayo E 143 B4
Villavella E 141 B3
Villaver de de
Guadalimar E . . . 158 C1
Villaverde del Rio
E. 162 A2
Villaviciosa E. 142 A1
Villaviciosa de Córdoba
E. 156 B3
Villaviciosa de Odón
E. 151 B4
Villavieja de Yeltes
E. 149 B3
Villayón E 141 A4
Villé F 93 C3
Villebois-Lavalette
F. 115 C4
Villecerf F 90 C2
Villecomtal F 130 A1
Villedieu-les-Poêles
F. 88 B2
Villedieu-sur-Indre
F. 103 C3
Ville-di-Pietrabugno
F. 180 A2
Villedômain F 103 B3
Villefagnan F 115 B4
Villefontaine F 118 B2
Villefort F 131 A2

Villefranche-d'Albigeois
F. 130 B1
Villefranche-d'Allier
F. 116 A2
Villefranche-de-
Lauragais F. 146 A2
Villefranche-de-Lonchat
F. 128 B3
Villefranche-de-Panat
F. 130 A1
Villefranche-de-
Rouergue F 130 A1
Villefranche-du-
Périgord F. 129 B4
Villefranche-sur-Cher
F. 103 B3
Villefranche-sur-Mer
F. 133 B3
Villefranche-sur-Saône
F. 117 A4
Villegenon F 103 B4
Villel E 152 B2
Villemaur-sur-Vanne
F. 104 A2
Villemontais F 117 B3
Villemur-sur-Tarn
F. 129 C4
Villena E. 159 C3
Villenauxe-la-Grande
F. 91 C3
Villenave-d'Ornon
F. 128 B2
Villeneuve
CH 119 A3
F 129 B5
Villeneuve-d'Ascq F 78 B3
Villeneuve-de-Berg
F. 131 A3
Villeneuve-de-Marsan
F. 128 C2
Villeneuve-de-Rivière
F. 145 A4
Villeneuve-la-Guyard
F. 90 C3
Villeneuve-l'Archevêque
F. 104 A2
Villeneuve-le-Comte
F. 90 C2
Villeneuve-lès-Avignon
F. 131 B3
Villeneuve-les-
Corbières F. 146 B3
Villeneuve-St Georges
F. 90 C2
Villeneuve-sur-Allier
F. 104 C2
Villeneuve-sur-Lot
F. 129 B3
Villeneuve-sur-Yonne
F. 104 A2
Villeréal F 129 B3
Villerias E. 142 C2
Villeromain F 103 B3
Villers-Bocage
Calvados F. 88 A3
Somme F 90 B2
Villers-Bretonneux
F. 90 B2
Villers-Carbonnel F . 90 B2
Villers-Cotterêts F . 90 B3
Villersexel F 105 B5
Villers-Farlay F . . . 105 C4
Villers-le-Gambon B 79 B4
Villers-le-Lac F . . . 106 B1
Villers-sur-Mer F . . 89 A3
Villerupt F 92 B1
Villerville F. 89 A4
Villeseneux F 91 C4
Ville-sous-la-Ferté
F. 105 A3
Ville-sur-Illon F . . . 105 A5
Ville-sur-Tourbe F . . 91 B4
Villetrun F 103 B3
Villetta Barrea I . . . 169 B3
Villeurbanne F 117 B4
Villeveyrac F 130 B2
Villevocance F 117 B4
Villiers-St Benoit F 104 B2
Villiers-St Georges
F. 91 C3
Villingen D 106 A3
Villmar D 81 B4
Villoldo E 142 B2
Villon F 104 B3
Villoria E 150 B2
Vilnes N 46 A1
Vilnius LT 13 A6
Vils
A. 108 B1
DK 58 B1
Vilsbiburg D. 95 C4
Vilseck D 95 B3
Vilshofen D 96 C1
Vilshult S 63 B2
Vilusi MNE 139 C4
Vilvestre E 149 A3
Vilvoorde B 79 B4
Vimeiro P 154 B1
Vimercate I 120 B2
Vimianzo E. 140 A1
Vimieiro P 154 C2
Vimioso P 149 A3
Vimmerby S 62 A3
Vimoutiers F 89 B4
Vimperk CZ 96 B1
Vimy F 78 B2
Vinadi CH. 108 C1
Vinadio I 133 A3

Vinaixa E 147 C1
Vinarós E 153 B4
Vinäs S 50 B1
Vinay F. 118 B2
Vinberg S 60 C2
Vinca F 146 B3
Vinča SRB 127 C2
Vinchiaturo I 170 B2
Vinci I 135 B3
Vindeby DK 65 A3
Vindelgransele S. . . 195 E9
Vindeln S 200 B5
Vinderup DK 58 B1
Vindsvik N 52 A2
Vinets F 91 C4
Vineuil F 103 B3
Vinga RO 126 A3
Vingåker S 56 A1
Vingnes N 48 A2
Vingrau F 146 B3
Vingrom N 48 A2
Vinhais P 149 A3
Vinica
HR 124 A2
MK 182 B4
SK 112 A3
SLO 123 B4
Viniegra de Arriba
E. 143 B4
Vinje
Hordaland N. 46 B3
Sør-Trøndelag N . 198 B6
Telemark N 53 A3
Vinkovci HR 125 B4
Vinliden S 200 B3
Vinninga S 55 B4
Vinnytsya UA. 13 D8
Vinon F 103 B4
Vinon-sur-Verdon
F. 132 B1
Vinslöv S 61 C3
Vinstra N 48 A1
Vintjärn S 50 B3
Vintrosa S 55 A5
Viñuela E 163 B3
Viñuela de Sayago
E. 149 A4
Viñuelas E 151 B4
Vinuesa E 143 C4
Vinzelberg D 73 B4
Viöl D 64 B2
Viola I 133 A3
Violay F 117 B4
Vipava SLO 122 B2
Vipiteno I 108 C2
Vipperow D 74 A1
Vir
BIH 138 B3
HR 137 A4
Vira CH. 120 A1
Vire F 88 B3
Vireda S 62 A2
Vireux F 91 A4
Virgen A 109 B3
Virgen de la Cabeza
E. 157 B3
Virginia IRL 27 C3
Virieu F 118 B2
Virieu-le-Grand F . .118 B2
Virje HR 124 A2
Virkkunen FIN 197 D10
Virklund DK 59 B2
Virovitica HR 124 B3
Virsbo S 50 C3
Virserum S 62 A3
Virtaniemi FIN . . . 193 D12
Virton B 92 B1
Virtsu EST 8 C3
Viry F 118 A3
Vis HR 138 B2
Visbek D. 71 B5
Visby
DK 64 A1
S 57 C4
Visé B 80 B1
Višegrad BIH 139 B5
Viserba I 136 A1
Viseu P 148 B2
Visiedo E 152 B2
Viskafors S 60 B2
Visland N 52 B2
Vislanda S 62 B2
Visnes N 52 A1
Višnja Gora SLO . . 123 B3
Višnjan HR 122 B2
Višnové CZ 97 C4
Visnums-Kil S 55 A5
Viso del Marqués
E. 157 B4
Visoko
BIH 139 B4
SLO 123 A3
Visone I 119 C5
Visp CH. 119 A4
Vissefjärda S 63 B3
Visselhövede D . . . 72 B2
Vissenbjerg DK . . . 59 C3
Visso I 136 C2
Vistabella del Maestrat
E. 153 B3
Vistheden S 196 D3
Vita I 176 B1
Vitebsk = Vitsyebsk
BY 13 A9
Viterbo I 168 A2
Vitez BIH 139 A3
Vithkuq AL 182 C2

Vitigudino E. 149 A3
Vitina
BIH 138 B3
GR 184 B3
Vitis A. 97 C3
Vitkov CZ. 98 B1
Vitoria-Gasteiz E. . 143 B4
Vitré F 101 A4
Vitrey-sur-Mance F 105 B4
Vitry-en-Artois F . . 78 B2
Vitry-le-François F . 91 C4
Vitry-sur-Seine F . . 90 C2
Vitsand S 49 B4
Vitsyebsk = Vitebsk
BY 13 A9
Vittangi S 196 B4
Vittaryd S 60 C3
Vitteaux F 104 B3
Vittel F 105 A4
Vittinge S 51 C4
Vittória I 177 C3
Vittório Véneto I . . 122 B1
Vittsjö S 61 C3
Viù I 119 B4
Viul N 48 B2
Vivario F. 180 A2
Viveiro E 140 A3
Vivel del Rio Martin
E. 152 B3
Viver E 159 B3
Viverols F. 117 B3
Viveros E 158 C1
Viviers F. 131 A3
Vivonne F 115 B4
Vivy F 102 B1
Vize TR. 186 A2
Vizille F 118 B2
Viziňada HR 122 B2
Viziru RO 17 C7
Vizovice CZ 98 B1
Vizvár H 124 A3
Vizzavona F 180 A2
Vizzini I. 177 B3
Vlachiotis GR 184 C3
Vlachovice CZ. 98 B1
Vlachovo SK 99 C4
Vláchovo Březi CZ . 96 B1
Vladimirci SRB . . . 127 C1
Vladimirovac SRB. . 127 B2
Vladislav CZ 97 B3
Vlagtwedde NL . . . 71 A4
Vlajkovac SRB 127 B3
Vlasenica BIH 139 A4
Vlašim CZ 96 B2
Vlatković BIH 138 A3
Vledder NL. 70 B3
Vlissingen NL 79 A3
Vlkolínec SK 99 B3
Vlorë AL 182 C1
Vlotho D. 72 B1
Vnanje Gorice SLO 123 B3
Vobarno I 121 B3
Vocín HR 124 B3
Vöcklabruck A 109 A4
Vöcklamarkt A 109 B4
Vodanj SRB 127 C2
Voderady SK 98 C1
Vodice
Istarska HR 123 B3
Šibenska HR 137 B4
SLO 123 A3
Vodňany CZ. 96 B2
Vodnjan HR 122 C2
Vodskov DK. 58 A3
Voe GB 33 A5
Voerså DK 58 A3
Voghera I 120 C2
Vogogna I 119 A5
Vogošća BIH 139 B4
Vogué F 131 A3
Vohburg D 95 C3
Vohenstrauss D. . . . 95 B4
Vöhl D 81 A4
Vöhrenbach D 106 A3
Vöhringen D 94 C2
Void-Vacon F 92 C1
Voiron F 118 B2
Voise F 90 C1
Voisey F 105 B4
Voiteg RO 126 B3
Voiteur F 105 C4
Voitsberg A 110 B2
Vojakkala FIN. . . . 196 D7
Vojens DK 59 C2
Vojka SRB 127 C2
Vojlovica SRB 127 C2
Vojnic HR 123 B4
Vojnice SK 112 B2
Vojnik SLO 123 A4
Vojvoda Stepa
SRB 126 B2
Volada GR 188 D2
Volargne I 121 B3
Volary CZ 96 C1
Volče SLO 122 A2
Volda N 198 C3
Volendam NL 70 B2
Volga RUS 9 C11
Volimes GR 184 B1
Volissos GR. 185 A6
Volkach D. 94 B2
Völkermarkt A 110 C1
Volkhov RUS 9 C8
Völklingen D 92 B2
Volkmarsen D 81 A5
Voll N 198 C4
Vollenhove NL. 70 B2

Vollore-Montagne
F. 117 B3
Vollsjö S 61 D3
Volodymyr-Volyns'kyy
UA 13 C6
Volokolamsk RUS . . 9 D9
Volos GR 182 D4
Volosovo RUS. 9 C6
Volovets UA. 13 D5
Voltággio I 120 C1
Volta Mantovana I . 121 B3
Volterra I 135 B3
Voltri I. 133 A4
Volturara Áppula I . 170 B3
Volturara Irpina I . . 170 C2
Volvic F. 116 B3
Volx F 132 B1
Volyně CZ 96 B1
Vonitsa GR. 182 E2
Vönöck H. 111 B4
Vonsild DK. 59 C2
Voorschoten NL . . . 70 B1
Vopnafjörður IS. . . 191 B11
Vorau A. 110 B2
Vorbasse DK 59 C2
Vorchdorf A 109 B4
Vorden
D 71 B5
NL 71 B3
Vordernberg A 110 B1
Vordingborg DK . . . 65 A4
Vorë AL. 182 B1
Voreppe F 118 B2
Vorey F. 117 B3
Vorgod DK 59 B1
Vormsund N 48 B3
Vormus DK 59 C2
Voskopojë AL. . . . 182 C2
Voss N 46 B3
Votice CZ 96 B2
Voué F 91 C4
Vouillé F 115 B4
Voulx F 90 C2
Voussac F 116 A3
Vouvray F 102 B2
Vouvry CH 119 A3
Vouzela P. 148 B1
Vouziers F 91 B4
Voves F 103 A3
Voxna S 50 A2
Voy GB 33 B3
Voynitsa RUS 3 D12
Voznesenye RUS. . . 9 B9
Vrå
DK 58 A2
S 60 C3
Vráble SK 98 C2
Vračenovići MNE . . 139 C4
Vračev Gaj SRB . . . 127 C3
Vraćevsnica SRB . . 127 C2
Vrådal N 53 A4
Vrakneika GR 184 A2
Vrana HR 123 C3
Vranduk BIH 139 A3
Vrångö S 60 B1
Vrani RO 127 B3
Vranić SRB 127 C2
Vraniči BIH. 139 B4
Vranja HR. 123 B3
Vranjak BIH 125 C4
Vranje SRB 16 D4
Vranovice CZ. 97 C4
Vranov nad Dyje CZ 97 C3
Vransko SLO 123 A3
Vrapčići BIH. 139 B3
Vratimov CZ. 98 B2
Vratsa BG. 17 D5
Vrbanja HR 125 C4
Vrbanjci BIH. 124 C3
Vrbas SRB 126 B1
Vrbaška BIH 124 B3
Vrbnik
Primorsko-Goranska
HR 123 B3
Zadarsko-Kninska
HR 138 A2
Vrbno pod Pradědem
CZ 85 B5
Vrboska HR 138 B2
Vrbov SK 99 B4
Vrbovce SK 98 C1
Vrbové SK 98 C1
Vrbovec HR 124 B2
Vrbovski SRB 127 C2
Vrbovsko HR 123 B4
Vrchlabí CZ 84 B3
Vrčin SRB 127 C2
Vrdy CZ 97 B3
Vrebac HR 137 A4
Vreden D 71 B3
Vreoci SRB 127 C2
Vretstorp S 55 A5
Vrginmost HR 123 B4
Vrgorac HR 138 B3
Vrhnika HR 123 B3
Vrhovine HR 123 C4
Vrhpolie SRB. 127 C1
Vriezenveen NL. . . . 71 B3
Vrigne-aux-Bois F . 91 B4
Vrigstad S 62 A2
Vrlika HR 138 B2
Vron F 78 B1
Vroomshoop NL . . . 71 B3
Vroutek CZ. 83 B5
Vrpolje HR 125 B4
Vršac SRB 126 B3
Vrsar HR 122 B2

Vrsi HR 137 A4
Vrtoče BIH 124 C2
Vrútky SK 98 B2
Všeruby CZ 95 B4
Všestary CZ 85 B3
Vsetín CZ 98 B1
Vučkovica SRB 127 D2
Vught NL 79 A5
Vuillafans F 105 B5
Vukovar HR 125 B5
Vuku N 199 B8
Vulcan RO 17 C5
Vulcăneşti MD 17 C8
Vuoggatjålme S 195 D7
Vuojärvi FIN 197 B9
Vuolijoki FIN 3 D10
Vuollerim S 196 C3
Vuotso FIN 197 A10
Vuzenica SLO 110 C2
Vyartsilya RUS 9 A7
Vyborg RUS 9 B6
Výčapy CZ 97 B3
Výčapy-Opatovce SK 98 C2
Východna SK 99 B3
Vydrany SK 111 A4
Vyerkhnyadzvinsk BY 13 A7
Vyhne SK 98 C2
Vy-lès Lure F 105 B5
Vylkove UA 17 C8
Vynohradiv UA 17 A5
Vyshniy Volochek RUS 9 D9
Vyškov CZ 97 B5
Vysokánad Kysucou SK 98 B2
Vysoké Mýto CZ 97 B4
Vysokovsk RUS 9 D10
Vyšší Brod CZ 96 C2
Vytegra RUS 9 B10

W

Waabs D 64 B2
Waalwijk NL 79 A5
Waarschoot B 79 A3
Wabern D 81 A5
Wąbrzeźno PL 69 B3
Wąchock PL 87 A5
Wachow D 74 B1
Wachów PL 86 B2
Wächtersbach D 81 B5
Wackersdorf D 95 B4
Waddington GB 40 B3
Wadebridge GB 42 B2
Wadelsdorf D 84 A2
Wädenswil CH 107 B3
Wadern D 92 B2
Wadersloh D 81 A4
Wadlew PL 86 A3
Wadowice PL 99 B3
Wagenfeld D 72 B1
Wageningen NL 70 C2
Waghäusel D 93 B4
Waging D 109 B3
Wagrain A 109 B4
Wągrowiec PL 76 B2
Wahlsdorf D 74 C2
Wahlstedt D 64 C3
Wahrenholz D 73 B3
Waiblingen D 94 C1
Waidhaus D 95 B4
Waidhofen an der Thaya A 97 C3
Waidhofen an der Ybbs A 110 B1
Waimes B 80 B2
Wainfleet All Saints GB 41 B4
Waizenkirchen A 96 C1
Wakefield GB 40 B2
Wałbrzych PL 85 B4
Walchensee D 108 B2
Walchsee A 109 B3
Wałcz PL 75 A5
Wald CH 107 B3
Waldaschaff D 94 B1
Waldbach A 110 B2
Waldböckelheim D 93 B3
Waldbröl D 81 B3
Waldeck D 81 A5
Waldenburg D 83 B4
Waldfischbach-Burgalben D 93 B3
Waldheim D 83 A5
Waldkappel D 82 A1
Waldkirch D 106 A2
Waldkirchen D 96 C1
Waldkirchen am Wesen A 96 C1
Waldkraiburg D 109 A3
Wald-Michelbach D 93 B4
Waldmohr D 93 B3
Waldmünchen D 95 B4
Waldring A 109 B3
Waldsassen D 95 A4
Waldshut D 106 B3
Waldstatt CH 107 B4
Waldwisse F 92 B2
Walenstadt CH 107 B4
Walentynów PL 87 A5
Walichnowy PL 86 A2
Walincourt F 90 A3
Walkenried D 82 A2
Walkeringham GB 40 B3
Wallasey GB 38 A3
Walldürn D 94 B1
Wallenfells D 82 B3
Wallenhorst D 71 B5
Wallers F 78 B3
Wallersdorf D 95 C4
Wallerstein D 94 C2
Wallingford GB 44 B2
Wallitz D 74 A1
Walls GB 33 A5
Wallsbüll D 64 B2
Walmer GB 45 B5
Walsall GB 40 C2
Walshoutem B 79 B5
Walsrode D 72 B2
Waltenhofen D 107 B5
Waltershausen D 82 B2
Waltham Abbey GB 45 B4
Waltham on the Wolds GB 40 C3
Walton-on-Thames GB 44 B3
Walton-on-the-Naze GB 45 B5
Wamba E 142 C2
Wanderup D 64 B2
Wandlitz D 74 B2
Wanfried D 82 A2
Wangen im Allgäu D 107 B4
Wangerooge D 71 A4
Wangersen D 72 A2
Wängi CH 107 B3
Wanna D 64 C1
Wansford GB 40 C3
Wantage GB 44 B2
Wanzleben D 73 B4
Waplewo PL 77 A5
Wapnica PL 75 A4
Wapno PL 76 B2
Warburg D 81 A5
Wardenburg D 71 A5
Ware GB 44 B3
Waregem B 79 B3
Wareham GB 43 B4
Waremme B 79 B5
Waren D 74 A1
Warendorf D 71 C4
Warga NL 70 A2
Warin D 65 C4
Wark GB 37 A4
Warka PL 87 A5
Warkworth GB 37 A5
Warlubie PL 69 B3
Warminster GB 43 A4
Warnemünde D 65 B5
Warnow D 65 C4
Warnsveld NL 70 B3
Warrenpoint GB 27 B4
Warrington GB 38 A4
Warsaw = Warszawa PL 77 B6
Warsingsfehn D 71 A4
Warsow D 73 A4
Warstein D 81 A4
Warszawa = Warsaw PL 77 B6
Warta PL 86 A2
Wartberg A 110 B1
Warth A 107 B5
Warwick GB 44 A2
Warza D 82 B2
Wasbister GB 33 B3
Washington GB 37 B5
Wąsosz PL 85 A4
Wasselonne F 93 C3
Wassen CH 107 C3
Wassenaar NL 70 B1
Wasserauen CH 107 B4
Wasserburg D 108 A3
Wassertrüdingen D 94 B2
Wassy F 91 C4
Wasungen D 82 B2
Watchet GB 43 A3
Waterford IRL 30 B1
Watergrasshill IRL 29 B3
Waterloo B 79 B4
Waterville IRL 29 C1
Watford GB 44 B3
Wathlingen D 72 B3
Watten
F 78 B2
GB 32 C3
Wattens A 108 B2
Watton GB 41 C4
Wattwil CH 107 B4
Waunfawr GB 38 A2
Wavignies F 90 B2
Wavre B 79 B4
Wearhead GB 37 B4
Węchadlow PL 87 B4
Wedel D 72 A2
Wedemark D 72 B2
Weedon Bec GB 44 A2
Weener D 71 A4
Weert NL 80 A1
Weesp NL 70 B2
Weeze D 80 A2
Weferlingen D 73 B4
Wegeleben D 82 A3
Weggis CH 106 B3
Węgierska-Górka PL 99 B3
Wegliniec PL 84 A3
Węgorzyno PL 75 A4
Węgrzynice PL 75 B4
Wegscheid D 96 C1
Wehdel D 72 A1
Wehr D 106 B2
Weibersbrunn D 94 B1
Weichering D 95 C3
Weida D 83 B4
Weiden D 95 B4
Weidenberg D 95 B3
Weidenhain D 83 A4
Weidenstetten D 94 C1
Weierbach D 93 B3
Weikersheim D 94 B1
Weil D 108 A1
Weil am Rhein D 106 B2
Weilburg D 81 B4
Weil der Stadt D 93 C4
Weilerswist D 80 B2
Weilheim
Baden-Württemberg D 94 C1
Bayern D 108 B2
Weilmünster D 81 B4
Weiltensfeld A 110 C1
Weimar D 82 B3
Weinberg D 94 B2
Weinfelden CH 107 B4
Weingarten
Baden-Württemberg D 93 B4
Baden-Württemberg D 107 B4
Weinheim D 93 B4
Weinstadt D 94 C1
Weismain D 82 B3
Weissbriach A 109 C4
Weissenbach A 108 B1
Weissenberg D 84 A2
Weissenbrunn D 82 B3
Weissenburg D 94 B2
Weissenfels D 83 A3
Weissenhorn D 94 C2
Weissenkirchen A 97 C3
Weissensee D 82 A3
Weissenstadt D 83 B3
Weisskirchen im Steiermark A 110 B1
Weisstannen CH 107 C4
Weisswasser D 84 A2
Weitendorf D 65 C5
Weitersfeld A 97 C3
Weitersfelden A 96 C2
Weitnau D 107 B5
Wéitra A 96 C2
Weiz A 110 B2
Wejherowo PL 68 A3
Welkenraedt B 80 B1
Wellaune D 83 A4
Wellin B 91 A5
Wellingborough GB 44 A3
Wellington
Somerset GB 43 B3
Telford & Wrekin GB 38 B4
Wellingtonbridge IRL 30 B2
Wells GB 43 A4
Wells-next-the-Sea GB 41 C4
Wels A 109 A5
Welschenrohr CH 106 B2
Welshpool GB 38 B3
Welver D 81 A3
Welwyn Garden City GB 44 B3
Welzheim D 94 C1
Welzow D 84 A2
Wem GB 38 B4
Wembury GB 42 B2
Wemding D 94 C2
Wenden D 81 B3
Wendisch Rietz D 74 B3
Wendlingen D 94 C1
Weng A 109 A4
Weng bei Admont A 110 B1
Wengen CH 106 C2
Wenigzell A 110 B2
Wennigsen D 72 B2
Wenns A 108 B1
Wenzenbach D 95 B4
Weppersdorf A 111 B3
Werben D 73 B4
Werbig D 74 C2
Werdau D 83 B4
Werder D 74 B1
Werdohl D 81 A3
Werfen A 109 B4
Werkendam NL 79 A4
Werl D 81 A3
Werlte D 71 B4
Wermelskirchen D 80 A3
Wermsdorf D 83 A4
Wernberg Köblitz D 95 B4
Werne D 81 A3
Werneck D 94 B2
Werneuchen D 74 B2
Wernigerode D 82 A2
Wertach D 108 B1
Wertheim D 94 B1
Wertingen D 94 C2
Weseke D 80 A2
Wesel D 80 A2
Wesenberg D 74 A1
Wesendorf D 73 B3
Wesołowo PL 77 A5
Wesselburen D 64 B1
Wesseling D 80 B2
West Bridgford GB 40 C2
West Bromwich GB 40 C2
Westbury
Shropshire GB 38 B4
Westbury *continued*
Wiltshire GB 43 A4
Westbury-on-Severn GB 39 C4
Westendorf A 108 B3
Westensee D 64 B2
Westerbork NL 71 B3
Westerburg D 81 B3
Westerhaar NL 71 B3
Westerholt D 71 A4
Westerkappeln D 71 B4
Westerland D 64 B1
Westerlo B 79 A4
Westerstede D 71 A4
West Haddon GB 44 A2
Westheim D 94 B2
Westhill GB 33 D4
Westkapelle
B 78 A3
NL 79 A3
West Kilbride GB 34 C3
West Linton GB 35 C4
West Lulworth GB 43 B4
West Mersea GB 45 B4
Westminster GB 44 B3
Weston GB 40 C1
Weston-super-Mare GB 43 A4
Westport IRL 28 A2
Westruther GB 35 C5
West-Terschelling NL 70 A2
Westward Ho! GB 42 A2
West Woodburn GB 37 A4
Wetheral GB 37 B4
Wetherby GB 40 B2
Wetter
Hessen D 81 B4
Nordrhein-Westfalen D 80 A3
Wetteren B 79 A3
Wettin D 83 A3
Wettringen D 71 B4
Wetzikon CH 107 B3
Wetzlar D 81 B4
Wewelsfleth D 64 C2
Wexford IRL 30 B2
Weybridge GB 44 B3
Weyerbusch D 81 B3
Weyer Markt A 110 B1
Weyersheim F 93 C3
Weyhe D 72 B1
Weyhill GB 44 B2
Weymouth GB 43 B4
Weyregg A 109 B4
Węzyska PL 75 B3
Whalton GB 37 A5
Whauphill GB 36 B2
Wheatley GB 44 B2
Whickham GB 37 B5
Whipsnade GB 44 B3
Whitburn GB 35 C4
Whitby GB 37 B6
Whitchurch
Hampshire GB 44 B2
Herefordshire GB 39 C4
Shropshire GB 38 B4
White Bridge GB 32 D2
Whitegate IRL 29 C3
Whitehaven GB 36 B3
Whitehead GB 27 B5
Whithorn GB 36 B2
Whitley Bay GB 37 A5
Whitstable GB 45 B5
Whittington GB 38 B4
Whittlesey GB 41 C3
Wiązów PL 85 B5
Wick GB 32 C3
Wickede D 81 A3
Wickford GB 45 B4
Wickham GB 44 C2
Wickham Market GB 45 A5
Wicklow IRL 30 B2
Wicko PL 68 A2
Widawa PL 86 A2
Widdrington GB 37 A5
Widecombe in the Moor GB 42 B3
Widemouth GB 42 B2
Widnes GB 38 A4
Widuchowo PL 74 A3
Więcbork PL 76 A2
Wiefelstede D 71 A5
Wiehe D 82 A3
Wiehl D 81 B3
Wiek D 66 B2
Większyce PL 86 B1
Wielbark PL 77 A5
Wiele PL 68 B2
Wieleń PL 75 B5
Wielgie
Kujawsko-Pomorskie PL 77 B4
Łódzkie PL 86 A2
Mazowieckie PL 87 A5
Wielgomłyny PL 87 A3
Wielichowo PL 75 B5
Wieliczka PL 99 B4
Wielka Łąka PL 76 A3
Wielowies PL 86 B2
Wieluń PL 86 A2
Wien = Vienna A 111 A3
Wiener Neustadt A 111 B3
Wiepke D 73 B4
Wierden NL 71 B3
Wieren D 73 B3
Wieruszów PL 86 A2
Wierzbica
Mazowieckie PL 77 B6
Mazowieckie PL 87 A5
Wierzbie PL 86 A2
Wierzbięcin PL 75 A4
Wierzchowo PL 75 A5
Wierzchucino PL 68 A3
Wierzchy PL 86 A2
Wies A 110 C2
Wiesau D 95 B4
Wiesbaden D 93 A4
Wieselburg A 110 A2
Wiesen CH 107 C4
Wiesenburg D 73 B5
Wiesenfelden D 95 B4
Wiesensteig D 94 C1
Wiesentheid D 94 B2
Wiesloch D 93 B4
Wiesmath A 111 B3
Wiesmoor D 71 A4
Wietmarschen D 71 B4
Wietze D 72 B2
Wigan GB 38 A4
Wiggen CH 106 C2
Wigston GB 40 C2
Wigton GB 36 B3
Wigtown GB 36 B2
Wijchen NL 80 A1
Wijhe NL 70 B3
Wijk bij Duurstede NL 70 C2
Wil CH 107 B4
Wilamowice PL 99 B3
Wilczęta PL 69 A4
Wilczkowice PL 77 B4
Wilczna PL 76 B3
Wilczyn PL 76 B3
Wildalpen A 110 B1
Wildbad D 93 C4
Wildberg
Baden-Württemberg D 93 C4
Brandenburg D 74 B1
Wildegg CH 106 B3
Wildendürnbach A 97 C4
Wildeshausen D 72 B1
Wildon A 110 C2
Wilfersdorf A 97 C4
Wilhelmsburg
A 110 A2
D 74 A2
Wilhelmsdorf D 107 B4
Wilhelmshaven D 71 A5
Wilków PL 77 B5
Willebadessen D 81 A5
Willebroek B 79 A4
Willgottheim F 93 C3
Willhermsdorf D 94 B2
Willich D 80 A2
Willingen D 81 A4
Willington GB 37 B5
Willisau CH 106 B3
Wilmslow GB 40 B1
Wilsdruff D 83 A5
Wilster D 64 C2
Wilsum D 71 B3
Wilton GB 44 B2
Wiltz L 92 B1
Wimborne Minster GB 43 B5
Wimereux F 78 B1
Wimmenau F 93 C3
Wimmis CH 106 C2
Wincanton GB 43 A4
Winchcombe GB 44 B2
Winchelsea GB 45 C4
Winchester GB 44 B2
Windermere GB 36 B4
Windischeschenbach D 95 B4
Windischgarsten A 110 B1
Windorf D 96 C1
Windsbach D 94 B2
Windsor GB 44 B3
Wingene B 78 A3
Wingham GB 45 B5
Winkleigh GB 42 B3
Winklern A 109 C3
Winnenden D 94 C1
Winnica PL 77 B5
Winnigstedt D 73 B3
Winnweiler D 93 B3
Winschoten NL 71 A4
Winsen
Niedersachsen D 72 A3
Niedersachsen D 72 B2
Winsford GB 38 A4
Wińsko PL 85 A4
Winslow GB 44 B3
Winsum
Friesland NL 70 A2
Groningen NL 71 A3
Winterberg D 81 A4
Winterfeld D 73 B4
Winterswijk NL 71 C3
Winterthur CH 107 B3
Wintzenheim F 106 A2
Winzer D 95 C5
Wipperdorf D 82 A2
Wipperfürth D 80 A3
Wirksworth GB 40 B2
Wisbech GB 41 C4
Wischhafen D 64 C2
Wishaw GB 35 C4
Wisła PL 98 B2
Wisła Wielka PL 98 B2
Wislica PL 87 B4
Wismar D 65 C4
Wisniewo PL 77 A5
Wiśniowa PL 99 B4
Wissant F 78 B1
Wissembourg F 93 B3
Wissen D 81 B3
Witanowice PL 99 B3
Witham GB 45 B4
Withern GB 41 B4
Withernsea GB 41 B4
Witkowo PL 76 B2
Witmarsum NL 70 A2
Witney GB 44 B2
Witnica PL 75 B3
Witonia PL 77 B4
Witry-les-Reims F 91 B4
Wittdün D 64 B1
Wittelsheim F 106 B2
Witten D 80 A3
Wittenberge D 73 A4
Wittenburg D 73 A4
Wittenheim F 106 B2
Wittichenau D 84 A2
Wittighausen D 94 B1
Wittingen D 73 B3
Wittislingen D 94 C2
Wittlich D 92 B2
Wittmannsdorf A 110 C2
Wittmund D 71 A4
Wittorf D 72 A2
Wittstock D 73 A5
Witzenhausen D 82 A1
Wiveliscombe GB 43 A3
Wivenhoe GB 45 B4
Władysławowo PL 69 A3
Wleń PL 84 A3
Włocławek PL 77 B4
Włodawa PL 13 C5
Włodzimierzów PL 87 A3
Włosień PL 84 A3
Włostow PL 87 B5
Włoszakowice PL 75 C5
Włoszczowa PL 87 B3
Wöbbelin D 73 A4
Woburn GB 44 B3
Wodzisław PL 87 B4
Wodzisław Śląski PL 98 B2
Woerden NL 70 B1
Woerth F 93 C3
Wohlen CH 106 B3
Woippy F 92 B2
Wojcieszow PL 85 B3
Wojkowice Kościelne PL 86 B3
Wojnicz PL 99 B4
Woking GB 44 B3
Wokingham GB 44 B3
Wola Jachowa PL 87 B4
Wola Niechcicka PL 86 A3
Wolbórz PL 87 A3
Wolbrom PL 87 B3
Wołczyn PL 86 A2
Woldegk D 74 A2
Wolfach D 93 C4
Wolfegg D 107 B4
Wolfen D 83 A4
Wolfenbüttel D 73 B3
Wolfersheim D 81 B4
Wolfhagen D 81 A5
Wolfratshausen D 108 B2
Wolfsberg A 110 C1
Wolfsburg D 73 B3
Wolf's Castle GB 39 C2
Wolfshagen D 74 A2
Wolfstein D 93 B3
Wolfurt A 107 B4
Wolgast D 66 B2
Wolhusen CH 106 B3
Wolin PL 67 C3
Wolka PL 87 A4
Wolkenstein D 83 B5
Wolkersdorf A 97 C4
Wöllersdorf A 111 B3
Wollin D 73 B5
Wöllstadt D 81 B4
Wolmirstedt D 73 B4
Wolnzach D 95 C3
Wołów PL 85 A4
Wolsztyn PL 75 B5
Wolvega NL 70 B2
Wolverhampton GB 40 C1
Wolverton GB 44 A3
Wombwell GB 40 B2
Woodbridge GB 45 A5
Woodhall Spa GB 41 B3
Woodstock GB 44 B2
Wookey Hole GB 43 A4
Wool GB 43 B4
Woolacombe GB 42 A2
Wooler GB 37 A4
Woolwich GB 45 B4
Wooperton GB 37 A5
Worb CH 106 C2
Worbis D 82 A2
Worcester GB 39 B4
Wördern A 97 C4
Wörgl A 108 B3
Workington GB 36 B3
Worksop GB 40 B2
Workum NL 70 B2
Wörlitz D 83 A4
Wormer NL 70 B1
Wormhout F 78 B2
Wormit GB 35 B5
Worms D 93 B4

Worpswede D . . . 72 A1
Wörrstadt D . . . 93 B4
Wörschach A . . . 110 B1
Worsley GB . . . 38 A4
Wörth
 Bayern D . . . 93 B5
 Bayern D . . . 95 B4
 Bayern D . . . 95 C4
 Rheinland-Pfalz D . 93 B4
Worthing GB . . . 44 C3
Woudsend NL . . . 70 B2
Woumen B . . . 78 A2
Woźniki PL . . . 86 B3
Wragby GB . . . 41 B3
Wrangle GB . . . 41 B4
Wręczyca Wlk. PL . 86 B2
Wredenhagen D . . 73 A5
Wremen D . . . 72 A1
Wrentham GB . . . 45 A5
Wrexham GB . . . 38 A3
Wriedel D . . . 72 A3
Wriezen D . . . 74 B3
Wrist D . . . 64 C2
Wróblewo
 Mazowieckie PL . 77 B5
 Wielkopolskie PL . 75 B5
Wrocki PL . . . 69 B4
Wrocław PL . . . 85 A5
Wronki PL . . . 75 B5
Wroxham GB . . . 41 C5
Września PL . . . 76 B2
Wrzosowo PL . . . 67 B4
Wschowa PL . . . 85 A4
Wulfen D . . . 80 A3
Wülfen D . . . 83 A3
Wulkau D . . . 73 B5
Wünnenberg D . . . 81 A4
Wünsdorf D . . . 74 B2
Wunsiedel D . . . 95 A4
Wunstorf D . . . 72 B2
Wuppertal D . . . 80 A3
Wurmannsquick D . 95 C4
Würselen D . . . 80 B2
Wurzbach D . . . 82 B3
Würzburg D . . . 94 B1
Wurzen D . . . 83 A4
Wust D . . . 74 B1
Wusterhausen D . . 73 B5
Wusterwitz D . . . 73 B5
Wustrau-Altfriesack
 D . . . 74 B1
Wustrow D . . . 66 B1
Wuustwezel B . . . 79 A4
Wye GB . . . 45 B4
Wyględów PL . . . 87 A5
Wyk D . . . 64 B1
Wykroty PL . . . 84 A3
Wylye GB . . . 43 A5
Wymiarki PL . . . 84 A3
Wymondham GB . . 41 C5
Wyrzysk PL . . . 76 A2
Wyśmierzyce PL . . 87 A4
Wysoka
 Dolnośląskie PL . 85 A4
 Wielkopolskie PL . 76 A2
Wyszanów PL . . . 86 A2
Wyszogród PL . . . 77 B5

X
Xanten D . . . 80 A2
Xanthi GR . . . 183 B6
Xarrë AL . . . 182 D2
Xátiva E . . . 159 C3
Xeraco E . . . 159 B3
Xert E . . . 153 B4
Xerta E . . . 153 B4
Xertigny F . . . 105 A5
Xilagani GR . . . 183 C7
Xilokastro GR . . . 184 A3
Xinzo de Limia E . 140 B3
Xixón = Gijón E . . 142 A1
Xove E . . . 140 A3
Xubia E . . . 140 A2
Xunqueira de Ambia
 E . . . 140 B3
Xunqueira de
Espadañedo E . 140 B3
Xylophagou CY . . 181 B2

Y
Yablanitsa BG . . . 17 D6
Yağcılar TR . . . 186 C3
Yahyalı TR . . . 23 B8
Yakoruda BG . . . 183 A5
Yalova TR . . . 187 B4
Yalvaç TR . . . 189 A6
Yambol BG . . . 17 D7
Yampil UA . . . 13 D8
Yaniskoski RUS . 193 D12
Yantarnyy RUS . . 69 A4
Yarcombe GB . . . 43 B3
Yaremcha UA. . . . 13 D6
Yarm GB. . . . 37 B5
Yarmouth GB . . . 44 C2

Yarrow GB . . . 35 C4
Yasinya UA . . . 17 A6
Yatağan TR . . . 188 B3
Yate GB . . . 43 A4
Yatton GB . . . 43 A4
Yavoriv UA . . . 13 D5
Yaxley GB . . . 41 C3
Yazıköy TR . . . 188 C2
Ybbs A . . . 110 A2
Ybbsitz A . . . 110 B1
Ydby DK . . . 58 B1
Yddal N . . . 46 B2
Ydes F . . . 116 B2
Yealmpton GB . . . 42 B3
Yebra de Basa E . 145 B3
Yecla E . . . 159 C2
Yecla de Yeltes E . 149 B3
Yelsk BY . . . 13 C8
Yelverton GB . . . 42 B2
Yena RUS. . . . 197 B14
Yenice
 Ankara TR . . . 23 B7
 Aydın TR . . . 188 B3
 Çanakkale TR . . 186 C2
 Edirne TR . . . 183 C8
Yenifoça TR . . . 186 D1
Yeniköy TR . . . 186 D4
Yenipazar TR . . . 188 B3
Yenişarbademli
 TR . . . 189 B6
Yenişehir TR . . . 187 B4
Yenne F . . . 118 B2
Yeovil GB . . . 43 B4
Yepes E . . . 151 C4
Yerköy TR . . . 23 B8
Yerólakkos CY . . 181 A2
Yeroskipos CY . . 181 B1
Yerseke NL . . . 79 A4
Yerville F . . . 89 A4
Yeşilada TR . . . 189 B6
Yeşilhisar TR . . . 23 B8
Yeşilova TR . . . 189 B4
Yeşilyurt TR . . . 188 A3
Yeste E . . . 164 A2
Yezerishche BY . . 9 E6
Y Felinheli GB . . 38 A2
Ygos-St Saturnin
 F . . . 128 C2
Ygrande F . . . 104 C1
Yialousa CY . . . 181 A3
Yığılca TR . . . 187 B6
Yli-li FIN . . . 197 D8
Yli-Kärppä FIN . . 197 D8
Yli-Muonia FIN . . 196 A6
Ylitornio FIN . . . 196 C6
Ylivieska FIN . . . 3 D9
Ylläsjärvi FIN . . . 196 B7
Ymonville F . . . 103 A3
Yngsjö S . . . 63 C2
York GB . . . 40 B2
Youghal IRL . . . 29 C4
Yoğuntaş TR . . . 186 A2
Yozgat TR . . . 23 B8
Yport F . . . 89 A4
Ypres = Ieper B . . 78 B2
Yssingeaux F . . . 117 B4
Ystad S . . . 66 A2
Ystalyfera GB . . . 39 C3
Ystebrød N . . . 52 B1
Ystradgynlais GB . 39 C3
Ytre Arna N . . . 46 B2
Ytre Enebakk N . . 54 A2
Ytre Rendal N . . 199 D8
Ytteran S . . . 199 B11
Ytterhogdal S . . 199 C11
Yttermalung S . . . 49 B5
Yunak TR . . . 187 D6
Yuncos E . . . 151 B4
Yunquera E . . . 162 B3
Yunquera de Henares
 E . . . 151 B4
Yushkozero RUS. . 3 D13
Yverdon-les-Bains
 CH . . . 106 C1
Yvetot F . . . 89 A4
Yvignac F . . . 101 A3
Yvoir B . . . 79 B4
Yvonand CH . . . 106 C1
Yxnerum S . . . 56 B2
Yzeure F . . . 104 C2

Z
Zabor PL . . . 75 C4
Żabowo PL . . . 75 A4
Zabrdje BIH . . . 125 C4
Zábřeh CZ . . . 97 B4
Zabrže e SRB. . . 127 C2
Ząbrowo PL . . . 67 C4
Zabrze PL . . . 86 B2
Zabrzeż PL . . . 99 B4
Zacharo GR . . . 184 B2
Zadar HR . . . 137 A4
Zadzim PL . . . 86 A2
Zafarraya E . . . 163 B3
Zafferana Etnea I . 177 B4
Zafra E . . . 155 C4
Żaga SLO . . . 122 A2
Zagajica SRB. . . 127 C3
Żagań PL . . . 84 A3
Zaglav HR . . . 137 B4
Zaglavak SRB . . 127 D1
Zagnańsk PL . . . 87 B4
Zagora GR . . . 183 D5
Zagorc SLO . . . 110 C2
Zagorje SLO . . . 123 A4
Zagórów PL . . . 76 B2
Zagradje SRB . . 127 C2
Zagreb HR . . . 124 B1
Zagrilla E . . . 163 A3
Zagvozd HR . . . 138 B3
Zagwiździe PL . . . 86 B1
Zagyvarekas H . 113 B4
Zagyvaróna H . . 113 A3
Zahara E . . . 162 B2
Zahara de los Atunes
 E . . . 162 B2
Zahinos E . . . 155 C4
Záhna D . . . 83 A4
Záhoří CZ . . . 96 B2
Zahrádka CZ . . . 97 B3
Zahrensdorf D . . . 73 A3
Zaidin E . . . 153 A4
Zaječar SRB . . . 16 D5
Zákamenné SK . . 99 B3
Zákány H . . . 124 A2
Zákányszék H . . 126 A1
Zakliczyn PL . . . 99 B4
Zaklopača SRB . . 99 B3
Zakroczym PL . . . 77 B5
Zakrzew PL . . . 87 A5
Zakrzewo PL . . . 76 B3
Zakupy CZ . . . 84 B2
Zakynthos GR . . 184 B1
Zalaapáti H . . . 111 C4
Zalabaksa H. . . . 111 C3
Zalaegerszeg H . . 111 C3
Zalakomár H . . . 111 C4
Zalakoppány H . . 111 C4
Zalamea de la Serena
 E . . . 156 B2
Zalamea la Real E . 161 B3
Zalaszentgrót H . . 111 C4
Zalaszentiván H . . 111 C3
Zalău RO . . . 17 B5
Zalavár H . . . 111 C4
Zalcsie PL . . . 86 A3
Zaldibar E . . . 143 A4
Zalec SLO . . . 123 A4
Zalesie PL . . . 77 A5
Zaleszczyki UA . . 13 D6
Zalewo PL . . . 69 B4
Zalishchyky UA . . 13 D6
Zalla E . . . 143 A3
Zaltbommel NL . . 79 A5
Zamárdi H . . . 112 C1
Zamarte PL . . . 68 B2
Zambra E . . . 163 A3
Zambugueira do Mar
 P . . . 160 B1
Zámoly H . . . 112 B2
Zamora E . . . 149 A4
Zamość PL . . . 13 C5
Zamoście PL . . . 86 A3
Zams A . . . 108 B1
Zandhoven B . . . 79 A4
Žandov CZ . . . 84 B2
Zandvoort NL . . . 70 B1
Zangliveri GR . . 183 C5
Zánka H . . . 111 C4
Zaorejas E . . . 152 B1
Zaovine SRB . . . 127 D1
Zapadnaya Dvina
 RUS . . . 9 D8
Zapfend D . . . 94 A2
Zapole PL . . . 86 A2
Zapolyarnyy RUS . 193 C14
Zapponeta I . . . 171 B3
Zaprešić HR . . . 124 B1
Zaragoza E . . . 153 A3
Zarasai LT . . . 13 A7
Zarautz E . . . 144 A1
Zarcilla de Ramos
 E . . . 164 B3
Zaręby PL . . . 77 A6
Żarki PL . . . 86 B3
Żarki PL . . . 77 B6
Żarnow PL . . . 87 A4
Żarnowiec PL . . . 68 A3
Zaroisice CZ . . . 97 B4
Żarów PL . . . 85 B4
Zarren B . . . 78 A2

Zarrentin D . . . 73 A3
Żary PL . . . 84 A3
Zarza Capilla E . . 156 B2
Zarza de Alange E . 156 B1
Zarza de Granadilla
 E . . . 149 B3
Zarza de Tajo E . . 151 B4
Zarzadilla de Totana
 E . . . 164 B3
Zarza la Mayor E . 155 B4
Zarzuela del Monte
 E . . . 150 B3
Zarzuela del Pinar
 E . . . 151 A3
Zas E . . . 140 A2
Zasavica SRB . . 127 C1
Zasieki PL . . . 84 A2
Zásmuky CZ . . . 96 B3
Žatec CZ . . . 83 B5
Zaton HR . . . 139 C4
Zatonie PL . . . 84 A3
Zator PL . . . 99 B3
Zauchwitz D . . . 74 B2
Zavala BIH . . . 139 C3
Zavalje BIH . . . 124 C1
Zavattarello I . . . 120 C2
Zavidovići BIH . . 139 A4
Zavlaka SRB . . . 127 C1
Zawady PL . . . 77 C5
Zawadzkie PL . . . 86 B2
Zawdy PL . . . 86 A2
Zawidów PL . . . 84 A3
Zawidz PL . . . 77 B4
Zawiercie PL . . . 86 B3
Zawoja PL . . . 99 B3
Zawonia PL . . . 85 A5
Zázrivá SK . . . 99 B3
Zbarazh UA . . . 13 D6
Zbąszyń PL . . . 75 B4
Zbąszynek PL . . . 75 B4
Zbehy SK . . . 98 C2
Zbiersk PL . . . 76 C3
Zbiroh CZ . . . 96 B1
Zblewo PL . . . 69 B3
Zbójno PL . . . 77 A4
Zbrachlin PL . . . 76 A3
Zbraslav CZ . . . 96 B2
Zbraslavice CZ . . 97 B3
Ždala HR . . . 124 A3
Žďánice CZ . . . 98 B1
Žďár nad Sázavou
 CZ . . . 97 B3
Zdbice PL . . . 75 A5
Zdenci HR . . . 125 B3
Ždiar SK . . . 99 B4
Zdice CZ . . . 96 B1
Zdirec nad Doubravou
 CZ . . . 97 B3
Zdolbuniv UA . . . 13 C7
Zdounky CZ . . . 98 B1
Ždrelo SRB . . . 127 C3
Zduńska Wola PL . 86 A2
Zduny
 Łódzkie PL . . . 77 B4
 Wielkopolskie PL . 85 A5
Żdżary PL . . . 87 A4
Zdziechowice
 Opolskie PL . . . 86 A2
 Wielkopolskie PL . 76 B2
Zdziszowice PL . . 86 B2
Zeberio E . . . 143 A4
Žebrák CZ . . . 96 B1
Zebreira P . . . 155 B3
Zebrzydowa PL . . 84 A3
Zechlin D . . . 74 A1
Zechlinerhütte D . 74 A1
Zederhaus A . . . 109 B4
Žednik SRB . . . 126 B1
Zeebrugge B . . . 78 A3
Zeewolde NL . . . 70 B2
Zegrze PL . . . 77 B6
Zehdenick D . . . 74 B2
Zehren D . . . 83 A5
Zeil D . . . 94 A2
Zeilarn D . . . 95 C4
Zeist NL . . . 70 B2
Zeithain D . . . 83 A5
Zeitz D . . . 83 A4
Želatava CZ . . . 97 B3
Żelazno PL . . . 68 A2
Zele B . . . 79 A4
Zelenoborskiy RUS . 3 C13
Zelenogorsk RUS . 9 B6
Zelenograd RUS . 9 D10
Zelenogradsk RUS . 12 A4
Železná Ruda CZ . 96 B1
Železnice CZ . . . 84 B3
Železnik SRB . . 127 C2
Železniki SLO . . 123 A3
Železný Brod CZ . 84 B3
Zelhem NL . . . 71 B3
Želiezovce SK . . 112 A2
Żelkowo PL . . . 68 A2
Zell
 CH . . . 106 B2
 Baden-Württemberg
  D . . . 93 C4
 Baden-Württemberg
  D . . . 106 B2
 Rheinland-Pfalz D . 92 A3
Zella-Mehlis D . . 82 B2
Zell am See A . . 109 B3

Zell am Ziller A . . 108 B2
Zell an der Pram A . 96 C1
Zell bei Zellhof A . 96 C2
Zellerndorf A . . . 97 C3
Zellingen D . . . 94 B1
Zelovce SK . . . 112 A3
Zelów PL . . . 86 A3
Zeltweg A . . . 110 B1
Zemberovce SK . . 98 C2
Zembrzyce PL . . . 99 B3
Zemianske-Kostol'any
 SK . . . 98 C2
Zemitz D . . . 66 C2
Zemné SK . . . 112 B1
Zemst B . . . 79 B4
Zemun SRB . . . 127 C2
Zemunik Donji HR . 137 A4
Zenica BIH . . . 139 A3
Zennor GB . . . 42 B1
Žepa BIH . . . 139 B5
Žepče BIH . . . 139 A4
Zepponami I . . . 168 A2
Zerbst D . . . 73 C5
Zerf D . . . 92 B2
Zerind RO . . . 113 C5
Żerków PL . . . 76 B2
Zermatt CH . . . 119 A4
Zernez CH . . . 107 C5
Zerpen-schleuse D . 74 B2
Zestoa E . . . 144 A1
Zetel D . . . 71 A4
Zeulenroda D . . . 83 B3
Zeven D . . . 72 A2
Zevenaar NL . . . 70 C3
Zevenbergen NL . . 79 A4
Zévio I . . . 121 B4
Zeytinbaği TR . . 186 B3
Zeytindağ TR . . 186 D2
Zgierz PL . . . 86 A3
Zgorzelec PL . . . 84 A3
Zgošča BIH . . . 139 A4
Zhabinka BY . . . 13 B6
Zharkovskiy RUS . 9 E8
Zhashkiv UA . . . 13 D9
Zhlobin BY . . . 13 B9
Zhmerynka UA. . . 13 D8
Zhodzina BY . . . 13 A8
Zhytomyr UA. . . . 13 C8
Žiar nad Hronom
 SK . . . 98 C2
Zicavo F . . . 180 B2
Zickhusen D . . . 65 C4
Zidani Most SLO . 123 A4
Ziddorf D . . . 73 A5
Žídlochovice CZ . 97 B4
Ziębice PL . . . 85 B5
Ziegendorf D . . . 73 A4
Ziegenrück D . . . 83 B3
Zieleniec
 Dolnośląskie PL . 85 B4
 Warmińsko-Mazurskie
  PL . . . 77 A6
Zielona
 Łódzkie PL . . . 77 B4
 Wielkopolskie PL . 85 A5
Zielona Góra PL . 75 C4
Zieluń-Osada PL . 77 A4
Ziemetshausen D . 94 C2
Zierenberg D . . . 81 A5
Zierikzee NL . . . 79 A3
Ziersdorf A . . . 97 C3
Zierzow D . . . 73 A4
Ziesar D . . . 73 B5
Ziesendorf D . . . 65 C5
Ziethen D . . . 74 B2
Žihle CZ . . . 96 A1
Žilina SK . . . 98 B2
Ziltendorf D . . . 74 B3
Zimandu Nou RO . 126 A3
Zimna Woda PL . . 77 A5
Zimnicea RO . . . 17 D6
Zinal CH . . . 119 A4
Zinasco I . . . 120 B2
Zingst D . . . 66 B1
Zinkgruvan S . . . 55 B6
Zinkovy CZ . . . 96 B1
Zinnowitz D . . . 66 B2
Zirc H . . . 112 B1
Žiri SLO . . . 123 A3
Zirl A . . . 108 B2
Zirndorf D . . . 94 B2
Žirovnica SRB . . 127 C3
Žirovnice CZ . . . 97 B3
Zistersdorf A . . . 97 C4
Žitište SRB . . . 126 B2
Zitsa GR . . . 182 D2
Zittau D . . . 84 B2
Živaja HR . . . 124 B2
Živinice BIH . . . 139 A4
Zlatar HR . . . 124 A2
Zlatar Bistrica HR . 124 A2
Zlaté Hory CZ . . 85 B5
Zlaté Klasy SK . . 111 A4
Zlaté Moravce SK . 98 C2
Zlatná na Ostrove
 SK . . . 112 B1
Zlatniky SK . . . 98 C2
Zlatograd BG . . . 183 B7
Žlebič SLO . . . 123 B3
Zlín CZ . . . 98 B1
Złocieniec PL . . . 75 A5

Złoczew PL . . . 86 A2
Zlonice CZ . . . 84 B2
Złotniki Kujawskie
 PL . . . 76 B3
Złotoryja PL . . . 85 A3
Złotów PL . . . 68 B2
Złoty Stok PL . . . 85 B4
Zlutice CZ . . . 83 B5
Zmajevac BIH . . 124 C2
Zmajevo SRB . . . 126 B1
Żmigród PL . . . 85 A4
Zmijavci HR . . . 138 B3
Žminj HR . . . 122 B2
Żnin PL . . . 76 B2
Znojmo CZ . . . 97 C4
Zöblitz D . . . 83 B5
Zocca I . . . 135 A4
Zoetermeer NL . . 70 B1
Zofingen CH . . . 106 B2
Zogno I . . . 120 B2
Zohor SK . . . 111 A3
Zolling D . . . 95 C3
Zolochiv UA . . . 13 D6
Zomba H . . . 112 C2
Zomergem B . . . 79 A3
Zoñán E . . . 141 A3
Zonguldak TR . . 187 A6
Zonhoven B . . . 79 B5
Zonza F . . . 180 B2
Zörbig D . . . 83 A4
Zorita E . . . 156 A2
Żory PL . . . 98 A2
Zossen D . . . 74 B2
Zottegem B . . . 79 B3
Zoutkamp NL . . . 71 A3
Zovi Do BIH . . . 139 B4
Zreče SLO . . . 123 A4
Zrenjanin SRB . . 126 B2
Žrnovica HR . . . 138 B2
Zruč nad Sázavou
 CZ . . . 97 B3
Zsadány H . . . 113 C5
Zsámbék H . . . 112 B2
Zsámbok H . . . 112 B3
Zsana H . . . 126 A1
Zschopau D . . . 83 B5
Zuberec SK . . . 99 B3
Zubieta E . . . 144 A2
Zubiri E . . . 144 B2
Zubtsov RUS . . . 9 D9
Zucaina E . . . 153 B3
Zudar D . . . 66 B2
Zuera E . . . 144 C3
Zufre E . . . 161 B3
Zug CH . . . 107 B3
Zuheros E . . . 163 A3
Zuidhorn NL . . . 71 A3
Zuidlaren NL . . . 71 A3
Zuidwolde NL . . . 71 B3
Zújar E . . . 164 B2
Żukowo PL . . . 69 A3
Žuljana HR . . . 138 C3
Žulová CZ . . . 85 B5
Zülpich D . . . 80 B2
Zumaia E . . . 144 A1
Zumárraga E . . . 143 A4
Zundert NL . . . 79 A4
Županja HR . . . 125 B4
Zurgena E . . . 164 B2
Zürich CH . . . 107 B3
Žuromin PL . . . 77 A4
Zurzach CH . . . 106 A3
Zusmarshausen D . 94 C2
Zusow D . . . 65 C4
Züssow D . . . 66 C2
Žuta Lovka HR . . 123 C4
Zutphen NL . . . 70 B3
Zvikovské Podhradi
 CZ . . . 96 B2
Zvolen SK . . . 99 C3
Zvolenská Slatina
 SK . . . 99 C3
Zvornik BIH . . . 139 A5
Zwartsluis NL . . . 70 B3
Zweibrücken D . . 93 B3
Zweisimmen CH . 106 C2
Zwettl A . . . 97 C3
Zwettl an der Rodl
 A . . . 96 C2
Zwickau D . . . 83 B4
Zwiefalten D . . . 107 A4
Zwieryn PL . . . 75 B4
Zwierzno PL . . . 69 A4
Zwiesel D . . . 96 B1
Zwieselstein A . . 108 C2
Zwoleń PL . . . 87 A5
Zwolle NL . . . 70 B3
Zwönitz D . . . 83 B4
Żychlin PL . . . 77 B4
Zydowo
 Wielkopolskie PL . 76 B2
 Zachodnio-Pomorskie
  PL . . . 68 A1
Żyrardów PL . . . 77 B5
Żytno PL . . . 86 B3
Żywiec PL . . . 99 B3
Zyyi CY . . . 181 B2